THE

EVERY DAY BOOK

OF

HISTORY AND CHRONOLOGY:

EMBRACING THE

Anniversaries of Memorable Persons and Events,

IN

EVERY PERIOD AND STATE OF THE WORLD,

FROM THE CREATION TO THE PRESENT TIME.

BY JOEL MUNSELL.

"What hath this day done? What hath it deserved?"

NEW YORK:
D. APPLETON & CO., 346 BROADWAY.
1858.

PREFACE.

The object of this work, as will be seen, is to bring together the great events of each day of the year, in all ages, as far as their dates can be ascertained, and to arrange them chronologically. It has been necessary to observe brevity in its compilation, in order to reduce it within a proper compass. Hence notices of the most eminent men are often confined to two or three lines, while individuals of less note have occasionally received more attention, on account of the absence of ready reference to them in books.

The dates are in accordance, it is believed, with the best authorities. Great care has been taken to make them so, and nothing has been inserted for which there was not at least some authority. Occasionally authors have been found to disagree in days, months, and even years, and it has been necessary to reconcile, as well as possible, such discrepancies. Much of this confusion arises from the change in the calendar; some authors following the old, others the new style, without informing us which they adhere to. The protestant countries did not all adopt the new style till 1777, about two centuries after the catholic authorities had reformed the calendar. The Russians still use the Julian era, and are now consequently twelve days behind the true time. With these difficulties in the way, no ordinary vigilance ensures an entire freedom from error in a work like this. The dates here, however, are made to conform to the new style as far as practicable. In some cases where different dates have been given, and it has been found impossible to determine the true one, the article has been inserted under different days with cross references. Repetitions have crept in however, which could only be discovered in preparing the index. Errors of this kind are perpetuated by a succession of authors following a wrong date, and are exceedingly difficult to detect, or when suspected, not easily traced to their origin. When dates have been taken from computations of time other than the Christian era, it should be understood that the corresponding day has been made to conform to our own era, and consequently perfect accuracy can not be claimed for them.

It has been said that geography and chronology are the eyes of history; in aiding to promote one of these sciences, the reader will not fail to discover how great and varied is the amount of facts brought together, rendering the work of use to persons of every age and calling. A reference to the index will show more clearly the extent of the work.

EVERY DAY BOOK

OF

HISTORY AND CHRONOLOGY.

JANUARY 1.

154 B. C. It was fixed that the Roman consuls should always enter upon their office on this day, and the years were named after them. On this occasion they went in solemn procession to the Capitol to sacrifice to Jupiter Capitolinus; after which the senate held a solemn session. Those who had discharged the office of consul enjoyed the pre-eminence of rank over the other senators. They were annually elected by the people till the time of Tiberius, who ordered that they should be chosen by the senate. The last consul after whom the year was named, was Barsilius, in the year 541, in the reign of Justinianus.

38. B. C. The Spanish era, or era of the Cæsars, commenced, being the year following the conquest of Spain by Augustus. It was much used in Africa, Spain and the south of France; but was abolished by one kingdom after another during the fourteenth century, and by Portugal 1555.

404. TELEMACHUS, or St. Almachus, whose story is the foundation of Fenelon's famed work *Telemaque,* suffered martyrdom at Rome.

1109. The Festival of Fools was instituted at Paris, and continued prosperous for 240 years. This, with the Lords of Misrule, and the Abbots of Unreason, was doubtless designed to ridicule the Druidic saturnalia.

1308. WILLIAM TELL, the Swiss patriot, associated himself on this day with a band of his countrymen against the tyranny of their oppressors.

1349. EDWARD III, king of England, defeated the French before Calais with great slaughter.

1504. Birthday of CASPER CRUCIGER, an extensive and multifarious scholar, and a follower of Luther. He died 1548.

1515. LOUIS XII of France, surnamed *the father of the people,* died. Notwithstanding the faults of his education, which had been purposely neglected, he became a wise and politic monarch, who had the welfare and improvement of his country in mind. Though extensively engaged in wars, he avoided burdening the people with taxes—was economical, just and magnanimous.

1513. JUAN DIAZ DE SOLIS, coasting the southern continent, discovered the mouth of a river on this day, which in consequence he called Rio Janeiro.

1516. JUAN DIAZ DE SOLIS again entered the Rio de Solis which he had discovered three years previous. In attempting a descent on the country he was slain by the natives, who in sight of the ship cut his body in pieces, and roasted and devoured it. He was reputed the ablest navigator in the world.

1523. Knights of Malta driven from the island of Rhodes by the Turks.

1537. JAMES V of Scotland married Magdalen, daughter of Francis I of France.

1617. HENRY GOLTZIUS, a distinguished Dutch painter and engraver, died. His father was a painter on glass, and gave his son instructions in the art; but it was his own genius and application that raised him to the rank he ultimately held among the best artists of the time.

1618. Charter of the first New Netherland company expired by its own limitation.

1618. Birthday of BARTHOLOMEW ESTEBAN MURILLO, the greatest of all the Spanish painters. He was employed by the churches and convents of Seville a great number of years, which were enriched by the masterly productions of his pencil, and procured for himself an independent fortune. Having been invited to Cadiz, he there executed his grand picture of St. Catharine; but just as he was about to finish it he was dreadfully wounded on the scaffolding, and died at Seville, 1682.

1630. THOMAS HOBSON, the celebrated

carrier of Cambridge, England, died. One of the most general proverbial expressions in England originated with him. He let to students and others horses, and his practice was to secure equal portions of rest as well as work for each horse. Hence when applied to for any, none but that which had its due proportion of rest could be let. "This or none" was the answer. Hence the phrase "Hobson's choice; this or none."

1644. MICHOB ADER, calling himself the Wandering Jew, appeared at Paris, where he created an extraordinary sensation among all ranks. He pretended to have lived sixteen hundred years, and that he had traveled through all regions of the world. He was visited by the literati of the city, and no one could accost him in a language that he was ignorant of; he was also familiar with the history of persons and events from the time of Christ, so that he was never confounded by intricate or cross-questions; but replied readily and without embarrassment. The learned looked upon him as a counterfeit, or madman, yet they took their leave of him bewildered and astonished.

1651. CHARLES II crowned king of Scotland at Scone.

1661. A parliament met in Scotland.

1700. The Russians began their new year.

1715. WILLIAM WYCHERLEY died, aged 81, an eminent English dramatic writer and comic poet.

1727. CLAUDE ADRIAN HELVETIUS died; a celebrated Dutch physician, who, having obtained celebrity by introducing the use of ipecacuanha in dysentery, was made inspector general of military hospitals, and died at London.

1729. Great fog in London, persons lost their way in St. James' park, and many fell into the canal.

1730. SAMUEL SEWALL, chief justice of the supreme court of Massachusetts died.

1731. EDWARD CAVE printed the first number of the well known *Gentleman's Magazine.*

1748. Birthday of GODFREY AUGUSTUS BURGER, a celebrated German poet, and the writer of that whimsical satire, *Munchausen's Travels.*

1748. JOHN BERNOUILLI, a Swiss mathematician, died. He was born at Basil in Switzerland, and educated for a merchant, but afterwards studied medicine, and finally devoted his attention to mathematics with great success. He was the contemporary of Leibnitz and De L'Hopital, and of Newton. His labors in the science were indefatigable, and his works contain an immense mass of discovery. But the details of his private life exhibit an unusual degree of acerbity and disingenuousness.

1752. The new style commenced this day in England by act of parliament. (See March 25.)

1757. Calcutta surrendered to the British under Admiral Watson, Colonel Clive and Captain Coote.

1761. Great hurricane in the East Indies, destroying a part of the British fleet; of the crews of three of the ships lost but 14 were saved out of 1100.

1776. Norfolk Burnt. Lord Dunmore, the royal governor of Virginia, having abandoned the town and retired on board his ships, became distressed for provisions; and on the arrival of the Liverpool man of war, the inhabitants refusing to supply his majesty's ships, the place was reduced to ashes. The provincials themselves destroyed the houses and plantations near the water, to deprive the ships of every resource of supply.

1781. Revolt of the Pennsylvania line at Morristown, N. J. They had enlisted for three years, and that term having expired they wished to be discharged.

1787. ARTHUR MIDDLETON, a signer of the Declaration of Independence, died. He was a native of South Carolina, born 1743, and educated in England; and at the age of twenty-two made the tour of Europe. On the breaking out of the war he engaged warmly on the side of the colonies. In 1779 he distinguished himself in the defence of Charleston against the British, who afterwards ravaged his plantation and rifled his mansion, by which he suffered an immense loss of property; and in the following year he was taken prisoner. On the termination of the contest he returned to his native seat, and spent the remainder of his life in elegant and philosophical ease—a model of private wealth and public virtue; a firm patriot and an enlightened philanthropist.

1793. A beginning was made upon the Pennsylvania state canal, at Conewago falls; seventeen rocks being blasted—one for each stockholder of the canal company.

1794. The French convention abolished flogging in the army and navy and substituted other punishments more congenial with the spirit of the times.

1794. THOMAS PAINE and ANACHARSIS CLOOTS arrested by order of Robespierre and sent to prison in Paris.

1797. ZEMAUN SHAH made his triumphal entry into Lahore, the capital of the Sikhs, where he formed an army of 100,000 men with a view of marching upon Delhi.

1798. Athenæum at Liverpool was opened.

1799. The French drove the king of Naples from his capital and forced him to take refuge on board of a British man of war, in which he sailed to Palermo.

1801. Union of Great Britain with Ireland.

1801. Ceres discovered by Piazzi, the astronomer, at Palermo.

1804. The numerous army which France had sent against the negroes of Hayti being compelled by disasters to fly to St. Domingo, the general and chiefs of the Haytian army entered into a solemn compact, in the name of *the people of Hayti;* renouncing all dependence on France, and appointed Dessalines, the oldest general, governor for life, with very extensive powers.

1806. The French republican calendar abolished, and the Christian era and reformed calendar restored.

1806. The elector of Wurtemberg proclaimed king of Swabia, and the elector of Bavaria king of Bavaria.

1807. Curacoa surrendered to the British under Sir Charles Brisbane.

1810. There had died in Philadelphia during the year ending this day 2004 persons; the population including the Liberties was about 100,000.

1810. Married at East Haddam, Conn., nine young ladies, being all that were marriageable at that time in the town.

1811. Tortosa in Valencia surrendered to the French under Suchet, who took nearly 8000 prisoners, 177 cannons, and a large quantity of provisions.

1811. Hamburgh formally annexed to France.

1811. Spanish cortes forbid the people obeying any act of Ferdinand XII, while a prisoner of Bonaparte.

1813. Jean Mourtrie, a Frenchman, died at the age of 115. He was a tile-maker, and continued his occupation to the age of 109. He was a pattern of honor and integrity; his gaiety made the young fond of his society; and his mild and even temper and kind disposition gained him the love of all who knew him.

1814. Great fog in London, which had commenced on the 27th of December, was now at its greatest density, extending seventy miles from the metropolis. Many persons lost their lives by falling into the river, and canals, and other places.

1814. The allied army entered France.

1814. American dragoons under Capt. Stone advanced on Buffalo, accompanied by Lieuts. Riddle, Totman and Frazer, of the United States regiment; the militia retiring, Totman was killed, and Riddle narrowly escaped being captured.

1815. William Creech, bookseller and twice lord provost of Edinburgh, died. He was a spirited writer.

1815. The British under Gen. Packenham opened a battery of two 18 pounders on the Americans at New Orleans; it was silenced the same day. The Americans had a boat loaded with military stores sunk; 34 men killed and wounded, and two caissons blown up by rockets. Gen Thomas joined Gen. Jackson same day with 660 men from Baton Rouge.

1816. William Hillhouse died, aged 88; for more than 50 years a member of the council and legislature of Connecticut.

1817. Martin Henry Klaproth, a German chemist and philosopher, died. He was born at Wernigerode 1743 and followed the profession of an apothecary till 1788, when he became chemist to the Academy of Sciences at Berlin.

1817. The new Bank of the United States opened at Carpenter's hall, Philadelphia; Wm. Jones president, Jonathan Smith cashier.

1818. William Harrod, an eccentric bookseller in Leicestershire, died.

1823. The French language abolished in the law courts of Holland, where it had long been in use, and was prevalent in society.

1825. Great Britain acknowledged the independence of the South American republics.

1835. Charles Lamb died. He was the author of the beautiful stories of *Elia*, which are universally admired. His exquisite humor, fancy, feeling and wit, have given an endurable character to his essays. The bettering of the condition of mankind was his great aim, and he was in the esteem of every philanthropist.

1835. First daily paper in Buffalo, New York.

1837. Samuel Hulse died at Chelsea Hospital, England, of which he had been governor since 1820, aged 90. He entered the British army in the year 1761, and at the time of his death had been upwards of three quarters of a century in the military service, and was then field marshal.

1837. Saphet in the Holy Land nearly destroyed by an earthquake. It is said that this and a subsequent shock were both predicted by a Walachian almanac maker.

1848. Girard college opened with appropriate ceremonies at Philadelphia.

1848. The state of Maryland repudiated repudiation, and resumed payment of interest on her debt at the Chesapeake bank, Baltimore.

1852. Frederick Philips Robinson, an American officer, died, aged 89; he had been scarcely less than 75 years in the military ranks.

1854. Great fire at Constantinople destroyed 400 houses; among which were those of the Greek patriarch, and the patriarch of Jerusalem.

JANUARY 2.

17. Titus Livius died at Padua. His history of Rome, to which he devoted twenty years, rendered him so celebrated, that a Spaniard is said to have gone from Cadiz to Rome for the purpose merely of seeing him. His history was written in 140 books, of which only 35 are extant. Five of these were discovered at Worms 1731, and some fragments are said to have been since found at Herculaneum. Few particulars of his life are known, but his fame was great even while he lived, and his history has made him immortal.

17 Publius Ovidus Naso, the Roman poet, died in exile at Tomos (a town on the inhospitable coast of the Black sea), aged 60. He exhibited an unconquerable predilection for poetry, and the ease and the enjoyments of life, which his fortune placed within his power. He traveled in Greece and Asia which added to his accomplishments; his works were adapted to the public taste, and he was esteemed by the learned; Horace and Virgil were his friends, and he was a welcome visitor at the court of Augustus. Until his fiftieth year he appears to have lived almost solely for poetry and pleasure. He might have hoped to pass the remaining years of his life in peace, under the shadow of his laurels, but he was suddenly banished by Augustus, for some unknown cause. His *Metamorphoses*, and *Art of Love* are often republished in our language. He painted nature with a masterly hand, and his genius imparted elegance to vulgarity; but impurity defiles the sweetness of his numbers, and his finest productions are sullied with licentiousness.

1547. Conspiracy of Genoa, headed by John Lewis Fiesco; his being drowned in the night, occasioned the failure of the scheme, in the very moment of success.

1604. The Jesuits reinstated in France.

1731. A reprieve sent to a prisoner at Newgate on condition he would suffer Mr. Chiselden to make an experiment on the tympanum of his ear. The experiment was never performed.

1741. John Barber, printer to the city of London, and the first printer that rose to the rank of mayor, died.

1757. Calcutta retaken by the English and permitted to be fortified by the subah.

1758. The Whitefield methodists observed this day in thanksgiving for the victories of the king of Prussia in favor of England.

1759. The French surprised and captured Frankfort on the Maine.

1766. James Edward Francis Stuart, the Pretender, died. He was the eldest son of James II, born at London 1688. He was five months old when his father was dethroned, and the royal family fled to France. His elder sister Anne afterwards came to the throne, and some effort was made to secure his own succession; but it does not appear that he entered into the project with much spirit.

1771. Lewis Cæsar, count d'Estrees, marshal of France, and minister of state, died aged 76. He distinguished himself in the war against Spain, and afterwards in 1741, wherein his bravery was conspicuous and his services meritorious. In 1756 he was placed at the head of the French forces in Germany, but was superceded by Richelieu through intrigue.

1774. The coffin of Edward I opened by a deputation from the society of antiquarians, after it had been buried 467 years. In a coffin of yellow stone they found the royal body in perfect preservation, enclosed in two wrappers; one of them was gold tissue, strongly waxed and fresh; the other and outermost considerably decayed. The corpse was habited in a rich mantle of purple lined with white and adorned with ornaments of gilt metal, studded with red and blue stones and pearls. Two similar ornaments lay on the hands. The mantle was fastened on the right shoulder by a magnificent *fibula* of the same metal, with the same stones and pearls. His face had over it a silken covering, so fine, and so closely fitted to it, as to preserve the features entire. Round his temples was a gilt coronet of *fleur de lys*. In his hands, which were also entire, were two sceptres of gilt metal; that in the right surmounted by a cross fleure, that in the left by three clusters of oak leaves, and a dove on a globe. The feet enveloped in the mantle and other coverings were sound and the toes distinct. Its length was 6 feet 2 inches.

1777. Cannonading at Trenton; the British repulsed in their attempt to cross Sanpink creek bridge. In the night Gen. Washington retired leaving his fires burning.

1780. The Dutch admiral, Count Byland, refusing to permit the British admiral, Fielding, to search his convoy, an action ensued, and the Dutch ships, two of the line and two frigates, surrendered; after detaining seven of the convoy, the Dutch admiral had permission to proceed; but he refused without the whole of his charge, and therefore sailed into Spithead.

1788. Georgia ratified the Constitution of the United States, without amendment, being the fourth state to do so.

1795. JOSIAH WEDGEWOOD, the inventor of the scale that bears his name in the thermometer for determining the different degrees of metallic heat, died at his residence in England.

1801. JOHN GASPER CHRISTIAN LAVATER died. He was born at Zurich, in Switzerland, where his father was a physician of skill and reputation. In 1763 he traveled in Germany; in 1767 appeared as a poet; and in 1769 as a preacher of much popularity. All his activity was devoted to religion until he undertook his work on physiognomy. This great work in 4 vols. quarto, in which he had collected the features of distinguished persons from all parts of the world, made him known throughout Europe. He published several other works, and became so popular that his journeys resembled triumphs. On the capture of Zurich by Massena, he received a shot while assisting the wounded in the street, which although he lived more than a year, and wrote several works, was the cause of his death.

1809. Two French ships of war and eleven victualers, proceeding to Barcelona, were captured in the port of Caldagues by the British under Lord Cochrane.

1809. Penguin island, at the cape of Good Hope, sank, and is now only known to mariners by name.

1810. Orders were received from Paris by Murat, king of Naples, to seize and immediately dispose of all American vessels and cargoes.

1814. Dantzic surrendered to the duke of Wurtemberg.

1815. The prince regent of England extended the military order of Bath, and divided it into three classes, namely: 1. Knights grand crosses; 2. Knights commanders; 3. Companions.

1816. LOUIS BERNARD GUYTON DE MORVEAU, a French chemist, died. He was born at Dijon 1737, and distinguished himself in 1773 by the invention of the method of purifying the air by means of chlorine. He was an upright, able, eloquent and business man; and founded a school at Dijon for the study of his favorite science, chemistry. He was a member of the national assembly and convention at the time of the revolution, and assisted to establish the polytechnic school.

1827. JOHN MASON GOOD, an English physician, poet and philological writer, died. At the age of 15 he was apprenticed to a surgeon; in 1793 removed to London, and by talent and perseverance, succeeded in establishing both a literary and professional fame. He was a voluminous writer, and the extent and variety of his works evince the greatest industry, and a retentive and orderly mind. He acquired thirteen European and Asiatic languages, and at the time of his death had just completed a translation of the Psalms.

1829. Forty men and thirty horses destroyed by an explosion of fire damp in a mine near Lyons, France.

1831. BERTHOLD GEORGE NIEBUHR the historian, died. He was the son of Niebuhr the traveler, born at Copenhagen 1777, and finished his education at Edinburgh. He traveled much and received great attention wherever he went. In 1810 he delivered his lectures on Roman history at Berlin; and in 1815, on the death of his father, planned and published his biography. In 1827 he published the first volume of a remodeled edition of his Roman history; the second volume appeared a few months before his death, leaving the third unpublished.

1835. ROBERT HINDMARSH, the most distinguished among those who supported the religious views of Emanuel Swedenborg, died at Gravesend.

1837. JOHN CUFFEE, a negro slave, died at Norfolk, Va., at the remarkable age of about 120 years. He was a native of Africa, was sold as a slave in the island of Barbadoes, and brought to Norfolk about 1740.

1850. GEORGE BLATTERMAN, professor of modern languages in the Virginia university, died at Charlottesville.

1853. A new and stringent law against the liberty of the press was published in Spain.

1857. ANDREW URE, author of the *Dictionary of Arts*, died at London, aged 89.

JANUARY 3.

456. B. C. MYRONIDES the Athenian general defeated the Bœotians at Enophyta.

106. B. C. Birthday of MARCUS TULLIUS CICERO, the Roman orator.

1641. JEREMIAH HORROX, an English astronomer, died. He seems to have been the first to observe the transit of Venus over the sun's disc, from which he deduced many useful observations, though not aware of the full importance of that phenomenon.

1661. Secretary PEPYS seeing the comedy of the *Beggars' Bush* performed at Lincoln Inn Fields, says: "And here the first time that ever I saw women upon the stage."

1670. GEORGE MONK, duke of Albemarle, died. He entered the British army at an early age; and in 1639 was engaged in the unfortunate expedition of Charles I against the Scots. He was confined three years in the Tower under the parliament, during which he wrote a work on military and political affairs; but finally accepted a commission in the republican army against the Irish, the Scotch and the Dutch. But at the death of the Protector he employed his influence to reinstate the Stuarts. In 1666 he was again employed against the son of his old antagonist Tromp, in which the English fleet was much damaged, and both claimed the victory.

1717. LAMBERT BOSS, an eminent Dutch philologist, died. He was born in Friesland 1670; studied under his father who was a clergyman, became private tutor in a family of rank, and subsequently professor of Greek in the university of Franeker. He was an indefatigible student, and regretted every moment which could not be devoted to his favorite pursuit. The number and character of his works mark his industry.

1724. PHILIP V of Spain abdicated the throne in favor of his son Louis; but he dying the same year, Philip resumed the crown again.

1730. The Turks began to learn the art of war and fortification after the European model, from Count Bonneval of France, who became a Musselman.

1777. Battle of Princeton, N. J., between the British and a division of the American army. under General Washington. The British lost 100 men, and 300 more who had taken refuge in the college, were forced to surrender.

1795. JOSIAH WEDGEWOOD died. His father was a Staffordshire potter, to whose business he succeeded, and soon distinguished himself by his discoveries and improvements, insomuch that in a few years England, instead of importing the finer earthen wares, was enabled to supply her neighbors. He was a scientific, as well as an active and enterprising man—and benevolent withal.

1797. Three of the large stones in the antique pile at Stonehenge in England fell, the smallest of which weighed 20 tons. They were loosed, it was supposed, by the severe frost of that season.

1805. CHARLES TOWNLEY, an English antiquarian, died. He employed his liberal fortune in the collection of rare manuscripts and relics of ancient art, and died at the age of 68, bequeathing his collection of antiquities to the British Museum.

1805. ALEXANDER WEDDERBURN, lord of Rosslyn, died. He distinguished himself as a lawyer, and was appointed solicitor general in 1771, in which office he is *remarkable* for having insulted Franklin in arguing on American affairs before the privy council. He joined the administration under Pitt, in 1793, and succeeded Lord Thurlow as chancellor; from which office he retired in 1801, with the title of Earl of Rosslyn. He is the author of a work on the management of prisons.

1815. British frigate Junon, Capt. C. Upton, captured the American privateer Guerrier, of 4 guns and 60 men, from Portsmouth, N. H.

1844. LEVI HEDGE, author of a treatise on logic and editor of an improved abridgment of Dr. Brown's *Lectures on the Philosophy of Mind*, died at Cambridge, England.

1847. JOHN SHEPHERD, a soldier of the revolution, died at Royalton, Ohio, aged 119.

1853. The Pantheon in Paris reopened as the church of St. Genevieve.

JANUARY 4.

100. TITUS, disciple of St. Paul, died at Crete.

1569. Burial of ROGER ASCHAM, at St. Sepulchre's, London. He was a man of learning, and author of numerous works, among others, *The Schoolmaster*.

1649. Some barrels of gunpowder exploded and destroyed 60 houses in Tower street, London. A child in its cradle was found alive and unhurt on the roof of Barking church.

1689. Col. HENRY SLOUGHTER appointed govenor of New York.

1698. The palace, except the banqueting house, of White-hall palace, in England, destroyed by fire.

1707. LOUIS WILLIAM I, marquis of Baden-Baden, died. He was born at Paris 1655, where his mother wished to educate him; but his father and grandfather stole him away at the age of three months, that he might pass his childhood among the people whom he was destined to govern. He served his first campaign under Montellucco against Turenne. He was in Vienna when that city was besieged by the Turks, and subsequently commanded against the Turks in the Danube. He was one of the greatest generals of his time; made 26 campaigns, commanded at 25 sieges, fought at 13 battles, yet was never really defeated.

1753. The first number of *The World* appeared, conducted by Coleman, Bonnel, Thornton, Chesterfield, and others.

1762. England declared war against Spain.

1773. The town meeting of Petersham, Mass., adopted a kind of manifesto of grievances, drafted by Josiah Quincy and signed by Sylvanus How.

1775. A circular letter from the British secretary of state was addressed to the governor of the several colonies, forbidding the election of delegates to the congress proposed to be held in May. The order was disregarded, and the country has not been without its annual sessions of congress since 1774.

1778. The British, under Col. Campbell, landed at the mouth of Savannah river, Ga., and defeated the Americans under Gen. Robert Howe. They took the city of Savannah, together with 38 officers, 415 privates, 48 cannons, 23 mortars, the fort, amunition and stores, the shipping in the river, and a large quantity of provisions.

1781. British ship Courageux, Capt. Phipps, captured in one hour the French frigate Minerva 32 guns. Minerva had 50 killed, 23 wounded; Courageux 10 killed, 7 wounded.

1784. Treaty signed between the United States and Great Britain; by which the latter relinquished her right to the sovreignty of the revolted colonies.

1789. THOMAS NELSON, a signer of the Declaration of Independence, died. He was born at York, Va., 1738. His father was an opulent merchant and sent him to England for an education. He returned 1761, and in 1774 had become a statesman of some note. Three years afterwards he was appointed brigadier general and commander in chief of the Virginia forces, and in 1781 succeeded Jefferson as governor of the state. His services elicited the public thanks of Washington.

1793. The Alien bill passed in the British parliament. During the debate on this measure the great Burke threw upon the floor a Sheffield dagger to enforce his oratory.

1795. The French crossed the Waal near Bommel, and took possession of Tiel. They also captured Rosas and 540 of the garrison.

1796. Message from Gen. Washington to congress, accompanied by the French flag presented by the committee of public safety, which was deposited among the archives.

1804. CHARLOTTE LENOX, the popular author of the *Female Quixotte*, &c., died.

1814. JOHN GEORGE JACOBI, a German poet, died. He was the son of a wealthy merchant; studied theology; became professor of theology and eloquence at Halle, where he published a periodical for the ladies called the *Iris*. He was afterwards connected with several periodicals. His works are published in 7 vols.

1825. FERDINAND IV of Naples died. The life of this prince is remarkable for the uncommon length of his reign, and its many vicissitudes, embracing a period of 65 years, and being closely connected with all the great events of Europe during the last half century. He was born 1751, and came to the throne at the age of eight. The first thirty years of his reign were attended with peace and happiness; but in 1798 the country was invaded by Bonaparte, before whom Ferdinand fled to Sicily: and afterwards in 1820 the Carbonari effected a revolution which again banished the royal family. The interposition of the Austrians, however, restored the ancient order of things, which continued till the death of the king, four years after.

1827. JAMES CHAMBERS, an eccentric poet, died in misery at a farm-house in Stratbroke, England. From the age of 16 to 70 he wandered about the country, gaining a precarious subsistence by selling his own effusions, of which he had a number printed in a cheap form. His compositions were mostly suggested to him by his muse, during the stillness of the night while reposing in some friendly barn or hay-loft. When so inspired, he would arise and commit the effusion to paper. He continued through life in hopeless poverty, and was a lonely man and a wanderer, who had neither act nor part in the common ways of the world.

1835. Thermometer 40 deg. below zero, at Lebanon, N. Y., the mercury becoming solid. It was severely cold throughout the United States.

1843. STEVEN THOMPSON MASON, formerly governor of Michigan, died at New York, aged 31.

1845. BENJAMIN RUSSELL, chiefly known as the conductor of the *Columbian Centinel*, died at Boston.

1849. SAMUEL JENKINS, a negro died at Lancaster, aged 115. He drove his master's provision wagon over the Alleganies in Braddock's expedition, and was supposed to be the last survivor of that expedition.

1849. The town of Moultan in India, after a long siege was taken by the British, but with great loss.

1852. ELIOT WALBURTON, an author of considerable note, perished in the Amazon steamship, on his way from Southampton to the West Indies.

1853. Mr. INGERSOLL, the American envoy to England, was feted by the chamber of commerce at Liverpool.

1854. Albion college, Michigan, destroyed by fire.

1856. JEAN PIERRE DAVID, a celebrated French sculptor, died at Paris, aged 65.

JANUARY 5.

62. B. C. LUCIUS SERGIUS CATILINE, the Roman conspirator, killed in Etruria. The history of his life unfolds a series of most revolting crimes; but there is reason to believe that some of them are unreal. Murder, rapine and conflagration were the

first pleasures of his life. Pompey, Crassus and Cæsar favored his schemes with a view to their own aggrandizement. Only two Romans remained determined to uphold their falling country—Cato and Cicero. The speeches of the latter in the Roman senate on the crisis of affairs are imperishable monuments of eloquence and patriotism, and produced the overthrow of the conspirators. Five of them were put to death, and Catiline being surrounded by the army under Petreius resolved to die sword in hand. The battle was fought with desperation, and the insurgents fell, with their leader at their head.

1066. Edward the Confessor, king of England, died. He was called to the throne 1041. He was not the immediate heir, but his claim was supported of Godwin, earl of Kent, whose daughter Editha he married. He was a weak and superstitious prince, and acquired the title of *Saint* or *Confessor*, by abstaining from nuptial connection with his queen. He was the first English monarch who undertook to cure the *king's-evil* by touching the patient. With him ended the Saxon line of kings.

1477. Charles the Bold, duke of Burgundy, killed in battle on this or the following day. This prince, the son of Philip the Good and Isabella of Portugal, early displayed a violent, impetuous and ambitious disposition; and in after life was constantly embroiled in unjust and cruel warfare, in which he performed many daring exploits. But having turned his arms against the Swiss, the fortune of war turned against him; and being deserted by his allies, with his usual temerity risked a battle with only 4000 men against a vastly superior force, was defeated and killed by the thrust of a lance in the 44th year of his age. His body covered with blood and mire, and his head imbedded in the ice, was not found till two days after the battle, when it was so disfigured that his own brother did not recognize it. With him expired the feudal government of Burgundy.

1531. The electoral college assembled at Rome and elected Ferdinand, brother of Charles V, king of the Romans. He was crowned a few days after at Aix-la-Chapelle.

1536. Catharine of Arragon, the repudiated queen of Henry VIII, died. She was the youngest daughter of Ferdinand and Isabella, born 1483. She was first married to Arthur, prince of Wales, who died five months after; and the king unwilling to return her dowry caused her to be contracted to his remaining son, Henry. The prince, at the age of 15, made a public protest against this proceeding, but finally consented to the match. Notwithstanding the inequality of their ages and the capricious disposition of the king, they had been married 20 years when the division took place. This separation led to a divorce from the pope also, and was the cause of mighty effects.

1559. Catharine de Medicis died. She was born at Florence 1519; married, 1533, the dauphin, afterwards Henry II, of France. She was three times regent of France, and during her administration made a conspicuous figure in the annals of Europe by her political genius. By her was begun the palace of the Tuilleries; but the lasting monument of her fame and iniquity is the massacre of St. Bartholomew's, which was brought about by her intrigues, when more than 50,000 protestants were massacred in one day.

1621. Paul Van Somer died in London. He was born at Antwerp, 1576, and arrived at great proficiency as a painter. His pencil was chiefly employed on portraits of royal and eminent personages, and is said to have equalled Vandyke.

1639. De Vries, who had recently arrived from Holland in the capacity of a patroon, sent his colonists over to Staten island from fort Amsterdam, to commence the colony and buildings.

1675. Turenne defeated the imperialists at Turkheim.

1705. Second volcanic opening of the peak of Teneriffe, in the ravine of Almerchiga, a league from Icore. It closed on the 13th of the same month.

1722. Bell, the Traveler, arrived at Moscow on the return from China. (See July 14, 1719.) The account of this journey, and of what he saw and learned at Pekin, is the most valuable part of his book, and one of the best and most interesting relations ever written by any traveler.

1724. Czartan Petrarch died, aged 184, at a village near Temeswar, in Hungary. He was born in the year 1539; and at the time the Turks took Temeswar from the Christians he was employed in keeping his father's cattle. A few days before his death he had walked with the help of a stick to the post house to ask charity of the travelers. His hair and beard were of a greenish-white color, like mouldy bread; and he had a few of his teeth remaining, and enjoyed a little eyesight. His son, who was ninety-seven years of age, declared that his father had married at an extreme age, for the third time, and that he was born in this last marriage. He had descendants in the fifth generation, with whom he sometimes sported, carrying them in his arms. His son, though ninety-seven, was still fresh and vigorous. The commandant of Temeswar on learning of his sickness, caused his portrait to be painted, and it was nearly finished when he expired.

1757. Damiens attempted the assassination of Louis XV, for which he was condemned to the most cruel tortures, and finally quartered by four horses. (See March 28.)

1764. A comet was first seen at Tewkesbury, England, near two small stars in the hand of Bootes.

1776. The New Hampshire provincial convention resolved to change the form of government.

1781. Arnold invaded Virginia with 1500 British troops; he marched to Richmond, destroyed the public stores and buildings, the rope-walk, and much private property.

1781. The British ship Warwick, Capt. Elphinstone, captured the Dutch ship Rotterdam, 50 guns and 300 men; the first material capture during that war.

1782. Trincomalee in the island of Ceylon, taken by the British under admiral Sir Edward Hughes.

1783. Onore, situated between Panian and Bombay, taken by assault by the British Gen. Matthews; the garrison and many of the inhabitants were cruelly slaughtered.

1795. The French attacked the British Gen. Dundas at Geldermalsem, and compelled him to fall back to Buren; and afterwards the whole force of Gen. Walmoden to cross the Leck.

1795. The British ships Bellona and Alarm captured the French ship Le Dumas of 20 guns, off Deseada.

1796. Samuel Huntington, one of the signers of the Declaration of Independence, died. He was born at Windham, Ct., 1732; his father being a farmer could allow him only a common school education; but his own assiduity made up the deficiency, so that at the age of 22 he commenced the study of the law with borrowed books; in 1764 he was sent to the general assembly; 1765 appointed king's attorney; 1774 raised to the bench of the supreme court; 1775 sent a delegate to the general congress of the colonies, and in 1779 succeeded John Jay as president of congress. At the time of his death he was governor of Connecticut.

1797. British ship Polyphemus, Capt. Lumesdaine, captured the French ship L'Uranie, 38 guns, off Ireland.

1798. A bill passed the house in congress paying Kosciusko $12,800; and the four daughters of count de Grasse $400 each per annum for five years.

1799. Treaty of defensive alliance between England and Turkey.

1806. Breslaw surrendered to the French under Vandamme; Lieut. Gen. De Thile, Maj. Gen. Krafti and 5500 Prussians taken.

1807. British sloop Nautilus, Capt. Palmer, lost on a rock near Peri, in the archipelago of the Seven islands. The captain refused to leave the vessel, and was lost in his 26th year.

1809. The British rear guard under Sir John Moore attacked by the French van guard under Soult. Gen. Colbert, aged 30, was mortally wounded, and the French were compelled to fall back.

1812. The French Gen. Leval was compelled to abandon the siege of Tariffa, defended by the British, Col. Skerritt.

1814. Gluckstadt surrendered to the British.

1814. British ships Bacchante and Saracen captured the fortress of Cattaro after a cannonade of ten days.

1827. Frederick, duke of York, died. He was the second son of George III, born in 1763; 1787 took his seat in the house of peers; 1789 fought a duel, firing his pistol in the air; 1791 married the eldest daughter of the king of Prussia, from whom he afterwards separated; 1793 went to Flanders at the head of the British army, and in the end showed himself unequal to the station; 1809 was called to account by the house of commons for the follies committed in the army through the influence of a female favorite; 1818 was appointed the *keeper of his father*, with a salary of £10,000. Although enjoying princely salaries and pensions he died universally lamented by his tailors and other creditors to the amount of some hundred thousands of pounds.

1841. James Abraham Hillhouse, an eminent American poet, died at New Haven, Ct., aged 51.

1845. The national debt of England amounted at this time to £794,193,645.

1849. The discovery of the magnetic clock by Dr. Locke of Ohio, announced to the secretary of the navy by Lieutenant Maury of the National observatory.

1852. Eugene Levesque died at Paris, aged 81; author of travels in America.

1852. Benjamin La Rochi died at Paris, aged 54; French translator of Shakespeare.

1852. Baron Kemenyi, a Hungarian chief, eminent for his patriotism and exploits in the struggle with Austria and Russia, died aged 53.

1853. Charles W. Morgan, an American commodore, died, aged 63. He was a nephew of Gen. Morgan of the revolution, and distinguished himself in the action between the Constitution and the Guerriere.

1853. Revolution in Mexico; Gen. Arista resigned, and Cevallos elected president ad interim.

1854. The steamer San Francisco, which had withstood a heavy gale, was foundered at sea. Of 700 persons on board 247 had been washed overboard before assistance arrived.

1855. Gen. CASTILLA defeated Pres. Echenique and entered Lima in triumph.

1855. The entire Victoria bridge across the St. Lawrence, carried away by the ice.

JANUARY 6.

1402. Birthday of JOAN OF ARC.

1540. HENRY VIII married Anne, daughter of John, duke of Cleves. This was his fourth wife. He had asked her hand in marriage after having seen a portrait of her by Holbein; and becoming disgusted with her in six months bestowed upon her the epithet of *Flanders mare*, and sent her home. She retired, not much disconcerted, to her own country, where she died 1557.

1649. ANNE OF AUSTRIA, queen regent of France, obliged to fly from Paris to St. Germain.

1698. Birthday of METASTASIO, the celebrated Italian poet.

1711. CHRISTOPHER BATEMAN, a noted English bookseller, died. He suffered none to open a book in his shop till it was bought.

1724. The bishop of London preached a sermon against masquerades, which produced a decree that no more than six masquerades, the number already subscribed for, should be held.

1725. Pope BENEDICT XIII, in great state and measured ceremony, opened with a golden hammer the *holy gates* of the four great churches which had been shut 25 years, for obtaining indulgences, &c.

1734. JOHN DENNIS, an English dramatist and critic, died. He was the son of a saddler, born in London 1657, and liberally educated. His first play appeared in 1697, and was followed by many dramatic pieces and poems which were sufficiently worthless to procure their author an imperishable notoriety in the *Dunciad*, where Pope has gibbeted him. He squandered a fortune which had been left him by an uncle, and not being able to subsist by his pamphlets and criticisms for the magazines, depended upon his friends for a living; and even those whom he had made his enemies joined in the benefit for him at the Haymarket theatre, after he had become blind and partially insane. One of his plays, which was condemned, is famous for a new kind of thunder introduced in it; a few nights after its representation, the players made use of the contrivance in Macbeth, when the author rose in the pit and with an oath claimed it as his thunder. His *thunder* is said to be that still used in the theatres.

1738. JEAN BAPTIST LABAT, a missionary and traveler, died. He was born at Paris 1663, and became a Dominican priest in Norway, where he taught mathematics and philosophy also. In 1693 he embarked for Martinique as a missionary; and during several voyages in service of the mission, visited all the Antilles. When the English attacked the island of Guadaloupe, he rendered his country important services as an engineer. He afterwards traveled much in Europe, and published his travels. His voyage to the West Indies has been translated into several languages, and is a truly scientific work.

1763. Unsuccessful and very disastrous attack by two English ships on Buenos Ayres. The commodore and nearly 300 of the crew were drowned.

1766. The wild man PETER taken in the Hartz forest and presented to George II, was brought from Cheshunt and shewn to George III and his queen. Like Shakspeare's Caliban, he could bring wood and water but not articulate any language.

1777. The American army, under Gen. Washington, went into winter quarters at Morristown, N. J.

1781. ARNOLD detached Lieut. Col. Simcoe, from Richmond to Westham, Va., who destroyed the cannon foundry and a quantity of public stores which had been removed from Richmond.

1785. The Halsewell, East Indiaman, Capt. Richard Pearce, wrecked on the island of Purbeck; of 240 persons but 74 were saved.

1794. The duke of Brunswick resigned his command as generalissimo of the coalition against France.

1795. French frigate La Pique, 33 guns, captured off Marigalante by the British frigate Blanche, Capt. Faulkner, who was shot through the heart; also 7 of his crew killed and 21 wounded. La Pique had 76 killed, 113 wounded, and 30 were lost when her mast went overboard.

1810. JAMES RICHARD DACRES died of a fall from his horse. He was vice-admiral of the Red, and father of the Capt. Dacres captured by Hull.

1813. ALEXANDER issued his ukase at Wilna, directing the foundation stone of a new church to be instantly laid in Moscow, dedicated to *Christ our Savior*, as a perpetual monument to future generations of the deliverance of Russia from the French, and the devotion of his people.

1816. FRANCIS NORODSKY, a Polish gentleman, died at Warsaw, aged 125. The Polish government allowed him a pension of 3000 florins, which the emperor Alexander continued till his death.

1817. General THOMAS died, at Milledgeville, Georgia, of cancer in the mouth.

1823. The siege of Missolonghi raised. Mavrocordato, the commander in chief, had thrown himself into the town on the 5th of November with 380 men, and 22 Suliots under Marco Botzaris, and though almost destitute of artillery and ammunition, defended it against the Turkish forces. On the 23d November it was relieved by sea, and the enemy were repulsed in several assaults, when they finally abandoned the walls.

1831. Died at Geneva, RODOLPHE KREUTZER, a distinguished violinist and musical composer.

1836. ABRAHAM VAN VECHTEN died at Albany, aged 75. He was a highly respected man, an eminent lawyer, and one of the fathers of the New York bar.

1839. A tremendous gale or hurricane in the west of England, which did great damage at Liverpool.

1840. Madame D'ARBLAY, the well known novelist, Miss Burney, died at Bath. Lord Chancellor Thurlow said her *Cecilia* was worth all the books in his library.

1841. Great freshet in the Hudson river and tributaries.

1849. GEORGE SINNET, a native of Germany, the last survivor of Gen. Wolfe's army, died at Brighton, Nova Scotia, aged 120.

1854. Russians defeated at Citale, near Kalafat, with a loss of 2500 men.

JANUARY 7.

1328. EDWARD II of England deposed by parliament, and his son, Edward III, proclaimed king.

1558. Calais, in France, retaken by the French after a short siege of one week, having been in the possession of the English 200 years, during which it had become a thriving place, and the seat of a considerable trade in wool.

1610. GALILEI discovered the satellites of Jupiter.

1657. THEOPHILUS EATON, first governor of the colony at New Haven, died. Before coming to America he was employed by the king as an agent at the court of Denmark. He was one of the original patentees of Massachusetts. On the settlement of New Haven he was chosen governor, for which office his integrity, dignity and wisdom peculiarly fitted him, and which he filled till his death.

1681. The commons of England resolved that till a bill be passed, excluding the duke of York from the throne, no supplies could be granted without danger to the state.

1692. The philosophical ROBERT BOYLE died leaving a sum of money for a monthly sermon against atheism.

1715. FRANCOIS DE SALIGNAC DE LA MOTTE FENELON, died. He preached his first sermon at the age of 15; and he was distinguished for learning and piety. The celebrated romance, *Telemaque*, was published against his will by the treachery of his servant, and involved him in difficulties with the king, who considered it a satire upon his reign. During the revolution of 1793 his coffin was dug up to furnish lead for bullets. In 1819 a monument was erected to his memory by public subscription, and in 1826 a statue by the sculptor David was placed at Cambray. The age in which he lived could not appreciate his worth.

1740. A rock fell on a large number of young people while at play on the first Monday of the year, at Kirkaldy, Scotland.

1758. ALLAN RAMSAY, a Scottish poet and author of the *Gentle Shepherd*, died.

1767. THOMAS CLAP, an American mathematician and natural philosopher, died. He graduated at Harvard college, and by singular industry made great acquisitions in almost every branch of learning. In 1739 he was elected president of Yale college, and continued in that office till the year before his death. He constructed the first orrery in America.

1779. LAFAYETTE embarked at Boston, in the frigate Alliance, for France.

1779. *The Mirror*, appeared at Edinburgh, to which Mackenzie the novelist was a principal contributor.

1782. The Bank of North America opened for business in Philadelphia. It was the first bank regularly established in America.

1785. Mr. BLANCHARD, the æronaut, accompanied by Mr. Jeffries, an American gentleman, made the bold attempt to cross the British channel, from Dover to Calais, in a balloon filled with inflammable air, then beginning to be used. They left the English coast at 10 o'clock, and at half-past two, reached the French side, a distance of twenty-three miles.

1798. The French army under General Menard, entered Switzerland with a design to revolutionize the cantons after the model of the French republic.

1806. PAULINUS, better known as John Philip Werdin, died at Rome. He was one of the first Europeans who acquired a knowledge of the Sanscrit language.

1807. British order in council prohibiting neutrals from trading from one port of France or her allies to another, or to any other where Great Britain was refused that privilege.

1811. Ship Rapid, of Boston, Capt. Dorr, with $280,000 on board, totally lost off the coast of New Holland; captain and crew saved.

1812. Joseph Dennie, an American editor, died. He was born at Boston 1768, and educated for the bar; but his literary taste and habits interfered with his profession, which he resigned and established at Boston a weekly paper called *The Tablet;* and subsequently edited the *Farmers' Museum* at Walpole, in which he published a series of popular essays under the signature of The Lay Preacher. He was afterwards editor of the *Port Folio* at Philadelphia, where his superior endowments would have procured him an independence, but for some unfortunate propensities which deprived him of health and happiness.

1817. First paper in Chautauque co., N.Y.

1822. Liberia in Africa colonized under the direction of Dr. Ayres. Cape Montserado with a large tract of adjoining country was purchased of the natives by the American colonization society, and a ettlement commenced by 28 colonists; in six years the number had increased to 1200 under the care of Ashmun.

1830. Thomas Lawrence, a distinguished English portrait painter, died. By industry and force of talent he rose in his profession, till on the death of Sir Joshua Reynolds he was made painter to the king, and in 1815 was knighted. His income for the last twenty years of his life was from 10,000 to 20,000 pounds; but he died poor, owing to his purchasing the best productions at the most extravagant prices.

1841. Louis Edward Bignon, Napoleon Bonaparte's historian, died.

1843. Mrs. Wingate, died at Stratham, N. H., aged nearly 101 years.

1850. John H. Kyan, a native of England, and inventor of Kyanized wood, died at New York.

1850. Samuel Miller, an eminent American theologian and sometime president of Princeton college, died, aged 91.

JANUARY 8.

1167. Edgar, king of Scotland, died, and was succeeded by his younger brother, Alexander I.

1536. Catharine of Arragon, died; queen of Henry VIII and mother of Mary, queen of England.

1642. Galileo Galilei, the astronomer, died, aged 78.

1676. French Admiral Duquesne defeated the Dutch and Spanish fleets under De Ruyter, who had both legs shattered.

1704. Laurentio Bellini, a Florentine anatomist, died, aged 61. He was held in great estimation by prince and pontiff. His theory and practice are out of date now, and his works also, in consequence of the vast improvements in medicine and surgery since his day.

1775. John Baskerville, an English printer and type founder, of rare celebrity, died. As a philanthropist he was also well known to large circles.

1777. British evacuated Elizabethtown, N. J.; Gen. Maxwell fell on their rear, and took 70 prisoners and a schooner loaded with baggage.

1780. British Admiral Rodney captured 22 sail of Spanish ships. One of these, the Guipuscaio, of 64 guns, was named the Prince William, from a son of George III who was in the action.

1784. Whitestown, N. Y., settled about this time.

1795. French ship Esperance, 22 guns, captured off Cape Henry by British ship Argonaut, Capt. Ball.

1796. Samuel Huntingdon, governor of Connecticut, and one of the signers of the Declaration of Independence, died aged 64.

1796. French took by surprise the British camp at Mount William, island of St. Vincent, West Indies. British lost 54 killed, Brig. Gen. Strutt and 109 wounded, and 200 missing.

1799. French privateer cutter La Rancune, from St. Maloes, captured by the British cutter Pigmy, Capt. Shepheard, who at the same time recaptured two British brigs, prizes to La Rancune.

1815. Battle of New Orleans. The city was attacked by the British under Packenham, consisting of 15,000 disciplined troops, and was defended by 6000 militia and volunteers, under Gen. Jackson, prepared to die in its defence. The result was a brilliant victory over the British. Packenham was killed, and 5,000 men surrendered—the rest fled to their vessels. The loss of the Americans was trifling, 13 killed and wounded, that of the British 2,600.

1815. Total loss of the Americans in this war up to the last battle, 1344 killed, 2673 wounded, 651 missing, 1351 taken prisoners.

1817. Two shocks of earthquake at Charleston, S. C., and at Savannah, Ga.

1825. Eli Whitney, inventor of the cotton gin, died.

1848. The lives of thirty persons lost by the bursting of the boilers of the steamer Blue Ridge on the Ohio river. The boilers had been in use nine years.

1849. The pope threatened all who should take part in electing a new assembly, with excommunication.

1850. First ship in the United States dry dock at Brooklyn.

1853. CHARLES HUMPHREY ATHERTON, an eminent New Hampshire lawyer, died, aged 79.

1854. WILLIAM CARR BERRESFORD, a distinguished British field officer and nobleman, died, aged 85.

1854. Metropolitan hall and Lafarge hotel, two of the finest buildings in New York destroyed by fire.

JANUARY 9.

1514. ANNE OF BRETAGNE, queen of France died, aged 37.

1584. WILLIAM CARTER, a daring London printer, hanged, boweled, and quartered at Tyburn, for printing lewd pamphlets, popish and others, and particularly a *Treatise on Schisme.*

1596. FRANCIS DRAKE, the English navigator, died. He served with distinction under his relative Sir J. Hawkins; and having lost all his property in an action with the Spaniards, he conceived an inveterate hatred against them. He signalized himself in the destruction of the Spanish Armada; and finally died on the coast of America in a war against the Spanish settlements. He made the first voyage round the world. To him is attributed the introduction of the potatoe into Europe. The day of his death is differently stated.

1621. The Plymouth colonists commenced the erection of their projected town, which they built in two rows of houses for greater security. The same street still exists, leading to the water side.

1658. Birthday of NICHOLAS COUSTON, a famous French sculptor, from whose labors the art of statuary received a noble impulse. He died at Paris 1733.

1757. BERNARD LE BOVIER DE FONTENELLE, a French author of great repute, died. He was born at Rouen 1657; his mother was the sister of Corneille. Although his works are now obsolete in consequence of the advancement of science, no learned man exerted a more decided influence on the age in which he lived than Fontenelle.

1766. THOMAS BIRCH, an English historian and biographer, died. He was of quaker parentage, and by unwearied industry educated himself. His literary labors were prodigious, which early rising and a strict economy of time enabled him to perform. He bequeathed his library to the British museum; it contained an incredible number of MSS. in his own handwriting.

1770. CATHARINE TALBOT, authoress of *Reflections on the Seven Days of the Week*, and a contributor to the *Rambler*, died.

1779. JOHN REINHOLD FOSTER, author of *Northern Voyages*, and who circumnavigated the globe, with Cook died in his 70th year.

1788. Connecticut, the fifth state which adopted the constitution of the United States without amendments.

1792. Treaty of peace signed at Jassy between Russia and Turkey.

1793. MR. BLANCHARD, the French æronaut, made the first balloon ascension in the United States, at Philadelphia, in the presence of General Washington.

1795. Thiel in Holland taken by the French under Macdonald.

1799. The habeas corpus act suspended in Great Britain.

1805. NOBLE WIMBERLY JONES, a revolutionary character, died. He came to America under Gen. Oglethorpe, and at the breaking out of the war was a practicing physician in Savannah. He was elected to the Georgia legislature a number of years and then resumed his practice again, at the solicitation of many of his former patients.

1809. Congress passed laws to enforce the embargo.

1810. The Diocesan court of the officiality of Paris pronounced a nullity of marriage between Bonaparte and Josephine.

1811. The Spanish cortes published a manifesto declaring their determination not to enter into a treaty with Bonaparte until his troops should have entirely evacuated the Peninsula.

1811. The whole militia of New Orleans ordered into immediate service by Gov. Claiborne to suppress a negro insurrection.

1812. Valentia in Spain surrendered to the French under Suchet, with 374 cannons, 18000 troops and stores of all kinds.

1813. British manifesto against the United States.

1815. Truce between Gen. Jackson and Gen. Lambert to bury the dead of the battle of the previous day.

1815. The British began the bombardment of the American fort St. Philip, defended by Major Overton, which was kept up daily until the 17th.

1815. A society instituted at Trenton, N. J., for forming a colony of blacks.

1818. OLD JOHN died. During eighty years, from the premiership of Walpole to that of Liverpool, he acted as messenger in the Royal printing office, London. He styled himself King's messenger.

1827. ELIZABETH OGILVY BENGER, an English authoress, died. In her 13th year she wrote a poem, and afterwards attempted the drama. Her reputation is based upon her *Historical Biographies*, which were originally published in 10 vols.

1828. FRANCIS DE NEUFCHATEAU, a French statesman, died. He was born 1750, and in his 13th year published a volume of poems, which indicated more for the future than was realized. He took part in the affairs of the revolution, but was condemned for his moderation. Napoleon took him into favor; his pursuits were chiefly literary, however.

1843. Great fire at Port-au-Prince; 600 houses burnt and property to an immense amount destroyed. The blacks who inhabited the mountains rushed down and completed the work of destruction, by firing and plundering such houses as the fire had not reached, and committing every sort of excess.

1854. The Astor library in New York opened to the public.

JANUARY 10.

1640. MAURICE ABBOT, a distinguished London merchant, died. He acquired great consequence by his own efforts in commercial affairs, and was employed in 1624 in establishing the settlement of Virginia. At the time of his death he was mayor of London.

1645. WILLIAM LAUD, archbishop of Canterbury, beheaded on Tower hill, aged 70. Sentenced to be hung for political misdemeanors, he was pardoned by the king; but parliament overruled the pardon, and substituted the *privilege* of being beheaded instead of hanging. He acquired so great an ascendency over Charles as to lead him, by the facility of his temper, into a conduct which proved fatal to that prince, and by which he lost his kingdom, and met the same fate four years after at Whitehall.

1661. A proclamation issued by the king of England prohibiting conventicles for religious meetings.

1661. The fifth monarchy men, headed by Venner, a wine cooper, arose to proclaim "King Jesus against all the powers of the earth." But King Charles's power was found too strong for them.

1754. EDWARD CAVE died, an English printer and founder of the *Gentleman's Magazine*. When his indentures expired as a printer's apprentice, he was employed in the post office, and occupied his leisure in writing for the newspapers. In 1731 was first published the Magazine, and it has continued to this day, more than a century, amid the crowd of magazines which have perished around it; and is one of the most successful and lucrative periodicals that history has upon record.

1756. FRANCOIS, marquis de Beauharnois, died at Paris. He was a member of the national assembly, and took part in the king's favor; subsequently joined the army under Conde; and was banished by Napoleon in 1807. The heroic wife of Lavalette was his daughter.

1757. The British under Admiral Watson took by assault, Houghley, situated about thirty miles above Calcutta.

1761. EDWARD BOSCAWEN, the English admiral, died. He was born 1711, and entered the navy at an early age. He acquired honorable distinction under Vernon, and afterwards signalized himself in many important contests with the French, in which he had the singular fortune to take the French commander, M. Hoquait, a prisoner three times, viz. in 1744, 1747 and 1755. On his return to England in 1759, after destroying the Toulon fleet in the Mediterranean, he was rewarded with a pension of £3000 a year.

1763. CASPER ABEL, a voluminous German historian and antiquary, died.

1765. Stamp Act passed the British Parliament. How little did that body anticipate the consequences that were to follow their decision on that subject.

1776. The New Hampshire convention dissolved itself and assumed legislative powers, chose twelve counselors as an executive branch, and delegates to Congress, which were recognized.

1782. GEORGE COSTARD died. A classical, mathematical and oriental scholar, whose reputation as an author is chiefly derived from a *History of Astronomy*, highly appreciated in Europe.

1791. Vermont, the last of the thirteen original states which composed the Union, adopted the constitution and took her place in the confederacy.

1795. The French frigate Iphigenie, 32 guns, captured by the Spanish fleet off Catalonia.

1797. French sloop Atalante, 16 guns, captured off Scilly by the British frigate Phœbe, 36 guns, Capt. Barlow.

1800. The first soup establishment for the poor was opened at Spitalfields, London.

1806. The Dutch surrendered the cape of Good Hope to the British.

1808. PHILLIPS COSBY, British admiral of the Red, died aged 78.

1809. Samana taken by the British, together with two privateers, and four vessels laden with coffee.

1812. London involved for several hours in impenetrable darkness. The sky, where any light pervaded it, showed the aspect of bronze. It was the effect of a cloud of smoke, which, from the peculiar state of the atmosphere, did not pass off. Were it not for the peculiar mobility of the atmosphere, this city of a hundred thousand chimneys would be scarcely habitable in winter.

1815. The British under Gen. Lambert having abandoned the enterprise on New Orleans began to re-embark their artillery and munitions, prepartory to a general retreat.

1816. The schooner Eliza cast away near Newport; the captain and crew saved by Com. Perry, who with part of the crew of the frigate Java, went five miles in a boat to their relief.

1824. THOMAS EDWARD BOWDITCH, the African traveler, died. He went to Africa at the age of 21, and engaged in a series of expeditions into the country. In 1822 he went out from England with a view of devoting himself to the exploration of the African continent. He had only arrived at the mouth of the Gambia when a disease occasioned by fatigue and anxiety of mind put an end to his existence.

1833. ADRIEN MARIE LEGENDRE, so well known as a profound mathematician, died at Paris. His work on geometry is much used.

1840. The uniform penny postage commenced in England; the number of letters despatched from London on this day being 112,000; the average for January, 1839, being 30,000.

1840. Battle between the Russian and Khivian cavalry; the latter commanded by the khan in person were completely routed and pursued to the city of Khiva.

1848. Miss CAROLINE HERSCHEL, member of the Royal astronomical society, London, died at Hanover.

1855. MARY RUSSEL MITFORD died, aged 68; a distinguished English authoress.

1856. THOMAS H. PERKINS, a wealthy and liberal Boston merchant, died aged 89. His was the first American firm engaged in the China trade.

JANUARY 11.

395. THEODOSIUS THE GREAT, emperor of Rome, died. He was born about the year 346, and on coming to the throne distinguished himself by his orthodoxy, and his zeal against heresy and paganism. His public and private virtues, which procured him the name of *The Great*, will scarcely excuse the fierceness of his intolerance, or the barbarity of his anger and revenge.

1569. The first English lottery drawn at London. It continued day and evening four months. The prizes were money, plate and merchandise. It had been advertised two years at the time it took place.

1698. PETER, the czar of Russia, arrived in England and wrought as a mechanic in the dockyard at Deptford, as well as in the workshops of various mechanics, with a view of carrying the English arts into his own country. He was well received by William III.

1751. A globular bottle of glass was made at Leith measuring 40 by 42 inches the largest ever made in Britain.

1753. Sir HANS SLOANE, the eminent English naturalist, died, aged 93. He was born at Killileagh in Ireland; studied medicine in London, and settled there in the practice of his profession. He was the second learned man whom science tempted to America. His museum, composed of the rarest productions of nature, he bequeathed to the public, on condition of the payment of £20,000 annually to his family, and was the foundation of the British Museum.

1775. The first provincial congress of South Carolina met at Charleston.

1778. CHARLES LINNE (or Linnæus), the Swedish botanist, died, aged 71. In his twenty-fourth year he conceived the idea of a new arrangement of plants, or a sexual system of botany. In 1732 the Academy of Sciences at Upsal appropriated 50 Swedish dollars to send him on a tour through Lapland, and with this small sum he made a journey of more than 3500 miles, unaccompanied, traversing the Lapland desert, and enduring many hardships. A series of offices and honors were conferred upon him, till in 1753 he was created a *Knight of the Polar Star*, an honor never before conferred on a literary man; and in 1761 he was elevated to the rank of nobility.

1778. A collection amounting to £3815 was made for the 924 American prisoners in England. Dr. Franklin, at Paris, applied to the British ambassador for an exchange of prisoners, but his lordship was pleased to return only the following answer: "no application received from rebels unless they come to implore his majesty's pardon."

1782. Ostenburg, near Trincomalee, in the island of Ceylon, taken from the Dutch by the British Admiral Hughes.

1795. The French, under Pichegru, crossed the Waal on the ice at different points.

1800. WILLIAM NEWCOME, archbishop of Armagh, died, aged 79. He rose gradually in the church to the primacy of Ireland; was a worthy man, and author of a great number theological works.

1801. CIMAROSA, the celebrated Italian musician, died.

1803. The Hindostan, East Indiaman, lost on the Culvers, off Margate, in a dreadful storm.

1805. Letters of marque and reprisal issued by Great Britain against Spain.

1807. Breig in Silesia surrendered to the French and Bavarians; 3 generals, 1400 Prussians, and considerable magazines were captured.

1810. In the night the mercury in three thermometers froze at Moscow and withdrew into the ball. At Iraish it was observed at 44½° of Fahrenheit immediately before it froze.

1811. Marie Joseph de Chenier, a French poet, died. By flattering the passions of the people he soon gained great popularity, and during the revolution was one of the most violent democrats.

1815. Cumberland island, Georgia, taken possession of by Capt. Barrie of the British ship Dragon. Same day British sloop of war, Barbadoes, Capt. Fleming captured privateer schooner Fox, of 7 guns and 72 men from Wilmington.

1817. Timothy Dwight, president of Yale college, died, aged 65. He entered Yale college at the age of 13, and became a tutor at 19. His health becoming impaired by the advice of his physicians he traveled, walking 2000 and riding 3000 miles in the course of a year. It had the effect to restore his constitution completely. His published works consist of theology, poetry and travels. His biography is interesting; he was an uncommon character.

1829. Gregorio Funes, a patriot of La Plata, died at Buenos Ayres. He was actively engaged in the South American revolution from its commencement. He was also an author.

1839. Alexander Coffin, the last survivor of the original proprietors who settled the city of Hudson in 1784, died, aged 99. He was highly respected for his talents, integrity and usefulness.

1839. Earthquake at Martinique, which did great damage, particularly at Fort Royal, where only 18 houses were left standing, of 1700, and 900 hundred sufferers were dug out of the ruins.

1843. Francis S. Key, district attorney of the United States and author of the national song, the *Star Spangled Banner*, died in Baltimore.

1853. Russia, Austria and Prussia, after considerable delay, finally acknowledge Napoleon III as emperor of France.

1853. The caloric ship Ericsson made her trial trip from New York to the Potomac.

JANUARY 12.

400. B. C. Xenophon, with the 10,000, forced a passage through the defiles of Armenia.

1519. Maximilian I, emperor of Germany, died. He was elected king of the Romans 1486, and ascended the imperial throne 1493. Under him the Turks were checked in their enterprises against Germany, and repelled from his hereditary territories.

1598. The Marquis De la Roche received from Henry IV a commission to conquer Canada. He sailed from France with a colony of convicts from the prisons. He landed them on the Isle of Sable, and sailed for Acadie, from whence he returned to France. The survivors of the colony twelve in number, were taken off seven years afterwards, and presented to the king in their sealskin clothes and long beards. He gave them fifty crowns each and pardoned their offences.

1640. An engagement of four days' duration near the island Tamaraca, Brazils, between the Dutch and Portuguese, in which the latter were defeated and the Dutch admiral killed.

1678. A remarkable darkness at noon in England.

1777. General Mercer died of the wounds of the battle of Princeton.

1781. The states general of Holland issued letters of marque and reprisal against England.

1793. Arthur Lee, a distinguished American statesman, died at Urbana, Va. The long and faithful services which he rendered his country during his arduous struggles for independence, in the alternate character of ambassador and statesman, are universally known and acknowledged.

1794. John George Adam Forster died, aged 40. He was of Scotch descent, born in Prussia, studied at St. Petersburg, taught German and French in England, accompanied Cook in his voyage round the world, accepted the professorship of natural history at Hesse Cassel, was appointed historiographer of a Russian expedition round the world; this project being frustrated by the Turkish war, he went to Germany, and residing at Mentz when the French took that city 1792, was sent by the republicans to request a union of that city with France. During his absence the Prussians retook the city, by which he lost all his property, including his books and papers, and died soon after. The Germans number him among their classical writers.

1795. In consequence of a great thaw the communication of the main army of the French under Pichegru and the four divisions that crossed the Waal the day before on the ice, was totally interrupted during two days.

1795. Mr. Pitt recommended in the British parliament that a premium be given by government to large families.

1805. British frigate Doris, Capt. Campbell, lost on the Diamond rock, Quiberon bay. The crew saved themselves and blew up the frigate.

1805. The thermometer at Danbury, Ct., stood at 19° below zero; being the coldest weather known there since 1780.

1807. A fatal explosion at Leyden, in Holland. A vessel containing 40,000 pounds of powder, moored before the house of Prof. Rau, exploded with a tremendous crash. Upwards of 200 houses were overthrown, besides churches and public buildings, 150 persons killed and 2000 wounded.

1809. Cayenne surrendered by the French, to the British and the Portuguese under Capt. Yeo.

1815. National fast in the United States.

JANUARY 13.

857. Ethelwulf, son of Egbert, sometimes styled the first king of England, died. In his reign the tax called Peter's pence was levied.

1399. The Tartars, under Tamerlane, pillaged the imperial city of Delhi, and two days after wantonly massacred the entire Indian population.

1400. Richard II of England murdered. He came to the throne at the age of 11, and after a turbulent reign of 22 years, was deposed and imprisoned.

1404. It was enacted at this short parliament of Henry's that no chemist shall use his craft to multiply gold or silver.

1560. John de Lasci, a learned Pole, died.

1618. Galileo discovered the fourth satellite of Jupiter.

1669. John Bochius, a Dutch poet, died. He excelled in Latin, and is called the Virgil of the Low Countries.

1691. George Fox, founder of the sect of quakers, died, aged 67. His father was a poor weaver, and George was apprenticed to a shoemaker; but he left his employment and wandered about the country in a leather doublet, and finally set up as a teacher. He visited different countries, and had the satisfaction to see his tenets taking deep root in his life time.

1705. A house in London where fireworks were manufactured, blew up, and destroyed 120 houses,and killed 50 persons.

1711. The last No. of the *Tatler* appeared (No. 271).

1715. Great fire in Thames street, London; many lives lost.

1716. Elizabeth Patch died at Salem; the first female born in the old colony of Massachusets.

1717. Maria Sybilla Merian, the distinguished painter, and writer on entomology, died at Amsterdam.

1738. The famous convention of Pardo signed.

1759. Execution of the conspirators against the life of the king of Portugal. The whole family of the Marquis Tavora was executed, and the name suppressed for ever.

1797. British ships Indefatigable, 44 guns, and Amazon, 42 guns, had a night action of six hours, in the bay of Audierne, with the French 74 gun ship Les Droits des Hommes, 1600 men; the latter was driven on shore, and the crew made prisoners; Gen. Renier and 750 men were lost in the action. The Amazon was also lost in the action.

1798. Lieut. Lord Camelford shot Lieut. Charles Peterson, at English harbor, Antigua, for disobedience of orders, was afterwards tried and acquitted.

1798. The Swiss cantons armed against France.

1809. The French under Marshal Victor defeated the Spanish under Castanos at Cuenca.

1811. The British merchant ship Cumberland, Captain Barrat, beat off 4 French privateers, and took 170 men who had boarded her.

1814. British and Prussians repulsed in an attack on Antwerp; part of the suburbs were burnt.

1814. The emperor of Russia and king of Prussia crossed the Rhine to invade France; the emperor of Austria, who had arrived the evening before at Cassel, went out to meet them, and they entered Basil, in Switzerland.

1814. General thanksgiving throughout Great Britain for the successes gained over Bonaparte.

1814. Capt. Barrie of the British ship Dragon, took the fort on Point Peter and the tower of St. Mary's, in Georgia; they afterwards destroyed the fort.

1817. The ship Georgianna, of Norfolk, experienced a tremendous shock in the Gulf stream supposed to be by earthquake; the day was calm.

1822. Johann Gottlieb Schneider, a German philologist and naturalist, died, aged 72; a voluminous author.

1836. Karl Chr. Traug. Tauchnitz, an eminent German printer, died, aged 75. At the age of 35 he commenced business for himself with a single press; but his establishment soon became very extensive, including a letter foundry and book store. He was most indefatigable in improving and perfecting whatever he undertook, as his publications attest. His founts of oriental type were unsurpassed in Germany.

1838. Chancellor Eldon died.

4

1840. Steam boat Lexington burnt, on her passage from New York to Stonington. Of 145 persons on board, only four escaped with their lives. Among the sufferers were many highly esteemed and valuable members of society.

1848. A severe battle took place at Chillianwallah between the British and Sikh forces without decisive results.

1854. An earthquake at Finana in Spain, crumbling down the Alcazaba, an ancient Moorish castle, prostrating houses and causing chasms in the streets, and loss of lives.

JANUARY 14.

1526. Treaty of Madrid between the emperor Charles V, and Francis I of France, by which the latter obtained his liberty.

1604. The episcopal divines and puritans held a conference at Hampton court in the presence of King James.

1611. EDWARD BRUCE, a Scottish statesman, died. He occupied some of the highest offices under the government, and his services were important in establishing the peaceable accession of James to the English throne.

1622. PIETRO SARPI, better known as Father Paul of Venice, died, aged 90. He employed the latter part of his life in writing a history of the council of Trent, in which he has developed the intrigues connected with the transactions of that famous assembly, with a degree of boldness and veracity, which renders the work one of the most interesting and important productions of the class to which it belongs.

1634. Of seven sailors left at Spitzbergen in the fall of 1633, by the Dutch fishermen, for the purpose of wintering there, the first of the number died. The journal which they kept relates that they sought in vain for green herbs, bears and foxes, in that desolate region. In November the scurvy appeared among them. Their journal ended February 26, and they were all found dead on the return of their countrymen in spring. (See April 16.)

1696. MARIE DE RABUTIN SEVIGNE, a French woman of quality, died, aged 70. Her *Letters* (11 vols. 8vo.) are models of epistolary style, and have been translated into English.

1738. The famous convention of Pardo signed.

1739. The pope issued an edict against the assemblies of freemasons, under penalty of the rack and condemnation to the galleys.

1742. EDMUND HALLEY the astronomer, died, aged 86. He devoted himself to mathematics with great success, and spent much time abroad in astronomical observations and experiments. His astronomical pursuits tended greatly by their results to improve the art of navigation.

1753. GEORGE BERKLEY, bishop of Cloyne in Ireland, died, aged 85. He appeared as an author before his twentieth year. He devoted seven years and a considerable part of his fortune in an effort to establish a college at Bermuda, for the education of Indian preachers, which miscarried. He published several philosophical, mathematical and theological works, and is said to have been acquainted with almost every branch of human knowledge.

1781. French took the island of Nevis.

1783. CERVETTO, an Italian of extraordinary musical genius, died at London, aged 103. He was a member of the orchestra of Drury lane theatre.

1784. Congress ratified the definitive treaty of peace.

1792. JOSEPH JACKSON, a celebrated English type founder, died. While an apprentice his master had carefully kept from his view the mode of making punches, but by boring a hole through the door he got an occasional glimpse of the art, and succeeded.

1795. Intense frost in Holland, which enabled the remainder of the French army to cross the Waal.

1795. The French were repulsed in an attack on all the posts of the allies, from Arnhem to Amerongen. In the night the allies retreated to Amersfoort, leaving 300 sick behind them.

1797. Battle of Rivoli in Italy. The contest was continued three days, and decided the fate of Mantua. The French under Joubert were victorious over the Austrians.

1798. Five English gentlemen who had been sent to investigate the title of Vizier Ally, were by his orders assassinated at Benares in India.

1801. ROBERT ORME died, aged 73; historiographer to the East India company.

1801. An embargo laid in England on all Russian, Swedish and Danish ships. More that 100 Swedish and Danish vessels were immediately seized.

1809. Formal treaty of peace, friendship and alliance between Great Britain and Spain.

1813. An engagement off Pernambuco between the United States privateer schooner Comet, Capt. Boyle, 14 guns and 120 men, and three British vessels of 24 guns, convoyed by a Portuguese ship of 32 guns and 165 men. The Portuguese were beaten off, and the British vessels captured. She also captured three other vessels on the passage.

1814. Treaty of peace signed at Kiel between Denmark and England.

1814. CHARLES BOSSUT, a French mathematician, died, aged 84. He studied under D'Alembert, and rose to eminence. On the breaking out of the French revolution he lost the offices he had acquired, and subsisted by his writings. He was a contributer to the *Encyclopedie*.

1815. Com. DECATUR, sailed from New York in the frigate President.

1822. The Grand Duke CONSTANTINE declined, by letter to his brother Alexander, the succession to the throne of all the Russias.

1831. HENRY MACKENZIE, the novelist, died, aged 86. He studied the law, at the same time cultivating elegant literature. His first effort was a tragedy, which was favorably received; his first novel appeared in 1771, in which he was eminently successful. Scott entitles him the Scottish Addison.

1834. WILLIAM POLK, a revolutionary officer, died. He held the rank of colonel at the close of the war, and was the last surviving field officer of the North Carolina line. He was among the small band of patriots who declared independence in Mecklenburg county, N. C., May 20th, 1775.

1838. Navy island evacuated by the Canadians, &c., under Mackenzie and Van Rensselaer, 510 in number. The arms belonging to the United States were surrendered, as also the cannon belonging to the state of New York.

1852. T. HUDSON TURNER died, aged 37; one of the ablest of the British archæologists.

1854. JOSHUA BATES, a distinguished New England clergyman, died, aged 77. He was twenty-three years president of Middlebury college.

JANUARY 15.

69. SERGIUS GALBA, the Roman emperor, assassinated, at the age of 72. He was the successor of Nero, and reigned but three months.

936. RODOLPH, king of France, died, in the 14th year of his reign, and was succeeded by Lewis the Stranger.

1549. The liturgy of the English church established by parliament. All the divine offices were to be performed according to the new liturgy, and infringements were to be punished by forfeitures and imprisonments, and for the third offence imprisonment for life. Visitors were appointed to see that it was received throughout England. From this time we may date the era of the Puritans.

1655. DANIEL HEINSIUS, a Dutch philologist, died. He made great progress as a student, under Scaliger, and was appointed to a professorship at Leyden. He was also successful as a Greek and Latin poet.

1559. Queen ELIZABETH crowned at Westminster, by the bishop of Carlisle, who was the only person that could be prevailed upon to perform the ceremony.

1672. JOHN COSIN, bishop of Durham, died; a lover of literature and prodigal in his expenditures on book-binding. He ordered that all his books should be rubbed once a fortnight to prevent their moulding.

1693. An army of six or seven hundred French and Indians set out from Montreal to invade the Mohawk castles. (See Feb. 6.)

1730. Gov. MONTGOMERIE granted the city of New York a new charter. Although that city had been put under the government of a mayor in 1665, it was not regularly incorporated until 1686.

1773. At Duff house, the residence of the countess dowager of Fife, the first masquerade ever seen in Scotland was exhibited.

1777. Vermont declared itself a free and independent state. It had been settled as a part of New Hampshire, but was claimed as a part of New York, and so decided to be by the British crown. But by the dissolution of the bonds which had held America in subjection to the crown of Britain, they considered themselves free from New York, to which the most of them had never voluntarily submitted; and being, as they said, reduced to "a state of nature," they assumed the right to form such connections as were agreeable to themselves. Accordingly they formed a plan of government and a code of laws, and petitioned congress to receive them into the Union.

1778. Nootka sound and the Sandwich islands discovered by Captain Cook.

1780. First exportation of woolen goods from Ireland to a foreign market.

1780. Unsuccessful attack by the Americans under Lord Stirling on the British at Long island.

1781. The traitor ARNOLD succeeded in burning some stores at Smithfield.

1783. WILLIAM ALEXANDER, Lord Stirling, an officer in the revolutionary army, died at Albany, aged 57. He was of Scotch descent, and from early youth a mathematician. Throughout the war he acted an important part, and was warmly attached to Washington. He left behind him the reputation of a brave, discerning and intrepid officer, and an honest and learned man. He was generally styled Lord Stirling, and was considered the rightful heir to the title and estates of that earldom in Scotland.

1794. A desperate engagement off the island of Corsica between three Sardinian ships and two Barbary xebecs. One of the xebecs was captured, but the other, rather than surrender, was blown up; upon which the prisoners taken, Turks and Algerines, 92 in number, were put to death.

1795. The French attacked the British outposts at Rhenen.

1795. The French national convention liberated Gen. Miranda and Capt. Lacrosse from prison.

1799. A revolution at Lucca in Italy, without bloodshed. Titles and exclusive privileges were abolished, the sovereignty of the people proclaimed, and a contribution of two millions of livres levied on the nobility alone, which was immediately presented to the French general Serrurier.

1805. ABRAHAM HYACINTHE ANQUETIL DU PERRON, the French orientalist, died, aged 74. He studied theology, but afterwards devoted himself with ardor to the study of the eastern languages. In 1754 he embarked for India, and with difficulty succeeded in finding some priests to instruct him in the sacred language of the Parsees. He returned to Paris in 1762 with a number of manuscripts, and proceeded to arrange them for publication. During the revolution he shut himself up with his books; but continued labors and an abstemious diet exhausted his constitution. He was a learned and excellent man.

1807. Battle between the forces under Christophe and Petion for the governorship of Hayti, which had been assumed by Christophe as the oldest general, on the death of Dessalines; but Petion had been subsequently duly elected. Christophe was defeated after a fierce encounter. A separation of the republic followed. Petion instituted a pure republic, while Christophe founded a monarchy.

1810. Masquerades and masked balls prohibited in the city of New York.

1815. The United States frigate President, Com. Decatur, captured by four British vessels, after a sharp action, and a chase of 18 hours. Loss of the Americans 22 killed, 59 wounded; British loss 11 killed, 14 wounded.

1825. ROBERT GOODLOE HARPER, an American statesman, died. He was born in Virginia, of poor parentage; acquired the rudiments of a classical education; served a campaign in the revolutionary army; after which he entered Princeton college. He subsequently settled in South Carolina, in the practice of the law, and acquired great reputation as a professional man and a politician.

1827. JEAN DENIS LANJUINAIS died. He was a staunch defender of liberal principles, and opposed first the arrogant pretensions of the privileged class, although himself one of their number: afterwards he arrayed himself against the intrigues of Mirabeau, the violence of the mountain party, and the usurpations of Bonaparte, in the face of destruction. The object of his wishes was constitutional liberty. He escaped the axe of the revolution, and was even promoted to office by Napoleon.

1834. The city of Leira, in Portugal, taken by Count de Saldanha, and the garrison, of Miguelites about 1500 in number, made prisoners.

1836. CHARLES LEWIS, one of the most eminent book binders in Europe, died. The splendidly bound books in the duke of Sussex's library are of his workmanship.

1842. JOSEPH HOPKINSON died. His speeches in congress on the Seminole war were much admired. He was author of the song, *Hail Columbia.*

1844. The Fontaine Moliere, a monument to the great French dramatist, at Paris, inaugurated. It combines a public fountain with a monument, and stands opposite the house in which Moliere died.

1849. Reporters excluded from an adjourned meeting of a convention of the southern states.

JANUARY 16.

1543. An act of the English parliament was passed forbidding women, apprentices, &c., &c., to read the New Testament in English.

1556. CHARLES V of Germany, (Don Carlos I of Spain) resigned the crown of Spain to his son Philip, after a reign of 40 years. Of all his vast possessions he only reserved to himself an annual pension. It was under him that Cortez conquered Mexico.

1580. An act of the English parliament inflicting a penalty of 20 pounds for absenting from church.

1599. EDMUND SPENCER, the English poet, died, aged 46. His first poem, the *Shepherd's Calendar*, appeared in 1576. He went to Ireland as private secretary to the lord lieutenant, and commenced the *Faery Queen* while in that country. The rebellion took place with such fury that he was obliged to leave the country in so great confusion, that an infant child was left behind, and burnt with his house. The unfortunate poet died soon after his arrival in England, in consequence of these misfortunes.

1643. Parliament of England forbid free commerce, and ordered no wagon or carriage to go to Oxford without a license.

1668. The earl of SHREWSBURY slain in a duel by the duke of Buckingham, who had lived in open adultery with Shrewsbury's wife. It is said that she, in the habit of a page, held Buckingham's horse when he was fighting with her husband.

1706. Articles of union between England and Scotland ratified by the Scottish parliament 110 to 69.

1715. ROBERT NELSON died, an English gentleman of fortune, which he employed in works of benevolence and charity. Few works on devotional subjects were more popular than his.

1748. The bottle conjuror imposed on a great multitude at the Haymarket theatre, by announcing that he would jump into a quart bottle.

1760. Pondicherry, defended by the French under General Lally, taken by the English under Colonel Coote.

1772. A revolution in Denmark which terminated in the imprisonment of the royal family, and finally the banishment of the queen, sister to George III of England.

1780. The Spanish fleet of 11 sail, under Langara, destroyed off St. Vincent by the British fleet of 19 sail, under Rodney. Langara was dangerously wounded and taken prisoner. One of the Spanish ships with 600 men on board was blown up, and all perished. The British lost 32 killed and 102 wounded.

1790. The bean-fed friars ejected from their convents by an augean labor of the French revolution.

1794. EDWARD GIBBON, the historian, died, aged 57. During his visit to Rome in 1764, he formed the plan of writing the *Decline and Fall of the Roman Empire.* In 1774 he obtained a seat in parliament, and two years after appeared the first quarto volume of his history. A disorder which he had endured twenty three years terminated in a mortification.

1795. Retreat of the British from Utrecht, in Holland, upon which the inhabitants capitulated to the French.

1796. The first theatre at Botany bay opened by the convicts at Sydney cove.

1809. Battle of Corunna in Spain, between the French and English, and death of Sir John Moore, who fell mortally wounded by a cannon shot, at the moment of victory achieved by the troops under his command. His men buried him in his cloak, and the French, in testimony of his gallantry, erected a monument over his remains. He was unmarried and in his 47th year.

1812. The king of Sicily, on account of ill-health, abdicated the throne in favor of his son, until he should recover. It is remarkable that Great Britain, Spain, Portugal and Sweden were governed by regents or viceroys at the same time.

1813. LEWIS BARNEY died at Champlain, New York, aged 105. He had 24 children by one wife.

1815. HENRY THORNTON, founder of the Sierra Leone company, and a writer on the credit of Great Britain, died.

1816. The bridge at the falls of the Schuylkill fell with the great body of snow upon it.

1816. JOHN WRIGHT, the first constable of Cumberland county, Virginia, died, aged 107.

1817. ALEXANDER JAMES DALLAS, an eminent lawyer of Philadelphia, died. He filled the office of secretary of state in Pennsylvania many years; and also that of secretary of the treasury of the United States a short time previous to his death.

1838. DOROTHY TORREY died at Windsor, Conn., aged 107.

1843. State lunatic asylum, at Utica, New York, went into operation.

1854. ALDEN PARTRIDGE died at Norwich, Vt.; nearly fifty years engaged in military instruction, and some time principal of West Point academy.

JANUARY 17.

86. B. C. CAIUS MARIUS, the Roman consul, died. He was the son of a farmer in indigent circumstances; but by his talents and energy raised himself to the highest dignity of the greatest state in the world.

395. The Emperor THEODOSIUS died at Milan, soliciting his heirs faithfully to execute his will.

1009. ABD-EL-MALEK, a Moorish prince, crucified by his conqueror.

1380. An act of parliament passed, by which foreign ecclesiastics were incapacitated from holding benefices in England.

1467. JOHN CASTRIOTTO, (or Scanderbeg) prince of Albania, died. His father placed him as a hostage with the sultan of Turkey, by whom he was educated in the Mohammedan faith, and at the age of 18 placed at the head of a body of troops. He afterwards deserted to the Christians, and on ascending the throne of his fathers renounced the Mohammedan faith. He obtained repeated victories over the Turks. After his death, when Albania submitted to the Moslem dominion, the Turks dug up his bones which they wore to transfer his courage to themselves.

1524. VERRAZANO sailed from a desolate rock near Madeira, with fifty men and provisions for eight months, arms, munitions and other naval stores, on his voyage westwardly, expecting to reach Cathay.

1546. Martin Luther preached his final sermon at Wittemberg.

1556. Philip Nerli, the Florentine historian, died.

1684. Wentworth Dillon, earl of Roscommon, died at Rome. The early part of his life was spent in dissipation, but he afterwards conducted with more discretion, and became distinguished among the wits of the day. Johnson calls him the most correct writer of English verse before Dryden.

1694. A powder magazine of 218 barrels exploded at Dublin, doing much damage.

1701. Roger Morris, an English chaplain, died, aged 73. He was a diligent collector of ecclesiastical manuscripts relating to the history of the English church, whereof, says Strype, "he left vast heaps behind him."

1705. John Ray, an English naturalist, died. He was the son of a blacksmith; received a liberal education at Cambridge, and devoted himself to science and literature. His publications were numerous.

1706. Birthday of Benjamin Franklin.

1733. George Byng, an English admiral, died. He entered the navy at the age of 15, and gradually rose to the highest honors and distinctions.

1746. Battle of Falkirk, in which the forces of the Pretender were victorious over the royal army.

1750. The singular ceremony of the Greek church of consecrating the water in memory of Christ's baptism, performed at St. Petersburg.

1766. Frederick V, king of Denmark and Norway, died.

1781. Battle of the Cowpens, in South Carolina, and defeat of 1100 British under Tarleton, by an inferior force of Americans under Morgan. British loss 100 killed and wounded, and 500 prisoners; 800 muskets, 2 field pieces, 35 baggage wagons, and 100 dragoon horses fell into the hands of the conquerors. The loss of the Americans was 12 killed and 60 wounded.

1783. Action between the British frigate Magicienne and the French frigate Sybille. The latter lost her masts, and was captured a few days after by the Hussar.

1789. John Ledyard, the traveler, died. He was born at Groton, Conn., 1751; entered Dartmouth college at the age of 19, but for some reproof resolved to escape: accordingly he felled a tree on the bank of the Connecticut, of which he constructed a canoe, and descended the river 140 miles to Hartford: studied theology a while, and then enlisted as a common sailor for a voyage to Gibraltar; accompanied Capt. Cook in one of his voyages, of which he published an account. Not meeting with assistance to prosecute any of the daring enterprises he proposed, he finally determined to make the tour of the globe from London east, on foot; and had proceeded as far as Yakutsk in Siberia, when he was arrested by order of the queen as a French spy and hurried back to the frontiers of Poland. He returned to London, he says, "disappointed, ragged, pennyless, but with a whole heart." He had scarcely taken lodgings when Sir Joseph Banks proposed an African expedition. He accepted the offer and proceeded as far as Cairo, where he was attacked by a disease which carried him off.

1789. Charles IV proclaimed king of Spain.

1791. Lord Dungarvon, an Irish peer, was tried at the Old Bailey, London, for stealing three and a half guineas from a poor woman in town, but was acquitted.

1792. George Horne, bishop of Norwich, died. His *Sermons* and *Commentary on the Psalms*, are well known.

1795. The stadtholder, William V, obtained permission from the States General to withdraw from Holland.

1800. The church at Chelmsford, England, fell; it was first built in 1424.

1804. Charles Nisbet died, aged 67. He was a Scotch clergyman, and the first president of Dickinson college in Pennsylvania.

1806. An iris or lunar rainbow was seen for one hour (9½ to 10½) at Wakefield in Yorkshire, England.

1810. Masquerades and masked balls prohibited by the authorities in the city of Philadelphia.

1811. The Mexican patriots under Hidalgo totally defeated near Guadalaxara by the Spaniards under Calleja.

1813. Capture of the United States brig Vixen, 12 guns, Capt. Henley, by the British frigate Narcissus.

1815. The king of Spain issued an edict against freemasonry.

1817. At Philadelphia and Albany the singular phenomena of snow, clear weather, rain, snow, thunder and lightning, hail and snow, was observed in succession.

1836. Two engagements in the mountains of Arlaban, between the forces of the queen of Spain under Gen. Cordova and the Carlists, in which the latter were defeated.

1841. Rezin P. Bowie died at New Orleans, aged 48; "well known in the southwest by his many deeds of valor in its early history, among the Mexicans and savages."

1851. Spencer Compton, marquis of Northampton, died, aged 61. He was president of the Royal society; was associated with Wilberforce in the anti-slavery-cause, and with Macintosh as a criminal law reformer.

1854. Two rail road bridges and crossings at Erie, Pa., destroyed by a mob of women, who were afterwards escorted through the town with banners, headed by a band of music.

1856. ZADOCK THOMPSON died, aged 59; author of several historical works relating to Vermont, and a naturalist.

JANUARY 18.

1486. HENRY VII married the princess Elizabeth, eldest daughter of Edward IV. Thus uniting the houses of York and Lancaster, blending the Roses.

1534. Lima, the present capital of Peru, founded by PIZARRO; thirty years before a single town was founded within the limits of the United States, St. Augustine, Florida, being founded 1565.

1546. The council of Trent assembled and agreed upon a confession of faith.

1561. The first English tragedy performed, at Whitehall, before the queen. It was entitled *Gorboduc*, from the name of a supposed ancient British king, and was written by Thomas Sackville and Thomas Norton. It consists of five acts, each preceded by a dumb show, prefiguring what is to occur; the first four acts close by choruses in rhyme, and the fifth by a didactic speech of nearly two hundred lines. Sir Philip Sydney pronounced it "full of stately speeches and well-sounding phrases, climbing to the height of Seneca his stile, and full of notable morality, which it doth most delightfully teach."

1701. FREDERICK III of Brandenburgh crowned first king of Prussia, by the title of Frederick I.

1703. THOMAS HYDE died. He was an Oriental interpreter during the reigns of Charles II, James II, and William III.

1713. ARCANGELO CORELLI, an Italian composer, died. He became so great a master in the science of music, that his countrymen bestowed on him the cognomen of *Il Divino.*

1718. SAMUEL GARTH, an English poet and physician, died. He settled in London where by his professional skill he soon acquired a very extensive practice; and by his wit and conversational powers distinguished himself among the literati of the day.

1739. SAMUEL BERNARD, one of the richest and most celebrated financiers of Europe, died at Paris. His funeral procession equaled that of a prince in point of magnificence and in the train of distinguished attendants.

1775. JOHN BASKERVILLE, an eminent English printer, died. He was a man fertile in invention, and effected improvements in the art which could scarcely have been expected from the exertions of a single individual.

1777. Battle of Kingsbridge, N. Y., between the Americans under Gen. Heath and the Hessians.

1782. DUMITER RADULY died at Haromszeck, at the remarkable age of 140.

1793. GEORGE GORDON, an English nobleman, after five years' imprisonment, appeared to give bail; but the attorney-general refused to accept of it. He was therefore remanded.

1795. The French under Salm took Utrecht in Holland, and Gen. Van Damme took Arnhem; the prince of Orange and his family escaping to England.

1797. FRANCIS LIGHTFOOT LEE, an American statesman, died at his residence in Virginia, aged 63.

1804. Goree taken by the French from the English.

1806. EUGENE NAPOLEON BEAUHARNAIS married to Augusta Amelia, daughter of the king of Bavaria.

1810. LYON LEVY, a jeweler, threw himself from the monument in London.

1811. Gen. JUNOT wounded in the face by a musket ball, while reconnoitering the British lines.

1813. Battle at Frenchtown in Michigan, between the United States troops and the British and Indians, when the latter were defeated. American loss, 12 killed, 55 wounded.

1815. The British decamped from before Fort St. Philip, on the Mississippi, which they had bombarded from the 9th. About 12 o'clock at night they took to their boats, leaving 80 of their wounded, 14 pieces heavy artillery, and a great quantity of shot.

1815. STANISLAUS, chevalier de Boufflers, died at Paris, aged 78. He was the son of the marchioness de Boufflers, mistress of Stanislaus, king of Poland. He distinguished himself in the army, which however he left to give his attention to literature. He was considered one of the most ingenious men of his time, and was noted for the elegance of his manners and conversation. The epitaph on his tomb, written by himself, is characteristic of him: *Mes amis, croyez vous que-je dors?*

1816. Thanksgiving throughout England on the restoration of peace.

1819. JOHN WILLSON, died in London, aged 52. He sometime held the chief command at Ceylon, and subsequently administered the government of Upper Canada.

1826. OMMEGANCK, one of the most celebrated Dutch landscape painters, died at

Antwerp. His pieces are distinguished for good taste, and for freshness and warmth of coloring.

1829. JOHN GEORGE HENRY HASSEL, a distinguished German geographer and statistical writer, died at Weimar.

1834. NATHANIEL AMES died at Providence. He was the son of Fisher Ames, and a seaman by profession. He is the author of *Mariners' Sketches*, *Nautical Reminiscences*, and *Old Sailor's Yarns*.

1848. JOHN DEIDRICH PETERSON died at Markham, Canada. He was the pioneer pastor of that town.

1854. JUDAH TOURO died at New Orleans, aged 78; bequeathing nearly two millions of dollars to the public institutions of that city.

1854. WILLIAM WALKER proclaimed the republic of Sonora.

JANUARY 19.

1472. Birthday of COPERNICUS, at Thorn in Prussia.

1514. VASCO NUNEZ DE BALBOA returned to his colony at Darien, after having made the discovery of the Pacific ocean. His expedition occupied four months and a half; his triumph was complete. The whole population poured down to the shore to meet him, to hail him as the author of their fortunes, as less a man than a gift of heaven, to guide them into the possession of glories and riches incalculable. The expedition had been undertaken in consequence of the extravagant representations by the Indians, of a people who lived on the borders of that ocean, six suns distant, who owned large ships, and whose eating and drinking vessels were of pure gold. They referred to the Peruvians.

1535. Date of the probate of the will of the famed early English printer, Wynkyn de Worde.

1547. HENRY HOWARD, earl of Surrey, a soldier, scholar and poet, beheaded on Tower hill for treason. In his youth he made the tour of Europe, and at Florence signalized his courage and romantic spirit, by publishing, in the style of a knight-errant, a challenge to all comers, Christians, Jews, Saracens, Turks and Cannibals, in defence of the surpassing beauty of his mistress, the fair Geraldine; and was victorious at the tournament instituted by the grand duke on the occasion. He served in the army sent against Scotland in 1542, and in 1544 accompanied the troops with which the king invaded France. For his services he was promoted, but being defeated in an attempt to seize a convoy, he was superseded. This unmerited disgrace was the beginning of his ruin. He is said to have aspired to the hand of the Princess Mary, and on some frivolous charges was tried by a common jury, by whom he was obsequiously found guilty of treason. Thus perished a man "no less valiant than learned, and of excellent hopes," aged 27.

1565. JAMES LAYNEZ, one of the founders of the Society of Jesus, died. He was born in Castile, 1512. His intimacy with Loyola was formed in Paris, where they matured the plan of the society. Loyola was chosen the first general, and in 1558 was succeeded by Laynez.

1576. HANS SACHS, the famous German master-singer, died. He was born at Nuremberg 1494; his occupation that of a shoemaker. At the age of 14 he began to write poetry, and made verses and shoes, plays and pumps, with equal assiduity, to the age of 77, when he took an inventory of his literary stock in trade. It consisted of 4200 songs, 508 comedies, and other pieces, in all 6048, making 32 folio volumes written by his own hand. From these a selection was published in 5 volumes folio. His poems are distinguished for *naïveté*, feeling, and striking description.

1643. Battle of Liscard, in Cornwall, England.

1657. MILES SYNDERCOMBE and others convicted of plotting the death of Oliver Cromwell.

1706. CHARLES SACKVILLE, earl of Dorset and Middlessex, died. He was an accomplished scholar and a good speaker, but declined all public employment, being wholly engrossed in gallantry and pleasure. He was the patron of poets and men of wit: his own productions are those of a man of wit, vigorous, gay and airy. He served in the Dutch war of 1665 as a volunteer, and on the night before an engagement, composed the celebrated song, beginning, "To all you ladies now at hand."

1728. WILLIAM CONGREVE, the English dramatist, died. He was educated for the bar, but like many others similarly situated, gave up the law for the pursuit of polite literature, in which he was eminently successful. His first work, *The Incognita*, was written at a very early age, and he produced his first comedy at the age of 21.

1730. PETER II of Russia died of the small pox. He was the grandson of Peter the Great, and ascended the throne by the will of Catharine, when but 13 years old.

1757. THOMAS RUDDIMAN, a celebrated Scottish printer and grammarian, and who excelled in many learned treatises, died.

1776. Great eruption of mount Vesuvius.

1777. HUGH MERCER, an officer of the revolution, died. He was a Scotchman by birth, and was in the memorable battle of Culloden. Soon after, he emigrated to

America, and was engaged with Washington in the Indian wars of 1755. He joined the patriots of the revolution, and distinguished himself at Trenton and Princeton; was wounded in the latter engagement, of which he died. His funeral was attended by 30,000 people.

1778. FRANCIS FURGLER, the New Jersey recluse, died. During 25 years, without fire, he lived in a cell in the form of an oven, about four miles from Burlington.

1782. The emperor JOSEPH pardoned all those who kept out of his dominions on account of religion, provided they returned within a year; he also abolished several religious orders, and absolved the monks and nuns from their vows, and at the same time disclaimed all subordination to the pope in secular affairs.

1795. Insurrection in the island of Granada.

1795. The French under Devinther took Amersfoort in Holland, and the advance of the French army entered Amsterdam.

1796. The brass coffin, containing the bones of Columbus and the chains with which he had been loaded at Cuba, were removed from St. Domingo to Havana, by the direction of his descendants. They are now preserved in a silver urn on the left of the altar of the cathedral.

1806. JAMES JACKSON, an officer of the revolution, died. He came from England only two years before the war, and although but 19 years of age in 1776, he displayed great intrepidity at the attack upon Savannah. He continued in the service throughout the war, and in 1782 was presented by the legislature with a house and lot in Savannah. He held various civil offices in the state, and at the time of his death was a senator in congress.

1809. The French entered Corunna.

1812. Ciudad Rodrigo, a town and fortress in Spain, eight miles from the Portuguese line, garrisoned by 1700 Frenchmen, taken by storm by the British under Wellington, after a siege of 11 days.

1817. Riot and rebellion of the students of Princeton college.

1819. CHARLES IV, king of Spain, died. He was born at Naples 1740, and came to the throne of Spain 1788. Too imbecile to govern, he was always ruled by his wife and ministers. He was dethroned by Napoleon 1808, and died a pensioner at Naples of a relapse of the gout.

1836. JOHN BUTLER, "the celebrated huntsman," died, in Wake county, N. C. He was supposed to be at least 110 years of age, and left a wife surviving equally as old.

1840. The United States exploring expedition under Lieut. Wilkes reported the discovery of a new antarctic continent on this day. A subsequent British expedition sailed over its site without being able to discern any vestige of it. It is supposed to have been a series of icebergs.

1843. THOS. W. WHITE, editor of the *Southern Literary Messenger*, died at Richmond.

1847. PETER R. LIVINGSTON, a prominent man in the counsels and politics of the state of New York, died at Rhinebeck.

1848. ISAAC D'ISRAELI, author of the *Curiosities of Literature*, died aged 82.

1853. C. B. ADAMS, an eminent American naturalist, and professor in Amherst college, died.

1854. GEORGE MCFEELY, died at Carlisle, Pa., aged 73. He distinguished himself on the Niagara frontier in 1813.

JANUARY 20.

1265. The earl of Leicester having defeated Henry III, summoned a new parliament, in which the commons were first represented.

1546. FREDERICK, elector palatine, established without any acts of violence, the protestant religion.

1662. Three women condemned at Hartford, Conn., as witches, one of whom was hanged.

1706. HUMPHREY HODY died, an eminent English writer. A dissertation on the resurrection of the body asserted is one of his most useful works.

1745. CHARLES VII of Germany died at Munich, aged 48.

1764. Mr. WILKES was expelled the British house of commons for writing the *North Briton* No. 45. This famed individual was subsequently outlawed; disregarded his outlawery; was three times elected for Middlesex, and his election as often voted void by the commons, though returned by large majorities.

1770. Lord Chancellor YORKE committed suicide in the 48th year of his age. He was a distinguished English politician, and his death is ascribed to remorse for neglecting a promise he had made to his brother to accept of no office from court.

1776. Gen. SCHUYLER disarmed the Highlanders at Johnstown, N. Y., and took six hostages.

1777. Gen. DICKINSON, with 400 militia and 50 Pennsylvania riflemen, defeated a British foraging party, took 9 prisoners, 100 horses, 40 wagons and a number of cattle.

1779. BENEDICT ARNOLD condemned to be reprimanded by the commander-in-chief, for misdemeanor at Philadelphia.

1779. DAVID GARRICK, the actor, died. He formed a new era in the English stage, a reform both in the conduct and license of the drama, which was honorable to the genius that had the power to effect it.

1781. A revolt of 160 of the Jersey line at Morristown. It was suppressed and two of the ringleaders executed.

1783. The Independence of the United States acknowledged by Great Britain.

1788. George Joachim Zollikofer, a Swiss divine, died. He was born 1730, and became one of the most eminent preachers of the last century. His sermons have been published in 15 vols.

1788. Australia first colonized, nearly three centuries after the discovery of the Ladrones by Magellan, which constitute a part of it. Governor Philip arrived with a number of convicts from England, and established a colony at Port Jackson in preference to Botany Bay.

1790. John Howard, the philanthropist, died at Cherson in Russia, aged 63. He had taken up his residence at this settlement on the Baltic sea; a malignant fever prevailing there, he was prompted by humanity to visit a patient laboring under the contagion, when he received the infection, and died in consequence.

1790. Lafayette, in the assembly of the states general supported the motion for the abolition of titles of nobility, from which period he renounced his own, and never afterwards resumed it.

1795. The French under Pichegru entered Amsterdam, and Geertruidenberg capitulated to Gen. Bonneau.

1795. A great fire occurred at Bergen in Norway, when 60 houses and a great many stores were burnt.

1796. Pichegru attacked Kaiserslautern, but was repulsed with the loss of 2000 men and several cannon. Austrian loss about 700 killed and wounded.

1798. The frigate Crescent sailed from Portsmouth, N. H., as a present from the United States to the dey of Algiers; she also carried out presents to the amount of $300,000.

1800. Thomas Mifflin, an officer of the revolution, died. He was a member of the first congress, and for many years governor of Pennsylvania.

1813. Christopher Martin Wieland, a German author of great repute, died aged 80. He was the father of 14 children, and 42 quarto volumes of books! by the sale of which last he was enabled to purchase an estate. He was knighted by Alexander of Russia, and by Napoleon.

1817. The weather had been so moderate that up to this time no ice had been seen on the Delaware at Philadelphia.

1817. James Anthony, of Hanover co., Va., died, aged 104.

1823. The British government received advice that a Bengalee newspaper had been issued, edited by a learned Hindoo. Its title was *Sungband Cowmuddy*, or the *Moon of Intelligence*.

1835. The city of Mocha taken by the Egyptians under Achmet Pacha; by which the whole of Arabia was rendered subject to Mehemet Ali, pacha of Egypt.

1836. Xavier Saubert, the celebrated fire-king, being engaged in making some experiments in chemistry, with phosphoric ether, it exploded and scattered his body into a thousand pieces.

1836. Treaty of peace and commerce signed between the United States and the republic of Venezuela.

1839. The army of the confederation of Bolivia and Peru, commanded by Santa Cruz in person, was entirely defeated and destroyed, at Yungay, with a loss of 2,600 killed and 3,400 prisoners. Santa Cruz immediately resigned his office.

1843. A report fully approving of the conduct of Com. McKenzie and his officers on board the United States brig of war Somers, was brought in by the court appointed for that purpose.

1848. Christian VIII, king of Denmark, died in the 62d year of his age and 9th of his reign. A constitution was offered the same day by his successor.

1854. A tornado in Ohio half a mile in width demolished every thing it encountered, and almost entirely destroyed the town of Brandon.

This day in the calendar of Hesiod, is most propitious for the birth of men.

JANUARY 21.

988. Adalbero, archbishop of Rheims, died. He assisted in placing Hugh Capet on the throne of France.

1582. Ferdinand Alvarez de Toledo, duke of Alva, a Spanish general and minister of state, died, aged 74. It is said of him that during nearly sixty years of warfare against different enemies, he never lost a battle, and was never taken by surprise. He was undoubtedly the ablest general of his age; had a proud mien, a noble aspect and a strong frame; slept little, labored and wrote much. But pride, severity and cruelty tarnished his renown, so that he became odious even to his own countrymen.

1609. Joseph Justus Scaliger died, aged 69. His education commenced early, and he was one of the most indefatigable students through a long life, that was ever known. So entirely immersed was he in his studies, that he passed whole days in his chamber without eating or drinking, and paid very little attention to the common affairs of life. He may be called the founder of the science of chronology.

1647. The plague broke out at Edinburgh. A writer of the time says, that the last plague they had raged so violently that the fortieth person lived not of those who dwelt there four years before, but that it was peopled with new faces.

1666. SHAH JEHAN, a Mogul emperor, died, aged 74. He was the son and successor of Jehangir, but did not inherit much of the talent and spirit of that powerful ruler. During a severe illness the government was usurped by his son, and on his recovery he was removed from Delhi to Agra, where he died, probably by poison.

1692. King WILLIAM and his court issued a proclamation against vice and profaneness.

1702. The affirmation allowed by Queen Anne to the quakers in England, extended to those of Pennsylvania.

1707. AURUNGZEBE, (*ornament of the throne*,) died; the last powerful and energetic sovereign that ruled over the Mogul empire of Hindostan. From his 20th year, military duties devolved upon him; he raised a body of troops, and obtained the government of the Deccan. He invited his old friends the fakirs, or religious mendicants, to a feast, and compelled them to put on new and decent clothing. The gold and silver pieces which he found on burning their old garments, was of great service to him in prosecuting the war against his elder brother for the sovereignty. He stirred up dissensions among his brothers, by which they were put out of his way, shut up his father in his harem, and in 1659 ascended the throne. Notwithstanding his cruelty he governed with much wisdom, and consulted the welfare of his people. Two of his sons endeavoring to form a party in their own favor, he caused to be put to death by slow poison. In the midst of his activity he died at Ahmednagar, and with his death terminated the brilliant epoch of the Moguls.

1721. FRANCIS PAGI died, author of a chronological history of the popes.

1733. BERNARD DE MANDEVILLE, an English author, died. He was born at Dort in Holland, and went to England to practice medicine. Meeting with poor encouragement, he turned author; but his topics, though professedly intended for the promotion of the public morals, introduced him to the notice of the grand jury. His pen procured the means of subsistence, but acquired for him an unenviable notoriety.

1750. JOHN BLAND, the renowned writing master, died at his academy in London.

1759. Battle of Wandewash, in India. The French under Lally defeated with the loss of 800 killed and wounded, by the British under Col. Coote, who lost 262 do.

1769. The first letter of JUNIUS appeared in Woodfall's *Public Advertiser;* and the last number was also published on this day, 1772.

1773. ALEXIS PIRON, a French dramatist, died. His first effusions were satires, which procured him so many enemies that even in the latter part of his life he could not get admission into the Academy. He revenged himself by calling them *les invalides du bel esprit*, and composing his own humorous epitaph:

> *Ci-git Piron, qui ne fut rien,*
> *Pas même académicien.*

1774. MUSTAPHA III, emperor of Turkey, died, and was succeeded by his brother Abdul Hamet.

1775. PUGATCHEF, the daring chief of the Tartars, defeated by the Russians, into whose hands he fell and was put to death.

1780. Admiral RODNEY of the English fleet arrived with his prizes and transports for the relief of Gibraltar; the garrison was short of provisions.

1782. Grand fete in Paris on the birth of the dauphin.

1793. LOUIS XVI beheaded at Paris, aged 38. He had reigned 17 years and 7 months, and is now represented as an amiable and benevolent man, anxious to make his subjects happy; who in turn treated him in the vilest manner, and executed him as a tyrant and a traitor. His behavior on many trying occasions vindicated him effectually of timidity, and showed that the unwillingness to shed blood by which he was particularly distinguished, arose from benevolence, and not from pusillanimity. Upon the scaffold he exhibited a firmness that became a noble spirit.

1814. JACQUES BERNARDIN HENRY DE ST. PIERRE, a French philosophical writer, died, at his estate near Paris. He is best known as the author of *Paul and Virginia*, which appeared in 1788, and passed through fifty editions in one year. It has been generally translated in Europe.

1815. MATTHIAS CLAUDIUS, a German poet, died. His prose and poetry are said to bear a peculiar stamp of humor, frankness and cordiality, and many of his songs, set to music by the first composers, have become a part of the national melodies. He filled several public offices.

1816. Day of general mourning in France, on account of the death of Louis XVI, twenty-three years after his execution.

1820. AMBROISE MARIE FRANCIS JOSEPH PALISOT DE BEAUVAIS, a French naturalist, died. He came to America in the pursuit of science, and while at Philadelphia learnt that he had been proscribed by the revolutionists as an emigrant. He supported himself as a teacher of music and languages until the arrival of the French minister, who afforded Palisot the means of prosecuting inquiries into the natural history of America. He was employed to arrange Peale's collection. On returning to France with his rich collections, he was admitted into the Institute, in the place of Adanson.

1824. CHARLES MACARTHY killed. He commanded at the Cape-Coast against the Ashantees. Whilst making preparations to repel these savages in 1821, the king sent his compliments to him, and said he hoped to have his head as an ornament to their great war drum. Subsequently Sir Charles marched against the enemy with a mixed force of Europeans and blacks; the latter ran away, and the whites being defeated and their commander captured, the ferocious menace was realized. The trophy however was afterwards recovered.

1839. Great conflagration at Constantinople, in which the grand vizier's palace, called the Sublime Porte, including the ministerial and administration offices, was destroyed. Loss estimated at 20,000,000 piasters.

1847. Major JAMES MORTON, died at High Hill, Virginia, aged 90. In the revolutionary war he acquired the cognomen of *Solid Column*, by which soubriquet he was recognized by La Fayette in 1824, at Richmond.

1854. The magnificent British vessel Tayleur on its voyage to Melbourne, wrecked on the Irish coast, and 370 persons lost.

JANUARY 22.

The *Catagogia*, an erotic and bacchanalian festival celebrated at Ephesus by its licentious devotees, about the first century.

97. TIMOTHY, to whom St. Paul addressed several epistles, is said to have been killed at Paris (Ephesus).

1265. First English parliament constituted of members from counties, &c., as at present, met.

1528. HENRY VIII and FRANCIS I declared war against Charles V of Germany.

1552. The duke of SOMERSET beheaded on pretence of inciting others to imprison Dudley, the duke of Northumberland. He was a distinguished writer of that age.

1561. Birthday of FRANCIS BACON, the English philosopher.

1562. The two houses of convocation subscribed the 39 articles of the English church.

1575. Queen ELIZABETH granted to Thomas Tallis and William Birde an exclusive patent for printing music, for the term of twenty-one years.

1683. ANTHONY ASHLEY COOPER, first earl of Shaftsbury, died. The career of this able, but dubious and versatile statesman was cast in a stormy period, and his acts have been severely reprehended. Yet much of it is to the attributed to the odium excited by opposing party feelings. His vices appear to have been redeemed by corresponding virtues, and had he appeared in a different age, it is likely he would have developed a different character.

1689. The British parliament having met under the name of a convention, declared that the king, James II, had abdicated the throne. William and Mary succeeded him.

1696. Birthday of JAMES BRUCKER, a German scholar, remembered by his *Critical History of Philosophy*, 6 vols. 4to. He gives an account of every school, from the Hebrew, Chaldaic and Egyptian, down to the Huron in America.

1749. MATTHEW CONCANEN, some time attorney-general of Jamaica, and a dramatic writer, died.

1788. Birthday of Lord BYRON.

1795. The French under Macdonald entered Naarden, Holland.

1800. GEORGE STEVENS died, best known as the editor of Shakspeare, though to the versatility and richness of his talent there are numerous testimonials. His literary collections were extremely curious, and as regards the days that are gone, of great value.

1809. Naval action off Guadaloupe between the British frigate Cleopatra and sloop of war Hazard, and the French frigate Topaz, 40 guns. The engagement lasted 45 minutes, and resulted in the capture of the Topaz, which was laden with provisions to relieve the garrison at Cayenne.

1810. The French forced the passage of the Sierra Morena, in Spain.

1812. Madame REICHARD ascended in a balloon to a great height at Kœnigsberg in Prussia. The balloon was totally destroyed by a hurricane, and the aeronaut precipitated to the earth, yet escaped with life.

1813. Second battle of Frenchtown in Michigan. The van of Gen. Harrison's army, about 750 men, was attacked at day break by 2000 British and Indians under Proctor and Tecumseh. Notwithstanding the superiority of the latter in numbers, the Americans fought with desperation six hours, when they surrendered. British loss, as stated by Proctor, 24 killed, 128 wounded; the loss of the Indians is supposed to have been greater. American loss, 200 killed, 522 prisoners, 27 escaped. Proctor was promoted.

1815. The remains of LOUIS XVI and his queen taken up from the burial ground, and deposited with much solemnity in the royal church of St. Denis.

1815. American commodore PATTERSON captured a British transport schooner, and took 63 prisoners. His own force was 53.

1815. United States privateer schooner Tomahawk 9 guns and 84 men, captured by the British ship Bulwark.

1818. CASPAR WISTAR died, a distinguished physician of Philadelphia. He was of German parentage, and a member of the society of Friends; became eminent as an anatomist, and corresponded with Cuvier and other eminent naturalists of Europe. He held scientific meetings at his own house, and was an active contributer to knowledge of all kinds. He died of a slow fever, caught by attending a poor family in a close apartment.

1822. JOHN JULIUS ANGERSTEIN died, celebrated as the founder of the British national gallery, which was purchased by the government after his death for £40,000, (*Cyclopedia Americana* says £60,000) and was first exhibited in May, 1824. He was born at St. Petersburg, 1735.

1830. Great fire at Pera, Constantinople, extinguished by the exertions of the crew of an English ship.

1834. Great earthquake in South-America; the cities of Popayan and Pasto almost entirely destroyed, and many lives lost.

1835. ANDREW WALLACE died at New York, aged 105. He emigrated from Scotland in 1752, enlisted in the American army in 1776, and continued in it till 1813, when he was honorably discharged, on account of his disability, having suffered a stroke of paralysis.

1840. JOHN FREDERICK BLUMENBACH died at Göttingen, aged 88. He was long a distinguished professor at the university, and a very eminent naturalist. His collection of skulls was said to be the richest in the world. The 50th year of his professorship was celebrated in 1826.

1849. JOHN C. CALHOUN'S draft of an address to the people of the United States adopted in preference to Berrien's, and the Southern convention adjourned sine die.

1854. PATRICK O'DONAHOE died at Brooklyn, N. Y.; one of the Irish exiles who escaped from Van Diemen's Land.

JANUARY 23.

1401. TAMERLANE introduced his troops into the city of Damascus, in violation of a truce; and after levying an enormous contribution in gold, massacred the inhabitants, and reduced the city to ashes, in revenge of the murder of the grandson of Mahomet, seven centuries before, by the Syrians.

1516. FERDINAND V of Spain died. He inherited the crowns of Aragon and Sicily, and united to them the kingdom of Castile by marriage. In 1492 he added to these the kingdom of Granada, the last possession of the Moors, by conquest; at the same time Columbus was discovering for him the new world. By force and treachery he acquired the kingdom of Naples, and by similar means Navarre was also added to his dominions. Thus the whole of Spain was united under him; so that he may be considered as the restorer if not the founder of the Spanish monarchy. He was the most powerful monarch of his time; but his conduct was characterized by a total want of faith, and a recklessness of principle of which he made no scruple of boasting. He was the founder of that fearful tribunal, the Inquisition.

1570. Earl MURRAY, regent of Scotland, shot by Hamilton of Bothwellhaugh. The latter, after the battle of Langside hill, had been condemned to death as a rebel, and pardoned. A part of his estate, however, was bestowed upon one of the regent's favorites, who seized Hamilton's house and turned his wife out into the fields naked in a cold night, by which she became deranged. This injury induced him to seek revenge on the regent, after which he escaped to France.

1722. HENRI DE BOULAINVILLIERS, count of St. Saire in Normandy, died. Having finished his studies he entered the army, which however, he soon left to devote his attention to literature. A marked antipathy to revelation pervades his writings, and exhibits itself in singular contrast with a superstitious reverence for judicial astrology, and the mystic sciences, which he cultivated with much diligence.

1733. O. S. Birthday of BENJAMIN LINCOLN, a revolutionary general, at Hingham, Mass. Great reliance was placed in his abilities by Washington, and many important commissions entrusted to him. In 1781 he was appointed secretary of war, which office he held three years, and then retired to his farm. He died 1810.

1761. Action between the British frigate Minerva, 22 guns, Capt. Hood, and French ship Warwick, 34 guns, M. de Bellair, near cape Pinas, which resulted in the capture of the latter. French loss 14 killed, 32 wounded; British loss 14 killed, 33 wounded, 3 of whom died.

1765. The British under Capt. Byron colonized the Falkland islands.

1766. WILLIAM CASLON, an eminent English type founder, died. He was induced to attempt letter-cutting by a friend, and such was the perfection to which he carried the art, that the beauty of his type exceeded all others of the day, and was sought for from other countries on the continent. He was employed to cut characters for several languages of Asia.

1772. Mrs. CLUM died near Litchfield, England, aged 138. She had lived 103 years in one house.

1775. The Pennsylvania convention declared their determination, in case the arbitrary laws of England were attempted to be executed by force, to repel the same by the most determined resistance.

1780. The British ship Culloden of 74 guns lost off Long island.

1789. FRANCES BROOKE died, an English lady, remarkable for her literary accomplishments. Her works consist of novels, periodicals, tragedies, musical dramas, and translations.

1789. JOHN CLELAND died; author of the notoriously immoral romance, *Fanny Hill.*

1790. The mutineers of the ship Bounty having arrived at Pitcairn's island, and landed all their effects, set fire to the vessel and destroyed every vestige that could lead to the discovery of their retreat. The island was then divided into nine equal portions between them, and the natives were reduced to the condition of slaves. (See Oct. 3.)

1795. JOHN SULLIVAN, a distinguished general in the revolutionary army, died. He was of Irish descent, and before the revolution practiced law in New Hampshire. He was among the first to take an active part in the contest; resigned his seat in the first congress to enter the army; was conspicuous at several engagements; and terminated his military career in laying waste the country of the Six Nations, in order to puta stop to their depredations. After the peace he filled several important state offices.

1795. The French took possession of the Hague and Helvoetsluis, made 800 Englishmen prisoners, and liberated 600 Frenchmen.

1799. The French under Championnet entered Naples.

1800. A convention signed between Gen. Kleber and the grand vizier for the evacuation of Egypt by the French troops.

1800. EDWARD RUTLEDGE, one of the signers of the Declaration of Independence, died. He was a member of the first congress and acted a conspicuous part during the war. While the British beleaguered Charleston, his native city, he commanded a company of troops, and was taken prisoner. On the restoration of peace he returned to the practice of law, and a short time previous to his death was elected governor of the state of South Carolina.

1802. HUMBOLDT and his companions ascended Chimborazo to the height of 18,576 feet above the surface of the sea. The blood started from their eyes, lips and gums, and they became almost torpid with cold. A narrow deep valley prevented them from reaching the summit, which was 1344 feet higher.

1806. WILLIAM PITT, second son of the earl of Chatham, died. He was born 1759, and at the age of 23 became chancellor of the exchequer and the next year prime minister. It was during the early part of his career that the American war was concluded. Notwithstanding the emoluments of his offices were great, so far from acquiring wealth, he died involved. Parliament decreed him a public funeral, and £40,000 to pay his debts.

1813. GEORGE CLYMER, one of the signers of the Declaration of Independence, died. By the death of his parents he was left an orphan at the age of 7 years; but he was taken care of by his uncle, who left him a large fortune, with which to continue the business of a merchant in Philadelphia. His services to the country during the revolution, in raising supplies and devising ways and means to continue the struggle, were of incalculable importance.

1813. Horrible massacre of the United States prisoners taken by the British and Indians at the battle of Frenchtown the day before. The houses in which the helpless wounded lay were set on fire, and those who were too feeble to continue the march were shot or tomahawked on the road. It is morally certain that the British generals Proctor and Elliott were culpable for this wanton sacrifice of human life to satiate the revenge of the savages.

1813. ROBERT JAMISON died in South Carolina, aged 104. His eyesight, which had failed him some years previous to his decease, returned again just before his death in all its strength.

1815. Thanksgiving day in New Orleans, and a solemn *Te Deum* on account of Jackson's victory.

1820. EDWARD, duke of Kent, died. He was the fourth son of George III. In 1802 he was appointed governor of Gibraltar, but his rigid discipline produced a mutiny, and he was recalled. The present queen of England is his daughter.

1824. STEPHEN ACOUR KOVER, an Armenian writer of distinction, died, aged 84.

1833. BANASTRE TARLETON died, aged 78. He commanded the British cavalry in the Carolinas, in the revolution.

1841. SARAH ANN DAVIS sentenced at Philadelphia for murder; the first capital conviction of a female in Philadelphia.

1844. WILLIAM GASTON died at Raleigh, the capital of his native state. The prudence and energy of his mother made a disposition, naturally volatile and irritable, become a pattern of patience and perseverance. His speeches when a member of congress were highly finished.

1853. Junius Smith died, aged 74; having devoted a considerable portion of his life to the establishment of transatlantic steam-navigation, and the naturalization of the teaplant in the United States.

1854. Alexander de Bodisco died at Georgetown. He was seventeen years Russian minister at Washington, and was very popular with the American people.

1855. There was an earthquake in a part of New Zealand, by which the surface of the earth was raised between three and four feet, and the shellfish attached to the rocks died.

JANUARY 24.

41. Caius Caligula, the Roman emperor, assassinated. He commenced his reign with every promise of becoming a good monarch. But at the end of eight months he was attacked with a fever, which appears to have left a frenzy upon his mind, for his disposition was totally reversed. After committing the most atrocious acts of cruelty and folly, he was assassinated by a tribune as he came out of the amphitheatre, in the 29th year of his age, and the 4th of his reign.

76. Birthday of Publius Ælius Adrian, the Roman emperor. He was a renowned general and great traveler; who, on a visit to Britain, built the famous wall or rampart, which still retains his name, extending from the mouth of the Tyne to the Solway frith, 80 miles, to prevent the incursions of the Caledonians into England.

1559. Christian II, king of Denmark, died. His history affords a series of cruelties and usurpations almost without a parallel, from 1515, when he ascended the throne, until 1523, when he was deposed. The remainder of his life was passed in imprisonment.

1709. George Rooke, an English admiral, died. He took the fortress of Gibraltar, by surprise, 1704; since which it has continued in the hands of the British, and is considered impregnable.

1712. Birthday of Frederick the Great of Prussia.

1727. Philip de Vendome, a French general, died. He distinguished himself in the army of Louis XIV.

1762. James Ralph, a voluminous writer of poetry, politics and history, died. He was an American by birth, but went over to England about 1729. He wrote a history of England, commencing with the Stuarts.

1781. The British garrison at Georgetown, South Carolina, surprised and taken by General Lee.

1793. The French minister, M. Chauvelin, ordered to quit England before the 1st of February.

1795. Lord Hood sailed from England, on an expedition against Corsica.

1797. At a dinner complimentary to Charles J. Fox, the chairman, the duke of Norfolk, gave as a toast, "Our sovereign's health, the majesty of the people;" for which offence he lost all his offices.

1812. Daniel McDonald died at Canajoharie, aged 102. He was a native of Ireland, born in the reign of Queen Anne, and had seen four monarchs on the English throne. He took an early and active part in the revolutionary war; and was possessed of a most remarkable degree of activity, both of body and mind, until the morning he expired.

1834. William Donnison, an officer of the revolution, died. He was appointed adjutant and inspector-general of the Massachusetts militia by Gov. Hancock in 1788, which office he held until 1813.

1838. Joseph Gouge, a revolutionary soldier, died, aged 109.

1838. Defeat of the Indians at Loche-Hatchee by the United States troops under Gen. Jessup; loss of the latter, 7 killed and 32 wounded.

1841. Matthias Denman, an enterprising western pioneer, and in early life one of the first owners of the land on which Cincinnati now stands, died at Springfield, N. J., aged 91.

1851. G. L. P. Spontini died in Italy; a celebrated dramatic composer, in the line of opera.

1857. Dr. Medhurst, English missionary to China, died, aged 71. He was also a noted linguist, and author of a work on China, a Chinese dictionary, and a Japanese and English vocabulary.

JANUARY 25.

275. Lucius Domitius Aurelianus, emperor of Rome, assassinated. He was the son of a peasant; his mother a priestess of the Temple of the Sun. He enlisted as a common soldier, and rose from that humble station to the highest military offices during the reigns of Valerian and Claudius, the latter of whom, on his death bed, recommended Aurelian to the choice of the troops. He delivered Italy from the barbarians, and conquered the famous Zenobia queen of Palmyra. He had planned an expedition against Persia, and was

waiting in Thrace for an opportunity to cross the straits when he fell a victim to a conspiracy.

1327. EDWARD II of England, then a prisoner in Kenilworth castle, compelled to resign his crown in favor of his son, Edward III.

1533. HENRY VIII privately married to Ann Boleyn in a garret at Whitehall.

1640. ROBERT BURTON, an English divine, died. He is known principally by his *Anatomy of Melancholy*, a rare book, which it is said he wrote to divert his own thoughts from that feeling.

1692. The Indians, accompanied by some French, attacked the town of York in Maine, killed 50 and carried away 100 of the inhabitants, and destroyed the town.

1717. The episcopal clergy of Scotland, who had before been fined for not praying for King George by name were forced to abscond or fly their country.

1726. WILLIAM DE LISLE, a distinguished geographer, died at Paris. His maps are still of great authority.

1730. A fire which broke out in the archduchess's apartments at Brussels, consumed the palace, with the national records and state papers.

1745. Action in the straits of Banca, (Sumatra) between the British ships Debtford and Preston, Com. Barnet, and three French company ships, in which the latter were captured.

1759. Birthday of ROBERT BURNS.

1782. DE GRASSE attacked the van of the British fleet under Admiral Hood. The French were drawn from their anchorage ground, and by a masterly manœuvre the British succeeded in obtaining it.

1786. CHARLES PRICE, one of the most successful counterfeiters ever known, committed suicide in prison, London. He had continued to practice forgeries on the Bank of England to an incredible amount during six years, contriving all the while to elude the most cunning devices of the police to detect him, although the notes were traced in every quarter to have proceeded from one man, always disguised and always inaccessible.

1787. Battle with the insurgents under Shays, at Springfield, Mass., who retreated with the loss of 3 killed.

1791. GEORGE SELWYN, a noted English wit, died, aged 72.

1804. JEAN JACQUES DESSALINES declared emperor of Hayti.

1807. Battle at Mohringen, in Prussian Poland, in which Bernadotte defeated the Russians under Pahlin and Salitzin, who lost 1200 killed and 300 prisoners.

1813. Concordat signed at Versailles, by which Napoleon allowed the pope to exercise the pontificate in France and Italy, in the same manner as his predecessors.

1834. Castle of St. Louis at Quebec, the residence of the British governor-general, destroyed by fire.

1836. General PAEZ gained a victory over the rebels at Venezuela near Porto Cabello.

1838. Earthquake in the eastern part of Europe. Seven severe shocks occurred during a few days, by which 300 houses were thrown down in the city of Bucharest, and 60 persons killed.

1841. The shock of an earthquake was felt in the city of New York and vicinity to such a degree as to excite considerable alarm.

1843. EDWARD DRUMMUND, private secretary to Sir Robert Peel, was assassinated in the streets of London. For nearly 20 years he discharged duties second to those of a cabinet minister, because less conspicuous.

1845. ALBIGAIL LEONARD died at Raynham, Mass., 101 years old. She was the fifth in descent from John Alden, who first landed from the Mayflower on the Plymouth rock.

1849. The usual convention of the two houses of congress declared that the people had elected Zachary Taylor their president and Millard Fillmore vice-president.

JANUARY 26.

477. Subterranean thunders were heard simultaneously from the Black to the Red sea, and the earth was convulsed without intermission for the space of six months after. In many places the air seemed to be on fire. Towns and large tracts of ground were swallowed up in Phrygia, during this convulsion, the particulars of which would seem incredible, were they not corroborated by contemporary historians.

1564. The pope confirmed by a bull the decrees of the Council of Trent.

1630. HENRY BRIGGS, an English mathematician, died.

1679. Keel of the Griffin, the first vessel in the western waters, laid 6 miles west of Niagara falls, by La Salle.

1679. The invaluable library of Elias Ashmole destroyed by fire at his chambers in London, together with his collection of coins and other curious antiquities.

1681. Two Cameronian women hanged at Edinburgh for calling the king and bishops "perjured, bloody men."

1699. Peace of Carlowitz concluded between Leopold I of Austria, and Mustapha II sultan of Turkey, after fifteen years of hostility.

1721. PETER DANIEL HUET, a celebrated French critic and classical scholar died. He was engaged twenty years in publishing an edition of the Latin classics, which extended to 62 vols.

1730. A leaden pot containing a human heart preserved in spirits dug up at Waverly in Surrey, England, supposed to have been there 700 years.

1733. A negro for an assault upon a white woman was burnt alive in New Jersey.

1737. All the prisoners for debt in White Chapel jail, England, were discharged by the executors of the will of the late Mr. Wright who paid their debts.

1769. JOHN WHITE, printer and publisher of the *Newcastle Courant*, died, aged 81. At his decease he was the oldest master printer in England.

1779. ARNOLD sentenced by court martial to be reprimanded by Gen. Washington.

1782. DE GRASSE with the French fleet, 29 sail, attacked the British under Hood, 22 sail, but was repulsed with the loss of 1000 killed and wounded. British loss trifling.

1787. The assembly of notables met at Paris, having been called together to assist the king, Louis XVI, and M. Calonne, to raise a revenue to meet the exigencies of the times. M. Calonne presented his new plan of reform and taxation, imposing a share of the burden upon the privileged classes: but as the assembly was composed of these classes they could not make up their minds to impose taxes upon themselves which had hitherto been borne by the lower classes. The assembly was called to help the king and his minister out of a dilemma, but plunged them deeper in trouble, and accelerated the revolution.

1793. The stadtholderate of Holland abolished, and the Batavian republic under the protection of France established.

1793. The senate of Venice acknowledged the French republic.

1795. The French national convention declared Marseilles in a state of siege.

1795. The assembly of the states of Holland met and chose Peter Paulus their president for the term of fifteen days.

1814. The Russians under Blücher passed the Marne and marched upon Troyes. Bonâparte at the same time entered Vitry.

1820. HENRY ANDREWS, a self-taught English mathematician, died. For more than forty years he produced an almanac for a company of stationers under the name of Francis Moore, physician, and astonished the simple and ignorant by his marvelous predictions. His prophecies were as much laughed at by himself as by the worshipful company of stationers for whom he annually manufactured them in order to render their almanacs salable among the ignorant, with whom a lucky hit covered a multitude of blunders. A few years before his death he predicted that the people would soon know better than to be influenced by the prophecies which his employers required him to write. He did not live to see the publication of the *British Almanac*, which effected the downfall of *Poor Robin* (the title of one of his almanacs), which ceased to exist in 1828.

1823. EDWARD JENNER died, aged 74, celebrated for having introduced the practice of vaccination as a preventative of the small pox. He was the youngest son of a clergyman, born in England 1749. He commenced his investigations concerning the cow pox about the year 1776, and twenty years afterwards the practice was introduced into London hospitals. The success of this discovery procured him honorary titles, and a grant from parliament of £20,000.

1838. JOHN O'NEIL died at Havre de Grace, Md., distinguished for the resistance which he made at that place, to the British under admiral Cockburn, during the last war.

1839. STEPHEN VAN RENSSELAER died at Albany. He was born in the city of New York 1764, and graduated at Cambridge, Mass. He was the fifth in descent from Kilian Van Rensselaer, the original proprietor and patentee of the colony of Rensselaerwyck, a territory 48 miles long and 24 broad. He filled several offices, civil and military; was a man of great wealth, and distinguished for his magnificent charities and Christian virtues.

1839. Tremendous gale and heavy rain in the United States. The river at Philadelphia rose 17 feet above low water mark, and at Kenebec 13 feet above high water mark. New York and Albany were considerably flowed.

1850. FRANCIS JEFFREY, a Scottish jurist, celebrated by his long connection with the *Edinburgh Review*, died, aged 77.

1853. SYLVESTER JUDD died, aged 40; a unitarian clergyman at Augusta, Me., author of several works which found many admirers.

JANUARY 27.

438. St. JOHN CHRYSOSTOM, one of the Fathers and archbishop of Constantinople, died.

1673. JEROME LALLEMANT, superior of the Jesuits in Canada, died, aged 80; leaving behind him a high reputation in his order. He furnished seven of the *Relaçons.*

1676. The Narragansetts, in retreating from their country in Rhode island, drove off from one of the inhabitants of Warwick, 15 horses, 50 oxen and 200 sheep.

1696. The Royal Sovereign burnt by accident. She was the first great ship built in England, and became one of the best men of war in the world. For sixty years she was so formidable to her enemies that none of the most daring of them willingly ventured an engagement. The levies of money for building this noble vessel caused the rebellion.

1733. THOMAS WOOLSTON, an English divine, died in prison. He imbibed a fondness for allegorical interpretations of scripture from reading some of the early writers—particularly Origen. His speculations finally led to an indictment for blasphemy, and being unable to pay the fine imposed, he was retained in prison. He was a learned man, but held notions peculiar to himself, which was a high offence in those days.

1760. The ice carried away one of the dykes of the Rhine, in consequence of which the neighboring country was inundated.

1783. The British under Gen. Mathews took possession of Bednapore and Candapore, without firing a gun, and the whole country, except Mangalore, yielded in consequence.

1795. PICHEGRU made a requisition upon the Dutch for the French army of 200,000 quintals of corn, 5,000,000 rations of hay, 5,000,000 measures of oats, 200,000 rations of straw, 150,000 pairs of shoes, 20,000 pairs of boots, 20,000 cloth coats and waistcoats, 40,000 pairs of stocking breeches, 150,000 pairs of linen pants, 200,000 shirts, 50,000 hats, to be furnished within a month, and 12,000 oxen to be furnished within two months.

1800. King John's castle, at Old Ford near Bow, in England, was blown down by a storm. It was built in 1203 and afforded the king a sleeping place after signing the magna charta.

1807. BURR's conspiracy communicated to congress.

1807. BONAPARTE confiscated the possessions of Ernest Frederick Anthony, hereditary prince of Saxe Coburg, for holding a commission in the Russian service.

1807. Action between the British ship Caroline and the Spanish ship St. Raphael, which resulted in the capture of the latter, bound from Lima to Manilla, with 500,000 Spanish dollars, 1,700 quintals of copper, and a valuable cargo.

1814. Camp Defiance attacked by the Indians at day break. The United States troops and friendly Indians were commanded by Gen. Floyd, who repulsed the assailants with great slaughter.

1823. CHARLES HUTTON, an eminent English mathematician, died. He was born 1737; his father, a viewer of mines, intended him for the same employment; but he rose by his own energy and application to a high degree of fame and fortune.

1832. AUGUSTIN DANIELS, count de Billiard, died, a French statesman and soldier. He fought at Jemappes, was with Bonaparte through the Egyptian campaign; at Austerlitz; in all the great battles in Prussia; at Moskwa; and lost an arm at Leipsic. He made himself useful under Louis XVIII and Louis Philippe.

1832. ANDREW BELL, founder of the Bell or Madras system of education, died. It has been made a subject of dispute whether Bell or Lancaster is the progenitor of the monitorial or mutual system of instruction. In 1796 Dr. Bell returned from Madras, and submitted his system to the public. It has since been widely diffused over the civilized world.

1836. FREDERICK DAVID SCHAEFFER died, pastor of the German Lutheran church in Philadelphia. He was born and educated in Germany, but came to this country in early life. He was a man of learning, and distinguished for his knowledge of languages.

1840. ISAAC CHAUNCEY, a distinguished American commodore, died at Washington.

1841. McLEOD arrested within the limits of the state of New York. Though engaged in burning the steamboat Caroline in 1837, yet being a British subject and that government having assumed the responsibility of that act, his arrest threatened a rupture of the peace between the two nations.

1850. WILLIAM ATKINS COLEMAN, for more than thirty years connected with the literature of New York, died.

1856. CHARLES MORRIS, a commodore in the United States navy, died, aged 71. He was the acknowledged chief of the navy in administrative wisdom and in varied professional attainments; had displayed great heroism and intrepidity in the capture of the Philadelphia and Guerriere; in the latter action he was shot through the body by a musket ball.

JANUARY 28.

814. CHARLEMAGNE, or Charles I of France, died. He was an illustrious sovereign, as well in the cabinet as in the

field; and though he could not write his name, was the patron of men of letters and the restorer of learning. He wanted the virtue of humanity.

1547. HENRY VIII of England having grown so unwieldy and corpulent that he was raised up and let down the stairs by a machine, after an illness of some weeks, sank under his disease, and died in the 38th year of his reign, and the 56th of his age. He repudiated his first wife 20 years after marriage, and in the course of about ten years espoused five others. Henry's reign was one of the most remarkable in the annals of the kingdom. He made himself so much feared, that no English king had fewer checks to his power. No hand less strong than his could have snapped the chain which bound the nation to papacy, and have resisted successfully the power and influence of the pope.

1588. THOMAS CARN died in London, aged 207; an instance of longevity exceeding any other on modern record, but well authenticated in the parish register of St. Leonard, Shoreditch. An old man died at Ekaterinoslaf, Russia, in 1813, between 200 and 205 years of age; and Don John Taveira de Lima died in Portugal, 1738, aged 198.

1596. FRANCIS DRAKE, the first Englishman that circumnavigated the world, died on board his own ship. (See Jan. 9.)

1612. THOMAS BODLEY died. He was actively employed during the last fifteen years of his life in collecting manuscripts and books for the library at Oxford which bears his name, and which by his perseverance came to be one of the most celebrated in Europe.

1687. JOHN HEVELIUS died, an eminent German astronomer.

1725. PETER the Great, of Russia, died, aged 53. He devoted his life time to civilize his subjects, and raise the nation from barbarism and ignorance, to politeness, knowledge and power. He spared no pains or fatigue to obtain knowledge which he thought would be beneficial to his subjects.

1732. The protestants of Saltzburg being driven out of their country, settled by invitation of the king of Prussia in Brandenburg.

1738. The first stone of Westminster bridge over the Thames laid.

1782. JOHN BAPTISTE BOURGUIGNON D'ANVILLE, the French geographer, died. He was esteemed as well for the gentleness and simplicity of his manners, as for his extensive knowledge. He labored at his maps fifteen hours a day for fifty years.

1782. JAMES MURRAY, a very eminent historical writer, and pastor, died at New Castle upon Tyne, England.

1790. The Jews of Spain, Portugal and Avignon admitted to the privileges of French citizens.

1794. JOHN GOTTLOB IMMANUEL BREITKOPF died at Leipsic. He acquired great celebrity as a printer and type founder. His foundry contained punches and matrices for 400 alphabets. He improved the printing press, and discovered a new method for facilitating the process of melting and casting. From his foundry types were sent to Russia, Sweden, Poland, and even America. With the interruption of only five or six hours for sleep, his whole life was devoted to study and useful employment.

1796. Prince of Wales, regent of England, attacked in his carriage by the populace.

1797. Battle of Unroomster, in India; Zemaun Shah attacked the Seicks at 8 o'clock in the morning, by opening his *shutah renauls*, or wall pieces mounted on camels, and a heavy fire was kept up until 2 o'clock, when the Seicks gave a signal for a general charge, and agreeable to their mode in close combat, flung away their turbans, let loose their hair, put their beards in their mouths, and dashed into the midst of the Huddalah army. The two armies continued engaged in close combat four hours, when Zemaun's troops gave way, and were pursued to the very gates of Lahore. The loss of the Seicks was 15,000; that of the Shah 20,000 killed.

1803. Madame CLAIRON, a French actress, died. She evinced when very young a predilection for the stage, and adopting the theatrical profession, soon became the first tragic performer of her age, and long remained without a rival. She published *Mémoires et Réflexions sur la Déclamation Théatrale.*

1804. JOSEPH NICHOLAS D'AZARA, a Spanish diplomatist, died, aged 73. He became acquainted with Napoleon in 1796, who conceived great admiration of him. He was an ardent admirer of the arts and sciences, and collected an elegant library and a rich collection of paintings and antiques, which however he lost in the political changes of the times.

1816. RICHARD JOACHIM HENRY VON MOELLENDORF, a Prussian general, died. He commanded the Prussian troops employed in 1793 in the disgraceful dismemberment of Poland, on which occasion he did every thing consistent with his commission to alleviate the misfortunes of the Poles.

1818. NATHAN BIRDSEYE died at Stratford, Conn., aged 103. His funeral was attended by 100 of his descendants; the whole number of which was 258.

1836. WILLIAM SCOTT, Baron Stowell, died. He filled the office of judge of the court of admiralty in England, thirty years with distinguished ability. He is represented to have been the charm and ornament of every society of which he formed a part; and his unbounded charities acquired for him universal regard and esteem.

1841. WILLIAM HOGG died at Brownsville, Pa., aged 86, leaving an estate of one million dollars to his heirs. Fifty years previous to his death, he crossed the Alleganies with a pack of goods on his back, which was his whole property, and opened a small store soon after at Brownsville, the first in that region of country.

1842. The first stone of the Anglican cathedral at Jerusalem laid, at a depth of 35 feet from the surface. It stands upon mount Zion, and the state of the rubbish which had accumulated since the time of David, rendered it necessary to excavate to the depth of 42 feet to the natural rock.

1854. LEWIS W. CHAMBERLAYNE, a Virginia physician, died; one of the founders of the Richmond medical college, of which he was a distinguished professor.

1854. A ball-cartridge manufactory at Ravenswood, L. I., blew up killing 20 workmen and destroying 50,000 ball-cartridges.

1854. The steamer Georgia, from Montgomery, Ala., having 200 passengers and 1000 bales of cotton on board, took fire at New Orleans, and 60 passengers lost their lives.

1855. The Panama railroad being completed, the first train passed over it this day.

JANUARY 29.

164 B. C. ANTIOCHUS EPIPHANES, the great enemy of the Jews, died.

1559. THOMAS POPE, the founder of Trinity college, Dublin, died.

1597. ANTHONY SHIRLEY, commanding a British squadron, landed at Jamaica, and marched six miles to the principal town, which submitted to his mercy.

1720. JOHN ADAMS, a celebrated English preacher, died.

1728. Dean Swift's STELLA died at Dublin.

1743. ANDREW HERCULE DE FLEURY, cardinal and prime minister of Louis XV, died, aged 90. He was 73 years of age when he was placed at the head of the ministry, at which time the state was in a miserable condition. He healed the wounds of his country, and without bloodshed or cruelty established and increased the internal happiness of France, and its national glory.

1762. From Christmas to this day the weather was severely cold in England. The ice on the Thames it is said was over five feet thick!

1780. The coldest day for 25 years at Philadelphia.

1812. Desperate attempt by a black man, a negro, to fire the British privateer Speedwell. He was killed after 7 shots had been fired at him.

1814. Battle of Brienne, in which the French under Napoleon gained an inconsiderable victory over the allies under Blücher, who narrowly escaped being taken prisoner. It was at this place that Bonaparte acquired the rudiments of that skill in the military art with which he had almost prostrated the world.

1820. GEORGE III died. It was during his reign that the discontents in America burst into an open flame, and an empire was lost to the British throne. In 1810 he retired from the government, and the interval which elapsed from that time until his death was a period of insanity. He died in the 82d year of his age and the 59th of his reign.

1824. LOUISA MARIA CAROLINE, countess of Albany, died at Florence, aged 72. She was the daughter of a German prince, and married Charles Stuart, the English pretender, whence she derived the title of countess of Albany. They resided at Rome, and had a little court, and were addressed as king and queen. The connection, however, was an unhappy one, and to escape from the barbarity of her husband she retired to a convent, and afterwards went to France. On the death of Charles, 1788, she returned to Italy. She was then secretly married to Alfieri, the poet; the French court conferred on her an annuity of 60,000 livres. Alfieri confesses that to her he owed his inspiration, and that without her friendship he should never have achieved anything excellent. Their ashes repose under a common monument in the church of Santa Croce, between the tombs of Machiavelli and Michael Angelo.

1829. PAUL FRANCIS JEAN NICHOLAS DE BARRAS, a French revolutionist, died. As a member of the national convention, he voted for the king's death; and subsequently, having offended Robespierre, he headed the force that captured the tyrant. As commander-in-chief of the troops of the convention, he entrusted Bonaparte with the post in which he first distinguished himself, on the 5th Oct., 1795. His political career ended 1799, when he received a passport to his estate from Napoleon, then first consul.

1829. TIMOTHY PICKERING, an American soldier and statesman, died. In public life he was distinguished for energy, ability and disinterestedness; as a soldier he was brave and patriotic; and his writings bear ample testimony to his talents and information. He was one of the leaders of the federal party.

1834. Duel at Paris between Gen. Bugeaud and M. Dulong, members of the chamber of deputies; Dulong was killed.

1855. NICHOLAS ordered the formation of a general militia of the Russian empire.

JANUARY 30.

422 B. C. A census of the inhabitants of Athens was taken, and reported the number of males to be 20,000.

405 B. C. Sophocles died at Athens.

1560. A phenomenon observed at London, called the *burning spears*, being one of the earliest records of that appearance now well known by the name of aurora borealis.

1601. SCIPIO AMMIRATI, an Italian historian, died. He wrote a history of Florence, published in 2 vols. folio.

1606. EVERARD DIGBY hanged, drawn and quartered at the west end of St. Paul's church, London. He was concerned in the gunpowder plot, having offered £1500 towards defraying the expenses of that dreadful affair. He also entertained Fawkes, who was to have executed it in his house, and was taken in open rebellion with other papists after the plot was detected and had miscarried.

1644. WILLIAM CHILLINGWORTH died; celebrated for his skill as a religious controversialist, and a defender of protestantism against popery.

1647. King CHARLES I delivered up to parliament by the Scots for £200,000. Some think it unworthy of the nation.

1649. CHARLES I beheaded. He was born in Scotland 1600, and succeeded to the British throne 1625. His reign was signalized by a struggle with his parliaments, in procuring supplies, which finally ended in his execution. He was tried for treason against the people, and condemned with only three days' grace.

1660. WILLIAM OUGHTRED, an English divine and mathematician, died, it is said, in consequence of excess of joy at the restoration of Charles II, whom he called Christ's anointed.

1661. The heads of Oliver Cromwell, John Bradshaw, and Henry Ireton set on poles at Westminster hall, and their bodies buried under the gallows at Tyburn, where their disinterred bodies had been hung.

1678. The expense of the equestrian statue of Charles I at Charing Cross, London, was defrayed with part of £70,000, voted for his funeral celebration.

1691. Pope ALEXANDER III died, after a reign of only 15 months.

1735. GEORGE GRANVILLE, viscount Lansdowne, an eminent English poet, died. Having vainly endeavored to get employment in arms for the defence of James II, to whose cause he was warmly attached, he retired to private life, enjoying the company of his muse, which he employed in celebrating the reigning beauties of the age, in imitation of Waller.

1757. Calcutta retaken by Col. Clive.

1766. JAMES BARTHOLOMEW BECCARIA, an Italian physician and professor of natural philosophy, died. His writings are highly esteemed.

1766. SUSANNA MARIA CIBBER died. She was not only considered the best actress in England, but supposed by many to excel the celebrated Madame Clairon, of Paris, her contemporary.

1805. JOHN ROBINSON, a celebrated Edinburgh mathematician, died.

1809. Assault upon Saragossa in Spain by the French under Junot, Lannes and Mortier. The Spaniards made a most desperate resistance; a corps of women even being formed for its defence. The houses were taken one by one; they were compelled to undermine upwards of 600 in order to get possession of them.

1810. Several meteoric stones fell in Caswell county, North Carolina.

1826. The mails were first carried over the Menai suspension bridge, which connects the island of Anglesey with the Welch shore.

1833. JOSEPH BLUYDENBURGE died at Smithtown, L. I., aged 101, retaining the vigor of perfect health to the last week of his life.

1834. Attempt to assassinate the president of the United States, Andrew Jackson, made by Richard Lawrence.

1834. RUDOLPH ACKERMAN, who so much improved lithography, and the first to use gas-light in England, died.

1837. Explosion of the magazine of the French garrison at Bona in Algiers, containing 12,000 pounds of powder and 1 million musket cartridges. The commandant with 108 men were killed, and 102 wounded.

1837. The town of Jaffa in Palestine destroyed by an earthquake. Of 15,000 inhabitants, only 2,000 escaped burial in the ruins.

1837. ADAM AZELIUS, the last remaining pupil of Linnæus, died; celebrated for his travels in Asia and Africa.

1841. The town of Mayaguez, Porto Rico, consisting of about 600 buildings, was consumed by fire. Loss estimated at from two to four millions of dollars.

1852. The king of Naples by decree confiscated the property of Neapolitan emigrants.

1855. Herman Knickerbacker died, aged 75; known as the prince of Schaghticoke, being the third in descent from the original settler there.

JANUARY 31.

1000 B. C. It is usual to fix the finishing of the temple of *Hercules* at *Tyre* on this day, and the death of *Anchises*, 183 years earlier.

1574. Birthday of Ben Jonson.

1578. Battle of Gémblours, in the Netherlands, by which the Spanish recovered their superiority in the Walloon provinces which were zealously catholic.

1606. Guido Fawkes executed. He was an officer in the Spanish service, concerned in the gunpowder plot, and discovered in the vault below the House of Lords, prepared to fire the train which was to involve the enemies of the catholic religion in one common ruin.

1616. Jacob Le Maire, a Dutchman, discovered cape Horn, the southern extremity of the American continent.

1686. In Norway, Courland and Pomerania, there fell a great quantity of a membraneous substance, friable, and blackish, somewhat like burnt paper. Baron Grotthus analyzed a portion of this substance, which has been preserved in a cabinet of natural history, and it is found to consist of silex, iron, lime, carbon, magnesia, a trace of chrome and sulphur, but not a particle of nickel.

1692. Massacre of Glencoe, Scotland. King William, whose chief virtue was not humanity, signed and countersigned the warrant, which was transmitted to the secretary for Scotland, who particularly charged the ministers of destruction to take no prisoners. The population was barbarously massacred, and the spot disemboweled of every social appearance.

1718. Ashton Lever died at Manchester, England. He was a collector of specimens in natural history, and possessed one of the finest museums in the world.

1750. The *Student*, a paper of much merit, issued at Oxford, England, appeared this day.

1754. The 1st number of the *Connoisseur* appeared, conducted by Coleman, Bonnell, Thornton, Chesterfield and others.

1775. Capt. Cooke discovered Southern Thule, soon after Sandwich land which from the vast quantities of ice seen he conjectured might be a continent.

1787. The attorney general stated to the Irish parliament that an insurrection existed in the county of Kerry, the people having taken an oath to obey the laws of *Captain Right* (a fictitious name), and to starve the clergy.

1788. Charles Stuart, the pretender to the throne of England, died at Rome. He was the grandson of James II, born at Rome 1720. In 1745 he landed in Scotland, with only seven companions, and marched south gaining strength and carrying every thing before him till he arrived within 100 miles of London. Here his career was arrested, and the battle of Culloden decided his fate. He wandered about the wilds of Scôtland five months, often without food, and the price of £30,000 set upon his head. He finally escaped in a French vessel, and ended his days in dissipation.

1795. The assembly of the states of Holland passed at the Hague the first public instrument in the shape of a declaration of rights.

1801. Sale of fine wheaten bread prohibited in London and that of brown substituted.

1813. Samuel M'Keehan, surgeon's mate in the Ohio militia, ordered by General Harrison, with a flag of truce, and money for supplies, for the wounded prisoners taken January 22d, put up for the night in a cave at the foot of the Miami, leaving his horse and cabriole at the entrance, and the flag stuck up; about midnight a party of Indians fired on them, wounded the doctor in the foot, killed and scalped his companion, Mr. Lamont, and stripped him, they took the money, horse, blankets, &c., and compelled the doctor to travel 20 miles that night on foot.

1826. François D'Etienne Lantier, a dramatic writer of no small celebrity in France, died at Marseilles.

1828. Alexander Ypsilanti, a Greek patriot, died at Vienna, aged 36. He attempted the liberty of his country, but was discountenanced by the emperors of Russia and Austria, and imprisoned by the latter seven years. His early death is attributed to his incarceration.

1833. Otho, prince of Bavaria, arrived at Napoli di Romania as the first king of restored Greece; at which time he had not attained his 18th year.

1838. Osceola, the celebrated Seminole chief, died at Charleston, S. C., aged 35. From a vagabond child he became the master-spirit of a long and desperate war. He was a subtil and sagacious savage, who established gradually and surely a resistless ascendancy over his adopted tribe, by the daring of his deeds, the constancy of his hostility to the whites, and the profound craft of his policy.

1839. James Byles died at Oyster bay, N. Y., aged 118. He was a native of France, came to this country while a boy was a soldier under Wolfe, and in the battle of Quebec.

1843. Was living at Caraccas, South America, MARIA DE LA CRUZ CARVALLO, aged 144. Her hair, which had been white with age, returned to black at the age of 133; and her sight, which was entirely lost at the age of 118, returned at the age of 138, so that she could thread a needle.

1854. The rail road track at Erie, Pa., torn up the second time by a mob.

1855. The western rail roads blocked with snow, and travel almost wholly obstructed for several days. No communication was had between St. Louis and Chicago for eleven days. Seventeen locomotives were frozen in or buried by the snow on the Chicago and Mississippi rail road.

FEBRUARY.

FEBRUARY 1.

107. St. Ignatius died, or was murdered.

1461. Battle of Mortimer's Cross, in which Edward, duke of York (afterwards Edward IV), revenged his father's death by a signal victory over the royalists, commanded by Jasper, earl of Pembroke.

1642. Edward Finch died. He was vicar of Christ church, London, from which he was expelled for preaching in a surplice and associating with women.

1681. John Edward Nidhard, an Austrian jesuit, died. He was appointed inquisitor-general and minister of Spain.

1684. Robert Leighton, a Scotch prelate, died. He for a number of years employed his talents and influence in a vain endeavor to bring about a reconciliation between the presbyterians and episcopalians. As a preacher he was admired beyond all his contemporaries, and his works have not yet lost their popularity.

1686. Francis Blondel died; eminent for his knowledge of geometry and belles-lettres; was professor of mathematics and architecture, and tutor to the dauphin of France.

1702. Marshal Villeroy, general of the French and Spanish armies in Italy, surprised in his bed at Cremona, and taken prisoner by the imperialists under Prince Eugene.

1708. Captain Rogers discovered Alexander Selkirk on the island of Juan Fernandez, where he had lived alone four years and four months.

1718. Daniel Francis Voisin, chancellor of France, died. He was eminent for his talents, integrity and virtue.

1733. Frederick Augustus, elector of Saxony and king of Poland, died. His court was one of the most splendid and polished in Europe, and he filled with dignity his station among the European powers. In his character generous ideas were united with despotic feelings; a taste for pleasure with the cares of ambition; and the restlessness of a warlike spirit with the effeminacy of a luxurious life. Instances of his prodigious strength are recorded, which appear almost incredible.

1775. The new congress of Massachusetts met at Cambridge and chose John Hancock their president.

1781. Lord Cornwallis with the British army, passed the Catawba at M'Cowan's ford. His passage was disputed by Wm. Davidson, lieut. col., commandant of the North Carolina line, and brigadier general of militia, with 300 militia. Davidson was overpowered, and killed by a ball in the breast. Cornwallis had his horse killed under him.

1789. The first president of the United States elected.

1793. War declared against England and Holland by the French.

1796. A stone was thrown at the carriage of George III, king of England, as he was returning from Drury lane theatre. It hit the queen in the face.

1800. Battle between the United States frigate Constellation, Capt. Truxton, and the French frigate La Vengeance of 54 guns. The action lasted from 8 o'clock in the morning until after noon, when the Vengeance was completely silenced; but taking advantage of a squall made her escape to Curacao, where she arrived in a shattered condition, having lost 160 men killed and wounded.

1801. Daniel Nicholas Chodowiecki, a German painter and engraver, died. He practiced miniature painting with great assiduity to support his mother. His first trials at engraving excited the astonishment of connoisseurs; and at length scarce a book appeared in Prussia for which he did not engrave at least a vignette. He was universally esteemed forhis integrity.

1804. J. Packer died at Spinningfield, England, aged 33, weighing 29 stone.

1813. American privateer schooner Hazard, Capt. Le Chartier, of 3 guns and 38 men, captured the British merchant ship Albion of 12 guns and 15 men; on the 23d she was re-captured by the British cutter Caledonia of 8 guns and 38 men; on the 26th the Hazard fell in with and took both of them; but succeeded in bringing the Albion only into St. Mary's. The Hazard had her first lieutenant and 6 men wounded, but she was much shattered. Great part of the Caledonia's crew were killed or wounded.

1814. Bonaparte defeated by the allied army near Chaumenil.

1814. A destructive eruption of Albay in Luconia, one of the Phillipines.

1815. Eruption of the volcano of Albay, in the province of Camarines, on the southern part of one of the Phillipine islands, in the Indian ocean; by this awful catastrophe five populous towns were entirely destroyed and more than 1200 of the inhabitants perished.

1824. Henry Bate Dudley died. He was born in England 1745, educated for the pulpit, and succeeded to his father's benefice. He established the *Morning Post*, and subsequently several other papers, and manifested his literary abilities by the production of several successful comedies. He obtained a baronetcy, and at the time of his decease was a magistrate for eleven counties.

1824. John Lempriere died, author of the *Biographical Dictionary*. He was an English prelate, and an excellent classical scholar.

1833. Elizabeth Moore died, in Pitt county, North Carolina, aged 101.

1837. A memorial was presented to congress, signed by 56 authors of Great Britain, praying that body to secure to them the exclusive right to their respective writings in the United States.

1837. Edward Donovan died, near London, a celebrated author on natural history.

1837. Simpson, in the service of the Hudson Bay company, reached Athabasca, having completed since the first of December a journey of 1277 statute miles, the *preliminary* step of the expedition.

1845. Samuel McGwinn, known as the *Caithness Veteran*, died at Andover, New-Hampshire, aged 110.

1851. Mary Wolstonecraft, widow of Percy Bysshe Shelley, died, aged 53; known in authorship by her *Travels* and *Frankenstein*.

1852. Ohio state house burnt, and a large mass of valuable papers perished with it.

1854. Silvio Pellico died near Turin in Italy. In 1820 he was seized by the Austrians as a carbonaro, while employed as a tutor, and confined in the fortress of Spielberg ten years. On his release he was employed as librarian by the Marchesa Barolo until his death.

1854. The splendid Parliament house at Quebec, with the government library and philosophical apparatus, were destroyed by fire.

1855. The United States surveying steamer Water Witch, ascending the Paraguay in violation of the ordinance that no man of war should enter that river, was fired at from the fort, and one man killed. The Water Witch returned the fire and backed down the stream.

1856. Ivan Fedorowitch Paskiewitsch, vice-roy of Poland, died, aged 74. He distinguished himself in all the wars of the Russian empire, beginning with that of the invasion of 1812.

FEBRUARY 2.

1141. Battle of Lincoln, and defeat of Stephen, king of England, by the earl of Gloucester. The king, whose valor deserved a better fortune, was taken prisoner, loaded with irons, and Matilda proclaimed queen.

1421. Henry V entered London from the complete conquest of France, which had been accomplished in about five years, and was received by the people amidst such pageants and popular rejoicings as that capital had never witnessed.

1461. Battle of Mortimer's Cross near Ludlow, where the king's forces were defeated, Owen Tudor taken and beheaded.

1529. Balthazar Castiglione, an Italian nobleman and poet, died. He was also so well skilled in painting, sculpture and architecture, that it is said Raphael and Michael Angelo, though incomparable artists, never thought their works perfect unless they had his approbation.

1626. Charles I of England crowned at Westminster. He wore the white rather than the purple robe, and to prevent the increase of the plague omitted the usual ceremony of riding in state.

1643. Prince Rupert took Cirencester for Charles, by storm; 200 slain.

1653. New York city incorporated.

1682. John Pautre died; an eminent French designer and engraver. His works were published in 3 vols. folio, and contained more than 1000 engravings.

1688. Abraham du Quesne died. He was a native of Normandie in France, and distinguished himself in the navy by a series of valorous and successful engagements.

1705. A new eruption of the peak of Teneriffe, forming the third volcanic mouth.

1723. Richard Sare, an eminent printer, died. A sermon preached at his death was well received and went through many editions.

1745. A conspiracy of 900 negroes to murder their masters in Jamaica was discovered by a negress to her mistress, because the plotters would not save a child she had nursed.

1752. The contributors to the Pennsylvania hospital, having rented a house, admitted their first patients.

1768. ARTHUR ONSLOW died. He was 33 years speaker in the English house of commons and the third of his family that had been nominated to that office.

1771. JOHN LOCKMAN, an English dramatic writer, died.

1787. Gen. ARTHUR ST. CLAIR elected president of the American congress.

1788. JAMES STUART died; sometimes called Athenian Stuart, a very celebrated traveler and delineator of Athenian architecture.

1794. The French convention decreed it treason for any officer to surrender his ship to a force less than double his own!

1797. Mantua surrendered to the French, who now became entire masters of the pope's dominions; whereupon Napoleon dictates to his holiness those pious terms of pacification signed ten days after.

1798. The Federal street theatre, in Boston, entirely destroyed by fire.

1799. THOMAS PAINE, often called the *Literary Merchant*, died. Few mercantile men become literary men.

1799. ELIZABETH WOODCOCK, an English woman, returning home from market in one of the most stormy nights ever known in England, was overwhelmed in a snow drift, where she remained eight days without sustenance. When discovered her mental faculties were unimpaired, but she had lost the use of her feet, and died some months after.

1801. The first imperial parliament of Great Britain assembled in London.

1804. GEORGE WALTON died, one of the signers of the Declaration of Independence. He was a native of Virginia, served an apprenticeship to a carpenter, removed to Georgia and studied law. He was foremost among the patriots of that state who assembled to devise measures of resistance to the acts of parliament in relation to American taxations.

1806. MIRANDA sailed from New York on his expedition to revolutionize South-America.

1806. THOMAS BANKS died. He was bred a wood carver, to which he served an apprenticeship. But having taken several premiums for models of sculpture he turned his attention to that art, and was sent to Rome to study at the academy's expense. From Italy he repaired to Russia, where he stayed two years; but not meeting with any adequate encouragement, he returned to his own country. A colossal statue of Achilles mourning the loss of Briseis is his masterpiece. He closed a life of arduous exertion, at the age of 70; and there are monuments, both in Russia and England that will long attest his skill.

1807. Battle of Bergfried near the lower Vistula. Bonaparte defeated the Russians after a severe and sanguinary contest, in which Soult, Augereau, &c., distinguished themselves very highly. The French took four pieces of cannon and 1700 prisoners. Same day, the French general Guyot captured the whole of the Russian magazines at Guttstadt.

1808. The French subverted the papal government at Rome.

1814. BONAPARTE defeated at Brienne with the loss of 173 cannons and 4000 men.

1817. The Scottish regalia, which had been deposited in a chest in 1707, (see March 26) was examined by a deputation. The doors were removed, and the floor was found covered with 6 inches of dust. No keys being found, the oaken chest was forced open, and found to contain the ancient crown, scepter and sword of state, as they had been deposited 111 years previous.

1820. BENJAMIN TRUMBULL died, aged 92, author of a *History of Connecticut.*

1831. A. BONPLAND, the celebrated traveler, permitted to leave Paraguay, where he had been detained about nine years, by the dictator Francia.

1834. RICHARD LANDER, the enterprising traveler and discoverer of the course of the Niger, died at Fernando Po, in Africa, of wounds received from the natives. All his papers were lost. The British government allowed his wife and daughter a pension of £150.

1834. LORENZO DOW died, aged 57; an eccentric traveling preacher. He was born in Connecticut and had a good elementary education; but in his youth acquired vicious habits which however he overcame at about the age of 14. At an early age he believed himself called to preach, and in obeying the impulse he commenced a career which has probably never been equaled; and in spite of acute bodily disease performed an amount of labor in traveling and preaching never before known. Before he had completed his twenty-fifth year, he once rode 1500 miles and held 184 meetings in ten weeks and two days; and about a year afterwards, traveled 4000 miles in the southern states, constantly preaching, in seven months, and finished his tour without stockings, shoes, or outer garment, and almost without a horse. For several years after he traveled from seven to ten thousand miles and held six or seven hundred meetings annually. It is thought that during the thirty-eight years of his public life he must have traveled two hundred thousand miles, including three voyages to England and Ireland. During these flying journeys he constantly refused donations and contributions, except for immediate want; and his traveling expenses exceeded his receipts more than one half, the first eighteen years. Afterwards, however, his books became a source of profit to him, and finally he became the maker and vender of a *family medicine!* which was a matter of speculation purely. He was twice married; his second wife survived him. He was familiar to every body throughout the United States, for there were few places however obscure which he had not visited.

1839. Deborah Logan died at Stanton, Pa. She was a member of the Pennsylvania historical society, and more intimately acquainted with the early history of that state, than any other person living.

1840. Olinthus Gregori, an English mathematician, died, aged 67. He was more than thirty years professor of mathematics in the royal military academy at Woolwich, and had the whole of the general superintendence of the almanacs published by the stationers' company, which had been for a long period conducted by Dr. Hutton. He published mathematics, biography and religion.

1841. William Bartlett, an eminent and wealthy merchant of Newburyport, and a munificent benefactor to the theological seminary at Andover, died, aged 93.

1851. Joanna Baillie, a Scottish dramatic authoress, died, aged 85.

1852. A priest, aged 63, attacked the queen of Spain with a dagger, as she was returning from church; for which he was executed.

1855. G. Fletcher, an English Wesleyan preacher, died, aged 108. Until within six months of his decease he preserved an astonishing activity of mind and body, often preaching without fatigue three times a day.

1856. The house of representatives at Washington elected a speaker after a contest of nine weeks.

FEBRUARY 3.

1014. Sweyn, king of Denmark, died.

1399. John of Gaunt, duke of Lancaster, died. He was the son of Edward III; was a prince of distinguished valor and prudence, and a patron of the poet Chaucer.

1497. "Johannes Cabotus Venetus et Sebastianus illius filius," commissioned by Henry VII of England to take six ships of 200 tons burden from any port in the kingdom for the purpose of making a western voyage of discovery. This expedition was got ready by the beginning of May, and consisted of two caravals freighted by the merchants of London and Bristol, and some smaller craft.

1619. By letters patent dated this day, James I granted Ben Jonson a pension of 100 marks during life, "in consideration of the good and acceptable service heretofore done and hereafter to be done by the said B. J."

1649. Charles II proclaimed king by the Scots.

1660. Charles X of Sweden died. He ascended the throne 1654, and was a prudent though a warlike monarch.

1698. Ernest Augustus, duke of Hanover, bishop of Osnabruck, and father of George I of England, died.

1700. Filippo Acciaguoli, an Italian dramatic poet and composer, died. He effected many improvements in the machinery and internal arrangements of theatres.

1730. Elizabeth Thomas, an English poetess, died. She is known by the name of *Corinne*.

1761. Richard Nash, commonly called *Beau Nash*, died, aged 87. He was the most accomplished *gentleman* in England.

1779. The American Gen. Moultrie defeated 200 British at Port Royal island, South Carolina, and drove them off that island. Moultrie had 1 lieutenant and 7 privates killed and 22 wounded. The British lost most of their officers.

1779. Mutiny suppressed on board the United States frigate Alliance, bound to France with M. de Lafayette and several French gentlemen of distinction on board. Half the crew were concerned in it, and measures were taken to quell it but a few hours before it was to have been carried into effect. Great inhumanity was meditated towards the officers and the French. This was the first organized mutiny ever known in the American service. The mutineers were 36 in number.

1781. The Americans, closely pursued by the British, after the battle of the Cowpens, crossed the Yadkin and secured their boats on the north side, when a sudden rise of the river arrested the pursuit of the enemy. In this retreat the Americans endured extreme hardships with admirable fortitude, and their remarkable escape confirmed them in the belief that their cause was favored of heaven.

1781. St. Eustatia, one of the West-India islands, taken by the British under Rodney. The plunder amounted to above £3,000,000, besides 6 Dutch armed frigates and 150 vessels, many of them richly laden. The British kept the Dutch colors hoisted, by which means several Dutch, French and American vessels were decoyed and captured.

1782. Demerary and Essequibo surrendered by capitulation from the French.

1783. The ratification of the preliminary articles of peace exchanged at Paris.

1786. GASPARD RISBECK, a German author, died.

1794. GEORGE III and Queen CHARLOTTE went to Hay Market theatre, which attracted so great a crowd, that more than 15 persons were trampled to death.

1794. The French convention received the deputies from St. Domingo, one of whom was a black, one a mulatto, and one a white; and at the same time decreed that all men of color whom a tyrannical force had made slaves, were still free and equally citizens with whites.

1795. A tableaux of the victories of the French from Sept. 8th, 1793, to this date, presented to the convention by Carnot, gives the following result: 27 victories, 6 of which were gained in pitched battles; 120 combats of less importance; 80,000 enemies killed, and 91,000 taken prisoners; 117 important fortresses, 36 of which were taken after a close blockade; 230 forts; 38,000 pieces of artillery; 17,000 muskets; 19,000 pounds of powder, and 90 stands of colors.

1797. Faenza in Italy carried by assault by the French under Victor, afterwards duke of Belluno.

1800. Four British ships, carrying in all 106 guns, captured off Seven islands, after a close action of 2 hours 10 minutes, the French frigate Pallas of 42 guns and 350 men. British loss, 10 killed, 34 wounded.

1807. Montevideo taken by storm by the British.

1808. The Neapolitan garrison of Reggio surrendered to the French.

1809. The French national ship l'Iris, 24 guns, captured by the British ship, l'Amiable.

1809. The Spanish junta in Seville issued orders to their troops to give no quarter to the French found in Spain.

1810. British ship Valiant of 74 guns captured the French frigate Cannoniere, 14 guns, with a cargo worth $800,000.

1810. The French destroyed the quicksilver mines at El Almoden del Azoque, near Seville.

1810. Guadaloupe surrendered to the British.

1813. The Spanish cortez abolished the inquisition.

1814. BONAPARTE entered Troyes. Same day the Russians and Prussians bombarded Vitry, defended by the French under Gen. Montmartre.

1831. The duke of Nemours elected king of Belgium.

1832. GEORGE CRABBE died; one of the most popular of the modern British poets.

1832. CHARLES VICTOR DE BONSTETTEN died, aged 87; a distinguished Swiss moralist, politician, metaphysician, geologist and traveler.

1836. MARIE LETITIA BONAPARTE, mother of Napoleon, died. She was born at Ajaccio 1750; her maiden name Romolini; was one of the most beautiful women of Corsica; married, in the midst of civil discord, Charles Bonaparte, an officer who fought with Paoli; was left a widow 1785, having borne 13 children, of whom 5 sons and 3 daughters survived their father, and became celebrated. Madame Bonaparte was a woman of great force and energy of character.

1844. Continued cold weather in the northern parts of the United States. Long Island sound was frozen over a few miles above New York, and a canal, seven miles in length, was cut through the ice at Boston to allow the British steamer to go to sea.

1852. Battle of Santos Lugares, near Buenos Ayres, between the army of Urquiza, 30,000 men and 50 cannon, and Rosas, 25,000 men and 90 cannon. Rosas was defeated, and took refuge on board an English steamer. The city was saved from pillage by ships of war of all nations then in the harbor.

1856. Thermometer at 30° below zero in Kansas; and the cold extended over the United States, in some parts to a degree unknown before.

FEBRUARY 4.

211. LUCIUS SEPTIMUS SEVERUS, emperor of Rome, died at York, England. His sons, Geta and Caracalla, were by this event recalled from Scotland, where they were debating with Fingal over heath and mountain, her ancient stubborn independence.

836. EGBERT, the last king of the Saxon heptarchy, and the first of England, died.

856. MAGNENTIUS MAURUS RABANUS, a learned German divine, died. His works on theology are numerous.

1194. RICHARD, *Coeur de Lion*, released from his imprisonment.

1536. The parliament of England abolished every thing relative to the pope's power in their realm.

1555. JOHN ROGERS, prebendary of St. Paul's, and the protomartyr, burned at Smithfield.

1607. JAMES MENOCHIUS died; a civilian of Pavia, of distinguished abilities.

1644. A very large comet which had terrified the straight-bodied folks of New England with its prodigious length of tail, disappeared on this day, to their great relief.

1648. George Abbot, an English statesman and religious author, died. He was one of the judges who sat at the trial of Charles I, and signed his death warrant.

1660. Gen. Monk, famous as the restorer of Charles II, marched into London and recommended a government moderately presbyterian.

1665. The first number of the *London Gazette* appeared, published by Sir Roger l'Estrange.

1687. Francis de Crequi, marshal of France, died. He was distinguished for his military enterprises and heroic courage.

1692. Goree taken from the French by the English under Gen. Booker.

1693. Earthquake of Sicily, which swallowed up Catania and 1800 citizens.

1746. Robert Blair, a Scottish clergyman and poet, died. The only production of his, which we possess, is *The Grave*, a poem, striking and vigorous.

1749. John James Heidegger died at London. He was born in Switzerland, and came to England, where by his taste and judgment in operatic amusements, he was appointed to the management of the opera house and the masquerades. He was the ugliest featured man in the kingdom, but good-humored, benevolent and charitable.

1756. A mummy disinterred near Auvergne in France.

1762. Samuel Davies, an American divine, died, aged 36. He labored some years as a presbyterian pastor in Virginia, where the act of uniformity was enforced with great rigor, and was the founder of the first presbytery in that state. His sermons have passed through many editions on both sides of the Atlantic.

1774. Charles Marie de La Condamine died. He was possessed of a daring spirit, which led him to enter the army. But the restoration of peace cut off his hopes of promotion, and he traveled in Turkey and Asia. On his return to Paris, the academy were making arrangements to send a deputation to the equator for scientific purposes. The very desire of being connected with so perilous an undertaking made him an astronomer. The fatigues and hardships which he encountered in South-America, were heightened by the discord and jealousy which arose among his companions. He died while undergoing an operation for the removal of a malady contracted in Peru. He bore an excellent character, and left many valuable works.

1779. John Hamilton Mortimer, an eminent English historical painter, died.

1783. Cessation of hostilities with Great Britain, and final conclusion of the seven years' war of the revolution, which freed the American colonies from the claims of the mother country, and gave a new nation to the world.

1787. Jacob Wismer died, aged 103. He was a German by birth, came to America in Queen Anne's reign, and settled in Pennsylvania; here he married his third wife, with whom he lived 67 years, and left 170 descendants.

1790. Louis XVI took the oath to maintain the new constitution.

1793. An embargo laid on all French vessels in Great-Britain.

1794. The legislature of Massachusetts having repealed the law against theatrical amusements, the Federal street theatre was opened as a regular, lawful theatre, with *Gustavus Vasa* and *Modern Antiques*.

1796. British ship Aurora, one of Admiral Christian's fleet, having 160 men on board, who had kept her afloat three weeks by manual labor, was rescued by Capt. Hodges of the American ship Sedgley. The troops were principally Germans and offered Capt. Hodges 1000 guineas for his exertions in saving their lives, which he nobly refused.

1797. Earthquake at Quito, which threw down many valuable edifices, and destroyed several neighboring towns and plantations. A great number of persons were swallowed up.

1800. William Tasker died, aged 60. He was 30 years rector of a church, but deprived of its income by unmerited persecutions and litigations, until near the close of his life. The works which he published added to his reputation with the learned, but contributed nothing to his support, and he continued to struggle against poverty and oppression.

1804. Christian Joseph Jagemann, librarian to the duchess Amalia of Weimar, died. He was destined for the cloister, but escaped from the monastery, and became a distinguished writer on the fine arts and literature of Italy.

1804. The boats of the British ship Centaur cut out of Martinique the French corvette Le Curieux.

1805. The British sloop of war Arrow, 28 guns, and bomb vessel Acheron, 8 guns, having a fleet of merchantmen in convoy, were captured by two French frigates, but most of the convoy escaped.

1806. Gen. Philemon Dickinson, who was in the battle of Monmouth, died at Trenton, New Jersey, aged 69.

1808. First legislative proceedings in relation to the New York canals.

1811. Jonathan Lambert, of Salem, Massachusetts, took possession of the uninhabited island of Tristan d'Acunha, south of St. Helena. The British took possession of it in 1817, and fortified it.

1812. Peniscola, in Valencia, surrendered to the French under Suchet.

1813. The United States frigate Constellation chased into Norfolk, Virginia, by a British squadron.

1814. The ice formed on the Thames at London, above the bridges, and a fair was held upon it during eight days.

1817. LEWIS PENNOCK died at West Marlborough, Pennsylvania, aged 92; 11 of his survivors, within a mile, arrived at 83½ years.

1834. JOHN O'KEEFE, a British dramatic author, died at Southampton, England, aged 68.

1835. WADE HAMPTON died at Columbia, S. C., aged 81. He distinguished himself in the war of the revolution under Sumpter and Marion; and during the last war commanded a brigade on the northern frontier. He was reputed the most extensive planter in the United States; one of the wealthiest men in the whole southern country; and perhaps no other man in this country ever amassed so large a fortune by agriculture.

1836. WILLIAM GELL died at Naples. He was a classical antiquary, the illustrator of the ruins of Herculaneum and Pompeii, and author of various works on classical antiquity. He was admired alike for the depth and versatility of his erudition, the benevolence of his heart, and the suavity of his manners.

1850. Seventy-five persons killed by a steam explosion in Hague street, New York.

1854. Eight steamboats destroyed by fire at New Orleans, and 37 persons perished in the flames.

1856. Fort Nicholas at Sebastopol blown up by the allies, with the aid of 106,000 pounds of powder.

This day in the calendar of Hesiod, is auspicious for marriages and the repairing of ships; but a day of *troubles*.

FEBRUARY 5.

46 B. C. MARCUS CATO killed himself, at the age of 48. He was a lover of philosophy, in which he rigidly followed the doctrines of the stoics. He was a soldier, and his first campaign was against Spartacus; afterwards he led 1000 foot into Asia, where he was ridiculed for the small number of his attendants, but was wholly unmoved by it. He sided with Cicero against Catiline, and opposed Cæsar in the senate on that occasion. He endeavored to bring about a reconciliation between Cæsar and Pompey, but finding it in vain, sided with the latter. When Pompey was slain he fled to Utica, and Cæsar pursuing him, he advised his friends to be gone, and his son to trust to Cæsar's clemency; then lay down upon his bed, read Plato on the immortality of the soul twice over, and rose and thrust his own sword through his body.

41 B. C. AUGUSTUS, by a vote of the senate, in full assembly, their brows crowned with laurel, saluted with the title of *Father of his Country*.

1444. An eruption of Vulcano, one of the Lipari islands, which changed the entire face of the local navigation. Aristotle records a dreadful explosion, which is supposed to have formed the island as it stood in the time of Pliny.

1552. JAMES MEYER, a Flemish historian, died, aged 61.

1556. A truce for five years was concluded between Charles V, emperor of Germany, and Henry II of France.

1617. PROSPERO ALPINI, a famous Venitian physician and botanist, died, aged 64.

1626. Three new committees, viz, one on religion, one on grievances, one on secret affairs, were appointed in the parliament of Charles I.

1664. CHRISTIAN AAGAARD died, a distinguished Danish poet of the 17th century, aged 48.

1674. A parhelion or mock sun observed near Marienburg in western Prussia. It appeared in the horizon beneath the material sun, of a red color.

1679. JOOST VAN VONDEL, a Dutch poet of considerable eminence, died, aged 91.

1684. PHILIP DE MONTAULT, duke of Noailles, died. He renounced the protestant faith, and rose to a high rank in the army.

1684. About the beginning of December commenced a frost at London, which continued till this day. Coaches were run, oxen roasted, bulls baited, &c., on the Thames.

1693. The Mohawk castles burned by the French.

1718. ADRIAN RELAND died; a learned orientalist and professor at Utrecht.

1721. JAMES, earl of Stanhope, died. He distinguished himself in the field and in the cabinet, under George I.

1729. JOHN TRUCHET died at Paris. He was distinguished for his knowledge of geometry and hydraulics.

1751. The coffin and remains of a farmer were interred at Stevenage, England. He died in 1721, bequeathing an estate worth £400 a year to his two brothers, to be enjoyed by them during 30 years, at the expiration of which time he expected to return to life, when the estate was to be given up to him again. In order to his convenience on his reappearance, he ordered his coffin to be placed on a beam in the barn, with the key enclosed, that he might liberate himself. Four days grace being allowed him for his resurrection, beyond the time specified in the will, and not then presenting himself, his bones were consigned to the earth and his estate forfeited.

1757. Battle of Plassy, in Hindostan, in which the British under Col. Clive achieved an important victory.

1776. Georgia adopted a new government.

1780. The first shock of the earthquakes in Sicily and the two Calabrias, was felt at Scylla on the same day. In the night a tremendous wave swept from the coast 2473 inhabitants, with the prince of the place. The work of destruction and terror continued for almost four months, accompanied by incessant rains and bursts of thunder. Of 375 villages in Calabria, 320 were destroyed. It is estimated that 35,521 persons lost their lives in 33 towns only.

1782. The garrison at Minorca, 2692 men under Gen. Murray, surrendered to the French and Spanish, 16,000, under the Duc de Crillon.

1788. Massachusetts adopted the federal constitution, proposing some amendments. This was the sixth state in the list (ratified on the 6th, q. v.)

1790. William Cullen, a celebrated Scottish physician and medical writer, died, aged 77. He settled at Glasgow, and was for some time a professor of the university there, which he left on an invitation to Edinburgh. He successfully combatted the specious doctrines of Boerhaave, depending on the humoral pathology; founding his own views on an enlarged view of the principles of Hoffman.

1791. John Beard, an eminent and popular English theatrical vocalist, died. He ultimately became joint proprietor and acting manager of Covent Garden theatre, and continued on the stage till the loss of his hearing forced him to leave it.

1792. John Eardly Wilmot, an English miscellaneous writer, died.

1795. Report of the committee of the assembly of the states of Holland, respecting the state of the bank of Amsterdam, by which it appeared that the bank had been for 50 years receiving as securities for large sums advanced by it, a very considerable number of bonds instead of specie.

1795. The royal assent was given to the bill for suspending the habeas corpus in Great Britain.

1796. Negombo, in the East Indies, captured by the British under Admiral Elphinstone.

1797. The post of Corne, at the bridge head of Hueningen, was surrendered to the Austrians by the French general, Sisce, Gen. Abbatucci having died a few days before. Two days were allowed to withdraw the garrison and every movable appertaining to the place.

1799. Lewis Galvani, an Italian philosopher, died, aged 62. His favorite studies were anatomy and physiology. In his pursuits he was led fortuitously to the discovery of a new branch of science, called *Galvanism*. His manners are said to have been most unostentatious and retiring, and his mind of a melancholy turn.

1802. The French and Spanish troops landed at Hayti and captured forts Dauphin, Bizoton and St. Joseph. Christophe, the black general, set the town on fire and massacred many of the white inhabitants.

1805. The East Indiaman, earl of Avergavenny, wrecked on the shambles off the bill of Portland, and sunk in twelve fathoms of water. Of 402 persons on board, only 139 were saved. Her cargo was valued at £200,000, exclusive of 275,000 ounces in dollars.

1807. Pascal de Paoli, a celebrated Corsican general, died near London. While endeavoring to rescue his native island from the tyranny of the Genoese government, and defending its liberties against Gallic encroachments and invasion, being overpowered by the French, he retired with a few of his followers to England, where in a few years he ended his illustrious career.

1807. The French under Soult, Davoust and Ney, surrounded and cut to pieces a Russian column of 9000 men, took 1000 prisoners and 16 cannon.

1809. British ship Loire, Capt. Schomberg, captured the French national ship Hebe, 20 guns, with 600 barrels of flour.

1810. The French under Sebastiani and Milhaud defeated the Spaniards and took Malaga with its immense stores, 171 cannon, &c. The same day two French frigates of 40 guns each, full of troops, destroyed off Guadaloupe.

1811. Royal assent given by commission to the act appointing a regent of Great Britain, in the person of the prince of Wales.

1813. British Admiral Warren declared the ports and harbors of the bay of Chesapeake to be in a state of blockade.

1814. Seventeen British officers put in close confinement at Chilicothe, on the principle of retaliation.

1814. The advance of Gen. De York made a successful charge upon the rear of Macdonald's army at La Chaussee, between Vitry and Chalons, took 3 cannon, and 100 Frenchmen prisoners.

1815. British ship Grannicus, Capt. Wise, captured the American privateer brig George Little, 8 guns, 58 men.

1816. Richard, Viscount Fitzwilliam, died, leaving to the university of Cambridge his splendid library and £60,000 for the erection of a museum for its reception and exhibition. In his collection there are more than 10,000 proof prints of the first artists, a very extensive library of rare and costly works, among which are nearly 300 Roman missals, finely illuminated. There is also a very curious collection of the best ancient music, containing the original *Virginal* book of Queen Elizabeth, and many works of Handel in the handwriting of that great master.

1818. CHARLES XIII of Sweden died. He was the second son of Adolphus Frederick, and appointed at his birth high admiral of Sweden. His education was directed chiefly to naval tactics, but the revolutions of the time called him finally to the throne, where he conducted with great prudence, and gained the confidence of the people.

1822. ALI, pacha of Yanina, generally called Ali Pacha, killed. He was a bold and crafty rebel against the Porte; an intelligent and active governor of his province; as a warrior, decided and able; as a man, a very fiend. His early life was unfortunate, but his extraordinary strength of mind, which shrank from no danger or crime, united to great address, raised him to princely independence. His enormities at length attracted the wrath of the sultan. Finding it vain to withstand so powerful a foe, he sued for pardon, gave up his fortress, and was treacherously cut down, with six of his companions.

1823. Yates county, New York, erected.

1823. JUAN ANTONIO LLORENTE died. He was induced by Bonaparte, who placed in his hands the papers of the inquisition, to write a history of that tribunal. When the fortunes of the Bonapartes declined, he was banished from his country, and lived in France in indigence, supporting himself by teaching Spanish in the boarding schools; but the university at last forbid him that means of support. The rage of his enemies was raised to the highest pitch by the publication of his *Portraits Politiques des Papes*, and the old man was ordered in the middle of winter to leave Paris in three days, and France in the shortest possible time. He was not allowed to rest one day, and died exhausted, a victim to the persecutions of the 19th century, a few days after his arrival in Madrid.

1824. HENRY CALLISEN, a German physician and surgeon, died. He was the son of a poor clergyman; educated himself; served in the army and in the fleet; afterwards in the hospitals in Copenhagen; and finally accepted a professorship in the university.

1831. The Russian army of 160,000 men enter Poland at several points, Count Diebitsch commander-in-chief.

1835. Tremendous eruptions of volcanoes, attended with destructive earthquakes, occurred in Central America, sinking several towns and villages, and destroying a large part of St. Miguel and St. Salvador.

1837. JAMES CERVETTO the younger died, aged 90. He first brought the violincello into favor in England. He excelled his father as a musician, was leader of the orchestra of Drury lane theatre in the time of Garrick, and 72 years member of the royal society of musicians.

1839. ASAHEL STEARNS, professor of law at Cambridge, died, aged 64. He published a learned and accurate work on real actions, and was one of the revisers of the statutes of Massachusetts.

1841. The Pennsylvania bank of the United States, after having, from the time of the resumption of specie payments on the 15th January, paid out an amount little if at all short of six millions of dollars in coin or specie funds, again suspended specie payments. The exhibition of its affairs, which soon followed, were so unfavorable as to cause great surprise. The suspension was followed by that of nearly all the banks south and west of New York and New England.

1851. JOHN PYE SMITH died, aged 77; a religious controversial author of note, and nearly half a century principal of a dissenting college in England.

1853. The Sloo treaty signed at Mexico, for opening a communication across the isthmus of Tehuantepec.

1854. JAMES B. COOPER, an American naval officer, died, aged 94. He was a member of Lee's legion in the war of the Revolution, and served in the navy during the war of 1812.

A day of dire calamity, says Hesiod, in which certain *Greek* ladies, called "the Furies," make their round, "*about, about, about.*"

FEBRUARY 6.

129 B. C. Three ambassadors from John Hyrcanus, the Jewish pontiff, were received at Rome, when the senate decreed a renewal of the league of amity and assistance with that "good and friendly people," and dismissed the delegates with presents.

1554. JOHN WYATT and a number of others executed for an insurrection and riot, on account of Queen Mary's marriage with Philip II of Spain.

1593. JAMES AMYOTT, grand almoner of France, died; a writer on various subjects, but chiefly known as the translator of *Plutarch's Lives and Morals.*

1623. JUAN MARIANA, a Spanish historian, died. He wrote several works, theological and historical; the most considerable of which is his *History of Spain*.

1649. The Rump parliament voted the house of peers to be useless and dangerous, and accordingly that branch of the legislature and the office of king, were abolished by two brief resolutions.

1685. CHARLES II, king of England, died. At the time of the death of his father he was a refugee at the Hague, on which he immediately assumed the royal title. In 1660 he entered London amidst the universal acclamations of the people. He was a confirmed sensualist and voluptuary, says Lardner, and owing to the example of him and his court, his reign was the era of the most dissolute manners that ever prevailed in England. His career was terminated by a fit of apoplexy, at the age of 55. It was during this reign that the great plague and the great fire of London occurred. He was the twenty-sixth king of England.

1693. A party of about 700 French and Indians fell upon the Mohawk villages near Schenectady, and took about 300 prisoners in the English interest, without doing much other damage. They were pursued by Col. Schuyler with a party from Albany, and several skirmishes ensued. The French escaped by crossing the north branch of the Hudson, on a cake of ice. They lost in this enterprise 80 men killed, and were reduced to great want before they got home.

1696. A plot to assasinate WILLIAM III of England, was discovered.

1736. Earthquake in New England.

1738. JOSEPH MITCHELL, a Scotch dramatic poet, died.

1740. CLEMENT XII (Laurence Corsini), pope of Rome, died. He was very popular, and corrected many abuses in the church.

1755. MAURICE JOHNSON, a noted English antiquary, died.

1756. Birthday of AARON BURR, at Newark, N. J. His father was the Rev. William Burr, second president of New Jersey college at Princeton, and his mother a daughter of the celebrated Jonathan Edwards, third president of that institution. His wife is well known.

1777. Great Britain granted letters of marque and reprisal against America.

1778. The French avowed the independence of the United States, by concluding a treaty of defensive alliance with them.

1778. New York acceded to the confederation.

1783. LAUNCELOT BROWN died. He invented a new system of horticulture, and carried ornamental gardening to a high degree of perfection. Many delightful places of resort in England will stand for ages as memorials of his superior taste and abilities.

1783. The first ship which displayed the thirteen stripes in any British port, was recorded at the London custom house. She was loaded with 587 butts whale oil, belonged to the island of Nantucket, and was manned wholly with American seamen.

1788. Massachusetts adopted the constitution of the United States, being the 6th state which ratified that instrument. The vote stood 187 to 168.

1792. The city of Morocco, which had shut its gates against the emperor Muley Yazid, was attacked by his forces and carried. The greatest excesses were committed by the soldiery, against friends as well as foes, and the Jews were as usual given up to be plundered. (See 12th and 16th.)

1796. The state of Vermont adopted its constitution.

1798. The bank of England subscribed £200,000 to assist government to repel the threatened invasion. By the assistance of manufacturers, &c., this sum was increased to £1,500,000.

1799. British ship Arago, Capt. Bowen, captured off Mahon, at midnight, the Spanish frigate Santa Teresa, 42 guns and 350 men.

1800. The duke of ORLEANS (Louis Phillip, afterwards king,) asked pardon of Louis XVIII, and swore that he was ready to shed the last drop of his blood in his service. He was graciously received.

1803. GIAMBATTISTA CASTI, a Florentine historian, died, aged 82. His works are full of wit and originality, and some of them have been translated into English.

1804. JOSEPH PRIESTLY died. He was the son of a Calvinistic clothier, in whose rigid principles he was educated. His heresy ripened into unitarianism. His publications had already made him extensively known, when in 1766 he became acquainted with Franklin, by whom he was encouraged to compose a work on electricity. This was followed by several scientific works, till in 1794, on the anniversary of the capture of the Bastile, the mob at Birmingham, where he then resided, proceeded to his house, which with his library, manuscripts and apparatus, fell a prey to the flames. Finally, goaded by party enmity, he sought an asylum in the United States, and took up his residence at Northumberland, Pa. Here his devotion to his favorite pursuits brought on a disease, which hastened the end of his existence, in the 71st year of his age. His works amount to about 70 volumes, octavo.

1806. Action between the British fleet under Admiral Duckworth, and the French under Lessiegues, off St. Domingo, which resulted in the destruction of the latter, consisting of four large ships of war.

1807. The French under Murat, defeated the Prussians under Hoff, in Prussian Poland.

1811. The prince regent of Great Britain took the oath prescribed by the regency act, and was installed.

1813. The United States government ordered all alien enemies to report themselves to the marshals of the districts in which they resided.

1814. Lord CASTLEREAGH, with other diplomatic characters, met at Chartillon-sur-Seine, for the negotitation of peace.

1815. Full pardon granted to the Barratarian pirates by the president of the United States, in consequence of their fidelity and courage in the defence of New Orleans.

1832. The crew of the United States frigate Potomac, made an attack upon Qualla Battoo, in Sumatra. The town was destroyed and 150 Malays killed; loss of the Potomac 2 killed, 14 wounded.

1833. PIERRE-ANDRE LATREILLE, a French naturalist, died at Paris. He particularly distinguished himself in entomology.

1834. The celebrated and enterprising traveler, Lander, died of a shot wound in Africa.

1853. President CAVALLOS resigned, and Gen. Lombardini chosen president of Mexico with dictatorial powers.

1853. The insurrection of Mazzini at Milan, which was unsuccessful.

1853. WILLIAM PETER, British consul at Philadelphia, died. He translated the *Prometheus* of Æschylus, was an accomplished scholar and talented poet.

FEBRUARY 7.

1451. B. C. The Jews place the death of Moses on this day.

1642. WILLIAM BEDELL, bishop of Kilmore, died; one of the most exemplary prelates of the 17th century. He was so greatly respected even by the papists, that when the Irish rebellion of 1641 broke out, his was for some time the only English house in the county that stood unviolated. But refusing to submit to the orders of the council of state, interfering with his religious duties, he was thrown into prison, and his death was occasioned by the rigors of confinement. He translated the old testament into Irish.

1674. MARGARET LUCAS, dutchess of Newcastle, died; authoress of plays, poems, letters, essays, and philosophical fancies, filling 12 folio volumes, and the biography of her husband, William Cavendish, earl of Newcastle. She was a very singular character, and has been both ridiculed and extolled by the best English authors.

1693. PAUL PELISSON FONTANIER died. He gave a history of the French academy from its establishment.

1778. DANIEL BOONE, the first settler of Kentucky, taken by the French and Indians near the Blue licks. This was the second time he had fallen into the hands of the Indians. He made his escape about ten days after, and reached home in safety.

1788. The settlement at Botany bay abandoned, and this day the regular form of government was adopted, under Gov. Arthur Philip, and settlement made at Sydney cove, Port Jackson, New South Wales.

1791. Saratoga and Rensselaer counties in New York, erected.

1792. ATHANASE AUGER, a celebrated linguist, died. He was born at Paris, 1734, and became a clergymen. His studies of the Greek and Roman writers were indefatigable; the study of Cicero and of Roman history occupied the last thirty years of his life. His translations, &c., were published in 30 vols. Learning proved its worth in his character and life.

1796. The British admiral, Sir FRANCIS GEARY, died, aged 86.

1799. JOHN HEDWIG died; a German botanist, whose researches respecting the cryptogamia class of plants have established his name.

1807. Schweidnitz in Silesia surrendered to the French general Vandamme.

1810. British General PICTON tried for ordering Louisa Calderon to be put to the torture. He was killed at the battle of Waterloo.

1812. Earthquake at Philadelphia; duration 30 seconds. It was also observed in various parts of the United States to a less extent.

1813. Capt. FORSYTHE with 200 volunteers from Ogdensburgh, crossed at Morristown to Elizabethtown, surprised the British guard and took 52 prisoners, 140 guns and some munitions, and liberated from jail 16 British deserters.

1821. The Caxton printing office, on Copperas-hill, Liverpool, the property of Henry Fisher, totally destroyed by fire. It was the largest periodical warehouse in Great Britain.

1823. ANNE RADCLIFFE died. She was born in London, 1764, and married at the age of 23, William Radcliffe, editor of the *British Chronicle*. The *Romance of the Forest*, her third novel, gave her much celebrity, and the *Mysteries of Udolpho* placed her at the head of a department of fiction then rising into esteem. These works still maintain their place among the more modern and fashionable productions of the kind.

1828. Henry Neele, an ingenious English poet and novelist, died by his own hand, in a fit of insanity, supposed to have originated from too intense an application to study. He was the son of an engraver, and educated for the bar. His literary remains were published after his death.

1834. Cadwallader D. Colden, so favorably known as a philanthropist and scholar, died at Jersey city.

1837. Gustavus Adolphus IV, ex-king of Sweden, died. He came to the throne at the age of 14, on the assassination of his father, 1792; but on account of his violent and impolitic conduct, he was deposed in 1809, and his heirs excluded from the throne. He afterwards traveled in different countries of Europe under different names, and died at St. Gall in Switzerland. The latter years of his life were spent in poverty; he was badly clothed and fed, and possessed only an annuity of £300.

1837. The royal palace at Naples took fire and was partially destroyed. The library and the magnificient collection of paintings belonging to the king were burnt.

1839. Karl August Nicander, a recent Swedish poet of no small celebrity, died.

FEBRUARY 8.

293 b. c. Papirius Cursor dedicated a temple to Quirinus, on which he placed a sun-dial, the first ever seen in Rome.

291 b. c. Esculapius, the Sanitary god, as it was fabled, was enshrined as a serpent on an island in the Tiber. As a physician he used the probe, cathartics, bandages, &c., hence the respect.

1250. Robert, count of Artois, killed. He was brother to Louis IX of France, refused the empire of Germany offered him by the pope, and accompanied his brother to the Holy Land, where he conducted himself with great valor. He fell in the battle of Massourah.

1574. Geoffrey Vallee, a French writer, author of *Bêatitude des Chrêtiens*, which drew upon him the censure of the inquisition, burnt at Paris.

1587. Mary Stuart, queen of Scots, beheaded in the great hall of Fotheringay castle, at the age of 44. She was the daughter of James V, of Scotland. The misfortunes which it was the destiny of this beautiful and accomplished woman to undergo are well known. After an imprisonment of 19 years in England, she was brought to the scaffold on a conviction of conspiracy against the queen, Elizabeth.

1594. Edmund Bonnefoy, a writer on oriental law, died at Geneva in Switzerland, at the age of 38. He was appointed professor in the university of Valence, in France, where he narrowly escaped assassination at the massacre of St. Bartholomews. He bore an excellent character, independent of his talents and learning.

1637. Ferdinard II of Germany, an enterprising monarch, died.

1664. Moses Amyrault, an eminent French divine, died. He was a man of such remarkable benevolence, that he bestowed the whole of his salary upon the poor, without distinguishing between catholics and protestants.

1674. A resolution was adopted by the house of commons in England, that a standing army is a grievance; that the king should have no other guard than the militia.

1690. A party of about 300 French and Indians made an assault on Schenectady about 12 o'clock at night. The inhabitants were taken by surprise, and 60 men, women and children massacred, and the town destroyed. They took 27 prisoners, the remainder of the inhabitants fled to Albany, nearly naked through a deep snow, of whom 25 lost their limbs from the severity of the frost.

1716. Earthquake in Peru.

1724. Peter I, emperor of Russia, died.

1727. George Sewell died; an English dramatic poet, physician and miscellaneous writer.

1750. An earthquake in London.

1750. Aaron Hill, a celebrated dramatic and miscellaneous writer in the time of Garrick, died.

1752. Gasper de Real died at Paris, author of a valuable work on government.

1772. The princess dowager of Wales died in her 53d year. She is said to have given the peculiar tone to the first years of her son's administration by her laconic exhortation "George be king."

1779. Moses Allen, chaplain to the Georgia brigade, was drowned in attempting to escape from a British prison ship. He was a native of Northampton, Mass.; his age 31.

1807. Battle of Preussish Eylau, between the French army of 90,000 under Bonaparte, and 60,000 Russians under Benningsen. The battle commenced at the dawn of day. At noon a storm arose, which drifted the snow in the eyes of the Russians. The contest ended at 10 o'clock at night, when each army, after 14 hours hard fighting, occuppied the same position as in the morning. Twelve of Napoleon's eagles were in the hands of Benningsen, and the field between was strewed with 50,000 dead, dying and wounded. The Russians finally retreated, leaving 15,000 prisoners in the hands of the French.

1815. The congress of Vienna determined to abolish slavery.

1817. Francis Horner died, aged 39. He was distinguished alike for his spirited report of the bullion committee, and his rich contributions to the *Edinburgh Review*.

1819. John David Ackerblad died; a Swedish scholar, who distinguished himself by his researches in Runic, Phœnician, Coptic and Hieroglyphic literature.

1820. Charles Justus Gruner, a Prussian police officer, died. He was an active opponent of Napoleon during the whole of his career, and was finally imprisoned to appease the French. After the second fall of Bonaparte he was made Prussian director of the police for Paris and the environs, in which capacity he counteracted with great decision and dexterity, the cunning of Fouche, who employed every means to retain the works of art which had been collected at Paris. He wrote several valuable works on subjects connected with politics and the police.

1820. Robert Cowley, an African, died at Richmond, Va., aged 125. He had been for many years door-keeper to the Capitol of Virginia, which office was bestowed upon him as a reward for revolutionary services.

1827. William Mitford, an eminent historical and philosophical writer, died. He is best known as the author of a popular history of Greece.

1842. Great earthquake at the Windward islands. Point Petre, in Guadaloupe, totally destroyed, and 10,000 lives lost. It extended over 46 degrees of latitude.

1851. Nicholas Van Sittart, a British statesman, died, aged 85.

1856. M. Chacornac discovered the thirty-ninth asteroid.

FEBRUARY 9.

1450. Agnes Sorel died. She was the mistress of Charles VII, of France, distinguished for her beauty, strength of mind, and the influence she possessed over the king, whom she incited to deeds of glory.

1547. Henry VIII was succeeded on the throne of England by his only son, Edward VI, in the ninth year of his age, who was crowned with great state at Westminster.

1555. John Hoopfr, bishop of Gloucester, burnt. He was a dissenter in the time of Mary, and refusing to recant his opinions, was burnt in the city of Gloucester, and suffered death with admirable constancy.

1555. Rowland Taylor burnt at Hadleigh, in England, for resisting the establishment of papal worship in his church. Great efforts were made to induce him to recant, which he firmly rejected, and proceeded on his way to the stake with great courage and apparent unconcern. During the burning he stood without crying or moving, till one of the executioners struck him on the head with a halberd, when his corpse fell down into the fire.

1577. Philibert de Lorme, an eminent French architect and antiquary, died. He left several works on architecture greatly esteemed.

1636. Philemon Holland died at Coventry, England. He was a laborious translator of the Greek and Latin authors.

1660. The gates and portcullis, of London destroyed by Monk, who soon discovered his error.

1670. Frederick III, of Denmark, died. He succeeded his father, Christian IV, and improved the condition of his people by making them more independent of the nobles; the crown he also made hereditary.

1671. A speech on the enormous subsidies granted to Charles II, by Lord Lucas; though delivered in the king's presence, it was published, and burned by the common hangman.

1674. The city of New York surrendered to the British by the Dutch governor, Anthony Colve.

1674. Treaty of peace between England and the States General.

1675. The French fleet, under the duke of Vivonne, of 9 men-of-war and several fire ships, defeated the Spanish blockading fleet at Messina, and entered that port in triumph.

1680. J. Claude Dablon, a Jesuit missionary in Canada, died. He contributed the two last volumes of the *Relacions*, which were sent to Europe; valuable for the geographical information they contain.

1734. Peter Poliniere died at Coulonces in France. He was a mathematician, philosopher and chemist, and the first who read lectures on those sciences at Paris.

1751. Henry Francis d'Aguesseau, a French statesman, died. At the early age of 21 he was appointed to the office of advocate-general, ten years after solicitor general, and finally, in 1717, succeeded to the chancellorship. He retired from this office 1750, at the age of 82, when an annuity of about $25,000 was settled upon him. Voltaire pronounced him the most learned magistrate that France ever produced. His published speeches and pleadings form 13 quarto volumes.

1752. Frederick Hasselquist, a Swedish botanist and natural historian, died at Smyrna.

1765. The peruke makers, distressed that people wore their own hair, and that foreigners were employed, petitioned the king for redress. But the populace, not seeing the consistency of being compelled to take off their hair while the peruke makers wore their own, rose upon them, and cut it off.

1767. Hubert Drouais died; a painter of Normandy, who by pencil raised himself from obscurity to fame and opulence.

1773. John Gregory, an eminent physician of Edinburgh, died. He taught that the medical art, to be generally admired and respected, needed only to be better known; and that the affectation of concealment retarded its progress, rendered it a suspicious art, and tended to draw ridicule and disgrace on its profession. His writings are spirited and elegant; among them *A Father's Legacy to his Daughter* is well known and appreciated.

1778. Two clergymen having preached in a chapel in Clerkenwell street, London, without leave of the bishop, were prosecuted, and the chapel shut by a writ of monition.

1779. William Boyce died; an eminent English musician and composer, chiefly of sacred pieces.

1782. Benjamin Martin died in London; one of the most celebrated mathematicians and opticians of the age in which he lived.

1795. Ferdinand III of Austria recognized the French republic, and made peace with it. This was the first power that acknowledged the new dynasty.

1795. The first parliament opened in Corsica, then subject to England.

1795. Treaty of peace signed between France and Tuscany.

1799. A naval action between the United States frigate Constellation, 36 guns, Capt. Truxton, and the French frigate Insurgent, 48 guns and 410 men. The engagement resulted in the capture of the Frenchman in one hour and a quarter. French loss, 29 killed, 44 wounded; American, 1 killed. 2 wounded. This was the first opportunity offered to an American frigate to engage an enemy of superior force.

1799. British ship Dedalus, captured the French frigate La Prudente in 57 minutes. French lost 27 killed, 22 wounded; British had 2 killed, 12 wounded.

1801. Definite treaty of Luneville signed.

1810. The French occupied Zafra in Estramadura.

1811. Nevil Maskelyne died at London, aged 79. This eminent mathematician and astronomer ardently devoted a long life to science, and mariners owe to his discoveries the method of finding the longitude at sea by lunar observations.

1815. Claudius Buchanan died. In scriptural erudition he had very few superiors. Deeply versed in oriental literature, he conceived the plan of giving every man to read the scriptures in his own tongue, and died while superintending an edition of the Bible in the Syriac language.

1834. Benjamin B. Wisner, a distinguished Calvinistic clergyman, of Boston, and for several years secretary of the A. B. C. F. M. died.

1845. Job Palmer, one of the fathers of the city of Charleston, S. C., and a worthy of the relvolution, died, aged nearly 98.

1849. On account of revolutionary movements the grand duke of Tuscany fled from Florence. The glorious Roman republic proclaimed.

FEBRUARY 10.

1024. Abdurrahman IV, sultan of Cordova, dethroned by a relative and put to death. He was a patron of science, which he cultivated with success, and a poet.

1306. John Comyn murdered by Robert Bruce in the convent of the minorite friars. They were rival nobles, who had recently settled their differences, and agreed upon a revolt from the dominion of England. Comyn had treacherously revealed the matter to Edward. Bruce hastened to accuse him of it, and after some altercation struck him with his dagger, and he was immediately despatched by Bruce's attendants.

1402. Walleran, count of St. Pol, issued against Henry IV, of England, his famous cartel of defiance.

1519. Hernando Cortez sailed from Cuba for the conquest of Mexico. His armament consisted of 11 ships, 508 soldiers and 109 mariners. This force was divided into 16 cavalry, 13 musketeers, 10 brass field pieces, 4 falconets, and 32 crossbows. This miniature army was destined to oppose more than 500,000 warriors before it reached the capital of the great Montezuma.

1539. John Stephen Duranti killed. He was the first president of the parliament of Toulouse; and made himself conspicuous by his efforts to preserve that city from the plague of 1538. He was killed by a mob.

1567. Henry Stuart, Lord Darnley, murdered, aged 21. The house in which he lay sick was blown up, it is supposed with the privity of his wife, Mary queen of Scots, by her favorite, the earl of Bothwell. Darnley had murdered Rizzio, the queen's musician, before her own eyes, whose blood was thus avenged. Mary perished on the scaffold, and Bothwell was taken by the Norwegians, and died insane after ten years' imprisonment.

1640. De Vries commenced a plantation about four miles above the fort at New Amsterdam, and complains that the director of the West India company had failed to send him people for his colony on Staten island, as had been agreed upon.

1658. Gerard Langbaine, an English

writer, died. He acquired literary celebrity by his edition of Longinus.

1676. Attack on Lancaster, Mass., by the Indians under Pocanoket. The village contained 60 families; most of the houses that were not garrisoned were burnt; and the house of the clergyman, although defended by a competent number of inhabitants, was fired by the Indians, the women and children carried away, and the men either killed on the spot or reserved for further misery. Mrs. Rowlandson and her children, the family of the clergyman, were afterwards redeemed. The town was saved from entire ruin by the appearance of a company of 40 men from Marlborough.

1676. Alexei Michaelowitz, czar of Russia, died. He was father of Peter the Great; distinguished for his wars, his munificence, and his improvements in the state.

1680. A great comet, which had alarmed the inhabitants of New England since the 18th November, disappeared. It was also observed in Europe, and Henault says that it was the largest which had ever been seen, and struck terror into the minds of the people of France. It was by the observation of this comet that Newton ascertained the parabolic form of the trajectory of comets, and demonstrated their orbits. This discovery contributed to the removal of those terrors with which the phenomenon had always been attended, in all ages, and among all nations, who viewed it as the presage of some direful event.

1686. William Dugdale, an eminent English antiquary and historian, died.

1689. Isaac Vossius, a German scholar, died. He is the author of various learned works in German, and edited several Latin and Greek works. In 1670 he visited England, was admitted to the degree of LL. D., and presented to a canonry at Windsor by Charles II, who afterwards took occasion to say that he was a strange divine, for he believed every thing but the Bible.

1711. Richard Duke died. He was a poet of some credit in the last century, and by Dr. Johnson included among the classics.

1743. British sloop Squirrel captured the Spanish ship Pierre Joseph, with 195,000 pieces of eight on board and a valuable cargo of cochineal, indigo, &c.

1747. Thomas Chubb died. He was bred a glover, but when he arrived at the age of manhood, devoted great attention to the sciences and divinity, and gained great celebrity by a work on the latter subject.

1755. Charles de Secondat, Baron Montesquieu, an illustrious Frenchman, died. His *Spirit of Laws* has immortalized his name.

1763. Treaty of peace signed at Paris between France, Spain and Great Britain, by which the latter retained possession of Canada and Florida, besides many important islands in the West Indias, and along the coast, which had been recently captured by the British.

1773. James Forthon died at Grenada, one of the West India islands, aged 127.

1775. Lord North, the prime minister, introduced a bill to restrain the trade and commerce of the New England states, which finally passed by a large majority on the 30th.

1783. James Nares, a celebrated English musical composer, died. His anthems manifest great power of genius, and with his other works will perpetuate his name, and ever rank him with the first of his profession.

1786. John Cadwallader, an officer of the revolution, died, aged 44. He commanded the Pennsylvania troops, and was in several important engagements as a volunteer; he enjoyed the confidence and esteem of Washington.

1786. Cardinal De Solis died, aged 110. He was a native of Andalusia in Spain, and at the time of his death was in the enjoyment of every faculty but strength and quickness of hearing.

1787. Charles Chauncey, a Boston divine, died. He was eminent for learning, independence and attachment to the civil and religious liberty of his country. His productions are numerous.

1790. The celebrated chess-player Phillodor won two games which he played with skilled players while he was blind folded. The moves being made by his directions.

1794. The British under Admiral Jarvis took Pigeon island, Martinique.

1795. The English garrison at Bergen-op-Zoom disarmed and sent prisoners to France. The French also took Groningen the same day.

1795. The tower of Martello in Corsica taken by the British under Admiral Hood.

1797. The French pillaged Loretto, a fortified town in Italy. The soldiers entered the cathedral which contains the *holy house*, in which it is said the Virgin Mary lived at Nazareth, and laid their republican hands upon the madonna, the famous *Lady of Loretto*, which they found standing upon an altar, in a niche of silver, surrounded by numerous gold and silver lamps, and adorned with jewels. She was sent to Paris.

1799. Bonaparte set out from Cairo on his disastrous expedition to Syria.

1802. Port au Paix in Hayti taken by the French. The blacks set it on fire and blew up two forts.

1803. Jean Francois de la Harpe, an eminent French orator, critic, poet and dramatic writer, died.

1804. His catholic majesty, Charles IV, renounced his protest against the alienation by France of Louisiana to the United States.

1807. Bill for abolishing the British slave trade passed the house of lords.

1808. Russia declared war against Sweden.

1809. Portugal invaded by the French under Soult.

1809. George Zoega, a celebrated Danish antiquary, died.

1818. Thomas Morris, a British officer, died, aged 74. He fought by the side of Montgomery in Canada during the French war, was taken by the Indians, and narrowly escaped burning at the stake. On quitting the army he published an account of his captivity, and in the retirement of a small cottage passed some years in the pursuits of literature.

1841. Union of Upper and Lower Canada; Lord Sydenham taking the oath of office as governor of the united provinces.

1852. Gold medal presented to Henry Clay at Washington by New York friends.

1854. Gen. Herrera, ex-president of the republic of Mexico, died. He was one of the veterans of the war of independence, and as a statesman, had given proofs of the loftiest patriotism and disinterestedness.

1856. President Rivas decreed the annexation of the whole Mosquito territory to Nicaragua.

FEBRUARY 11.

641. Heraclius, emperor of the East, died. He was the son of a governor of Africa, conspired against Phocas, whom he beheaded, and ascended the throne of Constantinople.

1225. Henry III subscribed the great charter of English liberties, which was witnessed by 13 bishops, 20 abbots, and 32 earls and barons.

1451. Amurath II, emperor of the Ottomans, died. He was the first Turk who used cannon in battle.

1502. Elizabeth of York, queen of Henry VII, died in childbirth, in the tower of London, on her birth day, aged 36. She married Henry in 1486, by which the antagonist houses of York and Lancaster were united.

1503. James Tyrell supposed to be one of the murderers of Edward V, executed as a traitor. He is said to have confessed his agency in the death of both the young princes.

1543. An alliance was formed between Henry VIII of England, and the emperor Charles V.

1573. Drake the navigator was conducted by the Symerons to a tree notched with steps, which served them for a watch tower, and from the summit of which he had a view of the two oceans, one of which no English vessel had ever yet navigated.

1650. Rene Descartes, a celebrated French philosopher and mathematician, died, aged 54. His superior intellect early manifested itself. He embraced the military profession, and served in various countries, the better to make observations and form satisfactory conclusions on scientific subjects. He finally settled in Holland, where during the last 20 years of his life, the greater part of his works were written. It is said of him that he extended the limits of geometry as far beyond the place where he found them, as Sir Isaac Newton did after him.

1659. Francis Osborne died; an English writer of great abilities.

1733. John Perry, a celebrated English engineer, died. He was patronized by czar Peter of Russia, of which country he wrote a history.

1761. A usurer fined at Guildhall, London, £300 for having exacted six guineas to discount £100 for six weeks.

1763. Peter Carlet de Mariveaux, a French romancer, died. The great characteristic of his works, is to convey a useful moral under the veil of wit and sentiment.

1763. William Shenstone died, aged 50. His father was a gentleman farmer, who cultivated a moderate estate, called the *Leasowes*, which were rendered celebrated by the taste of the son. Having finished his studies, and come into possession of the paternal property, he gave himself up to rural embellishments and the cultivation of poetry. He wrote for fame, which was not awarded him by his cotemporaries and he died broken hearted. "He was a lamp that spent its oil in blazing." His principal poem is *The Schoolmistress*.

1771. Jean de Beuarain died; a French negotiator and geographer. He was made geographer to Louis XV at the age of 25.

1771. John Burton, a learned English divine, died, leaving some ingenious writings, collected under the title of *Opuscula Miscellanea*.

1780. The British under Sir Henry Clinton landed in St. John's Island, about 30 miles from Charleston, S. C.

1793. Great Britain issued letters of marque and reprisal against France.

1797. Francis Lightfoot Lee, one of the signers of the declaration of indedence, and a brave officer in the American revolution, died at Richmond, Va., aged 63.

1807. Revolution in St. Domingo, in which a profusion of blood was shed.

1810. The spire and part of the tower of St. Nicholas' church at Liverpool, fell through the roof and killed several in the church.

1811. Battle of Laffesat, in which the Prussians defeated the Turks, after a sanguinary contest.

1814. Battle of Montmirial between the French under Bonaparte, and the Russians under D'Yorck.

1815. Fort Boyer, Mobile, with a garrison of 375, surrendered to 5,000 British under Lambert, with a fleet of 13 ships of the line and 25 smaller vessels. Col. Lawrence received a wound, and seeing that it was useless to contend against such odds, struck his flag. British loss 31; American 10.

1821. Adam Walker died. He was apprenticed to a weaver; but ultimately became a lecturer on philosophy, which he adopted as a profession, and traveled in England for the purpose of lecturing on that science.

1827. Jose Maria Abrantes, a Portuguese nobleman died in exile. He was the friend of Don Miguel, of infamous memory,

1828. De Witt Clinton died at his residence in Albany, aged 59. He was born in the town of Little Britain, Orange county, N. Y., 1769, and educated for the bar. He was at an early age elected to a seat in the legislature, and continued to hold offices of honor and emolument until the day of his death, at which time he was governor of the state of New York. It is to his perseverance in a great measure, that we owe the construction of the Erie canal. As a public character he is entitled to durable renown, and no one was ever more ambitious of a reputation for science and literature.

1837. John Latham, an eminent English naturalist and ornithologist, died, aged 97. He was one of the founders of the Linnean society, and commenced the publication of his last work at the age of 82.

1844. Henry Kifer, a soldier of the revolution, died at North Woodbury, Pa., aged 110 1-2 years.

1856. Caroline Lee Hentz, a well known American novelist, died.

FEBRUARY 12.

590. Pelagius II, pope of Rome, died. In his time a plague raged at Rome of so strange a nature, that persons seized with it died sneezing and gaping.

1401. William Sawtry, a Lollard, condemned and burned to death at London for heresy.

1448. A general poll tax of 6d. with 6s. 8d. on every merchant stranger, and 20d. on their clerks, granted by parliament to Henry VI.

1542. Catharine Howard, fifth wife of Henry VIII, beheaded. The execution of this ungrateful woman excited no commiseration, as she had been the principal instrument in the accusations against Anne Boleyn, her predecessor.

1554. Jane Grey beheaded, at the age of 17. She was the daughter of Mary, youngest sister of Henry VIII, and a woman of uncommon beauty, talents and learning, for her years, to which she added great amiability of disposition, and fortitude of mind. Her disastrous fate created an extraordinary interest in her favor, which has continued unabated. "Good Christian people, you come here to see me die; not for any thing I have offended, for I will deliver to my God a soul as pure from trespass, as innocence from injustice."

1589. Blanch Perry died, chief gentlewoman to Queen Elizabeth, and a great lover of antiquities, besides a very tasteful writer.

1640. William Alexander, Lord Stirling, died; a dramatic poet and statesman in the time of James and Charles I. His poetry, for purity and elegance, is far beyond the generality of the productions of the age in which he lived.

1660. General Monk, now reconciled to the citizens of London, drew up his forces in Finsbury fields, makes an apology which is the signal of rejoicing. Burning lamps the principal pastime.

1689. The parliament of England chose William and Mary king and queen.

1706. Battle of Fraustadt, in Prussia, in which the Saxons and Muscovites under Gen. Schullemberg, were defeated by the Swedes under Marshall Renschild.

1733. The colony of Savannah commenced, under Gen. Oglethorpe. This was the first settlement in Georgia.

1744. The elector of Bavaria chosen emperor of Germany under the title of Charles VII.

1746. Birthday of Thaddeus Kosciusko, the Polish warrior.

1757. Peace concluded between the English and Sourajah Dowlah.

1771. Adolphus Frederick II, king of Denmark, died. He was the founder of the academy of belles-lettres at Torneo.

1782. The British surrendered the island of St. Christophers to the French, under the marquis de Bouille.

1787. Joseph Roger Boscovich, an Italian mathematician, died at Milan. He was also an elegant poet.

1789. Gabriel Brotier died at Paris; an illustrious and amiable Frenchman, and one of the most distinguished ornaments of the belles-lettres in that country.

1792. Battle on the plain of Morocco, between Yezid and Ishem, two brothers, contesting for the throne. The forces of the latter, about 30,000, were defeated by about half the number under the former. Both commanders were badly wounded. Ishem lost 1,300 killed, and 800 prisoners, who were all put to death by being nailed to the walls and floors and left without food.

1793. John Manley died, aged 60. He was appointed by Washington a captain in the navy, was very successful in his captures, but was finally taken prisoner by the British and confined in the Mill prison.

1797. Anthony d'Auvergne died at Lyons. He was director of the opera at Paris, and an eminent composer.

1799. Lazarus Spallanzani, an Italian writer, died. He is considered as one of the greatest naturalists of that age.

1802. A messenger from England to lord Cornwallis was attacked by two wolves near Boulogne, which tore off the lips of his horses.

1804. Immanuel Kant, a Prussian metaphysician, died. He was the son of a harness maker in the suburbs of Koningsberg. He continued by persevering industry to obtain a good education, and at the age of 22 successfully attacked the doctrines of the most eminent metaphysicians of the day. He was an original and profound thinker, as his numerous works attest: and his philosophy has been taught in all the German universities except some Catholic ones.

1807. Battle of Marienwerder, in Polish Prussia, in which the Prussians were defeated by the French under Lefebre.

1808. Remarkable duel at Bonnau, in Austria, between the Bavarian general Von Wrede, and a former Swedish minister, Von Duben. It was occasioned by the latter having cast reflections upon the Bavarian troops in 1805, in his dispatches to the Swedish government, and was fought in presence of a vast number of people.

1810. Badajos in Spain summoned to surrender by the French marshal, Mortier. The govenor returned the summons unopened.

1814. Battle of Chateau Thierry, between the French and Russians, in which the general of the latter, Fredenrich, was taken prisoner.

1814. General Wilkinson burned his barracks at French Mills.

1817. Battle of Chacabuco, in Chili, in which the patriots under San Martin and O'Higgins, gained a decisive victory over the Spaniards under Maroto. This, with the victory of Maypu, which occurred afterwards, achieved the independence of the country.

1826. Deodatus Bye, died. He edited *Cruden's Concordance*, *Diversions of Purley*, &c. Some fugitive pieces in the *Gentleman's Magazine* bear his signature.

1831. Great solar eclipse (annular), visible in most parts of the United States.

1832. The cholera made its appearance in London.

1834. Frederick Schliermacher, a celebrated Prussian divine, died. He was professor of theology at Halle, and distinguished for the energy of his character and the extent of his acquirements.

1837. Edward Turner, professor of chemistry, London, died, aged 40. He was an eminent chemist, a popular and much esteemed professor, and a very exemplary and benevolent character.

1840. Astley Paston Cooper, a highly distinguished English surgeon, died at London, aged 72. He was one of the first operators of his time, and carried on a practice unexampled for extent and emolument in the annals of surgery. His income from his practice was nearly one hundred thousand dollars per annum. In one instance he received a fee of one thousand guineas for an operation for the stone.

1855. The island of Cuba declared by the captain-general to be in a state of siege, and the coasts and circumjacent waters in blockade.

FEBRUARY 13.

This day was kept by the Jews as a fast, instituted by Esther in memorial of the day appointed by Haman for the extirpation of her countrymen. The same day was afterwards decreed as a feast for the death of Nicanor, the Syrian captain, who was slain at Bethhoron, B. C. 161.

1098. London bridge carried away by a flood and tax imposed to erect another.

1570. Benvenuto Cellini, a Florentine sculptor, engraver and goldsmith, died. His works in gold and silver are sold now at immense prices. In his autobiography, which has been translated, he claims to have aimed the balls which killed the constable of Bourbon, and the prince of Orange, at the siege of Rome.

1579. John Fowler, an eminent English printer, died at Louvain, in Belgium, where he had a press and issued various controversial treatises, leveled at protestantism. He was well skilled in languages, a tolerable poet and orator, a theologist not to be contemned, and well versed in criticism and polite literature.

1585. Alphonsus Salmeron, of Toledo, died. He wrote commentaries on the scriptures, was a zealous follower of Loyola, the founder of the Jesuits and distinguished for his learning.

1602. Alexander Nowell, an English divine, died. His *Catechism*, published 1572, was in extensive use and much admired.

1662. Elizabeth, queen of Bohemia, and eldest daughter of James I, of England, died and was buried in Henry VII's chapel.

1689. Revolution in England; William, prince of Orange, and the princess Mary, a daughter of the abdicating monarch, were proclaimed, by the lords and commons, sovereigns of England. (Holmes says 16th.)

1694. The highland massacre at Glencoe, in Scotland.

1699. The government of England sent an order to the play-houses that nothing should be enacted contrary to religion or good manners.

1726. William Watton died; an English divine, critic, historian, and miscellaneous writer of great learning.

1727. The British under Col. Campbell precipitately evacuated Augusta, Georgia, in the night.

1727. The Spaniards under the marquis de la Torras, commenced the siege of Gibraltar. This was the twelfth siege, and proved unsuccessful.

1727. Cotton Mather died at Boston, aged 65. He was the most learned man in America, and one of the most superstitious. His achievements in one year were 72 sermons, 60 fasts, 20 vigils and 14 books. His publications amounted to 382, some of them being of large dimensions. The *Magnalia* is his chef d' œuvre. He lived in the age of witchcraft, and fell in with the delusion, hand, heart and pen.

1752. Samuel Croxall, an English author and translator of good repute, died.

1781. A troop of Tarleton's dragoons, under Capt. Miller, were cut to pieces by Lieut. Col. Lee: the captain and all were taken, except two; 18 were killed. Lee had ordered his Lieut. Lewis, to give no quarters, on account of Miller's having refused quarter to Lee's bugler, an unarmed boy, whom they had overtaken and sabred. Lee halted his men at a farm, was suddenly come upon by the advance of Cornwallis, but escaped by a sudden and bold movement.

1784. Jeremiah Miles died; an eminent English divine and antiquary. He was ardently engaged in the Chattertonian controversy, and the author of the supposed Rowley's poems.

1787. Charles Gravier, count de Vergennes, a French statesman, died. As secretary of state for foreign affairs to Louis XVI, he assisted the Americans in their struggle for independence.

1789. Ethan Allen, an officer in the revolutionary army, died. He took Ticonderoga and Crown-Point; was himself captured near Montreal, sent to England, and after experiencing much cruelty, exchanged. He sustained the character of an infidel, and in his writings ridiculed the scriptures.

1790. The French convention abolished monastic establishments, and confiscated their lands. (See Jan. 16.)

1794. The French convention ratified the treaty of peace with the grand duke of Tuscany.

1794. The canal of Merthyr Tydvil, in Wales, opened, another great improvement.

1798. Christian Fredrick Schwartz, an eminent German missionary to Hindostan, died. His labors were of nearly half a century's duration, and had a great influence over the affairs of the country.

1801. British frigate Success, 40 guns, captured by a French squadron.

1805. Action between the British ship St. Fiorenza and the French frigate Psyche 36 guns, and the prize ship Thetis, which resulted in the capture of the two latter. French loss 57 killed and 70 wounded; British 12 k., 36 w.

1814. General Wilkinson burned his boats in Salmon river, and broke up cantonment at French mills; Gen. Brown went to Sacketts harbor, and Gen. Macomb to Plattsburg; the snow being 2 feet 10 inches deep.

1817. George Rogers Clarke died; an officer in the service of Virginia against the Indians in the revolutionary war, where he distinguished himself greatly, and was for some time the protector of the people of the frontiers of Virginia and Pennsylvania against the inroads of the tribes.

1817. The elegant sword voted by the state of New York to Com. McDonough, was presented to him at Hartford.

1820. Charles Ferdinand duc de Berri, assassinated. He was the youngest son of Charles X., a man of talents and intrepidity, and popular with the army. His assassin was actuated to the deed by a desire to exterminate the Bourbon family, which he had vowed to accomplish, and had begun with the duke, in whom the line was to be perpetuated. (See July 7, Louvel.)

1833. Stanislaus Poniatowski died at

Florence. He was a nephew of Stanislaus Augustus, the last king of Poland. Having defended the interests of his country with manly eloquence in the diet of Poland, he retired to Florence, and was noted as a liberated patron of the arts and literature. This prince was the first who set the example of a useful and glorious reform by emancipating the serfs of his extensive domains.

1840. WILHELM WILLINK, a friend of Washington and of the United States, died at Amsterdam, aged 91. He furnished the first loan to the colonies after their revolt from the British dominion.

1843. Gen. ROBERT PORTERFIELD died at Augusta county, Va., aged 90. He served in the Revolutionary army.

1843. ISAAC HULL, a distinguished American commodore, died, aged 68.

FEBRUARY 14.

1543. The parliament of Paris caused the *Institutiones Religionis Christianæ* of Calvin, to be publicly burned at Paris.

1554. BRETT the commander of the London train bands with 58 others, hanged for joining with sir Thos. Wyatt and his Kentish men, who tried to resist the Spanish influence.

1623. The floor of Black friars' church broke down while the people were at mass, killing 100.

1668. LOUIS XIV took Dole, in Franche Compte.

1696. English assassination plot to favor the interests of James II, discovered by Pendergrass.

1713. ANTHONY ASHLEY COOPER, earl of Shaftsbury, and author of the *Characteristics*, died. He was grandson of the earl who figured so conspicuously in the reign of Charles II; and possessed a spirit of liberty which displayed itself in his political character throughout his life, and by which he uniformly directed his conduct on all occasions.

1713. WILLIAM HARRISON, an elegant English poet, died.

1737. CHARLES TALBOT, an eminent English statesman and chancellor, died.

1756. Three hundred recruits sailed from New York for the army, under the command of Gov. Shirley, quartered at Albany; the river being free of ice.

1760. ISAAC HAWKINS BROWNE died. One of the most popular productions of this ingenious poet, is his *Pipe of Tobacco*, in imitation of Cibber, Ambrose, Philips, Thompson, Young, Pope and Swift, who were all living.

1762. Martinique and the other Caribee islands delivered up to the British under Monkton and Rodney, by the French governor, M. de la Touche. The entire reduction of Martinique was effected with the loss of 107 killed and 150 wounded. The French lost 1000 of their best men. Before its reduction the island could raise 10,000 white inhabitants fit to bear arms and 40,000 negroes.

1764. PETER RESTAUT died; an advocate at Paris, distinguished for his learning and integrity.

1764. Mr. WILLIAMS a printer was put in the pillory for republishing the North Briton, No. 45, at London. But the spectators made a contribution for him of over 200 guineas.

1779. JAMES COOK, the English navigator, killed by the natives of Owhyhee. He was born 1728, of indigent parentage; entered the royal navy in 1755; had the command of a vessel sent against Quebec 1759, after the capture of which he assisted at the taking of Newfoundland. After making several voyages for scientific purposes, he sailed in 1776 on his grand enterprise for the discovery of a northwest passage, during which he met his fate.

1779. Battle of Cherokee Ford, in which Col. Pickens attacked and defeated a body of tories, killed 39 of them and their leader, Col. Boyd, and took about 70 prisoners. Of the last 5 only were executed. Pickens lost 9 killed.

1780. WILLIAM BLACKSTONE died. He was born in London, 1723, and was called to the bar 1746. In 1765 he published the first volume of his *Commentaries on the laws of England*, a production by which his name will descend to all posterity. His private character is said to have been exceedingly mild and amiable, and he was throughout life assiduously addicted to business.

1780. A Russian manifesto announced the coalition called the "armed neutrality," formed on the basis that free trade makes free goods.

1781. The American army under Gen. Greene, which had continued to retreat since the battle of the Cowpens, crossed the Dan, leaving the whole of North Carolina in the hands of the enemy. So close was the pursuit, that the van of the British reached the river, as the rear of the continentals had crossed, after a march of 40 miles that day.

1782. The island of Nevis surrendered to the French, under count de Grasse.

1785. KIENLONG, emperor of China, made a feast for the ancients of his kingdom. Those who had attained 100 years, received 50 bushels of rice and 2 pieces of silk; those who had reached 90 years, received 30 bushels rice and 2 pieces of inferior silk, and others in the same proportion, down to 50 years. Presents, to a large amount, were also made to the poor throughout the empire. He likewise exempted all the people from taxes that year, which was the 50th of his reign. On the occasion of the feast, 3000 aged men of quality sat down to it, and the emperor sat at the head of the table to do the honors.

1793. BRASS CROSBY died. He rose from a humble attorney to be lord mayor of London. Being implicated in some difficulties with the printers, in 1771, and stoutly avowing his partialities, he was sent to the tower, notwithstanding the dignity of his office; but his liberation was attended with great marks of respect and attention from the citizens.

1797. Action between the Spanish fleet of 27 sail and 12 frigates, admiral Langara, off St. Vincent, and the British under Admiral Jervis, 15 ships and 6 frigates. Four of the Spanish ships were captured, (two of 112 guns each) and the remainder completely defeated. British loss, 300 killed and wounded; Spanish loss 603.

1808. JOHN DICKINSON, an American political writer, died. He practiced law in Philadelphia until 1765; was deputed to attend the first congress at New York, and prepared the draft of the bold resolutions of that congress. He opposed the Declaration of Independence, believing that compromise was still practicable; but soon after entered into it with ardor. His public services were eminent.

1814. Battle of Vauchamp, between the French and Russians, in which the latter were defeated. At 8 in the evening Marmont attacked and defeated the Russians at Etoges, who lost 9 cannon and 1300 men killed.

1831. Insurrection at Paris in consequence of an attempt by the priests to celebrate a funeral mass for the duke de Berri. Several churches were destroyed or injured.

1831. GUERRERO, ex-president of Mexico, shot.

1834. JOHN SHORE, Lord Teignmouth, died, aged 82. He went to India in his youth, in the service of the East India company and succeeded Lord Cornwalllis as governor, there. He returned to England 1798; and on the formation of the British and Foreign Bible society, he was chosen the first president, and held the office during life.

1843. Mr. JOHN MARTIN, aged 105, died at Augusta, Georgia. He came with a company of salt buyers to Georgia, under the direction of Oglethorpe.

1852. Dr. RAE, the arctic explorer, arrived at St. Pauls, Minnesota, having returnedfrom a search for Sir John Franklin, without discovering any trace of that ill-fated adventurer.

FEBRUARY 15.

Feast of Supercalia at Rome, in honor of the god Pan, the defender from wolves.

1564. Birthday of GALILEO GALILEI, at Pisa, in Italy.

1600. JOSEPH D'ACOSTA, the Spanish historian, died. He was born in Leon, 1539, and became remarkably efficient in literature and science at an early age. In 1571 he was despatched as a missionary to South America, where he remained till 1588. During his residence at Peru he wrote the *Historia Natural y Moral de las Indias*, which has been translated into nearly all the European languages, and is valuable for its information on the early condition of the continent.

1632. DUDLEY CARLETON, on English statesman and political writer, died.

1664. JOHN TWYNNE was convicted of high treason and executed. His offence was printing the matter called libelous written by Milton and others.

1682. CLAUDE DE LA COLOMBIERE, a famous Jesuit, died. He became very popular as a preacher before James II, of England, and was the inventor of "The Solemnity of the Heart of Jesus."

1694. BRADFORD paid for printing the first book in the city of New York.

1708. JOHN PHILLIPS, an elegant English poet, died, aged 32.

1730. THOMAS BRAY, an English divine, died. He made himself eminent by his unwearied attention to the practice of benevolence; many charitable societies and good designs in London are formed on plans which he projected.

1732. FRANCIS ATTERBURY died. He was the son of a parish rector, educated for the minstry, and made himself conspicuous by his eloquence as a preacher. His ambition was gratified by preferments, honors and emoluments, till, in the reign of Anne, 1713, he reached the seat of the bishop of Rochester, the acme of his greatness. On the accession of George I, his prospects began to wane; and being suspected of some treasonable acts, he was condemned to perpetual exile. He settled in Paris, and died there. His literary fame rests on his sermons, and his correspondence with Pope.

1763. Peace of Hubertsburg concluded at the electoral palace of that name, which concluded the seven years' war between Austria, Prussia and Poland.

1765. CHARLES ANDREW VANLOO, a highly distinguished French painter, died.

1766. JOHN HELLOT, a French philosophical writer, and distinguished chemist, died.

1781. GOTTHOLD EPHRAIM LESSING, one of the most distinguished German authors, died. He contributed more than any other individual to the regeneration of German literature, and was remarkable for the versatility of his genius.

1782. Battle off Fort St. George, East Indies, between the British under Admiral Hughes, and the French under Admiral Suffrein.

1784. SCIPIO BEXON died at Paris. He assisted Buffon in his natural history, and was also an author in his own name.

1788. GEORGE ANN BELLAMY, an English actress of the time of Garrick, died at Edingburgh, aged 55. She drew the attention of the town for a number of seasons, particulary when she played Juliet with Garrick at Drury-Lane, against Mrs. Cibber and Barry at Covent Garden. She published her own memoirs in 6 vols.

1794. JOHN FENN, a learned antiquary, died. He greatly distinguished himself by his application to the study of natural history and antiquities; and made a large collection of curious original letters, written during the fifteenth century, which were published in 4 vols. quarto.

1796. The British under Admiral Elphinstone, captured Colombo in the East Indies, which is at present the seat of the British government in the island of Ceylon.

1798. Rome declared a republic.

1801. Concordat between Bonaparte and Pius VII, for the reestablishment of religion in France, signed at Paris.

1804. A squadron of the East India company ships under Capt. Dance, convoying the China fleet, beat off in the China seas, the French ship Marengo, 80 guns, Admiral Linois, 2 heavy frigates, a corvette of 28 guns, and a Dutch brig of 18 guns.

1806. JOSEPH BONAPARTE entered Naples, upon the capitulation of the garrison, and was soon after chosen king.

1808. The king of Prussia renounced all connection, political and commercial, with Great Britain, in compliance with the treaty of Tilsit.

1710. Birthday of LOUIS XV, of France, under whose reign the corruption of morals and principles spread to an alarming extent among all classes, and were followed by a general poverty, national humiliation, and ruined finances, which prepared the way for the explosion that took place under his unfortunate successor.

1813. Battle of Pietra Nera, on the coast of Calabria, between the French and the Sicilians.

1814. Battle of Montmirail in France, between the French under Bonaparte and the Russians under Blucher, in which the former gained a small advantage after a hard contest.

1815. British sloop of war Barbados,

1817. Cold day throughout the United tates; thermometer 8° below zero in Philadelphia, and 20° at Salem, Mass. Heavily laden teams crossed from Boston to Fort Independence.

1817. A wagon loaded with specie for the bank of Pennsylvania, overturned near Pittsburgh, and Thomas Wilson was killed by a box of coin falling upon him.

1818. FREDERICK LOUIS, prince of Hohenlohe-Ingelfingen, a general in the Prussian service, died. He acquired distinction in the almost constant scene of war in Europe, from 1793 to 1806, and contributed greatly by his superior skill and valor to several important victories.

1820. WILLIAM ELLERY, one of the signers, expired in his chair while reading Cicero, aged 92. He was born at Newport, R. I.; graduated at Harvard in his 20th year; and practiced law at Newport until he was sent to the first congress. His house at Newport was burnt by the British. He had filled the office of collector of the customs since the term of Washington.

1826. SCIPIONE BREISLAK, an Italian geologist, died at Milan, universally regretted, both for his scientific merit and his personal qualities. His rich collection of minerals passed into the hands of the Borromeo family.

1832. The legislature of Maryland appropriated $200,000 for the removal of free blacks over the age of 18; and enacted penalties against the settlement of colored persons in that state.

1835. NATHAN DANE died at Beverly, Mass., aged 82. He was the framer of the celebrated ordinance of congress of 1787, for the government of the territory of the United States northwest of the Ohio river, an admirable code of constitutional law, by which the principles of free government, to the exclusion of slavery, were extended to an immense region, and its political and moral interests secured on a permanent basis.

1836. JOHN GILLIES, historiographer to the king for Scotland, died, aged 90; author of a popular history of Greece, besides many other valuable works.

1836. MARGARET BURGEOIS died, on Prince Edward Island, aged 110.

1836. FIESCHI and his accomplices, Pepin and Moray, who attempted to take the life of the French king by the explosion of an infernal machine, executed at Paris.

1840. HARRIETT CAMPBELL, a Scottish author of distinguished talents, died at Montrieux in Switzerland, aged 34.

1843. NATHANIEL CHIPMAN, some time justice of the supreme court of Massachusetts and a senator of the United States, died in the 91st year of his age. He was a vigorous writer.

captured the United States letter of marque brigantine Vidette, 3 guns, 30 men.

FEBRUARY 16.

309. Pamphilius, presbyter of Cæsarea, died. He was of an eminent family, of great wealth and extensive learning, and ardently devoted to the scriptures. He collected a library of 30,000 volumes, solely for the promotion of religion. Traces of this library still remain at Paris and elsewhere.

1009. Abdurrahman, hajib, or chamberlain, of Hisham, king of Cordova, beheaded. He was entrusted with the civil and military powers of government, but aspiring to the throne itself, was destroyed by the people.

1279. Alonzo III of Portugal, died. From an exile in poverty he was raised to the throne by the pope, who had deposed his brother for attacking the immunities of the church.

1497. Birthday of Philip Melancthon, at Britten, in the palatinate of the Rhine His proper name was Schwartzerd (black-earth), but according to the custom of the learned of that time, he changed it into the Greek term for the same word, *melancthon*.

1510. The Portuguese under Alphonso Albuquerque entered Goa in Hindostan.

1532. Richard Rouse, the bishop of Rochester's cook, poisoned the soup and caused the death of several persons. An act was immediately passed making poisoning treason, and the punishment boiling to death. Rouse was boiled.

1560. John du Bellay, bishop of Paris, died. He was engaged as a negotiator between Henry VIII and the pope, with respect to the divorce of the former.

1639. Teixeira having ascended the Amazon and arrived at Quito, reembarked on his return this day, in a fleet of 45 canoes, with 70 soldiers, and 1200 native rowers.

1656. Spain declared war against England.

1736. Owing to an unprecedented tide, the council at Westminster hall, London, were carried out in boats to their coaches.

1741. George Raphael Donner, an Austrian sculptor, died. His works, to be seen in many Austrian churches and palaces, are masterpieces.

1749. Great riot at the Hay Market, London, occasioned by the failure of a conjurer to leap, as he promised, into a quart bottle.

1754. Richard Mead died, aged 81. He studied at the German universities at the same time as Bœrhaave, with whom he was intimate, and distinguished himself as a practitioner on his return to England. He introduced inoculation for small pox about the year 1720; his preliminary experiments were made upon condemned criminals. He did not live to see the great improvement by vaccination, introduced by Jenner.

1760. The Cherokees under Ocunnastota attacked Fort Prince George in Virginia, garrisoned by the British and Americans. The Indians were repulsed, and 20 hostages residing in the fort, and who attempted to rise on the garrison, were put to death.

1770. Bruce, the traveler, entered Gondar, the capital of Abyssinia, and was introduced into the palace of the emperor.

1784. Peter Macquer, a physician and chemist of great reputation, died at Paris.

1791. Herkimer and Otsego counties, N. Y., erected.

1792. Muley Yezid, emperor of Morocco, died of wounds received in battle on the 12th; when an end was put to a scene of slaughter which had continued since the 6th, such as the city had seldom known. It was computed that 20,000 of every age and sex, were destroyed.

1794. Tioga county in New York erected.

1795. The stadtholdership abolished in Holland. The stadtholder, Prince William of Orange, was then in England.

1796. John Romilly died at Paris. He was an ingenious mechanic and clockmaker at Geneva, and author of the articles on clockmaking in the *Encyclopedie*.

1796. Amboyna, the Dutch metropolis of the Moluccas, taken by the British under Admiral Rainer.

1798. Stephen Charles Lomenie de Brienne, archbishop and minister of state of France under Louis XVI, died. He early associated himself with the instigators of the revolution; but while he attempted to reduce the power and wealth of the monasteries, he was liberal in assisting those who were in need. Failing to keep pace with the ultra party, he was thrown into prison, where he died of ill treatment.

1802. Toussaint L'Overture and Christophe, black generals of St. Domingo, declared rebels by the French general, Le Clerc.

1804. United States frigate Philadelphia burnt in the harbor of Tripoli. This splendid action was achieved in 15 minutes by 70 volunteers under Lieut. Stephen Decatur, in the ketch Intrepid, with the loss of 1 killed. Decatur was promoted, and a sword and thanks voted him.

1807. Battles of Rossega and Ostrolenka, between the French and Russians, in which the former were victorious in both instances

1810. St. Martins surrendered to the British.

1812. Battle of Cartama in Spain; the French under Gen. Maransin defeated by the Spaniards, under Ballasteros.

1813. An elegant sword and thanks voted to Decatur and Biddle, by the legislature of Pennsylvania, for their distinguished gallantry and skill. They were presented to those officers at New London, on board their respective ships.

1826. LINDLEY MURRAY, the grammarian, died in England, aged 81. He was born in Pennsylvania, of quaker parentage, and studied law; but during the revolutionary war he turned merchant, and before its close acquired sufficient property to retire upon. He visited England for the benefit of his health, where he finally settled, about a mile from the city of York, and employed his leisure in the production of those works of education, which acquired such popularity as to have maintained their places more than forty years.

1826. The *Liberia Herald* appeared at Monrovia, the first paper printed in Africa. It was edited by Charles L. Force, from Boston, and like the early newspapers of New England, was printed on one side only.

1829. FRANCIS JOSEPH GOSSEC, an eminent music composer, died, aged 96. He was first attached to the cathedral at Antwerp; but in 1751 went to Paris, where he passed the remainder of his life, and acquired a reputation seldom surpassed.

1839. JAMES BOADEN, an English dramatic author and biographer, died, aged 70.

1843. Great land slide at Troy, N. Y.; 18 persons killed.

1852. Homoepathic college at Cleveland, Ohio, mobbed, and the windows and interior of the building destroyed, in consequence of the discovery of the remains of subjects which had been taken from the burial ground there.

1852. State lunatic asylum at Lexington, Ky., destroyed by fire, in which one of the inmates perished.

1853. GEORGE MANNERS died, aged 75; many years British consul at Boston, and author of several dramas of merit, and other poetical works.

1853. WILLIAM GIBBS MC NEIL died, aged 51; a military officer, who, during the Dorr excitement in Rhode Island, commanded the state troops, acting throughout with great prudence and judgment.

1853. The steamer Independence from San Juan del Sud to San Francisco, wrecked on Margaretta island, and also took fire, by which 140 lives were lost.

1854. The boiler of the Kate Kearney bursted at Louisville, Ky., killing and wounding a great number of people.

1856. JOHN STODDARD, an English author, died, aged 84. He for many years contributed leading articles to *The Times* newspaper, and was some time chief-justice of Malta.

1857. ELISHA K. KANE, the arctic explorer, died at Havana, Cuba.

FEBRUARY 17.

364. FLAVIUS CLAUD JOVIANUS, the Roman emperor, died at Dadastana, aged 33. He was elected by the army, on the death of Julian, and accepted the throne upon the assurance that the soldiers would embrace Christianity. He was suffocated in his bed by the fumes of a fire which had been made to dry the chamber, after a reign of only eight months.

1461. Battle of St. Albans, 21 miles from London, between the Lancastrians headed by the queen, Margaret, and the Yorkists under the earl of Warwick. The latter were defeated.

1564. MICHAEL ANGELO BUONAROTTI, the painter and architect, died at Rome, aged 89. He was of an illustrious family; studied painting and sculpture; and for a great number of years was employed by the popes in decorating the most superb edifices of Rome. At the age of 60 he was induced to attempt the *Last Judgment*, which is his master-piece. In architecture, St. Peter's and the Capitol are monuments of his ability. As a sculptor and poet also he is entitled to no mean place in the niche of fame. He was one of those favorites of nature, who combine in their single persons the excellence of many highly gifted men.

1571. An earthquake in Herefordshire, England, removed a hill containing 26 acres to a considerable distance, overturning every thing before it and continuing in motion several days.

1600. GIORDANO BRUNO, an Italian philosopher, burnt at Rome. He entered the order of the Dominicans, but his satires upon the lives of the monks drew upon him their persecutions, and he fled to the Calvinists. These in turn were excited against him by his paradoxes. After visiting Paris, London and Wurtemberg, he returned again to Italy, and fell into the hands of the inquisition, by whom he was condemned to be burnt, and suffered death, which he might have averted by a recantation, with the greatest fortitude. His philosophical writings, which have become very rare, display a classical cultivation of mind, a deep insight into the spirit of ancient philosophy, wit and satire, as well as a profound knowledge of mathematics and natural philosophy. With all his talent and erudition he was a pantheist.

1621. The Plymouth colonists met for the purpose of settling military affairs, and chose Miles Standish their captain.

1673. JEAN BAPTISTE POQUELIN DE MOLIERE died. At Narbonne, where the French theatre at that time began to flourish, through the talents of the great Corneille, he imbibed a strong passion for the stage. He became a distinguished comedian and dramatic writer, and died within four hours after personating a character in his play of the *Hypochondriac.*

1680. DENZIL, Lord Hollis, an eminent English patriot, died. He nobly maintained and defended the rights and privileges of the house of commons, of which he was a member, against the arbitrary measures of Charles I and his favorites. He was also a political writer.

1710. GEORGE BULL, an eminent English writer and preacher, died.

1720. JOHN HUGHES, an English poet and dramatist, died. He was a contributor to the *Tatler*, *Spectator* and *Guardian*. His last production, the *Siege of Damascus*, was performed with splendid success on the very night the author died suddenly. He was eulogized by Pope.

1735. NICOLO FORTIGUERRA died, an Italian prelate, and one of their best poets of the early part of the last century.

1739. GEORGE WHITFIELD, the celebrated Methodist, preached from a field pulpit to coalliers in Kingswood, near Bristol.

1758. JOHN WATKINS died at Bristol, England, aged 78. He was heir to a considerable estate, which being denied possession of, he made a vow never to shave till he enjoyed it; and kept his promise to the day of his death. He went by the name of Black John; after his death there was found upwards of 200 weight of half pence and silver, besides a quantity of gold, which he had amassed as a public beggar.

1759. THOMAS SIDDAL, a gardener at Chester, England, dug up a potatoe weighing 17 lbs. 4 oz., measuring 38 inches in circumference, and 47¼ in length.

1772. Convention between Frederick II of Prussia and Catharine II of Russia signed, for the partition of Poland. This was afterwards acceded to by Austria, and ratified by the Polish diet.

1773. An appearance similar to the aurora borealis first witnessed in the southern hemisphere, by Mr. Forster, who accompanied Capt. Cook.

1782. Action between the British fleet, Admiral Hughes, and the French fleet, M. de Suffrein, in which the British suffered severely.

1794. Fornelli in Corsica attacked and carried by the British under Lord Hood.

1796. JAMES MACPHERSON, the Scottish poet, died; distinguished for his translations and imitations of Gaelic poems, the principal of which is Fingal.

1797. The Spanish Admiral APODACA compelled to burn several large battle ships in the gulf of Paria, to prevent their falling into the hands of the British fleet under Harvey.

1804. Gen. MOREAU arrested at Paris, on an accusation of being concerned in the conspiracy of Pichegru and Georges.

1805. Action between the British frigate Cleopatra, 32 guns, and the French frigate Ville de Milan, pierced for 52 but mounting 26 guns. The Cleopatra was captured, with the loss of 20 killed and 38 wounded.

1810. Amboyna, the capital of the Moluccas, surrendered to the British, together with 49 merchant vessels in the harbor. It was not the first time it had fallen into the hands of the British.

1810. Rome annexed to France; the city to rank as the second in the French empire.

1814. Battle of Nangis, between Napoleon and the Russians under Count Witgenstein; same day, the Russians under Pahlen attacked the French at Marmont under Georges.

1814. The castle of Jaca in Arragon capitulated to the Spanish chief Francisco Espon y Mina, who took 84 brass cannon.

1818. HENRY OBOOKIAH, a Sandwich islander, died at Cornwall, Ct., aged 26. He was a member of the foreign mission school and has been made the subject of a memoir.

1827. JOHN HENRY PESTALOZZI, one of the most distinguished men of modern times for his efforts in the cause of education, died at Brugg. He was born at Zurich, in Switzerland; and devoted his life and property to the education of poor children. His system is not the best in use.

1828. HENRY GOTTLOB TSCHIRNER died, aged 50; an eminent German theologian.

1835. Five volcanoes burst forth simultaneously in Central-America, attended with tremendous earthquakes, which sunk three large towns, besides many villages. The air was so obscure with smoke, that the inhabitants were obliged to grope their way with torches for eight days. The lava in some places ran the distance of 60 leagues, destroying every thing in its course. In Alancho they thought the day of judgment had come, and more than 300 marriages took place among people who had previously lived in a state of concubinage.

1836. CORNPLANTER, (*Garyan-wah-gah,*) a celebrated Indian chief, died at the Seneca Reservation, aged about 100. At an early period of the revolutionary war he took an active part on the side of the Americans, and ever after manifested great friendship for the whites. He and his associate Red-Jacket, were for many years the counsellors and protectors of the interests of their nation.

1839. WILLIAM ADAM, a Scottish statesman, died. As member of parliament he opposed conciliatory measures with the refractory American colonies.

1840. JOSEPH CHITTY, a very eminent special pleader and author of many laborious and learned works in the profession of the law, died in London, aged 65.

1843. In British India 2,800 British troops defeated 22,000 Beloochees.

1852. WILLIAM THOMPSON, a distinguished naturalist, died, aged 46. He published the *Birds of Ireland*, and had undertaken to write the natural history of that country.

1852. Eruption of Mount Loa, Sandwich islands, which continued a long time undiminished.

1855. The Russians under Osten Sacken attacked Eupatoria, defended by the Turks under Omar Pasha, and were repulsed with loss.

1856. JOHN BRAHAM, a celebrated English vocalist, died, aged 82. He was the son of a German Jew, and his proper name was Abraham. He made his first appearance at Covent garden in 1787.

FEBRUARY 18.

3102, B. C. According to the tables of Trivalore, the great Hindostan epoch, *Callyhougham*, began at sunrise this day; that is, A. M. 902, and before the death of Adam!

1478. GEORGE, duke of Clarence, executed by drowning in a butt of Malmsey wine. He was the brother of Edward IV, against whom he had been induced to take up arms. He had the privilege of choosing the mode of his death.

1519. CORTES sailed from cape St. Antonio where he had stopped to complete his preparations. When all were brought together the vessels were found to be 11 in number; one of them of 100 tons burden, and three others from 70 to 80 tons; the remainder were caravels and open brigantines. His forces now amounted to 110 mariners, 553 soldiers, including 32 crossbowmen, and 13 arquebusiers, besides 200 Indians of the island, and a few Indian women for menial offices. He was provided with 10 heavy guns, 4 lighter pieces, called falconets, and a good supply of ammunition. He had besides 16 horses.

1546. MARTIN LUTHER, the reformer, died at Wittemberg. He was born at Eisleben in Saxony, 1483. His father was a miner, and Martin, to support himself at school, sung songs at the doors of the citizens. Yet this humble individual was destined to shake the papal throne to its foundations. His translation of the Bible, completed in 1534, was a labor of 13 years, amidst dangers 'and difficulties of every kind.

1639. THOMAS CAREW died; one of the wits of the court of Charles II. In the midst of a life of affluence and gaiety he found time to cultivate his taste for polite literature; and finally became a repentant devotee. He has been coupled with Waller as an improver of English versification, and was esteemed by Jonson and Davenant.

1645. RICHARD BAKER, an English historian, died. Having become security for the debts of some of his wife's relatives, he was thereby reduced to poverty, and thrown into the Fleet prison. During this imprisonment, and as a means of subsistence, he wrote his *Chronicle of the Kings of England*, and various other works, mostly devotional. He died in prison, where he had spent the last twenty years of his life, at the age of 77.

1652. GREGORIO ALLEGRI, an eminent musical composer, died at Rome. His compositions, the chief of which is the *Miserere*, are still performed in the pontifical chapel.

1653. Naval action off Portland, England, between the British under Blake, Dean and Monk, and the Dutch under Van Tromp and De Ruyter. The latter was defeated, with the loss of 2000 killed, 1500 prisoners, and 11 ships of war, besides a number of other vessels, principally merchantmen.

1654. JOHN LEWIS GUEZ DE BALZAC, historiographer of France, died. He acquired great celebrity by his publications.

1662. An unprecedented storm in severity passed over England, chiefly felt at London.

1672. JOHN LABADIE died at Altona; a celebrated French enthusiast.

1694. Several ships of war, &c., lost in a storm east of Gibraltar. The Sussex on board of which was Sir Francis Wheeler, the admiral, foundered with the whole of her crew.

1695. WILLIAM PHIPPS died at London, aged 45. He was born at Pemaquid, Maine; was apprenticed to a ship carpenter, and afterwards went to sea. Hearing of a Spanish wreck near Bahama, he gave such an acccount of it in England that he was fitted out in 1683 to search for it, but was unsuccessful. The duke of Albemarle fitted him out a second time, and he returned with a treasure of £300,000, of which his share was 16,000. He was subsequently sent over as governor of Massachusetts, but his administration was short and unpopular.

1702. THOMAS HYDE, an eminent English divine and orientalist, died. He published a work on the religion of the ancient Persians, which threw many new lights on the most curious and interesting subjects.

1709. Sir EDWARD SEYMOUR died. He had been a member of every parliament since 1661.

1710. PHILIP VERHEYEN, a medical author, died at Louvain, in Belgium, where he was professor of anatomy.

1712. LOUIS, duke of Burgundy, died, aged 30. He was educated under Fenelon, and as heir to the throne and counsellor of state, France expected to enjoy a long rest from her troubles, under this administration. He died suddenly of a disease which had taken away his wife and eldest son only a few days before.

1719. GEORGE HENRY GOERTZ, a Swedish statesman, beheaded. He joined Charles XII on his return from Turkey, and was placed at the head of affairs. The desperate state of Sweden gave full employment to his extraordinary talents; but on the fall of the king he was sacrificed to the hatred of the nobility and condemned without a trial.

1724. GEORGE WHEELER, an English traveler and antiquary died. He visited Greece and Asia, for the purpose of copying inscriptions and to describe antiquities, in company with Dr. Spon, an account of which was published in 6 vols. folio. The work is highly valued for its authenticity and antiquities.

1730. CHARLES BECKINGHAM, an English dramatic writer, died. His pieces were received with much applause.

1750. GEORGE BERNARD BILFINGER, professor of philosophy at Petersburg, and afterwards at Tubingen, died at Stutgard. He was eminent as an author.

1758. JOSEPH ISAAC BERRUYER, a French Jesuit, died; author of some theological works.

1772. JOHN HARTWIG ERNST, count Bernstorff, died at Hamburg. He settled in Denmark, where he became prime minister, and in this office devoted the whole energies of his powerful mind to the improvement of his adopted country. He set the example of manumitting the peasantry, who were in a state of bondage and gave the fourth part of his income to the poor. He is represented as a model of intelligence, wisdom and benevolence.

1777. Col. NIELSON of New Jersey, with a party of American militia, defeated the British Major Stockton, killed 4 and took him and 59 of his men prisoners.

1778. JOSEPH MARIE TERRAY, minister of state of France, died. He was a man of great integrity and patriotism; and on retiring from office, carried with him the gratitude of his country.

1791. Vermont admitted into the Union. (see March 4).

1793. Action between British ship Juno, Capt. Hood, and the French privateer schooner, L'Entreprenant, Capt. Vaniere. The latter was taken, together with a prize which she had captured. Vaniere shot himself.

1795. British squadron under Warren captured near the isle of Aix, 8 French vessels, and destroyed 10 brigs and a lugger, laden with provisions and clothing for the French fleet and army.

1797. Trinidad, another of the West India isles, surrendered to the English under Sir R. Abercromby.

1800. Action off Malta, between the British squadron under Nelson, and Le Genereux, a French 74, and a frigate which resulted in the capture of the two latter.

1800. LOUIS LE FROTTE, the Vendean chief, with 7 of his officers, shot by order of the French convention. They all refused to have their eyes covered.

1808. Austrian declaration of non-intercourse with England.

1811. French port of Tamĕtivi, in Madagascar, surrendered to a British force.

1812. The prince regent of England, afterwards George IV, invested with full legal powers.

1814. Battle of Montereau, in France; Chateau, who commanded the French, was repulsed and mortally wounded; but Gen. Gerard, the second in command, sustained the combat until 2 P. M., when being reinforced by Bonaparte, the Russians were in turn discomfited.

1815. The king of Candy, in Ceylon, surrendered to the British under Gen. Brownrigg.

1815. Treaty of peace between the United States and Great Britain ratified by President Madison.

1834. WILLIAM WIRT died, aged 62. He early became acquainted with Jefferson, Madison and Monroe, and filled several important offices under them with distinguished reputation. As a public and professional man, he was ranked among the first of his time.

1843. The Ameers of the punjaf in India wholly defeated by the British troops under Sir Charles Napier.

1851. VICTOR FALCK, a distinguished French ornithologist, died at Stockholm.

1852. CHRISTOPHER ANDERSON died, aged 73; known by his *Annals of the English Bible.*

1853. An attempt made to assassinate the emperor of Austria by a Hungarian named Lebenyi, who was executed.

1856. HEINRICH HEINE, the celebrated German poet, died at Paris.

FEBRUARY 19.

198. DECIUS CLAUDIUS ALBINUS, a Roman who assumed the imperial purple in opposition to Severus, was slain in battle on the river Rhone.

1401. WILLIAM SAUTRE, an English clergyman, was burned for heresy, by the clergy, with the permission of Henry IV. This is said to have been the first execution in England on account of religion. (Timperley says March 10.)

1549. A bill passed the English parliament allowing clergymen to marry, on the ground that it was a less evil than compulsory chastity.

1553. ERASMUS REINHOLD died; an eminent German astronomer and mathematician, and professor at Wittemberg.

1567. MILES COVERDALE, bishop of Exeter, buried. He was ejected from his see by queen Mary, and thrown into prison, from which he was liberated by Elizabeth. He assisted Tindal in the English version of the Bible, 1537.

1592. EDWARD COKE chosen speaker of parliament.

1597. THOMAS BENTHAM, an English bishop, died; celebrated for his knowledge of the Chaldee and Hebrew tongues.

1619. LUCILIO VANINI, a learned Italian, burnt. He early devoted himself with ardor to letters, studying philosophy, law, theology and astrology, at Rome and Padua. He traveled throughout every country of Europe, occupying himself with instruction; but wherever he appeared, he became obnoxious to suspicion on account of his religious views. In 1617 he went to Toulouse, where he was accused of atheism and sorcery, and condemned to the flames. He was drawn to the place of execution, when after his tongue was torn out, he was strangled, and burnt at the age of 34. His punishment appears to have been entirely undeserved, and has given him more celebrity than his writings.

1622. HENRY SAVILE died, a learned English divine, historian and critic; Greek tutor to Queen Elizabeth.

1638. Insurrection of the Edinburgh presbyterians, who threw off their allegiance, and entered into a covenant or association against the government, which they compelled all people to subscribe; several Scotch bishops were forced to fly to England.

1644. The Scots, consisting of 18,000 foot, 2,000 horse, and above 500 dragoons, passed the Tweed at Berwick in behalf of the parliament.

1671. CHARLES CHAUNCEY, president of Harvard college, died, aged 80. He was a nonconformist divine, who emigrated to America; a learned and venerated man.

1697. FRANCIS BERNARD, an English physician, died; eminent for his learning, and his valuable collection of books.

1717. PETER ANTHONY MOTTEUX, died in London on his birthday (supposed to have been murdered). He was a French refugee, settled in England, where he became an eminent dramatic writer, and translated Don Quixotte.

1734. Battle of Gaustalla between the French and the imperialists under count Konigsegg; the latter of whom were defeated with the loss of 5,000 men including the prince of Wirtemberg.

1743. La Guaira, in South America, attacked by the British under Knowles. He captured one ship, and blew up a magazine but did not succeed in his principal object, which was the total destruction of the shipping. Spanish loss 700.

1767. FRANCIS BOISSIER DE SAUVAGES, a French physician and botanist, died. His reputation was so great that he was called the Boerhaave of Languedoc.

1778. Capt. JAMES WILLING took possession of Natches in the name of the U. S.

1788. THOMAS CUSHING, of Massachusetts died. He was early engaged in polical life, and in 1763 appointed speaker of the council where, by his moderate and conciliatory conduct he was enabled to effect a great deal of good as a mediator between the contending parties. On the breaking out of disturbances he was sent to the first congress, and continued to fill some office till his death, when he was lieutenant governor.

1790. Marquis DE FAVRAS executed. His judges were intimidated by the mob shouting during the trial, *a la lanterne.*

1792. MATTHEW TAIT died at Auchinleck, aged 123.

1793. Lieuts. GIBBS and MOUNTESY with 21 men of the Lowestoffe frigate seized the tower of Martelli in Corsica, and hoisted the British flag for the first time in that island.

1794. French frigate La Fortunee burnt to prevent her falling into the hands of Lord Hood.

1797. JAMES DODSLEY the renowned and rich London bookseller died. He sold 18,000 copies of Burke's *Reflections on the French Revolution.*

1798. The Irish rebellion, as the discontents were called, commenced.

1799. JEAN CHARLES BORDA, a French mathematician, died. He made many improvements in hydraulics, and his experiments for the advancement of science were numerous and successful.

1801. Action off Gibraltar between the British frigate Phebe 36 guns, and the French frigate L'Africaine, 44 guns and 715 men. The Frenchman lost 200 men killed and 143 wounded, and was captured. British loss 1 killed and 12 wounded.

1802. NICHOLAS JOSEPH SELIS, a distinguished French poet, died.

1806. ELIZABETH CARTER, an English poetess, died, aged 89. She acquired nine foreign languages; but the reputation of this learned lady was established by a complete translation from the Greek of the works of Epictetus, with notes.

1807. Admiral DUCKWORTH, with 8 ships of the line and 4 frigates, together with fire ships and gun boats, effected the daring pass of the Dardanelles, without loss, and appeared before Constantinople, which until then had never seen an enemy's fleet. The Turks fired stone shot from their batteries upon the fleet, some of them weighing upwards of 800 pounds. The Turkish squadron, consisting of a 64 gun ship, 4 frigates, 3 corvettes, a brig and 2 gun boats, were burnt.

1811. Duke of Albuquerque, ambassador to England from the regency of Spain, died at London.

1816. WM. REESE died in Dublin district, Md., aged 108.

1816. A bridge of wire, 400 feet in length, for foot passengers having been constructed over the Schuylkill, was passed for the first time.

1821. Florida ceded to the United States by Spain.

1837. THOMAS BURGESS, bishop of Salisbury, died. He was the son of a grocer, and rose by his own merits. He was a man of extensive learning, and a voluminous author; was instrumental in founding the royal society of literature; and St. David's college founded by him for the education of Welsh ministers, is an enduring monument of his benevolence. To this institution he bequeathed the whole of his extensive library.

1843. MICHAEL J. QUINN, well known to general readers as the author of *A Visit to Spain*, &c., died at Boulogne-sur-mer, France.

1844. GILBERT, a servant of Washington at the great battle of the Monongahela, died at Stanton, Va., aged 112. He was also with the general at the surrender of Cornwallis, and was accustomed on holidays to appear in regimentals during his life, to the great edification of the boys.

1852. WILLIAM WARE, an eminent unitarian scholar and divine, died at Cambridge, Mass., aged 54.

1856. The ship John Rutledge from Liverpool to New York encountered an iceberg and sunk. Of five boats which left the ship, only one was picked up, with but one living man on board, the survivor of thirteen who had died one by one of cold and starvation.

FEBRUARY 20.

1413. THOMAS ARUNDEL, archbishop of Canterbury, died. He was consecrated bishop of Ely at the age of 21, and became infamous by the severity of his conduct towards the reformers.

1437. JAMES I, of Scotland, murdered, at the age of 44. He fell a martyr to his attempts to abolish the anarchy and disorder which prevailed throughout his kingdom. He was the first of the Stuarts, and stands on the catalogue of royal authors. (Is also dated 21st.)

1494. MATTEO MARIE BOIARDO, count of Scandiano, died. In his *Orlando Innamorato* he immortalized his own peasants and the charms of the scenery at Scandiano in the persons of his heroes and the beauties of nature.

1571. LEWIS CASTELVETRO, an Italian critic, died. He was famous for his parts, but more famous for spleen and ill nature. He distinguished himself chiefly by his *Commentary upon Aristotle's Poetics*, where, Rapin assures us, he always made it a rule to find something to except against in the text.

1579. NICHOLAS BACON, an English statesman, died. He was appointed lord keeper of the great seal on the accession of Elizabeth, and was an able and judicious counsellor of that queen during 20 years.

1579. DRAKE, after many profitable captures in the Pacific, arrived at Lima, where he plundered all the ships in the harbor, in one of which was found a chest full of reals of silver, and a good store of silks and linen cloth.

1648. THOMAS DAMME buried at Minshull, England, "being of the age of seven score and fourteen" (154 years).

1725. A party of 40 New Hampshire volunteers on an excursion for hunting Indians, discovered a party of ten encamped for the night round a fire. Advancing cautiously at midnight, the enemy were found asleep and the whole shot. They were marching from Canada well furnished with new guns and ammunition, and a number of spare blankets, moccasins and snow shoes, for the accommodation of the prisoners they expected to take, and were within two miles of the frontiers. The party entered Dover in triumph, with the ten scalps stretched on hoops and elevated on poles; and received a bounty of £100 for each scalp, at Boston, out of the public treasury.

1736. A bill was introduced into the British parliament, placing a duty of 20 shillings a gallon on spirituous liquors, and £50 license for selling them, in order to prevent their excessive use; but was defeated so far as to tolerate punch at a low rate, the merchants of Bristol and Liverpool fearing the lessening of consumption on rum and other things distilled from molasses.

1737. Elizabeth Rowe died; an English lady distinguished for her piety and literary talents.

1745. British ship Chester, Capt. Geary, captured the French ship Elephant with $24,000 on board.

1749. Usher Gahagan, executed at Tyburn. He was a gentleman by birth, and a scholar; he edited a beautiful edition of the classics, and translated Pope's *Messiah* and *Temple of Fame* into Latin verse. His crime was that of clipping coin!

1762. Tobias Mayer, a distinguished mathematician, died at Gottingen. His lunar and solar tables, as well as his original suggestions on the repeating circle are of much value.

1771. John James de Mairan, a French philosopher, died. He succeeded Fontenelle as secretary to the academy of sciences, and is the author of a *Treatise on Phosphoric Light*, &c.

1772. The royal marriage act of England was passed. This was another of those attempts to perpetuate regal domination.

1778. Laura Bassi died; she was honored with the degree of doctor of philosophy, for the great mental acquirements displayed in her lectures on that subject, and was distinguished as possessing every amiable virtue.

1780. British under General Clinton invaded South Carolina.

1781. Robert Morris appointed by congress superintendent of finance.

1790. Joseph II, emperor of Germany, died. He was an able and benevolent monarch, who devoted his attention closely to the affairs of the kingdom, and introduced many useful institutions.

1790. At Blackwall, England, while excavations were being made for a wet dock several hazel trees, with nuts, were found deeply imbedded below several strata of sand and clay.

1797. Treaty of Tolentino between Bonaparte and the pope.

1799. El Arish, and subsequently Gaza, with most towns in western Palestine, were taken by the French.

1799. Leopold II, died; grand duke of Tuscany 25 years, and elected emperor of Germany, 1790. He evinced great abilities.

1802. Joan Moore, a distinguished Scottish physician, and popular author, died. He wrote on the society and manners of different countries in Europe, which his accute discernment and lively imagination enabled him to describe with great accuracy and pleasantry.

1803. British evacuated Egypt.

1808. Gerard Lake died. He was made a peer of Great Britain for his successes as a general in India.

1809. Richard Gough, a learned and eminent English antiquary, died.

1809. Saragossa surrendered to the French. The garrison was reduced to 12,000 men, who, when they marched out of the city, had more the appearance of spectres than of human beings. During this second siege 54,000 perished, of whom one fourth were soldiers.

1810. Andrew Hofer, the leader of the Tyrolese insurrection, executed. He was a brave patriot, and met his fate with heroic firmness.

1811. Battle of San Christoval in Spain, in which general Mendizabal was defeated with the loss of about 12,000 killed and prisoners, by the French under Soult, whose loss was stated at 400 only.

1811. Francis II, of Germany, issued an edict, fixing the current value of bank paper at one fifth of its nominal value.

1817. Samuel Meredith died at his seat in Wayne county, Pa.; first treasurer of the United States under the federal constitution, which office he resigned in 1801.

1820. Arthur Young died; a distinguished English author on agriculture.

1822. John Stewart, commonly called *walking John*, died in London; to gratify the "amor videndi," he had perambulated much of the globe.

1835. A tremendous earthquake in Chili. The city of Conception, containing 25,000 inhabitants, was reduced to a heap of ruins, not a single house left standing; many other towns and villages were demolished. At first the sea retired and left the vessels in the harbor aground; but it soon rushed violently back 30 feet above its level.

1836. Mary Crawford, died at Castine, Me., aged 100 years and six months; widow of Dr. Wm. Crawford, chaplain and surgeon at Fort Point during the revolution.

1841. James G. Brooks died; known in early life as an American poet, and later as an editor of several newspapers.

1843. Peter Augustus Jay, well known in the state of New York as a statesman and historian, died.

1846. The first legislature of Texas under the U. S. met at Austin. Gen. Henderson was elected the first govenor.

1849. Newton M. Curtiss, author of a number of popular novels, died at Charlton, N. Y., aged 34.

1854. Elliott Cresson, president of the Pennsylvania colonization society, died, leaving $127,000 to charitable institutions.

1854. The most violent snow storm that had occcured since 1831, commenced at Washington, and extended over the Middle and New England states.

1855. JOSEPH HUME, the English statesman died, aged 78. He was a member of the house of commons 37 years.

FEBRUARY 21.

1340. The king of England assumed the title of the king of France, quartering his arms with the motto, "Dieu et mon Droit."

1513. GIULIANO DELLA ROVERA, (pope Julius II,) died. He was originally a fisherman. He built St. Peter's at Rome, to procure means for which he ordered the sale of indulgencies, which was one of the immediate causes of the reformation; so that it may be said without paradox, that St. Peter's is the great monument of protestantism. He is considered one of the most immoral of the popes, though a generous patron of the polite arts.

1595. ROBERT SOUTHWELL, called sometimes the English jesuit, died. He was esteemed no inferior poet in his day.

1633. Order of the privy council to stay several ships in the Thames, ready to sail for New England with passengers and provisions. The jealousy of the government was early directed towards the infant colony of Massachusetts. It was observed by one of the kings, that the *wheat* of the population was sifting across the Atlantic. These orders were ineffectual, for great numbers continued to emigrate, and scarce a vessel arrived in the colony that was not crowded with passengers.

1660. The secluded members of the long parliament again took their seats and voted Monk to be general of the English, Scotch and Irish forces.

1668. JOHN THURLOE, secretary of state to the two Cromwells, died. He was a man of very amiable character, and exercised all possible moderation towards persons of every party.

1676. Two or three hundred Indians principally Narragansetts, surprised the town of Medfield, Mass., killed 18 men, women and children, and burnt half of the town.

1682. The following appears in the minutes of the governor and council of Virginia: "John Buckner called before the Ld. Culpepper and his counsel for printing the laws of 1680, without his excellency's license, and he and the printer ordered to enter into bond in £100 not to print anything hereafter until his majesty's pleasure shall be known."

1684. CHARLES SPON, an ingenious and learned French physician, died at Lyons. He wrote Latin verse with ease and elegance, and corresponded with most of the learned men of Europe.

1717. PETER ALIX, a French protestant of eminent piety and learning, died. He resided in England, where he was greatly esteemed and honored.

1730. BENEDICT XIII, pope of Rome, died. He was a Dominican of Venice, and before his elevation bishop of Benevento, where his palace was destroyed by an earthquake, and he narrowly escaped. He filled the pontifical office six years, and sustained an excellent character.

1746. Le Bourbon and La Charite, French ships, captured by Com. Knowles in a heavy gale. The military chest belonging to the French vessels contained £5,000.

1759. Action between the British frigate Vestal, Capt. Hood, and the French frigate Bellona, which resulted in the capture of the latter, with the loss of 42 killed. British loss 2 killed and 22 wounded.

1760. The neighborhood of Mt. Vesuvius overflowed by burning lava.

1760. Commodore THOUROT arrived in the bay of Carrickfergus with a 43 gun ship and two sloops of war, and having landed 800 men, attacked the town, which, with the castle, he carried after a smart action. The French embarked a few days after, and meeting with a British squadron, an action ensued in which Thourot and 300 of his men were killed.

1792. JACOB SCHNEBBELIE died at London. From the profession of a Swiss confectioner, he rose to be one of the best draughtsmen in England, but too intense application to his studies hastened his death.

1796. Field Marshal CLAIRFAIT, the Austrian general, resigned, and was succeeded by the Archduke Charles, for whom a new rank was created, that of field-marshal-general, being the highest military rank in the empire.

1799. GILBERT WAKEFIELD was fined £100 and condemned to two years confinement, for his pamphlet against the bishop of Landaff.

1805. Dominica attacked by a French squadron, which was repulsed by the British under Gen. Provost.

1810. Action between the British ship Horatio, and French frigate Necessity, 21 guns, which last was captured in one hour.

1812. Action between the British ship Victorious, Capt. Talbot, and the Venitian ship Rivoli, 74 guns. The latter was captured, after an engagement of 5 hours, with the loss of 400 killed and wounded; British loss 42 k. 99 w.

1813. Ogdensburgh, N. Y., taken by the British.

1814. The British, about 2000 in number, under Col. Scott, crossed over to the French mills, burnt the arsenal at Malone, N. Y., pillaged the town and carried off some provisions. The enemy retreated in great haste, and lost 200 men by desertion. Gen. Wilkinson endeavored to come up with him, but was prevented by the weather.

1818. David Humphreys, an officer of the revolution, died. He was a native of Connecticut, and successively aid to generals Putnam, Greene and Washington. He is also known as a poet of very fair pretensions.

1824. Eugene de Beauharnais, duke of Leuchtenberg, died. He was the son of Josephine Tacher de la Pagerie, afterwards wife of Napoleon. He distinguished himself in the army, and was made viceroy of Italy, the government of which he managed with great prudence. With the fall of Napoleon he lost his titles and offices, but was in a measure idemnified by the articles of Fontainbleau,the congress of Vienna, and the duke of Bavaria. Under a simple exterior prince Eugene concealed a noble character and great talents.

1831. Robert Hall died at Bristol, England; a very eminent man and a celebrated preacher.

1838. Anthony Isaac Sylvestre de Sacy died, aged 80; renowned principally for his extensive critical knowledge, particularly in oriental languages and literature; esteemed, in this department of learning, the first scholar of his age.

1839. Charles Rossi, a celebrated sculptor, died at London, aged 77.

1840. William Frend, died in London, aged 84; a writer on algebra, taxation and various other subjects.

1845. Sydney Smith, canon of St. Paul's in London, and well known to Pennsylvania repudiators, died in London.

1855. Charles Roger Dod, assistant editor of *The Times* newspaper, died aged 62.

1856. The students of South Carolina college, armed with rifles, surrendered to the governor of the state and a posse of armed citizens.

FEBRUARY 22.

1371. David II of Scotland died. He was the son of Robert Bruce, was taken prisoner by the English in 1346 and detained in the tower 10 years.

1609. Ferdinand I, grand duke of Tuscany, died. He was eminent for the wisdom and energy of his government.

1630. The first day of public thanksgiving in Massachusetts. The day had been appointed for a general fast. No ship had arrived in a great length of time, and their stock of provisions was nearly exhausted. At this critical moment a vessel arrived from England laden with provisions; and they immediately changed the day of public fasting into one of public feasting. And it is quite probable that the day was observed with something more than an outward show of thanksgiving on that occasion.

1644. Charles I, having summoned a royal parliament, they met this day at Oxford to the number of 44 lords and 118 commoners; the session was opened with a speech from the king.

1674. Jean Chapelain, died. He attracted the notice of Cardinal Richelieu by a preface which he wrote for the *Adonis* of Marini. Chapelain was talented and learned, obsequious and discreet, and these made his fortune, for he could be of service to the cardinal, who had the weakness to set up for a *bel esprit*. He became one of the first members of the *Academie Francaise*, received a large pension, and became the oracle of the poets of the time, and was universally esteemed. It would have been better if he himself had not set up for a poet. In 1630 he commenced an epic, *La Pucelle*. It was announced twenty years before its appearance, and the public expectation was greatly disappointed; it soon became an object of ridicule.

1717. Great snow in New England; 6 feet deep in Boston. It commenced on the 20th, on which day Dr. Brattle was buried, and many who attended his funeral were unable to get home for several days.

1731. Frederick Ruysch, an eminent Dutch anatomist, died.

1732. Birthday of George Washington. He was the third son of Augustus Washington, and was born at Bridges Creek, Va.

1744. Partial action off Toulon between the combined French and Spanish fleets under M. De Court, and the British fleet under admirals Matthews and Rowley. The Poder, a Spanish 60 gun ship, was burnt. British loss 92 killed, 185 wounded.

1746. William Couston, director of the French academy of painting and sculpture, died.

1766. British stamp act repealed.

1770. A mob, principally boys, attacked the house of Mr. Richardson, Boston, owing to his having attempted to remove the mark set against the house of one Lille, who had contravened the non-importation law. Richardson fired upon the mob and killed Christopher Snider, a boy 11 years of age, who was recorded in the public prints as the first martyr to American liberty.

1780. An ox roasted on the ice at Philadelphia, the ice being 17 inches thick.

1782. The island of Montserrat surrendered to the French under Count De Grasse.

1787. The assembly of notables of France assembled.

1797. The French made a descent on Wales.

1806. JAMES BARRY, an Irish painter, died. He was patronized by Burke. His greatest effort is a series of allegorical pictures in possession of the Society of arts, London.

1809. LOUIS, count of Cobentzel, died at Vienna. He was born at Brussels 1753. He entered into the military service of Austria at an early age, and was employed as an embassador to the court of Copenhagen before he had attained his twentieth year; and was continued in that capacity at some one of the European courts during the whole of his life.

1810. CHARLES BROCKDEN BROWN, an American novelist, died aged 39. He holds a distinguished rank among American authors.

1810. The island of St. Eustatia surrendered by the Dutch to the British.

1811. The British ships Cerberus and Active captured 22 vessels from Otranto, with provisions and troops.

1812. Ogdensburg, New York, attacked by the British and Indians under Frazer and McDonnell. Forsythe was compelled to evacuate it. The British took 12 cannons, 1400 stands of arms, 300 tents, some provisions, and all the vessels and boats. American loss 27; British loss 64 killed and wounded.

1814. BLUCHER defeated by the French under Boyer; the former set the bridge and town of Mery on fire and fled.

1816. ADAM FERGUSON, an eminent Scottish writer, died. He was sent to America as secretary to the mission in 1778 to effect a reconciliation between the two countries.

1835. JANE JARMON died near Wadesborough, N. C., aged 105.

1836. JOICE HETH died at New York; a blind negro woman, who had been carried about the country as a show, under the pretence that she was 162 years of age and had been the nurse of General Washington. On a post mortem examination it was found that she could not have been more than 80 years old.

1841. A land slide in the commune of Gregano in Italy, by which 113 persons lost their lives. The town of Reggio, in Calabria, nearly destroyed by an earthquake.

1855. The San Francisco bankers suspended payment, causing a panic.

FEBRUARY 23.

303. The soldiers of Diocletian demolished the principal church of Nicomedia, and committed the sacred volumes to the flames.

1447. GABRIEL CONDOIMERO (Pope Eugenius IV), died. He was elected to the papal throne 1431, afterwards unjustly deposed, and again restored.

1545. FRANCIS DE BOURBON, Count Enghien, killed. He was a celebrated general in the service of Francis I, and was killed by accident.

1555. THOMAS WYAT beheaded. He took the lead in an unsuccessful insurrection against the "bloody Queen Mary."

1589. ANDREW DUDITH, a Hungarian divine, died. He was employed by Ferdinand II, in important affairs of state, wrote on physic, poetry, &c., and was a highly esteemed character.

1603. ANDREAS CÆSARALPINUS, an Italian philosopher and physician, died at Rome.

1619. BARTHOLOMEW ZIEGENBALG, a celebrated German missionary, died. He was sent to India by the king of Denmark, but meeting with some opposition from the Danish authorities there, he placed himself under the countenance of the British East India company, published a dictionary of the Malabar language, and was fulfilling the object of his mission with great zeal and success, when he was suddenly interrupted by death at the age of 36.

1679. THOMAS GOODWIN, a theological writer of the puritan school, died, aged 80. He was one of the members of the assembly of divines at Westminster, and attended Cromwell on his death bed.

1717. MAGNUS STEINBOCK, an illustrious Swede, died at Fredrickshaven. He distinguished himself by his valor under Charles XII, and in the absence of the king from Sweden, he managed the affairs of the government with uncommon wisdom and moderation.

1750. A brilliant borealis appeared at Cork, about seven in the evening. The tide at the same time rose far above its ordinary height.

1766. STANISLAUS I, king of Poland and elector of Saxony, died. He was an author, and a good ruler, though an unfortunate one.

1775. The daily consumption of *pulque*, the fermented juice of the maguei, in the city of Mexico, according to the custom house record, was 6000 arrobas (150,000 lbs.), and the daily consumption of tobacco for smoking, was reckoned at 1250 crowns. The population then exceeded 200,000.

1779. St. Vincents surrendered with considerable stores, to the Americans under Col. Clarke. British taken, 79.

1780. Action between the British ship Resolution, 74 guns, and French ship La Prothee, 64 guns, which resulted in the capture of the latter.

1792. JOSHUA REYNOLDS, the English painter, died in London, aged 69. He rapidly acquired opulence by his profession, and on the institution of the royal academy, was elected president. The lectures which he delivered before this society have become a standard work.

1796. NICHOLAS STOFFLET, the celebrated Vendean chief, shot at Angers. At the beginning of the French revolution he was a private soldier, but became one of the most intrepid and daring chiefs of the royal army of La Vendee, and had been in no less than 150 actions, 10 of them pitched battles; and in more than 100 of them he proved victorious. He met his fate with characteristic fortitude.

1796. BONAPARTE appointed commander-in-chief of the army of Italy.

1798. Rockland county N. Y., erected.

1798. The pope withdrew from Rome to Sienna, having been deprived of his temporal possessions by the French.

1800. JOSEPH WARTON, an English prelate, died. He was also an ingenious poet and critical writer.

1805. British frigate Leander, fell in with and captured the Ville de Milan, and her prize the Cleopatra, captured a few days previous. (See 17th.)

1814. The blacks under Christophe, took by assault fort Sabourin, in St. Domingo.

1821. The counties of Monroe and Livingston N. Y., erected.

1822. BENAVIDES executed; an outlaw and pirate, who for several years proved the scourge of the southern part of Chili, where he perpetrated the most horrid cruelties upon every age and sex that fell in his way. In 1818 he had been condemned to be shot, and was supposed to have been killed; but although shockingly wounded and left for dead, he recovered and became a fiend incarnate.

1827. WALTER SCOTT disclosed himself publicly for the first time as the *Great Unknown*, at a dinner of the Edinburgh theatrical fund, himself in the chair.

1831. GERTRUDE ELIZABETH MARIA, a favorite German vocalist, celebrated the anniversary of her 83d year at Reval, where Goethe offered her a poetical tribute.

1836. Battle of fort Alamo in Texas, in which the Mexican army of 4000, who made the assault, were repulsed.

1840. JAMES MAURY died at New York, aged 95. He was the first consul from the United States to Liverpool, to which office he was appointed by Washington, and which he held for nearly half a century.

1847. Battle of Buena Vista in which the Mexican army, numbering more than four to one of the Americans, was completely defeated. Many of the American officers were slain.

1848. JOHN QUINCY ADAMS, ex-president of the United States, died in the Capitol at Washington. It may well be questioned whether any statesman in the world was better informed.

1851. JOANNA BAILLE, the Scottish poetress, died, aged 89. She was born at Bothwell, near the Clyde, and lived in seclusion with her maiden sister.

1854. The steamer from Stonington arrived at New York, having been detained in the sound by ice during three days.

1856. A freshet commenced in the Ohio, which caused great destruction of property, among which were several steam boats.

FEBRUARY 24.

303. DIOCLETIAN issued the first general edict of persecution against the Christians, by which all their religious edifices in the empire were to be leveled to their foundations, and the church property confiscated and sold to the highest bidder. This abominable decree was instantly torn from its column by a Christian of rank, who for his audacity was burnt or rather roasted, by a slow fire.

1383. JOHN WICKLIFFE presented seven articles to parliament containing his doctrines.

1468. JOHN GUTENBERG, the inventor of printing, died. In connection with Faust he contributed greatly to the improvement of the art, then in a very rude state.

1495. JEM, son of Bayazid I the Osman sultan, died. He was defeated by his brother in a contest for the throne, and took refuge with the knights of St. John at Rhodes, who sent him to France, where he was kept in confinement several years, and then delivered up to the pope, Alexander VI, by whom he was poisoned.

1525. Battle of Pavia in Italy. The imperialists under Bourbon, Pescara and Lannoy defeated the French and captured their king, Francis I, whom they sent prisoner to Madrid. The king fought with heroic valor, killing 7 men with his own hand.

1540. CHARLES V of Germany entered Ghent, which had been in a state of insurrection; 26 of the principal citizens were put to death. He was born at this place on this day 1500.

1541. Pedro de Valdivia, having been sent by Pizarro with 200 Spaniards and a numerous body of Peruvians to Chili for the purpose of settling such provinces as he should conquer, succeeded in overcoming the resistance of the natives and founded the city of Santiago.

1563. Francis of Lorraine, duke of Guise, assassinated. He distinguished himself in the wars with Charles V and the English; and in the reigns of Henry II and Francis II of France, completely governed the kingdom. After the death of Francis, he espoused the side of the catholics in the civil wars.

1587. Thomas Cavendish passed the straits of Magellan.

1645. A treaty of peace, which was begun at Uxbridge on the 30th January, between the commissioners of Charles I, and those of the parliament, was broken off.

1665. A Dutch imposter whipped thro' the streets of London; possibly only a little eccentric.

1665. Deerfield, Mass., purchased of the Indians. The deed, which is still extant, was given "for the use and behoof of Major Eleazar Lusher, Ensign Daniel Fisher, and other English at Dedham, their associates and successors," by Chauk alias Chague, the sachem of Pocomptuck, and his brother Wassahoale, and witnessed by Wequonnock. It reserves to the Indians the right of fishing in the rivers, hunting wild animals, and gathering nuts. It is capable of proof, that the early settlers in New England, as well as New York, made it a matter of course to purchase the lands upon which they settled, in nearly all instances, and at prices which were considered a fair equivalent at the time by the Indians. It may be mentioned as a matter of curiosity, that the salary of the first minister settled at this place was £60, to be paid in wheat at 3s. 6d., peas at 2s. 6d., corn at 2s. per bushel, and salted pork at 2¼d. per pound.

1667. Thomas Adams died. He was born at Wem in England; went to London, where he established himself in business as a draper; and in 1645 rose to the high honor of lord mayor of that city.

1676. Attack on Medfield, Mass., by a party of about 300 Indians. The loss of Lancaster, a short time previous, had put the neighboring towns on their guard, and Medfield had obtained a small garrison of soldiers for greater security, although within 22 miles of Boston. The Indians during the night had secreted themselves, according to custom, under the fences and behind trees about the villages, so that the people were shot down as they came out of their doors and their houses immediately set on fire. The soldiers being lodged in different parts of the town, could not get together until about 50 buildings were on fire. Some were killed as they attempted to pass to their neighbors for shelter, and in some instances, the husband flying with one child and the wife with another, one of them fell into the hands of the savages or was killed, while the other escaped. Two or three discharges of a field piece put the whole horde to flight, who as they passed the river fired the bridge to prevent pursuit. Loss 18 killed, and many wounded and carried away for torture. (Holmes says Feb. 21.)

1684. Birthday of Handel, the music composer, at Halle.

1684. Boundary line between New York and Connecticut partially run.

1716. The earls of Derwentwater and Kenmuir beheaded on Tower hill, for treason in favoring the cause of the Pretender.

1721. John Sheffield, duke of Buckingham, died; a celebrated general, critic and poet.

1724. A great storm attended with an uncommon tide, was experienced in New England. The tide in some places rose ten feet higher than it was ever known before, and rendered many of the streets of Boston navigable.

1740. Providential delivery from death of a society of monks at Palermo.

1752. Isaac Wood, an English painter, died. His principal pieces are in oil and black lead upon vellum.

1758. Battle of Hoya in Westphalia, between the allies and French.

1762. Tremendous hurricane and fall of snow in England. Nearly 50 persons perished in the fields, and several whales were driven on the Essex and Kentish coasts.

1766. Stanislaus, the last duke of Lorrain and Bar, as an independent Duchy, died in consequence of burns from his robes de chambre having accidentally caught fire.

1777. William Dodd, an English divine, convicted of forgery, and sentenced to be hanged.

1777. Joseph, king of Portugal, died. He was of the house of Braganza, ascended the throne in 1750; his reign was turbulent and unfortunate.

1781. Edward Capell died; known as the editor of an edition of Shakspeare in 10 vols., and 4 large quarto vols. of "Notes and various readings of Shakspeare.

1785. Charles Bonaparte, father of Napoleon, died, leaving his family in straightened circumstances.

1797. Resumption of hostilities in Italy between the French and Austrians.

1799. George Christopher Lichtenberg, a famous German writer, died. His commentary on Hogarth is said of itself to immortalize his fame.

1809. Drury-lane theatre burnt. It had been previously burnt, and rebuilt 1671 by Sir Christopher Wren at a cost of £200,000.

1810. Henry Cavendish, an English philosopher, died. He made the important discovery of the composition of water. Of diffident and retiring manners, he devoted his days to experiments and improvements in the arts and sciences. It has been said that he was the richest among the learned, and the most learned among the rich men of his time. He left a fortune of £5,000,000.

1813. Action between United States sloop Hornet, Capt. Lawrence, and British man-of-war brig Peacock, Capt. Peake, off Demarara. The action commenced at half past 5 p. m. and continued 15 minutes, when the Peacock showed signals of distress. Exertions were made to keep the vessel afloat till the prisoners could be got off, but she sunk carrying down 13 of her crew and 3 Americans. The loss of the crew of the Peacock could not be ascertained; but the captain was killed in the latter part of the engagement, and the vessel was literally cut to pieces. The Hornet lost 1 killed and 4 wounded; and the vessel received trifling damage, except in her rigging.

1815. Robert Fulton died, aged 50. He was born at Little Britain, Pa., and early discovered a genius for painting and mechanics; and he subsequently studied painting in London, under Benjamin West. He also resided several years in Paris; after which he returned to America, and presented to the world the phenomenon of the steam boat.

1821. John Keats, an English poet, died, aged 25. He was of humble origin, but was possessed of a fine genius. His productions were made the subject of severe and unmerited criticism by Gifford, who had leaped from a cobbler's bench into an editor's stool, and presided over the pages of the *Quarterly Review*. These gross attacks preyed upon his mind and hastened his death.

1821. Iturbide issued his proclamation, called the plan of Iguala, for the pacification of the state of Mexico. It contemplated the independence of Mexico, and still to preserve its union with Spain.

1826. Richard Dale, an American naval officer, died. He was born in Virginia, 1756, and at the age of 12 went to sea. During the war of the revolution he was captured, and imprisoned, but found means to escape, and joined the celebrated Paul Jones. Under Jones he distinguished himself in the sanguinary and desperate engagement between the Bon Homme Richard and the British frigate Serapis, and was the first who reached the deck of the latter when she was boarded and taken. In 1802 he settled in Philadelphia, where he passed the remainder of his days.

1828. Jacob Brown, who acted so prominent a part in the war of 1812 between England and the United States, and for some time commander-in-chief of the United States army, died at Washington.

1838. Carl Heinrich Ludwig Politz, died at Leipsic. He was professor in the university, and an eminent writer on statistics, history and politics.

1843. John Owens, a soldier of the old French war and also of the American revolution, died, aged 107.

1848. Revolution at Paris.

1852. David Kennison, the last of the Boston tea party, died at Chicago, aged 117.

1854. Robert Armstrong died, aged 64; proprietor of the *Washington Union* newspaper.

1854. At Niagara falls two men fell from the suspension bridge, a distance of 240 feet and were dashed to pieces.

FEBRUARY 25.

52 b. c. Pompey elected sole consul of Rome.

1030. Adalbero, a French ecclesiastic, died. He has left a character suited to bold and unscrupulous intrigue.

1464. The Lancasterians defeated by the Yorkists at Heagley Moor, the *white rose* triumphing over the *red*.

1523. William Lily, an English grammarian, died at London of the plague. He is highly praised by Erasmus, who revised the syntax of his grammar, for his uncommon erudition in the languages, and admirable skill in the instruction of youth.

1601. Robert Devereux, earl of Essex, executed. He obtained the favor of the queen, Elizabeth, and distinguished himself on many occasions. But having committed some indiscretions which required reprimanding, his pride was wounded, which led him to open rebellion. His fate has formed the subject of four tragedies.

1634. Albert, count Wallenstein, generalissimo of the Austrian army during the thirty years war, assassinated.

1643. A barbarous massacre in the night of the Indians who were encamped at Pavonia, opposite the Dutch fort of New Amsterdam, instigated by Gov. Kieft. About 80 Indians lost their lives, and many enormities were enacted by the Dutch.

1676. The Indians assaulted the town of Weymouth, Mass., and burned several houses and barns. This was a disastrous year with the colonists. The Indians had risen in their utmost power, with the determination of utterly extirpating the English, and almost every day witnessed the smoke of a town or cluster of dwellings on fire.

1703. DANIEL DE FOE prosecuted as the author of a book entitled, *The shortest way with the dissenters*, and his book burned by the hangman.

1712. NICHOLAS CATINAT, an illustrious French general under Louis XIV, died.

1713. FREDERICK I, of Prussia, died. He was elector of Brandenburg, and ambitious of raising his duchy into a kingdom. To accomplish this object, he joined Leopold, emperor of Germany, in a war against several states.

1723. CHRISTOPHER WREN, the English architect, died, aged 91. He built St. Paul's and fifty other churches and monuments, which had been destroyed by the great fire of 1666.

1724. Pope INNOCENT XIII died.

1754. RICHARD MEAD, an eminent English physician and patron of learning, died, aged 81. His library sold for about $75,000. His income from his profession was about $25,000 a year.

1761. JOSEPH FRANCIS DESMAHIS, a French author of great celebrity, died.

1768. Mangalore, a seaport belonging to Hyder Ally, taken by the British.

1776. Battle of Trenton. The American army under Washington crossed the Delaware in the night during a violent storm of snow and rain, and attacked the British on the north and west parts of the town. A detachment had been ordered to cross the river and secure a bridge to prevent the escape of the enemy; but owing to the extreme difficulty of crossing, this part of the plan failed, and about 500 escaped. British loss 20 killed, 1000 prisoners; American loss 2 killed, 2 frozen, 5 wounded.

1779. The splendid bridge at Puerto Santo, in Spain, fell and killed a great number of persons while the priests were in the act of consecrating it.

1781. Battle near Haw river in North Carolina, between the Americans under Pickens and Lee, and a considerable body of royalists under Col. Pyle. The latter were cut to pieces, without the loss of a man by the former.

1781. The French and Spanish fleets encountered a furious storm off cape Francois in the West-Indies. Several ships sunk or foundered, and about 2200 men perished.

1782. Denmark acknowledged the independence of the United States.

1798. The French under Brune entered the canton of Berne in Switzerland.

1799. El Arish in Egypt surrendered to the French under Bonaparte.

1805. WILLIAM BUCHAN, an eminent Scottish physician, died near London. He was educated for the pulpit, but made choice of the medical profession, which he pursued during a long life. In 1771 he published his *Domestic Medicine;* it has been attended with a degree of success scarcely equaled by any other book in our language, and is translated into every European tongue.

1807. Battle of Peterswalde, between the French and Russians, in which the latter were defeated, with the loss of their general, Baron De Korff, his staff and 400 men prisoners.

1814. Action between the British frigate Erotas and French frigate Clorinde, 44 guns. The captain of the Erotas and 4 men were wounded and 22 killed. The Clorinde was captured the next day by the British ships Dryades and Achades, her loss supposed to have been 120 men.

1816. A number of sailors belonging to the American squadron in the Mediterranean, having been permitted to go on shore at Port Mahon, were attacked by the Spanish guard and several killed and wounded.

1816. FREDERICK WILLIAM BULOW, count von Dennewitz, a Prussian general, died. He is famous for his victories in the last French and German war, the art of which he had learnt scientifically in early youth. He was also devoted to literature and the fine arts, and esteemed as a citizen and a man.

1817. Schooner Ocean of New York sunk at sea. Isaac Roget, a merchant of high standing in New York, was convicted in conjunction with others, of having loaded her at Havre de Grace with 97 boxes of stones, with a view to defraud the insurance officers of $58,000.

1819. FRANCESCO MANUEL, a Portuguese poet, died. His opinions being rather too liberal for the times, he was summoned to appear before the inquisition, but instead of obeying the mandate he resisted the officer sent to arrest him, and fled to Paris, where he resided till his death. It has been said of him that no poet or writer since the time of Camoens had done so much for the language.

1822. WILLIAM PINCKNEY, a distinguished American statesman, died. It is said that he possessed almost unequaled legal science and eloquence.

1829. A violent hurricane in the island of Barbadoes, by which the whole of the eastern end of the island was devastated, and great damage done to the shipping.

1831. The Poles defeated near the walls of Warsaw by the Russians, with the loss of 5000 men. Russian loss 4,500.

1841. PHILIP P. BARBOUR, an eminent

American statesman and judge, died at Washington, aged 60.

1841. The Bogue forts and the city of Canton captured by the British. The number of Chinese killed and wounded was very great; 1000 were captured. Canton was almost deserted by its inhabitants.

1850. TAU KWANG, emperor of China, died, aged 69.

1856. Peace congress met at Paris, and agreed upon an armistice till the 31st of March.

FEBRUARY 26.

747 B. C. The era of Narbonassar (a king of Babylon) called also the Egyptian year, began on the first day of the month Thoth, corresponding with this day in the Julian calendar. The years are vague, containing 365 days without intercalation, so that in the year 31 B. C. the beginning of the year fell on the 29th August, and at the end of 1460 years it ran through all the Julian months.

The Mexican year began also on the 26th February. It is also certain that the Mexican calendar conformed greatly with the Egyptian.

387. In consequence of a sermon preached by John Chrysostom on drunkenness and blasphemy, a sedition broke out at Antioch. The statues of Theodosius and the imperial family were thrown from their pedestals and demolished by the tumultuous citizens.

398. JOHN CHRYSOSTOM, or the preacher with the golden mouth, elected archbishop of Constantinople.

1426. JOHN DE BROGNI died; originally a swine herd in Savoy; he distinguished himself for learning, virtue and piety, and was raised to the dignity of cardinal.

1512. ROBERT FABYAN, an English historian, died. He was brought up to a trade, became a merchant, and an alderman of London. His *Chronicle* was burnt by Wolsey.

1553. Four English noblemen, namely, RALPH VANE, MILES PARTRIDGE, MICHAEL STANHOPE and THOMAS ARUNDEL, were executed as accomplices to the duke of Sommerset.

1611. ANTHONY POSSEVIN, a Jesuit, died at Ferrara. He was distinguished as a preacher, and employed by the pope in embassies to different countries.

1616. GALILEO appeared before Cardinal Bellarmine to renounce his heretical opinions; and having declared that he abandoned the doctrine of the earth's motion, and would neither defend nor teach it, in his conversation or his writings, he was dismissed from the bar of the inquisition.

1638. CLAUDE MEZIRIAC, a Jesuit, died; known as a poet in several languages.

1686. GODFREY, count d'Estrades, died.

1696. CHARLES SCARBOROUGH, an eminent English physician and mathematician, died. He succeeded Dr. Harvey as lecturer on anatomy and surgery.

1723. THOMAS D'URFEY, an English poet, died. He was a man of sparkling talents, but his poetic and dramatic pieces are now forgotten. His *Pills to Purge Melancholy* is yet upon the shelves of many English libraries.

1726. EMANUEL MAXIMILIAN, elector of Bavaria, died. He distinguished himself under the emperor Leopold, was placed at the head of the Hungarian army, and made governor of the Low Countries by the king of Spain.

1729. The British parliament resolved that it was an indignity and a breach of privilege for any one to publish the debates or report the proceedings of the house.

1767. HYDER ALLY and the nizam of Deccan defeated by the British at Errour, near Trincomalee, in Ceylon.

1769. WILLIAM DUNCOMBE, an English dramatic author, died. He translated Horace.

1770. JOSEPH TARTINI died at Padua; an Italian musician, distinguished for his extraordinary performances on the violin.

1774. JOHN TICE died at Hagley, England, aged 125.

1775. Gen. GAGE despatched 140 soldiers under Col. Leslie to seize the military stores collected at Salem. The people foiled the expedition by drawing up a bridge and causing other delays till it was too late to effect any thing, and they returned bootless.

1789. The Cayugas sold their lands to the state of New York.

1802. ALEXANDER GEDDES died at Paddington, England. He was a catholic and is represented as a man of profound research in biblical literature, and employed himself many years in a new translation of the Bible, which he did not live to finish.

1807. Battle of Braunsberg in Prussian Poland, in which a division of 10,000 Russians were overthrown by the French, who took 2,000 prisoners and 16 cannon.

1810. JOHN DALRYMPLE, a Scottish author, died, aged 84. He was for many years baron of the exchequer in Scotland.

1813. ROBERT R. LIVINGSTON, an American statesman, died. He was one of the committee which drew up the Declaration of Independence. He was afterwards chancellor of the state of New York, and minister to France. He assisted Fulton with means to carry his experiments into effect, which gave to this country the honor of the first successful steam boat.

1815. BONAPARTE escaped from the island of Elba, accompanied by 1000 of his old guards, who had followed him into exile.

1823. JOHN PHILIP KEMBLE died; one of the most eminent tragedians of the British stage since the days of Garrick. He possessed talent and learning, and was an author.

1826. JOHN KAY, caricaturist, engraver, barber, and miniature painter, died in Edinburgh. His small shop in Parliament close, was a great lounging place for the idlers of the town.

1827. WILLIAM KITCHENER, an English physician, died. He is distinguished for his experiments in cookery; he treated eating and drinking as the only serious business of life, and promulgated the laws of the culinary art, under the title of the *Cook's Oracle*, professedly founded on his own practice. He possessed an ample fortune, which enabled him to follow the bent of his eccentricities.

1831. JOHN BELL, who gave direction and name to *Bell's Weekly Messenger* at London, died.

1833. ELIZABETH PEARCE died in Johnson county, North Carolina, aged 111.

1833. The spasmodic cholera appeared at Havana, and in about one month from that time had destroyed 7000 persons.

1834. ALOYS SENEFELDER, inventor of lithography, died at Munich, aged 63.

1852. THOMAS MOORE, the celebrated Irish poet, died, aged 73.

1854. The gallery of the French opera house at New Orleans fell during the performance, carrying away the second tier, by which the occupants were precipitated into the parquette, killing 3, and badly wounding 56 persons.

1854. Three shocks of an earthquake at Manchester, Kentucky, by which the houses were violently shaken.

1855. Gen. JACKSON'S sword presented to congress by the heirs of Gen. Armstrong.

1855. HENRY PIERPONT EDWARDS, an American judge, died at New York, aged 46.

1856. At the breaking up of the ice on the Mississippi at St. Louis, 23 steam boats were wrecked.

FEBRUARY 27.

212. GETA, emperor of Rome, slain by his brother Caracalla, who was incited to the deed by jealousy.

1411. The charter of the university of St. Andrews, at Aberdeen in Scotland, granted.

1642. TOBIAS CRISP died; a controversial writer on divinity, and a great champion on antinomianism.

1697. JOHN BERKLEY, baron of Stratton, died; a noted commander in the English fleet.

1706. JOHN EVELYN, the English diarist, died. He is ranked among the greatest philosophers of England, who turned his pen readily to almost every topic. His *Diary* is a curious book, extending nearly from his childhood to his death, and contains much information not elsewhere to be found.

1735. JOHN ARBUTHNOT, a Scottish physician, died. He was attached to the court of Queen Anne, was eminent in his profession, and distinguished as a wit in an age abounding with men of wit and learning.

1738. HENRY GROOVE, an English divine, died. He belonged to the dissenters, and wrote several valuable theological treatises.

1746. THOMAS FAUNCE died at Plymouth, aged 99. He knew the rock on which the pilgrims landed, and learning that it was covered in the construction of a wharf, was so affected that he wept. His tears, perhaps, saved it from oblivion.

1776. Battle of Moor's creek bridge, in which the tories and Highlanders under McDonald, were defeated with the loss of their bravest officers. They fled leaving 350 guns, 1500 rifles, 13 wagons, and 150 swords in the hands of the victors, as well as their general. This defeat depressed the spirits of the royalists in North Carolina, and prevented their making any further efforts.

1794. Of the crews of 13 American vessels captured by the Algerines, four were redeemed, leaving 126 still in the hands of their captors as slaves. Two of these vessels were captured in 1785, and the rest in 1793. A great effort was made throughout the land to raise money for their redemption by charitable contributions.

1797. Bank of England suspended specie payments. Twenty years after it resumed on one and two pound notes.

1806. Action between the British ship Hydra, and French brig La Furet, off Cadiz, in which the latter was captured.

1814. Battle of Orthes, in France, between the British under Wellington and the French.

1817. Two shocks of an earthquake felt at Kingston, Upper Canada.

1829. Battle of Tarqui between the Colombian army of 5000, and the Peruvian of 8000, in which the latter were defeated with considerable loss. Articles for the cessation of hostilities were signed on the field of battle, and mutual differences referred to the arbitration of the United States government.

1844. NICHOLAS BIDDLE, celebrated as the

president of the United States bank for a number of years, died near Philadelphia, aged 58. He graduated at Princeton at the early age of 15, and was a man of great ability, of rarely equaled scholarship, and of the most polished and courtly manners. On the ruin of the bank he retired into private life, where however the creditors of the bank did not allow him undisturbed repose.

1853. PAUL FREDERICK AUGUSTUS, reigning duke of Oldenburgh, died, aged 70.

FEBRUARY 28.

509 B. C. Battle of the Œsuvian fields, in which the Tarquins were vanquished and expelled from Rome, with the loss of more than 11,000 citizens on the side of the victors.

509 B. C. LUCIUS JUNIUS BRUTUS, the avenger of the rape of Lucretia, and founder of the Roman republic, fell at the battle of the Œsuvian fields. So great was the fury of the encounter between him and his adversary, that their shields were mutually pierced, and each fell dead from his horse transfixed by the lance of his enemy.

628. CHOSROES II, king of Persia, died. He carried his arms into Judea, Libya and Egypt, and made himself master of Carthage. He forced the Roman emperor Heraclius, to sue for peace; but his country was soon after penetrated by the Romans, his palace pillaged and burnt, and himself dethroned and cast into prison by his own son, after witnessing the massacre of 18 other sons.

1408. Battle of Bramham Moor.

1447. HUMPHREY, duke of Gloucester, murdered. He was the rival of Cardinal Beaufort, as the head of affairs in England, and was the friend and patron of learning. The cardinal lived to enjoy his triumph but six weeks.

1582. GEORGE BUCHANAN, a Scottish poet and historian, died. He occupied the last twelve years of his life in writing a history of his country in Latin.

1594. WILLIAM FLEETWOOD, an English lawyer, died. He was recorder of the city of London in the reign of Elizabeth, and the author of several law treatises.

1604. JOHN WHITGIFT, archbishop of Canterbury, died. He was unwearied in his efforts to make the puritans conform to the national church.

1610. The house of commons complained of the king's profusion, especially in the immense sums lavished on Scotch favorites.

1642. CHARLES I of England sent to the house of commons his reasons for refusing the militia bill; the house declared his advisers public enemies, and passed a vote of approval on the counties which had put themselves in a posture of defence.

1648. CHRISTIERN IV of Denmark, died. He sustained the character of an able and wise sovereign.

1680. DECAN and HENNESSIN were sent out from fort Crevecoeur on the Illinois, to trace the Mississippi to its source. They ascended the river to the 46th degree, where they were stopped by a fall, to which they gave the name of St. Anthony.

1703. JOHN BAPTIST THIERS, died; a doctor of the Sorbonne, and professor of the belles lettres at Paris.

1734. Battle in Syria between the Turks, 45,000, and the Persians under Kouli Khan. The Turks were marching to succor Babylon, but were defeated with the loss of 20,000 killed on the field or taken prisoners. The victory cost the Persians 10,000 men.

1735. Large statute of GEORGE II set up in the royal hospital at Greenwich, Eng., at the expense of Sir John Jennings and sculptor Mr. Rysbrack.

1736. A proposal submitted to the house of commons in England, to levy a duty on distilled spirituous liquors, so as to prevent the ill consequences of the poorer classes drinking them to excess. It was stated that some signs where they were sold had the following inscription: "Drunk for a penny; dead drunk for two pence; clean straw for nothing!"

1757. EDWARD MOORE died; an English fabulist and dramatic writer of considerable note.

1758. Action between the French fleet under Du Quesne and the British, under Saunders, near Carthagena. The British captured the Foudroyant, 80 guns, and Orphee, 64 guns; the Oriflamme, 50 guns, was driven on shore under the castle of Aiglos, coast of Spain.

1759. The pope permitted the Bible to be translated into all the languages of the Catholic states.

1760. Action between the French fleet under Thourot and the British, Capt. Elliot. Three French frigates were captured and Thourot killed. So great a terror had he created in the seaports of Great Britain, that his defeat was celebrated with the greatest rejoicings.

1771. RICHARD GREY, a learned English divine, died. He was a polemical and miscellaneous writer.

1781. WILLIAM STOCKTON died; a signer of the Declaration of Independence from New Jersey.

1783. JOHN BAPTIST D' ESPAGNAC, a French general, died. He signalized himself in the campaign of Italy.

1795. Five hundred emigrant sleighs passed through the city of Albany between sunrise and sunset, on their way to the Genesee country. It was estimated that as many as 1,200 sleighs, freighted with men, women, children and furniture, had passed up State street in the space of three days, destined for the Genesee valley, the *far west* of the emigrants of that day.

1799. BONAPARTE reached the city of Gaza in Palestine.

1799. Action between the British frigate Sybille, and French ship La Forte, 50 guns. The later was captured in 1 hour 40 minutes. The British lost two of their highest officers.

1804. PICHEGRU, the conquerer of Holland, arrested at Paris by order of Bonaparte.

1815. Action between the United States frigate Constitution, 44 guns, Capt. Stewart, and British frigate Cyane and sloop Levant, 54 guns, Capt. Falcon; British loss, 40 killed, 80 wounded; Constitution lost 4 killed, 11 wounded. The Cyane and Levant were captured.

1823. WILLIAM W. VAN NESS, an eminent judge of the N.Y. supreme court, died.

1834. MODESTE MALHIOT, the Canadian giant, died. His height was 6 feet 4 inches, and his weight 619½ pounds.

1837. ADAM BINKLEY, died in Davidson co., Pennsylvania, aged 138. He was an officer of the revolution and served throughout the war, at which time he had a wife and 11 children.

1843. A remarkable comet first observed in the northern states, which caused considerable controversy whether it was a comet or the zodiacal light. It was first seen at noon, and was distinctly observed with the naked eye from 7 to 9 o'clock in the evening during the month of March. Its train extended about 70° to 100°.

1851. The Spanish government of Manilla, totally destroyed the forts of the pirate Sultan of Sooloo.

1853. Doncaster church, England, built in 1070, destroyed by fire.

1854. Earthquake at Lexington, Ky., and surrounding country, attended by a loud roaring noise.

1854. American steamer Black Warrior, seized by the Cuban authorities at Havana.

1855. An earthquake at Broussa killed or wounded about 800 people, and was succeeded by a fire which destroyed nearly one-third of the houses.

FEBRUARY 29.

1631. The president and counsel for New England, made a grant to Robert Aldworth and Giles Elbridge of a hundred acres of land for every person whom they should transport to the province of Maine within seven years, who should continue there three years; and an absolute grant of 12,000 acres as their proper inheritance for ever, to be laid out near the river commonly called Pemaquid.

1704. Deerfield, in Massachusetts, burnt. Hertel de Rouville with 200 French and 140 Indians, after a tedious march through deep snow from Canada, made an attack upon this place, which was the northern frontier on Connecticut river. A watch had patrolled the streets until about two hours before day, when he incautiously fell asleep, and the snow was of such depth as to admit of an entrance over the pickets of the fort. The whole settlement was burnt with the exception of one house, which was standing until quite recently; 47 were slain, 112 carried into captivity, including among the latter, the Rev. John Williams and his family. Of the captives, 17 died or were killed on the march; 57 were redeemed, among whom were the minister and his family (his wife was killed soon after the capture), except one daughter who could not be persuaded to return; but adopted the manners and customs of the Indians, became a catholic, and married a savage. The bell taken from the church, it is said, still hangs in an Indian church at St. Regis.

1744. JOHN THEOPHILUS DESAGULIERS died. He was the son of a French protestant clergyman, who resided in England. Having been educated for the ministry, he settled in London; there he acquired a turn for natural philosophy, and was the first person who lectured on experimental philosophy in the metropolis. He was a man of rare ability, and his income enabled him to keep an equipage. His coachman, Erasmus King, from the force of example, became a kind of rival to the doctor; for he also undertook to read lectures, and exhibit experiments in natural philosophy. The terms of admission to the *lyceum* of the latter philosopher were in proportion to the humble station he had filled.

1793. The French convention passed a decree of accusation against Marat, and by so doing tore off the cloak of inviolability which covered its members, and constituted itself its own jury of accusation.

1808. Denmark declared war against Sweden.

1810. Battle of Vique, in Spain, in which the Spanish General O'Donnel attacked the French under Souham. The impetuosity of the charge made by the Spanish troops lost them the battle.

1844. Fatal explosion of the great gun, Peacemaker, on board the American war steamer, Princeton, by which several government officers lost their lives, and many persons were seriously injured.

MARCH.

MARCH 1.

509. B. C. Valerius Publicola pronounced a funeral oration over the body of Junius Brutus, which was the first institution of that generous tribute to the memory of the virtuous dead.

1554. In the household expenses of Queen Mary 15 shillings are given to a yeoman for bringing her majesty a leek on this day.

1562. The catholics under the duke of Guise fell upon a body of Calvinists at Bassi in France, who were singing the psalms of Marot in a barn. The latter were insulted, and induced to come to blows: when nearly 60 of these unhappy people were killed and 200 wounded. This unexpected event lightened the flame of civil war throughout the kingdom.

1564. Printing introduced again into Moscow. Some 12 years previous it had been used there, but the burning of the city by the Poles suspended it.

1625. John Robinson died; minister of the first English church in Holland, to which the first settlers of New England belonged. He fled to Holland with his congregation to avoid persecution, and at the time of his death was preparing to follow with the remainder of the brethren to America. He was distinguished for his learning, liberality and piety.

1645. Battle of Pontefract, in which Sir Marmaduke Langdale defeated the lord Fairfax.

1663. Adam Adami, a French ecclesiastic, statesman and historian, died.

1682. Thomas Herbert, an English author of *Travels in Asia and Africa*, died. He was engaged in the civil wars between the parliament and the royalists, and on the restoration was created a baronet.

1689. The odious hearth stone tax ordered to be taken off by William, prince of Orange.

1711. The *Spectator*, a daily critical, satirical and literary paper made its appearance in London, under the conduct of Addison and Steele principally, with the assistance of some of the master spirits of the day, and had a reputation which has never been equaled by any other periodical of the kind.

1733. That mysterious person, the *oldest* inhabitant, witnessed a great flood in the north of England, wholly unprecedented in his life time.

1766. Zabdiel Boylston, an American physician, died. He was the first to introduce inoculation for small-pox into New England. This mode of treating a virulent disease brought upon him the ridicule of his medical brethren; but he outlived these prejudices and realized a handsome fortune by his profession.

1774. Prince A. D. Kantemir, died; a Turk by birth, but subsequently a distinguished oriental scholar.

1781. Maryland ratified the articles of the confederation of the United States being the last state to do so.

1786. The first No. of the *Observer* appeared, conducted by Cumberland, the dramatist.

1791. The annual masquerade held at Rutland square rooms, Dublin, was the cause of a great riot and the death of many of the police.

1792. Leopold II of Germany, and I of Tuscany, died. He made the latter the happiest and best governed state of Italy. In 1790 he succeeded to the imperial crown, and was noted for the wisdom of his measures, his affability, strict justice and kindness to the poor.

1793. Battle of Aldenhoven, between the French under Dumourier, and 40,000 Austrians under Gen. Coburg. The French were defeated with the loss of 6,000 killed and 4,000 prisoners.

1799. Essex county, N. Y., erected.

1811. Massacre of the Mamelukes in Egypt by order of the pasha.

1814. Treaty of Chaumont, between Austria, Russia, Prussia and Great Britain, against Napoleon.

1815. Bonaparte landed at Frejus in France from Elba, and resumed the imperial crown.

1816. Ontario co., N. Y., erected.

1838. The Patriots of Canada, about 600 in number, under Nelson and Cote, surrendered to Gen. Wool of the United

States army, near Alburg Springs, Vt., and the frontier became tranquilized.

1845. Texas admitted into the Union as an independent State.

1854. The steam ship city of Glasgow left Liverpool for Philadelphia with more than 300 passengers, and was never more seen.

1855. THOMAS DAY, an eminent Connecticut jurist died, aged 78. He published 26 volumes of law reports, and his entire works number about 40 volumes.

1856. The colossal bronze statue of Beethoven, the gift of Charles C. Perkins, inaugurated at the music hall, Boston.

MARCH 2.

986. LOTHAIRE, king of France, died of poison, said to have been administered by his wife Emma.

1492. The Jews banished from Spain by an edict of Ferdinand V. They numbered 800,000 souls.

1585. Dr. PARRY executed for a design to assassinate Queen Elizabeth. She had formerly released him from imprisonment, on a charge of justifying Romanism.

1611. BARTHOLOMEW LEGGAT, convicted of the Arian heresy and delivered over to the secular power.

1617. ROBERT ABBOTT, bishop of Salisbury, died, aged 58. He was active and pains-taking in his office; a profound scholar, and an industrious author.

1619. QUEEN ANNE, consort of James I, died at Hampton Court.

1622. JOHN MARION AVANTIO, a learned Italian civilian, died at Padua.

1629. The speaker of the house of commons, in England, refusing for fear of the king's displeasure to put the question of reading the remonstrance against the king's usurpations, is held in his chair, the doors of the house shut, and the remonstrance read.

1711. DESPREAUX NICHOLAS BOILEAU, the French poet, died. He was born 1636, and in early youth gave indications of the future bent of his genius, by his fondness for the great poets of antiquity. His works are frequently republished in France, though some of his satires are little to the taste of the present day. Bruyere has said of him, that his verses will be read when the language is obsolete, and will be the last ruins of it!

1713. The first No. of the *Guardian* appeared, conducted by Steele during the temporary suspension of the *Spectator*.

1714. Peace proclaimed with Spain, and a special privilege granted to the English of supplying the West Indies with negro slaves at the rate of 4800 a year.

1714. Gibraltar and Minorca also ceded to the English.

1715. EMANUEL THEODOSIUS BOULLION, a cardinal and ambassador of Louis XIV of France, died.

1729. FRANCESCO BIANCHINI, an Italian antiquary and astronomer, died. He devoted his life to intense study, and in his character extensive learning was united with great modesty and amiability of manners. He was patronized by the pope, and received marks of respect from the Roman senate.

1738. JOHNSON and GARRICK started from Litchfield for London as literary adventurers. The former had two pence half penny in his pocket, and the latter something less.

1767. JAMES DRAKE, an English political and medical writer, died. He is chiefly known now by his *System of Anatomy*.

1768. The extensive copper mine in the isle of Anglesey was discovered.

1776. The Americans cannonaded Boston from Cobble hill and Lechmere point.

1786. JOHN JEBB, an eminent English non-conformist divine and physician, died. His publications, theologial, medical and political, gained great approbation.

1788. SOLOMON GESNER, a Swiss bookseller, poet and painter, died at Zurich. Of his writings the best known, in English, is the *Death of Abel*.

1791. JOHN WESLEY, founder of the methodists, died, aged 88. He was born at Epworth, England, and at the time of finishing his studies, was distinguished for his classical attainments, skill in dialectics, and talent for poetry. The origin of the sect called methodists is to be attributed to the circumstance of a club of kindred spirits, who used to meet on week days and read classics, and on Sundays divinity, but shortly their meetings became exclusively religious. This society consisted of fifteen members, who from the strictness of their manners and deportment, obtained the name of *Methodists*, an appellation which they sanctioned and retained. He visited America, and afterwards Germany, and on his return commenced the systematic labors by which he became the founder of a numerous religious sect. He joined with Whitfield in field preaching, but their opinions being at collision on some point, they finally separated. He continued his active labors till within a week of his death. His works on various subjects amount to upwards of thirty volumes octavo.

1793. Breda, a city of Holland, noted for its numerous sieges, was taken by the French.

1793. Congress passed a law making appropriations for purchasing two lots of ground with buildings, and other materials and necessaries for a mint, $1,279·78; and for the salaries of its officers from July to Dec. 1792. $2,694·88.

1794. Great scarcity of provisions in Paris.

1797. Battle of Monte di Savaro, between the French and Austrians, in which the former under Joubert attacked and carried the posts of the latter.

1797. HORACE WALPOLE, an English author, and son of Robert Walpole the statesman, died.

1799. Corfu, one of the Ionian islands taken by the Turco Russian squadron.

1799. Manheim, a strong German city, taken by the French.

1801. CHARLES ALBERT DEMOUSTIER, a French poet, died. He was first a successful lawyer, but subsequently turned his attention to literature, and wrote comedies, operas and poems. His pieces are distinguished for spirit, delicacy and ease, and some of them have maintained a place upon the stage.

1802. FRANCIS RUSSEL, duke of Bedford, died, aged 37. He distinguished himself by his endeavors to improve every branch af agriculture, and was a worthy man.

1830. Great freshet at Vienna, in Austria; the Danube rose twenty-three feet, and the houses of 50,000 inhabitants were inundated.

1835. FRANCIS I of Austria (II of Germany), died. His disposition was mild; his dress plain and homely; his manners gentle and familiar; and he was greatly beloved by his German subjects.

1835. SAMUEL BLACKBURN died; an officer of the revolution, an eminent lawyer and for many years a conspicuous member of the Virginia legislature. At his death he liberated his slaves, 46 in number, charging his estate with the expense of transporting them to Liberia.

1839. ZERAH COLBURN died at Norwich, Vt., aged 35. At the age of 6 years he attracted great attention in Europe and America by his marvelous powers of calculation. At that time he was unable to read or write, and ignorant of the name or properties of a single figure traced upon paper. Yet his talent for mental arithmetic was so extraordinary as to be wholly incredible, were it not supported by unquestionable evidence. This faculty he lost before he left England, which was in 1824; and on his return he became a methodist preacher, having acquired a respectable education while abroad.

1840. HENRY WILLIAM MATTHEW ALBERS, a celebrated astronomer, and practicing physician at Bremen, died, aged 81. He acquired a lasting reputation by the discovery of the planet Pallas, in 1802, and of Vesta, in 1807.

1841. First daily paper in Brooklyn published.

1843. ASA PACKARD, aged 84, died at Lancaster, Mass. He was a soldier of the revolution, and for nearly 70 years carried a musket bullet in his body.

1845. JUDAH ALDEN, a distinguished officer of the American revolutionary army, died at Duxbury, Mass.

1849. JAMES MORIER, the celebrated author of *Hajji Baba*, and other works, died.

1852. The town of St. Bartholomew, one of the Antilles, nearly destroyed by fire; 120 houses and stores having been burned in the space of four hours.

1852. MARMONT, duke of Ragusa, died at Venice, aged 78. He was the last of Napoleon's marshals.

1855. NICHOLAS I, emperor of Russia, died, aged 59. He came to the throne in 1826, and his reign was devoted to strengthening the power and extending the domain of Russia.

1856. An earthquake in the island of Great Sangor, one of the Moluccas, by which 2,806 lives were lost.

MARCH 3.

1589. JOHN STURMIUS, a learned German grammarian and rhetorician, died. He was called the Cicero of Germany.

1633. GEORGE HERBERT, an English divine and poet, died. Lord Bacon had so high an opinion of his judgment that he would not suffer his works to be published until they had been submitted to Herbert's examination.

1634. First colony arrived at Potomac for the settlement of Maryland, under Lord Baltimore. It consisted of 200 Catholics from England. The soil was purchased of the natives, and the foundation of the province was laid on the broad basis of security to property and of freedom in religion.

1703. ROBERT HOOKE, an English mathematician and philosopher, died. He is noted for many useful inventions and improvements in mechanics; and his writings are numerous and valuable.

1722. CAMPEGIO VITRINGA died; a learned author of Friesland, in the Netherlands.

1728. CAMILLO D'HOSTUN, count de Tallart, died. He was a brave general of the French, taken prisoner by the duke of Marlborough.

1760. Unsuccessful attack on the fort at Ninety-Six, by 200 Cherokee Indians.

1776. The Americans under Col. Bull burnt the British ship Inverness and six other vessels, near Savannah, laden for England.

1779. Battle of Briar Creek, when the Americans were surprised by the British under Provost, and lost 150 killed and 162 prisoners.

1780. JOSEPH HIGHMORE, an eminent English painter, died. He was also a writer of considerable merit.

1791. The church plate in France was sent to the mint for coinage.

1792. ROBERT ADAM, a Scotch architect, died. In connection with his brother, he built some of the first mansions in London; but the work for which they are chiefly celebrated, is the elegant range called the *Adelphi*, a Greek word denoting the relationship of brothers.

1796. Civic festival at the Hague on occasion of the installation of the Batavian national assembly.

1799. The advance guards of the French army arrived before Jaffa (the ancient Joppa) in Syria, and invested the city.

1802. County of St. Lawrence, in New York, erected.

1808. JOHANN CHRIST FABRICIUS died, one of the most celebrated entomologists of the eighteenth century. He was born 1742 at Sleswic in Denmark; studied medicine; but was afterwards induced to make an especial study of entomology, a science at that time in its infancy. He adopted a new arrangement of the insect tribe by choosing for his divisions, the modifications observable in the parts of the mouth.

1808. The French West India island Marigalante taken by the British. It was colonized by the French, 1647; twice taken by the Dutch, and twice before by the British, and restored to the French, 1763.

1810. The great Elm tree at Kensington, Philadelphia, under which William Penn held his first treaty with the Indians in 1682, was blown down.

1815. War declared between the United States and Algiers.

1817. LESCURE died at Beaulieu in France, aged 118. He enjoyed, at the time of his death the vigorous use of his intellect.

1843. Com. PORTER, a gallant American naval officer, died at Constantinople, where he was minister from the United States to the Sublime-Porte.

1845. Florida admitted into the Union as an independent state.

1846. HENRY PURKITT, one of those who assisted in the destruction of the tea in Boston harbor, died, aged 91.

1855. ROBERT MILLS died, a civil engineer and architect, under whom the Washington Post office, Treasury building and Patent office were erected.

MARCH 4.

1193. SALADIN the Great died at Damascus.

1530. CHARLES V granted to the knights of St. John, who had recently been expelled from the island of Rhodes by the Turks, the ownership of all the castles, fortresses, and isles of Tripoli, Malta and Gozo. Malta at the time was a shelterless rock, and the inhabitants, 12,000 in number, in a wretched condition.

1583. BERNARD GILPIN, an eminent English prelate, died. He came near falling a victim to the fury of Bonner, and was only saved from the stake by the death of the queen. His life was spent in well doing.

1629. Massachusetts patent confirmed by CHARLES I, by the name of "the governor and company of Massachusetts bay in New England," Matthew Cradock first governor.

1674. The governing charter of Dundalk, in the county of South Ireland, bears this date. This town was the Dundalgan of the Irish *Ossianic* poems, and is of great antiquity.

1681. The charter of Pennsylvania signed and sealed by Charles II, constituting William Penn and his heirs true and absolute proprietaries of the province, saving to the crown their allegiance and the sovereignty.

1744. JOHN ANSTIS died; an English antiquary, and a very eminent writer on heraldic subjects.

1765. WILLIAM STUKELEY, an English antiquary, died. He wrote ably as a divine, physician, historian and antiquary; was profound in British antiquities; a good botanist; erudite in ancient coins; drew well, and understood mechanics. The footsteps of the Romans were traced by him, and the temples of the ancient Britons explored. His antiquarian researches acquired him the name of Arch Druid.

1776. The Americans took possession of Dorchester heights, which were so far completed by day light as to excite the astonishment of the British, and render their position in Boston extremely hazardous.

1776. New Providence taken from the British by the American Commodore Ezekiel Hopkins. The governor, together with considerable military stores, fell into the hands of the victors.

1778. American frigate Alfred, 20 guns, taken by the British ships Ariadne and Ceres.

1782. The house of commons resolved that it would "consider as enemies to his majesty and the country, all those who should advise or attempt the further prosecution of offensive war on the American continent."

1789. The first congress of the United States assembled at New York.

1791. Vermont admitted into the Union. (See Feb. 18.)

1794. HENRY DE LA ROCHEJAQUELIN, the hero of La Vendee, killed. The peasants of the neighborhood having risen in the royal cause, he placed himself at their head, with this laconic harangue, "*Allons chercher l'ennemi; si je recule, tuez moi; si j'avance, suivez moi; si je meurs, vengez moi.* After gaining sixteen victories, he fell in single combat with a republican soldier.

1797. One pound or 20 shilling notes first issued by the bank of England. They were designed to take the place of the specie drained from the vaults to pay the foreign contracts.

1806. Action between the British fleet, Com. Popham, and the French frigate La Voluntaire, 46 guns. The latter was captured with 360 men and 217 British prisoners.

1811. First report of canal commissioners in New York.

1811. The French under Massena retreated before Lord Wellington upon Santarem, in Portugal, leaving their killed and wounded behind.

1812. The charter of the first bank of the United States expired by its own limitation.

1814. Battle of Longwood, about 100 miles from Detroit, in which the United States troops defeated a superior British force. British loss 80; American loss 8.

1814. Battle of Troyes, between the French under Oudinot and the Allies under Schwarzenberg, in which the former were defeated, with the loss of 10 cannon and 3,000 prisoners.

1815. United States letter of marque brig Aspasia, 3 guns and 25 men, captured by the British ship Voluntaire.

1815. FRANCES ABINGTON, a celebrated English actress, died. She was the original Lady Teazle.

1832. JOHN FRANCIS CHAMPOLLION, the French archæologist, died at Paris, aged 42. Having devoted much attention to the study of Egyptian antiquities, he was, in 1826, appointed to superintend that department in the royal museum at Paris, and in 1828, went with an expedition of learned men to Egypt, at the expense of the king, Charles X. The results of this journey were regarded of so great importance in relation to the hieroglyphics, that his manuscripts on that subject were purchased by the French government at about $9,300.

1838. Carlists under Cabanero, entered Saragossa, but were driven out by the national guards with the loss of 120 killed and 700 prisoners.

1847. A telescopic comet was discovered at the Cambridge university at 7 P. M. by G. P. Pond, assistant observer, being the fourth first discovered in this country by this young gentleman.

1856. The free state legislature of Kansas assembled at Topeka.

MARCH 5.

13. B. C. MARCUS EMILIUS LEPIDUS, one of the Roman triumvirs, with Augustus and Anthony, died at Cerceii.

493. ODOACER, chief of the Heruli, murdered. It was reserved for him, at the head of a tribe of barbarians almost unknown, to strike the decisive blow that overthrew the great mistress of the world—imperial Rome.

1223. ALONZO II of Portugal died. His career was begun by an attempt to deprive his sisters of their estates, and ended by robbing the church. The pope, however. interfered, and compelled him to promise to be civil to the ecclesiastics; but death overtook him before he had time to fulfill his engagements by making restitution.

1495. HENRY VIII granted a patent to John Cabot and his three sons Lewis, Sebastian and Sanchius, empowering them to sail under the flag of England in quest of countries yet unoccupied by any Christian state, to take possession of them in the name of Henry, and plant the English banner on the walls of their castles and cities, and to maintain with the inhabitants a traffic exclusive of all competitors, and exempted from customs; under the condition of paying a fifth part of the free profit on every voyage to the crown. They embarked two years after.

1534. ANTONI ALLEGRI, an illustrious Italian painter, died. He lived at Parma, where without any instruction he executed some of the most perfect pictures in the world. He is better known as Corregio, from his birth place.

1546. ISABELLA LOSA died; a native of Cordova in Spain, so illustrious for her acquirements that she was honored with the degree of D. D.

1605. CLEMENT VIII (Hippolitus Aldobrandi), pope of Rome, died. He was a liberal minded and benevolent pontiff.

1660. MONK'S parliament ordered the printing and setting up in churches the solemn league and covenant.

1686. JAMES II forbade the bishops to preach on controverted points.

1695. HENRY WHARTON died; an English divine and historian of uncommon abilities.

1701. ROBERT, earl of Bellamont, govenor of the province of New York, died, two years after his installment into that office.

1708. WILLIAM BEVERIDGE, an English divine, and bishop of St. Asaph, died, leaving many learned and valuable works.

1710. JOHN HOLT died. He had been for more than 20 years lord chief justice of the king's bench court in England.

1737. The servants called footmen occasioned a riot at Drury lane theatre, London, alleging that they had been shut out of the gallery, to which they were entitled.

1744. At Huddersfield, Yorkshire, a Roman temple was discovered and an altar inscribed to Antonius Modestus of the sixth conquering legion.

1770. Boston massacre. This occurrence, which is variously stated, is supposed to have arisen as follows: a crowd surrounded a corporal's guard in the evening, and commenced pelting them with snow balls, which exasperated his majesty's legions to such a pitch of valor, that they turned their muskets upon the citizens. The leaden balls of the soldiers were more than a match for those of the people, and five men fell mortally wounded. Their names were Mattucks, Gray, Caldwell, Maverick, and Carr.

1773. PHILIP FRANCIS died at Bath, England; distinguished as a translator of Horace and Demosthenes.

1775. PETER LAURENCE BUYRETTE DU BELLOI died; a French comedian and tragedian, who by his own pieces became extremely popular in his day.

1775. The citizens of New York held a town meeting, in which it is said the question of congress or no congress was carried in the affirmative by the aid of hoop poles obtained from a neighboring cooper's yard.

1778. THOMAS AUGUSTUS ARNE died; an English musician and opera writer. He received the degree of doctor of music.

1785. JOSEPH REED died at Philadelphia, aged 43. He was one of Washington's aids in the revolutionary war, and subsequently an adjutant-general, member of congress, and govenor of Pennsylvania.

1794. County of Onondaga, in New York, erected.

1798. An Algerine barque arrived at Baltimore, 85 days out, manned by Algerines; being the first that ever entered an American port.

1811. Battle of Barrosa in Portugal, between the French under Victor, and the English, Spanish and Portugese allied army, under Graham. The French were defeated with the loss of 3,000; allied loss 2,742.

1827. PIERRE SIMON LAPLACE, the French mathematician, died. His principal work, which will render him an object of admiration to posterity, the *Mechanique Celeste*, has been translated by our countryman Nathaniel Bowditch, in a manner creditable alike to the author, to himself and the literature of his country.

1827. ALESSANDRO VOLTA died. He was born at Como, Italy; devoted his attention to experiments in electricity, and made many important discoveries.

1829. Battle near the river Natonebi, in Asiatic Turkey, between the Turks and Russians, in which the former lost 1,000 and the latter 200 men.

1837. OLIVER ELLIOT died at Mason, N. H., aged 103. He was a soldier of the French war of 1756, and of the revolutionary war.

1846. JOHN PICKERING, president of the American Oriental society, &c., &c., died at Boston.

1849. The emperor of Austria, after a series of decrees, promulgated a new constitution.

1853. GERVINUS tried at Manheim for high treason, published in a work on the history of the nineteenth century, was found guilty of exciting to sedition, and sentenced to ten months imprisonment, and his book ordered to be destroyed.

1856. Covent garden theatre, London, burnt at the close of a masked ball.

MARCH 6.

13 B. C. AUGUSTUS CÆSAR assumed the office of high priest, in which capacity he destroyed 2,000 books of prophecy, for want of authority!

1393. JOHN HAWKWOOD, an Englishman, died at Florence. He was bred a tailor, but signalized himself so greatly in the wars in Italy, that he was promoted to the highest posts; and after his death the Florentines erected a black marble statue as an acknowledgment for the services he had done them.

1521. MAGELLAN, in the service of the king of Spain, on his voyage round the world, discovered the Ladrone, or Marian islands, and may be considered as the first discoverer of that portion of the world called Australia. This opened the way for the subsequent discoveries made in that quarter.

1557. Lord STOURTON hung at Salisbury in a halter of silk, to mark his dignity. His crime was the murder of two persons whom he had decoyed to his house.

1577. REMI BELLEAU, one of the seven poets called the Pleiades of France, died. He excelled as a pastoral writer.

1615. The yacht Halve Maan, 80 tons burden, in which Hudson entered the river which bears his name, was wrecked and destroyed on the island of Mauritius.

1716. Aurora Borealis first seen in England, and was gazed upon with every degree of alarm till nearly three o'clock in the morning.

1754. PELHAM, premier of England, died suddenly in the meridian of life. He was much opposed to the German alliances of the kingdom, but had not influence enough in the face of a hostile court to break them up.

1762. The ghost that had for so long a time alarmed the people of Cocklane, London, was detected.

1767. JAMES MALFILLASTRE, a French poet, died.

1781. Battle of Whitsell's mill, an important pass of Reedy fort creek, in which the British were worsted.

1784. FRANCIS XAVIER HALL, a Jesuit, professor of belles lettres and ecclesiastical law in several German universities, died.

1796. WILLIAM FRANCIS RAYNAL died. He was a French Jesuit, who distinguished himself as a historian of the European settlements in both Indias, and as a political writer.

1799. The French under Bonaparte took Jaffa by assault. The garrison consisted of 1,200 Turkish artillery and 2,500 Magrubins or Arnauts who were put to the sword.

1812. JAMES MADISON, an eminent American prelate, died, aged 63. His great attainments placed him in the presidential chair of William and Mary college at the early age of 28, and the reputation of the institution advanced under his charge.

1815. LEWIS XVIII declared Napoleon Bonaparte a traitor and a rebel, for having entered by main force the department of the Var.

1815. A great riot around the British parliament house, on account of the corn bill. A great many lives lost.

1817. Insurrection at Pernambuco, Brazils, headed by Domingos Jose Martins. The insurgents took possession of the town, and the governor fled to Rio de Janeiro.

1822. Owing to a strong south-west wind the tide in the Thames near London bridge was so low, that several persons forded the river and picked up many valuable articles that had laid for years on the bottom of the river.

1825. SAMUEL PARR, an eminent English divine and critic, died. He was possessed of a prodigious memory, and in curious and elegant classical knowledge he seems to have been at the head of the English scholars of his day.

1838. VILETTE EASTON, a colored woman, died at Providence, Rhode Island, at the age of 110.

1854. The block of marble sent by the pope as a contribution to Washington's monument, was destroyed by unknown persons at night.

MARCH 7.

161. ANTONINUS PIUS, emperor of Rome, died at Lorium, aged 23.

1274. THOMAS AQUINAS died. He was descended from the counts of Aquino, in Italy. There was a great contest for him between his family and the monks when he was a youth; but he eluded the vigilance of his keepers, became a theologian, and was called the evangelical doctor. His works have been often reprinted in 17 vols. folio.

1575. The general assembly of Scotland enacted that no comedies, nor tragedies, or such plays, shall be made on any history of canonical scriptures, nor on the Sabbath day.

1589. WALTHER RALEIGH, having expended £40,000 in attempting the colonization of Virginia, without realizing the expected gain, made an assignment of his patent to Thomas Smith and others, with a donation of £100 for the benefit of the colony.

1661. Goffe and Whalley, the regicides, arrived at New Haven, where by the connivance of the deputy governor and clergyman, they effectually eluded discovery during the remainder of their lives.

1755. THOMAS WILSON died; bishop of Sodor and Man, an excellent prelate and an eminent writer on theology.

1769. SAMUEL DERRICK died; originally a linen draper in Dublin; subsequently a writer of pamphlets in London, and finally master of ceremonies at Bath and Tunbridge.

1771. THOMAS MARTIN, an English antiquarian, died. He wrote a history of his own native town, and made a valuable collection of antiquities, &c.

1777. JAMES AITKEN, alias John the painter, was hanged on a gallows 60 feet in height for setting fire to the rope yard at Portsmouth. He confessed his having set fire to the vessels at Bristol quay and that he was stimulated to these acts by Silas Dean of the American congress.

1778. American frigate Randolph, Capt. Nicholas Biddle, 36 guns and 305 men, blown up about 9 at night, in an action of fifteen minutes with the British ship Yarmouth, 64 guns. Capt. Biddle perished, at the age of 27; only 4 of the crew were saved.

1781. A British soldier jumped over the pallisades at Gibraltar, and notwithstanding 1143 musket balls were fired at him, succeeded in reaching the Spanish lines, waving his hat.

1788. Clinton county, in New York, erected.

1794. Revolution at Warsaw. The Russians with Gen. Inglestrom and their ambassador, driven out of the city by the Poles.

1794. The mulatto Gen. Bellegarde and his second, Pelocque, with 300 followers, surrendered to the British at St. Domingo. The chiefs were sent to the United States.

1795. The British squadron, Sir Edward Pellew, captured near the Penmarks, 8 French vessels, burnt 2 ships, 3 brigs and 2 sloops.

1801. The British expedition under Lord Keith, consisting of nearly 200 sail and an army of 15,330 men, arrived in Aboukir bay, Egypt.

1803. Francis Edgerton, duke of Bridgewater, died. He was the projector of the Medway canal in England.

1804. British and Foreign Bible society founded in London. A clergyman of Wales, whom the want of a Welsh Bible led to London, occasioned its establishment.

1808. The Portuguese royal family arrived in Brazil, fleeing before the arms of Napoleon to the colonies.

1809. Schenectady county, New York, taken from Albany.

1810. Cuthbert Collingwood, the English admiral, died in his ship off Minorca. He entered the British navy at an early age, and by his talents rose to the highest rank. His most distinguished service was the part he bore at the battle of Trafalgar. On the fall of Nelson in that conflict, the command devolved on him. The victory on that occasion was attributable to the nautical skill, prudence and courage of Collingwood; and his ship was the first to break through the French line.

1814. Battle of Craonne in France, in which the French under Victor and Ney defeated the allies, took 6 generals and about 6,000 prisoners.

1828. Richard Stocton, a son of the signer of the Declaration of American Independence of that name, died at Princeton, New Jersey. He was one of the foremost supporters of Washington's administration.

1844. Florida admitted into the Union. (Query 3d.)

MARCH 8.

1096. Walter the Pennyless departed from France with the van of the Crusaders.

1639. Dudley Digges, master of the rolls under Charles I, died. He was noted for his patriotism, and was the author of several literary performances.

1663. The great frost at Paris, which had endured three months, broke up on this day.

1702. William III of England, died. He was celebrated as a politician, and formidable as a general. (16th?)

1721. Pope Clement XI died, aged 72. He reigned over twenty years.

1748. The British squadron, Admiral Knowles, attacked and carried Port Louis, in St. Domingo, which he also destroyed. The French lost about 130 killed; British loss 20 killed and 50 wounded.

1750. An earthquake at London which shook the whole city. It occurred at half past five in the morning, awoke people from their sleep, threw some persons out of bed and rung the bells.

1757. Thomas Blackwell, an eminent Scottish writer, died. His modesty was such that he published his works anonymously.

1766. The bill repealing the American stamp act received the royal assent, and was passed.

1766. William Chambers, the architect, died. He was born in Sweden, but was brought over to England at two years of age. As an architect, the building of Somerset house will place his name with the best of the British schools. He was the author of several works, principally on architecture.

1775. An inhabitant of the town of Billercia, Mass., tarred and feathered by the British troops. The British were the first to introduce this practice, which afterwards became a popular mode of punishing tories.

1793. The French national convention abolished imprisonment for debt, and decreed that all actually confined for debt in the republic should be set at liberty. From this law however were excepted all defaulters in public money.

1793. The city of Liege in Belgium, taken by the Austrians.

1796. A viscid and resinous substance fell near Bautzen, in Upper Lusatia, composed of carbon, hydrogen and oxygen. Several distinguished men of science examined specimens of it. It had the smell of the yellowish and very much dried gum of the juniper.

1796. Banda, an East India island, taken by the British under Admiral Rainer. A large quantity of spices and considerable money fell into the hands of the victors.

1799. Cayuga county, New York, erected.

1799. Massena took by assault the fortress of Luciensteig, cut out of the rock in the channel of the Rhine. This opened a passage through the Rhætian Alps.

1801. The British effected a landing in Egypt, at Aboukir bay, with the loss of 700 men. The French under Menou opposed their landing with great bravery.

1803. Francis Egerton, duke of Bridgewater, died. He is styled the father of canal navigation in England. He planned the Worsley canal, near Manchester, which he completed with the assistance of Brindley. He died immensely rich.

1804. Goeree, an island of the Netherlands, which had fallen into the hands of the French a few weeks previous, was retaken by the British on this day.

1807. Sawrey Gilpin, an English painter, died. He excelled particularly in delineating animals. His masterpiece is a group of tigers.

1808. Third day's action between the British frigate St. Fiorenza and the French frigate Piedmontaise, 50 guns, off cape Comorin. The action lasted one hour and twenty minutes, when the French struck, having 48 killed and wounded. The British lost 17 killed besides their commander, Capt. Hardinge.

1814. Lord Wellington defeated the French and entered Bordeaux.

1814. Unsuccessful attack by the British under Gen. Skerret upon Bergen-op-Zoom. Of 4,500 British it is supposed that not more than 1,500 escaped.

1815. Action between the British ship Tiber, Capt. Dacres, and the American privateer Leo, 7 guns, 93 men, Capt. Hemes, which resulted in the capture of the latter.

1819. Regnault de St. Jean d'Angely, a French statesman under Bonaparte, died at his ancient seat, on the day following his return from exile, of gout in the stomach.

1844. Charles John Bernadotte, king of Sweden, died, aged 81. He rose from the humble rank of a sergeant in the army, to the highest rank under Bonaparte; and in 1810 founded a new dynasty in Sweden. Having fortunately joined the allied powers in 1812 against Napoleon, he survived the overthrow of the other newly erected dynasties, and transmitted the crown to his son, Oscar I.

MARCH 9.

1403. Bajazet I, sultan of Turkey, died. He was celebrated as a warrior, but his disposition was cruel and tyrannical. Being conquered by Tamerlane, and exposed by him in an iron cage, he dashed his head against the bars of his prison, and killed himself.

1405. Battle of Grosmont, in which Henry IV defeated the Welch under Griffith Glendowr.

1566. David Ricci (or Rizzio), an Italian musician, residing at the court of Mary, queen of Scots, assassinated in her presence. His skillful performance of the national melodies of Scotland, tended not a little to their general improvement with the higher classes.

1609. William Warner, an English poet, died; author of *Albion's England.*

1615. Francis Beaumont, an English dramatist buried. He was jointly concerned with Fletcher in the production of several excellent plays, and assisted Jonson in some of his. He died under 30 years of age.

1649. The duke of Hamilton, earl of Holland and Lord Capel beheaded with others who were suspected of royalism. Bad faith is attributed to their judges.

1661. Julius Mazarin died; cardinal and prime minister of France under Louis XIV. His name is identified with the history of his time.

1678. Ghent surrendered to Louis XIV of France.

1679. A declaration forbidding pardon to be granted to any who killed another in a duel, issued by the council of England.

1694. Gaspard Sagittarius, a German historian, died. He was an able supporter of the doctrines of the reformation.

1735. Violent hurricane occurred at Kilverton in Norfolk rolling the lead of the roofs of houses and doing in the few minutes it lasted, incredible damage. A strong smell of sulphur followed.

1762. Joseph Calas, a merchant of Toulouse, executed on the wheel. He was unjustly condemned for the murder of his own son. His innocence was confirmed by a public *arret*, on this day the next year.

1770. William Guthries, a voluminous Scottish writer, died. He became celebrated as a bookmaker, and lent his name to the works of less popular authors.

1778. Great council at Johnstown between the Six nations and New York company.

1782. Mangalore, a seaport of Hindostan, surrendered to the British under General Matthews.

1783. Michael Etmuller, a German physician, died. His works have been published in 5 vols. folio.

1793. Congress passed the act to organize the militia; enacting the enrollment of every able bodied white male citizen between the ages of 18 and 45.

1795. The Fingal, or 118th regiment, mutinied at Birmingham, England.

1796. Charette, the famous Vendean chief, tried and shot at Nantes, aged about 33. He refused to have his eyes bandaged, and gave the signal to fire himself.

1801. Johann Christian Ackermann, a celebrated German physician and bibliographer, died, aged 45.

1810. London rendered impassable for several hours by a heavy rain.

1811. Battle of Pombal, in Portugal, in which the French were defeated with the loss of 470, by the British.

1812. John Henry's plot to dismember the Union disclosed to congress. Henry received $50,000 public money for disclosing it, and sailed immediately for France.

1814. Battle of Laon, in which Napoleon was defeated by Marshal Blucher.

1822. Edward Daniel Clarke, professor of mineralogy at Cambridge and a celebrated traveler and tourist, died.

1823. John Henry Van Swinden, a Dutch philosopher, died. He was an author on various subjects, and a man of great erudition.

1825. Anna Letitia Barbauld, an English authoress of great reputation in her day, died. She was early taught the languages, and became distinguished for her learning. She retained great vigor of mind and body to the extreme age of 90.

1834. Snow fell at Rome, the first event of the kind on record in 240 years. (See March 25, 1595.)

1840. George Gleig died at Stirling, Scotland, aged 87; distinguished for more than half a century as a scholar, critic, metaphysician and theologian.

1847. Battle of Vera Cruz.

MARCH 10.

222. Heliogabalus, emperor of Rome, assassinated. He was a cruel, vindictive and licentious tyrant.

1333. Ladislaus III of Poland died. He oppressed the people till they revolted and placed Wenceslaus upon the throne. On the death of the latter he was reinstated and governed with justice and moderation.

1668. John Denham, a British poet, died. One of his poems, *Cooper's Hill*, is commended by the ablest critics.

1673. Henrietta Coligni, a French poetess of much celebrity, died.

1683. The first council and assembly of Pennsylvania met at Chester. The session occupied 22 days.

1686. James II granted a general pardon to many of his subjects, excepting among others the girls of Taunton who gave a Bible and sword to Monmouth. James never favored the Bible.

1726. The Lyford giant born; when five years of age he could lift one hundred weight with one hand.

1736. William Cosby, captain general and commander in chief of the province of New York, died, almost universally detested.

1774. William Browne, an English physician, died. The active part he took in the contest against the licentiates, occasioned his being introduced by Foote into his play of the *Devil upon Two Sticks*. He is distinguished by many lively essays in English and Latin prose and verse.

1776. Elias Catherine Freron, a French *litterateur*, died. He was the constant subject of Voltaire's satire, who called him the tyrant, rather than the king of literature.

1776. The British soldiery, contrary to orders, plundered Boston.

1783. Anthony Loydi, a farmer of Amezquet, Spain, died, aged 114. He had never been sick until a few days before his death, always abstained from wine and tobacco, and retained his senses, his teeth and hair until he died.

1785. N. Sablier, an eminent French author, died at Paris.

1789. The city of London brillantly illuminated on account of the convalescence of the king.

1792. John, earl of Bute, died. He was made prime minister of England, from which he voluntarily retired to enjoy a life of learned leisure.

1797. The city of Albany made the capital of the state of New York.

1797. Delaware county, in the state of New York, erected.

1812. Bonaparte issued a decree *denationalizing* all flags that should submit to the British orders in council.

1813. Action at night in Chesapeake bay between the United States schooner Adeline and the British schooner Lottery; the latter it is supposed was sunk.

1819. Frederick Henry Jacobi, a German philosophical writer, died.

1820. Benjamin West, the painter, died at London, aged 82. He was born at Springfield, Penn., 1738. The first indications of his genius were elicited at the age of seven years, by drawing the portrait of his sleeping sister in red and black ink. He began painting as a profession at the age of 18, and four years after went to England. He was subsequently induced by Sir Joshua Reynolds to take up his residence in London, where he acquired a reputation seldom attained, and at the time of his death was president of the Royal academy.

1826. John Pinkerton, an eminent and voluminous Scottish author, died at Paris, aged 68.

1829. The William and Anne, a British trading vessel, wrecked at the mouth of Columbia river, on the north-west coast of America, and the whole crew, 16 Europeans and 10 Sandwich islanders, murdered by the natives.

1833. Samuel Tucker, an American revolutionary commodore, died at Bremen, Maine. He was distinguished as a brave and able commander, and at the time of his death, was supposed to have been, next to Lafayette, the highest surviving officer of the revolution.

1855. JAMES BROWN, an eminent book-publisher of Boston, Mass., died, aged 55. He not only was eminent in his profession, but possessed the taste and spirit of a scholar.

1855. CARLOS, the claimant of the Spanish throne from the time of the death of Ferdinand in 1833, died at Trieste, where he was known as the conde de Molina.

1855. The college building at Princeton, N. J., known as Nassau hall, was destroyed by fire. It was built in 1756. and in the Revolutionary war was used for barracks, by both the British and Americans.

MARCH 11.

1302. The marriage of ROMEO MONTOCCHIO with JULIET CAPELLETTO was solemnized at the church of the Minorites, at Citadella. These were Shakespeare's Romeo and Juliet.

1444. The university of Paris issued a circular addressed to all the French clergy, expressing the opinion of the church, that the *feast of fools*, about the calends of January, was a well imagined institution, connected with Christianity, and that those who attempted to suppress it should be curst and excommunicate.

1513. JOHN MEDICI elected pope and assumed the title of Leo X. From his grave appearance it was often said he seemed never to have been a child.

1544. Birthday of TORQUATO TASSO, styled the prince of Italian poets.

1669. The memorable eruption of Mount Etna began at sunset.

1722. JOHN TOLAND, a very famous English political, polemical and miscellaneous writer and antiquary, died at Putney.

1732. PETER CHIRAC, a French author and physician to the king, died.

1732. KOULI KHAN, usurped the Persian throne.

1738. It was ascertained that 12,000 persons were convicted in London in a few months for selling gin without a license, and 3,000 paid a fine of £10 rather than be committed to the house of correction.

1744. Action off Toulon between part of the British fleet under Matthews and Lestock, and the combined French and Spanish fleets.

1797. Two discharged servants informed the police that Ladies Buckinghamshire, Luttrel and Stuart played faro, in consequence of which their ladyships were fined.

1800. The Royal institution of London for the promotion of the fine arts held their first sitting.

1808. Franklin, Chatauque, Cattaraugus and Niagara counties in the state of New York, erected.

1809. HANNAH COWLEY died, aged 66. She was born at Tiverton, England, and distinguished as a poetress, and a dramatic writer.

1811. Badajos in Spain surrendered to the French under Soult. About 9,000 prisoners were taken, 170 cannon, 80,000 quintals of gunpowder, a large quantity of infantry cartridges,and two complete bridge equipages.

1812. PHILIP JAMES DE LOUHTERBOURG, a distinguished landscape painter, died at London. He was born at Strasburgh, 1740, and studied under Casanova. He gained considerable reputation by his paintings at Paris, after which he went over to England. Here he got up under the name of *Eidophusikon*, a novel and highly ingenious exhibition, displaying the changes of the elements and their phenomena, in a calm, a moonlight, a sunset and a storm at sea.

1813. Action off Surinam river between the United States privateer schooner Gen. Armstrong, 18 guns, and a British 24 gun frigate. The privateer sustained the attack 45 minutes within pistol shot, and succeeded in escaping with the loss of 6 killed and 16 wounded.

1848. HENRY WHEATON, an American statesman, philanthropist and classic writer, died at Roxbury, Mass.

1856. President RIVAS, of Nicarauga, declared war against Costa Rica.

MARCH 12.

1470. Battle of Erpingham, in England, and defeat of the rebels under Sir Robert Welles.

1507. CÆSAR BORGIA killed by a cannon shot before the castle of Biano. He was the natural son of Pope Alexander VI, and by him invested with the purple. He was a man of such conduct and character that Machiavel has thought fit to propose him, in his famous book, called *The Prince*, as a pattern to all princes who would act the part of wise and polite tyrants. He allowed no one to stand in his way to promotion from any scruples to removing them by the foulest means.

1578. ALEXANDER PICCOLOMINI died; author of dramatic and other pieces. He was the first who used the Italian language in philosophical subjects,

1581. WILLIAM FULKE preached a sermon within the tower of London in the hearing of such obstinate papists as were there imprisoned.

1612. The third charter of Virginia granted, by which new privileges and immunities were given for the encouragement of the colony.

1664. Charles II, of England, granted to his brother the duke of York, all Mattawacks, now Long Island; all Hudson's river, and all the lands from the west side of Connecticut river to the east side of Delaware bay, together with the royalties and rights of government.

1676. Action between the French fleet under Duquesne, and the Spanish and Dutch fleets under De Ruyter, who was mortally wounded.

1682. Chelsea hospital, England, founded.

1683. The first assembly of Pennsylvania was holden at Philadelphia, two years from the time that Penn obtained the charter.

1697. Ludovick Muggleton, a schismatic English tailor, died. He entertained notions peculiar to himself, and damned all who differed from him. He was pilloried and imprisoned, and his books burnt by the hangman.

1703. Aubrey de Vere died. His father was the valiant Robert de Vere, who married the daughter of a Friesland boor, named Beatrix Van Hemims. He was lord of the bed chamber to Charles I; was found so passive under Cromwell, that he escaped even the fine; conformed to the manners of the court of Charles II; went over from James II to William the conqueror; and was graceful in old age at the court of Queen Anne. He had been privy councilor to each of these sovereigns, and was hereditary lord chamberlain, senior knight of the garter, and premier earl of England.

1713. Steele commenced his paper *The Guardian.*

1716. Isaac Briand was fined £2000 by the court of aldermen, London, for marrying Miss Elizabeth Watson, an orphan of 13 years of age and a great fortune, without their consent.

1761. The shock of an earthquake felt in Massachusetts and the adjoining states, at half past two in the morning.

1768. Six students of Edmund hall, Oxford, were expelled the university for methodism. Their crime was praying, expounding the scriptures and singing psalms.

1772. Montgomery (originally Tyron) county, N. Y., erected.

1775. The earl of Effingham resigned his command in a regiment ordered to America. He refused to bear arms against his fellow subjects in the colonies.

1780. The British garrison at Mobile, Capt. Durnford, capitulated to the Spaniards under Don Bernardo de Galvez. The garrison consisted of 284 regulars, 54 inhabitants and 51 armed Indians.

1797. The French under Serrurier crossed the Piave, having defeated the Austrians who opposed their passage.

1801. The British fleet sailed from Aboukir bay, Egypt, and the army under Abercrombie, having effected their landing, took up their line of march for Alexandria.

1807. British order in council, interdicting all trade between port and port in France.

1809. Gustavus Adolphus IV, king of Sweden, dethroned, and the reigns of the government assumed by his uncle the duke of Sudermania, afterwards Charles XIII. (By some authorities, March 15.)

1811. The French under Massena attacked at Redinha, Portugal, by the duke of Wellington, and compelled to fall back.

1813. Warren county, N. Y., erected.

1814. The allied British and Portuguese, under Marshal Beresford, took possesion of Bordeaux in France, in the name of Louis XVIII.

1819. Robert Watt, author of the *Bibliotheca Britannica*, died. His family were severe sufferers by the failure of Constable & Co., of Edinburgh.

1837. M. de Pradt, archbishop of Malines, died at Paris, aged 78. He bore a conspicuous part in the political history of France, was often employed in important missions, and was the author of many political publications.

1843. Littleton Hunt, aged 107, died at Guinett, Ga. When a soldier of the revolutionary army he was severely wounded at the battle of Eutaw springs.

1844. Edward R. Shubrick, a brave and accomplished American naval officer, died on board his ship, the Columbia, off the coast of Brazil, aged 50.

1846. Jonathan Elliot, a well known newspaper editor and political writer, died at Washington, D. C.

1854. Hugh Macpherson died, aged 86; for 61 years professor of Greek at the university of Aberdeen.

1857. Rail road accident on the Great Western railway in Canada, by which a great number of persons were killed at a bridge over the Des Jardins canal.

1857. John Johnson, an old revolutionary soldier, died in Alleghany township, Westmoreland county, Penn., aged 103. He served in the continental army during the whole of the revolutionary war; fought at the battles of the White plains, Trenton, Princeton, Brandywine, Germantown, Monmouth, Stony point, Guilford court house, and Yorktown where Lord Cornwallis capitulated and surrendered to Gen. Washington, in all the battles and skirmishes of Gen. Anthony Wayne; and at the storming of Stony point by Wayne, he formed one of the *forlorn hope.*

MARCH 13.

565. Belisarius, a distinguished Roman general, died. He is memorable for his signal and momentous victories, and for his misfortunes. He was degraded to beg alms at the gates of Constantinople by the ungrateful emperor Justinian, to whom he had rendered the most important services.

1470. Battle near Stamford, England, in which Edward IV gained an important victory over his adversaries.

1493. Columbus arrived at Palos, from his first voyage of discovery.

1519. Cortez, on his expedition for the conquest of Mexico, landed at the mouth of the river Tabasco, and prepared to attack the town of the same name, in which about 12,000 warriors had assembled. Calling upon *St. Jago*, he fell upon the Indians, who were repulsed.

1521. Magellan discovered the Phillipine islands, on one of which he was killed by the natives.

1573. Michael de l'Hospital, chancellor of France, died. He was distinguished for the ability, integrity and mildness of his administration, which was cast in the midst of turbulence and faction.

1604. Arnaud d'Ossat, a celebrated French cardinal and statesman, died. His *Despatches* is highly recommended to the ambassador who hopes to succeed in his object.

1614. Bartholomew Legat burnt at Smithfield for the heresy of Arianism, under the reign of James I.

1676. Attack on Groton, Mass., by a body of 400 Indians, who had concealed themselves as usual in every part of the town during the night, in order to shoot down the inhabitants as they issued from their doors. The town was gathered into five garrisons, as those houses were called which were palisaded and otherwise protected from assault. Every man went constantly armed; and thus on a moment's warning, two of the enemy having been accidentally discovered, pursuit was made until they were drawn into an ambush and compelled to retreat. Another ambush in the meantime fell upon the opposite part of the town, and the flames arose from every unprotected building. Having pillaged every thing that fell in their way, and cast every indignity upon the bodies of their victims, they gave the garrison two or three volleys and disappeared. About 40 dwellings were burnt, with their outhouses; the town soon after broke up, and the inhabitants scattered to other settlements of greater safety.

1695. John de la Fontaine, the French poet, died. His compositions are characterized by a faithfulness to nature, and are totally unaffected.

1695. Peter Mignard, an eminent French painter, died. He was director and chancellor of the royal academy of painting.

1717. John Bell, the traveler, arrived at Ispahan, the residence of the Persian court, being in the retinue of the Russian ambassador, in the quality of physician. They were nearly two years on their journey from St. Petersburgh.

1726. Michael Bernard Valentin, a German botanist and professor of medicine at Giessen, died. He was an author on both sciences.

1775. George III gave his assent to the act restraining the commerce of New Jersey, Pennsylvania, Maryland, Virginia and South Carolina.

1778. Charles le Beau, an eminent French scholar, died. He was professor of belles lettres at Paris, and author of a history of the lower empire, in 22 vols.

1779. Kerim Khan, king of Persia, died a natural death, an extraordinary circumstance in the modern history of that country. He was of the family of an obscure tribe of robbers, the Zunds of Kirdistan.

1781. Herschel discovered the planet which bears his name, then the most distant of all the known planets, its revolution round the sun occupying a period of not less than 83 of our years. He had devoted 18 months in surveying the heavens star by star, with a seven feet reflector when he made the discovery of this primary planet.

1798. The body of a hair dresser at Newport, England, was buried in the highway; reason assigned, his gluttonous eating, whereof he died.

1799. A fire broke out at Constantinople which destroyed 1300 houses, including the hotels of the British minister, and Austrian internuncio, and several other magnificent edifices.

1801. Battle near Lake Maadie in Egypt, between the British and French forces, in which the former were the greatest sufferers, losing 143 killed and 946 wounded.

1808. Christian VII of Denmark, died. He may be said to have been virtually dead for many years.

1813. Edward Long died. During a residence in the West Indies he collected materials for his *History of Jamaica*, in 3 vols. quarto. It contains a large mass of valuable information, and many spirited delineations of colonial scenery and manners. He returned to England and spent the remainder of his long life in literary pursuits.

1815. The allied powers engaged to aid Louis XVIII and declared Bonaparte to be without the pale of social and civil relations.

1815. General JACKSON having received the ratification of the treaty of peace, revoked his order relative to martial law, ordered a final cessation of hostilities, and granted a general pardon for all military offences. The British took with them 199 negroes.

1824. SOPHIA LEE, an English dramatic writer and poetess, died, aged 74. The profits of her comedy of the *Chapter of Accidents*, were of great benefit to herself and sisters.

1835. A remarkable eruption of Vesuvius took place.

1845. JOHN FREDERICK DANIEL, who contributed so much to lighting the cities of Europe with gas, died of apoplexy while attending a meeting of the royal society, in London.

1848. AMBROSE SPENCER died at Lyons, Wayne co., N. Y.; one of those jurists who gave such a preeminence to the supreme court of the state of New York.

1852. Ninety-five Americans who were engaged in the Lopez expedition against Cuba, and captured and sent to Spain, arrived in New York, having been pardoned by the queen and sent home.

1853. The funeral of Madame RASPAIL, at Paris was the occasion of a formidable socialist demonstration; 40,000 persons marching in procession to Pere la Chaise.

1854. A convention signed between England, France and Turkey, against Russia.

1855. The floor of the new town hall, at Meredith, N. H., gave way, while 800 persons were present attending an election; 300 were precipitated below, several killed and a large number had their bones broken.

MARCH 14.

1262. HUGO DE ST. CARO, a Dominican, died. He deserves to be placed in the first rank of sacred critics and patrons of literature. The Dominicans are indebted to him for their celebrated *Correctorium Bibliorium*, and the first concordance of the Bible, that is of the Latin Vulgate; a comment on the old and new testament, and for the division of the Bible into chapters. He undertook to procure a union of the Greek and Roman churches.

1369. PETER THE CRUEL, king of Castile, killed. He manifested the most wanton inhumanity in his private and public life, by which he became odious to the people, and was killed by his brother.

1471. EDWARD IV of England returned from exile, and landed at Ravenspur; in his bonnet he wore an ostrich feather as prince of Wales; and his Fleming followers carried hand-guns, which is the first account of them in England.

1519. FERNANDO CORTEZ, having taken possession of the Indian town of Tabasco on the day of his landing in the country of Mexico, now marched out with his troops to a plain, where he was attacked by an immense body of Indians, who wounded above seventy of his soldiers at the first discharge of their weapons. The Spanish artillery did great execution, but when the cavalry came to the charge, the Indians, imagining the horse and rider to be one, were extremely terrified, and fled to the woods and marshes, leaving the field to the Spaniards.

1640. MANASSES DE PAS died; a French general, distinguished for his valor. His abilities were equally displayed in the cabinet, as ambassador to the courts of Sweden and Germany. He died of the wounds he received at the siege of Thionville.

1644. ROGER WILLIAMS having been sent to England as agent for Rhode Island and Providence, obtained of the earl of Warwick a patent for the incorporation of the towns of Providence, Newport and Portsmouth, with the power of governing themselves, but subject to the laws of England.

1660. WILLIAM LEDRA, a quaker, hanged by the puritans of Massachusetts, on conviction of having returned from banishment, to which he had been condemned for his faith.

1676. Attack on Northampton, Mass., by a body of Narraganset Indians, of Philip's party. The town had been fortified by palisades, set up a little while before for their better security against the savages. The Indians broke through these in three places, and succeeded in killing six persons and firing a few dwellings; but a company of soldiers being at that time quartered in the town, the enemy were speedily repulsed with the loss of many of their lives.

1710. MICHAEL BEGON, a French *avocat*, died. He also distinguished himself in the marines, and as governor of the French West India islands.

1712. MARY, countess of Falconberg, daughter of Oliver Cromwell, died. She possessed great beauty, spirit and activity; and on the deposition of her brother, exerted herself for the restoration of Charles II.

1745. Fort Augustus blown up by the forces of the pretender to the crown of England.

1754. PETER CLAUDE NIVELLE DE LA CHAUSSE, an admired French poet, died. Though favored by fortune, he preferred the honors of literature to all other distinctions, and acquired celebrity by his dramatic pieces, which possess great merit.

1757. JOHN BYNG shot at Portsmouth. He served under his father admiral George Byng, and rose to the same rank himself. His attempt to relieve Fort St. Philip in Minorca proving abortive, when blockaded by a French fleet under La Glassionere, and his hesitation in engaging the enemy when a bold attack might perhaps have gained him the victory, excited the clamor of the nation against him, and he was doomed to meet the penalty of cowardice.

1758. GENERAL WADE died. In 1715, he commanded against the forces of the pretender to the throne, and remained in Scotland as commander-in-chief after the war was ended. It was during this period that he cut the celebrated military road through the highlands, which facilitated the improvement and civilization of the country more than all the measures resorted to before the reign of George I. It was he who introduced the bill into parliament which disarmed and changed the dress of the highlanders.

1793. Battle of Tirlemont, in which the prince of Saxe Coburg defeated the French under Dumourier, who lost 33 cannon and 3,000 men.

1795. Action off Genoa between the British and French fleets, in which the latter were defeated, with the loss of the Caira, 80 guns, 3,000 men, and the Censeur, 74 guns, 1,000 men.

1799. WILLIAM MELMOTH died. He distinguished himself as the translator of the Epistles of Pliny and Cicero, and was the author of poems, letters and memoirs.

1800. DAINES BARRINGTON, an English lawyer, antiquary, and miscellaneous writer, died. He abandoned his offices, which he discharged with great dignity, to devote himself to literary pursuits, which he loved. His writings are numerous.

1803. FRIEDRICH GOTTLIEB KLOPSTOCK, died. He was born at Quedlinburg, 1724; studied the languages, became familiar with the classic writers, and formed the resolution of writing a great epic poem. In 1745 he studied theology at Jena, where he commenced in solitude the first canto of *The Messiah.* This work he finished about 1790. It procured him great celebrity in the north of Europe, so that he was received with great respect and veneration wherever he went. His funeral was attended by the principal men of Hamburg, in 126 carriages.

1813. Delaware river blockaded by the British ships Poictiers, Belvidere, &c.

1813. On this and the preceding day snow and hail of a red color, with much red dust and red rain fell over all Tuscany.

1823. General DUMOURIER, a name that fills some interesting pages of modern history, died in his 85th year, at Turville park, near London.

1835. Treaty with the Cherokee Indians, by which they ceded all their lands east of the Mississippi, and agreed to retire to a territory guarantied to them in Arkansas, in consideration of the sum of $5,262,-251.

1836. JOHN MAYNE, a Scotch poet, died near London, at an advanced age. His chief poem is *The Siller Gun*, four cantos.

1854. Steam boat Reindeer burst a flue at Cannelton, Indiana, by which 50 persons were killed.

1855. The new suspension bridge at Niagara falls crossed for the first time by a locomotive and train of cars.

MARCH 15.

44 B. C. CAIUS JULIUS CÆSAR, the Roman general, assissinated in the senate house. He perished at 5 o'clock in the afternoon by 23 wounds. As a *soldier*, he was unquestionably the greatest except one in the history of mankind; his character as a *citizen* is variously stated by different factions. He is said to have fought 500 battles, conquered 300 nations, taken 800 cities, defeated 3,000,000 men, and slain 1,000,000 on the field of battle.

35. LONGINUS, the penitent, who is said to have pierced the side of Christ, was killed at Cappadocia, probably in this year.

1079. A reformation in the Persian calendar effected by a general assembly of the Eastern astronomers. It is called the Gelalean era, but is only a renovation of that of Zoroaster, which had been neglected after the fall of the Magian empire.

1527. Pope CLEMENT VII concluded a treaty with Lannoy, viceroy of Naples, which the duke of Bourbon disregarded, and marched for Rome.

1573. MICHAEL DE L'HOSPITAL died. Few French statesmen were more liberal than him. He narrowly escaped the Bartholomew massacre, and his daughter, who had embraced the reformed religion was saved by the widow duchess of Guise, who concealed her.

1617. THOMAS EGERTON, an eminent and learned English lawyer, died. He was chancellor under James I.

1655. THEODORE MAYERNE, an eminent physician, died. He was born in Switzerland, studied in France, and settled in England in the service of James I, where he died.

1660. Dr. WREN, bishop of Ely, released after fifteen years' imprisonment.

1665. JAMES, duke of York, established at Gunfleet the first regular system of naval warfare in England.

1672. The famed act of indulgence, passed by Charles II, containing a clause for liberty of conscience.

1743. JOHN BAPTIST MOLINIER died; a distinguished preacher and theologial writer of Toulouse.

1754. DENYS FRANCIS SECOUSSE, a learned Frenchman, died. He was one of the first pupils of Rollin, and left the bar for the study of literature.

1781. Battle of Guilford court house, in North Carolina, in which 4,400 Americans, principally militia, under Gen. Greene, were defeated by 2,400 British regulars under Cornwallis. Loss of the Americans 400 killed; British loss 532 killed.

1784. THOMAS FRANKLIN, an English scholar and divine, died. He was possessed of no inconsiderable share of learning and poetical abilities, and was long a favorite in the literary world; translated Sophocles, Phalaris, Lucian and Voltaire, and is the author of a comedy and two tragedies, which were received with great applause.

1798. Chenango co., N. Y., erected; and the following year (1799) Oneida was formed.

1804. The Duke D'ENGHIEN seized by a party of French cavalry and hurried away to Paris, where he was tried in the night by a military tribunal, and condemned on vague and unsubstantial charges of carrying on a correspondence with the enemies of the republic, and shot immediately.

1809. GUSTAVUS ADOLPHUS IV, king of Sweden, arrested and deprived of his functions of goverment. (By some authorities, March 12.)

1818. HECTOR MCNEIL, a most deservedly popular poet of Scotland, died. *Scotland's Scaith* or the *Waes of War*, met with the unprecedented sale of 10,000 copies in one month.

1820. Maine entered the confederacy of the United States.

1823. JOHN JERVIS, earl of St. Vincent, an English admiral died, aged 90. He entered the navy at the age of 10, and gradually arose to the highest rank, and was raised to the peerage. His courage, skill and activity rendered him an admirable officer.

1838. The city of Bahia, in Brazil, taken from the rebels or insurgents, by the imperial troops, with loss of blood on both sides. The rebels fired the city; about 3000 of them were taken prisoners.

1839. Battle of Tuspan; the Mexican government troops, (Centralists) under Gen. Cos, defeated at Tuspan by the Federalists under Gen. Mexia, with a loss of 300 killed and several hundred prisoners.

1840. JAMES RILEY, an American sea captain, died at sea, aged 63. He is well known as the author of *Riley's Narrative*, which contains an account of his captivity and sufferings in Northern Africa.

1856. The steam ferry boat, New Jersey, while crossing the Delaware from Philadelphia to Camden, took fire and a large number of persons perished.

MARCH 16.

404 B. C. Athens was taken by Lysander and the tyranny of the 30 commenced.

37. CLAUDIUS DRUSUS NERO TIBERIUS, emperor of Rome, died. On his accession to the throne, he gave promise of a wise and happy reign, but soon became unrestrained in his conduct, and after a reign of 23 years, died in odium with the people.

455. FLAVIUS PLACIDUS VALENTINIAN, emperor of Rome, assassinated. He was a profligate and licentious ruler.

1190. The Jews of York lawlessly massacred for their wealth by the citizens.

1286. ALEXANDER III king of Scotland, killed. He succeeded his father, Alexander II, at the age of eight years. An enterprising and virtuous ruler; he introduced many good regulations of government, and under his sway the country seems to have enjoyed a tranquility to which she had long been a stranger. As he was riding in a dark night between Bruntisland and Ringhorn, on the banks of the frith of Forth, he was thrown with his horse over a precipice and killed on the spot.

1532. JOHN BOURCHIER died at Calais in France, of which he was the English governor. He translated Froissart's *Chronicle* into English

1621. The Plymouth colonists received the first Indian visit to their town. This was Samoset, sagamore of a country lying five days' journey from thence, called Patuxet. He informed the English that all the inhabitants had died of an extraordinary plague about four years before, and that there was neither man, woman or child remaining. Of course there was no one to dispute their possession.

1649. An army of 1000 Iroquois armed with guns fell upon the Huron village at the eastern extremity of the lake, and nearly massacred the entire population. The Hurons defended themselves bravely, but were forced to yield before the fire arms and superior numbers of the Iroquois, who lost more than a hundred of their best warriors. The French missionaries, Brebeuf and Lallemant, who labored with the Hurons, were taken, and suffered death by torture.

1660. The long parliament dissolved by its own act.

1675. Under a pair of stairs in the tower of London two bodies were found, supposed to be those of Edward V and his brother, whom their uncle Richard III murdered nearly two hundred years before.

1680. The first assembly of New Hampshire met at Portsmouth; John Cutts first president.

1689. The Habeas corpus act suspended for the first time in England.

1691. Jacob Leisler, who had exercised the office of governor of New York nearly two years by the election of the freeholders and the consent of the British ministry, was barbarously executed by some malcontents, as a traitor.

1738. Captain Jenkins, the master of a Scottish ship, exhibited his ear in a piece of cotton, which he affirmed had been torn off by a guarda costa. This is alluded to by Burke as the fable of Capt. Jenkins.

1751. James Madison, fourth president of the United States, born.

1781. Action off cape Henry between the British fleet, admiral Arbuthnot, and French fleet under d'Estouches. Both sides claimed the victory. British loss, 30 killed and 73 wounded.

1781. French surrendered the island of St. Bartholomews to the British.

1782. Action off cape Spartel, between British frigate Success and Spanish frigate Santo Catalina, 34 guns. The latter was captured, having 25 killed. British loss 1.

1792. Gustavus III, king of Sweden, shot by Count Ankerstroem at a masquerade.

1795. Clausel, adjutant general of the army of the Eastern Pyrennes, presented to the national convention 25 pairs of colors and a standard taken from the Spaniards at Figuieres.

1797. Battle of Cainin in Italy. The French under Murat passed the Tagliamento and attacked the Austrians, who were driven from the village, where the archduke had established his head quarters.

1799. John Dussaulx died. He distinguished himself in the war of Hanover under Richelieu, after which he devoted himself to literary pursuits. He took part in the French revolution, and was among the 73 proscribed deputies.

1799. A portion of the pavement in front of the Royal exchange, London, suddenly sunk and a well of water was discovered which had not been used in 600 years.

1802. A military institution established by government at West Point, which was the origin of the present academy there.

1808. Joseph Bonomi, an Italian artist, died at London. He was distinguished particularly by his architectural knowledge and genius, was an associate of the royal academy, and patronized by Sir Joshua Reynolds.

1810. On a pane of glass at an inn near London, under this date, is the following inscription. "Thomas Mount Jones dined here, ate six pounds bacon, and drank nineteen pots beer." It is a question for discussion, whether in this frail memorial, the love of distinction and desire for fame were not as great as the love of brutal gluttony.

1813. Captain Berresford of the British ship Poictiers, 74 guns, demanded of the inhabitants of Lewistown, Delaware, 25 oxen and vegetables and hay, otherwise he threatened to destroy the town. The demand was refused.

1817. William Thompson, an industrious Scottish writer and compiler, died. He possessed ability, but his writings bear the marks of haste and want of care.

1838. Nathaniel Bowditch died at Boston, aged 65. His father and ancestors in several generations were by profession shipmasters. Notwithstanding the very limited advantages of his education, and his laborious employment through life for the support of his family, yet by his extraordinary genius and economy of time, he made great acquisitions in learning and science, gained most of the languages, and made himself the most eminent mathematician and astronomer that America has produced. He published the *Practical Navigator*, a standard book; but the great work on which his fame will rest, is the copious and profound commentary upon the *Mechanique Celeste* of La Place, of which he made the first entire translation, and published at his own expense in 4 vols. quarto; saying that he preferred spending a thousand dollars a year in that way to keeping a carriage.

1853. Anthony Dumond Stanley, an American mathematician, died, aged 42. Profoundly versed in the science, he had begun a series of works which would have placed his name high on the scroll of fame.

MARCH 17.

49 b. c. Pompey abandoned Italy, and took the sea with his legions, at Brundusium.

45 b. c. Battle of Munda, in Spain, between the armies of Cæsar and Pompey, which decided the fate of the Roman republic. These men did not consider the Roman empire sufficiently large for two of them.

180. Marcus Aurelius Antoninus, sur-

named the philosopher, died on an expedition against the Marcomanni. He was so extremely popular with his Roman subjects, that they placed him among the gods, and kept his statue in their houses.

464. St. Patrick, the tutelar saint of Ireland, died. He was carried away with many of his father's vassals by pirates, from whom he made his escape to Gaul and Italy. He received a commission from Pope Celestine to convert the Irish to Christianity, in which mission he was eminently successful.

807. A large spot noticed upon the sun's disc, which continued there eight days.

1072. Adalbert, archbishop of Bremen, died. He became very powerful in Denmark, and even obliged the king to divorce his wife Gutha, because she was somewhat allied to him. Though intriguing and violent, he possessed some good qualities, and formed many wise regulations in civil and ecclesiastical affairs.

1562. Diego Esquivel Alava, a learned Spanish bishop, died. He was at the Council of Trent, and published a work on councils.

1565. Alexander Ales, a Scottish theologian, died. He first opposed the tenets of Luther, but afterwards embraced them, and suffered persecution. He wrote commentaries on some of the books of the old and new testament.

1632. Treaty of St. Germain, by which Canada and Nova Scotia were restored to the French. The capture of Quebec was unknown at the time peace was re-established, or perhaps those territories would not have been so generally given up.

1634. Thomas Randolph, an English poet, died. He was the friend of Jonson, and his works have been several times reprinted.

1640. Philip Massinger, an English dramatic poet, died. Some of his comedies still keep the stage. He was courted by the wits and learned men of his time.

1657. An offensive and defensive league concluded between France and England.

1676. Warwick, R. I., destroyed by the Indians. Only one house was left unburnt.

1677. Valenciennes, in France, taken by assault by the army under Louis XIV, in person.

1681. The members of the English parliament from London came to Oxford, the place of their meeting, armed and with ribbons on their hats inscribed with "No popery, no slavery."

1695. Augustin Lubin, an Augustine friar, died. He was geographer to the French king, and author of various works.

1715. Gilbert Burnet, bishop of Salisbury, died. He was a zealous promoter of the revolution in England, which placed the present family on the throne, and of which he wrote the history.

1740. Mrs. Stevens received £5,000 from the English parliament for making public her medicine for the stone.

1741. John Baptist Rousseau, an eminent French poet, died. He possessed a fine genius, but an unhappy temper embittered his life by stimulating him to abuse those whose friendship would have procured him a place above dependence.

1767. Birthday of Andrew Jackson, seventh president of the United States.

1776. Boston evacuated by the British. By four in the morning the king's troops, with those Americans who were attached to the royal cause, began to embark, and before ten all of them were under sail. As the rear embarked, General Washington marched into the city, where he was joyfully received as a deliverer. The British left 250 cannon and 25,000 bushels of wheat.

1781. Johannes Evald died: the most distinguished poetical genius of Denmark, in the eighteenth century. Being left to his own reading by his tutor, his imagination was captivated with *Tom Jones* and *Robinson Crusoe.* Proposing to himself the latter hero for a model, he eloped at the age of thirteen with a view of proceeding to Batavia, but was overtaken, and his project frustrated. He next conceived the scheme of entering the Prussian army, and enlisted at Magdeburg; but being received only as a foot soldier, instead of a hussar, he deserted to the Austrians. On quitting the army he devoted himself to the study of theology, but having suddenly become violently enamored with a young lady, who regardless of his passion, bestowed her hand on another, a permanent melancholy settled upon his mind, and under this influence he took up his pen. His first work *Fortune's Temple*, a vision, at once stamped his reputation. In 1772 he executed his literary chef-d'œuvre, *Balder's Död*, a drama of extraordinary poetical beauty, and greatly superior to anything which had then appeared in the Danish language. His after life was embittered by poverty and sickness; and it was under the hospitable roof of Madame Skou that he breathed his last, after having been confined to his bed or armchair two years, and almost deprived of the use of his limbs.

1782. Daniel Bernouilli, a German philosopher, died. He studied medicine as a profession, but was at the same time engaged with mathematics. At the age of twenty-four, he was offered the presidency of an academy at Genoa, but gave the preference to an invitation from St. Petersburgh. He returned to Basle in 1733, where he spent the remainder of his days, so much respected by the inhabitants, that to bow to Daniel Bernouilli, when met in the street, was one of the first lessons which every father gave his children.

1790. The government of France issued assignats to the amount of 170,000,000 francs. This system of assignats, while it gave more strength to the public, yet was the source of more private suffering than any other measure during the French revolution.

1793. Battle of Neerwinden, or Linden, between the French under Dumourier, and the Austrians under Coburg and Clarifayt. Dumourier was obliged to retreat.

1794. French sloop Avenger, 16 guns, taken by Admiral Jervis's squadron off Martinique.

1795. A number of the Parisians complained to the national convention of the *scarcity of bread* in Paris.

1798. Thomas Jackson, an English actor, died. His epitaph is ingenious: "Sacred to the memory of Thomas Jackson, comedian, who was engaged 21st December, 1741, *to play a comic cast of characters* in the great theatre, the world; for many of which he was *prompted* by nature to excel. The *season* being ended, his *benefit* over, the charges all paid, his account closed, he made his *exit* in the *tragedy of Death* on the 17th of March, 1798, in assurance of being called once more to *rehearsal*, where he hopes to find his *forfeits* all cleared, his *cast of parts* bettered, and his situation made agreeable by him who paid the great *stock debt*, for the love of *performers* in general."

1799. The French army arrived before St. Jean d'Acre, and to their no small chagrin and astonishment, beheld the town prepared for a siege, and the English colors flying in the harbor.

1800. The British ship Queen Charlotte, 110 guns, destroyed by an explosion off Leghorn. More than 800 persons perished with her.

1806. William Rowley, an eminent British physician, died. He was a man of great skill and experience in his profession, and his benevolence and humanity were conspicuous; yet was he one of the most obstinate opponents to the introduction of vaccination as a preventive of small pox that ever impeded the might of his authority to that experiment.

1808. Rupture of the negotiation at Washington between the British minister and the American government.

1811. Charles IV, of Sweden, resigned the government of his kingdom in favor of his adopted son, Bernadotte.

1828. James Edward Smith, an eminent English naturalist and physician, died. He was one of the founders of the Linnean society, and published several valuable works on natural history and botany.

1843. George Turner, aged 93, died at Philadelphia. He was a native of England, but joining the American revolutionary army, he distinguished himself in many severe actions and endeared himself to Gen. Washington.

1849. William II, king of Holland, died.

1855. The French and Russians at Sebastopol contended fiercely for the rifle pits which the latter had established between the French advance and the Mamelon.

MARCH 18.

251. St. Cyril, archbishop of Jerusalem, died.

979. Edward the Martyr, died. He was the son of Edgar, and succeeded his father as king of England at the age of 15. The young king paid little attention to any thing but the chase; and hunting one day, he got separated from his attendants, and repaired to Corfe castle, where his stepmother, Elfrida, resided. Having procured a draught of liquor, he was drinking it on horseback, when one of Elfrida's servants gave him a deep stab behind. He immediately spurred his horse, but fainting from loss of blood, was dragged in the stirrup till he died. The pity caused by his innocence and misfortune induced the people to regard him as a martyr.

1350. In the national roll of accounts for glazing St. Stephen's chapel, Westminster, Edward III ordained that the wages for artists be from 5d per day to one shilling, except for John Barnaby, his wages should be twopence.

1552. Maurice of Saxony took up arms against the emperor Charles V.

1629. Charles James, prince of Great Britain, born, baptized and died.

1629. Charles I, of England, issued a proclamation that he would account it presumption in any one to prescribe a time for him to call a parliament.

1635. Patrick Forbes, a Scotch prelate, died. He was a great and a good man; a benefactor particularly to Aberdeen university, of which he revived the professorship of law, physic and divinity.

1696. Bonaventure Baron, professor of divinity at Rome, died. He was a native of Ireland, but spent 60 years of his life in Rome; and was a learned and voluminous writer.

1718. Mary Wortley Montague made the first experiment of inoculation for small pox upon her own son at Belgrade, in Turkey. It was tried in England upon criminals, with complete success, about nine years after. This disease first made its appearance at Mecca, where it is stated to have destroyed the invading Ethiopian army, and thus terminated in 360, what is denominated *the war of the elephant.*

1728. GEORGE STANHOPE, an able English divine, died. His theological works were numerous and popular.

1741. Conflagration of the chapel and buildings in the fort at New York, which was followed immediately by the *negro plot.*

1745. ROBERT WALPOLE died, aged 69. He became heir to the family estate by the death of his elder brother, and in the jovial life of a country gentleman, soon lost his early inclination to literature. In 1700 he was returned to parliament, and warmly espousing the whig interest, rose to a high promotion in the offices of the government, and in 1742, was created earl of Oxford, on his resignation of the premiership. He is the reputed author of the saying that "all men have their price."

1754. The first theatre established in the city of New York, closed with the *Beggar's Opera* and the *Devil to Pay*, when the following notice appeared in the prints, which managers now-a-days have little occasion to repeat: "Lewis Hallam, comedian, intending for Philadelphia, *begs the favor* of those who have any demands against him to bring in their accounts and receive their money."

1766. Stamp act repealed by the British government, reserving however, the right to make laws binding on the colonies in all cases whatsoever. News of this repeal excited great joy in America, where it was celebrated by the ringing of bells, fireworks and festivals.

1768. LAURENCE STERNE, an eccentric English author and divine, died. His romance of *Tristram Shandy* and the *Sentimental Journey*, are well known.

1775. British Gen. GAGE seized 13,425 musket cartridges and 3000 pounds of ball, all of it private property, stored on Boston Neck.

1776. The British troops having evacuated Boston, Sir Archibald Campbell, unaware of this movement, on entering the harbor with 1700 men, was made prisoner by Washington.

1780. Congress resolved to call in by taxes in one year and burn all the continental money emitted prior to that time, and to issue ten million dollars new money, redeemable in specie within six years.

1781. ANNE ROBERT JAMES TURGOT, an eminent French statesman, died. He studied divinity, but his talents recommending him to the notice of the government, he was appointed to a civil office, where he displayed so great ability that he was appointed comptroller of the finances. His measures were grand, liberal and useful: but being ridiculed by the profligate and the vicious, who rioted on the miseries of the people, he retired from public life.

1796. Steuben county erected in south western New York.

1797. Palma Nuova, a frontier town in Italy, evacuated by the archduke Charles, who had wrested it from the Venitians only ten days before. The French under Bernadotte and Serrurier, on entering it found 30,000 rations of bread, and a million quintals of flour.

1805. BONAPARTE assumed the title of king of Italy.

1814. JOHN VINT, editor of the *Isle of Man Gazette*, and a distinguished philanthropist, died.

1817. An earthquake in Spain, Portugal, and Sicily, destroyed whole villages.

1817. CHARLES COMBE died; an eminent English physician and critic, and highly distinguished as a medalist.

1836. ABATE FEA, a celebrated archæologist, died at Rome, aged 88. He is known as the translator of Winckelman.

1839. The Chinese imperial commissioner, Lin, issued a proclamation at Canton, ordering the foreign opium dealers to deliver up all the opium in their possession, to have it burnt and destroyed, and forbidding its importation to all eternity, under pain of death.

1840. Dr. PARISH, favorably known to the medical world, died in Philadelphia.

1846. First steam boat arrived at Austin, Texas.

1846. WILLIAM M. CRANE, of the United States navy, died by his own hand.

1848. The emperor of Austria published by proclamation, at Milan, abolition of censorship, and a convention of the states. But the people wanting more, troubles began.

1854. A terrible gale at Albany, N. Y.; fifty houses unroofed, many chimneys and walls blown down, and great damage done.

1856. HENRY POTTINGEN, lieutenant general in the East India company's service, died aged 67. He distinguished himself in the Affghanistan war, and settled the opium difficulty with the Chinese.

1856. The Cunard steamer Curlew, from Halifax, ran on a reef north of the Bermudas, and was lost, with a part of her mail.

MARCH 19.

720. B. C. The first eclipse of the moon on record (by Ptolemy) happened on this day.

478. B. C. The history of Herodotus terminates with the siege of Sestos.

235. ALEXANDER SEVERUS, emperor of Rome, murdered by his soldiers. He was

a Phœnician by birth, led an exemplary life, and governed ably both in peace and war.

717. Chilperic, king of France, surprised in his camp, in the forest of Arden, by the duke of Austrasia, afterwards Charles Martel.

1355. Pressing for seamen to man the English navy, commenced in the reign of Edward III.

1521. Insurrection and massacre in the island of Majorca, in the Mediterranean sea.

1584. Iwan IV, Vassilivitz, first czar of Muscovy, died. He was denominated by the Russians the terrible, and by foreigners the tyrant.

1621. The complaint against lord Bacon for corruption, drawn up by Sir Edward Coke and others, presented to the house of lords. The chancellor was sick, but addressed a letter to his peers, requesting them not to prejudge his case from "any number of petitions against a judge that makes two thousand decrees and orders in a year; but that he may answer them according to the rules of justice, severally and respectively."

1626. Peter Coton, a French Jesuit, died. He was confessor to Henry IV, whose confidence he possessed, and it was a common expression that the king was good but that he had *cotton* in his ears. He was distinguished for eloquence and zeal.

1628. Patent for Massachusetts sold to Sir Henry Roswell, Sir John Young and "four other associates in the vicinity of Dorchester, England."

1631. The original patent of Connecticut made by Robert, earl of Warwick, to William, Viscount Say and Seal, Robert lord Brook and their associates.

1643. Battle of Hopton-Heath, between the forces of Charles I, and those of the parliament, in which the latter were defeated with the loss of a great part of their artillery.

1643. Spencer Compton, the friend of Charles I, killed at the battle of Hopton-Heath. He was the only son of William, first earl of Northampton; and refusing to accept quarter, was despatched by the parliament forces.

1687. Daniel Gookin died; for many years superintendent of the Indians in Massachusetts, whose interests he watched with so much zeal as to draw upon himself the abuse of the populace, whose outrages he constantly opposed. He published some historical collections of the Indians in New England.

1688. John Denham, one of the minor British poets, died. He was born at Dublin, in 1615, and first became known in 1641 by his tragedy of *The Sophy*. In 1643 appeared his first addition of *Cooper's Hill*, a justly celebrated poem, of which Dryden says, for majesty of style is, and ever will be, the standard of good writing.

1691. Col. Henry Stoughter published his commission from the Duke of York, appointing him governor of the province of New York.

1711. Thomas Ken, chaplain to Charles II of England, died. He survived several reigns, and in all, his firmness and consistency, added to his piety and learning, procured him respect and patronage.

1719. An extraordinary meteor seen from all parts of Great Britain about 8 o'clock in the evening. Its light exceeded that of the sun at noon-day. It exploded over the sea near the coast of Britany, at an altitude it is supposed of about 30 miles. It broke like a skyrocket into sparks of red fire, and was succeeded by a tremendous report.

1736. Nicholas Hawksmoor, died; an English architect of fame, pupil of Sir C. Wren.

1755. A cluster of houses in the village of Bergemoletto, near Piedmont, Italy, was overwhelmed by two vast bodies of snow that fell from the neighboring mountain. Three women, the only occupants of the houses at the time of the catastrophy, were dug out alive seven days after.

1759. Nicholas Verdier, a French anatomist, died. His character as an author and a man, are entitled to respect.

1781. Cornwallis retreated from Guilford court house, where he had defeated Greene on the 15th; leaving at the quaker meeting house all the wounded Americans he had taken, and about 70 wounded British officers.

1786. Hugh Pelliser, an English admiral, died. He was at the storming of Quebec; and at the battle of Ushant, 1778, on which occasion a dispute between him and admiral Keppel saved the French fleet from destruction.

1788. Francis Joseph Desbillons, a French Jesuit, died. He devoted many years to study, and at the abolition of his order published his *Fables*, and some other works, and left in manuscript a history of the Latin tongue.

1796. Stephen Storace, an English music composer, died. His productions are confined to the drama, and are remarkable for their spirit.

1797. Gradisca, a strong town in Austria, capitulated to the French under Bernadotte and Serrurier; 3,000 prisoners, 60 cannon and 8 standards fell into the hands of the French.

1801. Novalis, (the literary name assumed by Frederick Von Hardenberg,) died. He belonged to the religious society of Hernhutters.

1808. CHARLES IV, abdicated the throne of Spain in favor of his son Ferdinand VII.

1809. GUSTAVUS ADOLPHUS IV, the deposed king of Sweden, signed a formal deed of abdication. He assumed the title of count Gottorp.

1812. Constitution of the Cortez signed and proclaimed in Spain.

1814. SIMON SNYDER, governor of Pennsylvania, rejected the bill establishing 40 banks. It however became a law, two-thirds of the legislature having agreed to it.

1814. Rheims, in France, taken by the Russians.

1842. First newspaper at Flushing, Long Island.

1853. Nankin taken by the rebels; the Tartar garrison of 20,000 men massacred, except 100, who effected an escape.

1853. Battle of Donabew, Burmah; the British under Gen. Cheape defeated Mea Toon.

1855. An explosion took place in the Midlothian coal pits in Virginia; of fifty persons in the pits 35 were killed and 10 wounded beyond recovery.

MARCH 20.

268. PUBLIUS GALLIENUS, emperor of Rome, assassinated at Milan.

1413. HENRY IV of England, died. He usurped the throne 1399, and thereby excited the civil war between the houses of York and Lancaster, called the war of the roses.

1516. BAPTIST SPAGNOLI, a general of the Carmelites, died. He was a native of Mantua in Italy, and distinguished himself by the sound and virtuous regulations which he attempted to introduce among the corrupted members of his order. His works have been published in 4 vols.

1549. THOMAS SEYMOUR, lord high admiral of England, attainted and beheaded without being heard. His offence was alleged to be equal if not superior in power to his brother the protector.

1586. RICHARD MAITLAND, lord of session in Scotland, died. He reported the decisions of that court till he became blind at about the age of 60; when he commenced writing and collecting Scottish poetry. He sustained the character of "a maist unspotted and blameless judge, and valiant, grave and worthy knight;" but it is in his character of a writer and collector of Scottish poetry that he is now chiefly remembered.

1643. JOHN KIRCHMAN, a learned German, died at Lubeck.

1677. GEORGE DIGBY, an English nobleman of great ability, died. During the civil wars he espoused the cause of Charles I; but though romantically brave, was always an unsuccessful commander.

1687. SAMUEL PARKER, an English prelate, died. He was educated a puritan, but for the reward of place, it is believed, became an anti-puritan and was made bishop of Oxford. He wrote a history of his own times, which appeared in Latin and English.

1727. ISAAC NEWTON, the celebrated philosopher and mathematician, died, aged 84. He was so small and weak at the time of his birth, that his life was despaired of; and in his youth, his mother, finding him of no service in the management of the farm, sent him to finish his studies. From the success of his pursuits in after life, he has been styled the *creator* of natural philosophy. The last few years of his existence were spent in utter neglect of those studies which had engrossed fifty years of his life.

1730. ADRIENNE LA COUVREUR, a French actress, died. She is one of the few of her profession whose reputation has survived the age in which they lived.

1737. NICHOLAS HOOKER, *gentleman*, died at Conway, North Wales; celebrated as being the forty-first child of his father; and being himself the father of twenty-seven children. His tombstone, attesting the above facts, is to be found in the churchyard adjoining Conway castle.

1741. PETER BURMAN the elder died. He was professor of history and eloquence at the university of Leyden, and published editions of many of the Latin classics.

1744. France declared war against England.

1750. The first No. of the *Rambler*, by Dr. Johnson, appeared.

1750. FREDERICK, prince of Wales, and father of George III, died suddenly in his 45th year. He died in the arms of his violin player, who was playing for his amusement.

1767. FIRMIN ABAUZIT, a learned French writer, died. He became distinguished for his superior progress in every branch of polite learning, but particularly in mathematics and natural history; and was consulted in difficult questions by the most learned men of the age.

1775. DANIEL BOONE, employed, in forming a settlement in the then wilderness of Kentucky, was attacked by the Indians, near where Boonsborough now stands, and two of his men killed and two wounded.

1780. Action between the French fleet, admiral Piquet, and 3 British ships, off Monte Christie. The action continued till the next day, when the French suffered so much that they were compelled to lie by and repair.

1792. The French government adopted

the instrument since known as the guillotine; it had been in use in various countries several centuries before.

1793. WILLIAM MURRAY, lord Mansfield, died. He was eminent as a lawyer, and dignified as a judge; as an elegant scholar, of highly cultivated and vigorous intellect, he shone in the constellation of great men which arose in the reign of queen Anne; in eloquence and beauty of diction he outrivaled his predecessors, and has not been excelled by any successor in the high office he held.

1797. Battle of Larvis, between the Austrians and the French under Joubert, in which the former were defeated, after an obstinate battle. Austrian loss, 2,000 k., 4,000 taken.

1799. BONAPARTE opened the siege of St. Jean d'Acre, in Palestine.

1799. Battle of Pfullendorf, in Germany, in which the French under Jourdan sustained the attack of the Austrians under the archduke, who had the advantage in point of numbers and artillery, having no less than 300 pieces.

1800. Battle of Heliopolis, Egypt, in which the French under Kleber defeated the Turks under the grand vizier.

1801. The British, under admiral Duckworth, took the island of St. Bartholomews, in the West Indies. It was again restored on the dissolution of the armed neutrality.

1809. The populace rose and plundered the French in the Havana.

1811. MASSENA gave up the command of his army to Marmont, and retired into France.

1811. Birthday of NAPOLEON, duke de Reichstadt, son of the emperor of France. He was christened emperor of Rome.

1812. JOHN HORNE TOOKE, an English politician, died. He was educated for the ministry, with a great predilection for politics. In 1771 he induced the printers of two newspapers to publish the debates of the house of commons in violation of their rules, which led to proceedings that finally resulted in the defeat of the house, and the practice of those publications ever since. He was a warm opponent of the American war, and was prosecuted for sedition, for the wording of a resolution by which the Constitutional society voted £100 to the relief of the widows and children of the Americans who fell at the battle of Lexington, and was sentenced to a year's imprisonment and a fine of £200. In 1786, appeared his *Diversions of Purley*, which raised him to a high rank as a philologist. His political life ended with the dissolution of parliament, in 1802, and the remainder of his days were spent in the society of his friends.

1814. Battle of Arcis, in which the prince of Wirtemberg defeated the French and captured that place.

1815. BONAPARTE ascended the throne of France on his return from Elba.

1831. The Austrian troops entered Bologna, and in a few days overrun the revolted part of Italy.

1831. Insurrection of the slaves at Antigua. Suppressed on the 25th.

1843. CHARLES G. CORLISS was shot dead in a street near Broadway, New York, by a woman who escaped.

1844. PETER B. PORTER died, aged 71. His name is connected with most of the important events in the history of western New York; and as an officer in the army during the last war with great Britain he rendered important services to his country. He was some time secretary of war of the United States.

1849. NEWTON M. CURTISS, author of a number of novels, died, aged 34. He some time printed a political paper at Ballston, before his talent as a writer of fiction was developed. His subjects were mostly of Indian and revolutionary scenes and incidents.

1853. The French fleet sailed for the Turkish waters, to act against the Russians, if necessary.

1854. Two shocks of an earthquake at Macon, Ga.

1856. DAVID CONNER, a United States commodore, died. He entered the service in 1809, and was wounded in the action between the Hornet and Penguin.

1856. A party of 500 Costa Ricans attacked Col. Schlessinger who commanded 400 of Walker's men, at the hacienda Santa Rosa, and entirely defeated them. Mora had 16 killed and 25 wounded; of Gen. Walker's men 90 were killed and several perished in the woods. The action lasted but 14 minutes. The Costa Ricans shot 19 prisoners.

MARCH 21.

1140. A remarkable eclipse of the sun in England, which caused total darkness.

1491. The new epoch and sacred year of the Jews established, corresponding with the first day of Abib, (Nisan) the day of Pharaoh's overthrow.

1512. JUAN PONCE DE LEON landed in Florida, and claimed the honor of the discovery; although Sebastian Cabot sailed along the coast in 1497. He was led to undertake the expedition by the Indian tradition in Cuba, that in the interior of the country was a spring which made those who drank it young and perpetuated their youth. At a great loss of his men in the swamps and marshes, he penetrated into the interior, but was driven back by the Indians without discovering the miraculous fountain.

1556. Thomas Cranmer, archbishop of Canterbury, burnt for heresy at Oxford. He was born 1489, and educated for the ministry. His first promotion arose from his remarking that the meditated divorce of Henry VIII from his first wife, Catharine of Arragon, might be decided by learned divines without an appeal to the pope. The king, on hearing of it exclaimed "by G—d, the man has got the sow by the right ear!" He was sent for to court, and immediately preferred. On the accession of Mary, he was tried before commissioners, sent from Rome on charges of blasphemy, perjury, incontinence and heresy, and sentenced to be degraded and deprived of office, and finally burnt for the confessions he was induced to make with the hope of pardon. He contributed far more than any other individual to the establishment of the independence of the English church, and was a great patron of learning and the universities.

1604. Peter Ernest, count de Mansfield, died at Luxembourg. He was an able statesman in the service of the emperor of Germany. His conduct was considered so meritorious that he was appointed governor of Brabant.

1639. Thomas Campanelli, an Italian philosopher of great eminence, died at Paris. So great was his learning and eloquence, that his rivals and enemies procured the interference of the inquisition on an accusation of sorcery and magic. He was afterwards put to the rack and condemned to perpetual imprisonment, but found means to escape to France, where he was protected.

1644. Prince Rupert defeated the parliament forces in England, and relieved Newark.

1656. James Usher, archbishop of Armagh, died. He enjoyed a reputation seldom acquired, in every department of knowledge, and received pressing invitations to France and Germany, at a time when his own country was in a state of anarchy, and his property falling a prey to the fortunes of war.

1663. Charlotte Tremouille, countess of Derby, died. She was the wife of the earl of Derby who was treacherously beheaded during the civil war of England, and imitated his heroic conduct by defying the attacks of the parliament forces, and was the last person who submitted to them.

1673. The castle formerly standing at the entrance of Boston harbor, accidentally destroyed by fire. It was constructed of timber, since replaced by a new one of stone.

1676. A hissing, detonating meteor passed over Italy two hours after sunset. Its apparent diameter was greater than that of the moon; its real diameter about three quarters of a mile; and the velocity was calculated at 160 miles a minute.

1684. Nathaniel Highmore, an eminent English anatomist, died. He is the author of the first systematic treatise on the structure of the human body, in the English language, and was indefatigable in the pursuit and improvement of anatomical science.

1733. Stanislaus, king of Poland, sent his abdication by express, to Warsaw.

1766. Richard Dawes, an English scholar, died; celebrated as the author of the *Miscellanea Critica.*

1772. James Nicholas Bellin, a learned and laborious geographical engineer of Paris, died.

1776. The duke of Bridgewater's canal from Manchester to Liverpool completed, a great achievement for the time.

1778. The American ministers, Franklin, Dean and Lee, were publicly received at the French court.

1788. A fire occurred at New Orleans, by which seven-eighths of the city waslaid in ashes.

1797. John Parkhurst, an English divine, died aged 69; well known as a lexicographer.

1797. The French entered Goritz in Austria, where they found 1500 sick, and a great quantity of provisions and stores.

1799. Battle of Asterach, between the French under Jourdan, and the Austrians under the archduke, in which the latter were defeated. Austrian loss 2160.

1800. The Ionian republic, formed under the protection of the porte. Corfu, Zante and other Venitian isles formed the confederation.

1801. Battle of Aboukir, or Alexandria, in Egypt, between the French under Menou, and the British and Turks under Abercrombie. The French were defeated with the loss of 3000 killed, and the standard of the invincible regiment taken, the officer bearing this famous banner being killed, and nearly the whole of those celebrated soldiers annihilated. British loss 1376, and their commander, Abercrombie, mortally wounded.

1803. Edward Marcus Despard, an Irish officer, executed for treason. He was appointed superintendent of the English colonies in the West Indies, where his conduct led to a recall; out of his subsequent treatment grew a desire for revenge, which led him on to his fate.

1804. Duke d'Enghien, shot at Vincennes by torch light. (See p. 104.)

1806. Madison county, New York, was formed.

1815. BONAPARTE entered Paris, the Bourbons having previously evacuated it, on the news of his landing from Elba.

1821. MICHAEL BRYAN, an eminent connoisseur in the fine arts, died. He is the author of a biographical and critical dictionary of painters and engravers.

1829. Duel at London between the duke of Wellington and the earl of Winchelsea.

1829. Great earthquake in the provinces of Murcia and Oriheula, in Spain. Upwards of 20 churches and 4,000 houses destroyed, and great numbers of the inhabitants killed. A considerable portion of the former province was converted into a barren waste.

1839. LOUISA, the last surviving daughter of Linnæus the naturalist, died at Upsala, aged 90.

1843. HERARD, the successful general of the insurgents in Hayti, made a triumphal entry into Port au Prince.

1843. ROBERT SOUTHEY, an eminent English poet, died, aged 68, in a state of mental darkness, from an excess of labor.

1845. BENJAMIN BUSHE died at Greensboro, Vt., aged 115.

1849. BENJ. F. THOMPSON, the historian of Long island, died, aged 64. He was distinguished by an ardent love for historical research, and left a large collection of materials for the illustration of the local history of New York state.

1852. ARMAND MARRAST, one of the leading and ablest journalists of France, died. His name was conspicuous in the revolution of February, 1848, which made him mayor of Paris, and a member of the provisional government. He was the author of the French constitution of 1848.

1856. The fortieth asteroid, named Lætitia, discovered by Mr. Goldschmidt, at Paris.

MARCH 22.

387. THEODOSIUS degraded Antioch, the metropolis of the east, from the rank of a city, and subjected it to the jurisdiction of Laodicea, on account of a sedition.

1270. LOUIS IX, king of France, died. He displayed the magnanimity of the hero, the integrity of the patriot, and the humanity of the philosopher. By his order a translation of the whole Bible was made into French.

1312. The order of Knights Templars suppressed by a papal decree.

1520. LEO X gave permission for the publication of the *Complutensian Polyglott*, a magnificent edition of the Bible, prepared and printed at the expense of Cardinal Ximenes of Toledo. The work was commenced in 1502, and prosecuted without interruption fifteen years, at an expense of more than 50,000 crowns of gold.

1530. Diet of Augsburg, in Germany, at which Melanchton drew up a creed known by the name of the *Augsburg Confession*.

1595. WALTER RALEIGH, in search of the fabulous golden city of Manoa del Dorado, arrived at Trinidad. He had fitted out a fleet at great expense; leaving his ships at Trinidad he proceeded with 100 men in boats 400 miles up the Oronoque; but the river beginning dangerously to swell, he returned without effecting the great discovery.

1621. The colonists at Plymouth received a visit from Masassoit, the greatest king of the neighboring Indians. A league of friendship was agreed upon which was inviolably observed more than fifty years.

1646. Battle of Stowe, in which the royalists under Lord Astley, 3000 in number, were defeated by Col. Morgan. This was the last body of men that appeared on the field for King Charles.

1687. JEAN BAPTISTE LULLY, an Italian musician, died at Paris. He was born of obscure parentage, and at the age of ten was sent by the Chevalier Guise to France as a page to Mad'lle de Montpensier. The lady, however, was so little pleased with him, that she sent him into the kitchen, where he officiated as under-scullion, till his musical talent became accidentally known. From this time he rose rapidly, and contributed much to the improvement of the science of music in France. He is said to have been the inventor of the overture.

1717. MATTHEW HUBERT, an eloquent French preacher, died. His sermons are published in 6 vols. and highly esteemed.

1740. Porto Bello, on the isthmus of Darien, taken by the English under Admiral Vernon.

1758. JONATHAN EDWARDS, the most celebrated of American metaphysicians and theologians, died of small pox, aged 55. There have been three great editions of his works published, one in England and two in this country.

1765. Stamp act passed by the British parliament, the first attempt to tax America without allowing her a representation in the parliament.

1772. JOHN CANTON, an English natural philosopher, died. He was a cloth-weaver, and first devoted his leisure moments to mathematics. He became a member of the royal society, and obtained their gold medal by his experiments on the Leyden phial.

1797. Battle of La Chinse, in Austria.

The French under Guieux drove the imperialists before them until they fell in with Massena at Tarwis and were defeated. The French took 5000 prisoners, 400 wagons and 30 cannon.

1797. The French under Joubert crossed the Adige at Newmark, in Saxony, defeated Gen. Laudohn, entered Botzen, and marched directly for Claufen. The French took 1500 prisoners.

1806. Murat proclaimed at Dusseldorf, "Prince Joachim, duke of Cleves and Berg."

1821. Stephen Decatur, a distinguished American commodore, died at Washington, aged 41.

1828. Louis Choris, an eminent Russian painter and draftsman to Kotzebue's circumnavigating expedition, was killed in company with his traveling companion, near Vera Cruz in Mexico.

1832. The bill banishing the families of Napoleon and Charles X, passed the chamber of peers by a vote of 80 to 30.

1832. John Wolfgang von Gœthe, "the patriarch of German literature," died, aged 83. He early gave indications of genius and a taste for the fine arts; acquired several languages, and made some proficiency in drawing, engraving, &c.; and first attracted attention as an author by the drama of *Gœtz* in 1773, and the *Sorrows of Werther* the next year. The activity and versatility of his genius were prodigious, and his productions amounting to 50 vols., embrace every branch of literature and science. He died at Weimar, quietly seated in his armchair, and apparently without suffering.

1842. Condy Raguet, author of the *Free Trade Advocate*, and many other political productions, died at Philadelphia.

1851. Mordecai Manasseh Noah, for over forty years connected with the press of New York and prominent as a writer and politician, died.

1851. Isaac Hill, one of the most influential political writers in America and for many years editor of the *New Hampshire Patriot*, died.

1851. John Stuart Skinner, editor of the *Plow, the Loom and the Anvil*, died at Baltimore, aged 63. He was the pioneer in the establishment of American agricultural journals, although he had been educated for the law.

1855. Ramon Pinto, an eminent Cuban lawyer, suffered death by the garotte, at Havana, for conspiring to take Concha's life and overthrow the existing government.

1855. The Russians, in a night sortie upon the French lines at Sebastopol, were driven back after a contest of two and a half hours.

MARCH 23.

1208. The pope laid the churches of England under an interdict. King John in retaliation banished the bishops that obeyed.

1534. Clement VIII issued his bull rescinding Cranmer's sentence, and confirming Henry VIII's marriage with Catharine; in consequence of which the pope's authority was abolished in England, and the king declared the supreme head of the church.

1556. Julius III (John Marie du Mont), pope of Rome, died. He is notorious for having dissolved the council of Trent, and is characterized as a weak and narrow-minded pontiff, little calculated to uphold the dignity and power of his office.

1606. Justus Lipsius died; a most acute and learned Flemish critic and commentator on ancient authors. His works were published in 6 vols. folio.

1621. John Carver, first governor of Plymouth colony, died. He was among the English emigrants to Leyden; and when a removal to America was contemplated, he was sent over to negotiate for a suitable territory. He conducted the affairs of the colony with great prudence, and discovered great address in the management of the natives.

1650. The English army commanded by Oliver Cromwell, laid siege to the town of Kilkenny in Ireland. The defence was obstinate, but the garrison surrendered in a few days.

1776. Robert James, an English physician, died; known as the inventor of James' Fever Powders, a preparation which has acquired great celebrity and proved an inexhaustible source of opulence to his family, and benefit to the public.

1776. Congress issued letters of marque and reprisal against England.

1777. The British under Bird landed at Peekskill on the Hudson river for the purpose of seizing the military stores; but on the news of his approach the guard stationed there under Gen. McDougal, fired the principal store houses and retired.

1793. Spain declared war against England.

1797. The French under Dugua entered Trieste, the most important seaport town of Austria; at the same time another French army took possession of the mines of Ydria.

1801. Petrowitz Paul, emperor of Russia, assassinated. He was the son of Catharine II, who treated him with great rigor, during her life. In 1780 he traveled with his wife through the southern part of Europe under the title of *Count of the North*. In 1796 he ascended the throne, and among the first of his acts were the discontinuance of the Persian war, and the liberation of the Poles confined in Russia. But his conduct was suddenly reversed, and his indiscretions and tyranny finally produced a conspiracy among the nobles, by which it is supposed his sons were accessory to his death. In the official publication of his death, it was ascribed to apoplexy.

1806. The exploring party under Captains Clarke and Lewis, left fort Clatsop on their return up the Columbia river to the United States.

1808. MURAT, at the head of 40,000 French soldiers, taking advantage of a faction among the populace, entered Madrid and took possession of it.

1809. THOMAS HOLCROFT, an English dramatic writer, died. His father was a shoemaker in low circumstances, which occupation the son also followed till he resolved to try his fortune on the stage. Besides his dramas he produced several novels and translations from the German and French. He suffered imprisonment for republicanism, with Tooke and others.

1815. Action off the island of Tristran d'Acunha, between the United States brig Hornet, 16 guns, Capt. Biddle, and the British brig Penguin, 18 guns and a 12 pound carronade, 132 men, Capt. Dickinson. Capt. Dickinson was killed and the Penguin captured in 22 minutes; she was so much injured that it was found necessary to sink her. Penguin had 14 killed, 28 wounded; Hornet 1 killed, 11 wounded. After the surrender a British soldier wounded Capt. Biddle in the neck with a musket ball; he was immediately shot by two of the marines.

1819. AUGUSTUS FREDERICK VON KOTZEBUE, a celebrated German dramatist, assassinated at Manheim. *The Stranger* and *Pizarro* are translated and popular at our theatres. His works are numerous. He was assassinated by a fanatical student named Sandt, who at the same time stabbed himself; but recovered and was beheaded.

1840. WILLIAM MACLURE, a distinguished naturalist, formerly of Philadelphia, and twenty years president of the academy of natural sciences in that city, died near the city of Mexico. He wrote on the geology of the United States and the West Indies.

1849. BENJAMIN SIMPSON died at Saco, Maine, aged 94; one of the party engaged in throwing the tea overboard in Boston harbor, at the opening of the revolution.

1849. CHARLES ALBERT, king of Sardinia, in consequence of his defeat by the Austrians, abdicated his crown in favor of his eldest son, the duke of Savoy.

1849. ELIZABETH HUGHES, well known in England as a fortune-teller and familiar with angels, died at Fowdon in her 89th year.

1850. JOHN W. WEBSTER, professor of chemistry in Cambridge university, found guilty of the murder of his friend Benjamin Parkman; a case which excited community for a long time.

1854. A treaty of commerce concluded between Commodore Perry of the United States squadron, and the emperor of Japan.

MARCH 24.

1426 B. C. The 24th Nisan is marked as a feast in the Jews' calendar for the death of Joshua. He was buried, full of honor, on the border of his capital in Mount Ephraim.

1455. Pope NICHOLAS V, the friend of ancient literature and the protector of the learned exiles of Greece, died.

1495. COLUMBUS with an army of 200 men, 20 horses and 20 dogs! commenced a campaign against the natives of Hispaniola, who in consequence of the excesses of the Spaniards had raised an army of 100,000 men to destroy the colony at Isabella. The admiral spent a year in ranging the island; and reduced it to such obedience that every inhabitant was subjected to a quarterly tribute to the king of Spain in gold dust or cotton.

1545. Diet at Worms assembled. The protestants disclaimed all connection with the council of Trent.

1564. PIUS IV issued a bull denouncing the perusal of certain books, and establishing new rules by which to judge books.

1581. JAMES DYER, an eminent English judge, died. He was distinguished for his learning and excellence; a volume of law reports which he left in manuscript and were not published till 20 years after his death, have been often reprinted.

1588 (1580?). Bombs first used at the siege of Wachtendonk in Holland. The invention of bombs is disputed among several countries, and there are good reasons for believing that some contrivance of the kind had been made use of long before this event. Galen, bishop of Munster, is said to have been the inventor of bombs; while Strada in his account of the wars of the Low Countries, attributes the invention a few days before this siege to an inhabitant of the town of Venloo, and that the people of the city, wishing to exhibit it in presence of the duke of Cleves, discharged a bomb, which falling on one of the houses, set fire to it, and three-fourths of the town were destroyed before the flames could be extinguished.

1603. ELIZABETH, queen of England,

died, aged 70. She was the daughter of Henry VIII and Anne Boleyn. On the death of Mary, 1558, she was proclaimed queen, at the age of twenty-five, and held the sceptre forty-five years with uncommon ability. Her reign was a period of great prosperity for England. Her treatment of the queen of Scots can never be defended, and some other foibles tarnish her fame; but the splendor of her reign and the strength of mind displayed in the conduct of the government overbalance those weaknesses which few crowned heads are devoid of.

1638. Canonicus and Miantonimoh gave Roger Williams a deed of Providence.

1645. The parliament voted that the clause for the preservation of his majesty's person should be left out of Sir Thos. Fairfax's commission. This was a bad omen for King Charles.

1674. Jonathan Goddard, an English physician and chemist, died. He was a favorite with Cromwell; but on the restoration his abilities were not in sufficient estimation to preserve him from being disgraced. He was an able writer and a liberal patron of learned men, and one of the promoters of the royal society.

1698. John Evelyn, distinguished as a poet and translator, died, aged 45. At the age of 15 he wrote the elegant Greek poem which accompanies the second edition of the *Sylva*, written by his father.

1718. On the island of Lithy, India, there fell a ball of fire, containing gelatinous matter.

1720. John Peringskioll, a Swedish antiquary and historian, died. He was professor of antiquities at Upsala, and secretary and councilor to the king. His works amount to 17 vols. folio.

1726. Daniel Whitby, an English prelate, died. He was, like many of his profession, totally unqualified for the common pursuits of business; but was engrossed with matters of religion and learning. His publications are more than 40 in number; one of which gave offence to the clergy and was publicly burnt.

1730. The British parliament passed an act prohibiting any subject lending money to a foreigner or other nation.

1740. The English Capt. Knowles took from the Spaniards the castle of St. Lorenzo in South America; a large amount of spoil fell into the hands of the conquerors.

1742. Peter Sabbathier, a French Benedictine, died. He was engaged 23 years in making a collection of the Latin versions of the Bible, which was published 1743 in 3 vols. folio.

1744. War between France and Great Britain declared.

1751. Fredrick, prince of Wales, died.

1754. John James Wetstein, a learned Swiss divine, died. He traveled through several countries of Europe to examine the various manuscripts of the Greek Testament, and on his return to Basel published his *Prologomena;* he was immediately persecuted as a Socinian, and compelled to flee his country. He found protection at Amsterdam, where he died.

1764. Thomas Slack commenced the *New Castle Chronicle*, a paper still well sustained in England.

1773. Philip Dormer Stanhope, earl of Chesterfield, died, aged 79. He was one of the most celebrated wits of his age, an eminent statesman, political, epistolatory and miscellaneous writer. His *Letters*, containing advice to his son, prove him to have been an excellent scholar; but the critical reader will find that they insidiously inculcate the loosest principles.

1773. Stephen Leake, an ingenious writer on coins and heraldry, died at Thorp, England.

1776. John Harrison, an eminent English mechanic, died. He was the son of an obscure mechanic, but made himself famous by the invention of a time-keeper, in the form of a watch, for ascertaining the longitude at sea, for which he received from parliament about $90,000.

1782. Spain acknowledged the Independence of the United States.

1782. A blockhouse situated on Toms' river, New Jersey, attacked by a body of royalists. Capt. Huddy defended the place while his ammunition lasted, and on surrendering was executed without a trial.

1783. Robert Saunders, a self created LL. D., died. His *Notes on the Bible* profited him very little, though in a pecuniary point of view they profited others.

1794. Insurrection of the Poles. The Russian troops evacuated Cracow, and the patriot Kosciusko took possession.

1794. Charles Philip Ronsin, with a number of his *confreres*, guillotined at Paris. The revolution brought him out from obscurity only to display the natural deformity of his character. He was promoted to the office of minister of war, and then to the command of an army. He met his fate at the hands of Danton and Marat, who had raised him up.

1797. Battle in the passes of Eisach in Saxony, between the Austrians under Gen. Laudohn, and the French, who captured 8 cannon and 1500 soldiers.

1801. Paul, emperor of Russia, assassinated. His reign was remarkable for its caprice and eccentricity.

1804. The county of Seneca, in Western New York, formed.

1838. Thomas Attwood, an eminent English musical composer, died, aged 73.

MARCH 25.

1409. The schism of the church was ended by the council of Pisa.

1519. First regular battle of the Spaniards under Cortez with the Indians, on the plains of Ceutla, near Tabasco. The Spaniards were victorious, with the loss of 1 killed and more than 60 wounded. The loss of the Indians was very great; 800 were left dead on the field; the Indians being unable to carry off all their dead, as was their custom.

1595. Snow fell at Rome. There is no other record of such an event occurring there till 1834—exhibiting the curious phenomenon of a space of 240 years without snow.

1609. Henry Hudson sailed from Amsterdam on the voyage in which he discovered the North or Hudson river, and explored it as far as Albany.

1661. The Savoy conference, concerning the liturgy, between 12 bishops with 9 assistants, and a like number of presbyterians appointed by King Charles II.

1678. Ypres, in Belgium, surrendered to the French after a siege of 7 days.

1688. First establishment of charity schools in England.

1693. Printing ordered to be introduced into New York.

1711. Nehemiah Grew, a London physician, died. His merits and skill procured him a very extensive practice; he was also an author on subjects connected with his profession.

1741. The British under Admiral Vernon took the castle of Bocca Chicca, in Carthagena, by assault.

1751. The commencement of the year in England was altered from this day to the first of January, to conform with the custom of other European countries, which had long before adopted the Gregorian calendar. For this purpose there was passed an act of parliament, directing that the year should commence on the first of January, and that eleven days, from the 2d to the 14th September, 1752, should be omitted, so that the 3d of September should be dated the 14th. This occasioned great perplexity and confusion of dates, arising from the computations by the old and new styles.

1754. William Hamilton, an ingenious Scottish poet, died. His pieces are distinguished for liveliness of imagination and delicacy of sentiment.

1761. The first tree cut towards clearing land for cultivation in the town of Bennington, Vt. The honor of the act belongs to Samuel Robinson, who on that day began the settlement of the town. In 1790 it contained 4,000 inhabitants, and by actual return their industry produced 26,000 yards of linen cloth, made in private families from flax of their own raising.

1763. Elias Farneworth, an English prelate, died; distinguished as the translator of Machiavelli and several other European authors.

1792. Lake Harantoreen, in the county of Kerry, Ireland, sunk into the earth.

1792. The British under Gen. Campbell carried by storm the batteries at Port Royal in Grenada.

1793. Hebert, Anacharsis Cloots and 18 others, chiefs of the *Cordelier Club*, executed at Paris.

1799. Florence and Leghorn in Italy, fell into the hands of the French.

1799. Battle of Stockach in Germany. The princes of Furstenberg and Anhalt-Bernburg killed.

1800. The county of Greene, in New York, erected.

1801. The British army in Egypt reinforced by the Turks.

1808. Charles IV of Spain wrote to Bonaparte protesting against his abdication in favor of Ferdinand VII, as having been extorted from him by force, at the same time offering to place himself and the royal family in Bonaparte's power.

1809. Anna Seward, an English poetess, died. She exhibited an early taste for poetry, and her poems were popular in their day, and often republished. She held a correspondence with the literati of her time, and her letters were published in six volumes, octavo.

1810. Bonaparte issued a decree giving liberty to all state prisoners in France, and a free pardon to all deserters.

1811. Battle of Campo Mayor in Portugal, in which the British under Gen. Beresford defeated the French, took 600 prisoners, and drove them to Badajos.

1811. British frigate Amazon destroyed off cape Barfleur by part of the Cherbourg squadron.

1811. Every printing press in Paris obnoxious to Bonaparte, suppressed by the police.

1812. George Frederick Cooke, an eminent English actor, died. He was first engaged as a printer, and afterwards in the navy; but left these for the stage, and acquired a reputation seldom attained, in the highest walks of the drama.

1815. Confirmatory pact signed at Vienna, by which the allied powers solemnly united their forces to maintain the treaty of Paris against Bonaparte.

1815. Richard Dowell, the famed organist at Dulwich college, died.

1820. Alexander of Russia banished all Jesuits from his dominions, because they interfered with the government and the peace of families.

1836. Henry Roscoe died, near Liverpool, England. He was distinguished for his legal and various abilities and learning, and was the author of several professional and other works.

1843. Ceremony of opening the Thames tunnel. Its length is 1200 feet, its cost about two and a half millions of dollars, and it was 18 years in building, under Brunel. The number of persons who visited it during the two following days was about 50,000, at a revenue of one penny each is nearly $1000.

1849. George Cooke, an artist of some note in the south, died of Cholera at New Orleans.

1852. Jane West died, aged 93; a very fruitful authoress, in the beginning of the present century, of poems, tales and novels, long since forgotten, though much in vogue for a time.

1855. An unsuccessful attempt at revolution made in San Domingo with the intent to recall ex-president Paez.

MARCH 26.

1546. Thomas Elyot, an eminent English scholar, died. He published the first *Latin and English Dictionary* in that country.

1602. Bartholomew Gosnold sailed from England in a shallop with 32 persons to effect a colony in the northern part of Virginia. He was the first Englishman who came in a direct course to this part of America, instead of making the circuit by the Canaries and the West Indies. After a passage of 7 weeks they made land in 43 degrees.

1630. Charles I renewed the patent granted by his father to Ben Jonson, as poet laureate. The pension was augmented from 100 marks to 100 pounds, with the grace cup of "one tierce of Canary Spanish wine," to be delivered annually from the royal cellars at Whitehall.

1644. The English parliament made an ordinance to enjoin every family one meal per week, and to contribute the value thereof to the kingdom.

1649. John Winthrop, first governor of Massachusetts colony, died at Boston, aged 63. He came out to America 1630, as governor of the colony; to which he continued to be re-elected, with a few years intermission, till his death. He kept an accurate journal of the events of the early colony from its foundation to the time of his death, two volumes of which were published at Hartford 1790; and the third, which had been a long time lost, appeared in 1826.

1662. Brian Duppa, an English bishop, died. He was distinguished for his learning and virtues, and the firmness of his adherence to the cause of the Stuarts during their misfortunes.

1676. Marlborough, Mass., destroyed by the Indians. So completely did the enemy finish their horrid purposes here, that the inhabitants deserted their dwellings and sought shelter elsewhere. On the following evening a party of about forty men went out in search of the Indians; and coming upon them towards morning lying around their fires to the number of about three hundred, fired in upon them. Although it was so dark at a short distance from the fires that "an Indian could not be discerned from a better man," yet they discharged several volleys upon them, and came off without the loss of one of the band. The few houses which escaped the brand on this occasion were razed by the enemy soon after.

1688. Winston Churchill, an English historian, died; better known as the father of the great duke of Marlborough.

1699. "After an extraordinary storm," says Evelyn, "there came up the Thames a whale which was 56 feet long. Such and a larger of the spout kind, was killed there 40 years ago. *That year died Cromwell.*" The reverend antiquary probably considered this a *prodigious* omen of the usurper's dissolution.

1702. William Courten died; a collector of whatever was curious and important in medallic and antiquarian history. He left 38 vols. folio, and 8 quarto, which together with his collection were purchased for the British museum at £20,000; scarcely the value of the coins and precious stones.

1707. The *regalia* of Scotland deposited in an oaken chest, at the Edinburgh castle.

1711. Engagement between the British ship Lion, 60 guns, Capt. Walpole, and 4 French ships, in which the latter were beaten off. Walpole had his right arm shot off; and it may be mentioned that Lord Nelson had the same sword in his hand when his right arm was shot off, 1797.

1719. A Spanish fleet under the duke of Ormond, intended for the invasion of England in favor of the pretender, was dispersed by a storm.

1726. John Vanbrugh, an English dramatist and architect, died. He was knighted by Queen Anne, and held several lucrative offices; but a want of economy in the management of his income kept him in indigence, and his dramas were produced in rapid succession to retrieve his credit.

Few of his pieces, although popular at the time, still keep the stage.

1729. Robert Moss, a popular London preacher, died. His sermons have been published in 8 vols.; and he is the author of some poems, and small tracts.

1730. The landgrave of Hesse Cassel, father of the king of Sweden, died. The Swedish monarch was declared successor.

1756. Gilbert West, an English poet, died. He was a man of polished manners and great erudition.

1772. Charles Dineau Duclos, historiographer of France, died. He was also a distinguished member of the French academy, and was engaged in the *Dictionary* and *History of the Society*.

1784. Thomas Bond, a distinguished American physician, died. After spending considerable time in preparatory study at Paris, he returned and commenced practice in Philadelphia, where he acquired a great reputation in his profession, and as a man of letters.

1794. Congress passed an embargo law.

1799. Battle of Verona, between the French and Austrians. The battle continued from morning till night, and the loss on both sides was so great, that each army found it necessary to retreat.

1806. Broome county, in New York, erected.

1812. Earthquake in Venezuela, South America; the town of St. Philip with a population of 1,200 souls was entirely swallowed up, and it is supposed that about 20,000 persons perished in the whole province. Caraccas, with a population of 40,000, was destroyed, and from 10,000 to 40,000 persons perished, authorities differ.

1813. The American batteries at Black Rock opened their fire on the British, and silenced their lower battery.

1814. Gen. Hull, tried at Albany by court martial for surrendering Detroit, was found guilty and sentenced to be shot. His punishment was remitted by the president.

1814. Battle of St. Dizier in France, in which Bonaparte defeated Winzingerode.

1814. Engagement in the bay of La Hogue, between the British ship Hebrus and French frigate L'Etoile. French loss, 40 killed, 71 wounded; British 13 killed, 25 wounded.

1832. The Asiatic cholera appeared in Paris. During its prevalence 1 in 33 of the population died. In the whole of France 229,534 persons were attacked, and 94,665 died.

1838. William H. Ashley died near Boonville, Missouri. He was the first lieut. governor of that state, and a man highly respected for his great enterprise, talents, integrity and principle. He emigrated from Virginia at the age of 30, and settled near the lead mines. In 1822 he projected the scheme of uniting the Indian trade of the Rocky mountains with the hunting and trapping business; and having enlisted about 300 hardy men, they, after various successes and reverses, realized handsome fortunes.

1839. Power Le Poer Trench, archbishop of Tuam and primate of Connaught, in Ireland, died. He was distinguished for his talents, eloquence and learning, and greatly revered for his benevolence and piety.

1850. Samuel T. Armstrong, a distinguished American bookseller, died in Boston.

1852. While the engineer Maillefert and his assistants were engaged in submarine blastings at Hellgate, New York harbor, by accident a charge exploded and instantly killed Capt. Southard and 2 others. Maillefert and others were raised several feet, and fell into the water; but were rescued with few injuries.

1854. Jonathan Harrington died, aged 85; a fifer for the minute men who assembled on Lexington Green on the morning of the 19th of April, 1775, and the last survivor of the gallant band who were engaged in that first conflict of the American revolution.

MARCH 27.

47 B. C. Ptolemy Dionysius, king of Egypt, drowned in the Nile. His name is rendered execrable to the latest posterity for the murder of Pompey, his benefactor.

1306. Robert Bruce crowned king of Scotland at Scone. Edward had carried off the national diadem, so that one was manufactured for the occasion, which was placed upcn the head of the liberator by Isabella, countess of Buchan, a descendant of Macduff.

1350. Alphonso II of Castile died at Gibraltar. He is famous for his wars with the Moors, in which 200,000 of them were slain.

1546. John Diaz, a Spaniard, murdered at Neuberg, Germany. He embraced the doctrines of the reformers, and while on a visit to Calvin was met by his brother, who, being unable to reconvert him, hired an assassin to dash out his brains with an axe while in bed at night.

1563. A bill brought into the house of commons, permitting the Bible and church service to be translated into the Welsh or British tongue and used in the church of Wales. The New Testament in Welsh appeared in 1567, in quarto, 339 pages in black letter.

1614. An octroy passed the States General of the United Netherlands, for regulating voyages to America, under which Adrian Block, Hendrick Corstiaensen, and Cornelis Jacobsen Mey, distinguished themselves by their adventures.

1617. Francis Bacon made lord chancellor of England, in place of Ellesmere, who died within a fortnight of his resignation. The new chancellor soon disgusted the public by his vanity, love of show, meanness and corruption.

1622. The Indians, by a preconcerted conspiracy, fell upon the Virginia colony, 347 of whom, unresisting and defenceless, were massacred with indiscriminate barbarity. This massacre was plotted by Opecancanough, and was followed by an exterminating war between the parties.

1625. James VI of Scotland (I of England) died, aged 59. He was the son of Mary and Lord Darnley, and succeeded to the throne at an early age. In 1603 he succeeded to the crown of England, on the death of Elizabeth. It was during his reign that the famous plot was concerted for blowing up the king and parliament. It was also during his reign, and through his weakness; that Walter Raleigh lost his life. He was an encourager of learning, though a pedant himself. The translation of the Bible in present use bears his sanction and authority.

1634. Leonard Calvert, having been appointed governor of Maryland by his brother Lord Baltimore, arrived with two hundred settlers, and settled the town of St. Marys, establishing religious liberty and granting lots of fifty acres to each emigrant.

1654. Monsieur Bourdeaux, ambassador extraordinary from the king of France to Cromwell, arrived in London, and on obtaining an audience, recognized the principle that God shows his love to men by giving them wise rulers.

1660. Tobias Venner, an English physician, died. His medical works were popular, and for talent are above mediocrity.

1669. Mount Trumento formed of an indurated mass of lava by the great eruption of mount Etna.

1676. Battle of Patuxet, between fifty English and twenty friendly Indians under Capt. Pierce, and six hundred of Philip's Indians. The English were drawn into an ambush, or deceived in the force of their enemies, and making an error in drawing down by the side of the river to prevent being surrounded, the Indians crossed over, and galled them from the opposite side, so that they were constrained to fight it out to the last.

1699. Edward Stillingfleet, an eminent English prelate, died. His first work was entitled *Weapon Salve for the Church's Wounds*, which was ably written, notwithstanding the quaintness of the title. His works were principally polemical, and were published in 6 vols. folio.

1710. Sacheverell's two sermons burnt before the Royal Exchange in the presence of the lord mayor of London, and he himself forbid to preach for 3 years.

1718. Mary Beatrix Eleonora d'Este, queen dowager to King James II of England, died at St. Germain en Laye.

1729. Leopold, duke of Lorrain, died. He was noted for his military abilities, by which he recovered his country, and governed his subjects with wisdom and justice. He was also a liberal patron of the arts and sciences.

1756. French burnt fort Bull, Oneida county, New York.

1771. A. McDougal discharged by the supreme court of New York, after having been subjected to imprisonment as the author of a newspaper article signed *A Son of Liberty*.

1778. Nicholas Sebastian Adam, a French sculptor, died. He was the second of three brothers who enjoyed some reputation as sculptors in France in the early part of the last century. His principal works are the tomb for the wife of Stanislaus of Poland, and Prometheus chained.

1782. Caraccioli, the viceroy of Sicily, abolished the inquisition there, and destroyed the archives.

1793. The French Gen. Dumourier, in a conference with Austrian Col. Mack, at Ath, resolved to march back on Paris and establish the constitutional monarchy of 1791.

1794. Jacob Nicholas Moreau, historiographer of France, guillotined at the age of 77. He was also librarian to the queen, an able writer, and attached to the royal cause.

1794. Convention between Denmark and Sweden, for the mutual defence of their rights.

1802. Treaty of Amiens signed between England, Spain, France and the Batavian republic.

1805. The county of Lewis, in northern New York, erected.

1809. Sullivan county, New York, erected.

1809. An eruption of mount Etna.

1811. Battle of Anhalt in the Cattegat strait. The island was attacked by 4000 Danes, who were repulsed by 350 British, with the loss of 5 cannon and 500 prisoners.

1814. Battle of Horse-Shoe, at the bend of the Tallepoosie river, between the United States troops under Gen. Jackson, and the Creek Indians. The latter were defeated with the loss of about 800 killed; U. S. loss 91 killed, 268 wounded.

1829. The zoological society of London in Bruton street incorporated.

1839. All the opium belonging to British subjects in China, amounting to 20,283 chests, valued at about $9,000,000, was surrendered up to Capt. Elliot, superintendent of the British trade, for the purpose of being destroyed, in obedience to the orders of the Chinese government.

1847. Methuselah Baldwin died at Scotchtown, New York, aged 84; he was licensed to preach 1791 by the presbytery of Newark.

1854. William Henry Cavendish Scott Bentinck, duke of Portland, a British statesman, died, aged 84.

1856. N. S. Prime, a New York divine, died, aged 70; known as the author of a history of Long Island.

1857. Charles III, duke of Parma, aged 31, died at Turin of a wound given by an assassin in the streets the night previous.

MARCH 29.

168 b. c. The Roman senate assembled at eight o'clock in the morning, a few days after Paulus Emilius had assumed the immortal consulate. The English house of commons usually sat at the same hour five centuries ago.

193. Publius Helvius Pertinax, emperor of Rome, assassinated. He was of obscure origin, and was elected on the death of Commodus. His virtues were too great for the time in which he lived, and he was destroyed by the same hands which had raised him up; and the imperial diadem was offered at public auction.

1134. Stephen Harding, an Englishman, and one of the founders of the Cistercians, died. In the year 1098, he retired with twenty companions to Citeaux, a marshy wilderness in France, where they founded a monastery. A valuable manuscript copy of the Bible in four volumes, still preserved, attests the assiduity of the monk.

1318. The town and castle of Berwick taken by the generals of Bruce.

1380. Gunpowder is said to have been first used in Europe on this day, by the Venetians against the Genoese. The discovery of the power of powder is attributed to Berthold Schwartz, a monk of Mayence, about 1300, though it is said to have been known in India very early, and obtained from them by the Arabians, who employed it in a battle near Mecca in 690. The use of gunpowder at the battles of Cressy and Poitiers in 1346 is questioned. Rabelais says that the art of printing was invented about the same time by divine inspiration, as a match for the devil's suggestion of artillery.

1480. William Caxton, the first English printer, finished the *Cordial* in folio. The fact is thus set forth in his own words: "*The Book named Cordyale: or Memorare Novissima: which treateth of The foure last Thinges. Began on the morn after the Purification of our blessid Lady* (*2d Feb.* 1478), *&c. And finisshed on the even of thannciacion of our said blessid Lady, fallying on the Wednesdaye the xxiiij daye of Marche In the xix yere of Kyng Edwarde the fourthe.*"

1520. Sanzio Raphael, an illustrious Italian painter and architect, died. He is by general consent called the prince of modern painters, and was probably the best painter the world ever produced.

1636. James Callot, an eminent French engraver, died. He carried the art to a greater state of perfection than any other before him, and attained all that it then seemed possible for human industry to reach.

1638. William Kieft arrived at New Amsterdam as governor of the colony.

1663. At Laucha, near Naumburg, in Prussia, there fell a great quantity of a fibrous substance, represented as resembling blue silk.

1676. The Indians attacked Rehoboth, Mass., and burnt 40 houses and about 30 barns.

1677. Wentzel Hollar, a Bohemian engraver, died. His talents were noticed by Arundel, the English ambassador, by whom he was induced to visit England, where he executed a great number of portraits and views; but though his graver gave celebrity to so many, he was himself the victim of want, and was barely permitted by his creditors to die on his own bed.

1678. James Dixwell, one of the regicides, died at New Haven, Conn.

1678. Claudius Francis Milliet Dechales, a French mathematician, died. His works, published in 3 vols. folio, are a complete course of mathematics.

1741. The British Capt. Knowles destroyed the batteries at Passa Cavallo, Carthagena.

1745. Ventilators, invented by the Rev. Dr. Hales, ordered by the council of England to be introduced into Newgate.

1757. Robert Francis Damiens executed at Paris for an attempt to assassinate Louis XV. He was the son of a poor farmer, and from his vicious inclinations acquired the title of *Robert le Diable.* As the king was getting into his carriage at Versailles, surrounded by his train, Damiens stabbed him in the right side with a knife. He was seized, tried and condemned to a death of torture. Being drawn on a sledge to the Place de Greve, he there had the flesh of his thighs and arms torn off with red hot pincers, and the hand which held the knife cut off. Afterwards his body was drawn and quartered by four horses, his members and corpse burnt and the ashes thrown into the air.

1758. Action in the North Sea between 2 French and 2 British frigates; one of the former escaped, the other was captured with 40 guns and 340 men.

1760. MARGARET WOFFINGTON, an eminent Irish actress, died. Her talents and good sense were greatly aided by extraordinary beauty of features and form.

1778. LOUIS XVI issued letters of marque and reprisal against England.

1783. A hill 500 feet in height was carried four miles from its site by the great Calabrian earthquake.

7191. HONORE GABRIEL RIQUETTI, count DE MIRABEAU, the distinguished French revolutionist but debauched man, died. The French directory decreed a public mourning of eight days; and all the places of amusement in Paris were shut on the day of his death.

1794. J. B. V. GUILLOTINE was beheaded at Lyons. There is some mistake about this event; the authority from which it is derived stating that he was the inventor of the guillotine. (See March 20, and April 25, 1792; also May 26, 1814.)

1794. JOHN ANTHONY NICHOLAS CARITAT, marquis de Condorcet, died. His mathematical essays at an early age procured him a seat in the academy of sciences, of which he was afterwards elected secretary. He published the lives of several eminent men of his day, and was an active contributor to the famous *Encyclopedie*. He unfortunately took part in the revolution, and failing to keep pace with the ultra views of the Robespierre party, was proscribed, and died in prison either from want or by his own hand.

1801. RALPH ABERCROMBY died. He rose from a common soldier, through all the gradations, to the highest rank in the army; was appointed commander in chief of the expedition to Egypt, and landed after a severe contest at Aboukir bay. He was wounded and unhorsed at the battle of Alexandria, notwithstanding which he disarmed his antagonist, and kept the field during the day and was victorious. He was conveyed on board the admiral's ship where he lingered a few days, and died. He was buried beneath the castle of St. Elmo, in Malta.

1802. The planet Pallas discovered by Dr. Olbers, at Bremen. Its revolution round the sun occupies 4 years, 7 months and 11 days.

1805. The county of Jefferson, in northern New York, erected.

1811. A hereditary monarchy established in Hayti, and Christophe declared king by the title of Henry I.

1814. Action in the neutral port of Valparaiso between the United States frigate Essex, Capt. Porter, 52 guns, 255 men, and the British ship Phebe and sloop of war Cherub, in all 81 guns and 500 men. After a most sanguinary conflict of more than 2 hours, the Essex was captured, with the loss of 58 killed.

1818. ALEXANDER SABES PETION, president of Hayti, died. He joined the revolution at the age of 20, and when the blacks had succeeded in gaining their independence, he was appointed governor of the western province, and in 1807 elected president.

1836. RICHARD VALPY, an eminent Greek and Latin scholar, died, aged 82, at Kensington, England.

1838. THOMAS MORTON, one of the most successful of modern dramatists, died at London, aged 74.

1849. The king of Prussia elected emperor by the German parliament at Frankfort. He did not accept.

1852. JOHN HAVILAND, an eminent architect, died at Washington, aged 60. He was born in England, and commenced his career in Russia. He came to this country highly recommended by J. Q. Adams, and constructed many public works. He paid especial attention to the construction of jails and prisons.

1853. A peace address signed by 4000 English merchants, bankers and traders, presented to Napoleon III at the Tuilleries.

1854. War formally declared against Russia by Great Britain and France.

1855. The United States marshal at Philadelphia arrested 12 men who had enlisted in that city for a foreign legion.

MARCH 28.

403. Battle of Pollentia and defeat of the Huns under Alaric their leader.

1069. ABBA'D ABU' AMRU, surnamed the ornament of the state, died; a Moorish king of Seville, who made extensive conquests of the neighboring states, and was an extraordinary character in his day.

1208. Notwithstanding the pope's interdict, King John gave a receipt to the sacrist of Reading, for books which had been in the custody of the abbot of that monastery.

1315. RAYMOND LULLY stoned to death by the natives of Mauritania, in Africa, whither he had gone to convert the Mohammedans, at the age of 80. He was born at Majorca, 1235, and became attached to the gay court of James I of Arragon. He afterwards became the most celebrated chemist and alchymist of his time. At the age of 30 he commenced the study of theology, for the purpose of converting infidels. He went over to Africa to convert the Mohammedan doctors to Christianity, from whence he narrowly escaped with his life. He made a second attempt several years after, which resulted in his banishment from that region; but he returned a third time, and was stoned to death.

1405. Prince JAMES of Scotland, on his passage to France, was seized by an English corsair at Flamborough head, and conducted to the English court.

1461. Battle of Towton, which decided the fate of the houses of York and Lancaster. The battle commenced at break of day in a snow storm, and was maintained with deadly obstinacy till three in the afternoon. It is said 38,000 bodies were left dead on the field, of whom the herald appointed to number the slain, returned that 28,000 were Lancastrians. The duke of York, who won the day, made a triumphal entry into York, where he ordered the death of several prisoners, while Henry who lost his crown, escaped with difficulty to the borders.

1562. PHILIP II of Spain and the Netherlands to prevent the circulation of the scriptures and books favorable to the reformation, issued a placard ordering the officers not only to visit the houses of booksellers, but diligently to watch that no pedler went about with books for sale.

1629. TOBIAS MATTHEWS, an able divine in the reign of James I, died. His talents and worth raised him to the office of archbishop of York.

1644. Battle of Cherington, where the forces of Charles I, 14,000 strong, under Hopeton, were defeated by the parliament forces under Waller.

1672. The test act of England passed, which required all officers of government to receive the sacrament according to the church of England.

1675. A large body of Indians attacked the town of Providence, R. I., and burnt 29 houses. The records of the town were partially saved by being concealed in a mill pond. The town did not recover from this disaster in more than sixty years.

1689. THEOPHILUS BONET, a noted Swiss physician, died. He spent several years at the best universities of Europe, in the study of his profession, and became eminently successful. He published several medical treatises in his old age, valuable in their day, for the facts and observations which they contained.

1710. HENRY BASNAGE, a French lawyer, died at the Hague. He was a member of the parliament of Rouen, who upon the proscription of the protestants fled to Holland.

1726. JAMES PIERCE, an eminent English divine, died. He was attached to a congregation of presbyterians; but becoming an Arian was expelled from the desk.

1730. VINCENT HOUDRY, a French Jesuit, died, aged 99. He was an eloquent preacher, and his writings comprise about 30 vols. His last moments were embittered by the reflection that he could not be permitted to reach his 100th year!

1751. THOMAS CORAM, projector of the foundling hospital, died. He was captain of a colonial trading vessel, and was prompted to this charitable project, by frequently seeing children exposed in the streets of London by the cruelty of their parents. He persevered in this humane design 17 years, and at last obtained a charter by his sole application. He was accustomed to spend so much of his time and money in charitable services, that in his old age he was dependent upon the charities of others, when his principal benefactor was the prince of Wales.

1772. EMANUEL SWEDENBORG, founder of the New-Jerusalem church, died in London, aged 84. His father was a Swedish Lutheran bishop, and the son received a scientific education, and became eminent as a mathematical and philosophical writer, was ennobled, and shared the favor of the king. From the pursuit of philosophy he subsequently turned his attention to heavenly things, and became equally celebrated for his mystical reveries. His followers have multiplied in Europe and America since his death.

1792. GUSTAVUS III, king of Sweden, died. He succeeded to the throne 1771. His reign was a turbulent one, in which all the arts and stratagems to which he was obliged to resort, scarcely secured him in power. He formed a plan for uniting Sweden, Russia, Prussia and Austria, with himself at the head of the confederacy. While he was maturing his plans, a plot was formed among his nobility for assassinating him. A masquerade at Stockholm was chosen for the perpetration of the deed. He was shot in the back by Ankerstroom, a disbanded officer.

1796. LA CHERETTE was executed; this closed the Vendean or civil war at the commencement of the French revolution.

1797. The Mohawks relinquished all their claims to land in the state of New York.

1799. The legislature of the state of New York passed a law for the gradual abolition of slavery in that state, providing that every child born of a slave after the fourth of July in this year, should be free at the age of 28 if a male, and 25 if a female.

1807. The planet Vesta discovered by Dr. Olbers. Its revolution is completed in 3 years, 66 days and 4 hours.

1809. Oporto, in Portugal, taken by the French under Soult, and pillaged in spite of that general's endeavors to prevent it.

1814. BONAPARTE had his head quarters at Troyes, from whence he moved by forced marches to Paris, by the road of Sens.

1815. BONAPARTE abolished the slave trade in the French dominions.

1829. The castle of Rumelia in Turkey surrendered to the Greek army under Capo d'Istria.

1837. The *Akhbar Vekai*, (News and Events) the first Persian newspaper, made its appearance at Teheran. It consisted of two closely written and lithographed pages, one devoted to oriental, the other to foreign intelligence. Its conductor had been an envoy to London, whence he carried home with him and executed the idea of a newspaper—the most efficient missionary for the spread of civilization and intelligence the world has ever known.

1844. E. PENDLETON KENNEDY, of the United States navy and commander of the battle ship Pennsylvania, died at Norfolk, Va.

1848. JOHN JACOB ASTOR, founder of the Astor library, died in New York, aged 80. He was a native of Germany, and during a residence of nearly 60 years in America, amassed a fortune of about twenty millions of dollars. He landed in this country with a trifling sum in his pocket, and early commenced business as a trader in fur, and when the state of New York was a wilderness, made frequent voyages up the Mohawk, to trade with the Indians. As his wealth increased, he enlarged his business until by the formation of the American Fur Company, he was a competitor with the great capitalists of Europe, the proprietor of the North Western and Canadian fur companies. Such was his enterprise, that he extended his business to the mouth of the Columbia river and formed the first fur establishment there, known as Astoria. Several expensive expeditions were fitted out by him, of overland journeys, to the Pacific, some of which were executed by individuals with great suffering. For many years previous to the war of 1812, and subsequently, Mr. Astor was extensively engaged in the Canton trade, and during the war was so fortunate that several of his ships arrived here with valuable cargoes in safety. The profits on those ships were enormous. Mr. Astor made large investments in American stocks, which he purchased duing the war with Great Britain, at sixty to seventy cents on the dollar, and which after the peace, went up to twenty per cent. above par. His great estate, however, accumulated more from the purchase of real estate, than from any other source.

1849. The Lahore war being finished, the Punjaub was formally annexed to the British crown.

1849. LOURIANA THROWER died in Georgia, aged 137. Her sight had failed, 20 years before her death, but returned, so that she could read the finest print, and her faculties remained almost unimpaired.

1853. The jail at Chesterfield, S. C., destroyed by fire, and 8 prisoners burned.

1853. A democratic conspiracy discovered at Berlin, in Prussia, and 86 persons arrested.

MARCH 30.

1756 A. M. The ark of Noah grounded on the 17th of 2d month, Marchesvan (corresponding with this date), after the waters had prevailed upon the earth 150 days, (*See Nov.* 2.)

317 B. C. PHOCION, the Athenian general, executed by poison. He was of an obscure family, and rose by his own merits. He was placed at the head of the Athenian armies 45 times, and on all occasions displayed great ability; nor was he less illustrious for his virtues. Yet neither his virtues nor his services could shield him from the malace of his enemies, and he was condemned on a false accusation of treason.

1280. HUGH BALSAM, bishop of Ely, endowed his foundation of Peterhouse, the first college in the University of Cambridge.

1282. Massacre of 8,000 French by the people of Sicily. It began at Palermo as the bell was tolling for evening service, and hence it has taken the quaint title of the *Sicilian Vespers.*

1296. Berwick, on the borders of Scotland, taken by assault by the English under Edward I, and about 17,000 of the inhabitants put to the sword.

1323. A truce for 13 years concluded at Thorpe, between Edward II, who had been recently defeated at Biland Abbey, and Robert Bruce.

1327. EDWARD III, then newly inaugurated, in his fifteenth year, convoked his splendid and gallant rendezvous at York, of 60,000 men at arms, including 500 belted knights, animated by the presence of the queen mother, and fifty ladies of the highest rank, to revenge the breach of the treaty made by the Scots with his father.

1363. EDWARD III first distributed the Maunday for the purification of the poor.

1587. RALPH SADLER, an English statesman, died. He filled some of the highest offices of state under Henry VIII and Elizabeth, with ability.

1601. Henry Cuffee, celebrated for his wit, learning and misfortunes, was executed at Tyburn. An epigram alluding to his Greek, says:

Thy alpha was crowned with hope,
Thy omega proved but a rope.

1612. John Wower, a distinguished German politician and literary character, died at Gottorp.

1621. John King, an English prelate, died. He was chaplain to Queen Elizabeth, and so popular a preacher, as to acquire the title of "the king of preachers." Coke declares him "the best speaker in the star chamber of his time."

1638. John Davenport, a celebrated preacher of Coleman street, London, and several of his followers, having purchased of the natives all the lands lying between the rivers Connecticut and Hudson, sailed from Boston for Quinnipiack, now New Haven. The colony was organized under a tree, and they agreed to be governed in civil matters by the laws of God until they could make better!

1647. Mutiny in the parliamentary army on account of arrearages of pay due to the soldiery, many of them having twelve months' pay due.

1669. William Somner, an English antiquary, died. He was indefatigable in his researches, and acquired the old Gaelic, Irish, Scotch, Danish, Gothic, Saxon, and other northern dialects, that he might with greater accuracy and success develop the records of ancient times. He published a Saxon dictionary and some other works.

1707. Sebastian le Prestre, seigneur de Vauban, a celebrated French engineer, died. He was taken prisoner in the service of Spain, and persuaded to enter the French army, in which he distinguished himself by a most unexampled career. During his life he had been engaged in 140 actions, conducted 53 sieges, assisted in repairing 300 ancient citadels, and erected 33 new ones. His publications were principally on fortifications, and he left 12 large volumes in manuscript, containing observations, thoughts, &c., which he called his *oisivétés* (idlenesses).

1756. Stephen Duck, an English poet, committed suicide. He was a persevering character, entirely self taught, and his poems were above mediocrity. The queen bestowed upon him a pension, which enabled him to take orders, and he obtained "a living;" in which office he sustained himself with credit. Notwithstanding his good fortune, his spirits became depressed, and he was led to cut short his existence by throwing himself into the Thames.

1761. At Tregony, in Cornwall, was discovered a coffin 11 feet 3 inches long, 3 feet 9 inches deep, inclosing a skeleton of gigantic size.

*1781. Mutiny disclosed on board U. S. frigate Aliance, Capt. Barry, on return from France to Boston. The plot was disclosed by an Indian named Mahomman, on the eve of its being carried into effect. It was intended to murder the officers and take the ship to England or Ireland. This was the second mutiny in the service, the first having occurred on the same vessel, two years before (see Feb. 3d). The third was seasonably disclosed on board the Somers in 1842.

1783. William Hunter, an eminent British anatomist, died. He was educated at the University of Glasgow, and in 1746 established himself in London as a teacher of anatomy, where he distinguished himself; and his works on medical subjects, which appeared at short intervals, added to his reputation. He built an anatomical theatre and museum, and ultimately collected there a library of Greek and Roman classics, and a valuable cabinet of medals, now deposited in the university of Glasgow.

1793. The English under General McBride took possession of Ostend in France.

1796. The French army under Beaulieu entered the Genoese territory.

1798. Ireland declared in a state of rebellion, and orders issued for disarming the United Irishmen, and all disaffected persons, by the most summary and effectual measures.

1799. Second battle of Verona (March 26). The French under Moreau were again successful, but the division under Scherer having being beaten again by the imperialists were obliged to halt to cover the main body of the army.

1800. Action between the French ship Guilleaume Tell, Admiral Dacres, 84 guns, 1000 men, and three British ships of 180 guns, Capt. Berry. The Frenchman was the last ship of the Nile fleet that remained uncaptured, and was taken after a most determined resistance, with the loss of 200 killed. British loss, 101; among the wounded was Capt. Berry.

1801. Jail liberties for the first time established in the state of New York, and prisoners entitled to the benefit of them, on giving a bond and sufficient sureties to the sheriff, that they would remain true and faithful prisoners, and not at any time or in anywise escape.

1806. Joseph Bonaparte proclaimed king of Naples.

1810. Luigi Lanzi, a modern Italian archeologist and writer on art, died of apoplexy.

1813. The prince regent of England notified to foreign ministers in London, that effcient measures had been pursued to place New York, Delaware, Port Royal, Charleston, Savannah, and the river Mississippi in a state of blockade.

1814. Battle of La Cole Mills, Canada; Gen. Wilkinson was repulsed with the loss of 13 killed and 123 wounded; British loss, 13 killed, 45 wounded.

1814. The allied army after a sanguinary resistance from Marmont, and Mortier, advanced to the gates of Paris, and offered terms of capitulation, which were agreed to.

1834. Rudolph Ackerman died; the originator of the British annuals, and the first to introduce the lithographic art into England, and lighting by gas into London.

1844. Thorwaldsen, the sculptor, buried at Copenhagen with regal honors; the king and princes and chief officers of state acting as mourners, followed by troops and processions of the different guilds and orders of citizens, and a concourse of thousands. The streets were lined with soldiers as at a royal funeral; and the queen and princesses attended the service in the church. At the end of the ceremony, the king headed a subscription for a monument on a magnificent scale by the regal donation of $25,000.

1849. General Haynau assaulted Brescia, which, after great slaughter, was taken and sacked.

1854. A fight took place 12 miles from Loar, between a company of 60 dragoons under Lieut. J. W. Davidson, and a party of nearly 300 Apache and Utah Indians. The dragoons lost 21 killed and 18 wounded; the Indian loss unknown.

1856. Treaty of peace between the French, English, and Turks on one side, and the Russians on the other, signed at Paris.

MARCH 31.

32 B. C. Titus Pomponius Atticus, a distinguished Roman, died. He understood the art of conducting himself so well, that amidst the civil wars and party strife of the time in which he lived, he preserved the respect and esteem of all parties. He reached the age of 77 without sickness; but finding himself at last attacked by a slight disease, he resolved to put an end to his life by abstaining from food, and expired in five days.

1474. The first book printed in England finished by Caxton as appears by the following entry: "*The Game and Playe of the Chesse;* translated out of the French and emprynted by William Caxton. Fynished the last day of Marche, the yer of our Lord God a thousand four hundred and lxxiiij."

1547. Francis I of France died. He was the rival and opponent of Charles V of Germany, with whom he was involved in war during almost his whole reign, with various success, and to whom he was once a prisoner, with his two sons. He was a patron of literature and the arts.

1605. An expedition fitted out by the earl of Southampton and Lord Arundel, under the command of George Weymouth, sailed from the Downs with a view to the discovery of a north-west passage to India, the passion for which was now in its full vigor.

1621. Philip III of Spain died. He ascended the throne of his father at the age of 20. The war with Holland, which had revolted, was continued with great spirit, and the siege of Ostend maintained three years, at great expense, and the loss of 80,000 men before it was reduced. He imprudently banished the Moors from his kingdom, and thus deprived himself of a million of peaceable and useful artists; a loss which the country has never recovered from.

1631. John Donne, an English poet and divine, died. He embraced protestantism at an early age, which together with his shining talents, procured him favors and emoluments. Dryden styles him "the greatest wit, though not the greatest poet, of the nation," and his eloquence as a divine is also attested to.

1654. Cockfighting prohibited in England by the parliament (called an act of the usurpation).

1656. James Usher, archbishop of Armagh, died, aged 76. He was advanced by James I and Charles I, and courted by Cromwell.

1665. The English authorities issued an order to imprison George Fox, the founder of the sect called Quakers, for his sermons against the awful crime of building meeting houses with steeples.

1698. Peter Joseph d'Orleans, a French Jesuit, died. He professed belles-lettres, and wrote several valuable histories and biographies.

1713. Peace of Utrecht concluded, which placed England at the head of the European states, and humbled the ambition of France.

1763. Mr. Harrison was granted £5,000 for the construction of a chronometer to determine with more accuracy the longitude at sea.

1765. The Jesuits expelled from Madrid and all Spain. The order was finally suppressed by the pope, 1773.

1774. The bill for closing the port of Boston received the royal assent.

1783. Nakita Ivanowitz, count de Panin, a Russian statesman, died. He was raised from the rank of a horse soldier, under Elizabeth, became a general under Peter, and prime minister of the great Catharine. He possessed great powers of mind, and other qualifications for the high places which he occupied, but his business habits were lax, his conduct haughty, and his manners dissolute.

1791. Matthias Ogden, a revolutionary patriot, died. He was one of the first that joined Washington at Cambridge; he penetrated the wilderness with Arnold to Canada, and was wounded in the attack on Quebec. On his return he was promoted by congress, and remained in the army through the war.

1794. The national convention of France, in the plenitude of omniscience, decreed *that there was no God!*

1795. The British museum purchased the oriental manuscripts of Mr. Halstead, the disciple of the prophet Brothers.

1797. Daniel Bull Macartney, an Irish gentleman, died, aged 112. He married his fifth wife, who survived him, at the age of 84, when she was 14, by whom he had 20 children in 20 years. His constitution was so hardy that no cold affected him, and he could not bear the warmth of a sheet in the night time for the last 70 years of his life. In company he drank freely of rum and brandy, which he called *naked truth;* and retained his activity to the time of his death.

1797. Bonaparte, from his head quarters at Klagenfurth, offered peace to the archduke Charles.

1801. The island of Santa Cruz, in the West Indies, surrendered to the British under Admiral Duckworth. It was afterwards restored.

1806. George Macartney, a celebrated British statesman, died. He was employed in several important embassies and other offices, till in 1792 he was selected as ambassador extraordinary to China, a mission which occupied three years, and engaged much attention in Europe; and an account of which has been published in 3 vols. quarto by Sir G. Staunton.

1807. Slave trade abolished by the British government.

1812. Wells, the pedestrian, undertook for 5 pounds, to walk from Westminster bridge, London, to Croydon and back, in two hours, a distance of 19 miles. He performed it in 2 minutes less than the time, but dropped down with fatigue, and was unable to walk home.

1813. Battle of St. Antonio, Mexico, between the royalists and patriots. The former were defeated with the loss of 100 killed, their camp equipage, 6 cannon, and great quantities of stores, &c.

1814. Paris capitulated to the allied army, about 2 o'clock in the morning, and the French troops evacuated it at 7, hostilities to commence in 2 hours. At 11, the conquerors entered the city with the emperor of Russia and the king of Prussia at their head.

1827. Ludwig Von Beethoven, a German musical composer, died. His works are numerous, and universally known and admired. His musical talents procured him wealthy patrons among the nobility, by whom he was munificently supported. He was extremely deaf, and eccentric in his manners.

1831. Edward Augustus Holyoake, a venerated New England physician, died, aged 100. He was born at Salem, Mass., 100 years after its settlement, and was a practicing physician there 79 years. He enjoyed uninterrupted good health during life, and at a dinner given by a number of the profession on his centennial anniversary, he appeared among them with a firm step. On a post mortem examination, all the vital organs appeared to have been unimpaired by age and capable of sustaining life much longer, except the stomach, which was divided by a stricture, leaving an aperture less than an inch in diameter.

1831. Battle of Praga, between the Poles under Skrzynecki, and the Russians of 8000 under Geismar, in which the latter were almost totally destroyed, with the loss of 4000 prisoners and 1600 cannon.

1831. An Irish scholar and divine, Rev. Hynes Halloran, chaplain to the Britannia in the battle of Trafalgar, was transported for seven years, for forging a frank, value 19 pence.

1835. John Whitcomb, a soldier of the revolution, died at Swanzey, N. H., aged 104.

1836. Matthew Lumsden died; an eminent orientalist.

1837. The president at interim of Mexico protested "in the most solemn manner, before all civilized nations, against the acknowledgment of the pretended republic of Texas made by the United States."

1839. Battle of Pago Largo in South America, between the troops of Corrientes and Entre Rios, two provinces of the Argentine republic. The former were defeated with a loss stated at 1960, including the commander-in-chief.

1851. John Caldwell Calhoun, one of the most distinguished American statesmen, died, aged 68, a senator from South Carolina.

1852. Tremont Temple, Boston, entirely destroyed by fire.

1854. THOMAS NOON TALFOURD, an English judge and dramatist, died, aged 57. He cultivated literature as a refreshing relief from the labors of his profession. He died while charging the jury.

1854. Gen. CANROBERT and more than 1000 French troops landed at Gallipoli.

1854. The artisans of Barcelona, Spain, to the number of 1500 proceeded to the municipality and demanded that the price of provisions should be reduced and wages increased.

APRIL.

APRIL 1.

168 B. C. EMYLIUS PAULUS passed from Brundusium to Corcyra (the modern Corfu) on his famous Macedonian expedition, and on the 6th, sacrificed at the shrine of Delphi.

1386. JAMES AUDLEY, an English warrior, died. He distinguished himself under Edward III in the wars with France, and on their return was liberally rewarded by his sovereign for the deeds of heroism he had displayed in the service.

1405. TAMERLANE, chan of the Tartars, died. He is supposed to have been the son of a shepherd, and raised himself by his courage and prudence to the sovereignty of nearly three quarters of the world. He was preparing for the invasion of China when death put a stop to his career at the early age of 36.

1506. ERASMUS was entertained at London by the great and learned men of the day.

1614. HENRY DE MONTMORENCY, constable of France, died. He distinguished himself in several famous battles. Catharine de Medici found means to disgrace him, when he retired to Savoy, and made successful war upon his country. He lived to be promoted to the highest office under the king.

1672. ARCHIBALD ARMSTRONG, privileged jester or fool of Charles V, died. There is a little book high priced and of little worth entitled *Archibald's Jests.*

1696. Pere GERBILLON, the Jesuit missionary (see May 30th), accompanied the imperial Chinese army into Tartary, in the suite of the emperor, being his fifth journey into that country.

1696. JOHN BIGG, an English hermit, died, aged 97. He begged pieces of leather, which he nailed to his clothes, till he became a truly grotesque figure. One of his shoes is preserved in the Bodleian museum, and is made up of about a thousand patches of leather.

1712. Lord BOLINGBROKE stated in parliament, that in the great contest, called "the glorious wars of Queen Anne," the duke of Marlborough had not lost a single battle, and yet the French had carried their point, the succession to the Spanish monarchy, the pretended cause for so great an enterprise. Dean Swift called this statement "a due donation for *all fools day.*"

1720. JOHN LEAKE, an English admiral, died. He fought against the far famed Van Tromp, but the battle at La Hogue most distinguished him.

1729. The grand jubilee began at Rome.

1732. JOHN BURCHARD MENCKE, a learned German author, died at Leipsic, where he had conducted the *Acta Eruditorum* 25 years, a valuable work begun by his father in 1682, and which established a correspondence with the learned men of Europe.

1764. An annular eclipse of the sun was observed at London.

1764. At Monmouth assizes a girl, aged 18, was burned for murdering her mistress. This was among the last punishments by burning in England.

1775. Col. DANIEL BOONE, the Kentucky pioneer, began to erect the fort of Boonsborough, at a salt lick, 60 yards from the Kentucky river.

1779. JOHN LANGHORNE, an English poet and divine, died. Besides poems, sermons and miscellanies, by which he is favorably known, the translation of Plutarch in common use bears his name.

1789. First meeting of congress under the federal constitution.

1794. The British under Sir John Jervis took the island of St. Helena.

1794. JOHN LEWIS LOMBARD, a German professor of artillery, died. He wrote several works on the movement of projectiles and the principles of gunnery.

1797. The French under Bernadotte entered Lauback, the capital of Carniola. At the same time Massena, commanding the advance guard of the French army, attacked the imperialists in the defiles near Neumark; the strife being between the flower of the Austrian army and the French veterans of Italy, was most obstinately contested. The French, however, carried the day.

1799. Assault upon the works of St. Jean d'Acre, in Palestine. The French were repulsed with great loss.

1808. Russian ukase prohibiting the introduction of British goods into the Russian ports.

1810. State marriage of Napoleon Bonaparte with the archduchess Maria Louisa of Austria celebrated at St. Cloud. The emperor caused a medal to be struck on the occasion, with the singular device of Love bearing a thunderbolt.

1826. Isaac Milner, an English mathematician and theological writer, died. He was brought up to the weaving business, but occupied his leisure with the classics and mathematics. He was the tutor of Wilberforce and Pitt.

1832. War broke out between the Winnebago and other Indian tribes and the United States.

1832. The London *Penny Magazine*, under the superintendence of the society for the diffusion of useful knowledge, commenced.

1833. John Hooker Ashmun, professor of law in Harvard university, died. He had not attained his 33d year, yet he had gathered about him all the honors which are usually the harvest of a riper life.

1837. Robert Hawker, an English divine, died at Plymouth, England. In 1814 he published the holy scriptures in penny numbers for the use of the poor.

1843. John Armstrong, aged 84, died at Red Hook, N. Y. He was the author of the celebrated *Newburgh Letters*, and a prominent soldier in the war of the American revolution, and for some time secretary of war under President Madison.

1844. Peter S. Duponceau so favorably known as a scholar and statesman, died at Philadelphia, aged 84. In his 78th year he published his *Dissertation on the Chinese Language*.

1853. Santa Anna arrived at Vera Cruz, having been elected president of Mexico by the vote of 19 out of 25 states.

1856. Isaac McKeever, an American commodore, died at Norfolk, Va., where he commanded the navy yard.

1856. The Emperor Alexander published at St. Petersburg a proclamation announcing the signing of the treaty of peace with England, France and Turkey which terminated the struggle between Russia on the one side, and England, France and Turkey on the other, and prolonged the salvation of the latter country.

APRIL 2.

1081. Constantinople besieged by Alexius Commenus.

1507. Francis, of Paula, founder of the order of Minims, died.

1512. Florida discovered by Ponce de Leon.

1594. A skirmish at Edinburgh between the earl of Bothwell and the cavalry of King James.

1640. Matthias Sarbieuski Cassimir, a Polish Jesuit, died. He was so excellent a Latin poet that his poems have been thought to be equal to some of the best Latin authors, not excepting Horace and Virgil. He had begun an epic in the style of Virgil, called *The Lesciades*, but died before it was completed. Many editions of his poems have been published.

1640. Paul Flemming, one of the best German poets of the 17th century, died.

1683. William Penn gave his colonists in Pennsylvania a new charter.

1696. There fell in many parts of Ireland a thick dew, which the country people called butter, from the consistency and color of it, being soft, clammy, and of a dark yellow. This phenomenon had for some time been of frequent occurrence; it fell always in the night, and chiefly in moorish low grounds, on the top of the grass, and on the thatch of the cabins. It frequently lay a fortnight without changing its color, and had a bad odor, like that of church yards or graves.

1698. The earl of Bellemont arrived at New York to succeed Fletcher as governor.

1736. Jacob Tonson the elder, a noted English bookseller, died.

1743. Birthday of Thomas Jefferson, third president of the United States.

1747. John James Dillenius, a German botanist, died in England. He is considered as the father of cryptogamic botany. His works were illustrated with plates, admirably drawn and engraved by himself.

1754. Thomas Carte, an English historian, died. He was engaged several years in writing a history of England, which was published in four vols. folio, and esteemed a work of great merit.

1755. Severndroog castle, on the coast of Malabar, the rendezvous of the celebrated pirate Angria, taken by the British under Com. Jones.

1768. John Baptist Boyer, a French physician, died. He distinguished himself by the skill which he displayed during the plague at Marseilles.

1784. County of Washington, in the state of New York, erected.

1791. Honore Gabriel Riquetti, count de Mirabeau, the French revolutionist, died. He was an extraordinary character, of great talent and ambition, but whose genius was controlled by the worst propensities. He was the master spirit of the revolution, and had he lived might have given it a different character. His funeral was conducted with great pomp by the enthusiastic populace.

1793. Dumouriez, the French general, arrested the minister of war and the commissioners of the convention, who had been sent to arrest him, and delivered them to the Austrian general, Clairfait.

1794. The British took the island of St. Lucia, in the West Indies, belonging to the French. It was ceded to the British in 1814.

1794. William Jones, a distinguished oriental scholar, died in India.

1801. Battle of Copenhagen, between the Danish and British fleets, the latter under Nelson and Parker. The Danish ships and batteries were entirely destroyed, with the loss of 1600 men killed and wounded. British loss, 254 killed, 689 wounded. Nelson was created viscount on his return home, and his honors made hereditary, even in the female line.

1804. Jean Mossequin died at Portieu, in France, aged 103. He was married the day before to his ninth wife, Marie Vascois, aged 19. He left twenty-nine children.

1817. Mrs. McCowen, aged 77, died at Lewistown, Pa. She was one of the first white women that came up the long narrows to that wilderness which is now a fruitful field.

1817. Kosciusko abolished servitude in his domain of Siechnowieze, in Poland, and declared his ancient serfs free, exempted from all charges and quit-rents, and fully entitled to their chattels and lands.

1821. Erie county, New York, erected.

1823. First paper in Syracuse.

1839. Hezekiah Niles died, at Wilmington, Delaware, aged 63. He is known as the founder, and for twenty-five years the intelligent and laborious editor of *Niles's Weekly Register*, a valuable journal published at Baltimore. In private life he was one of the most amiable of men.

1840. Richard Phillips, a self-educated English author, and editor of various publications, died, aged 73. His original name is said to have been Philip Richard, and he was many years an eminent London bookseller. He established the *Monthly Magazine*, which at one time had a great circulation. He was afterwards elected sheriff, and received the honor of knighthood.

1855. George Bellas Greenough, an English geologist, died, aged 77. He was one of the founders of the Geological society, of London, and constructed several valuable maps, the most celebrated of which is a geological and physical map of all India, giving the geological attributes of each district between the plateaux north of the Himalaya and cape Cormorin.

APRIL 3.

13. Augustus, emperor of Rome, signed his will, bequeathing to the Roman people 40,000,000 sesterces, (about $1,600,000,) and divorced the two Julias, his daughter and grand-daughter, from his sepulchre. It was written upon two skins of parchment.

33. Jesus Christ, our Savior, crucified.

68. Galba accuses Nero before the people of his enormities, and elects himself lieutenant of the state.

1068. William, the conqueror, again imposes the tax of Danegelt which occasioned an armed opposition at Exeter.

1143. John II (*Commenus*), emperor of the East, died. He ascended the throne of Constantinople on the death of his father; was victorious over the Mohammedans and other foes; and swayed the sceptre with wisdom and ability.

1367. Battle of Navarette, and victory of Edward the black prince, by which Peter the cruel was replaced on the Castilian throne.

1421. Battle of Beauge, in France, when the duke of Clarence and 1500 English were slain.

1617. John Napier, baron of Merchiston, died. He was born in Scotland, in 1550, and after completing his education traveled on the continent. On his return he devoted himself to the cultivation of science and literature, became a distinguished mathematician, and was regarded by Kepler as one of the greatest men of the age. He is known as the inventor of logarithms for the use of navigators.

1646. Thomas Lydiat, an English chronologer, died. He early devoted himself to literature, became an able scholar, and was deservedly esteemed by the learned of the times.

1707. Edmund Dickinson, a learned English physician, died. He was appointed physician to Charles II and his successor; and retired from practice to become an author.

1717. James Ozenham, an eminent French mathematician, died. He taught mathematics at Paris, and acquired property; but the Spanish war reduced his finances, and the death of his wife and twelve children embittered his last days. His works are numerous and valuable.

1736. JOHN ALBERT FABRICIUS, a learned German, died at Hamburgh. He was an indefatigable scholar, of great modesty and simplicity of manners, and so highly esteemed by the citizens of Hamburgh, that when invited elsewhere, the senate prevailed on him by a superior salary, not to relinquish his residence among them.

1760. JAMES BENIGNUS WINSLOW, an eminent Danish anatomist, died. He went to Paris, where his talents were appreciated and rewarded.'

1763. All the gibbets on the Edgeware road, on which many malefactors were hung in chains, near London, were cut down by unknown persons.

1764. The archduke JOSEPH chosen and crowned king of the Romans.

1775. New York colonial legislature held its last session.

1783. Treaty of amity and commerce for fifteen years between the United States and Sweden concluded by Franklin.

1791. JOHN BERKENHOUT, a literary and medical character, died. He was the son of a Dutch merchant, and experienced many vicissitudes; first served in the Prussian and afterwards in the English army; studied medicine at Leyden; and in 1778 came with certain commissioners to America, where he was imprisoned by congress, on which account he enjoyed a pension from the British government.

1792. GEORGE POCOCKE, an English admiral, died. He signalized himself by the capture of Havana, and many other important services.

1793. DUMOURIEZ, the French general, who escaped from the lines, under the repeated fire of three battalions, joined the Austrians, accompanied by several other officers.

1811. Partial action on the Coa, near Sabugal, between the advanced posts of the British, and a division of the French army under Massena, who was defeated, and the French expelled from Portugal.

1813. Action near Urbanna, on the Chespeake, between 17 British barges and 2 schooners, and 3 letters of marque and 1 privateer of Baltimore; the latter were captured.

1814. The French conservative senate solemnly decreed that Bonaparte had forfeited the throne, and released all persons from their oaths of allegiance to him.

1815. Eruption of mount Tomboro, on the island of Sumbawa, distant about 800 miles from Batavia, in the Indian Ocean.

1816. Treaty of peace concluded by Lord Exmouth, commanding a British fleet before Algiers, between the Dey and Sardinia, and 51 Sardinian prisoners liberated.

1816. THOMAS MACHIN, an officer of the revolution, died at his residence in Schoharie county, N. Y., aged 72. He was a British officer at the battle of *Minden*, and an American officer during the whole war of the revolution. The chain across the Hudson at West Point was constructed under his direction, and he was wounded at Bunker Hill and Fort Montgomery.

1826. REGINALD HEBER, bishop of Calcutta, died. He was zealous in his calling, and no doubt accelerated his death by his devotion to the cause of his master. He ranks high among the British poets.

1829. Safety banking fund in the state of New York established.

1833. NICHOLAS IPSILANTI, an officer of the Greek revolution, died, at the age of 35.

1838. M. ANTOMARCHI, physician of Napoleon at St. Helena, died at St. Jago de Cuba. He was a native of Corsica, and left a professorship at Florence, in order to accompany the exiled emperor. He attended him in his last moments, of which he has given an account, and received a legacy of 100,000 francs. He afterwards practiced medicine in Paris, where he published a series of beautiful and expensive anatomical plates. On the revolt of the Poles he hastened thither, and took the direction of the medical establishments.

1854. JOHN WILSON, a Scottish author, died, aged 69. He is well known as the Christopher North of *Blackwood's Magazine*.

1856. GORHAM A. WORTH, a New York financier, died, aged 72.

1856. President COMMONFORT returned to the city of Mexico after a triumph at Puebla, where the rebel army surrendered to him, and where the rebel generals were reduced to the rank of privates.

APRIL 4.

357. B. C. A transit of the moon over the planet mars observed by Aristotle.

397. AMBROSE, archbishop of Milan, died. He was famous for the zeal which he manifested in the cause of the church, and the severity with which he censured the emperor Theodosius, who had barbarously ordered several innocent persons to be put to death at Thessalonica. The *Te Deum* is attributed to him.

1284. ALPHONSO X, of Castile, died. He was elected emperor of Germany 1258, but neglecting to visit the empire, Rodolphus was chosen in his place. He was dethroned by his own son, and compelled to seek protection among the Saracens. His fame as an astronomer and a man of letters, is greater than as a monarch. He is the first Castilian king who had the public laws and the scriptures drawn in the vulgar tongue.

1581. DRAKE, the navigator, was knighted on board his famous ship, the Pelican, at Deptford.

1588. FREDERICK II, of Denmark, died. He was a liberal and enlightened ruler, who enlarged the happiness of his people and patronized learning. The astronomer Tycho Brahe, particularly, was indebted to him for munificent protection and advancement.

1589. Lady BURLEIGH, eldest daughter of Sir Anthony Cooke, and a highly distinguished literary character, died, aged 63. This age was prolific of literary women.

1593. Three Samuels of Warboys condemned for bewitching the children of Mr. Throgmorton at Huntington, England.

1594. SYLVESTER WYET, of Bristol, England, made a voyage up the gulf of St. Lawrence, for the barbs or fins of whales and train oil. He met with 60 sail of French, and 28 sail of Englishmen, engaged in fishing at this early day.

1634. ROBERT NAUNTON, an English statesman, died. He was secretary of state to James I, and published some curious anecdotes of the reign of Elizabeth, under the title of *Fragmentia Regalia.*

1638. Massachusetts patent demanded. A quo warranto having been brought by the attorney general of England against the governor and corporation of Massachusetts, and judgment given that the liberties and franchises should be seized into the king's hand, the council made an order requiring that the charter should be returned by the next ship. Arbitrary measures were pursued in reply to the petitions of the colony, and 8 ships prepared to sail for New England were detained in the Thames by order of the privy council. By this order, Oliver Cromwell, Arthur Hazelrig, John Hambden and other malcontents, were forcibly prevented from emigrating to America. How little did Charles anticipate that by this high-handed measure he was detaining the very men who were destined to overturn his throne, and terminate his career by a violent death.

1643. SIMON EPISCOPIUS, an able Dutch divine, died. He embraced the doctrines of Arminus in relation to predestination, which exposed him to much persecution and obloquy, and finally led to his banishment from the commonwealth: he afterwards was permitted to return, and became minister of the remonstrant church. His death happening at the moment of an eclipse of the moon, was considered as an emblem of the departure of the brightest ornament of the church.

1656. ANDREW RIVINUS, (alias Barchmann) a Saxon physician, died. He became professor of poetry and philosophy at Leipsic, and published several works of considerable merit.

1669. JOHANN MICHAEL MOSCHEROSCH, a German writer, died. His celebrity consisted chiefly in some satirical pieces entitled *Wunderliche und wahrhafte Geschichte Philanders von Sittewald.*

1704. The first newspaper printed in the United States, appeared at Boston, called the *Boston News Letter.*

1706. JOHN BAYLES, an English buttton-maker, died, aged 130. He used to walk to the neighboring markets with his buttons till he was 120 years of age.

1720. KNIGHTLY CHETWODE, dean of Gloucester, died. He wrote several poems, and a life of lord Roscommon.

1743. ROBERT AINSWORTH, an English teacher, died. In 1714 he was invited by the English booksellers to undertake the compilation of an English and Latin dictionary, on the plan of Faber's *Thesaurus.* The task proved to be more difficult than had been anticipated, and was not completed till 1736.

1747. Number Four (Charlestown, N. H.) attacked by a large body of French and Indians under M. Debeline, and gallantly defended by 30 men, under major Stevens. The enemy kept up a brisk assault night and day; when, on the third day, being in a starving condition, and finding it impracticable to force or persuade a surrender, they retired and were seen no more. This was considered one of the most chivalrous feats of the time.

1764. MICHAEL LOMONOZOF, a Russian poet, died. From the occupation of a fishmonger he rose to be the "father of Russian poetry," and a philosopher of no mean pretensions. He published a history of the Russian sovereigns, and an ancient history of Russia, from the origin of the nation. His odes are greatly admired for the originality of invention, sublimity of sentiment, and energy of language.

1769. HYDER ALLY, the adventurous East India chief, compelled the English to form a treaty with him.

1770. JAMES PARSONS, an eminent English physician, died. He was the correspondent of Buffon and other learned characters on the continent, and an able writer on physic, anatomy, natural history, antiquities, language, and the fine arts.

1774. OLIVER GOLDSMITH died, aged 46. He received a partial education at Dublin college, after which he strayed from home, and making a tour on the continent, afoot and alone, with a flute in his hand, fixed himself, on his return, in London, as a *builder of books.* The details of his life are interesting, chequered as they are with vicissitudes. As a bookseller's hack he was particularly successful; but the liberality of his disposition and want of economy, contributed to keep him in want, and sometimes brought him to starvation. He died about £2,000 in debt. His works, though most of them were produced on the spur of the moment, to procure the necessaries of life, are still found in almost every library.

1777. JOHN SWINTON, an English antiquary, died. His literary productions, which are numerous, appeared originally in the Philosophical Transactions, and relate principally to antiquities.

1786. Columbia county, in the state of New York, erected.

1793. General DUMOURIEZ, accompanied by General Valance and young Egalite (Louis Philip), afterwards king of France, narrowly escaped to the Austrians.

1794. Battle of Raclawice, Poland, between the Russians and 4,000 Poles under Kosciusko, mostly armed with scythes. The battle lasted five hours, and ended in the defeat of the Russians, who left 3,000 killed on the spot.

1795. BARRERE a lawyer, VARENNES a monk, COLLOT DE HERBOIS a comedian, and VADIER a counsellor, members of the French convention, sentenced by a decree of that body to be transported to Guiana. Barrere was president of the convention, and as such passed sentence of death upon the king; and they all voted for the king's death.

1799. Battle of Tauffers and St. Marie, in Germany. The French under Jourdan lost upwards of 4,000 men, and fell back to the heights of Villengen.

1802. LLOYD KENYON, an English judge, died. He filled the offices entrusted to him with distinguished integrity, and to him England is indebted for much of that reform which has been introduced into the practice of the law.

1807. JOSEPH JEROME LA FRANCAIS DE LALANDE died at Paris, aged 70. He received a minute religious education, and displayed his abilities while quite young by his sermons and mystical romances. His attention was first drawn to astronomy by the remarkable comet of 1744; and he pursued the study with so great success that he was sent to Berlin by the academy at the age of 19, to make some observations on the moon's parallax, when Frederick the Great could not conceal his astonishment at the phenomenon of so young an astronomer. He became editor of the *Connaissance des Temps*, published several works on astronomy, and wrote all the astronomical articles for the great *Encyclopedie*. In 1778 he published a folio volume on canals, containing a general history of all the ancient canals which had been previously undertaken, accomplished and even projected. Although a sceptic, he is said to have been "religious, in his own way."

1809. The legislature of Pennsylvania passed a law directing the poor to be sent to the most convenient school and their tuition paid.

1812. Congress passed an embargo law for 90 days.

1814. Bonaparte having received the opinions of his marshals abdicates the imperial throne in favor of his son, only to be succeeded the next day by a relinquishment in favor of his heirs also.

1815. Hostilities between France and the allied powers ceased. Alexander I, in the name of the allies, recommended Bonaparte to choose a place of retreat for himself and his family.

1817. ANDREW MASSENA, prince of Essling, one of the ablest of Bonaparte's field marshals, died. He commanded in chief in the memorable campaign in Switzerland; when at the battle of Zurich he had to contend against the archduke Charles and prince Suwaroff; yet the fruits of this campaign were 70,000 prisoners. He ended his military career in 1810, by the command of the army of Portugal, where he was defeated by Wellington.

1831. ISAIAH THOMAS, a distinguished American printer, died. He was born in Boston, 1749, served an apprenticeship of 11 years, and commenced business at a very early age at Newburyport. In 1770 he printed the *Massachusetts Spy* at Boston, where he annoyed the provincial officers by the boldness and freedom of his articles on the difficulties that agitated the country. He was also one of the most active and dexterous of the skirmishers on the plains of Lexington. A few days after that affair he removed his paper to Worcester; and gradually established presses and bookstores in different parts of the Union, to the number of twenty-four; so that he nearly supplied the entire country with books. His Bibles, school books and almanacs, were in great repute for a long time. He was the founder of the American antiquarian society, and author of the *History of Printing in America*, a valuable work to the profession and the antiquary.

1841. WILLIAM HENRY HARRISON, president of the United States, died at Washington, aged 69. He was a distinguished patriot of the revolution, one of the signers of the declaration of independence, governor of Virginia, and long a leader of the United States armies in the severe contests with the British and Indians.

1855. The Baltic fleet, fitted out by the French and British governments to act against the northern ports of Russia, sailed from Portsmouth.

APRIL 5.

2348 B. C. The ark of Noah rested on mount Ararat.

347 B. C. PLATO, the Athenian philosopher, died. He was the pupil of Socrates, and on the death of his master went into foreign countries in search of knowledge. His works have come down to us, and confirm the opinions of his contemporaries by whom his talents and learning were highly appreciated.

33. The day of our Savior's resurrection called Easter.

1242. Battle of lake Peipus, in Russia; the Russians under Alexander Jaroslawitz gained a decisive victory over the Swedes under Eric XI. The battle was fought on the ice; 400 Teutonic knights were slain, and 50 made prisoners. The German knights were pardoned, but the Esthonians were ordered to be hung as Russian rebels.

1470. An instrument similar to a warranty deed given to William Tourneville, bishop of Angers, with a copy of Faust and Schoeffer's Bible for the sum of 40 crowns, bears this date.

1605. JOHN STOW, an English antiquary and historian, died, aged 80. He was born in London, 1525, and initiated by his father into all the mysteries of tailoring as practiced at that period. But he discovered a penchant for musty relics and antiquarian lumber, and finally quitted his business to compose a history of England. He at length got together such a medley of antique and diabolical books and parchments, that he became suspected of some heretical designs against religion, so that the bishop of London ordered an investigation of his library. He published *A Summarie of the Englyshe Chronicles*, and in 1598 a *Survey of London*, on which he was long employed, and which has been often reprinted. He was reduced to live by charity, and at length fell a victim to poverty and disease. His labors formed a rich legacy to future historians.

1621. JOHN CARVER, first governor of Massachusetts, died. He conducted the colonists over from Leyden, and managed the affairs of the settlement with great prudence and address.

1676. JOHN WINTHROP, first governcr of Connecticut, died. He was the eldest son of the governor of Massachusetts, and a man of great learning and talents. He was one of the founders of the Royal society, distinguished as one of the greatest chemists and physicians of the day, and one of the most noted men in New England. In 1635 he came over to settle a plantation on Connecticut river, and began the town of Saybrook at the mouth of that river.

1677. Cambray, a fortified city of France, surrendered to Louis XIV, who commanded in person.

1684. WILLIAM BROUNCKER, an English mathematician, died. He is celebrated for his attachment to the royal cause during the civil wars. On the institution of the Royal society, he was the first president, and adorned the office by his polite manners and extensive erudition.

1707. Battle of Almanza, in Spain; the allied British, Dutch and Portuguese army defeated with the loss of 1000, attributed to the bad conduct of the Portuguese troops.

1725. BENJAMIN IBBOT, an eloquent English divine, died. A selection of his sermons was published after his death by his friend Dr. Samuel Clarke.

1735. WILLIAM DERHAM, an able English philosopher and divine, died. He accomplished much in the advancement of science by a long life of industry; his publications amounting to not less than 40, mostly on philosophical subjects.

1746. THOMAS HANMER, an English statesman, died. He was for 30 years a distinguished member of Parliament, from which he retired to devote himself to literary pursuits.

1748. Unsuccessful attempt by the British under admiral Knowles on St. Jago de Cuba.

1753. Parliament passed an act to raise £20,000 by lottery to purchase the library of Sir Hanse Sloane, of his daughters, for the public use. It formed the basis of the British museum.

1758. The first number of Johnson's *Idler* appeared.

1762. Granada surrendered to the British.

1776. GRAINGER, vicar of Shiplake, and author of the *Biographical History of England*, died suddenly while administering the sacrament.

1779. The refugees plundered Nantucket and carried off with them two loaded brigs, and several other vessels.

1780. ALEXIS HUBERT JAILLOT, a French geographer, and sculptor to the king, died.

1790. ELIZABETH WELSH died at New York, aged 104.

1794. GEORGE JAMES DANTON, a French revolutionary leader, guillotined. Robespierre, dreading the dauntless intrepidity of Danton, Fabre d'Eglantine, Bazire, Chabot, and others of the most noted of his fellow desperadoes in the convention, caused them to be arrested as conspirators against the republic, and after a summary trial, they were executed by the guillotine on this day. The government of France was now almost entirely vested in one man, under whose sanguinary administration the prisons of Paris contained at one time more than seven thousand persons, and a day seldom passed without sixty or eighty executions by the revolutionary axe.

1794. MARIE JEAN HERAULT DE SECHELLES, a French statesman, guillotined. He conducted before the revolution as an able and upright officer; but as the scene progressed he became identified with the terrorists, and went to the scaffold with Danton, Desmoulins, (q. v.) and others. The two conducted with as much levity in their last moments as if they had been going to a party of pleasure.

1794. BENEDICT CAMILLE DESMOULINS, one of the founders of the Jacobin club in France, guillotined. He was the friend of Danton, and one of the most bloody and reckless of the revolutionists. When arraigned by order of Robespierre, he was asked his age, to which he replied "33 *ans, l'age du sans culotte Jesus Christ.*" His wife, whom he adored, a beautiful, courageous and spirited woman, desired to share her husband's fate, which Robespierre seems not to have been slow to grant.

1795. Treaty of peace concluded at Basle, Switzerland, between France and Prussia.

1795. County of Schoharie, in New York, erected.

1797. The first Turkish ships arrived at London.

1799. The British forces under Gen. Harris, called the Madras army, arrived at Seringapatam, within Tippoo Saib had retreated after the defeat of Seedasere.

1799. Battle of Villingen and Rothweil in Germany; the French under Joubert defeated by the Austrians under the archduke Charles.

1800. British captured Goeree; admiral Duckworth's squadron on the same day, fell in with and captured two Spanish frigates and eleven merchantmen from Lima. The admiral's share of the spoil amounted to £75,000.

1804. ROBERT RAIKES, an English printer and philanthropist, died. He succeeded his father in the printing business and having realized a good property, he employed it, with his pen and his influence, in relieving such objects as stood in need of his benevolent assistance. He is however best known as the originator of sabbath schools.

1811. HENRY I (Christophe), king of Hayti, created an hereditary nobility, consisting of 4 princes, 7 dukes, 21 counts, 9 barons and chevaliers, and appointed persons to those ranks.

1811. JAMES TRAQUAIR died; the first man in America who procured busts to be carved in American marble. They were likenesses of Washington and Penn, and executed by an Italian.

1814. BONAPARTE accepted the island of Elba as his residence, and renounced for himself and heirs the throne of France.

1815. Continued eruption of Tomboro, which began April 3. (See April 12.)

1817. Battle of Maypu, which sealed the independence of Chili. The patriots under San Martin and Las Heras defeated the royalists, 5000, under Osorio; 2000 were killed and 2500 taken.

1830. The bill to remove the civil disabilities of the Jews introduced into the British parliament.

1832. Ratification of the treaties of commerce, navigation and limits, between the United States and Mexico, exchanged at Washington.

1837. HENRY BATHURST, bishop of Norwich, died in London, aged 93. He was distinguished for the liberality of his principles, and was exemplary in the exercise of his duties—the father of 36 children, 22 by his first wife, 14 by his second.

1842. PATRICK KELLY died at Brighton, England. He is well known for his valuable writings on science, but his great work the *Universal Cambist* entitles him to lasting distinction.

1843. VALNIER, a native of St. Domingo, died at Merida, Yucatan, aged 117. He retained his sight until the age of 105, and his intellect was unimpaired till the time of his death.

1844. JOHN SANDERSON of Philadelphia, who wrote an account of the lives of the signers of the declaration of American independence, died. He had some reputation for wit.

1852. FELIX VON SCHWARTZENBERG died at Vienna, aged 52. He represented the Austrian empire at various courts, at different periods, the earliest being at the age of 15. In a military capacity he took the field in 1843 against Charles Albert of Sardinia, and half a year later succeeded prince Metternich, on his fall, as prime minister of the empire.

1853. A new planet was discovered by Prof. de Gasparis, at Naples.

APRIL 6.

323 B. C. ALEXANDER (*the Great*,) of Macedon, died of intemperance. The death of this famous hero took place at Babylon, on the 6th day of the Athenian month Thagelion, which then corresponded with the 28th of the Macedonian month Dæsius. He lived 32 years and 10 months, and

reigned, computing from the Olympiad six months prior to the death of Philip, 12 years and 10 months—a brief career of extraordinary, but profitless glory.

1190. Richard I (*Cœur de Lion*), killed at the siege of Chalus, in France. He commenced his career by rebellion against his father. On ascending the throne of England, he plundered and massacred the Jews, and set sail for Palestine with the bravest of his subjects. Taking the lead in the crusade, he gained a series of victories over the Moslem. On his way home he was seized and imprisoned, and ransomed by his subjects with 150,000 marks. He was preparing for another crusade, when his career was suddenly terminated by a wound from a cross-bow, in the 42d year of his age.

1348. Laura de Noves, Petrarch's mistress, died. She was descended of a Provencal family which became extinct in the 16th century, inherited a large fortune by the death of her father, and married Hugh de Sade of Avignon. She was considered the most beautiful woman of the city. Petrarch says it was 6 o'clock in the morning of the 6th April, 1327, that he first saw her in the church of the nuns of St. Clara; and it was at the same hour of the same day, 1348, that she died of the plague. Nearly two centuries after, some antiquarians obtained permission to open her grave. They found a parchment enclosed in a leaden box, containing a sonnet bearing Petrarch's signature.

1453. Mohammed II besieged Constantinople, which terminated in the overthrow of the Christian empire.

1528. Albrecht Duerer, a celebrated German painter and engraver, died. He is still esteemed in Germany as one of the brightest jewels in her crown of fame. He was the reformer if not the founder of the German school of painting, and was the first to bring the art of engraving to any degree of perfection.

1574. Paul Manutius, a learned Venetian printer, died, aged 62. He wrote valuable commentaries on Cicero, and four treatises on Roman antiquities.

1580. Earthquake which was felt throughout England. The bells rang, and chimneys toppled down.

1590. Francis Walsyngham, an English statesman, died, aged 90. He flourished in the reign of Elizabeth, and was of infinite service to the state, by the energy and zeal with which he performed the duties of his offices. Yet he died so poor that his remains were privately buried by night, without any ceremony.

1609. Henry Hudson departed from the Texel on his famous voyage of discovery, the object of which was to find a northern passage to India. Meeting with obstructions he determined to attempt a north-west passage; and this also being attended with disasters, he shaped his course south along the American continent, and discovered the noble river which bears his name, and gave him immortality.

1645. William Burton, an English antiquary, died. He published a history of the county of Leicestershire, which is valuable.

1655. David Blondel, a French protestant minister, died. He had the misfortune to lose his sight by close application to study, but even under that calamity he dictated two folio volumes on the genealogy of the kings of France. He was a man of great learning.

1686. Arthur Annesley, earl of Anglesey, died. He was a statesman of great ability, sagacity and learning, under Charles I.

1695. Richard Busby, a celebrated English schoolmaster, died. He was educated by the bounty of the parish, and became head master of Westminster school, which place he held during half a century. He educated most of the eminent men who flourished about the period of his death. They regarded him as a father, though a severe one.

1707. William van der Velde (the younger), a Dutch painter, died. He was an admirable artist, distinguished for his excellence in marine subjects, painted in black and white, on a ground so prepared on canvas, as to give it the appearance of paper. It is said he has had no equal in his line.

1717. James Perizonius, a German professor at Leyden, died. He published various works in Latin, on history, classical literature and antiquities; and was a man of extensive erudition, great application and sound judgment.

1739. The workmen at Stocks market, England, disinterred a grave stone with antique letters, supposed to have been buried 297 years.

1743. William Melmoth, (the elder,) a learned English lawyer, died. He is better known by a treatise on religious life, of which immense editions have been published.

1751. Frederick, king of Sweden and landgrave of Hesse Cassel, died.

1755. Richard Rawlinson, an English antiquary, died. He was an indefatigable collector, and made himself useful to his cotemporary antiquaries in the completion of their works. The sale of the printed books and pamphlets of his library occupied 60 days.

1760. Charlotte Charke, the last surviving daughter of Colley Cibber, died.

1776. Action between the British ship Glasgow, of 20 ninepounders, and her tender, Capt. Howe, and American brigantine Cabot, 20 nines and 10 sixes; Columbus, 18 nines, 10 sixes; Annodine brig, 6 guns, and Providence sloop, 12 sixes, under Com. Hopkins. The British made the attack, and continued the engagement 3 hours, when the tender was captured, but the Glasgow escaped.

1793. The French army evacuated Antwerp and Mons in Belgium, and retreated towards Valenciennes and Lisle.

1794. The French took Oneglia, in Sardinia, where they captured 2 frigates and a few galleys.

1796. David Allan, a Scottish painter, died. He practiced history, portrait and landscape; but exercised his talents chiefly on works of humor. Some of his pieces have been engraved.

1796. David Campbell, a Scottish divine, died. He was professor of divinity at Aberdeen, translated the gospels, and answered Hume on the miracles.

1799. Clayton Mordaunt Cracherode, an English antiquary, died. He was a man of great wealth and literary attainments, and his library and cabinet was one of the most select and valuable in the kingdom. His immense collection of books, medals, drawings, &c., &c., he bequeathed to the British museum.

1804. Charles Pichegru, the French general, died. He was born 1761, of poor parents, educated in a monastery, and was a tutor of Bonaparte at Brienne. He came to America with a French regiment near the close of the revolution. At the outbreak of the revolution in France he distinguished himself so much that he rose to be the first in command, and achieved a series of most brilliant and important victories, which resulted in the conquest of Holland. He was detected in a plot for the restoration of the Bourbons, which cut short his career, and he died in prison by strangulation.

1808. Corner stone laid of the vault prepared for the relics of the American seamen, soldiers and citizens, who perished in the British prison ships at the Wallabout, during the war of the revolution.

1810. Three days' rioting commenced in London on account of Francis Burdett's budget.

1811. French privateer Revance de Cerfe, burnt at Norfolk, Va. She was fired by 15 men in 2 boats, at about 2 A. M.

1812. Badajos, in Spain, taken by storm, at ten at night, by the British and Portuguese troops under Wellington; loss of the allied army 4000; the defence made by the French governor was brave, determined and noble.

1813. Lewistown, Delaware, cannonaded about 20 hours by the British frigate Belvidere. The defence was conducted in such a manner that but little injury was done.

1814. The French provisional government proposed, and the conservative senate adopted the form of a constitution; a limited monarchy, founded on the French and American constitutions, and declared Louis XVIII king.

1815. The American prisoners in Dartmoor prison fired upon by their guard, and many of them killed and wounded. The prince regent pointedly disapproved of their conduct, censured the officers and soldiery, and offered to make provision for the widows and families of the sufferers; this, however, was rejected by president Madison.

1829. Henry Nicholas Abeel, one of the most acute mathematicians of the present age, died.

1831. Revolution in Brazil. Don Pedro abdicated in favor of his son, who was proclaimed Don Pedro II.

1853. The Mexican Governor Trias issued a proclamation at Chihuahua, relative to the possession of the Mesilla valley, threatening to resist the occupation of New Mexico by the United States.

1855. An asteroid was discovered by M. Chacornac, at the imperial observatory of France.

1856. The constitution of the new state of Deseret was established by a people's convention at Salt Lake city, Utah territory.

APRIL 7.

1118. Baldwin I, king of Jerusalem, died, and was buried on mount Calvary. He accompanied his brother, Godfrey de Bouillon, to Palestine during the crusades, and on the death of Godfrey was made king.

1141. Maud declared queen of England in a national synod.

1196. William Longbeard, a factious priest, executed. He was notorious for raising seditions in London, during the reign of Richard I. He was torn to pieces by horses, and then hung upon a gallows.

1498. Charles VIII, (*the affable*,) king of France, died. He was crowned king of Naples, and emperor of Constantinople, but afterwards met with reverses, and was driven back into France.

1521. Magellan erected the Spanish standard on one of the Phillipine islands.

1656. Jerome Bignon, a French statesman, died. He was born 1590, and his attainments were so rapid that at the age of 10 he published a description of Palestine, and at the age of 14 a treatise on the election of the popes.

1668. WILLIAM DAVENANT, an English poet and dramatist, died. He succeeded Ben Jonson as poet laureate, and obtained a patent for a theatre in Lincoln's Inn fields, which was in operation a number of years.

1684. Dublin castle in Ireland burned.

1710. THOS. BETTERTON, the actor, died. He was esteemed the greatest master of tragic action in his time.

1710. EDWARD CODRINGTON died at Barbadoes. He was a native of the West Indies, and distinguished himself by his learning, and by his courage in defence of the British islands against the French.

1712. RICHARD SIMON, a French critic and historian, died. His works are numerous, and evince extensive learning and strong judgment.

1766. TIBERIUS HEMSTERHUYS, a Dutch critic, died. He was appointed professor of mathematics and philosophy at Amsterdam at the early age of 19, and is the author of several learned works.

1776. CHARLES PETER COLARDEAU, a French poet, died. He translated a part of Pope and Young with great spirit and elegance, and also wrote for the stage.

1780. ROBERT WATSON, a Scottish historian, died; author of *Philip III of Spain*.

1785. First paper issued in Hudson, Columbia county, New York.

1786. The celebrated catacombs of Paris consecrated, with great solemnity. They lie under a part of the city which was undermined some centuries ago, to furnish stone for the ancient edifices of Paris, and at length became closed up. This cemetery had been used more than a thousand years by twenty parishes, and it is estimated that more than three millions of people had been inhumed within its inclosures. In process of time, as the city extended, palaces and churches were built over the subterranean caverns, and were in imminent danger of sinking into the pit below, before it was again discovered. The mighty city of Paris had until now but one burial place, where a pit was dug, and the bodies laid side by side, without any earth being put over them, till the first tier was full; then a thin layer of earth covered them, and another tier of dead came on; thus by layer upon layer, and dead upon dead, the hole was filled up. These pits were emptied every thirty or forty years to receive new tenants. The last grave digger, Francis Pontraci, had by his own register, in less than thirty years, inhumed more than 90,000 bodies in that ground. The great increase of burials rendered the cemetery still more inconvenient, and it was at last happily thought of converting the quarries under the city into a receptacle for the dead.

1788. The first settlement in Ohio began, at Marietta, by 47 persons from New England.

1789. PETER CAMPER, a Dutch physician and naturalist, died. He was distinguished for the extent of his knowledge. A splendid edition of his works was published in 6 vols. accompanied by 100 folio plates.

1789. ACHMET IV, one of the most enlightened of the Turkish rulers, died. The first act of his successor Selim was the execution of the grand vizier, on the pretext that he had occasioned the loss of Oczakov.

1796. The British squadron under Warren captured 3 French brigs and 1 sloop, laden with provisions.

1797. Suspension of arms between Napoleon and the Archduke Charles.

1797. WILLIAM MASON, an English poet, died. He was chaplain to the king till the American war, when his name was erased from the list in consequence of the sentiments he entertained in regard to the liberties of the subject.

1800. Action between the British ship Leviathan, admiral Duckworth, and the Spanish frigates Carmen and Florentia, 36 guns each, and 650 men, with 3000 quintals of quicksilver on board. The Spaniards were captured, together with 7 vessels under convoy.

1806. Alleghany county in western New York erected.

1807. LALANDE (see April 4: by some authorities his death is put down on the 7th.)

1812. Capt. AGAR, a celebrated English pedestrian, undertook to walk a distance of 59 miles in 8½ hours, for 200 guineas. He won the match 3 minutes within the time.

1812. Mrs. BUMBY died at Ekring, England, aged 80; remarkable for a horn growing from her forehead in a spiral form to the length of nearly six inches.

1814. About 200 British marines and sailors landed at Saybrook, in Connecticut, spiked the cannon and destroyed several vessels, and escaped in the night to their shipping.

1817. The county of Tompkins in the state of New York erected.

1835. JAMES BROWN, an American statesman, died. He rose to a high rank at the bar, and was several years minister to France.

1836. WILLIAM GODWIN, an English novelist, and political and miscellaneous writer, died, aged 81. He commenced his career as a dissenting minister, which station he relinquished to gain a subsistence by literature. His works are numerous, and acquired him much celebrity, though tinctured more or less with skepticism.

1844. Morgan Lewis, a distinguished American military officer and statesman, died at New York, aged 90. He served with fidelity under the colonial government, and with honor and gallantry in the war of the revolution, and in the war of 1812. He held various important civil offices from 1791 to 1810.

1849. Irvine Shubrick, an American naval officer, died. He had been thirty-five years in the service, and fought under Decatur and Downes. He commanded the expedition against the island of Sumatra in 1832, which captured Qualla Battoo, and broke up a horde of pirates who molested vessels there.

1850. James Emott, a distinguished member of the New York bar, died at Poughkeepsie, aged 80.

1854. All English and French vessels were ordered out of the port of Odessa.

1856. The steamship Adriatic, the largest vessel of the kind that had ever been built, was launched at New York.

APRIL 8.

431 b. c. A body of 300 Thebans surprised the town of Platæa, in Greece, in the dead of night, and were all destroyed or captured by the inhabitants.

46. Battle of Thassus, in Africa; Scipio and Juba defeated by Julius Cæsar.

217. Caracalla, the Roman emperor, assassinated at Edessa.

1341. Petrarch crowned with laurels at Rome, with great pomp. This distinction was awarded him on the appearance of his Latin poem entitled *Africa*, in which he celebrates Scipio, his favorite hero. This poem he considered his best, yet it was never finished. His reputation now rests as a poet, on his Italian poems.

1364. John I, king of France, died. He was taken by Edward III at the battle of Poictiers, and conducted to England, where he was retained in captivity four years. He returned from France in 1363, which he had visited on parole, and died at his palace in London, aged 45, after a reign of 14 years, which had been extremely calamitous to France.

1492. Lorenzo de Medicis, surnamed *the Great*, and the father of letters, died at Florence. He was a great merchant, and an eminent statesman; whose public services so recommended him to the Florentines that he was declared chief of the republic; and whose wisdom and judgment were so conspicuous, that foreign princes made him the arbiter of their differences.

1546. The council of Trent declared against the Lutheran system, and adopted the Latin or vulgate translation of the Bible by St. Jerome.

1663. The first play bill issued from Drury Lane theatre. The play was advertised to be acted "by his majesty's company of comedians," and was entitled the *Hvmovrovs Lievtenant*, and was to commence at three o'clock precisely.

1679. Bosia, a village near Piedmont, in Italy, suddenly sunk into the earth, by which about 200 persons perished.

1702. Thomas Gale, an English divine, died. Though engaged the best part of his life in active and laborious employments, he yet found much time to devote to literature and classical learning. His publications are numerous and display great ability.

1704. Job Ludolphus, a German linguist, died, aged 80. He was one of the most eminent orientalists of his time, and the first European who acquired the Ethiopic language, of which he published a grammar and dictionary, and a history of the country. He was well versed in twenty-five languages.

1704. Henry Sidney, earl of Romney, died. He was brother to the famous Algernon Sydney, and an accomplished statesman.

1731. Elizabeth Cromwell, granddaughter of the lord protector of England, Oliver Cromwell, died at Bedford row in her 82d year.

1735. Francis Leopold Ragotzki, prince of Transylvania, died. He wrote an interesting memoir on the revolutions in Hungary.

1793. Edmund C. Genet, first minister from the French republic to the United States, arrived at Charleston. He was superseded by Fauchet at the request of Washington the next year.

1801. The French surrendered Rosetta, in Egypt, to the British troops under Col. Spencer.

1803. Louis Frederick Antoine Arbogast, a French mathematician, died. He was a member of the national convention, but appears not to have taken any active part in politics, his name appearing only to some report on scientific subjects. His works place his name high among the distinguished men of the day; his character was blameless.

1806. Herring, aged 60, and his wife, executed at Newgate, London, for coining money.

1808. County of Cortland in New York state erected.

1811. First law passed by the New York legislature respecting the Erie canal.

1812. Louisiana became a member of the United States confederacy.

1821. SIMON ASSEMANNI, one of the most learned of Maronites in modern times, died at Padua, where he had long been a professor. His explanation of the Arabian antiquities is much esteemed.

1832. ROBERT SIMSON died at Montreal, aged 101. He was at the attack on Quebec under Wolfe.

1835. Mr. CLAYTON, an American æronaut, made an ascension at Cincinnati, which proved an extraordinary affair. The spot at which he came to the earth was on Stevenson's knob, a mountain in Virginia, 3000 feet above the level of the sea, and 350 miles from Cincinnati, which distance he was wafted in 9½ hours.

1835. WILLIAM VON HUMBOLDT, a distinguished philologist, died, near Berlin, Prussia. He was elder brother of the celebrated traveler of that name, and distinguished as a statesman and a scholar.

1838. JOHN, a negro, drowned at Washington, aged 115.

1854. An explosion on the steam boat Gazelle, at Canemah, Oregon, destroyed the boat and killed 21 persons.

1854. A fire at Salonica, in Greece, destroyed 600 houses and warehouses.

1854. The Ganges canal, a work of vast magnitude, was opened by the lieutenant-governor of Agra, with great ceremony and a display of troops.

APRIL 9.

1483. EDWARD IV, of England, died. He disputed the crown with Henry VI and involved the kingdom in war and bloodshed, till the death of the latter, when he ascended the throne unmolested. He became a voluptuary, and died from excessive eating.

1483. Dr. SHAW, brother to the lord mayor of London, preached a sermon on the text "*Bastard slips shall not thrive.*" It was not productive of many converts.

1547. EDWARD VI succeeded to the throne of England on the death of Henry VIII.

1589. THOMAS SAMPSON, a noted English nonconformist divine, died. During the reign of Mary, he fled to Geneva, where he was engaged in the translation of the *Genevan Bible.*

1609. HUDSON left the Texel on his memorable voyage of discovery, in the yacht "Halve Maan," of forty lasts (80 tons) burden; a size which easily admits the supposition that he ascended the river as far as Half-Moon, or Waterford.

1626. FRANCIS BACON, an English philosopher, died, aged 66. At the age of 13 he entered the university, where he made the most astonishing progress in all the sciences then taught, and at the age of 16 attacked the Aristotlean philosophy. He succeeded rapidly in office under government, and in 1619 was appointed lord high chancelor of England and baron of Verulam. Here, unfortunately, he sullied his name, and was fined, imprisoned and degraded, for bribery and corruption. This extraordinary man is justly entitled to the appellation of "the father of experimental philosophy."

1648. A great insurrection of the people of London by reason of the parliament abolishing holydays.

1670. SAMUEL SORBIERRE, a French writer, died. He was educated for the protestant ministry, but abandoned that faith for popery, without much advantage to himself, as his sincerity was suspected. His literary reputation is also somewhat tarnished.

1697. WILLIAM, earl of Craven, died in his 89th year. The nobility of England are famed for longevity.

1747. SIMON FRAZER, Lord Lovat, executed on Towerhill, aged 80. He was a Scottish statesman, educated among the Jesuits in France. His life was a scene of treachery and misdemeanor, which compelled him to fly from one country to another. Finally, joining the rebellion of 1745, he was seized and condemned, and died like a martyr.

1754. CHRISTIAN WOLFF, a Prussian philosopher, died. In consequence of a Latin oration on the Chinese, which gave offence to the clergy, he was expelled from the country; but the honors conferred upon him by other countries, led to his recal by the king, when his merits were duly rewarded, and his former injuries obliviated. His whole life was devoted to advance the interests of science and virtue.

1759. NICHOLAS HARDINGE died, an eminent English scholar, and author of some Latin poems.

1761. WILLIAM LAW, an English dissenting divine, died. He is well known as the author of the *Serious Call.*

1780. Charleston invaded by the British land and naval forces under Sir Henry Clinton.

1790. NICHOLAS SYLVESTER BERGIER, a French ecclesiastic, died. He is the author of several learned and valuable works. His talents and worth commanded preferments, until he declined any more, replying that he was rich enough!

1795. An act for the encouragement of common schools passed by the legislature of New York.

1796. A British squadron under Sir Edward Pellew captured a large French convoy, under the protection of La Volage, 25 guns, which was driven on shore.

1804. James Necker, a Swiss statesman, died. He was sent as ambassador to France, where his abilities were so much respected, that he was twice elevated to the rank of prime minister. But the revolution destroyed his popularity, and he retired to Copet, where he died. He is the author of a work on the finances of France.

1807. John Opie, an eminent English painter, died. He was the son of a humble carpenter, and was drawn from obscurity by the patronage of Dr. Wolcott (alias *Peter Pindar*). He not only became an excellent artist, but also an admirable writer on the art.

1813. The Chesapeake frigate, Capt. Evans, returned to Boston from a cruise, having captured during an absence of four months, 2 British brigs and 1 ship, 1 American brig with a British license, and a schooner.

1831. Battle near Siedlce, in Poland, in which the Russians were defeated.

1854. The English and French vessels on the coast of Thessaly were directed to search all vessels suspected of having munitions of war on board, and to seize such as were so found.

1855. All the English and French batteries opened on Sebastopol, and continued incessantly through the night and following day. The Russian loss was acknowledged by Gortschakoff at 833 killed and wounded.

APRIL 10.

879. Louis II. of France, died. He is characterized as a weak prince, who had not sufficient firmness to maintain his rights.

1534. James Cartier sailed from France with two small ships and 122 men, with a view to the establishment of a colony. He arrived at Newfoundland in May, and named the gulf St. Lawrence, from his entering it on the day of that festival. He returned without effecting a settlement.

1563. The city of Goa in India introduced printing.

1599. Gabrielle d' Estrees, a mistress of Henry IV, died. She was descended from an illustrious house, and was 20 years of age when her beauty captivated the king. He procured a divorce from Margaret of Valois, in order to raise Gabrielle to the throne; but her sudden death, probably by poison, frustrated the plan, and plunged him in excessive grief. Her amiable disposition, gentleness of character and modesty, won her general favor, and she was universally lamented by the French.

1603. A couple of vessels, fitted out by the mayor and aldermen of Bristol, under the command of Martin Pring, to make discoveries on the north of Virginia, and collect sassafras, sailed for the American coast. The sassafras, which was greatly overrated for its medicinal virtues, formed a profitable article of traffic, and is still extensively exported to Great Britain. Of this, they procured a cargo near Bristol, Rhode Island.

1606. The colony of Virginia, as it was called, divided by the king into two colonies. Although 109 years had elapsed since the discovery of the country by the Cabots, in the service of Henry VII, the English had made no effectual settlement in the new world. Twenty years had elapsed since Walter Raleigh attempted the settlement of a colony in Virginia, but not an Englishman was now to be found in the country.

1630. William Herbert, earl of Pembroke, died. He was the son of the illustrious Mary Sidney, and united in himself the virtues of his mother with the manners and accomplishments of a scholar. He is the author of a volume of poems.

1651. Birthday of Ehrenfried Walter von Tschirnhausen, an ingenious Lusatian mathematician, and founder of the celebrated Dresden porcelain manufactory. He also constructed, about the year 1687, an extraordinary burning mirror.

1653. Oliver Cromwell, having turned out the long parliament, locked the doors upon them.

1703. Andrew Morel, a Swiss antiquary died. He was a diligent and curious collector of medals, and in a work published in 1683 promised to give a description of twenty thousand medals, exactly designed. A part of this great work appeared after his death, in two vols., folio, describing 3,539.

1728. Robert Woodcock, an eminent English musician and composer, died. He also excelled as a painter of sea pieces.

1736. Francis Eugene, prince of Savoy, died, aged 73. He was born at Paris, and destined for the church, against his own inclinations. He applied to the king for a company of dragoons, and on being refused, entered the Austrian service. His first campaign was in capacity of a volunteer against the Turks; where he acquitted himself with so much distinction, that he was appointed to the command of a company of dragoons. He finally rose step by step to the rank of commander in chief of the Austrian army, and achieved a succession of brilliant victories and enterprises in Europe, which humbled the arms of the French, and rendered his name immortal in the annals of fame. His successful campaign in conjunction with the duke of Marlborough, rendered him so popular in England, that a maiden lady bequeathed him £2500, and a gardener £100. [By some authorities, 21st.]

1741. Battle of Molwitz, between the Prussians and Austrians. The latter were defeated with the loss of 7000 men and 180 officers. The Prussians took 1200 prisoners; their loss was 1500 killed, and 3000 wounded.

1752. William Cheselden, an eminent English surgeon and anatomist, died. He acquired great professional reputation, and published several popular works. He was the first foreigner admitted into the French royal academy of surgery.

1756. Joseph Vaissette, a French eccleciastic, died. He published a *History of Languedoc*, and a *Universal Geography*.

1774. John Saas, a French canon and librarian, died. He wrote an abridgment of the French *Historical Dictionary*, and other works.

1786. John Byron, the English admiral, died. He enjoys a high and merited reputation for courage and professional skill.

1794. The islands of the Saints, in the West Indies, captured by the British.

1795. Action between the British ship Astrea, Capt. Pawlet, and French ship La Glorie, 24 guns: the latter was captured.

1796. Battle of Montenotte, which was attacked by the Austrians under Beaulieu, and defended by the French under Rampon, with such desperate resistance that Bonaparte had time to come up and obtain a victory, taking 2000 prisoners.

1797. Miss Farren, the actress, took leave of the stage, after the performance of her part in the *School for Scandal*, to marry the earl of Derby.

1798. Bernadotte, the French ambassador at Vienna, in obedience to the Directory, displayed the tri-colored flag at his lodgings; but the populace in a rage tore it down. Not receiving the satisfaction he desired, he left the court.

1806. Horatio Gates, a distinguished officer in the revolutionary war, died. He came over from England as a soldier, and at the defeat of Braddock, 1755, was shot through the body. He joined the American army in 1775, and in 1777 captured Burgoyne. He was afterwards defeated by Cornwallis, at Camden. In 1790 he liberated his slaves in Virginia, and removed to New York, where he died.

1813. Von Berger and Fink executed at Oldenberg, Germany. When the Russians approached the town, the French magistrates fled, leaving a committee of regency of which the above were members. This committee were summoned before a court martial, at which Vandamme presided, and these two excellent men were unjustly condemned to death, although their accuser had only proposed their imprisonment.

1813. Joseph Louis Lagrange, a Sardinian mathematician, died. He went to Paris 1787, where he met with great favor, and under Bonaparte was invested with honors and dignities. His chief work is the *Méchanique Analitique*.

1814. Battle of Toulouse, at which the French under Soult were defeated by Wellington.

1816. The bank of the United States incorporated by act of congress, with a capital of $35,000,000.

1818. John Cleves Symmes, "of Ohio, late captain of infantry," promulgated "to all the world," his theory that the earth is hollow, containing a number of solid concentric spheres, one within the other, and that it is open at the poles 12 or 16 degrees. His theory amused the world for a number of years.

1823. Charles Leonard Reinhold, an Austrian philosopher, died. He was sent to study with the Jesuits, whose order was abolished while he was a student. In 1787 he settled at Jena, which owes much of its reputation to him, and in 1797 at Kiel, where he died. His works are numerous.

1835. Jacob Schmuck, a distinguished officer in the war of 1812 with England, died. He was a native of Pennsylvania, died at St. Augustine.

1842. John Sutherland, commonly called *Killyman*, died at Merigonisbe, aged 116. He was born in the last year of the reign of George I, and consequently lived under all the sovereigns of the house of Hanover, six in number. He emigrated to Nova Scotia about 1822, and continued to wear the kilt to the end of his life, declaring that he would never disgrace his country by adopting a foreign garb.

1856. The Americans under Lieut Green attacked 200 Costa Ricans, killed 27 of them and dispersed the rest. American loss 1 killed and 2 wounded.

1856. A company of 208 men left New York to join Gen. Walker in Nicaragua.

APRIL 11.

52 b. c. Trial of Milo for the murder of Clodius, in the consulship of Pompey. All the unwashed industry of the city was crammed within the forum on that momentous day; but neither Cato's candid ballot, nor the splendid labors of Tully, were sufficient to save the tyrant-killer; so that he was banished to Marseilles, and his estate confiscated.

44 b. c. Marc Antony recorded in the

senate a decree of Julius Cæsar, on behalf of the Jews, made thirty-four days before his assassination. The decree is addressed to the senate of Paros, who had forbidden the Delian Jews to worship in the manner of their forefathers.

1415. Pierre Plaont, bishop of Senlis, died. A large quarto Bible fairly written on vellum was presented by him to the House of the Sarbonne for the use of the poor, valued at £15.

1447. Henry Beaufort, brother of Henry IV of England, died. He held the highest ecclesiastical and civil offices in England, under the king; was created cardinal and pope's legate in Germany; and is characterized as proud, haughty and ambitious.

1512. Battle of Ravenna, in Italy, between the Spanish and papal troops, and the French under the brave Gaston de Foix. The French were victorious, with the loss of their general, who was killed in endeavoring to cut off the retreat of the Spaniards. He was but 24 years of age.

1544. Battle of Cerisoles, between the imperialists under the marquis del Geasto, and the French, count de Enguin, who obtained the victory. The marquis was wounded, and 10,000 of his men slain; his tents, baggage and artillery, and many prisoners taken.

1555. Thos. Wyatt beheaded; acquitting with his last breath the princess Elizabeth and the earl of Devonshire.

1585. Gregory XIII, (Hugh Buoncompagno), pope of Rome, died, aged 83. He was an able pontiff, and has rendered his name immortal by the reformation of the calander, and the adoption of the style which bears his name. This plan, necessary and useful, was long pertinaciously rejected by the protestants, and not adopted by them generally till about two centuries after, and not yet by Russia.

1644. The parliamentary forces under the two Fairfaxes victorious at Selby; 1600 common soldiers, 2000 stand of arms and 500 horses, the result. The parliament ordered a day of thanksgiving.

1669. Clifford, Arlington, Bucks, Ashley, Lauderdale, constituted the cabinet council of Charles II. From the initials of their names, this was called the king's *cabal*.

1713. The celebrated peace of Utrecht concluded, and with it the twelve years' war for the throne of Spain, in which the principal powers of Europe had been engaged, at a vast expense of life and treasure.

1733. The sheriffs of London and eminent merchants in 200 carriages, went to the house of parliament with a petition against the excise bill, then pending.

1737. Philip Hecquet, a French physician, died. He is the original of the immortal Sangrado of *Gil Blas*. He was a man of great simplicity of diet, and a friend to bleeding and the use of warm water at proper times, whence the caricature. He published several medical works.

1758. The wooden bridge over the Thames at London was burned down.

1766. Above 100 convicts left Newgate, in London, for the American colonies. They passed along with music playing before them.

1786. The first commencement of Columbia college, New York, when, the papers of the day say, "the public with equal surprise and pleasure, received the first fruits of reviving learning, after a lamented interval of many years."

1798. Stanislaus Augustus Poniatowski, the last king of Poland, died. He was elected to the throne in 1764 under the influence of Russian bayonets; was an elegant and accomplished gentleman, with good intentions, but without the energy and firmness of purpose necessary to sustain a tottering throne, and bridle a licentious nobility. The three great robbers, Russia, Prussia and Austria, divided his kingdom between them, and he retired to private life at St. Petersburgh, on a pension, where he died.

1799. Battle of Ledjars, in Syria; the French under Kleber defeated the Turkish and Arabian army, consisting of 4000 cavalry and 5000 foot, and compelled them to retreat across the river Jordan.

1801. Anthony de Rivarol, a French author, died. He was a man of great acquirements, and associated with the learned men of France before the revolution.

1804. James Thomas died in Tatnal county, Georgia, aged 134.

1805. Treaty signed between Great Britain and Russia, the basis of the anti-Gallican alliance.

1808. British order in council encouraging evasions of the United States embargo law.

1812. Four British barges taken in Hampton roads by the frigate Constellation and revenue cutter Jefferson; prisoners 80.

1814. Napoleon subscribed the treaty of abdication at Paris. On the same day the white banner was advanced by lord Wellington on the ramparts of Toulouse.

1816. Act of the British parliament regulating the intercourse with St. Helena during Bonaparte's confinement there. It legalized the detention of the fallen emperor as a prisoner of war during the king's pleasure; British subjects aiding or assisting him to escape, to suffer death.

1817. WILLIAM BELOE, an English divine and critic, died. He is principally known as the translator of Herodotus and Aulus Gellius, though his works are numerous and highly creditable.

1817. At Dartmoor, England, a man sold his wife in the market place. She stood as in olden times, with a rope round her neck. Her first lover was the purchaser at the price of two guineas.

1823. County of Wayne erected in western New York.

1824. JEAN BAPTISTE DROUET, who arrested Louis XVI in his flight, and was expelled from France as a regicide, died under the assumed name of Meyer, at Macon in France.

1829. The catholic relief bill passed the house of peers, in the British parliament after much discussion.

1832. RAFFAELE MORGHEN, a celebrated Italian engraver, died at Florence, aged 72.

1833. ROWLAND HILL, an able and eccentric preacher, died, aged 89. He usually spent a considerable part of the summer in visiting various parts of England, preaching in churches of every denomination that would admit of his services, and occasionally to large assemblies in the open air. He preached for the last time to an immense audience, but three days before his death.

1837. KIRK BOOTT died at Lowell. He was a native of Boston, and received an excellent education, partly in England; went to Spain, and joined the British army as an officer under Wellington; spent two years at the military school at Woolwich, Eng.; on his return to Boston he engaged in mercantile pursuits, and subsequently was called to superintend the erection of manufacturing establishments at Lowell, where, by his enterprise, energy and extraordinary talent, his name became identified with the prosperity of that new and flourishing city.

1840. ALEXANDER NASMITH, the father of the Scottish school of landscape painting, an eminent artist, and author of numerous productions, died at Edinburgh, aged 83.

1844. JAMES STEWART, commonly known as Jimmey Strength, died in England, aged 116. He was born at Charleston, S. C., 1728, and at the age of 20 enlisted as a soldier—was at the battle of Quebec and Bunker's Hill. He had five wives and 27 children. Ten of his sons were killed in battle. His strength was remarkable. During the last 60 years of his life he traveled the *borders* as a wandering minstrel, scraping upon a wretched violin.

1854. One of the college buildings of the Indiana University was destroyed by fire; it contained a library of 2700 volumes.

1854. The emperor NICHOLAS issued a manifesto to all his Russian subjects, stating the object of the war with Turkey and the allied powers.

1855. Broussa, in Asia Minor, again visited by an earthquake, and the wooden buildings in the place were mostly destroyed by fire.

1856. The great bridge over the Mississippi at Rock Island completed, and locomotives passed from the Illinois to the Iowa side.

1856. Battle of Rivas; General WALKER, with 400 Americans and 300 natives, attacked the Costa Ricans, numbering 3000 men, who after a long contest left the city. The latter acknowledged a loss of 200 killed and 400 wounded; Walker's loss, 80 killed and disabled, including almost all of his official staff.

APRIL 12.

205 B. C. The shrine of the potent goddess Cybele received at Rome from Pessinus, and deposited in the temple of Victory; Scipio Africanus and Crassus Dives, consuls. This was done in pursuance of an oracle in the sybilline books, which affirmed that if a foreign enemy invaded Italy, they might be vanquished by introducing the goddess Cybele into the capital.

65. LUCIUS ANNÆUS SENECA, the Roman philosopher, destroyed himself by order of Nero. He was born in the first year of the Christian era, received a careful education, and became a disciple of the stoic school of philosophy. He was the tutor of Nero, who, listening to the calumnies of his enemies, had him accused of treason and condemned. He professed a contempt for luxuries, but was not indifferent to wealth, for he acquired an immense estate. His *Morals* have often been republished in English.

276. MARCUS CLAUDIUS TACITUS, emperor of Rome, died, at Tyana upon Saurus. He claimed descent from Tacitus the historian, was a wise, benevolent and patriotic ruler, and had reigned but six months when he was snatched away by assassination or some violent disease.

1204. Siege of Constantinople by the French and Venitian crusaders. In the pillage which followed the conquest of this superb city, all the admirable monuments of Grecian art were demolished, including a colossal Hercules, by Lysippus. This deed by Christians is a great offset to the wanton depredations upon works of art of which the Turks and pagans are so often accused.

1443. Henry Chicheley, archbishop of Canterbury, died. His talents fitted him for the office; and the office enabled him to exercise his benevolence and charity with munificence. He founded the college of All Souls.

1520. Francis Alvares, a Portuguese priest, arrived at the court of David, king of Abyssinia, where he remained six years, and on his return published an account of his embassy.

1549. Joan of Kent, an anabaptist, condemned to be burned.

1646. Francis de Bassompierre, marshal of France, died. He was one of the most distinguished and the most amiable men of the court of Henry IV. Incurring the displeasure or the jealousy of Cardinal Richelieu, he was sent to the Bastile, where he remained 12 years, until the death of the cardinal. He wrote his own memoirs and a history of his embassies, while in prison.

1655. Francis Guyet, an eminent French critic, died. He employed many years in traveling and study, and finally settled in Paris, where he became so much esteemed that he might have risen to the highest honors, had he not preferred retirement.

1678. Thomas Stanley, a learned English writer, died, aged 34. He published a *History of Philosophy*, containing the lives and opinions of philosophers, of every sect, a work of great merit and popularity, and which was translated into Latin for the use of the German literati.

1695. Votes of the assembly of New York first published.

1695. John Kittlewell, an English divine, died. He acquired great reputation previous to the revolution, but refusing to take the oath of allegiance after that event, was deprived of his living, and devoted his time to writing.

1704. James Benignus Bossuet, bishop of Meaux, in France, died. He distinguished himself as a preacher and a writer of great erudition. His works were published in 12 vols. quarto.

1709. First number of the *Tattler* appeared.

1734. Thomas Fautet de Lagny died at Paris. His mathematical efforts and researches were directed more to subjects of curiosity than utility. He carried the quadrature of the circle to 120 decimal places.

1743. George Cheyne, a Scottish physician, died. He was studious and abstemious in his youth, but on coming to London, cultivated the society of free livers for the advantages of trade! till he became at length extremely asthmatic, lethargic, listless, and corpulent, exceeding 32 stone in weight. Finding the power of medicine unavailing, he returned to a milk and vegetable diet, and recovered his strength, activity and cheerfulness, with the free and perfect use of his faculties; and by a regular observance of this regimen, reached the mature age of 72. His writings are numerous, and principally on health and longevity.

1749. British ships Namur, 74 guns, 700 men; Pembroke, 60 guns, 400 men; Apollo, 40 guns, 300 men; and a great many merchantmen, lost on the coast of Coromandel; 23 men only saved from the Namur.

1749. Francis Bellenger, a learned doctor of the Sarbonne, died at Paris. He translated some of the ancient historians, and wrote criticisms on Rollin's works, to show his ignorance of Greek.

1757. Subsidiary treaty between England and Prussia; England to pay annually 4,000,000 crowns to Frederick II.

1765. Edward Young, the English poet, died, aged 84. He was educated for the church, but was unfortunately induced to abandon it for politics, in which he was unsuccessful. His *Night Thoughts* had their origin in a melancholy state of mind, produced by his misfortunes.

1770. George III gave his assent to the act for repealing the duties on glass, paper and colors, in America; but the duty was continued from a point of honor, and as a badge of sovereignty over the colonies.

1780. The British opened their fire upon the American batteries at Charleston, which they continued until the 20th.

1782. Pietro Metastasio, an Italian poet, died. He supplied the opera for a number of years with popular operas and oratorios. He has been styled the poet of love. In all his works he stands high; in his operas he is unrivaled.

1782. The French fleet under count de Grasse defeated by the British under Rodney, with the loss of 9,000 killed and wounded. A French 74 gun ship was blown up, and one of the same rate sunk; two 74's, one 64, and the Ville de Paris, of 110 guns, having on board the French admiral, were taken. Thirty-six chests of money, the whole train of artillery, battering cannon, and traveling carriages, were on board the captured vessels—a circumstance which totally disabled the French from carrying on offensive operations against the British possessions in the West Indies. British loss 1,050 killed and wounded. A new system of tactics for breaking through the line of an enemy was here made use of for the first time. It was invented by John Clerk, of Eldin, a country gentleman, unacquainted with navigation. His principles have since been applied by all the English admirals, and Howe, St. Vincent, Duncan and Nelson, owe to them their most signal victories.

1782. Action off Ceylon, between the French under Admiral Suffrein, and the British under Hughes. British loss, 144 killed and 400 wounded.

1784. JOSEPH RAULIN, an eminent French physician, died. He was induced by Montesquieu to remove to Paris, where he acquired great reputation, and was employed by government to write medical works.

1788. The first power loom began to work at Philadelphia, and on the first of November following the quantity of cloths manufactured was 3,719 yards jean, 580 corduroys, 67 federal rib, 57 beaver fustian, 3,672 plain cottons, 123 birdseye, and 2,879 linen; total 11,197, besides the quantity then in the looms.

1800. FREDERICK CONRAD HORNEMANN, a celebrated German teacher, who had undertaken a journey into Africa for discovery, wrote that he was on the point of setting out with the great caravan of Bornou, since which nothing certain has been learned of him.

1804. JOSEPH DACRE CARLYLE, an English orientalist, died. He devoted much attention to the study of Arabic, traveled in the east, and on his return was employed in the publication of the Bible in Arabic, when his constitution gave way under the task imposed upon it.

1809. The French fleet in Basque roads destroyed by the British under Admiral Cochran. The British lost but 10 killed and about 40 wounded. The loss of the French in vessels and men was tremendous.

1810. The French captured the East India company's settlement at Tapanooly, in Sumatra.

1814. Count D'ARTOIS, brother of Louis XVI, entered Paris; Bonaparte set off for the island of Elba; intercourse between France and England opened; and a grand illumination in London, on account of the restoration of the Bourbons, and peace with France, which was continued three days.

1814. CHARLES BURNEY, an English musical composer, died. He commenced the study of music as an organist. At the age of 31 he undertook to write a *General History of Music*, upon which he bestowed nearly 40 years of labor and travel. He visited all the institutions of Europe at which he could obtain important information for his work. He furnished the musical articles for Rees' *Encyclopedia*, and is the author of several other valuable works.

1815. Great eruption of Tomboro, which commenced on the 5th. The explosions resembled the firing of cannon, and were heard at Sumatra, not nearer than 900 miles. Such were the tremendous effects of the burning lava, the overflowing of the sea, the falling of houses, and the violence of the whirlwind, that out of 12,000 inhabitants on this island, only 26 survived. At Java, 300 miles distant, the air was so full of ashes, as to produce profound darkness at mid-day; and at Bima, 40 miles distant, the roofs of many houses were crushed by the weight of ashes falling on them.

1816. Hamilton county in northern New York erected.

1829. FELIX NEFF, a Swiss preacher, died. He undertook to improve the education and domestic habits of the peasants of the dreary regions called the High Alps of France. He persevered a number of years with much success; but his unremitting labors destroyed his constitution, and led to a premature death.

1834. N. G. DUFIEF, a French linguist, died. His mother was distinguished for her heroism in the Vendean war; and the son was driven to America by political disturbances, and resided at Philadelphia. He just survived the publication of his great work, the *Pronouncing Dictionary*.

1839. JOHN GALT, the novelist, died at Greenock, Scotland, aged 60. Being unsuccessful in business in London, he visited the south of Europe in 1809, and soon after commenced an active literary career, which continued till near the close of his life.

1839. The justly celebrated Dr. Black, of Mareschall college, Aberdeen, Dr. Keith so well known as a writer on prophecy, with the devoted Messrs. McCheyne and Bonar of the Scottish church, sailed from Dover in England to inquire into and devise measures for the amelioration of the state of the Jews in Palestine. This mission proved of much benefit.

1840. FRANCIS ANTHONY, chevalier de GERSTNER, a distinguished Austrian engineer, died at Philadelphia, aged 44. He commenced at his own risk, the first rail road on the continent of Europe, from Budweis on the Moldau, to Lintz on the Danube, 130 miles. He suggested to the emperor Nicholas the project of a rail road from St. Petersburg to Moscow, a portion of which was undertaken under his direction, and first opened in 1837, and since prosecuted by the government.

1848. New code of New York laws adopted.

1849. Signor GASPARIS, at Naples, discovered a new planet, making the fourth added to our system in four years.

1850. ADONIRAM JUDSON, a celebrated baptist missionary died at sea.

1854. A review of 25,000 troops in Paris, before the British officers.

1854. The French squadron under Admiral Parseval-Deschenes, sailed from Brest to join the British fleet in the Baltic.

1855. The United States gave the twelve months' notice to Denmark of their intention to terminate the treaty of 1826, by which the payment of sound dues was recognized.

APRIL 13.

58 B. C. JULIUS CÆSAR finished his famous wall of entrenchment, 16 feet in height and 17 miles in length, from Geneva to St. Claude; being a labor of only 6 days.

1436. Paris surrendered to the French under Charles VII, having been almost 14 years in the possession of the English.

1517. Cairo taken by the Turks under Selim, after a gallant resistance, and 50,000 of its inhabitants barbarously massacred. The sultan was hanged on one of the gates, Egypt was reduced to a province, and the power of the Mamelukes crushed, who for more than 260 years had swayed the land.

1584. An expedition fitted out by Sir Walter Raleigh took possession of Wowoken, on the coast of America, since called Virginia. A colony was left there, but they were cut off by the Indians, and every one put to death.

1598. HENRY IV of France published at Nantes the memorable edict of toleration; it was revoked 1685, by Louis XIV.

1605. BORIS GODOONOFF, czar of Moscow, died. He was called to the throne by acclamation, on the death of Fedor, the last of the dynasty of Ruric. In abilities and vigor of character, he resembled Peter the great; and might be called one of the greatest of princes, was not his name tarnished by a crime that led his way to the throne.

1638. HENRY, duke of Rohan, a French warrior and historian, died. He signalized himself under Henry IV, both in the field and in the cabinet, but the jealousy of Richelieu drove him to Geneva. He joined the duke of Saxe Weimar against the imperialists, and was wounded in the battle, of which he died.

1640. The English parliament again met by royal mandate, after a refusal on the part of the king to call one for 12 years.

1641. RICHARD MONTAGUE, a learned English prelate, died. He published several controversial works.

1684. NICOLAO ANTONIO, a Spanish author, died. He published an account of all the Spanish writers, in 4 vols. folio, entitled *Bibliotheca Hispania*. He spent his income, which was large, in acts of charity, and in collecting a library, which at his death amounted to 30,000 volumes.

1686. ANTONIO DE SOLIS, a Spanish author of note, died, aged 76. He was appointed historiographer of the Indies, and wrote the *Conquest of Mexico*, on which his fame as an author principally rests.

1699. Birthday of MARIA CATHARINA WALTER, in Germany. She died in Philadelphia, 1802, aged over 103, having lived in three centuries.

1722. CHARLES LESLIE, an Irish theologian, died. He was a magistrate under James II, and respected for his talents and integrity. His writings were numerous, and sought for with avidity.

1726. VELASCO Y. PALOMINO, a highly admired Spanish painter, died at Madrid.

1742. OLIVER REYLOF died at Ghent, eminent as a Latin poet.

1748. CHRISTOPHER PITT, an English poet, died. His translation of Virgil's *Æneid* is said to be superior to Dryden's.

1759. GEORGE FREDERICK HANDEL, the illustrious German musical composer, died at London, aged 75. His grand oratorio, the *Messiah*, appeared in 1741.

1759. Battle of Bergen, in which the duke of Broglio defeated the allies under Prince Ferdinand of Brunswick, who lost 2,000 men and the Hanoverian prince Ysemberg.

1777. Battle of Boundbrook, New Jersey, in which 500 Americans under Gen. Lincoln were attacked by 2000 British under Cornwallis, and effected a retreat with the loss of 60.

1782. Third action off Ceylon, between the British under Admiral Hughes, and the French under Suffrein; latter defeated.

1787. Board of regents of the university of the state of New York established.

1788. Great riot in New York, occasioned by the imprudent manner in which the physicians procured subjects from the burying grounds; several lives lost.

1794. PETER GASPARD CHAUMETTE, a French revolutionist, executed. He was the son of a cobbler, displayed great courage at the taking of the Bastile, and became one of the most sanguinary and reckless characters of the time, till his career was arrested by the guillotine.

1795. Riots in England on account of the high prices of food.

1796. Battle in the defiles of Millesimo, Italy, in which the French under Augereau and Joubert defeated the imperialists, who retreated to the mountains of Cossaria.

1799. Schaffhausen, on the Rhine in Switzerland, taken by the imperialists.

1801. The canal at Alexandria, Egypt, cut by the British, and the country inundated.

1804. Makey, a Malay settlement on the coast of Sumatra, destroyed by the British.

1807. Robert Heron, an erudite and popular writer, died. By unwearied industry he raised himself from an obscure to a prominent situation in society.

1813. Battle of Castilla, in Spain; the British under Sir John Murray, defeated the French under Suchet.

1815. The bill for the construction of the Erie canal from the Hudson river to lake Erie, passed the house of assembly, 84 to 15.

1818. Thomas Hatchcock died in Richmond county, North Carolina, aged 125, leaving a son aged 93 and another 16, and a great progeny besides.

1827. Hugh Clapperton, a Scottish traveler, died. He was employed by the British to explore the interior of Africa, and died at Sackatoo, on his second journey thither.

1832. Shadrach Bond, first governor of Illinois, died at Kaskaskia.

1839. Robert Hillhouse, an English poet, died. He was a stocking-weaver of Nottingham, and had no advantages of education but such as were afforded by Sunday schools. His works "will insure his celebrity as a poet of no mean grade."

1850. Pope Pius IX returned to Rome.

1853. William R. King, vice-president of the United States, died. He was for many years a diplomat abroad, and his career furnished a remarkable instance of the eminent and deserved success of probity, fidelity, industry, gentlemanly spirit and bearing, and inflexible honor.

1855. Henry Thomas de la Beche, an eminent English geologist, died, aged 59 He was the author of many geological works, and director-general of the geological survey of the united kingdom, and was knighted in 1848, in recognition of his valued and long-continued services.

1856. Philadelphia visited by a tornado, 150 houses unroofed.

APRIL 14.

979. Ethelred II, crowned at Kingston by the famous Dunstan, then archbishop of Canterbury. This was the first king in England who took a coronation oath, and the first it is said to institute trial by jury. In this reign priests were forbidden to marry.

1040. Harold I (*Harefoot*), king of England, died. He was succeeded by his brother Hardicanute, whose first act was to order the body of Harold to be dug up and thrown into the Thames.

1293. Naval engagement in the British channel, between the French and English fleets, by mutual agreement, with the whole of their respective forces. The English, under Edward I, were victorious, carrying off more than 250 sail of their opponents.

1293. The mariners of Portsmouth and the Cinque Ports captured the Norman fleet, of 200 ships, off Brittany, and massacred the crews.

1322. Fitz-Simeon and Hugh the illuminator, two friars of Dublin, commenced their pilgrimage to the holy sepulchre.

1345. Richard Aungerville, an English scholar and statesman, died; better known as Richard de Bury. He may be classed as the first bibliomaniac upon record in England. He purchased thirty or forty volumes of the *Abbot of St. Albans*, for fifty pounds weight of silver; and so enamored was he of his collection, which became very large for that period, that he expressly composed a treatise on the love of books, entitled *Philobiblon*.

1471. Battle of Barnet, between Edward IV and the great earl of Warwick, in which the latter was defeated and slain, together with his brother and 10,000 men. Margaret (the queen of Henry VI, who was confined in the tower,) landed from France on the same day with troops, only to hear the tidings of the disaster which had befallen her cause.

1558. Marriage of the dauphin of France with Mary Stuart, queen of Scots, to whom he had been affianced ten years.

1619. John Van Oldenbarneveldt, a statesman in the time of Elizabeth, beheaded for his praiseworthy attempts to limit the power of the stadtholder Maurice, which were construed into crimes. His noble lady, who witnessed his death without emotion, was afterwards solicitous for the pardon of a son, telling the astonished Maurice that she did not ask pardon for her husband for he was innocent, but she entreated for her son for he was guilty.

1662. William Fiennes, Lord Say and Sele, died. He was a troublesome subject under Charles I and Cromwell; but became tractable under Charles II (as he had been under James I), and was promoted, instead of others who had been more devoted to the royal cause.

1685. Thomas Otway, an English dramatist, died. His tragedy of *Venice Preserved* still keeps the stage; and though his pieces were generally successful, he died at a public house (where he had secreted himself from his creditors) in a state of great destitution, at the early age of 34.

1707. Battle of Almanza, in which the combined English and Portuguese armies were totally defeated by the French and Spaniards under the duke of Berwick, with the loss of 5,000 killed and wounded, and 10,000 prisoners.

1711. Louis, the dauphin of France, died of smallpox, aged 50.

1743. Thomas Rundle, a learned English prelate, died. He was the intimate friend of the learned and polite of his age. A volume of his letters has been published.

1760. Louis Silvester, an eminent French painter, died. He was ennobled by the king of Poland.

1769. John Gilbert Cooper, an English miscellaneous writer, died. He was a man of wealth, who made literature his amusement. His works, original and translated, are lively and elegant.

1780. Battle of Monk's Corner in South Carolina; the American cavalry surprised and defeated by Tarleton.

1783. Michael Francis Dandre-Bardon, a French painter, died. He was professor in the academy of painting, and admired for his historical writings.

1785. William Whitehead, an English poet, died. His principal works are the *Roman Father* and *Creusa*, dramas, which were received with great applause.

1793. Action between the British ship Phæton and French privateer Dumourier, with a Spanish prize in tow. The prize was taken; her cargo was valued at £1,300,000, and £935,000 was adjudged salvage for her recapture.

1793. John Baptist Gobel, a French bishop, guillotined. He took an active part in the revolution, abjured religion, and was *condemned by Robespierre for atheism*, and executed.

1795. A cargo of boards arrived at Newburyport, the first arrival through the locks and canals on Merrimack river—an expensive project of inland navigation, which was the best then in vogue.

1796. Battle of Millesimo, Italy; the French under Napoleon defeated the Austrians and Sardinians, who lost 2,500 killed, about 8,000 prisoners, and 22 cannon.

1801. Lemuel Hopkins, a Connecticut physician and poet, died. He was singular in his appearance and habits, but possessed great skill and assiduity in his profession; and as a man of learning and a poet entitled to more fame than is awarded him.

1803. John F. Hamtramck, an officer of the revolution, died at Detroit, where he was stationed as colonel of the first regiment of United States infantry, and commandant of Detroit and its dependencies. He served during the whole war of the revolution, with such distinguished merit as to receive the particular approbation of Washington.

1809. Beilby Porteus, bishop of London, died. His talents and acquirements procured him honors and wealth; and his writings will perpetuate his name.

1814. Congress repealed the embargo law of Dec., 1813.

1855. The office of the *Industrial Luminary* in Parkville, Missouri, was broken into, and ransacked, and the press thrown into the Missouri river, and the editors ordered to leave the state. The mob voted that no person belonging to the northern methodist church should preach in Platte county under "the penalty of tar and feathers for the first offence, and a hemp rope for the second."

APRIL 15.

1491 b. c. The Israelites arrived at the wilderness of Sin, on the 15th of Jiar, just a month after their departure from Ramasses.

43 b. c. First battle of Mutina, the modern Modena, in which Marc Antony was repulsed by the two consuls Hirtius and Pansa, assisted by Octavius Cæsar. Pansa died of the wounds he received in this conflict, and Hirtius was slain after he had achieved a second and more decisive victory.

1053. Godwin, earl of Kent, died. He was a powerful Saxon baron, who distinguished himself under Canute in the war with Sweden.

1205. Baldwin I, emperor of Constantinople, defeated by Joannices, king of the Bulgarians, and taken prisoner.

1415. Emanuel Chrysoloras, a learned Greek, died. He was employed by John Palæologus as ambassador to different courts of Europe, where he acquitted himself with honor.

1513. The English fleet under sir Edward Howard defeated off Brest by the French.

1521. The faculty of divines of the university of Paris, after many meetings held in the Sorbonne, drew up a *censure* of the heresies of Luther, which was solemnly proclaimed in a general assembly on this day.

1558. A volcano burst out near a spring in the isle of Palma, one of the Canaries.

1570. William Alley, bishop of Exeter, died. During the reign of Mary he retired, and kept a school and practiced physic, in order to avoid persecution; but on the accession of Elizabeth he was promoted. He wrote the *Poor Man's Library*, and other works.

1611. Richard Mulcaster, a celebrated scholar and English writer, died at Stanford Rivers, where he was rector.

1632. George Calvert, lord Baltimore, died. He was a learned, amiable and accomplished man, who resigned his offices under James I on embracing the catholic faith. The king, however, raised him to the Irish peerage of Baltimore. He obtained a grant for a plantation in Newfoundland; but the invasions of the French obliged him to abandon it, after he had spent £25,000 in its settlement. In the place of it, he received a territory on the continent, now known as the state of Maryland.

1642. Battle of Killrush in Ireland, in which the Roman catholic army was signally defeated by the duke of Ormond.

1659. Simon Dach, a German poet, died. He lived in a humble condition until he was appointed professor of poetry in the university of Konigsberg. His secular songs are said to be lively and natural; his sacred songs distinguished for deep and quiet feeling.

1670. John Daillie, a distinguished French protestant divine, died. His works evince great learning and judgment, and excited much interest.

1697. Charles XI of Sweden died. He was successful in war, and respected as a just prince.

1702. The proprietaries of East and West Jersey surrendered the government to queen Anne, after which it continued under one government, called New Jersey.

1715. The Yamasses, a powerful tribe of Indians in South Carolina, having meditated the extirpation of the English settlements in that state, fell upon Pocataligo and the neighboring plantations, and massacred all who fell into their hands.

1719. Frances d'Aubigne, madame de Maintenon, a celebrated French lady, died. From a state of want and dependence she rose to be the wife of the king of France, though not publicly married. Her examplary life and extensive charity after that event, made amends for many errors committed in reaching the height of her ambition.

1720. Luke Melbourne, an English divine, died. He was a prose and poetical writer of considerable ability, and his name is frequently introduced by Dryden and Pope in their works.

1754. The first theatre opened in Philadelphia, at the west corner of Cedar and Vernon streets, with the *Fair Penitent* and *Miss in her Teens*.

1755. The counters of the bank of England were broken down by the crowd in their eagerness to obtain lottery tickets.

1756. James Cassini, a French astronomer, died. He succeeded his father as astronomer royal, and made many important discoveries.

1758. The strong fortress of Schweidnitz, in Prussia, taken by assault, by the Prussians, and count Theirhaimb with 5,000 Austrians surrendered.

1761. James Cawthorne, an English poet, died. His poems were collected and published quarto, in 1771.

1761. William Oldys, a famous English antiquary, died. He was well versed in English antiquities, a correct writer and a good historian.

1764. Jane Antoinette Poisson, marchioness de Pompadour, died. She was the favorite of the licentious Louis XV. The patronage she extended to literature and the arts in some degree atoned for the follies she committed.

1764. Archibald Laidlie, having accepted a call from the reformed protestant Dutch church in New York, preached the first English sermon before that congregation.

1768. The populace at Peterborough, England, demolished a house that had been opened for the inoculation for small pox. The pretence was to prevent the spreading of a new disease.

1776. James Granger, a learned and ingenious English divine, died. He is the author of a valuable *Biographical History of England*, 4 vols. quarto.

1777. A party of 100 Indians attacked the settlement of Boonesborough, in Kentucky, and killed 4 of colonel Boone's men.

1777. Congress resolved that no distinction be made between the troops, and that the titles of Congress's Own Regiment, Washington's Life Guards, &c., be abolished.

1777. British picket near Bonumtown, N. J., stormed by a detachment under captain Patterson.

1786. Andrew Wilson executed at Edinburgh. This execution occasioned the subsequent Porteous mob.

1788. Mary Delany, an ingenious Irish lady, died, aged 88. She corresponded with some of the learned men of the day; but is chiefly known by an ingenious *Flora* which she commenced at the age of 74, and labored at with taste and assiduity nearly ten years, when her sight began to fail her. It was constructed of paper, cut and painted to resemble nature, with great accuracy of form and color.

1791. The first corner stone in the district of Columbia was laid at Jones's point, near Alexandria, with the imposing masonic ceremonies of the time, and a quaint address by Rev. James Muir. By the retrocession of Alexandria, a little more than fifty years after, the corner stone was no longer within the district.

1793. Forster Powell, the celebrated English pedestrian, died, aged 59. His favorite walk was from the monument in London to the cathedral in York and back again, a distance of 340 miles, in less than six days.

1793. Philibert Francis Rouxelle de Blanchelande executed; distinguished in the American war, and at the taking of Tobago.

1796. Second battle of Dego, Italy. The Austrians under Beaulieu surprised the French and carried the village. Massena, who attempted to stop their progress, was repulsed; Bonaparte with Victor and Lannes finally succeeded in driving them out.

1813. ALEXANDER MURRAY, a Scottish linguist, died. His *History of European Languages*, which was published after his death, is a work of great research and merit. His application hastened his death, which took place at the early age of 37.

1816. A brick-red snow fell on Tonal and other mountains in Italy.

1817. The memorable law upon which the system of internal improvement of the state of New York is based, passed the legislature.

1820. JOHN BELL, an eminent surgeon of Edinburgh, died at Rome. He is well known for his valuable works on surgery and anatomy.

1825. HENRY FUSELI, a Swiss painter, died. He was induced to visit England, where he distinguished himself.

1828. MICHOFSKY, a Russian farmer, died at Pleskow, in the government of Novogorod, aged 165. He led a very sober life, though occasionally he partook of ardent spirits. He never ate meat more than twice a week. At 120 he still labored in the field. His mother lived to the age of 117, and one of his sisters 112, but his father died at 52.

1834. AYLET HAWES, a distinguished philanthropist, died in Culpepper county, Virginia. He manumitted his slaves, 110 in number, and provided for their removal to Liberia.

1840. JAMES BROWNE, a Scottish author, died at Edinburgh; a man distinguished for his learning and research, for several years editor of the *Caledonian Mercury*, and a writer of valuable articles in the *Encyclopedia Britannica*, particularly on grammar, history, biography, &c.

1843. CHARLES BULFINCH, an eminent American architect, died in Boston, Mass. The state house at Boston and the capitol at Washington were built after his designs.

1846. At an eruption of mount Hecla the pillars of fire rose from a new crater to the height of 14,000 feet. The ice and snow which had covered the mountain for many centuries were wholly melted, and pieces of scoriæ weighing 200 pounds were thrown a league and a half.

1852. ALEXANDER MACKAY, an English political economist and reformer, died, aged 33. He was many years connected with the *Morning Chronicle* newspaper; traveled in the United States in 1846–7, and published his observations in three volumes, under the title of *Western World*.

1854. JAMES MOORE died at Metrechin, N. J., aged 100. His death was occassioned by a fall, before which he was accustomed to walk 12 miles a day.

1854. The steam boat Secretary, while crossing San Pablo bay, from San Francisco to Petaluma, burst her boiler, by which the boat was blown to pieces, and more than 50 persons perished.

1856. An affray occurred at Panama between the passengers of the American transit company and the natives, in which 30 passengers were killed and 20 wounded.

APRIL 16.

29 B. C. OCTAVIUS CÆSAR entered Rome and celebrated the grand triple triumph of nine days, for his victories at Dalmatia, at Actium and Alexandria, and shut the gates of the temple of Janus Quirinus the second time. This is also the anniversary of his being saluted *Emperor*. The city at this time was 50 miles in circumference, containing 4,000,000 inhabitants, and the annual revenue of the state amounted to about $180,000,000,000!

66. The massacre and crucifixion of 3600 Jews took place at Jerusalem, on the 16th Artemisius, (Jiar) under the procuratorship of Gessius Horus.

1546. Paul III excommunicated the bishop of Cologne for heresy in countenancing Lutheranism. The bishop resigned rather than expose his people to the miseries of war.

1548. Evening prayer began to be read in English in king Edward VI's chapel.

1551. A pestilence broke out at Shrewsbury, in England. It reached London in July, and the weekly mortality was upwards of 700. It ravaged the eastern and northern parts of the kingdom till September, when it stopped suddenly.

1564. Birthday of WILLIAM SHAKSPEARE, at Stratford-upon-Avon.

1629. The lord treasurer's warrant issued, giving liberty for 60 women and maids, 26 children, and 300 men, with victuals, arms, apparel and tools, 140 cattle, some horses, sheep and goats, to go to America. They sailed in 6 ships, and landed at Naumkeak, in Massachusetts, now Salem, a name which was chosen in place of the aboriginal one, as expressive of the peaceful asylum they found in the American wilderness.

1634. Of seven sailors left by the Dutch on the coast of Greenland, for the purpose of establishing a wintering place, the first one died. These sailors were amply supplied with every article of clothing, provisions and utensils thought necessary or useful in such a situation. A journal was kept by them, by which it appears that on the ninth October they began to make a constant fire to sit by; and soon after it was remarked that they experienced a considerable change in their bodies, with giddiness in their heads. At the time of the death of this man, they were all disabled but one person. This poor wretch continued the journal till the last day of April, when they were praying for a speedy release from their miseries. On the return of their countrymen in the spring, they were all found dead. (See Jan. 14th for a similar event.)

1639. WILLIAM KIEFT having become governor of New Netherland, took the affidavit of sundry persons to the effect that under the administration of his predecessor the public interests had been neglected, and the fortifications allowed to go to decay.

1644. WILLIAM BREWSTER, one of the leading members of the Plymouth colony, died. He possessed a large property in England, which he lost in escaping from ecclesiastical tyranny, and supported himself in Holland by teaching a school.

1662. Three of the judges who condemned Charles I, namely Miles Corbet, John Ohey and John Barstead, were arrested in Holland, and sent to England for execution.

1681. The province of New Jersey offered for sale, at about $25,000. An original letter is still in existence, from the earl of Bath to lord Norbury, since sold by auction as a curious manuscript, containing a proposal for the sale, in which it is represented as "a country almost as large as England, belonging to the late George Carteret."

1689. APHARA BEHN (alias *Astrea*) an English authoress, died. At Surinam, where her family resided, she became acquainted with the African prince Oroonooko, on whose story she founded a novel, which Southey has dramatized. Her works consist of novels, poems and 17 plays.

1743. CORNELIUS VAN BYNKERSHOEK, an eminent Dutch lawyer, died. He published several law works, which display great talents and research, and is characterized as "one of the most learned among modern civilians."

1746. Battle of Culloden, which terminated the Scottish rebellion. The forces of the pretender were defeated, with the loss of 1,200 slain, by the English under the duke of Cumberland, second son of George II, and the pretender himself compelled to flee to France.

1781. Naval action in the harbor of St. Jago, Cape de Verde, between the British fleet under Johnstone, and the French under admiral Suffrein, in which the latter were compelled to retire with considerable loss.

1788. GEORGE LOUIS LECLERC, count de Buffon, died. He was the greatest naturalist of the 18th century. His *Natural History*, to which he devoted fifty years of his life, was published in 36 vols. and opened a new science to the world.

1796. SAMUEL PINNOCK, a negro, died at Kingston, Jamaica, aged 125.

1796. Battle of Cera; the entrenched Piedmontese camp attacked by the French under Augereau and Joubert; the former fought all day, and then evacuated their camp.

1799. Battle of Esdrelon and Mount Tabor; the Syrian army defeated by Bonaparte, with the loss of 5,000 men.

1811. A plantation at Port-Royal mountains, Jamaica, on which were about thirty acres of coffee, sunk down and disappeared, so that only the ridge of the house was discernible.

1812. HUGH WHITE, founder of Whitestown, near Utica, New York, died.

1813. Part of the British squadron anchored off Petapsco river, within sight of Baltimore.

1814. CHARLES PHILIP, count d'Artois, declared the Capetan, or French monarchy, to be re-established.

1820. ARTHUR YOUNG, a celebrated English agriculturist, died. He traveled extensively in Great Britain and on the continent with a view to the improvement of husbandry. Besides his works on agriculture he published his tours.

1823. WILLIAM ASPINWALL, an American physician, died, aged 80. He was a surgeon in the revolutionary army, and was famous for his skill in the treatment of smallpox. He erected hospitals, where he received patients to be inoculated for the disease; but on becoming convinced of the efficacy of vaccination, he closed them.

1830. Earthquake in Central America; several towns destroyed.

1831. National congress of Belgium dissolved.

1832. MUZIO CLEMENTINO, the father of pianoforte music, died in England. He was born at Rome, 1752, and practiced in his profession as a musician with great applause in the principal cities of Europe.

1840. WILLIAM PITTS, an eminent sculptor, died at London, aged 50.

1847. JOHN BURNHAM, aged 93, and his wife, Mehitable, aged 90, died in Essex, Mass., and were buried in one grave. Two days previous Benjamin Burnham, aged 92, died at the same place. They were the three oldest inhabitants of that town.

1854. The city of San Salvador was wholly destroyed by an earthquake, causing the loss, in less than one minute, of more than 200 lives, and four millions worth of property.

1854. The ship Powhatan, from Havre for New York, having on board 311 emigrants, went ashore in a gale on Long Beach, near Egg Harbor, was totally wrecked, and not a single passenger was saved.

1856. THACHER MAGOUN, a noted American ship builder, died, aged 81. He laid the first keel of a ship at Midford, Mass., in 1802, and during half a century built a fleet.

APRIL 17.

1013. ABDULLAH, a Moorish historian, was killed at the taking of Cordova, his native city.

1421. An inundation of the rivers at Dort, in Holland, which swept away 100,000 persons, and destroyed 72 villages.

1434. The ice broke up at Paris, which had continued from the first of January. Snow fell in Holland forty days successively during the same winter.

1492. The Spanish sovereigns, Ferdinand and Isabella, signed at Granada their grant to Columbus, constituting him hereditary admiral and viceroy over all the islands and continents he should discover during his expedition, with the benefit of a tithe of the profits arising from the merchandise found within his admiralty.

1537. The river Simeto, in Sicily, overflowed its banks, and destroyed 500 houses with the neighboring castles, and all the wood was uprooted by a storm.

1575. WILLIAM DAVENANT, a learned German, died. He was the friend and confidant of the leaders of the reformation, as well as of every man of learning and consequence of the age. His works are numerous.

1610. HENRY HUDSON sailed on his last voyage.

1613. A "prodigious monster" born at Adlington, England, with two bodies joined to one back. It was described by a reverend gentleman, in a pamphlet entitled *Strange News*.

1670. ERIC DANIEL ACHRELIUS, a Swedish philosopher and professor at Abo, died, aged 66.

1688. GEORGE VILLIERS, duke of Buckingham, died. He distinguished himself as a statesman, a poet and dramatic writer; but his character both in public and private life was extremely reprehensible.

1697. CHARLES XI, king of Sweden, died; successful as a warrior and accounted a just prince.

1704. *The Boston News Letter*, the first newspaper printed in the North American colonies, was commenced at Boston, by John Campbell, who was a bookseller and postmaster, and printed by B. Green.

1711. JOSEPH I, 15th emperor of Austria, died. He was crowned king of Hungary, 1687; elected king of the Romans, 1690, and succeeded to the empire of Germany, 1705.

1761. BENJAMIN HOADLEY, bishop of Winchester, died, aged 85. He was a great controversialist, and started a question which occupied the press a number of years. His works comprise 4 volumes folio.

1765. Lord BYRON convicted before the house of peers in London of manslaughter in slaying Mr. Chaworth in a duel. Being a privileged peer, burning in the hand was dispensed with, and he was discharged on the payment of fees.

1770. Great illumination of the city of London, on account of the liberation of the celebrated politician, Mr. Wilkes, from prison.

1777. HENRY WOODWARD, a celebrated English comedian and harlequin, died, aged 60. His death was occasioned by an accident as he was jumping upon a table in the character of Scrub!

1780. Engagement between the British fleet under Rodney, and the French, admiral De Guichen, in the West Indies. The French took shelter under Guadaloupe, where the British were too much crippled to follow.

1784. Universal religious equality created by law in New York.

1790. BENJAMIN FRANKLIN, the American printer, statesman and philosopher, died. He was born at Boston, 1706, and went to Philadelphia at an early age, where he spent the remainder of his life. His public career is well known; his private life, written by himself, is full of counsel, and cautions, and examples of prudence and economy, and is the largest work he ever composed.

1794. The Russians expelled from Warsaw by the Poles.

1796. The French convention decreed that all printers of journals should be personally liable for the contents of their papers, as well as the hawkers, sellers and posters of periodical papers.

1816. An act for improving the internal navigation of the state of New York, embracing the Erie and Champlain canals, became a law. Stephen Van Rensselaer, De Witt Clinton, Samuel Young, Joseph Ellison, and Myron Holley, were created commissioners, and seventy thousand dollars appropriated to the purpose.

1817. Seven Luddites hanged at Leicester, England. Luddites was a name given to malcontents who went about destroying labor-saving machinery.

1830. Navigation of the Black sea opened to American vessels.

1834. Ivan Petrovitch Martos, died; formerly director of the academy of fine arts at St. Petersburg, and one of the most eminent sculptors of the age. His works are found in the principal cities of Russia.

1835. William Henry Ireland died. He rendered himself notorious by an attempt to impose on society some dramatic compositions of his own, as relics of those of Shakspeare. He confessed himself the author, and fully exonerated his father who had been implicated in the fraud.

1837. Joseph Anderson, an American statesman, died at Washington, aged 80. He was a native of Pennsylvania, and served in the New Jersey line throughout the revolutionary war.

1837. Henry Vose died at Woodville, Mississippi, of small pox. He was distinguished at the West Point school as a proficient in mathematics, and was subsequently connected with the press in Mississippi, to which he contributed extensively in geography, statistics and history.

1837. United States sloop of war Natchez captured a Mexican brig of war, after having made a formal demand upon the Mexican authorities to release six American vessels which had been illegally captured.

1838. John Reilay died at Troy, aged 104.

1843. Alexander Proudfit, pastor of the Associate reformed church at Salem, Washington co., N. Y., and secretary of the New York Colonization society, died, aged 75.

1849. The steamer General Pike burnt on the Mississippi, when Col. Butler of Texas, with several others, perished in the flames.

1850. James Thom, the sculptor, died at New York.

1852. Etienne Maurice Gerard died in Paris, aged 74. He entered the army in 1791, and was engaged in the battles of Fleurus and Austerlitz, and in those of the disastrous Russian campaign; became a marshal and peer of France, and twice held the place of minister of war.

1854. Riot at Saginaw, Michigan; some 300 armed men attempted to burn the jail, and rescue certain prisoners. The sheriff and others were killed.

1854. The Winchester, an emigrant ship from Liverpool for Boston, was wrecked, and a large number of passengers lost.

1855. A new planet of the eleventh magnitude was discovered by Luther, at the observatory of Bilk, near Dusseldorf.

1855. Petropaulowski deserted by its inhabitants, and its fortifications destroyed, and what stores could not be removed were burned.

1856. The peace conference at Paris terminated, for the settlement of the war in the Crimea between Russia on the one side, and England, France and Turkey on the other.

APRIL 18.

515 B. C. The Jewish passover, a festival in commemoration of the destruction of the first born of the Egyptians, while the houses of the Jews were spared, was celebrated in the new temple.

1551. Nicholas Udall obtains a patent to print the works of Peter Martyr and the English Bible.

1552. John Leland, styled the father of antiquaries, died in London. He applied himself to his favorite pursuit with so much ardor as to impair his reason. He was the most accomplished writer of the age.

1556. Lewis Alemanni, a Florentine statesman, died. He was at the head of the faction that sought to expel the Medici; but finding himself unable to keep his popularity, he fled to France, where he was employed as a diplomatist.

1587. John Fox, the martyrologist, died, aged 70. His attention was early turned to the reformation, and he studied the early writers with so much devotion that his seclusion and frequent absence from church excited the persecution of his enemies, and occasioned him a great deal of misfortune.

1593. Shakspeare's poem of *Venus Adonis* entered in the books at Stationer's Hall.

1610. Robert Parsons, an English Jesuit, died at Rome. His abilities procured him the patronage of the pope, and he was employed in educating missionaries to convert protestants in England. He possessed the elements of turbulence and intrigue to a great extent, but his operations were entirely unsuccessful.

1630. Manors in America created.

1640. Peter Kirstenius, a German physician, died at Upsal. He applied himself with great assiduity to literature and science, acquired 26 languages, and published among other things an Arabic grammar.

1676. Sudbury, Mass. attacked by the Narragansetts. Several houses and barns were burnt, and a small party who had hastened from Concord to their relief were intercepted and cut off. Another party of 50, sent from Boston for the relief of Marlborough, which the Indians had totally destroyed the day before, went in pursuit of the enemy, were drawn into an ambush and suddenly surrounded by a body of 500. The gallant leader and his brave band fought with desperate valor to the last man: but they fell a prey to the numbers, the artifice, and the bravery of their enemies. The Indians lost about 120.

1689. Sir Edmund Andros, governor of Massachusetts, seized and imprisoned by the people, and the old magistrates reinstated. This revolution was brought about after the colonists had borne the impositions of the new administration about three years, on the circulation of a rumor that a massacre was intended by the governor's guards.

1689. George Jeffreys, baron Wem, the infamous lord chancellor under James II, died. He was never formally admitted to the bar, yet continued to practice unrestrained until he attained the highest employments in the law. He was one of the advisers and promoters of all the oppressive and arbitrary measures of the reign of James II, till the revolution transferred him to the tower, where he died.

1710. Alexander Lainez, a French poet, died. His pieces possess great vivacity and elegance.

1710. Four Indian chiefs from eastern New England and Canada, arrived at London and were carried in the royal coaches to their audience with the queen.

1768. Madame Bontems, a French poetess, died at Paris. She was respected for her wit and knowledge; she published a translation of Thompson's *Seasons*.

1781. British evacuated Camden, S. C., after burning the jail, mill, several houses, the greater part of their baggage and stores, and a large quantity of private stores. They left 31 American and 58 British soldiers, and 3 officers, all too badly wounded to be removed.

1782. Naval action between the French and British fleets, in which Rodney of England defeated and took prisoner Count de Grasse of France.

1791. Louis XVI and the royal family arrested by the populace, while on their way to St. Cloud, and compelled to return to Paris.

1794. Charles Pratt, earl of Camden, died, aged 80. He was an eminent English statesman and judge, and particularly distinguished himself by his animation and eloquence in parliament.

1794. Jean Joseph de Laborde, a wealthy French merchant, guillotined. At the breaking out of the American revolution, he alone furnished the government with twelve million livres in gold at Brest, which enabled the expedition under Rochambeau to set sail. He sustained an admirable character and bestowed immense sums for charitable and benevolent objects. He fell a sacrafice to the fury of the revolution, at the age of 70, for no offence but that of being rich.

1796. Sidney Smith was taken prisoner on the French coast, and sent strongly guarded to Paris.

1797. Austria made peace with France, ceding the Netherlands, free navigation of the Rhine, &c., to France.

1802. Erasmus Darwin, an English poet, died. He studied medicine at Edinburgh, and first appeared before the world as a poet in 1781, by the publication of the *Botanical Garden*. He has left behind him the character of an able man of great eccentricity. His publications tended to materialism, and although popular for a time, have nearly fallen into oblivion.

1831. John Abernethy, an eminent English surgeon, died. During his studies he was remarkable rather for the oddity of his conversation and manners, than for any indications of genius; and passed by the name of the *ostler*, on account of his attending the lectures in the dress of a groom. His medical and surgical works are numerous, and his eccentricity was proverbial.

1838. Enactment of the New York general banking law.

1842. Charles Bell, a distinguished medical author, and brother to the anatomist, John Bell, died at Edinburgh.

1847. The American army carried the heights of Cero Gordo with much loss, but took many prisoners.

APRIL 19.

481 B. C. An eclipse of the sun noticed by Herodotus.

1110. Robert, abbot of Molesme, founder of the Cistersians, died. The Cistersian monks allotted several hours of the day to copying books, or sacred studies and manual labor. (See March 28, 1134.)

1390. Robert II, of Scotland, died, aged 84. He was the first of the house of Stuart who reigned, and was crowned in 1371. On the accession of Richard II of England a war commenced which continued during the greater part of his reign.

1529. The elector of Saxony, marquis of Brandenburg, landgrave of Hesse, dukes of Lunenburg, prince of Anhalt, together with 14 imperial cities, entered a solemn protest against the decree of the diet of Spires condemning their nonconformity to the Romish church by abolishing the mass, &c., declaring the decree unjust and impious. Hence they were distinguished by the name of *protestants*.

1560. Philip Melanchthon, a celebrated German divine, died. He was a coadjutor with Luther in the reformation, and one of the wisest and greatest men of his age.

1593. Giles Bays died; a celebrated Parisian printer, and the first after Ramas to make a distinction between j & i and u & v in printing.

1598. HENRY IV of France published the memorable edict of Nantes, by which protestantism was tolerated in his dominions.

1608. THOMAS SACKVILLE, an English statesman and poet, died. He distinguished himself as a writer by the tragedy of *Gorboduc*, the first regular play on the English stage. As a statesman he has left a fair character.

1618. THOMAS BASTARD died; a poet and preacher of England, of considerable learning and ability.

1669. GEORGE BATE, an English physician, died. He had the talent and address to keep his situation as court physician to Charles I, Cromwell and Charles II. He wrote an account of the civil wars in Latin.

1684. The Synod of Edinburgh changed the year of confirmation for children from 8 to 16 years.

1689. CHRISTINA, queen of Sweden, died. She resigned the sceptre, 1654, became a catholic, and resided at Rome. She was a woman of great abilities and learning, and corresponded with the learned men of the day in different languages.

1689. The toleration act, so famous among dissenters and others in England, was passed.

1710. The 5 Mohawk chiefs, who were taken to England by Col. Schuyler, attended an audience of great state with the queen, and made a speech.

1739. NICHOLAS SAUNDERSON, an English mathematician, died. He lost his sight from smallpox, at the age of one year; notwithstanding which he acquired a knowledge of Greek and Latin, pursued his studies with the assistance of friends, and was sent to Cambridge University, where he became acquainted with Newton, and was finally chosen professor of mathematics. His eminence in the science of certainties has rarely been equaled.

1747. THOMAS COXETER, an English antiquary, died. He was a faithful and industrious collector of old English literature, amassed materials for a biography of the English poets, and assisted Ames in his *History of English Typography*.

1751. JOHN BANKS, an English author, died. He was originally a weaver's apprentice.

1751. LA CAILLE arrived at the cape of Good Hope, for the purpose of observing the southern hemisphere. He remained there three years, during which period he determined the exact position of ten thousand stars, and fixed the situation of the isles of France and Bourbon.

1765. While at dinner with his family at Redriffe, in England, a blacksmith was killed by a cannon ball projected from an old cannon thrown into a neighboring furnace for fusion.

1775. Battle of Lexington, which commenced the revolutionary war. About 800 British grenadiers and light infantry, proceeding to destroy the military stores at Concord, fell in with about 70 militia, upon whom they fired and killed 8. The British proceeded to Concord, where they partially effected their purpose, but were compelled to retreat before the gathering provincials, although reinforced by 900 men and 2 pieces of cannon. In this excursion the British lost 65 killed, 180 wounded, and 28 prisoners. The provincials lost 88 killed, wounded and missing.

1779. Col. VAN SCHAICK marched from fort Schuyler and destroyed Onondaga, N. Y., killed 12 Indians, took 34 prisoners, together with a large quantity of stores, arms, horses, &c. He returned without losing a man.

1782. Holland acknowledged the independence of the United States.

1783. Cessation of hostilities was proclaimed in the American army, just eight years from the day on which the war commenced. The loss of lives to the Americans during this war was estimated at 70,000 men, vast numbers of whom died on board of prison ships; not less than 11,000 died in the Jersey prison ship alone.

1787. Dr. HERSCHEL observed three lunar volcanoes.

1791. RICHARD PRICE, an eminent English divine, died; celebrated for his great abilities in arithmetical calculations, and for very numerous and valuable writings, theological, political and scientific.

1797. Battle of Diersheim, between the Austrians under the veteran Gen. Kray, and the French under Hoche, &c. The former were defeated with the loss of 4000 prisoners, and all their cannon, baggage, ammunition, &c.

1797. The French under Moreau defeated the Austrians and entered Kehl. The Austrians fled, abandoning everything to the enemy.

1813. BENJAMIN RUSH, a distinguished American physician and statesman, died. He was a member of Congress in 1776, and a signer of the declaration of independence. Few men have been greater ornaments to the country, and very few have acquired greater reputation both at home and abroad.

1824. GEORGE GORDON, lord Byron, died aged 36. At the age of 19 he published a volume of his juvenile poems, which were the precursors of some of the rarest productions which the language affords.

His career was marked by singularities and dissipation. Having embarked in the struggle of the Greeks for liberty, he was attacked by fever and died at Missolonghi.

1833. James Gambier, a British admiral died. He commanded the fleet which took possession of the Danish navy in 1807. He was characterized by great piety and benevolence.

1837. M. Ancillon, a Prussian minister, died at Berlin, aged 70; eminent as a statesman, philosopher and publicist.

1839. Aaron Ogden. an American statesman and patriot, died. He served as an officer during the whole of the revolutionary war; after which he practiced law for many years with great reputation, and held important civil offices.

1854. John Davis, a Massachusetts statesman of great ability, died, aged 67.

1856. Thomas Rogers, a noted manufacturer of cotton machinery, died in New York, aged 64. He early turned his attention to the construction of iron work and machinery for rail roads, and in 1835 began the manufacture of locomotives, in the construction of which he became greatly distinguished.

APRIL 20.

69. Marcus Salvius Otho, emperor of Rome, died. He ascended the throne after the murder of Galba and Piso, and three months after, being defeated by Vitellus, killed himself, rather than fall into the hands of the conqueror.

332. Battle of Mæsia, in which Constantine defeated the Goths under Alaric, and compelled them to recross the Danube.

1314. Clement V (Bertrand de Goth), pope of Rome, died. He was a Frenchman, bishop of Bordeaux, elected pope, 1305; was accused of licentiousness and extravagance.

1534. Elizabeth Barton (*the Holy Maid of Kent*), and several other persons, hanged at Tyburn, and their heads set up in several parts of London, for practicing an imposture.

1558 (or 9). John Bugenhagen, a learned coadjutor of Martin Luther in translating the scriptures, and author of commentaries thereon, died.

1566. John Mason, an English statesman, died. He rose from obscurity to places of honor under Henry VIII, and maintained his influence at court under Edward, Mary and Elizabeth.

1579. A man named Hammond was burnt in a ditch at Norwich, England, for the crime of obstinate heresy, as charged by the bishop of Norwich.

1626. St. Salvadore, capital of Brazil, surrendered by the Dutch to the Portuguese.

1657. Naval battle in the harbor of St. Cruz, Teneriffe, in which Admiral Blake attacked and destroyed the Spanish fleet of 16 ships, under the protection of the batteries on shore. This was his last and greatest achievement.

1708. Damaris Masham, a learned English lady, died. She was an authoress, and deservedly respected, not only for her learning, but for every virtue.

1718. James Petiver, an English botanist, died. He collected a valuable museum, and wrote several works on botany.

1743. French seigniories on Lake Champlain.

1750. John Lewis Petit, a celebrated French surgeon, died. He was invited to visit the king of Poland, and afterwards went to Spain to attend on Ferdinand. He invented some valuable surgical instruments, and published several works on surgery.

1775. General Putnam joined the patriot band at Concord, having rode his horse about 100 miles in 18 hours.

1777. First constitution of New York state adopted.

1792. French declared war against Francis I, as king of Hungary and Bohemia.

1795. Treaty between the French convention and the Chouans.

1798. Jenkins, known in London as the *tall clerk*, died. His outer coffin measured 8 feet. He was buried under the floors of the banking house which covered a part of St. Christopher's burying ground. £200 had been offered for his body.

1798. Engagement between the British ship Mars, 74 guns, Capt. A. Hood, and French ship L'Hercule, 74 guns, and 700 men. The British captured the Frenchman, but with the loss of Capt. Hood killed.

1809. Battle of Abensburgh; the Austrian army defeated by Napoleon, who took about 10,000 prisoners and 40 cannon. This defeat broke the lines of the Austrians, and exposed them to farther misfortunes.

1810. Great fire at Constantinople, 8,000 houses burnt.

1812. George Clinton, vice-president of the United States, died. He was a member of the colonial assembly at the breaking out of the revolution, when he received the appointment of brigadier-general. He was reelected governor of New York five times.

1813. The advance of the British and Indians appeared before Fort Meigs.

1821. Frederick Charles Achard, a Prussian naturalist and chemist, died. He is principally known as the inventor of a process of manufacturing sugar from beets, which has since been brought to great perfection.

1835. Samuel Slater, "father of the cotton manufacturing business in the United States," died. The first cotton manufactory in this country was built by him at Pawtucket, R. I.; it was standing and in operation at the time of his death.

1838. A meteoric shower observed at Knoxville, Tenn.; 154 meteors being counted by two observers between the hours of 10 at night and 4 in the morning.

George Nugent, general and field-marshal, died in England at the age of ninety-two. He was the oldest field officer in service, having entered it in 1773. He served throughout the American revolutionary war, and was employed in the expedition up the Hudson for the relief of Burgoyne's army. He was also present at the capture of Forts Clinton and Montgomery.

1842. Bertrand Cassel, who for a time was a resident of the United States, and during that period was sentenced to death by the French government, died at Toulouse.

1845. William Read, a member of Gen. Washington's staff, died at Charleston, S. C., aged 91.

1847. Battle of Cherubusco.

1854. An offensive and defensive alliance was signed between Austria and Prussia.

1854. The bill of Miss Dix, the philanthropist, granting ten millions of acres of the public lands to be distributed among the states, to ameliorate the condition of the indigent insane, was vetoed by the president.

1856. Robert L. Stevens died at Hoboken, N. J., aged 68. He devoted much time to the improvement of steam machinery and steam boat models; was one of the projectors of the Camden and Amboy rail road, and at the time of his death was engaged by government in building an immense steam battery for harbor defence.

APRIL 21.

753 b. c. Anniversary of the foundation of Rome, in the 3d year of the 6th olympiad, 431 years after the destruction of Troy, and 116 years from the building of Carthage. Romulus was in his 17th year when he received the regal title, and his subjects consisted of a legion of 3,000 foot and 300 horse.

753 b. c. Remus, the brother of Romulus, slain by the workmen who were building Rome, for ridiculing the weakness of the walls. Thus marked with blood at the outset, the city became the sanctuary of refugees and criminals, and to increase the population, neighboring females were dragged within its boundaries.

323 b. c. Diogenes, *the cynic*, died at Corinth, aged 90. He was expelled from his native city, Synope, for coining false money. His smart sayings and repartees were taken for wisdom, and his misanthropy and residence in a tub for philosophy! He *snarled* at the follies of men—wherein he differed from two other *great philosophers*, one of whom laughed at, the other wept for, the foibles of the world.

248. The thousandth anniversary of the foundation of Rome celebrated, in the reign of the emperor Philip, when Pompey's famous theatre was burnt.

1073. Alexander II, pope, died. He possessed *one* Christian virtue, that was charity for the Jews, whom he protected from murder and rapine.

1109. Anselm, archbishop of Canterbury, died. He was no sooner invested with the robes, than he began a quarrel with the king, in which he was worsted. He was a haughty prelate, and the first who insisted on the celibacy of his clergy in England. He was canonized under Henry VII.

1143. Peter Abelard, a learned Frenchman, died. His love and misfortunes have saved his memory from oblivion; and the man whom his own century have admired as a profound divine, is now celebrated as the martyr of love. The letters of Abelard and Heloise are frequently republished, and there is a voluminous life of the lovers by Berington.

1284. Alfonzo X (*the wise*), king of Castile and Leon, died. He was a man of great learning, and was the first king who had the public documents written in Spanish, which he did with a view to polish and enrich the language. His son usurped the throne, and it was with the greatest difficulty that he got it back again, by calling in the troops of the Moors; and the excommunication of the pope.

1480. William Caxton, the first English printer, finished the translation of *Ovid's Metamorphoses*, as we learn from his own memorandum, as follows: "*Ouyde his booke of Metamorphose Translated and fynnysshed by me William Caxton at Westmestre the xxii day of Apryll, the yere of our lord m. iiijc.iiijxx. And the xx yere of the Regne Kynge Edward the fourthe.*" This work is not known to have been printed, but there are several fragments of the work preserved in manuscript.

1519. The armament under Cortez arrived on the coast of Chalchiucuechan, a part of the Mexican empire.

1526. Battle of Paniput, in Hindostan, between Ibrahim Lodi, sultan of Delhi, and the Tartar prince Raber. Ibrahim was defeated and killed, which decided the conquest of Hindostan by the Tartars.

1545. The mines of Potosi opened. They were discovered by an Indian peasant, while hunting. A shrub which he had laid hold of to support himself, was torn up by the roots, and disclosed to the hunter a rich mass of silver. The population of the city increased so rapidly that in 1611, a little more than half a century afterwards, there were 160,000 inhabitants, but in 1826 they had decreased to 12,000. There are at present less than 100 mines worked, and these conducted with great ignorance and disadvantage.

1671. Anthony Godeau, a French divine, died. He was one of the first and brighest ornaments of the academy of belles-lettres, an active and attentive prelate, and exemplary in every part of his conduct. He wrote a valuable *Ecclesiastical History*, 3 vols. folio.

1679. The council of 30 constituted by Charles II. They consisted of 15 whigs and 15 tories—chosen by their property to balance the commons, the former valued at £300,000, that of the latter at £400,000.

1696. Brigadier Ambrose Rockwood with two others, convicted at Tyburn for high treason and executed on the 29th. They were the first prisoners having the benefit of council, &c.

1718. Philip de la Hire, a French mathematician, died, aged 78. He is characterized as a great and good man whose days were employed in study, and his nights frequently in astronomical observations. His scientific pursuits were various, and his works numerous and valuable.

1757. Battle of Reichenberg, in Bohemia; the Prussians under Schwerin defeated the Austrians under Count Konigseg. Austrian loss 1,000 killed, 400 prisoners; Prussian loss, 100 killed and wounded.

1765. David Mallet, a Scotch poet, died. His name is familiar as an author, although his place is not very high on the roll of fame; there is no species of composition in which he was eminent.

1770. Marriage of Louis XVI and Maria Antoinette, archduchess of Austria; when 4,000 persons perished in the crowd that assembled to witness the procession.

1773. Ali Bey, governor of Egypt, died. He was the son of a Greek sold by a band of robbers to the Janisaries, who raised him to power; and was finally enabled to throw off his obedience to the Porte. He was humane and generous, and possessed an elevated mind.

1794. Guadaloupe and its dependencies, Marigalante and Deseada, surrendered to the British.

1809. Battle of Landshut, in Bavaria, when Napoleon following up his victory of the previous day, attacked the Austrian army and defeated it. The Austrians lost 30 pieces of cannon, 9,000 prisoners, baggage, &c., and retreated to concentrate their forces at Eckmuhl.

1818. New York state library established.

1836. Battle of San Jacinto, in Texas, between the Mexicans, 1,500, under Santa Anna, and the Texians, 783, under Gen. Houston. The Mexicans were defeated, with the loss of 630 killed, 208 wounded, and 730 prisoners, among whom were Santa Anna and Gen. Cos; also 600 muskets, 390 sabres, 260 pistols, several hundred horses, and $12,000 in specie, fell into the hands of the victors, who lost 2 killed, 23 wounded.

1843. Augustus Frederick, duke of Sussex, died in London. He was an untiring patron of the deserving aspirants in any art.

1844. Henry Baldwin, one of the judges of the United States supreme court, died at Philadelphia.

1853. Lewis C. Beck, noted for his attainments in natural science, died at Albany, aged 53. He published works on botany and chemistry, and one on the mineralogy of New York.

1855. A riot broke out at Chicago, occasioned by the license question; the military were called out.

APRIL 22.

1369. Corner stone of the bastile, (a name used to denote a fortress or prison,) laid at Paris, by Hugues d'Aubriot, provost des marchands, and the founder of the Huguenots. It was not completed till 1383. It was demolished 1789.

1509. Henry VII of England died. The victory of Bosworth field and the death of Richard III left him in peaceable possession of the throne. He was an able and wise king, but insatiably covetous.

1519. Cortez arrived at San Juan Ulloa, in Mexico, where he received ambassadors from Montezuma, with rich presents, offering his services to the Spaniards, but declining to receive their visits at his court; and finally, after mutual messages and presents, refused to consent that foreign troops should appear nearer his capital, or remain longer in his dominions. "Truly this is a great monarch, and rich," said Cortez to his attendants; "with the permission of God we must see him."

1522. Battle of Villalar; count de Haro defeated Padillo, chief of the holy junta. Padillo was taken and executed next day, with John Bravo and Francis Maldonado, two of his chiefs.

1555. Sienna, in Tuscany, reduced by

famine, surrendered to the Florentines, after a siege of 10 months.

1608. HUDSON sailed from England on his second voyage of discovery; but returned after spending about four months in the search of a northwest passage to England.

1638. WOUTER VAN TWILLER, having been superseded in the government of New Netherland, leased the farm or bouwery No. 1, belonging to the West India company, for three years, at an annual rent of 250 guilders ($100).

1697. Birthday of BELINDA CRAUFORD, who died in the beginning of June, 1812, aged 115, at Richmond, Galway county, Ireland. It is said that at the time of her death she could read and sew without spectacles, and what was more remarkable, looked as youthful as a girl of eighteen years, had a blooming complexion, her eyes animated and lively, and walked occasionally a distance of two miles to church.

1699. HANS ASSMAN VON ABSCHATZ, a German statesman and poet, died.

1699. JEAN RACINE, a French tragic poet, died. His pieces were received with great applause, and he came to be generally preferred to his contemporary Corneille, who had been previously looked upon as inimitable.

1702. FRANCIS CHARPENTIER, a Frenchman of learning and abilities, died. He greatly contributed to the noble series of medals struck in the reign of Louis XIV.

1715. Total eclipse of the sun in England. It occurred at 9 in the morning, when the stars appeared, and the birds sunk within their nests.

1730. A public library founded in New York.

1741. MATTHEW ELIAS, a painter, died; who, under the patronage of Corbeen, rose to great eminence in his profession.

1751. One, OSBORNE, and his wife accused by a publican at Tring, in Hertfordshire, England, of witchcraft, were brutally murdered by the populace.

1758. ANTHONY DE JUSSIEU, an eminent French botanist, died. He traveled over several countries of Europe in the pursuit of his favorite science, which he greatly improved.

1764. EDWARD COBELEN, an eminent English divine and theological writer, died. Although he enjoyed several clerical offices, he restricted himself to a small income, on which he lived with simplicity and contentment.

1792. ISAAC RENE GUY DE CHAPELLIER, a native of Rennes, in France, and a zealous advocate of liberty, died.

1794. CHRISTIAN WILLIAM DE LAMOIGNON MALESHERBES, an able French advocate and author, beheaded. After serving his country 25 years he retired; but was recalled by Louis XVI to be minister of the interior. When the unfortunate king was dragged before the revolutionary tribunal, Malesherbes boldly appeared to defend him. He was himself condemned by the same tribunal, and ascended the scaffold with his daughter and a grandchild.

1796. Demerara and its dependencies in Guiana, surrendered to the British.

1801. MURAD BEY, the celebrated Mameluke chief, died of the plague, while descending the Nile to join the English. He was succeeded by Tambourji, so named from having been a drummer.

1809. Battle of Eckmuhl, in which Bonaparte, having routed one division of the Austrian army two days in succesion, executed a variety of movements, considered as among the most admirable displays of his science, by which he brought the whole of his force upon the army of the archduke Charles, which he had concentrated at Eckmuhl. The battle is said to have been one of the most splendid which the art of war could display. The Austrian army, of upwards of 100,000 men, were dispossessed of all their positions, by the combined attack of the French, whose divisions appeared on the field, each in its due place and order, as regularly as the movements of the various pieces in the game of chess. The battle commenced at two in the afternoon and continued till nightfall. It resulted in the complete overthrow of the Austrians; all their wounded, a great part of their artillery, fifteen stands of colors, and 20,000 prisoners, remained in the power of the French to which their loss in the field may be added. Their retreat was also attended with corresponding loss.

1826. Missolonghi taken by the Turks. It had been besieged several months, and was reduced to a heap of ruins by continued bombardments. The heroic garrison forced a passage through the besiegers, leaving the sick, aged and wounded in a mill containing a quantity of powder. An old wounded soldier took his seat on the mine, and fired it as soon as the Turks entered.

1829. Lepanto surrendered by capitulation to the Greeks.

1839. THOMAS HAYNES BAYLY, an English lyric poet, died. He is the author of about 30 plays, and many beautiful and popular songs.

1846. The Chilian ship Maria Helena arrived at Edgartown, Mass., from Valparaiso Dec. 7th; said to have been the first Chilian ship that ever visited the United States.

1850. The last publication of the bans

of marriage in Massachusetts. It was the case of a black man who declared his intention to marry a white woman.

1853. An insurrection attempted at Freiburg, in Switzerland, by the Jesuit party; but was soon suppressed, with some loss of life.

1854. Odessa was bombarded by the allied fleets, and in ten hours a large part of the city was laid in ruins.

APRIL 23.

997. Adalbert, the apostle of Prussia, murdered. He was archbishop of Prague, preached the gospel among the Bohemians, and afterwards among the Poles, where he was killed.

1016. Ethelred II, king of England, died. To deliver himself from the heavy tribute which he paid the Danes, called *Danegelt*, he caused them to be put to death; whereupon England was invaded by Sweyn, and Ethelred obliged to fly to Normandy, where he remained till Sweyn's death.

1349. The order of the Garter instituted by Edward III.

1408. The heroic earl of Warwick, Richard Beauchamp, on his way to the Holy Land, is challenged at Verona by Pandulph Malet, whose shoulder the English knight cleaved with his battleaxe.

1500. Brazil discovered by Pedro Alvarez Cabral, a Portuguese adventurer; who immediately sent home a ship with the intelligence, and the king took possession of it. But as the pope had given all the western infidels to the Spaniards, it is probable a great deal of trouble would have arisen out of the case, had not the two monarchs been kinsmen and friends.

1547. Battle of Mulhausen, in which the emperor Charles V defeated the Saxons, who lost 1200 killed, and the elector was wounded and taken prisoner.

1557. Peter Danes, professor of Greek at Paris, died. He was a prelate of great eloquence and extensive learning.

1616. William Shakspeare, the English dramatist, died, aged 52. His history is shrouded in obscurity; but the success of his dramas, with the sobriety and moderation of his views, enabled him to retire early with a competence. The writings of this great poet of nature are found in the libraries of the greatest foes of the drama. This is also the anniversary of his birthday, 1564.

1616. Michael de Cervantes Saavedra, the Spanish novelist, died, aged 67. His life was attended with poverty and misfortune. The immortal *Don Quixote*, which wrought so great a change in the fashionable literature of the day, is still read and admired in almost every language.

1625. Maurice of Nassau, prince of Orange, died. He succeeded his father in the government of the Low Countries, added to his dominions by conquest, and was considered the ablest general of his time.

1662. Charter of Connecticut granted, with ample privileges, by Charles II. John Winthrop was appointed governor until a new election should be made. The colony of New Haven was included in the charter, but did not consent to be united with the other colonies under one government. The fact was, they considered their civil and religious code rather superior to any thing else of the kind in the world, and were exceedingly jealous of contamination.

1676. Engagement off Aosta, in Sicily, between the French fleet under admiral du Quesne, and the Dutch fleet under De Ruyter, who was mortally wounded.

1709. The first number of the *Tatler* was published by Steele, Addison and Swift.

1729. Jean Barbeyrac, an eminent French jurist, died. He has distinguished himself by many learned works, which show a high degree of erudition and a liberal spirit.

1740. Thomas Tickell, an English poet, died. He was the friend of Addison whose works he published, and translated the Iliad in opposition to Pope.

1750. Andrew Baxter, a Scottish metaphysician, died. His writings are highly lauded by Warburton. By one of them we learn that dreams are caused by the agency of separate immaterial beings.

1774. Battle between the forces of Rohilcund in Afghanistan, and the subahdar of Oude backed by a British force. The Rohilcas showed great bravery and resolution, and exhibited a considerable share of military knowledge; but after a cannonade of two hours and twenty minutes, they retreated with the loss of 2000 killed, including many of their chiefs; the country became tributary, and the people robbers and plunderers.

1775. A captain Sears and Mr. Lamb assembled the citizens of New York, shut up the custom-house, and prevented the sailing of vessels to Boston, Quebec and Georgia. They sent an express to Philadelphia, where the same measures were adopted.

1781. Fort Watson, in South Carolina, taken from the British, by the provincials under colonel Lee. The fort was built on an Indian mound 30 feet high; but the besiegers speedily erected a work which overlooked the fort, and fired into it with such effect that the garrison surrendered.

1794. JAMES DUVAL D'EPREMENIE, a French advocate, executed. He was remarkable for the violence of his proceedings during the revolution, and was sent to the scaffold with his old opponent Chapellier.

1795. WARREN HASTINGS acquitted after a trial of 7 years. His crime as charged by the house of commons to the peers was maladministration in India.

1808. MURAT, at the head of 40,000 French soldiers, taking advantage of a faction among the people, entered Madrid and took possession of it.

1809. Battle of Ratisbon. The Austrians, having sustained defeat and losses four days successively, made some attempt to fortify this city, in order to protect the retreat of the army. The French, who had advanced to the storm, were cut down by the musquetry of the besieged. There was at length difficulty in finding volunteers to renew the attack, when the impetuous Lannes, by whom they were commanded, seized a ladder and rushed forward to fix it himself against the wall. "I will show," exclaimed he, "that your general is still a grenadier." The French rallied and carried the ramparts—the contest was renewed in the street, and the city fired. The Austrians were driven out of Ratisbon, leaving cannon, baggage and prisoners in the hands of the French. Thus in five days, in spite of the inferiority of numbers and the imperfect manner in which his troops were combined, Bonaparte, by the sole energy of his genius, triumphed over the main forces of his opponent, and opened the road to his capital. At no period of his momentous career, says Scott, did the genius of Napoleon appear more completely to prostrate all opposition; at no time did the talents of a single individual exercise such an influence on the fate of the universe.

1810. Fort Matagorda, having been reduced to a heap of ruins, was evacuated by the British, in consequence of which the French were enabled to bombard Cadiz; 500 officers and 900 men fell into the hands of the French.

1810. DINAH, a black woman, died in Bucks county, Pennsylvania, aged 116.

1823. AARON ARROWSMITH, hydrographer to the king of Great Britain, died. He was distinguished as a constructor of maps and charts, and published a new *General Atlas* to accompany the *Edinburgh Gazetteer*.

1823. JOSEPH NOLLEKINS, an eminent sculptor, died. He gained great reputation as an artist during his residence in Italy, and on his return to England was so extensively patronized that he acquired a large fortune.

1833. The foundation laid of the first protestant episcopal church ever built in France.

1838. The English steam packets Great Western and Sirius arrived at New York, forming a new era in navigation, and commencing a new and expeditious mode of intercourse between England and the United States. The Great Western, measuring 1,340 tons, made the passage in 14½ days, against head winds and a rough sea.

1839. H. V. DUCOUDRAY HOLSTEIN died at Albany; formerly a distinguished officer under Bonaparte. After the fall of the emperor he came to this country, and gained a subsistence by teaching the French and German languages.

1847. N. P. AMES, the celebrated manufacturer of fire arms, swords, &c., died at Cabotville, Mass.

1848. The United States exploring expedition reached the Dead sea, which was circumnavigated for the first time in a boat. It was sounded to the depth of 600 fathoms, and the bottom found to be crusted with crystalized salt.

1850. WM. WORDSWORTH, an eminent English poet, died, aged 80.

1852. SOLOMON VAN RENSSELAER, an officer in the war of 1812, died at Albany, aged 78. He commenced his military career at the age of 18, and was with Wayne in the battle of Miami, where he was dangerously wounded. He received six balls at the battle of Queenstown, one of which he carried to the time of his death. He also held several civil offices with distinction.

1852. ARTHUR CONDORCET O'CONNOR died in France, aged 87. He was a native of Ireland, and one of the most conspicuous leaders of the rebellion in 1798, which made him an exile in France. He married a daughter of Condorcet, and adopted the name of the philosopher within his own.

1854. Fifteen firemen lost their lives by the sudden fall of a large store in Broadway, New York, while in the discharge of their duty.

1854. Great tornado at Burmah, which swept over several hundred miles of country, causing great loss of life on the Irrawaddy.

1856. A grand review of the fleet took place off Plymouth, England; it consisted of 240 ships of war, all but 2 being steamers.

1856. JOSEPH ROBERTS died, aged 81. He was cashier for the trustees of the first bank of the United States, the affairs of which institution he conducted to its final winding up.

APRIL 24.

1184 B. C. The conquest and destruction of the city of Troy by the Greeks, took place on the 24th of Thargelion.

339 B.C. TIMOLEON defeated the Carthagenians at the river Crimesus, near the mount Giuliano, in Sicily.

1016. ETHELRED II buried in St. Paul's, London.

1254. LOUIS IX of France, embarked from Acre, in Palestine, on his return from the crusade, with his queen, children and troops, in 14 vessels, and arrived in Vincennes in September, after an absence of six years, and a most disastrous campaign.

1345. RICHARD AUNGERVYLE, bishop of Durham, died. He was the tutor of Edward III, a learned man, and the author of a work on the right use of books.

1474. In Edward prince of Wales's procession there was a station with three patriarchs standing with Jacob's 12 sons, and many other personifications of scripture characters,—such was the amusement of the times.

1500. Brazil discovered by Pedro Alvarez de Cabral, who left two convicts.

1556. OSEP NAPEA, the first ambassador from Russia to England, made his appearance at the court of Elizabeth, and delivered his master's presents.

1557. GEORGE RORAR (Rorarius), a learned corrector of the press at Wittemburg, died, aged 65. He had been the amanuensis of Luther, and assisted in editing some of the works of the great reformer.

1599. Birthday of OLIVER CROMWELL.

1603. JAMES BEATON, bishop of Glasgow, died. He was raised to the see before the age of 25; when the reformation broke forth, he fled to France, with the records and sacred vessels of his cathedral, which were deposited with the Scotch college of Paris. He left a history of Scotland in manuscript.

1617. D'ANCRE CONCINI, marechal of France, assassinated. He was a Florentine by birth, and acquired his offices by intrigue. The day following his burial, the body was taken from the grave, mutilated and dragged through the streets of Paris.

1645. CROMWELL defeated the king's forces at Islip bridge, near Oxford, taking the king's standard and 200 prisoners.

1667. MATTHEW WREN, bishop of Hereford, died. During the civil wars his property was confiscated and himself confined in the Tower 18 years without being brought to trial.

1704. The *Boston News Letter*, the first paper printed in America, made its appearance at Boston, published by John Campbell, the postmaster. It was printed on a half sheet of writing paper. It was continued until the British evacuated Boston, in 1776.

1731. DANIEL DEFOE, a popular English author, died, He is best known as the author of *Robinson Crusoe*, which was supposed at first to be a true narrative, and afterwards as erroneously to have been founded upon the papers of Alexander Selkirk. It still enjoys an old age of honor and renown, which it is impossible for any eulogium to exalt. Like its hero, it has traveled into the most distant regions, and worn the costume of literature and the garland of fame in almost every civilized country of the globe.

1735. "Here lyes inter'd ye remains of deacon CHRISTOPHER HUNTINGTON of Norwich, November 1st, 1660, and ye first born of males in ye town. He served near 40 years in ye office of a deacon, and died April ye 24th, 1735, to ye 75th yr. of his age. Memento mori."

1763. CHARLES STEPHEN PESSELIER, a French dramatist and financier, died. He was early assiduously devoted to literature and the muses; but when entrusted with the finances of the kingdom, his application ruined his constitution, and he fell a victim to excessive mental fatigue.

1773. PHILIP DORMER, earl of Chesterfield, died. He was a polished courtier, and a writer on, rather than a practicer of, good manners.

1775. JOSIAH QUINCY, Jr., an eminent American patriot, died. He was employed by the British officers, together with John Adams, to defend their cause in the case of the Boston massacre, and although warmly opposed to the measures of the British ministry, he conducted the defence with great propriety. He fell a victim to intense application, at the age of 31, and died at sea on his return from England.

1778. Action in the roads opposite the town of Carrickfergus, in Ireland, in which the British sloop of war Drake was captured by the United States ship Ranger, under Paul Jones.

1780. CLAUDE JOSEPH DORAT, a French poet, died. He entered the military service as a musketeer, but abandoned it to pursue his favorite study. His works comprise 20 vols.

1780. JOHN NOURSE, a distinguished bookseller and mathematician, died.

1799. WILLIAM SEWARD, an English antiquary, died. He was the son of a brewer, and being possessed of a competency devoted himself to literature. He published 7 volumes of anecdotes and notices of distinguished characters, compiled from scarce and curious books.

1799. PETER AUGUSTIN CARON DE BEAU-

MARCHAIS, a French dramatist, died. He was a watchmaker, and made some improvement in the escapement of a watch. His dramas are numerous, and some of them still popular.

1814. The British army took the city of Washington by surprise, and burnt the public buildings. The library of congress consisting of 3000 volumes of rare books was destroyed.

1824. RICHARD PAYNE, died at London; an eminent Greek scholar and antiquary.

1841. GEORGE BAXTER, one of the most eminent of Presbyterian ministers, died at his residence in Virginia, aged 77.

1856. The sheriff of Kansas, who had been engaged in arresting some Free State men, as they were termed, was shot while sitting in his tent.

APRIL 25.

68. Saint MARK, the evangelist, died at Alexandria.

1199. JOHN, the 6th son of Henry II of England, seized the treasures of his late father, preparatory to taking possession of his throne and dukedom.

1284. EDWARD II born at Caernarvon, and styled the *prince of Wales*, the first who received that appellation.

1342. BENEDICT XII (James de Nouveau, *the baker*), died. When elected, unanimously, by the cardinals, pope of Rome, he had so little confidence in himself that he told them they had chosen an ass. His conduct, however, was firm and dignified, and gained him universal respect.

1513. EDWARD HOWARD, an English admiral, celebrated for his bravery, killed in an action with a French ship.

1520. FERDINAND MAGELLAN, the Portuguese navigator killed in one of the Phillipine islands, fighting for the king of the country, who had become his ally. Of all his fleet, only one ship and 18 men returned to Spain, from whence the expedition sailed.

1536. Conflagration of mount Ætna, which overwhelmed the church of St. Leon, and the physician Piazzi.

1576. Treaty between Holland and Zealand, being the two first provinces that united for their liberty. William of Nassau, prince of Orange, drew up the treaty, and may be considered as the founder of the United Provinces.

1595. TORQUATO TASSO, an illustrious Italian poet, died. He was excellent in every kind of composition, but the *Jerusalem Delivered* procured him the offer of the laurel crown. He expired on the day appointed for the coronation.

1636. JAMES HAY, earl of Carlisle, died. He was the first Scotchman raised to the English peerage, and was employed by James I in various embassies.

1660. HENRY HAMMOND, an English divine, died. He published a commentary on the New Testament; and begun a paraphrase and commentary on the Old Testament, which he did not live to finish.

1671. The city of Oxford, England, nearly destroyed by a great fire.

1728. JOHN WOODWARD, an English natural philosopher, died. He was bound apprentice to a linen draper, but was attracted from the business by the charms of science.

1732. The corpse of bishop Atterbury who died in France arrived in the Thames. Four pieces of French silk brocaded with silver were found with the body, which the custom house officers seized!

1734. JOHN CONRAD DIPPEL, a German chemist and physician, died. He was an eccentric character, who pretended to have discovered the philosophers' stone, and yet was confined for debt. In pursuing his alchemical researches, he discovered Prussian blue, and the animal oil which bears his name.

1735. SAMUEL WESLEY, an English poet, died. His writings made up in quantity what they lacked in quality. He wrote the *Life of Christ*, a heroic poem, in folio, and a history of the Bible in verse, 3 vols.

1764. JUDAH MONIS, an Italian Jew, died at Northborough, Mass., aged 82. He was converted and baptized, and was the first Hebrew instructor at Harvard college.

1770. JOHN ANTHONY NOLLET, a learned Frenchman, died. His writings are valuable, and his experiments contributed much to the advancement of science.

1775. The Baltimoreans received the news of the battle of Lexington, and immediately seized upon the provincial magazines, containing 1500 stand of arms, &c.

1781. Battle of Camden, between the provincials, about 1200, and the British under lord Rawdon. In the beginning of the action the Americans had essentially the advantage; but the premature retreat of two companies occasioned a total defeat. Greene retreated in such order as to bring off all his wounded and cannon, and took 50 prisoners.

1781. British under Arnold and Philips took Petersburg, Va., after a smart action with baron Steuben. They burnt 400 hogsheads of tobacco, a ship, and several small craft.

1782. ADRIAN BALBI, the Venitian geographer, was born at Venice. The work by which he is best known is his *Abrégé de Géographie.*

1792. The convention having determined on adopting the proposition of M. Guillotin, to substitute decapitation for hanging, the first criminal was executed by this mode on this day. M. Guillotin was actuated by benevolent motives in proposing the machine, which was called from him *guillotine*, and from which himself narrowly escaped.

1800. WILLIAM COWPER, an excellent English poet, died. He commenced publishing at the age of 50, and three years after produced the *Task*, which excited universal admiration. He was subject to religious delirium, and died in a state of absolute despair.

1805. THOMAS POWNALL, an English antiquary, died. He was successively governor of New Jersey, Massachusetts and South Carolina under the crown. His works are numerous, and display a great deal of information.

1810. Sweden excluded British goods, conformably to the continental system established by Bonaparte.

1812. Baltimore privateer schooner Surprise, Capt. Cothell, of 10 guns, captured the British brig Kutousoff, of 12 guns, laden with coffee, &c., and brought her safe to port.

1820. PATRICK COLQUOHUN, a distinguished Scottish magistrate, died. He was a writer on police and political economy, and his works possess great merit.

1832 & 1833. Spring navigation of the Erie canal opened.

1835. JONATHAN P. CUSHING, president of Hampden Sidney college, died, aged 40. The institution, over which he had presided 14 years, was greatly indebted to his services, and he was highly esteemed for his virtues.

1838. The second centennial celebration of the settlement of New Haven.

1838. The steamboat Moselle burst her boiler with a tremendous explosion. She had just left the wharf at Cincinnati for Louisville, with 225 passengers on board, of whom but 124 were saved.

1839. SAMUEL SMITH, an officer of the revolution, died at Baltimore, aged 87. His name is connected with some of the most important events of that struggle for freedom, and is identified with the history of the city of Baltimore for a great number of years; that city being indebted to his enterprise for a large share of its commercial thrift.

1840. M. POISSON, a peer of France, and president of the academy of sciences, died at Paris, aged 58. His life was devoted to analytical discovery and scientific investigation, and he was styled the first geometrician of Europe.

1849. The parliament house and library of the British provinces, at Montreal, burned by a mob.

1849. The French republican armament against republican Rome reached Civita Vecchia.

1854. The slaves of Venezuela became freemen by virtue of an act previously passed for their emancipation.

1855. Lieut. Col. ST. VRAIN, with a detachment of United States troops, came up with and captured a camp of Apacha Indians, on the Purgatory, near the Raton mountains.

APRIL 26.

871. ETHELRED I defeated the Danes, but died of his wounds. In his reign a great plague occured.

1478. LORENZO DE MEDICI, duke of Florence, rescued by the populace from the hands of assassins. His brother Julian was less fortunate; he fell beneath their daggers. The duke was conducted back to his palace by the multitude with every demonstration of regard, while the archbishop, who became the tool of the pope for executing this foul and impious conspiracy, was suspended in his pontifical robes from the window of his own sanctuary.

1566. DIANA DE POITIERS, duchess of Valentinois, died, She captivated the heart of the king of France, Henry II, and for many years remained sole mistress, not only of his affections, but of the kingdom. Her unusual powers of mind, and firmness and dignity, constituted her the fitest sovereign of the two.

1595. MICHAEL NEANDER, a learned German protestant, died. He was rector of the university of Ilfeldt 40 years, and published several learned works.

1607. CHRISTOPHER NEWPORT, with three vessels and 100 emigrants, forming the first permanent English colony, stood into Chesapeake bay, "which seemed to invite his entrance."

1616. JOHN SOMERS, an English statesman, died. He was a patriot of the noblest and most extensive views, and justly celebrated as a man of learning, eloquent and refined.

1665. The great plague of this and the subsequent year broke out at St. Giles, London.

1726. JEREMY COLLIER, an English divine, died. In 1698 he made an attempt to reform the stage, which engaged him in a controversy, and exposed him to the satire of the wits of the day; but after a ten years' struggle he accomplished his object, and actually produced an amendment.

1734. JOHN BAPTIST MORVAN DE BELLEGARDE, a French Jesuit, died. He was expelled from the order at Nantes, for being a Cartesian.

1777. Danbury, Conn., burnt, and the military stores destroyed, by a detachment of 2,000 British under Tyron. The place was guarded by 100 soldiers, who retired to await reinforcements. Eighteen houses, 800 barrels of flour, 800 barrels of pork and beef, 2,000 bushels of grain, and 1,700 tents were destroyed. The enemy were pursued and annoyed by a few hundred of the citizens under Wooster and Arnold; the former was killed.

1783. EYRE COOTE, a celebrated commander of the East India Company's forces, died. He gained great renown by his victories over Hyder Ally; in one of which, near Porto Novo, with 10,000 men he defeated Hyder's army of 150,000.

1794. The Vendeans under Charette defeated by the French.

1794. Battle of Prisches; Austrians defeated by the French.

1794. Grand attack of the French upon the allies, from Trevers to the sea.

1805. WILLIAM WOODVILLE died; a distinguished English physician and medical writer.

1807. The planet Vesta observed in England by Groombridge, an ingenious and active astronomer, who had successfully devoted his leisure and fortune to the advancement of astronomy.

1815. CARSTEN NEIBUHR, a Danish traveler, died, aged 82. He was employed by the Danish government in 1761, with four other learned men, to explore Arabia; was the only one of the company who returned, after an absence of six years, and was liberally rewarded. His publications were, *Travels in Arabia* and *Description of Arabia.*

1816. GEORGE HARDINGE, an eminent English lawyer, died. He rose rapidly in his profession, became council for the East India Company, and attorney-general to the queen, and had a seat in parliament. His speeches and writings were numerous.

1831. Imprisonment for debt abolished in the state of New York.

1835. HENRY KATER died at London. His experiments on the pendulum and Geodesic surveys rendered him famous.

1836. St. Jean d'Arc, in Palestine, surrendered to the Egyptian troops under Ibrahim Pasha. The governor of the fortress was provided with a safe residence in Egypt, and an annual pension of 75,000 piasters.

1837. The trial of MEUNIER for an attempt to assinate the king of the French, terminated in his conviction. His sentence was commuted to perpetual banishment.

1838. Battle near Brugos, between Gen. Espartero and the Carlists under Negri, in which the latter were defeated, with the loss of 2,000 prisoners, their baggage and artillery.

1840. BACCHUS, a negro slave, died at Friedland, in Virginia, aged 110. He had been in the family of his last owner more than 40 years; was employed as a teamster during the war of the revolution; and was in attendance with his team at the glorious and final siege of Yorktown. He saw Gen. Braddock as he passed on to his defeat, and could give a succint account of that sanguinary action. The evening previous to his death he was walking about the farm, in the full possession of all his faculties of mind and body.

1840. JOHN THORNTON KIRKLAND, president of Harvard university, died, aged 70. His father was more than 40 years a missionary among the Oneida Indians, during which he was born at Little Falls, 1770. His rank was with the most eminent among the constant and serviceable friends of good principles, good learning and good men. Some of his productions will continue to be esteemed among the gems of our literature.

1843. HODIJAH BAYLIES died; a soldier of the revolutionary war, and for some time an aid to Gen. Washington. Like others of that noble band, he too was a distinguished civilian.

1853. RUSSELL JARVIS died in New York, aged 63; widely known as a politician, and co-editor with Duff Green, of the *United States Telegraph,* at Washington.

1854. A day of humiliation was observed throughout England; divine service was performed in all the places of public worship, and collections taken for the benefit of the wives and children of the soldiers engaged in the war of the east.

1854. GABRIEL ROSETTI, an Italian poet and painter, died, aged 71. Setting up for a reformer, he was obliged to fly to England, where he spent the remainder of his days in teaching Italian.

1854. HENRY T. COCHRANE, a Scottish jurist, died; known as the biographer of his friend Lord Jeffrey.

1855. The emperor and empress of the French, having visited the queen of England, returned to France on this day.

APRIL 27.

1124. ALEXANDER I of Scotland, son of Malcom Canmore, died. He ascended the throne on the death of his brother Edgar, 1107, and from the energy and impetuosity of his character he was called the *fierce.* There were several rebellions and insurrections against his reign, which he put down with vigor. A conspiracy was formed against his life, and the traitors got admission into his bed chamber at night. He cut his way through them, and after killing six made his escape.

1192. CONRAD DE MONTFERRAT assassinated at Tyre.

1296. Battle of Dunbar, in which Edward I, of England, defeated the Scots under the king, John Baliol, who lost 20,000 slain. Baliol was taken prisoner to England, and confined in the tower.

1404. PHILIP (*the bold*), duke of Burgundy, died. He was a just and brave prince, but so profuse in his expenses, that his body was seized after death by his creditors, and it was with difficulty that his duchess could redeem it.

1573. The army of the States General seized Flushing, and hanged the Spanish commander.

1603. King JAMES I, on his way to take possession of the English crown, was magnificently entertained at Winchinbrook by Sir Oliver Cromwell.

1610. Patent for Newfoundland granted to the earl of Northampton and 44 other persons, by the name of the treasurer and company of adventurers and planters of the cities of Bristol and London, for the colony or plantation of Newfoundland, from lat. 46 to 52 deg., together with the seas and islands lying within ten leagues of the coast.

1667. MILTON disposed of the copy right of the *Paradise Lost* for £5! It was with much difficulty that he could find any one to undertake the publication of it.

1702. JOHN BARTH died; who by his bravery and skill rose to a high rank in the French navy.

1717. The Dissenters received £5,000 for damages done their meeting houses during the rebellion on account of the pretender to the English throne.

1742. NICHOLAS AMHERST, an English political writer, died. He for a considerable time published the *Craftsman*, a paper conducted with unusual spirit and success, which guided the public taste and awed the administration.

1762. The Irish levelers suppressed by Lord Halifax.

1775. The Bostonians delivered up a large quanity of guns, &c., to the British general Gage.

1782. EDWARD CHAMBERLAYNE, an English statesman, died. He was one of the best scholars of his age.

1785. Prince LEOPOLD of Brunswick, son of the reigning duke, having gone to the relief of the inhabitants of an inundated village on the Oder, near Frankfort, was upset in his boat and drowned. Thus dying as he had lived, in the highest exercise of humanity.

1792. JOHN JAMES ANKERSTROOM, a Swedish officer, executed for the murder of Gustavus, king of Sweden.

1794. WILLIAM JONES died, a man who rose by the superiority of his genius, from a low station to a high judicial office in Bengal. By his unwearied industry and skill in the Asiatic languages, he successfully explored the hidden sources of oriental science and literature, and to whose translations we are indebted for many beautiful effusions of the Persian muse. As a linguist he has seldom if ever been surpassed. He was master of almost every language of Europe and Asia.

1794. JAMES BRUCE, the celebrated Scottish traveler, died. Being consul at Algiers, he found leisure to study the oriental languages, and formed the project of exploring the interior of Africa. He discovered the sources of the Nile.

1796. CHARLES TOWNSEND, an English nobleman, was found dead in a post chaise on his return from Great Yarmouth, for which borough his brother Frederick had been elected to parliament. They both had exhibited marks of insanity, and in one of these paroxyms Charles shot himself.

1799. Battle of Cassano, in Italy; the French under Moreau totally defeated by the Russians and Austrians under Suwarrow.

1803. TOUSSAINT l'OVERTURE, a mulatto chieftain of St. Domingo, died. He possessed unbounded influence over the blacks of that island, and became the head of all power, civil and military, among them. He was treacherously betrayed by the French, and thrown into prison where he died.

1804. JONATHAN BOUCHER, an English archæologist, died. He was an episcopal preacher in America, till the revolution drove him back to England. He prepared a glossary of provincial and archæological words, intended for a supplement to Johnson's Dictionary.

1806. The squadron under Miranda, intended to begin a revolution in South America, engaged two Spanish guardacostas. The Spaniards captured two schooners, having on board 22 officers and 30 men, all of whom were hanged or sent to the mines.

1813. The American army under Gen. Pike took York, the capital of Upper Canada. The British blew up the works, by which Gen. Pike was killed, as well as about 50 of the British, and 200 American soldiers killed or wounded.

1830. City of Guatamala nearly destroyed by an earthquake.

1834. THOMAS STOTHARD died; celebrated for his illustrations to the *Canterbury Tales*, *Rogers' Italy*. *Pilgrims' Progress* and *Robinson Crusoe*.

1836. John Hart, an American physician, died. He joined the army at the outbreak of the revolution, and continued in it until it was disbanded. He was afterwards a member of the Massachusetts senate, and much esteemed as a physician and a patriot.

1836. Battle near Fort Brook, Florida, between the United States volunteer troops and the Indians. The Indians were defeated with the loss of 200 killed. Loss of the U. S. troops, 2 killed, 24 wounded.

1836. The celebrated Bible presented by Alcuin to Charlemagne, was sold at auction in London for £1,500 ($6,666). See Dec. 1, 801.

1838. Baroness Schopenhauer died at Jena; a woman of talent and celebrity, and author of various works, which were collected in 24 vols.

1838. Great fire at Charlestown, S. C., "which laid waste 145 acres of the most populous part of the city."

1849. William B. Cooper, ex-governor, and a highly respected citizen of the state of Delaware, died at his residence, Laurel hill.

1850. The Atlantic, first steamer of the Collins line, sailed from Liverpool.

1855. Col. Kinney arrested in New York on a bench warrant, for beginning a military entreprise against Nicaragua.

1856. Ratification of the treaty of peace between England, France and Turkey, and Russia, which terminated the Crimean war.

1856. Robert Kelly, a New York merchant, died, aged 47. Having acquired a fortune and a high reputation as a merchant, he devoted his attention to science, acquired eight languages, and filled many important offices. His superior talents and untiring industry were under the direction of philanthropic and Christian impulses.

APRIL 28.

1060 b. c. The 28th Jiar is kept as a fast by the Hebrews for the death of Samuel, which took place two years before the destruction of Saul.

492 b. c. Menenius Agrippa, a Roman patrician died; celebrated for appeasing a sedition by a fable of the belly and the limbs.

357. Constantius, the third and surviving son of Constantine the great, visited Rome for thirty days, when he displayed the magnificence of a triumph.

1489. Henry Percy, earl of Northumberland, murdered.

1494. Joan Boughton, a widow, was burned for heresy; said to be the first female martyr of England.

1521. Cortez having constructed 13 brigantines with sails and oars, and transported them on the backs of 8000 Tlascalans, they were launched on this day in the lake of Mexico, with religious ceremonies under a discharge of the artillery and small arms, followed by the singing of *Te Deum* to the music of military instruments. They were provided with sails and twelve oars each, and a falconet, or small brass cannon. The final success of the enterprise was greatly indebted to these vessels.

1535. Albert Pio, a Spanish ecclesiastic buried with extraordinary pomp at Paris, in the church of the Cordeliers.

1552. The council of Trent was prorogued for two years; it did not assemble again until 1562.

1636. Julius Cæsar, an English statesman under Elizabeth, died. He was a man of great learning and integrity, charitable and benevolent.

1710. Thomas Betterton, an English tragedian, died. He was a bookbinder previous to going upon the stage; and acquired a high degree of reputation as an actor.

1721. An order of the English council was issued to suppress Hellfire clubs.

1738. Shakspeare's tragedy of *Julius Cæsar* performed at Drury Lane theatre, for the purpose of raising a fund for the erection of a monument to his memory at Westminster.

1751. Thomas Gibson, an eminent English painter, died.

1752. Francis Oudin, a French Jesuit, died. He was professor of theology at Dijon, and an author.

1754. Washington attacked a French encampment at the confluence of the Allegany and Monongahela. The night was dark and rainy, and the enemy completely secure. His troops having surrounded the camp, fired and rushed upon the French, who immediately surrendered.

1760. Battle of Sillery, in Canada, between the British garrison at Quebec, 3000, under Gen. Murray, and the French under Levi, consisting of 10 battalions of regulars, 6000 Canadian militia, and a body of Indians. The British general finding himself in danger of being outflanked, retreated to his fortifications, with the loss of 1000 men. The French loss was still greater, and they reaped no essential advantage from the victory.

1772. The counts Struensee, and Brandt, the favorite of the king of Denmark, executed at Copenhagen. Their alleged crime was an intrigue with the queen of Denmark, princess Caroline Matilda, sister of George III, of England.

1779. Simon Barnard, a celebrated aid-du-camp of Napoleon, and for some time chief of the engineer corps of the United States, was born at Dôle, in France.

1786. Gustavus, king of Sweden, read the eulogy of Creutz, the poet and statesman, who died a short time previous. Creutz signed with Franklin a treaty of amity between the United States and Sweden, 1783.

1788. Maryland, the 7th state in succession, adopted the constitution of the United States; votes 63 to 12.

1789. Mutiny on board the ship Bounty on her voyage from Otaheite, whither she had sailed to procure fruit trees to stock the West India islands. The vessel had on board 1015 plants of the bread fruit tree. Lieut. Bligh and 19 of the crew were compelled to go into an open boat; "they reached the island of Timor in June, after a perilous voyage of 1200 leagues."

1789. Thomas Hutchins, geographer-general of the United States, died. He was a native of New Jersey, and was in England at the commencement of the revolutionary war, where he refused some excellent offers, and was subsequently imprisoned and lost £12,000 on suspicion of holding correspondence with Franklin in Paris. He afterwards returned to America, served under Greene in South Carolina, and published several historical and geographical works, with charts and maps.

1793. Battle of Duren; the French defeated by the Austrians under Clairfait, with a loss of 2000, and their military chest, 12 cannon, and 13 ammunition wagons.

1796. Action off Lizard point, between the British ship Indefatigable, sir Edward Pellew, and French frigate La Virginia, 44 guns; the latter captured.

1796. Charette, the Vendean chief, executed at Nantes. This afforded General Hoche an opportunity to subdue the royalists in France.

1797. Robert Parker hanged for burglary at Knoxville, Tennessee.

1799. The French ambassadors were assassinated at Radstat. The infamy of this base action is shared by the French emigrants and Austrians.

1799. Battle of Adda, in Italy; the Russians under Suwarrow defeated the French under Serrurier, who, with his division, was taken prisoner.

1804. Surinam, or Dutch Guiana, in South America, taken by the British; the Dutch surrendered 2000 prisoners, 282 cannon, and several vessels.

1813. Spesutie island taken possession of by the British, situated near the head of Chesapeake.

1813. Privateer Yorktown, Capt. Riker, of New York, captured the British brig Avery, with a valuable cargo, and brought her safe to port.

1813. Michael Lavrionovitch Golenitcheff Kutusoff-Smolenski, the famous Russian field-marshal, died. He commanded the Russian army destined to oppose the invasion of Bonaparte in 1812.

1814. Bonaparte embarked for Elba from Frejus. He had landed at this place on his return from Egypt, when about to commence that astonishing career, which will be remembered in the history of Europe to the end of time: but which now, to all appearance, was about to terminate, and that at the very point from which it had started.

1851. Edward Codrington, a British admiral, died, aged 81. He distinguished himself under Howe and Nelson, but his name is chiefly renowned by the famous action of Navarino, where he had chief command.

1854. The American barque Hespar, bound for Antwerp, came in collision with the Bremen barque Favorite, for Baltimore, having 180 passengers on board, all of whom perished.

1854. William Henry Pagot, marquis of Anglesey, died, aged 86. He distinguished himself in several campaigns, especially in the Peninsular war, and was raised to the rank of field marshal.

1855. Giovanni Pianori, a hired bravo, attempted to shoot Louis Napoleon while riding in the Champs Elysees.

1856. The receipt of the ratification of the treaty of peace by all the foreign powers was announced officially in England, and a day of thanksgiving throughout the United Kingdom was appointed.

1857. Frederick Emerson, an eminent American instructor, died, aged 68. He was the author of a popular arithmetic used in the public schools.

APRIL 29.

997. Adalbert, archbishop of Prague, murdered. His zeal led him among foreigners as a missionary; after visiting Bohemia, he went among the Poles, by whom he was killed. Boleslaus purchased his body for its weight in gold.

1075. Waltheof, earl of Huntingdon and Northampton, executed by William the conqueror. He had married Judith, William's niece; and being considered by the English as the last resource of their nation, they most grievously lamented his death.

1205. King John, along with wine of various kinds to be transmitted to Windsor, ordered to be sent immediately the romance of the *History of England*.

1594. Thomas Cooper, an English prelate, died; highly commended for his great learning and eloquence.

1643. Ferdinando, lord Fairfax, the father of the famous General Fairfax, defeated at Bramham moor, by the earl of Newcastle.

1649. Dockier, a prominent leader of the *Levelers*, in the times of the English commonwealth, was shot by order of the government.

1652. A great eclipse of the sun in England. The almanacs of the day did not let so favorable an opportunity escape for exercising their power over the ignorant, and accordingly their prognostics created such a terror among the inhabitants "and so exceedingly alarmed the whole nation," says Evelyn, "that hardly any one would work, nor stir out of their houses. So ridiculously were they abused by ignorant and knavish star-gazers."

1659. John Cleveland, an English poet, died. He was contemporary with Milton, and preferred before him by critics of the day, but has now sunk into oblivion.

1676. Michael Adrian de Ruyter, the famous Dutch admiral, died. He began his military career at the age of 11, and continued in the service nearly 60 years.

1685. Luc d'Acheri, a French ecclesiastic, died. He displayed great learning as an antiquary and an author.

1688. Frederick William, elector of Brandenburg, died. Posterity awards to him the character of a brave, generous and patriotic prince, who devoted his attention to the commerce and general welfare of his people.

1735. The Turks defeated by the Persians under Thamas Kouli Khan, 60,000 slain.

1740. Charles Drew, executed at St. Edmundsburg, in Suffolk, for the murder of his father.

1740. The English parliament prorogued. It was at this parliament that the famous acts against horse racing and deceitful gaming were passed.

1743. Charles Irenæus Castel de Saint-Pierre, a French ecclesiastic, died; distinguished as a politician, a man of letters, and an author.

1746. Curtis Barnet, a British commodore, died.

1758. Action off fort St. Davids, East Indies, between the British under admiral Pococke, and the French fleet under count d'Ache. British loss, 29 killed, 89 wounded; French loss, 600 killed and wounded, and one of their vessels sunk.

1762. The book of Cornelius Nepos in Latin was issued from the Russian press, being the first in that language ever printed in Russia.

1779. John Ash, an English dissenting minister, died. His *Complete English Dictionary*, until the appearance of Mr. Todd's octavo edition of Johnson's, was the best compendium of words that could be referred to.

1783. Bernard de Tanucci died; professor of jurisprudence in the university of Pisa, and prime minister of Naples, an office which he sustained with dignity, ability and integrity, for 50 years, when he resigned.

1788. Election of representatives from New York to consider the federal constitution held.

1793. A French privateer with her prize, the Spanish ship San Jago, was captured by the English. Cargo valued at £1,500,000.

1805. The constitution of the Batavian republic changed for the third time; the state was divided into 8 departments, and a legislative body of 19 members, with a pensionary (Schimmelpenninck), chosen for the term of five years, who administered the executive power.

1810. Augustenburgh, crown prince of Sweden, and heir to the throne, seized with an apoplexy while reviewing some corps of cavalry, fell from his horse and expired immediately.

1813. United States frigate Essex, Capt. Porter, captured, near Albemarle island, in the Pacific, British ships Montezuma and Policy, of 10 guns each, and Georgiana, of 6 guns and 4 swivels.

1813. British admiral Cockburn burnt the store-houses at Frenchtown, Chesapeake bay, in which was a great quantity of goods belonging to Philadelphia and Baltimore merchants. He also burnt two vessels, and plundered the private houses.

1814. Action between the United States sloop of war Peacock, 20 guns, 160 men, and British king's brig of war Epervier, 18 guns, 128 men, off cape Carnaverel. The Epervier was captured in 42 minutes, with the loss of 8 killed and 15 wounded; the Peacock had 2 wounded. The Epervier had on board $118,000, exclusive of $10,000 which the crew plundered before she was boarded. The Epervier was sent in 1815 from Algiers, with American prisoners, liberated there, but never arrived.

1827. Rufus King, an American statesman, died. He was many years a senator in congress, and twice minister to England. All parties have borne testimony to the value of his services, and the eminence of his talents.

1849. The republicans at Rome repulsed the French republicans under the city walls.

1849. The emperor NICHOLAS of Russia declared, by ukase, his purpose to assist Austria. (See April 26th.)

1851. C. C. PEPYS, earl of Cottenham, died in Italy, aged 70. He passed through all the honors of the law, and in 1836 became lord chancellor.

1854. Great excitement at Louisville, occasioned by the acquittal of Matthew F. Ward, who murdered Prof. Butler.

1855. ROBERT HAMILTON BISHOP died, aged 78. He was a native of Scotland, was licensed to preach in 1801; on coming to this country, he assisted in rearing several institutions of learning in the western states.

1855. JOHN WILSON, a celebrated landscape and marine painter, died at Folkstone, aged 81.

1855. The United States troops under Col. Fauntleroy, attacked a camp of Utah Indians near the Arkansas river, twenty miles north of the Puncha pass, killed 40, captured 6, and took a large amount of Indian property and plunder.

APRIL 30.

65. MARCUS ANNÆUS LUCANUS, the Latin poet, died. He was the friend and favorite of Nero, but afterwards joined a conspiracy with Piso against the tyrant, and was compelled to destroy himself, which he did by suffocation in a bath.

313. Battle of Heraclea, in which the emperor Galerius Maximus was defeated by Lucinus.

534. AMALASONTHA, queen of the Ostrogoths, murdered by her husband Theodatus. She was universally regretted; as for learning and humanity she had few equals.

711. TARIK, a freed man of the Arabian viceroy of Africa, landed at the foot of the rock Calpe called afterwards by his name Gebal-Tarik (Gibraltar), and two days after by a great battle fought on the banks of the Guadalete put an end to the Gothic empire in Spain.

1156. The city of Moscow founded by Duke George I. Its present population is about 400,000.

1262. ALEXANDER NEWSKI, grand duke of Russia, died. He signalized himself by a great victory which he obtained on the banks of the Neva, over the northern powers.

1439. RICHARD DE BEAUCHAMP, the famous earl of Warwick, died at Rouen, in Normandy. He was the most distinguished warrior in the reign of Henry VI.

1483. The duke of Gloucester (afterwards Richard III), arrested the lords Rivers and Gray at Stony Stratford, on their passage with the young king to the capital.

1513. EDMUND DE LA POLE, earl of Suffolk, on account of his near relationship to the house of York, beheaded.

1519. A skirmish at Edinburg, called "Cleanse the Causeway," between the earls of Arran and Angus.

1524. PIERRE DU TERRAIL, chevalier de Bayard, buried. He was a distinguished warrior under Francis I, mortally wounded at the battle of Marignan.

1542. The new creed, called the *King's Book*, approved by the houses of convocation, and made the standard of English orthodoxy.

1544. THOMAS AUDLEY, an English statesman, died; appointed chancellor in the place of sir Thomas More.

1572. PIUS V (Michael Ghisleri), died. He was an Italian of the Dominican order. It was under his auspices that the battle of Lepanto was fought, in which the Turks were so signally defeated.

1598. The edict of Nantes signed and sealed by Henry IV of France, re-establishing the protestant religion where it had been interrupted, and restoring its churches, houses and revenues.

1614. Captain JOHN SMITH arrived on the coast of New England, it being his first voyage to North Virginia, as the country was then called. He explored the coast in open boats, from Penobscot to Cape Cod, and trafficked with the Indians. It was on his return from this voyage that he presented a map of the country to prince Charles, who declared that it should be called New England.

1632. Battle of Ingolstadt, in Bavaria; the imperial troops of Germany, under count de Tilly, defeated by the Swedes under Gustavus Adolphus, and the general mortally wounded in defending the pass of the Lech.

1632. JOHN TZERCLAES, count de Tilly, died; a Dutch officer, who distinguished himself in the wars with the Turks, and with Denmark.

1637. The puritans forbid by royal proclamation to emigrate to New England.

1655. EUSTACHE LE SUEUR died; one of the best French historical painters of his time.

1655. CHRISTOPHER BENNET died; a distinguished London physician, and writer on medical subjects.

1667. The Dutch fleet attacked Burnt island, in Scotland, but were repulsed.

1690. RENE LE PAYS, a French poet, died; well known at court by his miscellanies.

1696. ROBERT PLOT died; an eminent English philosopher and naturalist.

1707. GEORGE FARQUHAR, an ingenious comic writer, died. He was the son of an Irish clergyman, and held a commission in the army. His comedies are sprightly and diverting.

1712. PHILIP LIMBORCH died; a Dutch professor of divinity, and author of a history of the inquisition.

1724. WILLIAM DAWES, an English nobleman and prelate, died. He was learned, benevolent and pious, and author of several religious works.

1735. DANIEL DUNCAN died; one of the most eminent physicians of his time. He was known in almost every part of Europe as a practitioner and an author.

1745. Battle of Fontenoy, in Belgium, between the British and Hanoverians, under the duke of Cumberland, and the French under count de Saxe. The allies were defeated with great loss.

1758. German Flats in the colony of New York attacked by French Indians.

1762. The celebrated JOHN WILKES committed to the tower as the author of the *North Briton*, the 45th number of which was burnt by the common hangman.

1769. Battle of Choczine between the Russians and Turks.

1776. The eccentric EDWARD WORTLEY MONTAGUE died. He was the son of Lady Mary the author of the celebrated letters.

1781. ARNOLD, the traitor, made war upon 1,200 hogsheads of tobacco at Manchester, Va., and on his return to Petersburg conflagrated a large range of rope walks, a magazine of flour, all the vessels on the stocks, a number of warehouses, &c., and several fine mills. His progress was like that of the cannibal!

1789. WASHINGTON inaugurated first president of the United States.

1795. JEAN JACQUES BARTHELEMI, "the Nestor of French literature," died, aged 80. His principal work is *Travels of Anacharsis in Greece.*

1796. GEORGE ANDERSON, an English self-taught mathematician, died. His parents were peasants and he wrought as a day laborer till he attracted attention. He translated Archimedes' treatise on measuring the sands, and wrote a general view of the variations which have taken place in the affairs of the East India company. His intense application proved fatal to him at the age of 36, after which his widow received a pension, as a reward due to the merits of her husband.

1802. Lotea, in Spain, destroyed by the bursting of a reservoir, which inundated more than twenty leagues of the surrounding country, and "upwards of 1,000 *persons* perished, *exclusive of cattle, &c.*"

1810. The prince regent of Portugal prohibited the exportation of wine.

1812. Eruption of the Souffriere mountain, in St. Vincent, one of the Caribee islands. It was preceded by repeated earthquakes for 11 months. No flames had been emitted since 1718.

1812. SAMUEL ABBOT, a Boston merchant, died. He was one of the founders of Andover theological seminary, and contributed altogether about $125,000 to that institution.

1812. HENRY LEMOINE died. He was a bookseller, but better known as a translator of the German contributor to the *Gentleman's Magazine, &c.*

1816. A spot on the sun visible with the naked eye at Philadelphia. It was seen for several days.

1840. GEORGE BRUMMELL, the celebrated *Beau Brummell*, died at Caen, in France, aged 62. He was the associate of George IV when prince of Wales, and was for a long time at the head of fashion and manners in England. He passed the latter part of his life in poverty, and towards the close of it, was confined in a madhouse.

1843. JACOB RIDGWAY, a wealthy mechanic, died at Philadelphia. He was in early life a shipcarpenter, and subsequently American consul at Antwerp. His property was estimated at $6,000,000. He was noted for liberality to mechanics and tenants.

1854. The first rail road opened in Brazil, the emperor and empress being present at the inauguration.

1854. JAMES MONTGOMERY, the poet and journalist, of Sheffield, died, aged 82.

1855. HENRY ROWLEY BISHOP, a noted English music composer, died, aged 68. He was the most distinguished representative of the English school of composition, and was knighted in 1842.

1857. W. B. BUCHANAN, an American poet, died, aged 63. He was long a correspondent of the *National Intelligencer*, and other papers, residing in Virginia.

MAY.

MAY 1.

305. Diocletian, the Roman emperor, abdicated the throne in the presence of the soldiery and a multitude of people, at Nicomedia, in the 21st year of his reign. When afterwards solicited by a friend to resume the purple, he calmly replied, that if he could show the *cabbages* which he had planted at Salona with his own hands, he should no longer be urged to relinquish the enjoyment of happiness for the pursuit of power.

475. Henghist, the Saxon, caused 300 English noblemen to be murdered.

1119. Henry I of England obtained a great victory over the Normans at Brenville.

1291. All the Italian merchants in the realm of France, called money lenders, seized by order of Philip the fair, for their ransoms.

1308. Albert I, emperor of Germany, assassinated by his nephew, John, duke of Swabia. The Swiss were led by his oppressions to assert their liberty.

1515. Henry VIII and queen attended by nobles went a maying and were entertained by the noted forester Robin Hood.

1517. A riot among the London apprentices, against foreign artisans, which resulted in the death and mutilation of many of the latter, principally Frenchmen. It commenced at 9 o'clock in the evening, and continued till 3 in the morning. The exertions of the city authorities, who had notice of the meditated riot, were unable to prevent or quell it. The next morning, several hundred youths, from 13 years upwards, were arrested, and ten gallows, constructed to move from street to street, prepared for their execution. The ring leaders were drawn, hanged and quartered; when an order came from the king to suspend the execution, and the remainder were pardoned.

1557. England made her first commercial treaty with Russia.

1607. Henry Hudson sailed from Gravesend on his first voyage for the discovery of a northwest passage to India. In this voyage he discovered the island of Spitzbergen.

1619. The famous Calvinistic convocation, the synod of Dort, caused their decrees to be publicly read, and dissolved the council. (May 9? 29?)

1637. A court was summoned at Hartford, Conn., to take measures to secure the colony against the depredations of the Pequot Indians. They determined that an offensive war should be carried on against them, and voted to raise 90 men! The Pequots then numbered 5000 fighting men.

1660. The convention parliament having heard Charles's letters read by sir John Granville, voted that the government of England should be by king, lords, and commons.

1683. Robert Fitzgerald received a patent in England for making salt water fresh.

1701. John Dryden, an illustrious English poet, died. "What he has done in any one species or distinct kind of writing would have been sufficient to have acquired him a great name."

1703. Battle of Pultusk, in Poland, in which the Swedes under Charles XII defeated 10,000 Poles.

1707. Union of England and Scotland consummated.

1708. Claude de Vert died; he devoted much attention to the ceremonies of the church of Rome, of which he wrote a history.

1727. Francis Paris, a French ecclesiastic, died. He retired from office, bestowing his property upon his brother, in order to devote himself to the austerities of a religious life. After his death crowds flocked to his grave to touch his holy monument, till the authorities caused the church yard to be shut.

1737. John Alphonsus Turretini died; professor of ecclesiastical history at Geneva, distinguished for his learning.

1755. John Baptist Oudri died; an admired French painter.

1760. William Duncan died; an ingenious Scottish critic, professor of philosophy at Aberdeen, and translator of *Cæsar's Commentaries*.

1771. Louis Petit de Bachaumon died; a native of Paris, known as the author of several literary works.

1772. Gottfried Achenwall, an eminent German lecturer on statistics, history and the laws of nature, died at Göttingen.

1774. William Hewson died; an eminent English anatomist, and medical author.

1775. Israel Lyons died; a celebrated English mathematician.

1776. Dr. Adam Weishaupt, professor of canon law at Ingolstadt, founded the secret society of the illuminati.

1785. Miles Cooper died; a learned English divine and poet.

1786. Gibbon concluded the fourth volume of his *History*, immortal as its subject.

1789. The states general of France met at Paris, convened by the king to calm the troubles of the state, which he had not power to quell, and which had now assumed a menacing appearance towards royalty itself.

1790. Indian war commenced between the British and Tippo Saib, sultan of Mysore.

1807. Slave trade in the West Indies proscribed in the British parliament.

1808. A volcano broke out in the island of St. George, one of the Azores. A crater was formed in the centre of the island, amidst fertile pastures, 3,500 feet in height, and this beautiful island, before rich in cattle, corn and wine, became a scene of ruin and devastation.

1809. Gottlieb Conrad Pfeffel, one of the best poets of Germany, died. He became blind at the age of 21, a misfortune which he bore more than 80 years, and rendered himself a useful citizen by conducting a school where many excellent scholars were educated.

1813. British and Indians opened their fire upon fort Meigs, from a 24, a 12 and a 6 pounder, and a howitzer. They fired 260 shot, and wounded 8 men, 1 mortally.

1813. John Baptist Bessiers, duke of Istria, killed. He distinguished himself under Napoleon, by whom he was greatly lamented. He was killed in the combat that preceded the battle of Lutzen.

1813. James Delille, one of the most celebrated of modern French poets, died.

1814. Pierre Van Cortlandt, a distinguished revolutionary patriot, died at his seat at Croton river, aged 94. He was a member of the first provincial congress, and eighteen years lieutenant governor of the state of New York.

1823. The skeleton, entire, of a mammoth, was discovered at Ilford, in Essex, England.

1830. The Comet started on her first trip up the Arkansas, being the first steam boat that ascended that river.

1837. An official return stated that there were 70,000 English residents in France, and over 24,000 in Paris alone.

1838. Battle of Rio Pardo, in Rio Grande, between the troops of the emperor of Brazil, about 1,800 in number, and the republican forces; the former were completely routed.

1839. Herbert Marsh, professor of divinity in the university of Cambridge, England, died. He was the author of many learned theological works and controversial publications.

1848. Insurrectionary movements at Rome in consequence of the pope's refusal to declare war against Austria.

1854. Great flood in the Connecticut valley; the water was 29½ feet above low water mark, and 2½ feet higher than during the great flood of 1801. Hundred of persons were driven from their dwellings and drowned.

1855. The French under Gen. Pelissier carried the Russian works at Sebastopol, in front of the central bastion, and held them against vigorous sorties, taking eight small mortars, and 200 prisoners.

1855. An extraordinary eruption of mount Vesuvius commenced, which in ten days had advanced ten miles from its original source.

1856. Ogden Hoffman, a distinguished member of the New York bar, died, aged 62. He served as a midshipman in the last war with Great Britain, after which he studied law, and took the front rank in his profession, and showed an eminent fitness for the public offices which he filled.

1856. George James Guthrie, an eminent British surgeon, died in London, aged 71. He published several valuable works on surgery.

MAY 2.

373. Athanasius, patriarch of Alexandria, died. His parents were pagans; he became a Christian, and distinguished himself by his learning, and the zeal with which he opposed the Arian heresy.

1450. The duke of Suffolk, prime minister to Henry VI of England, beheaded in a boat at Calais. During his ministry England lost most of her possessions in France. Yet his murder was resented by the formidable rebellion of *Jack Cade*.

1487. Lambert Simnel, an impostor, crowned at Dublin, by the title of Edward VI.

1494. Columbus discovered the island of Jamaica.

1519. LEONARDO DA VINCI, a celebrated Italian painter, died. He distinguished himself in early youth by the variety of studies which he accomplished. He afterwards became the head of the Florentine school of painting.

1520. SEBASTIAN BRANDT died; counsellor of Strassburg, a lawyer, and author of a curious poem.

1550. JOAN BOCHER, of Kent, England, burnt for heresy.

1568. MARY, queen of Scots, aided by the gallant George Douglass, escaped from the castle of Lochleven, where she was confined after the murder of Darnley.

1595. ANTHONY, titular king of Portugal, died at Paris, a fugitive from the victorious arms of the Spaniards.

1606. FERNAND DE QUIROS discovered the New Hebrides islands.

1611. The Half Moon, in which HUDSON made his memorable voyage of discovery, sailed in company with another vessel to the East Indies, under captain Laurens Redel, and was lost. (March 6.)

1635. HORACE VERE, an English general, died. He was created baron Tilbury by Charles I for meritorious services.

1667. GEORGE WITHERS, an English pastoral poet, died. He was so zealous a partisan of democracy, and of Cromwell, that the authorities frequently placed him in a straight jacket. His poems were numerous and quaint.

1679. JAMES SHARP, archbishop of St. Andrews, assassinated for his zeal in the cause of the episcopacy in Scotland.

1691. GEORGE MACKENZIE, a Scottish lawyer, died. He figured conspicuously in trials of witchcraft, which puzzled the best heads in those days, and it is probable that he dealt with that sin most thoroughly, for he received the appellation of "the blood thirsty advocate." He was a literary character, however, of no small note, and was among the first Scotchmen who wrote the English language in a style approaching to purity.

1711. LAWRENCE HYDE, earl of Rochester, died; deservedly respected as an able statesman.

1753. LEONOR JEAN CHRISTINE SOULAS D'ALLAINVAL died; a native of Chartres, in France, and author of several comedies of merit.

1774. Permission was given to the society of antiquaries to open the stone coffin of Edward I, and it was found that the body was in a perfect state of preservation, and measured 6 feet 2 inches. It had been placed in wax.

1777. DAVID WOOSTER, a revolutionary officer, died of a wound received in pursuing the British from Danbury (April 27). He graduated at Yale college, and at the commencement of hostilities was appointed to the chief command of the Connecticut troops.

1785. JOHN LEWIS MOREAU DE BEAUMONT, a French political author, died. His works are much and deservedly admired.

1795. The number of prisoners confined in the 12 prisons of Paris amounted to 2338.

1802. BONAPARTE constituted first consul for a second term of ten years.

1808. Embargo laid on American shipping in France.

1808. The royal family of Spain sent prisoners to France. At the sight of this procedure, there was a general insurrection of the inhabitants of Madrid, who attacked the French soldiers with knives, and a bloody contest took place, which was only quelled by scouring the streets with grape shot. The Spaniards finally desisted on seeing their resistance fruitless. It is estimated that 4,000 French and 6,000 Spaniards lost their lives.

1808. JOHN COLLINS died; author of *The Evening Brush*, an oral entertainment of story, song and sentiment, which he delivered many years with great success, in all the principal towns in Great Britain. In this sort of entertainment he has had many followers, among whom the most noted was Charles Matthews.

1809. Battle of Amaranta, in Portugal, in which the Portuguese were defeated by the French under Soult.

1813. Battle of Lutzen, between the French army under Bonaparte, and the allies, under the kings of Russia and Prussia. The attack was commenced by the allies under Blucher upon the French centre, with a fury irresistible. The battle was for a long time maintained by both armies with obstinate energy. It was the more desperate and deplorable, says sir Walter Scott, that on the one side fought the flower of the Russian youth, which had left their universities to support the cause of national honor and freedom; and on the other, the young men of Paris, many of them of the best rank, who bravely endeavored to sustain their country's long pre-eminent claim to victory. Both combatted under the eyes of their respective sovereigns, maintained the honor of their country, and paid an ample tribute to the carnage of the day. The victory finally resulted to the arms of the French, by the superior generalship of their great leader, and the determined bravery of his troops. The allies sustained a loss of 20,000, and among them several experienced officers. The French loss was severe.

1817. CATHARINE RUSH died at Philadelphia, aged 110 years, 11 months.

1821. HESTER LYNCH PIOZZI, an English

authoress, died. She is known as Mrs. Thrale, the friend of Dr. Johnson.

1825. ADAM SEYBERT, an American statistical writer, died at Paris. He was a member of congress from Philadelphia, and a man of science.

1836. JEREMIAH HOLME WHIFFEN, an English poet, died. He belonged to the society of friends, published a variety of miscellaneous poems, a translation of the Spanish poet Garcilasso de la Vega, and of Tasso.

1840. THOMAS MANNING, a eminent English linguist, died, aged 67. Having made several ineffectual attempts to penetrate China, his services were solicited by the British government, to accompany lord Amherst in his embassy to that country. He made himself one of the first Chinese scholars in Europe, and collected one of the finest Chinese libraries to be found in that quarter of the world.

1844. WILLIAM BECKFORD, author of the Arabian tale entitled *Vathek*, with many other works, died at Fonthill, England.

1855. GEORGE HEAD, a British commissariat, died, aged 73. He published several valuable works, relating to different parts of the world, where his duties called him, and was knighted in 1831.

1856. JAMES GATES PERCIVAL, an eminent American poet and philosopher, died in Wisconsin, aged 60. He was a native of Connecticut, graduated at Yale college, and studied medicine, but devoted himself to the cultivation of poetry, and the pursuit of science. He assisted in preparing *Webster's Dictionary* for the press, and superintended the publication of *Malte Brun's Geography*. He afterwards made a geological survey of Connecticut, and in 1854 was appointed state geologist of Wisconsin, in which service he died. Although distinguished for his attainments in philology and general science, he will be chiefly remembered as one of the eminent American poets.

MAY 3.

1324. A poetic festival at Toulouse called *jeux floraux*, to which all the poets of the *Langue d'Oc* were invited, where the composer of the best poem was to receive a violet of fine gold. The celebrated troubadour, Arnaud Vidal, won the prize.

1381. JOHN BALL, a priest and compeer of the notorious Wat Tyler, preached to Tyler's army from the proverbial rhyme:

"When Adam dalfe and Eve span,
Who was then a gentleman?"

1410. ALEXANDER V, pope, died. He was originally a beggar, but found means to cultivate his mind, and rose by degrees in the church till he reached the pontifical chair. He is distinguished as a man of great firmness, liberal and munificent.

1481. MAHOMET II, sultan of Turkey, died. He took Constantinople from the Christians, thereby driving many learned men into the West, which was a great cause of the restoration of learning in Europe.

1493. The pope issued a *great bull*, by which the infidel world was divided between Ferdinand and Isabella on the one hand, and the Portuguese on the other. That is, the Spanish were granted the full right to all countries inhabited by infidels which they should discover west of an imaginary line drawn from pole to pole, at a distance of 100 leagues westward of the Azores, while the Portuguese were to have all east of that line.

1568. DOMINIQUE DE GOURGES, having destroyed the Spanish settlements in Florida, embarked for France. The Spaniards had seized the French settlements in the same places, and murdered the inhabitants. Gourges fitted out three vessels and 150 soldiers at his own expense to revenge their death, and repair the honor of his nation. The Spaniards were well fortified to the number of 400 in their forts; but de Gourges resolutely pressed forward, and after a desperate assault carried the forts. Those who escaped the massacre were hung upon the same trees on which the Frenchmen had previously been hung. The Spaniards had placed over their victims a label, signifying, "*I do not this as to Frenchmen, but as to Lutherans.*" De Gourges replaced it with a tablet of fir wood, on which was graven the following: "*I do not this as to Spaniards, nor as to mariners, but as to traitors, robbers and murderers.*"

1573. A border feud at Reedsquair, between the English and Scottish marchmen, in which the former were completely beaten. This skirmish was the last of any note between the two nations.

1621. Sentence of fine and imprisonment passed upon lord Bacon in the house of peers for bribery.

1649. ISAAC DORISLAUS assassinated; a Dutchman who went from Leyden to England and read lectures on history at Cambridge. He was alternately royalist and republican during the civil wars; and was stabbed to the heart by some enthusiastic royalist while on an embassy to Holland.

1655. The English took the island of Jamaica from the Spanish.

1664. The earl of Tiviot, governor of Tangier, surprised and defeated by the Moors.

1697. KALDAN, khan of the Eleuts, who had for several years eluded the formidable armies sent against him annually from

China, accompanied by the emperor himself, being finally reduced to the last extremity, and abandoned by his best subjects, put an end to his life by poison.

1702. Lord Cornbury commenced his administration of the government of New York.

1711. Richard Chiswell, a noted English printer and an extensive publisher, died.

1733. Richard Cox, lord chancellor of Ireland, died. He published a history of that kingdom.

1747. Naval battle between the English fleet under Anson and Warren, and the French fleet under M. de la Jonquiere, which was convoying six East India ships and a number of transports and merchantmen to Canada. After a regular and well fought battle, the French struck their colors. The loss of the French killed and wounded was 700; that of the British 500. The trophies of the victory were six men of war and all of their East India ships, and between four and five thousand prisoners. The treasure taken on board these vessels was afterwards conveyed to the bank of England in 20 wagons. The French loss by this defeat was estimated at one million and a half.

1759. A young woman in England who had laid a considerable wager that she could ride 1000 miles in 1000 hours, finished her match in a little more than two-thirds of that time. At her coming in the country people strewed flowers in her way.

1763. George Psalmanazar, a literary impostor, died. He was a native of France, and obtained a thorough education. After various adventures he arrived at London under the character of a Japanese converted to Christianity, was patronized by the great, and undertook to translate the catechism into Japanese, and wrote a history of the country. Some absurdities were detected, when he confessed himself an impostor, and afterwards subsisted by turning his pen to better employment.

1765. Sujah ul Dowlah defeated at Calpy, in India, by the British.

1776. Sir Peter Parker's squadron of 20 sail arrived at Cape Fear river, with lord Cornwallis.

1784. Anthony Banezet, a philanthropist of Philadelphia, died. He was a native of France, and early engaged in mercantile pursuits, which he abandoned to devote his attention to objects of benevolence and philanthropy, in which he continued during a long life.

1793. Battle of Famars, in which the allies drove the French from their camp with great loss.

1794. James William Thouret guillotined; he was president of the national assembly when Louis XVI accepted the constitution of 1791.

1797. The first commencement of Union College for conferring degrees in the arts and sciences.

1797. Bonaparte invaded Venice pretending that the Venetians had illtreated the French. This issued in republicanizing Venice and Genoa.

1799. Benjamin Flower, printer of the *Cambridge Intelligencer*, was fined £100 and ordered by the house of lords to be imprisoned 6 months, for some freedom with the speech of bishop Llandaff.

1802. Peter Elmsly, a partner of the celebrated Paul Valliant, and himself an importer of books and no mean critic and linguist, died.

1810. Lord Byron, in emulation of Leander, swam the Dardanelles, from Abydos to Sestos. The distance, including the length he was carried by the current, was upwards of four miles; though the actual breadth is barely one.

1813. Havre de Grace, Maryland, burnt by the British.

1814. Bonaparte arrived at the island of Elba, and Louis XVIII made his entrance into Paris.

1814. Thomas Coke, a methodist bishop in the United States, died. He became one of the assistants of Mr. Wesley, and was active in the service of the church. He wrote a *Commentary on the Bible*, *History of the West Indies*, &c.

1816. James McHenry, confident of Gen. Washington, and for some time secretary of war, died at Baltimore.

1818. Capt. Ross sailed from Shetland, on his first voyage for the discovery of the north-west passage.

1839. Fernando Paer, an Italian dramatic composer, died at Paris. He was a native of Parma; his pieces have been performed in Germany, France and Italy, with success.

1840. James Morison, self-styled *The Hygeist*, died at Paris, aged 70. He was the inventor of the vegetable universal medicines, known as *Morison's Pills*, from which he realized great profits, and is said to have paid the English government in ten years £60,000 for medicine stamps.

1849. A serious insurrection occurred at Dresden, in Saxony, but was in a few days put down.

1852. Sarah Coleridge died; the accomplished and only daughter of S. T. Coleridge. She translated from the Latin the curious works of Dobrizhoffer on Paraguay, 3 vols., and completed the editorial care of her father's *Literary Remains*, begun by her husband.

1853. John B. Gibson, an eminent Pennsylvania jurist, died at Philadelphia, aged

73; at which time he was judge of the supreme court.

1856. ADOLPHE CHARLES ADAM, the noted French music composer, died at Paris, aged 54.

MAY 4.

1471. Battle of Tewkesbury, between the York partisans and the Lancastrians, in which the latter were defeated, and queen Margaret and her son Edward taken prisoners. The young prince was basely murdered on the spot, by the dukes of Gloucester and Clarence.

1605. ULYSSES ALDROVAND, a Bolognese philosopher, died. He was the most celebrated naturalist of the 16th century, and spent his life and exhausted his resources in the pursuit of science. He lost his sight, and ended his days in a hospital at the age of 80.

1643. LOUIS XIII (*the just*), king of France, died. He was guided in his conduct by the celebrated cardinal Richelieu, who, from motives of ambition, kept him at war during most of his reign.

1655. GIOVANNI FRANCESCA ABELA, a historian and ecclesiastic of Malta, died.

1668. A riot in London under pretence of destroying brothels. Four of the leaders taken and executed for treason. In the reign of some of the English kings the demolition of such houses would not have been adjudged treason.

1673. RICHARD BRATHWAITE, an English poet and miscellaneous writer, died. His works are numerous.

1677. ISAAC BARROW, an eminent English mathematician and divine, died. His writings are numerous and valuable, and chiefly on mathematical subjects; his sermons are highly esteemed, and have been frequently edited.

1702. War declared against France and Spain, by England, Germany and Holland.

1729. LEWIS ANTHONY DE NOAILLES, a French cardinal, died. Though by birth duke of St. Cloud, he preferred the ecclesiastical state to political distinction.

1734. JAMES THORNHILL died; an English historical painter.

1737. EUSTACE BUDGELL, the friend of Addison, drowned in the Thames. He turned his attention to polite literature, contributed to the *Spectator*, *Tatler*, *Guardian* and *Craftsman*, and published two volumes of biography.

1768. CHARLES STEPHEN LOUIS CAMUS died, a learned French mathematician.

1786. GEORGE GORDON, an English nobleman, who it is said submitted to circumcision, avowed Judaism, and was excommunicated from the church of Mary le Bone

1791. The pope burnt in effigy at Paris.

1799. Seringapatam, a city of Hindostan, taken by storm by the British, under Gen. Harris. Tippoo Saib was slain, with 8,000 of his men. The treasure found in the city amounted to £3,000,000; 2,200 cannon, and an immense booty, fell into the hands of the conquerors, and the once powerful kingdom of Mysore was extinguished.

1804. The conservative senate sent a deputation to Bonaparte, expressing their desire that he would accept the title of emperor.

1813. Heavy rain retarded the firing on fort Meigs; 220 cannon shot were fired; 2 killed, several wounded. The rifle was more used this day than on any other.

1831. MEHEMET ALI, pasha of Egypt, employed upwards of 70,000 men in excavating, cleansing and lining canals in his territories.

1842. Great fire at Hamburg, in Germany, destroyed 2,000 houses.

1843. JAMES P. PRESTON, formerly governor of Virginia, died at Smithfield, aged 69. He commanded a regiment in the war of 1812, and was maimed for life in the battle of Chrystler's fields.

1854. ALEXANDER WITHERSPOON, a New York physician, died at Washington, aged 37; a medical writer remarkable for the exactness of his observations and the clearness of his statements.

1854. JOHN MATTHEWS died, aged 70. He served with distinction as a general officer in the war of 1812-15; and for a period of fifteen years was a representative in the state legislature of Maryland.

1856. JOHN COLLINS WARREN, a distinguished Boston physician, died, aged 77. He was the first successful competitor for the Franklin medal. He had a long and brilliant career as a physician, and during the latter years of his life devoted much time to the study of the natural sciences, and collected a valuable museum, among which was the most perfect skeleton of the mastodon known to exist.

MAY 5.

1421. A holy convocation at Canterbury decreed that a bishop's barber should not receive a fee from any one on whom the bishop had conferred holy orders.

1432. FRANCESCO BUSSONE DI CARMAGNOLA, count de Castlenuovo, executed. He was a celebrated Italian general, first in the service of the duke of Milan, afterwards led the Venetian army to repeated victories. His fortune at length turned, when the senate suspecting him of treachery, he was tortured and condemned to death.

1526. FREDERICK (*the wise*), elector of Savoy, died. He was one of the first and most zealous friends of Luther.

1529. PAULUS ÆMILIUS, a learned Italian, died. He was invited to France, where he employed a great number of years in writing a history of the French kings, but did not live to finish it.

1556. The company of London stationers received their first charter from Philip and Mary, under the title of "The master and keepers or wardens, and commonalty, of the mystery or art of the stationers of the city of London."

1586. HENRY SIDNEY, an English statesman, died. He was the favorite of Edward VI, and afterwards employed by Mary and Elizabeth.

1618. One WILLIAMS, a barrister, arraigned for libeling the king, was executed.

1643. Parliament of England ordered the *Book of Sports* to be burned by the common hangman.

1670. FRANCIS ANNIBAL D'ESTREES, a French statesman, died, aged 98. He distinguished himself by several military exploits, and wrote some valuable historical works.

1682. WILLIAM PENN, published in England his frame of government for the colony of Pennsylvania.

1687. A proclamation was issued by government to establish a manufactory for white paper in England.

1700. STEPHEN MORIN, a French protestant divine, died at Amsterdam. He was professor of oriental languages; his dissertations on various subjects of criticism and antiquity were highly esteemed.

1705. LEOPOLD I, emperor of Germany, died. He was long engaged in sanguinary war with the Turks and the French, who pillaged and destroyed his frontier towns.

1706. Lateral eruption of the peak of Teneriffe. A volcano opened at the south side, towards the port of Garachico, and in a few hours not an edifice of that populous city was left standing.

1710. NICHOLAS JOSEPH POISSON, a French priest, died. He was the friend of Descartes, and a philosopher; distinguished for his eloquence and as an author.

1751. JOHN PICHON died; a French Jesuit and an author.

1757. Battle of Prague, between the Prussians under Frederick the great and the Austrians. The Prussians were victorious, after a bloody contest, in which the distinguished general, count Schwerin, was killed. Austrian loss 24,000; Prussian loss 18,000.

1760. LAWRENCE SHIRLEY, earl of Feraro, executed at Tyburn for the murder of his steward. He was a man of no mean mental acquirements, but passionate and often inflamed by inebriety.

1776. Congress declared the authority of England over the thirteen colonies abolished.

1785. THOMAS DAVIES (alias *Honest Tom Davies*), an English author, died. He was educated at the university of Edinburgh, became an actor, afterwards a bookseller, turned strolling player, married Miss Yarrow, an actress of great beauty, returned to bookselling, became bankrupt, was relieved by the assistance of Dr. Johnson, wrote the *Life of Garrick*, several other biographies and innumerable miscellanies, and was entrusted with the publication of Granger's *Biographical History of England.*

1789. JOSEPH BARETTI, an Italian lexicographer, died. He emigrated to England, where he published an Italian and English dictionary, and assisted Dr. Johnson in compiling his dictionary.

1789. Assembly of the states general of France, at Versailles. This may be called the first day of the revolution, although the object of the meeting was to prevent such a catastrophe.

1795. The law went into operation in England imposing a tax on wearing hair powder.

1802. Cleopatra's coffin, head of the Theban ram, and other Egyptian curiosities, arrived in England.

1804. France formed into an empire.

1808. PETER JOHN GEORGE CABANIS, a French physician, died. He was the friend of Mirabeau, sat in the council of 500, and in the senate of Napoleon acquired great reputation for talent, learning and benevolence. His works are published in 7 volumes.

1811. Battle of Fuentes d'Onor, in Portugal; the French repulsed with great loss, by the British under Wellington.

1813. Battle at Fort Meigs; Gen. Clay arrived with 1,000 Kentucky militia and volunteers, attacked the British, carried their batteries and spiked their cannon; but having pressed too far in pursuit, were met by a reinforcement of Indians, and in turn defeated, so that only 150 escaped. The British had fired 143 cannon shot into the fort before the arrival of Gen. Clay. American loss, 64 killed, 124 wounded, exclusive of Clay's loss. British stated their loss at 103, killed, wounded and missing, and that they had taken 495 American prisoners.

1814. NAPOLEON landed at Elba at an early hour in disguise, with a sergeant's company of marines. He made a formal landing at 2 in the afternoon, and was welcomed by the people with acclamation.

1821. NAPOLEON BONAPARTE died at St. Helena, in the 52d year of his age, and the

6th of his exile, to the great relief of the British nation. He commenced in 1795 that unparalelled career of military achievements, which continued to agitate Europe for 20 years, and terminated with the battle of Waterloo, 1815.

1822. THOMAS TRUXTON, an American naval officer, died. He distinguished himself in the revolutionary war, and also in the war with France of 1799, after which he retired from the navy, and died in Philadelphia.

1827. FREDERICK AUGUSTUS I, king of Saxony, died, aged 77; a wise and benevolent monarch, who devoted the energy of his mind to promote the welfare of his subjects.

1846. JOHN PICKERING, an eminent American philologist, died at Boston, aged 60. He commenced the practice of the law, and distinguished himself as a jurist; but his reputation rests chiefly on his attainments as a scholar, and on his literary and scientific labors, which were of great service to the cause of learning in this country. He published a vocabulary of Americanisms, and a Greek and English lexicon.

1848. Opening of the national assembly of France, after the abdication of Louis Philippe.

1853. His other demands having been conceded, prince Menschikoff sent in an ultimatum to the Turkish divan, demanding for the emperor of Russia the protectorate of the Greek church Christians in Turkey.

1853. A new planet was discovered at the observatory of Bilk, at Dusseldorf, by Prof. Luther.

MAY 6.

356. B. C. MARCIUS RUTILUS, the first dictator elected from the plebeians, entered Rome in triumph from his victories over the Etrurians.

1527. The imperialists under the duke of Bourbon, took Rome by assault and plundered it. The duke was killed by a musket ball. He had been disgraced at the French court, and was now in the service of Charles V of Germany.

1540. JOHN LEWIS VIVES, a learned Spaniard, died. He resided some time at the court of Henry VIII of England, where he was imprisoned for opposing the divorce of Catharine of Arragon.

1562. PAUL DE LA BARTHE, lord of Thermes, a French general, died, aged 80. He was distinguished in the wars of his country by several important victories.

1569. The first English lottery, which commenced drawing on the 11th January (q. v.), and had been continued day and night, finished on this day. It consisted of 400,000 lots of 10s. each. The prizes were plate, and the profits were to be expended in repairing the havens of the kingdom.

1631. ROBERT BRUCE COTTON, an eminant English antiquary, died. His writings are numerous and valuable, and he did great service to learning by leaving his valuable library to the use of posterity, in the British museum.

1643. Battle of Stratton, in which the parliamentary army under the earl of Stamford was attacked by the Cornish royalists, who, although far inferior in numbers, gained a complete victory, taking the camp of the enemy, all their artillery, baggage and provisions, and many prisoners.

1667. SAMUEL BOCHART, a learned French protestant divine, died. He was distinguished as an oriental scholar, and died while delivering an oration at the academy of Caen.

1673. The island of St. Helena retaken by the English.

1712. GARIEN DE SIEUR DE SANDRAS COURTLITZ, a French author, died. His works were numerous, and some of them political, for which he was confined in the bastile nine years.

1739. KOULI KHAN, after pillaging the capital of Hindostan, and slaughtering 150,000 of its inhabitants, departed from the city, leaving his son Mohammed Schah on the throne.

1743. ANDREW MICHAEL RAMSAY, a Scottish historian and philosopher, died. He spent much of his time in France, with Fenelon and Turenne, where he died.

1763. JOHN WILKES released from the tower by the memorable sentence of chief justice Pratt. (See April 30).

1766. SAMUEL SQUIRE, bishop of St. David's died; a poetical, historical and antiquarian writer of note.

1766. Lord HOWE and Gen. HOWE appointed commissioners for restoring peace to the British colonies.

1766. THOMAS ARTHUR LALLY, an Irish officer in the service of France, executed. He fought against the British in the East Indies with great bravery, but had become so unpopular, that on being defeated he was imprisoned and condemned for treason.

1780. Fort Moultrie, on Sullivan's island, surrendered to the British, who bombarded Charleston at the same time.

1782. STEPHEN MIGNOL DE MONTIGNI died at Paris; eminent as a mechanic and a man of science, who introduced several useful manufactures into France.

1790. JOHN JAMES GESNER died; professor in the university at Zurich, and a noted Swiss author.

1796. ADOLPHUS F. F. L. KNIGGE, a German author, died. His works were various, and his novels once popular. He was a member of the illuminati, and implicated in some of the disputes relating to that order.

1801. Action of Barcelona, between British ship Speedy, 14 guns, 54 men, lord Cochrane, and Spanish frigate El Gamo, 32 guns 319 men. British loss, killed and wounded 11, Spanish loss, 55.

1802. SAMUEL McDONALD died, aged 40. He served under the British with the Sutherland fencibles, and afterwards as fugleman in the royals. He was six feet ten inches in height, and his strength is represented to have been prodigious. He continued active till his 35th year, when he began to decline, and died of water in the chest.

1811. WILLIAM BOSCAWEN, an English poet and miscellaneous writer, died. His translation of Horace is preferred by some critics to that of Dr. Francis.

1814. Battle of Oswego. The town was attacked the second time by the British, 1,600 soldiers and sailors, and two companies of Glengarians, under Gen. Drummond. The Americans, about 300, under Col. Mitchell, gallantly defended the place, till they were compelled to retreat before an overwhelming force, after securing their stores. American loss, killed 6, wounded 38, missing 25; British, 94.

1839. WILLIAM LENOIR, an officer of the revolution, died. He bore a distinguished part in the war in South Carolina, and was closely identified with the early history of the state. He held various civil offices, was a justice of the peace about 60 years, and for many years a member of the state legislature. He was distinguished for integrity, firmness and patriotism.

1840. DEMETRIUS AUGUSTINE GALITZIN, son of prince de Galitzin, one of the first nobility of Russia, died in poverty at Loretto, Pa., aged 70. He left the princely halls of his ancestors, and spent thirty years in a rude log cabin in America, almost denying himself the comforts of life, that he might devote his days to religion, and assist the poor and distressed. Few have left behind them such examples of charity and benevolence.

1840. FRANCISCO PAULA DE SANTANDER, formerly president of the republic of New Granada, died at Bogota, aged 48. When the revolution began to agitate the country he embarked in the cause of independence, and soon rose to distinction as an officer in the army.

1844. Fearful rioting in Philadelphia between the native Americans and Irish.

1848. Engagement between the Austrians and Piedmontese before Verona; great loss on both sides.

1848. Gen. FOLQUE, a veteran officer, died at Lisbon, Portugal, aged 102.

1853. The drawbridge of the New York and New Haven rail road having been carelessly left open at Norwalk, the cars were thrown into the water; forty-five persons were killed, and many severely injured.

1856. An accident occurred on the Panama rail road, recently put in operation, by which 43 persons were killed, and 60 wounded.

1856. WILLIAM HAMILTON, a distinguished Scottish metaphysician, died at Edinburgh, where he was professor of logic and metaphysics, and became more widely known by his volume of *Essays*.

MAY 7.

431 B. C. The war which wasted the Athenians for 27 years, commonly called the Peloponnesian war, began May 7th.

399 B. C. SOCRATES, the greatest of the ancient philosophers, died. He was put to death by the Athenians on a charge of atheism, and corrupting the youth.

973. OTHO (the great), emperor of Germany, died. He was an active and valiant prince, who made himself respected by the powers of Europe.

1253. RUBRUQUIUS (or Ruysbroeck) landed at Soldaia, on the Black sea, on his way to discover a Christian people, who were said to inhabit the centre of Tartary. On this embassy he explored that country, and though unsuccessful in the object of his mission, he brought back a fund of curious information, which after the lapse of centuries is still about the best picture we possess of Tartar life. But few have been among them in their native wilds since then, and those who have, like Marco Polo, John Bell and Timkowsky, confirm most of his details.

1402. Battle of Nisbeth, between the English and Scottish forces, in which 10,000 of the latter were slain.

1588. Lord BURLEIGH, as chancellor of Cambridge, issued rules for reforming the apparel and other "disorders" of the scholars: "and that the excess of colored shirtbands and ruffs, exceeding one inch and a half (saving for the sons of noblemen), be avoided presently; and that no scholar do wear any long locks of hair upon his head, but that he be polled after the manner of the gravest scholars, under pain of 6s. 8d."

1621. JOHN GUILLIM died; rouge-croix pursuivant at arms, and author of a celebrated work called *The Display of Heraldry*.

1621. JOHN SUCKLING, an English poet, died. He also signalized himself as a soldier under Gustavus Adolphus.

1660. The king's statue was again set up in Guild hall, London, and the states arms taken down.

1768. Patrick Delany died; an eminent divine and theological writer of Ireland, better known now as the friend and correspondent of Dean Swift.

1676. Henry de Valois (Henricus Valesius) died; a French critic of great abilities and learning.

1776. The American army under Gen. Thomas, on their retreat from before Quebec, took up their line of march at 1 in the morning, and reached Point de Chambault. At Jaques Cartier they had but one batteau to cross the army over with, and were fired upon during the whole time by two frigates.

1777. Charles de Brosses, president of the parliament of Burgundy, died. He is the author of several useful works.

1778. British took possession of Bordentown, N. J. They burnt 4 store-houses and about 40 vessels.

1794. Robespierre appeared before the French convention as the *Champion of the Supreme Being!* It was thought advisable to found a religion, and it was necessary first to enact a supreme being, for *God had been abolished by a decree of the convention.* The tyrant made an eloquent speech, and concluded by declaring the real temple of the supreme being to be the universe; his worship, virtue; his festivals the joy of a great nation. His propositions were carried by acclamation, and a solemn festival proclaimed, which under the arrangement of David, the painter, was a magnificent affair.

1795. Anthony Quentin Fouquier Tinville, a notorious French revolutionist, guillotined. As public accuser, he caused the death of immense numbers, of all ages and either sex.

1796. Bonaparte and the army of the French republic crossed the Po at Placenza.

1800. Nicholas Piccini, an eminent musical composer, died at Naples.

1811. Richard Cumberland died; eminent as a British poet, essayist, novelist and dramatic writer. The number of his works is very extraordinary, as was also his vanity.

1825. John Gabriel Chasteler, governor of Venice, died. He was a Spanish grandee of the first rank, entered the Austrian service, and distinguished himself in several engagements with the French. He possessed a chivalrous and cultivated mind, and spoke 12 languages.

1830. Treaty between the United States and Turkey signed at Constantinople, securing to the United States the free navigation of the Black sea, and the trade of the Turkish empire.

1838. Mary Sprouse died in Albemarle county, Va., aged 99. She was in the practice of carrying poultry, vegetables, &c., to market at Charlottesville, a distance of 8 miles, on foot, till within a few weeks of her death.

1838. Thomas Bradford, the oldest master printer in America, died at Philadelphia, aged 94. He was the successor of Dr. Franklin as editor, and entered upon the business in 1763. During the revolutionary war he was commissary-general to the Pennsylvania division, and printer to congress. He was long known as a distinguished printer, editor and publisher.

1840. A tremendous tornado passed over the city of Natchez, very destructive to life and property. Almost every building in the city was more or less injured, many being utterly demolished. The amount of property destroyed was estimated at $1,-500,000; and 317 persons were killed.

1840. Thomas Barnes, principal editor of the *Times* newspaper, died in London, aged 56. He was unquestionably the most accomplished and powerful political writer of the day, and particularly excelled in the portraiture of public men.

1842. The island of Hayti destroyed by an earthquake. Not a single town escaped without some casualty. Thousands of lives were lost, and property to an incalculable extent was destroyed. Cape Haytien was entirely leveled with the ground, and of 12,000 inhabitants, one half were buried under the ruins, and of those which escaped, a great part perished by fire and other disasters which followed. Bands of armed negroes came in the next day to plunder, and stabbed and shot the wounded wherever they found them, for the jewels and clothing they wore.

1844. It was discovered that all the watches on board the British schooner Henry Curwen, and the chronometer, had stopped, and on referring to the three compasses on board, they were found to point different ways, and were entirely useless. In about two hours afterward the watches and chronometer recommenced going, and the compasses resumed their position. This occurred in 44° north, and 32° 35′ long., at 4 A. M.

1848. The Polish insurgents surrendered to the Prussian troops, after great slaughter, at Posen.

1848. Insurrection at Madrid, when many lives were lost.

1848. The Indians, who were in a state of insurrection in Yucatan against the Spanish population, entered the town of Marie, and butchered 200 of the inhabitants, besides committing other outrages.

1849. Gen. Worth died at San Antonio de Bexar of cholera.

1849. Macready, the English tragedian,

hissed from the stage of the Astor opera house in New York.

1852. JAMES SAVAGE, a distinguished London architect, died, aged 74. The *Gentleman's Magazine* contains a long list of the bridges and churches which attest his reputation and skill.

1854. The gallery of the Catholic church at Erie, Pa., fell, crushing the people below, and killing and wounding several persons.

MAY 8.

685. Pope BENEDICT II died.

1360. The treaty called the *great peace* signed at Bretigni, by which Edward III renounced all his claims to the French crown and its territories.

1429. The siege of Orleans was abandoned. At dawn, the English army was discovered at a small distance from the walls, drawn up in battle array, and braving the enemy to fight in the open field. After waiting for some hours, the signal was given; the long line of forts, the fruit of 7 months' labor, was instantly in flames and the soldiers, with mingled feelings of shame and regret, turned their backs to the enemy. This was one of the inexplicable feats of Joan d'Arc.

1493. FERDINAND and ISABELLA confirmed, at Barcelona, the appointment of Columbus, on his return from the new world. "The office of admiral of the said ocean, *which is ours*, commences by a line, which we have ordered to be marked, passing from the Azores to the cape de Verd islands, from the north to the south, from pole to pole; so that all which is beyond the aforesaid line to the west is ours, and belongs to us; and of all this we create our admiral, you and your children."

1532. FRANCIS ALVAREZ PAEZ died; a Portuguese divine of the order of the Cordeliers, and an author.

1535. HENRY VIII of England had his *head shaved*, and commanded all about his court to follow his example.

1538. EDWARD FOX, an English prelate and statesman, died. He was the principal pillar of the reformation in England.

1572. Dame DOROTHY PACKINGTON sent the trusty and well beloved Thos. Lichfield and George Borden to be her burgess in parliament, informing the queen that whatever they might do in her service in parliament should receive her (Dorothy's) approval.

1638. CORNELIUS JANSENIUS died; founder of the Jansenists, who gave the pope and the Jesuits much trouble in Europe.

1655. EDWARD WINSLOW died; one of the first settlers of Plymouth colony, Mass., and afterwards its governor. He joined the fleet sent over by Cromwell to attack St. Domingo, the only place of strength which the Spaniards had in Hispaniola, and died at sea, aged 60. His marriage was the first that was celebrated in the colony.

1657. CROMWELL refused the title of king of England.

1659. A remnant of the long parliament assembled during the anarchy, and has been termed the *rump*.

1662. PETER HEYLIN, an English historian, died. He was an able and indefatigable writer, principally known by his *Descripton of the great World*, and *History of the Reformation*.

1676. Bridgewater, Mass., invaded by the Indian enemy, and 17 buildings laid in ashes.

1703. VINCENT ALSOP died; a presbyterian clergyman, who attacked Dr. Sherlock with great wit and some seriousness.

1725. Capt. JOHN LOVEWELL, with a party of 36 men, encouraged by his former success against the Indians (see Feb. 20), undertook an expedition against Pigwacket, on Saco river, was ambuscaded, and himself and a great part of his men killed. They made a brave resistance, determined to die rather than yield, and by their well directed fire thinned the number of the savages so that their cries became fainter, and they finally left the field, carrying off their dead.

1729. WILLIAM KING, archbishop of Dublin, died; author of a celebrated treatise on the origin of evil.

1744. GILES JACOB died; an English law writer, biographer, and lexicographer.

1758. BENEDICT XIV (Prosper Lambertini), pope, died. His character was that of a learned, liberal-minded and benevolent man. His works fill 16 vols. folio.

1775. The great tunnel at Norwood hill, through which the Chesterfield and Trent canal was to pass, was opened; its length nearly 1¾ miles.

1779. CHARLES HARDY, an English admiral, died. He was two years governor of New York, and was appointed commander in chief of the western squadron, 1779.

1782. SEBASTIAN JOSEPH CARVALLO DE POMBAL, a Portuguese statesman, died. He displayed great wisdom and abilities in the offices to which he was promoted; and under his munificence and patriotism the city of Lisbon rose from her ruins by the earthquake, in new splendor and increased magnificence.

1793. Battle of Vicogne, the French defeated by the Austrians under Clairfait, after an obstinate action and great carnage.

1793. JAS. RIDGWAY and H. D. SYMONDS,

booksellers in London, severely fined and sentenced to 4 years imprisonment for selling the books of Thomas Payne.

1794. Anthony Lawrence Lavoisier, a French chemist, guillotined. His philosophical researches were of great service to science, and of practical utility to his country; he was condemned on the most frivolous pretexts.

1799. Bonaparte made an unsuccessful attempt to carry St. Jean d'Acre by assault.

1806. Robert Morris, one of the signers of the Declaration of Independence, died. He was one of the most extensive merchants in America, and in 1781 was appointed to the control of the government finances, where the services he rendered the country were of the utmost importance. The army was frequently supplied by his own personal credit. It is painful to add, that the latter years of his life were passed in prison, where he was confined for debt.

1813. The Americans evacuated York, Upper Canada, after burning the blockhouses, barracks and king's stores.

1815. David Ramsay, an American physician and historian, died. By unwearied industry and economy of time he was enabled, amidst an extensive practice, to publish several important histories, and left others in manuscript.

1815. Saxony dismembered, and a great part of the kingdom given to Prussia.

1816. The United States ship Washington, 74 guns, put to sea, being the first American ship of the line afloat.

1822. John Stark, a major general in the revolutionary army, died, aged 93. By his skill and intrepidity the first step was achieved towards the capture of Burgoyne, by the defeat of colonel Baum in the battle of Bennington.

1829. Charles Abbot, lord Colchester, died; a British statesman.

1842. More than 70 lives lost by a rail road accident between Versailles and Paris among whom were the celebrated navigator, admiral Dumont d'Urville and his wife and children.

1846. Battle of Palo Alto. The Americans, 2,000, under Gen. Taylor, were attacked on their return from Point Isabel, by 5,000 Mexicans. The former fought their way through the Mexican lines, dispersing the enemy, capturing their baggage and artillery, and several of their superior officers.

1848. Great hail storm at Charleston, S. C.; some of the stones that fell were 7½ inches in circumference.

1852. The emperor of Russia visited the emperor of Austria at Vienna, and two days afterwards reviewed the Austrian troops, consisting of 20,000 infantry and 10,000 artillery and cavalry.

1853. John Farrar, a distinguished American mathematician, died, aged 54. He gave the active portion of his life to the service of Harvard college, to which he brought great natural tastes and aptitudes, habits of persevering labor, and deep conscientiousness.

1854. The sultan of Turkey gave a grand banquet in honor of Napoleon.

1855. Jane Davy, widow of sir Humphrey Davy, died in London; conspicuous in literary circles for her accomplishments, unwearied conversation and physical activity.

MAY 9.

1502. Columbus sailed from Cadiz, with four vessels and 140 men and boys, in search of a passage to the South sea, being his fourth voyage across the Atlantic. It was a disastrous expedition for the admiral, against whom the elements seem to have joined his countrymen, to complete the ruin of his fortunes.

1657. William Bradford, second governor of Plymouth colony, died. He removed to America with the first settlers of the colony, and was their governor thirty years. He wrote a history of the colony from 1602 to 1646, which was deposited in the library of the old south church in Boston, where it fell a sacrifice to the fury of the British, 1775.

1657. A secret treaty signed at Paris between Louis XIV and Cromwell, for "the ruin and destruction of the proud and tyrannical monarchy of Spain."

1760. Nicholas Lewis Zinzendorf, a German count, died; founder of the sect of Moravians, or Hernhutters.

1767. Cassini observed, by the position of certain spots, the revolution of the planet Venus on its axis.

1768. Bonnel Thornton died; an English poet, essayist and miscellaneous writer, and translator of Plautus.

1776. Ellen Ellis at Beumaris in Anglesey gave birth to a child in her 72d year.

1781. British generals Arnold and Philips took Wilmington, Va.

1781. Spaniards took Pensacola and all Florida.

1791. Francis Hopkinson, one of the signers, died. He was judge of the admiralty court of Pennsylvania; his writings abound with wit, humor and satire.

1794. Charles Henry d'Estaing, a French admiral, guillotined. He was commander of the French squadron in the American war; and at the revolution in France became member of the assembly of notables.

1799. Sally from the garrison of St. Jean d'Acre, when they succeeded in spiking 4 cannon within the French lines.

1803. Robert Chambers died at Paris; a learned English judge and orientalist.

1805. Frederick Schiller, an eminent German dramatist, died. He is also the author of a history of the revolt of the Netherlands from Spain.

1813. The siege of fort Meigs raised. It had continued 13 days, and it was computed that 1760 cannon balls and shells had been fired at the fort, by which 17 were killed and 66 wounded.

1832. Israel Thorndike, a Boston merchant, died. He possessed a talent for business which enabled him to accumulate the largest fortune ever acquired in New England, amounting to nearly two millions. In 1818 he purchased the valuable library of professor Ebeling, of Hamburg, 4,000 vols., and presented it to Harvard university. This library is considered the most valuable and extensive in American history and antiquities, ever collected.

1832. Camillo Philip Louis Borghese, an Italian prince of immense wealth, died. He was an officer under Bonaparte, whose sister he married. After the abdication of the emperor, he broke up all connection with the Bonaparte family, and separated from his wife.

1836. Caleb P. Bennett, governor of the state of Delaware, died, aged 78. He was the last surviving officer of the Delaware regiment in the revolutionary army.

1846. Battle of Resaca de la Palma and death of major Samuel Ringgold, whose place of sepulture in Baltimore is surrounded by an inclosure of Mexican bayonets.

1846. Charles Turner Torrey died in the jail at Baltimore, Maryland, while sustaining an imprisonment for a breach of the laws of Maryland in relation to kidnapping slaves.

1853. An earthquake completely destroyed Schiraz in Persia; 12,000 lives were lost.

1854. An imperial ukase in Russia called for nine men out of every thousand souls of the "eleventh ordinary partial levy in the eastern portion of the empire," and, independently of this, three recruits out of every thousand souls to bring up arrears; the Jews furnishing ten men out of a thousand.

MAY 10.

664. The memorable pestilence in Ireland began.

1307. Battle of Loudown hill; Bruce defeated Aylmer de Valence, earl of Pembroke.

1422. Henry V reduced Meaux, after a siege of 7 months.

1503. Columbus discovered the Tortugas islands.

1547. Charles V summoned Wittenberg, defended by Sibylla, wife of the elector of Saxony; refusing to surrender, he ordered a court-martial who condemned her husband, then a prisoner, to death.

1574. Queen Elizabeth issued her royal license under seal, for the performance of stage plays; the first establishment of a regular company of players in England.

1611. Sir Thomas Dale arrived at the Jamestown colony, with 3 ships, 300 people, 12 cows, 20 goats, and all things needful. Lord Baltimore had previously left for England on account of his health, and Dale took command. Sir Thomas Gates arrived in August following, with 6 ships, 280 men, 20 women, 100 cattle, 200 hogs, and military stores, and assumed the government. These added to the 200 left by lord Baltimore, swelled the number to 800.

1631. Magdeburg taken by the Austrians under general Tilly, by assault, and given up to pillage, massacre and fire, only two churches and some ruins remaining.

1632. Louis de Marillac, marechal of France, beheaded. He conspired against Richelieu, to whom he was indebted for much of his good fortune, and to whose resentment he fell a victim.

1641. John Bannier died; a Swedish general under Gustavus Adolphus.

1646. Manuel d'Almeida, a Portuguese Jesuit, died; a missionary to India 40 years, and author of a work on Ethiopia.

1649. Governor Endicott, and other influential men in Massachusetts, formed an association against wearing long hair!

1671. The English admiral Sprague destroyed 12 Algerine pirate ships at Bugea, a seaport of Algiers.

1696. John de la Bruyere, a noted French author, died. His *Characters*, in imitation of Theophrastus, is a work of established excellence, and descriptive of the manners of that age.

1733. Barton Booth died; a celebrated tragedian in the reign of queen Anne, author of some songs and minor pieces.

1773. An act of parliament passed, authorizing the East India company to export their own tea, duty 3d. per pound; in consequence of this act they determined to send it to New York, Philadelphia and Boston. In October of the same year the Americans refused to receive it.

1774. Louis XV of France died, in the 60th year of his reign. He outlived the respect of his subjects.

1775. Colonels Allen and Arnold surprised Ticonderoga, which surrendered, without the loss of a man. Crownpoint was taken by them the same day.

1775. Carolina Matilda, the divorced queen of Denmark, died at Zell, aged 24: youngest sister of George III.

1779. Portsmouth and Norfolk, Va., taken by the British, and many vessels, stores and houses destroyed.

1781. Lord Rawdon evacuated Camden, after destroying the public and private houses, and much of his own baggage.

1784. Anthony Court de Gebelin, a French writer, died; celebrated as the author of *The Primitive World compared with the Modern*, a work which the French academy were so well satisfied with that they twice decreed him the annual prize of 1,200 livres for the best work.

1790. The *Gabelle Tax* in France was abolished. This was a duty on salt capricious and unequal in its operation, which notwithstanding had continued since the beginning of the 14th century.

1793. Clairfait attacked and carried the wood of Hasnon; the slaughter of the French was great.

1794. Battle of Tournay and defeat of the French by the British and Austrians under the duke of York.

1794. Elizabeth of France, sister of Louis XVI, guillotined.

1796. Battle of Lodi, in which Bonaparte gained an important victory over the Austrians, under the veteran general Beaulieu. The long narrow bridge which led to the city, was defended by 30 pieces of cannon. The French generals put themselves at the head of 3000 grenadiers, and in the face of a murderous fire crossed the bridge over the dead bodies of their comrades, who were mowed down by hundreds, and took possession of the Austrian batteries. The loss was about 3,000 men on each side. This was one of the most striking military achievements of Bonaparte. It was on this occasion that he received the title of *the little corporal.*

1796. The Babeuf conspiracy was discovered by the council of 500 in Paris. Babeuf and Darthe, the principal leaders were secured and executed, which completely crushed the Jacobin power.

1809. The Swedish diet renounced all allegiance to Gustavus IV, and deprived him and his heirs of the crown.

1811. French evacuated Almeida, after destroying everything, and the next day they abandoned Portugal entirely.

1824. John Guthrie, the celebrated Edinburgh bookseller of the firm of Guthrie & Jait, died. Like Benjamin Franklin he wheeled home his own purchases.

1831. John Trumbull, an American poet, died. He was for many years judge of a court in Connecticut, and is known as the author of the popular poem, *McFingal.*

1831. Battle of Terlepe; 20,000 Albanians under the pasha of Scodra defeated by the Turks under the grand vizier.

1837. All the banks in the city of New York without exception, and by common consent, stop specie payments. The banks throughout the Union adopted the same course.

1848. A very destructive fire occurred in Detroit, Michigan. The houses were of wood principally on leased land.

1849. The city of Leghorn taken by the Tuscan troops.

1849. Astor house opera riot in the city of New York.

1853. Ashbel Strong Norton, an American preacher, died, aged 87. He was born in Farmington, Ct., graduated at Yale college in 1790; filled the pastoral office at Clinton, N. Y., with distinguished usefulness and success forty years, during which he was largely concerned in laying the foundations of social and religious institutions in central New York.

1853. The pope prohibited the circulation of *Uncle Tom's Cabin*, an American novel, in his dominions.

1855. A mob of armed men destroyed the Birch creek reservoir, in Clay county, Indiana, connected with the Wabash and Erie canal.

MAY 11.

1491 b. c. The Egyptians under Pharaoh drowned in the Red sea.

1153. David I, of Scotland, died. He was earl of Northumberland and Huntington, and married the daughter of the king of England, for whom he claimed the throne on the death of her father. He was a mild and popular king.

1310. James de Molai, grand master, and 54 knights of the temple, publicly burned at Paris, under the decree of an archiepiscopal council. They were condemned on confessions of Islamism and paganism, extorted by the rack, and afterwards retracted.

1537. A terrible and destructive eruption of Mount Ætna.

1553. Three vessels sailed from England, under Sir Hugh Willoughby, to explore the northern seas. By this voyage an inlet was discovered to the White sea and the bay of Archangel, and an almost exclusive commerce established with Russia in that quarter.

1554. Francisco de Orellana sailed from St. Lucar, in Spain, with 4 ships and 400 men, for the purpose of exploring the river Amazon. He forced his way up about 120 leagues, and meeting with disasters by which he lost his ships and the greater part of his men, he turned about and died on his way back. "Orellana was very *warmly* received by armed swift-footed females, which originated the fanciful name *Amazonia.*"

1676. The Indians assaulted the town of Plymouth, Mass., and burned 11 houses and 5 barns; and two days after they burned 7 houses and 2 barns, and the remaining houses in Namasket.

1686. OTHO GUERICKE, a Prussian philosopher, died. He was the most celebrated mathematician of his time, and invented the air pump.

1690. Charlemont, in Ireland, taken by the English.

1696. The Reformed Dutch church at New York incorporated.

1723. JEAN GUALBERT DE CAMPISTRON, a French poet, died. He is thought to be little inferior to Racine in the merit of his dramatic compositions.

1743. Several tons of leaden pipe were dug up in Fleet street, London, laid down 300 years before.

1749. CATHARINE COCKBURN, an English poetress, died. She produced the tragedy of *Agnes de Castro* in her 17th year, which was followed by several others. She possessed also a great and philosophic mind, and wrote an able defence of Locke.

1776. At an action near Charleston, S. C., between count Pulaski and the British, Major Huger of the American army was killed by mistake.

1778. WILLIAM PITT, earl of Chatham, a most illustrious English statesman, died. He was the friend of liberty and justice, and eloquent in their cause.

1781. Orangeburgh surrendered to the American Gen. Sumpter; prisoners taken, 82.

1782. RICHARD WILSON died; an English landscape painter of great merit.

1799. PHILIP NICHOLAS PIA, a French chemist, died. He was sheriff of Paris, 1770, and employed his leisure in objects of benevolence, till the revolution overwhelmed him.

1807. Action in the Dardanelles, between the Russian and Turkish fleets; 3 of the latter stranded.

1810. Hastalrick, in Catalonia, evacuated for want of provisions; the garrison cut their way through the French troops.

1813. SPENCER PERCEVAL, prime minister of Great Britain, shot in the lobby of the house of commons.

1814. ROBERT TREAT PAINE, one of the signers, died. He was a distinguished lawyer, of learning and integrity, member of the first congress, and judge of the supreme court of Massachusetts.

1821. GEORGE HOWE, editor of the *Sydney Gazette*, died. His paper commenced in March, 1803, in the 15th year of the colony, and was the first Australian periodical.

1838. ANDREW THOMAS KNIGHT died. His horticultural writings were exceedingly beneficial, as well to the gardeners as farmers.

1839. THOMAS COOPER, president of South Carolina college, died, aged 80. He wrote on law, medical jurisprudence and political economy, and translated Justinian and Broussais.

1844. STEPHEN WOOD, died at Miami, Ohio, aged 82. He was the last survivor of those who were associated with John Cleves Symmes in the settlement of North Bend.

1848. An expedition under Sir James Ross, sailed for the Arctic regions, in search of Sir John Franklin.

1853. PETER HITCHCOCK, an eminent civilian, died at Painesville, Ohio, aged 70. He was a member of the Ohio senate, and of the house of representatives at Washington; also for twenty-five years a judge of the supreme court of Ohio.

1854. The packet Pike, from St Louis to Louisville, struck a snag, and sank in a few minutes, by which about fifty passengers lost their lives.

1854. J. DELIUS, of Bremen, assistant professor of English literature at Berlin, fell into the crater of Vesuvius, and perished there.

MAY 12.

48 B. C. Battle of Pharsalia, between Cæsar and Pompey, in which the latter was defeated, and escaped on foot. This battle forms an important era in the history of the world.

824. PASCHAL I, pope, died; distinguished for his benevolence and toleration.

1264. Battle of Lewes and defeat of Henry III by Leicester.

1294. EDWARD I of England met at Norham the states of Scotland, when they acknowledged his sovereignty, and engaged to deliver up to him their castles.

1430. The famous JOAN OF ARC, or maid of Orleans, pretended to be sent from God to save the kingdom of France.

1539. FERDINAND DE SOTO sailed from Havana with ten ships for the conquest of Florida.

1618. The Calvinists of Bohemia entered the castle of Prague, cast the leading members of the council from the windows, and took possession of the capital.

1621. The first marriage in the colony at Plymouth took place, between Edward Winslow and Susanna White.

1641. THOMAS WENTWORTH, an English statesman under Charles I, beheaded on a false charge of treason. The king was compelled by the clamors of the populace to order his execution.

1663. The books of the London stationers company record the names of 59 persons exercising the trade as master printers.

1690. John Rushworth, an English writer, died in the king's bench prison, where he had been confined 6 years; author of *Historical Collections*, in 7 vols. folio.

1763. John Jackson died; an English divine and historian, author of *Chronological Antiquities*.

1763. John Bell, the distinguished anatomist of Scotland, was born at Edinburgh.

1771. Christopher Smart, an English poet and miscellaneous writer, died; known by a popular translation of Horace. By some authorities his death is placed in 1770.

1780. Charleston, S. C., surrendered to the British; 2,500 prisoners and 400 cannon fell into the hands of the enemy.

1781. Fort Motte surrendered by the British to the American generals Marion and Lee.

1785. Mr. McGuire having ascended from Dublin in a baloon, was carried with great velocity towards the sea, into which he descended, and was taken up nearly lifeless.

1791. Francis Grose died; author of the *Classical Dictionary of the Vulgar Tongue*, a complete collection of British technicals, vulgarisms, and billingsgate used by gamblers, ostlers, servants, fishwomen, &c., which, though not very popular, or creditable to him, is yet quite a curiosity. He produced some other works of great merit, which mark him a profound antiquary.

1795. Ezra Stiles, president of Yale college, died. He was eminent as a divine, and an indefatigable scholar. His publications were few, but he left 40 vols. in manuscript.

1796. The French under Bonaparte defeated the Austrians with great slaughter, who were compelled to abandon their guns and baggage, and take refuge under the cannon of Mantua.

1797. Bonaparte took possession of Venice, boasting an independence of fourteen centuries.

1798. Sidney Smith escaped from France after two years imprisonment.

1809. Vienna capitulated to the French, and Napoleon established his head quarters in the imperial palace of Schoenbrunn. The emperor had already quitted it, with all his family except his daughter the archduchess Maria Louisa, afterwards wife of Napoleon, who was confined to her chamber by sickness—on learning which, Bonaparte ordered that there should be no firing in that direction.

1809. Lord Wellington took Oporto by assault, and the French under Soult were compelled to retreat to Amarante.

1809. Alcantara, in Spain, taken by a division of the French under Victor, together with the British garrison.

1848. Alexander Baring, lord Ashburton, died in England, aged 78. He passed much of his youth in America, and was British embassador at Washington, to settle the Maine boundary in 1842. He acquired great wealth, and was a highly accomplished man.

1848. Posen incorporated with Germany, and the insurgent Poles disarmed.—Violent earthquake at Sienna, Italy.

1849. A crevasse was made in the levee above New Orleans flooding much of the city.

1854. The British ship Tiger, 16 guns, was captured near Odessa by the Russians, with 226 prisoners.

1855. D. J. McCord, an American lawyer, died at Columbia, S. C. He published law reports, and edited the *Statutes at Large*, on the death of Dr. Cooper, to whom the work was first entrusted.

MAY 13.

432. b. c. Meton, the Athenian astronomer, began his famous *lunar cycle* of 19 years (then marked by successive letters in gold, which are now called the golden numbers), with the new moon nearest to the summer solstice falling upon the 16th of Scirophion.

48 b. c. Pompey, in passing through the Archipelago, stopt at Mitylene to receive his wife, the exemplary Cornelia, and there conversed with Cratippus, the philosopher, *on the nature of providence*.

1213. King John received Pandulph, the pope's legate, in whose presence he subscribed an instrument by which the sentences of interdict, excommunication and deposition were revoked, conditionally that he reversed all his formeracts of oppression.

1520. Massacre of the Mexicans by Alvarado, during the absence of Cortez. This happened on the great festival of their god *Huitzilopochtli*, in the month Toxcatl, the emperor being then a prisoner of the Spaniards in his palace, and the principal nobles gathered there for the dance, when the Spaniards fell upon them with the utmost fury. The victims were unable to defend themselves or escape by flight, and the slaughter was terrible. An insurrection immediately followed, and the quarters of the Spaniards were assaulted with such determined energy that they were compelled to hasten the return of Cortez, and led to the disaster of the 1st July (q. v.)

1539. A bill brought into the English parliament vesting in the crown all the property of the monastic institutions. This was followed by the fall of 644 monasteries, 90 colleges, 2,374 chantries, and 110 hospitals. The revenue of these establishments amounted to £161,000.

1568. Battle of Langside hill, Mary queen of Scots defeated by the regent Murray, and fled to England.

1607. Jamestown, Virginia, settled. Three small ships, with 105 persons intended to form a settlement, under Sir Christopher Newport, took possession of a peninsula in Powhatan river, and gave it the name of Jamestown. Though they had to strive against appalling difficulties, and were several times on the verge of losing or abandoning the enterprise, they were ultimately established, mainly through the great exertions and talents of Capt. John Smith, one of the most remarkable persons connected with the early history of the country, and indeed one of the most remarkable of an age prolific of memorable men. Jamestown was for a long time the capital of the state, but has sunk into ruin, and is almost desolate. Two or three old houses, the ruins of an old steeple, a churchyard, and faint marks of the rude fortifications, are the only memorials of its former importance.

1614. Marguard Freher died. His books on law, criticism and history are numerous and respectable.

1619. John Van Oldenbarneveldt, a Dutch statesman, beheaded. Zeal for his country led him to oppose the arbitrary measures of the stadtholder, for which he was accused of treason and condemned at the age of 72. (See April 14.)

1625. Charles I issued a proclamation for "settling the plantation of Virginia." The colony was reduced under the immediate direction of the crown, and the commission to the new governor and council was accompanied with arbitrary instructions. "The commerce of the colony was restrained, and the persons of the colonists enslaved."

1649. William Chappel, bishop of Cork, died. His works have been translated into English. To him is ascribed, among others, the authorship of the *Whole Duty of Man*.

1704. Louis Bourdaloue died; esteemed the best preacher that France ever produced.

1728. Counsellor Hagen, formerly secretary to the famous baron Gortz, shot himself through the head. He left a letter to king George II, and a paper stating "I am quite weary of eating and drinking, of shunning my creditors, weary of being burthensome to my friends, weary of being vexatious to my enemies, and lastly tired with myself."

1734. James Thornhill, an eminent English historical painter, died.

1736. The foundation of the Ratcliffe library laid at Oxford, England.

1781. Roger Byrne, the Irish giant, was buried. He weighed with his coffin 578 lbs., and died of no other disease than suffocation occasioned by a superabundance of fat, which stopped the play of his lungs, and put a period to his life in the 54th year of his age. His height, it is believed, was nearly 8 feet.

1760. A copy of Tendall's testament sold at Oxford for 20 guineas, supposed to be the only copy of that edition unburned by Tonstall. This book occasioned some prelates to say that they must root out printing or printing would root out them.

1783. Society of Cincinnati established; originated by Gen. Knox, and composed exclusively of officers who had served in the regular army during the revolutionary war.

1790. Action in the port of Revel, between the Swedish fleet of 23 ships and 18 frigates, and the Russian fleet of 11 sail and 5 frigates, protected by several batteries and fortifications. A furious storm raged at the time, which destroyed two Swedish ships.

1799. Bartholomew Mercier, abbot of St. Leger, died; a learned French author and a worthy man, whom the revolution reduced to poverty and wretchedness.

1806. Broome county in the state of New York erected.

1814. Madam Murat surrendered the fleet and arsenal at Naples, and Ferdinand returned to his capital.

1814. British cannonaded and bombarded the town of Charlotte at the mouth of Genesee river. It was successfully defended by Gen. Peter B. Porter, with 150 volunteers and 350 militia.

1816. Treaty between the United States and the Sac Indians of Rock river.

1825. Charles Whitworth, an English earl, died; employed by the government as ambassador to different courts of Europe—a man of much private worth and unquestioned talent.

1832. George Leopold Cuvier, the French naturalist, died. His grand work, the *Animal Kingdom*, forms an imperishable monument of his genius.

1835. Elizabeth Cook, widow of Capt. James Cook, the circumnavigator, died near London, aged 94. She survived her husband 55 years, and was highly esteemed for her virtues.

1835. John Nash, the architect of Regent street, Buckingham palace, &c., London, died.

1836. Sir Charles Wilkins, an eminent oriental scholar, died.

1838. Zachary Macauley, a distinguished philanthropist, died at London, aged 70. He edited the *Christian Observer* from 1802 to 1816, with ability, and for more than 40 years dedicated his eminent talents and active energies in conjunction with other distinguished men to the abolition of African slave trade.

1839. Joseph Fresch, archbishop of Lyons, died. He was the uncle of Bonaparte, and after the fall of the emperor resided at Rome in the enjoyment of immense wealth, and one of the first picture galleries in that city.

1841. The American Bible Society celebrated its 25th anniversary at New York. The whole amount of receipts during the year preceding, was $118,860·41; the number of Bibles and testaments published and circulated through the efforts of the society since its organization, *three millions*.

1849. A revolution at Carlsruhe, and the grand duke of Baden fled.

1852. George Dolland, an English astronomer and optician, died, aged 78. His father and grandfather followed the same pursuits. He is the author of the *Atmospheric Recorder*.

MAY 14.

1097. The siege of Nice, the Turkish capital of Soliman, sultan of Roum, opened by the French crusaders, whose camps formed an imperfect circle of more than 6 miles.

1501. Amerigo Vespucci sailed with three ships furnished him by Emanuel of Portugal. This was his third voyage, which he extended as far as Patagonia.

1602. Bartholomew Gosnold, after a passage of 7 weeks direct west from England, discovered land on the American coast, and fell in with a shallop with sails and oars, manned by Indians, with whom they had friendly intercourse. They are represented as naked, "save neere their wastes seale skins tyed fast like to Irish dimmi trouses;" and the chief wore a few things of European fabric, described the coast with a piece of chalk, and "spake diverse Christian words." Their vessel is supposed to have belonged to some wrecked fishermen of Biscay.

1610. Henry IV of France assassinated by Ravaillac. Above 50 historians and 500 panegyrists, poets and orators, have spoken in his praise; but the *Henriade* of Voltaire is the most likely to immortalize him.

1652. British commodore Young fell in with a Dutch convoy, and demanded that according to an act of king John (A. D. 1200) they should strike their flag to the British flag. This being refused, a severe action ensued, which ended in the Dutch flag being struck, after which they were permitted to proceed!

1667. Joan Henry Ursinus died; a Lutheran divine, eminent for his learning in sacred and profane history.

1692. Sir William Phips arrived at Boston with the new charter by William and Mary, where he was received with great pomp, and conducted by the military, magistrates, ministers, and principal men of the country to the town-house, where the charter was published. This charter included the whole of old Massachusetts, Plymouth colony, the provinces of Maine and Nova Scotia, the islands of Elizabeth, Nantucket and Martha's Vineyard, as the province of Massachusetts, of which Phips was appointed governor.

1731. A final settlement was made of the boundary line between New York and Connecticut; 60,000 acres called the Oblong being ceded to New York in exchange for lands near the sound.

1761. Thomas Simpson, an eminent English mathematician, died. He was a weaver in the lowest circumstances, who raised himself to distinction by close application to science.

1780. Peter Montan le Berton died; an eminent French musician, and manager of the operas at Paris.

1781. Lieut. col. Christopher Greene (the conqueror of count Donop) and major Flag, surprised and murdered at Croton river, by a party of refugees.

1785. Canal opened between the Baltic and North seas.

1796. Vaccination for cowpox first applied by Dr. Jenner.

1796. Bonaparte made his public entry into Milan under a triumphal arch.

1798. David Ruhnkenius died; professor of belles-lettres and history, and librarian in the university at Leyden, and a learned and able critic.

1805. Robert Bisset died; a Scottish historian, biographer, and novelist.

1810. Lerida, in Spain, surrendered to the French general Suchet, who found large quantities of stores. Same day, Catalonians defeated the French, whose loss is stated at 45,000, and that of the Catalonians 25,000.

1814. British fleet on lake Champlain commenced a heavy cannonade on the American batteries under colonel Davis, at the mouth of Otter creek. The British were compelled to retreat.

1814. French defeated at Madrid by lord Wellington.

1814. Spanish squadron belonging to Monte Video, defeated by the Buenos Ayrean squadron under com. Brown.

1820. Henry Grattan, an Irish statesman, died. He warmly espoused the interests of his country, and many important measures were effected by his eloquence.

1826. State prison at Sing Sing, New York, commenced.

MAY 15.

164 B. C. The Jews, upon the 15th Sivan, celebrate a feast for the victory of Judas Maccabæus over the people of Bethsan, or Scythopolis.

67. VESPASIAN invested Jotopata, in Galilee, defended by Josephus, the historian, a very interesting siege as it respects the latter.

392. VALENTINIAN, emperor of Rome, strangled at Vienne, in Milan, by order of Arbogastes, his rebellious general.

1213. King JOHN, oppressed with guilt and despair, resigned the kingdoms of England and Ireland to the pope, to be held of him and of the Roman church in fee, by the annual rent of 1,000 marks.

1464. Battle of Hexham, on the banks of the Dilswater, and defeat of the Lancastrians under the duke of Somerset, by Edward IV. The fate of the royal family after this defeat was extremely singular and distressing.

1494. COLUMBUS discovered a great number of small islands in the West Indies, which he called the *Queen's Garden*. These were in his opinion the 5,000 islands which Marco Polo and Mandeville described as the boundary of India.

1548. The emperor CHARLES V laid before the diet of Augsburg a *rule of faith*, which he compelled them to acquiesce in, notwithstanding that it was disapproved by both protestants and papists.

1567. Marriage of Mary, queen of Scots, and the earl of Bothwell.

1571. Moscow burnt by the Tartars, who had surrounded the city, and set it on fire at all points. The entire city was burnt down, and upwards of 200,000 of the inhabitants perished in the flames.

1602. BARTHOLOMEW GOSNOLD, in search of a suitable place to settle a plantation, discovered a head land in 42 deg., where he came to anchor; and taking a great number of cod at this place, they called it cape Cod, which name it still retains.

1618. The celebrated KEPLER discovered his canon for the periodical motion of the planets.

1645. Battle of Alderne, in which the earl of Montrose defeated the Scots under Urrey with great slaughter.

1664. The Dutch governor surrendered the island of Cayenne to the French, by treaty.

1674. Besançon, an ancient city of France, taken by Louis XIV.

1679. The Ashmolean museum, at Oxford, England, founded for the purpose of receiving the antiquary's "twelve cartloads of rarities."

1716. JOHN BAGFORD, an English antiquary, died. He was originally a shoemaker, became a bookseller, and an amateur of old English books and curious prints, with which he enriched several famous libraries.

1719. FRANCIS MALAVAL died; a Frenchman, who, although he lost his sight when 9 months old, acquired celebrity as a mystical writer on quietism.

1737. ALEXANDER CUNNINGHAM, a Scottish historian, died. He wrote a valuable *History of Great Britain* in Latin, which remained in manuscript till 1787, when it was translated by Thompson, and published in 2 vols. quarto.

1740. EPHRAIM CHAMBERS, an English encyclopedist, died. He was apprenticed to a globemaker, and during his minority projected his *Dictionary of the Arts and Sciences*, which appeared in 1728 in 2 vols. folio. It was extended by Dr. Rees to 45 vols. quarto.

1747. British fleet under Anson captured 1 French ship of 74 guns, 5 of 64, 4 of 60, 1 of 50, and 20 merchantmen.

1766. JOHN ASTRUC, a French physician, died; author of several useful and curious works.

1772. ANTONY FRANCIS RICCOBONI died; an Italian actor, author of *Art du Théatre*, a work of great merit.

1773. ALBAN BUTLER died; director of the English college of St. Omer's, and author of the *Lives of the Fathers, Saints and Martyrs*, with valuable notes.

1775. Congress resolved to issue paper money.

1776. American fort at the Cedars, 43 miles above Montreal, surrendered by maj. Butterfield, with 390 men, to capt. Foster, with 650 British and Indians. (See May 20, 27.)

1781. Fort Granby surrendered by the British to col. Lee.

1789. The number of emigrants which had passed through Muskingum to settle in Kentucky since the first of Aug., 1786, (not including those who passed in the night unnoticed) was 19,882. These were accompanied by 8,884 horses, 2,297 cattle, 1,920 sheep, 627 wagons, and 1,067 boats.

1800. JAMES MALLET DU PAN died in England, where he took refuge from the revolutionary mania of France. He was a literary and political writer, distinguished by the extent of his knowledge and vigor of style, as well as probity and independence of character.

1800. BONAPARTE crossed the mount St. Bernard. Each man, says sir Walter Scott, carried from sixty to eighty pounds, up icy precipices, where a man totally without encumbrance could ascend but slowly. Probably no troops but the French could have endured the fatigue of such a march; and no other general than Bonaparte would have ventured to require it at their hands.

1802. The Portuguese frigate Cine captured by the Algerines, after a smart action. The crew having ran below, the officers were all cut to pieces.

1814. The British plundered Poultneyville, on lake Ontario. They were driven off by general Swift.

1817. David Irving died at Philadelphia. He was taken prisoner on board the United States frigate Philadelphia at Tripoli and imprisoned there two years.

1821. John Wall Callcott died; an English musical composer, and author of a *Musical Grammar*.

1821. John Bonnycastle died; an English mathematician, whose works are in use in this country. He contributed the mathematical articles for *Rees's Cyclopedia*.

1830. An extensive shower of red dust extending over Italy, Malta, Sicily, Sardinia, &c., observed by Dr. John Davy.

1833. Edmund Kean, a celebrated English tragedian, died. It is ascertained that the total sum which he received for acting from 1814, was £177,000, averaging nearly $40,000 per annum for 19 years; yet he died poor.

1836. The village of Roanoke, on the Chatahoochee, Ga., attacked and stormed by 300 Indians, and burnt to ashes.

1838. John Murphy died in Fauquier county, Va., aged 106.

1847. Daniel O'Connel, the Irish agitator, died at Genoa, on his way to Rome. His heart was sent forward and his body carried back to Ireland.

1848. Attempted communist counter revolution in Paris.

1848. Richard H. Toler, a distinguished writer and for 23 years editor of the *Lynchburgh Virginian*, died at Richmond.

1854. George Perkins, a retired Boston merchant, was murdered by the Chinese crew of a boat which he had engaged to take him ashore at Macao, whither he had just arrived from San Francisco.

1854. The ship Townsend, from Boston to San Francisco destroyed by fire, and several lives lost.

1854. An explosion took place in the Blackheath coal mines, Virginia; by which of the twenty-three workmen only one escaped death.

1855. The universal industrial exhibition was opened at Paris by Louis Napoleon.

1855. A destructive tornado swept over a portion of Lapeer county, Michigan.

MAY 16.

1277. John XXI, pope, killed by the fall of a building. He was a Portuguese, and wrote on philosophy, medicine, &c.

1525. Thomas Munzer, a Saxon divine, executed. In conjunction with Stork, he pulled down all the images in the churches which Luther had left standing, and finally at the head of 40,000 men, commenced leveler of all ranks and distinctions, as usurpations on the rights of mankind. He was at length defeated in battle, when 7,000 of his followers were slain and himself captured.

1568. Mary, queen of Scots, crossed the frith of Solway, the *irremeable stream*, and landed in England.

1681. Female dancers first introduced on the Parisian stage, in a court opera, called *Le Triumphe dè l'Amour*.

1691. Leisler and Milbourne hung as the cause of the Schenectady massacre.

1710. Thomas Smith died; a learned English writer on the manners and religion of the Turks, &c.

1725. Paul de Rapin de Thoyras, an eminent French historical writer, died. He served in the English army, and devoted 17 years to a *History of England*, which was published in 10 vols. quarto.

1747. M. Buffon, the celebrated naturalist, communicated to the Academy of sciences the results of some experiments on burning glasses, asserting the account of Archimedes burning the Roman ships at Syracuse, were neither absurd nor false.

1770. Louis XVI of France espoused Maria Antoinette, archduchess of Austria. A violent tempest on that day was regarded as an omen of future misfortunes.

1776. The French navigator, De Pages, passed the 81st degree of north latitude, in an attempt to reach the pole.

1776. John Hoadley, an English poet and dramatic writer, died. He was the son of bishop Hoadley, took orders and was loaded with preferments.

1782. Daniel Charles Solander, a celebrated Swedish naturalist, died. He was the pupil of Linnæus; visited England, and went with Cook on his voyage round the world.

1793. Edmund C. Genet, the French minister, arrived at Philadelphia. He was received with much enthusiasm by the citizens. (See July 14.)

1795. The Batavian republic formed, by the aid of the French, in imitation of France; being governed by a legislature and a directory of five.

1796. Earthquake in Syria; Lataka, the ancient Laodicea, was laid in ruins, and more than 3,000 persons buried under the fallen mass. The village of Gibel was totally destroyed, and many houses in Tripoli were tumbled down.

1801. Battle of Heliopolis; the French under Belliard defeated by the Turks under the grand vizier.

1806. Blockade of the Elbe and of Brest, a coast of 1000 miles, with no place invested by land, and before many of the ports no blockading ships.

1809. The rear guard of the French army attacked at Salamonde in Portugal, and compelled to retreat before superior forces, with the loss of their artillery and baggage; having lost about 8,000 men, 2,000 of whom were slaughtered by the Portuguese. The army was a fortnight without clothing, shoes, provisions, &c., excepting those procured by marauding, and they must all have been destroyed but for the great military talents of Soult.

1811. Battle of Albuera, in Spain; the allies defeated by the French under Soult; about 20,000 men fell in this battle.

1811. Action between the United States frigate President, Rogers, and British ship Little-Belt, which was captured.

1813. Battle of Mignano, Italy, and defeat of the French.

1828. William Congreve, a British officer, died; inventor of the Congreve rocket, a hydro-pneumatic canal lock, and a new method of manufacturing gun powder, &c.

1830. The bill to remove the civil disabilities of the Jews rejected in the British parliament by a vote of 288 to 165.

1830. Great eruption of mount Ætna; seven new craters were formed, and eight villages were destroyed, to which the lava had never before extended.

1835. Felicia Dorothea Hemans, a celebrated English poetess, died. Her poems were extremely popular during her lifetime, and have been published in 2 vols.

1838. New York state banks resumed specie payment.

1841. A constitution of the republic of Yucatan decreed by the legislature and published at Merida, the capital; Yucatan having declared its absolute independence of the republic of Mexico.

1842. Count de Las Casas, author of the *Memoirs of Napoleon*, died near Paris.

1849. The city of Bologna capitulated to the Austrians after a conflict of eight days.

1850. William Hendricks, for some time governor of Indiana, died at Madison, aged 67.

1854. Tornadoes occurred in Alabama, Missouri and Illinois, accompanied with extensive damage to property.

1855. General Canrobert resigned the command of the French troops in the Crimea, and was succeeded by general Pelissier.

MAY 17.

1039. Harold I, the second Danish monarch of England, died, at Oxford. A heavy tax which he imposed on his people made him unpopular. He was buried at Winchester; but by the cruel edicts of his brother the body was dug up, beheaded and thrown into the Thames; recovered and again buried only to be a second time disinterred and committed to the Thames; found and privately buried at Westminster.

1163. Heloise, abbess of the Paraclete, died; celebrated as the mistress of Abelard, and for her learning. She was entombed with her husband. At the dissolution of the monasteries in 1792, the principal inhabitants of Nogent-sur-Seine went in grand procession to the Paraclete, to transfer the remains of the lovers to a vault in their church. In 1800 they were transported to Paris, and one of the most picturesque and interesting ornaments in the cemetery of Pere la Chaise, is the sepulchral chapel covering their remains, constructed from the ruins of the Paraclete.

1498. Vasquez de Gama discovered the continent of India. On his return he again doubled cape Good Hope, which had long been regarded as the *ne plus ultra* of navigation.

1536. George Boleyn, an English statesman, beheaded. He was a man of learning and ability, whose elevation followed that of his sister Anne as queen; and when she fell, he too was degraded and unjustly condemned.

1575. Matthew Parker, second protestant archbishop of Canterbury, died. He was deeply versed in Saxon literature and published a work on the antiquity of the English church.

1610. Gervase Babington died; bishop of Worcester and an eminent theological writer.

1617. Jacob Augustus Thuanus (alias De Thou) died; an illustrious French statesman and historian.

1664. The English conventicle act was passed forbidding more than five persons meeting for religious purposes except those regulated by the book of common prayer.

1690. A party of French and Indians under the sieur Hertel, returning from a marauding excursion among the English settlements, attacked and destroyed the fort at Casco, Me.

1723. Joseph Bingham, an English ecclesiastic, died; author of *Antiquities of the Christian Church*, a learned and laborious work, in 10 vols.

1727. CATHARINE ALEXIEVNA, empress of Russia, died. She was the daughter of a peasant of Livonia, married a Swedish dragoon, who was killed on the same day in battle. The Russian general Bauer made her his mistress, after which she lived a short time with prince Mentschicoff. In her 17th year she became the mistress of Peter the Great, who afterwards married her and presented her with the diadem and the sceptre. After his death she was proclaimed sovereign empress of all the Russias, and showed herself worthy of her high fortune.

1729. SAMUEL CLARKE, a famous English divine, died; celebrated also for his writings on mathematics, &c.

1732. WILLIAM LOWTH died; a celebrated English theological writer and commentator.

1738 o. s. BELL, the Scottish traveler, returned to St. Petersburg from his embassy to Constantinople, whither he went at the earnest solicitation of the Russian cabinet, and the British minister. This was the last of his expeditions, and was undertaken in the midst of winter, through a country exposed to all the horrors of a barbarous warfare, attended by only one servant, who understood the Turkish language.

1740. PETER JULIAN ROUILLE, a French Jesuit, died; professor of theology and philosophy to his order, and co-editor of the *Roman History*, 21 vols. quarto.

1742. Battle of Czaslau, or Chatusitz, in Bohemia; the Prussians defeated the Austrians, who lost 7,000; Prussian loss, 3,000.

1749. SAMUEL BOYSE, an Irish poet, died. His talents were amply rewarded, but he unfortunately had a disposition to practice the meanest deceptions to procure benefactions, which brought him to wretchedness and contempt.

1767. ROGER WOLCOTT, governor of Connecticut, died. He never attended school a single day of his life, yet gradually rose by his own efforts to the highest military and civil honors.

1772. The theatre at Amsterdam, in Holland, took fire and burned to death 31 persons.

1774. At a town meeting of the inhabitants of Providence, R. I., the subject of a general congress was acted upon, being the first act of the kind by a public assemblage.

1776. Captain MUGFORD in a vessel of 4 guns captured British ship Hope, 4 guns, with 1,500 barrels powder and military stores, and brought her into the port of Boston.

1794. Battle of Surcoign; British defeated by the French after a sanguinary conflict.

1797. Revolution in Venice, and a democratic government formed under the direction of the French general Angereau.

1797. LOUIS XVIII compelled to quit the Venetian territory.

1797. MICHEL JEAN SEDAINE, a French dramatic writer, died, aged 78. Bred to the occupation of a stone mason, by application to study he won a place in the French academy.

1801. A French convoy of 560 men with 1 cannon and 550 camels, in Egypt, captured by the British.

1801. WILLIAM HEBERDEN died; an English physician and medical writer.

1809. BONAPARTE issued from Vienna a decree declaring the temporal sovereignty of the pope to be wholly at an end, and incorporating Rome with the French empire. The "holy father" instantly fulminated a bull of excommunication against the daring emperor, but it did not avail; his holiness was taken in his palace and conveyed away at midnight, under pretence that a life so sacred in the eyes of all Christians, might be endangered!

1817. SAMUEL JESSUP died; an opulent English grazier, of pilltaking notoriety. An apothecary's bill, which was given in evidence on a trial a short time previous to his death, affords a table of statistics which will not be exceeded by the memorabilia of the life of any man. In 21 years he took 226,934 pills. He began with a moderate appetite, which increased as he proceeded, so that in the last five years he took them at the rate of 78 a day, and in the year 1814 swallowed not less than 51,590. Notwithstanding this, and an addition of 40,000 bottles of mixtures, he attained the advanced age of 65 years.

1829. JOHN JAY, a distinguished American statesman, died, aged 84. His public services commenced in 1774, and continued till 1801, when he retired to private life; distinguished as a man of great discernment, extensive information, and fine talents as a writer.

1829. Battle between the Russians under general Diebitsch, and the Turks; the latter of whom, 5,000 in number, were defeated and driven into Silistria, with heavy losses on both sides.

1829. Battle of Pravadia, between the Russian army under general Roth, and the Turks under the grand vizier. The Turks are said to have lost 2,000, and the Russians 1,000. The latter maintained their ground, but no important advantage was gained by either party.

1831. NATHANIEL ROCHESTER, an officer in the revolution, died at Rochester, New York, from whom the town took its name.

1838. Charles Maurice de Talleyrand Perigord, one of the most distinguished statesmen and diplomatists of modern times, died at Paris, aged 84. His name was intimately associated with French politics, from the commencement of the revolution in 1789.

1841. About 250 feet of the cliff on which the defences of the city of Quebec stand, fell away, causing the ruin of several buildings, and the death of about 30 persons.

1843. Peter W. Gallaudet died at Washington, D. C., aged 88. The Washington manual laborer school and the Howard institution can bear testimony to his industry and patriotism.

1848. Massacre in Naples, justified by the king, on the ground of necessity; 1777 bodies were found, 400 troops killed, and the city given up to pillage.

1849. A severe and very destructive fire at St. Louis, Missouri.

1850. Gallinas, the noted slave factory on the west of Africa, purchased by the Liberian republic.

1856. Redwood Fisher, an American author, died, aged 73. He began business as a merchant in Philadelphia; subsequently edited a daily paper in New York, and took an active part in public affairs. He published several volumes on political economy, and was much interested in statistics.

MAY 18.

975. Edward (the martyr), murdered by his step-mother. He was the son of king Edgar who enacted laws against excessive drinking, ordaining a size with pins in the cup with penalties on any who should presume to drink *deeper* than the mark. Hence the phrase *drinking deep*.

1291. The city of Acre, in Palestine, taken by the Turks; after a siege of 30 days the double wall was forced by the Moslems, the principal tower yielded to their engines, the Mamelukes made a general assault, the city was stormed, and death or slavery was the lot of 60,000 Christians, and the Holy Land was again in the hands of the Turks.

1410. Robert, emperor of Germany, died, just as a powerful combination had been formed to deprive him of the crown.

1539. Ferdinand de Soto, governor of Cuba, sailed for the conquest of Florida with nine vessels, 900 men besides sailors, 213 horses and a herd of swine. He landed on the west coast of the peninsula, with 300 men, and pitched his camp; but about day break the next morning they were attacked by the natives, and obliged to retire.

1565. The Turks under Mustapha, pasha, to the number of 30,000 choice troops, landed on the island of Malta, with a view to extirpate the knights. But the desperate resistance they encountered compelled them to abandon the island with the loss of 25,000 men. Loss of the knights 7,000.

1596. Heemskerk, accompanied by Jan Cornelissen Ryp, with two vessels again attempted the discovery of a northern passage to India. In this voyage he became embayed in ice, and passed the winter in the arctic regions, exposed to the rigors of the climate, and other perils. The ill success of this expedition destroyed all hope with the Dutch of finding a northern passage to China.

1652. Naval action near Dover, England; admiral Van Tromp refusing to pay honor to the British flag by lowering his own, brought on a furious battle between him and admiral Blake. One of the Dutch ships taken, and one sunk.

1663. Samuel Des Marets, a French protestant divine, died; celebrated for his controversies, in which he was diligently engaged 18 years, and displayed astonishing knowledge and erudition.

1664. "His sacred majesty," Charles II, advertised that he would attend to healing his people of the king's evil, by *touching*, during the month of May.

1675. Stanislaus Lubienietski, a celebrated Polish Socinian, died in exile at Hamburg. His theological works are numerous, but he is better known by a work on comets, entitled *Theatrum Cometicum*, which was written to show that comets portend both good and evil, in opposition to the prevailing notion that they were the harbingers of misfortune only! It contained an elaborate account of all the comets recorded in history (415), down to the year 1665.

1676. Indian battle at Turner's falls, on Connecticut river above Greenfield. The Indians having planted nothing, were unwilling to lose the fishing season also, and had encamped here in great security; when three of the towns below hearing of their position mustered about 150 men, mounted on horses, and set out for their camp. Arriving towards morning, they tied their horses, and proceeding about a quarter of a mile farther, found them sleeping in their huts, without any sentinels or guard. The attack was so sudden and unexpected that they fled, many into the river where they perished, and others were killed under the banks where they had concealed themselves. The Indians at first supposed they had received a visit from their *friends* the Mohawks, but the daylight disclosing the error, and the fewness of their assailants, they rallied and turned upon their pursuers. The English retreated in turn, unable to resist the superiority of numbers, and not managing their retreat well, thirty-eight were cut off and lost. The Indians acknowledged a loss of 300.

1692. ELIAS ASHMOLE, a noted English antiquary, died. His valuable collection of coins, to the number of 9,000 besides books and other curiosities, were destroyed by fire; but his most valuable gold coins and manuscripts escaped. He was an indefatigable laborer in the cause of science.

1701. FREDERICK SPANHEIM died; a noted divinity professor at Leyden, and a voluminous writer.

1724. Cardinal VINCENT MARIA ORSINI elected pope and took the name of Benedict XIII.

1733. EDMUND CHISHULL, an English traveler, died; author of a book of travels in Turkey.

1742. RICHARD JOY (*the English Samson*), died; a man of wonderful strength.

1769. Virginia entered into the non-importation agreement.

1773. Boundary line between New York and Massachusetts agreed upon.

1787. First attempt made to engrave on glass by M. de Puymaurin, at Toulouse.

1794. Battle of Bullion; French under Jourdan defeated by the Austrians under Beaulieu with the loss of 1,200 killed.

1794. Battle of Tournay; British defeated by the French.

1794. Battle of Lannoy, in France, between the French under Pichegru, and the British under the duke of York; the latter defeated with the loss of sixty pieces of cannon.

1800. PETER ALEXIS WASILIOWITSCH, count Suwaroff-Rimnitskoy, died; a Russian general, known in the wars of Europe as Gen. Suwarrow; distinguished for his bravery and abilities, and equally so for his inhumanities.

1803. War was again declared between France and England. Who, asked Bonaparte, is responsible for the consequences. Ah! who indeed.

1804. The conservative senate of France declared Bonaparte emperor.

1805. Battle of Derne, in Barbary, which was attacked by the Tripolitan army, and defended by the American general Eaton, who repulsed the assailants with great slaughter.

1807. JOHN DOUGLAS, bishop of Salisbury, died. He was one of the first literary characters of the age, and the last surviving member but one of the *beef steak club*, celebrated by Goldsmith in his poem of *Retaliation*.

1821. TIMOTHY BIGELOW, an eminent lawyer of Massachusetts, died. He was 11 years speaker of the assembly, and during a practice of thirty-two years, argued 15,000 causes.

1822. ITURBIDE declared emperor of Mexico by the army under the title of Augustin I.

1832. CASSIMIR PERRIER, prime minister of France, died. He left the army in 1800 to become a banker, in which capacity he acquired an immense fortune, with the advantages of which he combined great mental capacity, talent for business and habits of public speaking. He was one of the few victims of cholera in the higher ranks of life.

1843. CHARLES BAGOT, governor-general of the British North American provinces, died at Kingston, in Canada.

1848. Commander HENRY PINCKNEY, of the United States navy, was drowned by the swamping of a boat.

1850. Great fire at the village of Corning, Chemung county, New York.

1855. JOHN C. SPENCER, an American statesman, died at Albany, aged 67. He was a man of intellect and energy, and was in public life from an early age. He achieved his highest fame from his connection with the revision of the statutes of New York.

MAY 19.

804. FLACCUS ALCUINUS, an English ecclesiastic, died in France. He may be considered as one of the learned few whose genius dissipated the gloom of the 8th century. His writings, most of which are extant, were published 1617. (See Dec. 1)

1122. Lincoln in England destroyed by fire.

1217. Battle of Lincoln; the French defeated, and England effectually secured from the dominion of Lewis the Dauphin, who was then holding his court within the walls of London.

1218. OTHO IV (*the proud*), emperor of Germany, died. He laid claim to some of the territories of the pope, by whom he was excommunicated and deposed.

1242. HENRY III of England embarked for France, taking with him 30 hhds of silver.

1494. COLUMBUS, proceeding towards Cuba, named the headland Cabo de Cruz on this day. He now ascertained from the natives that Cuba was an island, but after coasting it 335 leagues from the eastern point, renounced the idea; and but for the scarcity of provisions, would have attempted to return to Europe by way of the Red sea, under the impression that he was on the coast of India.

1536. ANNE BOLEYN, queen of England, executed. She was crowned at Westminster 1533 with unparalleled splendor, and in a few weeks after became the mother of the famous Elizabeth.

1610. THOMAS SANCHEZ, a Spanish Jesuit, died, and was buried with extraordinary magnificence. His works are ingenious.

1613. King JAMES issued *farthing tokens* by proclamation.

1622. OSMAN I, sultan of Turkey, strangled by his soldiery. He undertook an expedition against Poland, in which he lost 80,000 men and 100,000 horses: these misfortunes were attributed to the Janizaries, who thereupon hurled him from the throne.

1643. Battle of Rocroy, between the French and Spaniards, in which the French under the duke d'Enghein gained a signal victory.

1651. PETER WRIGHT, chaplain to the marquis of Winchester, executed. Romanist priests were viewed in the same light as highway robbers.

1656. JOHN HALES died; an English author, so much admired for his wit and learning, that he is called the *ever memorable*.

1670. FERDINANDO UGHELI, a Florentine monk, died; distinguished for his learning and his virtues.

1676. JOHN GREENHILL died; an eminent English painter.

1692. Battle of La Hogue; the combined English and Dutch fleets defeated the French of 50 sail, who lost 20 of their largest men of war, and were prevented from making a descent on England.

1715. CHARLES MONTAGUE, earl Halifax, died; an eminent English statesman, orator and poet.

1769. Cardinal GANGANELLI proclaimed pope under the title of Clement XIV.

1776. Captain MUGFORD having secured his prize (see May 17) and put to sea again, was attacked by 13 British boats, whom he beat off; but was himself killed, being the only person injured.

1780. Dark day in New England, occasioned by a thin cloud or vapor. The people dined by candlelight, and the darkness of the night is represented as *Egyptian*.

1788. SAMUEL BADCOCK, an English divine and writer, died; admired as a pulpit orator and a man of literary talent.

1788. Congress ordered two cannon to be named, one John Hancock, and the other Adams; being one moiety of four cannon which constituted the whole train of artillery possessed by the colonies at the commencement of the war. The other two were taken by the British.

1795. JAMES BOSWELL, died, aged 55; a Scottish lawyer, rendered famous as the friend and biographer of Dr. Johnson, with whom he lived in the closest intimacy.

1795. JOSIAH BARTLETT, one of the signers, died. He was a delegate from New Hampshire in the first congress, and his was the first name called on the vote of the declaration of independence.

1798. BONAPARTE with an immense armament sailed from Toulon for the conquest of Egypt. The sunrise was splendid and similar phenomena were called the suns of Napoleon.

1798. Intelligence having been received by the British that a number of transports fitted out at Flushing were intended to be sent round by the canals to Ostend and Dunkirk, for the purpose of invading England, an expedition was despatched to destroy the sluices and basin of the Bruges canal at Ostend. The direction of the enterprise was entrusted to general Coote and captain Home Popham, who on this day disembarked their troops, and in a few hours the sluices were blown up, and several vessels in the canals destroyed; but on returning to the beach, the wind and surf were so high, that it was impossible to re-embark; meanwhile the country being alarmed, the enemy advanced upon them with a superior force, and the British, after a spirited resistance, were compelled to capitulate. Of 1000 forces landed more than 100 were killed or wounded, among whom was general Coote.

1808. Action in the night between British ship Virginia, and Dutch frigate Gelderland; the latter captured.

1810. Explosion of a powder magazine at New Haswell in Hungary, which destroyed 300 houses, killed 80 persons, and 300 were dug out of the ruins alive.

1831. FRANCIS MASERES, an English mathematician, died, aged 93. He was not only an author, but devoted a part of his income to reprinting such works as he thought useful either in illustration of mathematical history or of that of his country. Penny Cyclopedia says 1824, which agrees with the 93 years from the date of his birth.

1838. THOMAS T. BIDDULPH, an eminent English clergyman, died. He was the author of various publications, one of which, *Sixteen Short Sermons*, has been translated into 15 languages.

1850. A body of Americans under gen. Paredez landed on the island of Cuba, with a view to revolutionize it, and took the town of Cardenas.

1853. The Chinese rebels captured the city of Amoy.

1854. WILLIAM HULME COOPER, a lieutenant in the British navy, died, aged 26, from the effects of exposure and privation during four years arctic service in search of sir John Franklin. He commanded a cutter in an expedition from Icy cape to the Mackenzie; for three days he was lost in a snow storm, and for two winters he and his boat's crew were isolated near the northern shores of America. The hardships he endured caused the pulmonary disease of which he died.

1856. JOHN KEATING died at Philadelphia, aged 96. He was a native of France and in early life was an officer in the service of Louis XVI. He came to the United States after the death of that monarch, with about thirty families of the French noblesse and military, and founded the colony of The Asylum, near Towanda, in Pennsylvania.

MAY 20.

526. Earthquake at Antioch, by which 250,000 persons are said to have perished.

1499. ALONZO DE OJEDA sailed from Cadiz on a western voyage of discovery, accompanied by Amerigo Vespucci. It is uncertain in what station Amerigo sailed, but he appears to have had a chief share in directing the voyage, and on his return published an amusing account of the country they visited; which having a rapid circulation, he was supposed to be the discoverer, and it came gradually to be called by his name.

1506. CHRISTOPHER COLUMBUS, the discoverer of the new world, died at Valladolid in Spain, aged about 70. He had devoted his whole life to the study and accomplishment of his grand enterprise, and its complete success embittered the remainder of his days by exciting the perfidy and ingratitude of a base and treacherous nation.

1521. CORTEZ mustered his army in the great market place of Tezcuco, to make a division of it, appoint commanders, assign to each the station where they were to form their camps, in order to invest the city of Mexico. (See May 30.)

1610. NICHOLAS SERARIUS, a French Jesuit, died. His works, 16 vols. folio, display great labor and extensive erudition.

1618. King JAMES publicly declared his pleasure, "that after the end of divine service, the people should not be letted from any lawful recreation on Sundays, such as dancing, archery, vaulting, May-games, Whitsun-ales, morris-dances, and the setting up of May-poles, and other sports therewith used."

1690. JOHN ELIOT, the apostle of the Indians, died, aged 86. He was the first protestant clergyman who preached the gospel to the North American Indians.

1713. THOMAS SPRAT, an English prelate and poet, died; he was distinguished as a writer, and rewarded with preferments.

1726. NICHOLAS BRADY died; an Irish divine of good ability and learning, translated Virgil and wrote a new version of the Psalms in conjunction with Tate.

1728. JAMES LE QUIEN DE LA NEUFVILLE, a French historian, died; author of an excellent history of Portugal, &c.

1732. THOMAS BOSTON, a Scottish divine, died; author of the well known book, *Human Nature in its Fourfold State.*

1735. The Turks defeated by the Prussians, and more than 60,000 killed and wounded.

1736. The body of one Samuel Baldwin, of England, in compliance with his will, immersed in the sea at Lymington. His motive for this extraordinary mode of interment was to prevent his wife from dancing over his grave, which she had threatened to do in case she survived him.

1756. Naval action at Fort Philip, Minorca, between the French fleet, 12 ships 5 frigates, and the British, 13 ships 5 frigates. Admiral Byng was afterwards shot in England, on an unjust charge of cowardice in this affair.

1758. The scenery and wardrobe of the Bath theatre burned by the wagons taking fire on which it was being transported over Salisbury plain.

1774. British parliament passed an act for transporting Americans to England for trial.

1775. Articles of confederation and union agreed on by the American colonies.

1776. Major SHERBURNE, with 140 Americans, marching to relieve the post at the Cedars, in Canada, was attacked by 500 Indians, and after an obstinate battle, the party surrendered. The Indians having lost a chief and 21 warriors, massacred as many prisoners.

1778. Gen. GRANT with 7000 British, made an attempt to surprise La Fayette, then posted at Barren-hill, Pa., with 2500 men. The latter escaped by a masterly retreat.

1783. WILLIAM ROBERTSON, the Scottish divine, died.

1789. The French clergy renounced their privileges.

1793. CHARLES BONNET, a noted Swiss naturalist, died at Geneva.

1796. BONAPARTE passed the river Po; MARCEAU and CHAMPIONNET drove the Austrians from Hunsruch; they were also defeated on the Sieg, with the loss of 2400.

1799. BONAPARTE raised the siege of St. Jean d'Acre; it had lasted 60 days.

1799. JOSEPH TOWERS died; a printer, bookseller, and afterwards a preacher with the title of LL. D. He wrote *British Biography*, 7 vols. and other works of merit.

1800. BONAPARTE passed mount St. Bernard, among the Alps, after astonishing efforts.

1813. Battle of Bautzen, between Russians and Prussians under Barclay de Tolly, and French under Bonaparte.

1813. American frigate Congress, capt. Smith, captured British brig Jean, 10 guns, took out 40 tons copper and sunk her.

1815. MURAT, king of Naples, left the city in disguise, while his queen sought the security which had been promised her on board a British man of war.

1820. CHARLES LOUIS SAND executed; the murderer of Kotzebue.

1840. JOSEPH BLANCO WHITE, an English preacher and controversial writer, died, aged 67. He was the author of various works, and distinguished himself by the zeal and ability with which he opposed the catholic religion.

1841. WILLIAM P. DEWEES, a distinguished medical writer, died at Philadelphia.

1848. A treaty of peace made with the Navajo Indians and the United States.

1855. The king of Hanover issued an ordinance annulling the constitution settled in 1848, and the provincial electoral law of 1850.

1856. JAMES KING, editor of the *Evening Mirror*, at San Francisco, California, died of a pistol wound inflicted in the street a few days before by Casey, editor of the *Sunday Times*. Casey was arrested and conveyed to jail under great popular excitement. Subsequently the vigilance committee, numbering 3000 men, proceeded to the jail, and took Casey and another murderer to the committee rooms, where they were tried, and soon after hung.

MAY 21.

216 B. C. Battle of Cannæ, in Italy, in which the Roman consuls were vanquished by Hannibal, with a loss of 40,000 men, including Paulus Æmylius, and 5,630 knights. The Carthaginians seemed not to know the use of victory.

987. LOUIS V (*the lazy*), king of France, poisoned by his wife, Blanche.

1342. JOHN CANTACUZENUS, the historian of his own times, and a defender of the faith, inaugurated emperor of Constantinople.

1420. Treaty of Troyes, by which Henry V of England was to marry Kate, daughter of Charles VII of France, and the two kingdoms to be united under Henry on the death of Charles.

1502. The island of St. Helena discovered.

1542. FERDINAND DE SOTO, a Spanish adventurer, died at the confluence of the Guacoya and Mississippi. He was a companion of Pizarro in his Peruvian expedition, and amassed great wealth; after which he became governor of Cuba. He fitted out an expedition to search Florida for more gold, and lost his life.

1643. Battle of Wakefield; the forces of Charles I defeated by the parliamentary troops.

1647. PETER CORNELIUS HOOFT, one of the most eminent poets and prose writers of Holland, died.

1649. The commonwealth of England proclaimed.

1650. JAMES GRAHAM, marquis of Montrose, executed. He fought with great bravery in the royal cause; but being at length captured he was hung on a gallows 30 feet high at Edinburgh, and his quartered remains exposed over the city gates.

1682. MICHAEL ANGELO RICCI, an Italian cardinal, died; celebrated as a mathematician.

1718. GASPARD ABEILLE, a French poet and wit, died. His writings are not much esteemed.

1723. JAMES MABOUL, an eloquent French preacher, died; author of *Orationes Funebres*.

1724. ROBERT HARLEY, earl of Oxford, died; an English statesman and literary character.

1745. British squadron captured French ship Vigilant, 64 guns, and 560 men, with a cargo valued at £60,000.

1762. British ships Active and Favorite captured the Spanish ship Hermione from Lima, with a cargo of $2,308,700. The four highest British officers shared $288,000 each.

1780. Village of Johnstown, New York, burnt by the tories.

1781. British fort Dreadnought surrendered to the Americans under Gen. Lee.

1782. American general Wayne defeated a considerable body of British under Col. Brown, near Savannah.

1789. JOHN HAWKINS, an English writer, died; author of a *History of Music* in 5 vols. quarto.

1790. THOMAS WARTON, an English poet died; author of a *History of Poetry*, 3 vols.

1794. French under Dumas scaled mount Cenis.

1794. Bastia, in Corsica, surrendered to lord Hood.

1796. Battles of Tombio and Codogno; the French defeated the Austrians; the gallant French gen. La Harpe killed.

1799. Archduke CHARLES crossed the Rhine into Switzerland.

1804. The first interment in the cemetery of Pere la Chaise; it was laid out and prepared by order of Bonaparte.

1807. Dantzic surrendered to the French after a siege of 51 days. Its garrison at first consisted of 16,000; 4000 deserted; only 9000 were taken; 800 cannon and immense stores fell into the hands of the French.

1809. Battle of Essling, in Austria. It began by a furious attack upon the village of Asperne, which was taken and retaken several times. Essling sustained three attacks also. Night interrupted the action; the Austrians exulting in their partial success, Napoleon surprised that he should not have been wholly successful. On either side the carnage had been terrible, and the pathways of the village were literally choked with the dead.

1813. British attacked Sacketts Harbor.

1813. Battle of Bautzen, which had continued two days; the Prussians were driven from their position, and Napoleon advanced to Breslaw, leaving 12,000 Frenchmen in the searching claws of their *executors*—the crows.

1826. George Reichenbach, a distinguished mechanical artist, died at Munich, where he had a noted manufactory of astronomical instruments, unsurpassed in the world.

1830. Leopold of Saxe Coburg declined the throne of Greece, except on terms which the allied sovereigns would not accede to.

1832. George W. Rogers, an American commodore, died on board ship Warren, off Buenos Ayres.

1849. Maria Edgworth, the popular and distinguished authoress, died at her residence in Edgworthstown, Ireland.

1855. The ship canal round the falls of St. Mary's river, Michigan, was completed and accepted.

1855. The allied fleet of the French and English entered the Russian port of Petropaulowski, and found it deserted.

MAY 22.

334 b. c. Battle of the Granicus, in Bythinia, in which Alexander of Macedon defeated the Persians.

337. Constantine (*the great*), emperor of Rome, died. He was an able general and a sagacious politician; celebrated as the builder of Constantinople on the site of Byzantium, and as the first emperor who embraced Christianity.

1424. James I, of Scotland, crowned 18 years after his accession, since which he had been in captivity.

1498. Vasco de Gama landed at Calicut, the first Indian port visited by a European vessel.

1542. Paul III, summoned the council of Trent; but was compelled to prorogue it, his own ecclesiastics only attending.

1555. John Peter Caraffa elected pope, and assumed the title of Paul IV.

1604. The first settlement made on the coast of Guiana, by captain Charles and sir Oliver Leigh.

1611. James I, instituted the order of Baronets, and elevated 75 families to that dignity.

1659. Richard Cromwell's parliament dissolved by commission under the great seal, at the instance of Desborough.

1661. The solemn league and covenant burned by the common hangman at London, and afterwards throughout the country.

1667. Alexander VII (Fabio Chigi), pope, died; characterized as little in great things, and great in little ones. He was liberal towards men of letters, and embellished Rome with some splendid edifices.

1680. A vast luminous meteor appeared at Leipsic.

1688. John Andrew Quenstedt died; a German divine, author of a Latin account of learned men down to 1600.

1690. Naval action at Cherbourg; British admiral Ashby destroyed 3 French ships of the line and several frigates, being part of Tourville's squadron.

1692. Action off La Hogue, commenced the night previous, between the combined English and Dutch fleets, admiral Russell, and the French fleet, which lost 16 sail.

1707. Battle of Stolhoffen, on the Rhine; French under Villars forced the lines of the allies.

1722. Sebastian Vaillant, a French botanist, died. He was originally organist to a convent.

1725. Robert Molesworth, an able English statesman, died. He rendered himself obnoxious to the clergy by insinuating that "religion is a pious craft, a useful state engine, but far inferior to the principles which in the school of Athens and Rome, incited their attentive youth to the love of their country, and to the practice of the moral virtues."

1734. Kouli Khan, defeated the Turkish army in Persia.

1745. Battle Jagernsdorf; Prussians defeated the imperialists.

1773. John Entick, an English clergyman and schoolmaster, died; author of the *Spelling Dictionary*, and other works.

1775. Meeting of provincial congress at New York.

1780. Sir John Johnson, with a party of British and tories, burnt a mill and 33 houses at Johnson Hall, killed about a dozen persons, destroyed all the sheep and cattle, and having dug up his silver plate decamped.

1781. JOHN BAPTIST BECCARIA, a learned Italian monk, died.

1782. Formosa, a large island in the Chinese sea, almost wholly inundated by volcanic agency, during a storm.

1794. Battle of Esperes; French defeated by the British, who took 500 prisoners and 700 cannon.

1795. MUNGO PARK, sailed from England on his first expedition to Africa, for the purpose of tracing the course of the Niger, and procuring information relative to the city of Timbuctoo, of which little more than the name was known.

1798. BONAPARTE and the French fleet sailed from Toulon; at the same time lord Nelson's fleet was in a storm in the gulf of Lyons, not many leagues distant.

1809. Second battle of Essling; French recrossed the Danube.

1810. CHARLOTTE GENEVIEVE LOUISA AUGUSTA ANDREA TIMOTHEE DU BEAUMONT D'EON, a French diplomatist, died, aged 82; memorable as a politician, but more so for having been discovered to be a female while on an embassy to England, in the year 1777.

1812. Action off the coast of France, between 2 British ships and 2 French 44 gun frigates, and a brig of 18 guns; the latter were destroyed.

1813. Battle of Reichenbach; 1500 French cavalry charged and overthrew the allied cavalry; but many divisions coming to their aid, the French were reinforced by 14,000 horse and cuirassiers and the allies compelled to retreat.

1813. MICHAEL DUROC, a distinguished French general, killed by a cannon ball, which struck him as he stood conversing with Mortier and Kirgener, the latter of whom was also killed instantly.

1813. United States frigate Congress, Capt. Smith, captured the British brig Diana 10 guns.

1814. JOSEPH WHITE, an eminent English divine, and oriental scholar, died. He was a weaver in humble life till his self-acquired attainments attracted patronage.

1819. The steamship Savannah, started from Savannah, Ga., for Liverpool, being the first passage of the Atlantic attempted by steam. She arrived in Liverpool on the 22d June, having consumed her fuel in ten days. She visited Stockholm and St. Petersburg before her return, which was in December following.

1819. HUGH WILLIAMSON, an American physician, scholar and statesman, died, aged 83. He assisted in framing the federal constitution, and made himself useful to his country in various ways.

1854. Rail road inaugurated in Sardinia, running between Turin and Susa; the king and queen, the government officials, and a great concourse of people participating.

1855. The convent suppression bill passed the Sardinian senate.

1856. PRESTON S. BROOKS, a South Carolina member of congress, wickedly and cowardly assaultted Charles Summer, senator from Massachusetts, while seated at his desk in the senate chamber, and felled him to the floor with a cane, in retaliation for abusive language in debate.

MAY 23.

1270 B. C. LARCHER places the chronology of the fall of Troy upon this day.

63 B. C. Jerusalem taken by Pompey on the 23d day of the Hebrew month Sivan, in the consulate of Cicero, a day that was then observed as a fast, in remembrance of the defection and idolatry of Jeroboam, *who made Israel to sin.*

37 B. C. Jerusalem fell into the hands of Herod, in the consulate of Agrippa; it being one of those septenniary periods called sabbatic years.

683. LEO II, pope, died; an able and resolute pontiff; established the kiss of peace at the mass, and the use of holy water.

1125. HENRY V of Germany died; leaving an odious character.

1430. The town of Compiegne in France was besieged by the combined forces of England and Burgundy, and defended by Joan of Arc.

1455. Battle of St. Albans (first of the roses), between the Lancastrians under Henry VI, and the Yorkists. The former were defeated with the loss of 3 earls, 49 barons and about 5,000 men killed, and the king himself was wounded in the neck and taken prisoner. Loss of the other party 500.

1498. GERONIMO SAVANAROLA, an Italian monk, burnt. His influence was so great at Florence, that for several years he guided the state as its sovereign; but when he attacked the corruptions of the church of Rome and the infamous conduct of pope Alexander VI, neither his purity nor his popularity could save him from destruction.

1533. CRANMER pronounced sentence of divorce between Henry VIII and Catharine of Arragon.

1609. The company of South Virginia not realizing the expected profit from its colony, obtained from king James a new charter, with more ample privileges. Their territory extended 400 miles on the Atlantic coast, and "from the Atlantic westward to the South sea."

1610. The English wrecked on the island of Bermudas (see July 24), having built two small vessels and paid the seams with lime and tortoise oil, arrived in them at the settlement of Jamestown; they found the inhabitants reduced from 500 to 60, by famine; and seeing no other means of preserving them than by abandoning the country, they took them all on board, with the intention of returning to England. At this juncture lord Delaware arrived with three ships, 150 men, and plenty of provisions, and settled the colony.

1679. It was discovered that 27 members of the English parliament had been pensioners on the government.

1692. Third action off La Hogue, between the British and French fleets; 6 ships of the latter burnt.

1701. WILLIAM KIDD with others executed at Execution dock, London, for piracy. In America every reminiscence of Kidd has yet an air of romance.

1706. Battle of Ramilles, in Belgium, between the French under Villeroy, and the allies under the duke of Marlborough, in which the latter were signally victorious. The armies contained about 60,000 men each; the loss of the French was 15,000, that of the allies 4,000.

1720. The French Mississippi scheme, projected by John Law, dissolved, like those bright floating circles which amuse and vex the hopes of children of a lesser growth.

1752. WM. BRADFORD, a noted American printer, died, aged 94. He established the first printing office in Philadelphia, and also in New York. He was government printer more than fifty years, and is said to have walked over a great part of the city of New York on the day he died.

1764. FRANCIS ALGAROTTI died; an Italian, eminent as a connoisseur and critic in every branch of belles-lettres, and an author of repute.

1783. JAMES OTIS, an American patriot and statesman, killed by lightning. He was one of the most zealous and active promoters of the revolution.

1785. WILLIAM WOOLLET, a celebrated English historical and landscape engraver, died. The death of general Wolfe from West's painting is probably his best.

1786. MAURITIUS AUGUSTUS BENYOWSKY, an extraordinary Hungarian adventurer, killed on the island of Madagascar in an action with the French.

1783. South Carolina adopted the federal constitution, recommending amendments, being the 8th state in succession; votes 149 to 73.

1793. Battle of Famars; the French defeated by the allies, consisting of Austrians, Prussians, British, Hanoverians, Hessians and Dutch.

1794. CECILE REGNAULT attempted to assassinate Robespierre and Collot d'Herbois.

1798. The rebellion of the united Irishmen commenced.

1798. Lady EDWARD FITZGERALD, the celebrated Pamela, daughter of the duke of Orleans, ordered to quit the kingdom.

1808. Riots among the English weavers on account of wages.

1812. LOUIS DUTENS, a French miscellaneous writer, died.

1815. G. HENRY ERNEST MUEHLENBURGH, an American Lutheran divine, died. He was a man of extensive science, particularly eminent as a botanist.

1816. Massacre of the Christians by the Turks at Bona in Algiers.

1836. EDWARD LIVINGSTON, an eminent American jurist, died. He was a native of New York, and after holding various offices, removed to New Orleans, where on the invasion of Louisiana by the British, he offered his services to general Jackson, and acted as aid. He was afterwards secretary of state at Washington and minister to France, in which offices he manifested distinguished ability.

1841. SAMUEL DALE, an eminent pioneer in the settlement of the southwest, died in Lauderdale county, Mississippi. He was remarkable for his courage and bodily strength, and distinguished for his contests with the Indians, and as an officer in the last war with England.

1848. Freedom of the negroes proclaimed at St. Pierre, Martinique; an insurrection followed, and several houses and 32 persons were burnt.

1850. GRINNELL'S ships of discovery sailed from New York in search of sir John Franklin.

1851. RICHARD LALOR SHEIL, a British statesman and dramatist, died at Florence, aged 59. He was minister of queen Victoria at the court of Tuscany.

1855. The state of siege and blockade of the island of Cuba was withdrawn.

MAY 24.

1085. GREGORY VII (Hildebrand), pope, died. He was the son of a carpenter, and when raised to the papal throne embroiled himself in disputes and dissensions till he was compelled to retire.

1153. DAVID I, king of Scotland, died. He married Maud, daughter of William the conqueror, and is characterized as a mild and popular king.

1276. A capitation tax of three pennies

laid on every Jew in England above the age of 12 years, and all above the age of 7 to wear a yellow badge.

1357. EDWARD the *black prince*, conducted his captive, John, king of France, through the city of London, in triumph.

1430. JOAN OF ARC, after performing prodigies of valor, deserted and alone, was taken prisoner by the English, after her horse was slain, in a sally from Compiegne.

1543. NICHOLAS COPERNICUS, the great astronomer, died, aged 70. After a constant devotion of 43 years to the study, he produced his immortal work, *De Orbium Cœlestium Revolutionibus*. The work was excommunicated by the pope, and although the planets continued their revolutions, it was not till 278 years after, namely, in 1821, that the papal court annulled the sentence!

1551. VON PANNIS, an eminent surgeon of England, burnt to death for denying the divinity of Christ.

1572. DRAKE sailed from England on his voyage of reprisal to the West-Indies, against the Spanish.

1612. ROBERT CECIL, earl of Salisbury, died; an English statesman, the ablest minister of his time.

1651. LOUIS XIV of France purchased of the West-India company, for the benefit of the knights of Malta, the islands of St. Christopher, St. Bartholomew, St. Martin and San Cruz, for the sum of 120,000 livres turnois. (See August 10, 1665.)

1663. South Carolina erected into a separate province. First permanent settlement began in 1669; original charter included North Carolina and Georgia.

1686. An eruption of mount Ætna, which extended its ravages four leagues around, and buried several persons alive.

1689. Passage of the well known toleration act of England, which so greatly relieved the dissenters.

1692. Four days' action off La Hogue; the remainder of the French ships, seven in number, and a great many transports and ammunition ships burnt.

1698. Pere GERBILLON, a Jesuit missionary, set out on his eighth and last journey to Tartary, in the train of the Chinese grandees, sent by the emperor to hold an assembly of the Kalka Tartars, who had been several years in rebellion, and to regulate the affairs of the country. (See April 1, Oct. 13.)

1715. WILLIAM READ died; originally a cobler, became a mountebank, and practiced medicine by the light of nature! Queen Anne and George I honored him with the care of their eyes! He could neither write nor read, but such was the success of his practice, that he rode in his own chariot, and "dispensed good punch from golden bowls."

1775. JOHN HANCOCK elected president of congress; he succeeded Peyton Randolph in that office.

1777. Colonel MEIGS made a successful attack on the British stores at Sag harbor, destroyed 12 British brigs and schooners, and great quantities of stores, and brought away 90 British prisoners, without sustaining any loss.

1786. CHARLES WILLIAM SCHEELE, an eminent Swedish chemist, died. His discoveries were numerous, though his experiments were made under great disadvantages.

1792. GEORGE BRYDGES, lord Rodney, a celebrated British admiral, died, aged 74.

1794. Battle of the Sambre, in the Netherlands, in which general Kaunitz defeated the French, who lost 3,000 taken prisoners, and 50 cannon.

1798. Several battles were fought at different places between the English troops and United Irishmen, in which the latter were generally defeated.

1811. The Seringapatam, prize to the United States frigate Essex, capt. Gamble, captured by the British sloop of war Cherub, at the Sandwich islands.

1814. Pope PIUS VII, whose powers had been abridged by Napoleon, made his grand public entry into Rome, to resume the throne.

1822. Battle of Pichinca, fought near the volcano of that name. The Columbians under Sucre succeeded in gaining the vicinity of Quito by marching over the frozen mountains of Cotopaxi, by which, and several other daring movements, the Spaniards were compelled to hazard a battle, and sustained a total defeat. The patriots thus became possessed of the entire province, with all the Spanish magazines and stores, and the road to Peru was left open to Bolivar.

1833. JOHN RANDOLPH, of Roanoke, an American statesman, died, aged 60. He was a descendant in the 7th generation, from Pocahontas, the Indian woman who saved the life of capt. Smith, and was distinguished for genius, eloquence and eccentricity.

1839. WILLIAM LEGGET, an American poet, and miscellaneous writer, died. He was a man of talent, and employed by government as charge d' affaire to Central America.

1844. JAMES THATCHER, a surgeon of the revolutionary army and author of the *Military Journal* and *History of Plymouth*, died at Plymouth, Mass.

1845. WILLIAM RAMSAY died in Boone county, Mo., aged 104. Early a pioneer and Indian fighter in Kentucky.

MAY 25.

535 B. C. The foundations of the second temple at Jerusalem, laid by the *children of the captivity*, by permission of Cyrus, on the twenty-fifth of Sivan.

67 B. C. TITUS VESPASIAN took the city of Joppa, in Galilee, by assault, on the 25th of the month Dæsius.

337. CONSTANTINE the Great died, having divided the empire among his children and nephews.

709. ALDHEM, an English divine, died; said to have been the first Englishman who cultivated poetry.

1261. ALEXANDER IV, pope, died. He bestowed the crown of Sicily on Edmund, son of the king of England, and attempted to unite the Greek and Latin churches.

1315. EDWARD BRUCE invaded Ireland with 6000 men. "He fought many battles and gained them all," and was for a brief period king of the country.

1427. ALEXANDER, lord of the isles, performed penance of submission to king James in his shirt and drawers, before the congregation of Holyrood church.

1510. GEORGES D'AMBOISE, a French cardinal and statesman, died; a great benefactor to France.

1622. PETRUS PLANCIUS, who with others contributed so much to the discovery of New Netherland and other countries, died at Amsterdam.

1625. WILLIAM BARLOWE, died; celebrated as the discoverer of the nature and properties of the loadstone.

1630. Eight Englishmen left by mischance in Greenland by their ship, were found on this day by their countrymen, having by good economy and wise expedients, succeeded in passing the winter without loss of life. (See Jan. 14, 1634, and Ap. 16, 1634.)

1681. DON PEDRO DE LA BARCA, a noble Spanish dramatist, died; who together with Lope de Vega, gave law to and polished the Spanish theatre. His works comprise 10 vols. quarto.

1743. JAMES ANTONY ARLAUD, a celebrated Swiss painter, died.

1760. Insurrection of the negroes in Jamaica. The loss to the island, in human flesh and blood, was $500,000.

1775. Sir GUY JOHNSON, called an Indian council at Guy Park, where the Mohawks alone attended; his object being to provide against a rumored attack upon his person by the revolutionists.

1775. Generals Howe, Clinton and Burgoyne, arrived at Boston.

1776. Congress resolved to engage the services of the Indians.

1778. About 500 British and Hessians from Rhode Island destroyed at Kickmut river, 70 boats and other property; burnt the church and several dwellings at Warren, and a church and 22 hosses at Bristol.

1780. Two regiments of Washington's troops mutinied; but were persuaded to return to their duty.

1798. CHARLES JAMES FOX, had his name stricken by the king from the list of privy councillors, for giving as a toast at the meeting of the Whig club, "The sovereignty of the people."

1798. ASMUS JACOB CARSTENS, a distinguished German artist, died. He was the son of a miller, and raised himself to eminence by his great talent and genius as a painter.

1798. A party of United Irishmen defeated near Dublin with great slaughter; many of those taken were executed.

1802. GEORGE FORDYCE, died; an eminent Scottish physician and writer on medicine and chemistry.

1803. BONAPARTE constituted all Englishmen between 18 and 60 years of age, found in the French territory, prisoners of war, and ordered the capture of British vessels.

1805. WILLIAM PALEY died; a learned English divine and writer on ethics. His *Evidences of Christianity* is one of the ablest defences of the Christian religion that has ever appeared.

1812. EDMUND MALONE, an Irish attorney, died. He is celebrated as the editor of Shakpeare, and published several biographies.

1818. DAVID MITCHELL, a major-general in the war of the American revolution, died, aged 77. He was the friend of Logan, the Indian, and had fought the Indians in 27 battles.

1830. The French expedition against Algiers sailed from Toulon, consisting of 34,160 men, under the command of General Bourmont, and succeeded in reducing that barbarous kingdom to a French province.

1840. Singular phenomenon in lake Erie, at Toledo; the water rising to the height of four feet above its ordinary level in the space of a few hours, without any apparent cause. The water and the weather were calm and still, and no unusual commotion was observable, as the bay gradually rose nearly a foot higher than ever before known.

1843. One hundreth anniversary of the Am. Philosophical Society, founded by Franklin at Philadelphia. It is the oldest scientific association this side of the Atlantic.

MAY 26.

604. AUGUSTINE (*alias Austin*), first archbishop of Canterbury, died. He was originally a monk, and was sent into Britain with 40 others to convert the English Saxons to Christianity.

735. BEDE (*the venerable*), a learned English monk, died. He passed his life in severe study, and wrote an ecclesiastical history from Julius Cæsar to his own age.

946. EDMUND I, king of the Anglo Saxons, killed by an outlaw named Liof, at the age of 23. He was distinguished for personal courage, as well as taste for elegance and splendor, whence he was called *the munificent*.

1416. JEROME of Prague made the fearless declaration that he was a supporter of the doctrines of Wickliffe and Huss, for which he suffered martyrdom.

1512. BAYAZID II, sultan of Turkey, died on the journey to Denitoka, his birth place, whither he was retiring, having resigned the government to his son, Selim, who had rebelled against him.

1536. FRANCISCO BERNI, a Tuscan poet, died. He is the principal writer of Italian jocose poetry, which has ever since retained the name of poesia Bernesca.

1568. An *estoddfod* of the Welsh bards and minstrels held at Cayroes by commission of queen Elizabeth, when the great prize of the silver harp was adjudged to Simon ap Williams ap Sion.

1595. PHILIP NERI, founder of the oratorians, died. He was noted for his benevolence, and established a *hospice* for the accommodation of pilgrims, which has become one of the finest in Rome.

1608. Sir THOMAS SACKVILLE, that great servant of Apollo and the state, interred with pomp at Westminster. "There never was a better treasurer," observes sir Richard Baker, "both for the king's profit and the good of the subject."

1623. FRANCIS ANTHONY, an English chemist, died; who took advantage of his knowledge to impose upon the credulous and unwary, by selling his panacea of potable gold.

1637. Fort Mistic, garrisoned by a large body of Indians under their grand sachem Sassacus, taken by assault, and about 70 wigwams burnt.

1689. Battle at the pass of Killicrankie, remarkable for the defeat of king William's troops by the Highlanders under lord Dundee.

1685. JOHN MARSHAM died; a learned English chronologist.

1703. SAMUEL PEPYS, a learned Englishman, died; celebrated for his collection of valuable documents, &c.

1746. THOMAS SOUTHERN, an English dramatist, died.

1766. JOHN LAURENCE BERTI, a learned monk of Tuscany, died; author of about 20 quarto volumes of divinity.

1781. Congress resolved to establish the bank of North America, being the first regularly established bank in the country.

1782. WILLIAM EMERSON, an eminent English mathematician, died. His knowledge was very extensive, and his works accurate.

1784. Musical festival in Westminster abbey, in commemoration of the birthday of Handel. This was the greatest concert ever known; the number of performers was 525; 275 vocal, 250 instrumental. The sum produced was over $12,000.

1794. The French convention decreed that no quarters be given to British and Hanoverian soldiers. But the French troops refused to execute the decree.

1795. The Ottoman Porte acknowledged the French republic.

1798. Battle of Tarah and defeat of the United Irishmen.

1799. JAMES BURNETT, lord Monboddo, died. He was one of the lords of session in Scotland, and a philosophical writer of considerable learning, but of peculiar notions.

1809. FRANCIS JOSEPH HAYDN, the celebrated musical composer, died. His works are numerous and highly valued.

1811. JAMES PULTENEY, a wealthy English baron, died; whose income was $250,000 per annum.

1813. Cannonade between forts George and Niagara, and bombardment from all the batteries.

1814. JOSEPH IGNACE GUILLOTIN, a French physician, who revived the use of the instrument known as the maiden, died at Paris, aged 76.

1824. CAPEL LOFFT, an English poet and miscellaneous writer, died in Italy. He was the patron of Bloomfield.

1831. Battle of Ostrolenka, between 55,000 Russians and 20,000 Poles, in which the latter were defeated.

1836. WILLIAM YOUNG OTTLEY, keeper of the prints in the British museum, died. He was for half a century actively devoted to his favorite pursuit of the fine arts, and is honorably known as an artist, a collector, and an author.

1838. WILLIAM BUTLER died at Philadelphia, aged 108.

1840. WILLIAM SIDNEY SMITH, admiral of the red, died at Paris, aged 76. He was one of the most celebrated naval officers of the last age, and distinguished himself on various occasions by his talents and courage.

1844. Jacques Lafitte, the French banker, died.

1848. By a fire which occurred in the omnibus establishment of Kip & Brown, New York, 130 horses were burnt.

1852. Samuel Nott, for a long time regarded as the patriarch of the clergy of New England, died in Franklin, Conn., aged 98. He graduated at Yale college in 1780, and two years after settled at Franklin, where he spent the remainder of his protracted life. He was also engaged in the business of instruction, and was a maker of public men. He was injured by a burn, and died of the effects of the accident.

1853. The yellow fever made its appearance at New Orleans; the number of victims during the season was 8,186, the greater part of whom died in August and September.

1854. Angus Patterson, for a long time president of the senate of South Carolina, died at Barnwell, in that state.

1854. A great crowd in Boston, excited by inflammatory speeches, attacked the court house and attempted to rescue the negro, Anthony Burns, under arrest as a fugitive from servitude. A special assistant of the United States marshal was killed, but the object of the riot was not effected.

1855. An imperial ukase ordered that all the serfs in certain of the Russian states, between the ages of 30 and 35, should be enrolled.

MAY 27.

346 b. c. Philip of Macedon took possession of Phocis upon the 27th Scirophorion, and the towers were soon after dismantled, which terminated the ten years' war.

1199. Hubert, archbishop of Canterbury, made lord chancellor in consideration of his services in crowning king John.

1257. Richard, brother to Henry III, crowned at Aix la Chapelle, king of the Romans.

1520. Cortez, with 250 men, without horses, or any other arms than pikes, swords, shields and daggers, attacked the well appointed expedition under Narvaez, sent against him by the governor of Cuba, consisting of about 1400 men, which was defeated and gained over to his party. Thus the almost dispirited adventurer suddenly found himself again at the head of a more numerous army than ever, consisting of nearly 2000 Spanish troops, about a hundred horses and 18 vessels, and a great sufficiency of ammunition.

1538. Anthony Fitzherbert, an able English judge, died; author of several works on the law.

1541. Margaret, countess of Salisbury, beheaded in the tower, at the age of 70. She was the mother of the celebrated cardinal Pole, and the last of the royal line of Plantagenet.

1564. John Calvin, the great reformer, died. He was a man of eminent talents, solid judgment and extensive learning. His great rigor, however, procured him many enemies; indeed it ill became a reformer to defend, as he did, the burning of heretics.

1600. Matins of Moscow, so called from the time of the day when prince Demetrius and all his Polish adherents were massacred at 6 in the morning.

1602. The colony accompanying Gosnold fixed upon a place of settlement, on the western part of Elizabeth island in Narraganset bay. On a rocky islet in the centre of a fresh water pond two miles in circuit they commenced erecting a fort and store house. (See June 18.)

1610. Francis Ravaillac, the fanatic who assassinated *Henri Quatre*, (see May 14,) was executed by being drawn and quartered by four horses.

1647. Peter Stuyvesant, a man of learning and a soldier, the last Dutch governor of New York, arrived at New Amsterdam, and superseded Kieft.

1648. Vincent Voiture, an elegant French writer, died. He wrote verses with elegance in French, Spanish and Italian, and was a polisher of his native language in a barbarous age.

1679. English act of habeas corpus passed; the act suspending it was repealed, probably forever, 1818.

1681. "The sweet singers" of the city of Edinburgh renounced the printed Bible at the Canon gate tolbooth, and all unchaste thoughts, words and actions, and burned all story books, ballads, romances, &c.

1694. The French under marshal de Noailles defeated the Spaniards near the river Ter, and took Gerona.

1702. Dominic Bouhours, a French Jesuit, died; celebrated as a learned writer and critic.

1703. St. Petersburg founded by Peter the great. Its present population is about one-third that of London.

1721. The *Weekly Journal or Saturday's Post* of this date adjudged to contain libelous matter against the government of England.

1723. George I assented to the bill for the banishment of bishop Atterbury, whose great virtues are now remembered.

1725. Charles de la Rue, a French Jesuit, died; distinguished as an orator and poet and a professor of belles-lettres.

1728. CHARLES LEOPOLD, duke of Mecklenburgh, deposed by the emperor of Germany.

1775. Battle at Noddle's island, near Boston; the British defeated by the Americans under Putnam and Warren, who had but 3 men wounded. British loss 200, together with an armed schooner and some stores.

1776. ARNOLD with about 900 Americans captured the British post at the Cedars without any resistance, and retook 500 American prisoners.

1777. BUTTON GWINNETT, one of the signers, died of a wound received in a duel.

1779. THOS. NUGENT, a distinguished lexicographer, died. His French and English dictionary has much merit.

1781. Lord CORNWALLIS, with a vastly superior force, compelled the marquis La Fayette to evacuate Richmond.

1794. Battle of Kaiserslautern, in which the Prussian general Mollendorf surprised the French camp, killed 1000, and took 2000 prisoners, and 20 cannon.

1798. Battle of Oulart Hill; the United Irishmen under father Murphy defeated the English, and massacred all but five. Same day, a large body of Irishmen defeated at Kilthomas hill, 150 killed, and 100 cabins and 2 chapels burnt.

1799. Addison's library sold by auction in London on this and the three following days, 70 years after his death, when it brought about $2,000.

1811. RICHARD PENN, one of the proprietors, and governor of Pennsylvania before the revolution, died in England.

1811. HENRY DUNDAS, lord Melville, a distinguished British statesman, died.

1813. The American army landed in Canada under cover of the fire from Chauncey's fleet, and carried fort George by assault. The vanguard landed first, consisting of Forsyth's riflemen, and the Albany and Baltimore volunteers, under Col. Scott.

1817. A Tunisian corsair of 12 guns, with two prizes, under Oz Maney, were captured near Dover, England, by two British revenue cutters.

1832. St. Jean d'Acre in Palestine taken from the Turks by the pasha of Egypt.

1840. Great freshet in the Savannah river; the city of Augusta and town of Hamburgh entirely submerged; the water rising 35 feet above low water mark. The destruction of property was very great.

1840. Baron PAGANINI, the most celebrated violinist the world ever produced, died at Nice, in Italy, aged 57, leaving a large fortune. (See June 27, 1819.)

1848. The princess SOPHIA, 12th child of George III of England, died, aged 71; an amiable and benevolent lady.

1850. The temple of Nauvoo, erected by the Mormons, finished in 1845, partially burnt in October 1848, having but its four walls left—all its timber works having been consumed by the flames—was destroyed by a hurricane.

MAY 28.

812. St. WILLIAM, of Aquitaine, died. He distinguished himself by his valor against the Saracens, under Charlemagne.

1089. LANFRANC, archbishop of Canterbury, died. He was an Italian, and has the character of a great statesman, as well as a learned prelate.

1220. Pope HONORIUS issued a decree that no person in England should keep in his hands more than two of the royal castles; intended to check the encroaching barons.

1357. ALPHONSO IV, of Portugal, died. He was an able prince, benevolent, and warred with the Moors.

1500. DE CABRAL'S fleet encountered a violent storm; 4 of his vessels ran foul of each other and sunk. Bartholomew Diaz, the Portuguese navigator, who first doubled the cape of Good Hope, was lost here.

1576. The first newspaper printed in England was the *Liverpool Times* of this date; it is said to be published at the present day.

1583. The printing of the *Vandalie Bible* commenced at Wittemberg, by Samuel Seelfish, at the expense of the state of Carniola, which paid 8,000 florins for 1,500 copies.

1661. The marquis of ARGYLE beheaded at Edinburgh and his head set upon the Tolbooth.

1672. Battle of Southwold bay, in which the Dutch admiral De Ruyter with 91 ships of the line and 44 frigates and fireships, engaged the combined fleets of France and England, consisting of 130 sail, under the command of the duke of York, afterwards James II, and the admiral count d'Estrees. The conflict was terrible. The allies had a trifling advantage, and the Dutch retired to the coast of Holland.

1672. EDWARD MONTAGUE, earl of Sandwich, drowned in the confusion of the battle of Southwold bay. He was distinguished as a statesman, general, admiral, and writer.

1672. War declared in Boston against the Dutch; the first declaration of war in the colonies.

1673. Action between the English and French fleets, under prince Rupert, and the Dutch under De Ruyter, at Schonvelt; both sides claimed the victory.

1701. ANNE HILARION DE COSTENTIN DE TOURVILLE, a French admiral, died. He distinguished himself against the Algerines and the Spaniards, but the battle of La Hogue was fatal to his glory.

1708. Com. WAGER attacked and destroyed the Spanish fleet near Carthagena.

1736. Madamoiselle SALLE, a famous *danseuse* at Paris, who piqued herself upon her reputation, instituted an order there, of which she was president, by the name of the *Indifferents*. Both sexes were indiscriminately admitted, after a nice scrutiny into their qualifications. They had rites, which no one was to disclose. The badge of the order was a ribbon, striped black, white and yellow, and the device something like an icicle. They took an oath to fight against love, and if any of the members were particular in their regards, they were excluded the order with ignominy.

1745. JONATHAN RICHARDSON died; a celebrated English painter of heads, and an author.

1754. Battle at fort Duquesne; the French and Indians defeated by the Americans under Washington.

1781. American frigate Alliance, 32 guns, Capt. Barry, captured British sloops of war Atalanta, 16 guns, and Trespasser, 14 guns.

1793. ANTHONY FREDERICK BUSCHING, a distinguished Prussian geographer, died.

1794. Lord HOWE's first action with the French fleet under Joyeuse. British ship Russell captured the Revolutionaire, 110 guns.

1795. WILLIAM, prince of Orange, issued a manifesto against the French and Batavian republics, protesting against their right to abolish the stadtholdership.

1797. Toulon, which had been seized by the French royalists, surrendered to the conventional troops.

1798. JAMES DUNBAR, professor of philosophy at Aberdeen, died; author of an essay on the history of mankind in the rude and uncultivated ages.

1798. Father MURPHY, at the head of the United Irishmen, took Enniscorthy, killed 90 of the king's troops, and set the town on fire.

1803. British ship Victory captured the French frigate Ambuscade, formerly belonging to the British.

1803. RICHARD HOLE, an English poet and divine, died. He published Ossian in a poetic dress and other works.

1808. The bones of the American prisoners who had perished on board the Jersey and other British prison ships at New York during the revolutionary war, solemnly inhumed in a vault erected at the Wallabout.

1808. RICHARD HURD, bishop of Worcester, died, aged 89. He was a learned man, author of several literary productions, and was offered the primacy, which he declined.

1810. The crown prince of Sweden killed by a fall from his horse. A circumstance which led the way for the elevation of Bernadotte.

1818. First steam boat on lake Erie (Walk in the Water), launched at Black Rock.

1839. MICHAEL BUFF, a soldier of the revolution, died in Oglethorpe co., Ga. He was under Gen. Forbes, 1758, and fought at the battles of Brandywine and Germantown.

1840. THOMAS HARVEY, a distinguished officer in the British navy, died at Bermuda, aged 65.

1841. Capitulation of the city of Canton, which had forfeited previous stipulations with the British and resumed hostilities. The Chinese agreed to pay six millions of dollars in one week as a ransom for the city, and that their troops should be withdrawn 60 miles into the interior, and that all losses sustained by the partial destruction of the factories, should be paid. The sum was paid as stipulated.

1843. NOAH WEBSTER, the American lexicographer, died, aged 85.

1850. JOHN N. MAFFIT, the well known and eccentric methodist preacher, died at Mobile.

1852. THOMAS FRANCIS MEAGHER, a political exile from Ireland, and convict at Van Dieman's land, arrived at New York.

1853. The French legislature passed an act restoring capital punishment for attempts on the life of the emperor, or to subvert the imperial government.

1854. A riot occured at the park in New York, between a party of Catholics and the friends of a street preacher; several persons were badly injured.

MAY 29.

71 B. C. The range of embankments thrown up by Titus against the wall of Jerusalem, the work of 17 days, was undermined and consumed, or buried in a pit of fire, with all the Roman engines. This was effected by the skill and conduct of John, the high priest.

1379. HENRY II, of Castile, died. He ascended the throne by the murder of Peter the cruel, which he perpetrated with his own hand. He was one of the bravest princes of his time, and won the good will of his subjects.

1405. Battle of Shipton moor; prince

Henry dispersed the 8,000 insurgents under Scroop, by seizing the persons of their leaders.

1453. Constantinople taken by the Turks under Mohammed II, which terminated the Greek empire, after an existence of ten centuries. Constantine XIII (Paleologus), was killed, and the beautiful Irene, whose fate is dramatized by Johnson, was one of the captives.

1545. DAVID BEATON, archbishop of St. Andrews, assassinated. He was a great persecutor of heretics, and united with great talents equally great vices.

1588. The Spanish armada, intended for the annihilation of England, sailed from the Tagus, under the duke of Medina Sidonia. The armament consisted of 92 galleons, or large ships of the line, 4 galliases, 30 frigates, 30 transports for horse, and 4 galleys; on board whereof were 8,350 marines, 2,080 galley-slaves, and 19,290 land-forces. The fleet was dispersed by a storm, and compelled to rendezvous at Corunna for repairs.

1593. JOHN PENRY, an English controversial writer, executed for heresy against the episcopacy.

1660. CHARLES II made his entry into London, after a long series of misfortunes and exile, and re-established the royalty, which had been suspended about 12 years.

1672. The new conduit erected in London by sir Thomas Vyner, ran with wine for a few hours in honor of the birthday and restoration of Charles II.

1691. CORNELIUS TROMP died; a Dutch admiral in the service of the republic, succeeded de Ruyter, 1670, as admiral of the fleets of the United Provinces.

1700. MICHAEL ANTHONY BAUDRAND, a French ecclesiastic, died; author of a *Geographical Dictionary*, 2 vols. folio.

1715. Great riot in London; the whigs complaining that unless they shouted high church and the duke of Ormond, they were insulted by the tories.

1758. Action between the French ship Raisonable, 64 guns, prince di Mombazon, and British ship Dennis, 70 guns. The Frenchman was captured with the loss of 61 killed, 100 wounded.

1762. The duke of Newcastle on resigning his premiership in the British ministry being offered a pension declined, saying, "if he could no *longer* serve he could not *burden* his country."

1780. Battle of Waxhaws, S. C., col. Tarleton, with 700 cavalry and infantry, came up with 300 continentals under col. Buford, who surrendered after a short action. A few continuing to fire after the main body had surrendered, an indiscriminate slaughter ensued. Tarleton states that 113 Americans were killed, 153 too badly wounded to proceed, and 53 taken prisoners.

1780. Great meeting of the protestant association was held in Coachmakers' hall, London, lord George Gordon presiding, saying that he would not present the petition unless signed by 20,000.

1785. ANDREW COLTEE DUCAREL, a French antiquary, died. His researches were confined to England.

1790. ISRAEL PUTNAM, a revolutionary officer, died. He was one of the most daring, brave and intrepid officers of the army, and his adventures almost border on romance.

1790. Rhode Island adopted the constitution of the United States, adding the 13th pillar to the federal edifice, by a majority of only 2—34 ayes, 32 noes; recommending amendments.

1793. The general assembly of Corsica, consisting of 1,009 delegates, unanimously expelled the Bonaparte family.

1796. The floor of the methodist meeting house at Leeds, England, gave way during service, and 18 persons were killed, and about 80 dreadfully wounded.

1811. Battle of Taragonna, in Spain, which was assaulted by the French under Suchet. The garrison consisted of 2,500 men, of whom only 903 prisoners were taken; the remainder were put to the sword.

1813. Attack on Sacketts Harbor, by the British under Yoe and Provost: they were repulsed with the loss of 260; American loss 156.

1814. British repulsed by maj. Finney of the Accomac militia, at Pongoteague creek.

1814. JOSEPHINE, ex-empress of France, died.

1820. CHRISTIAN WILLIAM VON DOHM, a Prussian statesman and scholar, died.

1823. JOHN PHILLIPS, an eminent lawyer in Boston, died, aged 53.

1829. HUMPHREY DAVY, the noted English chemist, died. He made several important discoveries in the science, and invented the miner's safety lamp.

1832. GEORGE BURDER, an English divine, died, aged 80; author of the *Village Sermons*, now so popular.

1837. JOHN AFZELIUS, an eminent Swedish chemist, died at Upsal, aged 84.

1839. DAVID KIRKPATRICK, an officer of the revolution, died. He entered the army at the commencement of the war, was in the battles of Monmouth, Germantown, Brandywine, Trenton, Cowpens, &c., and was the last surviving officer of the Delaware line.

1840. WILLIAM LEGGET, a well known political writer, died at Rochelle, near New York, when preparing for a diplomatic mission to Guatemala.

1848. Thomas Dick Lander, a distinguished Scottish literary writer, died.

1849. Sarah J. Howe, an American poetess and literary writer, died at Louisville.

1855. Jesse Chickering, an American statistician, died at Roxbury, Mass., aged 57. He studied theology, and afterwards medicine, but after a practice of ten years devoted himself to literature, and produced works on population and immigration.

1856. The president transmitted to congress the announcement that he had ceased to hold diplomatic intercourse with the British minister, Mr. Crampton, on account of his attempting to make enlistments for the British service among the citizens of the United States.

MAY 30.

542. Arthur, a British prince, died. He was a victorious warrior against the surrounding nations, and is celebrated as the founder of the knights of the round table at Winchester.

1216. Louis of France, at the invitation of the rebel English barons, crossed the channel with 680 sail, and landed at Sandwich.

1252. The epoch of the Alphonsine tables, constructed by Hazan, a Jew, by order of Alphonso the wise, commencing with the day of his accession to the throne of Leon and Castile.

1416. Jerome of Prague, burnt for the heresy of protestantism, at Constance, and suffered with great fortitude.

1431. Joan of Arc, the Maid of Orleans, burnt at Rouen, for sorcery and intercourse with infernal spirits, by the English. Chapelaine celebrated her in 12 times 1200 verses; Southey has made her the subject of an epic, and Schiller of a tragedy.

1484. Charles VIII (*the affable*), inaugurated at Rheims, in his 15th year. He was met at the gates by a young damsel, habited as Flora, who delivered him the keys of the city.

1498. Columbus sailed from the port of St. Lucar de Barrameda, with a squadron of six vessels, on his third voyage of discovery, with additional powers. The Indians were to wear a mark of brass or lead coin about their necks, which were to be *exchanged* for others on the payment of their tribute money.

1521. The Spaniards under Cortez, invested Mexico with 917 Spaniards and 75,000 Indians, which were soon increased to 200,000. He had 86 horses, 3 large iron cannons, and 15 smaller of copper, 1000 Castilian pounds of gun powder and a large quantity of balls and arrows, the strength of his little army having doubled by the supplies from Spain and the Antilles. The Spanish troops, in proceeding to their posts, in commencing the siege, had several engagements with the Mexicans. In attempting to break the aqueduct of Chapoltepec to cut off the water from the city, a powerful resistance was made. At one assault, so thick was the shower of arrows, darts and stones, which were shot at them, that 8 Spaniards were killed, and more than fifty wounded, and they were with difficulty able to retreat to Tlacopan, where they encamped.

1539. Ferdinand de Soto, landed on the West coast of Florida, in search of gold. He is supposed to have wandered over many of the southern states; but being disappointed in his great object, he returned without effecting a settlement.

1574. Charles IX, of France, died, aged 25. It was during his reign that the fatal massacre of St. Bartholomews took place, which renders his name odious.

1577. Martin Frobisher, the English navigator, sailed on his second voyage for the discovery of a north-west passage to India. He coasted Greenland and Labrador, and returned with 200 tons of glittering stones and sand, which he had mistaken for gold ore.

1640. Peter Paul Rubens, the celebrated Flemish painter, died. He was also a statesman, and a man of learning.

1654. Christina of Sweden abdicated the throne, on which occasion she caused a medal to be struck, with the motto, "Parnassus is worth more than a throne."

1658. Prince of Conde, at the head of 2000 cavalry, threw himself into Cambray, then besieged by marshal Turenne.

1663. Denis de Sallo, the inventor of literary journals, published the first number of the French *Journal des Savans.*

1676. Hatfield, Mass., burnt by the Indians. The town was attacked by about 600 of the enemy, while the men were all out in the fields at work except one who was very old. They burnt 12 houses and barns without the fortification, and drove away the cattle and sheep. The news of this affair having reached the neighboring town of Hadley, 25 resolute young men hastened to the scene of desolation, and charged the savages with such undaunted courage, that five or six of them fell at the first shot; and making their way through the thickest of the Indians, they threw themselves into the garrison, with the loss of five of their number, who fell as they were entering the town. The enemy, amazed at the resolution of this little band, and having lost 25 of their number, fled from the place immediately, with their booty.

1688. Pere GERBILLON, one of the French Jesuit Missionaries who accompanied Du Halde to China, set out on his first journey into Tartary. His travels are published at length in the great work of Du Halde. (See Ap. 1, 96; May 24, 98; Oct. 13, 98.)

1718. BERNARD NIEUWENTYD, a Dutch writer on mathematics, died.

1744. ALEXANDER POPE died: the celebrated English poet and epistolary writer.

1756. ELIZABETH ELSTOB, an English literary lady, died. She was skilled in eight languages, and published a Saxon grammar.

1764. SIMON SACK, died at Trionia, aged 141.

1770. Fire works in honor of the marriage of Louis XVI, of France, when about 1100 persons were crushed to death in the crowd.

1775. Americans burnt the mansion house on Noddles island, and carried off the cattle.

1778. MARIE FRANCIS AROUET DE VOLTAIRE, the celebrated French philosopher, died. He was an extraordinary man, of whom it has been said, he was a free thinker in London, a Cartesian in Versailles, a Christian in Nancy, and an infidel in Berlin. In society, he was alternately an Aristippus and a Diogenes. For versatility of talent, his equal has, perhaps never appeared.

1796. Battle of Borghetto; Bonaparte defeated the Austrians.

1799. The editor, printer and publisher of the *London Courier*, were fined and imprisoned for saying that the emperor of Russia was a tyrant among his own subjects and ridiculous to the rest of Europe.

1801. JOHN MILLER, who wrote a historical view of the English government, died at Glasgow.

1804. JEFFERSON issued a proclamation erecting the district of Mobile.

1806. Bonaparte issued a decree calling an assembly of Jewish deputies, for the purpose of forming a Sanhedrim.

1813. American privateer Yankee, 16 guns, captured British brig Thames, 14 guns; cargo sold for $180,000.

1814. Treaty of Paris, between Louis XVIII, and the allied sovereigns. The latter left Paris the same day, on a visit to England.

1826. JOHN BEATTY, a general officer in the war of the American revolution, died.

1832. JAMES MACKINTOSH, an English statesman, died; known by his *History of England*. He was employed principally in the affairs of India, during which he found time for literary pursuits.

1833. JOHN MALCOLM, a general in the India service, died. He distinguished himself as a soldier, statesman and scholar, He contributed much information respecting the history and present condition of Persia.

1837. CHRISTOPHER BROWNE, a soldier of the revolution, died at Philadelphia, aged 107.

1844. The Irish agitator DANIEL O'CONNEL, sentenced to fine and imprisonment.

1848. Battle of Goito, Italy; the Austrians defeated by the king of Sardinia.

1848. Ratifications of the treaty between the United States and Mexico exchanged with the latter government at Quaretaro.

1848. General HERRERA elected president of Mexico by 11 states against 5.

1854. Three British steamers destroyed the ships, dockyards and stores at Brahestadt, in the north of the gulf of Bothnia.

1854. The Turks made a sortie from Silistria, and killed 3000 Russians in the trenches.

1854. PEREGRINE MAITLAND, a British officer, died, aged 76. He served at Walcheren, in the Peninsula at Corunna, and at Waterloo. For his services on the Nive as commander of the first brigade of guards, he received a medal. He had been lieutenant-governor of Upper Canada and Nova Scotia, and commander-in-chief of the Madras army.

1856. The ship Pallas, sailing from Cork to Quebec, struck the breakers off St. Paul's island and bilged; of 120 passengers 72 were drowned.

MAY 31.

1434. LADISLAUS IV, king of Poland, died, aged 80; universally respected for all those virtues which should grace a throne.

1521. The siege of Mexico having been begun by Cortez, Sandoval with a division of the Spaniards and more than 35,000 allies marched to the assault of the city of Iztapalapan, situated about 8 miles from Mexico, on the eastern border of the lake. Great havoc was made upon the people and the city, devastated by fire. The inhabitants attempting to escape by water, were met by Cortez, who rushed among their frail boats with his brigantines, and destroyed immense numbers of them.

1589. WALTER MILDMAY, an English statesman, died; founder of Emanuel college.

1658. Kingston, Ulster county, N. Y., founded.

1672. Union between the colonies of Massachusetts, Connecticut and Plymouth.

1680. CHRISTOPHER DAVENPORT, died; a learned Englishman, who became a Franciscan, and published several theological works.

1707. SIMON PATRICK, an English bishop, died, aged 80. He rose from the lowest condition by his own worth.

1723. WILLIAM BAXTER, an English critic and grammarian, died, aged 73. Few *litterateurs* have commenced their career more unpromisingly; for at the age of 18 he could neither read a word, nor could he speak any thing but Welch; yet he became a noted linguist, translated several Latin authors, and compiled a *Dictionary of British Antiquities.*

1731. PHILIP WHARTON, died; an English nobleman, remarkable for his eccentricities.

1740. FREDERICK WILLIAM, king of Prussia, died. He was a wise and politic monarch, who sought the prosperity of his subjects and the kingdom.

1745. Shah NADIR, defeated the Turks at Erzeroum.

1775. The Americans landed on Pettick's island, near Boston, and carried off 500 sheep and 30 cattle.

1778. Col. ETHAN ALLEN arrived from England, and was received with discharges of cannon.

1779. Stoney Point evacuated by the Americans, and taken possession of by Gen. Clinton.

1791. Punishment by the wheel abolished in France.

1793. An armed force beset the palace of the Tuilleries, and demanded the arrest of the Brissotine party.

1796. BONAPARTE dissolved the great council and took possession of Venice.

1830. FREDERICK A. WILSON, inventor of gaslight, died at Paris.

1832. MAXIMILIAN LAMARQUE, died at Paris; a dintinguished French officer, and defender of liberal principles.

1833. JOHN MALCOLM, a distinguished philanthropist and faithful servant of the English East India Company, died. A tasteful obelisk 100 feet high is raised to his memory in his native Eskdale, Scotland.

1835. WILLIAM SMITH, an English statesman, died. He was 46 years a member of the British parliament.

1839. Great Western steamship arrived in New York from Bristol, in 13 days 8 hours, the shortest voyage from Europe to America theretofore made.

1847. THOMAS CHALMERS, the eminent Scottish divine, whose powers of oratory were the admiration of the world, died at Edinburgh, aged 67.

1853. THOMAS M. PETIT, director of the United States mint, died at Philadelphia.

1853. The second American arctic expedition left New York in search of Sir John Franklin, and for scientific purposes.

1854. The British transport Europa, having troops on board, was totally destroyed by fire opposite Brest, and 21 lives lost.

1854. Three wagon loads of powder, 11,250 pounds, exploded in the street at Wilmington, Delaware, killing several persons, and badly injuring 75 houses in the vicinity.

1855. CHARLOTTE NICHOLLS, died; an English authoress under the *nom de plume* of Currer Bell. Her fame was established by the novel of *Jane Eyre.*

1855. The propeller Arctic and barque Release, left Brooklyn navy yard under command of Lieut. Hartstein, in search of Dr. Kane and his companions in the Arctic sea.

1856. JOHN M. NILES, a Connecticut statesman, died, aged 68. He commenced the practice of the law in Hartford, in 1816, and was concerned in establishing the *Hartford Times*, which he principally edited. He held various offices with distinction; among others that of post master general under Mr. Van Buren.

JUNE.

JUNE 1.

67 B. C. Jotopata, in Judea, captured by the Romans under Vespasian, on the first of Panemus, in the 13th year of Nero. The city was demolished, entombing 40,000 Jews, the number of slain.

1205. HENRY DANDOLO, duke of Venice, died. He was a brave admiral, who took Constantinople, 1203, and had the moderation to refuse the imperial dignity.

1204. Rouen, the capital of Normandy, conquered by the French, which with the Dutchy had been separated from France for 300 years.

1450. JACK CADE's rebellion broke out in England.

1533. ANN BOLEYN crowned queen of England.

1571. Dr. JOHN STORY, an unrelenting persecutor of the protestants, was executed at Tyburn. On the accession of Elizabeth he fled to Flanders, and used all the influence he possessed to injure the trade of his native country.

1572. *Ovid's Elegies* burned at Stationer's hall by the order of the bishops of Canterbury and London.

1572. THOMAS, duke of Norfolk, executed for high treason. He was the first subject in England by rank, and the qualities of his mind corresponded with his high station. He fell a victim to love and ambition, in attempting to marry Mary Stuart.

1593. CHRISTOPHER MARLOWE, an English dramatist and poet, murdered in an affray. He was accounted an excellent poet in his time.

1603. A man was whipped through London for going to court when his house was infected by plague. In this visitation 30,244 persons died. James I, to avoid this plague retired to Wilton.

1638. Earthquake in New England; it occurred in the afternoon, and was so violent as to shake down movable articles in houses, and formed a memorable epoch in the annals of the country.

1660. MARY DYER executed. She was a quakeress, who had been banished from Massachusetts, and on her return was sentenced to death for "rebellious sedition and obtruding herself after banishment on pain of death."

1666. Great naval action between the Dutch under de Ruyter and Tromp, and English prince, Rupert, which continued four days with great fury, and the victory was claimed by both parties.

1679. GRAHAM of Claverhouse defeated by the Scottish covenanters at Drumclog, Scotland.

1740. SAMUEL WERENFELS, a Swiss professor and author, died; respected for his learning and many virtues.

1743. ROBERT LE LORRAINE, a celebrated French sculptor, died.

1764. The French carried off all the inhabitants of Turk's island, in the West Indies, with 9 English vessels.

1769. EDWARD HOLYOKE, president of Harvard college, died; an excellent mathematician and natural philosopher.

1774. Boston port bill went into operation. Business closed at noon, and the harbor was shut against all vessels. The citizens, on a short notice of 20 days, were deprived of the means of gaining a subsistence. Contributions were raised in other cities for their relief, and the inhabitants of Marblehead offered the merchants the use of their wharves. Universal indignation spread through the colonies against this high handed measure of the British king and parliament.

1780. American privateer Pickering, 16 guns, Capt. Harridon, captured British ship, Golden Eagle, 22 guns.

1783. CHARLES BYRNE, the Irish giant, died. His height was 8 feet 2 inches. (See May 13, 1781, Roger Byrne).

1785. JOHN ADAMS, the first minister of the United States of America to England, was presented to the king.

1791. The United States army under gen. Chas. Scott entered the Kikapoo villages, on the Wabash, and taking the Indians by surprise, extirminated their villages, killed and took many prisoners. He returned without the loss of a man killed by the enemy. These savages committed great depredations on the frontiers, and refused all terms of peace.

1792. Kentucky admitted into the Union with the consent of Virginia.

1793. The armed Parisians again assembled with cannon around the convention, and demanded the arrest of the Brissotine party. The decree of accusation was passed.

1793. The death of Richard Crutwell, the well known editor of the *Bath Chronicle*, took place at Cheltenham, England.

1794. Action between the French fleet, 26 ships of the line, under Joyeuse, and the British fleet, 25 ships, under lord Howe. The French were defeated with great loss.

1795. PETER JOSEPH DESAULT, a noted French surgeon, died.

1796. Tennessee admitted into the Union.

1797. Desperate engagement between an Algerine cruiser of 18 guns, well manned, and a Corsican frigate of 26 nine and twelve pounders. The action began at 7 in the morning, and was continued with unremitted obstinacy until 3 in the afternoon, when a sloop and cutter coming up, the frigate was towed off in a disabled condition, and the pirate being completely riddled, they fired the magazine, and blew themselves up. The Algerine had a number of Christian captives on board, and was commanded by Sidney Beder, the terror of the Spanish coast.

1805. Detroit destroyed by fire. The houses on 25 streets were consumed; 16 persons lost their lives, and the cattle, generally shared the same fate.

1807. Niesse, a Prussian fortress in Silesia, taken by the French under Jerome Bonaparte, with 3,000 prisoners, and about 300 cannon.

1811. WILLIAM EATON, an American general, died; celebrated for his heroic achievements in the expedition against Tripoli, 1798.

1813. Action between the United States frigate Chesapeake, 36 guns, Capt. Lawrence, 2 days out from Boston, with a raw crew, and British frigate Shannon, 38 guns, and a picked crew. The Chesapeake was captured, with the loss of Capt. Lawrence and 146 killed and wounded, British loss 84.

1815. ALEXANDER BERTHIER, a distinguished French officer, killed. He served in America during the revolutionary war, and afterwards signalized his talents and bravery under Bonaparte, who placed unlimited confidence in him.

1832. THOMAS SUMTER, a distinguished officer of the revolution, died, aged 97.

1833. RENE SAVARY, duke of Rovigo, died; one of the ministers of France under Bonaparte.

1833. OLIVER WOLCOTT died; a statesman under Washington, and 10 years successively governor of Connecticut.

1833. Cholera broke out at Lexington, Ky., number of deaths to August 1st, 502.

1835. OTHO, king of Greece, his minority having ended, ascended the throne at Athens, with appropriate ceremonies.

1839. Port Gibson, Miss., destroyed by fire.

1841. DAVID WILKIE, an excellent Scottish painter, died at Gibraltar, on his return from Egypt, aged 56. He was the author of many celebrated works in his profession.

1843. Dr. JAMES HAGAN, a native of Ireland, but for several years a citizen of the United States, fell in a street fight in Vicksburgh, Miss., provoked by the violence of his language as an editor.

1846. Pope GREGORY XVI died. His pontificate was 15 years.

1846. A convention of delegates to revise the constitution of New York met at Albany.

1847. The steamer Washington, first of the Collins or American line, sailed from New York.

1848. Defeat of the Danes by the Germans.

1852. A submarine telegraph wire coated with gutta percha, was laid across the channel, from Holyhead, a distance of 80 miles, by which telegraphic communication was completed from London to Dublin.

1854. Four British steamers attacked and destroyed the ships, dockyards and stores at Uleaborg.

1854. EMILY CHUBBUCK, widow of Adoniram Judson, died at Hamilton, N. Y.; better known as Fanny Forrester, an accomplished woman, and a writer of considerable celebrity.

1855. The republic of Nicaragua issued a manifesto, proclaiming "martial law and prohibiting the adventurers Kinney and Fabens," on pain of death from entering the republic for any cause.

JUNE 2.

193. DIDIUS JULIANUS, emperor of Rome, executed after a reign of 60 days, which he purchased of the soldiers.

1581. JAMES DOUGLAS, earl Morton, was guillotined at Edinburgh for the supposed murder of lord Darnley.

1609. Seven ships, attended by two small vessels, with 500 people, sailed for Virginia, under sir Thomas Gates, sir Geo. Somers, and Christopher Newport. (See May 23.)

1627. CHARLES I granted to James Hay, earl of Carlisle, by letters patent, all the Caribbean islands.

1653. Action between the English fleet under Monk, and the Dutch under Tromp. The action continued 2 days, and resulted in the defeat of the Dutch, who lost 20 ships taken or destroyed.

1656. Corner stone of the Dutch church, laid in the centre of State street, in the city of Albany, N. Y., by Rutger, Jacobsen one of the magistrates.

1671. EDWARD LEIGH, a learned Englishman, and member of the long parliament, died.

1676. Indian battle near Mount Hope. About 300 of the English, mounted on horses, with a number of friendly Indians, in pursuit of Philip and his regiment of Wampanoags, came upon their camp, which had been newly pitched in a swamp. The friendly Indians upon a given signal ran down upon them from one side, while the mounted soldiers attacked them from the opposite side, so that many of those who fled were taken prisoners. The fruits of this expedition were 3,000 of the enemy killed and taken, and among the prisoners a Narraganset squaw called the old queen. None of the English, and but few of the allies were hurt in this assault. Philip escaped this pursuit, although it was an irreparable blow to his plan of a general extermination of the English settlements, and nearly completed his ruin.

1754. Earthquake at Cairo, in Egypt, which nearly destroyed the city, and buried 40,000 of its inhabitants in the ruins.

1779. Verplank's point, with a garrison of 70, and 4 cannon, surrendered to the British gen. H. Clinton.

1780. Great riots in London. Lord Gordon, at the head of 50,000 protestants, went to parliament to present a petition against popery.

1781. French under BOUILLE took Tobago.

1782. Battle of Arnee, in India, and defeat of Hyder Ally, by the British under sir Eyre Coote.

1783. WASHINGTON furloughed the soldiers of the war.

1789. Baron KNYPHAUSEN, a Hessian general in the British service during the war of the American revolution, died at Berlin, in Prussia, aged 59.

1791. The city of Anapa, in Asia, stormed and taken from the Turks by the Russians. In the assault many were put to the sword, and a pasha and 14,000 made prisoners.

1793. BRISSOT and several other members of the convention arrested in Paris.

1795. M. DAMBOURNEY died at Rouen; distinguished as a merchant and a man of science.

1802. British house of commons voted Dr. Jenner £10,000 for his discovery of the vaccine inoculation.

1803. THOMAS PETT, an English miser, died. He went to London at the age ot 10, with a solitary shilling in his pocket. He lodged 30 years in one gloomy apartment, which was never lighted up with coal, candle, or the countenance of a visitant. It is said he never eat a morsel at his own expense, and left about $35,000 to relatives whom he had never seen.

1805. British surrendered Diamond rock, Martinique, to the French.

1811. CHRISTOPH, and MARIA LOUISA, his sable consort, crowned at Cape Francois, sovereigns of Hayti.

1812. JOHN WILLIAM DE WINTER, a noted Dutch admiral, died at Paris.

1814. Peace between Great Britain and France proclaimed in London.

1843. JOHN CARY, a negro, died at Washington, aged 114. He accompanied Washington as his personal servant in the old French war, and preserved a dress coat presented to him by the general, which he had worn at the siege of Yorktown.

1854. The military force of Boston was called out to protect the government marshal in delivering Anthony Burns, a fugitive slave, on board a Virginia vessel. No serious outbreak occurred, though crowds thronged the streets, and hooted and hissed and groaned, and threw missiles at the military, and at the marshal and his assistants.

1855. There was a riot at Portland, Me.; a crowd attempted to seize with violence certain liquors, claimed to be owned by the city; and, persisting, the military were called out and fired, killing one man and wounding others.

JUNE 3.

1098. Capture of Antioch, the capital of Syria, by the first crusaders. The sword of Godfrey, says an eye witness, divided a Turk from the shoulder to the haunch; and one half of the infidel fell to the ground, while the other half was carried by his horse to the city gates.

1137. Cathedral of Rochester, in England, burned.

1162. THOMAS A BECKET made archbishop of Canterbury.

1594. JOHN AYLMER, a learned and benevolent English prelate, died. He was tutor to lady Jane Grey, and more noted for his severity against the Puritans than for his learning.

1609. MARY ELLIS died at Leigh, England, aged 119. Her inscription informs the reader that "she was a virgin of virtuous courage and very promising hopes."

1611. Lady ARABELLA SEYMOUR escaped from confinement in the tower of London by stratagem.

1647. King CHARLES I of England arrested by Joyce with 500 cavalry, at Holdenby.

1649. FARIA E. SOUSA, a Castilian historian and lyric poet, died. He devoted himself with great ardor to literature, and wrote, by his own account, 12 sheets daily. He labored 25 years on a commentary on the *Lusiade*, which was prohibited by the inquisition.

1657. WILLIAM HARVEY, an English physician, died; celebrated as the discoverer of the circulation of the blood.

1665. Naval action between the British fleet, 114 sail, besides fire ships, under the duke of York and prince Rupert, and the Dutch under admiral Opdam. The latter were defeated, with the loss of 19 ships sunk or taken. The admiral's ship was blown up with himself and all the crew. The English lost but one ship.

1689. Six captains with 400 men in New York, and a company of 70 men from East Chester, joined Leisler in holding the fort at New York for the prince of Orange.

1694. The duke of SAVOY, at the instance of England and Holland decreed the free exercise of their religion to the Vaudois.

1732. EDMUND CALAMY died; an eminent English divine among the non-conformists.

1740. JETHRO TULL died; celebrated as the first Englishman who bestowed particular attention on agriculture, and endeavored to reduce it to a science.

1759. Admiral RODNEY bombarded Havre de Grace, France, 52 hours without intermission.

1769. Transit of Venus over the sun's disc. Capt. Cook sailed from England to Otaheite with scientific men, to take an observation there. As it had never been seen but twice before by any inhabitant of our planet, and could never be seen again by any person then living, it caused considerable excitement among the scientific in Europe. It was also observed by our countryman David Rittenhouse, at Philadelphia.

1770. The city of Port-au-prince, St. Domingo, destroyed by an earthquake.

1776. During the celebration of a wedding at Mantua, the floor of the house gave way, and 66 persons were killed, among whom was the bride.

1780. THOMAS HUTCHINSON, a governor of Massachusetts, died. He published a valuable history of the colony from 1628 to 1749, and a third volume has been compiled from his manuscripts, extending it to 1774.

1788. Lord MANSFIELD, of England, resigned his chief justiceship of the king's bench, a station he had occupied with distinguished reputation for 32 years.

1789. PAUL EGEDE died, aged 81; author of an *Account of Greenland*, and a zealous missionary there.

1790. Action between the Swedish and Russian fleets, in which the former were defeated with great loss.

1802. Madame MARA, the celebrated vocalist, took leave of the English stage.

1805. Peace concluded between the United States and Tripoli; the American prisoners to be liberated.

1808. PHILIP SCHUYLER, an officer of the revolution, died at Albany, aged 73. He possessed a mind of great vigor and enterprise, and was characterized by integrity and amiableness.

1826. NICHOLAI MIKHAELOVITCH KARAMSIN died. He was one of the most eminent Russian writers that country has yet produced.

1832. JEAN PIERRE ABEL REMUSAT died; a distinguished French orientalist, and professor of the Chinese and Tartar languages in the college of France.

1836. BARRY EDWARD O'MEARA died; formerly surgeon to Napoleon, and author of *Napoleon in Exile*, and other works.

1840. The steam packet Unicorn, the first steam vessel from England to Boston, arrived in the latter port in 18 days from Liverpool.

1844. ALEXANDER J. DALLAS, an American commodore, died on board his frigate in Callao bay, having been in the naval service 39 years.

1848. Gunpowder explosion at Vera Cruz, by which several buildings were injured and 20 persons killed, mostly women.

JUNE 4.

1137. The greater part of the city of York, its cathedral, and 39 churches burned.

1453. ALVAREZ DE LUNA, a Spanish statesman, executed. He acquired such an ascendancy over the king that he was himself the monarch more than 30 years.

1520. A famous interview between the kings of England and France, near Guisnes.

1561. St. Paul's, London, burnt, having stood nearly four centuries. Its dimensions were 960 feet in length, 130 in breadth, and surmounted by a spire 520 feet high.

1585. MARK ANTHONY MURETUS died; a French critic and poet.

1663. WILLIAM JUXON, archbishop of Canterbury, died. He was the friend of Laud, by whose influence he was promoted, and by whose fall he was a great sufferer. He was exemplary in his conduct and irreproachable in the discharge of his duties; and on the restoration was raised to the see of Canterbury.

1665. JOHN LAWSON, an English admiral, killed.

1691. Baltimore in Ireland taken by the English under general Ginkle.

1711. The fleet of transports containing 5,000 troops from England and Flanders, designed for the reduction of Canada, arrived at the port of Boston, under sir Hoveden Walker, after a passage of one month's duration.

1725. A general assembly of the kirk of Scotland met at Edinburgh.

1731. A person sentenced at the old Bailey court of London to be hanged for forgery; said to have been the first capital punishment for that offence.

1737. FRANCIS LE MOINE, an excellent French painter, ran himself through with a sword in a fit of lunacy.

1738. Birthday of GEORGE III of England. He began his reign at the age of 22, and occupied the throne 60 years.

1744. ANSON arrived in England after a voyage of three years round the world.

1745. Battle of Hohenfriedberg, between the army of Frederick II of Prussia, and that of prince Charles of Lorrain, in which the latter was defeated with the loss of 4,000 killed and 7,000 prisoners.

1745. ALEXIS NORMAND, advocate of the parliament of Paris, died; justly celebrated for his love of justice.

1746. Battle of San Lazaro; the French defeated in an assault upon the Austrian camp, with the loss of 15,000 killed, wounded, and prisoners, 60 colors and 10 cannon.

1792. First legislature of Kentucky met.

1792. Route between Pennsylvania and the Genesee country in New York explored.

1792. JOHN BURGOYNE, a British officer and dramatist, died. He was "tint at Saratoga."

1794. Port-au-prince, St. Domingo, taken by the British. They found 131 cannon, &c., 13 ships and 9 brigs laden, and other vessels.

1796. Battle of Altenkirchen; the French under Kleber defeated the Austrians and took much booty.

1798. Battle of Tubberneering; the united Irishmen defeated the English under colonel Walpole, who was shot through the head.

1799. Battle of Zurich between the French under Massena, and the Austrians under the archduke Charles.

1800. Cisalpine republic re-established by Bonaparte.

1800. The English squadron under Pellew attacked Quiberon in France, destroyed the forts and brought off several vessels.

1800. FRANCIS BULLER, an eminent English judge, died.

1801. Genoa united to France; Eugene Beauharnais appointed viceroy of Italy, by Bonaparte, who at the same time appointed the order of the *iron crown*.

1803. FRANCIS XAVIER TALBOT died; a French ecclesiastic, and author of some poems.

1804. Vaccination for the cowpox introduced with great success in Persia.

1805. The American prisoners at Tripoli liberated.

1807. EDWARD DILLY, a benevolent and distinguished bookseller, died. His purse and advice were always at the service of the deserving.

1808. A new constitution formed for Spain by Bonaparte.

1813. The French under Joseph Bonaparte and Jourdan evacuated Valladolid, Spain.

1816. Treaty between the United States and Weas and Kickapoo Indians.

1817. CLOTILDA TAMBRONI, an Italian poetess, died.

1819. Washington lodge of independent order of Odd Fellows organized at Baltimore, Md., the first lodge of the order in the United States.

1823. LOUIS NICHOLAS DAVOUST, duke of Auerstadt and prince of Eckmuhl, died; one of Napoleon's bravest generals.

1829. Steam frigate Fulton blown up, and 26 persons killed.

1835. OWEN PUGHE died in Wales; author of a *Welsh and English Dictionary*, and styled the Johnson of Wales.

1837. ABIEL HOLMES, a learned American clergyman, died, aged 74; known principally by his *American Annals*, one of the most valuable historical publications that has been written in this country.

1843. ANDREW BELL died at Perth Amboy, N. J., for many years surveyor for the proprietors of that state.

1844. JESSE SMITH died at Salem, Mass., aged 88. He fought at Bunkers hill, and also at almost every other scene of conflict during the war of the American revolution.

1848. MATTHEW GREGORY died at Albany, aged 91; a revolutionary soldier, who was at the capture of Cornwallis; the noted keeper of the Tontine in the early part of the century.

1854. A riot occurred at Brooklyn, N.Y., between the advocates of street preaching and the catholics, when many persons were killed and wounded, and quiet was only restored by the aid of the military.

1856. ALEXANDER CRICHTON, an English physician, died near London, aged 93. He was for many years physician in ordinary to the emperor Alexander I, of

Russia, and was the oldest member of the Royal society.

JUNE 5.

1402. HENRY IV tried to dispel by proclamation the rumors of Richard VI having appeared in Scotland.

1465. ENRIQUE IV, a weak king of Castile, deposed and solemnly degraded in the public square at Avila, and his brother Alonzo proclaimed king in his stead.

1480. CAXTON completed the printing of the history of England, which he thus announced: *The Chronicles of England, &c. Enputed by me William Caxton. In thabbey of Westmynstre by London, &c., the v day of Juyn the yere of thincarnacion of our lord god m.cccc.lxxx, &c.,"* folio.

1508. LAMORAL EGMONT, count of Holland, beheaded by order of the Spanish duke of Alva, at Brussels. He was a renowned general in the Spanish armies, but they were jealous of his partialities for his own country's liberty.

1594. Three ships fitted out by some Amsterdam and Zealand merchants, for the purpose of discovering a passage to India by the Northern ocean, sailed from the Texel under Willem Barentszoon and Jacob Heemskerk, shaping their course around Nova Zembla.

1603. The English merchants trading to the Levant surrendered their patent to the king. They paid £4,000 annually for this commercial monopoly.

1667. JOHN HENRY HOTTINGER, a learned Swiss orientalist, drowned in the Limmat. Notwithstanding the assiduity with which he applied himself to his numerous avocations he found time to write several works.

1672. An Indian deed under this date granted to the inhabitants of Schenectady a territory of three miles (12 English miles) all around that town.

1690. THOMAS BAKER, an English mathematician and general scholar, died at Bishops Nymmet, where he lived a retired and literary life.

1716. ROGER COTES, an English mathematician and astronomer, died, aged 33. He was rapidly acquiring distinction in science, and his loss was much regretted.

1724. HENRY SACHEVERELL, a notorious English prelate, died. He made himself obnoxious to parliament by the intemperance of his sermons. The mob took up his cause, and the ministry was overturned. He does not seem to have deserved much of the adulation bestowed upon him.

1745. Battle of Placentia, in which the Spaniards and French were defeated.

1757. CHARLES VINER died; an eminent English law writer.

1781. Fort Cornwallis, at Augusta, Ga., surrendered with 300 men to the Americans under Pickens and Lee. The latter had 40 killed during the siege which lasted 17 days.

1783. First public ascension of a balloon. It was made at Annonay, in France, by John and Stephen Montgolfier. An immense bag of linen lined with paper, and containing 23,000 cubic feet, was provided for the occasion. It was inflated by burning chopped straw and wool under the aperture of the machine, which immediately began to swell; and on being set at liberty ascended 6,000 feet into the air. As yet no individual had ascended.

1790. The steam boat constructed by John Fitch, left the city of Philadelphia at 4 o'clock in the morning for Trenton landing; from which place she returned to Philadelphia again at 5 in the afternoon, performing 80 miles against a strong head wind all the way down, and 16 miles against current and tide. It was propelled by 12 oars, and was the first successful experiment in America, and the most successful one in the world at that time—16 years before the triumph of Fulton.

1792. DAVID HENRY, an English printer, died. He was for more than half a century an active manager of the *Gentlemen's Magazine*, and published several other valuable works.

1794. Battle near Schecketschine, beyond the Vistula, in which the Russians defeated the Poles under Kosciusko.

1794. A small island emerged from the sea near the island of Tenedos. It was about half a mile in circumference.

1798. United Irishmen repulsed with great loss in an attack on New Ross. The British, on the score of retaliation put to death 221 prisoners, men, women and children.

1799. Bonaparte reached Jaffa on his retreat from St. Jean d'Acre, where he remained three days; during which time the French burnt the neighboring villages, carried away all the grain and cattle; they also destroyed all the fortifications at Jaffa, and threw the artillery into the sea.

1799. The archduke CHARLES compelled the French under Massena to evacuate Zurich.

1800. A signal defeat of five columns of Austrians by two French, on the Iller.

1806. NAPOLEON proclaimed his brother Louis Bonaparte king of Holland.

1807. Battle of Spandau, in which the Russians attacked the French under Bernadotte, and were repulsed with the loss of 1,200 killed.

1811. Venezuela in South America declared itself independent.

1813. Battle of Stoney creek, Canada, in which the Americans were attacked by the British in the night. American loss 30 killed and about 180 taken. British loss about 250.

1816. JOHN PAISIELLO, an Italian composer, died at Naples. His reputation extended over the whole continent, and his presence was courted by the sovereigns of Europe. His works are numerous and in high repute.

1826. CARL MARIA VON WEBER, the celebrated German musical composer, died at Paris. He is one of the best of the modern authors.

1827. The academy of sciences at Paris had presented to them at their sitting this day, the phenomenon of a woman with a breast in her left thigh, with which she suckled her own and several other children.

1828. HARRY STOE VAN DYCK, a poetical and miscellaneous writer, of Dutch descent, died near London. In conjunction with Bowring he translated specimens of the Dutch poets, under the title of *Batavian Anthology*, which procured each of them a handsome medal from the king of Holland.

1847. The celebrated African farmer of Cedar creek, Del., died, almost 118 years of age.

1852. JACQUES PRADIER died near Paris, aged 54; the most distinguished sculptor of his day in France.

1852. JOHN HOWARD PAYNE died at Tunis, Africa, aged 60. He was a native of New-York, and long styled on English boards the American Roscius. He was British consul at Tunis at the time of his death.

1854. A large elephant attached to a menagerie, while going from Providence, R. I., to Fall River, Mass., broke loose from his keeper, and before he could be captured attacked all the carriages that he encountered on the road, killing the horses, tearing the wagons to pieces, and severely injuring several persons.

1854. JOHN FRYALL SNODGRASS, a distinguished and successful Virginia lawyer, died at Parkersburg, aged 50. He was an influential and valuable member of the convention for revising the constitution in 1850, and fell dead in court while trying a cause.

1855. The National Know-nothing, or American convention assembled at Philadelphia.

1855. The British frigate Cossack appeared off Hango Udd, and sent a boat on shore under a flag of truce, and the men landed; when the boat was fired on and sunk, and the crew killed or wounded and taken prisoners.

1856. Governor JOHNSON, of California, declared San Francisco to be in a state of insurrection.

1856. ASA CUMMINGS, an American divine, died at sea, aged 65. He was editor of the *Christian Mirror* at Portland, Me., from 1826 to 1855, and was deeply interested in the cause of missions and education.

JUNE 6.

356. B. C. Birthday of ALEXANDER, *the Great*, on the sixth day of *Lous* (*Hecatombœon*) during the Olympic games, in the first year of the 106th Olympiad, at Pella. This joyful *deliverance* was notified to Philip at the falling of Potidæa; and two other messengers reached his camp on the same day, announcing that his race horse had gained the prize at the games, and that Parmenio his captain had defeated the Illyrians. It was on the night of this very day that the celebrated temple of Diana was burnt to the ground by Eratostratus, an Ephesian youth who fondly panted for an infamous reputation.

1210. King JOHN, landed in Ireland, and received the homage of twenty native princes.

1439. The act of union between the Greek and Latin churches, took place in the cathedral of Florence, where the contracting parties met, at the instigation of John Palæologus; but was sundered by the act of Russia.

1481. BATTISTA FRESCOBALDI and others engaged in a conspiracy to assasinate Lorenzo de Medici, executed at Florence.

1487. Battle of Stoke; the earl of Lincoln defeated and slain by the king Henry VII.

1527. Pope CLEMENT VII, surrendered the castle of St. Angelo, and gave up himself a prisoner to the imperialists, under Philbert de Chalons, prince of Orange, who succeeded the duke of Bourbon.

1533. LUDOVICO ARIOSTO, the Italian poet, died. His *Orlando Furioso* procured him the laurel crown at Rome, which was placed upon his brow by the emperor Charles V.

1577. On Corpus Christi's Eve, the usual celebration greatly aggrieved the perth weekly assembly. The play being judged idolatrous.

1597. WILLIAM HUNIS, one the contributors to the metrical theology of the times of Edward VI, died. Edward himself was no mean writer. Hunis versified the whole book of Genesis, calling it a hive full of honey.

1650. ANTHONY ASCHAM a friend of Cromwell, and member of the long parliament, assassinated. He was at the time envoy to Spain, and the deed was perpetrated by six exiled royalists there.

1660. Charles II, issued a proclamation for the regicides to surrender, that they might not be excepted from the general pardon: 19 availed themselves of the proclamation, but 19 others doubting the sincerity of the government, disobeyed the summons.

1693. Dr. Pitcarine, published at Leyden his dissertation on the circulation of the blood through the veins.

1710. Louise Francoise Valliere, wife of the duke of Orleans, and mistress of Louis XIV, died. She spent the last 35 years of her life in a cloister in acts of piety and devotion.

1745. A body of Silesian peasants, at Landshut, 2000 in number, sought permission of the king, Frederick II, to massacre the Roman catholics. He refused to allow the barbarous demand.

1749. Conspiracy of the Turkish slaves at Malta to exterminate the order of knights.

1761. British under lord Rolla took Dominica.

1762. George Anson, the circumnavigator, died, aged 62. His life was spent upon the ocean, and he rendered important services to his country, for which he was rewarded.

1780. Riots in London continued, occasioned by the property act. The rioters liberated the prisoners confined in the prisons, and totally destroyed Newgate by fire.

1794. Point a Petre, Guadaloupe, stormed by the French.

1799. Patrick Henry, an eminent Virginian patriot, orator and statesman, died, aged 63. He was chosen the first governor of Virginia, on the abdication of lord Dunmore.

1800. Sir Edward Pellew's squadron landed and destroyed the forts at Morbihan, in France, blew up the magazines, destroyed the guns, took 100 prisoners, 2 brigs of 18 guns, 2 sloops and 2 gun vessels.

1807. Battle of Deppen, in which the French cut to pieces a body of Russians.

1807. Battle of Eylau, between the French and Russians; 30,000 of the latter were killed.

1808. Spanish Junta declared war against Bonaparte. Same day he issued a degree at Bayonne, declaring his brother Joseph king of Spain and the Indies.

1832. Riots commenced in Paris between the Carlists and republicans united, and the National guards. The rioters were finally overpowered, after several days' resistance and great slaughter.

1832. Jeremy Bentham, a celebrated English jurist, died, aged 85. He was a man of great learning and eccentricity, and devoted his long life to laborious study.

1853. The Italian ecclesiastic Gavazzi, lectured at Quebec, and gave rise to a riot.

1854. John Speed Smith, a highly intelligent and cultivated Kentucky gentleman, died. He was repeatedly a member of the Kentucky legislature, and served two years in congress.

1855. The bombardment of Sebastopol was reopened with 157 guns and mortars on the part of the British, and above 300 on the part of the French.

JUNE 7.

218. Marcus Opilius Severus Macrinus, emperor of Rome, beheaded by his soldiers. He was an African, and rose from the obscurest situation to the throne on the death of Caracalla.

632. Mahomet (*or Mohammed*), founder of the Islam religion, died, aged 62. His followers are now computed at one hundred millions.

1099. The army of Christians comprising the first crusade, encamped before Jerusalem. The first army led on by Peter the Hermit, numbered at the outset 300,000; another of 600,000 followed, burning with zeal to rescue the holy land from the Moslem dominion. Battle, desertion and disease had thinned their ranks so that now there remained scarce 22,000 fit for the field, of all that vast host that had marshaled in Europe.

1329. Robert Bruce, king of Scotland, died. He succeeded by repeated and arduous efforts in freeing his country from the English yoke, and when he had accomplished his purpose, he devoted himself to advance the prosperity of his subjects.

1520. Famous interview between Henry VIII of England and Francis I of France, upon "the field of the cloth of gold," on English ground. It continued eighteen days.

1546. Archbishop Cranmer and the queen accused of heresy, but protected by Henry.

1565. Sir Thomas Gresham, laid the foundation of the Royal Exchange, London, on the model of the Mart at Antwerp, then the centre of commerce.

1593. Lopez, a Jew, the queen's physician, convicted and with others executed, for conspiring to destroy Elizabeth.

1629. Charters graned to patroons in the colony of New Netherland, now New York.

1660. An order of council that the Stationers' company do seize and deliver to the secretary of state, all copies of Buchanan's *History of Scotland*, and *De Jure Regni apud Scotus*, "which are very pernicious to monarchy, and injurious to his majesty's blessed progenitors."

1663. Second war at Esopus, now Kingston, in Ulster county, New York.

1673. Action between the Dutch admiral de Ruyter, and the French and English fleets, commanded by d'Estrees.

1692. Great earthquake in Jamaica; nine-tenths of Port Royal buried under water, and terrible devastations were made over the whole island. About 1000 acres were sunk northward of the city, and 2000 persons perished; and 3000 white inhabitants perished of pestilential diseases ascribed to the putrid effluvia issuing from the apertures.

1711. HENRY DODWELL, a learned English writer, died, aged 70. His writings, which are very numerous, and which prove him to have been a man of indefatigable diligence and extensive learning, are on controversial, theological and classical subjects.

1731. WILLIAM AIKMAN, an eminent Scottish painter, died. He was the intimate friend of the most distinguished characters of the day in England, whose portraits he painted, and thus unwittingly added much to their celebrity.

1751. JOHN MACHIN, a noted English astronomer, died. He is the author of a method of determining the quadrature of the circle.

1753. ARCHIBALD CAMERON, brother of Lochiel, executed; recently the estates of this attainted family have been restored. The execution of this gentleman has always been held as a specimen of ministerial cruelty.

1761. Belleisle, on the coast of Brittany, surrendered to the British. Its reduction cost an immense sum, besides the loss of 2000 choice troops, who perished in the expedition. British had 313 killed and 494 wounded.

1769. ANTHONY ALEXANDER HENRY POINSINET, died; a French dramatic writer.

1775. The general court of Massachusetts met at Salem, and chose delegates to the first congress.

1779. WILLIAM WARBURTON, bishop of Gloucester, died; an English prelate of great abilities.

1780. London riots continued. King's bench, Fleet prison, New Bridewell, and the toll gates on Blackfriar's bridge, &c., burnt. The military fired on the rioters, killed 210 and wounded 258.

1780. Unsuccessful attempt of the Spaniards with 10 fire ships to burn 3 British ships in the new mole, Gibralter bay.

1780. About 5000 British under Knyphausen, Tryon and Stirling, left Staten Island and entered Elizabethtown, N. J.; continuing their march five miles farther to Connecticut farms, they shot the minister's wife in the midst of her children, burnt the house and church, and had much other pastime of the like character.

1786. A small manuscript volume of prayers composed and written by queen Elizabeth, sold at auction for 100 guineas.

1794. Battle of Chelm; the Poles defeated by the Russians.

1795. The royalist expedition against Quiberon, assisted by English munitions and money, terminated disastrously for the royal cause. The Republicans obtained possession of clothing and equipments which had been landed for 40,000 men.

1795. Luxemburgh, in Belgium, under marshal baron de Bender, surrendered to the French under Gen. Hatry.

1798. Battle of Antrim; lord O'Niel killed with a pike.

1805. The Antigua convoy for England, captured and burnt by the combined French and Spanish fleets.

1811. Tremendous hail storm at Alexandria, Virginia.

1826. JOSEPH VON TRAUNHOFER, died; a celebrated German optician.

1831. SARAH SIDDONS, a celebrated English tragic actress, died. She was the daughter of Roger Kemble, manager of a strolling company, married Siddons in her 18th year, and in 1782, appeared at Drury Lane in the character of Isabella. Her course from that time was a perpetual triumph, and in 1812 she retired to private life with an ample fortune.

1836. NATHAN DRAKE, an English physician, died; also a highly respectable and voluminous author.

1836. JOHN PRINCE, an American clergyman, died at Salem, Mass., aged 85; distinguished for his talents and literary acquirements, and for his improvements in the air pump.

1840. FREDERICK WILLIAM III, king of Prussia, died, aged 70. He is characterized as an honest, just and economical ruler. Destined to take an active part in the great events which followed the French revolution, his reign was distinguished by great vicissitudes of ill fortune and success. He left a fortune of nearly twenty millions of dollars.

1848. GEORGE TRIPNER, an officer of the revolution, died at Philadelphia, aged 87. He was at many of the severest battles of the war, and throughout the entire campaign rendered no little service to his country.

1848. Whig convention at Philadelphia

nominated Gen. Zachary Taylor for the presidency.

1852. Hosea Ballou, a distinguished universalist preacher, died, aged 80. He was excluded from the baptist church, and began to preach in 1791.

1853. Important amendments were made to the New York city charter, restraining the power of municipal officers in money matters, which were adopted by a vote of 36,672 against 3,351.

1855. The allies attacked and carried some of the Russian outworks at Sebastopol; the French, those in front of the Mamelon, and the British the quarries in of the Redan. The Russians made six front attempts in the course of the night to recover them, but without success. British loss in killed and wounded 30 officers and 433 men; French loss in killed and wounded estimated at 400; 75 guns and 502 prisoners were taken from the Russians.

1856. Christian Wulf, a Danish naval officer, died at Beaufort, N. C., aged 46. He was sometime at the head of the naval academy at Copenhagen, and inheriting the literary taste of his father, admiral Wulf, he translated Shakspere, and Bancroft's *History of the United States*, and at the time of his death was making the tour of the United States.

JUNE 8.

68. Claudius Domitius Nero, emperor of Rome, destroyed himself at the age of 32, and the 14th of his dominion. He had committed every enormity, and finding himself at last the inevitable victim of a conspiracy, he was doomed to see his own grave prepared, and died with his eyes standing out of his head, to the terror of all that beheld him.

1042. Hardicanute died at a nuptial feast of a Danish lord. By his death the connection between the kingdoms of England and Denmark was severed.

1316. Louis X (*Hutin*), king of Navarre, died, aged 26. During his short reign the Jews were protected and encouraged in his dominions.

1376. Edward, prince of Wales (called the *black prince* from the color of his armor), died, aged 46. He distinguished himself as a warrior under his father Edward III in the war with France, in several famous battles, and was the idol of the nation.

1405. Archbishop Scroop beheaded at York, England, for insurrection.

1536. Henry VIII's new parliament passed an act of attainder against Anne Boleyn, and declared both divorces legal, and the issue illegitimate.

1590. Thomas Randolph, an English diplomatist under Elizabeth, died. He wrote an account of his embassy in Russia, 1568, which may be found in *Hakluyt's Voyages*.

1683. John Durell, an eminent English divine, died. His writings are chiefly controversial.

1692. Henry Arnauld, a French ecclesiastic, died. He was nearly half a century bishop of Angers, and devoted himself incessantly to the duties of his office.

1695. Christian Huygens, a celebrated Dutch mathematician, died. He made several astronomical discoveries, and improved the air pump. His works comprise 6 vols. 4to.

1709. Paper money first authorized and issued in New York.

1711. Catharine Lascaille, daughter of the celebrated Holland printer, James Lascaille, who herself was so famed as a poet, as to be called the Dutch Sappho, or the *tenth muse*, died in Holland.

1714. The princess Sophia died; fourth daughter of the king of Bohemia by Elizabeth, only daughter of James I, of England. She was the mother of George I.

1727. Augustus Herman Francke died; professor of oriental languages and of divinity at Halle, and distinguished for his learning and piety.

1747. Thamas Kouli Khan, the Persian conqueror, assassinated. He rose from the humble rank of a shepherd boy, to be the captain of a band of robbers, which in time became sufficiently formidable to place him on the throne of Persia. He extended his conquests into India, and overran some of its richest provinces.

1755. Action off Newfoundland, between the British ship Dunkirk, 60 guns, and 420 men and boys, and the French ship Alcide, 64 guns, 700 men. The Alcide struck in about 30 minutes; the slaughter on board of her was very great, the first broadside killing 47 men and officers. The governor of Louisburg and 4 officers of note were taken, and £30,000.

1764. William Pulteney, an English statesman, died. He was many years the friend of Walpole, finally opposed his measures and was disgraced. He continued his opposition with so much zeal and spirit, that Walpole was in turn disgraced, and himself rose in his place.

1768. Abbe John Winckelman, a celebrated German antiquary, assassinated at Trieste. He was the son of a shoemaker, and sometime engaged in the same business himself. His labors were indefatigable, and his works possess great merit.

1768. Andrew Millar, the most distinguished bookseller of his times, died in London. Dr. Johnson said he had raised the price of literature.

1776. Unsuccessful attempt of 800 Americans to surprise the British at the village of *Trois Rivieres*, Canada; 200 were taken prisoners. Same day the Americans under col. De Haas, burnt St. Annes, on the St. Lawrence.

1781. A reinforcement of 1,500 French troops landed at Boston, and marched to join Rochambeau at White plains.

1782. HYDER ALLY surrounded and cut off the advanced body of the British army under sir Eyre Coote.

1788. £1,340,000 voted on motion of Mr. Pitt for the benefit of American loyalists.

1793. British order in council to capture vessels bound to France with corn meal or flour, the cargoes to be paid for.

1794. Festival in Paris dedicated to the Supreme Being.

1794. Corsica united to England.

1794 GODFRED AUGUSTUS BURGER, a German poet, died, aged 46.

1795. LOUIS XVII (*the dauphin*), died. The unhappy prince was put in charge of a wretch, on the execution of his father, by the name of Simon, a cobbler, with the instructions that he was to be got rid of. Accordingly, by the most severe treatment, by beating, cold, vigils, fasts, and ill usage of every kind, he sank to the grave.

1806. GEORGE WYTHE, a signer from Virginia, died, aged 81. He was a learned and upright man.

1807. Battle of Gutstadt, in which the French under Bonaparte defeated 10,000 Russian cavalry, and 15,000 infantry, taking 1,000 prisoners.

1809. THOMAS PAINE, a political writer of great force during the revolution, died, aged 72. His writings were deemed of so much service that the legislature of Pennsylvania voted him £500, and New York made him a grant of land. His life and conduct subsequently was extremely imprudent and reprehensible.

1809. Battle of Viga; the French, 8,000, under Ney, attacked 12,000 Spaniards under Carera, and were repulsed.

1810. Mequienza, in Arragon, surrendered to the French under Suchet. This terminated the fourth campaign in the north of Spain.

1811. Extraordinary agitation of the sea and earthquake at Cape Town.

1813. Americans under general LEWIS broke up their encampment by order of general Dearborn, and returned to Fort George. The British succeeded in dispersing the boats with the baggage belonging to his command, and captured 12 of them.

1832. The first case of cholera asphixia in America occurred on this day at Quebec.

1838. JOHN LUSK, a soldier of the revolution, died, aged 104 years. He was born on Staten island, of Dutch parentage, and was a soldier in the regular service nearly 60 years. He died in Warren county, Tennessee, and was the last survivor of the old French war in Canada.

1842. HENRY BROOK PARNELL, famed as a political writer and liberalist, died by his own hand.

1842. JAMES BARBOUR, a distinguished American statesman, died in Orange co., Virginia.

1844. JAMES WADSWORTH, a distinguished and wealthy citizen of western New York, died at Geneseo.

1845. ANDREW JACKSON, an American general and statesman, died, aged 78. He was the seventh president of the United States.

1854. GEORGE H. TALCOTT, a captain of ordinance in the United States army, died at Indian springs, aged 43. He was a native of Maryland, and graduated at Westpoint in 1831.

1856. HENRY WARE WALES, an American linguist, died at Paris, aged 37, bequeathing a large and valuable library to Harvard college.

1857. DOUGLAS JERROLD, an English dramatist and journalist, died, aged 54. He was an extraordinary genius, and contributed to almost every department of literature.

JUNE 9.

587 B. C. On the 9th *Thammug*, an especial fast of the Jews was observed for the taking of Jerusalem under Nebuchadnezzar, king of Babylon, on that day.

597. COLUMBA, the founder of the famous monastry of Iona, or Icolmkill, in the Scottish Hebrides, died. This island was in that age the luminary of the Caledonian regions.

911. LEO VI (*the philosopher*), emperor of the east, died. He was a politic monarch, the patron of men of letters, and an excellent author himself.

1075. HENRY IV defeated the Saxons at Thuringia.

1099. The siege of Jerusalem opened by the first crusaders. Godfrey of Bouillon erected his standard on the first swell of mount Calvary; to the left as far as St. Stephen's gate the line of attack was continued by Tancred and the two Roberts, and count Raymond established his head quarters from the citadel to the fort of mount Sion.

1496. COLUMBUS returned to Spain from his second voyage.

1536. Dr. HEYLIN says: On this day the clergy of London agreed upon the form of a petition to king Henry, for permission to the people to read the Bible.

1553. Battle of Sieverhausen in the Duchy of Lunenberg, in which Albert of Brandenburgh was defeated by the confederates. His camp equipage taken and 4,000 killed.

1586. Great earthquake in Lima.

1625. First child of white parents born in Brooklyn, New York.

1674. The English parliament prorogued on account of the differences between the lords and commons. It is said more than £200,000 was spent in bribing the commons.

1681. William Lilly, a famous English astrologer, died. He made quite a snug fortune out of the cavaliers and roundheads by predicting for both parties. The parliament under Cromwell gave him £100 a year for flattering their prospects, and he was complimented with a gold chain and medal by the king of Sweden. He also made a handsome business by his almanacs and other publications.

1696. Antoine Varilas, a French historian, died. His works were popular for a time, until they were discovered to be very inaccurate, and carelessly compiled.

1724. Benedict Pictet, a Swiss professor of theology at Geneva, died. He possessed great abilities and learning, and published several valuable works.

1758. The English effected a landing at Louisbourg.

1770. British settlers expelled from the Falkland islands by a large Spanish force. They were restored the following year, when the dispute was ended.

1775. Force of the American army assembled at Cambridge, 1,581 officers, 6,063 privates; total 7,644.

1776. John Ives, an eminent English antiquary, died, aged 25. He had accomplished much at his early age, but had published only three papers from his collection.

1779. William Kenrick, an English dramatist and miscellaneous writer, died. He was originally a mechanic, and became an author of great popularity and merit.

1790. Robert Robinson, a self-taught English preacher, died. He was an apprentice to a wig and curl maker, when Whitefield attracted his attention, and he became a methodist preacher. He soon after became a baptist, and preached that doctrine a number of years, and was extremely popular. He finally became a unitarian, and died at Birmingham while on a visit to Priestly, before he had time to shift his opinions to any thing else.

1795. The only son of the unfortunate king Louis XVI died in the Temple in his 12th year. The convention agreed to exchange his sister for the commissioners, betrayed by Dumourier to Austria.

1798. Battle of Arklow, in Ireland, between the United Irishmen and British. More than 20,000 of the insurgents, under father Murphy, advanced against the town, which was defended by only 1,600 men. The contest was continued with great obstinacy till nightfall, when the rebels retired. Father Murphy was killed by a cannon ball.

1798. An eruption of the peak of Teneriffe. It continued 4 months and 6 days, had 4 mouths, and projected rocks 3,000 feet.

1811. Second unsuccessful attack on fort San Christoval, Badajos, by the British under lord Wellington.

1814. United States brig Rattlesnake, lieut. Renshaw, captured and destroyed British brig John, laden with English goods.

1824. William Oxberry, the comedian, died by apoplexy, the consequence of over living. This was acting tragedy.

1825. Abraham Rees, the cyclopedist, died. He was born in Wales, and educated for a dissenting minister, and officiated as such more than 40 years. He published sermons, and contributed to the *Monthly Review*, but is best known as the editor of the *Cyclopedia*, 47 vols. quarto.

1826. Jedediah Morse died, aged 65; author of the geography so well known.

1829. Battle of Oriva, in Turkey; the Russians, under general Geismar, assaulted and took the town.

1834. William Carey, the devoted and pious missionary, died.

1836. Battle of Micanopy; about 200 Indians defeated by a detachment of United States troops under Heilman.

1839. War declared by the sultan of Turkey against Mehemet Ali of Egypt, and his son Ibrahim, deposing them from the government of Egypt and Syria.

1846. The water in lake Ontario had fallen 14 inches since the 24th March. (See Aug. 21.)

1849. Charles Albert, ex-king of Sardinia, died on his arrival at Portugal, soon after his abdication.

1850. John Melcher, the oldest printer in N. H., died at Portsmouth, aged 90.

1853. Father Gavazzi, an emissary of the pope to America, caused a riot by his preaching at Montreal. A mob attacked him in the pulpit; the military fired upon the people, and 10 persons were killed and 16 wounded.

1854. The emperor and empress of France attended the first agricultural exhibition ever held in Paris.

JUNE 10.

312. CONSTANTINE (*the Great*) called the first council of Nice to determine on the Arian heresy.

1190. FREDERICK I (Barbarossa), emperor of Germany, died in Syria, in consequence of bathing imprudently in the Cydnus. He was frequently engaged in quarrels with the popes, but was at last persuaded to turn his arms against the Saracens. He marched a numerous army into Asia and was victorious over all that opposed him.

1429. Battle of Jargeau; the place was carried by storm by the French, who were lead on by Joan of Arc. On reaching the top of the wall she received a blow on the head, which precipitated her into the ditch. Being unable to rise, she continued to exhort her friends, assuring them that the Lord had delivered the English into their hands.

1530. The college of Bologna determined that the marriage law in the book of Leviticus, being a part of the law of nations, as well as of the law of Moses and of God, is binding on the whole Christian church, as well as infidels; and therefore, gave their decision against the legality of Henry's marriage with Catharine of Arragon.

1584. Two barks fitted out by Raleigh, under the command of Barlow and Amidas, arrived in the West Indies, upon a voyage of discovery. They returned to England about the middle of September, having taken possession of a new country, which so pleased the queen, Elizabeth, that she named it Virginia.

1593. Date of the Leghorn or Livorno indulto, by which merchants of all nations and of every religion were invited to settle in the town. Many Jews from Spain availed themselves of this privilege.

1604. ISABELLA ANDREINI, a famous Italian actress, died. She distinguished herself equally as a poetess, and possessed, with great personal beauty, wit and genius in a superior degree.

1610. The first Dutch emigrants to America landed at Manhattan, now New York.

1654. ALEXANDRE ALGARDI, a Bolognese sculptor, died. He was employed to restore the garden of Sallust; many of his original pieces have been engraved.

1667. The Dutch fleet, commanded by de Ruyter, sailed up the river Medway, in England, as far as Chatham, and destroyed several men of war.

1692. BRIDGET BISHOP hanged at Salem, Mass., for witchcraft.

1692. An army of French and Indians made a furious attack on the garrison at Wells, in Maine, commanded by captain Wells, who, after a brave and resolute defence, drove them off with great loss.

1710. The German emigrants, who fled from the devastations committed in the palatinate of the Rhine, by Louis XIV, arrived in New York.

1719. Battle of Glenshields in Scotland, which ended the Spanish invasion.

1724. A party of volunteers at Oyster river, in New Hampshire, discovered an Indian ambush, which they attacked, killed one, and wounded two others, who made their escape, though pursued and tracked by their blood to a considerable distance. The slain Indian was a person of distinction, and wore a kind of coronet of scarlet-dyed fur, with an appendage of four small bells, by the sound of which the others might follow him through the thickets. His hair was remarkably soft and fine, and he had about him a devotional book and a muster-roll of 180 Indians. His scalp produced a bounty.

1726. ANTHONY ALSOP, an English prelate and poet, died.

1735. THOMAS HEARNE, an English antiquary, died. He edited nearly forty works, some of them classics, but principally relative to ancient English history and antiquities.

1739. Grosvenor square centre house valued at £10,000, was raffled for and won by Mrs. Hunt, a grocer's wife in Piccadilly.

1761. Indian battle; the Cherokees defeated by the British under colonel Grant, and their town Etchoe utterly destroyed, together with their magazines and cornfields.

1768. Riot in Boston, headed by captain Malcom, on account of the seizure of the sloop Liberty, belonging to Mr. Hancock, by the commissioners of the king's customs.

1772. The Gaspee, an armed British schooner, having exacted some degrading terms of the American vessels entering the port of Providence, a body of the inhabitants boarded her, put the officers and crew ashore, and burnt the vessel with all her stores.

1792. Russians attacked a detachment of Poles, under general Judycki, between Mire and Swierza; but were defeated, with the loss of 500 dead on the field.

1798. BONAPARTE attacked Valetta, in Malta, and in a sortie the Maltese lost the standard of their order.

1800. Battle of Montebello, in Italy, in which the Austrians were defeated, and compelled to retire to Voghera.

1801. The pasha of Tripoli declared war against the United States of America.

1806. The British house of lords resolved to abolish the slave trade.

1807. Battle of Heilsburg, in Prussia. The French, under Bonaparte, defeated the Russians, who fell back into their entrenchments. About 4,000 Russians were taken prisoners. Roussel had his head carried off by a cannon ball, and Murat had two horses shot under him. The Russians retreated the next night.

1809. Pope PIUS VII excommunicated Bonaparte.

1811. Lord WELLINGTON raised the siege of Badajos. The French governor, Phillipon made a brave and noble defence.

1831. FRANCIS ABBOT, the *Hermit of Niagara Falls*, drowned while bathing in the river. He was a native of England, of quaker parentage. He arrived at the falls in June, 1829, on foot, in a very singular costume, and after a week's residence became so fascinated with the place that he determined on fixing his abode on Goat island. He sought seclusion, and wished to erect a hut, but the proprietor not thinking proper to grant his request, he took a small room in the only house, where he was occasionally furnished with bread and milk by the family, but more generally providing, and always cooking his own food. In the second winter of his residence, the house changed tenants, at which he quitted the island and built himself a small cottage on the main shore, about thirty rods below the fall. He was a person of highly cultivated mind and manners, a master of languages, and deeply read in the arts and sciences, and performed on various musical instruments with great taste; his drawings were also very spirited. He had traveled over Europe, and parts of the East, and possessed great colloquial powers when inclined to be sociable. On entering his hut, his guitar, violin, flutes, music books and port folio were scattered round in profusion; but not a single written paper of any kind was found to throw the least light on this extraordinary character.

1831. General DIEBITSCH, commander of the Russian forces in Poland, died, by the official accounts of cholera; it is supposed by poison.

1836. JEAN MARIE AMPERE, famed as a mathematician and natural philosopher, died. Near the close of his life he busied himself with a classification of the sciences, a work from which great minds before him had shrunk.

1837. The plague at Smyrna committed great ravages; about 300 died daily for some time.

1839. JOHN RIDGE, a Cherokee, murdered. He was educated at the Cornwall school in Connecticut, where he married a respectable white woman. He was a practicing attorney among the Cherokees, and a man of talents.

1851. ROBERT DUNDAS, viscount Melville, British statesman, died, aged 80. He was for many years in the ministry, especially as first lord of the admiralty.

1854. The Crystal palace at Sydenham, England, was opened by the queen, Victoria; 40,000 persons being present.

JUNE 11.

1656 A. M. The tops of the mountains were seen, 73 days after the waters of the deluge began to subside, 1st of 10th month, answering to this day.

1184 B. C. The destruction of Troy is placed commonly by English chronologists in the night of this day; an event which Homer has invested with unrivaled importance, and a gorgeous immortality. (See April 24.)

534 B. C. SERVIUS TULLIUS, sixth king of Rome, assassinated. He is celebrated for his laws on the subjects of rank and property. He was murdered by his son-in-law, the second Tarquin.

90 B. C. The consul RUTILIUS LUPUS was destroyed with his forces, by an ambuscade, near the river Livis, during the social war.

816. LEO III, pope, died. A conspiracy was formed against him in 799, and it was only through the power of Charlemagne that he was enabled to keep the pontifical chair. He was an able pontiff.

1183. Prince HENRY, son of Henry II of England, died, aged 27. He is sometimes called Henry III, on account of his rebellion against his father.

1258. The great council of reform, called the mad parliament, assembled at Oxford. Every member was sworn to allow no consideration, "neither of gift nor promise, profit nor loss, love nor hatred, nor fear," to influence him in the discharge of his duty.

1289. Battle of Campaldino, in Italy, in which the Florentines defeated the people of Arezzo. The poet Dante, then in his 24th year, was present, and served in the foremost troop of cavalry. He says, "the Uberti, Lamberti and Abati, with all the excitizens of Florence who adhered to the Ghibelline interest, were with Aretini; while those inhabitants of Arezzo, who, owing to their attachment to the Guelph party, had been banished from their own city, were ranged on the side of the Florentines."

1294. ROGER BACON, an eminently learned monk of the Franciscan order, died, aged 80. He was a miracle of the age in which he lived, and the greatest genius, perhaps, for mechanical knowledge, that ever appeared in the world since Archimedes. (1292 by some authorities.)

1381. WAT TYLER assembled his followers at Blackheath, amounting to 100,000 men.

1520. A grand tournament between Henry VIII of England and Francis I of France, at Guines. "At the houre assigned," says Holinshed, "the two kings, armed at all peeces, mounted on horssebacke, and with their companies, entered the field; the French king on a courser barbed, covered with purple sattin, broched with gold, and embroidered with corbin's feathers. All the parteners of the French king's chalenge were in like aparell, everie thing correspondent in cloath of silke embrodered. On his person were attendant on horssebacke noble persons, and on foot foure persons, all apparelled in purple sattin."

1526. Holy league against the emperor Charles V.

1543. Nicholas Copernicus, the astronomer, died on this day, according to Lalande, who says, in his *History of Astronomy for* 1798, "The death of the great Copernicus was, till lately, a problem. I resolved it in my tour. Copernicus died on the 11th of June, 1543, although Gassendi and Weidler date this circumstance on the 24th May, and Planche the 11th of July." (See May 24.)

1567. Flight of Mary, queen of Scots, and her husband, Bothwell, from Borthwick castle to Dunbar.

1576. Anthony Cooke, preceptor of Edward VI, died. He also educated his own daughters, who were "learned above their sex in Greek and Latin."

1576. Martin Frobisher was despatched with three pinnaces to discover a northwest passage, but compelled by the ice to return. He was the first navigator who attempted to find a northwest passage to China.

1578. Queen Elizabeth granted letters patent to Humphrey Gilbert for the discovery and settlement of "barbarous lands in America, undiscovered by any Christian prince or people." This was the first charter granted by the crown of England to a colony.

1665. Kenelm Digby, an eminent English philosopher, died. He was also in the employ of the government as a soldier and a statesman. He was brave, learned and eloquent, but somewhat visionary.

1685. The duke of Monmouth landed at Lyme, Dorsetshire with men and arms in opposition to James II.

1693. An expedition fitted out in England against Canada and Martinique, arrived in Boston. During the voyage, 1,300 out of 2,100 sailors, and 1,800 out of 2,400 soldiers, had died of a malignant disease. On the arrival of the fleet the disease spread into the town, and proved more malignant than any other epidemic which had ever been known in the country.

1695. Andrew Felibien, counselor and historiographer to the king of France, died. He was also celebrated for his taste and judgment in the fine arts, and his *Dialogues upon the Lives of the Painters* has done him great honor.

1698. Balthazar Bekker, a Dutch divine, died. His writings got him into trouble with the church, which was alarmed at some very harmless notions he entertained about spirits and devils.

1712. Lewis Joseph, duke de Vendome, died. He was a descendant of Henry IV of France, and distinguished himself under Philip V of Spain, whom he succeeded in raising to the throne, in opposition to the claims of Charles III, archduke of Austria.

1719. A terrible earthquake happened at Pekin, in China, throwing down houses and burying more than 1,000 inhabitants in the ruins.

1727. George I, king of England, died in his carriage near Osnabruck, in Germany, aged 68. He was the first king of England of the house of Brunswick, and had reigned 13 years.

1756. Cæsar Chesneau du Marsais, a French grammarian, died. He was engaged in the *Encyclopedie*, and his articles on grammar are drawn up with great precision, correctness and judgment.

1776. Congress appointed Thomas Jefferson, John Adams, Benjamin Franklin and Robert R. Livingston, a committee to prepare a Declaration of Independence.

1783. Great eruption of the Scaptar Jokul, in Iceland, commenced, and continued several days (see 18th).

1792. The first bank in New Hampshire commenced discounting at Portsmouth.

1792. Battle of Mire; the Polish general Judycki, surrounded by the Russians, defeated, and compelled to retreat.

1793. N. Gouvion, a French officer, killed at Maubeuge, on the Sambre. He served in America in the war of the revolution, and at the time of his death was a general in the army of the north.

1793. William Robertson, the Scottish historian, died. His works are popular, and the *History of Charles V* will be long read with admiration.

1796. St. Vincent, Grenada, and St. Lucia islands in the West Indies were taken by the British.

1798. Bonaparte seized Malta, the key of the Mediterranean, which he garrisoned, and proceeded with the fleet, carrying 20,000 regular troops, to the Egyptian coast.

1800. Samuel Ireland, an ingenious English mechanic, died. He distinguished himself by his skill in drawing and engraving. He was unjustly accused of an attempt to impose upon the world a spurious volume of letters and papers in the name of Shakspeare. (See April 17th, 1835.)

1812. A great skirmish of cavalry in Estremadura, Spain, between the English under general Slade, and the French under general Lallemand.

1825. DANIEL D. TOMPKINS, a distinguished New York statesman, died, aged 51. He was vice-president of the United States under Mr. Monroe, and governor of the state of New York.

1828. DUGALD STEWART, an eminent Scottish philosopher and writer, died. His philosophical works are well known.

1829. Battle of Schoumla; the Turks under the grand vizier defeated by the Russians under general Diebitsch, with the loss of 6,000 killed, 1,500 prisoners, and 60 pieces of cannon. Russian loss, 1,400 killed, 600 wounded.

1842. ALEXANDER CROMBIE died at London. As a scholar and a critic, a metaphysician and a theologian, his name stands high among the first writers of the age.

1845. THEODORE DWIGHT, secretary of the Hartford convention, died, aged 81. He was editor of the *Connecticut Mirror*, published at Hartford, and in 1815 established the *Albany Daily Advertiser*, the first daily paper in that city. In 1817 he became editor of the *New York Daily Advertiser*.

1849. Great excitement at Paris, and a proposition to impeach the president for his aiding the cause of the pope, signed by Ledru Rollin and 141 others.

1849. Ancona capitulated to the Austrians after a very destructive bombardment.

1853. GUERAZZI, ex-minister of Tuscany, tried for high treason at Florence, and found guilty, was sentenced to fifteen years' imprisonment, which was subsequently commuted to perpetual exile.

1854. THOMAS H. BOTTS died at Fredericksburg, Va., aged 54; a lawyer, and one of the leading men of his profession.

JUNE 12.

456 B. C. HERODOTUS recited his celebrated *History* at Athens, during the Olympic games, in his 29th year, on the 12 Hecatombæon. He had traveled with his work from Caria. Thucydides was then a boy; Æschylus died in that year; Cimon was recalled from exile, and the Athenians completed their long walls.

455. MARCUS CLODIUS PUPIENUS MAXIMUS, emperor of Rome, murdered by the soldiery, after a reign of 15 months. He was of humble birth, but rose by his merits to the most eminent posts of the state, and was raised to the imperial dignity on the death of Gordian. He made salutary laws and reformed abuses.

1099. The army of crusaders who had encamped before Jerusalem, made a furious attack on this city, and amid a storm of arrows and fire balls, burst the first barrier, and strove to surmount the walls by escalade. The want of proper instruments rendered the assault abortive, and the followers of the cross were driven back with shame and slaughter to their camp. This defeat was followed by suffering and privations, from the scarcity of provisions and water.

1211. Battle of Tolosa, in Spain, between the Christians and Moors. Mohammed Abu Abdallah, at the head of a powerful army, one of the five divisions of which, according to the Arabic and Spanish historians, amounted to 160,000 men, made a descent from Africa, with the design of conquering the whole Spanish peninsula. Such was the terror which this vast armament inspired among the Christians, that Innocent III, proclaimed a crusade, and several bishops went from town to town to rouse the Christian princes. The kings of Castile, Arragon and Navarre, with a numerous body of foreign volunteers, advanced to stop the progress of the Moslems. The two armies met in Las Navas de Tolosa, between Castile and Andalusia. The result of the engagement was so complete a victory over the Africans, that Mohammed had a narrow escape, and left no less than 170,000 men in the field; the rest fled for safety.

1268. BILBARS, the sultan of Syria, took possession of Antioch. The Latin principality was extinguished, and the whole existence of the Franks was now confined to the city of Ptolemais.

1402. Battle of Melienydd, in Radnorshire, Wales, in which Owen Glendour, the last of the native Welsh princes, defeated and captured sir Edmund Mortimer.

1418. Massacre at Paris, at night, by the direction, if not under the eye of John, duke of Burgundy, called the fearless. In the course of three days, 3500 persons were sacrificed.

1488. JAMES III, king of Scotland, killed. He put his brother John to death, and attempted the life of his other brother, Alexander; he escaped, however, and levied war against the tyrant, who had rendered himself odious by his cruelties. James was defeated in battle, and put to death in a mill, by the daggers of his own subjects.

1565. Adrian Turnebus, a French critic, died. Great encomiums have been passed upon his genius and learning, as well as the amiability of his private character.

1630. John Winthrop, the first governor of Massachusetts, arrived at Salem, with the charter of the colony. He settled at Shawmut, which was finally determined upon for the metropolis, and named Boston.

1647. Thomas Farnaby, an English grammarian, died. His works display great erudition.

1660. William Oughtred, an English divine and mathematician, died. He was disturbed in his retirement by the partisans of Cromwell, and escaped sequestration only by the interference of influential friends. His works were small, but of great value to subsequent mathematicians.

1665. The city of New York incorporated by governor Nichols; a mayor, 5 aldermen and a sheriff were appointed. Prior to this, it had been governed by a schout, burgomasters and schepens.

1672. The French under Louis XIV, crossed the Rhine. The prince de Conde was wounded for the first and only time during all his campaigns; but the young duke de Longueville was killed.

1672. The government of England issued a proclamation to restrain the spread of false news and licentious talking of matters of state and government.

1676. Attack on Hadley by the Indians, to the number of 700, who were resolved on a grand effort to carry this post. The attack was commenced at day-light, with great spirit; they gained possession of a house, and fired a barn; but were in a short time driven back with loss. The attack was renewed on other points, the enemy appearing to be determined on carrying the place; but the discharge of a piece of ordnauce cooled their ardor, and they drew off; and on assistance coming from Northampton, the foe was driven into the woods, with a loss of two or three of the English. It is supposed to have been on this occasion that general Goffe, one of the judges of Charles I, who was at that time concealed with the minister at Hadley, made his appearance in so mysterious a manner. At a moment when the people were in the greatest consternation, there appeared a man of venerable aspect, differing from them in his apparel, who assumed the command, put them in order for defence, and by advice and example animated them throughout the attack. When the scene was over, on looking about for the stranger, he had disappeared, and was seen no more—leaving the inhabitants to form the strangest conjectures.

1683. The Rye house plot discovered. It was headed by Monmouth, Essex, and lord John Russell, and their object seems to have been to oppose the succession of the duke of York. Russell and many others suffered on the scaffold, Essex was found with his throat cut in prison, and Monmouth was in a short time reconciled to the king.

1734. James, duke of Berwick, killed by a cannon shot at the siege of Phillipsburgh, in Germany, while standing between his two sons. No general of his time excelled him in the art of war, except his uncle, the duke of Marlboro'.

1759. William Collins, an English poet, died. He was entirely neglected, and his *Odes*, which possessed great merit, failed to attract any attention during his life time.

1775. General Gage, issued a proclamation at Boston, offering the king's pardon to all who would lay down their arms and return to their peaceable occupations, excepting Samuel Adams and John Hancock, and at the same time he proclaimed martial law.

1778. Philip Livingston, a signer and a strenuous advocate for the declaration of independence, died. He was a New York merchant, and became a prominent character in that city before the revolution.

1788. Settlement made at Sierre Leone by blacks from England. The town lots were drawn for and apportioned this day.

1794. Couthon reported, and the French convention decreed, the organization of the revolutionary tribunal, consisting of a president, 3 vice-presidents, a public accuser, 4 deputies, 12 judges and 50 jurors.

1796. Battle between the Chinese and Eleuths, in a desert which the Chinese had attempted to penetrate in pursuit of the retreating army. The Tartars under Kaldan, taking advantage of the exhausted state of their enemy, gave them battle; but were defeated and totally routed, with the loss of 2000 killed, and all their women, children, baggage and cattle, taken by the Chinese.

1798. The French troops took possession of the fortifications of Malta, and the fleet anchored in the ports. They found two line of battle ships belonging to the Maltese, a frigate, three galleys, two galliots, and several guard boats; 1500 pieces of artillery, 35,000 stand of small arms, 12,000 barrels of powder, and a large quantity of shot and shell. The order of knights from this day became virtually extinct; from a position of political importance it fell to the level of an obscure association, and such, as far as human foresight goes, it is destined to remain.

1798. The Irish rebels defeated with great slaughter at Ballynahinch by general

Nugent. This quelled the insurrection in the north.

1799. A division of the French army, under Olivier, took Modena, and drove the Austrians beyond the river Po.

1805. American ship Atahualpa, captain Porter, treacherously attacked by the Indians while bartering for skins in Sturgis's cove. Captain Porter and 8 of the crew were killed, and 11 wounded.

1812. Putnam county in New York erected.

1813. Major CHAPIN and other American prisoners taken at the head of the lake, and sent in boats for Kingston, when arrived near York rose upon the guard, and after a short struggle took the boats and returned to Niagara.

1816. PIERRE FRANCOIS CHARLES AUGEREAU, duke of Castiglione and marshal of France, died. He was the son of a fruit merchant, and served as a carabineer in the French army. He first distinguished himself in 1794, after which his career for a number of years was brilliant, and full of honor and glory.

1829. A large body of Turkish cavalry and infantry defeated near Kuganoff, and 600 killed.

1843. HENRY R. CLEVELAND, aged 34, died at St. Louis, Mo. He was an elegant and graceful writer, and the author of the well written life of Henry Hudson, in Sparks' Biography.

1843. SAMUEL KIDD, professor of oriental and Chinese literature in University college, London, died, aged 42.

1846. More than 6000 persons driven from their houses by a disastrous fire in St. Johns, Newfoundland.

1848. GEORGE POZER, a wealthy merchant of Quebec, died, aged 95.

1848. Insurrection at Prague; the princess of Windichgratz shot by the insurgents.

JUNE 13.

1483. ANTHONY WIDVILLE, earl Rivers, beheaded at Pontefract.

1502. OLIVER MAILLARD, a French divine of the order of Cordeliers, died. He was an eminent preacher, and published several volumes of Latin sermons.

1584. JOHN SAMBUCUS, a learned German physician, died. His learning attracted the attention of the emperor Maximilian II, and he was appointed counselor of state and historiographer of the German empire. He wrote several learned and useful works.

1605. Riot at Moscow, when Fedor Godonoff, the reigning czar, who had been but two months on the throne, was dragged with his family from the palace, and shut up in one of his own private houses, where he was murdered a few days after.

1633. Lord Baltimore obtained a grant for a tract of land in America, now the state of Maryland, which was first settled by a colony of catholics.

1666. Second charter granted to South Carolina by Charles II. It was an enlargement of the previous charter, making the colony independent of any other province.

1678. HENRY SCOUGAL, an eminent Scottish divine, died, aged 28. His great exertions to sustain himself as a professor of theology at St. Andrews, and as a preacher, threw him into a consumption, and he died greatly lamented.

1710. Second great immigration of Palatines.

1721. A treaty concluded at Madrid with Great Britain. The ships employed for the traffic of negroes by the Royal company of Great Britain, were to be admitted, without hindrance, to trade freely.

1757. Decree of pope Benedict XIV, prohibiting the use of any version of the Bible in the common language.

1767. JAMES WORSDALE died; an English painter and dramatic writer.

1769. Corsica seized by the French. General Paoli fled, and embarked at Corsica for England, where he remained until 1790.

1770. WOODFALL, the publisher of the *Letters of Junius*, was prosecuted and found by the jury guilty of printing and publishing only, which was tantamount to an acquittal.

1777. WILLIAM BATTIE died; an eminent English physician and medical writer.

1780. Major-general Gates ordered by congress to take command of the southern department.

1780. A society formed in Philadelphia, under the name of the American daughters of liberty, for the purpose of supplying the soldiery with clothing. The city was divided into 10 districts, and four appointed to each district to solicit subscriptions. Their donations amounted to 2030 shirts, and they obtained 77 shirts and 380 pairs of stockings from New Jersey.

1788. GEORGE LUKINS dispossessed of seven devils by the same number of clergymen, in the Temple church, Bristol, England.

1794. Battle of Ghent; the Austrians defeated by the French.

1794. Violent earthquake and eruption of Mt. Vesuvius, which did much damage.

1796. Action between British ship Dryad, lord Beauclerc, and French frigate La Proserpine, 45 guns; which last was captured in 44 minutes, with the loss of 30 killed, 45 wounded. British loss 2 killed, 7 wounded.

1797. SIMON ANDREW TISSOT, a celebrated Swiss physician, died. He was the advocate of experimental rather than theoretical systems of medicine, and early adopted the practice of inoculation. His fame was not confined to his own country.

1810. BONAPARTE prohibited the exportation of grain.

1813. Battle of Carcagenta, in Valencia; the Spaniards under general Elio attacked the French, and were defeated with the loss of 1500 men, of whom 700 were taken prisoners.

1817. RICHARD LOVELL EDGEWORTH, an English philanthropist and practical philosopher, died. He invented the telegraph, which was generally adopted during his lifetime. He spent a great part of his life in improving and experimenting on various instruments used in agriculture and the arts.

1833. JAMES ANDREW died; principal of the East India company's seminary at Addiscombe, and author of a Hebrew grammar and dictionary.

1843. CHARLES STERNS WHEELER, of Massachusetts, a good scholar, died at Leipsic, Germany, aged 23.

1848. PIERRE VAN CORTLAND died, aged 86; a gentleman who filled many important public stations, civil and military, in the state of New York.

1848. GAMALIEL S. OLDS, a distinguished American scholar, died at Circleville, Ohio, aged 71.

1855. The anti-slavery branch of the American party, called the Know-somethings, assembled in convention at Cincinnati.

1857. Whirlwinds occurred in several parts of the state of New York, and in other states. This was the day in which the astrologers of Europe had predicted the destruction of the earth by a comet, and much alarm existed even in this country, insomuch that deaths actually occurred from fear. The village of Pania, Ill., was wholly destroyed.

JUNE 14.

510 B. C. The Roman republic established and the first consuls elected, according to the Capitoline marbles This noble political fabric subsisted for a period of 462 years, until the battle of Pharsalia.

1631. FRANCIS GARASSE, a French Jesuit, died. As a preacher he was eloquent and popular, but his writings were gross, and kindled a violent feud between his order and the Jansenists. He lost his life by attending the sick during the pestilence at Poictiers.

1636. HUMPHREY LYNDE, an English author, died. He wrote various books against popery, one of which was translated into several languages, and often reprinted.

1636. JOHN CAYLARD DE ST. BONET, marquis de Toiras, a French general, killed before the fortress of Fontanette, in Italy. His services were important to his country, but he was nevertheless disgraced by Richelieu, and found in Italy a just respect for his abilities and merits.

1637. BURTON, a clergyman, BASTWICK, a physician, and PRYNNE, yet a prisoner in the Tower, ordered to be pilloried, lose their ears, and be fined £5,000 each, for a libel on the government of Charles I of England.

1645. Battle of Naseby, in which the forces of Cromwell obtained a bloody victory over the army of Charles I, under prince Rupert, and obliged him to retire into Wales.

1654. Battle of Dunes; the French defeated the Spaniards under prince de Conde and don John of Austria.

1662. HENRY VANE, an English statesman, beheaded. He was vascilating in his politics, and characterized as a dangerous man.

1683. The Rye house plot to assassinate king Charles II of England, discovered by Joseph Keeling.

1704. RALPH BATHURST, an English physician, divine and Latin poet, died. He was a man of great erudition.

1710. Gen. HUNTER arrived at New York from England in the capacity of governor of the province, bringing with him 3000 Palatines, who formed a Lutheran church in New York.

1723. CLAUDE FLEURY, a French advocate, died, aged 82, greatly respected for his learning and virtues. His works are numerous and valuable.

1743. JAMES VILLOTTE, a French Jesuit, died. He traveled in Armenia, and published commentaries on the gospels.

1746. COLIN MACLAURIN, an eminent Scottish mathematician and philosopher, died. His writings are very numerous, and highly valuable for the purposes of navigation and geography.

1754. A convention was held at Albany, for the purpose of concluding a treaty with the Six Nations. It was attended by about 150 Indians.

1756. PROSPER MARCHAND, a French author, died in Holland, at a great age. He left France on account of religious views, and published a *Journal Litéraire*. He also wrote a history of printing, and published a new edition of Bayle's *Dictionnaire*.

1769. The general court of Massachusetts having remonstrated to governor Hutchinson against their place of meeting being surrounded with an armed force, and Boston being invested by sea and land, he adjourned the court to Cambridge.

1776. Americans evacuated Sorel, in Canada, and the British under Gen. Burgoyne entered it.

1776. The Americans cannonaded the British fleet from Moon and Long islands, and compelled it to leave the bay and open the intercourse with Boston.

1777. Congress resolved that their flag should consist of 13 stripes alternate red and white; that the union be 13 stars, white on a blue field, representing a new constellation.

1787. ABDULWAHLAB, an Arabian reformer, and founder of the Wahabbites, died, aged 95. He founded a temporal empire, which ceased A. D. 1818, but his religious doctrines are still cherished.

1792. Battle of Lubar on the river Sluez, in which the Polish cavalry under Joseph Poniatowski defeated the Russians.

1792. A plot was discovered in London to blow up the King's bench prison.

1792. The stockholders of the Hartford bank held their first meeting for the choice of directors. John Caldwell was the first president. This was the first bank in Connecticut.

1799. The French, commanded by Gen. Macdonald, on the Trebia, were defeated with immense loss by Suwarrow.

1800. JEAN BAPTIST KLEBER, commander in chief of the French army in Egypt, assassinated while walking in his garden, by a Turk named Souliman. He had conquered the country and was forming plans for its peaceful government and improvement.

1800. Battle of Marengo, in Italy; Bonaparte defeated the Austrians, who lost 1700 killed and prisoners. The French acknowledged the loss of 500 killed and wounded.

1800. LEWIS CHARLES ANTHONY DESSAIX, a distinguished French general, killed at the battle of Marengo. He arrived on the field of battle with a fresh battalion at a moment that decided the victory for the French, but received a shot in the breast, of which he instantly died.

1801. BENEDICT ARNOLD, the traitor, died in England. He was a brave officer in the American service, from the commencement of the war of the revolution; but some imprudent conduct subjected him to a reprimand from the commander-in-chief, after which he sought an opportunity to desert. He joined the British army, and committed great cruelties upon his countrymen during the remainder of the war.

1807. Battle of Friedland, in ancient Prussia; the Russians and Prussians were defeated, with the loss of 17,500 men and 80 cannon, by the French under Bonaparte. The battle commenced at 10 in the morning, and the Russians withstood the superior force of the French till nearly 5 in the afternoon; when Bonaparte, putting himself at the head of the army, commanded a general assault, which was executed with overpowering effect. Benningsen was compelled to retreat, destroying the bridge behind him.

1829. Battle of the defile of Pozzoy; the Turkish troops, 15,000, entirely defeated, and their camp taken by storm by the Russians.

1833. ABRAHAM BOGARD died in the poor-house, Maury county, Tennessee, aged 118; a native of the state of Delaware.

1846. Nearly 50 persons killed by the burning of the theatre at Quebec.

1848. A revolt at Hayti, and a tumult at Berlin.

1851. THOMAS MOULE died in London, aged 67; a well known writer to the extent of many volumes on topographic and heraldic antiquities.

1854. A great fire occurred at Worcester, Mass., destroying property valued at half a million of dollars, and throwing a thousand mechanics out of work.

1856. Mr. MARCY, secretary of state, formally notified the Danish minister that the United States would not make forcible resistance to the collection of the Sound dues for a year from this day.

JUNE 15.

1381. WAT TYLER treacherously killed at Blackheath, where he had assembled the malcontents in great numbers, and the insurrection was suppressed.

1467. PHILIP (*the good*), duke of Burgundy, died. His life was spent in war; and the title which he acquired seems to have been forfeited by his last act, the burning of the town of Dinan, which he was carried on his bed to witness, at the age of 72.

1520. MARTIN LUTHER excommunicated by Leo X.

1530. CHARLES V made a public entry into Augsburg, where the members of the diet had assembled. The famous decree, called the *Confession of Augsburg*, drawn up by Melancthon, was then read.

1560. The massy spire of St. Paul's church, London, was burned down by lightning.

1568. GILES CORROZET died at Paris; a French bookseller, and author of several works of merit.

1643. ABEL JANSEN TASMAN, the Dutch

navigator, arrived at Batavia, after having sailed round the southern side of the globe. He started in September, 1642, and discovered Van Dieman's land and the island of New Zealand, which he called Staten island.

1735. Rene Aubert de Vertot d'Auboeuf, an elegant French historical writer, died, aged 80. He united the virtues of private life to great intelligence, deep penetration, and an elegant taste.

1744. Anson arrived at Spithead, after a voyage of three years and nine months round the world. The treasures of the famous Acapulco galleon were conveyed to London in 32 wagons, and the booty divided among those brave men who had shared his glory and toils.

1746. Battle of Placentia, between the allies and Spaniards.

1749. The fleet of sir Edward Cornwallis, having on board over 3000 British colonists, dropped anchor in the spacious harbor of Halifax, Nova Scotia.

1756. The nabob of Surajah Dowla invested Calcutta at the head of 70,000 horse and foot, and 400 elephants.

1768. James Short, a celebrated Scottish optician, died. He was of humble origin, but became a noted and wealthy man. His telescopes were long surpassed only by those of Herschel.

1768. The commissioners of the customs at Boston requested Gen. Gage to support them in the execution of their office with a military force.

1775. Washington appointed commander in chief of the American army.

1776. The legislature of New Hampshire voted unanimously that their delegates in congress should join with the other delegates in declaring the 13 united colonies a free and independent state.

1776. The British under sir Henry Clinton attacked Sullivan's island, and were repulsed by Gen. Lee.

1785. Pilatre de Rosier, a French æronaut, killed. He was attempting to cross the English channel from Boulogne; but the balloon took fire soon after its ascent, and he was precipitated to the earth.

1794. A memorable eruption of mount Vesuvius.

1811. A marine volcano burst through the sea in 40 fathoms of water, at the west end of St. Michaels, one of the Azores, about three miles from land.

1815. Battle of Fleury, in which Bonaparte with 150,000 men, attacked the Prussians and English of 200,000, and drove them back, and the next day defeated them at Ligny.

1826. The sultan of Turkey defeated and abolished the ancient corps of Janizaries. This military body, consisting of trained captives, was first instituted by the third Amurath, in 1362.

1836. Arkansas admitted into the Union.

1840. Francis Beauguard died at Grey Nun's hospital, Montreal, aged nearly 108.

1841. The town of Praia, in the island of Terceira, completely destroyed by an earthquake. Much damage was also done to other places in the island by a series of earthquakes.

1844. Thomas Campbell, a distinguished British poet, author of the *Pleasures of Hope*, died at Boulogne, in a state of imbecility, aged 67.

1852. Queen Victoria issued a proclamation against "Roman catholic ecclesiastics wearing the habits of their order, exercising the rites and ceremonies of the Roman catholic religion in highways and places of public resort."

1852. Roger Jones, an American military officer of distinction, died at Washington. He commenced his military career in 1809, and as a lieutenant of marines, and served in the war of 1812. His zeal and activity in the arduous campaigns on the Niagara frontier, and his distinguished gallantry as a major of the staff in the memorable conflicts of Chippewa, Lundy's Lane, and the sortie of fort Erie, won for him universal respect and admiration, and the marked approbation of the government.

1854. James Kendle Browne died in Mark lane, London, aged 82; the father of the corn exchange.

1856. John Dicks Eccles, an eminent North Carolina lawyer and orator, died at Fayetteville, aged 64.

1857. The citizens of Halifax, Nova Scotia, celebrated the 108th anniversary of the settlement of that place.

JUNE 16.

632. The Persian era began, recording the fall of the Sassanian dynasty, and the religion of Zoroaster. This famous era, as amended by the sultan Geluleddin, is now in use by the parsees of India.

1381. John Ball, in order to be chancellor under Wat Tyler, gave his followers a sermon.

1487. Battle of Stoke, England. Lambert Simnel, who had been crowned in Ireland, received the king's pardon, and was made a scullion in the royal kitchen.

1575. Adrian Junius, a learned Dutch author, died; he is quoted by the people of Harlem to establish the right of Lawrence Coster to the honor of being the inventor of printing in that city, about 1430.

1658. Edward Capellus, a learned French protestant divine, died. He was engaged in a long and learned controversy concerning the antiquity of the Hebrew points, his adversary maintaining that they were coeval with the language, while he showed that they were unknown before the dispersion of the Jews, and were invented about 600 years after Christ. He was engaged 36 years on the *Critica Sacra*, a work of prodigious labor and great merit.

1666. RICHARD FANSHAWE, an English statesman, died. He was actively engaged in political affairs, yet found time to produce several works of much credit.

1719. LEWIS ELLIS DUPIN, a learned French critic, died. He devoted himself to a biographical dictionary of ecclesiastical authors, which was brought down to the end of the 16th century, and has been translated into English. His works are numerous.

1722. JOHN CHURCHILL, the renowned duke of Marlborough, died. He stands unrivaled among the British generals, and during several years gained a series of the most splendid victories. It has been said that he gained every battle which he fought, and took every town which he besieged.

1743. Battle of Dettingen, in which the French suffered a severe defeat, losing 6000 men; the allies, under George II, 1000.

1752. JOSEPH BUTLER, an eminent prelate and theological writer, died. He is celebrated as the author of the *Analogy of Religion*.

1755. Fort Beausejour, in Nova Scotia, surrendered to the British, the French garrison being permitted to march out with the honors of war.

1760. At Glen, in Leicestershire, England, the populace threw two old women into the water to try by their sinking or swimming whether or not they were witches.

1772. The banking house of Neal and Fordyce, in London, failed, and it was counted an extraordinary feat to carry the intelligence to Edinburgh, a distance of 425 miles, in 43 hours.

1777. JOHN BAPTIST LOUIS GRESSET, a celebrated French poet, died. His poems were elegant, lively and interesting, and obtained for him, among other honors, letters of nobility.

1779. Manifesto presented to the British court, announcing that Spain had taken decided part with France and America against Great Britain.

1789. The states general of France formed themselves into the national assembly.

1793. Unsuccessful attack of the British on Martinique.

1794. Battle of Josselies; the hereditary prince of Orange attacked and defeated the French, who lost 7000 men and 22 cannon, and were compelled to retreat across the Sambre.

1806. Total eclipse of the sun at Philadelphia and other cities in the United States.

1808. JOSEPH BONAPARTE proclaimed king of Spain. "Your princes," said Napoleon, "have ceded to me their rights to the crown of Spain. Your nation is old; my mission is to restore its youth."

1810. LEWIS AUGUSTUS PHILIP AFFRAY, first magistrate of Switzerland under Napoleon, died. He was in early life an officer in the Swiss army; and when elevated to civil office, he conducted with the ability, the intelligence and the experience of a thorough statesman.

1812. BONAPARTE joined his great army on the Vistula, destined to invade Moscow.

1813. Action off Presque isle, between the United States schooner, Lady of the Lake, lieut. Chauncey, and the British schooner, Lady Murray, laden with provisions and ammunition, for York, Canada, which was captured.

1814. The editors of the *Gazette Universal* having said something about the constitution of the Cortes, were condemned by their monarch, Ferdinand VII, to the galleys.

1815. BONAPARTE attacked the Prussian posts of Sombref, St. Amand and Ligny, under prince Blucher. The contest was very severe, and the Prussian loss very great; they notwithstanding kept their position until after night, when they retreated upon Wavre. Blucher had a horse killed under him, and narrowly escaped with his life. Ligny was taken and retaken several times. At the same time Bonaparte attacked the British troops under Wellington, at Quartre Bras, and compelled him to fall back upon Gemappe. The loss of the allies was very severe.

1818. The village of Bagnes, in Switzerland, overwhelmed by the giving away of an ice barrier.

1818. Irruption of lake Mauvoisin, in the Alps, occasioned by the bursting of its icy mound, by which six hundred millions cubic feet of water were in an instant let loose upon the beautiful valley of the Drana, carrying before its overwhelming torrent every vestige of civilized life which stood within its reach.

1819. An earthquake near Poonah, in the East Indies, swallowed up a large district and more than 2000 persons.

1821. JOHN BALLANTYNE, the confidential printer of sir Walter Scott's Waverly novels, died at Edinburgh. He also established the *Kelso Mail*, a respectable provincial paper, yet in existence.

1830. An eruption of mount Etna, which destroyed eight villages, and buried many of the inhabitants under the ruins of their houses.

1831. The president of Hayti ordered all the French white inhabitants to leave the island before the 15th July.

1843. Died at Boston, whither he had accompanied president Tyler to attend the Bunker Hill celebration, HUGH S. LEGARE, a distinguished American statesman.

1843. Count WITTGENSTEIN, the Russian field marshal, who distinguished himself in the wars with Napoleon, died at St. Petersburg, aged 87.

1851. TOM JOHNSON, a Norwegian, died at the Naval asylum, Philadelphia, aged 100; the last survivor of the gallant crew who fought with Paul Jones, in the desperate conflict with the Serapis in 1799.

1852. The sultan of Turkey issued a firman granting new rights and privileges to his Christian subjects.

1854. The siege of Silistria raised; the Turks made a sortie, causing a complete defeat of the Russians, forcing them to recross the Danube in all haste, took several standards and a great quantity of baggage, and killed or severely wounded five Russian generals.

1857. A riot took place in the city of New York, occasioned by a dispute about the public offices, there having been two sets appointed by different authorities. Mayor Wood was arrested for assault and battery.

JUNE 17.

431 B. C. The dictator TUBERTUS POSTHUMUS gained a victory over the Æqui and Volsci, inconsiderable but noxious enemies of the commonwealth.

1081. ROBERT GUISCARD opened the famous siege of Durazzo, now in European Turkey, on the gulf of Venice.

1272. An attempt made to assassinate Edward I of England in his tent at Acre, by a messenger of the emir of Joppa. He received the blow on his arm, grappled with the assassin, and throwing him on the ground despatched him with his own dagger. The life of the prince was saved by his wife, who sucked the poison from the wound.

1458. ALFONSO V, of Arragon (*the magnanimous*), died. He made himself master of Naples and Sicily; aside from his exploits as a warrior, he was a learned man and the patron of learning, and the father of his people.

1614. WILLIAM BATHE, an Irish Jesuit, died. He was rector of an Irish school at Salamanca, and a writer on music and divinity.

1639. The king and his Scottish subjects met at Dunse, in Scotland, and agreed that matters ecclesiastical should be decided by an assembly, civil matters by parliament.

1658. Dunkirk surrendered to the French, and by them put into the hands of the English.

1673. Father MARQUETTE, and JOLIET a citizen of Quebec, employed by M. Talon for the discovery of the Mississippi, entered that noble river. They descended to within three days' journey of the gulf of Mexico.

1685. The unfortunate duke of Argyle taken in a morass.

1696. JOHN SOBIESKI, king of Poland, died. He distinguished himself on many occasions in the Polish wars but the greatest of his exploits was the raising of the siege of Vienna, by which Europe was saved from the calamities consequent upon an irruption of the Turks.

1719. JOSEPH ADDISON, editor of the *Spectator*, died. He was the ornament of his age and country, and his writings will long continue to be read and admired.

1734. LOUIS HECTOR VILLARS, peer of France, died, aged 82. He early adopted the profession of arms, and distinguished himself through a long life as a brave and efficient officer.

1740. WILLIAM WYNDHAM, an eminent English statesman, died. His abilities led to his promotion to the highest offices in the state.

1745. Louisbourg, cape Breton, taken from the French by the British and Massachusetts forces, under governor Shirley and admiral sir Peter Warren.

1761. The first English "navigation canal" opened, extending from Worsley to Manchester, 18 miles. It originated with Scroope, duke of Bridgewater.

1775. Battle of Bunker's hill, and burning of Charlestown by the British. The Americans were defeated with the loss of 453 killed, wounded and missing. The killed, and those who died of their wounds were 139, including general Warren. British loss, 1,054, of whom 226 were killed, and among them colonel Abercromby and major Pitcairn, who occasioned the first shedding of blood at Lexington.

1776. British transports, George and Arabella, captured in Boston bay by six American privateers. Among the prisoners taken was the honorable Archibald Campbell, and 271 Highlanders.

1780. Bank opened in Philadelphia for supplying the army with provisions, and £189,000 subscribed, payable in gold and silver.

1788. Convention at Poughkeepsie, N. Y., to consider the federal constitution.

1789. The tiers etat, of France, were joined by the whole body of inferior clergy with some nobles. They constituted themselves into a legislative body, and took the name of national assembly.

1791. SELINA, countess of Huntington, died. From habits of gaiety and dissipation, she became suddenly grave and pious, and was distinguished by very extensive charities.

1792. Battle of Zielime, in which the Polish army was defeated by a superior force of Russians. The action lasted from 7 in the morning till 5 in the evening. Loss of the Russians 4,000; that of the Poles 1,100.

1794. Ypres, in Belgium, surrendered to the French under Moreau. Four battalions of Austrians, 6 of Hessians, 2 of Baden, 200 horse chasseurs, 150 Austrian cannoniers, were taken prisoners, with 140 cannon.

1799. First day's battle of the Trebia, between the French under Macdonald, and the Russians and Austrians under Suwar row. The French were compelled to fall back.

1807. Konigsberg, the capital of Prussia proper, taken by the French under Soult. Immense stores, with nearly 300 loaded vessels, 160,000 stand of arms, &c., were taken.

1810. JAMES CHALMERS, printer to the city and university of Aberdeen, and proprietor of the *Aberdeen Journal*, died.

1812. The *Decameron* of Boccacio, a single volume small folio, printed in 1471, sold at the sale of the duke of Roxburgh's library to the marquis of Blandford, for £2,260.

1814. HENRY TRESHAM died; an Irish poet and painter of merit.

1815. The allied army under Wellington fell back on Waterloo, and Blucher to Wavre. The earl of Uxbridge made a brilliant charge of cavalry at Gemappe.

1815. British order in council, forbidding the Americans to use the British territories for purposes connected with the Newfoundland fisheries.

1825. Corner stone of Bunker hill monument laid with great and enthusiastic ceremonies; Lafayette being present.

1839. WILLIAM BENTINCK, an English statesman, died. He had sustained many high public offices, was a general in the army, and ten years governor-general of India.

1850. The steamer Griffith on lake Erie was burnt and 300 lives lost.

1852. THOMAS BUFFUM died, aged 75; an active man in the political history of Rhode Island, who had filled with credit many offices of honor and trust.

1852. JOHN TRIMBLE, a Kentucky judge, died, aged 69; having sustained the character of an able and upright man.

1852. WILLIAM KING, first governor of Maine, died, aged 84. He removed to Bath early in the present century, and his name is identified most intimately with all that relates to the separation from Massachussetts, and the adoption of the state constitution. He held various civil offices with ability and fidelity.

1852. The city of Sonora, in California, was nearly destroyed by fire.

1854. SEWARD BARCULO, a New York jurist of distinction, died, aged 50. He was chosen justice of the supreme court at the first judicial election held under the new state constitution.

1854. JOSIAH HOLBROOK, a distinguished advocate of popular education, died, aged 65. He was a native of Derby, Ct., and graduated at Yale college in 1810. He was very successful in diffusing among the young a love for the study of mineralogy and geology. He lost his life by accidently falling into Blackrock creek, near Lynchburg, Va., while on a geological excursion.

JUNE 18.

64. The conflagration of Rome, attributed by Nero to the Christians, which was the ostensible cause of the first persecution. (See 24th June.)

741. LEO III (*Isaurian*), emperor of Constantinople, died. He was the son of a cobbler, and disgraced the imperial dignity by acts of barbarity and tyranny. He was the enemy of learning and learned men, and set fire to the valuable library of his capital, by which 30,000 volumes were destroyed, besides many of the choicest paintings and medals.

1053. Battle of Civitella; the forces of the pope, Leo IX, routed by Robert Guiscard, the Norman.

1314. EDWARD II marched upon Scotland from Berwick, with his vast army.

1429. Battle of Patray, in France; the English under Talbot defeated by Joan of Arc, with the loss of 1,500 slain, and 1,000 taken. It was in this conflict that the notable sir John Falstaff, considering discretion to be the better part of valor, dropped his *thirsty lance*, and ran away.

1538. Truce for 10 years between Charles V of Germany, and Francis I of France. Hostilities were renewed three years after.

1580. The colony of Virginia discouraged with their losses and various misfortunes embarked for England.

1588. ROBERT CROWLEY, a scholar, preacher and printer, died. One of his principal works was in metre, entitled:

Pleasure and pain, heaven and hell,
Remember these four and all shall be well.

1602. The fort and store house built by Gosnold on Elizabeth island for a settlement, was abandoned in consequence of discontents arrising among those who were to have remained in the country, and the whole company returned to England. The ruins of this ephemeral settlement were seen as late as 1797.

1616. THOMAS BILSON, a celebrated English divine, died. He was distinguished for his eloquence as a preacher, and his learning as a theological writer and controversalist. He was one of the two final correctors of the present translation of the Bible.

1621. The first duel in New England fought by two servants with sword and dagger, both of whom were wounded. For this outrage they were sentenced to lie 24 hours with their heads and feet tied together.

1633. CHARLES I, of England, crowned king of Scotland at Holyrood house, by the archbishop of St. Andrews.

1667. WILLIAM RAWLEY, an English divine, died. He was chaplain to Charles I and II, and also to Bacon, whose works he edited.

1675. Battle of Fehrbellin ; the elector Frederick William, at the head of 6,000 cavalry, attacked the Swedish invading army under the celebrated Wrangel, and gained a complete victory.

1684. The English court of chancery gave judgment for the king against the governor and company of Massachusetts ; their charter was declared forfeited, and their liberties were seized into the king's hands.

1697. RICHARD, earl of Bellomont, was appointed to succeed colonel Fletcher as governor of New York.

1718. An earthquake extended through several inland provinces of China, by which the gates and walls of cities were thrown down. The city of Yong-ning-tchin was entirely swallowed up, and several mountains were thrown over a plain to the distance of about two leagues.

1741. FRANCIS POURFOUR died ; a French physician and skillful herbalist.

1749. AMBROSE PHILIPS, an English poet, died. He wrote also for the stage with some success, although his performances were ridiculed by Pope.

1756. Calcutta, in India, taken by Surajah Dowla: of 146 prisoners put into a dungeon called the "black hole," 123 were suffocated.

1756. Minorca surrendered to the French by the British general Blakeney. The British had taken it from the Spaniards in 1708.

1757. Battle of Kolin ; the Prussians under Frederick II defeated by the Austrians under count Daun, with the loss of 8,000 killed and wounded. Frederick lost his battle through the rash bravery of one of his generals.

1764. Lighthouse at Sandyhook first put in operation.

1772. GERARD VAN SWIETEN, a Dutch physician, died. He settled in Vienna, where he became a distinguished practitioner, and his memory is still held in great veneration by the profession there.

1776. Gen. BURGOYNE entered St. Johns, Canada, the Americans having evacuated it, and burnt the fort and barracks.

1779. British West India island St. Vincent, surrendered to the French under Romain and d'Estaing.

1783. The volcano of Skaptar Jokul, in Iceland, which had recently become very active, poured out an immense amount of lava, which, taking a new direction, dammed up the streams, and caused great destruction of property and lives. After flowing several days it was precipitated down the cataract of Stapafoss, where it filled a profound abyss, which that great waterfall had been excavating for ages, and thence the fiery flood continued in its course.

1783. WASHINGTON announced to the governors of the several states his intended resignation of the command of the army.

1793. British frigate La Nymphe, capt. Pellew, captured French frigate Cleopatra, after an action of 55 minutes. French captain and about 60 of his men killed or wounded. The British loss 25 killed, 27 wounded. This was the first capture made after the declaration of war.

1795. Russian manifesto issued by gen. Thimothie Tutomlin, on taking possession of Russian Poland.

1799. Second day's battle of Trebia ; French under Macdonald obliged to retire across the river by the Russians under Suwarrow.

1805. ARTHUR MURPHY, an English dramatic writer of eminence, died. Many of his plays still keep the stage. His translation of Tacitus is also in common use.

1811. RUTH PIERCE, the mother of sir Benjamin Thompson, count Rumford, died at Baldwin, Maine.

1812. United States declared war against England.

1815. Hostilities ceased between England and the United States throughout the world.

1815. Battle of Waterloo, in the Netherlands. The forces of the two armies are differently stated, but are supposed to have been about 75,000 each. The battle began about noon, and continued with great obstinacy till night, when the French were completely defeated with the loss of more than 30,000 men, 210 cannon, several military chests, and all Napoleon's baggage.

The loss of the allies was probably upwards of 20,000. This great battle gave peace to Europe.

1823. WILLIAM COOMBE, a British author of considerable merit, died. He did not attach his name to his works.

1832. The duke of Wellington attacked by a mob in the streets of London—the anniversary of his victory at Waterloo.

1835. WILLIAM COBBET, an English poetical and miscellaneous writer, died. He was a self-taught and self-made man, who for many years made a conspicuous figure in the politics of England, and was finally elected to parliament.

1841. The constitution of the newly constituted state of the isthmus of Panama publicly sworn to, and Dr. Thomas Herrara elected president.

1848. HENRY TOOLEY, a consistent member of the methodist episcopal church, the first masonic grand master in Mississippi, and a son not only but the father of temperance in Natchez, died there, aged 75.

1848. The city of Prague, which had revolted on the 12th, was bombarded and reduced to ruins.

1848. The Austrians defeated by the Piedmontese near Rivoli.

1848. Venice garrisoned by 13,000 Romans.

1848. Carlowitz bombarded.

1854. HENRIETTA SONTAG, one of first lyric artists of the day, died at Mexico, aged about 50.

1855. The allies made a combined attack upon the Malakoff and Redan towers, at Sebastopol, without success, and with a loss of 56 officers killed, 146 wounded and 17 prisoners; and 1,694 men killed or missing, and 2,690 wounded.

JUNE 19.

325. The first council of Nice began and continued to 25th August; present 318 bishops.

1215. JOHN, king of England, signed the famous magna charta, and the charter of the forests, in a meadow at Runnimede between Staines and Windsor. (See 29th.)

1312. PIERS GAVESTON, the favorite of Edward II, executed. In his elevation he was proud, overbearing and cruel, and the barons rose up against him, and accomplished his destruction.

1566. JAMES VI of Scotland and I of England, was born in a small room in Edinburgh castle.

1579. Maestricht, in Holland, taken by the Spaniards under the duke of Parma, after a siege of four months, during which about 8000 persons perished miserably. It was given up to pillage.

1619. The first assembly of Virginia met at Jamestown. The settlements had now become so numerous that 11 corporations appeared by their representatives to exercise the noblest function of freemen, the power of legislation.

1690. EZEKIEL HOPKINS, a learned English prelate died, aged 57.

1707. WILLIAM SHERLOCK, an eminent English divine, died, aged about 66; famous for his controversial works, in which he took sides against the dissenters, as also against Dr. South on the subject of the trinity.

1709. ISAAC PAPIN, a French divine, died. His views differed a hair from those of his sect, and persecution followed him from one country to another, till he finally took refuge with the catholics.

1715. NICHOLAS LEMERY, a French chemist, died, aged 70. He was ardently devoted to the science, and contributed much to spread a correct knowledge of it among the people by his lectures.

1720. JOHN MATTHEWS, aged about 18, was executed at Tyburn, for, while an apprentice, printing a political work.

1729. ROBERT KNELL, the compositor, and JOHN CLARK, the pressman, of *Mist's Journal*, were pilloried, but protected by their friends from being pelted by the mob.

1741. Admiral VERNON seized the castles of Carthagena, South America. The British were afterwards compelled to retire on account of pestilence.

1754. A convention of the states at Albany proposed a union for defence against the common enemy. Delegates were present from New Hampshire, Massachusetts, Rhode Island, Connecticut, Pennsylvania, Maryland and New York.

1755. WILLIAM HAY died in England; remarkable for his deformity, on which he wrote an essay. He was a member of parliament, and an author of some merit.

1757. Action between British ship Experiment, 20 guns, 142 men, and French ship Telemaque, 26 guns, 460 men, in which the latter was captured with the loss of 125 killed, 110 wounded. It had been fitted out expressly to capture the Experiment, which had 12 killed, 36 wounded.

1781. Assault on fort Ninety-six, by the Americans under Gen. Greene, who were repulsed with the loss of 185. The Americans then abandoned the siege. British loss 85.

1783. HENRY LOYD, a military officer and writer, died. He was born in Wales, entered the service of Austria, and afterwards served in the armies of Prussia and Russia. On his return to England he produced several military works of great merit.

1786. NATHANIEL GREENE, an officer in the revolutionary army, died, aged 46. He was of quaker descent, born in Rhode Island. He distinguished himself at the battles of Trenton, Princeton, Germantown and Monmouth, and finally covered himself with glory at the battle of Eutaw Springs, which closed the war in South Carolina.

1794. French general DUMOURIER, arrived in London on his escape from the convention, but was ordered to depart the British dominions immediately.

1794. The Corsicans accepted their new constitution, and acknowledged George III their king.

1794. RICHARD HENRY LEE, a revolutionary patriot, died. He originated the first resistance to British oppression, and during the struggle continued to hold some important civil office, where his talents were conspicuous.

1798. BONAPARTE left Malta at the head of the French expedition which was destined for Egypt, leaving behind him 4,000 men under Gen. Vaubois, to regenerate the island after the pattern of the French republic.

1799. Third day's battle of Trebia. The French under Macdonald crossed the river and attacked the Austrians and Russians. But after an obstinate and bloody conflict they were compelled to fall back with a loss of 1700 killed and 500 prisoners.

1799. Five French frigates bound from Jaffa to Toulon, with 1340 men, were captured by a British squadron.

1800. Battle of Blenheim; the French under Moreau, after a short but obstinate action, defeated the Austrians under Gen. Starray, and obliged them to abandon Ulm and retire into Franconia.

1807. Naval action off Lemnos between the Russians and Turks, in which the latter were defeated with the loss of an 80 gun ship and two other ships of the line taken, and five burnt.

1808. Action off the Nase of Norway; the British sloop Seagull sunk by a Danish brig and several gun boats. Several of the Danes went down with her.

1809. Congress renewed the non-intercourse act.

1811. SAMUEL CHASE, a judge of the United States supreme court, died. He was a distinguished member of the congress of 1774.

1813. British landed from their shipping on lake Ontario, and destroyed the public stores at Sodus; they burnt several of the best houses and stores in the village.

1818. PATRICK BRYDONE, a Scottish traveler, died. He published a narrative of his travels in Sicily and Malta, which has been often republished.

1820. JOSEPH BANKS, an eminent English literary and philosophical writer, died. He made several voyages in pursuit of science, one of which was with captain Cook.

1821. Battle of Dragashan, in Turkey, between the Greeks and Turks. The Greeks were commanded by the brave Ypsilanti; but owing to the treachery of the Arnauts, who abandoned their posts, the Greeks were totally defeated, and the "sacred band" of the *hetaireia*, the flower of the Greek youth, were annihilated. This affair nearly proved fatal to the cause of the Greek revolution.

1829. JOHN CLEVES SYMMES, an American officer, died. He is to be remembered for the enthusiasm with which he maintained the theory that the earth was hollow, with an opening at each of the poles.

1830. Battle of Strouli, between 50,000 Algerines, Turks and Arabs, and 25,000 French under Gen. Bourmont, in which the former were defeated.

1853. RICHARD TAYLOR, second chief of the Cherokee nation, died at Tahleguah, Arkansas. He commanded under Gen. Jackson in the war against the Creek Indians.

JUNE 20.

404. The illustrious JOHN CHRYSOSTOM banished from his patriarchate to the remote and desolate town of Cucusus, among the ridges of mount Taurus, by a command of the empress Eudoxia. The day of this his final exile was marked by the conflagration of the cathedral, senate-house, and the adjacent buildings, and by the destruction of the incomparable statues of the Muses from the temple of Helicon.

840. LOUIS I (*Debonnaire*), king of France and emperor of the West, died. He had not sufficient ability to manage the conflicting interests of his large dominions, and was harrassed by the rebellion of his brothers and sons.

981. ADALBERT, bishop of Magdeburg, died. He converted the Sclavonians, and penetrated far into Pomerania as a Christian missionary.

1333. Battle of Halidon hill. The regent of Scotland, six earls, and many barons fell in the field; the fugitives were pursued by king Edward and a party of horse, and also by lord Darcy and his Irish auxiliaries. The slaughter is said to have exceeded that of any former defeat.

1472. King HENRY VI of England murdered in the Tower by order of the duke of Gloucester, afterwards Richard III, as is supposed.

1632. The patent of Maryland, designed for George Calvert, lord Baltimore, was on his decease, filled up to his son, Cecilius Calvert. When king Charles signed it, he gave to the new patent the name of Maryland in honor of his queen Henrietta Maria. Lord Baltimore held it of the crown of England as part of Windsor manor, paying yearly forever, two Indian arrows, which may now be seen at the castle.

1649. Richard Brandon, the hereditary hangman, and the executioner of Charles I and the earl of Strafford, died in misery. He was interred the next day amidst execrations and vulgar insults, which he could not feel.

1698. The summit of Carguairazo, a burning mountain near Quito, 1800 feet high, crumbled together, so that nothing more than two enormous rocky horns of the crater's edge remained, and the country for nearly two square miles, was desolated with liquid tufa, and argillaceous mud, enclosing dead fishes.

1719. The Spaniards defeated the Imperialists at Franca-Villa in Sicily, with the loss of their general, Merci, and 4000 men.

1743. John George Keysler, a German traveler and antiquary, died. On his visit to England he was admitted fellow of the Royal society, and deserved it by his explication of Stonehenge.

1743. Action near Manilla, between the British ship Centurion, lord Anson, and the Acapulco ship, the *Nostra Signora de Cabadonga*, 36 guns and 550 men, commanded by don Geronimo de Montoro, a Portuguese officer. The cutter was captured, with the loss of 67 killed, 84 wounded; British loss 2 killed, 17 wounded. The property on board this prize amounted to $1,500,000.

1747. Nadir Shah, for some time monarch of Persia, was assassinated by his men, whom he had designed the next day to massacre.

1752. The trustees of Georgia, finding that the province languished under their care, and weary of the complaints of the people, surrendered their charter to the king.

1756. Calcutta taken by Surajah Dowla, and 145 Englishmen incarcerated in the *black hole*, including Holwell, the governor of Bengal; all of whom were suffocated but 23. (See June 18.)

1779. Battle of Stono-Ferry, in which the Americans under Gen. Lincoln were defeated, owing to the mismanagement of a part of the forces, who did not come up. Loss 146.

1781. Cornwallis evacuated Richmond, Virginia.

1787. Charles Frederick Abel died; an eminent musician, whose performances attracted much attention in Europe.

1789. The national assembly of France having been refused admission into the usual place of meeting, assembled in the rain in a tennis court.

1790. Titles of nobility and feudal right abolished in France.

1791. Louis XVI and the royal family made their escape from Paris with the intention of proceeding to Germany, to avoid the disturbances which threatened the country.

1792. The assembly of the sans culottes appeared in Paris with their arms and colors.

1793. The negroes and mulattoes of cape Francois began an indiscriminate massacre of the whites. A company of 2000 men were sent on shore from the French fleet to arrest their depredations, but were compelled to embark again. (See 23.)

1794. Felix Vicq d'Azir, an eminent French physician and anatomist, died at Paris.

1798. Jeremy Belknap, a Boston divine, and historian of New Hampshire. died, aged 58. He also published two volumes of *American Biography*, a work which his death abridged.

1813. British made an attack on Oswego, but were repulsed by the militia under Col. Carr.

1815. That questionable monster, the sea-serpent, observed at Plymouth, Mass. Its extension above the surface of the water was supposed to be more than a hundred feet. The serpentine animal noticed in the Norway seas is of much larger proportions, with large blue eyes, "which looked like a couple of *bright pewter plates.*"

1818. Joseph Adams, an eminent London physician and medical writer, died.

1819. The first steam vessel which crossed the Atlantic arrived at Liverpool.

1830. Battle between the French and Algerines, near Sidi Khalef; the latter were defeated.

1836. Edmund Joseph de Sieyes, a French statesman, died, aged 88. He long acted a conspicuous part in the affairs of France, but on the fall of Napoleon was banished, and some years previous to his death was reduced to a state of idiocy.

1837. William IV of England, died, aged 72. His reign was brief, but was distinguished for various important measures of reform, and the abolition of colonial slavery.

1837. Michigan entered the United States confederacy.

1840. Pierre Claude Francois Daunou, peer of France, and eight years editor of the *Journal des Savants*, died at Paris, aged

79. He was a laborious writer, in which he was distinguished by his great learning and elegance of style.

1843. HENRY DOGGETT, an officer of the revolutionary army, died at New Haven, aged 86. He was the son of Naphtali Doggett, president of Yale college during the revolution, and was the oldest surviving graduate of the college.

1843. HUGH S. LEGARE, attorney-general of the United States, died at Boston, aged about 50. He was eminent for his acquirements as a scholar, his fine taste as a writer, and his learning and eloquence as a lawyer and advocate. He was acting secretary of state at the time of his death, and experience showed that he was amply fitted for the highest trusts, and adorned every station which he was called to fill.

1844. JOHN PINTARD died in New York, aged 87. He was one of the originators of the New York historical society, and of the Savings bank.

1848. PAREDES raised the standard of revolt in Mexico, assisted by padre Jurauta.——A portion of Washington's library, consisting of 450 bound volumes, and about 1000 pamphlets, presented to the Boston atheneum by the citizens.——A loan negotiated at Washington by the government, of sixteen million dollars, at a premium of half a million.

1852. WILLIAM BIDDLE SHEPARD, a noted lawyer and politician, died at Elizabeth City, N. C., aged 51. He distinguished himself, by his abilities, and was ten years in congress.

1854. GEORGE W. MARTIN, an efficient military officer, died at Tallahatchie, Missouri. He served in the war of 1812, and accompanied Gen. Jackson throughout the campaigns of three years, and in the Creek war.

1856. TANCRED FLORESTAN ROGER LOUIS GRIMALDI, prince of Monaco and duke of Valentinois, died at Paris. On the death of his brother in 1841 he became sovereign prince of Monaco, under the title of Florestan I.

JUNE 21.

545 B. C. THALES, a Grecian philosopher, died. He was the chief of the seven sages of Greece, and founder of the Ionic sect of philosophers. He divided the Grecian zodiac into seasons, and the year into 365 days.

1339. Battle of Laupen; the citizens of Bern, in Switzerland, defeated an army of 18,000 from its rival cities, headed by 700 of its own nobility and 1,200 knights, who were totally vanquished.

1377. EDWARD III, of England, died, aged 65, having reigned 51 years.

1529. Trial of CATHARINE, first queen of Henry VIII of England.

1529. JOHN SKELTON, an English poet, died. He wrote sonnets and satires, and was invested with the laureate.

1585. HENRY PERCY, the 8th earl of Northumberland (exclusive of Dudley), was found in the tower, dead, his breast pierced with three pistol bullets—alleged suicide, but supposed violence.

1596. Naval victory of the English over the Spaniards, at Cadiz, when the earl of Essex, in a fit of delight, threw his hat into the sea!

1611. HENRY HUDSON, having wintered in the bay which bears his name, and pursuing the object of his voyage, a northwest passage, a conspiracy broke out on this day among the ship's crew, when Hudson, his son, and five others, most of whom were sick and lame, were forced into the shallop, with a small quantity of meal, one gun and ammunition, two or three spars and an iron pot, and with the most savage inhumanity turned adrift. This is the last account of Hudson.

1631. JOHN SMITH, one of the early settlers of Virginia, died. He was a brave and daring man, and it was mainly owing to him that the colony was made permanent.

1652. INIGO JONES, a celebrated English architect, died. He surpassed most of the great men of his age in learning and ability.

1675. Foundation laid of the cathedral of St. Paul's, London. It stands upon upwards of two acres of ground, and its height is 404 feet.

1738. GEORGE WILLIAM FREDERICK, the young English prince, *re-baptized* by the bishop of Oxford, with great pomp. Private baptism at his birth was first administered, fearing his immediate death.

1747. British fleet under commodore Fox captured 48 sail of French West-Indiamen.

1759. Fort George erected at the head of lake George.

1764. British commodore Byron sailed from the Downs in the Dolphin, on his voyage round the world.

1768. JOHN LINDSAY died; a learned English divine, and a historical and theological writer.

1770. Fete on account of the marriage of Louis XVI of France, when 15,000 persons were trampled to death.

1770. WILLIAM BECKFORD, one of the most popular mayors of London, died.

1773. GEORGE JUAN, a Spanish knight of Malta, and an able mathematician, died. His writings have been translated into various languages.

1782. The British government sent Mr.

Woodyear in the Tiger man-of-war, to the West Indies to determine the longitude.

1783. About 300 American troops with fixed bayonets, surrounded the house in which congress was sitting, and demanded a redress of grievances.

1788. New Hampshire adopted the federal constitution, recommending amendments, being the ninth state to do so; votes 57 to 46.

1791. A flood near the Havanna, swept away 3,000 persons.

1792. An immense body, headed by Santerre, forced their way into the Tuilleries, and compelled Louis XVI to wear the red cap.

1797. Andrew Peter Bernstorff died; a German who settled in Denmark, became a distinguished statesman, and a great favorite with the people.

1797. Peter Thellusson, a rich London merchant, died. His will, devising lands to the amount of £4,500 per annum and £600,000 personal property to be funded to aid in liquidation of the national debt, gave rise to the act regulating devises.

1798. Battle of Vinegar hill, at which the Irish rebels were completely routed and the insurrection crushed.

1809. Daniel Lambert, an English giant, died at Stamford, aged 36. His weight was 739 lbs. when last weighed, but at the time of his death, it was supposed to have been full 800. His coffin contained 112 superficial feet of Elm timber.

1813. Battle of Vittoria, in Spain, between the French under Joseph Bonaparte and Jourdan, and the allies under Wellington. French met with a disastrous defeat, losing 15,000 killed and wounded, and 3,000 prisoners, 150 cannon, 400 wagons of ammunition, 14,000 cattle, and the military chest, containing 42,000,000 reals. Loss of the allies 4,645.

1814. John Martin Miller, a professor of oriental languages, and poet of some note, died at Ulm.

1816. The king of the Netherlands acceded to the holy alliance.

1828. Leandro Fernandez Moratin died at Paris. He was a dramatic writer of much merit.

1832. Simon Waronzow, a Russian statesman, died in London. He had been for 30 years Russian ambassador to Great Britain.

1832. Anna Maria Porter, an English novelist, died. Her works, together with those of her sister Jane, had gained a great degree of popularity, which was in a measure swept away, with every thing else, before that splendid series, the Waverly novels.

1848. About 3,000 houses destroyed by fire in Constantinople; damage estimated at $100,000,000.

1850. Matthew L. Davis, a distinguished citizen and printer in New York, died.

1850. Jacob Hayes, long a leading police officer of New York, died. His notoriety was very great.

1852. Mary Ann Clarke died at Boulogne, in France, aged 74; the notorious mistress of the duke of York, to whose name, for a time, much consequence was given, in parliament and in London society, by the charges against the duke in 1809.

1853. A boat's crew from the Austrian brig-of-war Huzzar, lying in the harbor of Smyrna, seized in that port a Hungarian refugee, named Martin Koszta, and carried him to the ship. The populace, excited by the outrage attacked three Austrian officers, of whom two were slain. Koszta having protection, in virtue of his primary declaration of an intention of becoming an American citizen, captain Ingraham, of the American sloop-of-war St. Louis demanded his release. The affair caused a good deal of excitement throughout the civilized world. (See July 2.)

JUNE 22.

168 b. c. Battle of Pydna; Perseus, the last king of Macedon, defeated by the Romans under Paulus Æmylius, who brought to Rome a great number of books and manuscripts. The date is settled by an eclipse which happened the preceding night. This battle terminated the independence of a country which had seen a succession of thirty legitimate monarchs and eight usurpers, since its foundation by Caranus 814 b. c., six years after the fall of Assyria.

431. Third Œcumenical council assembled at Ephesus, to execute the decree of pope Celestine as to the heresy of Nestorius. He was deposed from his see and banished to an oasis.

1191. A remarkable eclipse of the sun, when the crusaders were at Acre, at 8 o'clock in the morning. In that year a parhelion appeared undistinguishable by the naked eye from the real sun.

1298. Battle of Falkirk; Edward I with 80,000 English defeated the Scottish army under Wallace, with great slaughter.

1415. John Huss, a Bohemian clergyman who had adopted the opinions of Wickliff, was burnt at the stake.

1476. Battle of Morat, in Switzerland, and defeat of Charles the Bold, duke of Burgundy. Philip de Comines, speaking of this celebrated conflict for liberty, mentions arquebusiers as troops.

1483. Accession of the usurper Richard III.

1527. NICCOLO MACHIAVELLI, a Florentine writer, died. His works are numerous, but that called *The Prince* is the most famous, and has generally given him a bad character, though defended by Bacon and Clarendon.

1535. JOHN FISHER, an English prelate, beheaded at the age of 77. He pertinaciously opposed the measures of the king, in relation to his wives. He was the opponent of Erasmus, who, however, gives him a superior character.

1596. The combined English and Dutch fleets under lord Effingham and admiral Van Duvenwoord, attacked the Spanish fleet in Cadiz bay, burnt 3 galleons, captured two, and drove a great number on shore. To save the latter the Spaniards agreed to pay 2,500,000 ducats.

1602. "Lent unto Benjamy Johnsone, at the apoyntment of E. Allen and William Birde, in earnest of a booke [play] called *Richard Crook-back*, and for new adycions of *Jeronimo*, the sum of *xlb*."—*Henslowe Manuscripts.*

1632. GALILEO and his books condemned by the inquisition.

1664. CATHARINE PHILIPS, an English poetess, died.

1679. Battle of Bothwell bridge; the Scottish covenanters defeated by the English under the duke of Monmouth.

1691. MAHOMET IV, of Turkey, assassinated in prison. In the beginning of his reign he was eminently successful in war; but the resistless valor of John Sobieski drove the Turks within their own dominions. These calamities were attributed to the sultan, and the janizaries deposed him.

1691. SOLYMAN III, of Turkey, brother of the preceding, died. He was taken from prison and placed on the throne, on the deposition of his brother, Mahomet, 1687. He was indolent and superstitious.

1714. MATTHEW HENRY, an eminent English dissenting divine, died. His writings are highly valued, particularly the *Expositions of the Bible*, 5 vols. folio.

1734. EDMUND POURCHAT died; a French professor of philosophy, and a man of extensive learning.

1741. This day is memorable for the impressment of seamen into the British service. Nothing could protect the unhappy individuals; in 36 hours the names of 2370 were enrolled.

1763. JOHN PETER DE BOUGAINVILLE died; a French author, of great acquirements, whose application hastened his death, at the age of 41.

1770. PHILIP CARTERET WEBB died a distinguished English lawyer and antiquary.

1772. Chief-justice MANSFIELD, of England, gave judgment that the master of a negro slave which had been brought to England had no right to send him back to the plantations.

1775. Congress resolved to emit $2,000,000 in bills of credit.

1777. British evacuated New Brunswick and retired to Amboy; they suffered severely from Morgan's riflemen and Wayne's brigade.

1780. The forts on Licking river attacked by 600 Indians and Canadians under colonel Bird, with 6 field pieces; they took all the inhabitants captives, and loaded them with heavy baggage; such as failed on the journey were tomahawked and scalped.

1803. WILLIAM HEINSE, a German author, died. His works are in 10 vols., and manifest great ability.

1807. British ship Leopard, 50 guns, attacked American frigate Chesapeake, 36 guns, captain Barron. The Chesapeake struck in 30 minutes; 3 men killed, 18 wounded. Four men were taken out of the Chesapeake, when she was permitted to proceed. One of these was hanged. Barron was suspended for five years.

1813. Battle of Craney island, in Chesapeake bay. British under sir Sidney Beckwith and admiral Warren defeated by 480 Virginia militia and 150 sailors. British loss 1200 killed wounded or drowned. None of the Americans were injured.

1815. BONAPARTE'S second abdication. He announced that his political life had terminated, and proclaimed his son, Napoleon II, emperor of the French.

1835. CHARLES BUTLER, the reminiscent, died.

1834. FERDINAND WILHELM BECKER died; a distinguished German physician.

1835. FRANCISCO TACON Y ROSISQUE died; a Spanish statesman, and minister from Spain to the United States. He had filled many distinguished offices, and was greatly respected and esteemed for his talents and amiable qualities.

1839. DEBORAH KNIGHT died at Sumner, Me., aged 105.

1848. The difficulties and disturbances occasioned by the disbanding of the operatives in the national workshops at Paris began.

1848. Civil war in Paris; barricades erected, and a terrible slaughter of the people; general Cavaignac declared dictator.

1848. MARTIN VAN BUREN nominated for president of the United States at a convention at Utica.

1849. ELIZABETH GRINDELL died in Goshen, N. H., aged 104¼ years, leaving a descendant of the *fifth* generation.

1852. Charles C. Berry, commander of the steamship United States, died at Brooklyn, N. Y., aged 39. He had been connected with the mercantile marine of New York from an early age.

1854. Jeremiah M. Scarritt, a United States military engineer, died at Key West. He was a native of New Hampshire, graduated at the military academy of West Point in 1838, served with distinction in the war with Mexico, and was brevetted for gallant and meritorious conduct.

1855. Samuel Sumner Wilde died, aged 84. He was one of the delegates to the Hartford convention, and the last survivor of that assemblage; he also held the office of a justice of the supreme court of Massachusetts 35 years. His judicial career was distinguished by great legal learning and stern integrity.

1855. William Henry Stone, the correspondent of the *London Times* from the seat of war, died at Balaclava, aged 30. He was employed by the British government in administering the fund for the relief of the sick and wounded, and was a young man of brilliant promise.

JUNE 23.

217 B. C. Battle of Thrasymene, in Italy, between the Romans under Caius Flaminius, and the Carthaginians under Hannibal. The Romans were defeated, and Flaminius killed.

303. St. Alban, the first martyr for Christianity in England, beheaded at Verulam in Hertfordshire. Nearly five hundred years after his death his memory was honored by Offa, king of the Mercians, who built a stately monastery over him, whence the town of St. Albans receives its name.

1137. Albertus, archbishop of Mentz, died. He abused the confidence and liberality of the emperor, Henry V, by raising a conspiracy, for which he was imprisoned.

1281. A terrible convulsion of Mount Etna, about sunset.

1485. Richard III published his famous proclamation, stating that Henry Tudor intended to "change and subvert the laws of the realm, and to do the most cruel murders, slaughters, robberies and disherisons, that were ever seen in any Christian country."

1579. The famous union of Utrecht effected. It included Gelderland, Holland, Zealand, Friesland and Utrecht. Ghent and Ypres afterwards acceded.

1596. Cadiz surrendered to the English by capitulation. A ransom of 120,000 crowns was paid by the inhabitants for their lives, and the town and merchandise were abandoned to the rapacity of the conquerors.

1606. Henry Garnet, provincial of the Jesuits, executed for the *gunpowder* plot.

1645. Viera's plot discovered, to deliver Olinda and the other Dutch possessions into the hands of the Portuguese. He was originally a butcher's boy.

1650. Charles II arrived on the coast of Scotland, but was compelled to take the covenant before landing.

1654. Southworth, a catholic clergyman, executed in his 72d year. He reproached his persecutors for arming themselves for liberty of conscience, and killing him for differing with them.

1664. The duke of York conveyed a part of his tract in North America to John lord Berkley, baron of Stratton, and sir George Carteret, by the name of Nova-Cæsarea, or New Jersey. Thus the New Netherlands became divided into New York and New Jersey.

1687. M. Denonville, with 1,500 French and 500 Indians marched from Canada for the purpose of humbling the Seneca Indians. When he had reached the foot of a hill about a mile from the principal village of the Senecas, he aroused an ambush of 500 Indians, which at first threw his army into confusion, but they soon rallied again and the Senecas were defeated, with the lose of 80, and laid their own village in ashes. The French found only two old men, whom they cut in pieces and boiled to make soup for their allies.

1707. John Mill, a learned English divine, died; editor of a *Greek Testament*, with various readings and critical notes; a labor of thirty years, and which was published only a fortnight before his death.

1728. Gabriel Daniel, a learned French Jesuit, died. His books were rapidly republished, and several translated.

1736. Achmet III, ex-emperor of Turkey, died, aged 74. He waged war with Russia, Persia and Venice successfully, and is entitled to some regard for the hospitality he showed to that unfortunate madman, Charles XII of Sweden.

1757. Battle of Plaissey, in Hindostan; the British under lord Clive defeated Surajah Dowla, and took his camp, baggage, and 50 cannon.

1758. Battle of Crefelt; French defeated with the loss of 600 by the allies under Ferdinand of Brunswick, who lost 1,500.

1759. Battle of Kay, on the Oder; the Prussians under Wedel attacked the Russians, and were defeated with the loss of 4,000.

1760. Battle of Landshut; the Austrians assaulted and carried the town with great loss on both sides.

1764. Joseph Barry, a French ecclesiastic and author, died. His *History of Germany*, 11 vols. quarto, is reckoned the best work in French on the subject.

1770. Mark Akenside, an English poet, died. He wrote also on medicine; and possessed an original and powerful mind.

1780. Battle of Springfield, N. J.; the British took the town and burnt it, and retreated.

1791. Catharine Macauley (Graham), an English historian, died. She wrote several histories, essays and political works, which are now nearly obliviated.

1793. New declaration of the rights of man by the French convention.

1793. Cape François burnt by the negroes and mulattoes, after an indiscriminate massacre of the whites, which had been in progress since the 7th, by which several thousands perished. (See 20th.)

1795. Action between the British and French fleets off L'Orient, in which the latter were defeated, with the loss of several large ships.

1824. Stephen Aignan, a French poet and dramatic writer, died. He filled several offices under Napoleon.

1824. Wilson Lowry, an English artist, died. He made many improvements in the art of engraving.

1836. James Mill, a Scottish divine, died; celebrated for his literary and philosophical works, author of a *History of British India, &c.*

1839. Hester Stanhope, a learned English lady, died at D'Joun, in Syria. She had resided in Syria nearly thirty years, and was celebrated for her eccentricity and singular mode of life. She was a niece of William Pitt, and abandoned civilized society to reside among Arabs, over whom she acquired great command.

1854. A terrible hurricane occurred at Manteno, Illinois, extending from six to eight miles in width, prostrated many houses, and caused much other damage.

1854. Daniel Wells, chief justice of the court of common pleas of Massachusetts, died at Cambridge, aged 63. He was born in Greenfield, Mass., and in 1837 was appointed district attorney for the western district, the duties of which office he discharged with marked ability, propriety and success until appointed chief justice.

1855. The Russians, 30,000 men, under general Mouravieff, invested Kars in the Crimea; the Turkish garrison was commanded by general Williams, an Englishman.

1856. Prince Esterhazy, an eminent Austrian ambassador, died at Berlin, in Prussia, where he was envoy.

JUNE 24.

64. The first Christian persecution under Nero.

79. Titus Flavius Vespasianus, emperor of Rome, died, after a popular reign of 10 years. He was the first of the Roman emperors who died a natural death.

1203. The third, or Boniface's crusade, reached Chalcedon.

1314. Battle of Bannockburn in Scotland. The English army of 100,000 men under Edward II totally defeated by the Scots, 30,000, under Bruce. The loss of the English was 154 earls, barons and knights, 700 gentlemen and upwards of 10,000 common soldiers.

1340. Battle of Sluys: the English under Edward III, with 240 ships, defeated the French fleet of 400 ships. The French lost 230 vessels and 30,000 men killed.

1450. Battle of Seven Oaks, in England, when Cade, the rebel, turning on his pursuers, put them to flight, killed sir Humphrey Stafford, and arrayed himself in the knight's panopli and spurs.

1497. John Cabot and his son Sebastian, in the service of England, first descried land on the continent of America, which they called Prima Vista, and is generally supposed to have been some part of Newfoundland. No one had yet reached the continent.

1534. John Boccold (of Leyden) a journeyman tailor, crowned king of Sion at Munster, in Germany, by the anabaptists. The German princes took the city by surprise on this day the year following, and deposed the king, and afterwards put him to death.

1577. Sebastian III of Portugal embarked at Lisbon against the Moors in Africa, with 1,000 sail.

1637. Nicholas Claude Fabri Peiresc, a distinguished French antiquary, died. He was a learned man, and highly esteemed by his cotemporaries.

1643. John Hampden, an English statesman, died. He was a leader of the parliamentary forces, and mortally wounded at the battle of Chalgrove field.

1675. King Philip's war began at Swanzey, in the Plymouth colony, not far from mount Hope. Having sent their wives and children to the Narragansetts for safety, a party of the Wampanoags advanced to Swanzey, where they menaced the people, and proceeded to rifle their houses, and even to kill the cattle. An Indian was shot, whereupon the party rushed forward and slew eight or nine of the inhabitants; thus opened the bloody scene, which for more than a year spread terror and devastation over the New England colonies, and shed a deluge of human blood. It was a contest for extirpation, and ere it ended the flower of the English and the chivalry of the Indians were laid low.

1711. Queen ANNE's fleet, sent to reduce Canada, arrived at Boston, New England.

1724. Great tumult in Glasgow, occasioned by a tax on malt. Preparations of malt liquor were at that time deemed essential articles of comfort.

1736. English act of parliament against witchcraft, passed in the reign of James I, repealed.

1741. A daily mail first instituted in London.

1750. Pension of £30 per annum conferred on Hannah Snell, the female soldier, who under the name of James Gray, served king George more than 5 years.

1762. Battle of Graebenstein; the allies under prince Ferdinand, defeated the French under Soubisse, and d'Estrees, who lost 300 men.

1770. CHRISTOPHER DRAKENBERG died in Norway, aged 146.

1782. JOHN BLAIR, a Scottish chronologist, died. His principal work is a chronology and history of the world.

1796. DAVID RITTENHOUSE, an American natural philosopher, died. From a manufacturer of clocks and mathematical instruments he became, by his own exertions, one of the most scientific men of the day.

1799. Division of the territory and treasures of Tippo Saib, by the English.

1803. MATTHEW THORNTON, a signer of the declaration, died. He was a practicing physician in New Hampshire, when the war of the revolution broke out.

1804. The spire of Hanslope church, Buckinghamshire, England, fell immediately after divine service and crushed down the roof also; no lives were lost.

1810. Battle of Beaverdams; 570 Americans surprised and taken by the British.

1812. The grand imperial army of Napoleon, consisting of 470,000 men, consolidated into three masses, began the Russian campaign by the passage of the Niemen.

1817. THOMAS M'KEAN died; a signer of the declaration, and governor of Pennsylvania.

1821. Battle of Carabobo, in Colombia; the royalist army totally defeated by the republicans, with the loss of their artillery, baggage, and 6,000 prisoners.

1839. Battle of Nezib, in Syria, between the Turks, 70,000, under the seraskier, Hafiz pasha, and the Egyptians, 80,000, under Ibrahim. The Turks were defeated, with the loss of 6,000 killed and many prisoners.

1840. The 400th anniversary of the discovery of the art of printing celebrated at Boston and various places in Europe.

1848. ANTONIO GAGNA, a Mexican military officer, died at Puebla, aged 64 years, 52 of which he had spent in the service, and acquired the reputation of a gallant, benevolent and courtly gentleman.

1852. CHRISTOPHER EDWARDS GADSDEN, bishop of the episcopal diocese of South Carolina, died at Charleston, aged 68.

1852. The first national agricultural convention assembled at Washington, consisting of 151 members, representing 22 states; Marshall P. Wilder, of Massachusetts, president.

1853. A courier arrived at St. Petersburg, bringing the refusal of the sultan of Turkey to the note of the czar, whereupon orders were issued for the invasion of the Danubian principalities.

1855. Forty-seven Russian ships, of from 200 to 700 tons each, were destroyed near Nystadt, in the gulf of Bothnia, by boats from the allied squadron.

JUNE 25.

1208. PHILIP, duke of Swabia, assassinated. He was elected emperor of Germany, but was obliged to give room to Otho, who had the most powerful supporters. His memory is still respected in Germany.

1520. The assaults of the Mexicans upon the Spaniards in the centre of their capital, which had continued without intermission since the massacre of the 13th May, (q.v.) was made with increased fury on this day. The Spaniards defended themselves with 12 pieces of artillery, which made terrible havoc upon their enemy; but as the number of them was infinite, they covered the sight of their dead with fresh numbers. The Spaniards with Cortez at their head made a sally into one of the principal streets, carrying fire and sword among the dense mass, destroying men and houses before them.

1526. An imperial diet assembled at Spires, and observed the rites of the reformed church. It was at this sitting that Charles V proposed the meeting of a general council for reforming the abuses of the church.

1634. JOHN MARSTON died; an English dramatic author. He was a chaste and pure writer, avoiding the ribaldry and obscenity of the age.

1644. THOMAS WESTFIELD died; a learned English divine, whose eloquence and pathos procured him the appellation of the weeping prophet.

1663. JOHN BRAMHALL, lord primate of Ireland, died. He was highly serviceable to the royal cause during the English civil wars.

1667. JOHN HARMAN with 16 ships defeated a French fleet of 30, near Martinico.

1672. The king of France at the head of 120,000 choice troops, commanded by the ablest generals in the world, entered Utrecht in triumph, and advanced within 9 miles of Amsterdam. At this crisis the inhabitants of Amsterdam opened the sluices and laid the country under water. Fertile fields, numerous villas and flourishing villages were overwhelmed by the inundation. They even formed the design of migrating to their settlements in the East Indies, and erecting a new empire in the southern extremity of Asia. It was found that there were vessels in the harbor sufficient to transport 150 families, but a favorable turn in their affairs, prevented the necessity of having recourse to that desperate expedient.

1689. WILLIAM THOMAS, an English bishop, died; author of an *Apology for the Church of England*, and other works.

1695. Namur in Belgium taken from the French after a long and bloody siege.

1725. JONATHAN WILD, the noted thief catcher, hanged at Tyburn. The evening previous he tried to poison himself, but lived to be stoned and hooted by the populace on his way to the gallows.

1744. ROGER GALE, an English antiquary, died; esteemed one of the most learned and polite scholars of the age.

1767. GODFREY SELLIUS, a Prussian historian, died.

1781. The wives, children and dependents of those inhabitants of Charleston, who resided in the rebel colonies, ordered by the British to quit the place by the 1st of August. More than 1,000 persons were thus exiled.

1782. Action between the French and Spanish fleet, 25 sail, and the Newfoundland and Quebec fleets; 18 of the latter, laden chiefly with provisions, were captured.

1784. Judge WHITE, with his family, having ascended the Mohawk river, landed at the mouth of the Sauquoit. Hence the origin of Whitestown. The country then was an unbroken wilderness.

1788. Virginia, the tenth state, adopted the federal constitution, 89 to 79, the least majority of any state except New York.

1794. CHARLES BARBAROUX, a noted French revolutionist, guillotined. He attacked the usurpations of Robespierre and the machinations of the Jacobins, by which he fell.

1794. Charleroi surrendered to the French under Jourdan, seven days after the trenches had been opened. General Reinach and 3,000 Austrians who defended the fortress, were made prisoners of war.

1795. WILLIAM SMELLIE, a Scottish naturalist, died. He was a printer by profession, wrote for the *Encyclopedia Brittannica*, translated *Buffon*, and conducted the *Edinburgh Review* and *Magazine*.

1807. An armistice between the emperors of France and Russia, when they held a personal conference upon a raft moored in the river Niemen, near Tilsit. The sovereigns embraced each other, and retiring under a canopy, had a long conversation, to which no one was a witness.

1813. British under admiral Cockburn, with 2,000 troops, took Hampton, Va., and pillaged it for two days.

1815. BONAPARTE's farewell address to his soldiery.

1816. HUGH HENRY BRACKENRIDGE, a Pennsylvania judge, died; known as the author of *Modern Chivalry*, a poem, and by other works.

1823. ALEXANDER GRIFFITHS, at once a parricide and suicide, was buried in the cross roads near London; the last so interred, as the act giving suicides Christian burial then took effect.

1841. ALEXANDER MACOMB, commander in chief of the army of the United States, died at Washington. He entered the service of the United States in 1799 as cornet of dragoons; was raised to the rank of brigadier general in 1814, and commanded at the successful battle of Plattsburgh.

1842. M. SISMONDI, the historian, died near Geneva, aged 69.

1844. JARVIS CUTLER, the first white man that cut down a tree for a settlement in Ohio, died at Evansville, Indiana.

1852. DUDLEY MARVIN, an eminent lawyer of western New York, died, aged 65, at Ripley, Chautauque county. He was a native of Lyme, Ct., studied at Canandaigua, and was several times returned to congress.

JUNE 26.

285 B. C. DIONYSIUS of Alexandria began his astronomical era. He was the first to find the exact limits of the solar year, which he made to consist of 365 days, 5 hours, 49 minutes.

44 B. C. The memorable conference between Brutus and Cassius, and Cicero at Antium.

363. JULIAN, emperor of Rome, died, aged 32. He was elected by his soldiery, on the death of Constantius, and soon declared himself a pagan. He was learned and in his private character respectable.

1276. INNOCENT V (Peter de Tarantaise), pope of Rome, died.

1541. FRANCISCO PIZARRO, the Spanish adventurer, assassinated in his own palace, at noonday, by the friends of Almagro, at the age of 63.

1569. VICTORIUS STRIGELIUS died; a learned professor at Leipsic, and one of Luther's first disciples.

1574. GABRIEL DE MONTGOMERY, a zealous protestant nobleman, beheaded at Paris by order of Catharine, who sacrificed him to her unjust revenge. (See June 29, 1559.)

1657. OLIVER CROMWELL solemnly inaugurated lord protector.

1685. RUMBOLD, the maltster who contrived the Rye house plot taken and executed at Edinburgh.

1688. RALPH CUDWORTH, a celebrated English divine, died. He was a man of extensive erudition, well skilled in the languages, an able philosopher, an acute mathematician and a profound metaphysician.

1691. JOHN FLAVEL died; an English divine, author of *Navigation and Husbandry Spiritualized*, &c.

1696. Portsmouth plain, N. H., attacked by the Indians; five houses were assaulted at once, early in the morning, and 14 persons killed on the spot. One was scalped and left for dead, but afterwards recovered.

1708. The act vacating extravagant grants of land in New York confirmed.

1719. ALEXIS PETROVITZ, only son of Peter the great of Russia, died in prison. His intemperance alienated him from his father, and he died in prison under sentence of death.

1748. Indian battle of Marlborough, Vt. Captain Hobbs with 40 men from No. 4, (Charlestown) on his march through the woods was attacked by a large body of Indians. Without the least knowledge of their force, Hobbs instantly gave them a well directed fire, which checked their impetuosity. A sharp action ensued of four hours, without either side yielding an inch of their original ground. Sacket, who led the Indians, finally ordered a retreat, carrying off the dead and wounded. Three of the English were killed, and as many wounded. This defence was considered at the time a masterpiece of bravery; the Indians being estimated four to one of the English.

1749. A conspiracy discovered at Malta against the knights; 125 slaves suffered death.

1752. GIULIO ALBERONI, a Spanish statesman, died, aged 89. He was the son of a gardener, and became a great and ambitious man.

1782. Slavery entirely abolished in Austrian Poland.

1784. CÆSAR RODNEY, president of Delaware, died, aged about 54. He voted for the declaration of independence, and was enabled to afford efficient aid to Washington in the prosecution of the war. His death is usually placed in 1783.

1793. GILBERT WHITE, an English naturalist and antiquary, died.

1794. Battle of Fleurus, in Belgium; the allies defeated by the French under Jourdan, after a contest of 15 hours. On this occasion, Coutel, an æronaut, with 2 officers, reconnoitered the contending armies in an air balloon.

1795. PETER DEMOURS died; a French surgeon and oculist, known for his dexterity, and author of some professional works.

1799. The first newspaper at Brooklyn, New York, issued.

1799. Naples surrendered to lord Nelson; on which occasion Ferdinand created him duke of Bronte. *Bronte* was the forge of Cyclops, on which he forged the thunder of Jove. He also presented him with an estate worth $18,000 per annum, and a sword valued at 60,000 ducats.

1807. British order in council, blockading the Ems and rivers on the Baltic.

1807. Conference on the river Niemen between Bonaparte, Alexander of Russia and Frederick William of Prussia.

1810. JOSEPH MONTGOLFIER, the celebrated inventor of balloons, died.

1814. Attack of the American flotilla and marines under commodore Barney, upon two British frigates moored at St. Leonard's creek, which were compelled to retire.

1830. GEORGE IV, of England, died.

1831. Cholera made its appearance at St. Petersburg. The number of cases in the first 18 days, 4,916; deaths, 2,219.

1834. GILBERT BLANE, a distinguished Scottish physician, died, aged 85. His career was marked by a zeal for the mitigation of the evils of war and a sea life, and a diligent cultivation and exertion of solid talents.

1835. ENOCH CROSBY, the *Harvey Birch* of Cooper's *Spy*, died. His services were of great benefit to the commander in chief during a part of the revolutionary war.

1848. JOHN J. DE GRAFF died at Schenectady; formerly a representative in congress.

1848. EDWARD B. PHILLIPS died at Brattleborough, leaving an immense fortune, which he did not know how to enjoy. He bequeathed Harvard university $100,000.

1849. Panama rail road stock ($1,000,000) subscribed, without effort, in New York city.

1849. The great crevasse in the levee of the Mississippi river was stopped.

1852. RALPH WORMLY, a British admiral, died at Utica, New York. He was retired from actual service, and had resided for some time in Boston.

1853. The czar of Russia issued a manifesto respecting the Turkish question to his own subjects, pretending to act as the champion of Christianity.

1855. JOHN J. GUION, a Mississippi jurist, died, aged 54. He held various important offices of state with ability.

JUNE 27.

432 B. C. The estival solstice of Meton, the Athenian, corresponds with this day, in the 87th Olympiad. From the time of Solon the Attic months were lunar, composed alternately of 30 and 29 days.

1137. The city of Bath in England destroyed by fire.

1299. Pope BONIFACE VIII issued an authoritative rescript, directed to Edward I, claiming the feudal sovereignty over Scotland. Edward received it in his camp, and in reply formally deduced his claim to the superiority, from *Brute the Trojan*. His holiness rejoined that the Scots cared not for Brute the Trojan, as they were derived from *Scota*, the daughter of Pharaoh, who landed in Ireland, and whose descendants became kings of Albany by conquest.

1506. FERDINAND of Arragon resigned the government of Castile, and Philip and Joanna were enthroned.

1534. The University of Oxford unanimously determined that the jurisdiction of the pope of Rome did not exceed the ministry of any other English bishop.

1627. VILLIERS, duke of Buckingham, sailed from England on his expedition against the French coast, from which he returned in disgrace, with the loss of the flower of his army.

1627. JOHN HAYWARD, an English historian, died. He wrote also biographies of some of the kings, and several religious works.

1630. FREDERICK MOREL, a learned French printer, died. Some of his predecessors had been directors of the king's printing house, and his descendants were also distinguished for their learning, and as elegant printers.

1651. "Milton's book" burnt at Toulouse by an *arrêt* of the parliament. The famous *Defence of the People of England*, was twelve days later burnt by the common executioner, at Paris, under a judicial sentence.

1689. Dover, N. H., attacked by the Indians. The houses were garrisoned, but some squaws got permission to sleep by the fire in two of them, who gave the Indians admission in the night. Several houses were burnt, 23 persons killed, and 29 captivated.

1694. The French under Du Casse, attacked the island of Jamaica, and laid it waste.

1699. SEBASTIAN JOSEPH DE PONTCHASTEAU, a French author, died; remarkable for the singularity of his acts of devotion and charity.

1709. Battle of Pultowa in Russia, between the Russians under Peter the Great and the Swedes under Charles XII, in which the latter were totally defeated, after a desperate conflict of two hours.

1720. The *Mississippi bubble* burst in France; amount about $450,000,000.

1724. A party of 13 Indians, called French Mohawks, attacked the house of John Hanson, a quaker, in Dover, N. H., killed and scalped two small children, and carried off his wife, three children and the nurse. The quakers could not be persuaded to use any means for their defence though equally exposed with their neighbors to an enemy who made no distinction between them.

1725. CHRISTIAN HENRY HEINECKEN, an extraordinary German boy, died. He spoke his maternal tongue fluently at ten months; at one year old he knew the principal events of the Pentateuch; in two months more he was master of the entire histories of the Old and New Testament; at two years and a half he answered the principal questions in geography, and in ancient and modern history. He spoke Latin and French, German and Low Dutch, with great facility, before the commencement of his fourth year, 1725, in which he died. His constitution was so delicate that he was not weaned till a few months before his death.

1742. NATHAN BAILEY, the English lexicographer, died. Besides his well known dictionary, he was the editor of school editions and translations of several of the ancient classic poets and historians.

1774. NICHOLAS TINDAL, an English historian, died; known as the translator of Rapin's history.

1777. WILLIAM DODD, an English divine, hanged for forgery.

1780. I. H. WASER, a Swiss ecclesiastic, executed at Zurich, for some strictures in a newspaper on the administration of justice in that city.

1785. SAMUEL MATHER, a learned New England divine, died, aged 79. He wrote the life of his father, Cotton Mather.

1788. Virginia adopted the constitution of the United States, recommending amendments; tenth state which ratified that document.

1789. Union of all the orders in the national assembly of France.

1794. SIMON NICHOLAS HENRY LINGUET, a French writer, guillotined. The freedom of his writings drove him from one country to another to escape prosecution, till he finally came under the revolutionary axe at Paris. The number of his works is thirty-five.

1794. The populace of Warsaw put eight of their principal noblemen to death as traitors to their country.

1800. WILLIAM CUMBERLAND CRUIKSHANK, an eminent Scottish anatomist, died in London, where he distinguished himself as a surgeon and medical writer.

1801. Cairo surrendered by the French to the Anglo-Turkish army; conditioned to be sent to France. The army consisted of 13,754 men, of whom 600 were Greeks and Copts, and 100 Mamelukes.

1806. The British took possession of Montevideo only to be made prisoners of war.

1817. Fort Bizoton, Port-au-Prince, blown up by its commandant, in revenge of some supposed injuries received from his superiors. He was the only one killed.

1819. The commune of Grignoncourt, in the arrondissement of Neufchateau in France was desolated by a hail storm. M. Jacoutot, the mayor, collected and melted several weighing upwards of a pound each and having a transparent stone in the centre, flat, round and polished, and perforated in the centre. Wherever the hail had fallen, there were found, when it had melted, many similar stones, hitherto unknown in Grignoncourt.

1820. JOSEPH VON HAGER, an eminent Chinese scholar, died. He was born in Italy, studied in Germany, and resided some time in London. He published several works on Chinese literature, and detected the historical fraud of Vella, a Sicilian monk.

1826. PETER EDWARD LEMONTEY, a French dramatist, died. He was also an able statesman, and censor of the theatre.

1828. ABIEL ABBOT, an American clergyman, died; author of *Letters written in the Interior of Cuba*, and various pamphlets.

1829. Erzroum, in Turkey, captured by the Russians. Among the prisoners were the seraskier and 4 pashas, 150 cannon.

1832. Cholera appeared in New York.

1840. LUCIEN BONAPARTE, younger brother of Napoleon, died at Viterbo, in Italy, aged 66, of a cancer in the breast, the same disease of which Napoleon died.

1843. JOHN MURRAY, a distinguished London publisher, died. He not only maintained an eminent position in his profession for a long series of years, but was much esteemed in private life.

1849. The steamer Europa came in collision with the American bark Charles Bartlett, on the ocean; the latter was sunk with the loss of 134 persons.

1857. ——— MITCHELL, a North Carolina geologist, was killed by a fall into the Caney river, while engaged alone in scientific explorations.

JUNE 28.

1059. ABDULLAH, founder of the dynasty of the Almoravides, which ruled Africa and Spain during a century, died of a wound received in battle.

1598. ABRAHAM ORTELIUS, a Dutch geographer, died. He traveled over a considerable portion of Europe, and for his knowledge was styled the Ptolemy of his age.

1632. The original charter of Maryland granted to Cecil, lord Baltimore. The draft being in Latin, the country was called *Terra Mariæ*, in honor of the queen.

1650. JOHN DE ROTRON, a distinguished French poet, dramatic writer and magistrate, died. He lost his life by administering to the necessities of the poor at a time of plague.

1675. An attack on the head quarters of king Philip, the celebrated sachem, by a body of the Plymouth colonists, who succeeded in routing the savages.

1681. First general yearly meeting of the quakers in America, held at Burlington, New Jersey.

1700. THOMAS CREECH, an eminent English translator, died by his own hand.

1734. General OGLETHORPE arrived in London from the colony of Georgia, with several Indian chiefs, among whom was Tomo Chichi.

1748. JOSEPH DE MAILLA, a French missionary, died at Pekin. His great knowledge of Chinese led to his employment at Pekin, where he became a great favorite with the emperor, at whose request he constructed a map of China and Chinese Tartary, and had it engraved in France.

1776. British under Clinton and admiral Parker made an unsuccessful attempt upon Sullivan's island. The American force was 344 regulars and a few volunteers. The British made the attack in 10 ships, one of which was abandoned and burnt. After the action was over 7,000 balls were picked up.

1778. Battle of Monmouth, between the British under Cornwallis, and the Americans under Washington. Owing to some mistakes on both sides, the action was delayed and the day far spent without much fighting. The Americans were prepared to renew the engagement in the morning, but the British had retreated during the night in great silence. British loss 246 killed, 59 died of fatigue; American loss 142 killed, 160 wounded. The day was excessively hot, and many died of fatigue on both sides.

1785. Treaty of fort Herkimer, between the Oneidas, Tuscaroras and the state of New York.

1794. Battle of Fleurus and capture of chateau de Namur, by the French. The allies lost more than 7000 men killed, and 1500 prisoners. The conquest of the Netherlands was greatly influenced by the result of this battle.

1794. The Poles under Kosciusko, armed with scythes rose upon the Russians at Cracow and defeated the regular troops.

1796. Battle of Renchen; Moreau victorious over the Austrians.

1797. George Keats died; author of *Ancient and Modern Rome*, a poem, and an account of the Pelew islands.

1802. Thomas Garnet died; an English physician and chemist, and an author on chemistry, &c.

1802. M. Garnerin ascended in a balloon from Chelsea, England, and made an ærial voyage of more than 50 miles at the rate of 70 miles an hour. This was the most memorable ascent in England from the time of Leonardi.

1808. Valencia, in Spain, assaulted by the French under Moncey; they were repulsed with the loss of 1000 men.

1809. First steam boat on lake Champlain, arrived at St. Johns, Canada, from Burlington, Vt. She was 120 feet long, 10 wide, and drew 3½ feet water.

1811. Battle of Tarragona, in Spain; the city carried by the French under Suchet, with horrible slaughter; 10,000 prisoners taken, 384 cannon, 40,000 balls, and 500,000 quintals powder, &c.

1814. United States sloop of war Wasp, 20 guns, Capt. Blakeley, captured in 19 minutes British sloop of war Reindeer, 19 guns, 118 men. British loss Capt. Manners and 24 killed, 42 wounded; American loss 9 killed, 17 wounded.

1815. Commodore Decatur arrived off Algiers with the American squadron.

1815. Russians under Blucher defeated the French at Villers Coterets, took 1500 prisoners and six cannon.

1815. Allies under Colloredo engaged the French near Befort; allies lost 300.

1815. French 8000 strong driven through Chevannes at the point of the bayonet.

1815. General Creneville attacked Carouge, crossed the Arve near Geneva, which was also taken.

1815. Troops of Gen. Bubna passed mount Cenis, one of the loftiest peaks of the Alps, in Savoy.

1815. The head of the bridge of Arly in Savoy carried by assault by the allied Sardinians, Piedmontese and Austrians, with the loss of 1000 men.

1835. Charles Matthews, an eminent English comedian, died, aged 79; author of a monodramatic entertainment called *Matthews at Home*, which was extremely popular in England and America.

1836. James Madison, 4th president of the United States, died, aged 86. He was distinguished for his great talents and acquirements, for the important offices which he filled, and for his virtues in private life.

1838. Coronation of Victoria celebrated in London with great splendor and parade.

1839. Indian battle in Arkansas between the Ross and Ridge parties of Cherokees; about 50 were killed on both sides, and among them John Ross, head of the Ross party; John Ridge the leader of the other party, having been previously killed. (See June 10.)

1847. Alexander Hill Everett died at Canton, China. He was some time editor and principal proprietor of the *North American Review*, and at his death commissioner of the United States to China.

1848. The revolution in Wallachia ended in the flight of the prince and the establishment of a provincial government.

1854. A military insurrection broke out in Spain.

1855. Battle of Rivas, in Central America. Col. Walker arrived in brig Vista and landed his forces and those of Gen. Castillon; but was forced to retire.

1855. Fitzroy James Henry Somerset, baron Raglan, commander of the British forces in the Crimea, died of cholera at Sebastopol, aged 66. He served with Wellington on the Peninsula, and lost his right arm at the battle of Waterloo. During the arduous duties of the campaign in Turkey, he won the confidence of the army by his calmness, quick perception and fortitude, and performed great and brilliant services. He was succeeded by Maj. Gen. James Simpson.

JUNE 29.

65. Peter, the apostle, crucified at Rome, in the reign of Nero. On the evening of this day, St. Peter's church at Rome is splendidly illuminated.

455. The sack of Rome under Genseric, the Vandal, terminated. It had continued 14 days. The spoils of Jerusalem were removed to Carthage.

794. Offa, a powerful English king, died. He corresponded on flattering terms with Charlemagne, and fixed a seal to his charters.

1033. A great eclipse of the sun was observed. In France it caused almost midnight darkness at noon.

1215. King John signed magna charta,

or the great charter of liberties, which is esteemed the basis and palladium of British freedom, on this day, at Runemede, a meadow on the banks of the Thames, between Staines and Windsor, now occupied as a race course. Of 26 barons who subscribed this document, only 3 could write their own names. (This event is attributed to various days.)

1450. WILLIAM ASCOUGH, bishop of Sarum, murdered at the altar by Jack Cade and his followers.

1502. COLUMBUS arrived at Hispaniola on his fourth voyage.

1509. MARGARET OF LANCASTER, mother of Henry VII, died. She was a munificent patron of learning, and the founder of St. John's and Christ's colleges at Cambridge. She sustained an excellent character.

1519. CHARLES V declared emperor by the electoral voices.

1559. HENRY II of France wounded in the eye with a spear, at a famous tournament, by the English count de Montgomery, of which he died. (See July 10.)

1573. GASPARD SANLY DE TAVANNES, a distinguished French general, died. He was an honor to the military profession, and by his exertions the king of Navarre and the prince of Conde escaped the massacre of St. Bartholomews.

1586. PRIMUS TRUBER, a Lutheran minister, who gave the first edition of the Vandalie scriptures, died.

1612. A lottery drawn in London for the benefit of the Virginia plantations, the profits of which amounted to nearly £30,000.

1644. Battle of Cropredy bridge; the parliament forces under Waller, defeated by the royalists.

1667. The French, Dutch and Danes concluded a peace with England at Breda.

1674. CHARLES II granted to his brother, the duke of York, the territory of the state of Delaware, then a part of New Netherland.

1678. Grenadiers introduced into England.

1716. ERNESTUS AUGUSTUS, duke of Brunswick, Lunenburg, and bishop of Osnabruck, brother to George I, created duke of York and Albany, in Great Britain, and earl of Ulster in Ireland.

1734. Battle of Parma, in Italy; the imperialists defeated by the French, and their general and 5,000 men killed.

1754. Lieutenant-governor DELANCEY opened at Albany a treaty with the Indians, who had been tardy in assembling at the convention of the provinces. A preconcerted speech was delivered, and the presents were distributed in the name of all the colonies.

1779. ANTHONY RAPHAEL MENGS, an eminent Bohemian painter and author, died at Rome.

1793. FRANCIS CHARLES VIVOT DE SOMBREUIL, a French general, guillotined at Paris, together with his eldest son, for their attachment to the king.

1794. MOREAU entered Bruges—British quitted Ostend—French defeated at Guadaloupe.

1810. British ships Amphion, Cerberus and Active, burnt 26 vessels in the harbor of Grao, Spain, and brought off 26 with their cargos.

1811. French took fort Olivo by stratagem, and captured 900 Spaniards without firing a gun.

1813. British sloop of war Persian, wrecked on the Silver keys, in chasing the American privateer Saucy Jack.

1813. VALENTINE GREEN, an English mezzotinto engraver, died. Besides his great merit as an artist, he is also known as the author of a valuable work on antiquities.

1816. Pope PIUS VII issued his bull against Bible societies, and prohibited the circulation of Bibles published by heretics, as eminently dangerous to souls.

1816. DAVID WILLIAMS, an English miscellaneous writer, died. He founded the literary fund.

1836. EDWARD SMEDLEY, prebendary of Lincoln, died; author of several poems, a history of the reformed religion in France, and editor of the *Encyclopedia Metropolitana.*

1837. HOFRATH ALOYSIUS HIRT died at Berlin, Prussia, aged 78; an eminent archæologist, distinguished for his attainments in literature and the fine arts, one of whose chief works was on the architecture of the ancients.

1840. THOMAS SIMPSON, companion of Mr. Dean in the discovery of the northwest passage, died by his own hand at Turtle river, aged 32. He was a native of Scotland, and for four years had been actively engaged in the prosecution of the discoveries which will immortalize his name, and for which he is represented to have possessed uncommon qualifications.

1848. Croton aqueduct bridge over the Harlem completed; 1,400 feet long, resting on 15 arches, 8 of them 80 feet span; a work of surpassing skill and magnitude.

1850. Part of the Table rock at Niagara falls gave way.

1852. HENRY CLAY, an eminent American statesman, died, aged 75. Having received a common school education, he commenced the study of the law at the age of 19, and became one of the most distinguished orators of his day. He was an earnest supporter of the colonization society, and twice an unsuccessful candidate for the office of president of the United States.

JUNE 30.

1513. HENRY VIII embarked with his forces at Dover for the invasion of France, appointing his "most dear consort, queen Catharine, rectrix and governor of the realm."

1520. MONTEZUMA, the Mexican monarch, died. The situation of the Spaniards becoming desperate, Cortez persuaded the captive monarch to address his people from a terrace, and request them to desist from their attacks and allow the Spaniards to evacuate the city. The Indians were silent while he spoke, but answered that they had promised their gods never to stop till the Spaniards were totally destroyed. A shower of stones and arrows then fell about the spot where he stood, which were warded off by the shields of the soldiers. At the moment they removed their shields, that the king might renew his address, three stones and an arrow struck him to the ground. He died, less of his wounds than of sorrow and indignation, at the age of 54.

1543. Battle of Atherton moor, in England; lord Fairfax defeated by the royalists, and totally routed.

1607. CÆSAR BARONIUS, an Italian cardinal, died. His works are numerous and valuable, especially the *Ecclesiastical Annals*, 12 vols. folio.

1666. ALEXANDER DE BROME, on English poet, died; author of innumerable odes and sonnets written during the English revolution, in which the round heads are treated with great keenness and severity.

1670. HENRIETTA, duchess of Orleans, and sister to king Charles II, died in her 26th year. Suspicions were entertained that she had been poisoned by her husband for infidelity.

1685. ARCHIBALD CAMPBELL, duke of Argyle, beheaded at Edinburgh for seditious measures. His father was also beheaded there 24 years before, as a traitor.

1690. Battle of Fleurus, in the Netherlands; the allies defeated by the French under Luxembourg, with the loss of 6,000 killed, 8,000 prisoners, and all their artillery and baggage.

1690. The Dutch and English fleets under Torrington, engaged the French fleet off Beachey head, and were defeated. English loss 2 ships, 400 men; Dutch loss 2 admirals, 6 ships; the king, William, was wounded by a cannon ball.

1694. ADAM LITTLETON, an excellent English philologist and grammarian, died.

1697. THOMAS POPE BLOUNT died; an eminent English writer and a man of great learning and research.

1703. Battle of Eeckeren, between the French and confederated armies of the English and Dutch, in which the slaughter on both sides was very great.

1733. Twenty sail of merchant ships destroyed by a hurricane at St. Christophers.

1734. Dantzic, in Prussia, surrendered to the Russians.

1777. British evacuated Amboy, N. J., and encamped opposite, on Staten island.

1785. JAMES OGLETHORPE, the first governor of Georgia, died in England, aged 97. He took an active part in the settlement of Georgia, and founded the town of Savannah. He displayed great courage and address in protecting the colony from incursions of the Spaniards.

1797. RICHARD PARKER hanged; author of the noted rebellion in the English fleet at the Nore.

1797. The chief officers of the Cisalpine republic installed by Bonaparte. This like the French republic, was but of short continuance.

1802. Treaty of Buffalo creek, when the Senecas sold their land west of Genesee river to the state.

1803. Two British ships captured off St. Domingo the French frigate Creole, 44 guns, having on board 100 blood hounds for the French army against the blacks.

1815. Action in the strait of Sunda, between United States sloop of war Peacock, and British king's ship Nautilus. The latter was captured in 15 minutes, but was given up next day, as hostilities had ceased twelve days before between the two countries.

1815. Treaty of peace concluded between the United States and Algiers, in which the dey relinquished the payment of tribute to the Algerines, released the prisoners, and made restitution for American property captured by his cruisers.

1815. Allied army from the heights of Belleville, commenced their attacks on Paris.

1817. The Prussian government prohibited the further use of the term *protestant* in the country, as being obsolete and unmeaning, since the protestants did not any longer protest, and ordered the word *evangelical* to be substituted for it.

1817. CHRISTOPHER DANIEL EBELING, a German geographer, died. His great work, the *Geography and History of North America*, was completed and published at Hamburg 1799, in 5 vols. His collection of books in relation to America, nearly 4,000 in number, were purchased by Israel Thorndike of Boston, and presented to Harvard college.

1821. JOSE FERNANDEZ ABASCAL died, aged 78; long engaged in the military service of Spain, and viceroy of Peru during the early part of the war of independence in South America.

1831. William Roscoe, an English biographer and miscellaneous writer, died. He was of humble parentage, but his lives of Lorenzo the Magnificent, and Leo X, give him an exalted and enduring reputation.

1832. Silistria, in Bulgaria, surrendered to the Russians. The trophies were 8,000 prisoners, 2 three-tailed pashas, 250 cannon, &c.

1835. Benjamin Pritchard, the Kentucky giant, died. His disease was dropsy; his weight 525 pounds.

1840. The sub-treasury, or independent treasury bill passed the house of representatives in congress, by a vote of 124 to 105.

1855. The yellow fever became epidemic in New Orleans.

JULY.

JULY 1.

1452 B. C. **Aaron**, the Jewish high priest, died on the first day of the month Ab, at the age of 123.

1190. The crusaders under Richard Plantagenet and Philip de Valois, amounting to 100,000 warriors and pilgrims, assembled in the plains of Vezelai.

1270. **Louis** IX of France sailed from Aigues Mortes, on his fatal crusade against the infidels of Tunis.

1413. **Pierre des Essars**, a French nobleman, executed. He served in the Scottish army against England, 1402, and was taken prisoner. On his return to France he became a statesman, but was suspected of some political heresies, which forfeited his life.

1450. **Jack Cade** took possession of Southwark, and two days after entered London, cutting the ropes of the draw bridge with his sword.

1520. **Cortez** secretly evacuated the city of Mexico with the remains of his army. The Spaniards commenced their retreat a little before midnight, which was soon discovered by the Mexicans, who assailed them on all sides, so that it was with the utmost hazard of entire destruction that they effected their escape, with the loss of 600 Spaniards and 4,000 allies. All their artillery, all the riches they had amassed, the manuscripts of Cortez, were lost; together with 40 horses, most of their prisoners, and the men and women in the service of the Spaniards, were killed. It was one of the most horrible and disastrous scenes on record, and acquired the name among the Spaniards of the *noche triste*.

1555. **John Bradford**, an English martyr in the reign of queen Mary, and an eloquent preacher, burnt at Smithfield for heresy.

1582. **James Crichton** (*the admirable*) assassinated at Mantua. He was a native of Scotland, and altogether a most extraordinary character, about whom authors differ also most extraordinarily, some even treating his existence as fabulous. Urquhart places his death on the 27th February, at the carnival.

1614. **Isaac Casaubon**, a celebrated Swiss critic and theologian, died at London. Nearly all the ancient classics are indebted to his valuable researches.

1626. Chaplains first appointed to each ship in the British navy.

1627. King **Charles** I of England dismissed his queen's French servants, which occasioned a war with France.

1643. The great assembly of divines met at Westminster in the Jerusalem chamber; 118 preachers and 26 laymen.

1676. New Jersey divided into East and West Jersey; the former granted to George Carteret, the latter to William Penn and others.

1681. **Oliver Plunket**, primate of Ireland, executed at Tyburn. It was afterwards discovered that he was guiltless of the crimes imputed to him, and that he fell a sacrifice to the intrigues of some of his priesthood.

1690. Battle of the Boyne, in Ireland, which decided the fate of James II and the Stuart dynasty, and established William III on the British throne. The duke of Schomberg, one of the ablest generals of the time, was killed, at the age of 82. Also the Irish rector, George Walker, famous for his heroism. The forces of James were but 27,000, opposed to 36,000 strong.

1709. **Edward Lhuyd** died; a celebrated antiquary and linguist, and keeper of the Ashmolean museum.

1731. **John Montgomery**, governor of New York, died. He possessed a kind and human disposition, and his death was much lamented.

1743. Action between the British ship Centurion, 60 guns, 400 men, Com. Anson, and Spanish ship Acapulco, 64 guns, 550 men. The latter was captured, with above a million and a half of dollars on board. Spanish loss 67 killed, 84 wounded; British loss 2 killed, 17 wounded. (See June 15, 1744.)

1762. **John Baptist Nolin**, a French geographer, died at Paris.

1766. **John Francis Lefevre de La-**

BARRE, a young French nobleman, executed. A wooden crucifix had been defaced on a public bridge, at which the bishop of Amiens was greatly enraged, and demanded a disclosure of the perpetrators. Labarre was arraigned on the false accusation of his enemy, Duval de Saucourt, and the indictment also charged him with having passed a procession of monks without taking off his hat. He was sentenced to have his tongue cut out, his right hand cut off, and to be burnt alive. This sentence the parliament of Paris commuted, by a small majority, into decapitation before burning. Labarre was scarcely nineteen years old, and was one of the latest victims of that religious fanaticism in France which led to the revolution. Voltaire exerted himself as warmly against this infamous act, as he had against the execution of Calas.

1780. Action off cape Finisterre between British ship Romney, 50 guns, and French frigate Artois, 40 guns, 460 men. The Artois was captured in 45 minutes, 20 killed, 40 wounded; British 2 wounded.

1780. JOHN BELL, a celebrated Scottish traveler, died, aged 91. He commenced his travels about the year 1714, in the employ of Peter the Great of Russia, with whom he was on terms of great intimacy; and extended his travels into many different countries; was afterwards for several years a merchant at Constantinople, and finally in 1747 returned to his native country to spend the remainder of his life in ease and affluence on his estates of Antermony.

1781. Battle of Porto Novo, in Hindostan; 7,000 British under sir Eyre Coote defeated Hyder Ally and 150,000 men. English loss about 400 killed and wounded; Hyder lost many of his best officers and 4,000 killed.

1782. The marquis of ROCKINGHAM, first lord of the English treasury, died. His merit was his patriotism, and his patronizing such men as Burke, and bringing them into influence.

1798. Alexandria, in Egypt, taken by the French under Bonaparte, who issued a proclamation, stating that he venerated God, the prophet, and the koran, and more than the Mamelukes did.

1800. JEAN CLAUDE D'ARCON, a French general and engineer, died. He invented the floating batteries, which were intended to reduce Gibraltar.

1810. LOUIS BONAPARTE abdicated the throne of Holland, and retired to Austria as a private individual.

1814. Peresque Isle surprised by the United States troops under lieutenant Gregory.

1818. THOMAS BERNARD, founder of the British gallery, died. He was eminent as a philanthropist.

1820. Toll first demanded and received on the Erie canal.

1832. Rite of suttee abolished in Hindostan by the British authorities.

1835. JAMES GIBBON, the hero of Stony point, died at Richmond, where for several years he had been collector of customs.

1839. MAHMOUD II, sultan of Turkey, died in the 54th year of his age and 31st of his reign.

1839. About 150 Chippewa Indians treacherously massacred at the falls of St. Anthony, and 20 on the St. Croix, by the Sioux, who had invited the Chippewas to meet for the purpose of forming a treaty of peace. About 50 of the Sioux were killed.

1850. SERGEAT S. PRENTISS, a distinguished American lawyer, died, aged 40.

1853. ARTHUR LIVERMORE, a New Hampshire jurist, died at Campton, N. H., aged 87.

1854. WALDO J. BURNETT died at Boston, aged 25; a distinguished physician and naturalist, and author of several tracts on medical subjects.

1855. There was a second Sunday demonstration in Hyde park, London, by a large and excited mob, against sir Robert Grosvenor's Sunday bill.

1856. A heavy gale on the coast of Labrador, when of a fleet of 30 vessels, 29 were driven on shore and lost.

JULY 2.

928. JOHN X, pope of Rome, suffocated in prison. Better fitted for heading an army than governing the church, he was victorious over the Turks in battle.

936. HENRY I (*the fowler*), of Germany, died. He was successful in his wars, strengthened his empire, and promoted harmony and union among the German princes.

1296. JOHN BALIOL subscribed his abdication at Kincardin. For three years he had the tower of London and a circuit round the walls for twenty miles for his possession; and in 1299 was permitted to retire into Normandy, where he died forgotten six years afterwards.

1491. Madeira, an island in the Atlantic, covered with wood (whence its name), discovered by John Gonzales Zarco, in the service of Portugal. It was the next year colonized, and planted with the Cyprian vine and sugar cane of Sicily.

1492. ADOLPHUS, emperor of Germany, killed. He was a poor count, elected partly through intrigue, and his reign was a series of intrigues to maintain himself in power. The throne was finally given to Albert of Austria, and when the two emperors met in battle, they fought hand to hand, and Adolphus was killed by the lance of his rival. His abilities were inadequate to his station.

1566. MICHAEL NOSTRODAMUS died; an able French physician and celebrated astrologer.

1609. HUDSON on his first voyage, after various vicissitudes, through storm and ice, loss of foremast and sails, arrived off the banks of Newfoundland, and refreshed his men by a heavy *catch* of cod.

1644. Battle of Marston Moor; the parliament army under Cromwell and Fairfax, defeated the royalists under prince Rupert, who lost the whole of his artillery and left the northern counties in the hands of the confederates.

1692. ADRIAN DE VALOIS (or Valesius) died; a learned French historian and critic.

1704. Battle of Donauworth, in Bavaria; the French and Bavarians defeated by the duke of Marlborough. Loss about 6,000 on each side.

1730. LAURENCE CORSINI was elected pope by the conclave, after it had sat four months. He took the name of Clement XII.

1740. THOMAS BAKER, a learned and ingenious English antiquary, died. He wrote with great purity of style.

1741. THOMAS MORECROFT died; the person who figures in the *Spectator* as *Will Wimble.*

1775. WASHINGTON arrived at Cambridge, and took command of the American army, then consisting of 14,500 men.

1776. The memorable resolution, declaring the North American colonies independent, passed by congress, without one dissenting colony. It was proclaimed on the 4th, and hence that day is celebrated, instead of this, which is, perhaps, better entitled to the honor.

1778. A fanatic calling herself queen Beck, assaulted king George III as he was alighting from his carriage.

1778. JEAN JACQUES ROUSSEAU died at Paris. He was the son of a watchmaker at Geneva, and strayed to Paris while young, where he became one of the most celebrated authors of the day. His works are collected in 33 vols.

1782. DIONYSIUS DIDEROT, a noted French philosopher, died. He was the son of a cutler, educated by the Jesuits. Rejecting the ecclesiastical profession for literature, he became an author, and conceived the stupendous design of the *Dictionnaire Encyclopédique*, on which he labored 20 years. He was a Jacobin, and contributed his full share to the revolution.

1800. Bill for the union of Great Britain and Ireland signed by order of the king, George III.

1802. Colonel BARRE, so noted in the British parliament as an opponent to the American war, died. He had been blind for many years.

1805. PATRICK RUSSELL, a British physician, died at London; author of a valuable treatise on the plague, and several estimable works on natural history.

1807. JEFFERSON issued his proclamation forbidding all intercourse with British ships of war, and ordering all those within the American waters to withdraw therefrom. (See June 22.)

1812. American embargo expired by its own limitation. On the same day the frigate Essex, captain Porter, sailed from New York on a cruise against the British, on which occasion he hoisted a white flag, bearing the motto, "Free trade and sailor's rights."

1812. PETER GANSEVOORT, a distinguished American officer, died at Albany, aged 63.

1816. BENJAMIN THOMPSON died; formerly a timber merchant, translator of the *German Theatre*, and author of several other productions. His death was caused by extreme sensitiveness at the manner in which his play of *Oberon's Oath* was received. It was hissed on the first representation, at which he was extremely dejected; at its second representation it was received with universal applause, which elated him so much that he died of the excitement.

1830. Battle near Milliduse between the Turks and Russians. The Turks were defeated with considerable loss, and their general, Hadki pasha, taken prisoner.

1840. The port of Canton, in China, blockaded by the British under commodore Bremer.

1849. The city of Rome surrendered to the French.

1851. CAROLINE AMELIA HALSTED, an English authoress, died. Of three or four works which she published the principal one is a *Life of Richard III*, in 2 volumes, octavo.

1851. WILLIAM BERRY, an English author, died at Bristol, aged 77; author of various works on genealogy and heraldry.

1853. The Russian troops under prince Gortschakoff crossed the Pruth and invaded Turkey.

1853. A controversy having arisen between the consuls of Austria and America at Smyrna about Martin Koszta, an Austrian refugee, captain Ingraham of the American sloop of war St. Louis, hearing of a design to convey him to Trieste, demanded the surrender of Koszta before 4 o'clock, and brought his guns to bear on the Austrian brig. An engagement was prevented by the compromise that Koszta be delivered to the French consul at Smyrna for safe keeping.

1855. The legislature of Kansas met at Pawnee and organized; Thomas Johnson, president of the council, and John H. Stringfellow, speaker of the house.

1855. THOMAS WEAVER, an eminent English geologist, died at Pimlico, aged 82.

1855. CHARLES ELKINS, a British admiral of the red, died, aged 87. He published a review of the naval battles from 1744 to 1814.

1856. ROWLAND STEPHENSON, for many years a London banker, and also a member of parliament, died at Bristol, Pa., aged 83. He had resided in this country about thirty years.

JULY 3.

237. ANTONIUS AFRICANUS GORDIAN, killed near Carthage by a general of Maximinus, during whose reign he had been elected emperor, much against his will.

323. Battle of Adrianople and overthrow of Lucinius, when Constantine took possession of Byzantium, which he afterwards made the seat of his empire, and named it Constantinopolis.

987. Inauguration at Rheims of Hugh Capet, son of Hugo, duke of Burgundy, and founder of the third race in the French monarchy—the Capetan.

1437. The sacred play of *The Passion* represented in the park of Vexmeil, attended by the French nobility.

1521. CORTEZ attempted to retake the city of Mexico by storm, but was repulsed with the loss of 60 Spaniards, 1000 allies, 7 horses and 1 cannon. The Mexicans made prisoners of 40 Spaniards, who were immediately sacrificed in their great temple to the war god.

1608. CHAMPLAIN, who took the charge of conducting the French colony in Arcadie, after examining all the eligible places on the St. Lawrence, selected a spot at the confluence of that river and the St. Charles, about 320 miles from the sea, where he erected barracks, cleared the ground for tillage, and on this day laid the foundation of Quebec.

1642. MARY DE MEDICIS, of France, died; the promoter of the massacre of St. Bartholomews.

1672. FRANCIS WILLOUGHBY, an English naturalist, died. To rank and fortune he added great application, and had traversed the principal countries of Europe in pursuit of his favorite study, the history of animals, when he was cut off at the early age of 37.

1676. Indian battle near Narraganset; the main body of the Indians were surprised at a large cedar swamp, and attacked so suddenly that a considerable number were killed or taken on the spot, and those who fled into the thicket were surrounded. They lost 171 on this occasion.

1743. GABRIEL ROMANOVITCH DERSHAVIN, a celebrated Russian poet, died.

1769. The first theatrical performance enacted in Albany, by a company from New York, having gained permission "for one month only" from "his excellency the governor." The play was *Venice Preserved;* the place, the hospital.

1776. Three towns in Turkey, containing 10,000 inhabitants, destroyed by an earthquake.

1779. Grenada, in the West Indies, taken by the French under count d'Estaing.

1789. JAMES BERNOUILLI II, a learned German mathematician, died of apoplexy while bathing in the Neva at St. Petersburg.

1794. Earthquake in Natolia, Asia Minor, destroyed several large and populous towns and villages, one of which was Amasia, the birth place of Strabo.

1795. British squadron off St. Maloes captured a French brig and six merchantmen.

1797. Admiral NELSON, in his barge, captured a Spanish launch, after a severe engagement, in the course of which he narrowly escaped death, by the assistance of his coxswain.

1807. British Capt. DOUGLAS threatened to capture all vessels from Norfolk, unless the magistrates permitted him to have communication with the British consul at that place; they refused.

1811. American government resolved to occupy West Florida; the British government remonstrated against it.

1814. United States troops under Gen. Brown, effected a landing on the Canadian frontier, between Chippewa and Fort Erie, which latter surrendered.

1815. Commercial treaty between England and America signed at London.

1833. Naval battle between the fleet of Don Pedro, under the command of admiral Napier, and that of Don Miguel, in which the latter was defeated with the loss of 6 vessels.

1838. SAMUEL THORNTON, an English gentleman, distinguished for his benevolence and usefulness, died, aged 83. He was 53 years a director of the bank of England, and 40 years a member of parliament.

1849. The French republican army, commanded by Gen. Oudinot, entered Rome.

1851. Edward Quillinan, a British author, died. He married a daughter of the poet Wadsworth, and was particularly accomplished in Portuguese literature.

1853. Samuel Putnam, a Massachusetts judge and senator, died at Somerville, aged 85.

1853. The American expedition under commodore Perry, left Loo Choo for Japan.

1854. Princess de la Moskwa, widow of marshal Ney, died in Paris.

1854. Thomas Ritchie died, aged 75; celebrated as the editor of the *Richmond Inquirer* and the *Washington Union*. He wielded great political influence in Virginia, his native state.

1855. The Cunard steamer Persia was launched at Glasgow.

JULY 4.

1097. Battle of Dorylæum, in Phrygia, and rout of the Moslems under Soliman.

1450. Lord Say and Sele beheaded by order of Jack Cade, at Cheapside, London.

1533. John Fryth, an English preacher, burnt at Smithfield for the heresy of Lutheranism.

1563. Leeds bridge school was founded in the time of Henry VIII.

1584. Amidas and Barlow, two experienced commodores sent out by sir Walter Raleigh for the purpose of discovering and taking possession of the American continent north of Florida, arrived at the coast on this day. Sailing along the shore 120 miles, they entered the mouth of a river and took formal possession of the country for the queen of England, delivering it over to the use of sir Walter. (See June 10, 1584.)

1623. William Bird, a celebrated English musical composer, died, aged 80. His music outlived his history, few particulars of his life being known.

1653. The parliament, commonly called *Barebone's*, from a zealot of that name who was one of the 120 members, assembled at Whitehall, and Cromwell delegated to them their chairs for fifteen months.

1663. Charles II of England, reviewed his 4000 guards, then the whole regular force of the kingdom, yet deemed dangerous to liberty. The king and his brother imputed the misfortune of their father, Charles I, to the want of a regular army.

1669. Anthony Escoba de Mendoza, a Spanish Jesuit, died. He was for many years a popular preacher, and bequeathed to posterity 40 vols. folio of his own writings.

1670. George, duke of Albemarle, captain-general of his majesty's forces, died at the cockpit. Possibly some lessons of ferocity might be learned there.

1671. Meric Casaubon, a Swiss *litterateur* and critic, died in London. Considerable offers were made him by Cromwell to write the history of the civil war, which he refused.

1744. Thirty-two wagons, variously decorated, loaded with the treasure brought home by Anson, guarded by his seamen, passed St. James's in London to the Tower.

1749. Joseph Vanaken, a celebrated Dutch painter, died.

1754. The commissioners of the American colonies met at Albany for the purpose of holding a conference with the Indians, (see June 19,) proposed a plan for the union of the colonies, which was agreed to this day, exactly 22 years before the declaration of independence. Its fate was singular. It was rejected in America because it was supposed to put too much power into the hands of the king; and it was rejected in England, because it was supposed to give too much power to the assemblies of the colonies.

1757. John Joseph Vade, an excellent French poet, died. His youth was spent in dissipation, for which he made some amends in the brief space allowed him by his impaired constitution.

1761. Samuel Richardson, an English printer, died; known as the author of a series of moral romances, among which *Pamela* and *Sir Charles Grandison* are the most noted. The former suggested to Fielding his famous *Tom Jones*.

1776. Declaration of American independence adopted by congress. It was 39 times before that body previous to its adoption. It may be added that this event took place 264 years after the discovery of America by Columbus, 160 from the first effectual settlement of Virginia, and 150 from the settlement of Plymouth.

1777. Boonesborough attacked by 200 Indians, who killed and wounded 2 of the pioneer's men. All the settlements were attacked at the same time.

1778. Francesco Manoel, the most celebrated lyric poet of modern Portuguese literature, escaped the inquisition by disarming the officer sent to arrest him, and fled to Paris. He became obnoxious to the holy office by some expressions concerning toleration and monks, in his translation of Moliere's *Tartuffe*.

1780. British admiral Geary captured 12 French merchantmen from Port-au-Prince.

1781. Williamsburg, Va., evacuated by the British under Cornwallis.

1789. Gosen Van Schaick, a brigadier general in the United States continental army, died at Albany.

1790. Action between the Swedish and Russian fleets, in which the former under the king, Charles XII, were defeated with great loss.

1793. Action off the capes of Virginia, between the French privateer, Citizen Genet, and two armed English vessels with a convoy. The convoy was captured and the two vessels much damaged. The Genet had 30 men, not one of whom was wounded by the enemy.

1800. A Mr. RUSBY was found guilty of reselling grain (technically regrading) in the market of Mark Lane. The judge, lord Kenyon, remarking to the jury, "You have conferred by your verdict almost the greatest benefit on your country that ever was conferred by any jury!"

1803. A remarkable ball of fire fell upon a public house at Wapping, England. It was accompanied with thunder.

1804. Mail stage commenced running once a week from Pittsburg and Philadelphia.

1806. Battle of Maida, in Italy; the French defeated by the British and Sicilians, with the loss of 800 killed and 1000 taken prisoners; British loss 45 killed 282 wounded.

1808. FISHER AMES, an American orator and statesman, died, aged 50. He possessed a mind of great and extraordinary character.

1813. United States smack Yankee captured by boarding, without any loss, British sloop Eagle.

1814. A part of the United States forces under Gen. W. Scott, advanced from fort Erie towards the British works at Chippewa. A smart action was had with the British at Street's creek. The division which crossed under Capt. Turner was attacked by a very superior force; but they gallantly cut their way through to a house, where they made a stand until relieved.

1816. RICHARD WATSON, bishop of Landaff, died; known by his *Apology for the Bible*, in answer to Paine's *Age of Reason*.

1817. The construction of the Erie canal commenced, in the neighborhood of Rome, Oneida county, New York.

1826. THOMAS JEFFERSON, third president of the United States, and author of the *Declaration of Independence*, died, just 50 years from the date of that document, aged 83.

1826. JOHN ADAMS, second president of the United States, died, aged 91. He was one of those patriots who most warmly advocated the declaration of independence in congress, and was an able statesman.

1831. JAMES MONROE, fifth president of the United States, died, aged 73. He joined the revolutionary army in 1778, and after the close of the war was constantly in the service of his country, as a statesman, till the close of his life.

1845. Texas finally annexed to the United States, by a convention of its citizens ratifying the action of the United States senate.

1845. An Englishman by the name of SPEER, accompanied by three chamois hunters, set out from Interlachen to ascend the Wetterhorn, or peak of tempests, one of the highest of the Oberland Alps, which had never been trodden by the foot of man. They reached the summit on the 8th, after a tedious and dangerous effort. The height of the peak ascended is 12,000 feet and upwards.

1848. DE CHATEAUBRIAND, a distinguished French savan, died at Paris, aged 80.

1848. Treaty of peace with Mexico proclaimed at Washington.

1848. Ceremony of laying the corner stone of the Washington monument at Washington, conducted with great pomp.

1849. Two thousand and seventy-four immigrants arrived in the steerage at New York.

1850. KIRBY, an eminent entomologist, died at Suffolk, England, aged 91. His work on the bees of England described upwards of 200 wild species in that country.

1853. The first Norwegian rail road opened.

1854. A collision on the Susquehanna rail road, near Baltimore, by which 30 persons were killed, and a large number badly wounded.

1854. JAMES MURRAY, mayor of Alexandria, La., was killed while attempting to suppress a disturbance at a barbecue.

1855. WILLIAM TERRELL, an accomplished and useful citizen of Georgia, died at Sparta in that state. He took great interest in the promotion of agricultural science, and bestowed $20,000 for the establishment of an agricultural professorship in the University of Georgia.

1855. A convention of cotton planters assembled at Cooper's Well, Miss., to hear the report of a committee upon the subject of a direct trade between the southern states and Europe. They adjourned to meet at Jackson, in January.

1855. Svartholm, a fort of great strength, commanding the approach to Lovisa, on the gulf of Finland, which had been deserted by its garrison, was destroyed by the allies.

1856. The members of what was termed the Kansas free state legislature, assembled at Topeka, but were dispersed by the U. S. troops, by direction of Col. Sumner.

1856. The statue of Washington, in Union square, New York, was inaugurated.

1857. Anton Schmidt, a German literary celebrity, died at Salzburg, aged 71. He was custos of the imperial library at Vienna, and was a popular author.

1857. William L. Marcy, an American statesman, died, aged 71. He filled the offices of comptroller and governor of New York with ability; but distinguished himself as secretary of war under president Polk, and secretary of state under president Pierce.

JULY 5.

394 b. c. Agesilaus crossed the Hellespont, on his recal from the Persian satrapy, a march of thirty days, which had occupied Xerxes twelve months.—The great battle fought by the Spartans against their countrymen happened about the same day.

965. Benedict V, pope, died. He was elected in opposition to Leo VIII. His short reign was stormy, and he was carried to Hamburg by Otho, who favored the cause of his rival.

1044. Aba, king of Hungary, defeated by his own subjects and killed in battle.

1100. Jerusalem taken by the Crusaders, after a siege of five weeks, and given up to massacre and pillage. Every inhumanity was practiced; those who had surrendered upon terms of safety, were butchered in cold blood to the number of 10,000; and among the inhabitants, also, neither age nor sex escaped the merciless fury of the Christian swords.

1529. Paulus Æmilius, a Veronese historian, died at Paris. He had begun a Latin history of the kings of France, and although he spent many years at it, was able only to reach the reign of Charles VIII. (May 5?)

1535. Thomas More, a celebrated English statesman, beheaded. He was doomed, for his adherence to the papal supremacy, to descend from the highest office under the king to an apartment in the tower, and suffered death rather than yield his opinions. He wrote several works, the most noted of which is the *Utopia*.

1566. Robert Carnegie, a Scottish statesman, died. He was a lord of session, and often sent on important embassies to France and England.

1582. At Rockhausen, not far from Erfurth, in Prussia, there fell a great quantity of a fibrous matter resembling human hair. It was at the close of a great tempest, such as usually precede an earthquake.

1614. Peter de Bourdeilles (or *Brantome*), a French abbot and courtier, died. His memoirs are printed in 15 vols.

1623. William Bride, an English music composer, died. The grace *non nobis Domini*, composed by him, was first sung on the second anniversary of the gunpowder plot, 1607.

1641. Simon Baskerville, a learned and wealthy English physician, died. He obtained great distinction, honors and a large fortune, by his success in the practice of medicine.

1641. Battle of Lansdowne, between the parliamentary and king's forces; a sanguinary action.

1644. York taken by the armies of the parliament.

1685. Battle of Sedgemoore; the duke of Monmouth's rebel army defeated. The misguided nobleman was taken *napping* in a dry ditch, with the George and 200 guineas in his pocket.

1715. Charles Ancillon, an eminent French lawyer, died. He was made inspector of the French courts of justice in Berlin, and historiographer to the king.

1758. The English and provincials under Abercrombie embarked on lake George against Ticonderoga and Crown point, on board 125 whaleboats and 900 batteaux. The army consisted of nearly 16,000 effective men, of whom about 9,000 were provincials, and was attended by a formidable train of artillery.

1758. General lord Howe was killed in a skirmish before Ticonderoga. With him it is said "the soul of the army expired."

1767. John Key, said to have been the first person born in Philadelphia, died at Kennet, Pa., aged 85.

1770. A naval action between the Turks and Russians took place, and while two of the leading ships of each party were grappled together, they took fire and blew up, carrying destruction and death to all around.

1775. Birthday of William Crotch, a musical prodigy, who excited universal astonishment at London by his preformances on the organ, at the age of three years.

1779. New Haven, Conn., entered by the British under sir George Collier, and subjected to almost indiscriminate ravage and plunder till night.

1780. Action off cape Ortegal between British ships Prudent and Licorne, and French ship Capricieuse 32 guns. The latter was captured, but so much damaged that they were obliged to burn her.

1782. Fifth action between the British fleet, admiral Hughes, and the French, admiral Suffrein, in the East Indies.

1788. Mather Byles, a Boston divine, died; a man of talent and wit, who corresponded with Pope, Lansdowne and Watts. He was suspected of tory principles during the revolution, and frequently, on complaint, sentenced to be confined to his own house, with a sentinel over him; on one of these occasions he induced the sentinel to go on an errand for him, promising to take his place, and was seen very gravely marching before his own door, the musket on his shoulder, keeping guard over himself.

1792. Robert Strange died; styled the father of historical engraving in England. He studied in France, and had the first knowledge of the dry needle, an instrument which his genius improved and used with great success.

1797. Second bombardment of Cadiz by the British.

1807. Buenos Ayres assaulted by the British under general Whitelocke. They were forced to retire with the loss of 2,000 men, and soon after compelled to withdraw the armament.

1808. Cuenca, Spain, taken by the French under Caulincourt, and given up to pillage.

1809. Battle near Enzersdorff and Wagram. Massena having crossed the Danube during the night, which was stormy and tempestuous, compelled the Austrians under the archduke Charles to give Bonaparte battle. The action continued the whole day, but neither party gained any decided advantage.

1811. The seven provinces of Venezuela made declaration of indedendence.

1814. Battle of Chippewa; the United States troops under general Brown, defeated the British, and compelled them to retire within their works. British loss 198 killed, 100 wounded, and 137 taken prisoners—435; American loss 60 killed, 257 wounded, and 20 missing—337.

1816. Dorothea Jordan, an eminent English actress, died. Notwithstanding her popularity and patronage, she died in France in great obscurity and penury.

1817. The golden sovereign of England first put in circulation.

1830. Algiers surrendered to the French under general Bourmont, after a siege of six days. A rich booty fell into the hands of the conquerors, of gold and silver, besides 1,500 cannon, and 12 ships of war lying in the harbor. Loss of the French previous to effecting this conquest, 2,400 men; that of the Algerines 10,000.

1836. Daniel Cole, a native of Long island, N. Y., died in Canada, aged 106.

1839. The third centennary of the protestant reformation was celebrated with great parade and splendor at Dresden, in Saxony.

1848. The negroes at St. Croix revolted and compelled the governor to proclaim their freedom. The whites thereupon formed a provisional government, deposed the governor, attacked the negroes, and having captured 300, shot them immediately.

1852. The British minister at Washington, gave notice that to prevent encroachments of fishing vessels belonging to the United States and France, upon grounds reserved by the convention of 1818, directions had been given for stationing a force of vessels and steamers off New Brunswick, Prince Edward's island, and in the gulf of St. Lawrence, as would be deemed sufficient to prevent the infraction of the treaty.

1852. The steam boat St. James exploded her boilers on lake Ponchartrain, and burnt to the water's edge. About 20 persons were killed and 19 wounded.

1852. The convention for revising the constitution of Louisiana met at Baton Rouge; Duncan F. Kenner president.

1852. Isaac T. Preston, a distingnished jurist, died near New Orleans, aged 59. He was a native of Virginia; graduated at Yale college in 1812, and suspended his legal studies to serve as captain of a company in the war with Great Britain. He rose to high distinction in the legal profession, and was elected judge of the supreme court of Louisiana, which office he held at the time of his death. He was killed by the explosion of a steam boiler on lake Ponchartrain.

1854. A fire at Philadelphia consumed the National theatre, Chinese museum, and other edifices.

JULY 6.

63 B. C. The Roman capitol fired during the night by an incendary and consumed. The famous *sibyline verses* perished with it.

1189. Henry II, of England, died. He added Brittany and Ireland to his dominions, attempted to repress the ambition of the clergy, and died of a broken heart at the rebellion of his children.

1303. Benedict XI (*Nicholas Bacosin*), pope, died. He was the son of a shepherd, succeeded Boniface VIII, and was poisoned by his cardinals.

1439. The solemn act of reunion between the Greek and Latin churches subscribed in the cathedral of Florence, after a separation of 600 years, by the pope, the emperor of Constantinople, and principal members of both churches.

1483. Richard III, with his consort (Anne Beauchamp, widow of Edward, prince of Wales), inaugurated at Westminster. The train of the king was borne by the duke of Buckingham, that of the queen by the countess of Richmond, both of the opposing houses of Lancaster.

1553. Edward VI, of England, died of consumption, aged 16, and was succeeded by his sister Mary.

1568. John Oporinus, one of the most learned and eminent of the early German printers, died. He employed 6 presses and 50 men, and printed only his own works.

1583. Edmund Grindal, archbishop of Canterbury, died; an able theological writer.

1630. A fleet of 14 sail, with men, women and children, and provisions, intended to make a firm settlement in New England, arrived in Massachusetts bay. There were on board about 1,500 passengers of various occupations, principally from the vicinity of London; among whom was governor Winthrop and his lieutenant Dudley, with several other gentlemen of wealth and quality. The expense of this equipment and transportation was £21,200.

1653. Cromwell's first parliament met.

1660. Charles II, of England, resumed touching for scrofula; placing his hands on the neck of the patient, the chaplain saying "He laid his hands on them and healed them."

1759. William Pepperell died; an officer in the British service before the American revolution, and 32 years a member of his majesty's council. He was born in Maine, rose to the highest military honors, and in 1745 commanded the expedition against Louisburg, which was reduced. He was rewarded with the title of baronet of England.

1767. Michael Bruce, an elegant Scottish poet, died, aged 21.

1775. Congress issued a manifesto, setting forth the causes and necessity of taking up arms in defence of their rights, against England.

1777. Ticonderoga and mount Independence evacuated by the American general St. Clair, who retreated to fort Edward. At the same time the Americans at Skeenesborough were obliged to burn their vessels, and retreat to the same place. The British under Burgoyne had advanced their works so far as to threaten a complete inclosure of the continental army.

1779. Action off Granada between the British fleet, admiral Barrington, 21 ships, and French fleet, 27 ships, admiral d'Estaing. Although the French avoided a close action, it is supposed that their loss was 1,200 killed, owing to their ships being crowded with men. British loss 529 killed and wounded.

1781. Battle of James river; general Wayne with 800 men, intending to strike Cornwallis's rear guard, was deceived by a countryman, and met the whole army of 4,000 regulars, drawn up to receive him. He instantly attacked them and retreated. Cornwallis, from the daring singularity of the manœuvre, concluded it to be a feint to draw him into an ambuscade, therefore did not pursue him. Wayne, however, lost his artillery.

1782. Sixth action between the British fleet, admiral Hughes, and French, admiral Suffrein, in the night, in close action. Both fleets suffered much; French lost the Orient, crew saved.

1790. Some workmen engaged in digging near Donadea, Ireland, discovered a vault, 12 feet by 8, and 6 f. 3 in. deep, containing a stone coffin in which rested a skeleton measuring 8 feet 3½ in. in length, by the side of which was a spear 7 feet in length and two brass urns, having the sun and moon engraved on them in a most curious, though antique manner. The vault was seventeen feet from the surface of the ground and no clue could be found to the identity of the body, or the time of its deposit there.

1790. George Augustus Eliott, lord Heathfield, died. He gained much celebrity in the Prussian service, and during the seven years' war in Germany; but his constancy and talent in defence of Gibraltar during three years of constant investment, in which all the powers of Spain were employed, excited the admiration of the world.

1796. Adam Stanislaus Maruszewich, a Polish poet and historian, died.

1801. Action off Algesiras between the British and French fleets. A British 74 grounded and was captured.

1809. British sloop of war Bonne Citoyenne captured in 6 hours 50 minutes French frigate La Furieuse. British loss 1 killed, 5 wounded; French loss 35 killed, 37 wounded.

1809. Battle of Wagram, between the French army of 180,000 under Napoleon, and the Austrians under the archduke Charles, of about half the force. The battle commenced on the 5th, and was decided on the 6th. The Austrians were compelled to retreat, after having taken 7,000 prisoners and 12 eagles, and retired fighting three days in succession, leaving the field of battle covered with their slain. It is stated that 27,000 fell on both sides. The French reckoned their loss 15,000 killed, about 4,000 wounded. Of the Austrians 12,000 were wounded, and 20,000 taken prisoners; 19 generals were killed or taken, and 40 cannon lost.

1813. Granville Sharp, a learned English philanthropist, died. He interested himself in the abolition of slavery, and to his exertions "England owes the verdict of her highest court of law, that the slave who sets his foot on English ground becomes that instant free."

1815. Samuel Whitbread, member of the British parliament and one of the most extensive brewers in the world, died by his own hand.

1823. Pius VII (*Gregory Barnabas Chiaramonti*), pope, died. He was a prisoner under Napoleon from 1808 to 1814, during which time he rejected with firmness the offers of the emperor.

1835. John Marshall, chief justice of the United States, died, aged 80. He was an extraordinary man, and the object of universal respect and confidence, on account of his extraordinary talents, his unsuspected integrity, his exemplary private virtues, and his important public services, which by some are deemed second only to those of Washington. He wrote the *Life of Washington*, 5 vols.

1838. Alexander Aikman, late printer of the *Jamaica Royal Gazette*, died. His exertions spread much light in that island.

1839. Great fire at Eastport, Me., by which the larger portion of the business part of the town was destroyed.

1849. Successful sortie of the Danes besieged in the fort of Frederick by the Schleswig Holsteiners, of whom 3,112 were slain and taken prisoners.

1851. David Macbeth Moir, a Scottish writer, died at Dumfries, aged 53. He was the *Delta* of *Blackwood's Magazine*, to which he was long a contributor, and in whose pages first appeared *Mansie Wauch*, which was long ascribed to Galt.

1857. John Lauris Blake, an American divine, died at Orange, N. J., aged 68. His principal work is a *Biographical Dictionary*, of which several editions were printed.

JULY 7.

715 b. c. Romulus, founder and first king of Rome, disappeared on the *nones*, during the *quirinalia*, in a chariot of fire, *patriis equis*, as he was reviewing his people. There seems to be no other way of explaining this account, than that he was a victim of some of the elements.

587 b. c. The city of Jerusalem, with the temple, palaces and walls, razed to the ground, the inhabitants carried into captivity, and the entire Israelitish monarchy terminated (after it had stood 468 years from the accession of David), in the 11th year of Zedekiah, on the seventh day of the Hebrew month *Ab*. It is still observed as a day of lamentation.

1307. Edward I, ninth king of England, died in the 35th year of his reign, aged 69. He was distinguished for his wisdom and the equity of his laws, as well as for his military abilities. (See Jan. 2, 1774.)

1415. John Huss, a celebrated German reformer, burnt by the council of Constance. He was the first opposer of the doctrine of transubstantiation, and the defender of Wickliffe.

1520. Battle of Otumba; the retreating army of Cortez being hotly pursued by the Mexicans, that general resolved to halt and risk a battle. The Tlascalan allies were of incalculable service to the maimed and wretched band of soldiers, who now faced about to resist the whole Mexican force, determined not to leave a trace of the Spaniards upon the earth. This battle lasted four hours; the Spaniards performed prodigies of valor, and were victorious. The cavalry penetrated the masses of Mexicans and struck down the chiefs when they began to give way, and the Tlascalans mowed down all before them with the arms which were thrown away by the fugitives.

1572. Sigismund II, king of Poland, died, and with him the Jaghellon race became extinct.

1573. James Borazzio Vignola died; an eminent Italian architect.

1607. The national anthem, *God save the King*, written by Ben Jonson, and composed by Dr. Bull, first *vocalized* in Merchant Taylor's hall, by the choir of the royal chapel, the king being present.

1640. The inhabitants of Providence, 40 in number, united in forming a civil government, after their own model.

1647. Revolt in Naples against the Spanish authorities, headed by the famous Thomas Aniello (*Massaniello*) a fisherman.

1647. Thomas Hooker, an English dissenting divine, died. He emigrated to Holland to escape persecution, and thence to America, and settled in Connecticut. In 1647 he removed with his whole congregation to the banks of the river, and may be considered the founder of the town of Hartford. He was a rigid puritan, and a man of learning and talent.

1648. Battle of St. Neots in England.

1667. The British admiral sir John Harman destroyed the entire French fleet, 33 sail, at Martinique, and left the vessels to rot on the strand.

1696. A party of French and Indians under count Frontenac left the island of Montreal to invade the country of the Five Nations with a great army. The expedition was unsuccessful.

1708. Conrad Samuel Schurtzfleisch died; professor of history, poetry and Greek at Wittenberg, and counselor and librarian to the duke of Saxe-Weimar.

1713. William Compton, bishop of Oxford, died. He was a dissenter, and took a conspicuous part in the politics of the day, particularly in the cause of William of Orange, whom he crowned.

1721. Sir WILLIAM KEITH, governor of Pennsylvania, held a council with the Indians at Connestogo.

1725. Treaty of Vienna between the emperor Charles VI and Philip V of Spain concluded by the baron de Ripperda, of Pragmatic sanction memory.

1776. JEREMIAH MARKLAND died; a very learned and acute English critic.

1777. Action between the United States frigate Hancock, 32 guns, captain Manley, and three British ships, under sir George Collier. The Hancock was captured; she wanted upwards of 60 of her complement, they being on board her prize, the British frigate Fox, which was soon after recaptured.

1779. British under governor TRYON plundered and burnt at Fairfield, Conn., 2 churches, 82 dwellings, 55 barns, 15 stores and 15 shops; and at Green Farms 1 church, 15 dwellings, 11 barns, and several stores; and sailed thence to Norwalk.

1784. Fort Dauphin, St. Domingo, entered by a negro, Jean Francois, a lieut. general in the Spanish service, with several hundred men, who massacred the white French, about 771 in number. The town had been delivered to the Spaniards for protection, conditioned that the negroes should not be permitted to enter it.

1791. THOMAS BLACKLOCK, an eminent Scottish poet and divine, died. His talents and acquirements were the more extraordinary, when it is considered that he lost his eye sight at the age of six months, by small pox.

1797. Congress declared the existing treaties with France no longer obligatory.

1798. WASHINGTON appointed lieutenant general of the armies of the United States.

1799. WILLIAM CURTIS, a distinguished English botanist, died. His great work, the *Flora Londinensis*, gave him an enduring reputation.

1799. The Kennet and Avon canal in England was opened.

1808. Desperate action, at night, between the British ship Sea Horse and Turkish frigate Badere Zaffer, 52 guns and 500 men, and another Turkish ship of 24 guns. At daylight the Badere struck, having 165 killed and 195 wounded; the other escaped. Sea Horse had 5 killed, 9 wounded.

1809. Cuxhaven, a fortified town of Hanover, taken by storm, by the boats of a British squadron.

1809. St. Domingo surrendered to the British and Spaniards.

1814. The three estates of the British realm offer public thanksgiving at St. Paul's for the peace of Europe.

1814. The United States troops under major general Brown, attacked the British at Chippewa; the latter retreated, and in the evening the Americans occupied their works.

1816. RICHARD BRINDSLEY SHERIDAN, an English dramatist, wit and orator, died. His dramas were undertaken for a subsistence; afterwards, for thirty-two years, he pursued a splendid parliamentary career, but died in great poverty.

1820. PIERRE LOUIS LOUVEL executed for the murder of the duke de Berri.

1843. JOHN HOLMES died at Portland, Me. He was the first United States senator sent from that state.

1844. The disgraceful riots of Philadelphia again commenced; many were killed.

1848. JULIA RUSH, widow of Dr. Rush, died, aged 90.

1848. OLIVER W. P. PEABODY died; an accomplished scholar, and able contributor to the *North American Review*.

1849. During the week closing with this day, 21,297 immigrants arrived at the port of Quebec, Lower Canada.

1853. A plot to assassinate the emperor of France while on his way to the opera, was discovered. Many armed conspirators were seized near the theatre, of whom 21 were convicted on trial.

1854. Battle of Giurgevo; the Turks defeated the Russians, and drove them from their position, with a loss in the conflict of 1,700 killed and wounded.

1855. WILLIAM EDWARD PARRY, the noted Arctic explorer, died at Ems, aged 64. He succeeded in extending his expeditions beyond those of his predecessors, for which he received the parliamentary reward, and was knighted in 1829.

JULY 8.

17. The isle of Thia, one of the scattered cluster called the Sporades, in the Grecian archipelago, rose brightly from the sea.

1117. ADAM DE ST. VICTOIRE, a French ecclesiastic and writer, died.

1174. HENRY II of England performed severe penance before the shrine of Thomas a Becket in the cathedral of Canterbury.

1497. The Indian expedition of Emanuel, king of Portugal, sailed from the Tagus. It consisted of three vessels, under Vasco de Gama.

1520. The retreating and almost annihilated army of Cortez entered the dominions of their faithful allies, the Tlascalans. Here the Spaniards rested to repair their fortunes, and the Mexicans meanwhile employed themselves in restoring their devastated capital.

1524. JAMES VERRAZZANUS, the Florentine discoverer, dated his letter to the king of France from Dieppe, giving an account of his voyage along the coast of the United States, in which he is supposed to have visited the outer harbor of New York.

1533. LUDOVICO ARIOSTO, the Italian poet, is by some authorities said to have died on this day. (See June 6.)

1550. The king of Denmark entered into a written contract to bind the Danish Bible in whole leather with clasps, for two marks Danish a copy and lodging; and to complete 2,000 copies in a year and a day. It was a middle sized folio, of 1,090 pages and sold for three rix dollars a copy.

1560. A peace between England, France and Scotland concluded.

1623. GREGORY XV (Alexander Ludovisio), pope, died. He erected the see of Paris into an archbishopric, and assisted the emperor and the king of Poland in their wars.

1639. BERNARD, duke of Weimar, a German officer in the 30 years' war, died, supposed to have been poisoned by Richelieu. With him fell one of the chief supports of the protestants.

1709. Battle of Pultowa, in Russia, between the Swedes under Charles XII, and the Russians under Peter the Great. The Swedes were entirely routed, and forced to take refuge within the dominions of the sultan of Turkey. The czar had his hat pierced by a ball, and prince Menzikoff had three horses killed under him.

1716. ROBERT SOUTH, a celebrated English divine, died, aged 83, and was buried with great honors to his memory. He shone as a polite scholar and a wit, and is famous for his controversy with Dr. Sherlock on the subject of the trinity. His sermons were published in 11 vols. octavo.

1721. ELIHU YALE, the benefactor of Yale college, died. He was descended from an ancient and wealthy family in Wales; born in New Haven 1748; acquired an estate in the East Indies, and on his return was chosen governor of the East India company.

1738. JOHN PETER NICERON, a popular French preacher, died; also author of *Memoirs of Men illustrious in the Republic of Letters*, of which the 39th volume was finished in the year of his death. He addicted himself to laborious studies and had an extensive knowledge of ancient and modern languages.

1747. Unsuccessful attempt of the French and Spaniards to force the pass aux Exiles in Dauphiny; the chevalier Belleisle and 5,000 men were left dead on the field of battle.

1758. Battle of Ticonderoga, in which the British and provincial troops of 16,000 men under Abercrombie, were repulsed in attempting to storm the fort, then under the command of Montcalm. The British general was induced to this rash attack by the favorable report of the engineer, and from having learned that a reinforcement was expected from Canada. The French had felled a breastwork of trees in front of the fort with their branches pointing outward and sharpened, so as to form an almost impenetrable abatis: in this the assailants became entangled, and were exposed to a murderous fire. Abercrombie, finding the attack fruitless, ordered a retreat after a contest of near four hours. Nearly 2,000 of the British were killed or wounded. Of the Highland regiment nearly half were either killed or desperately wounded. The loss of the enemy, who were covered by their works, was inconsiderable.

1760. Action in the bay of Chaleur, between the British and French fleets, in which the latter were defeated with the loss of 3 large ships of war and 20 sail of schooners, sloops and small privateers.

1768. Thirty men boarded a schooner at Boston that had been seized by the officers of the customs, for having 30 hogsheads of molasses on board; they confined the officers and carried off the molasses.

1775. Lord DUNMORE, the royal governor of Virginia, with his family, took refuge on board the Fowey, British man-of-war, at Yorktown.

1776. The Declaration of Independence of the United States proclaimed from the steps of the state house at Philadelphia, and read to the army in the city of New York.

1777. Battle of fort Ann; the British defeated the Americans under colonel Livingston, who retreated to fort Edward. The Americans lost 128 cannon and considerable stores.

1778. The French fleet under count d'Estaing arrived off the Delaware, having been at sea 87 days.

1779. The British under governor TRYON plundered and burnt Norwalk, Conn. Two churches, 80 dwellings, 87 barns, 22 stores, 4 mills and 5 vessels were destroyed.

1784. TORBERN BERGMAN, a Swedish chemist and natural philosopher, died. He was the friend of Linnæus, and an able and successful investigator of the secrets of nature.

1790. RENWICK WILLIAMS, known in London as the *Monster*, was convicted of cutting the garments of Miss Porter. The judge reserved the case till he could determine whether the crime was felony or only a misdemeanor. Williams was a dancing master and for years a great nuisance in London.

1793. The dauphin, LOUIS XVII, taken from his mother and placed in the care of the *sans culotte* cobbler, Simon, under whose tender mercies he soon yielded up his life.

1797. EDMUND BURKE, a British writer, orator and statesman of great eminence, died. His complete works have been published in 16 vols. octavo.

1813. Outposts of the American encampment at fort George attacked by the British and Indians. A company under lieutenant Eldridge was sent to support the posts, but fell into an ambush, and after an obstinate struggle 13 were killed, 5 escaped; the remainder, including lieutenant Eldridge, were taken prisoners and put to death by the Indians with great barbarity. In consequence of this event and similar outrages, general Brown received into the service of the United States a party of Seneca and Tuscarora Indians, under young Cornplanter.

1814. The Americans under Gen. SCOTT succeeded in throwing a bridge over the Chippewa, and compelled general Riall to retreat to Ten-mile creek. General Brown occupied the British works the same evening.

1822. THOMAS FANSHAW MIDDLETON, bishop of Calcutta, died. He was the first to hold that office, and was distinguished for talents and acquirements, zeal and fidelity.

1838. Treaty of peace concluded between Russia and Turkey.

1847. The canal from the Durance to Marseilles in France completed. More than one-fifth of its length is through the Alps in tunnels.

1848. To test the effect of an eclipse upon animals five healthy linnets were put in a cage together and fed; at the end of it three of them were found dead; a dog which had long been kept fasting, and which was eating hungrily when the eclipse commenced, left his food as soon as the darkness set in; a colony of ants which had been working actively, suddenly ceased from their labors at the same moment.

1850. The Alabama historical society was organized at Tuskaloosa.

1852. A destructive fire at Montreal laid waste a considerable portion of the city.

1853. The American expedition under commodore Perry arrived at Japan.

1856. PRESTON S. BROOKS, indicted at Washington for an assault upon senator Sumner, was sentenced to pay a fine of $300.

JULY 9.

597 B. C. An eclipse of the sun, foretold by Thales.

518. ANASTASIUS I, the silentiary, died; who from obscure birth became emperor of the East by marrying the widow of the emperor Zeno.

551. The city of Berytus overthrown by an earthquake. It gave birth to Sanconiatho, the Phœnician historian, about the period of the Trojan war, in the time of Hercules.

552. The Armenians commenced their era, Tuesday. The year, like the Noetic, consists of twelve months of thirty days, with an insertion of five, or (in leap year) six days, after the 5th of August, when their ecclesiastical year commences. In their correspondence with Europeans, they usually adopt, as in Russia, the old Julian style, and the months.

1228. STEPHEN LANGTON, archbishop of Canterbury, died. He was a man of great abilities as a writer and a politician. He was nominated to the office of archbishop by the pope, 1207, which being considered as an usurpation of the rights of the king of England, lead to a quarrel between those dignitaries, which terminated disastrously to the king.

1386. Battle of Sempach, in the canton of Lucerne, which established the independence of Switzerland. Leopold II, duke of Austria, was killed in this battle.

1535. ANTHONY DUPRAT, a very eminent French statesman, died. He was president of the parliament of Paris, and a man who, to increase his fortune or enlarge his power, did not hesitate to sacrifice either fame or virtue.

1546. ROBERT MAXWELL died. He was chiefly instrumental in bringing and procuring the passage of an act in the Scottish parliament permitting the reading of the scriptures in the vulgar tongue.

1598. DAVID BOUCHARD, governor of Perigord, killed at the siege of Lisle. He was a famous chieftain under Henry IV of France.

1669. The encenia, or dedication of the incomparable theatre at Oxford, endowed and founded 1664, by archbishop Selden. The first act held in a secular building was kept there on the same day. Wren adopted his ground plan from the theatre of Marcellus at Rome.

1693. The English or confederated army defeated by the French at Landon.

1742. JOHN OLDMIXON, an English historian and poet, died. He was a man of learning and abilities, but a violent party writer, and a severe and malevolent critic.

1746. PHILIP V of Spain, died. His accession to the throne was opposed by the archduke of Austria, and gave rise to one of the most bloody wars on record.

1755. Memorable defeat of BRADDOCK on his march to fort Du Quesne. The English army of 1,200 was ambuscaded, the general having neglected all precautions against such an event, and totally routed by the French and Indians, about 900 in number. Of 85 officers 64 were killed, and about half the privates. The remains of the army were brought off by Washington, who was the only officer on horseback that escaped.

1762. Revolution in Russia, followed by the abdication of Peter III. The empress Catharine was declared autocratrix, and Peter imprisoned, where he died seven days afterwards.

1762. A substance called honey dew fell in the neighborhood of Rathiermuc, Ireland, which loaded the trees and long grass in such a manner that quantities of it were saved by scoops.

1766. JONATHAN MAYHEW died; a distinguished American clergyman, and missionary among the Indians.

1776. The leaden statue of George III, in New York, thrown down by the revolutionists, and sent to Litchfield, Conn., where the women manufactured it into bullets.

1781. Captain EGGLESTON, of Lee's legion, routed a British foraging party at Friday's ferry, Congaree river, and took 45 dragoons.

1785. WILLIAM STRAHAN, an eminent Scottish printer, died. Having served a regular apprenticeship, he settled in London, where he rose to great eminence in his profession, and finally sat in parliament.

1790. Action off cape Musalo, between the Swedish fleet under the king in person, and the Russian fleet. It continued into the following day, and resulted in the destruction of 5 Russian frigates, 15 galleys, 2 floating batteries, 9 galliots, and 2 other floating vessels. The Swedes lost but one of their galleys burnt.

1794. Seventy-one persons were guillotined at Paris.

1805. GEORGE WOLFGANG PANZER, a distinguished German bibliographer, died. He published a catalogue of all the works known to have been printed from the invention of the art of printing to the year 1536. The works in all languages are chronologically arranged, the place of printing given, also a short account of them, and the libraries and publications in which they are contained.

1806. Confederation of the Rhine signed at Paris, between Bonaparte and several of the smaller German states, who placed themselves under the protection of France, and renounced their connection with the German empire.

1810. The kingdom of Holland annexed to France; Amsterdam to rank as the third city in the empire, Paris being first and Rome second.

1814. United States army under general Brown left Riall's works on the Chippewa, and pursued the British to Queenstown, and encamped there.

1816. Rio de la Plata declared itself independent of Spain, and took the title of the United Provinces of South America.

1818. RICHARD BEATNIFFE, the well known author of the *Norfolk Journal*, died at Norwich, England.

1830. Erzeroum, the capital of Turkish Armenia, surrendered to the Russians.

1831. The Belgian congress acceded to the articles agreed on at London by the plenipotentiaries of the five great powers, and declared Leopold of Saxe-Coburg king of Belgium.

1838. ROBERT GRANT, governor of Bombay, died; a man greatly respected for his talents and his public services.

1843. WASHINGTON ALSTON, the great historical painter of South Carolina, died.

1850. ZACHARY TAYLOR, president of the United States, died, aged 65. He was a general in the United States army, and won laurels in the Mexican war.

1853. CHARLES CALDWELL, a medical writer and teacher of great celebrity, died at Louisville, Ky., aged 90.

1854. RICHARD SHUBRICK PINCKNEY, a naval officer of the United States, died at Charlestown, S. C., aged 57. He entered the navy in 1814, and was engaged in the operations against the Algerine pirates of the Mediterranean, where he was severely wounded. He commanded the Decatur during the Mexican war.

JULY 10.

70. Conflagration of the second temple of the Jews, in the night following the ninth day of Lous (Ab) the second year of Vespasian.

138. PUBLIUS ÆLIUS ADRIAN, emperor of Rome, died. He was a renowned general and great traveler; and on a visit to Britain built the British wall, extending from Newcastle to Carlisle, 80 miles in length.

983. Pope BENEDICT VII died.

1024. BENEDICT VIII, pope, died. To the arts of the politician he added the valor of the warrior, and exterminated the Saracens who invaded Italy. He also defeated the Greeks, who were ravaging Apulia.

1212. Burning of London bridge, when 3000 persons inhabiting that borough perished in the flames.

1440. An anniversary was held in Haarlem for two days, commemorating the invention of printing on movable wooden types in this year, by Lawrence Coster. The emblems on his monument are a branch of beech, a winged A, a wreathed snake and a lamp. It was also celebrated by the printers of Dortrecht and Rotterdam.

1460. Battle of Northampton, England; the forces of Henry VI defeated by earls Warwick, Salisbury and March, with great slaughter among the gentry and nobility on both sides, and Henry was taken prisoner.

1472. The siege of Beauvais, France, raised by Charles the Bold, duke of Burgundy, who had invested it with an army of 80,000 men. An anniversary is still held on this day in memory of the heroine Jeane Hachette, and her regiment of women, who signalized themselves at this famous siege.

1559. HENRY II, of France, died. He was a persecutor of the protestants, and during the thirteen years of his reign, much embroiled in war. He recovered Calais from the English, and was wounded at a tournament, of which he died. (See June 26, 1574; 29, 1559.)

1579. WILLIAM WHITTINGHAM, dean of Durham, died. He was one of the translators of the Genevan or German Bible, usually called the *Breeches Bible.*

1584. WILLIAM I, prince of Orange, assassinated. He is styled the father of the Dutch republic, having brought about the union of the provinces. He was shot in the breast with three balls by an assassin supposed to have been employed by the king of Spain, who claimed the sovereignty of the Netherlands.

1634. DE VRIES sailed from the Texel in the ship King David, 14 guns, with 25 head of cattle, and 30 planters, intending to form a colony on the coast of Guyana.

1680. LEWIS MORERI, a learned French writer, died, aged 37; author of the great historical dictionary, which appeared 1674, and was afterwards enlarged to 10 vols. folio, and greatly improved in the numerous editions it underwent.

1683. FRANCIS EUDES DE MEZERAI, a French historian, died. He entered upon the laborious character of historian of France at the age of 26, and his work was received with universal applause. Several other books were also published by him, reflecting great honor upon his integrity, candor and faithfulness.

1686. JOHN FELL, an English prelate, died. During the civil war he bore arms for the king, and lost his offices by his loyalty. He was distinguished for learning and assiduity, and published many excellent works.

1688. The city of Smyrna in Asia destroyed by an earthquake.

1689. "Here lyeth the Body of Mr. David Gardiner, of Gardiner Island, deceased IVLY 10, 1689, in the Fifty-fourth year of his Age. Well, sick, dead, in one hour's space. Hartford, Con." He was the first white child born in Connecticut.

1704. The fortress of Gibraltar in Spain taken by the British.

1733. Nearly 800,000 quarters of grain exported from England to Portugal; cost, £1,000,000 sterling.

1767. ALEXANDER MONROE, a Scottish physician, anatomist and writer, died. His *Osteology* has been translated into several languages.

1776. New York declared an independent state.

1777. Major-general Prescott, commander of the British army at Newport, surprised at night in his quarters, and carried off by a party of 40 Americans.

1780. French fleet under admiral Ternay, arrived at Rhode Island, having on board 6000 French troops under count Rochambeau, intended for the American service.

1791. Battle of Maclin; a body of 70,000 Turks under the grand vizier, defeated by the Russians. The Turks lost 4000 killed, and the whole of their camp; 30 cannon, and 15 standards were taken. The flower of the Asiatic troops, with their chiefs were in this battle.

1792. CHABANON, a French dramatist and translator, died. His best works belong to a species of criticism which is characterized by learning and taste.

1794. Battle in India between the British army, and the Hindoos under Viziaram Rauze, rajah of Vizigapatam. The rajah and most of his officers were killed; British loss 10 killed, 50 wounded.

1796. Island of Elba seized by the English under Duncan and lord Nelson.

1799. The French under LA GRANGE surprised the Mamelukes at Sababier, in Egypt, took their baggage, 50 horses and 700 camels.

1799. Action between American ship Planter, captain Watts, 18 guns and 43 men, and a French privateer of 22 guns, which was beaten off "after an action of 5 glasses." Two female passengers, Mrs. MacDowell and Miss Mary Harley, dressed the wounded and supplied cartridges. The Planter had 4 killed, 8 wounded.

1804. FRANCIS AMBROSE DIDOT, a learned and ingenious French printer, died. He made some important improvements in the printing press and paper mill, and is supposed to have hastened his death by a too close application to the revision of an edition of Montaigne's works.

1810. Ciudad Rodrigo surrendered to the French under Massena, with a garrison of 6000, after having been bombarded 25 days, a great quantity of artillery, ammunition and rich stores were taken. This fortress was built by the Spanish as a rampart against Portugal, from which it is distant only 8 miles. (See Jan. 19.)

1810. Holland incorporated with the French empire, by which all the 17 provinces of the Netherlands were united under the dominion of Napoleon.

1826. LUTHER MARTIN, an eminent lawyer and one of the delegates from Maryland in forming the constitution of the United States, died, aged 82.

1828. LOUIS AUGUSTIN GUILLAUME BOST, a well known French naturalist and professor at the Jardin du Roi, died.

1834. Abolition riots in New York.

1850. JAMES LOVEL, oldest member of the society of the Cincinnatti, died at St. Matthews, S. C., aged 92.

1852. A fire in Boston destroyed the Mariner's church, the Sailor's home, the Boylston school house, and many dwellings and stores.

1855. The British bombarded the Redan tower at Sebastopol, for one day.

1856. JOHN LOCKE, an American physician and naturalist, died at Cincinnati, aged 64. He was a native of Maine, but spent a considerable portion of his life in Cincinnati; was connected with the geological survey of the state, and of lake Superior, and seems to have had a knowledge of various other sciences.

JULY 11.

472. PROCOPIUS ANTHEMIUS, emperor of Rome, murdered. He acquired the title of Augustus by his valor. Ricimir, a general to whom he had given his daughter in marriage, burst the gates of Rome, and imbrued his hands in the blood of his father-in-law, while his barbarian followers were indulged without control, in the three-fold license of murder, rapine and indiscriminate pillage.

1103. ERIC (the good), king of Denmark, died at Cyprus.

1191. Acre, in Palestine, surrendered by the Saracens to the crusaders under Richard of England and Philip of France, who had besieged it two years. Nine battles were fought in the vicinity of mount Carmel, with such vicissitudes of fortune, that in one attack the sultan forced his way into the city, while in a sally the Christians penetrated the royal tent. There were slain, by the computation of the minister of Saladin, 100,000 Christians.

1450. JACK CADE, an Irishman who headed a rebellion in England, was slain near Lewes, and his head placed on London bridge.

1576. MARTIN FROBISHER, the navigator, descried Friesland "rising like pinnacles of steeples and all covered with snow;" and entered, with his two small barks, the strait which bears his name.

1628. WILLIAM DANIEL died; a famed Greek and Hebrew scholar, translator of the New Testament and liturgy into Irish.

1708. Battle of Oudenarde, in Belgium, between the French and the allied army under the duke of Marlborough and prince Eugene. The French were defeated with the loss of 15,000; loss of the allies 5000.

1724. MARY MANLEY died; an English authoress, of considerable reputation as a writer, but of a wanton and licentious character. She wrote principally plays and romances.

1754. The Indians, who had been assembled to attend the congress of the colonies at Albany, were dismissed apparently well pleased and had engaged their coöperation with the colonies against the French. One of the sachems chalked out a sketch of the interior forests, rivers and lakes, with a clear discernment of their relations, and made the judicious remark, that Louisburg was one key of the inland country, and New York another, and that the power which had both, would open the great chest, and have Indians and all.

1763. PETER FORSKAL died; a celebrated Swedish naturalist and oriental traveler.

1764. ANDREW CANTWELL died; an Irish practitioner and writer on medicine of considerable abilities.

1782. JOHN JAMES FLIPART, a French engraver of great merit, died.

1782. Savannah, Georgia, evacuated by the British, and taken possession of by general Wayne.

1789. JAMES NECKER, the prime minister and great financier, ordered to leave France.

1797. CHARLES MACKLIN, an Irish actor and dramatic writer, died, aged 107. His name was M'Laughlin, which he changed for one more euphonious. His last performance was at the age of 90, when his memory failed him, and he took leave of the audience forever. His comedies still keep the stage.

1804. A duel fought between Aaron Burr and Alexander Hamilton, at Hoboken, opposite New York. On the first fire Hamilton fell mortally wounded, on the same spot where, a short time previous, his eldest son had been killed in a duel. He lingered until the afternoon of the following day, when he expired.

1807. MICHAEL NEKITITCH MINAVIEW, a Russian author of much distinction, died. One of his most admired productions is *Oskold*, which describes the march of the northern nations against Constantinople.

1809. Battle of Znaim; the French under Marmont, duke of Ragusa, defeated the Austrians, took 2 standards, 3 cannon and 3000 prisoners.

1811. Earthquake at St. Michael's one of the Azores; an island was formed where the water had been 30 fathoms in depth.

1812. United States frigate Essex captured a British transport with a detachment of the first regiment of Royal Scots on board.

1813. Blackrock taken by the British, who burnt the barracks, blockhouse, and other buildings, spiked several cannon, and took off a quantity of provisions, leaving on the shore a part of their killed and wounded.

1814. United States brig Rattlesnake captured by a British 50 gun ship. The Rattlesnake had some time previous thrown overboard all her guns except two, to escape another British man-of-war.

1814. The fort at Eastport, Moose island, mounting six 24 pounders, commanded by major Putnam with about 80 men, surrendered to a large British force. In consequence of this capture, the whole of the islands in Passamaquoddy bay fell into the hands of the enemy.

1818. The use of the French language in judicial proceedings and by the public authorities abolished in the Netherlands, only allowing advocates to make use of it for a certain time.

1853. An earthquake destroyed the city of Teheran, the capital of Persia, having a population of 60,000.

1853. SAMUEL APPLETON, one of the most opulent, benevolent and public spirited citizens of Boston, died, aged 87. His charitable donations for many years exceeded $25,000 per annum.

JULY 12.

100 B. C. Birthday of JULIUS CÆSAR, the Roman emperor. Pliny says of him that he could employ at the same time his ears to listen, his eyes to read, his hand to write, and his mind to dictate.

1174. King WILLIAM of Scotland taken by the famous chief-justiciary, Glanville. This success of the arms of king Henry has been attributed to his having, on the Thursday previous, done penance at the tomb of Thomas a Becket.

1191. The Christians took possession of the city of Acre. The two western kings planted the royal standard each in his own portion of the conquest, and divided the booty of the Saracens between them.

1212. The Christians defeated the Moors at Toulouse.

1536. DESIDERIUS ERASMUS, the celebrated Dutch philosopher, died. He was the most learned man of the age in which he lived, and greatly contributed to the restoration of learning in Europe. The *New Testament* in Greek (of which he was the first actual publisher, 1516), written with his own hand, is, with other relics, including his sword and pencil, to be seen at Basil, where he died.

1543. Marriage of HENRY VIII with the protestant lady, Catharine Parr, his sixth queen. Kate was a *doctor*, and a lover of learning; and survived the queen-killer.

1566. First stone of the walls of the Tuilleries at Paris laid, in the presence of Charles IX and his mother, Catharine de Medicis. The site of this famous palace had been occupied by a manufactory.

1581. MAURICE CHAUNCEY died at Paris; a French historian prior of the Carthusians, and confessor to queen Mary.

1609. HUDSON having continued his course westward for some days, first obtained sight of the American continent, and on the 17th, the fog having cleared up, ran into Penobscot bay, in the state of Maine.

1625. PAUL BENI, a learned Italian author, died. He censured the dictionary of the della crusca academy at Florence, and refuted its opinions in his defence of Tasso and Ariosto. His works were collected in 5 vols. folio.

1676. HENRY STUBBE, a learned English author, drowned. His writings are very numerous and instructive, and evince great research; at the same time they abound in abuse, satire and malevolence.

1691. Battle of Aghrim in Ireland; the French under Gen. St. Ruth defeated and himself killed by the forces of William III under Gen. Ginckle. Of the French and Irish catholics 4000 were slain and 600 taken, with their baggage, artillery, &c.; English lost 800 on the field.

1691. Cardinal PIGNATELLI elected pope, and took the name of Innocent III.

1712. RICHARD CROMWELL died, aged 82. He assumed the protectorate of England on the death of his father, but found himself inadequate to sustain the office, and resigned it to retire to more peaceful pursuits. He inherited little of his father's ambition.

1637. JOHNSON, "a stranger in London," addressed Cave, editor of the *Gentleman's Magazine*, " having observed in his papers very uncommon encouragement to men of letters." In this letter he proposed a translation from the Italian of Sarpi.

1730. LAWRENCE CORSINE elected pope, the conclave having sat four months.

1776. Lord HOWE arrived from Europe with a formidable squadron and 30,000 men, chiefly Hessians, and joined his brother Gen. Howe on Staten island.

1776. Capt. Cook sailed on his third and last voyage of discovery.

1779. Biœrnstahl, a learned Swedish professor of the oriental languages, died at Salonica in Turkey.

1780. Sumpter with 133 men attacked and defeated a detachment of British at Williamson's plantation, South Carolina.

1791. Baba Mahomet, dey of Algiers, died, aged 80. He was one of the most singular characters of the age; raised himself from a common soldier to the throne, and governed a nation of barbarians more than 25 years with uncommon reputation. He was succeeded by Sidi-Hassan, his prime minister, whose succession was accomplished, for the first time, without bloodshed.

1793. The first official trial of the Clauda Chappe telegraph was made with complete success; transmitting despatches 'forty-eight leagues in 13 min. 40 sec.

1794. Battle of Edikhoffen commenced, which continued three days. The French lost 1000 killed, and 6000 prisoners fell into the hands of the Prussians; notwithstanding which the French finally obtained the victory, and obliged Moellendorf to retreat 60 miles.

1796. Ninety-four prisoners taken by the Algerines on board American vessels, were redeemed by the United States consul at Algiers.

1798. The knights of St. John at Malta surrendered to Bonaparte. They had possessed the island nearly 270 years, and under them it had risen from a state of destitution to a place of great opulence and luxury; and the military works which remain to this day, are a monument of their perseverance and power.

1801. Action off the coast of Spain between the British fleet, 5 sail of the line, and the combined French and Spanish fleet of 13 sail, and a considerable number of gun boats. Two of the Spanish ships, of 112 guns each, blew up, another of 74 was taken, and the remainder made their way into Cadiz.

1803. Charles Jordan died in Anson county, North Carolina, aged 114. His favorite amusement was hunting, and only four days before his death he killed two deer at a shot.

1804. Alexander Hamilton, an American statesman, died of a wound received in a duel with Col. Burr. Hamilton was born on the island of St. Croix 1757, and came to New York in 1773. At the commencement of the war he joined the army, and was an aid-de-camp to Washington, and afterwards a major-general. He continued in the service until the surrender of Cornwallis at Yorktown, where the troops under his command stormed and took the British works. He afterwards commenced the practice of law in New York, and rose to the highest eminence in the profession. He was appointed secretary of the treasury under Washington. As a statesman and a financier he revived the public credit, and placed the United States revenue on a permanent footing. Of all the coadjutors and advisors of Washington, Hamilton was doubtless the one in whose judgment and sagacity he reposed the greatest confidence, whether in military or civil career; and of all the American statesmen, he displayed the most comprehensive understanding and the most varied ability, whether applied to subjects practical or speculative. A collection of his works was issued in New York some time after his death, in 3 vols. octavo.

1807. Ratification of the peace between Bonaparte and the king of Prussia at Tilsit.

1812. The United States frigate Constitution completely manned and equipped, under the command of Com. Isaac Hull, left Anapolis in Chesapeake bay, for New York, and made a singular escape from the British squadron, consisting of a sixty-four gun ship, three frigates and a schooner, by running into Nantucket harbor. She was chased sixty hours, and escaped by *kedging*, an invention of Chas. Morris.

1812. Gen. Hull, with an army of United States volunteers invaded Canada.

1814. John Swift, a revolutionary soldier and brigadier general in the United States army, killed whilst reconnoitering the British positions at Queenstown. He had surprised an outpost, and was most basely shot in the breast by a soldier who had begged and received quarters. Swift however, killed the soldier himself.

1816. A slide from the bank of West Canada creek, near the village of Herkimer, carried nearly five acres of land into the creek.

1816. A dreadful storm burst upon the town of Worchestz, in Hungary, which injured every house in the place; damage estimated at four millions of florins.

1823. The Diana steam boat, built at Kidderpore, near Calcutta, launched; and on the same day she made her first voyage on the Ganges between Calcutta and Chinsoorah in six hours and a half. This was the first appearance of these boats in the east.

1832. The monolithic column, in honor of Alexander of Russia, was debarked at St. Petersburg. It measures 12 feet in diameter at the base, and is 84 feet in length; being the largest pillar of modern erection. It was raised upon its pedestal in September following.

1836. William Murray died near Jonesborough, Tenn., aged 111.

1838. John Jamieson, an eminent Scottish seceder, died, aged 80. He is the author of several theological and miscellaneous works, and of a celebrated *Etymological Dictionary of the Scottish Language.*

1841. Wm. James McNeveen, so celebrated as a physician and author, died at New York.

1851. Daguerre, inventor of the daguerreotype, died at Paris, aged 61.

1854. Louis Dwight died at Boston, aged 61. He was a native of Stockbridge, Mass., and graduated at Yale college in 1813. On the formation of the Prison discipline society, he was appointed corresponding secretary, and devoted the remainder of his life to the promotion of the interests of this important institution of public economy and Christian philanthropy.

1855. A convention of the friends of slavery was held at Lexington, Mo.

1855. A mob at Jonesville, Mo., seized a prisoner whom a jury had found guilty of murder, for which the statute punishment was imprisonment for life, and hung him on a tree.

1856. The Crimea was evacuated by the last of the allied forces of Great Britain and France.

1856. The submarine telegraph cable was laid across the St. Lawrence gulf, from cape Race cove, Newfoundland, and Ashby bay, cape Breton, a distance of 85 miles, and messages transmitted from place to place.

JULY 13.

325. The first œcumenical council, that is, council of the whole habitable earth, assembled at Nice, now Isnick, in Bythinia, where 318 fathers of the church subscribed the ordinances regulating the festival of Easter, and establishing the Godhead, in opposition to the dogmas of Arius.

573. Pope John III died.

1024. Henry II, emperor of Germany, died. He was successful in arms against the Greeks and Saracens, whom he drove from Calabria, restored peace and tranquility in Italy and Germany, and increased his popularity by various deeds of benevolence and kindness wherever he went.

1377. Isle of Wight taken by the French and plundered.

1568. Elizabeth committed Mary queen of Scots to the castle of Bolton, a prisoner.

1571. George Fabricius, a learned German poet and historian, died, aged 55.

1621. Thomas Hariot, an English mathematician, died. He accompanied sir Walter Raleigh to America, and wrote an account of Virginia. It is said that Descartes drew from his works many of his improvements in algebra.

1629. Gaspard Bertholin, a Swedish physician and divine, died. He is said to have learned to read perfectly in 14 days at the age of 3, and to compose with correctness Greek and Latin orations at the age of 13. His works are on anatomy, metaphysics, logic, and rhetoric.

1637. Battle with the Pequods, in which the last body of that formidable tribe was exterminated. They had secreted themselves in a swamp near where Fairfield now stands, in Connecticut; when some of the rangers who were in pursuit of them discovering their lurking place, rushed in upon them, in defiance of their arrows, and the hazard of being swallowed in the miry bogs. After a fruitless parley, the Indians refusing to come to terms, the soldiers were ordered to cut through the swamp with their swords, in order to hem them in, till they were begirt in a narrow space and remained all night sorely galled by the fire of their besiegers. Taking advantage of a dense fog, some of the stoutest made their escape, leaving the rest to the mercy of their conquerors. They were discovered in the morning sitting in crowds, sullenly refusing to ask for their lives, and were shot by dozens or cut in pieces. The male children which were taken were sent to the Bermudas, and the females distributed to the English towns. This overthrow of a great and powerful nation, cast a terror upon the arms of the colonists, which brought other tribes to a lasting peace.

1650. Dr. Levins, a civilian, was hanged for having in his possession blank commissions from Charles II, against the commonwealth.

1677. William Berkeley, governor of Virginia, died in England, after having administered the office nearly 40 years. His measures were generally bigoted and revengeful.

1730. Elijah Fenton, an English poet and divine, died. He assisted Pope in the translation of the *Odyssey.*

1750. The excessive heat of the weather at this time caused the fish in the Thames to assemble in shoals under the bank, where they were readily caught.

1759. Battle of Zullechan, in which the Prussians were defeated by the Russians.

1762. James Bradley, an English astronomer, died. He made some important discoveries, and greatly improved the instruments which enrich the celebrated observatory at Greenwich.

1772. Captain James Cook sailed on his second voyage round the world.

1774. Charles Frey de Neuville, a French Jesuit, died, aged 81. He was long known as an eloquent preacher; but on the suppression of his order he retired into privacy.

1774. William Johnson, Indian agent, died at his seat near Johnstown, during the sitting of a convention at his place. He was a man of stern and determined purpose, but urbane and conciliatory when necessary, and held a greater controlling influence over the Indians than any other individual since the settlement of the province.

1785. Stephen Hopkins, a signer from Rhode Island, died. He was a man of learning and a powerful speaker. His signature to the declaration is indicative of a tremulous hand, owing to a nervous affection, which compelled him, when he wrote, to guide his right arm with his left.

1788. An extraordinary and destructive hail storm happened in France, converting many of the richest autumnal prospects into arctic desolations.

1793. Jean Paul Marat, a notorious leader of the French revolution, assassinated. He was a humble physician in Paris when the storm of anarchy burst forth, and became the most insatiable advocate of human slaughter of all the blood-thirsty demons by whom he was surrounded. He endeavored to get up a general massacre, and publicly demanded 270,000 executions.

1795. Action between the British fleet, admiral Hotham, and the French fleet. French ship Alcide struck, but took fire and blew up with several hundred of her crew on board, who perished.

1807. James Bernouilli 3d, a Swiss astronomer, died. He was one of an illustrious family of scientific men.

1809. Senegal, in Africa, taken by the British.

1810. Francis James Jackson, British minister, burnt in effigy before the door of his lodgings in Albany.

1813. A British fleet of 11 ships, captured and plundered Portsmouth and Ocracoke, in North Carolina, and took the privateers Anaconda of New York, and Atlas of Philadelphia, then lying in port.

1831. James Northcote, an English artist of some celebrity, died in Argyle st. London.

1843. John Rowan, an eminent statesman and jurist, of Kentucky, died at Louisville.

1851. John Lingard, the well known catholic historian of England, died at Hornby, aged 82.

1854. San Juan bombarded by the United States sloop of war Cyane, captain Hollins; and a party landing from the sloop burnt the entire town, with the exception of two small buildings. A demand had previously been made upon the authorities, by Capt. Hollins, for satisfaction for alleged injuries, but without effect. A considerable portion of the property destroyed belonged to Americans. One British vessel of war in the harbor protested against the act.

1854. Battle of Gaymas, between some Frenchmen under count Raousset de Boulbon, and the Mexicans under Col. Yanez. The former were defeated, the count taken prisoner, and shot on the 12th August.

1854. A riot occurred at Buffalo growing out of street preaching.

JULY 14.

66. It was on the 14th of *Lous*, during the festival of Zylophory, or wood carrying, at Jerusalem, to feed the perpetual fire at the sacred altar, that the zealots destroyed the house of Ananias the chief priest, and the palaces of Agrippa and Berenice, with all the public archives, containing the bonds of debtors, "the nerves of the city."

1099. Jerusalem taken by the crusaders.

1420. Battle of Prague; 4000 Hussites under their celebrated leader Zisca, repelled the Bohemian army of 30,000 under the emperor Sigismund.

1514. Christopher Bainbridge, an English archbishop, poisoned at Rome. He was the envoy of Henry VIII to the pope, where he distinguished himself.

1584. Balthazar Gerard, the assassin of William prince of Orange, whom he shot through the breast with a pistol as he was going out of his palace at Delft, was executed in the same manner as Damiens (q. v.) and died, in his own conceit, a martyr of the church of Rome.

1675. Mendon, Mass., attacked by the Nipmuck Indians, and several persons killed. Mather says: "blood was never shed in Massachusetts, in the way of hostility, before this day."

1678. The expedition under M. de la Salle set out from Rochelle, consisting of thirty men, among whom were pilots, smiths, carpenters, and other useful artists.

1683. Mustapha, the grand vizier, sat down before Vienna with an army of 150,000 Turks, and opened the trenches.

1694. Bombardment and destruction of Dieppe, in France, by the English.

1699. William Bates, an English nonconformist divine, died. He was chaplain to Charles II, a man of great learning, and the intimate friend of the first men of the kingdom.

1711. The prince of Nassau, stadtholder of Friesland, was drowned in his coach while ferrying over the Hollandsdiep, near Moerdyk.

1719. Bell, the traveler, left St. Petersburg with Ismayloff the ambassador and a numerous retinue for China. They took the route by Moscow, Siberia and the great Tartar deserts, and did not reach Pekin until sixteen months after their departure from the Russian capital, having undergone great fatigue during the journey.

1741. EDWARD SYNGE, an Irish bishop, died. He distinguished himself for above twenty years as an active and laborious parish priest; and his tracts, written in a popular style, have been considered of so much value as to require frequent editions.

1742. RICHARD BENTLEY, a celebrated English divine and classical scholar, died. His editions of the ancient classics procured him a great reputation for learning, but they were made the medium for retorting upon his contemporaries, who assailed him on all sides.

1748. An eclipse of the sun observed at London. 10 digits eclipsed, and Venus seen in a crescent form through a telescope.

1762. PETER III (*Fedrowitch*), emperor of Russia, died in prison. He acquired the enmity of the nobility and clergy by trenching upon their privileges, and introducing foreign customs, and was hurled from his throne by a conspiracy, after a reign of six months, and probably murdered.

1766. The grand junction canal commenced, uniting the Trent with the Mersey, and opening a water communication with both the east and west coasts of England. This great improvement was originated with Brindsley, who is represented to have "handled rocks as you would plum pies, and made the four elements subservient to his will."

1774. Captain FURNEAUX, who sailed in the discovery ship Adventure with captain Cook, returned with the ship, having reached 67° 10′ north, and circumnavigated the globe.

1776. WASHINGTON refused to receive a letter from lord Howe, addressed to "George Washington, Esq.," and afterwards another addressed to "George Washington, &c., &c., &c." The British lion, on further study, gave his message the proper direction.

1780. CHARLES BATTEUX, a French philosopher, died; eminent for his erudition and his private virtues, and author of several works on classical literature.

1788. Congress ratified the constitution framed by the convention of which Washington was president, and it went into operation the ensuing March.

1789. Marquis DE MIRABEAU, an advocate of Quesnay's sect of political economists, and author of *Ami des Hommes*, died. He was father of the fiery orator, count Mirabeau.

1789. Destruction of the Bastile, at Paris. This awful fortress of despotism, of which the name had for ages inspired terror, and which had withstood a vigorous siege about two centuries previous, was invested by a mixed multitude of citizens and soldiers. De Launay, the governor, displayed a flag of truce and demanded a parley, but abusing the confidence which that signal inspired, he discharged a heavy fire of cannon and musketry on the besiegers. This act of treachery, so far from intimidating the people, inflamed their rage and rendered them desperate. They renewed the attack with frenzy, and carried the prison by assault. The governor was seized and massacred, and his head carried in triumph through the streets. The Bastile was razed to the ground, and with it the despotism of the French monarchy fell prostrate in the dust. It cost 200,000 livres to demolish this edifice to its foundations, and the materials were sold for 36,000.

1790. GIDEON ERNEST LAUDOHN, an Austrian field marshal, died. He was commander-in-chief of the Austrian forces, and so high was his reputation, that Frederic the Great of Prussia admitted that he feared nobody so much as Laudohn.

1790. Grand national confederation of France, at Paris, in the field of Mars, when the civic oath was administered. Accommodations were made for exhibiting at one view 350,000 persons on this occasion, in a vast amphitheatre.

1791. Commencement of the Birmingham riots, which were occasioned by the celebration of the anniversary of the French revolution, by some private individuals. The destruction of property was very great; Dr. Priestly's house, library, manuscripts and philosophical apparatus were totally consumed.

1794. British squadron captured, on the American station, 14 sail of French ships laden with provisions.

1795. The British took Simonstown, cape of Good Hope.

1796. The British post of Oswego delivered up to the Americans, agreeable to treaty stipulations. The British had continued to occupy stations within the state of New York since the revolution. As they marched out the United States troops marched in, planted a standard on the ramparts, and fired a salute of 15 guns.

1798. Congress passed the famous act for the punishment of sedition, &c., against the United States, commonly called the *gag law*.

1798. Battle of Chebriessa, in Egypt, the French under Bonaparte defeated the Mamelukes by land and water.

1807. George Saville Carey, an English dramatist and poet, died. He was bred to the profession of a printer, which he left for the stage. His writings all tend to awaken patriotic, generous and amiable emotions.

1808. Battle of Riosecco, in Spain; the French under Gen. Bessieres, came upon the united armies of Castile and Leon, and defeated them in a desperate action, in which 20,000 Spaniards perished. This calamitous battle opened the gates of Madrid to Joseph Bonaparte.

1813. The United States schooner Asp, of twenty men and two guns, attacked by five British barges; after a gallant resistance, in which she lost ten of her men and her commander, she was abandoned to the enemy.

1814. The British schooner Balaboo, of six guns, captured by the American privateer schooner Perry of five guns, after a running fight of fifty, and a close action of ten minutes.

1817. Anna Louisa Germaine Necker, baroness de Stael Holstein, died. Her talents were so early displayed that she was said never to have been a child, and she became distinguished at an early age as a writer, and by the spirit of her conversation. She was banished twice by Napoleon for attempting to thwart his government. Her works form 17 vols.

1834. Edmund Charles Genet, a French statesman, died. He was a minister to the United States in 1793, and when superceded he remained in the country, and settled on the Hudson river.

1836. Isabella James died at Montego bay, Jamaica, aged 110.

1848. A portion of the levee fell in at New Orleans, by which a number of persons were drowned and much property destroyed.

1852. The college of the Holy Cross, at Worcester, Mass., destroyed by fire, partially damaging the library, which was otherwise wholly saved.

1853. Com. Perry landed at Japan, and delivered to the imperial commissioners the letter from the American president.

1853. The crystal palace opened at New York, in presence of the president of the United States, and many other dignitaries.

1854. Duc d'Ecklingen, second son of marshal Ney, died at Gallipoli. He commanded a brigade of cavalry in the French army of the east.

1854. Abbas Pasha, viceroy of Egypt, died at Benha, a small town on the Nile. He had reigned over Egypt since 1848. He was very unpopular, and under his rule the population decreased, and those that remained lived in great wretchedness. The only remarkable work of his reign was the commencement of the railway from Cairo to Alexandria.

1856. Enoch Lewis, a prominent member of the society of Friends, died at Philadelphia, aged 81. He wrote much in explanation of the principles and practice of his sect, was for many years editor of the *Friend's Review*, and was also noted for his attainments in mathematics.

JULY 15.

496 b. c. Battle of Regillum, in which it is said the twin knights Castor and Pollux appeared upon white horses and assisted the Romans. In memory of this event an annual cavalcade was instituted at Rome, during which the knights, robed in purple, and crowned with olive wreaths, rode in solemn procession from the temple of Honor to the Capitol, where the censor, seated on his curule chair, passed judgment on their characters.

238. Maximus and Balbinus, emperors of Rome, murdered by the prætorian guards.

1099. Jerusalem taken by the crusaders on the 39th day of the siege. Two huge movable towers had been constructed, and rolled with great labor to the foot of the fortifications. From the tops of these they fought the besieged on even terms till afternoon, when a warrior named Letolde leapt upon the ramparts and was followed by all the other knights, and drove the Saracens down into the city. The standard of the cross was planted in triumph on the walls, and after 460 years of bondage, the holy city passed from under the Moslem yoke. The victory thus bravely won, was tarnished by the ferocity of the conquerors. The number who were slain in the city amounted to 70,000, and the Jews were burnt in their synagogues.

1535. Trajan's floating palace (which was sunk at a great depth in lake Nemi, Italy, 1340 years before) explored by Marchi in a diving machine. It was found in a tolerable state of preservation, measuring 500 feet in length, 270 in breadth and 60 in depth. This magnificent work was designed for the retirement of a prince celebrated for his magnificent taste, and were it possible to rescue it from its present position, or examine the interior, many valuable relics might be brought to light, to enrich the cabinet of the antiquarian if not to subserve the use of the sciences.

1546. The protestants having assembled a force of 70,000 foot, 15,000 horse, and 6,000 pioneers, with 120 cannon, 800 ammunition wagons, 8,000 beasts of burden, determined to support their cause by the force of arms. They issued a manifesto, and sent a letter to Charles V. (See July 20.)

They were, however, overcome without battle, in consequence of having separated themselves into small bodies early in 1547.

1557. ANNE OF CLEVES, one of the queens of Henry VIII of England, died. The king demanded her in marriage after having seen her picture. But the painter had flattered the beauty, and the king becoming disgusted with what he termed a *Flanders mare*, obtained a divorce and sent her home again. She retired, seemingly unconcerned, and no doubt considered it a matter of great good fortune to have escaped with life.

1557. A great dearth of breadstuffs in England; wheat £2 13s. 4d.; malt £2 4s.; peas £2 6d. per quarter.

1567. MARY, queen of Scots, unable by entreaties or threats, to induce her followers to fight any longer in her cause, surrendered herself up to her disaffected subjects, by whom she was imprisoned.

1570. IGNATIUS AZEVEDO, a Portuguese Jesuit, murdered. He relinquished the enjoyment of a large fortune to embark as a missionary to India, was captured by pirates, and with nineteen of his companions, barbarously massacred, near Palma.

1575. HENRY, duke of Anjou, divested of the Polish crown, in full diet, and the throne declared vacant.

1610. The Halve Maan, in which the first white man sailed up the Hudson river, arrived at Amsterdam on her return, having been detained in England since Nov. 7 of the previous year.

1614. PETER DE BOURDEILLES, lord-abbot of Brantome, in France, died. He served an apprenticeship in arms under Francis of Guise, and is supposed to have visited most of the countries of Europe, either in a military capacity or as a traveler. His memoirs or works were published in 1666, and several editions have since been printed. It is represented to be a rare work, but has never been translated into English. (*Biog. Univer.* says July 5, q. v.)

1685. JAMES, duke of Monmouth, beheaded. He was the natural son of Charles II, against whom he rebelled; and on the accession of James II, he invaded England, was defeated, (See July 5,) imprisoned and finally brought to the scaffold, after having made the most humiliating petitions for his life.

1715. BELL, the Scottish traveler, left St. Petersburg for Persia, with the Russian embassy, in the quality of physician. They were obliged by the severity of the weather to halt at Cazan and pass the winter, and were detained there till June 4, 1716. They then proceeded by Astraken, the Caspian sea and Tauris to Ispahan, where they arrived in 1717.

1716. The island of Corfu, besieged by 80,000 Turks, and defended by the Venetians, was attacked by the Turkish admiral with 22 ships, and an attempt was made by the land forces to storm the citadel; but the Venetian fleet destroyed that of the Turks, and the garrison, making a counter sally with 2000 men, took the Turks by surprise in the rear, who fled, leaving 4000 dead in the trenches.

1751. JOHN WILSON, an eminent English botanist, died. His occupation was that of a shoemaker, and he ranks among the self-elevated men, who without a liberal education have distinguished themselves by scientific and literary abilities. He became an expert and accurate botanist before Linnæus's method of discriminating species improved the science, and published a *Synopsis of British Plants.* He was the first writer that attempted a systematic arrangement of indigenous plants in the English language.

1761. DOMINICO PASSIONEI, a learned Italian cardinal, died. He made a valuable collection of books and manuscripts, and was particularly distinguished as the friend and patron of literature.

1769. The general court of Massachusetts refusing to make provision for the support of the British soldiery, with whose presence they were favored, governor Bernard prorogued that assembly.

1776. British king's ships Phœnix, Rose and two tenders, effected their passage to Tarrytown, on the Hudson, under a heavy cannonade from the New York batteries, &c.

1778. France declared war against England, and 40,000 men were assembled in Normandy for the invasion of England. The plan was not carried into effect, because the French and Spanish fleets, which were to protect the landing, were dispersed by contrary winds.

1782. WILLIAM DE BURE died; a Paris bookseller, famous for his knowledge of old, curious and valuable books.

1785. A new mufti of Constantinople prohibited the reading of foreign gazettes and newspapers, in whatever language they might be written, under severe penalties.

1789. LOUIS XVI, accompanied by his two brothers, went to the states general of France, and declared his determination to act in concert with the *national assembly*, a title which he then employed for the first time. They returned on foot to the palace, amid the shouts and blessings of an immense crowd.

1791. Great riot in Birmingham, England. Dr. Priestley's house and library destroyed by the mob. His philosophical apparatus was the best in the world, and his library and manuscripts above price, and not capable of being restored.

1795. Desperate engagement between a British private armed lugger of 12 guns, and 9 French vessels of 65 guns altogether. The French were beaten off after an incessant action of 18 hours.

1797. The exiled French ministers were permitted to return to France on taking an oath to support the constitution.

1800. BRYAN EDWARDS died; a British West India merchant, author of an elegant *History of the West Indies*, and other lesser productions, connected with the islands in that part of the world.

1802. THOMAS DERMODY, an Irish poet, died, aged 28. He was employed as Greek and Latin assistant in his father's school, at the age of 9 years; and is said to have written as much genuine poetry at 10, as either Cowley, Milton or Pope had produced at nearly twice that age. He was, at the same time, a depraved wretch, and died of intemperance.

1807. JOSEPH MCKEEN died; an American mathematician, and first president of Bowdoin college.

1808. MURAT placed upon the throne of Naples by Bonaparte, under the title of *king Joachim Napoleon*. He governed with prudence and vigor.

1815. BONAPARTE surrendered himself to captain Maitland, of the British ship Bellerophon.

1819. "A steam vessel entered one of our ports from America," says a British writer under this date.

1834. The inquisition again abolished in Spain.

1839. WINTHROP MACWORTH PRAED, an eminent English orator and statesman, died.

1853. An earthquake at Cumana, in Venezuela, South America, destroyed many edifices and killed 600 persons.

1855. The first legislature of the new state of Panama, formed of the provinces of Panama, Azuen, Veraguos and Chiriqui, met at Panama. Justo Arogemena was appointed superior chief.

JULY 16.

523 B. C. One hour before midnight at Babylon the moon was eclipsed 6 digits on her northern disk. This is believed to be the 5th eclipse on record.

622. The Hegira, or Mohammedan era, commenced. It was instituted by Omar, the second caliph, in imitation of the era of the martyrs, beginning with the first appearance of the new moon (the crescent), 68 days before the flight of Mohammed from Mecca to Medina.

1054. MICHAEL CERULARIUS, the Greek patriarch, excommunicated at Constantinople by the pope's legates. "Shaking the dust from their feet, they deposited on the altar of St. Sophia, a direful anathema, which enumerates the seven mortal heresies of the Greeks, and devotes them to the eternal society of the devil and his angels." The Greeks have never abandoned their errors, the popes have never repealed the sentence, and from this thunderbolt we may date the consummation of the scism between the two churches.

1212. Battle of Tolosa in Spain; the Moors defeated by Alphonso of Castile. This day became an anniversary festival called *The triumph of the Cross*.

1216. INNOCENT III died; he was a steadfast friend of king John of England.

1377. The baron PERCY created earl of Northumberland, by Richard II at his coronation.

1429. The town of Rheims in France was taken from the English by Joan of Arc, and on the following day the dauphin was crowned, an exploit which Joan had sworn to accomplish.

1439. Commencement of a direful pestilence and famine, which scourced England and France for two years, and caused an intermission of hostilities between the two countries.

1519. The first embassy sailed from Cortez to the king of Spain. He accompanied his letter by a present of all the gold he had received from the king of Mexico, including the two great wheels, one of gold, representing the Mexican century, curiously wrought, valued at 10,000 sequins, and the other of silver, representing the Mexican year, also wrought with figures in bas-relief. His object was to prepossess the king against the representations which might be made by the governor of Cuba.

1546. ANNE ASKEW (or *Ascough*), an accomplished protestant lady, after having been tortured, was burnt for heresy. It is remarkable that her husband was *accuser*, the lord chancellor *extortioner*, and the mayor of London *incendiary*, in that unmanly work.

1640. CORNELIUS VAN TIENHOVEN, secretary of New Netherland, at the head of one hundred men, made a rash attack upon the Raritans, who lived at a small river five miles behind Staten island; the soldiers committed excesses, which the Indians resented the following year.

1647. THOMAS ANELLO (or *Massaniello*), a fisherman of Naples, killed. He headed an insurrection, caused by the viceroy's laying a new tax on fruit, fish, &c. The sedition continued for ten days, when all kinds of barbarity were practiced, and Anello became supreme dictator over 150,000 people. He gave himself up to debauchery, and was despatched by four assassins and his body dragged through the streets with every mark of indignity.

1676. Maria Margaret de Brinvilliers, a French lady known for her intrigues and crimes, executed at Paris. She cut off her relatives by poison, and spared her husband only because he looked upon her crimes with indifference.

1691. Francis Michael le Tellier, a French statesman, died. He was a great favorite with Louis XIV, who on a certain occasion treated him with so much coolness that he returned home from the levee and died in his own apartment of vexation and grief. He was endowed with splendid talents, which he exerted for the benefit of his country.

1696. John Pearson, an English prelate, died; known by his valuable *Exposition of the Creed.*

1710. Battle of Alamanza, in Spain; Philip V of France defeated by the allies under Stanhope, with the loss of 1500 killed.

1717. Battle under the walls of Belgrade; the Austrians under prince Eugene defeated the Turks.

1719. James Keill, a Scottish physician, died in England; author of several valuable medical works.

1736. Thomas Yalden, an English poet and physician, died. His works are not the most polished, yet deserving of perusal.

1760. Battle of Exdorff; the prince of Brunswick defeated the Prussians, and took their commander Glaubitz, the prince of Anhalt-Cothen, and five battalions prisoners.

1761. Battle of Fillinghausen in the palatinate, between the allies under the hereditary prince Ferdinand, and the French under Broglio and Soubise. The French were defeated with the loss of 5000 and 9 cannon; loss of the allies 1200.

1767. Charles Molloy, an English dramatic writer, died. He also conducted *Fog's Journal*, and *Common Sense.*

1779. Stony point taken by the Americans. The assault was made at half-past 12 at night, when both columns rushed forward under a tremendous fire of musketry and grape shot, entered the works at the point of the bayonet. American loss 98 killed and wounded; British loss 63 killed, 543 prisoners, with 15 cannon and a considerable quantity of military stores.

1780. John Nicholas Hubert Hayer, a French ecclesiastic, died. His works display great zeal and learning.

1794. Mark Anthony Charrier, a French lawyer, beheaded at Paris. He was a member of the states general, and boldly opposed all innovations.

1786. Treaty of peace between the emperor of Morocco and the United States.

1789. The parliament of Paris insulted the king by a vote of thanks, but communicated their resolution only to the national assembly. The same day a great number of the nobility left France.

1794. Battle of Wigoya; the Poles defeated the Russians.

1795. Attack on the heights of St. Barbe at Quiberon, by the French emigrants, who were defeated by the French under Hoche, with the loss of 300.

1799. Aboukir in Egypt attacked and carried by assault by the Turks under Seid Mustapha Pasha, and the whole garrison, 700 in number, put to the sword. The castle of Aboukir with a garrison of 400, also surrendered immediately after.

1808. Battle of Baylen, in Spain, which terminated in the defeat and capture of general Dupont and his division, one of the first serious reverses of Napoleon in the peninsula.

1812. Colonel Cass with 280 men attacked and carried the bridge over the river Aux Canards, four miles from Malden. It was defended by a part of the British 41st regiment and some Indians.

1815. Bonaparte sent a flag of truce and entered the Bellerophon man-of-war, captain Maitland, who proceeded with his illustrious *ruin* to Torbay.

1832. The German diet, at Franckfort, issued a protocol suppressing the liberty of the press in Baden.

1833. Corner stone of New York University laid.

1838. George Domberger, a soldier under prince Eugene, died, aged 130. He married for the first time when in his 100th year. He was a special pensioner of the emperor of Austria.

1843. Samuel Hahnemann, founder of the homeopathic system of medical practice, died at Paris, aged 88.

1849. David B. Ogden, an eminent New York attorney, died. For more than half a century he was associated with the councils of the state and city of New York.

1849. Frost was seen at Pittsfield and vicinity, although the thermometer had been at 90° the day before.

1852. Louis Kossuth, the Hungarian revolutionist, left New York in the steamship Africa, for Liverpool, under the assumed name of Alexander Smith.

1854. Nathaniel Bowditch Blunt, an eminent New York attorney, died at Lebanon Springs.

1854. A day of humiliation and prayer observed at Bombay, and all over India, by the natives as well as the Europeans, for the success of the British arms.

1856 A formidable insurrection which had broken out at Madrid in Spain two days before, was suppressed after a sanguinary contest of 30 hours.

1857. Pierre Jean de Beranger, a French lyric poet, died, aged 77. His songs are at once a storehouse of gayety and satire, and a record of the history of his time.

JULY 17.

855. LEO IV, pope, died. He was a wise and courageous pontiff, who, when the Saracens approached Rome to pillage it, boldly marched out to meet them, unsupported by the emperors of the east or the west. The Saracens were defeated with great slaughter, and the captives employed to adorn and fortify the city they had come to destroy. The famous pope Joan succeeded for a few days to the papal chair.

1085. ROBERT GUISCARD, duke of Apulia, died at Corfu. He was a famous Norman knight, who assisted in the conquest of Naples from the Saracens.

1429. CHARLES VII, of France, crowned at Rheims. Joan of Arc, his supporter, was seated on horseback, helmeted, at his right side, with her triumphal banner unfurled.

1453. JOHN TALBOT, earl of Shrewsbury, killed. He distinguished himself in the reduction of Ireland, of which he was made governor by Henry V. This brave warrior, who was the terror of the French, and acquired the title of the English Achilles, accompanied the English army to France, and took several towns; but was finally killed in battle, near Castillon.

1525. An act of the English parliament was passed prohibiting the importation of any of Luther's books into England.

1530. TINDAL's translation of the *Pentateuch* was published at Marlborow (Marburg), in the land of Hesse. The violence of the times rendered concealment necessary.

1652. EDWARD SACKVILLE, earl Dorset, an English statesman, died. He was also sent with an army into Bohemia, and fought at the battle of Prague 1620.

1755. The British East India ship Doddington lost, and only 23 out of 273 persons saved.

1556. Battle of Valenciennes; the prince of Conde and don John of Austria, defeated the French under Turenne and La Ferte; the latter was captured. The French army was saved by the masterly manœuvres of Turenne.

1679. JAMES DUPORT, an English divine, died, whose great erudition as a classical scholar is evinced in the learned works which he published.

1786. Thirteen elm trees removed by a storm in Devonshire, Eng., 200 yards where they afterwards took root.

1791. The first bank in Albany began to discount, being the present bank of Albany.

1793. MARIE JOSEPH CHALIER, a French revolutionist, guillotined. He was an admirer of the sanguinary character of Marat, whom he determined to imitate at Lyons, where he was a merchant. He erected a guillotine, and had already marked 900 victims for sacrifice, when he fell into the snare himself.

1793. MARIE ANNE CHARLOTTE CORDAY D'ARMANS, the assassin of Marat, executed. She gained admittance to him while bathing, and when he declared some of his bloody designs, she plunged a dagger to his heart. She was 24 years of age, possessed rare charms of person, united with great courage, and was actuated by a sense of duty in ridding the world of a monster, at the expense of her own life.

1793. The crown revenue of Poland sequestered by order of the Russian ambassador.

1796. JOHN CHRISTIAN HARTWICK, a Lutheran divine, died at Clermont, N. Y., aged about 90. He was eminent for his classical knowledge and literary abilities, and spent 62 years in the gospel ministry. He left a large estate for the promotion of religious purposes.

1796. JOHN BAPTIST SECONDAT DE MONTESQUIEU, died. He was a son of the celebrated Montesquieu, and devoted himself to agricultural pursuits. He published several agricultural and scientific works.

1806. RICHARD JOSEPH SULLIVAN, an English writer, died. His works consist of travels, history, &c., &c.

1812. American privateer schooner Dolphin, 2 guns, captain Endicott, captured a British ship of 14 guns. She took six other prizes.

1812. *Fort Michilimackinac* with a garrison of 57 United States troops, capitulated to the British, 306 men, 715 Indians.

1812. United States frgiate *Constitution* fell in with a British squadron, from which she effected her escape by the masterly seamanship of captain Hull, after a chase of 60 hours.

1813. A small number of volunteers with 40 soldiers from fort George, in two row-boats, captured at the head of the river St. Lawrence, a British gun-boat, mounting a 24 pounder, and 14 bateaux laden with 230 barrels of pork, and 200 bags of bread, and took 4 officers and 61 men.

1813. British and Indians made an attack on an outwork of the garrison at fort George, but were repulsed.

1832. JOHN CARR, an English tourist, died at London; well known as a writer of tours and travels.

1853. An exhibition of relics was made at Aix-la-Chapelle, when more than 60,000 pilgrims entered the city to see them

1854. The first party sent out under the auspices of the Massachusetts emigrant aid society, left Boston for the territory of Kansas.

1854. The American steamer Franklin, from Cowes for New York, went ashore on Long island beach, and was lost; the mails and passengers were safely landed.

1854. GEORGE C. WASHINGTON, a nephew of general Washington, died at Georgetown. He had been twice a member of congress, from his district in Maryland, was president of the Ohio and Chesapeake canal, and commissioner for the settlement of Indian claims. All his duties were performed with faithful attention and marked ability.

1854. An insurrection broke out at Madrid, and barriers were erected by the people in all parts of the city.

1856. A collision occurred on the North Pennsylvania rail road, near Philadelphia, when a Sunday school excursion on one of the trains had 60 killed and 78 wounded.

1856. The steam boat Northern Indiana was burnt on lake Erie, and over 30 persons lost.

1856. While a fire was raging at Salonica, Turkey, a terrific explosion of gunpowder occurred, killing and wounding 700 persons, among whom were the Dutch, Russian and Sardinian consuls.

JULY 18.

390 B. C. Battle of Allia, a river in Italy; the Romans defeated by the Gauls under Brennus, who destroyed the city, except the capitol.

1009. JOHN XVIII, pope, died. He was a Roman; after him the right of election passed from the Roman people to the clergy. He resigned the dignity some time before his death, and died in the obscurity of a monastry.

1100. GODFREY DE BOUILLION, one of the heroes of the crusades, died. He was the son of a French count, defeated the armies of the sultan with great slaughter, and made himself master of all Palestine. He was elected king of Jerusalem, as a reward for his activity and heroism, which he declined for the humbler appellation of the duke of the holy sepulchre.

1390. On this and the two following days the parish clerks of London played interludes before Richard II and his queen, at Skinnerswells.

1566. WILLIAM RONDELET, a French anatomist, died. He wrote a Latin treatise on fishes, 2 vols. folio, and various tracts on medicine, afterwards collected into a volume. His death was occasioned by eating figs to excess.

1639. BERNARD, duke of Saxe-Weimar, died. He waged an active war with Austria, in which he was successful, till death stopped his career.

1656. Battle of Warsaw, which continued three days.

1675. The Narragansets, posted in a swamp were attacked by the colonists and defeated. They retreated to their recesses, where they remained till they discovered that it was determined to surround and starve them out, when they found means of escape.

1694. A body of 250 Indians under the sieur de Villieu fell with great fury on a village at Oyster river, in New Hampshire, and killed and captivated about a hundred persons, and burnt 20 houses.

1683. Battle under the walls of Vienna; the Turks defeated by the combined armies under John Sobieski of Poland. The vanquished fled with precipitation, leaving behind them the standard of Mahomet.

1705. The duke of MARLBOROUGH defeated the French near Tirelemont, for which victory a thanksgiving was ordered in England.

1761. THOMAS SHERLOCK, an eminent English prelate, died. His controversial works and sermons are well known. His private virtues were adorned with the purest acts of benevolence and humanity.

1775. A party of Americans under col. Ashe entered fort Johnson, on cape Fear river, in the dead of night, and burnt it, with the houses and other buildings. The governor, Martin, retired on board the king's ship Cruzier.

1782. GABRIEL FRANCIS COYER, a French writer, died. He was originally a Jesuit, but abandoned the society for literature. He wrote bagatelles, morals, history, biography, travels, &c., all in a popular style, and translated Blackstone.

1786. JOHN BASEILLAC DE ST. COSME, an eminent lithotomist, died at Paris. His instruments were much used formerly.

1790. ADAM SMITH, a celebrated Scottish philosopher, died. His *Wealth of Nations* procured him immediate fame and emolument. His *Life of Hume* marks him a deist.

1792. KOSCIUSKO at the head of 5,000 Poles, gave battle to the Russians, 14,000 in number, and was defeated with the loss of 1,100.

1792. JOHN PAUL JONES died in Paris. He was distinguished as a seaman. Yet though both in the United States and Russian service, he died in neglected poverty.

1794. The French under Moreau took Nieuwpoort, in Belgium; 300 emigrant prisoners taken were shot.

'1802. DUMARESQ, a British admiral, died, aged 73. He boasted that he had never employed a physician or a lawyer.

1806. Sale of the Leverian museum concluded. It was pronounced by those who had visited the most celebrated museums of Europe to be superior to any of them. The sale occupied 65 days. It was founded by sir Ashton Lever.

1806. The strong fortress of Gaeta surrendered to the armies of France, after a desperate resistance.

1814. Akim Nicholaevitch Makhimov, a Russian poet, died. His poem called the *Speaking Monkeys*, composed in derision of Napoleon's attempt to take Moscow, is much admired.

1817. Jane Austen, an English authoress, died. Her writings were principally novels, which have lately been republished.

1820. The first chain bridge in England thrown over the Tweed, captain Brown architect. The river 437 feet wide.

1835. William Cobbett, a powerful and original English writer, died. He was editor of the *Register* more than thirty years, during which time he made himself sufficiently conspicuous as a violent and somewhat fickle politician. He was an extraordinary man, and the oracle of a multitude of his countrymen.

1839. Rev. William White, bishop of Pennsylvania, died. He was one of the first elected as chaplain to the United States congress.

1844. Jesse Bushyhead, a person of great distinction among his tribe, and chief justice of the supreme court of the Cherokees, died. He was a correct translator.

1848. The Mexican agitator, Paredes, defeated by Bustamente at Guanajanto, and totally routed. The belligerent priest, padre Jurauta was captured and immediately shot.

1848. The Indians, in Yucatan, repulsed at all points, and the towns in their possession retaken by the whites. The Indians at this time were waging a war of extermination against the whites.

1853. The Atlantic and St. Lawrence rail road, from Portland to Montreal, was opened throughout its whole length of two hundred and ninety miles.

1854. A tremendous hurricane prevailed at Davenport, Ill., causing great destruction of life and property.

1854. A negro woman died in Virginia, aged 140.

1855. W. R. Henry, a late captain of the Texas volunteers, issued a proclamation to the people of Texas and the Mexicans, that he and his companions intended to cross the Rio Grande, to aid in overthrowing Santa Anna, and in establishing a government more favorable to the interests of Texas.

JULY 19.

64. The firing of Rome in the reign of Nero is placed by des Vignoles on the 19th July; the day also on which it was sacked by the Senonian Gauls. (See June 18.)

1203. Fall of Constantinople to the Venitian crusaders, when Isaac Angelus, feeble and blind, was solemnly reseated, with his son Alexius, upon the imperial throne.

1242. Battle of Taillebourg, upon the Charente, in France. The French king, at the head of a vast and superior force, carried the bridge, and the English under Henry, the royal palmer, after a desperate stand, gave way, and were driven with rapidity to Saintes.

1333. Edward III defeated the Scots at Halidown with great slaughter, which defeat was followed by the surrender of Berwick which Edward annexed to England.

1374. Francesco Petrarca, the celebrated Italian poet, died, aged 70. His talents and learning contributed greatly to the revival of literature, and he has been justly styled the father of modern poetry.

1573. John Caius, an English physician, died. He visited the most learned institutions in Europe to improve himself in his profession, and when he finally settled in London became extremely popular as a practitioner. He endowed a college, which bears his name.

1610. The foundation of the famed and valuable Bodlein library was laid at Oxford.

1629. Quebec capitulated to the English under Louis and Thomas Kerth. This was 130 years before its final conquest by Wolfe.

1693. Battle of Landon in which the confederates were defeated by the French with great slaughter.

1701. The confederated tribes of Indians surrendered to the English, at Albany, their beaver hunting country, lying between lakes Ontario and Erie, to be by them defended for the said confederated Indians, their heirs and successors forever.

1743. William Somerville, an English poet, died. On the completion of his education he settled on his paternal estate, became known as a magistrate and a country gentleman, and devoted his leisure to the muses.

1763. Nathaniel Hooke, an English historian, died. He is little known, except by his *History of Rome*, 4 volumes 4to.

1777. Logan's fort, Kentucky, besieged by 200 Indians. The garrison consisting of 16 men, who repelled the savages.

1779. Battle of Paulus Hook; the British garrison surprised and made prisoners by the Americans under general Lee. The commandant of the fort and a few Hessians escaped; 30 were killed and 161 taken. American loss 6 killed or wounded.

1783. Job Orton, an excellent English dissenting divine, died; author of many valuable works, among which is a life of Dr. Doddridge.

1794. A revolution commenced at Geneva in Switzerland, headed by two commissioners of the French revolution residing there.

1806. Action off Feroe islands, between British frigate Blanche and French frigate Guerrier, 50 guns, 317 men. The latter was captured in 45 minutes, with the loss of 26 killed, 30 wounded; British loss, 4 wounded. The Guerrier was taken from the British by captain Hull, in 1812.

1808. Battle of Baylen, in Spain; the French under Dupont defeated by the Spaniards. Dupont and 2,600 fell, after a desperate action from 3 o'clock in the morning till noon, when the French sued for terms. A convention was agreed upon, by which they were to lay down their arms, and be conveyed to France; accordingly 14,000 soldiers defiled before the Spanish army, laid down their arms, and all their military accoutrements, and were conducted to Cadiz. The officers were sent home, but the soldiers were placed in hulks, where they remained some years; until the few that survived the miseries of their confinement, driven to despair, cut the cables of their prison-ships, drifted out of the harbor, and were saved by their countrymen then besieging Cadiz.

1810. The king of Prussia issued a decree forbidding American vessels to enter his ports.

1812. Battle at the bridge Aux Canards. 150 volunteers under colonel M'Arthur while reconnoitering fell into an ambush and were fired upon by a party of Indians under Tecumseh. The Indians were routed.

1812. United States brig Nautilus, 12 guns, captured by a squadron of British frigates.

1814. Action off Sandy hook, between the United States privateer Gen. Armstrong and British sloop Henrietta; the latter was captured, laden with stores for the fleet in Chesapeake bay.

1814. Matthew Flinders, an English navigator, died. He explored a part of the coast of New Holland; but lost his ship in that enterprise, and on his return home was held a captive in the isle of France 6 years, and deprived of his papers.

1824. Augustin Iturbide, emperor of Mexico, shot. He entered the army at a very early age. In 1820 he took up arms for the cause of freedom, and led his army on to a series of splendid victories. He became suddenly popular, and was raised to the throne; but was as suddenly deposed and banished. His execution was occasioned by his return.

1836. Lefebure de Cheverus, arch bishop of Bordeaux, died. He came to America after the French revolution, and was consecrated first catholic bishop of Boston, 1810. He was a man of distinguished talents, and extensive scientific and literary acquirements. He returned to France at the invitation of Louis XVIII.

1848. Robert Swartwout died; quartermaster general in the war of 1812, and afterwards known as a politician.

1849. Harmanus Bleecker, a prominent and universally respected citizen of Albany, died, aged 70. He was minister for the United States at the Hague for several years.

1849. George Tibbits of Troy, well known in the councils and commerce of the state of New York, died.

1849. The excavation for the passage of the double track of the Utica and Schenectady rail way through the rock at Little Falls, Herkimer county, New York, was completed. 30,000 yards of granite were taken out and 1,600 kegs of powder consumed in the operation.

1853. The Danish parliament was prorogued, and a fundamental law issued, by which the government became an absolute one.

1854. The insurrection at Madrid (see 17th) triumphed, and the Rivas ministry resigned.

1855. Joseph L. Folsom, first collector of the customs at San Francisco, died, aged 38. He was educated at West Point, and after serving in Florida, went to California with a New York regiment in 1847. He was reputed the richest man in California.

1857. A fire broke out in Taiefa, Portugal, which spread over an immense district of agricultural country, consuming a vast quantity of standing grain, country houses, barns, &c.

JULY 20.

1322 b. c. The great Canicular cycle of the Egyptians, consisting of 1460 years, began with the sun in Cancer, 15 days after the summer solstice. Its first revolution was just completed with the reign of Adrian, 138 a. d.; its second in the time of Shakspeare, 1598. The famous expedition of the Argonauts, and the foundation of the Pythian games, are events which chronologists have placed *sixty years* afterwards.

44 B. C. The customary games in memory of Cæsar's victories were exhibited by Octavius upon this day, dedicated to Venus Mater, when he produced the hero's golden spectatorial chair. The anniversary is interesting from the fact of a comet having appeared near the *Great Bear*, which was visible for seven days.

1031. ROBERT (*the Wise*), king of France, died. He refused the crown of the empire and of Italy, satisfied to rule his own subjects, for whose happiness he labored earnestly.

1164. PETER LOMBARD, bishop of Paris, died; called *Master of the Sentences*, from a work of his by that name, which has been ably commented on by succeeding divines.

1546. The emperor CHARLES V placed the protestant confederates under the ban of the empire; whereupon they declared war upon him. (See July 15.)

1553. Lady Jane Grey's *nine days' usurpation* terminated.

1620. Massacre of the protestants in the Valteline in Switzerland. It began on this day and extended to all the towns of the district; it was a labor of three days.

1650. JOHN PRIDEAUX, an English prelate, died. He rose from the ranks of poverty and dependence to be bishop of Worcester; and sunk back again to his original level rather than compromise with the republicans.

1655. ROBERT BROOKE died; he was the first settler in Patuxent, Maryland.

1691. ADRIAN AUGUSTIN DE BUSSY DELAMET, a French ecclesiastic, died. He was of a noble family, and wrote among other things a *Dictionary of Cases of Conscience*, 2 volumes folio.

1704. PEREGRINE WHITE, the *first-born* of Plymouth colony, died at Marshfield, aged nearly 84.

1752. JOHN CHRISTOPHER PEPUSCH, an eminent Prussian musician, died in England. His abilities were so early displayed, that at the age of 14 he was employed to teach music to the prince royal at Berlin.

1759. The English general, PRIDEAUX, commanding the enterprise against Niagara, while directing the operations of the siege, was killed by the bursting of a cohorn.

1779. DOUGAL GRAHAM (*the Rhymer*), chronicler of the events of the rebellion of 1741, died.

1788. Action off Hoogland between the Russian fleet of 17 ships, and Swedish fleet of 15. It continued from 5 P. M. till near midnight, and ended in the defeat of the Russians, who had one ship sunk and one of 74 guns and 780 men captured. The Swedish fleet was inferior to the Russian in the size of the vessels as well as in number.

1794. A revolutionary tribunal established at Genéva, in Switzerland; about 2,000 persons arrested; 200 on the proscription list escaped.

1814. General BROWN moved his whole force upon fort George, but not being supported by the fleet on account of Com. Chauncey's illness, fell back on the 22d to Queenstown.

1814. The British fort St. Joseph taken possession of by colonel Croghan.

1814. Privateer general ARMSTRONG arrived at New York, having captured 11 vessels.

1819. JOHN PLAYFAIR, a celebrated Scottish mathematician, died. He was also eminent as a geologist and geographer. His largest work is a system of geography in 5 volumes.

1825. WILLIAM BROWN, a celebrated gem engraver, died. He was first patronized by Catharine of Russia, and subsequently by the king of France; but the storm of the revolution drove him from Paris to London, where he executed many excellent works.

1843. The Chinese city Chin-keang-foo was captured by the British forces under sir H. Pottinger.

1844. JOHN HALSAM, a British author on insanity, died in London.

1852. The obsequies of Henry Clay celebrated with the greatest pomp and magnificence in New York. The city was shrouded in mourning, business was suspended, and the shipping wore their colors at half-mast.

1854. CAROLINE BOWLES, widow of Southey, died at Buckland, England; a poetess of some merit.

1855. A great portion of the village of Chamouni, in Savoy, destroyed by fire.

1857. THOMAS DICK, a Scottish astronomer, died near Dundee, aged 83. His *Christian Philosopher* and some other works are popular in both continents.

JULY 21.

1756 A. M. The window of the ark opened 40 days after the appearance of the tops of the mountains, 1st of 10th month, (June 11). See Nov. 2.

330 B. C. DARIUS III (*Codomanus*), the last king of the ancient Persian empire, assassinated. He was conquered by Alexander the Great, and treacherously slain by Bessus, governor of Bactria, his own general, who hoped to succeed to the sovereignty. With his death the Persian empire became extinct, after a lapse of 228 years from its establishment by Cyrus.

365. A memorable earthquake which

shook the greatest part of the Roman world, and deluged the lower shores of the Mediterranean. The city of Alexandria annually commemorated the fatal day, in which 50,000 inhabitants lost their lives in that inundation.

1403. Battle of Shrewsbury, between Henry IV and Henry Percy (Hotspur). Their numbers were matched and the mutual slaughter was immense; several earls, 2,300 gentlemen, and 6,000 privates were slain. Hotspur was brained by an English *cloth yard*, and his rival in execution, Douglas, was taken prisoner. But for the disparity in prudence, the dynasty upon the English throne would probably have been reversed. (20th? 22d?)

1575. Francis Marullo, or Maurolico, abbot of Messina and an eminent astronomer, died. Owing to the illiberality of the age in which he lived much of his treatise on comets was suppressed.

1586. Thomas Cavendish sailed upon an American expedition, at his own expense, in three ships, with 123 persons, victualed for 2 years, and circumnavigated the earth. It was the second English voyage round the world, and was effected in two years and two months, with the loss of two of his ships. On his voyage he pillaged and burnt several Spanish settlements on the west coast of America.

1667. Treaty of Breda, between the English, French and Dutch, when New York was exchanged for Surinam, and Antigua and Montserrat restored to the British.

1601. Peter Airault died; a magistrate of Paris of great integrity and firmness, by which he acquired the title of *the rock of the accused.*

1637. Daniel Sennertus, a learned German physician, died. He was the son of a shoemaker, rose to great celebrity, and was one of the first to introduce the study of chemistry among his pupils.

1683. William Russel, duke of Bedford, executed. This was one of the arbitrary measures of the reign of Charles II. An attempt was afterwards made to satisfy the ends of justice in this affair by seeking out the instigators of the deed, and restoring his family to their privileges and estates.

1688. James Butler, duke of Ormond, died; a celebrated statesman and warrior in the reign of Charles II, to whose restoration he materially contributed.

1772. Peter Barral, a French ecclesiastic, died. He distinguished himself by the production of several useful works, and among them a historical dictionary.

1773. Pope Clement XIV signed the famous bull which pronounced the extinction of the society of Jesuits.

1788. Gaetano Filangieri died at Naples; one of the most celebrated political economists of the last century.

1789. M. Foulon and his son-in-law, Berthier, massacred at Paris; they are numbered as the 8th and 9th victims of the revolution.

1796. Robert Burns, the Scottish poet, died. In the humble employment of a ploughman, he discovered a most extraordinary genius, which has given to his productions an enduring fame.

1797. Peter Thelluson, a Swiss resident in London, died. He accumulated an immense property, the bulk of which he left to be funded till it should amount to £140,000,000, when, if he should have no lineal descendants, it was to be applied to the *sinking fund* of Great Britain.

1798. Battle of the Pyramids in Egypt. Murad with 22 other beys were defeated by the French under Bonaparte, with the loss of 40 cannon, 40 camels, and their whole baggage and provisions. Cairo surrendered to the *king of fire*, as the Mamelukes termed the combative Corsican, and the whole of Lower Egypt submitted to his arms.

1814. The inquisition reestablished in Spain by Ferdinand. It had been suspended during the reign of Bonaparte.

1815. Harriet Ackland died in England, aged 66. Her husband was wounded and taken prisoner at Saratoga in 1777, and the interest felt for her on the occasion, and the hardships and dangers she encountered have made her the subject of history.

1827. Archibald Constable, if not the most fortunate by far the most eminent publisher that ever adorned the Scottish capital, died. He directed the printing and publishing of the *Edinburgh Review*, &c.

1831. Leopold, king of Belgium, made his entry into Brussels, and took the oath of the constitution.

1832. The sultan of Turkey gave his assent to the extension of the Greek frontier, as required by the London conference, from the gulf of Arta to that of Volo, and recognized the independence of the Greek states.

1838. John Maelzel, an ingenious German mechanist, died. He visited many countries of Europe and America with Kempelin's automaton chess-player, which he improved by giving it the powers of speech. He also invented several automata of surprising powers, which are familiar throughout the country.

1848. The cities of Dublin and Waterford proclaimed by the lord lieutenant of Ireland to be under the coercion act.

1849. Elizabeth Dodd died at Stephens, New Brunswick, aged 111.

1849. Ebenezer Mack, long and favorably known as a distinguished printer and the conductor of the largest book establishment in western New York, died at Ithaca.

1853. Thomas P. Moore died at Harrodsburg, Ky., aged 57; an officer in the war of 1812, member of congress, minister to Colombia in 1829, and lieutenant-colonel in the regular army in Mexico.

1855. The fortress of Fredrickshamm was attacked by the allied fleet, and its garrison driven out.

JULY 22.

310 b. c. The Carthaginians defeated Agathocles, who nevertheless carried the war into Africa.

711. Roderick, the last of the Goths, is overthrown by Tarik, or Xeres, upon the Guadelete, in Spain.

1298. Battle of Falkirk; the Scots under Wallace defeated with great slaughter by the English under Edward I. Wallace escaped, but his sun had now sunk forever, and the remainder of his life was spent in his native forests, a fugitive. The number of slain in the Scottish army is by some represented as high as 50,000. Guy, earl of Warwick, "the black dog of Arden," then a young adventurer for fame, signalized his prowess in the ranks of Edward on this occasion.

1403. Battle of Shrewsbury, in which the forces under Douglas, Percy and Owen Glendower were defeated, and the earl of Northumberland's son, Henry Holspur, slain.

1461. Charles VII, king of France, died. He succeeded in driving the English from has kingdom, by the assistance of Joan of Arc; but having restored peace he relapsed into sensuality, and died of anguish and starvation at the undutiful conduct of his son.

1534. John Frith and Andrew Hewet burnt at Smithfield for heretical opinions relative to the sacrament; Henry VIII king.

1575. Peters and Turwert, two anabaptists, burnt at Smithfield, in presence of an immense crowed of spectators.

1581. Richard Cox, bishop of Ely, died. He was the chief framer of the liturgy, and translator of the Bible, called *The Bishop's Bible*, made in thereign of Elizabeth.

1589. Henry III, of France, assassinated. His reign was distracted by the quarrels between the catholics and protestants, till he fell a victim to the zeal of a priest named Clement, and the house of Valois became extinct.

1674. Gerbrant Vanden Eeckhout, a Dutch painter, died. He was a pupil ot Rembrant, whom he rivaled in merit and popularity.

1676. Pope Clement X died. He was a Roman, and in disposition mild.

1686. City of Albany incorporated.

1698. Claude Boyer, a dramatic writer, died at Paris.

1704. Gibraltar (*Gebel al Tarik*, the mountain of Tarik, where the Saracens landed), taken by the British under sir Geo. Rooke, in whose possession it has ever since continued.

1706. Treaty for the union of Scotland with England signed. It was ratified by parliament and queen Anne, and went into operation May 1, the following year.

1734. Peter King, chancellor of England, died. He was a grocer and salter in his boyhood, that being the trade of his father; but his genius soared to higher occupations, and he became a student. His abilities were appreciated and rewarded by a succession of high and responsible offices.

1763. John Dalton, an English divine, died. He prepared Milton's masque of *Comus* for the stage; sought out the poet's grand-daughter, then overwhelmed with age and poverty, and procured her a benefit which produced £120. His works consist of sermons, poems, &c.

1776. The foundation stone of the far-famed observatory on Calton hill, near Edinburgh, Scotland, was laid.

1779. Battle of Minisink.

1793. The city of Mentz surrendered to the Prussians.

1794. John Benjamin de la Borde, a French writer, guillotined. He was valet to Louis XV, upon whose death he was appointed farmer-general.

1802. Action between the United States frigate Constellation, captain Murray, and 9 Tripolitan gun boats. Four of them were driven on shore, and the remainder took shelter in Tripoli.

1802. Marie Francis Xavier Bichat, an eminent French physician and author, died, aged 31.

1805. Action off Feroll, between the British fleet, 11 sail, and the French and Spanish fleets, in which the latter were defeated with the loss of two large ships captured.

1807. Battle of Novoleski; the advance of the Russians under prince Bagration defeated a strong body of French chasseurs with great slaughter, taking only 150 prisoners. Bagration rushed on, and near Mohiloff a sanguinary action took place. French loss 4,000; Russians lost 3,000.

1812. Battle of Salamanca, in Spain; the British under Wellington defeated the French under Marmont, who lost an arm. Of the French, 7,000 were taken prisoners,

-and it was owing to the night and Clausel's skill and science that the army was saved from destruction. British loss 5,220.

1813. George Shaw died; an eminent English naturalist and writer on zoology, and principal keeper of natural history in the British museum.

1823. William Bertram, a distinguished American botanist died, aged 82. His father was the first American who conceived and carried into effect the design of a botanical garden, for the cultivation of American plants as well as exotics.

1826. Joseph Piazzi, a celebrated astronomer, died at Palermo. He made a new catalogue of the stars, consisting of 7,646, and in 1801 discovered an eighth planet, which he named Ceres Ferdinandia. He is the author of several scientific works.

1832. Francis Charles Joseph Bonaparte, duke of Reichstadt, died, aged 21. He was the only son of Napoleon Bonaparte and Maria Louisa; is said to have possessed distinguished talents, united with great kindness of disposition, and early gave indications that his ruling passion was military ambition.

1833. William Thompson died at Hickory hill, Baltimore county, Md., aged 112.

1836. Armand Carrel, a French republican. killed in a duel. He was principal editor of the *Nationel* of Paris. A monument by David is over his grave.

1839. Ghuznee, one of the strongest places in Asia, defended by a garrison of 3,500 Afghans, under a son of the exking of Cabul, was taken by the British under general Keane; 500 of the garrison being killed and the rest taken. British loss about 200.

1850. Sarah Margaret Fuller d'Ossoli, a distinguished American authoress, with her husband and child, perished near Fire island, on their homeward passage to New York.

1852. Excelmans, a noted French general, died at Paris, aged 77. He first gained distinction under Oudinot, in 1799; commanded a part of the cavalry at Waterloo, and was raised to the dignity of marshal of France.

1854. A new planet was discovered by the astronomer Hind, from the observatory at Regents park, London.

JULY 23.

1401. The city of Bagdad sacked by the Tartars under Tamerlane (*Timour the Lame*,) who erected on her ruins a pyramid of 90,000 heads.

1531. Treaty of Nuremberg between Charles V and the reformers, and soon after solemnly ratified by the diet of Ratisbon.

1562. Gœtz von Berlichingen (*with the iron hand*), a bold, restless and warlike German knight, died. He placed himself at the head of the rebellious peasantry in the war which they waged against their oppressors, but was soon taken prisoner.

1584. Elizabeth Russel died; an English lady, distinguished for a well cultivated mind and a taste for literature.

1584. John Day, an eminent English printer, died. He was the first who printed in Greek and Saxon characters in England, and is deserving of remembrance for his enterprise in the publication of many extensive works, the effect of which was to facilitate the progress of the reformation.

1588. Date of the oldest preserved newspaper in England, the *English Mercurie*, by queen Elizabeth. It had been printed at intervals before, as this was the fiftieth number, and is still preserved in the British museum. It is printed in the Roman character. (May 28.)

1602. The *lacteals* discovered by Caspar Asselli, while dissecting a dog. The discovery was accidental.

1627. Robert Shirley, a native of England, died in Persia. He made a visit to Persia, and was induced to settle there; became a favorite with the emperor, who gave him his niece in marriage, and sent him as his ambassador to Poland and England.

1637. The *cuttie* stool thrown by a woman at the head of the bishop, in St. Giles's church, Edinburgh.

1691. Henry Sloughter, governor of the province of New York, died, after a short, weak and turbulent administration, and was buried in Stuyvesant's vault, next to the old Dutch governor.

1692. Giles Menage, a learned French author, died. He acquired the title of the Varro of his time, and became so popular that Mazarin even was jealous of him. He left numerous valuable works.

1712. Achille de Harley died; first president of the parliament of Paris, and an upright magistrate.

1741. Battle of Williamstadt, in Sweden, between the Russians and Swedes.

1752. Alexander Politi, an Italian professor of great learning, died at Pisa. He published an edition of Eustathius's *Commentary on Homer*, with a Latin translation, and notes, 5 vols. folio; a labor of great value.

1757. Zittau, in Saxony, bombarded, taken and destroyed by the Austrians; the inhabitants, as well as the Prussian troops who defended it were put to the sword.

1758. Battle of Sangershausen; the Hessians defeated by the French under Soubise; who, although victorious, lost 2,000 men.

1765. In Lapland, 120 reindeer were struck dead by lightning.

1773. GEORGE EDWARDS, styled the father of ornithologists, died, aged 81. He was apprenticed to a trade, but as soon as his indentures expired he began to travel, and extended his researches into various countries of Europe. The first volume of his work appeared in 1743, and the whole was completed in 1764, in 7 vols. 4to, containing engravings and descriptions of upwards of 600 subjects in natural history never before delineated.

1779. The Minisink settlements in Orange co., N. Y., attacked by the Indians under Brant, by whom it was also plundered and burnt, and the inhabitants either killed or carried away.

1780. Battle in North Carolina, between 300 militia under colonel Lock, and the British and tories under Moore. The latter proposed a cessation of hostilities for one hour, which being agreed to, he decamped with his party.

1785. The Germanic union concluded; the last act of importance of the life of Frederick II.

1793. ROGER SHERMAN, one of the signers, died.

1794. ALEXANDER BEAUHARNAIS, a French general, guillotined. He served in the American war under Rochambeau, was some time president of the national assembly of France, afterwards commanded the army of the Rhine, and in 1793 was minister of war. He was condemned on a false accusation, and perished at the age of 34. His widow, Josephine, was the first wife of Bonaparte.

1800. JOHN FRANCIS VAUVILLIERS, a learned Greek scholar, died. He was for 20 years professor of Greek at Paris, but finally driven out by the revolution, and invited to St. Petersburg by the emperor, where he died.

1816. ELIZABETH HAMILTON died; an English lady of great talents and acquirements, who left several excellent works on various subjects.

1816. The Enterprise arrived at Charleston from Savannah; being the first steam boat ever seen in that city it excited a great deal of curiosity.

1832. Battle near Coimbra, Portugal, between the forces of Don Pedro, 8,000 men, and those of Don Miguel, 12,500, in which the latter were defeated.

1836. HUGH SHAW died, aged 113.

1838. FREDERICK CUVIER, the well known French naturalist, died at Strasburg.

1855. JOSEPH C. HART, American consul, died at Santa Cruz, Canary islands. He was a man of literary taste and an author.

1855. The insurgent Mexicans under general Vidauri, at Saltillo, defeated the government forces under generals Cruz and Guitian, and drove them from the city.

JULY 24.

634. ABUBEKIR, father-in-law of Mohammed, the Arabian prophet, died. He was elected caliph, and supported with energy the fabric already erected by the founder of the new religion. He subdued the disaffected tribes at home, and turned his arms successfully against foreign invaders.

1313. RALPH DE BALDOCK, bishop of London, died. He wrote a history of British affairs, now lost, and was a virtuous and charitable prelate, and a man of learning and judgment.

1322. BRUCE, after ravaging the western marches in England during 24 days, returned home with his wagons filled with plunder.

1411. Battle between the Gaelic and Lowland Scottish factions, led by the earl of Mar, and Donald of the Isles. This battle was of the highest importance, since it decided the superiority of the more civilized regions of Scotland over those inhabited by the Celtic tribes, who remained almost as savage as their forefathers, the Dulriads.

1520. HENRY STEPHENS, a celebrated French printer, the founder of the family of that name, died at Lyons.

1527. FRANCISCO ALVAREZ, a Spanish traveler, returned from an expedition to Africa. He accompanied an embassy from the king of Portugal to David, king of Abyssinia, in 1515. The expedition met with many obstacles, and did not arrive till 1520. He published an account of his travels at Lisbon, 1540, a work of great fidelity and merit.

1567. Queen MARY, a prisoner in Lochleven castle, subscribed the instrument by which she resigned the Scottish crown in favor of her son, James VI, afterwards king of England.

1590. STEPHEN TABOUROT (*sieur des accords*), a French writer, died.

1595. ANDREW DE BRANCAS DE VILLARS, a French general, murdered. He espoused the interests of the league against Henry IV, but afterwards abandoned it, was taken prisoner and despatched.

1595. CHARLES DE LORAINE D'AUMALE, a French nobleman, broken on the wheel at Paris, *in effigy*. After the assassination of the duke of Guise, he became the head of the league against the Calvinists, and secretly aimed at the throne. He even took possession of Paris, sent the members of the parliament to the Bastile, and compelled the king to fly. But meeting with reverses, he joined the Spaniards, was outlawed, and the parliament being unable to take him, executed their sentence upon his effigy. He resided principally in Flanders, till his death, which took place at Brussels, 1631, at the age of 77.

1609. The expedition under Somers, (see June 2,) overtaken by a tremendous tempest. The admiral ship was severed from the rest "by the *tail* of a mighty hurricane," but at length after having *drank to one another*, "as taking their last leaves, intending to commit themselves to the mercy of the sea, most luckily the ship was driven and *jammed between two rocks*."

1712. Battle of Denain; the French under Villars defeated the allies under Albemarle, who was taken, together with four German princes, and many other prisoners.

1722. The wearing of broadswords prohibited in Edinburgh.

1744. Alphonso de Vignoles, a French protestant, died. He retired to Prussia on the revocation of the edict of Nantes, where he was patronized by the king, and wrote several learned works.

1755. Elisha Williams, president of Yale college, died; esteemed for his learning and great moral worth.

1756. George Vertue, an English engraver and antiquary, died.

1758. John Dyer, an English poet, died. In 1727 he published the poem of *Grongar Hill*, and soon after he went to Italy to delineate the antiquities of that country, under the title of the *Ruins of Rome*, a poem which places him high on the scale of merit as a writer.

1759. Battle of Niagara. The English under sir William Johnson defeated the French and Indians with great slaughter, and took fort Niagara. The loss of this fortress effectually cut off all communication between Canada and Louisiana.

1768. Nathaniel Lardner, an eminent English divine, died. His literary labors, which have been published in 11 vols., were translated into various languages abroad, and procured him great distinction at home.

1779. An expedition fitted out by Massachusetts to take a British post at Penobscot, totally defeated by the unexpected arrival of the British fleet. The troops were dispersed in all directions, and found their way home with difficulty; 19 vessels were taken or destroyed, and 24 transports burnt.

1797. Unsuccessful attack of the British upon Santa Cruz, Teneriffe. Lord Nelson lost his right arm.

1804. Adolphus Charles Adam, afterwards a distinguished musical performer, born at Paris.

1813. An attempt made by several United States officers to blow up the British ship Plantagenet, in Lynnhaven bay, with a torpedo. It exploded without effecting their purpose, though so near the vessel as to injure it.

1817. About mid-day, after a loud detonation, the lake Canterno, or Porciano, in Italy, totally disappeared. A large opening was discovered in the bottom, through which the waters were supposed to have escaped into the sinuosities of the neighboring mountains.

1822. Ernest Theodore William Hoffman, a Prussian novelist, died. He possessed much imagination and talent, but was an irregular and unhappy man.

1830. The thermometer at noon in Boston stood at 95°, at sundown at 50°, and fires were made.

1833. Lisbon surrendered to the army of don Pedro, under the duke of Terceira.

1848. An intended insurrection at Cuba; the government becoming apprised of it, general Lopez, the head conspirator, escaped to the United States.

1849. John L. Lawrence died, aged about 67. He was one of the secretaries who assisted at the treaty of Ghent; well known in the councils and commerce of the state, and at the time of his death comptroller of the city of New York.

1853. Hezekiah C. Seymour, engineer in chief of the state of New York, died at Piermont, aged 42. His name is prominently associated with the New York and Erie rail road, and with the Ontario, Huron, and lake Simcoe rail road in Canada.

1854. Henry King, a British general, died, aged 77. He had been a soldier for sixty years, serving in the West Indies, Egypt, Walcheren, and the Peninsula. In Egypt he lost a leg, but that did not prevent him from subsequently taking part in the war.

1854. The American fishing vessel Ellen Morrill, was captured by the British cruisers, and carried into the port of Bathurst, causing much excitement among the fishermen.

1855. Violent and repeated shocks of an earthquake destroyed the Swiss villages of St. Nicholas and Viege, during this and the preceding day.

JULY 25.

306. Constantius Chlorus, emperor of Rome, died at York palace, and was succeeded the same day by his son Constantine the Great.

811. Nicephorus I, emperor of Rome, died. He was chancellor of the eastern empire, and seized the throne 807, banish-

ing the empress Irene to Mitylene. He overcame all opposition from his own subjects, but was vanquished by the Bulgarians, and fell in battle.

1139. Battle of Aurique, in Portugal; Alphonso I vanquished five Moorish kings and their barbaric heads were emblazoned in the arms of the monarchy.

1214. Battle of Bouvines, in France, in which the forces of Otho were overthrown by Philip Augustus, and peace restored.

1261. The Greek emperor, MICHAEL PALÆOLOGUS, expelled the Latins from Constantinople, who had taken possession of it nearly 60 years previous.

1441. ROGER BOLINGBROKE, chaplain to the duke of Gloucester, having been convicted of necromancy, was exposed, with his instruments, to the public finger, at St. Paul's, in London.

1471. THOMAS A KEMPIS (*Thomas Hammerken of Kempen*), a famous German theologian, died, aged 92. He displayed great piety and devotion, and instead of confining himself to transcribing books of devotion, like the rest of his brethren, composed works of divinity himself, one of which, *De Imitatione Christi*, has been translated into nearly all languages in the world.

1505. PHILIP BEROLDUS, a French professor of belles-letters, died. He was extremely dissipated in youth, but reformed after marriage, and produced several works, in prose and verse. He was a man of great learning for that age, and is noted for his valuable edition of the classics.

1535. CHARLES V, emperor of Germany, having assembled a powerful fleet, landed at Tunis, and carried by assault the fortress of Goletta. This gave him possession of Barbarossa's fleet of 87 galleys and 300 cannon. Having reinstated Muley Hassan and liberated more than 20,000 slaves, he returned to Europe.

1554. Queen MARY of England married to Philip of Spain at Winchester.

1564. FERDINAND I, emperor of Germany, died. He became king of Hungary and Bohemia 1527, and was elected king of the Romans 1531. On the abdication of his brother, Charles V, he succeeded to the empire, and governed with great moderation and prudence.

1593. HENRY IV, of France, formally renounced the protestant faith at St. Denys, rather than perish by the hand of an assassin.

1603. King JAMES and his queen crowned at Westminster by archbishop Whitgift.

1653. The assembly of the Scottish church being met at Edinburgh were dismissed by Cotterel for not having the authority of the parliament of England, and commanded that not three of them should be seen together.

1659. The pope, ALEXANDER VII, acknowledged by a papal brief, the king of France sovereign of the conquests and colonies which his subjects had made in the American isles. Hitherto the court of Rome had preserved inviolate the *universal grant* of that infamous man, pope Alexander VI, in 1493, to his catholic majesty, the king of Spain. (See May 3.)

1666. Engagement at the mouth of the Thames, between the English fleet under Rupert and Albemarle, and the Dutch under Van Tromp and De Ruyter. Each fleet consisted of about 80 sail. Three Dutch admirals were killed.

1722. New England declared war against the Indians. The small pox at that time was waging a war with both.

1724. A violent persecution of the protestants began in France.

1757. The duke of Cumberland defeated by d'Estrees at Hastenbeck.

1759. General JOHNSON took fort Niagara in America.

1790. WILLIAM LIVINGSTON, governor of New Jersey, died. He was a member of the New York bar, and a warm advocate of the rights of the colonies. He removed to New Jersey, and on the deposition of the royal governor, Franklin, he was elected to fill his place, which he held till the time of his death.

1790. JOHN BERNARD BASEDOW died; at one time professor of moral philosophy and belles-lettres, at Soroe in Denmark, from which he was expelled for some irreverent remarks on religion. He was the son of a barber at Hamburg, and acquired a reputation for learning and ability.

1794. FREDERICK VON DER TRENCK, a Prussian baron, guillotined at Paris. For some imprudent conduct he excited the indignation of the authorities, and was imprisoned a long time at Magdeburg. He finally escaped to France, where he became obnoxious to the guardians of the state, and suffered death at the age of 70. The account of his imprisonment and adventures, written by himself, and highly spiced with romance, is translated into English.

1795. WILLIAM ROMAINE, an eminent English divine, died; author of many valuable theological works.

1799. Battle of Aboukir, in Egypt, between the French under Bonaparte, and the Turks, Arabs and Mamelukes, under Mustapha. The Egyptians were defeated, with the loss of their general and 200 taken prisoners, with all their equipage and 20 cannon; 2,000 dead on the field, and about 10,000 driven into the sea and drowned.

1804. Georges and 11 of his companions guillotined at Paris for a conspiracy against Bonaparte.

1804. The American squadron, consisting of the Constitution frigate, 3 brigs, 3 schooners, 2 bomb and 6 gun boats, arrived in sight of Tripoli.

1812. Battle of Ostrovna; the Russians under Ostermann Tolstoy defeated by the French. The battle continued two days; the loss was about 4,000 on each side.

1814. Battle of Bridgewater, (alias Lundy's Lane,) near Niagara falls, between the British under Riall, and the Americans under Brown. It was a sanguinary action, and for the numbers engaged, perhaps unequaled in modern warfare; in which both the senior generals were wounded. British loss 878 killed and wounded and missing; American loss 860 do. The battle commenced at 5 P. M., and ended at 12 in the defeat of the British, 2,700 veteran regulars, exclusive of a large body of Indians.

1814. Charles Dibdin, a celebrated English song writer and dramatist, died. His songs amount to upwards of 1,200; he has scarcely an equal in the number and merit of this species of composition.

1824. William Sharp, an eminent English engraver, died. He rose to distinction in his art by his own unassisted exertions, but was in other respects a very simple character. His works are numerous and held in high estimation.

1830. Charles X of France ordained that the liberty of the periodical press was suspended, and five days after was himself suspended from the throne.

1833. James Martin, a soldier of the revolution, died at Knoxville, Tenn., aged 106.

1834. Samuel Taylor Coleridge, an eminent English poet, metaphysician and theologian, died. As a poet and author he was popular, but his conversational powers captivated the most learned men of his time, who visited him to enjoy his conversation. Two volumes of his *Table Talk* were published after his death.

1840. A couple of officers belonging to the United States exploring expedition having gone on shore at Malolo, one of the Fejee islands, were murdered by the natives. Lieut. Wilkes immediately attacked and burnt the town and fort, killed upwards of 70 of the natives, destroyed the plantations and laid the island waste.

1840. Andrew Laughlin died at Devrock, Ireland, aged 110. He saw five sovereigns successively ascend the British throne. The faculties of his mind were unimpaired until the last few months of his life.

1852. Baron Gourgaud, a distinguished French general, died at Paris, aged 69. He entered the French service in 1801, was engaged in most of the great battles of Napoleon, including Waterloo; attended the emperor to St. Helena, and was afterwards near being involved in a duel with Walter Scott, through his fervid zeal for his master.

1852. William Scroop, at eminent English naturalist, died at London, aged 81.

1852. James Spencer Cannon, a talented minister of the Dutch reformed church, died at New Brunswick, N. J., aged 60. He was 26 years professor of metaphysics in Rutgers college, and of pastoral theology and ecclesiastical history in the Theological seminary at that place, and was distinguished for strong and original powers of mind, urbanity of manners, and fervent piety.

JULY 26.

46 B. C. Julius Cæsar, arrived at Rome from Utica, celebrated the fourfold triumph in a quadriga of white horses, for the victories over the Gauls, over Ptolemy in Egypt, over Pharnaces in Pontus, and over Juba in Africa; entertained the people with naumachian and pentachlic or circensian games during 40 days; rewarded and feasted them at 22,000 tables; was declared consul the fourth time, and dictator for ten years; and to place him on the summit of human glory, his statue was erected in the capitol opposite to that of Jupiter, with the globe at his feet. He commenced in this year his reformation of the calendar, called, from the long intercalation, the year of confusion.

40. Petronius, in his account of Trimalchio, has preserved a *Roman newspaper*, (diurna acta) for this day. "On the 26th July 30 boys and 40 girls were born at Trimalchio's estate at Cuma. At the same time a slave was put to death for uttering disrespectful words of his master. The same day a fire broke out in Pompey's gardens, which began in the night, in the steward's apartments."

1346. The English under Edward III, captured the opulent city of Caen, in France, and pillaged the country around.

1469. Battle of Banbury (or Hedgecote), in which the royalists under Pembroke were defeated by the Yorkshire rebels. Pembroke was taken and put to death, and earl Rivers beheaded.

1470. Post office first established in Paris.

1471. Paul II (*Peter Barbo*), pope of Rome, died. He was a Venetian noble, and on coming to the throne gratified the cardinals with the purple habit, the red silk cap, and the mitre, which had hitherto been worn only by the sovereign pontiff.

1546. Emperor Charles V and pope Paul III secretly leagued against the protestants.

1560. James Bonfadius, a polite writer of Italy, executed. He incurred the enmity of some powerful families at Geneva by the freedom of his remarks in his writings, who wrought his ruin.

1581. Philip excluded by edict from all sovereignty over the united provinces of the Netherlands.

1592. Armand Gonrault de Biron, marechal of France, killed. From the humble rank of a page he rose through all the gradations of the army, to the highest dignity under the sovereign. He distinguished himself in the service, and was killed by a cannon ball at the siege of Epernai.

1630. Charles Emanuel (*the Great*), duke of Savoy, died; an ambitious prince and brave warrior.

1653. "This day," says Dugdalo, "the fair bell, called *Jesus's bell*, at Litchfield, was knocked in pieces by a presbyterian *pewterer*, who was the chief officer for demolishing the Cathedral."

1659. The island of Montreal invaded by 1200 Indians, who burned all the plantations, and made a terrible massacre of men, women and children, upon whom they committed every barbarity. "Ils ouvrirent le sein des femmes enceintes," says Charlevoix, "pour en arracher le fruit qu' elles portoient, ils mirent des enfans tout vivants à la broche, et contraignirent les mères de les tourner pour les faire rôtir." They killed 1000 and took 26, who were afterwards burnt.

1680. John Wilmot, earl of Rochester, died; a dissolute English nobleman of the reign of Charles II, and the favorite companion of the king. He was a poet, and one of the greatest wits of the day.

1687. A party of French built fort Niagara.

1691. Richard Ingolsby, captain of an independent company, was sworn into the office of president of the council of New York, or as lieutenant-governor, on the decease of Sloughter, instead of the administration coming to Dudley, as of right it should.

1738. William Thomas, an English divine, died; distinguished as a man of letters and an antiquary.

1758. Louisbourg, which had been restored to the French by treaty, was again taken by the British under admiral Boscawen and lieutenant-general Amherst, and its fortifications have since been demolished.

1759. Ticonderoga abandoned by the French, and occupied by the British under general Amherst.

1766. Wallis, the navigator sailed on his great voyage.

1772. John Græme died; a Scottish poet and miscellaneous writer of considerable merit.

1775. Maryland convention met at Annapolis, and resolved to support the measures of Congress. They also ordered $266,666 in bills of credit to be struck, and that 40 companies of minute men should be raised.

1775. Congress first established a post office: the route extended from Falmouth, New England, to Savannah, Georgia, and Franklin was appointed post master.

1788. The printing office of Thomas Greenleaf, in New York, was much damaged and his types taken away by a mob. When the two great political parties were forming, subsequent to the organization of the government, that which opposed the administration attacked the measures of Washington with a great degree of virulence in Greenleaf's paper. He was opposed to the federal constitution.

1788. New York adopted the constitution of the United States, recommending amendments. Ten states had already given their assent to it, nine being required before it could be adopted by congress.

1789. Lafayette added to his cockade the white of the royal arms, declaring at the same time that the tri-color should go round the world.

1793. Stanislaus Clermont Tonnere, a French nobleman, massacred at Paris for his opposition to the Jacobin club.

1798. A remarkable mirage was seen at Hastings, England. The French coast distant 50 miles was at 5 p. m. brought close to the feet of the observers.

1803. An iron railway from Wandsworth to Croydon, in England, was opened to the public for the conveyance of goods.

1803. British ship Thunderer, captain Bedford, captured the French privateer Venus, of Bordeaux, pierced for 28 guns, but mounting only 16.

1806. British frigate Greyhound and sloop Harrier captured off Macassar the Dutch frigate Pallas, 36 guns, and two large East Indiamen, laden with spices.

1812. Battle of Kobrine; the Saxons under general Klingel, defeated by the Russians, and himself, together with 70 officers, 2500 men, &c., captured; Russian loss 1000.

1814. The Americans under general Ripley and P. B. Porter burnt Bridgewater mills and bridge, and the British barracks there.

1830. Charles X, of France, issued three ordinances, dissolving the newly elected chamber of deputies, suppressing the liberty of the press, and altering the law of election. This gave rise to a revolution which terminated in his dethronement, and the elevation of Louis Philippe.

1838. The Bolivian troops under Moran having left Lima on the previous day, Nieto and Orbegozo entered the city with about 2000 men and declared the constitution of 1835, Orbegozo being named provisional dictator.

1847. JOB DURFEE, a jurist of Rhode Island, and author of *What cheer; or Roger Williams in exile, &c.*, died at Tiverton.

1848. FRANCIS R. SHUNK, governor of Pennsylvania, died, aged 60.

1848. After several days of hard fighting, the Piedmontese under Charles Albert were totally defeated by the Austrians under Radetsky, and retreated to Milan.

1852. The Irishmen in New York made an unsuccessful attempt to rescue Thomas Kaine, in the custody of the United States marshal, and claimed by the British government, under the treaty, as a fugitive from justice.

1855. The pope declared the laws which had been enacted in Piedmont, to the detriment of religion and the power and liberty of the church, to be void and of no effect; and that all who supported them incurred the greater excommunication; also that the recent laws in Spain concerning the church property to be null and void.

1856. The boiler of the steam boat Empire State, exploded on the passage from Fall river to New York, killing and wounding several passengers.

JULY 27.

1139. The country of Portugal erected into a monarchy.

1276. JAMES I (*the Warrior*), of Arragon, died. He conquered several Moorish kingdoms, and added them to his dominions, and supported himself against the encroachments of the papal power.

1586. Sir FRANCIS DRAKE arrived in England from a western expedition, accompanied by Lane, the commander of Raleigh's Virginian colony, who now first brought from his settlement, tobacco into England: that which sir John Hawkins brought home in 1565 was considered a medicinal drug merely, and as Stow observes, *all men wondered what it meant.*

1597. JACOB HUYCK, translator of the first authorized version of the catholic Bible, printed in Cracow, died there, aged 57.

1627. THOMAS GOFF, an English divine, died. He wrote among various other things, four tragedies.

1661. Schenectady purchased from the Indians.

1663. A bill for the better observation of the Sabbath, was stolen from the clerk's table in the English house of commons, ere it had received the assent of the king.

1675. HENRY DE LA TOUR D'AUVERGNE, viscomte de Turenne, the renowned French general, killed by a cannon shot at the village of Saltzbach, in Germany. He was preparing for a great battle with the Austrians under Montecuculli.

1694. The charter of the bank of England for 12 years, determinable upon one year's notice, signed by the dynarchs, William and Mary.

1704. STANISLAUS LECZINSKI elected king of Poland.

1706. The legislative union of England and Scotland completed; one of the most important events of the reign of queen Anne.

1712. A disgraceful quarrel between the French and Dutch plenipotentiaries at Utrecht.

1755. A party of Indians prowling about Hinsdale, N. H., ambushed three men, Caleb Howe, Hilkiah Grout and Benjamin Garfield, as they were returning from the field, only one of whom escaped. The Indians went directly to Bridgman's fort, where their families resided, and who had heard the report of guns. By the sounds of feet without, they concluded their friends had returned, and hastily opened the gate, when to their inexpressible surprise they admitted the savages and were all made captives. An interesting account of this affair is familiar to many.

1759. The English under general Amherst took Ticonderoga without firing a gun, the French having abandoned it on the approach of the former.

1759. PIERRE-LOUIS MAREAU DE MAUPERTUIS died at Basle. He was successful in many trigonometrical surveys, and was instrumental in determining the latitude and longitude of several places with much more accuracy.

1773. Captain C. J. PHIPPS, lord Mulgrave, reached nearly the 81° north latitude.

1774. SAMUEL THEOPHILUS GMELIN, a German botanist, died. He was professor of botany at St. Petersburg, and employed on a mission of discovery in the provinces bordering on the Caspian sea; was detained a prisoner by a Tartar chief, in which situation he died.

1775. Congress established a hospital for 20,000 men, and appointed Benjamin Church director and physician-general.

1778. Action off Ushant between the French and British fleets, each of 30 sail; the British claimed the victory. British loss 133: 373. French loss 165: 529.

1794. Overthrow of ROBESPIERRE and

the Mountain party, which put an end to the reign of terror.

1799. Mantua with a garrison of 10,00C men dishonorably surrendered to the Austrians.

1806. The United States exploring expedition under captain Lewis, had their guns seized while asleep, by a party of Minnetarre Indians. One of the Indians was stabbed to the heart, and Lewis shot another in the body, who fell on his knees and elbow, raised himself and fired; the ball grazed Lewis's head. The remainder of the Indians fled, leaving the explorers in possession of their baggage, provisions, and four horses.

1807. PETER AUGUSTUS MARIA BROUSSONET, a French naturalist, died. He introduced Merino sheep and Angora goats into France.

1809. First day's battle of Talavera; Wellington made a stand against the French army of double his number of men, under Jourdan, Victor and Mortier.

1828. RADAMA, king of Madagascar, died. He was an extraordinary character, and his reign constitutes the most important era in the history of the island; the slave trade was suppressed, Christianity and the art of printing, as well as other arts and sciences were introduced.

1830. The second French revolution began in Paris by a resistance of the decrees of Charles X. It burst forth on the following day, and continued three days, when the people were left undisputed masters of the capital. About 3000 victims fell in this glorious struggle.

1833. WILLIAM BAINBRIDGE, an American commodore, died, aged 60. He was a distinguished commander in the navy for a long series of years.

1840. CHARLOTTE OUELLET, a Canadian heroine, died, aged 100. She was one of a number of young women of St. Anne de la Pocatiere, who put on men's apparel and armed themselves to drive out the British regulars who were amusing themselves by firing the houses and barns of the village, during the siege of Quebec. She and the rest of her company fired upon the English, who fled, making temporary barrows in their flight, to rescue those who fell under the fire of these brave Canadian girls. A few days previous to her death she indulged in merriment at the thought that she was one who had made the best shots.

1843. FREDERIC HALL, of Washington, one of the most successful American geologists, died at Peru, Illinois.

1844. JOHN DALTON, an eminent English chemist, died, aged 79. He had devoted his whole life to laborious study. A public funeral was given him in Manchester, his native town. He worshipped with the Friends. He could distinguish but two colors, yellow and blue; red and green had the same appearance to his eye.

1849. The grand duke of Tuscany reentered his capital and resumed his authority.

1854. The cholera made its appearance in the Massachusetts state prison at Charlestown, over 70 convicts being attacked; but one died.

1856. The steam boat John Jay, running on Lake George, took fire on her passage from the landing near Ticonderoga to Caldwell, and was consumed, by which several of the passengers and crew perished.

JULY 28.

2348 B. C. NOAH, the Xisuthrus of Berosus, opened the windows of the ark and sent forth a dove and a raven, 40 days after the appearance of the mountains.

388. MAGNUS MAXIMUS, emperor of Rome, beheaded. He was a Spaniard, proclaimed emperor by his troops in Britain. On arriving at Aquelia, on his way to Rome, he was defeated by Theodosius I, and beheaded.

450. THEODOSIUS (*the younger*), emperor of Rome, died. He was successful in war against the Persians, who were defeated near their own dominions; but the Huns compelled him to sue for peace on terms not the most advantageous to the Romans. He was succeeded by his sister Pulcheria, and the empire for the first time submitted to a female reign.

1402. Battle of Angora near Constantinople, between the Tartars under Tamerlane and the Turks under Bajazet. It was an obstinate engagement, and continued three days. The Turks were defeated and Bajazet taken prisoner.

1492. INNOCENT VIII (*John Baptist Cibo*), pope, died. He was a Genoese nobleman of Greek descent; employed his influence to reconcile the quarrels of the Christian princes with one another, and left behind him the character of a high minded and benevolent man.

1540. THOMAS CROMWELL, earl of Essex, beheaded. He rose from the purlieus of a blacksmith's shop to those of the palace; from the pursuit of a humble calling to the dignity of lord chamberlain of England. But he fell a victim to the caprice of Henry VIII.

1541. The diet of Ratisbone closed its sittings.

1592. WILLIAM HACKET, an English fanatic of the reign of Elizabeth, hung and quartered for blasphemy.

1609. Sir GEORGE SOMERS, governor of

Virginia, with his crew, who were wrecked on the 24th, landed on Bermudas. They found "a huge and curious sort of fish," and having remained there about nine months, and built two cedar barks they quitted the *isle of Devils* on the 10th May following. (See May 23.)

1629. JOHN SPEED died; an English chronologist, historian and antiquary.

1635. RICHARD CORBET, an English bishop, died. He also wrote a volume of ingenious poems, which were published under the title of *Poetica Stromata.*

1667. ABRAHAM COWLEY, an eminent English poet, died. Addison observed of him, that no author ever abounded so much in wit, according to Locke's definition of it.

1718. STEPHEN BALUZE, a French writer, died, aged 87. He wrote the lives of the popes of Avignon, and was an indefatigable collector of curious manuscripts, &c.

1750. CONYERS MIDDLETON, a celebrated English divine and critical author, died. His writings are numerous, and display profound learning and extensive information.

1750. THOMAS GORDON, who in company with John Trenchard, for some time managed the *Independent Whig*, died at London. His knowledge of the classics was respectable and he translated Tacitus.

1789. The *Pittsburg Gazette* was printed, the first newspaper west of the Allegany mountains.

1790. The Forth and Clyde canal opened from the British to the Atlantic ocean, in Scotland.

1793. French general SEMONVILLE arrested on his route to Constantinople to bribe the divan; 64,000 louis d'ors and a great quantity of jewels were found on him.

1794. MAXIMILIAN ISIDORE ROBESPIERRE, the sanguinary demagogue of the French revolution, guillotined, aged 35. He rose from obscurity by his talents, but the demon of destruction seemed to sway his mind and urge him on to the most inhuman deeds that ever disgraced even a political demagogue. Twenty others perished at the same time by the same means.

1802. JOSEPH SARTI, an Italian music composer, died. He resided at the court of Catharine of Russia, where he was master of the chapel. He composed a *Te Deum* for the taking of Oczakow, the bass of which was accompanied by cannon of different calibre.

1804. POMPEY, a negro man, died at Dover, Delaware, aged 120.

1806. Buenos Ayres taken by the British.

1809. Second battle of Talavera, between the British and Portuguese under Wellington, and the French under Victor, in which the latter were defeated. Loss of the allies 8,167; French supposed to have lost more.

1813. Fourth battle of the Pyrenees; the French under Soult defeated the British under Wellington.

1813. ANDOCHE JUNOT, duke of Abrantes, died. He entered the army as a volunteer 1791, afterwards distinguished himself under Bonaparte in the Italian and Egyptian campaigns, and commanded in the campaign in Russia.

1817. VADAMME, a celebrated French general, a voluntary exile, arrived at Philadelphia.

1818. GASPARD MONGE died at Paris. He was preceptor to Lacroix and other distinguished mathematicians, and was the first to reduce the art of fortifications, &c., to geometrical rules. His *Géométrie descriptive* is much used.

1820. JOSEPH ZAJONCZECK, viceroy of Poland, died. He entered the army at an early age, espoused the cause of freedom, and fought bravely for his country. He afterwards served in the armies of Bonaparte; and was finally appointed by Russia viceroy of Poland.

1833. WILLIAM WILBERFORCE, a celebrated philanthropist, died at London, aged 74. He was a member of parliament and the intimate friend of Pitt. He began his efforts for the abolition of the slave trade as early as 1787.

1835. EDWARD ADOLPHE CASIMIR JOSEPH MORTIER, duke of Treviso, killed by the explosion of an infernal machine, intended to assassinate Louis Philippe. He joined the army 1791, and from that time his life was marked by combats, exploits and promotion during a term of nearly 30 years. "He is among a small number of Napoleon's generals, whose reputation for private worth has remained unquestioned through life." It was to him that Napoleon entrusted the hazardous undertaking of blowing up the Kremlin at Moscow.

1836. NATHAN MAYER ROTHSCHILD, a celebrated London banker, died. He was a Jew, whose financial operations pervaded the whole continent of Europe. His transactions were carried on in conjunction with his brothers in Paris, Vienna, Frankfort and Naples, all of whom possessed collosal fortunes of their own.

1840. JOHN GEORGE LAMBTON, earl of Durham, died, aged 48. He was made governor-general of Canada in 1838, but returned the same year, and published a valuable work on Canada. He was regarded as the leader of the reform movement which agitated the country, and his talents and merits were very differently estimated by different parties.

1849. The late king of Sardinia, CHARLES ALBERT, died at Lisbon.

1851. HORACE SEBASTIANI, a French marshal, died at Paris, aged 80. He was born in Corsica, and bore a part in most of the great battles during Bonaparte's career. He was in the ministry under Louis Philippe, and ambassador both at Naples and London.

1852. The steam boat Henry Clay, on her passage from Albany to New York, took fire about 3 o'clock in the afternoon, near Yonkers, and was consumed to the water's edge; 56 persons lost their lives, so sudden and rapid was the destruction of the boat. She had been racing with the Armenia.

JULY 29.

1108. PHILIP I, king of France, died. He came to the throne at the age of 8 years; was ambitious and unscrupulous in his acts; engaged in war with England and Flanders, and was defeated by both.

1218. LOUIS VAN LOON died; the husband of Ada, the expatriated queen of Holland.

1540. A statute was made confirming the seizures of the abbeys by Henry VIII.

1567. Prince JAMES, less than 14 months old, was crowned king of Scotland at Stirling.

1578. SEBASTIAN, king of Portugal, killed. He was unfortunate in his wars, and lost his life at Tangiers, in battle with the Moors. Camoens dedicated his *Lusiad* to this king, but he had the stupidity to treat the intended honor with contempt.

1603. BARTHOLOMEW GILBERT, in search of the lost English colony, having landed in a bay about the 40th degree of latitude, in a boat with four men, was attacked by the natives and every one killed. The rest of the crew immediately weighed anchor and returned to England.

1653. Admiral VAN TROMP killed and his fleet destroyed by the English fleet under Monk and Blake.

1644. URBAN VIII (Maffeo Barberini), pope, died. He was an excellent poet, and was called the *Attic Bee.*

1653. GABRIEL NAUDÆUS, a learned French author, died. He was patronized by Richelieu and Mazarin, and Christina of Sweden.

1654. THOMAS GATAKER, an English divine, died, aged 80. He was one of the most noted men of the age; who united to extensive erudition, great moderation and benevolence.

1678. ANDREW MARVELL, an English poet, politician and critic, died (*Penny Cycolpedia* says August 16th). He supported the civil and religious liberties of his country, against the encroachments of the court, by his writings and parliamentary interest; and though poor, declined the bribes of the king.

1693. Battle of Neerwinden (or Landon), in Belgium; the allies under William III, defeated by the French, with the loss of 60 cannon, 9 mortars and about 7,000 men. The king had his clothes penetrated by three bullets.

1714. MARTIN POLI, an Italian chemist, died at Paris. It is said that he communicated to the king some powerful agent of destruction for military use; but the king, at the same time that he commended and rewarded his ingenuity with a pension and an office, insisted that the secret should die with him.

1747. Dr. BLACKWELL, a Scotch physician and for some time a corrector of the press to Mr. Wilkins in London, beheaded at Stockholm. Being informed that his head was not properly laid on the block he replied as it was his first experiment no wonder he needed some instruction.

1759. Crown point abandoned by the French on the approach of the British and provincials under general Amherst.

1760. At Lidden near Canterbury in grubbing down an enormous ash tree two human skeletons were found in the centre.

1773. The city of Guatemala laid in ruins by an earthquake and the eruption of a volcano.

1794. Seventy-one members of the municipality of Paris guillotined.

1794. STANISLAUS AUGUSTUS, king of Poland, compelled by the Prussian, Austrian and Russian coalition to annul the Polish constitution, and deliver the army over to the Russian general Branicki.

1801. WILLIAM AUGUSTUS ERNESTI died; a distinguished German scholar and professor of eloquence at Leipsic.

1832. JOHN ANTHONY CHAPTAL, a celebrated French chemist, died. He produced numerous valuable works on chemistry and other practical branches of the arts and sciences, was made minister of the interior by Bonaparte, and successively filled many other important situations.

1839. GASPARD CLAIR FRANÇOIS MARIE RICHE DE PRONY, peer of France, died, aged 84. He was formerly professor of mechanics in the polytechnic school, an eminent engineer, and author of many scientific works.

1848. The long expected outbreak in Ireland; viscount Hardinge arrived to take command of the troops from England, the whole available force of which was sent over, supposed to be 50,000 in number.

1848. M. ELLETT, engineer of the Niagara suspension bridge, drove a two horse carriage over that part of the bridge which was laid down and partly finished.

1853. Jonathan Richmond, one of the pioneers of western New York, died at Aurora, aged 79. For forty years he was actively engaged in aiding the rising fortunes of his sections of the state.

1856. A fire in Boston destroyed a block in North street, where 80 families were burnt out, and 9 lives lost.

JULY 30.

578. Benedict I (Bonosus), pope, died. During his pontificate the people suffered the double calamity of famine and invasion, throughout which he interested himself to alleviate their condition.

911. Abu Abdillah assassinated; the principal actor in the revolution which established the dynasty of the Fatimites in Africa and Egypt.

1095. Ladislaus I, king of Hungary, died. He was an able statesman and general, and victorious in his wars with the surrounding nations. The Huns were driven from the country by him.

1388. Battle of Otterbourne, on Thursday, "about the Lammas tide," between sunrise and sunset. The youthful combatants were nearly of the same age. Douglas was slain, and the English Hotspur and his brother taken prisoners. The ancient song called *The Hunting a' the Cheviat*, refers to a private conflict 48 years after this, between the son of Hotspur and William Douglas; but *Richard Sheale*, with the license of a ballad-poet has mingled the two events together.

1540. Thomas Abel, a chaplain at the court of Henry VIII, executed. He incurred the resentment of the king by his attachment to the cause of the queen, Catharine. He was hanged, and then drawn and quartered.

1588. William Stuart killed in Edinburgh by earl Bothwell.

1609. Battle between Champlain and Indians in Essex county, New York.

1625. The week's plague bill in London returns 2,471.

1631. A French coin dated 1596, found in digging a well at Dorchester, Mass.

1673. New York taken by the Dutch. A small expedition, fitted out to destroy the commerce of the English in America, having effectually performed this service on the Virginia coast, made their appearance before New York, which submitted without exchanging a shot. New Jersey was also humbled.

1711. The British and colonial fleet, consisting of 12 men of war, 40 transports, and 6 store ships, with 40 horses, a fine train of artillery, and all manner of war-like stores, sailed from Boston for the conquest of Canada.

1718. William Penn, the founder of Pennsylvania, died, aged 74. At the age of 24 he became a preacher among the quakers; but by the grant of Pennsylvania he was placed in the position of a legislator, and well did he sustain it.

1743. Thomas Emlyn, an English dissenting divine, died. He enjoyed an imprisonment of two years' duration, as a reward for the publication of some religious opinions, which no man had a right to entertain in those days.

1746. Eight of those concerned in the pretender's rebellion hung, beheaded and disemboweled near London.

1750. John Sebastian Bach, a German musician, died; celebrated for his skill as an organist, and also as a composer.

1762. Moro fort, at the entrance of the harbor of Havana, stormed by the English under admiral Pococke; 400 Spaniards were either cut in pieces, or perished in attempting to escape by water to the city; the rest threw down their arms and received quarter. (See Aug. 12.)

1768. Captain Cook sailed from England in the Endeavor, on his first voyage of discovery.

1771. Thomas Gray, an eminent English poet, died. He was one of the most learned men of Europe, equally conversant with every department of science.

1775. Captain Cook returned from his second and most important navigation, having lost but one man by sickness, out of a crew of 118 men, during an absence of more than three years.

1777. General Burgoyne reached fort Edward, on the Hudson river, having with incredible labor and fatigue conducted his army through the wilderness. General Schuyler, whose forces did not exceed 4,400 men, retreated over the river to Saratoga.

1780. Rocky mount, a British post on the Catawba, stormed and taken by Gen. Sumpter, after three repulses.

1784. Earthquake at Port Royal and Kingston, Jamaica. Of 150 vessels in the harbors but 6 or 8 were saved, and the sugar works were blown down. A scarcity of provisions attended the calamity.

1789. Battle of Putna; the Turkish army of 30,000 defeated with the loss of 1,500 men and all their artillery, camp equipage, &c., by the Austrian and Russian army, whose loss did not exceed 200.

1800. The grand jury of York, England, recommended the enclosing of 7,800,000 acres of waste lands as the best preventive of future famines.

1809. The British under lord Chatham invaded Holland with 40,000 troops.

1813. Fifth day's battle of the Pyrenees. The French under Soult defeated by the allies under Wellington, after an obstinate engagement. Loss supposed to have been about 8,000 on each side.

1844. ZECHARIAH POULSON, for many years editor of *Poulson's Daily Advertiser*, died. He was the last link connecting the fraternity of publishers with those of the days of Franklin.

1845. LYNTHIA BROWNING, the Kentucky giantess, died at Flemingsburg, Ky. She was seven feet high.

1855. GEORGE JOHNSTON, an eminent British surgeon, died, aged 58. While engaged in the practice of his profession, he devoted his leisure to natural history, in which he attained great eminence.

1855. JOHN WOODS, an eminent Ohio lawyer, died at Hamilton, aged 61. As state auditor he did much to preserve the public credit at a time of general depression.

JULY 31.

1423. Battle of Crevant, in France, in which the armies of the infant king of England were victorious.

1481. FRANCISCUS PHILADELPHUS, a learned Italian, died. He was at the head of the learned men of the day, professor of eloquence at Venice, and the personal friend of Lorenzo de Medici.

1498. COLUMBUS discovered the island of Trinidad, resembling three mountains.

1556. IGNATIUS LOYOLA, founder of the Jesuits, died. He was a brave officer in the Spanish army, and while under the hands of a surgeon his mind was directed to the subject of religion by reading. After having made a pilgrimage to Jerusalem and studied theology he went to Paris, and laid the foundation of an order, which in time became sufficiently powerful and corrupt.

1592. Sir WALTER RALEIGH disgraced, and sent with his lady to the tower.

1602. CHARLES GONRAULT DE BIRON, a French admiral, beheaded in the bastile. He distinguished himself by flood and field, and was a great favorite at the court of Heny IV. His fondness of pleasure led to error and ruin.

1627. A terrible earthquake in Apulia, by which many thousands lost their lives.

1712. Marchiennes surrendered to the French.

1718. JOHN HUGHES and SARAH DREW, two rustic lovers, struck dead by lightning, under the shelter of a hay cock, in England. Pope, Thomson and Gay, have scattered flowers upon their graves.

1718. Fifteen Spanish ships destroyed near Syracuse, by admiral sir George Byng.

1719. Colonel HUNTER, departing the province of New York, the chief command devolved on Peter Schuyler, as the oldest member of the board of council.

1750. JOHN V, of Portugal, died. He devoted himself to the encouragement of commerce, literature and industry among his subjects.

1760. Battle of Warburgh; the allies under the hereditary prince Ferdinand, defeated the French, who lost 1,500 killed, and about the same number taken prisoners.

1777. The marquis LAFAYETTE received, by a vote of congress, the appointment of major-general in the American army, being then but 20 years of age.

1786. A booth, at Montpelier, France, where a play was performing, fell and killed 500 persons.

1790. JOHN EDWIN, an English comedian, died. It was to his extraordinary talents that O'Keefe's dramas were greatly indebted for their success.

1807. The fortress of Mongal, in Spain, carried by storm and destroyed by the British under Cochrane.

1808. JOSEPH BENCIRENNI, an Italian writer, died. He distinguished himself in the belles-lettres and public affairs.

1813. Plattsburgh taken by the British without opposition, all the public and much private property was destroyed.

1813. Com. CHAUNCEY took York, U. C., destroyed the public property and brought away the stores and provisions.

1831. London bridge completed, having occupied nearly 8 years in its construction. It is built of granite, 928 feet in length. The old bridge had stood, with propping and patching, six centuries.

1840. MULLER, the distinguished antiquary and historian, died at Castri Levadia.

1848. EDMUND SIMPSON died; thirty-eight years manager of the Park theatre, New York, during which time he paid John Jacob Astor half a million dollars rent.

1850. The great diamond called Koh-i-noor, or mountain of light, was brought to England. It is valued at $2,000,000.

1854. The defenders of the barricades, at Madrid, 3,000 in number, defiled before the queen's palace, her majesty appearing on the balcony, with the king on one side, and Espartero, who had entered the city the day before, on the other.

1855. The official announcement was made of the removal of governor Reeder, of Kansas, and the appointment of John L. Dawson as his successor.

AUGUST.

AUGUST 1.

30 B. C. Defection of the entire fleet of Marc Antony, at Alexandria, which suddenly passed over to Octavius, afterwards Augustus Cæsar.

117. MARCUS ULPIUS TRAJAN, emperor of Rome, died. He admired and copied the virtues of Nerva, his predecessor, and reigned nearly twenty years in the hearts of his people, when Hadrian received his mantle.

432. CELESTINE I, pope, died. The doctrines of Nestorius were condemned by him.

643. OSWALD, king of Northumberland, slain at Maserfield. Bede says he erected in the shape of a wooden cross the first altar to Christ among the Bernicians.

725. The old English tax called *Peter's pence*, was first laudably imposed by Ina, king of the west Saxons, for the support of an English college at Rome, but afterwards appropriated by the church for very different purposes.

1137. LOUIS VI, king of France, died. He was a wise and popular monarch, but during his reign, which continued nearly thirty years, the country was disturbed by external quarrels and internal factions.

1202. King JOHN of England obtained a victory over his nephew Arthur, whom with his sister Eleanor he took prisoner.

1221. The convent belonging to Westminster abbey destroyed ; which issued in several individuals being severely punished.

1464. COSMO DE MEDICIS, a Florentine merchant, died. He bestowed vast expense and attention in the promotion of learning, and presided over the commonwealth 34 years, with so much wisdom and popularity, as to acquire the title of *Father of the People*. (See Oct. 5, 1434.)

1498. COLUMBUS, on his third voyage, first set his foot upon the continent of America at Terra-Firma, mistaking it for an island. This was more than a year after the English expedition under the Cabots had reached its shores.

1560. The Scottish parliament assembled which overturned the Roman church in Caledonia, and established a new ecclesiastical system on a Calvinistic and presbyterian model.

1589. HENRY III, of France, assassinated. He was a weak and vicious prince, during whose reign the country was desolated with factions and civil and religious wars. He was the last of the house of Valois.

1605. EDMUND ANDERSON, an eminent English lawyer, died. He was one of the ablest and most learned of queen Elizabeth's judges; his law works are of great authority.

1625. The first parliament of Charles I, of England, on account of the plague, met at Oxford.

1714. ANNE, queen of England, died, in the 50th year of her age.

1716. JAMES BOILEAU, a celebrated French theologian, died; a doctor of the Sorbonne, and a man of great wit and learning.

1720. JOHN LEAKE, a brave English admiral, died. He signalized himself in many important victories in different parts of the world.

1732. WILLIAM COSBY arrived at New York as governor of that province and New Jersey.

1743. RICHARD SAVAGE, an eminent English poet, died in prison, aged 46. His great natural abilities were over-balanced by vices and follies which rendered him an unhappy man.

1759. Battle of Minden; the British and German forces under Ferdinand of Brunswick defeated the French, who met with great losses.

1766. France stipulated not to aid the Pretender if England would suffer a Romish bishop to be sent to Canada; it was acceded to.

1768. The merchants and traders of Boston entered into a non-importation agreement against Great Britain.

1769. JEAN CHAPPE D'AUTEROCHE, a French astronomer, died at California, whither he had gone to make an observation. He was distinguished for learning and abilities.

1770. Battle of Cahal; the Turkish

army of 150,000 defeated by 18,000 Russians under marshal Romanzow.

1772. A revolution was effected in Sweden by the army, and dissimulation of the crown.

1774. Dr. Priestly discovered *dephlogisticated air*, which has been called the birth day of pneumatic chemistry.

1780. The village of Canajoharie laid waste by the Indians.

1790. John Knox, the book seller, and the improver of the herring fisheries in Scotland, died.

1793. Action without the harbor of New York between the French frigate L'Ambuscade, and British frigate Boston. The battle was severe, and both vessels were greatly damaged; but the Boston would have been captured if she had not been enabled to retreat. The Ambuscade had 6 killed, 20 wounded. The British lost their captain and nearly all their officers killed. The crews of the two frigates were about the same, 350 each.

1798. Battle of the Nile; the French fleet of 13 sail and 4 frigates defeated by the British, 13 ships of 74s, and a 50 gun ship under Nelson. Nine of the French ships were taken and 2 burnt, and 2 of the frigates destroyed. Admiral Brueys was mortally wounded and blown up in the Orient, 120 guns and 1070 men. Of the French 3,105 were put on shore by cartel, and 5,225 perished.

1801. Jonathan Edwards, president of Union college, died; a man of uncommon powers of mind.

1803. William Woodfall, an English printer, died. He possessed a remarkably retentive memory, and was the first who gave a full and immediate detail of the proceedings of parliament.

1807. John Walker, the English lexicographer, died.

1819. James Forbes died; a civil servant in the East India company, and creditably known as the author of *Oriental Memoirs*, which were selected from a mass of manuscripts written during 17 years' residence in India, stated to occupy 52,000 folio pages, in 150 vols. The plates, from drawings of plants and animals made by the author, have rarely been surpassed in spirit and beauty.

1821. William Floyd, one of the signers, died.

1821. Elizabeth Inchbald, an English dramatic writer and actress, died. She possessed great beauty and talent, and an unsullied reputation; many of her pieces are still *stock plays*.

1829. Capture of Jambouli and destruction of the Turkish camp by a brigade of Hulans and Cossacks, after having defeated on the road a body of 15,000 Turks.

1834. Robert Morrison, an eminent English orientalist, at Canton, died. He was considered the best Chinese scholar in Europe. He translated the whole of the *New Testament* into Chinese, which was printed in 1813; but the great monument of his literary fame is his *Dictionary of the Chinese Language*, 6 vols. quarto.

1834. The slaves in the British colonies emancipated, and a temporary apprenticeship commenced.

1834. The bill admitting dissenters to the honors of the English universities, which had passed the house of commons, rejected in the house of lords by a majority of 102—a grand halt to the march of mind in England.

1838. John Rogers died; a distinguished naval officer, and senior commander in the American navy. He had been fifteen months a resident of the naval asylum, and the greater part of the time in close confinement as a confirmed lunatic.

1838. The entire emancipation of the negro apprentices in the islands of Jamaica, Barbadoes, Chevis, Montserrat, St. Christophers, St. Vincent and Tortola, took place, in compliance with the acts of the colonial legislatures.

1848. The city of Vera Cruz delivered up to the Mexicans by the United States; general Smith embarked for home.

1849. Henry A. Breckingham, known as the author of several historical sketches and other interesting reminiscences of the early days of the American colonies, died at Brooklyn, of cholera.

1849. Queen Victoria embarked at Cowes on her visit to Ireland.

1851. Harriet Lee, an English authoress, died, aged 95. Jointly with her sister Sophia, they were the authors of various works, chiefly novels or dramas. Harriet was almost the exclusive author of the *Canterbury Tales*, 5 vols., perhaps the best known of their labors.

1853. The Austrian government, in a circular addressed to the European courts, protested against the proceedings of Capt. Ingraham, in the port of Smyrna, in rescuing Martin Koszta, claiming to be a citizen of the United States.

1854. Kenneth Muschison formerly governor of Penang and Singapore, died in London, aged 60.

1854. The yellow fever became epidemic at New Orleans. It disappeared in November, when the number of deaths was 2441. There were 600 deaths in Savannah from the same disease.

AUGUST 2.

338 B. C. Battle of Cheronea, on the Cephisus, and defeat of the Athenians and Thebans by Philip of Macedon.

338 B. C. The army of Archidamus, the Spartan, overthrown in Lucania, and himself killed.

322 B. C. Joint victory of Antipater and Craterius, near the walls of Cranon, in Thessaly.

10. Three Roman legions under Varus cut off in Germany. "Quintilius Varus, give me my legions again," exclaimed the father of his country. Varus, however, had shared the fate of his legions.

44. King AGRIPPA (*the Great*), smitten with disease in the public theatre at Cæsarea, on the second day of the games exhibited in honor of Claudius.

1100. WILLIAM II (*Rufus*), king of England, killed by an arrow. He possessed vigor, decision and policy, and acquired great wealth, by which he was enabled to purchase two French provinces. He founded Westminster hall.

1553. The *peace of religion* signed at Passau, on the Danube, between the confederates under Maurice of Saxony and the emperor Charles V, which established the protestant church in Germany.

1563. That great scourge, the plague, began in London.

1651. CROMWELL, after a week's siege, erected the colors of the commonwealth on the walls of Perth.

1675. Brookfield destroyed by the Indians. This town was situated in the country of the Nipnets, whom Philip finally succeeded in engaging to himself in his plan of a general extermination of the English colonies. The inhabitants being alarmed had scarcely time to flee to the principal house in the village, before the savages came pouring in, and fired every other house. The whole number of people thus collected together was about seventy. They withstood the assaults of the Indians two days, who kept up the attack night and day, and endeavored to fire the house by means of poles with firebrands and rags dipped in brimstone tied to their ends. They also filled a cart with hemp and flax, and other combustibles, and having set it on fire thrust it backward with poles spliced together to a great length. A storm of rain defeated this last scheme; and several companies of soldiers came to the relief of the besieged so unexpectedly that the Indians, although they had surrounded the town to cut off assistance, were disheartened and fled.

1676. King PHILIP, the Wampanoag, surprised in his quarters by a party of the colonists under captain Church; 150 of his men were killed, his wife and sons were taken prisoners, and he narrowly escaped with his life.

1684. A treaty of peace concluded at Albany, between the colonists and the Five Nations, who, since the peace of 1761, had extended their arms southward, and conquered the country from the Mississippi to the borders of the plantations; involving Virginia and Maryland in the calamities of their Indian allies, whom they were unable to protect.

1689. INNOCENT XI died. He has been called the protestant pope.

1704. Battle of Blenheim, in Bavaria; the English and Austrians under the duke of Marlborough and prince Eugene, obtained a famous victory over the French and Bavarians, who lost 12,000 killed and drowned, and 13,000 prisoners, including marshal Tallard. (13th by some authorities.)

1713. MENSEN ALTING, a Dutch writer, died; author of an excellent description of the Low Countries.

1732. RIP VAN DAM, upon whom the government of the province of New York devolved, finished his administration, on the arrival of William Cosby, with a commission over New York and New Jersey.

1748. Attack on fort Massachusetts by 300 French and Indians. Captain Williams sallied with 30 men and drove the enemy before him, when an ambuscade arose and attempted to cut off his retreat to the fort. By a quick movement he regained the place, and returned their fire with so much spirit that the enemy withdrew, carrying off their dead and wounded.

1763. Battle of Nuncas Nullus; the English defeated the troops of Mir Cossim, 28,000, took all their artillery and 150 boats laden with grain and stores.

1770. The Russians under Romanzow, defeated the Turks with great slaughter on the Pruth.

1776. MATTHEW MATY, an English writer, died. He published at the Hague, during six years, the *Journal Britannique*, containing an account of the productions of the English press, in French.

1786. MARGARET NICHOLSON, supposing herself to be queen of England, made an attempt to assassinate George III. She was afterwards confined as a lunatic.

1788. THOMAS GAINSBOROUGH died; one of the most celebrated English landscape painters of the last century.

1793. MARIE ANTOINETTE, queen of France and daughter of an emperor, taken from the temple prison in the night, and removed to a cell in the Conciergerie, 8 feet square, and partly under ground. As a matter of favor she was permitted to take under her arm a small bundle of clothing.

1798. John Palmer, a popular English actor, died on the stage during a performance, immediately on uttering the words, "There is an other and a better world."

1802. Bonaparte declared consul of France for life.

1803. John Hoole, an ingenious English poet, died. He translated some of the best Italian poets, wrote three tragedies, and several other works.

1811. William Williams, one of the signers died, aged 81. He advanced money and obtained supplies for the army, and also contributed by his writings and speeches to arouse the spirit of freedom in his countrymen.

1813. Defence of fort Stephenson by 160 men with 1 six pounder, under Col. Croghan, then aged 21. The British, consisting of 500 regulars under Proctor, and about 800 Indians under Tecumseh, with 5 six pounders and 1 howitzer, were defeated with considerable loss.

1814. The remarkable steeple of Kelwinning, in Scotland, fell. It was built in 1140.

1815. Convention between the representatives of Great Britain, Prussia, Austria and Russia, who declared Bonaparte to be the prisoner of the allies, and entrusted his custody especially to Great Britain.

1830. Charles X, of France, subscribed his abdication in favor of his grandson the young duke of Bordeaux.

1842. John Clifford, a lieutenant in the revolutionary army, died at Bethlehem, Hunterdon co., N. J., aged 94.

1843. Francis W. P. Greenwood, pastor of King's chapel, Boston, died at Dorchester, Mass., aged 50. He was also an accomplished scholar and naturalist.

1843. James Richards, professor of theology in the Auburn theological seminary, died, aged 75; an eminently useful man.

1849. Mehemet Ali, pacha of Egypt, died at Alexandria, aged 80. He was a powerful sovereign, and gave the sultan much trouble. He did more than any of his predecessors towards introducing improvements into his territories.

1849. Garibaldi, the Roman chief, escaped on board some fishing vessels at Cesenatico, on the Adriatic, accompanied by 300 followers. The remainder of his band surrendered to the Austrians.

1849. Stephen Longfellow, a New England lawyer of note, died at Portland, Me., aged 73. He was a member of the Hartford convention from Massachusetts, and distinguished for great acuteness and penetration. He compiled 16 volumes of the *Massachusetts Reports*, and 12 of the *Maine*, extending over a period of thirty years.

1852. Thomas Thomson, a Scottish author, died, aged 60. He was professor of chemistry in the university of Glasgow, and established a highly scientific reputation. In 1812 he began the *Annals of Philosopy*, in London, which he conducted ten years.

1852. A violent earthquake occurred at St. Jago de Cuba, causing a great destruction of property.

AUGUST 3.

479 b. c. The fatal battle of Platea, between Mardonius the Persian and Pausanius the Spartan general. The other sanguinary victory over the Persians, on the promontory of Mycale was achieved the same day, third of Boedromion.

431 b. c. An eclipse of the sun noticed by Thucydides, eight days after the first invasion of Attica under Archidamus, king of Sparta, at the head of 60,000 Peloponesian confederates, and whilst Pericles was in the act of embarking against Epidaurus, the sacred city.

678. A morning comet, shaped like a fiery pillar, seen in England. It was visible during three months, and caused the conversion of the South Saxons from paganism.

1274. Edward I landed in England from Palestine. He sailed from his winter mansion, Trepano, Sicily, on the 20th April, 1271.

1414. James I of Scotland conveyed from the tower to Windsor; there this bird of song was *wired in* for three years.

1460. James II (*with the fiery face*), king of Scotland, killed by the bursting of a gun, aged 29, after a reign of 24 years.

1492. Columbus embarked in the carack Santa Maria, with two other vessels and 120 persons, from the Isle of Saltes, against Palos, in Andalusia, to find a western continent.

1546. Stephen Dolet, a learned Frenchman, a painter and a bookseller, burnt at Lyons for atheism.

1554. The first letter in Europe known to have been sealed with sealing wax bears this date, and was written at London, addressed to the rheingrave Philip Francis von Daun, from his agent in England, Gerhard Hermann. The wax employed in sealing this letter is of a dark red color, very shining, and the impress bears the initials of the writer.

1554. Battle of Marciano; the troops of Cosmo de Medici, under Medicini, defeated the French under Peter Strozzi, a Florentine nobleman, who was wounded.

1592. The English earl of Cumberland captured a Spanish carack, Madre de Dios (Mother of God), valued at $150,000.

1612. John Bond, a learned English commentator on the Latin classics, died.

1645. Battle of Nordlingen; the allies under Merci, defeated by the French under Turenne, Conde and Grammont. Merci was killed and Grammont taken prisoner.

1672. John Francis Senaudt, a Dutch theological writer, died.

1692. Battle of Steenkerken; the English under William III defeated with great slaughter by the French.

1712. Joshua Barnes died; an eminent English critic and professor of Greek. He wrote the *Life of Edward III*, and several Latin and English poems.

1715. A cobbler of Highgate, London, was whipped from Holloway to that place for reflecting on the government.

1720. N. Heinsius, an eminent Dutch statesman, died. He was 30 years grand pensionary of Holland, and exerted the energy of his mind and the resources of his country to abridge the power of the French monarch.

1721. Grinlin Gibbon died, an eminent English sculptor and carver in ivory and wood. The place or country of his birth is not known. He was discovered by sir John Evelyn, who walking by accident near a poor solitary thatched cottage, had the curiosity to look in at the window, when he saw him carving a large cartoon or crucifix of Tintoret, a copy of which Evelyn himself had brought from Venice. His performances in marble and ivory were so very fine, that they often required to be defended by a glass case. Many of his flower pieces are light almost as fancy, and shake to the rattling of passing carriages. There is no instance before him, says Walpole, of a man who gave to wood the loose and airy lightness of flowers, and chained together the various productions of the elements with the free disorder natural to each species.

1732. The first stone laid of the bank of England.

1761. John Matthew Gesner, a German scholar and critic, died. He published several valuable editions of the classics.

1763. Thomas Godfrey, an American poet, died, aged 27. He was a watchmaker, and said to have been the real inventor of Hadley's quadrant.

1768. Thomas Secker, archbishop of Canterbury, died; whose lectures and sermons are masterly compositions.

1777. Fort Schuyler, at the head of the Mohawk river, invested by the British, about 1,800, under St. Leger. The garrison consisted of 600 continentals under general Gansevoort, who maintained their position till the British abandoned the siege and returned to Canada, leaving their tents standing; their artillery, and ammunition and provisions fell into the hands of the Americans.

1780. Stephen Bonnot de Condillac, a distinguished French philosopher, died. His works are characterized by great clearness and sagacity, and were published in 1798 in 35 volumes.

1783. A new eruption of the Skaptar Jokul, in Iceland, poured forth fresh floods of lava, which taking different directions from the others, filled the bed of a river, and formed a large lake. By this single eruption, 9,000 persons lost their lives, being nearly one-fifth of the whole population of the island. This volcano, which commenced on the 11th June, continued for two years, and the lava was not cooled in some places, when visited eleven years after.

1787. John Baynes, an English politician, died, aged 29. He was distinguished for his early attainments and devotion to the cause of liberty.

1788. Louis Francois Armand du Plessis de Richelieu, marechal of France, died, aged 93. He had the courage, the fortune and the talents of a great general, the sagacity, prudence and penetration of a great statesman; but with these and many amiable qualities he chose to be nothing but a common courtier.

1792. Richard Arkwright died; inventor of the spinning jenny, one of the most useful machines in the world. He was originally a barber, but his invention enabled him at his death to leave a property worth £500,000.

1797. Jeffrey Amherst, a celebrated English admiral, died. He assisted in the conquest of Canada.

1802. Henry, prince of Prussia, died. He distinguished himself at the head of several Prussian armies, and in time of peace was engaged in literary pursuits. On the death of his elder brother, he was excluded from the throne by his nephew, and resided in France.

1804. The United States squadron under Com. Preble, attacked the shipping and batteries of Tripoli. During the action the Constitution was much injured; 13 were wounded and 1 killed; 3 of the enemy's boats were captured and 3 sunk.

1805. Christopher Anstey, an ingenious English poet, died.

1806. Miranda, having received a reinforcement from the British, landed in the gulf of Paria, for the purpose of effecting a revolution.

1806. Michael Adanson, an eminent French naturalist, died, leaving an immense mass of manuscripts which he had collected with the view of publishing an encyclopedia. He passed several years in

Africa making collections in natural history.

1812. Privateer schooner Atlas, of Philadelphia, captured in one hour British ships Pursuit, 16 guns, and Planter, 12 guns. The latter was recaptured.

1814. Fort Erie invested by the British, upwards of 5,000.

1814. 1,200 British crossed the Niagara, to attack Buffalo, but were repulsed by 250 riflemen under Morgan, and compelled to recross.

1814. Great disturbances in Spain, many members of the cortes arrested by order of the king.

1819. Barrow's straits rediscovered by Capt. Parry. He penetrated to Melville island. The lowest state of the thermometer was 55° below zero, Fahrenheit.

1823. Lazare Nicholas Marguerite Carnot, a distinguished French general, died. He possessed an uncommon talent for the mathematical and military sciences, and pursued a uniform and correct course in his politics, which enabled him to ride out the storm of the revolution, and the subsequent changes.

1848. Women's rights convention assembled at Rochester; demanded the rights of suffrage, property, preaching, teaching, &c., &c.

1849. Aaron K. Wooley, a Kentucky judge, died at Lexington, aged 49. He was a native of New Jersey, graduated at West Point, and studied law in Mississippi. He was some time state senator of Fayette county, Ky., and at the time of his death had been ten years professor of law in Transylvania university.

1849. General Oudinot surrendered the civil administration of the Papal states into the hands of the pope's three commissioners, who entered on the work of *reaction*.

1850. Jacob Jones, an American commodore, died at Philadelphia, aged 82. He stood nearly at the head of the list of post captains, two names only taking precedence. Capt. Jones, we believe, was a native of Delaware. He is one of the number who, in the war of 1812, contributed to establish the naval renown of our country. He fought in the Wasp one of the bloodiest naval battles in our history, and captured in 45 minutes the British brig-of-war Frolic of superior force, and under circumstances highly unfavorable to success. For this action the states of Delaware, Massachusetts and New York, each voted him a sword in commemoration of his gallantry, which was in no wise impaired by the subsequent capture of both the Wasp and the Frolic, when in a crippled condition, by a British 74. He was afterwards appointed to the Macedonian. Temperate himself, he deserves honorable mention as a promoter of temperance among his crew; many seamen were reclaimed by him.

1851. The steamer Pampero, with about 500 troops, composing the expedition against Cuba under general Lopez, left New Orleans at daybreak.

1854. Colonel Loring, a receiver of public moneys at Benicia, Cal., was murdered at the St. Nicholas hotel, New York, by Dr. Graham, of New Orleans.

1856. Edward Curtis, a prominent New York lawyer and politician, died. He was a native of Vermont, was graduated at Union college, and began his political career in 1834 in the New York common council. He was collector of the port under president Harrison.

1857. Eugene Sue, a celebrated French novelist, died, aged 49. *The Mysteries of Paris* and *the Wandering Jew*, are known in all Europe and America.

AUGUST 4.

57 b. c. The decree recalling Cicero from banishment, which passed the full senate, consisting of 417 members, was ratified in the field of Mars, by a vote of all the centuries; it was nearly the last genuine public act of Roman liberty.

882. Louis III, of France, died. He shared the throne with his brother Carloman, and ably defended himself against his enemies.

1060. Henry I, of France, died in consequence of taking an improper medicine; highly respected as a good warrior and a benevolent man.

1265. Battle of Evesham; the earl of Leicester defeated and killed by the forces under prince Edward, and the king released from confinement. No quarter was given, and the aged king only received his life by an unwonted energy of mind; exclaiming to his antagonist, "Hold, fellow, I am Harry of Winchester."

1347. The conquest of Calais by the third Edward, after a siege of 11 months, when the six citizens, with halters round their necks, surrendered the keys of their independence. The condemned lives of these men, whose patriotism has scarcely ever been equaled, were spared through the tears and intercessions of Philippa. The inhabitants were removed and the city repeopled with English, in whose possession it remained more than two centuries. The pay of the army was as follows: the marines and archers on foot received 3d.; the black prince £1; and the bishop of Durham, with the earls, 6s. 8d. per day.

1496. Bartholomew Columbus, the admiral's brother, laid the foundation of St. Domingo.

1578. Battle of the three kings, in the west of Africa, which was invaded by Sebastian of Portugal, in which the Moors were victorious, but the three kings engaged in it lost their lives.

1583. Sir HUMPHREY GILBERT landed at St Johns, Newfoundland, and took possession of it in the name of the queen of England.

1598. WILLIAM CECIL, lord Burley, died. He was an eminent English statesman, memorable for his virtue and integrity, as well as his great abilities.

1609. HUDSON discovered cape Cod, and under the supposition that it was an island, called it New Holland, in compliment to the country of his employers. The Dutch afterwards called it Staaten hoek. The Indians here were observed to have green tobacco, and pipes with clay bowls and copper stems.

1612. HUGH BROUGHTON, an eminent Hebrew scholar, died. So classical was his Hebrew that a Jew predicted the turning of the whole Jewish race if the New Testament would be printed in such pure Hebrew.

1633. GEORGE ABBOT, archbishop of Canterbury, died, aged 71. He rose from humble circumstances to great dignity.

1651. Stirling castle and town taken by Monk for Cromwell.

1666. A disastrous hurricane in the West Indies. Lord Francis Willoughby perished with his fleet of 15 sail. The poor fellows who escaped the wreck, were seized with exultation by the French.

1696. General FRONTENAC invaded the Onondaga country.

1713. WILLIAM CAVE, an eminent English scholar and divine, died. He published a great number of useful works.

1723. WILLIAM FLEETWOOD, an English bishop, died. "His character was great in every respect."

1747. MICHAEL MAITTAIRE, a learned French critic and bibliographer, died. He edited many of the classical authors, with useful indexes, and wrote several important works.

1759. Crown point on lake Champlain, taken from the French by Gen. Amherst.

1774. CHRISTOPHER COUDRETTE, a French ecclesiastic, died. His chief work was a history of the Jesuits; he was an opposer of that order, and of the pope's bull, unigenitus.

1781. ISAAC HAYNE, a patriot of the revolution, hanged at Charleston by order of the British lord Rawdon, an act, under the circumstances, extremely unjust and merciless, and which his lordship attempted to justify in a pamphlet.

1783. Captain JOHN DARBY, of the Astrea, arrived at Salem with the news of the ratification of the treaty of peace between the United States and Great Britain. He is said to have carried out the accounts of the first conflict at Lexington.

1789. Privileged classes abolished in France.

1792. JOHN BURGOYNE, a British general, died. He surrendered his whole army to general Gates at Saratoga, and returned to England. He was a member of parliament, and a successful dramatic author. (June 4, P. Cyc.)

1799. JOHN BACON, an English sculptor, died. He was apprenticed to a porcelain manufacturer, in which condition he devoted his leisure to statuary, and finally rose to great eminence in his profession.

1804. ADAM DUNCAN, a gallant English admiral, died; celebrated for the victory he gained over the Dutch fleet at Camperdown, for which he was rewarded with a peerage.

1806. MIRANDA arrived at Coro an hour before day; the place was abandoned, and through mistake his troops fired on each other.

1808. French assaulted Saragossa in Spain, and penetrated into a part of the town.

1808. The commencement of Wellington's famous retreat into Portugal.

1814. United States troops under Col. Croghan attacked the British and Indians at fort Mackinaw, but were repulsed with the loss of 50 killed.

1815. BONAPARTE delivered a written protest for the prince regent of England, against being sent to St. Helena.

1821. WILLIAM FLOYD, one of the signers of the declaration of independence, died at Western, New York.

1835. The Spanish ministry having suppressed the Jesuits and confiscated their property, a royal decree to this effect was signed. By this decree 900 convents were suppressed in Spain, and their property applied towards the payment of the debts of the state.

1836. The famous bell of Moscow, the largest in the world, raised from the ground, where it had laid a great many years. Its weight is about 440,000 pounds, is 21 feet in height and 23 in diameter.

1842. JOHN BANIN, a popular Irish novelist, died near Kilkenny, Ireland.

1846. FISHER AMES HARDING, one of the editors of the *Detroit Daily Advertiser*, died at Detroit.

1848. DANIEL WADSWORTH, a gentleman of highly cultivated taste and benevolence, died at Hartford, Ct., aged 77.

1848. Capital punishment except in cases of martial law, abolished in the

Prussian assembly, also in the German parliament at Frankfort.

1851. At Leon, Nicaragua, Gen. Munoz, late minister of war, with a small body of troops, took prisoners president Pineda and most of his cabinet, sent them to a port in Tigre islands, and elected Justo Albuanez president.

1852. ALFRED D'ORSAY, the mirror of fashion, letters and art, died in Paris, aged 54.

1854. A severe battle was fought between the Chippewa and Sioux Indians.

1854. BAILEY WASHINGTON, a surgeon in the navy, died at Washington, aged 67. He was a relative of general Washington, and entered the navy in 1810 as surgeon. He was with the Enterprise when she captured the Boxer, and was fleet surgeon under Rogers, Elliot and Patterson, in the Mediterranean.

1854. JOSE BARUNDIA, minister from Honduras, died at New York, aged 70. He was elected to the presidency of the confederation of Central America, when he adopted many of the laws of the United States, and devoted his salary to the promotion of public schools. He was the prime mover of the liberal party, and the first to raise the standard of rebellion against the Spanish government.

1857. JOSHUA FORMAN, founder of the city of Syracuse in New York, died in Rutherfordton, N. C., aged 71. He was one of the early promoters of the Erie canal, and first judge of the county of Onondaga, from which he removed about twenty years before his death.

AUGUST 5.

57 B. C. CICERO landed from Durazzo at Brundusium, and was met there by his excellent daughter Tullia, on the 20th anniversary of her birthday.

1100. Inauguration of Henry I, of England, who instantly granted a charter to the nation, restoring the laws of Edward *the Confessor* to the same state in which they had been settled by *the Conqueror;* and drove from his court the *effœminati* with their enormous and disgusting train.

1391. CHARLES VI, of France, surnamed the *Well-beloved*, seized by a mental distemper, which, as it deprived him of the sovereign authority, afterwards led, in bad hands to the ruin of his kingdom.

1407. ROBERT KNOLLES, so famed in the French wars of Edward III, died at Scenethorp, Norfolk, but was buried at White Friars church, London, which he had built.

1501. REGINALD BRAY, an English architect, died. He was also a distinguished warrior and statesman, and in the latter capacity acquired the title of "the father of his country."

1604. By royal proclamation this 5th day ot August was appointed a holiday in celebration of king James's delivery from the conspiracy of the Gowries.

1633. GEORGE ABBOT, archbishop of Canterbury, died. He assisted in the translation of the *Bible*, being one of the eight divines to whom it was committed.

1704. Sanguinary battle at Hochstädt, in which the French, &c., were defeated by the confederates under Marlborough.

1717. Battle of Peterwaradein; the Turks defeated by the Austrians under prince Eugene, with great loss. (1716?)

1754. JAMES GIBBS, an ingenious English architect, died; leaving a handsome property to public charities.

1759. Leipsic taken by the Austrians.

1778. The British burnt and destroyed their fleet off Rhode island on the appearance of the French fleet under count d'Estaing.

1781. Action off the Dogger bank, between the British fleet, 6 ships, 4 frigates and a cutter, under admiral Parker, and the Dutch, 8 ships, 10 frigates and 5 sloops, under admiral Zoutman. Both fleets were greatly damaged; the Dutch retired to the Texel; the British did not follow them.

1792. LAFAYETTE accused of treason before the national assembly. He had previously been burnt in effigy in the Palais royal by the Jacobins.

1792. FREDERIC NORTH, earl of Guildford, better known as *Lord North*, died, aged 60. As adviser to George III in the American war, he became and continued to his death unpopular.

1796. Battle of Castiglione, between the French under Bonaparte and the imperialists under Wurmzer. The latter were defeated, with the loss of 500 killed, 2,000 captured, and 8 cannon.

1799. RICHARD HOWE, a celebrated English admiral, died. He entered the navy at the age of 14; rose through the usual gradations to the highest rank, distinguished himself on many occasions, and died at the age of 75.

1812. Battle of Brownstown; the British regulars and Indians attacked the United States troops, 150 men, under Van Horne.

1813. American privateer Decatur, 13 guns, captured British schooner Dominica, 16 guns, by boarding.

1814. Division of the Scheldt fleet, in virtue of the treaty of Paris, between France and the allies.

1815. Massacre of the protestants at Nismes, in France; these enormities continued nine days.

1816. First state election held in Indiana.

1833. GEORGE GIBBS died near New York. He was a practical mineralogist, and the collector of the extensive cabinet of minerals in Yale college.

1835. THOMAS MCCRIE, a Scottish divine and ecclesiastical antiquary, died. He was distinguished for his patient research, candor and ability as a historian, and produced several works which have a high reputation.

1835. G. S. NEWTON, an eminent painter, died in England. He was a native of Halifax, N. S., became distinguished in his profession, and produced a number of works which are highly esteemed.

1839. The city of Cabul, Afghanistan, taken by the British, and the war in that country brought to an end.

1840. The city and island of Chusan, belonging to China, captured after a short resistance, by the British under brigadier general Burrell. The Chinese lost 25 killed; the British none.

1846. JOHN WARD (*Father of the City*) died at St. Johns, New Brunswick, aged 92. He was born near New York, and adhering to the British interest, entered the army in 1776, and was frequently in action. At the peace of 1783, he embarked with his regiment, the Loyal Americans, to New Brunswick, where the corps was disbanded. He then embarked in commercial pursuits, and at the time of his death was the senior half pay officer, as well as the oldest merchant in the province. He filled several civil offices, and sustained an estimable character.

1849. The number of births in Connecticut for the year ending this day was 7,373; marriages 2,757; deaths 5,016.

AUGUST 6.

1577. Queen ELIZABETH granted a license to John Day, and Richard Day, his son, during their lives, and that of the longest liver, to print the *Psalms of David* in metre.

1580. ANDREA PALLADIO, a very distinguished Italian architect, died; many specimens of his designs yet remain.

1585. DAVIS, the navigator, reached the strait which bears his name, and cast anchor in Exeter bay, "beneath that brave mount, the cliffs whereof were orient as gold."

1637. BENJAMIN JONSON, the English poet and dramatist, died, aged 63. He was a bricklayer at the outset of life; but his inclinations turned to the building of monuments more imperishable than those of brick and stone. (16th, N. S.)

1638. Birthday of NICHOLAS MALEBRANCHE, a distinguished French philosopher. His works were highly esteemed for their genius and style; and for his manners, which were amiable and simple, he was greatly venerated.

1660. DON DIEGO VELASQUEZ DE SILVA died; a distinguished Spanish painter.

1662. METACOM, sachem of Pokanoket, afterwards celebrated under the English title of king Philip, made his appearance at the court of Plymouth, and solicited the continuance of the amity and friendship which had subsisted between the governor of Plymouth and his father and brother; and promised for himself and his successors to remain subjects of the king of England.

1674. THOMAS WILLETT, the first mayor of New York, died. He is buried at Seekonk, Mass.

1695. FRANCIS DE HARLAY died; archbishop of Paris, the favorite of Louis XIV.

1701. ULRIC OBRECHT, a learned German critic and Latin historian, died. So extensive and various was his learning that he has been styled "the epitome of human science."

1706. JOHN BAPTIST DU HAMEL died; a celebrated French philosopher and divine.

1725. THOMAS RAWLINSON (*Tom Folio*), an English antiquary, died. The sale of his collection of books and manuscripts, which were put up at auction after his death, occupied several weeks.

1745. DAVID WILKINS died; an English librarian and antiquary, and a learned author.

1756. EUGENE ARAM, a self-taught English scholar, executed near York, for murder, and hung in chains on Knaresborough forest. He was a man of consummate abilities and wonderful erudition, but appears to have been a victim to covetousness.

1777. General HERKIMER, marching with the forces of Tryon county to relieve Gen. Gansevoort at fort Schuyler, was ambushed by a strong detachment of British and Indians, and defeated with the loss of 400. The Indians lost several of their great chiefs and 70 warriors.

1778. Sieur GERARD, ambassador from France, introduced to congress. He was the first ambassador from any nation to the United States.

1780. Battle of Hanging-rock; 600 Americans under Sumpter attacked and defeated the British, consisting of the prince of Wales' regiment and a large body of tories. The regiment was almost entirely destroyed; from 278 it was reduced to 9 men.

1788. The last *lit de justice* in France, assembled at Versailles, by Louis XVI, to enforce upon the parliament of Paris the adoption of the obnoxious taxes proposed by Calonne.

1796. Battle of Roveredo; the French under Bonaparte defeated the Austrians under Wurmzer, after an action of 16 hours, and entered Trent. Austrian loss 6,000 men.

1796. James Pettit Andrews died; author of several English histories and other works of merit.

1799. Marie Eliezer Block, an able German naturalist, died. He was of obscure parentage, and self-taught. Besides other valuable works on natural history and medicine, he published a *History of Fishes*, 6 vols. folio, colored plates.

1806. Francis II, emperor of Germany and king of Rome, resigned his titles and annexed his possessions in Germany to the Austrian empire. The *millenium* of the empire, founded by Charlemagne, fell upon the holiday of Christmas, 1800.

1815. Commodore Decatur arrived with his fleet off Tripoli.

1817. Pierre Samuel Dupont de Nemours, a French statesman, died. He was distinguished for his knowledge and talents, as well as his excellent character and principles. On the return of Bonaparte from Elba he came to America, where he died.

1818. David Ferguson, a Scottish soldier, died at Dunkirk, aged 124, very much respected and beloved.

1824. Battle of Junin, in Peru; the royalists defeated by the united Peruvian and Colombian forces, under Bolivar. The combatants fought hand to hand, with lance and sabre, those engaged being cavalry only.

1840. Louis Napoleon Bonaparte, son of the late king of Holland, accompanied by about 60 men, made an attempt to effect an hostile descent upon France. The party landed about two leagues from Boulogne, directed their march to that city, and were soon taken prisoners. The prince was soon after placed in the castle of Ham.

1843. The *Thousand Years' Jubilee* celebrated in Germany, in commemoration of the settlement by which the empire was divided between the three brothers, sons of Philip *the Devout*. The festival occurred on Sunday, and was very generally and appropriately celebrated, more particularly in the Prussian states.

1846. A revolution took place again in Mexico, in favor of the exiled Santa Anna. The troops in Vera Cruz and its vicinity first declared in his favor, and were soon followed by those at the capital, who deposed and imprisoned general Paredes, the president of the republic, and proclaimed Santa Anna, and the constitution of 1824.

1849. A treaty of peace was signed between Austria and Piedmont.

1851. An eruption having taken place in the volcanic mountains of Martinique, columns of smoke were seen to issue from eight distinct craters.

1855. A riot at Louisville, Ky., between the Americans and foreigners; several were killed on both sides, and rows of houses belonging to the foreign population were torn down and burnt.

AUGUST 7.

480 B. C. The immortal battle in the pass of Thermopylæ is placed upon this day; when Leonidas with 300 Spartans withstood the army of Xerxes. There was a skirmish also with the Grecian fleet at Artemisium. Diodorus fixes the victory of Gelon, under the walls of Himera, in Sicily, upon the same day.

445 B. C. Dedication of the walls of Jerusalem by Nehemiah, on the 7th of Elul, in the 21st year of Artaxerxes.

44. Herod Agrippa, king of Judea, died suddenly upon his throne. He was a great builder, whose expenses exceeded his income, for his generosity was boundless, saith Josephus. He persecuted the Christians, and was one of those scourges of mankind who have been cut off with their vices.

461. Julius Valerius Majorian, emperor of Rome, assassinated. He was successful in his war with the Vandals, and universally respected for his virtues.

1106. Henry IV, emperor of Germany, died. He was a brave, but unfortunate prince, who, having humbled his enemies in 66 battles, was finally dethroned and reduced to indigence by his own sons.

1485. Henry Tudor, earl of Richmond, afterwards Henry VII, landed at Milford haven from Normandy, for the invasion of England, with 2,000 men.

1588. The Spanish armada, becalmed before Dunkirk, completely discomfited by the appearance of eight ships filled with pitch, sulphur and other combustibles, and having been set on fire as the breeze sprung up were directed by the English admiral against the different divisions of the Spanish fleet. The darkness of the night lent terror to the awful appearance of the approaching flames; and the crews, anxious only for their own preservation, weighed anchor or cut their cables, and suffered their ships to drive before the wind. In this confusion many of them ran afoul of one another, and several of them received such damage as to be unfit for future use.

1613. Dorchester, in England, destroyed by fire.

1667. John Wilson, first minister of Boston, died. He came over with governor Winthrop, 1630, and was ordained under a tree in Charlestown.

1679. La Salle sailed from the foot of lake Erie in the first vessel built upon that lake, with a crew of thirty men. His vessel was lost on its return from Mackinaw with its crew of six men, and a cargo of peltries, valued at fifty thousand francs.

1771. John Daniel Schoepflin, an eminent German philosopher, historiographer and antiquary, died. His reputation was so great, that his residence was solicited by the sovereigns of different countries.

1793. The first patient of yellow fever in Philadelphia, which raged there with great fury this year, died on this day. The number that died of the disease during its prevalence was about 3,500.

1804. Second attack on Tripoli by the United States squadron under Com. Preble. One of the prizes previously taken was blown up by the passage of a red hot ball through her magazine.

1806. Elizabeth Smith, an accomplished English lady, died. She understood most of the learned languages, and had a knowledge of the sciences.

1807. Ignatius Mouradgea d'Ohsson, an Armenian diplomatist, died. He was in the service of the Swedish embassy at Constantinople, where he conceived the plan of a work on the Ottoman empire. It was completed, after a labor of 45 years, in 7 vols., and published at Paris.

1812. United States frigate Essex captured British king's brig George.

1819. Battle of Bojaca ; the revolutionists of Venezuela and New Granada, under Bolivar, totally defeated the Spaniards, whose destruction was so complete that the viceroy fled, leaving the public treasure a prey to the conquerors. This battle decided the independence of New Granada.

1820. Eliza Bacciocchi, sister of Bonaparte, died. She married a captain in the army, who on the conquest of Italy was created prince of Lucca and Piombino ; but she was the actual sovereign, and when she reviewed the troops, her husband discharged the office of aid-de-camp.

1821. Caroline Amelia Elizabeth, wife of George IV, of England, died, aged 53. She was abandoned by her husband, then prince of Wales, soon after their marriage, and the nation was repeatedly agitated by their disputes, for more than 20 years.

1830. The throne of France declared vacant by the chamber of deputies; after making various important modifications in the charter, they called to the throne Louis Phillippe, and his male descendants for ever.

1848. The great comet, whose revolution occupies 292 years, passed its perihelion in July, and was first seen on this day by a gentleman in Altona.

1854. The Turks entered Bucharest, which the Russians had previously evacuated.

1855. A severe and bloody riot occurred at St. Louis, Missouri, between the Irish and Americans, which continued for 48 hours, and resulted in the death of 10 persons, and the severe injury of 30 more.

1855. While two companies of militia were conducting to jail a prisoner named Debar, for the murder of a negro, at Milwaukie, the mob seized him and killed him without resistance.

1855. Richard Sheepshanks, a British astronomer, died, aged 61. He made great efforts in determining the latitude and longitude of places in England and Ireland, and contributed a series of papers to the *Penny Clyclopedia* on the science of astronomy.

AUGUST 8.

70. Capture of Jerusalem by Titus, the 8th day of the month Gorpieus, (Elul) upon his daughter's birthday.

1419. Peter d' Ailly, a French ecclesiastic, died. He was of an obscure family, and rose by his merit to the office of cardinal.

1503. Alexander VI (*Roderick Borgia*), pope, died. He was of infamous notoriety before his elevation to the pontificate, and is supposed to have been poisoned by a draught which he had prepared for some of his guests.

1540. Nuptials of Henry VIII and Catharine Howard, his fifth spouse. By "a notable appearance of honor, cleanness and maidenly behavior," she won the heart of old Harry, whose marriage with Anne of Cleves was annulled the 9th of July previous.

1588. Edwin Sandys, archbishop of York, died. He assisted in the translation of what is called the *Bishop's Bible*, and was one of the nine divines appointed by Elizabeth to dispute with nine catholics before the parliament.

1588. The English fleet under lord Howard attacked the Spanish armada. The engagement began at 4 o'clock in the morning and continued till 6 at night, and resulted in a total defeat of the armada. The Spanish admiral, apprehending the entire destruction of his fleet, resolved to sail northwards and make the circuit of the British isles. When he had rounded the Orkneys, the fleet was dispersed by a storm; horses, mules and baggage were thrown overboard to lighten the ships, some of which were wrecked, some sunk in the North sea, others wrecked on the coast of Scotland, and more than thirty were driven by another storm upon the coast of Ireland, where many of the crews were barbarously murdered. The duke of Medina finally reached Santardu with sixty-five sail in a shattered condition, out of 150 sail of noble vessels which entered the British channel, many of them of the largest class.

1641. Though Sabbath, both houses of the English parliament sat to prevent the king from going to Scotland.

1776. Force of the northern American army, under Washington, 10,514 fit for duty, 3,668 sick, 2,946 on command, 97 on furlough—total, 17,225. The small pox was committing great ravages at this time, 5,500 having died of it since April; inoculation being prohibited in general orders.

1778. Fort Boonesborough invested by 450 Canadians and Indians. The fort was garrisoned by 50 men, who defended it with great spirit against every stratagem till the 20th, when the siege was abandoned, and its capture never again attempted.

1780. The combined fleets of France and Spain captured five East Indiamen and fifty merchant ships bound for the West Indies.

1792. John Leake, an English physician, died; founder of the Westminster lying-in hospital, and an esteemed author.

1794. The entrenchments of Pellingen, a series of redoubts raised by the Austrians in the most advantageous situations, in order to cover Treves, were carried by the French.

1804. Robert Macfarlane, a Scottish miscellaneous writer, died. He translated Ossian into Latin.

1805. Richard Worsley, governor of the isle of Wight, died. During a tour in Europe he made a fine collection of statues and antiques, of which he published a description.

1808. John Broome, lieutenant-governor of the state of New York, died, and was buried in the presbyterian church yard in Wall street, in the city of New York.

1811. British under admiral Stopford took Batavia and a great part of the island of Java.

1812. The United States troops under general Hull evacuated Canada and entered Detroit.

1814. First meeting of the British and American commissioners at Ghent, to treat for peace.

1816. The meetings of freemasons and other secret societies prohibited by the king of Naples under penalty of banishment, fine and imprisonment.

1827. George Canning, an eminent English statesman, died. He was of humble origin, but rose to the premiership by his great talents, and sustained himself against a powerful opposition.

1828. Frederic Bouterwek, a German litterateur, died; author of *Geschichte der neueren Poesie und Beredsamkeit*, containing separate critical histories of the belles-lettres of Italy, Spain, Portugal, France, England and Germany, from the revival of letters to the close of the 18th century, 12 vols.

1836. Frederick Carl Ludwig Sickler died at Heldburghausen; an eminent archæologist, and author of various learned works on archæolology, antiquities and philology.

1838. The Chilian squadron of 32 vessels landed 5000 men at Ancon, and demanded two millions of dollars, which not being granted, they advanced and took Callao and Lima, after an action in which 2000 were killed. Gomarra was proclaimed president, and Orbegozo fled to the mountains. (See July 26.)

1840. Charles Ottfried Muller, of Gottingen, died at Athens, from an illness brought on by fatigue and exposure in copying inscriptions, and making excavations at Delphi. The object of his investigation was connected with a great work on which he was engaged, upon the general history of Greece. He was buried on the summit of a little hill above the academy. (July 31.)

1851. Samuel Emerson, an eminent physician, died at Kennebunk, Me., aged 87.

1853. A strike at Stockport, England, for an advance of ten per cent in wages, ceased, 20,000 workmen resumed their labors, having accomplished their object.

1856. Mrs. Matthews (madame Vestris), long a celebrated dancer and pantomimist, died in England, aged 59. Her maiden name was Lucia Elizabeth Bartolozzi; she married Armand Vestris in 1813, and it was under this name that she was well known in Europe and America. She married Matthews in 1838.

AUGUST 9.

357 b. c. An eclipse of the moon which preceded the departure of Dion from Zacynthus (Zante) upon his celebrated expedition against the tyrant Dionysius the Younger. He entered Syracuse with his little band of 800 veterans in September, and in three days became master of the empire. The deaths of Democritus and

Hippocrates, each 104 years old, and of Timotheus, the Milesian poet and musician, took place in that year.

378. The great and disastrous battle of Adrianople, second only to that of Cannæ, in which the Roman legions under Valens, were for the first time defeated by the Cythian Goths. The wounded emperor was removed to a cottage, which was fired, and he perished in the flames.

1342. Sir WALTER MANNY raised the siege of Hennebon in Brittany, so nervously and heroically defended by Jane, countess of Montford, against the power of France.

1611. JOHN BLAGRAVE died; an early English mathematician of considerable eminence and a laborious author on his favorite science.

1634. NOY, attorney-general to Charles I of England, died at London. He is supposed to have devised the plan of levying ship money, which went into operation the day after his death.

1641. DAVID BAKER, an English Benedictine monk and ecclesiastical historian, died. He collected the records of the ancient congregation of the black or Benedictine monks in England, 6 vols. folio, and his religious treatises filled 9 folio vols. in manuscript.

1694. ANTHONY ARNAULD, a French theological and philosophical writer, died. He was one of the most learned men of his age, and did much for the improvement of morality in the catholic church. His works were printed in more than 100 volumes of various sizes.

1710. French and Spaniards defeated at Saragossa, with the loss of 5,000 killed, 7,000 prisoners, and all their artillery, and the allies entered the city.

1718. Action off cape Passaro, between the British fleet, 20 sail, admiral Byng, and the Spanish fleet, 27 sail of the line. The Spaniards were defeated with the loss of 21 of their ships, either taken or destroyed.

1719. DOMINICO DE ANGELIS, an Italian scholar, died. He made the tour of France and Spain, and was everywhere received with honor by the learned.

1720. SAMUEL OCKLEY, an English divine, died; a very learned man, and well skilled in oriental literature.

1744. JOHN BRIDGES, duke of Chandos, died. Few particulars are known of this peer, except of his munificence. The earlier part of his manhood was spent in reflection and observation; his middle age in business, honorable and useful; and his advanced years in deeds of benevolence. He erected the princely seat of Canons, near London, where he lived in a splendor to which no other subject had ever aspired. His liberality was equaled only by his generous forgiveness of injuries. Pope made him the subject of his satire, which Hogarth punished by representing the poet on a scaffold whitewashing Burlington house, and bespattering the duke of Chandos's carriage as it passed. Yet Pope's verse respecting the short-lived magnificence of Canons was prophetic:

> Another age shall see the golden ear
> Embrown the slope, and nod on the parterre:
> Deep harvests bury all his pride has planned,
> And laughing Ceres reassume the land.

Three years after his death the stately mansion was sold by auction, piecemeal, such was the rage to buy something at Canons. Its site was soon an arable.

1746. Battle of Rotto Fredo, between the allies and the Austrians; the former defeated with the loss of 8,000; Austrian loss about half that number.

1748. ALEXANDER BLACKWELL, a Scottish physician, beheaded in Sweden, on suspicion of treason. His wife, to support him in prison, published a *Herbal* in two vols. folio, containing 500 plates, drawn, engraved and colored by herself.

1757. Fort William Henry with a garrison of about 2600 men under Col. Monroe, capitulated to Montcalm, who had invested the fort with an army of 11,500. The garrison was to be allowed the honors of war, and protected from the Indians; but with the characteristic perfidy of the French in all these colonial wars, the Indians were allowed to pillage and massacre the defenceless soldiers, so that their baggage was lost and 1500 slain or made prisoners.

1759. Birthday of JEAN BAPTIST ANNIBAL AUBERT DUBAYET, in Louisiana. He served in the American army during the war of independence, and went to France on the breaking out of the revolution there. He was appointed minister of war, and the next year ambassador to Constantinople, where he died.

1775. Captain LINZEE, of the British sloop of war Falcon, attempted to take an American schooner in Gloucester harbor, cape Ann, in two barges, a whale boat, schooner and cutter, all of which were captured by the Americans; in consequence of which he bombarded the town. American loss 1 killed, 2 wounded.

1778. General GREENE's army crossed over from Tiverton to the north end of Rhode Island.

1778. Lord HOWE's fleet arrived off Newport, in quest of count d'Estaing, who put to sea the next morning.

1782. DE LA PEROUSE, with a considerable French military and naval force, took fort Prince of Wales, at Hudson's bay, and soon after forts York and Severn; the settlements and forts were destroyed.

1787. The ship Columbia, captain GRAY, and sloop Washington sailed from Boston for the north west coast of America and China. They returned in 1790, being the first American vessels that circumnavigated the globe.

1793. ALEXIS BRULARD DE GENLIS, marquis de Sillery, a French general, guillotined at Paris. He was a deputy to the states-general, and an avowed enemy to the king, on whose trial he voted for detaining the royal family until the peace, and for their perpetual banishment after that event.

1796. Elba surrendered to the British under commodore Nelson.

1804. ROBERT POTTER, an English prelate, died; known by his elegant translations of Æschylus, Euripides and Sophocles, the three great dramatists of ancient Greece.

1805. Lieutenant ZEBULON M. PIKE commenced his voyage to the sources of the Missouri river, with a party of 22; they were taken by the Spaniards, and returned the next year.

1808. ROMANA, with 10,000 Spanish troops, deserted the French army under Bernadotte, and were conveyed to Spain in British transports.

1809. The president of the United States, THOMAS JEFFERSON, received official information of the non-ratification of the British treaty, and suspended all intercourse with that country.

1811. Battle of Baza; the Spaniards under Blake defeated by the French under Soult; of 20,000 Spaniards not more than 7,000 rallied again.

1812. Battle of Magauga; the British and Indians under major Muir and Tecumseh, defeated by the United States troops under general Miller, and driven into Brownstown, whence they escaped to Malden in boats. American loss 10 killed, 8 wounded.

1814. Bombardment of Stonington, by the British, commenced. It continued three days. British loss 21 killed, 50 wounded; American loss 6 wounded.

1815. Commodore DECATUR settled the differences between the United States and the dey of Tripoli. The dey made restitution of property and prisoners.

1815. The British ship Northumberland, 74 guns, admiral Cockburn, sailed from Torbay with the exiled Napoleon for St. Helena.

1818. Captain Ross discovered the Esquimaux tribe of Indians, situated at the north east corner of Baffin's bay, extending on the sea shore 120 miles, and not exceeding 20 miles in breadth, and bounded on the south by an immense barrier of mountains, covered with ice. They seemed utterly ignorant of other nations to the south, whence they are supposed to be the original race. They are destitute of boats, and furnish an unique instance of a fishing tribe unacquainted with the art of floating on the water.

1824. JOSEPH NIGHTINGALE, an English dissenting minister, died. He possessed great literary talent, and published many excellent works.

1839. Pera, a suburb of Constantinople, nearly destroyed by fire; 3700 houses burnt.

1841. The steam boat Erie, on her passage from Buffalo to Chicago, took fire and was totally destroyed. Of 200 persons on board, principally Swiss and German emigrants, only 28 were saved. The boat was valued at $75,000; merchandise $20,000; specie $180,000.

1842. Treaty establishing the boundary line between the United States and Canada across the state of Maine; the British acquiring thereby a good portion of the latter state that of right belonged to the United States.

1844. Imprisonment for debt abolished in England; the act taking effect on this day.

1853. SAMUEL JONES, a New York jurist, died, aged 80.

1855. SANTA ANNA left the city of Mexico with 2600 men, under pretence of putting down the revolution at Vera Cruz; but signed an abdication at Perote, and sailed to Havana. On his departure a mob destroyed a large number of houses.

AUGUST 10.

353. MAGNENTIUS, emperor of Rome, killed. He was a German, and rose from a private soldier to the throne.

1506. The island of Madagascar discovered by the Portuguese.

1519. FERDINAND MAGELLAN sailed from Seville with 5 ships and 234 men, on his voyage of discovery, which was continued round the world.

1543. The Turks under Barbarossa and the French under count d'Enguein assaulted Nice, but were repulsed by Montford, a Savoyard gentleman, and obliged finally to raise the siege.

1557. Battle of St. Quintin; the French under Montmorency defeated by the allies under Phillibert of Savoy and the earl of Pembroke. The duke d'Enguein, 600 gentlemen and 4,000 French were killed; several dukes and many other officers of distinction, 300 gentlemen and 4,000 men were taken prisoners, and all their standards, cannon and ammunition fell into the hands of the victors.

1607. JAMES MENOCHIUS died; an Italian author of great repute in his day.

1630. Staten Island was purchased of the Indians by Michael Pauw, a Dutch subject. It was the favorite spot of the primitive settlers. The Indians sold it twice afterwards.

1633. ANTHONY MUNDAY, an English dramatic author, died.

1637. EDWARD KING, a young English poet, drowned. His death gave rise to the beautiful poem of Lycidias, by Milton, his friend.

1653. MARTIN HARPERTZOON VAN TROMP, a Dutch admiral, killed in an engagement with the English fleet off the Texel. He entered the navy at the age of 8, and rose from the lowest station to the chief command. This brave man refused all titles except that of father of the sailors. (July 31, o. s.)

1665. The French West India company, purchased of the order of Malta, the islands of St. Christopher, St. Cruz and St. Bartholomew, for 500,000 livres turnois.

1669. HENRIETTA MARIA, queen dowager to Charles I, died at St. Colombe, near Paris, in France.

1672. JOHN DE WITT, the famous pensionary of Holland, killed by a mob. "He was the zealous patron of the glory and liberty of his native country; the greatest genius of his time; the ablest politician in war as well as peace; the Atlas of the commonwealth."

1674. HUGH PAULIN CRESSY, an English divine, died. He became a catholic, was much respected, and published some valuable works, particularly an able ecclesiastical history.

1675. Corner stone for the foundation of the royal observatory was laid at Greenwich, England. The edifice was erected by Charles II, under the superintendence of sir Christopher Wren, and Flamsteed appointed astronomer-royal.

1675. PETER BALES,, an early and eminent English writing master, finished a performance which contained the Lord's prayer, the creed, the decalogue, two short prayers in Latin, his own name, motto, the date, and the year of the reign of Elizabeth, within the circle of a penny, and so accurately wrought as to be plainly legible. It was enchased in a ring of gold, and presented to the queen.

1686. JOHN BAPTIST COTELERIUS, a learned Frenchman, died. He published the works of all the fathers in the apostolic age, with learned notes.

1702. Lord CUTTS carried, sword in hand, fort St. Michael, at Venlo, before any breach had been made. This was considered one of the greatest exploits during the wars of queen Anne.

1709. LEWIS ANTHONY PROSPER HERISSANT died; an eminent French poet and physician.

1723. WILLIAM DUBOIS, cardinal and prime minister of France, died. He rose from an apothecary's shop to rank, power, and immense wealth.

1749. THOMAS TOPHAM, an Englisman of remarkable strength, died. One of his feats was that of throwing his horse over the turnpike gate. He possessed the strength of six ordinary men.

1757. BENJAMIN HOADLEY, an English physician, died; distinguished by several able professional works, and a popular comedy, the *Suspicious Husband*.

1759. FERDINAND VI (*the Wise*), of Spain, died.

1760. Oswegatchie taken by the British.

1779. A destructive eruption of mount Vesuvius commenced and lasted several days. The country for several miles round was covered with lava.

1783. East India company's ship Antelope, wrecked on the coast of Oorolong, and the crew protected and aided by the king of the Pelew islands.

1790. Captain JOHN GORE, who circumnavigated the earth three times, on the third conducting home the ships after the death of Cooke and Clark, died, a captain in Greenwich hospital.

1791. WILLIAM CUNNINGHAM, captain of the British provost in Boston and New York during the revolutionary war, executed in England for forgery. He confessed to have starved more than 2,000 American prisoners in New York, by stopping their rations, which he sold; and to have hanged upwards of 270 in a private manner.

1792. The alarm bells rung in every part of the city of Paris, and the drums beat to arms, when an immense multitude attacked the palace of the Tuilleries. The Swiss guard at first repelled the populace; but the assailants redoubling their efforts, the palace was carried by storm, the apartments, the passages and courts soon streamed with blood. The king, the queen, and the royal family, fled for refuge to the national assembly. Of the besiegers 3,740 were killed, and 852 of those in the palace. The Swiss guards, who heroically defended the king, were inhumanily butchered by the *Marsellois*.

1792. LOUIS BOUGAINVILLE, the French navigator, massacred at Paris. His discoveries were of importance to the French, but neither his services nor his virtues could shield him against the fury of the mob.

1793. Destruction of the tombs of the kings of France, at St Denis, by order of the national convention. The body of marshal Turenne, deposited there 1675, was found apparently as fresh as ever.

1794. Calvi, in Corsica, surrendered to the British, lord Hood, with the whole of his army, after a siege of 51 days.

1796. Battle of Bassano, in Italy; Bonaparte defeated the Austrians under Wurmzer, took 5,000 prisoners, 25 cannon, &c.

1802. The sea at Teignmouth and coast of Devonshire, England, rose and fell several times two feet in *ten minutes.*

1812. The Russians under WITGENSTEIN attacked the French under Oudinot near Klaistitzy. The action continued into the following day, when the French were defeated with the loss of 5,000 killed, 3,000 prisioners, 2 cannon, and all their ammunition wagons.

1813. Partial action in the night, on lake Ontario, between the United States commodore Chauncy, and British commodore Yeo. The latter succeeded in capturing schooners Julia, 3 guns, and Growler, 5 guns.

1814. WILLIAM COWDROY, proprietor, editor and printer of the *Manchester Gazette*, died. Some of his best editorials were set in type without writing.

1821. Missouri became one of the members of the United States confederacy.

1821. The remains of the ill-fated Maj. Andre disinterred and taken to England.

1838. A papal decree issued at Rome by the congregation of the supreme inquisition, forbidding the introduction of infant schools into the pontifical states.

1843. ROBERT ADRIAN, a skillful mathematician, and for some time professor in Columbia college, N. Y., died in his 68th year.

1851. M. DAGUERRE, the inventor of the daguerreotype, died near Paris, aged 63. His peculiar process was published by him in the autumn of 1839, and the French government awarded him a pension of 6,000 francs for his discovery.

1854. FREDERICK AUGUSTUS, king of Saxony, died at Munich, aged 57. His carriage was overturned as he rode into the city, and he was killed by a kick from one of the horses.

1854. A fire destroyed 180 houses at Varna, in Turkey, and destroyed vast quantities of stores belonging to the allies.

1854. A violent tornado swept along the track of the Cleveland and Pittsburg rail road, between Bedford and Macedonia, covering the track with large uprooted trees, and causing great obstruction to the trains upon the road.

1855. Delegates met at the city of Mexico, and chose general Carrera president for six months, and ordained the freedom of the press.

1856. Last island, a summer resort in the gulph of Mexico, was destroyed by a terrible storm of three days' duration. The island was entirely submerged, the houses swallowed up, and 173 persons lost.

1856. JAMES MURDOCK, an eminent American linguist and theologian, died, aged 80. He studied under president Dwight in 1802, and after preaching sometime became a teacher, and finally an author and translator.

AUGUST 11.

50. The first of the month Thoth, in the movable Egyptian year, corresponded, as Pliny intimates, with this Julian day (798 of the era of Narbonasser); and with the 30th July, A. D. 97 (845 era Narb.), in the Greek month Metagitnion, as we collect from Plutarch.

1332. Battle of Gladsmuir, near St. Johnstown, in which David of Scotland was defeated by Baliol.

1454. NICHOLAS DE CUSA, an Italian cardinal, died. He rose from extreme indigence and obscurity by his own merit, to great dignity and fame. His talents and learning were extraordinary; for besides his profound knowledge of law and divinity, he was distinguished as a natural philosopher and geometrician.

1576. MARTIN FROBISHER entered the strait bearing his name.

1607. A party of English under George Popham landed at the mouth of the Sagadahock or Kennebec river. It consisted of 100 men, with ordinance and all provisions necessary until they might receive farther supplies. Only 45 remained, who built a store house on Parker's island, and fortified it.

1642. JOHANNES MEGAPOLENSIS, the first minister at Albany, arrived from Holland to take charge of his church.

1654. VIRGILIO MALVEZZI, an Italian author, died. He quitted the law to enter the Spanish service, at arms, and wrote in both languages.

1673. Sanguinary engagement off the Texel between the combined English and French fleets under Rupert and d'Estrees, and the Dutch under De Ruyter and Cornelius Tromp. Both sides claimed the victory. Admiral Sprague was drowned, his boat being sunk by a cannon shot.

1693. The Indians of New Hampshire sued for peace, after a long and bloody warfare with the English colonists, incited by the French.

1718. Action off the coast of Sicily, between the British fleet, admiral Byng, and the Spanish fleet, under Castanats; the latter lost 21 ships, captured and sunk

1744. SARAH, duchess of Marlborough, bequeathed to William Pitt £10,000, "upon account of his merit in the noble defence he had made for the support of the laws of England, and to prevent the ruin of his country."

1766. ANN SOWERBY was burnt at York, England, for poisoning her husband; one of the last relics of this mode of capital punishment.

1768. PETER COLLINSON died; an eminent English botanist and natural historian.

1772. A *charged cloud* at Java destroyed 2,000 persons.

1778. AUGUSTUS MONTAGUE TOPLADY died; an eminent English Calvinistic divine and theological writer.

1781. The British took into New York the American frigate Trumbull. Congress had then but two frigates left.

1782. British evacuated Savannah.

1787. First bishop appointed for Nova Scotia. First bishops in England, 694; Denmark, 939; form of consecrating bishops in England ordained, 1549; the office abolished by parliament, 1646; restored, 1660; first episcopal bishop in America, 1784; first catholic, 1789.

1794. Battle of Wilna; the Poles defeated by the Russians, and the town taken by assault.

1809. Battle near Almonacid; the Spaniards defeated by the French under Joseph Bonaparte, and compelled to retreat, after nine hours' hard fighting.

1810. Severe earthquake at St. Michaels, one of the Azores, which continued two days; 22 houses swallowed up.

1813. HENRY JAMES PYE, an English poet, died. Having ruined his fortune, he was gratified with the office of poet laureate, and left many poems, original and translated.

1818. NIKOLAI I. NOVIKOV, sometimes calledthe Franklin of Russia, died, aged 74. Certain it is that by his activity and taste he contributed not a little to the improvement of Russian literature.

1822. SAMUEL AUCHMUTY, commander-in-chief of the British forces in Ireland, died. He was a native of New York, who took the side of the British in the revolutionary contest, and held various honorable and lucrative stations under the British government.

1831. Barbadoes destroyed by a hurricane. It commenced at 3 P. M., and continued two hours; 5,000 persons perished; the houses were mostly destroyed, and the face of the country changed to a desert; neither trees nor vegetables were left standing.

1834. The Ursuline convent at Charlestown, Mass., destroyed by a protestant mob. The house was occupied by females, who were driven to seek shelter where they could find it, in the midst of night, while their valuables to a large amount were plundered.

1849. General GÖRGEY, to whom the Hungarian diet had confided its powers, surrendered his army to the Russian general, Rudiger, at Vilagos, and the conquest of Hungary was consumated.

1849. A proclamation was issued by the president of the United States, warning all citizens against connecting themselves with an armed expedition believed to be fitting out with the intention to invade the island of Cuba, or some of the provinces of Mexico.

1853. JOHN DOWNES, an American commodore, died at Charlestown, Mass., aged 69. He entered the navy in 1802, was in active service during the war of 1812, and commanded the Potomac, which bombarded the piratical town of Quallah Battoo, in reprisal for injuries done American sailors by the Malay pirates.

1853. Great heat from this day to the 14th throughout the United States, and Canada; the thermometer everywhere ranging at about 100° Fahrenheit; 200 deaths in New York on the last of these days, and the total deaths of the four days from that cause exceeded 400.

1855. SAMUEL J. PETERS died at New Orleans, aged 54. He held various offices, and the city owed much of its prosperity to his energy and enterprise.

AUGUST 12.

403 B. C. Act of amnesty, which restored the Athenian democracy, between Thrasybulus and the decemvirate, in the archonship of Euclides, 12th of Boedromion—the year when Thucydides returned from exile.

243 B. C. Liberation of Corinth, by Aratus, in his 2d prætorship.

1099. Battle of Ascalon; the Saracens under the sultan of Egypt defeated by Godfrey de Bouillon, and totally overthrown.

1204. BONIFACE, marquis of Montferrat, disposed of the isle of Candia, with the ruins of a hundred cities, to the Venitians, for 10,000 marks.

1241. GREGORY IX, pope, died. He incited the European powers to undertake a crusade, which was joined by Frederick of Germany, who had been twice excommunicated.

1332. Battle of Duplin moor; Edward Baliol defeated the Scots with terrible slaughter. Donald, earl of Mar, the new regent, fell with the host.

1417. HENRY V, by a letter to his chancellor, dated Tonques, in Normandy, gave directions for the sealing annuities of £6 13s. 4d. each, to seventeen masters of the "grete shippes, carracks, barges and balyngers," belonging to the royal navy.

1560. THOMAS PHAER, an English physician, died. He published various medical works, chiefly compiled from the French, and translated a part of the *Æneid.*

1577. THOMAS SMITH died; a learned English statesman, historian, and critic, and secretary of state under Edward VI, and Elizabeth.

1606. HENRY CHALLONS sailed in a ship of 50 tons to make farther discoveries on the coast of North Virginia, and if it should appear expedient to leave as many men as he could spare in the country. He was fitted out by lord chief-justice Popham, sir Ferdinando Gorges and others of the Plymouth company.

1652. Cardinal MAZARINE exiled the second time from France.

1652. An act of the protectorate for the *settlement of Ireland.*

1662. CHARLES SEYMOUR, "the proud duke of Somerset," died. He was in office under several succesive sovereigns.

1676. King PHILIP (or *Metacom*), killed at Mount Hope, in Rhode Island, whether he had been driven by the English, as a last refuge. One of his confederates proposing peace, so irritated Philip that he killed him. A brother of the murdered Indian repaired to the English camp, and offered to lead them to Philip's retreat. Captain Church set out with a small body of men, accompanied by a few friendly Indians, and attacked the chief in his den. He formed his men in extended order, placing an Englishman and an indian together, with orders to fire on any who should attempt to escape. At the dawn of day the sentinels alarmed the camp, when Philip seized his arms and attempted to escape; as he approached two of Church's guards, the Englishman leveled his gun, which missed fire; the Indian sent two balls through his body, one of which piercing his heart, laid him dead upon the spot. When the battle was over, the English repaired to the place where he lay. He had fallen on his face in a muddy spot of the ground, from which he was drawn; the head was taken off and the body left to be devoured by wild beasts. Thus fell a powerful chief, and a ferocious savage. It was then hailed with joy as the extinction of a virulent and implacable enemy; but is now often viewed as the fall of a great statesman and a mighty prince, who died in defence of his just rights. This was a war of extermination; it was a general rising of the Indians, under a powerful and sagacious warrior, against the English, not a vestige of whom would have been left had they been victorious. As it was, several of the tribes were annihilated; a miserable remnant of the others incorporated themselves with distant and strange nations. In this short but tremendous war, about 600 of the white inhabitants, composing its principal strength, were either killed in battle or murdered; 12 towns entirely destroyed, and 600 dwellings burnt. The English triumphed, indeed, but the ravages of the enemy left them in a deplorable condition.

1689. INNOCENT XI (*Benedict Odescalchi*), pope, died. He effected several important and useful measures and reformations during his reign.

1712. The first stamp on English newspapers used this day.

1715. NAHUM TATE, an English dramatic writer and poet, died. He succeeded Shadwell as poet laureate, and assisted in a version of the *Psalms.*

1724. Battle of Norridgewock, in New Hampshire, and death of Ralle. He was a Jesuit, and a principal agent in instigating the Indians against the English colonies; had resided at this place twenty-six years, and become thoroughly acquainted with the country. An expedition was fitted out to destroy his den. The place was attacked by 240 men, and carried. Ralle was found in his cabin firing upon the English; orders had been given to take him alive, if possible; but refusing to ask quarter he was shot down. Eighty were killed, among which were some of the most noted warriors of the tribe, and the remnant scattered. Ralle was a man of extensive learning, and of great service to the French; he wrote a dictionary of the Norridgewock language, which was taken, and is deposited in Harvard library. He was sent out as a missionary, had acquired the languages of nearly all the tribes in America, and spent thirty-seven years among them.

1728. WILLIAM SHERARD (*Sherwood*), an eminent English botanist and antiquarian, died. He spent the greater part of his life, abroad, in the pursuit of his favorite studies, and founded a professorship of botany at Oxford.

1759. Battle of Kunersdorf; the Prussians under Frederick II defeated with great loss by the Russians and Austrians. The allies by their own confession lost 24,000 men, says Gillies (Smollet says 10,000); the Prussians fought desperately and left 20,000 dead on the field, among whom were several generals. The king had two horses killed under him, and his clothes perforated by several balls. He lost his whole train of artillery.

1759. Ewald Christian de Kleist, a Prussian general and poet, killed at the battle of Kunersdorf.

1765. The great mogul constituted the East India company receivers of all the revenues of Bengal, Bahar, and Orissa.

1778. The French fleet under count d'Estaing dispersed in a gale off Rhode Island, and much damaged.

1778. Robert Goadby died; an English printer and bookseller, and author of several useful publications.

1801. Thomas Hastings, author of the *Wars of Westminster*, and other political papers, died. He was an itinerant bookseller.

1803. Agra taken by the British under the duke of Wellington. Among the trophies was an immense gun, 25 feet long, said to have carried shot into the camp of the British, though out of the range of all ordinary weapons, also a howitzer 14 feet long and 22 inches calibre, throwing a shot of 1,494 lbs.

1805. Capt. Lewis arrived at the head of the Missouri river, and having crossed the mountain this day struck the waters of the Columbia, in the Shoshone country, which he named Lewis's river.

1806. Spaniards recaptured Buenos Ayres, and made the British troops there prisoners.

1811. Miranda reduced New Valentia, in South America.

1812. Lord Wellington entered Madrid, Joseph Bonaparte having evacuated it the day before.

1812. Sanguinary battle on the heights, near Kobrine, between the allied French, Austrian and Saxon army, under Schwartzenberg, and the Russians under Tormozoff. The latter retired with the loss of 4,000; loss of the allies 5,000. Many officers of rank were wounded on both sides.

1813. Samuel Osgood, an officer of the revolution, and for a time postmaster-general, died, aged 65. He published several works of a religious character.

1814. Lodowick Morgan, major 1st U. S. rifle regiment, killed, with 10 of his men, in an attack on the British near fort Erie.

1822. Robert Stuart, lord Castlereagh, premier of England, committed suicide by opening the jugular vein with a penknife.

1828. William Blake, an English painter, died. He is described as a gentle visionary in shapes and fancies, and airy somethings upon paper.

1830. First American rail road, Mohawk and Hudson, between Albany and Schenectady, completed.

1849. Albert Gallatin, a statesman and scholar, died at Astoria, N. Y., aged 88. He was a native of Switzerland, and emigrated to America in 1780. He settled in Pennsylvania, and became soon a prominent member of the legislature, and then of congress. He was secretary of state under Jefferson, and spent many years abroad as American minister.

1851. The steamer Prometheus arrived in New York from San Juan, the Atlantic terminus of the Nicaragua route, now for the first time opened.

1854. Lord Jocelyn died in London, aged 38; military secretary of the Chinese expedition, and author of *Six Months in China*.

AUGUST 13.

582. Tiberius II, emperor of Constantinople, died. His character was conspicuous for humanity, justice, temperance and fortitude.

587. Radegonde, the queen of Clotaire of France, died. At the age of 18 she renounced paganism, and was celebrated for her personal charms, and devotedness to religious duties.

875. Louis II, king of France and emperor of Germany, died. He was a brave and virtuous monarch.

1415. Henry V of England sailed for the conquest of France with a fleet of about 1,300 vessels, and landed his force at Harfleur on the second day following, consisting of 24,000 foot and 6,500 cavalry.

1482. Sixtus IV (*Francis Albecola*), pope, died. He was the son of a fisherman at Geneva, became professor of divinity at Padua, and rose by degrees to the papal chair.

1521. Cortez retook the city of Mexico, assisted by 10,000 Tlascalans, and an innumerable host of other Indian allies from the neighboring nations, whom he had attached to his service. It was not, however, till after seventy-five days of fierce and almost daily fighting, that he accomplished his victory. On no occasion did native Americans so bravely oppose European troops; but the superior discipline of the Spaniards carried the day: and thus a daring adventurer, regarded and treated by his countrymen as a rebel, after a bloody struggle, gained possession of a country which for more than three centuries formed one of the brightest gems in the Castilian crown. It is computed that during this siege 100,000 Mexicans were slain and 50,000 died of sickness and famine. The inhabitants being ordered to leave the city without arms or baggage, the three roads leading from it were full of men, women and children, in the most wretched condition, for three days and nights, seeking an asylum in the open country. The city contained at this time 50,000 houses. Sixty dangerous battles were fought in which 100 Spaniards were killed, or taken and sacrificed, and some thousands of the allies slain.

1535. HIPPOLYTO DE MEDICIS, an Italian cardinal, died. He possessed great talents as a negotiator and military man.

1553. The chaplain of bishop Bonner preached a sermon at St. Paul's abusing the administration of the late Edward, whereupon the people very much abused him; but he was rescued by two protestant ministers.

1587. MANTEO, a friendly Indian, who had been to England, was baptized, according to a previous order of sir Walter Raleigh, and in reward of his faithful service to the English, was called lord of Roanoke and Desamonguepeuk.

1636. DE VRIES, who had been two years on the coast of America, with a view to settling a colony, entered on his diary this day, that he requested Wouter Van Twiller to put Staten island down to his name, intending to form a colony there, which was done, and two days after he sailed on his return to Holland.

1660. A proclamation was issued by Charles II against dueling.

1667. JEREMY TAYLOR died; an eminent English theological writer and controversialist.

1704. Battle off Malaga, between the British fleet of 33 ships of the line and several frigates, admiral Rooke and Cloudesley Shovel, and the French fleet of 54 ships and 24 galleys. The action continued all day, and at night the French bore off. No vessels were taken by either.

1743. FRANCIS PECK died; an eminent English antiquary, biographer and critic.

1762. Cuba surrendered to the British. The booty was great; £3,000,000 in specie, large quantities of goods and munitions of war, 9 ships of the line and 4 frigates. It was exchanged into the hands of the Spanish again the next year for the Floridas.

1775. WASHINGTON informed congress that the whole stock of powder in New England amounted to no more than 9,927 pounds, about 9 rounds to a man. Although this information was communicated to the British by a deserter, they could not believe it possible that the Americans possessed such consummate assurance as to continue to invest them in Boston, while so destitute of ammunition.

1778. The Languedoc of 90 guns, count d'Estaing's flag ship, having lost her rudder and masts in the storm of the day before, was attacked by the British ship Renown, 50 guns, which was beaten off. At the same time a British ship of 50 guns attacked another of d'Estaing's ships, of 80 guns, having only her mainmast standing, but was also beat off.

1782. HENRY LEWIS DU HAMEL died at Paris; eminent for his knowledge of mechanics, agriculture and commerce.

1786. GILBERT STUART, an eminent Scottish historian, died.

1794. Battle of Bellegarde, between the French and Spanish. The action was a severe one; both claimed the victory.

1806. MIRANDA abandoned his conquests on the Spanish main, and sailed to Aruba.

1808. The French in the night raised the siege of Saragossa, in Spain. It had been most nobly defended since July 2d, by general Palafox and the countess de Burita, who raised a company of ladies, that exposed themselves to the greatest personal dangers and fatigues.

1810. JAMES FRANCIS MENON, a French general and politician, died. He was in the employ of the national convention and of Bonaparte.

1812. The British sloop of war Alert, attacked the United States frigate Essex, captain Porter, and after an action of eight minutes struck her colors with seven feet of water in her hold, much cut to pieces and three men wounded. The Alert had been sent out to capture the Hornet, and mounted twenty 18 lb. carronades, and had 130 men.

1817. JOHN BEALE, aged 87, a member of the society of Friends, died at his residence in Bucks county, Pennsylvania, in the same house in which he was born, having never resided in any other.

1819. Just after a brilliant meteor a mass of gelatinous and very fetid matter fell at Amherst, Mass.

1822. An earthquake devastated the greater part of Syria. It began about half past nine in the evening, and in ten or twelve seconds, Aleppo, Antioch, and every village and detached cottage in the pashalic of Aleppo, and several towns in the adjoining territories, were entirely ruined. There were 20,000 people destroyed by it, and as many more maimed or wounded.

1826. LAENNEC died; author of the *Auscultation System of Ascertaining Diseases of the Lungs.*

1838. JOHN FARMER, an American archæologist, died. He published several works relating to the early history of the country, which evince great patience and industry, and bring to light many important facts which would have perished otherwise. For some time previous to his death he was engaged in arranging the state papers in the public offices at Concord, containing the old province and council records, and revolutionary papers. By supplying omissions, transcribing papers that were scarcely legible, and having them arranged and bound, the state of New Hampshire has a very complete set of its early records.

1841. J. B. RICHSONVILLE, principal chief of the Miami nation, died near fort Wayne, Indiana, aged 80. He is said to have left $200,000 in specie, besides immense quantities of valuable real estate.

1842. THOMAS P. EMMET, son of Thomas Addis Emmet, and a contributor to *Silliman's Journal*, died in New York, aged 47.

1851. The people of Litchfield county, Connecticut, celebrated the two hundredth anniversary of its settlement.

1854. General PAIXHANS died at his estate of Jouy-aux-Arches, near Metz, aged 72. He was renowned by his connection with the artillery, and especially with the celebrated gun which bears his name.

1854. At Marysville, Kentucky, a powder magazine, containing 800 kegs, was fired, and the explosion caused the entire destruction of 13 houses, involving a great loss of property.

AUGUST 14.

394 B. C. An eclipse of the sun noticed by Xenophon, which just preceded the battle of Coronea, where Agesilaus stood his ground against the Greek confederates. Xenophon, who fought under the Spartan, describes it as the most desperate conflict in his time.

376 B. C. CHABRAS defeated the Lacedæmonian fleet off Naxos, full moon of Boedromion. The youth Phocion here distinguished himself.

1211. LLEWELLYN, prince of Wales, made his submission to king John of England, and delivered 28 hostages at the foot of Snowden, for his good faith. These young noblemen were hanged the ensuing year.

1248. The great cathedral of Cologne commenced. It was prosecuted at intervals during 200 years, and then suspended 400 years. It was taken up again with new vigor in 1842, and became a popular enterprise of the day to strive for its completion.

1433. JOHN I, king of Portugal, died. It was under his reign that the Portuguese began their famous discoveries.

1457. JOHN FAUST and PETER SCHOEFFER published at Mainz the *Psalter*, supposed to be the first printed book of any magnitude, on record.

1464. PIUS II (*Æneas Sylvius*), pope, died; celebrated for his wise and witty sayings.

1613. JOHN HARRINGTON, an English nobleman, died, aged 22. He was distinguished for the talents and genius which he displayed at a very early age.

1621. An army of *fourteen men* sent out from Plymouth colony to awe the Indians. Corbitant, a petty chief, had seized Squanto, a friendly Indian, and threatened Massasoit; the menaces of revenge in case of any disturbances, are said to have settled all difficulties.

1678. Three days after the conclusion of a peace between France and Holland, the prince of Orange fell upon the marshal of Luxemburg, by which 4,000 lives were sacrificed.

1681. The Scottish parliament adopted a resolution asserting that difference in religion does not bar the right of succession, or make void the magistrate's just and lawful authority.

1711. Sir HOVEDEN WALKER, with the British and colonial fleet intended to invade Canada, arrived at the mouth of the St. Lawrence. A succession of untoward winds and accidents rendered it necessary to put back soon after, without accomplishing any thing.

1756. Fort Oswego capitulated to the French under Montcalm. It was commanded by colonel Mercer with 1,400 men. Montcalm besieged it with an army of 5,000. Colonel Mercer was killed by a cannon ball on the 13th, and there being no probability of aid, the fort surrendered on condition that they should be exempted from plunder, conducted to Montreal, and treated with humanity. The terms were agreed to, the garrison marched out, and the fort was demolished.

1761. Action between British ships Bellona and Brilliant, and one French ship and three frigates. The Frenchmen were captured with the loss of 240 killed and 110 wounded; British loss 6 killed, 28 wounded.

1775. The celebrated Liberty Tree of Boston *consecrated*, by exposing on it the effigies of the men who had rendered themselves odious by their agency in procuring the passage of the stamp act. A copper plate 30 inches by 42 was fixed upon it, bearing the inscription in golden letters—*The Tree of Liberty, Aug.* 14, 1765. Ten years afterwards the British cut it down, at which time it had been planted 119 years. They left nothing but the stump above ground—the *root* they could not exterminate. It produced fourteen cords of wood. One of the party engaged in demolishing it lost his life.

1775. ARNOLD left the camp at Cambridge, with a detachment of 1,000 Americans, to penetrate into Canada by way of Kennebec river and the wilderness. They reached Quebec after great suffering from fatigue, hunger and cold.

1776. Constitution of Maryland adopted.

1776. Lords DUNMORE and CAMPBELL, and sir PETER PARKER, joined lord Howe at Staten island, having taken from the Virginians about 1,000 negroes.

1779. American general LOVEL raised the siege of Penobscot, having sustained very considerable loss of stores, 19 armed vessels, besides transports, &c.

1787. EDMUND LAW, bishop of Carlisle, died, aged 84; an eminent theological writer.

1788. THOMAS SHERIDAN died, aged 67; an eminent English actor, philological writer, and lexicographer, son of Thomas Sheridan, the divine and poet.

1788. First newspaper in Goshen, Orange county.

1790. AGOSTINO CARLINI, a Genoese statuary, died at London, where he was keeper of the Royal academy. He was celebrated for the grace and skill with which he executed drapery.

1794. GEORGE COLMAN (*the elder*), died, aged 61; an eminent English scholar and dramatic writer.

1794. Le Quesnoy taken by the French republican army. The garrison consisting of 28,000 men, were made prisoners of war.

1799. Battle of Novi; between the French under Joubert and the allied Russian, Austrian and Piedmontese armies, under Suwarrow. Joubert wasmortall y wounded.

1813. Action between United States brig Argus, 20 guns, lieutenant Allen, and British brig Pelican, captain Maples. The Argus was captured in 43 minutes, with the loss of lieutenant Allen and 8 others killed, mostly officers. She had taken, prior to her capture, 19 British vessels prizes.

1814. British captured, off fort Erie, two United States schooners, laden with provisions for the garrison of that fort. The fort was bombarded same day.

1814. The Swedish army having obtained possession of several strong places in Norway, prince Christian resigned his pretensions to that crown, and his resignation was followed by the union of Norway and Sweden.

1819. ERIK ACHARIUS, an eminent Swedish physician and botanist, died, aged 82.

1837. A great fete for the inauguration of the statue by Thorwaldsen to Guttenberg, one of the inventors or improvers of the art of printing, at Mainz. It continued three days, and was attended by about 20,000 strangers from different parts of Germany.

1839. MARIE JEANNE ROBIN died at New Orleans, aged 108.

1840. The steam packet Britannia arrived at Liverpool in 10 days from Halifax, the quickest passage hitherto made between the American continent and England.

1846. JOSHUA L. WILSON, pastor of the first presbyterian church erected in Cincinnati, died there, aged 72. He was born in Virginia, and brought up in Kentucky as a blacksmith. He was a preacher of the highest character and influence, during a ministry of 38 years.

1850. GERARD TROOST died at Nashville, Tenn., aged 74. He was a native of Holland, who came to this country in 1810. He was first president of the Academy of natural sciences, at Philadelphia, and for a long time professor in the university at Nashville, and also geologist of the state.

1856. WILLIAM BUCKLAND, an English divine, died, aged 72. He is best known by his scientific pursuits, particularly in mineralogy and geology, upon which subjects he published valuable treatises.

AUGUST 15.

1356 B. C. The Eleusinia, or great Grecian mysteries, founded in this year, so celebrated throughout the classical world, were observed by the Athenians at Eleusis, every fifth year for nine days, commencing on the 15th Boedromion; introduced in memory of Ceres.

310 B. C. AGATHOCLES landed in Africa during an eclipse of the sun, not many weeks subsequent to his defeat by the Carthagenians at Himera. Epicurus began in that year to teach at Mitylene and Lampsacus.

423. HONORIUS, emperor of Rome, died; who, with his brother Arcadius, first divided the empire into east and west sovereignties.

718. The second and memorable siege of Constantinople (under the reign of Leo the Isaurian), by the Saracens, raised. It commenced, according to Theophanes, on the same day of the preceding year.

1038. STEPHEN I, of Hungary, died. He introduced Christianity into his kingdom, and enacted wise laws for the benefit of his people.

1096. The princes of the crusade began their march through Germany.

1118. ALEXIUS COMNENUS I, emperor of Constantinople, died. He usurped the throne 1080, and distinguished himself in his wars with the Turks.

1279. ALBERT (*the great*), of Brunswick, died; a monk who acquired great knowledge in an age of ignorance.

1369. PHILIPPA, of England, died; memorable for her humanity towards the six condemned citizens of Calais, when that city fell into the hands of Edward.

1635. Great storm in New England. The tide rose 20 feet, a great many houses and plantations were destroyed, and the Narragansetts were obliged to climb trees for safety; the tide of flood returning before the usual time, many of them were drowned.

1656. JAMES BOWELS, a native of Killingworth, England, died, aged 152.

1661. THOMAS FULLER, an English historian and divine, died. It is said of his memory, among other incredible things, that he could repeat a sermon verbatim on once hearing it.

1702. Unsuccessful attack of the British under admiral Rooke and the duke of Ormond, on Cadiz.

1702. Battle of Lauzara, in Italy, between the allies under prince Eugene, and the French under the duke de Vendome.

1725. GERARD NOODT, an eminent Dutch civilian, died.

1728. The queen of Sardinia died; she was the daughter of Charles I of England.

1729. BENJAMIN NEUKIRCH, a German poet, died. He deserves a place in history rather as having taken the first step to reform German literature, than as a good writer.

1733. A Roman pavement of mosaic work discovered in Little St. Helen's, Bishop gate street, London; supposed to have lain over 1700 years.

1741. BEHRING discovered East cape, the easternmost point of Asia.

1746. NICHOLAS HUBERT DE MONGAULT, an ingenious and learned French critic, died.

1751. THOMAS SHAW, an English divine and antiquary, died; a writer on Barbary and the Levant.

1758. Kustrin, the capital of the new march of Brandenburg, bombarded by the Russians, and reduced to a heap of ruins.

1758. PIERRE BOUGUER, a celebrated French mathematician, died. He was employed to measure a degree of the meridian in Peru, a difficult task, which he accomplished with great fidelity.

1760. LACY RYAN died; an English dramatic writer, but more eminent as an actor.

1764. IWAN, son of prince Anthony Ulric, of Russia, massacred in prison by his keepers. He was grandson of Peter the Great, and had been kept in prison almost from his birth.

1769. Birthday of NAPOLEON BONAPARTE, at Ajaccio, in the island of Corsica.

1771. Birthday of sir WALTER SCOTT, at Edinburgh.

1780. American general SUMPTER attacked and carried a redoubt on the Wateree, and intercepted a convoy from fort Ninety-six, with 40 wagons loaded with stores, and took 100 prisoners.

1782. Briant's Station, near Lexington, Ky., attacked by 500 Indians and Canadians, who were repulsed, and retreated on the third day, having lost 30 killed.

1786. THOMAS TRYWHITT, an English antiquary and critic, died; author of several learned works, and one of the many commentators on Shakspeare.

1793. *Levée en masse* was proposed in the French assembly which proved the foundation of the famous but tyrannical conscription act of Napoleon.

1794. French convention ordered the French and American flags to be united and hung up together in the hall of their sitting. James Monroe was received as minister from the United States.

1799. The French under MASSENA defeated the Austrians and Russians under the archduke Charles, at Richterswyl, Etzel and Schwindelezzi, in Switzerland. Lecourbe forced the famous pass of the Devil's bridge, took possession of St. Gothard, and seized on the Valois.

1801. CHARLES LOUIS L'HERITIER DE BRUTELLE, a French botanist, assassinated. He published *Stirpes Novæ*, a splendid book, and was engaged in preparing a work on English plants.

1802. BONAPARTE invested with the sole power of nominating his successor and of appointing two subordinate consuls, and nominating a large number of additional senators, &c.

1812. British general BROCK summoned the city of Detroit to surrender, occupied by general Hull.

1812. Battle of fort Chicago; the garrison, consisting of 54 regulars and 12 militia, was attacked by the Indians and after a resolute resistance of some hours, in which 26 of the regulars, all the militia, 2 women and 12 children, were killed, they surrendered on the promise of protection. The survivors, however, 25 men and 11 women, were brutally massacred.

1814. Assault on fort Erie by the British under colonel Drummond, who were repulsed with great loss. The attack commenced at 2 o'clock in the morning, and it was a part of the British orders that no quarters should be given. The action was desperate and bloody; the British lost by official report, 57 killed, 309 wounded, 539 missing—by another account they lost 222 killed, 174 badly wounded, and 186 prisoners, besides 200 killed at Snake Hill. Colonel Drummond was killed; acting up to his barbarous order, when a wounded American officer asked quarter, he shot him with a pistol, whereupon a soldier leveled his piece and shot Drummond in the breast. Total American loss, 93—killed 26, wounded 92, missing 11.

1815. JOHN MEERMAN, a celebrated Dutch author, died. Under Bonaparte he was made director of the fine arts and minister of public instruction, and became a count of the empire and senator. His library sold in 1824 for 131,000 florins.

1816. Great fire at Constantinople; 1200 houses and 3000 shops and magazines destroyed.

1844. WILLIAM LEET STONE, a New York editor, died, aged 52. He published memoirs of Brant, and of Red Jacket, and some other works, and edited for a long time the *New York Commercial Advertiser*. He was also superintendent of common schools in that city.

1849. Riot at Montreal; house of L. H. Lafontaine, head of the Canadian ministry, was assailed by a mob. Fire arms were discharged from the building, by which one person was killed, and the rest driven back.

1851. A violent and destructive tornado occurred at St. Louis, Missouri.

1853. A conspiracy discovered in Rome; 146 persons arrested.

1854. STEPHEN SIMPSON, died at Philadelphia. He was at one period of his life an editor, and gained considerable celebrity as a political writer, especially against the United States bank, over the signature of Brutus, in Duane's *Aurora*.

AUGUST 16.

1191. The Saracen hostages, 2500 in number, put to the sword beneath the walls of Acre, by order of Richard, with the sanction of his confederates. The galls of the murdered infidels were converted into Christian medicines.

1380. JOHN of Gaunt erected a *court of minstrels* at Tutbury, England, with legal jurisdiction over the men in that profession in five counties. It consisted of a king and four other officers, who had sovereign authority upon this day.

1424. Battle of Verneuil, in France; the French and Scotch under Buchan, constable of France, defeated by the English. The Scottish auxiliaries were nearly annihilated.

1494. FERDINAND and Isabella addressed letters of approbation to their high admiral of the Indian seas, Columbus, from Segovia, wishing "to know all the seasons of the year, such as they take place there in each month separately: some wish to know if there are two summers and two winters in the same year."

1513. Battle of the Spurs, in France, between the French, and the English under Henry VIII, at Guingette. It received its title from the flight of the French gendarmerie, and the pursuit of the English, in which the contest was one of speed.

1519. CORTEZ set out from his colony of Villarica on his expedition to Mexico, with 415 Spanish infantry, 16 horses, 200 Indians to transport his artillery and baggage, and some native troops, among which were 40 nobles, whom he took as auxiliaries in war, and hostages of the Totonecas.

1604. HUBERTUS GIFANIUS, a Dutch critic and civilian, died at Prague. He wrote notes and commentaries on Homer, Aristotle, Lucretius, and other authors, and was a noted professor of philosophy.

1654. Onondaga salt springs discovered.

1677. The second ship from England arrived at West Jersey, bringing 230 passengers, most of whom were quakers, some of good estates in England.

1681. NIKON, a celebrated person in the annals of Russia, died. He was the sixth patriarch in the Russian church.

1705. Battle between the French and Imperialists at Cassino in Italy. Both claimed the victory and sang a Te Deum.

1718. Action off Sicily, between the British and Spanish squadrons, in which the latter were defeated, and several large vessels taken or destroyed.

1721. No. 1 of the *New England Courant* was issued. James Franklin, brother to Benjamin, was the publisher. It lived only about six years.

1730. LAWRENCE ECHARD, an English historian and divine, died. His works were creditable performances.

1733. MATTHEW TINDAL, a celebrated English polemical writer, died.

1738. JOSEPH MILLER, better known as *Joe Miller*, died. He was an English comedian, and the compiler of a popular jest book.

1777. Battle of Bennington; general Stark with about 1600 New Hampshire militia, attacked and defeated a detachment of 1500 British regulars and 100 Indians, sent out by Burgoyne, under the command of the Hessian generals, Baum and Breymen, to take a magazine at Bennington. British loss 226 killed, and 33 officers and 700 privates prisoners; they lost four cannon, with all their baggage, wagons and horses. Americans lost less than 100 killed and wounded.

1780. Battle of Camden; the Americans under general Gates totally defeated by the British under Cornwallis. Baron De

Kalb received 11 wounds in this engagement, which proved mortal.

1792. First theatre opened in Boston. It was called the *New Exhibition Room;* the statute of the state prohibiting dramatic performances, they advertised to represent the moral lecture of *Douglas!* One evening, about two months after, as sir Peter and lady Teazle were representing their parts of the moral lecture of *School for Scandal*, the sheriff made his first appearance on that stage, and arrested them by virtue of a peace warrant.

1800. Samuel Barrington died; a distinguished admiral in the British navy.

1806. Action between the French ship Veteran, under Jerome Bonaparte, and 6 British vessels of the Quebec fleet, homeward bound, which were captured.

1812. Detroit surrendered by general Hull to the British under general Brock, without firing a gun from the fort or consulting an officer. The American force amounted to 1100 men. The British took about 40 cannon, 2500 stand of arms, 400 rounds 24lb. shot fixed, 40 barrels powder, 100,000 musket cartridges made, and 15 days' provisions.

1814. The United States fleet, employed in the expedition to Mackinaw having failed in its object, colonel Croghan reembarked his troops.

1824. Charles Thomson, died, aged 94. He was the first secretary of congress, in which office he continued 15 years. The Indians called him *The man of truth.* He translated the *Septuagint* in 4 vols. 8vo.

1825. The northern sea discovered by captain Franklin, who traced the Mackenzie river to its source.

1844. Turhand Kirtland, aged 89, died at Poland, Ohio. He was one of the pioneers of the Northern Ohio, then called New Connecticut.

1848. An immense conflagration at Constantinople consumed about 2500 shops and 500 houses.

1848. A serious insurrection took place at Ceylon against the British authorities, which was subdued by strong measures.

1851. George McClure, a general in the war of 1812, died at Elgin, Illinois, aged 80. He resided a long time at Bath, Steuben county, N. Y., was many years member of assembly from that county, and at different times judge, surrogate and sheriff.

1851. Stephen Olin, an eloquent Methodist divine, died at Middletown, where he was president of the University, aged 54. He held the presidency of Macon college also, in 1833; and is known as an author.

1851. The division of the forces of Lopez under colonel Crittenden having been driven to the coast, where they embarked in open boats, were captured and shot at Havana.

1854. The Russians blew up the fortifications at Hangho, in sight of the allied fleets; the evacuation of the Principalities by them was continued.

1854. The allied fleets in the Baltic accomplished the final conquest of the Bomarsund forts, situated on the largest of the Aland islands, accompanied by the capture of 2000 Russians.

1855. Battle of Tchernaya; the Russians under Gortschakoff attacked with great force the lines of the allies, and drove in the outposts, defended by the Sardinians; but after a severe contest were driven back with great loss; 4000 supposed to have been killed, and 2200 left prisoners and wounded. Loss of the allies 1200, of whom 200 were Sardinians.

1856. Henry Colburn, an eminent London publisher, died. He brought out the works of Bulwer, D'Israeli, Hook, Maryatt and James, and originated several very popular magazines.

AUGUST. 17.

1408. John Gower, an early English poet, died. He was a member of the bar, and a severe contemner of the vices of the age.

1483. Edward V of England, and his brother the duke of York, smothered in prison by order of the duke of Gloucester, their guardian.

1502. Columbus sent his brother Bartholomew on shore at Orejas, and took possession of South America in the name of Ferdinand and Isabella.

1544. St. Dizier surrendered to the emperor Charles V, after a noble defence made by the French governor.

1590. The governor of the colony of Roanoke returned from England, whither he had been for supplies (see August 27), and found the settlement deserted, the houses taken down, and the word Croatoan written upon the trees. He was compelled to return without finding the place of their removal.

1657. Robert Blake died; one of the most intrepid and successful admirals that have adorned the British navy.

1673. Regnier de Graaf died in France, where he acquired great celebrity as a physician and a writer; aged 32.

1679. Jonas Moore, an English mathematician, died; noted in the reigns of Charles I and II for his labor and enterprise in the cause of science.

1682. A comet made its appearance before the people of New England, with a tail of the very respectable length of 15 degrees; which that goodly folk did not see the last of till the 15th September.

1714. George I arrived in England to succeed on the throne.

1720. Anne le Fevre Dacier, a French lady of great learning, died. She translated the principal Greek and Latin poets into her native language, and was noted for her many virtues. (6th by some authors.)

1748. Jonathan Baxter performed the singular feat of crossing the Thames at Blackfriars in a butcher's tray in 1h. 10m., paddling with his hands.

1755. George Jeffreys, an English dramatic and miscellaneous writer, died.

1758. Richard Houseman, a laborer of Knaresborough, was committed to York castle on suspicion of having murdered Daniel Clark.

1765. Timothy Cutler, an Episcopal clergyman, died at Boston, aged 82; formerly president of Yale college.

1779. The independence of the United States declared at New Orleans by beat of drum.

1785. Jonathan Trumbull, governor of Connecticut, died. He bore a conspicuous part in public affairs during a period of 50 years; and retired at the close of the revolution.

1786. Frederick II (*the Great*) of Prussia, died. He distinguished himself as a warrior, and a man of letters, and was one of the most celebrated characters of his day.

1796. The Dutch fleet under admiral Lucas surrendered to the British at the cape of Good Hope.

1807. British army invested Copenhagen; at the same time the Danish gun boats attacked the British with grape and round shot.

1808. Battle of Roleia, in Portugal, between the French, 6,000, under Laborde, and a much superior force of British under Wellesley. The French were compelled to retreat with the loss of 1,500; British loss 500.

1809. Matthew Boulton, an English engineer, died. He erected an extensive establishment at Soho, and expended £47,000 in the course of experiments on the steam engine, before Watt perfected the construction and occasioned any return of profit.

1812. First day's battle of Smolianovo, on the Dwina; the Russians under count Witgenstein defeated the French under Oudinot, with great carnage. Oudinot was dangerously wounded, and St. Cyr took the command.

1812. Battle of Smolensko, on the Boristhenes. Upwards of 100,000 men were engaged, and the conflict was long and bloody. The French under Bonaparte and his best generals maintained their ground; the Russians retreated in the night, after having fired the city. The French are supposed to have lost about 13,000, and the Russians about half the number.

1813. Battle near lake George, between the United States troops under Gen. P. B. Porter and a body of British and Indians; the latter were defeated.

1818. James Constantine Perier, an able French machinist, died. He was the greatest manufacturer of machinery in France, having at one time no less than 93 establishments. Notwithstanding this weight of business, he found time for literary pursuits, and was an author.

1830. La Fayette created marshal of France.

1832. Jean St. Martin, an eminent French orientalist, died at Paris of cholera. He was principal editor of the *Journal Asiatic*, and particularly distinguished for his knowledge of the languages of western Asia.

1836. M. de Rayneval, an eminent French diplomatist, died. He was employed in important missions under Bonaparte, and after the restoration had a still more distinguished career in diplomacy.

1838. Lorenzo da Ponte died in New York, aged 89. He was an Italian by birth, but long a resident of the city of New York; distinguished for his attainments, particularly in Italian literature and art, and author of various publications, among which are some celebrated operas.

1840 Mordecai Moor, died at Clinton, Me., aged 104.

1848. Disastrous fire at Albany; several hundred buildings burned, and one million of property destroyed.

1849. Henry Colman, many years Unitarian minister at Salem, Mass., died in London. He had for some time devoted himself to agricultural inquiries, and published several volumes on the agriculture of foreign countries.

1850. Ashtabula county court house, Ohio, with all papers and records, destroyed by fire.

1852. Pompeo Litta, an Italian author, died at an advanced age. He began in 1819, a costly illustrated work on the genealogies of the principal Italian families, existing and extinct.

1853. A difficulty occurred at the Chincha islands between the Peruvian commandant and the American shipmasters in port.

1857. A block of pure chrystalline ice weighing 25 lbs. was discovered in a meadow near Cricklewood, England. On the day previous a destructive hail storm passed over the spot. Mezray, in his history of France mentions a block of ice that fell of the weight of 100 lbs., during a thunder and hail storm in the year 1510.

AUGUST 18.

332 B. C. Gaza, in Palestine, entered by Alexander the Great, and 10,000 of her inhabitants put to the sword. This was during the Isthmian games, and shortly after the fall of Tyre, which was taken in the month Hecatombæon.

328. HELENA, empress of Rome, died, aged 80. She was the mother of Constantine, and distinguished for her zeal in the cause of the Christian religion.

852. ABDURRAHMAN II, sultan of Cordova, died, aged 65. He was the patron of learning and scholars, though constantly engaged in war.

1187. GEOFFRY, son to Henry II, killed in a tournament at Paris.

1348. A three-fold scourge, which during this year visited the continent of Europe, first appeared in England upon this day; earthquakes, deluges of rain, and a vast ephemeral pestilence, traveling the belt of Asia from Cathay to Delta; over Greece to Italy, beyond the Alps into France, reached London in November.

1510. EDMUND DUDLEY, an English statesman, executed for treason; known as an instrument of Henry VII in the arbitrary acts of extortion practiced during the latter years of his reign.

1510. RICHARD EMPSON, another characteristic of the same stamp, perished at the same time.

1559. PAUL IV (*John Peter Caraffi*), pope, died. He ascended the throne at the age of 80, and conducted himself with so much haughtiness and indiscretion that his death was unlamented.

1587. The first English child born in America, at Roanoke, Virginia. She was the grand-daughter of the governor, and was baptized on the following sabbath, by the name of *Virginia.*

1609. The Half Moon having pursued a course south and west for ten days, arrived at the entrance of Chesapeake bay, where the first effectual attempt to plant an English colony had been commenced only two years before. (See Aug. 28.)

1642. GUIDO RENI, the celebrated Italian painter, died. His skill as an artist attracted great attention, and he was loaded with honors and wealth. His pictures are valuable, and adorn the collections of the great.

1655. CROMWELL, as *protector*, adopted the *We*, in answering a petition. Instead of the capital W, he had at first written the more familiar I; then a small w, which was finally erased with his finger for the royal character.

1670. DRYDEN created *laureate* by royal patent.

1707. WILLIAM CAVENDISH died; first duke of Devonshire, an able English statesman, who was active in procuring the invasion of England by William III.

1746. WILLIAM, earl of Kilmarnock, and ARTHUR BALMERINO, beheaded in London, as traitors for levying war against George II, in behalf of the pretender.

1659. Action between the British fleet, admiral Boscawen, and the French fleet, M. de la Clue, off the coast of Barbary. The French were defeated, and on the following day, five of their largest ships were taken or destroyed.

1765. FRANCIS I, of Germany, died. He commanded the Austrian armies in Hungary against the Turks, and his reign of 20 years' duration was distinguished by many memorable events.

1780. British under TARLETON attacked Sumpter on the Wateree, and killed, captured or dispersed the whole of his party, and retook 300 British prisoners.

1780. Battle of Musgrove's mills; 500 British and tories defeated by the Americans under colonel Williams, and 120 killed or wounded.

1783. JOHN DUNNING, lord Ashburton, died; noted for his extensive practice as a lawyer in London. He defended Wilkes and opposed the American war.

1783. BENJAMIN KENNICOTT died; an English prelate, well known in the learned world for his elaborate edition of the Hebrew Bible and other valuable works.

1798. General HUMBERT landed at Killala, Ireland, with 700 French; a few days afterwards they were all captured.

1803. JAMES BEATTIE died; a Scottish poet and miscellaneous writer, and professor of moral philosophy and logic.

1807. The Danish gun boats renewed their attacks upon the British army before Copenhagen, but were finally driven back into the harbor.

1810. CHARLES PETER CLAREL DE FLURIEU, a French hydrographer, died. He was also a statesman under Louis XVI and Napoleon.

1812. Second day's battle of Smolianovo. The French under St. Cyr defeated with great slaughter. The battle continued 12 hours. The French lost 2,500 killed and wounded, and 3,000 taken prisoners. Russian loss 1,000 hors du combat in both engagements.

1813. Battle of St. Antonio; the Spanish

royalists under Aredonda defeated the Mexican patriots.

1814. British admiral, COCHRANE, addressed a letter from on board the Tonnant, in the Patuxent, to the American government, declaring his determination to destroy and lay waste such towns and districts upon the American coast as might be found assailable, though contrary to the usages of civilized warfare.

1829. DAVID BAIRD, of Aberdeen, a distinguished British general, who led the storming party at the capture of Seringapatam, died.

1834. A tremendous eruption of Vesuvius, which continued several days, and destroyed about 1,500 houses.

1838. The first United States exploring expedition sailed, under Com. Wilkes.

1838. Battle of Morella, in Spain; the queen's troops defeated by the Carlists with the loss of 2,000 men; the victors left in possession of Lower Aragon.

1840. TIMOTHY FLINT, a noted missionary in the Mississippi valley, died, aged 60. He published an account of that region in two works, which are interesting and valuable.

1851. EBENEZER YOUNG, a Connecticut civilian, died at West Killingly, aged 67. He was often in public life, especially in the legislature of his native state, and in congress.

1853. JOHN TALIAFERO, librarian of the treasury department at Washington, died, aged 85. He had also been a member of congress fourteen years.

1855. JABEZ D. HAMMOND, an eminent New York lawyer, died, aged 77. He filled several important offices, and wrote a *Political History of New York*, and some other works.

1855. THOMAS METCALFE, an American officer of the war of 1812, died in Kentucky, aged 75. He also filled various civil offices with ability, under the state and general government.

1855. The queen, VICTORIA, and prince ALBERT, left Osborne at day break to visit Louis Napoleon; arrived at Boulogne, 96 miles, in 4¼ hours, and reached Paris the same evening.

1855. ABBOT LAWRENCE, a noted Boston merchant, died, aged 63. He was a liberal and public spirited citizen, and endowed the Lawrence scientific school at Cambridge with $100,000.

AUGUST 19.

335 B. C. The city of Thebes demolished by Alexander, during the mysteries.

14 (A. U. C. 766). OCTAVIUS CÆSAR AUGUSTUS, the great and virtuous emperor of Rome, died at Nola. This day is also the anniversary of his first exaltation to the consular dignity.

1493. FREDERICK III, of Germany, died. He was fifty-eight years emperor of Austria, and fifty-three emperor of Germany, during which time he was constantly embroiled in troubles, and suffered many humiliations and indignities from the neighboring princes, who took advantage of his imbecility. During his reign the Turks took Constantinople, and the art of printing was discovered.

1579. LOUIS DE CLERMONT BUSSY D' AMBOISE assassinated; a French nobleman distinguished for his bravery and his crimes.

1601. WILLIAM LAMBARDE, an eminent lawyer and antiquary, died at Westcombe, in England. His collection and translation of the Saxon laws was among the first of his works.

1617. Sir WALTER RALEIGH sailed from Cork on his last voyage, with fourteen vessels.

1646. Ragland castle, in Montgomeryshire, England, surrendered to the parliament forces. This was one of the last fortresses that held out for Charles.

1648. IBRAHIM, son of Achmet, sultan of Turkey, assassinated.

1662. BLAISE PASCAL, a French divine, died; noted for his mathematical abilities. His works are published in 5 vols.

1680. JOHN EUDES, the founder of the sect of Eudists, died at Caen, in France.

1692. Five persons executed at Salem, Mass., for witchcraft.

1699. GEORGE BURROUGHS, a New England minister, hung for witchcraft. He was a man of unblemished character, and fell a victim to one of the most astounding delusions that ever disgraced the name of religion.

1702. Action near Santa Martha, in South America, between the British fleet, admiral Benbow, and the French squadron, Du Casse. The cowardice of the English lost them the battle.

1708. The British under sir John Leake and major general Stanhope took Minorca, which was retained by the government.

1744. JOHN BAPTIST SILVA, a distinguished French physician, died at Paris.

1763. Under cover of a severe hail storm and an unusual darkness in the neighborhood of London, the populace attempted the rescue of a criminal to be executed, but though they detained the execution till eight in the evening, they were unsuccessful.

1772. GUSTAVUS, king of Sweden, effected a revolution, which totally overturned the Swedish constitution of government, without any bloodshed. It was a masterly stroke of policy, that placed him in the attitude of absolute master over the laws.

1772. Revolution in Poland; the prerogatives of the crown, lost more than half a century before, were restored.

1777. Nicholas Herkimer, a brave officer, wounded at the battle of Oriskany, died at his house near Little Falls, New York.

1782. Battle near the Blue Licks, between the Kentucky pioneers, 176 in number, under colonel Boone, and 500 Indians. The Indians were defeated with the loss of 71; Boone's loss 63 killed, 7 taken.

1782. British man-of-war, Royal George, 100 guns, sunk off Spithead. Admiral Kempenfeldt, with 400 seamen and 200 women, perished. The wreck was visited by means of a diving bell in 1817, and found to be a mass of shapeless timber.

1792. The grand army of the allies entered France.

1807. The Danish gun boats again attacked the British before Copenhagen. The latter gained some advantages.

1811. The French under Macdonald captured Figueras, in Spain, after a desperate resistance by its famished defenders.

1812. Action between United States frigate Constitution, captain Hull, and British frigate Guerriere, 49 guns, captain Dacres. The Guerriere was sunk in 30 minutes, with the loss of 15 killed, 61 wounded, 24 missing. Constitution lost 7 killed, 7 wounded.

1812. Battle near Gedeonovo, in Russia, between the French, 90,000 and the Russians, stated at 40,000. The French drew off at night with the loss of 600 killed, 2,500 wounded. The Russians admitted the loss of 1,000 killed, 3,000 wounded. Not a prisoner was taken.

1814. Gustavus Maurice, count of Armfelt, a distinguished Swede, whose chief misfortune was that of being in advance of his age, died at Czarshoesels.

1814. Benjamin Thompson, count Rumford, died. From the humble station of a yankee schoolmaster he rose by his talents to distinction and wealth. His inventions and discoveries will perpetuate his name.

1823. Robert Bloomfield, an English poet, died. He learned the trade of a shoemaker, but was constrained to write poetry by nature. The one sustained his body while the other was perpetuating his memory.

1825. Juan Diaz (or *John Martin*), a Spanish partisan officer, executed; distinguished for his conduct during the French invasions.

1826. Paul Allen, an American poet, historian and editor of considerable merit, died at Baltimore, aged 51.

1838. The United States exploring expedition, consisting of 6 vessels, sailed from Hampton roads.

1839. Aaron Ogden, an officer during the revolution, died at Jersey City, aged 83. He was governor of New Jersey in 1812; was also senator of the United States, and practiced law with reputation.

1851. "The great aggregate meeting" of Roman catholics from all parts of Great Britain, was held at Dublin for the inauguration of the catholic defence association.

1852. A destructive tornado, accompanied with hail, passed over an extensive district in Hancock county, Me. Utter devastation followed its track, which was a fourth of a mile wide, and 40 miles long.

1853. George Cockburn, who ordered the destruction of the public property at Washington, on the capture of the city by the English, died at the age of 82.

1854. Grisi and Mario, the two most renowned artistes of the old world, arrived at New York.

AUGUST 20.

480 B. C. Battle of Salamis, in Greece, and defeat of the Persians under Xerxes. This great achievement occurred on that day of the *mysteries* devoted to the solemnities of Bacchus.

332 B. C. Tyre taken by Alexander, which with the subsequent conquest of Gaza, gave to him Egypt.

984. John XIV, pope, died. He was imprisoned in the castle of St. Angelo, by Boniface VIII, where he died, either of poison or grief.

1153. St. Bernard, of Clairvaux, died, and was cannonized on this day. He was an extraordinary character, who obtained great influence over the ecclesiastical affairs of Europe, by the mere force of personal character, without any adventitious advantages, and is styled the last of the fathers.

1485. The earl of Richmond, afterwards Henry VII, halted with his army at Atherstone, two nights previous to the decisive battle of Bosworth field. The troops encamped in a meadow to the north of the church, which now bears the name of the Royal meadow. During the night, Henry held a conference in the town with the two Stanleys, when the measures were agreed upon which resulted in the defeat and death of Richard III.

1513. Norham castle taken by the Scots; its ruins yet remain about eight miles west from Berwick.

1580. Jerome Osorio, an able Portuguese divine and author, died.

1639. Martin Opitius, an elegant German poet, died of the plague at Dantzic.

1648. Edward Herbert died; an eminent English statesman, and writer on history, philosophy and criticism.

1648. Battle of Lens; the French under

Conde defeated the Spaniards and imperialists, under the archduke Leopold, of whom 3000 were killed, and general Beck and 5000 taken prisoners.

1660. JOHN LUGO died; a Spanish Jesuit, professor of theology at Rome. He introduced *Jesuit's bark* into France, was created cardinal, and wrote 7 vols. folio.

1677. PETER PETIT died; a learned Frenchman, celebrated for his mathematical and philosophical writings. (Penny Cyc. says 1667; other authorities 1687.)

1680. WILLIAM BEDLOE, the famous witness in the Titus Oates plot, died, charging the queen and the duke of York with being concerned in the plot, except the assassination of the king.

1694. WILLIAM PENN was reinstated in his province of Pennsylvania, which had been taken from him and annexed to New York.

1701. CHARLES SEDLEY, an English poet, died. He flourished at the court of Charles II. (1703?)

1704. Battle of Narva; the town taken by assault by Peter the Great, who on the occasion killed several of his soldiers with his own sword, for disobedience in committing excesses upon the inhabitants. He had been defeated here four years previous by Charles XII.

1724. LOUIS I, king of Spain, died of small pox; in consequence his father, the abdicated monarch, resumed the throne.

1746. Fort Massachusetts, situated in the town of Adams, surrendered to the French and Indians. It was garrisoned with 22 men under captain Hawks, when attacked by 900 French and Indians. The little band kept the horde at bay while their ammunition lasted, and then capitulated on promise of protection—to be humanely treated, and none delivered to the Indians. In violation of the terms, Vaudreuil delivered one half to the irritated savages. Hawks lost but one man in the siege; while the loss of the enemy was afterwards ascertained to have been 47.

1756. THOMAS WINSLOW, a native of Ireland, died, aged 146.

1760. JAMES M'DONALD, died at Cork, Ireland, aged 117, and 7 feet 6 inches in stature.

1768. JOSEPH SPENCE, an eminent English poet and critic, drowned in a canal in his garden.

1783. JOHN DEMESTE died; chaplain and chief surgeon in the army of the prince of Liege, and known as the author of *Letters on Chymistry.*

1785. JOHN BAPTIST PIGALLE, a eminent sculptor, died at Paris.

1794. Battle of Miami, in Ohio, between the United States troops under general Wayne, and the British and Indians; the latter were defeated and driven out of the United States. The most hostile tribes were the Wyandots, Delawares, Shawnees and Miamis. The number of Indians engaged in this battle was 2000; that of our troops did not amount to 900.

1799. Surinam surrendered to the British under admiral Seymour.

1801. The French garrison at fort Mirabou, at Alexandria, Egypt, surrendered to the British under general Coote.

1815. RICHARD ALZOP, an American poet, died at Middletown, Ct., aged 56.

1829. Adrianople captured by 28,000 Russians under general Diebitsch. The garrison of the city, amounting to 100,000 regular troops, laid down their arms immediately on the approach of the Russians, abandoning all their artillery, camp equipage, and munitions of war.

1840. MICHAEL WALSH died, aged 77; author of the *Mercantile Arithmetic*, formerly in extensive use in this country. He was a native of Ireland, and settled in America in early life.

1841. Dreadful explosion at Syracuse; 26 lives destroyed.

1847. The Mexican works at Contreras near the city of Mexico were carried by general Smith's command. Falling back on Cherubusco a severe battle was fought and the Mexicans completely routed. Many were slain on both sides.

1849. Major EMORY, in the United States service, gave information that a river forty feet wide and more than waist deep, with good drinkable water, broke forth from the desert about this time, between the river Gila and the mountains.

1852. The steam boat Atlantic came in collision on lake Erie with the propeller Ogdensburgh, and sunk in half an hour. Of 500 passengers, 250 were lost.

1854. FREDERICK WILLIAM JOSEPH VON SCHELLING, one of the most prominent among the philosophers of modern Germany, died in Switzerland, aged 79.

AUGUST 21.

638. Antioch in Syria taken by the Saracens.

1130. ABDULMUMEN, ibn Ali, elected sultan of eastern Africa by the following stratagem. Having trained a parrot and a lion, he assembled the chiefs in his tent, and urged upon them the necessity of naming a successor to their rising empire. In the midst of their deliberations the parrot perched himself upon one of the poles of the tent, and pronounced distinctly "Victory and power be the lot of the khalif Abdulmumen, commander of the faithful." The lion then made his way through the terrified assembly, licked his hand, and lay down at his feet. Deeply impressed with this wonder, and the manifest interference of heaven, the simple Almohades unanimously proclaimed him sultan.

1553. JOHN DUDLEY, duke of Northumberland, beheaded. He acquired almost unbounded authority after the death of Henry VIII, and by the abortive attempt to place lady Jane Grey on the throne, lost his own life and brought about the ruin of all concerned in the scheme.

1560. The great solar eclipse, which first turned the attention of Tycho Brahe, at the age of 14, to the science of astronomy.

1561. MARY (*the Myrtle of the South*), arrived in Scotland, after an absence of thirteen years in France. It was on her passage that she composed that simple and touching chanson, beginning, "Adieu, plaisant pays de France."

1621. A cargo of marriageable ladies consisting of one widow and eleven maids, consigned at London to the colony in Virginia, to be sold for tobacco, at the rate of 120 lbs. of the best leaf for each.

1682. WILLIAM PENN, to prevent any future claim, obtained a release from James, duke of York, of all his right to Pennsylvania.

1703. THOMAS TRYON died. He was the son of a tiler and plasterer at Bibury, England, and became a shepherd. At the age of 13 he learned to read, and at 14 he gave one of several sheep he had obtained, to be taught the art of writing. Afterwards, selling his stock, for three pounds, he went to London and apprenticed himself to a hat maker, where he spent the day in learning his trade, and most of the night in reading. He commenced business, and acquired a considerable fortune. He rejected animal food, lived in "temperance, cleanliness and innocency," and died at the age of 69.

1708. Haverhill burnt. A force of about 400 French and Indians made an irruption from Canada, and shaping their course to the Merrimack, fell upon the town in the morning, plundered and burnt the houses, killed about 40 persons, and captured many more. The enemy were pursued, and many of them killed, among whom was a brother of the French leader, Rouville. Among the captives was the clergyman; his two daughters 6 and 8 years old, were preserved by the servant, who concealed them under tubs in the cellar, which the Indians did not disturb.

1726. Great destroying earthquake at Palermo, in Sicily.

1762. MARY WORTLEY MONTAGUE, an English lady of great literary reputation, died. She introduced the practice of inoculation for small pox into England.

1770. A leaden equestrian statue of George III was erected in the Bowling Green, New York, near fort George, by Wilton, a celebrated statuary of the day. It being the birth day of the king's father, prince Frederick.

1775. The continental army under Gen. Montgomery arrived at Ticonderoga.

1780. French king abolished the application of torture to extort confession.

1791. The American army under Gen. Wilkinson arrived at the Rapids on the Ohio, returning from an expedition against the Ouiattanons, having destroyed their principal town, and a Kickapoo village, made many prisoners, and cut down 430 acres of corn. The army sallied from fort Washington, and made a march of 450 miles. Only 2 men were lost.

1792. LAFAYETTE abandoned the French army, of which he was commander in chief, and with his three friends surrendered to the Austrians. They met with a long imprisonment.

1805. Brest fleet attacked in Camaret bay, by the British under Cornwallis, who with an inferior force compelled them to retire into the inner harbor.

1808. Battle of Vimiera, in Portugal. The French army, 12,000, under Junot and Kellerman, made a desperate assault on the English and Portuguese, 20,000, under Wellesley. The French were defeated.

1810. Revolution in Santa Fe, South America.

1818. The renowned WARREN HASTINGS died.

1821. FRANCIS HARGRAVE, an eminent English law writer, died. His *State Trials* comprise 11 vols. folio. His library was purchased by parliament at about $40,000.

1823. MARCO BOZZARIS, the Leonidas of modern Greece, killed. He was a native of Souli, in the mountains of Epirus, and on the breaking out of the revolution headed a battalion of Suliotes. The pasha of Schodra advancing with a numerous force of Albanians to attack Missolunghi, Bozzaris with a handful of devoted followers attacked the camp by night, and fell.

1831. Insurrection of the negroes in Virginia, and massacre of the white population.

1835. JOHN McCULLOCH, distinguished for his geological writings and other works of merit, died in consequence of being thrown from his carriage.

1846. The water in lake Ontario had fallen since the first of December, 1845, 28 inches, and was lower than ever known before. Gulf island, which had been submerged seven years before, again appeared above water, and many rocks and sandbars never before known made their appearance.

1848. A hurricane devastated the islands of Antigua, St. Kitts, Nevis, and St. Thomas.

1849. A national convention of inventors met at Baltimore; Horace H. Day, of New York, president.

1850. DANIEL P. PARKER, a Boston merchant, died, aged 60. He gave close attention to the construction of merchant vessels, and had in his service many ships of superior model and sailing qualities.

1851. A prisoner under sentence of death at Sacramento, California, was reprieved by the governor; but was hung, notwithstanding, by some of the disaffected citizens.

1851. New Orleans riot, growing out of the Cuban expedition. The office of *La Patria*, the Spanish paper, was destroyed, as well as the cigar shops kept by Spaniards; and the Spanish consul was obliged to ask protection, and was placed in the city prison for safety.

1856. The famous Charter oak at Hartford, Conn., was blown down in a storm.

1857. A hurricane passed over the town of Woodland, Wisconsin, and destroyed every house in the place.

AUGUST 22.

1138. Battle of North Allerton, in England, and defeat of the Irish under king David.

1280. NICHOLAS III, pope, died. His reign is noted for a missionary expedition to Tartary.

1357. ISABELLA, queen of England, died in prison, where she had been confined 28 years.

1485. Battle of Bosworth field, in which the forces of Richard III were defeated and himself killed. The forces of Richard exceeded 16,000, while those of Richmond did not amount to 5,000. The battle lasted little more than two hours, and was determined by the defection of Stanley. He is the only English king since the conquest who fell in battle, and the second who fought in his crown.

1540. Burial of WILLIAM BUDÆUS, a learned French critic and commentator; styled by Erasmus ***Portentum Galliæ*** (the prodigy of France).

1567. Capt. GOURGES sailed from Bourdeaux to dislodge the Spaniards in Florida. (See May 3, 1568.)

1567. MURRAY proclaimed regent of Scotland.

1572. THOMAS PERCY, earl of Northumberland, beheaded at York.

1613. DOMINIQUE BAUDIUS died; advocate of the parliament of Paris, and author of some Latin poems.

1615. ARTHUR AGARD, a learned English antiquary, died.

1642. CHARLES I of England erected the royal standard at Nottingham. It was supposed equivalent to a declaration of hostilities.

1650. EUSEBIUS ANDREWS, an English barrister, and colonel in the army of Charles I, beheaded by Cromwell.

1651. CHRISTOPHER LOVE was beheaded at Tower hill. His offence was a desire to restore monarchy, that presbyterianism might succeed.

1711. An expedition from New England against Quebec, frustrated by the loss of a number of transports among the rocks, at midnight, about 9 miles up Canada river. About 1000 men perished.

1711. LEWIS FRANCIS DE BOUFFLERS, a distinguished French military character, died. He was opposed to prince Eugene, and celebrated for his defence of Lisle.

1739. JAMES VANIERE died; a French Jesuit and famous Latin poet.

1752. WILLIAM WHISTON, an eminent English divine, died. He was also a mathematician, and succeeded sir Isaac Newton as professor of mathematics at Cambridge.

1766. PHILIP CARTERET sailed from England in the sloop-of-war Swallow, on his voyage round the world, in company with captain Wallis in the Dolphin. They parted company April 10, 1767; the latter returned in 1768, the former March 20, 1769.

1773. GEORGE LYTTLETON, an elegant English poet, historian and miscellaneous writer, died.

1776. The British troops, 24,000, under lord and sir William Howe, landed on Long island, between Gravesend and Utrecht.

1777. The siege of fort Stanwix raised by St. Leger, who retreated in great confusion, losing his tents, most of his artillery and stores.

1777. An unsuccessful attempt was made by general Sullivan and colonel Ogden on Staten island. The latter took 130 privates and some officers, burnt a magazine of hay and 7 vessels, and destroyed some stores, &c. The general deviated from his original plan, whence his enterprise was not so completely successful.

1778. Count D'ESTAING sailed from Newport for Boston, which compelled general Sullivan to raise the siege of Newport and fall back; 2 or 3,000 volunteers having left him in consequence.

1779. General WILLIAMSON and colonel PICKENS entered the Indian country, and burned about 50,000 bushels of corn in eight of their towns.

1779. CHARLES CLERKE, the English circumnavigator, died of consumption off Kamschatka, and was buried at Paratounca. He had but a short time previous succeeded captain Cook in the command of the expedition.

1792. Longroy, in France, captured by CLAIRFAIT, with 3,500 troops and 71 cannon.

1795. French convention adopted a new constitution, by which a council of 500 was established, and a council of ancients consisting of 250.

1798. The French under general Humbert landed in Ireland and took possession of Killala. (18th.)

1808. Armistice signed by the French general JUNOT and sir ARTHUR WELLESLEY, by which the French agreed to evacuate Portugal.

1814. The inhabitants of Nantucket declared themselves neutral, under the protection of England. Same day 27 sail of square rigged British vessels arrived at Benedict; commodore Barney, in conformity to his orders blew up his flotilla and retreated to Nottingham. The British landed and marched to Marlborough.

1818. WARREN HASTINGS, an English statesman and scholar, died. He was employed in the service of the East India company, and by oppression and injustice raised the revenue of the company from three to five millions pounds.

1826. A barge belonging to Beechey's expedition reached longitude 156° 21′ west. Here they were embedded in ice some days, and were about to abandon the bark, and return on foot 120 miles, to the ship, when it was fortunately extricated, and made sail to rejoin the ship.

1828. FRANZ JOSEPH GALL, founder of the science of phrenology, died at Paris, aged 71. His works are voluminous; his style is characterized as vivid and powerful; his description as accurate and striking: and he may be looked upon as one of the most remarkable men of his age.

1848. The rail road train made the transit from Springfield to Hartford, 26 miles, in 33 minutes.

1849. The fortress of Moultan was destroyed by a freshet, "remaining an island of mud in an expanse of waters."

1849. A convention called the Peace congress, opened its sittings at Paris.

1849. Venice capitulated to marshal Radetsky.

1850. NATHANIEL BERRY died at Gardiner, Me., aged 94; a member of Washington's life guard.

1851. The American yacht America, at the regatta at Cowes, England, won the "cup of all nations."

1852. ÆNEAS MUNSON, the oldest graduate of Yale college, died at New Haven, aged 89. He was an assistant surgeon in the war of the revolution, afterwards became a merchant, and for a long period was president successively of several banks.

1853. PIETRO BACHI, a Sicilian exile, died at Boston, aged 66. Being implicated in Murat's attempt to reascend the throne in 1815, he was banished, and arrived in America in 1825. He was highly accomplished in ancient and modern languages, and became an instructor of Italian in Harvard college.

AUGUST 23.

634. ABDALLAH ATIK BEN ABI KOHAFAH, better known as Abu Bekr, died. He was the first caliph or successor of Mohammed in the government of the faithful. He enlarged the empire, and caused the precepts of the prophet to be collected in a volume, called *Al Koran*, which is the sacred and classical book of the Mohammedans.

1305. WILLIAM WALLACE, "the peerless knight of Ellerslie," at the age of about 35, executed on Tower hill, and his head set up on London bridge, to the public gaze.

1350. PHILIP DE VALOIS, king of France, died. His crown was disputed by Edward VIII of England, which gave rise to a disastrous war.

1400. Edinburgh, the Scottish capital, burnt by the armies of Henry IV of England.

1481. THOMAS LITTLETON died; a celebrated English judge in the time of Edward IV, and author of a treatise on tenures or titles, by which all estates were anciently held in England.

1500. DON FRANCISCO DE BOBADILLA arrived at St. Domingo, a royal commissioner to inquire into the conduct of Columbus.

1532. WILLIAM WARHAM, bishop of Canterbury, died; some time chancellor of England, from which office he was removed to make room for Woolsey.

1622. *The Certain News of the Present Week* is the title of a small quarto of 18 pages published this day in London, supposed to be the first weekly newspaper in England.

1628. GEORGE VILLIERS, duke of Buckingham, a noted English statesman, assassinated, at the age of 36.

1630. The first court of assistants held at Charlestown, Mass. They determined that ministers should be settled, houses built and salaries raised for them at the public expense. They settled the price of mechanical labor; carpenters, joiners, bricklayers, sawyers and thatchers, should take no more than 2*s*. a day, under a penalty of 10*s*. to giver and taker. At this court Edward Palmer was sentenced for extortion, in charging 2*l*. 13*s*. 4*d*. for the wood work of Boston stocks, to sit in them one hour and pay a fine of five pounds.

1642. JOHN GEORGE WIRSUNGUS, an Italian anatomist, assassinated. He was professor of anatomy at Padua, where he discovered and explained the pancreatic duct.

1679. WILLIAM OWTRAM died; an eminent English preacher and scholar in the reign of Charles II.

1686. Buda, the capital of Hungary, after being in possession of the Turks for 145 years, was taken by the imperialists.

1693. The first printing executed in New York, was a proclamation of governor Fletcher bearing this date.

1719. HENRY CLEMENTS, an eminent bookseller in London, died. His death was memorable on account of the occasion it furnished for the publication of his funeral sermon, entitled *the Christian's Support under the Loss of Friends*.

1720. JAMES VERGIER, a French poet, assassinated at Paris. He possessed great talents; but dissipation and licentiousness were unfortunately his distinguishing characteristics.

1723. INCREASE MATHER died; a New England clergyman during the witchcraft delusion, which he labored to mitigate. It is said that he usually spent 16 hours a day in study; the number of his publications was 85, the number of his years 84. (His tomb stone says Aug. 27.)

1727. HOSIER, the English admiral, died off Porto Bello. He had been sent out the year previous with 7 ships of war to intercept the Spanish galleons. On his arrival the galleons unloaded their treasure, and to prevent them from sailing the fleet lay off that pestilential coast until both the ships and their crews were desolated. Glover, author of a little poem called *Admiral Hosier's Ghost*, represents the number of dead at 3,000.

1756. Foundation stone of Columbia college laid at New York.

1782. HENRY LEWIS DU HAMEL died at Paris; eminent for his knowledge of mechanics, agriculture and commerce.

1782. Cape River fort surprised and carried by assault by the British captain Campbell with 150 negroes. He lost but 2 killed; Spanish loss 65 killed, 9 taken, mostly wounded.

1789. SILAS DEANE, minister of the United States to France in 1776, died in England in extreme poverty.

1793. Massacre of the French in St. Domingo.

1793. The British took Pondicherry from the French.

1795. French convention decreed that all assemblies known by the name of clubs or popular societies in France, should be suppressed immediately, their places of meeting shut up, and the keys delivered to the secretary of the town house.

1795. WILLIAM BRADFORD died at Philadelphia, aged 39; some time attorney-general of the United States, and known as an author and poet.

1804. Tripoli bombarded the third time by the American commodore Preble, from 2 P. M., until daylight the next morning, without much effect.

1806. CHARLES AUGUSTIN DE COULOMB, a French engineer, died. He is noted for his brilliant experiments and discoveries in electricity and magnetism.

1813. Battle of Gross-Beeren, near Berlin in Prussia; the French under Oudinot, about 80,000, defeated with considerable loss.

1813. ALEXANDER WILSON, the naturalist, died at Philadelphia; author of the *American Ornithology*, 7 vols. 4to, a work of great accuracy and comprehensiveness.

1818. First steamer from Buffalo to Detroit.

1820. OLIVER HAZARD PERRY, a distinguished American naval officer, died at Trinidad of yellow fever, on the anniversary of his birth day, which was the 23d August, 1785. His victory on lake Erie over a British force superior in men and guns to his own, has given his name a permanent place in the history of his country.

1826. KOLLER, an Austrian general, died. He accompanied Napoleon, where he had to protect him against the rabble infuriated by priests and ultras, which was done by an exchange of garments. He left a valuable collection of antiques.

1835. ISAAC POCOCKE died; one of the most successful dramatic writers of his day.

1835. Massacre at Para in Brazil by the Indians. The attack commenced on the 14th. The United States consul barely escaped with his life. It is supposed that the slaughter must have been immense, and a more complete sack of any city probably never took place.

1850. CHARLES DYER, a midshipman in the United States navy, was drowned at Pensacola, in nobly attempting to save the crew of a vessel in distress. ALEXANDER HALE, assistant engineer in the service and a graduate of Yale college, lost his life also in the same cause.

1855. HENRY LAWSON, an English astronomer, died at Bath, aged 81.

AUGUST 24.

79. First eruption on record of Vesuvius, which overwhelmed the towns of Herculaneum and Pompeii, and destroyed the *martyr of nature*. The younger Pliny, the nephew of that greater man, has described the terrific catastrophe in two letters to Tacitus.

93. Cneius Julius Agricola, a celebrated Roman general, died. He was governor in Great Britain, and by doubling the northern point of Scotland, first discovered it to be an island. (Sept. 1st?)

410. Alaric, at the head of the Goths, entered Rome at midnight, and gave up the town to be pillaged for six days, but with orders to his soldiers to be sparing of blood, to respect the honor of the women, and not to burn the buildings dedicated to religion. A part of the city was burnt, and many ancient works of art destroyed. The treasures of the city collected from all parts of the world fell a prey to the barbarians, and the once proud mistress of the world experienced a severe retribution for the sufferings which her heroes had caused to so many cities, countries and nations.

1227. Gengis-Khan, a renowned Mogul prince, died. He suddenly rose from the lowest fortunes, and in the space of 28 years subdued the greater part of Asia.

1344. Battle of Cressy, which gained Edward, the black prince, immortal honor. Here was slain the blind king of the Bohemians, the ornaments on whose sword were adopted as the coat of arms of the princes of Wales, *Ich Dien*, with three ostrich feathers.

1481. Alphonso V, of Portugal, died of plague. He was a great patron of learning, and conquered several places belonging to the Moors.

1525. Francis I, king of France, entered Madrid a prisoner to the emperor Charles V.

1572. Massacre of St. Bartholomews, which commenced in the city of Paris, and was continued throughout the kingdom during thirty days. The number of protestants who were butchered in this bloody affair, is estimated at 30,000, and by others at 70,000.

1572. Gaspard de Coligny, admiral of France, fell at the massacre of St. Bartholomews. He was distinguished for valor in battle, for strict discipline, and for his conquests over the Spaniards; and was feared by the court as the powerful leader of the Calvinist party.

1581. An assemblage of divines deputed by the states of Carniola, Styria and Carinthia, met at Laybach, to examine and revise the translation of the *Vandalic Bible*.

1605. The Turks having overrun the Persian provinces along the Caspian sea, their army of 100,000 was met by 66,000 Persians under schah Abbas, and completely overthrown.

1634. Abbasah, pasha of Erzerum, executed. He was the untiring enemy of the Janisaries, who succeeded in awakening the suspicions of the sultan Murad IV.

1653. An act passed by the parliament of the commonwealth of England permitting marriages to be solemnized by justices of the peace.

1662. The English act of uniformity in religion took effect; about 2,000 ministers were ejected from their benefices, without any provision for themselves or their families. Soon after they were banished five miles distant from every corporation in England. Several ultimately died in prison, for exercising their ministry in private, contrary to law; but a considerable number of them found an asylum in New England.

1682. The duke of York conveyed to William Penn all his right to the three lower counties on the Delaware river, now state of Delaware.

1683. John Owen, an English non-conformist divine, died, aged 63. He preached the first sermon before parliament after the execution of Charles I, was promoted to high places under Cromwell, which he lost at the restoration, by the influence of the presbyterian party. His works, which are of a high Calvinistic character, amount to 7 vols. folio, 20 quarto and 30 octavo. (See Oct. 15, 1651.)

1702. Sixth action between the British fleet, admiral Benbow, and the French under Du Casse. The brave English admiral had his leg carried off by a chain shot, and received two other wounds.

1756. Eighty Acadians arrived in New York from Georgia.

1777. General Washington marched his troops through Philadelphia for the Chesapeake.

1781. The allied French and American army under Washington and Rochambeau crossed the Hudson river and marched for Philadelphia.

1782. Jean de la Perouse, a distinguished French seaman and navigator, took fort York, on Hudson's bay, from the English. Here he found a manuscript of Hearne's journey to the Coppermine river, which Hearne received back as his private property on condition of publication.

1793. Marseilles subjected to the French convention, against which it had revolted.

1797. Thomas Chittenden, first governor of Vermont, died, aged 67.

1799. BONAPARTE left Egypt.

1803. GREGORY FONTANA, a Swiss mathematician, died; distinguished as a professor and an author, during a period of thirty years, in Italy.

1811. Swiss cantons recalled their troops from the British service, and voted 6,000 additional men for the French service.

1814. Battle of Bladensburg, and capture of Washington city by the British under general Ross and admiral Cockburn. The capitol, president's house and public offices were burnt in a spirit unworthy of any nation. A dreadful retribution, however, overtook them, by the explosion of a magazine, by which one half their number was either killed or wounded. American loss, 40 killed, 60 wounded.

1829. REUBEN KELSEY died at Fairfield, Vt., of voluntary starvation, after a fast of 52 days, during which he took no other nourishment than water.

1833. ADRIAN HARDY HAWORTH died of cholera in England: a distinguished botanist, entomologist and ornithologist; author of the *Lepidoptera Britannica*, and various other works.

1842. BENJAMIN WRIGHT, a distinguished American civil engineer, died. The great Erie canal afforded him an opportunity for the exercise of his mathematical knowledge.

1844. Great outrages committed in Rensselaer county, New York, by the tenantry on Rensselaerwick.

1845. SAMUEL HASKELL, the oldest episcopal minister of the state of New York, died at New Rochelle.

1848. The American ship Ocean Monarch burnt in the Irish channel, and more than 170 lives lost.

1849. JOHN PIERCE, of the Congregational church, Brookline, Mass., died. He was distinguished as a preacher and one of the earliest advocates of total abstinence from intoxicating drinks in the state.

1849. The chamber of representatives of Hayti, acting upon a petition which had been circulated one day, brought in a bill conferring the title and dignity of emperor upon Faustin Soulouque, the president of that government.

1851. JAMES McDOWELL, a Virginia statesman, died. He was sometime governor of the state, and representative to congress.

1851. A fire in Concord, New Hampshire, destroyed the best part of the business portion of the town.

1851. During devotional exercises at the jail in San Francisco, two prisoners, Samuel Whittaker and Samuel McKenzie, were taken from the jailer by force, and hung by the vigilance committee.

1852. JOSEPH VANCE, an Ohio statesman, died. He served the state in various stations, being governor in 1836.

1857. THOMAS CLAYTON, a Delaware judge, died at Newcastle, aged 76. He was sixteen years in congress and occupied the bench with ability for a long time.

AUGUST 25.

383. GRATIANUS, emperor of Rome, assassinated at the age of 24. He was a powerful Christian ruler, but of an unfortunate turn of mind to conduct a government.

1170. STRONGBOW, under king Dermot, carried Dublin by storm.

1270. LOUIS IX, of France, died. He made two crusades for the recovery of the Holy Land, and died of a contagion off Tunis, in Africa.

1313. HENRY VII, emperor of Germany, died. He entered Rome sword in hand, at a time when the country was distracted by the war of the Guelphs and Ghibelines, and was crowned by the pope.

1381. An eruption of Etna, which consumed all the olive yards around Catania.

1482. MARGARET, of Anjou, queen of Henry VI, of England, died. She became conspicuous by her heroism in battle for the rescue of her husband, and being taken prisoner was ransomed with 50,000 crowns.

1576. The earl of ESSEX died in Ireland, suspected to be poisoned by the earl of Leicester, who married his widow.

1585. Sir RICHARD GRENVILLE, planted the first English colony in America, on the island of Roanoke, consisting of 107 persons. This settlement was begun 17 years after the French had abandoned Florida, on the same coast, but far to the north of the settlements for which France and Spain had contended. The expedition was fitted out by Sir Walter Raleigh, and consisted of 7 ships.

1654. Battle of Arras, in France; the Spaniards under Conti defeated by Turenne.

1675. Battle of Sugarloaf hill, a few miles above Hatfield, on the Connecticut river. The Hadley Indians had betrayed their conspiracy with Philip's party, by fleeing from their dwellings, were pursued by captains Lathrop and Beers, and overtaken at this place, where a skirmish took place, in which 9 or 10 of the English fell, and about 26 Indians.

1725. A Hungarian picture of this date has the following inscription: "John Roven, in the 172d year of his age, and Sarah, his wife, in the 164th year of her age. They have been married 147 years, and both born and died at Stradovia. Their children, two sons and two daughters, yet live; the youngest son is 116 years of age."

1758. Battle of Zorndorf between the Prussians, 30,000, under Frederick the Great, and 50,000 Russians, under Fermor. The Russians were defeated, with the loss of 19,000 killed, and 3,000 taken, and 103 cannon. Prussian loss, 10,000 killed. This was the bloodiest and one of the most remarkable battles of the seven years' war.

1770. THOMAS CHATTERTON, an English poet of astonishing genius, died at the age of 18, by taking poison, to escape hunger and misery.

1776. DAVID HUME, the Scottish historian, died. His *History of England* is a work of great merit, and has long been the most popular work of the kind.

1782. A large foraging party of British attacked at Combahee, in South Carolina, by the Americans under general Gist and colonel Laurens, who captured a schooner. Laurens was mortally wounded, and died aged 27.

1788. Archbishop SENS, premier of France under Louis XVI, seeing the finances of the state utterly desperate, and fearing for the king and more for himself, retired from the administration, and left the monarch, while bankruptcy and famine threatened the kingdom, to manage as he might, amid the storms which the measures of the minister himself had provoked to the uttermost. He fled to Italy with the greatest expedition, after having sent his resignation to his unfortunate sovereign.

1789. MARY WASHINGTON, mother of the illustrious general, died at Fredericksburgh, Va., aged 82.

1796. LAFAYETTE and other prisoners released from the castle of Olmutz, at the requisition of the French government.

1797. JOHN BAPTIST LOUVET DE COUVRAY, a French advocate, died; distinguished as an actor in the revolution, and an author.

1799. JOHN ARNOLD, eminent for his improvements in the mechanism of timekeepers, died. He was the inventor of the expansion balance and detached escapement, and was the first artist who applied the gold cylindrical spring to the balance of a timepiece.

1800. ELIZABETH MONTAGUE died; an English lady of considerable literary celebrity.

1803. TATE WILKINSON died; an English comedian and manager, often noticed by the writers of his day.

1804. Fifth attack on Tripoli by the Americans under commodore Preble.

1805. JOHN SKEY EUSTACE, a distinguished officer of the revolution, died, aged 45. In 1794 he went to France, and commanded a division of the French army in Flanders.

1806. JOHN PHILIP PALM, a Nuremberg bookseller, shot for a publication against Bonaparte.

1807. EDWARD PREBLE died; the brave and intrepid commodore of the American fleet, which in 1804 subdued Tripoli.

1808. Action between the British and Swedish squadron under admiral Hood, and the Russian squadron, in which the latter was defeated.

1810. The solemn inauguration of the column to the glory of the *grande armée* in the place Vendôme, Paris, took place on the 15th.

1812. The French raised the siege of Cadiz, which had long resisted their efforts. Among the artillery abandoned, was a large mortar, which had been employed in throwing shells the immense distance of three miles.

1814. Washington city evacuated by the British under major general Robert Ross and admiral Cockburn.

1819. JAMES WATT, an eminent Scottish natural philosopher, died; celebrated for his improvements in the steam engine.

1822. WILLIAM HERSCHEL, the English astronomer, died. He discovered the planet Georgium Sidus, which sometimes bears his name.

1830. Insurrection of the Belgians commenced at Brussels. The populace attacked and destroyed several houses belonging to the most obnoxious individuals, and skirmishes followed between the inhabitants and the troops.

1834. MORRIS EVANS died at Raleigh, N. C., aged 105.

1835. Earthquake in Natolia, by which 2,000 houses were destroyed in the city of Kaisarieh.

1836. CHRISTIAN WILLIAM HUFELAND, an eminent Prussian physician and medical writer, died, aged 75. He was a popular lecturer, distinguished for his profound and extensive learning, and ingenious application of his theory to practice.

1837. The cholera raged at Rome, and was fatal to 300; the greatest number of deaths that occurred in any one day.

1849. The French admiral, de Tromelin, took possession of and dismantled the fortifications at Honolulu, Sandwich islands, the government having refused to comply with the demands of the admiral. He relinquished the possession three days after.

1854. The city of Troy, N. Y., visited by a destructive fire, which consumed more than a hundred houses and manufactories.

AUGUST 26.

331 B. C. Battle of Arbela, the modern Irbil, on the Lycus, between the Macedodians under Alexander, and the Persians under Darius (26th Boedromion). The Persians were defeated and the fate of Darius sealed.

55 B. C. JULIUS CÆSAR made a landing on British ground, at a point eight miles north of Dover.

55. A surprisingly great comet was seen by the inhabitants of China.

1278. Battle of Marchfeld, in Austria, between Ottocar and Rodolph of Hapsburg, in which Ottocar fell. This day laid the foundation of the house of Hapsburg, which is still seated on the throne of Austria.

1346. Battle of Crecy, in France; the English, less than 30,000 under Edward III, defeated the French, 90,000, under Philip VI, who received two wounds, and was one of the last who fled. It is estimated that of the French upwards of 30,000 soldiers, 1,200 knights, 80 bannerets and 9 princes fell in the battle and pursuit.

1595. ANTONIO, a pretender to the throne of Portugal, died. He was assisted in the struggle for the crown by several of the European powers, but was driven out, and died in exile.

1635. LOPEZ FELIX DE LA VEGA died; a Spanish divine, poet and a dramatic writer of great fertility of genius. His works form upwards of 70 volumes.

1693. PETER BARRIERE, a French soldier, who attempted to assassinate Henry IV, of France, broken on the wheel.

1723. ANTHONY VAN LEEUWENHOEK, a celebrated Dutch physician, died. He became famous throughout Europe by his experiments and discoveries with the microscope.

1762. Valentia de Alcantara, in Spain, taken by assault by the British, under Gen. Burgoyne.

1765. Riot in Boston occasioned by the stamp act; several private houses destroyed, and among them that of the lieutenant governor Hutchinson, one of the best in the province; his books and papers, which he had been 30 years in gathering, were destroyed, together with his plate, furniture, &c., and £1,000 in money.

1766. THOMAS WINSLOW, an English military officer, died, aged 146.

1775. The Americans opened their entrenchments on Plowed hill, near Boston. The British threw about 300 shells at them.

1775. JAMES BURGH, an ingenious English moral and political writer, died at Islington.

1776. GERMAIN FRANCIS POULLAIN DE ST. FOIX, a French historical tourist, died. He retired from the army to devote himself to literature, at Paris, and was appointed historiographer.

1777. FRANCIS FAWKES, an English poet, died. He translated several of the Greek poets, and wrote many miscellaneous poems, in a pleasing and elegant style.

1785. GEORGE SACKVILLE, an English nobleman, died. He was an officer under Marlborough, and present at several important engagements.

1794. Sluys, in Dutch Flanders, surrendered to the French under Moreau, 22 days after the opening of the trenches. The sudden capture of this fortress, exceedingly strong by nature and art, and defended by the brave general Vanderduyn, so intimidated the remainder of the Dutch and Hanoverian garrisons, that they thought only how to escape the fate of Sluys, and evacuated several fortresses equally strong; besides nearly 30 less important forts, and all Dutch Flanders.

1795. Trincomalee, a Dutch colony in the island of Ceylon, taken by the British under admiral Rainer.

1795. British squadron under Nelson, captured in the bay of Alaeso, 11 French vessels.

1806. EDWARD THURLOW, an eminent English lawyer, died. He became attorney and solicitor-general to the king, a member of parliament and lord high chancellor of England. He possessed a vigorous and active mind, which added to close application, gave him a high rank among the professional men of his day.

1813. Battle of Katzbach, in Silesia; the French defeated by the Russians and Prussians under Blucher. The day was so rainy that fire arms could not be used, and the battle was fought hand to hand. The French were driven into the river and perished in great numbers.

1813. Battle of Dresden. The citizens beheld a spectacle of an army of 60,000 troops marching through the streets to the field of battle, under Napoleon. An army of 120,000 allies were drawn up around the city.

1813. THEODORE KORNER, a German poet, killed in battlle. Many of his pieces have been set to music, and become national.

1832. ADAM CLARKE, an eminent English divine, died of cholera, aged 72. He commenced his career as a methodist preacher at the age of 18, and became so popular that few men have ever drawn so large congregations. He was a man of great talents and extensive learning, particularly in the oriental languages and Biblical literature, and author of a well known and learned commentary on the scriptures, and various other publications.

1836. Buffalo and Niagara rail road opened.

1838. Caleb Stark, an officer of the revolutionary war, died. He entered the army at the age of 15, and commenced his career at the battle of Bunker hill as an ensign in his father's regiment. He remained in the army till the close of the war, at which time he was a brigadier-general.

1848. A battle took place at the cape of Good Hope, between the British and Boors. The former were victorious, with the loss of 54 men killed and wounded; the Boors lost 199.

1849. The senate of Hayti, having concurred in the bill of the chamber of representatives, Faustin Soulouque submitted to the wishes of the people, and was crowned emperor of Hayti, under the title of Faustin I.

1849. J. A. Yates, an eloquent divine and learned professor of Union college, died, aged 49.

1850. Louis Philippe, the exiled king of the French, died at Claremont, England, aged 77.

AUGUST 27.

413 b. c. The Athenian army under Nicias lost on account of the general's fright at an eclipse of the moon.

524. Flavius Severinus Bœthius, a celebrated Roman philosopher, died in prison, probably executed by order of Theodoric.

1556. Charles V, emperor of Germany, resigned the government to his brother Ferdinand, and set out for Spain.

1565. William Rastal died; an eminent English judge of the sixteenth century, and author of a work on the statutes of England.

1587. At the urgent solicitation of the colony of Roanoke, Gov. White returned to England for supplies; but of his countrymen whom he left behind nothing was ever afterwards known. Thus, says Holmes, terminated the exertions of Raleigh for colonizing Virginia.

1590. Sixtus V (*Felix Peretti*), died; distinguished for the energy with which he extirpated the outlaws, and opposed the overgrown power of Spain. He embellished Rome with numerous and useful structures, among which is the present Vatican.

1630. The first church founded at Charlestown and Boston; their pastor was to receive a salary of £40.

1664. Articles of capitulation signed, by which the Dutch colony at New Amsterdam became subjects of England, with the privilege of continuing free denizens; to possess their estates undiminished; to enjoy their ancient customs with regard to inheritance, to their modes of worship and church discipline, and were allowed a free trade to Holland. The doughty governor, Stuyvesant, could not be prevailed upon to ratify it with his signature till two days afterwards.

1683. Thomas Dongan arrived as governor of the province of New York. He was a man of integrity, moderation, and genteel manners, and may be classed among the best of the provincial governors of New York.

1748. James Thomson, an eminent English poet, died; author of the *Seasons*.

1758. Fort Frontenac surrendered at discretion, to the English and provincials under Col. Bradstreet, after a siege of two days. They found in the fort 60 pieces of cannon, 16 mortars, a large number of small arms, a vast quantity of provisions, military stores and merchandise, together with 9 armed vessels in the harbor.

1770. John Jortin, an eminent divine of the English church, and writer on ecclesiastical history, died, aged 72.

1776. Battle of Flatbush, or Long Island; the Americans surprised by the British and Hessians, and defeated with the loss of about 500 killed and 1,100 taken prisoners; British loss about 70 killed, 350 wounded.

1791. Placidus Fixmilner died; an Austrian ecclesiastic, and writer on astronomy and the canon law.

1793. Adam Philip de Custines, a French nobleman and general, guillotined. He served in the seven years' war and in the American revolutionary war.

1794. Valenciennes, after Lisle the strongest place of the famous northern barrier of France, surrendered to the republicans at the first summons.

1813. Second day's battle of Dresden. The allies were defeated and forced to retreat, with the loss of 30,000. The French had 10,000 wounded; the number of killed not known. Moreau had both legs shot away by a cannon ball.

1816. Algiers bombarded by the British and Dutch fleets, under lord Exmouth. The dey's fleet and defences were utterly destroyed, and he was compelled to submit to a treaty on his enemy's terms.

1825. Lucretia Maria Davidson, an American poetess, died before completing her 17th year. Her pieces amount to 278, of which *Amir Khan* is the principal; some of them written at the age of 9 years.

1834. George Clymer, inventor and manufacturer of the Columbian printing press, died in London. He was instrumental in improving many other mechanical improvements.

1847. Silas Wright, an eminent American statesman, died at Canton, St. Lawrence county, N. Y., aged 52.

1849. Gabriel H. Ford, an American jurist, died at Morristown, N. J., aged 85. He was one of the most eloquent and efficient lawyers of New Jersey, and held the office of judge of the supreme court twenty-one years. His residence was the head quarters of Washington in 1777.

1850. Benjamin Chambers, died, aged 86. He was a native of Pennsylvania, who entered the revolutionary army at the age of 16, and afterwards settled in Indiana. He held various important civil and military appointments under the early presidents.

1854. The city of Louisville, Ky., was visited by a tornado, which blew down and unroofed a large number of buildings; a church fell upon the congregation while at worship; 25 were killed and 67 seriously injured.

1857. Rufus W. Griswold, a voluminous American author, died, aged 42. He wrote for numerous periodicals, and left several unfinished works.

AUGUST 28.

430. Aurelius Augustinus (or St. Augustin), one of the fathers of the Christian church, died at Hippo, in Africa.

876. Louis I, of Germany, died. He acquired the title of the pious, at the same time rendered himself powerful and formidable to his neighbors.

1443. John V, duke of Britanny, died, and was succeeded by his son Francis.

1595. Drake and Hawkins sailed from England with six of the queen's ships and twenty-one private ships and barks, on an expedition against the Spanish settlements in the West Indies.

1608. Francis Vere, died; an English general, who distinguished himself in the expedition to Holland, 1585.

1609. Hudson, having retreated his steps from Chesapeake bay, discovered another great bay, which has since acquired the name of Delaware. He anchored the Half Moon in eight fathom water, and took possession of the country.

1645. Hugo Grotius, an eminent Dutch philosopher, died. He was a man of great talent and laborious study, and notwithstanding he passed a stormy life, his works are very numerous.

1654. Axel Oxenstiern, a Swedish statesman, died. He was placed at the head of affairs on the death of Gustavus Adolphus, and owed his elevation to his merit and abilities.

1686. Cassini, an Italian astronomer, discovered the satellite of Venus.

1710. Joseph Keble, an English law writer, died. Besides his published works, which were few, he left 100 large folio, and 50 thick quarto volumes in manuscript.

1722. Port Royal in Jamaica, destroyed by a hurricane; 26 ships and many lives lost.

1731. Charles Boyle, earl of Orrery, died, aged 56. He made a figure from the age of 19 up, in literary, military, and almost every other kind of warfare.

1737. John Hutchinson, an English author, died: founder of a well-known philosophical sect, which opposed Newton's doctrine of gravitation. His theories are curious, but no longer in repute.

1754. An irruption of the French and Indians upon Hoosick and Schaghticoke, by which those settlements were broken up, two persons scalped, and the houses fired.

1775. George Faulkner, a celebrated Irish printer, died. He was the first to carry the art to a high degree of perfection in that country, and appears to have been a worthy and useful citizen.

1788. Elizabeth Chudleigh, duchess of Kingston, died at Paris; celebrated for her matrimonial speculations.

1792. Dumourier took his post at the head of 20,000 men, undisciplined and unorganized. Yet with these materials he arrested the progress of 80,000 Prussians and Hessians, and forced them to retreat with the loss of half their army.

1794. Battle of Powassin, between the Prussians and the Poles, in which the former lost their batteries and cannon, after a bloody engagement.

1798. James Wilson died, one of the signers of the declaration of independence. He was eminent for his talents and integrity, and continued in the discharge of some public office till his death.

1804. Margaret, widow of Benedict Arnold, died in London, aged 44. She was the daughter of Edward Shippen, of Philadelphia. It was said of her, that with a superiority and strength of mind seldom equaled, she possessed such polished and fascinating manners, as to convert every acquaintance into a friend.

1811. John Leyden, a distinguished linguist, died on the island of Java, in his 36th year. He was ordained as a minister, but never attained any popularity as a preacher.

1814. Bombardment of fort Erie continued by the British; a shell entered the roof of Gen. Gaines's quarters, and burst at his feet, by which he was so severely wounded as to be obliged to resign the command of the fort.

1816. Treaty signed between Algiers and England, by which Christian slavery was to be abolished, and all slaves, of whatever nation, to be delivered up. The number released was 1,033.

1839. WILLIAM SMITH, an eminent English geologist, died, aged. 70. In his employment as a land surveyor and engineer, he turned his attention to the geology of England, and published upwards of 20 geological maps of the counties. He is styled the *Father of English Geology.*

1839. A grand tournament appointed at Eglintoun castle in Ayrshire, Scotland. The day was very stormy, and the multitude from all parts of Great Britain who had assembled to witness the feats, estimated at 80,000, suffered greatly from the inclemency of the weather, and the impossibility of procuring shelter, food, or vehicles. An immense sum had been expended by the romantic nobleman in getting up the festival, which proved a total failure.

1851. The yacht America beat the iron yacht Titania, on a race of forty miles out and back, and left her eight miles astern.

1854. MARIA CHRISTINA, queen mother of Spain, left Madrid for Portugal, under escort of a body of government troops, but against the will of the people; she was indebted to the state 71,000,000 reals.

1855. SPENCER H. CONE, a Baptist minister, died in New York, aged 70. He was an actor, and on the stage for the last time when the Richmond theatre was burnt. He afterwards edited a newspaper, and finally became one of the most distinguished of the Baptist ministers.

1855. The vessel engaged to lay the submarine cable between cape Ray in Newfoundland and cape North in cape Breton, 55½ miles, began to pay it out. The cable afterwards broke, and a gale coming on, it was found necessary to let it go.

1856. The Dudley observatory was inaugurated at Albany.

AUGUST 29.

30 B. C. Conquest of Alexandria by Augustus; exactly three lustra or fifteen years preceding the great victory of Drusus over the Rhœtians and Vindelici, which concluded the Barbaric war.

30. St. JOHN (*the Baptist*) beheaded. The decollation of the Baptist determines the birthday of Herod, tetrarch of Galilee, called Antipas, who for his ambition was banished by Caligula to Spain or Lyons, with Herodias, in the year 38.

410. Alaric evacuated Rome and ravaged the provinces of Italy.

284. Era of Diocletian (or the martyrs), commenced, still used by the Copts and Abyssinians. It receives its name from the persecution of the Christians in the reign of Diocletian, and was much used by the Christian writers until the introduction of the Christian era, in the sixth century.

1350. Great naval battle in the English channel, off Winchelsea, between the English under Edward III and the mariners of Biscay. Fourteen Castilian ships were carried triumphantly into port.

1353. Action between the Genoese fleet under Antonio Grimaldi, and the combined Venitian and Catalonian fleets, under Pisani, in which the former suffered so great a defeat that only 17 vessels escaped.

1445. PAUL, of Burgos, a learned Jew, died. He was converted to Christianity, and was baptized at the same time with his three sons, who all distinguished themselves.

1527. Battle of Mohatz, between the Turks under Solyman, and the Hungarians under Louis II, in which the latter were defeated with the loss of 20,000 killed. The Turks carried nearly 200,000 persons into captivity.

1583. STEPHEN PARMENIUS BUDEIUS, a learned Hungarian, shipwrecked on the coast of Newfoundland. He accompanied sir Humphrey Gilbert's squadron of discovery, for the purpose of recording their discoveries and exploits in Latin. He was on board the Delight, which carried down more than 100 persons with her.

1657. JOHN LILBURNE, a famous English enthusiast, died. He was the ringleader of a party called the levelers.

1660. The act of indemnity signed by Charles II, out of which most of those called regicides were excepted.

1692. Col. BENJAMIN FLETCHER arrived at the port of New York, with a commission as governor of the province, which he published the next day.

1708. Haverhill, on the Merrimack, surprised by the French and Indians, who burnt part of the town, killed about 40, and carried away 100 prisoners.

1749. MATHIAS BEL, died at Presburg; a Hungarian ecclesiastic, ennobled for his literary.

1750. LETITIA PILKINGTON, a lady of great wit and literary celebrity, died at Dublin.

1764. JOHN BERNARD, a distinguished London merchant, died. He represented the city in parliament forty years, and was so highly esteemed by the public that his statue was placed in the Royal Exchange during his life time.

1769. EDMUND HOYLE died; author of a celebrated treatise on whist and other games.

1776. Americans retreated from Long

Island. Gen. Mifflin commanded the rear guard, with whom Washington remained until the retreat was effected. The army amounted to 9,000.

1778. The rear of the American army under Gen. Sullivan attacked by the British, who were repulsed. British loss 260; American loss 206.

1779. The Indians defeated by Sullivan at Elmira.

1780. James Germain Soufflot, an eminent French architect, died.

1782. British ship Royal George, 108 guns, sunk while careening. Admiral Kempenfelt and about 1,000 persons were lost, of whom 300 were women and children. (This is put down by other authorities on the 19th, and differently stated.)

1799. Pius VI (*John Angelo Braschi*), pope, died. He rendered his name famous by draining the Pontine marshes. Bonaparte entered his state twice, making him a prisoner the second time, and carried him over the Alps to Valentia, where he died of excessive fatigue, aged 82.

1804. Com. Preble's fifth attack on Tripoli. The Constitution fired upwards of 300 rounds, besides grape and canister: sunk a large Tunisian galliot, and silenced two of the batteries and the castle. American loss 3 killed, 1 wounded.

1816. Scheta, the celebrated astronomer of Liliennthal, died.

1833. Great fire at Constantinople, in which a circuit of three miles, said to comprise 12,000 houses and 50,000 inhabitants, was devastated, and many lives lost.

1843. A treaty of peace between Great Britain and China concluded. The Chinese to pay twenty-one millions of dollars, open 5 of their principal ports and cede the island of Hong-Kong to the British.

1849. The fortress of Achulga, the residence of Schamyl, a celebrated Circassian chief, was carried by assault by the Russians, after a siege of four months.

1851. Lopez, who had invaded Cuba with American volunteers, after sixteen days of reverses, and having lost nearly all his followers, was captured in the mountains by the aid of bloodhounds.

1851. A convention of twenty-five delegates assembled in Lewis county, Oregon, and appointed a committee to prepare a memorial to congress, to procure a division of the territory, and the organization of a separate territorial government.

1853. The Austrian minister, M. Hulsemann, addressed a note to the American government, complaining of the conduct of Capt. Ingraham in the Koszta affair.

1854. Petropaulowski, a Russian town, attacked and bombarded by the allied English and French fleet. The town was defended by 1,200 men and 120 guns.

1854. A new asteroid, named Euphrosyne, was discovered at the Washington observatory, by James Ferguson, assistant astronomer.

AUGUST 30.

30 B. C. Cleopatra, queen of Egypt, destroyed herself by the bite of an asp, to save herself from the disgrace of captivity.

526. Theodoric, first king of the Goths in Italy, died. He advanced commerce and the arts, and patronized literature, but committed great acts of cruelty.

1181. Alexander III, pope, died. He was an able pontiff, beloved by his subjects and respected by the world.

1483. Louis XI, of France, died. His ambition led him to the commission of the greatest crimes, by which he acquired the title of the Tiberius of France.

1563. Wolfgang Musculus, a celebrated German divine, died. He adopted the tenets of Luther, and by his eloquence gained over the city of Augsburg.

1566. Solyman II (*the Magnificent*), sultan of Turkey, died. He prosecuted war with various success in Europe and Asia, and took the island of Rhodes from the knights of Jerusalem.

1645. Treaty of peace between the New England colonies and the Narragansett Indians; by which the latter were to pay the expense of the preparations already made for war, estimated at 2,000 fathoms of wampum; restore to Uncus the prisoners and canoes taken from him; keep perpetual peace with the English and all their allies; and give hostages for the performance of the treaty. Formidable preparations were made for this contest with the heathen savages. They drew up a manifesto, containing such facts as they considered sufficient to justify them in making war against the Narragansetts. It was entitled, "a declaration of former passages and proceedings betwixt the English and the Narrohiggansetts, with their confederates, wherein the grounds and justice of the ensuing warr are opened and cleared." In this document it is affirmed that the English colonies, "both in their treaties and converse with the barbarous natives of this wilderness, have had an awful respect to divine rules." It was determined immediately to raise 300 men; Massachusetts to raise 190, Plymouth 40, Connecticut 40, New Haven 30.

1645. A formal treaty of peace between the Dutch in New Amsterdam, under William Kieft, and the Indians in the vicinity.

1645. Parliament ordered a fast for a

blessing on Scotland and sir Thomas Fairfax's army, and a cessation of the plague.

1690. King William forced to raise the siege of Limerick after sustaining great loss.

1717. William Lloyd, an English prelate, died, aged 91. He was a zealous promoter of the revolution, and a voluminous author.

1757. Battle of Norkettin; the Prussians forced the Russian camp and batteries, and killed 2,000 men with an equal loss on their own part.

1785. By the plague which raged at Tripoli, 30,000 persons had died up to this date, of which 3,300 were Jews. The brother of the bey, his two sons, and all the ministers of the bey were dead. All the Christians established in the city as merchants had died.

1794. The Austrian garrison of Conde laid down their arms as prisoners of war at the first summons of the French republican general Scherer. The garrison was strongly entrenched, and might have defied the enemy as long as their provisions lasted.

1795. Andrew Danican (*Philidor*) died; noted for his musical performances and compositions, by which he acquired the *sobriquet* from the king, of Philidor, after an Italian musician of that name, and by which he is generally known as a celebrated chess player. His fondness for the game grew into a passion, in order to indulge which he traveled over a great part of Europe, engaging everywhere with the best players. He remained some time in England, during which he printed his *Analysis of Chess*, a standard work. On his return to France he devoted his attention to the comic opera, of which he produced 21 pieces. A short time previous to his decease he played two games blindfolded at the same time against two excellent chess players, and won.

1797. In England, the Leeds methodist conference resolved to eject from their communion, a brother, who should propogate opinions in opposition to the established church.

1801. Cairo surrendered to the British, and Egypt evacuated by the French under Menou. He was the first French general who landed with Bonaparte, and the last who left it.

1804. Thomas Percival, well known for his writings on moral and medical subjects, died at Manchester, England.

1804. John Blair Linn, an American poet, died, aged 27. He published 2 vols. of miscellaneous pieces.

1810. John Philip de Cobentzl, an Austrian statesman, died. He was the last of that illustrious family.

1813. Battle of Nollendorf, in Bohemia, when Von Kleist made a daring descent from the mountains, upon the rear of Vandamme, and gaining a decisive victory saved Bohemia, against which Bonaparte had directed his masterly demonstrations.

1814. Alexandria, in Virginia, capitulated to the British, and delivered up the public stores, shipping, &c.

1814. The British under sir Peter Parker, having attacked the Americans at Moorsfield, were repulsed with considerable loss. Among the killed was sir Peter himself.

1832. Number of deaths in Paris from cholera since March, 18,000.

1834. Harding, an eminent astronomer, died at Gottingen; celebrated as the discoverer of the planet Juno.

1835. William T. Barry, postmaster-general under president Jackson, died at Liverpool on his way to Spain, as minister plenipotentiary of the United States.

1838. David Hume died, aged 82; baron of the exchequer in Scotland, and author of a celebrated work on criminal law.

1844. Francis Bailey, so favorably known as a stock broker and author, died in England. He was instrumental in founding the astronomical society of London.

1848. The United States district attorney of Arkansas had orders from government to discover and prosecute all those who were engaged in preparing a military expedition against Mexico, and establishing the republic of the Sierra Madre.

1849. The chamber of deputies at Turin voted 100,000 livres to relieve the refugees from different parts of Italy.

1850. John Inman, a New York editor, died, aged 46. He was educated for the law, but commenced his editorial experience about 1830, with the *Spirit of the Times*. He was also for a time connected with the *New York Mirror*, and in 1834 became assistant editor of the *New York Commercial Advertiser*, which he edited ably on the death of William L. Stone.

1852. John Camden Neild, an English barrister, died at London, aged 72. He was privately known by his eccentricities and miserliness, and after his death became more publicly known by the strange bequest of all his property, estimated at $2,500,000, to the queen.

1852. George Frederick Von Langsdorff, a noted botanist and traveler, died at Freidburg, in the duchy of Baden.

1853. The cholera, which prevailed very generally in the north of Europe, became nearly extinct at Copenhagen, where it destroyed 4,006 lives. In St. Petersburg the deaths during this visitation were 5,609.

1854. The British admiral Price engaged

in bombarding the Russian town Petropaulowski, was killed by a shot from his own pistol.

1855. Feargus Edward O'Connor, leader of the chartists in Great Britain, died at Notting hill, England, aged 59, in the custody of an institution for the insane.

AUGUST 31.

1130. Abu Abdillah Mohammed, founder of the sect and dynasty of Almohades, died. The empire founded by this imposter, lasted 140 years.

1290. Edward I, by a proclamation, exiled the whole race of English Jews forever, on penalty of death.

1422. Henry V of England died at Vincennes, in France. He had conquered the kingdom, and was received at Paris as the future master of the country.

1523. Ulric Hutten, an eccentric German poet, died.

1568. John de la Valette Parisot, grand master of the knights of Malta, died. He bravely defended the island against a formidable siege by the Turks in 1557.

1578. Frobisher embarked to return from his third voyage to the northernmost part of the American continent. His fleet was separated the next night, by a violent storm, but arrived safe, one ship after another, in England. Stow, the chronicler, says, "they fraught their shippes with the like pretended gold ore out of the mines," as on their last voyage, "but after great charges it proved worse than good stone, whereby many men were deceived to their utter undoings."

1615. Stephen Pasquier died; an eminent French advocate and poet.

1660. John Freinshemius, a learned German, died. He understood most of the languages of Europe, and his supplements to Livy and Quintus Curtius, go far to supply the loss of the originals.

1688. John Bunyan died, aged 60. From an abandoned youth he became a respectable preacher; the authorship of *Pilgrim's Progress* will perpetuate his memory.

1733. Fifty tons of half pence and farthings sent from the Tower of London to Ireland.

1772 William Borlase, an English writer on natural history, &c., died. He also devoted much attention to antiquities.

1805. James Currie, an eminent Scottish physician, died. He wrote on medicine, and published an edition of Robert Burns with an excellent memoir.

1813. Battle of St. Sebastian; Wellington having driven the French over the Pyrennes, carried this place by storm and achieved a victory on the heights of San Marceil. French loss 15,000.

1832. Everard Home, an English anatomist, died, aged 77. He was one of the most eminent medical men of his day, and his publications are numerous and in high repute.

1849. The convention for framing a state constitution for California, assembled at Monterey.

1852. James L. Kingsley, professor of languages and ecclesiastical history, died, aged 73. He was connected with the college in the department of classical literature, with high reputation, for half a century.

1853. The cholera appeared at Newcastle upon Tyne, in England, and caused 1538 deaths before its disappearance on the 26th October.

1853. A Roman circus of great size was discovered at Tours in France, where excavations were being made.

1853. The small pox raged at the Sandwich islands, having since May carried off 1,805 persons out of a population of 60,000.

1855. William H. Fry died at Philadelphia, aged 78. He was one of the magnates of the press in that city, and the founder of the *National Gazette.*

1855. Lewis Weston Dillwyn, a British naturalist, died at Swanse, Wales, aged 77. He produced several valuable works on natural history, and communicated various papers on fossils, shells and plants to the Royal society.

SEPTEMBER.

SEPTEMBER 1.

5508 B. C. The world was created, according to the *Septuagint*, followed by Julius Africanus, a chronologer of the third century, upon the first of September, five thousand five hundred and eight years, three months and twenty-five days before the birth of Christ. Of the 7,349 years which are thus supposed to elapse since the creation, we shall find 3,000 of ignorance and darkness; 2,000 either fabulous or doubtful; 1,000 of ancient history, commencing with the Persian empire and the republics of Rome and Athens; 1,000 from the fall of the Roman empire in the west to the discovery in America; and the remaining 349 will compose the modern state of Europe and mankind.

44 B. C. Divine honors decreed to the memory of Cæsar.

1159. ADRIAN IV (*Nicholas Brekespere*), pope, died. He was the only Englishman ever elected to the office.

1611. The crew of HENRY HUDSON, who had mutinied and put him adrift in an open boat, were picked up by a fisherman, in a wretched condition. Their best sustenance left, while on their voyage, was seaweed fried with candles' ends, and the skins of fowls. They were in such a state of starvation that only one of them had strength to lie on the helm and steer the ship. It appears that they had quarreled among themselves, and met with a fearful retribution.

1620. The English pilgrims sailed from Plymouth in the Mayflower, for the American continent, intending to find some place near Hudson's river for a settlement.

1633. ANTONIO QUERENGHI, an Italian poet, died.

1641. The Raritans made an attack upon the colony of Staten island, and murdered the colonists, in revenge for previous depredations by the Dutch.

1651. Dundee, in Scotland, taken by storm by general Monk. "Mounche commaundit all, of quhatsummever sex to be putt to the edge of the sword. There were 800 inhabitants and soldiers killed, and about 200 women and children. The plounder and buttie they gat in the towne, exceeded two millions and a half."

1675. The Indians under the notorious king Philip fell upon the town of Deerfield, in Massachusetts, killed one man, and laid most of the town in ashes.

1682. WILLIAM PENN sailed for America in the ship Welcome, 300 tons burthen, with about a hundred other emigrants, mostly quakers.

1685. LEOLINE JENKINS, an able English civilian and statesman, died.

1687. HENRY MORE, an English philosopher and poet, died. His works once enjoyed a high reputation.

1697. The imperialists, commanded by prince Eugene, defeated the Turks at Zentha; the grand vizier and upwards of 20,000 men killed.

1715. LOUIS XIV, of France, died. His reign is marked as an era of magnificence, learning and licentiousness, in France; and he left behind him monuments of unprecedented splendor and expense, in palaces, gardens, &c.

1715. FRANCIS GIRANDON, an eminent French sculptor and architect, died.

1720. EUSEBUS RENAUDOT, a distinguished French orientalist, died.

1721. JOHN KIELL, an eminent Scottish mathematician and philosopher, died. His works are numerous and in high repute.

1729. RICHARD STEELE, an English writer and politician, died; "justly celebrated as an essayist, just remembered as a dramatist, and almost forgotten as a politician."

1730. A new volcano opened at Temanfaya, in the isle of Lanzerota.

1731. French erected a fort at Crown point, on lake Champlain.

1755. MAURICE GREENE, an eminent English music composer, died. He undertook an important reformation in church music which he did not live to effect.

1766. PETER ANICH, a Tyrolese peasant, astronomer and geographer, died. He followed the occupation of a farmer till the age of 28, after which he commenced his scientific career.

1771. CUTHBERT SHAW died; an English poet of "humble origin, but of superior attainments, and inferior to no writer of ancient or modern times."

1774. General GAGE seized the powder at Charlestown, in consequence of which the people rose and compelled several officers of the king's government to resign.

1776. LEWIS HENRY CHRISTOPHER HOLTY, an Excellent German poet, died. "In tender elegiac or idylic poetry, he is peculiary successful."

1779. French fleet, count d'Estaing, captured off Charleston, S. C., British ship Experiment, 50 guns, and three frigates.

1784. JOHN FRANCIS SEGUIER, a distinguished French botanist, and president of the academy of Nismes, died.

1787. JOHN BAKE, an eminent Dutch philosopher and Latin writer, was born at Leyden. His last work was an edition of *Cicero de Legibus*.

1793. A fine marble bust of John Milton, the poet, was placed in the church at Cripplegate.

1801. ROBERT BAGE, an English novelist of considerable merit, died.

1804. The planet Juno discovered by Harding, of Germany. Her diameter is 1,425 miles, and she performs a very eccentric orbit round the sun in 4 years and 128 days.

1804. JAMES NICHOLSON, an officer in the American navy during the war of the revolution, died.

1806. PATRICK O'BRYEN, the Irish giant, died at Bristol, England. His height was 8 feet, 5 inches.

1814. Champlain village taken possession of by the British under Provost.

1814. Fort Castine, on the Penobscot, and several places taken by the British under Sherwood and admiral Griffith.

1814. United States sloop of war Wasp, captain Blakely, fell in with 10 sail of British vessels convoyed by a 74, and bomb ship. He cut out of the convoy a brig laden with military stores, and burnt her, and sunk the brig Avon, of 19 guns.

1818. The state prison at Auburn, N. Y., opened.

1831. GEORGE FULTON, author of an improved system of education and a popular pronouncing dictionary, died near New Haven, Scotland.

1838. WILLIAM CLARKE died; the companion of Lewis in the pioneer journey across the Rocky mountains. He was held in the highest estimation by nearly all the tribes of western Indians, however remote, whose character he well understood. He was several years governor of Missouri, and at the time of his death the oldest American settler residing in St. Louis.

1841. JOSEPH NOURSE died; a soldier of the revolution, one of the vice-presidents of the American Bible society, and 40 years register of the United States treasury.

1849. The deaths registered in London for the week, were 2,796; exceeding those of any previous week, and nearly three times the average of the season. Of the number, 1,663 were by cholera, and 234 by diarrhea.

1851. ANTONIO LOPEZ, who attempted to affect a revolution in Cuba, was garotted at Havana.

1851. The rail road in Russia from St. Petersburg to Moscow, was inaugurated.

1853. LOUIS CHITTI, an Italian exile, died in New York. He was secretary of finance to Murat, afterwards professor of political economy at Brussels; then commissioner to the United States from Belgium. During the troubles of 1821 at Naples, he was expelled, and resided in this country.

1855. WILLIAM CRANCH, an eminent American judge, died at Washington, D. C., aged 86. He published 9 vols. of cases in the supreme court, and was highly respected for his talents and learning.

SEPTEMBER 2.

44 B. C. CICERO delivered the first of those speeches against Marc Antony, called his *Philippics*.

31 B. C. Battle of Actium, off the promontory of Epirus, in which the fleet of Marc Antony was defeated and his hopes utterly prostrated.

1338. EDWARD III was invested by the emperor at Coblentz, with the title of his vicar, but refused to kiss the imperial foot.

1483. The renowned Caxton issued from his press a book entitled, *Confessio Amantis:* That is to saye in Englisshe, The Confessyon of the Louer.

1504. COLUMBUS sailed from Hispaniola to Spain—his final leave of the country which he had discovered—a discovery that had been to him a source of unutterable vexation and the vilest ingratitude.

1519. Battle of Zehuacingo, between 400 Spaniards under Cortez, and the whole force of the Tlascalan Indians, amounting to about 40,000 warriors. The Indians closed in upon the Spaniards in a dense mass, and bore down with determined bravery upon the sturdy little band of invaders. A body of them, wielding two-handed swords succeeded in killing one of the horses at a blow; but the rider was saved, and the saddle also at the cost of ten men wounded. The cannons and guns of the Spaniards made terrible havoc among the dense masses of the Indians, and they were compelled to retire with a great loss, leaving their enemy too much fatigued to follow them, and greatly rejoiced to find that they had escaped annihilation.

1591. RICHARD GRENVILLE, an English naval officer, died. He distinguished himself in battle against the Turks, and on the American coast against the Spaniards.

1592. ROBERT GREEN, an English poet, and one of the famous Grub street writers, died in London. So infamous was Grub street at that time, that Mr. Henry Welley says in his narrative, that he lived there 40 years without being seen of any one.

1666. Great fire in London, which consumed 400 streets, 13,200 houses and 89 churches—and destroyed the plague!

1685. ALICIA LISLE beheaded at Winchester. Her offence was harboring a nonconforming minister named Hicks.

1701. The court of chancery of the state of New York organized.

1746. JOHN BAPTIST COLBERT, marquis of Torrey, died; a French statesman, celebrated for his embassies.

1755. Sir CHARLES HARDY arrived in the port of New York, to succeed De Lancey as governor of the province, and his commission was published on the next day, with the usual solemnities, and was followed by an entertainment, bonfires, illuminations and other expressions of joy.

1766. ARCHIBALD BOWYER, a learned Scottish Jesuit, died. He wrote a *History of the Popes*, and some other historical works; but is accused of much imposture.

1784. JOHN BAPTIST ANTHONY VISCONTI, an Italian antiquary, died. In his researches for ancient monuments at Rome, he discovered the tomb of the Scipios.

1792. The prisons of Paris, filled with nobles, ecclesiastics and opulent citizens, suspected of favoring the court and aristocratical party, were burst open, and the inmates massacred to the number of 12,-487, during this and the following day. Neither age, rank nor sex were respected by the Jacobins, who urged the expediency of destroying these persons before the Austrians should reach the capital.

1792. MARIE THERESE DE LAMBALLE, an Italian princess, murdered in Paris. She escaped from Paris at the same time with the royal family, by another road, and reached England. But on hearing the fate of her friend the queen, hastened back to share her fortune, and met with a barbarous death from the hands of the mob.

1806. An immense rock forming the summit of the Rosenburg in Switzerland was precipitated into the valley with a vast amount of rubbish, overwhelming several villages, and partly filling lake Lauwertz. Upwards of 1,000 persons perished, and three villages totally disappeared.

1813. JEAN VICTOR MOREAU, one of the most distinguished generals of the French revolution, died of wounds received at the battle of Dresden.

1832. FRANCIS XAVIER DE ZACH died of cholera at Paris. He was a native of Hungary, and one of the most eminent astronomers of the age.

1832. JOHN OLDING BUTLER died; an English writer, author of a *Geography of the Globe*.

1834. THOMAS TELFORD, a distinguished architect and civil engineer, died at London. He was a self-made man, rising from a shepherd boy in Eskdale, Scotland, to rank with the most learned of his age.

1836. WILLIAM HENRY, a celebrated writer on chemistry, died.

SEPTEMBER 3.

1189. Inauguration of RICHARD I (*Cœur de Lion*), at Westminster, a most splendid pageant.

1328. CASTRACANI CASTRUCCIO, a famous Italian general, died. He was found, when an infant, in a heap of leaves, in Tuscany; and lived to attain the highest rank in military fame.

1332. A famous bull feast in the Coliseum at Rome, after the fashion of the Moors and Spaniards. The ladies were seated in three balconies, lined with scarlet cloth. Every knight assumed a livery and device. The champions who were left on the arena outnumbered the *quadrupeds*.

1588. RICHARD TARLETON, a celebrated jester and actor, and dramatic writer, was buried at Shoreditch, London—the *Yorick* of Shakspeare's Hamlet.

1592. ROBERT GREENE, an English dramatic author, died; notorious for his licentiousness.

1609. HENRY HUDSON, coasting northwardly, at 3 o'clock in the afternoon came to three great rivers, and stood for the northernmost.

1634. EDWARD COKE, the celebrated English judge, died. He was a clear and luminous writer on the laws and constitution of his country.

1642. Battle of Liscarrol, between the Irish army of 7,500, under general Barry, and the British, 2,400, under lord Inchiquin, in which the latter were victorious.

1650. Battle of Dunbar; the Scots under Leslie defeated with great slaughter by Oliver Cromwell; 3,000 of them slain and 10,000 taken prisoners, one half of whom were "driven, like turkeys, into England."

1651. Battle of Worcester; Cromwell defeated Charles II with great slaughter; the whole Scottish army being principally killed or taken.

1653. Claudius Salmasius, a French historian and critic, died. He was a man of most uncommon abilities and erudition, as his works, numerous and various, show.

1658. Oliver Cromwell died, on the anniversary of some of his most famous victories. The mighty conqueror, Death, snatched him in no ordinary manner, for Dan Æolus proclaimed it in *tempest* to all nations of Europe.

1660. James, duke of York, remarried to Ann Hyde; Clarendon, lord chancellor, pretending on account of the dignity of royalty, he would rather have seen her his concubine than his wife.

1662. William Lenthall, speaker of the parliament that levied war against Charles I, died.

1680. Paul Ragueneau, superior of the Jesuit missionaries in Canada, died at Paris, aged 75. He was a man of wonderful confidence in God, and of the most complete disengagement from temporal things.

1692. David Ancillon, a German divine, died; eminent for his learning, piety and eloquence. His library at Metz was a great curiosity to the learned.

1711. Elizabeth Sophia Cheron died; a French lady who obtained great celebrity by her talents for poetry, painting, the learned languages and music.

1715. The pretender proclaimed king James VIII by the earl of Mar at Aboyne, Aberdeenshire.

1729. John Hardouin, a French Jesuit, died; who distinguished himself for his criticism and extensive erudition, as well as by the singularity of his opinions.

1733. At Carlton, Yorkshire, England, a vault, 8 feet by 5, was discovered 18 feet below the surface, in which lay a skeleton of a large body with a helmet in a niche over the head, on the wall some Saxon characters and the date 992 were discovered.

1739. George Lillo, an English dramatic writer, died. Though a jeweler by profession, and a man of business, he cultivated the muses, and acquired great celebrity.

1752. New style; eleven days blotted from the English calendar; this, the 3d, being accounted the 14th. The Julian computation, either from ignorance or negligence, supposing a complete solar revolution in the precise period of 365 days and 6 hours, made no provision for the deficiency of 11 minutes per annum, which, however, in the lapse of 18 centuries amounted to a difference of 11 days.

1774. Antony de Ferriol, count Pont de Vesle, died; a French comic writer.

1777. British under Gen. Howe marched upon Philadelphia, and the Americans retreated across the Brandywine.

1782. Sixth action between the British, admiral Hughes, 12 ships and a 50 gun ship, and the French admiral Suffrein, 12 ships and three 50 gun ships, off Trincomalee. The action was bloody; the French on re-entering the harbor in the evening, lost a 74 gun ship.

1783. Definitive articles of peace signed at Paris, between England, France, Spain and America.

1791. New French constitution presented to Louis XVI by the national assembly.

1796. Battle of Wurzburg; the French under Jourdan defeated by the Austrians under the archduke Charles.

1801. British took possession of Alexandria, Egypt. They found there 312 cannon. The garrison consisted of nearly 12,000, who had subsisted a long time on horseflesh.

1803. Joseph Ritson, an English writer, died. Though a man of learning, he adopted a most singular and capricious form of orthography.

1804. Sixth attack on Tripoli by the American squadron under Com. Preble. The Constitution brought to in a situation where more than 70 guns could be brought to bear upon her. She silenced one of their batteries, and considerably damaged the town, castle and other batteries.

1807. Clara Reeve died, aged 70; an English writer of considerable literary talent.

1816. Kia King, emperor of China, dethroned by the guards of his palace, on account of a sentence he passed in relation to some affairs of religion.

1839. William Sullivan died at Boston, aged 64. He was an eminent lawyer, and sustained various civil and military offices, and was the author of *Familiar Letters, Political Class Book, &c.*

1852. George Richardson Porter, secretary of the board of trade, died at Tunbridge Wells, England, aged 60. He wrote upon the sugar cane, and other products and manufactures.

1855. Gen. Walker with 150 men, only 80 of whom were white, took up his quarters at Virgin bay. Gen. Mandiola attacked him with 400 men, but was defeated with the loss of 50. Walker's loss 1 white, 4 natives.

1855. Rachel, the noted French actress, made her first appearance in America at New York, and was enthusiastically received.

1855. Battle of Sand Hills; the United States troops under general Harney gained a complete victory over the Sioux Indians, killing 86 warriors, and capturing about 70 women and children, with a loss of only 4 of his own men.

SEPTEMBER 4.

1456. John Corvinus Hunniades died; a general in the Hungarian armies, distinguished for his bravery and his great success in the wars with the Turks.

1532. Pizarro, having landed in Peru and founded a colony, now began his march for the conquest of the country. His force consisted of 62 horse, and 106 foot, among whom were 20 crossbowmen, with which he went forth to encounter tens of thousands of fierce and warlike men. It is said that Pizarro incited his followers to this dangerous enterprise by the singular argument, that this main design was the propagation of the catholic faith, without injuring any person.

1588. Robert Dudley, earl of Leicester, died. He was a great favorite at the court of Elizabeth, and accounted a man of talents; but artful, ambitious, and criminal.

1598. Philip II of Spain died at the Escurial of a loathsome disease. By his own account, he expended 600,000,000 of gold ducats and sacrificed 20,000,000 of human lives.

1665. Naval action between the English and Dutch; the latter lost 12 war and 2 East India ships.

1676. John Ogilby, a Scottish writer, died. From the profession of a dancing master he became an eminent geographer, critic and poet.

1699. Christian V, king of Denmark, died, in consequence of a wound received in hunting, aged 53. He was much engaged in war. (August 25 ?)

1727. The body of George I of England was interred in the night at Hanover.

1745. The town of Perth occupied by the adherents to Charles the pretender, and he himself proclaimed king of Great Britain.

1753. Andrew Fountaine, an English antiquarian, died. He traveled over the European continent in search of pictures, medals, statues and inscriptions, with which he enriched the cabinets of England.

1759. Paul Francis Velli, a French Jesuit, died; author of a valuable history of France.

1780. John Fielding, one of the police justices of London, died at Bromton. Though blind from his youth he was a vigorous writer, and an efficient magistrate.

1784. Cæsar Cassini de Thury, an eminent French astronomer, died. He had acquired much knowledge on the science at the age of 10. He published a map of France in 182 sheets, which has served as a model for all subsequent works of the kind. This family had been at the head of the Royal observatory at Paris 113 years.

1785. A Mr. Sadler ascended at Oxford, England, in a balloon of his own construction. He was the first Englishman who undertook an ærial voyage.

1796. A quantity of rope was brought into the office of the secretary of state at London as the first specimen of the labor of convicts at Botany bay. It was two inches thick.

1797. On this day the majority of the French directory overthrew the opposite party; sixty-five deputies were condemned to deportation as guilty of a conspiracy for the restoration of the monarchy. The councils renewed their oaths of hatred against royalty on this occasion.

1800. Cayuga bridge over the lake finished.

1802. Garnerin, a French æronaut, made a descent of about 8,000 feet in his parachute. This was not so successful as a former experiment, the parachute not opening for some time after being cut from the balloon.

1804. Great hurricane in the West Indies; 274 vessels lost.

1805. Peter Francis Andrew Mechain, a French astronomer, died. He was a practical man, and accomplished much useful labor.

1808. John Home, a Scottish writer, died, aged 84. He was a preacher at the time his admirable play of *Douglas* appeared, which gave so much offence to the presbytery that he resigned.

1830. Donald McDonald died at Lynn, Mass., aged 108. He was born in Scotland, 1722, and during the last years of his life wandered about the country, a vagrant of the most intemperate habits. He was with Wolfe at the battle of Quebec.

1834. George Clymer, inventor of the Columbian printing press, died in London, aged 80; formerly of Philadelphia.

1836. The sultan of Turkey released all the inmates of his seraglio from the perpetual imprisonment within the precincts of his palace, to which they had considered themselves to be condemned for life.

1843. Capt. Ross landed at Folkstone on his return from a voyage of discovery in the southern polar circle, which had occupied four years.

1844. Metamoras destroyed by a hurricane. More than two-thirds of the houses in the city were prostrated, and 200 lives lost. This city was devastated in the same way in 1835 and 1837.

1850. Marshal Haynau, who commanded the Austrian forces in the Hungarian war, visited the brewery of Perkins & Barclay, London, and was attacked by a mob composed of the workmen in the establishment, and the draymen and coal heavers outside, and barely escaped with his life, by the assistance of the police. The cruelties of his acts had excited the indignation of all Christendom.

1852. The Hudson river steam boat Reindeer exploded, by which 28 lives were lost, and 20 others were injured.

SEPTEMBER 5.

1548. CATHARINE PARR, the sixth and last queen of Henry VIII, died. She was learned, and had sufficient prudence and sagacity to direct the caprices of the monarch in his dotage.

1569. EDMUND BONNER, bishop of London, died. He was of low parentage, and on coming to power, distinguished himself by a most cruel and bloody persecution of the protestants, 200 of whom he was instrumental in bringing to the stake, and is said to have whipped and tortured several with his own hands. On the accession of Elizabeth he was committed to prison, where he died.

1593. The river Thames in England almost dry from westerly winds and low tides.

1618. JACQUES DAVY DU PERRON, a French cardinal, died; celebrated for his learning and political knowledge.

1654. Cromwell's first parliament assembled at Westminster. The speech explaining his policy occupied three solemn hours.

1655. STUYVESANT sailed from New York against the Swedes on the South or Delaware river.

1685. FRANCIS NORTH, an English statesman, died. He rose through his abilities, and found time amidst his arduous duties to prepare and publish several works.

1701. EDMUND BOURSAULT, a French dramatist, died. He received little or no education, yet became a correct and popular author.

1745. SIMON JOSEPH PELLEGRIN, a French ecclesiastic and poet, died. He obtained the prize at the academy in 1704.

1752. The first play performed in America by a regular company of comedians, at Williamsburgh, then the capital of Virginia. The piece was the *Merchant of Venice*, and the afterpiece *Lethe*, written by Garrick. Thus Shakspeare had the first place, in time as in merit, as the dramatist of the western world, and Garrick the honor of attending on his master. Lewis Hallam made his "first appearance on any stage" at this performance. He had one line to speak, apparently an easy task, but when he found himself in presence of the audience, he was panic struck; he stood motionless and speechless, until bursting into tears he walked off the stage, making a most inglorious exit. It is scarcely necessary to add that he was afterwards the hero and favorite in tragedy and comedy for nearly half a century.

1765. ANNE CLAUDE DE CAYLUS, a French writer, died. His *Collection of Egyptian Antiquities*, 7 vols. 4to, is valuable. He also discovered, from a passage of Pliny, the ancient mode of encausting painting, and of tinging marble.

1774. The first congress met at Philadelphia. There were 52 members present from eleven colonies. (Sept. 4, ?)

1778. British under Gen. Grey landed at Bedford or Dartmouth, and destroyed above 70 sail of shipping, besides small craft. They burnt the magazine, wharf, storehouses, vessels on the stocks, the dwelling houses and mills, and levied a contribution of all the public moneys, 300 oxen and 10,000 sheep.

1781. An indecisive engagement took place off the Chesapeake between the British fleet, admiral Graves, and the French fleet under de Grasse. While the two admirals were manœuvering, count de Barras with a French fleet of eight line of battle ships passed the British at night and got within the capes of Virginia; by this combination the French had a decided superiority, and the British took their departure.

1785. LUNARDI made the first balloon ascent in Scotland. He ascended at Edinburgh, and traversed a distance of fifty miles over sea and land in one hour and a half.

1786. JONAS HANWAY, an English merchant and philanthropist, died. He undertook a laborious and dangerous course of travels through Russia into Persia, with a view of opening trade. The city of London owes many useful improvements and institutions to his enterprise and benevolence.

1794. JOHN HELY HUTCHINSON, an Irish lawyer and statesman, died. He was noted for his avidity after lucrative offices; of whom lord North remarked, that if England and Ireland were given him he would solicit the Isle of Man for a potato garden.

1800. The capitulation of the fortress of Valetta, at Malta, was signed, two years after it had been taken from the knights by the French. It was agreed that the French troops should march out with the honors of war as far as the sea shore, where they should ground their arms, and then be embarked for Marseilles as prisoners of war until exchanged, and Malta has remained in the hands of the British.

1808. CLEMENT CRUTTWELL died; an

English divine and author, whose literary performances, for labor, extent and utility, have rarely been equaled.

1812. First battle of Borodino, in Russia; the French under Bonaparte and his favorite generals; the Russians under Koutousoff. The Russians made a desperate resistance, till night separated the combatants.

1813. Action off Seguin between United States brig Enterprise, 17 guns, Lieut. Burrows, and British brig of war Boxer, 18 guns, Lieut. Blythe; the latter was captured in 40 minutes, with the loss of upwards of 20 killed and 14 wounded; American loss 4 killed and 10 wounded. Both commanders were killed, and were buried together at Portland, on the eighth.

1819. At Studein, in Moravia, at noonday, the atmosphere being serene and tranquil, there was a fall of little pieces of earth from a small cloud isolated and very bright.

1824. Peter Louis Lacretelle died; a distinguished French lawyer and writer.

1837. Borowlaski, a celebrated Polish dwarf, died in England, aged 98. His height was short of 36 inches, though his person was of complete symmetry. In former years he traveled on the continent, but for the last 40 years had resided in England. He excelled as a wit and humorist, was acquainted with several languages, and his company was much courted. He had brothers and sisters, some of whom were above six feet in stature.

1841. Grenville Millen, an American poet, died at New York, aged 41. He relinquished the profession of the law to devote himself to poetry and literature, of which he published a volume in 1833.

1848. The city of Messina, in Sicily, was bombarded and taken by the king's troops.

1848. An insurrection occurred at Leghorn, and the city was placed by the insurgents in the hands of a provisional government.

1849. Samuel Bunch, a congressman from Tennessee, died, aged 63. He commanded a regiment under Gen. Jackson in the Indian war, and in the charge of the battle of the Horse Shoe, was the first or second man over the breast works of the enemy.

1852. William Macgillivray died; professor in the university of Aberdeen, who published works upon birds, and in other departments of natural history.

1852. John Pitkin Norton, professor of agricultural chemistry at Yale college, died, aged 30.

1853. I. L. Mason, a United States engineer, died at San Francisco. He was born in Providence, educated at West Point, and constructed the fortifications at fort Adams, and was one of the most skillful and scientific officers of the engineer corps. He was sent out to superintend the construction of the fortifications at San Francisco.

1853. George Poindexter, a Mississippi statesman, died at Jackson. He was the second governor of Mississippi, and in 1811 killed Abijah Hunt in a duel.

1854. Robert M. Patterson, director of the United States mint, died at Philadelphia. He was president of the American philosophical society, and had been a professor in the universities of Pennsylvania and Virginia.

SEPTEMBER 6.

972. John XIII, pope, died. He was elected by the power of the emperor, against the wishes of the Roman people. A violent dissention was the consequence, and the new pontiff was banished the next year by the prefect of Rome; he was reinstated by the emperor, and his opponent in turn sent into exile.

1492. Columbus sailed from the Canaries, where he had been detained since the 12th of August, in refitting for the voyage.

1521. John Sebastian del Cano, having on the death of Magellan, been appointed captain of the Spanish expedition for the discovery of a western passage to the Molucca or Spice islands, conducted the remainder of the voyage, which was finished this day. This was the first voyage round the world. It sailed August 10th, 1519, from Seville, and consisted of five ships and 236 men. Only one ship of this squadron ever reached Spain. (8th ?)

1578. Drake having passed the straits of Magellan, entered the Pacific ocean, on his memorable campaign against the Spanish treasure ships.

1581. William Postel, a French mathematician, died. He possessed great learning, but was a visionary. His works are twenty-six in number, on curious and strange subjects.

1609. Hudson having anchored at Sandy Hook, sent forward five men in a boat, who passed through the Narrows, sounding as they went. They were attacked by two Indian canoes, and John Colman, an Englishman, who had accompanied Hudson in his polar voyages, was killed. This was the first European blood that was shed in these waters. The place where he was interred is still called Colman's point.

1620. The Mayflower, with its company, consisting of 101 passengers, sailed from Plymouth, England, for America; having been obliged to put back twice, on account of the leaky condition of the Speedwell, which was to sail with her. This was the company of Pilgrims which landed at Plymouth rock, and commenced the settlement of New England.

1645. A general thanksgiving was ordained by governor Kieft, to be observed through the limits of New Netherland, for the restoration of peace with the Indians; showing that this festival, which is by many asserted to be exclusively puritanical, was also observed by the Dutch occasionally.

1652. PHILIP ALEGAMBE died; a Dutch Jesuit whose works were in high estimation.

1676. The Massachusetts forces, having subdued Philip, turned their arms against the eastern Indians, and surprised about 400 of them at Cocheco, in Maine, who were all taken; those found accessory to the late rebellion, being about half the number, were sold into slavery, and several who had committed murders were hung.

1678. TONGE and OATES furnished a narrative of a plot to overturn the English government.

1683. JOHN BAPTIST COLBERT, marquis of Segnelia, died. He was an illustrious French statesman, deservedly respected as a minister who ably restored the navy, the commerce and finances of the country, patronized learning and science, and invigorated genius by his mild and active generosity.

1689. Mentz, in Germany, surrendered to the imperialists.

1748. EDMUND GIBSON, bishop of London, died; an eminent antiquarian, theological, political and controversial writer.

1769. Great jubilee at Stratford, England, in honor of Shakspeare. The pageant continued three days, and attracted much attention.

1775. JOHN BAPTIST BULLET, a French author, died. He possessed a most retentive memory, and his works are learned and useful.

1781. Fort Griswold taken by the British under Arnold, and the garrison put to the sword. Colonel Ledyard, who commanded the fort, was run through the body with his own sword, after he had surrendered. Of the garrison, 73 were killed, 30 or 40 wounded, and 40 taken prisoners. British loss 48 killed, and 142 wounded.

1781. New London was set on fire, 60 dwellings and 84 stores burnt.

1781. American privateer, Congress, captured British sloop of war Savage, 20 guns.

1783. ANNA WILLIAMS, a blind English authoress, died, aged 77.

1784. GEORGE ALEXANDER STEVENS, an English writer, died. He possessed the rare faculty of entertaining an audience four hours at a sitting. By his lectures on heads he realized about 50,000 dollars; but died finally in a mad house.

1796. WILLIAM BENWELL, an elegant English scholar, died.

1808. LOUIS PIERRE ANQUETIL DU PERRON, a French divine and historian, died. He traveled in Asia, where he acquired the language of the ancient Persians, and became acquainted with the original writings of Zoroaster, and brought home a large amount of literary spoil.

1810. Battle of Rudschuck; the Russians defeated the Turks, killed the seraskir and 5,000 men, and took an immense number of prisoners, with all their artillery and equipage.

1813. WILLIAM BURROWS, a gallant naval officer of the United States, was slain in the action between the Enterprise, United States, and British ship Boxer. (See 5th.)

1814. British under general Provost took Plattsburgh.

1816. THOMAS CLARKE died in London, aged 80. He came to the city at the age of 22, and obtained the place of a porter; by the strictest economy and well directed effort, he accumulated the fortune of one and a half million dollars.

1821. VICESSIMUS KNOX died; a learned English divine and miscellaneous writer.

1839. An insurrection at Zurich, in Switzerland, in consequence of the city government having enacted a new law, enforcing a system of government, independent of the clergy, and differed from the routine of the old catechism, and having called from Germany to fill the theological chair of the university, professor Strauss, whose neological doctrines had given much offence. Several thousand peasants assembled and marched into the city headed by their pastors. A few lives were lost, the government declared itself dissolved, the peasants withdrew, and the city became tranquil.

1848. The British forces under general Whish, besieged the city of Moulton, in northern India, and were forced on the 14th to withdraw with much loss.

1848. THOMAS TRENOR, an Irish exile, died in New York, aged 86. In 1798 he was a merchant in extensive business, joined the patriots, and became treasurer of the United Irish society. He was arrested for treason, and spent four years in prison. Ruined in fortune, and with impaired health, he came to America; for 17 years was occupied in the iron manufacture in Vermont, and for the last 15 years was employed in the New York custom house.

1855. Colonel HENRY L. KINNEY was

appointed by acclamation civil and military governor of San Juan del Norte, or Greytown, at a mass meeting of the citizens.

SEPTEMBER 7.

70. Jerusalem demolished, and her foundations broke up on this day, Gregorian time. The walls were crossed on Friday, the last day of August, the conquest was completed on the sabbath and the calends of September, and the havoc consumed about six days. There were slain or butchered one million *beards*. (See 8th Aug. Gorpeius is a tropical month, beginning 25th Aug.)

1069. The Danes again made a descent on England, and landed at Dover.

1134. Alfonso, king of Arragon, killed in battle.

1493. Frederick IV, of Germany, died. He was a weak, indolent and superstitious monarch, who saw his subjects revolt with indifference, and was afterwards reduced to beg his bread.

1533. Birthday of Elizabeth, afterwards queen of England; daughter of Henry VIII and Anne Boleyn.

1566. Nicholas Zrinyi, a Hungarian Leonidas, killed. He had thrown himself into the castle of Szigeth, with 3,000 men, and was besieged by the Turks. This number was dwindled down to 600 by repeated sallies. The sultan died of rage at his obstinacy, and the grand vizier made a general assault. Zrinyi rushed out at the head of his band, and was killed by three balls; the whole garrison shared his fate. Above 20,000 Turks had been killed during the siege.

1644. Grey Bentivoglio, an Italian cardinal, died. He wrote an account of Flanders, and a history of its civil wars.

1655. Nicholas Abram, a French Jesuit, died; distinguished for his proficiency in the dead languages.

1671. A great training in Boston, says Winthrop's journal, which lasted two days; 1,200 men in the field, not an oath uttered, nor any body drunk during the whole time, though there was much wine and strong beer in town.

1706. Battle of Turin; the French under count Marisin defeated by prince Eugene, with the loss of 2,000 killed, and all their baggage and ammunition, and the military chest.

1736. The door of the Tolbooth, of Edinburgh, burnt, and John Porteus, who had been sentenced to death, but reprieved by the queen, taken out of jail by a mob, and hanged on a lamp post.

1760. Montreal surrendered to the English. By the reduction of this place, Gen. Amherst completed the conquest of Canada, and the subversion of the French empire in North America, which was added to the British possessions.

1772. An unprecedent rain and consequent flood happened in Inverary, Scotland.

1776. George Smith, an eminent English landscape painter and author, died.

1779. John Armstrong, a celebrated Scottish poet, died.

1783. Leonard Euler, a Swiss mathematician, died. He possessed great erudition, and was perfect master of ancient mathematical literature; and had the history of all ages and nations, even to the minutest facts, ever present to his mind.

1784. Ann Lee, known by the appellation of the "elect lady," or mother of Zion, and head of the sect called Shakers, died at Nisqueunia, near Albany, N. Y.

1798. Peter Frederick Suhm, an eminent Danish historian and miscellaneous writer, died. His histories form 16 quarto volumes, and his other works 15 vols.

1799. John Ingenhouz, an eminent Belgian natural philosopher, died in England. His chemical discoveries were applied to medical aud agricultural improvements.

1799. Peter Charles le Monnier, a celebrated French astronomer, died. He was one of those who made the journey to the north in 1785, for the admeasurement of the globe.

1805. Thomas Butler died; he was a brave officer in the American revolutionary army, but refusing to comply with the general order, to cut the hair close to the head, he was involved in much difficulty with general Wilkeson.

1807. Copenhagen surrendered to the British after a long bombardment, in which six thousand were killed and wounded, and 1,800 houses destroyed.

1811. Peter Simom Pallas, a distinguished writer of Prussia, died. He accompanied empress Catherine's famous expedition to Siberia, for the observation of the transit of Venus, &c. He was subsequently tutor to the grand dukes Alexander (afterwards emperor) and Constantine.

1812. Battle of Borodino; the Russian army consisted of 120,000, and the French had an equal number. There were also 500 cannon employed by each. The slaughter was dreadful; of one of the Russian divisions that mustered 30,000 in the morning, only 8,000 survived. These had fought in close order under a fire of 80 cannon. It is computed that not less than 30,000 Russians, and 50,000 French were killed; and night found either army on the ground they had occupied at day break.

1820. Great solar eclipse in England.

1827. Abo, the capital of Finland, nearly destroyed by fire. Only 800 volumes of the public library escaped destruction, and nearly 100 persons perished.

1831. Warsaw captured by the Russians under Paskiewitch after two days' fighting. Russian loss estimated at 20,000.

1833. HANNAH MORE, a celebrated English authoress, died, aged 88. Her works are very numerous, by which she realized upwards of $140,000.

1836. JOHN POND, an eminent English astronomer, died. He was named by Dr. Maskelyne as the fittest man to succeed him as astronomer royal, which office he held during 25 years with consumate ability.

1838. WILLIAM COLFAX, an officer of the revolution, died. He was one of the life guards of Washington, and supposed to have been the last survivor of that corps.

1839. ANDREW HALLIDAY died; a Scottish medical and historical writer of merit.

1847. Letters from St. Petersburgh of the 7th Sept. state, that that city has been visited with the most terrific storm of wind and rain ever experienced within the memory of the oldest inhabitant. It rained incessantly for forty-eight hours, whilst the wind blew with intense violence. The result of this visitation was the destruction of above 400 houses. At one period fears were entertained for the safety of the entire city, and some timid and superstitious persons apprehended the end of the world was at hand.

1850. The bill admitting California as a state and Utah as a territory of the United States, passed the house of representatives.

1851. LEVI WOODBURY, an American statesman, died at Portsmouth, N. H., aged 64.

1855. The first Hebrew temple in the Mississippi valley was consecrated at St. Louis.

1855. LEONARD MAELZEL, the inventor of several musical and automatic instruments, and who exhibited the famous chess player in this country, died at Vienna, aged 79.

SEPTEMBER 8.

70. Jerusalem taken by TITUS after a most obstinate resistance on the part of the inhabitants. More than 1,000,000 are said to have perished.

1636. Harvard college founded at Cambridge, Mass.

1644. FRANCIS QUARLES, a celebrated English poet, died.

1650. The princess ELIZABETH, daughter of the unfortunate Charles, died at Carisbrook castle in the isle of Wight, aged 15.

1656. JOSEPH HALL, "the first professed English satirist," died. He was bishop of Norwich, and acquired the title of the Christian Seneca. He is universally allowed to have been a man of great wit and learning.

1664. The colony of New York surrendered to the English.

1705. According to De Foe, it was on this day that the apparition of Mrs. Veal appeared to Mrs. Bargrave, at Canterbury, to say that *Drelincourt on Death* was the very best book on that subject.

1755. Battle of lake George, between the English under colonel Johnson and the French and Indians under baron Dieskau. The French force was nearly 2,000; that of the provincials greatly superior. A detachment of 1,000 men and 200 Indians which were sent out from the fort were ambuscaded and narrowly escaped destruction. A grand attack was then made on the fort by the French regulars, the Canadians and Indians being employed on the English flanks. After a battle of four hours, the enemy was compelled to retreat in disorder, and were pursued by a party from the camp, which fell on their rear and precipitated their flight. Dieskau was taken prisoner, and the remnant of his army completely routed by a detachment of 200 New Hampshire militia, from fort Edward, who had been sent to the assistance of the main army. The loss of the provincials was 327 killed and wounded—that of the enemy about 600. King Hendrik killed here.

1756. The Indian village of Kettaning, in Pennsylvania, destroyed by the colonists under colonel Armstrong. The Indians had fortified their village and provided a supply of powder for 10 years, and great quantities of arms and merchandise. The place was surprised, the chief, colonel Jacobs, killed, and as the Indians refused to accept quarter, they were exterminated. This affair was of so great importance that the authorities caused a silver medal to be struck on the occasion.

1757. The duke of CUMBERLAND in behalf of England signed the convention of Closter Seven, by which the electorate of Hanover was left in the hands of the French and the whole army consisting of 40,000 Hessians, Brunswickers, &c., disarmed.

1760. Canada surrendered to the British at Montreal under lord Amherst. This was hailed with universal joy by the colonies, as the end of the cruel wars and bloody massacres which had hung over their towns and plantations nearly a century, in which the French and Indians had been uniformly the aggressors, and had vied with each other in murder, barbarity and rapine. Under the brief repose which followed the colonies rapidly increased in number and wealth, till the gigantic struggle for independence again plunged the country in scenes of desolation and ruin, in which the British armies in a degree emulated the French and Indian foe.

1761. BERNARD FOREST DE BELIDOR, a Spanish mathematician, died at Paris. He wrote on fortifications and engineering, several valuable works.

1772. The first court of general quarter sessions of the peace for the county of Tryon was held at Johnstown, so called after sir Wm. Johnson; Guy Johnson, judge.

1775. JOHN LEYDEN, afterwards a poet and famed oriental scholar, was born at Denholm, Roxburghshire.

1781. Battle of Eutaw Springs; the British regulars, 2,000 in number, under colonel Stewart, were defeated by the Americans under general Greene, 1,400 regulars and 500 militia. British loss in killed, wounded and prisoners about 1,000; American loss about 500. This battle closed the war in South Carolina.

1782. Tremendous cannonade and bombardment from Gibraltar with red hot balls and carcasses, upon the Spanish besiegers. Two floating batteries were consumed.

1793. The British under the duke of York raised the siege of Dunkirk, in France, defended with great bravery and resolution by Hoche.

1794. Battle of Brescia; the Poles defeated by the Russians under Suwarrow, with the loss of 8,000 men, and their whole park of artillery.

1795. A monument by FLAXMAN to the memory of Collins, the poet, was set up at Chichester, England.

1797. RICHARD FARMER died; a celebrated scholar and critic. He is noted for a single work, his *Essay on the Learning of Shakspeare*, in which he maintains that the bard obtained his knowledge of ancient history and mythology from translations and not from original classic authors. It is probably the best commentary which has been produced.

1798. The first number of the *Allgemeine Zeitung* (General Gazette) published at Augsburg, in Bavaria. Under the charge of baron Cotta, it is probably the most celebrated newspaper in the world. It has correspondents in all countries of Europe, and in America.

1798. Battle of Standtz, in Switzerland. The hardy mountaineers defended their homes against the French with clubs, spears and fragments of rock; but were forced to retire before the regular artillery and muskets of their enemy, their beautiful valley was destroyed by fire, and neither age nor sex spared by the furious soldiery.

1804. Great storm at Savannah, by which the city suffered to an immense amount in damages to buildings and other property, as well as loss of life. The storm extended to a considerable distance, carrying destruction with it in every quarter.

1817. JOHN CARTER, an eminent English antiquary, draftsman and critic, died. He was many years a laborious contributor to the *Gentleman's Magazine*.

1837. SAMUEL EGERTON BRIDGES, an English nobleman, died near Geneva, in Switzerland. He was a man of considerable talents and learning, and a voluminous writer in various branches of literature, but possessed of a most unhappy temper and disposition.

1838. BENJAMIN BOOTH ROYD, pastor of the independent church, Huddersfield, England, died. He was a lively example of piety and a life of industry.

1846. GEORGE MIFFLIN BACHE, lieutenant commanding United States brig Washington, died at sea off cape Hatteras. His hopes of thoroughly exploring the Gulf stream were thus cut off.

1847. Battle of El Molino del Rey, in Mexico, where many a brave American fell.

1847. MARTIN SCOTT fell at the battle of Molino del Rey. In early life he was one of the sharp shooters among the *Green Mountain Boys*, and it is storied of him that so unerring was his aim that a nail driven partway into a board, he could drive home by his bullet.

1849. AMARIAH BRIGHAM, a distinguished physician, died at Utica, New York, aged 51. He was superintendent of the State asylum for the insane.

1852. MARK H. SIBLEY, an eminent lawyer, died at Canandaigua, New York, aged 56. He had distinguished himself at the bar, in the state assembly and in congress, and on the bench.

1853. The first chamber in Holland adopted the much disputed law on religious liberty by a vote of 22 to 16.

1854. A violent storm at Charleston, South Carolina, which continued forty-eight hours, overflowing the wharves and damaging the shipping.

1855. ROBERT MULLER, a celebrated pianist and composer, died at Edinburgh, Scotland.

1855. WILLIAM HOLLAND DANIEL CUDDY, an experienced and efficient British officer, killed in the attack on the Redan, at Sebastopol, aged 41. He had served in India until 1841, and afterwards with distinction in the Chinese war.

1855. The allies having kept up an *infernal* fire upon the fortress of Sebastopol during three days and nights, attacked the works in three columns, and captured the Malakoff, whereupon the Russians blew up the remaining forts upon the south side of the city, sunk and destroyed their vessels, and under cover of the explosions and of the night, retreated to the north side of the city over a bridge recently constructed, leaving a large number of guns, and a vast amount of military stores in the hands of the victors, who lost 2,019 killed, and about 7,500 wounded and missing.

SEPTEMBER 9.

905. Olga, princess of Russia, received with great pomp and ceremony at Constantinople by the emperor Constantine Porphyrogenitus. The baptism and nomination of the empress Helena, established the era of Russian Christianity.

1087. William I (*the Conqueror*), king of England, died in consequence of a fall from his horse, near Rouen, in France. He invaded England from Normandy, 1066, and having defeated Harold, who was slain at the battle of Hastings, was crowned king.

1513. Battle of Flodden, in Scotland, among the Cheviot hills. The Scots were defeated with the loss of 5,000 killed. Admiral Howard reported 10,000 Scots that fell in the field and pursuit. The English are supposed to have lost about an equal number, but among their slain were no persons of note. The heroic king James was struck down by an arrow a spear's length from the feet of Surrey, the English general.

1576. Titian (*Tiziano Vezellio*), the Italian painter, died of the plague, aged 96.

1583. Humphrey Gilbert, on his return from a voyage of discovery to America, was foundered at sea in a violent storm when every person perished.

1607. Pompone de Bellievre, an eminent French statesman, died. He enjoyed the favor of princes and the reward of office, and in turn was disgraced.

1609. Henry Hudson arrived in New York harbor, which perceiving to be a good one for all winds, the ship rode all night.

1654. Peter Stuyvesant, with 700 men, approached the Swedish settlements on the Delaware. They were all reduced without bloodshed. (See Sept. 16.)

1677. About twenty Indians who had descended Connecticut river, fell upon Hatfield as the people were raising a house, killed and captured about twenty, among the latter some women and children. On their return the same day they halted at Deerfield, where several people were employed in rebuilding their houses. But being discovered, their mischief was confined to killing one and capturing two. These people were just returned to their farms which had been laid waste the year before. They were soon compelled again to abandon them.

1681. John Foster, the first Boston printer, died, aged 33. He graduated at Harvard, 1667, and it having been permitted to "have a printing presse elsewhere than at Cambridge," it was put under his charge.

1689. The famous treaty of partition was signed at the river Kerbechi, between China and Russia.

1703. Charles de St. Denis Evremond, a French nobleman, died in England, aged 95. He signalized himself by his valor in the army, and was equally eminent for his literary talents.

1734. An eagle whose expanded wings from tip to tip measured nine feet eight inches, was taken at Charlton, in Kent, England.

1770. Bernard Siegfried Albinus, an eminent Dutch anatomist, died, aged 88. He surpassed all his predecessors in the science of anatomy, and published 3 folio volumes of plates to illustrate the human body.

1771. Robert Wood, an English traveler and writer, died.

1776. United States first so called.

1781. British colonel Stewart destroyed a great quantity of his stores and abandoned Eutaw springs. He left 1000 stand of arms and 70 wounded men.

1782. Grand attack on Gibraltar by the Spaniards, from a floating battery of 64 heavy cannon, and their whole lines, together with 60 mortars and their shipping, which was continued during the whole day.

1790. Action off Codgia bay, between the Turkish and Russian fleets, which was begun the day previous, and ended in the defeat of the Turks, who lost two ships taken, and one in which was the admiral, blown up, and the admiral alone escaped death.

1792. Charles Xavier Joseph Franqueville d'Abancourt, minister of Louis XVI, perished at the massacre of the Orangery.

1797. Three men were suffocated in one of the famed Meux's brewvats at London, not having first used the precaution to let down a lighted candle.

1801. Gilbert Wakefield died; an eminent English polemical and classical writer.

1806. John Brand, an English antiquary, died. He was originally a shoemaker; but found means to acquire a liberal education and left several valuable works.

1814. Captain McGlassin with 50 Americans, forded the Saranac and reconnoitered the British works, drove in a party of 150 men, attacked and carried their battery, killed their commanding officer and 16 men, and having destroyed their works, returned with the loss of 1 wounded and 3 missing.

1814. British navy with a detachment of troops, 150 sailors and 250 Indians, captured the United States schooners Tigress and Scorpion, near St. Joseph, Michigan.

1816. Kilian Van Rensselaer, a general in the revolutionary army, died at Albany. He embarked early in defence of his country; in 1777 was attacked by a large body of Indians at fort Anne, where he was wounded in the thigh by a ball, which was extracted after his death, having been carried 39 years.

1824. An expedition, fitted out at Rangoon in Burmah, consisting of English and native troops to the number of 1,000, took the town of Tavoy, a place of considerable strength, with 10,000 fighting men, and many mounted guns. The viceroy of the province and many persons of distinction were among the prisoners. A new state carriage for the king of Ava, a magnificent vehicle surpassing anything of the kind in Europe in splendor and costly material, was taken, and conveyed to England.

1830. William Bulmer, an English printer, whose name is associated with all that is beautiful in printing, died.

1839. Second fire at Mobile (the first being on the 7th), by which the best part of the city was laid in ruins.

1839. The United States Bank of Pennsylvania refused to pay its liabilities, and all the banks in Philadelphia immediately suspended specie payments. The whole number of banks in the Union was 959; of which 343 suspended entirely, 62 in part, 493 did not suspend, and 56 never resumed.

1846. Magnetic telegraph between Albany and New York completed; by means of which New York and Buffalo were brought together also.

1848. Great conflagration at Brooklyn, New York; about 200 houses burnt, and property destroyed amounting to $750,000.

1851. Thomas H. Gallaudet, an American philanthropist, died at Hartford, Ct., aged 64. He opened the first establishment in this country for the education of deaf mutes at Hartford, in 1817, and devoted a large part of his active and most useful life to this work of benevolence.

1851. The funeral obsequies of the Spaniards and Cubans who fell in the contests with the forces of Lopez, was celebrated with great pomp at the cathedral in Havana; $70,000 were subscribed by the citizens for the benefit of their widows and children.

1852. J. D. Belin, consul for Belgium and Switzerland, died at New Orleans.

1853. The remnant of the famous table rock at Niagara falls broke off and tumbled into the abyss with a tremendous crash.

1854. Angelo Mai, an Italian cardinal, died at Albano, aged 72. He was chief librarian of the Vatican, and a learned correspondent of the academies at Paris and Munich; but is better known by his discoveries from palimpsest manuscripts, which were published in two collections of 10 volumes each.

SEPTEMBER 10.

954. Louis IV, king of France, killed by a fall from his horse, at the age of 38.

1167. Matilda, of England, empress of Germany, died. She was the daughter of Henry I of England, married Henry IV of Germany, and was afterwards acknowledged queen of England; but her conduct not suiting the nobles, she was deposed and Stephen placed on the throne.

1543. The small remains of the army which had sailed from Cuba in 1539 (see May 18) under de Soto, for the conquest of Florida, arrived at Panuco on their return. This great expedition ended in the poverty and ruin of all concerned in it. Not a Spaniard remained in Florida.

1547. Conspiracy of Placentia, when Peter Louis Farnese, son of pope Paul III, was assassinated. The place was taken by the conspirators and delivered to the troops of the emperor Charles V before daylight next morning.

1547. Battle of Pinkey, in Scotland; the English under the protector Somerset, defeated the Scots under the earl of Arran, and obtained one of the most finished victories on record. The Scots lost 10,000 men.

1604. William Morgan, bishop of Asaph, formerly of Landaff, died. He directed and superintended the translation of the scriptures into Welsh.

1621. King James gave sir William Alexander a patent of the whole territory of Acadia, by the name of Nova Scotia. It was erected into a palatinate, to be holden as a fief of the crown of Scotland. An unsuccessful attempt was soon after made to effect a settlement, and he sold it to the French in 1630. Twenty years afterwards three thousand families settled there from New England.

1649. Peter Goudelin, a poet of Gascony, died. He was so celebrated that he acquired the title of the Homer of Gascony.

1691. EDWARD POCOCKE died; a most learned English critic and commentator, and famous particularly for his great skill in the oriental languages.

1714. An agreement between the Van Hoorn or Berbice company, and the Dutch East India company, to furnish the former annually after this day, 240 negroes from Angola, or Ardrah (one-third to be females), at 165 florins a head.

1730. GUICHARD JOSEPH DU VERNEY died; professor of anatomy at Paris, of great celebrity.

1738. THOMAS SHERIDAN, an Irish divine and poet, died. He published a prose translation of *Perseus*.

1752. JOHN BAPTIST BERTRAND died; a French physician, known for his interesting account of the plague of Marseilles.

1759. Second action off Pondicherry, between the British fleet, admiral Pococke, and the French under admiral d'Auché. British loss 164 killed, 385 wounded. A deserter reported the French loss to have been 1500 killed and wounded.

1771. Birthday of MUNGO PARK, a celebrated Scottish adventurer. He twice attempted the discovery of the course and outlet of the Niger, so long a source of conjecture with geographers, in the second of which he lost his life in the 35th year of his age.

1779. Indian village of Canandaigua burnt.

1781. Count D'ESTAING returned with his fleet to the Chesapeake, and captured two British frigates of 32 guns each.

1782. The firing on Gibraltar from the isthmus continued by the Spaniards, at the rate of 6,500 cannon shot, and 1,080 shells in every 24 hours.

1785. Treaty of amity and commerce between the United States and Prussia.

1791. A great insurrection among the negroes in St. Domingo, attributed to the new opinions of liberty and equality, called in Paris *L'Ami des Noirs*.

1797. MARY WOLLSTONECRAFT GODWIN died; a lady of very superior literary accomplishments, who distinguished herself by many able productions, and the peculiarity of her views.

1802. A lunar rainbow observed at Matlock, in Derbyshire, England.

1806. JOHN CHRISTOPHER ADELUNG, a German professor at Erfurt, died; author of a grammatical and critical dictionary of the German language, in 5 vols. quarto. He was never married, and it was said of him that his writing desk was his wife, and the 70 volumes which he wrote were his children. His wine cellar, which was unique, he called his *bibliotheca selectissima*.

1809. AUGUSTUS LOUIS VON SCHLOETZER, a German historian, died. He wrote a *History of Lithuania*, &c.

1813. Battle of lake Erie, and defeat and capture of the entire British fleet under Com. Barclay, by the United States fleet under Com. Perry. The British force consisted of 6 vessels, 63 guns; Americans had 11 vessels, 54 guns. The action commenced at 15 minutes before 12, and ended about 3 P. M. The loss of the British was estimated at 200; Americans lost 27 killed, 96 wounded—123.

1827. UGO FOSCOLO, a distingushed Italian writer, died. His works are numerous, but giving offence to the authorities, he was driven from country to country, and died from disease and penury.

1845. JOSEPH STORY, one of the most distinguished American jurists, died at Cambridge, Mass., aged 66.

1851. The steamer Pampero, which had been used in the Lopez expedition against Cuba, was seized by the United States revenue officers, at Dunn's lake, Florida, and subsequently condemned.

1852. URQUIZA, director of the Argentine confederation, was deposed.

1852. The Burmese evacuated and burned Prome.

SEPTEMBER 11.

1069. The Danes under Harold and Canute landed in England, at the mouth of the Humber, and laid waste the country.

1297. Battle near Cambuskenneth, on the Forth, between the Scots under Wallace, and the English, in which the latter were defeated with the loss of 5,000 slain. The victors, to show their utter detestation of that tool of Edward, Cressingham, flayed his body, and converted his skin into thongs for their horses.

1539. Date of the will of Henry Pepwell, a distinguished book publisher, who died this year.

1609. HUDSON while at anchor in the harbor of New York, was visited by the natives, who made a great show of friendship, giving tobacco and Indian corn.

1649. Drogheda, in Ireland, taken by assault by the English, under Cromwell. A universal massacre was permitted during five days. "I believe we put to the sword," is the general's despatch, "the whole number of the defendants. *This is a marvellous great mercy.*" The garrison alone consisted of 2,500 foot and 300 horse. There was scarce thirty lives saved in the whole town, and these were by Cromwell reserved to be sent to Barbadoes.

1677. JAMES HARRINGTON, an eminent English political writer, died; author of the political romance of *Oceana*, in imitation of Plato's *Atlantic Story*.

1697. The famous peace of Ryswick proclaimed.

1709. Battle of Malplaquet, in Belgium; the allies under the duke of Marlborough and prince Eugene, defeated the French army of 120,000 men, under Villars and de Boufflers. This was a dear victory to the allies, who lost 20,000 of their best troops.

1745. MARY CHANDLER died; an English lady, distinguished for her poetic talent.

1776. Great tempest on the coast of Newfoundland; a large amount of shipping, and a great number of lives lost.

1777. Battle of Brandywine; the Americans under Washington and Green entirely defeated by the British, under Cornwallis. The Americans lost about 1,300 killed, wounded and prisoners. This was the first battle Lafayette was in; he was wounded in the leg.

1781. JOHN AUGUSTUS ERNESTI died; professor of theology at Leipsic, and author of numerous literary and theological works.

1798. The Sublime Porte, incensed at the invasion of Egypt, declared war against France, and joined with his old adversary, the emperor of Russia.

1799. Tortona surrendered to Suwarroff. Thus was Italy nearly reconquered.

1813. Running action between the United States commodore, Chauncey, on lake Ontario, and the British commodore, Yeo; the latter succeeded in getting into Amherst bay.

1814. The British, 8,000 strong, commenced disembarking their troops at North Point, about 12 miles from Baltimore, for the purpose of attacking that city.

1814. Battle of lake Champlain and Plattsburgh. The British fleet 95 guns, under commodore Downie, defeated and captured by the United States fleet, Com. Chauncey, 86 guns. British loss 57 killed, 72 wounded; American loss 52 killed, 58 wounded. At the same time the British troops under general Provost, about 14,000 veterans, the flower of the duke of Wellington's army, attacked the American lines at Saranac, Plattsburgh, and were defeated by general Macomb. American loss, killed 38; wounded 64; missing 20.

1820. HOME RIGGS POPHAM died; a distinguished British naval officer.

1823. DAVID RICARDO, a celebrated English writer on finance and statistics, died. He was of Jewish descent, and abandoned by his father at an early age for marrying a quakeress. His talents however, procured him wealth and distinction.

1826. WILLIAM MORGAN, a freemason in western New York, abducted by his fellows of the craft for revealing their secrets.

1833. Deaths by cholera in the city of Mexico, from the 5th August to this date, 10,000.

1840. LONG-KIEWA, a Chinese linguist, died at Calcutta, aged 59. He was inspector of the tea plantations established by an English company at Assam, but was obliged to exile himself on account of a family misdemeanor. He is represented to have been a man of immense knowledge. Besides his erudition in the sciences, he was proficient in all the principal languages spoken in Europe and Asia, as well as Hebrew, Greek and Latin. He made for the most part the Chinese translation of the scriptures published by Marshman, and left in MS. a Chinese-Latin-English dictionary. He bequeathed to the Asiatic society of Calcutta his library, containing 30,000 volumes, more than 20,000 of which are in the Chinese language.

1840. The town of Beyrout, in Syria, fired upon, reduced to a mass of ruins, and taken, by the British and Austrian fleets.

1842. A Mexican army 1,300 strong, took possession of Texas, but soon retreated.

1851. A riot at Christiana, Pa., upon the attempt to remove a fugitive slave. Mr. Gorsuch, the owner of the slave was killed and his son mortally wounded; the United States marshal and his posse were driven from the ground by armed negroes, and the slave escaped.

SEPTEMBER 12.

284. MARCUS AURELIUS NUMERIANUS, the Roman emperor, died, or was assassinated. He was admired for his learning and moderation, was naturally eloquent, and was esteemed one of the best poets of the age.

1362. INNOCENT VI (*Stephen Albert*), pope, died. He was of a peaceful disposition, and labored earnestly to reconcile the kings of England and France.

1382. LOUIS I, king of Hungary and Poland, died. One of his acts was to expel the Jews.

1504. COLUMBUS sailed from San Domingo—that great man's last voyage. His crazy and shattered bark, like his body, landed at St. Lucar in November.

1528. ANDREW DORIA, a noble Genoese, and the ablest seaman of his age, retook Genoa from the French, and restored its independence.

1553. ALBERT, of Brandenburgh, defeated by Henry of Brunswick. He was placed under the ban of the empire, and fled to France, where he died.

1609. HUDSON weighed anchor in the harbor of New York, and commenced his memorable voyage up the river which bears his name.

1651. The Scots prisoners taken at the battle of Worcester, &c., brought before Cromwell and the parliament at Acton, and sold to the West Indies for slaves or given away as dogs.

1660. JAMES CATS, a Dutch statesman and poet died, aged 83. His poems are much admired by his countrymen.

1665. JOHN BOLLANDUS, a Flemish Jesuit, died. His judgment, learning and sagacity led to his appointment to collect materials for the lives of the saints of the Romish church. He lived to complete 5 vols. folio, and the work was continued to 47 vols. by his successors.

1672. TANNEGUI LE FEVRE, a learned French author, died. He was the father of Madam Dacier.

1683. The allies under John Sobieski and the duke of Lorraine, routed the vast Turkish army under the walls of Vienna, and compelled them to raise the siege. Sobieski sent a post to his queen, saying that the grand vizier had made him his sole heir, including 70,000 dead men.

1683. ALPHONSO VI, king of Portugal, died. His conduct displayed the tyrant and the madman, and he resigned his crown.

1703. The emperor and king of the Romans, resigned their right to Spain to the archduke Charles, who was thereupon declared king of Spain.

1714. Barcelona surrendered to the duke of Berwick.

1729. Birthday of MOSES MENDELSOHN, a learned Jew of Berlin. He was of obscure origin, and became a merchant; but quitted commerce for literature, and acquired great reputation.

1764. JOHN PHILIP RAMEAU, a French musician, died. His writings on music procured him the title of the Newton of the science.

1776. WASHINGTON, with the remains of his army, entered Philadelphia, after his disastrous defeat at Brandywine. The same night a party of the British made an excursion to Wilmington, took the governor of Delaware out of his bed, and captured a shallop richly laden with public and private property, and the public records.

1784. The Spanish fleet under Don Barcelo, bombarded Algiers. The Spaniards fired 600 bombs, 144 balls and 260 grenades. The Algerines fired 202 bombs, and 1,164 balls. Great damage was done to the city.

1804. The American squadron captured near Tripoli, two vessels laden with wheat for that city.

1806. EDWARD THURLOW, an eminent English nobleman, died. He possessed a vigorous and active mind, added to close application, which gave him a high rank among the professional men of that day.

1812. Fort Wayne relieved by the troops under general Harrison. The Indians raised the siege with great precipitation.

1813. EDMUND RANDOLPH died; whose history is blended with that of his country.

1814. Battle of fort McHenry, near Baltimore. The British, 8,000 men, under general Ross, were arrested in their march upon Baltimore, and general Ross was killed. The fort was bombarded incessantly 25 hours. Total American loss in killed and wounded 173; British official loss 290.

1819. GEBBARAL LEBRECHT, prince von Blucher, a celebrated Prussian field-marshal, died. He had been 45 years in the army, and for his celerity in the field, was called *Marshal Forwards*.

1820. FRANCIS CHRISTOPHER KELLERMAN, a French marshal, died. He entered the army at the age of 17 as a huzzar, and rose to the highest honors under Napoleon.

1829. Surrender of the Spanish army at Tampico, under general Barradas, to the Mexicans under Santa Anna. The Spaniards were to transport themselves to Havana, and pledged not to serve against Mexico in future. This terminated the expedition to subdue Mexico after five engagements.

1832. PRISCILLA WAKEFIELD, an English authoress, died, aged 82. She wrote many popular and useful works for children and youth, and promoted the institution of savings banks.

1838. HENRY RYALLS died at Darien, Ga., aged 11C. He was a soldier of the revolution, and retained his faculties to the last.

1847. First day's battle of Chapultepec.

1849. MARIANO PAREDES, expresident of Mexico, died in that city, after a long and painful illness.

1850. The fugitive slave bill passed by the house of representatives at Washington, as it had come down from the senate.

1854. DAVID LANSBOROUGH, a Scottish divine, died at Ayrshire, aged 73. He was distinguished as a naturalist, and contributed much to the knowledge of fossils, botany and shells.

1857. Steamship Central America, from Panama to New York, having 626 persons on board, and nearly two millions in treasure, was totaly lost in a gale, and about 100 persons were saved.

SEPTEMBER 13.

507 B. C. The dedication of the Roman capital fell upon this day, about the full moon of the Greek month Matagitnion.

Horatius Pulvillus, as supreme prætor, drove the first annual *nail* in the wall of the temple, near the fane of Minerva.

44. CÆSAR executed his last testament at his seat near Lavicanum. He left the people his gardens near the Tiber, and 300 sesterces to each man.

81. TITUS FLAVIUS VESPASIANUS, emperor of Rome, died. He was an obscure native of Riti, who by his merits and virtues rose to consequence in the Roman armies, and headed the expedition against Jerusalem.

335. CONSTANTINE dedicated his great church of the Resurrection at Jerusalem, Saturday; and on Sunday exalted the relic of the cross.

1435. JOHN PLANTAGENET, duke of Bedford, regent of France, died. He was the brother of Henry V of England, and the most accomplished prince of Europe. He purchased and transported to London the Royal library of Paris.

1515. Battle of Marignano, in Italy, which lasted with great fierceness two days. The French commander, who had been in eighteen pitched battles, exclaimed that all other fights compared with this were but children's sports, that this was the war of giants. The French were victorious.

1529. Vienna besieged by the Turks.

1557. JOHN CHEKE, a learned Englishman, died. He was professor of Greek in the university, and held important state offices. On the accession of Mary, he preferred popery to the fagot, and abjured his faith.

1565. WILLIAM FAREL, a successful French reformer, died. He labored with great zeal against the Catholic church, and made many proselytes.

1592. MICHAEL DE MONTAIGNE died; a celebrated French writer, whose works are still quoted.

1598. PHILIP II, of Spain, died. He was made king of Sicily and Naples, 1554; became king of England by marriage with Mary, and two years after ascended the Spanish throne by the abdication of his father, Charles V. (See Sept. 4.)

1629. Nine sachems came to Plymouth and voluntarily subscribed an instrument of submission to the English, acknowledging themselves the loyal subjects of James, king of Great Britain, France and Ireland, defender of the faith, &c.

1629. JOHN BUXTORF, a German linguist, died. He was professor of Hebrew, at Basil, and is placed in the first rank of men who have been eminent for rabbinical learning.

1645. Battle of Philiphaugh near Selkirk, where the earl of Montrose was defeated.

1694. JOHN BARBIER D'ANCOUR, a French advocate and critic, died.

1748. The scaffolding used in Westminster Hall for the trial of the prisoners adhering to the pretender, Charles Edward Stewart, was pulled down and sold to the builder for £400.

1759. Quebec stormed and taken by the British under Wolfe, who was wounded and died in the arms of victory. The French lost 500 killed, and 1,000 taken; British loss 50 killed, 500 wounded.

1771. JOHN GAMBOLD, a noted Moravian preacher in London, died; a great enthusiast, but respected for his learning and abilities, and inoffensive manners.

1781. Combined attack on Gibraltar by 10 Spanish floating batteries, and about 300 cannon, mortars and howitzers from the isthmus. Two of their largest ships were burnt and 2 feluccas taken. The British saved from one of the ships about 350 men; 8 other ships blew up or were burnt.

1787. MOSES BROWN, an English poet and divine, died.

1794. JOHN PETER CLARIS DE FLORIAN, an eminent French author, died. His dramas, pastorals, novels and fables, gave him great popularity as a sentimental writer.

1795. Captain VANCOUVER returned from his voyage of discovery after an absence of four years.

1797. JOHN FELL, an English dissenting minister, died. He is known as the author of several respectable works.

1806. CHARLES JAMES FOX, an eminent English statesman, died.

1808. XAVIER BETTINELLI, an elegant Italian writer, died. His works are published in 24 vols., two of which are tragedies, and two poems.

1814. British approached within 700 yards of fort Bowyer, Mobile, and opened their fire on it.

1819. Completion of the Mahmudie or Alexandria canal, in Egypt. This vast undertaking was commenced in January of the same year by Mehemet Ali, pasha of Egypt, under the superintendence of six European engineers, with about 100,000 laborers, and their number, though more than 7,000 died of contagious diseases, was gradually increased to more than 290,000, each of whom received about 17 cents per diem. It extends from below Soane, on the Nile, to Pompey's pillar, is 47½ miles long, 90 feet wide, and 18 feet deep.

1831. Albany and Schenectady rail road opened; the first in the state of New York.

1839. JAMES MAITLAND, earl of Lauderdale, died, aged 80. He was the author of various publications on finance and political economy.

1842. An Affghan army under Akbar Khan, numbering 13,000, defeated by the British under Gen. Pollock, at Tetzeen. Three days after the city of Cabul occupied by British forces.

1843. The town of Port Leon in Florida, was almost entirely destroyed by an inundation and hurricane. The inhabitants selected a new site upon which to rebuild, a few miles higher up the St. Marks, which was called Newport.

1847. Levi Twiggs killed at Chapultepec, Mexico; a distinguished officer of the United States army.

1848. Alexander Slidell Mackenzie, an American naval commander, died at Tarrytown, N. Y., aged 45. In 1842 he made a cruise in the Somers, in which he felt constrained to hang several mutineers to the yard arm. He published several works, and was a man of integrity and devotional feelings.

1850. The Advance and Rescue, American vessels in search of sir John Franklin, were completely fastened in the ice.

1855. The expedition in search of Dr. Kane, who was in search of sir John Franklin, arrived at Lievely, isle of Disco, Greenland, where they found Dr. Kane and his companions, who had left their ship in the ice, and traveled 83 days to a Danish settlement.

SEPTEMBER 14.

258. Thascius Cæcilius Cyprianus, beheaded. He was bishop of Carthage, and a principal father of the Christian church.

407. John Crysostom, one of the most illustrious fathers of the church, died. His works were edited by Montfaucon in 13 vols. folio.

533. The Roman general Belisarius achieved the conquest of Africa, a chaotic waste of enslaved humanity, where the image of *intelligence* is unknown.

1321. Alghieri Dante, a celebrated Italian poet, died. His most considerable work is the *Inferno*.

1403. Battle of Homildon hill, in which the Scots were defeated.

1499. Vasco de Gama landed at Lisbon from his immortal adventure.

1523. Adrian VI, pope, died. He was of obscure birth, but his abilities raised him gradually to consequence.

1528. Richard Fox, bishop of Exeter and Durham, died. He was of obscure origin; besides his episcopal offices he was employed on several embassies.

1544. The English under the duke of Norfolk raised the siege of Montreuil in France.

1646. Thomas Howard, earl of Arundel, died; famous for the discovery of the Parian marbles which bear his name, and which he gave to the university of Oxford.

1661. The bodies of May the historian, the mother and daughter of Cromwell, Pym and several others, were removed from king Henry VII's chapel and buried in the churchyard.

1666. A French expedition, consisting of 28 companies of foot and all the militia of the colony, marched from Quebec for the purpose of destroying the Mohawks. This formidable army, entered the Mohawk country, after a march of 700 miles, and laid waste their villages; the Indians, retiring into the woods with their women and children, escaped. The expedition was commanded by M. de Tracy, then upwards of 70 years of age.

1677. Richard Atkins, a typographical author, who suffered much on account of his loyalty, died in Marshalsea prison, being confined for debt. His writings were all of the ultra kind.

1704. William Hubbard, a New England clergyman and historian, died, aged 83. He was settled at Ipswich, Mass., and was one of the best writers of the time in which he lived.

1711. The British fleet intended for the reduction of Canada having met with numerous reverses, arrived at Spanish-river bay, a council of land and sea officers, considering that they had but ten weeks' provisions, and could not depend upon a supply from New England, concluded to return home and abandon the enterprise.

1712. John Dominic Cassini, a celebrated Italian astronomer, died. He was invited by the senate to teach mathematics at Bologna, at the age of 15; and before his death had enriched science with a thousand new discoveries.

1714. Thomas Britton, a celebrated musical small coal man, died. He rented a house in London, commenced business, and occupied his leisure hours in learning chemistry and music. He became an adept in those sciences, and excelled in many curious arts and crafts, all which he had acquired without neglecting his business. During the day he was seen with his sack and measure crying small coal, and in the evening conducting a concert at his house, where men of fashion and well dressed ladies of high rank ascended to his room by a ladder, to regale their ears. He was a member of a weekly society of black-lettered literati, where leaving his sack at the door, he entered the room among noblemen in his checked shirt, and produced his books collected from stalls and shops in blind alleys. His death was occasioned by a ventriloquial friend, who during a musical conversation pronounced these words distinctly as coming from a distance: "Thomas Britton, go home, for thou shalt die." Honest Tom, supposing the voice to have proceeded from an angel, went home depressed in spirits, took to his bed and died. He was twice induced to sit for his portrait. In one he is represented in a blue frock, with a small coal measure in his hand; and in the other tuning a harpsichord. One of them is in the British Museum.

1716. The Thames both above and below London bridge nearly dry, supposed to be caused by a strong west wind keeping back the tide.

1726. The Senecas, Cayugas and Onondagas surrendered to the English their habitations and country, from Cayahoza to Oswego, and sixty miles inland.

1741. Charles Rollin, the celebrated French historian, died, aged 81. He was the son of a cutler, and became famous not only as a writer, but also for his eloquence.

1751. James Philip d'Orville, a Dutch critic, died; professor of eloquence, history and Greek at Amsterdam.

1772. A bow and quiver were found in the new forest, England, supposed to have lain since the time of William Rufus, who was killed by an arrow in this forest in 1100.

1777. Burgoyne, having collected about thirty days' provision, and thrown a bridge of boats over the Hudson, crossed and encamped on the heights and plains of Saratoga.

1778. During the celebration of mass at Bourbon-les-bains, in Bassigni, France, the vault under the church gave way, which occasioned the death of 600 persons.

1784. James Essex died; an Englishman famous for his skill in Gothic architecture.

1788. Jordan Noel de Vaux, a celebrated French general, died. He was made governor of Corsica in 1769, and completed the conquest of that island; he was afterwards raised to the dignity of marshal of France. He had been present at 19 sieges and 14 battles.

1792. John Vander Mersch died. He headed the insurgents of Brabant against the imperial forces, in 1789, and distinguished himself by his valor and prudence.

1795. The English drove the Dutch from their camp at the cape of Good Hope, and captured the Williamstad of 26 guns.

1811. James Grahame, a Scottish poet and divine, died.

1814. The French advance guard under Murat and Beauharnois entered Moscow. No defence was made except by the populace in the Kremlin, who fired the palace, and the whole city was wrapt in flames. Of 4,000 superb stone houses, only 200 remained; of 800 churches, all were destroyed or heavily damaged, and of 8,000 wooden houses, about 500 escaped.

1814. Gloutzk attacked and stormed by the Russians; the Poles and French under Dombrofsky retreated with the loss of 1,000 men.

1816. William Bawdween, an English vicar, died. He was an excellent Saxon scholar, and translated the two first volumes of that curious national work the *Domes-day Book*, which was published by a vote of the British parliament. He proposed to publish the whole work, and is said to have left the other 8 vols. prepared for the press.

1835. John Brinkley, bishop of Cloyne in Ireland, died. He was distinguished as a mathematician and astronomer.

1836. Aaron Burr, third vice-president of the United States, died, aged 81. He possessed very distinguished talents, but manifested a lamentable want of principle.

1839. Don Carlos abandoned Spain and retired with his family into France, by which the long protracted civil war in Spain was regarded as at length closed.

1847. Battle of Gareta San Cosme in Mexico, which preceded the entrance of the Americans into the city.

1848. The British forces under Gen. Whish had besieged for several days the city of Moultan, in northern India. After much bloody fighting, the desertion of Shere Singh, an important ally, they were compelled to withdraw.

1851. James Fennimore Cooper, a distinguished American novelist, died, aged 62. He was born at Burlington, N. J., graduated at Yale, and adopted the navy as his profession. He stands at the head of nautical novelists, and is the author of historical works besides.

1852. The world-renowned duke of Wellington, died at Walmer Castle, in Kent, England, aged 83; and the numerous honors concentrated upon him were scattered in various directions. (See Nov. 18.)

1852. Augustus N. W. Pugin, styled the *Christian architect*, died at Ramsgate, England, aged 41. The revival of Gothic architecture in England is associated with the names of himself and his father.

1853. The engine of a freight train on the Ohio and Pennsylvania rail road exploded while running, lifting the locomotive from the track and hurling it fifty feet.

1853. The first ground broken of the European and North American rail road, at St. John, by lady Head, assisted by the lieutenant-governor in the presence of 25,000 people.

1854. ALEXANDER W. STOWE, chief justice of the state of Wisconsin, died at Milwaukee.

SEPTEMBER 15.

1590. GERARD BONTIUS, professor of medicine at Leyden, died. He was the first who immortalized himself by pills, having invented a kind, the secret of which was long unknown.

1596. Cadiz taken and plundered by Howard and Essex. Loss computed at 20,000,000 ducats.

1607. HUDSON returned to England from his first voyage of discovery, having discovered the island of Spitzbergen, but failed in the great object, the discovery of a north-west passage to India.

1609. HUDSON, in his first ascent of the great river, came in view of mountains which lay from the river's side, and anchored, it is supposed, near the present site of Catskill landing.

1613. THOMAS OVERBURY, a polite English writer, poisoned in the Tower. He wrote in verse and prose. (See 17th.)

1623. NICHOLAS BERGIER, historiographer of France, died. He wrote a history of the great roads of the Roman empire.

1643. RICHARD BOYLE, the great earl of Cork, died. He went to Dublin with a small fortune, and by his great industry and ability enriched himself and benefited his country.

1678. The expedition under La Salle arrived at Quebec from France; count Frontenac being governor of Canada.

1712. SIDNEY, earl of Godolphin, died. He began his political life under Charles II; voted for the exclusion of the duke of York, but became minister to the same person when James II; voted for a regency when James fled; became minister to William III, and under queen Anne became premier.

1745. ARTHUR BEDFORD, a learned English clergyman, died. He made great exertions for the reformation of the drama.

1775. ANDREW FOULIS, a learned Scottish printer, died. From his press issued some of the finest specimens of correct and elegant printing that were produced in the eighteenth century.

1776. The British under general Howe took possession of New York.

1777. WASHINGTON left Philadelphia and crossed the Schuylkill with the remains of his army, determined to give battle to sir Wm. Howe wherever he could meet him.

1784. The first ærial voyage made in England by Vincent Lunardi, an Italian.

1793. Battle at Parmesans; the French defeated by the Prussians under the duke of Brunswick, with the loss of 3,000 taken prisoners, and 27 cannon. Same day Wurmser advanced upon the French lines at Lauter and Weissenburg, and carried by assault the different redoubts, took all their tents and 26 cannon, and would have destroyed the greater part of the army had not their retreat been favored by a fog.

1794. Battle of Boxtel; the French under Pichegru defeated the Prussians. The French under Jourdan also defeated the Austrians under Clairfait.

1797. LAZARUS HOCHE died; a brave and intrepid general in the French army during the revolution.

1810. A plot discovered to massacre the British at Lisbon, though defending the Portuguese cause.

1814. One of the large vats in the brew house of Meux & Co., London, burst, and demolished two houses; 3,500 barrels of beer were lost and four persons killed.

1814. British ship Hermes, destroyed in an attack on fort Bowyer, at Mobile point, and the other three ships compelled to put to sea. The fort was attacked at the same time by the British and Indians on the land side. The American garrison consisted of 130 men, of whom 4 were killed and 4 wounded. British loss, killed and wounded, 232.

1819 .An edict of the king of the Netherlands required, that in certain provinces, none other than the national language, the Flemish-Dutch, should be used in public business.

1829. Slavery abolished in Mexico by the president.

1829. JAMES HAMILTON died at Dublin; inventor of the Hamiltonian method of instruction.

1830. WILLIAM HUSKISSON, an English statesman, killed by a train of cars on the Liverpool rail road.

1833. JOHN GORDON SMITH, an eminent English scholar, died. He published a celebrated work on medical jurisprudence; became involved in pecuniary difficulties, and terminated his short and useful life within the walls of the Fleet prison.

1834. WILLIAM H. CRAWFORD, an American statesman, died. He was minister to France in 1813, and in 1825 a candidate for the presidency.

1838. ADALBERT VON CHAMISSO, one of the most popular modern poets of Germany, died at Berlin.

1843. Revolution in Athens, which, though not sufficient to eject king Otho from the throne of Greece, yet obliged him to concede much to the popular will.

1849. STRAUSS, the celebrated musical composer, died at Vienna.

1849. The sultan of Turkey formally refused to deliver up Kossuth and his colleagues, Hungarian refugees, on the demand of Russia and Austria, and diplomatic relations with the ambassadors of those powers were broken off.

1855. GEORGE T. NAPIER, a celebrated British general, died, aged 72. He first distinguished himself at Martinique in 1809, and afterwards in the Peninsula, where he lost an arm. He was seven years civil and military governor of the cape of Good Hope, where he introduced important measures and reforms.

SEPTEMBER 16.

1757 A. M. The covering of the ark removed by Noah on the 1st day of the 1st month, answering to our Sept. 16. (See Nov. 2.)

322 B. C. DEMOSTHENES, the Grecian orator, died by poison, on the most mournful day of the *Thesmophoria*, 16th of Pyanepsion.

36. HEROD AGRIPPA thrown into bonds at Rome by Tiberius.

655. MARTIN I, pope, died. He caused the doctrines of the monothelites to be condemned, and was afterwards sent to the Crimea by Constantine, where he died of ill treatment.

1186. A conjunction of all the planets at sunrise in Libra, on which occasion the astrologers had predicted great calamities.

1380. CHARLES V (*the Wise*), of France, died. By his abilities and energy, the English were dispossessed of nearly all their provinces in France.

1519. JOHN COLET, an English divine, died; known as the founder of St. Paul's school, London, for the gratuitous education of 153 pupils perpetually. His father had 22 children, yet at the time of making the above endowment, he had no near relative to inherit the property.

1589. MICHAEL BAIUS, an able French ecclesiastic, died. His writings are superior to the learning of the times in which he lived.

1655. The Swedish settlement on the Delaware, called fort Casimir, commanded by Suen Scutz, surrendered to the Dutch under Gov. Stuyvesant. The strength of the place consisted of 4 fourteen pounders, 5 swivels and some small arms, which were delivered to the conquered, who became possessed of the west side of Delaware bay, and the fortress was called New Amstel by the Dutch, and New Castle by the English.

1681. Action off cape Spartel between a British ship and an Algerine corsair with 327 men and 88 Christian slaves on board. The battle lasted from 2 till 8 P. M., within pistol shot, and was renewed again next morning, when the corsair, having lost two masts, called for quarter.

1686. FYCHAN GAUNOR died at Abercowarch, in Wales, aged 140. (1786?)

1701. JAMES II, of England, died in France. He was dethroned in 1688, and remained a pensioner on the bounty of the king of France till his death.

1732. The tide in the river Thames, England, flowed eight hours instead of four and ebbed five instead of eight.

1736. GABRIEL DANIEL FAHRENHEIT, a Prussian philosopher, died; eminent for his great improvement in the construction of thermometers.

1745. Bergen-op-Zoom surrendered to the French.

1775. ALLEN BATHURST, an English statesman, died. His biographers claim for him almost every talent and every virtue.

1776. Unsuccessful attack of the British on the Americans at Harlem Heights. British lost 20 killed and about 100 wounded.

1779. Count D'ESTAING summoned Savannah, Georgia, garrisoned by the British under general Provost, who amused the French until he received a reinforcement.

1782. CARLO BROSCHI (*Farinelli*), died; an Italian singer of great celebrity.

1784. ROBERT BELL the first who kept a circulating library in Philadelphia, died at Richmond, Va.

1785. Darkness so great at Quebec that no person could read at noonday. (See Oct. 16, 1783.)

1792. Three thousand French refugees had landed in England from the revolution in France; and in the course of the following year they were reckoned at 8000 priests and 2000 laymen. These were mostly destitute, and down to 1806, about two million pounds had been contributed to their support.

1795. Cape of Good Hope surrendered to the British by the Dutch.

1800. Battle of Lambach: the French took from the Austrians 1000 wagons of provisions, equipage and ammunition.

1804. WILLIAM TINDALL, an English divine and antiquary, died.

1805. An experiment with a calamaran made on a vessel of 300 tons burden opposite Walma castle, England, which succeeded and blew up the vessel.

1808. PETER ISAAC THELLUSON, a rich London merchant, died, leaving 500,000 pounds to accumulate till the male children of his grandsons are dead, which may extend to 120 years from his death, when it will amount to £140,000,000, and if there should be no lineal descendants, it goes to the benefit of the sinking fund.

1824. Louis XVIII, of France, died. During the reign of Napoleon he lived in England. He is represented as a mild and amiable prince, who consulted the wishes and happiness of his people.

1833. Calvin Edson, the *living skeleton*, died. His weight was about 40 pounds.

1833. The boundary line between New York and New Jersey settled.

1834. William Blackwood died in Edinburgh; eminent as a bookseller, and publisher of the well known periodical, *Blackwood's Magazine.*

1838. The entire rail way from London to Birmingham opened; when the passage including stoppages of 34 minutes, was performed in 4 hours, 48 minutes.

1839. The expedition under Dease and Simpson regained the Coppermine river after the longest voyage that had ever been performed by boats in the Polar sea—1631 statute miles. On the return of the party from the Red river settlement to England, Simpson perished by violence; but was more fortunate than Parke or Hudson, in leaving behind him his own record of his own achievements.

1848. John P. Cushman, an American jurist, died at Troy, N. Y., aged 64. He was born in Connecticut, graduated at Yale, and commenced the practice of law in Troy. He held various offices of trust, and was eminent in his profession.

1848. The populace of Frankfort attempted an insurrection, but were quelled. Prince Lichnowski and major von Auerswald were barbarously murdered by insurgents outside of the walls.

1851. Henry Whiting, an American general, died at St. Louis. He began his military career in 1808, and was among the oldest officers of the army. He served with reputation on the Niagara frontier, and in the war with Mexico, sharing in the glory of the field of Buena Vista. He was a contributor to the *North Am. Review.*

1852. Earthquake in Manilla and places adjacent, which continued until 18th October, doing great damage.

1854. Luzerne Rae, an American poet, died at Hartford, Ct., aged 43. After graduating at Yale, he became a teacher in the deaf and dumb institution at Hartford, where he found time to edit the *Religious Herald*, and the first six volumes of *Annals* of the deaf and dumb, to write poetry, and collect materials for a history of New England.

1855. Benedetto Pistrucci, medalist to the queen of England, died at Windsor, aged 73. He was a member of various learned European institutions.

SEPTEMBER 17.

1575. Henry Bullinger, one of the early reformers, died. He was one of the authors of the *Helvetic Confession*, and assisted Calvin in drawing up the *Formulary.* His works form 10 vols. folio.

1614. Thomas Overbury poisoned in the Tower with an envenomed clyster contrived by the earl of Somerset and his countess. (See Sept. 15.)

1621. Robert Bellarmin died; an Italian cardinal, and one of the most celebrated controversial writers of his time.

1651. Constantine Caietan (*Thomas de Vio*), an Italian cardinal, died. He made a literal translation of the Bible from the original.

1665. Philip IV, of Spain, died. He was unsuccessful in his wars with Holland and France; and the Portuguese also rebelled, and compelled him to acknowledge their independence.

1673. James Barrelier, a celebrated French ecclesiastic and naturalist, died. He traversed the south of France, Spain and Italy, and during a residence of 25 years at Rome, collected plants and other objects of natural history, with a view to their publication. Dying before the work was completed, he bequeathed his manuscripts to the library of a convent; but soon after his death all his collections were dispersed, and some were burnt, except the copperplates, which were collected and published by Jussieu.

1683. Controversy between lord Baltimore and William Penn. Lord Baltimore appointed Col. Talbot to demand of Penn all the lands lying on the west side of the river Delaware and south of the 40th degree, as a part of Maryland.

1690. A fire in Boston destroyed the printing office of Bartholomew Green, which was the best furnished in America.

1703. Gelders, a Prussian city, surrendered to the duke of Marlborough, after having been long blockaded, bombarded and reduced to a heap of ashes.

1720. William Burnet, son of the English bishop, took upon him the government of New York.

1753. The first theatre in New York opened in Nassau street by Lewis Hallam; the third stage on which the productions of the dramatic muse were exhibited to the inhabitants of the new world. The days of performance were Mondays, Wednesdays and Fridays, and so continued for near half a century.

1759. Quebec taken.

1762. Francisco Geminiani, died; an extraordinary performer on the violin, and composer for that instrument.

1767. Frances Sheridan died; an ingenious novelist and dramatic writer, and mother of Richard Brinsley Sheridan.

1771. The Prussians under Gen. Platten, destroyed the Russian magazines on the frontiers of Poland.

1775. Americans under Gen. Montgomery laid siege to St. John's Canada.

1782. Permacoli, in Hindostan, surrendered by the British to Hyder Ally and the French.

1785. Anthony Leonard Thomas, a French poet and prose writer, died.

1787. The constitution of the United States adopted by the federal convention at Philadelphia, and referred to the conventions of the separate states for concurrence.

1795. The French national assembly directed that a copy of the *Dictionary* of the academy, with the notes and additions in the margin, deposited in the library of the committee of public instruction, should be delivered to the booksellers, and that after a new one should be completed that it be returned; 15,000 copies to be printed.

1796. Battle of Altenkirchen, in which the celebrated French general Merceau was killed.

1802. Richard Owen Cambridge died; an elegant English poet, critic and miscellaneous writer.

1811. A beautiful annular eclipse of the sun was observed at Richmond in Virginia and other places adjacent.

1814. Sortie and battle of Fort Erie. The British *sine qua non*, totally defeated, and compelled to break up the camp and retire. British loss, killed, wounded and prisoners, 578; American loss, 82 killed, 216 wounded, 215 missing—513.

1837. Henry Brown, a soldier of the revolution, died at Boston, Ohio, aged 104. He was at the battle of Bunker Hill, and other engagements.

1839. Matthew Carey, a celebrated printer and bookseller of Philadelphia, died. He was a native of Ireland, and a man of great activity and benevolence. His writings are numerous and well known.

1840. Emma Roberts, an English authoress of considerable note, died at Poonah, in India.

1842. Henry Floyd, a bricklayer of Romsey, England, died, aged 47. He was remarkable for his great bulk, being the largest man in England. His weight was about 500 lbs. Notwithstanding the unwieldiness of his frame he was in constant attendance upon his business, was shrewd, intelligent and good natured, and much respected. His coffin contained nearly 200 feet of inch board.

1851. John Kidd, librarian to the Radcliffe library, died at Oxford, England, aged 76. He wrote upon medicine, mineralogy and geology, and furnished one of the best of the Bridgewater treatises.

1854. The steamer City of Philadelphia, seven days out from Liverpool, with 540 passengers, struck upon cape Race and became a total loss. The passengers were saved.

1855. The corner stone of the public library laid in Boston with appropriate ceremonies.

SEPTEMBER 18.

96. Titus Flavius Domitianus, emperor of Rome, died. He was the last of the Cæsars. Juvenal has shown him a buffoon, and history fixed his infamy.

1014. A violent storm caused the inundation of a large portion of Flanders.

1069. The city of New York burned by the Norman garrison.

1180. Louis VII, king of France, died. He made a crusade, with an army of 80,000 men, to Palestine, but was defeated by the Saracens.

1609. Hudson, ascending the river which bears his name, observing the water to become shoal, cast anchor in the neighborhood of the present town of Castleton, where he went on shore at the invitation of an old man, who appeared to be the governor of the country; who was chief over 40 men and 17 women; and who occupied a house made of the bark of trees, exceedingly smooth, and well finished, within and without. Here he found large quantities of Indian corn and beans, enough to load three ships, besides what were still growing in the fields.

1621. The Plymouth colonists sent an expedition consisting of ten men in a shallop, accompanied by Squanto and two other Indians, to the Massachusetts, to discover the bay, see the country, make peace, and trade with the natives.

1674. Gabriel Cossart died; a French writer, who assisted Labbe in his grand collection of councils, which extended to 28 vols. folio.

1675. Battle of Deerfield, Mass., with the Indians. A company of 96 men under captain Lathrop were escorting 3,000 bushels of corn to a place of security, when they were so suddenly set upon by about 800 Indians, that only 8 escaped. This was a choice company of young men culled from the towns of Essex county. Another company, coming, though too late to their rescue, marched through and through that great body of Indians, and after a fight of five or six hours, came off with a loss of only two, and eight wounded. It is thought that had Lathrop followed the same mode of fighting, he might have escaped with a smaller loss; but his mode was to fight the savages in their own way, by skulking behind trees, and picking off single persons, which enabled five or six of the enemy, which were so greatly superior in numbers, to surround a single man, and deliberately fire at him at once. The Indians afterwards acknowledged a loss of 96 that day.

1684. JOHN ANTONIDES (*Vander Goes*), an excellent Dutch poet, died.

1721. MATTHEW PRIOR died; an eminent English poet and statesman.

1722. ANDREW DACIER, a very celebrated French critic and philosopher, died. He translated many of the classics.

1759. The city of Quebec surrendered to the English under brigadier general Townshend, and was garrisoned by 5,000 men under general Murray.

1773. The Polish diet finally ratified the treaty of the partition of their country between Russia, Austria and Prussia.

1773. JOHN CUNNINGHAM died; an ingenious pastoral poet and dramatic writer.

1777. Americans under colonel BROWN attacked and defeated the British on the north end of lake George and Ticonderoga, took 293 prisoners, released 100 Americans, and retook the continental standard left there on its evacuation in July.

1777. Congress at Philadelphia adjourned to meet at Lancaster, on account of the approach of the British.

1790. HENRY FREDERICK, brother to George III, and duke of Cumberland, died. His marriage with Mrs. Horton gave rise to the famed *Marriage Act of England.*

1792. The south-east corner stone of the north wing of the Capitol at Washington, was laid by general Washington.

1794. Bellegarde, a strong and important fortress, commanding the road from France into Spain, surrendered at discretion to the French under Dugommier, although abundantly supplied with every thing required to hold out a siege of many months.

1798. NELSON being applied to for assistance by the Malthese, sent a Portuguese squadron, consisting of 4 ships of the line and 2 frigates, which appeared before Valetta on this day.

1800. The treaty between Bonaparte and the pope, called the *Concordat*, ratified. This was dictated by the first consul and in every article infringed on the pretensions of the papal dignitary.

1811. Dutch surrendered the island of Java to the British.

1811. Battle of Ximena, in Spain, and defeat of the French under Soult.

1816. BERNARD M'MAHON, an eminent botanist from Ireland, died at his botanic garden, near Philadelphia.

1819. JOHN LANGDON died; an active and powerful advocate of the American revolution. He was a member of the congress of 1775, and of the convention which framed the constitution; a senator in congress, and governor of New Hampshire.

1821. JOHN NICHOLAS CORVISART, a distinguished French physician, died. He was physician to Napoleon, and greatly promoted the progress of experimental medicine and pathological anatomy in France.

1830. WILLIAM HAZLITT, an elegant English writer, died. He is also known as an artist.

1834. KEATING SIMONS died, aged 82; aid-de-camp in the revolutionary war to general Marion.

1838. Great eclipse of the sun over the United States.

1840. C. S. RAFINESQUE, an eminent botanist, died at Philadelphia, where he had been for several years professor of botany and natural history in Transylvania university, and author of several works on various scientific subjects.

1842. JOHN C. COLT under sentence of death in New York for the murder of Mr. Adams, killed himself on the day appointed for his execution.

1853. ANDREWS NORTON, an American theologian, died, aged 68. He wrote several theological works, was a profound and accurate scholar, and for talent, acquirements and influence, one of the most remarkable men of New England.

1854. The British consul at the Sandwich islands presented his protest to the king, against the annexation of those islands to the United States.

1854. WILLIAM PLUMER, a New Hampshire statesman, died, aged 65. He graduated at Harvard, and while in congress opposed the Missouri compromise. He was a man of taste, had an attachment to historical researches, and collected a fine library. He published two small volumes of poems.

1855. JOHN F. W. JOHNSTON, an eminent English chemist and mineralogist, died at Durham, aged 59. He published several valuable works on agricultural chemistry and geology, and was a contributor to the reviews.

SEPTEMBER 19.

880. ABBATEGNIA decided the oblignity of the ecliptic to be 23° 25′.

1356. Battle of Poictiers, between the English army of 12,000 men, under Edward, the *Black Prince*, and the French, 60,000 under king John. The battle ended in the utter rout of the French army and the capture of their king, who was afterwards led in triumph through the streets of London.

1471. The first book known to have been printed in the English tongue bears this date, and is entitled *The Recuyell of the History of Troy*, translated from the French, and printed by William Caxton, at Cologne. (See Oct. 4.)

1524. The imperialists under Pescara raised the siege of Marseilles and retired with precipitation towards Italy.

1587. James Pamelius, a learned Flemish writer, died.

1650. Stuyvesant, the Dutch governor of New-Netherland, arrived at Hartford and demanded of the commissioners for the united colonies, a full surrender of the lands on Connecticut river. After an altercation of several days, articles of agreement in relation to boundaries were settled.

1665. The number of deaths by plague in London for the week ending on this day was reported to be 10,000; the greatest weekly mortality reported during the scourge.

1678. Bernard Van Galen, a Westphalian bishop and general died. His ecclesiastical office was of minor importance with him, and he contrived to keep up a perpetual war with one state or another; so that when he died, his loss was little regretted.

1681. Desperate engagement between a Moorish vessel, the Half Moon, 32 guns, from Angier, and the English galleys James and Sapphire. Of the Turks and Moors 93 were killed; English loss 95 killed and wounded.

1693. At St. Malo three hundred houses were unroofed by the blowing up of a fire vessel sent in by captain Benbow.

1710. Olaus Rœmer, a Danish astronomer, died.

1736. Mrs. Mapp, the famous bone setter, of Epsom, having set up a fine equipage, came to Kensington and waited on the queen.

1737. Gottingen university opened.

1745. The celebrated Jonathan Swift died, aged 78.

1761. Peter Van Musschenbroek, a distinguished Dutch philosopher, died.

1777. Battle of Stillwater, between the British under Burgoyne and the Americans under general Gates. The action was continued with great valor on both sides during 4 hours. The Americans retired to their camp at night, with the loss of 319 killed, wounded and missing. British loss over 500.

1778. Action between American privateer Hancock and British frigate Levant, 32 guns. The Levant blew up, and only 18 of her crew were saved.

1793. The new French calendar commenced. It divided the year into 12 months of 30 days each with 5 intercallary days, called *Sansculotides*.

1798. Elihu H. Smith, a physician and poet, died in New York.

1803. Dutch colonies of Demerara and Essequibo surrendered to the British.

1804. George Zabira, a learned Greek, died.

1810. James Cheetham, a noted political editor, died in New York, aged 37. He was the biographer of Thomas Paine, and published the *American Citizen*.

1814. The boats of the British ship Forth, under the direction of lieutenant Neville, carried by boarding and destroyed the American letter of marque brig Regent, 5 guns and 35 men, at the mouth of Little Egg harbor.

1851. Battle of Camargo, between the forces of the Mexican government and those of Carvajal, in which the latter were victorious.

1851. Frederick Whittlesey, a New York jurist, died at Rochester, aged 54.

1852. Great inundation in the valleys of the Rhine and the Rhone.

1854. The allied forces which had landed at Old Fort, to operate against Sebastopol, commenced their march to that fortress. They consisted of 25,000 British, 25,000 French, and 8,000 Turkish troops.

1855. A terrible gale swept lake Borgne and the Gulf coast, causing loss of life and great destruction of property at Pass Christian, Mississippi city, Biloxi, and other points in the vicinity.

SEPTEMBER 20.

377 b. c. On this day was fought the famous naval battle of Naxus, in which the Lacedemonians were totally defeated.

331 b. c. Alexander crossed the Tigris and entered Assyria. The army encountered great difficulties in the passage, both from the depth and force of the current, and the slippery nature of its bed. The cavalry formed a double line, within which the infantry marched with their shields over their heads, and their arms interlinked. In this manner they crossed without loss of lives. Their entrance into Assyria was signalized by an almost total eclipse of the moon, by which the date of the event is determined.

92 b. c. Lucius Lucinius Crassus died; a Roman orator, greatly commended by Cicero.

692. ABDULLAH IBN ZOBEYR, khalif of Mecca, having been besieged nine months in his capital until he was deserted by his friends and family, put himself at the head of five faithful followers, and rushed upon the besiegers, by whom he was slain, at the age of 72.

1142. MAUD, queen of England, besieged in Oxford by the forces of Stephen, but escaped on foot.

1384. LOUIS I, duke of Anjou, died at Paris, of a broken heart, in consequence of the ill success of his measures.

1415. OWEN GLENDOWER, a celebrated Welch warrior, died; he opposed the sovereignty of Henry IV of England more than fourteen years, by force of arms, declaring him to be an usurper and the murderer of Richard II.

1527. JANUS GRUTERIUS, an eminent Dutch philologer, died. He was an able critic, a man ot extensive erudition, and a very voluminous and respectable writer.

1581. HUBERT LANGUET, an eminent French statesman, died. He was a man of great political knowledge, and deservedly esteemed by the wisest and most eminent men of his age.

1586. ANTHONY BABINGTON with others cruelly executed in St. Giles's fields for a conspiracy against queen Elizabeth.

1639. JOHN MEURSIUS, a learned Dutch scholar, died. His works were printed at Florence in 12 vols. folio.

1643. Battle of Newbury, between the royalists under prince Rupert, and the parliamentary forces under the earl of Essex. Night put an end to the action, and left the victory undecided. Lucius Carey, lord Falkland, and the earls of Sunderland and Carnaervon, were killed.

1653. The New England colonies declared war against Ninigret, sachem of the Niantick Indians, and voted that 250 foot soldiers should be immediately raised in the four colonies: Massachusetts to send 166, Plymouth 30, Connecticut 33, New-Haven 21.

1662. JOHN GAUDEN, an English prelate, died. He published the *Icon Basilike* of Charles I, and had the good fortune to escape the search of the parliament for the publisher of that popular book.

1668. VINCENT WING died; a famous English astronomer and astrologer, who published *The Celestial Harmony of the Visible World*, and other works.

1736. JOHN BERNARDI died in Newgate prison, England, aged 79. He had been confined there 40 years on a false charge of plotting the assassination of William III.

1740. CHARLES VI died; sixteenth and last emperor of Germany of the house of Austria, in the male line; he was succeeded by his daughter Maria Theresa.

1746. The *Young Pretender*, CHARLES EDWARD, having been completely defeated at Culloden, embarked for France at Lochmannoch, in a privateer of St. Malo, and arrived safe. His followers were less fortunate.

1759. JULIAN LE ROY, a distinguished French mechanic, died. His watches acquired great celebrity.

1761. Auto-da-fé at Lisbon; there were 54 criminals, 3 of them in effigy.

1770. Captain PHIPPS returned to London from his voyage to the polar seas, being stopped by ice, latitude 81° 30′ north.

1783. Captain TURNER, the traveler, was received at Jikadze, the capital of the lama of Thibet.

1791. LOUIS XVI, for the first time after his return from Varennes, repaired to the hall of the national assembly, in order to give his adhesion, viva voce, to the new constitution.

1792. Battle of Valmy, between the French and allies. It is stated that although more than 40,000 cannon shot were fired in this engagement, not more than 400 men were killed.

1805. PIERRE FRANÇOIS ANDRE MECHAIN died at Castillon, in Spain. His theory of eclipses and other astronomical phenomena has much merit.

1814. The British under general DRUMMOND, in consequence of the losses sustained on the 17th, raised the siege of fort Erie.

1814. AUGUSTUS WILLIAM IFLAND, a German actor and dramatic writer, died at Berlin, and was interred with great pomp.

1815. WILLIAM HUTTON died; the historian of Birmingham, and author of various other works.

1831. JOHN HENRY HOBART, bishop of the protestant episcopal diocese of New York, died; a man of vigorous intellect and great decision of character.

1840. FRANCIA, dictator of Paraguay, died at Paraguay, at a very advanced age.

1842. WILLIAM MAGINN died in England. He was a contributor to the London *Literary Gazette*, and in 1818–20 to *Blackwood's Magazine* under the signature of O'-Doherty.

1849. JONATHAN H. HUBBARD, a distinguished American statesman, of Vermont, died, aged 81.

1852. PHILANDER CHASE, bishop of Illinois, died at Peoria, aged 76. He was a native of New Hampshire; was bishop of Ohio 12 years, of Illinois 17 years; laid the foundation of Kenyon college, and was president of Jubilee college.

1854. The allies attacked the Russians under Menschikoff, who 40,000 in number, were strongly entrenched upon the heights of Alma, and after a contest of four hours drove them from the ground with great loss. The allies had about 500 killed and 2,500 wounded; the Russian loss said to have been more than 7,000.

SEPTEMBER 21.

60. Saint MATTHEW, the apostle, died at Heliopolis, in Parthia.

1327. EDWARD II, 10th king of England, barbarously murdered at Berkley castle. Less wise and firm than his father, he forfeited the confidence of his people, and his wife Isabella joined the rebellion against him.

1520. SELIM I, sultan of Turkey, died. He came to the throne by causing the death of his father and two brothers. He conquered Egypt and crushed the power of the Mamelukes, which for 260 years had governed that country.

1534. ALCAZABA sailed from Cadiz on a voyage of discovery. He was murdered in the straits of Magellan by his crew, and the ship was wrecked at Brazil.

1558. CHARLES V, emperor of Germany, died. He ascended the throne of Spain 1518, and two years afterwards was elected to the empire. After a reign of 38 years he resigned and retired to a cloister. His death was caused by taking cold on getting out of his coffin after having gone through with a mock funeral, to gratify an idle whim.

1576. JEROME CARDAN died; an Italian physician, and one of the most extraordinary men of the age. His works were printed at Lyons in 10 vols. folio.

1609. HUDSON arrived in the vicinity of Albany, and having satisfied himself by despatching a boat seven or eight miles farther up, that he had gained the head of ship navigation, he prepared to retrace his course.

1659. First Esopus war began.

1704. BEAT DE ZURLAUBEN (*the younger*), a Swiss general in the French army, died at Ulm, in consequence of seven wounds which he had received at the battle of Hochstadt.

1723. The Irish house of commons addressed king George I on the evils of Wood's halfpence. For some time this subject was a theme for lampoons and Dean Swift's wit.

1733. NOEL STEPHEN SANADON, a learned French Jesuit, died; professor of rhetoric at Paris, and author of several much admired orations and poems.

1735. PETER ARTEDI drowned; a Swedish naturalist, so intimate with Linnæus that they made each other heirs of their manuscripts and other literary property.

1745. Battle of Prestonpans, in England, between the forces of the young pretender and those of the king. The former gained a complete victory with the loss of only 50; while 500 of the king's troops were killed on the field of battle, and lost their artillery, colors, tents, baggage and military chest.

1748. JOHN BALGUY died; an eminent English prelate, and controversial and metaphysical writer. He committed 200 of his sermons to the flames in presence of his son, afterwards prebendary of Winchester, whom he wished to excite to the same laudable application.

1757. ROBERT PARR died at Brignorth, England, aged 124. He was a great grandson of Thomas Parr who attained the age of 152. One of the sons of the latter attained the age of 109, and a grandson died at the age of 113. Their mode of living was simple and temperate.

1761. GABRIEL MALAGRIDA, an Italian Jesuit, burnt in Portugal as a false prophet. His zeal and eloquence rendered him popular, but he became obnoxious to the inquisition after the abolition of his order.

1776. Great fire in New York, then in possession of the British; 1,000 houses were burnt.

1777. British under general Grey, surprised the Americans under general Wayne in the night, killed about 300, and took a few prisoners and some baggage. The prudent dispositions of Wayne prevented their further success.

1780. Americans under colonel Davie surprised a party of British at Wahab's house, killed and wounded 60, and took 96 horses and equipments, and 120 stand of arms, with the loss of only 1.

1780. Major ANDRE, an adjutant-general in the British army, landed in the night from the British sloop of war Vulture, and proceeded to West Point to confer with Arnold.

1792. Royalty abolished, and France declared a republic, by acclamation, in the national assembly.

1795. The *Peep of day boys*, in Ireland, changed their name to *Orange men*, and opened their first lodge.

1802. Mons. GARNERIN ascended at London in a balloon about 4,000 feet, and descended in a parachute safely at St. Pancras. His balloon fell the next day near Farnham, in Surrey.

1803. ROBERT EMMET hanged in Dublin for high treason in conspiring the death of George III, and providing arms, &c., for the rebels. His speech in his defence is a masterly piece of eloquence.

1812. The Americans under captain Forsyth attacked and carried the village of Gananoque, in Canada.

1814. Action between the United States sloop of war Wasp, captain Blakely, and the British brig Atalanta, formerly the Siro of Baltimore. The Atalanta was captured, and made the 13th and last prize of the Wasp during that cruise; for nothing is known of her fate afterwards.

1814. The British under lieut. Drummond retreated from before fort Erie to Niagara.

1832. Walter Scott, the most popular writer of his age, and the most distinguished novelist in English literature, died at Abbotsford, in Scotland. His fictitious prose works comprise 75 volumes, and his complete works about 100 volumes.

1842. Jeremiah Smith, for many years a member of congress from and ex governor of New Hampshire, died at Dover, aged 62, highly respected as a statesman and a jurist, as well as a scholar.

1842. James Ivory, a distinguished Scottish mathematician, died near London. At the solicitation of lord Brougham, king William IV conferred on him the order of knighthood, with a pension of £300.

1846. First day's battle of Monterey.

1851. The stores of Spanish residents at Key West, Florida, were attacked and their contents destroyed, in consequence of the excitement about the Cuban expedition of Lopez.

1852. William Badger, a New Hampshire jurist, died, aged 73. He had long filled various offices of state with creditable ability.

1852. John Chambers, a pioneer Kentucky emigrant, died, aged 73. He was born in New Jersey, and went to Kentucky at the age of 13. He practiced law with success; was a volunteer aid-de-camp to Harrison at the battle of the Thames, and was one of the foremost in the pursuit of Proctor. He was the first governor of Iowa, and held other public offices.

1853. General Pineda, sometime president of Nicaragua, died at Rivas.

1854. Jonathan Mayhew Wainwright, a New York episcopal bishop, died, aged 63; esteemed a learned theologian and a ripe scholar.

SEPTEMBER 22.

479 b. c. Battle of Mycale, between the Greeks and Persians. This victory happened in the 24th of the Bœotian month Panemus, observed as an anniversary by the Greek confederates. The Persians, computed at 100,000 men, were completely defeated and despoiled.

479 b. c. The battle of Platæa is also placed on the same day, in which 300,000 Persians under Mardonius were defeated by 100,000 Greeks under Pausanius and Aristides. The loss of the the Greeks was inconsiderable; but of the Persians Mardonius was slain and scarcely one-tenth of his army escaped by flight. (See Aug. 3.)

19 b. c Publius Maro Virgilius, the most excellent of all the ancient Roman poets, died.

622. Flight of Mahomet; an imposing event, which took place, it is ascertained with certainty, sixty-eight days *after* the commencement of the great Arabian era, July 16th.

1193. Henry IV, of Germany, and his captive, Richard the Lion, addressed letters from Spires to the primates and magnates of England, notifying the severe terms of ransom "agreed" upon between them.

1298. Battle of Stirlingbridge, between the Scots under Wallace and the English under Warrenne; the latter defeated and obliged to retire into England.

1415. Henry V took Harfleur, in France, reducing it to an English colony.

1536. William Tyndale, one of the first publishers of the Bible in English, was burnt at the stake at Antwerp.

1554. The duke of Northumberland with sir John Gates and sir Thomas Palmer executed.

1559. Robert Stephens, the celebrated and learned Parisian printer, died, aged 56.

1604. Ostend, a seaport in Flanders, surrendered to the Spanish under general Spinola, after a close siege of upwards of three years. The Spanish are supposed to have lost 80,000 men during this siege; and not less than 50,000 English and Dutch perished in the town during that time.

1632. Frederick Borromeo, archbishop of Milan, died. He sustained an excellent character, and founded the Ambrosian library.

1646. John Francis Niceron died; an eminent French mathematician and optician; and author of some valuable works.

1662. John Biddle, styled the father of the English unitarians, died in prison, a martyr to principle.

1688. Francis Bernier, a celebrated French traveler and physician, died at Paris. He extended his travels to the Mogul empire, where he became physician to Aurungzebe.

1692. Two men and seven women executed at Salem for witchcraft. One of them was pressed to death for standing mute.

1703. VINCENT VIVIANI, a famous Florentine mathematician, died. He was the pupil and friend of Galileo.

1708. Battle near Smolensko, in which the Swedes under Charles XII, consisting of six regiments of horse and 4,000 infantry, attacked and defeated 10,000 horse and 6,000 Calmucks. The king killed above a dozen with his own hand.

1735. PETER BROWNE, bishop of Cork, died. He distinguished himself by some philosophical writings.

1738. JOSEPH AVERANIUS died; a Florentine philosopher, of great powers of mind.

1741. In the north of Ireland wheat sold at sixpence a stone of 14 lbs., and beef at one penny a pound.

1742. BENOIT, a learned Phœnician, died. He became a Hebrew professor at Pisa, and edited the works of Ephrem Syrus.

1743. GEORGE CLINTON arrived at New York, as governor of the province, "seeking nothing more than a genteel frugality and common civility, while he was mending his fortunes, till his friends could recall him, and with justice to their own characters and interests, to some indolent and more lucrative station."

1761. GEORGE III and his queen CHARLOTTE, crowned at Westminster.

1769. ANTHONY GENOVESI died; a native of Castiglione, who acquired great celebrity as a lecturer on philosophy at Naples; and much odium by adopting the theories of Galileo, Grotius and Newton.

1770. Convention of the people of Massachusetts, consisting of delegates from 96 towns and 8 districts, met at Faneuil hall to consider the grievance of standing armies, &c.

1770. THOMAS LE SUER died at Rome, where he taught theology, philosophy and mathematics with great applause.

1774. CLEMENT XVI (*John Ganganelli*), pope, died. He was studious in his youth, and recommended himself to office by his abilities and merits.

1788. The Oneidas ceded all their lands to the state of New York.

1792. Commencement of the French republican era. It computes from midnight: "the 1st of the 1st decade of the 1st month (Vendemaire) of the 1st year of the French republic, one and indivisible."

1796. The English frigate Amphion blown up at Plymouth. Out of 220, 16 only saved.

1803. ANGIOLO FABRONI, an Italian ecclesiastic, died. He wrote an account of the learned men in Italy in the 17th and 18th centuries, in 21 vols.

1814. The celebrated colossal statue of sir William Wallace, the Scottish chief, finished under the direction of the earl of Buchan. This statue overlooks the grave of sir Walter Scott.

1837. DAVID UNWINS, a distinguished London physician, died. He was a man of literature and science, and author of several valuable medical works.

1846. The battle of Monterey, in Mexico, was fought. The Americans though signally victorious, yet lost many brave officers and men. It began on the 21st and was concluded on the 23d.

1851. LOUIS KOSSUTH, the Hungarian chief, and thirty-five of his country men, were sentenced to death *in contumaciam*, at Pesth, for not appearing after citation.

1851. MARY MARTHA SHERWOOD, an English writer of juvenile books, died at Twickenham, aged 77. Her works number about fifty, and were valuable and popular, particularly *Little Henry and his Bearer*.

1852. PHILIP MILLEDOLER, president of Rutgers college, died at Staten Island, aged 77. He was one of the framers of the American Bible society, and was an eminent minister of the Dutch reformed church.

1854. JOHN PURVIANCE, a Maryland jurist, died, aged 81. He was judge of the county court of Baltimore nearly thirty years, and left a fine library which was dispersed by auction after his death.

1854. THOMAS DENMAN, an English judge and peer, died, aged 75. He distinguished himself in parliament, and also in the trial of queen Caroline. He presided in the court of queen's bench more than 17 years.

SEPTEMBER 23.

67. Gamala, supposed impregnable, fell before Vespasian on the 23d Hyperberetеus (Tisri), nor age nor sex was spared.

768. PEPIN (*the Short*), king of France, died. He maintained respect at home and abroad by the valor and heroic firmness of his conduct.

1459. Battle of Bloreheath, in England. The Yorkists, under the earl of Salisbury, defeated lord Audley, who was slain.

1519. CORTEZ entered the Indian city of Tlascala; having in the short space of twenty-four days subdued a powerful nation.

1571. JOHN JEWEL, bishop of Salisbury, died; one of the most learned and prominent divines under Elizabeth.

1641. Irish rebellion and massacre. The number of protestants slain is variously estimated, probably, however, not less than 150,000. O'Niel was the instigator.

1641. The Merchant Royall, a fine ship,

"having in her a world of treasure," was wrecked near Land's end.

1642. Battle of Worcester; the parliament forces under Sandys defeated by the royalists under Rupert.

1657. JOACHIM JUNGE died; a German philosopher of great ability, who arrayed himfelf against the Aristotelian philosophy.

1675. VALENTIN CONRART died; to whose influence, taste and love for literature, the French ascribe the origin of their academy, of which he is styled the father.

1709. Newburgh on the west side of the Hudson river settled.

1727. JAMES ABBADDIE, a learned French protestant minister, died. He was an elegant preacher, and his works were unusually popular.

1737. The Hebrews disfranchised by a vote of the New York legislature.

1738. HERMAN BOERHAAVE, an eminent Dutch physician, died. From his multifarious knowledge he has been styled the Voltaire of science.

1746. Namur, in Belgium, taken by the French, and with it 7,000 Austrians surrendered.

1777. The British army under general Howe crossed the Schuylkill.

1779. American frigate Bon Homme Richard, 40 guns, 375 men, captain Paul Jones, engaged and captured the British frigate Serapis, captain Pearson, 44 guns. While engaged, the American frigate Alliance, 36 guns, frequently sailed round the Serapis and poured in a raking fire, both fore and aft, but as they were close alongside of each other, her fire frequently did execution on board Jones's ship, 11 of whose men and an officer were killed by one broadside. The loss on both sides was very great. At the same time, in company, the British ship Countess of Scarborough engaged the French frigate Pallas, and after an action of two hours struck her colors and was made prize of.

1780. JOHN ANDRE, the British spy, intercepted near Tarrytown, about 25 miles above New York, and taken into custody.

1784. Some Americans in Savannah, not to be behind the age, fitted up a balloon in which 6 men with 600 bushels of corn and necessaries for the trip, started from that city for Jamaica.

1792. Dr. PRIESTLY and THOMAS PAINE were elected to the national convention of France.

1794. French national convention decreed the formation of a company of *ærostats* to superintend the military balloons.

1795. The Dutch colony at the cape of Good Hope taken possession of by the English.

1803. Battle of Assaye, in Hindostan, between the British, 4500 men, under Wellesley, and Scindea's army consisting of 38,500 cavalry, 10,500 regular infantry, 500 matchlocks, and 500 rocket men—total, 50,000 men, with a train of 90 cannon. The latter were defeated.

1806. The American exploring party under captains Lewis and Clarke, returned to St. Lewis, having lost but one of their party.

1807. The British withdrew their troops from Egypt, after having sustained a loss of more than one half by climate and combat.

1813. American frigate President, Com. Rodgers, took the British schooner Highflyer, 5 guns, without any action.

1823. MATTHEW BAILLIE died; an eminent English physician, author of a superior work on the morbid anatomy of the human body.

1824. Major CARTWRIGHT, an enthusiastic English reformer, died, aged 84. So early as 1775 he published a tract entitled American Independence the Glory and Interest of Great Britain.

1835. BELLINI, a celebrated Italian musical composer, died at Paris, aged 29.

1836. MARIA FELICITAS MALIBRAN DE BERITAS, a celebrated vocal actress, died. She possessed extraordinary endowments, and a remarkable combination of fine qualities rendered her the admiration of all who saw or heard her. She was heard to sing in one evening in six different languages, and with unqualified admiration in all.

1842. A great fire took place in Liverpool, England; 500,000 pounds sterling worth of property destroyed and 20 persons killed.

1846. The new planet predicted by M. Leverrier was discovered at Berlin by Dr. Galle. On the 29th it was seen in London; 21st Oct. at Cambridge, Mass.; 23d Oct. at Washington.

1846. Last day's battle of Monterey, in which the arms of the United States troops were gloriously victorious.

1852. The barque Cornelia, having cleared at Havana, was brought to and boarded at the mouth of the harbor, and the mail bags rifled in the expectation of detecting a conspiracy.

1854. The Russians closed the passage to the harbor of Sebastopol by sinking in the entrance five ships of the line and two frigates.

1855. The island of Guam visited by a terrific tornado, nearly every house on the island was destroyed, and 8,000 persons left houseless.

SEPTEMBER 24.

366. LIBERIUS, pope, died. He subscribed, very reluctantly, the condemnation of Athanasius.

867. MICHAEL III (*the Drunkard*), emperor of Rome, assassinated. His minority was governed by his mother, a woman of great ability; but on assuming the reigns of government, his profligate conduct led to his death.

1143. INNOCENT II, pope, died. He was elected to the office in 1130, but excluded by a rival for several years.

1332. JOHN BALIOL crowned king of Scotland at Scone, by the bishop of Dunkeld.

1404. WILLIAM OF WYKEHAM, bishop of Winchester, died. He rose from obscurity, and before his death appropriated the large possessions which he had acquired to endow two new colleges, New College Oxford, and Winchester.

1427. Lady RAVENSWORTH devised to her children the following things: "I wyl yat my son Robert (bishop of London) have a sauter covered with red velvet. My doghter Margory a primer covered in rede," &c., &c.

1635. ANTHONY BRUNI, an Italian poet, died.

1650. CHARLES DE VALOIS, duke de Angouleme, died; a French militaire.

1664. Fort Orange, now Albany, surrendered to the English under colonel Cartwright. The title of Jeremiah Van Rensselaer to the manor of Rensselaerwyck was confirmed.

1664. The first convention was held in Albany between the English and the Iroquois, who were now the predominant race, holding sway over every savage nation. The Iroquois continued the allies of the English until the revolution.

1680. SAMUEL BUTLER, an English poet, died; author of *Hudibras*.

1693. Bayonets first used at the battle near Turin on loaded muskets, which has been practiced ever since. In 1620 they were first constructed at Bayonne. Hence the name.

1722. JAMES WATSON, author of the *History of Printing in Scotland*, died at Edinburgh.

1757. AARON BURR, president of New-Jersey college, died. He was an able divine and an accomplished scholar.

1793. Foundation laid of the Iron bridge over the river Wear, at Sunderland, England. It was finished in 1796.

1803. Berbice, a Dutch colony in Guiana, celebrated for its fine coffee, surrendered to the British.

1805. WILLIAM BYRNE, a distinguished British landscape engraver, died.

1811. French under general MARMONT forced Wellington to raise the siege of Ciudad Rodrigo in Spain.

1816. EUSEBIUS VALLI, an eminent Italian physician, died a martyr to science. He visited Smyrna and Constantinople to make observations on the plague, and the West-Indies to study the nature of the yellow fever. In both instances he voluntarily subjected himself to the disease, and in the latter made a fatal experiment in exposing himself to the infection with a dead body, so that in three days the scene closed upon him in death.

1821. The Hetærists, a Greek brotherhood, extirpated. On the breaking out of the Greek revolution they hastened from all parts of Europe and formed a legion of heroes. The last band of them were attacked and defeated at the monastery of Seck, where their leader Jordaki, being wounded, and to escape falling into the hands of the Turks, set fire to the monastery, and perished in the conflagration.

1825. PETER PAUL DOBREE died; an eminent professor of Greek and Latin, who succeeded Porson at Cambridge, and was one of the most finished classical scholars in Europe.

1831. Mount Auburn, a retired and ornamental place of sepulture about four miles from the city of Boston and containing about fifty acres, was publicly dedicated, the first of the kind in the United States.

1835. JOHN PITT, earl of Chatham, died. He was the eldest son of the great earl of Chatham and brother of the prime minister. As he left no heir, the peerage became extinct.

1839. ROBERT Y. HAYNE, a distinguished American statesman and orator, died.

1841. Mr. BROOKE, an enterprising Englishman, became rajah, or governor, of Sarawak, the first footing obtained by the English on the island of Borneo, it is believed.

1842. Mrs. ELIZABETH AYLETT, daughter of the celebrated Patrick Henry, died at King William county, Virginia.

1847. WILLIAM POPHAM, an officer of the revolution, died in New York, aged 95.

1847. Col. DAVID FOLSOM, a chief of the Chocktaws, died.

1852. General CASTANOS, duke of Baylen, died, aged 95. He was the companion in arms of Wellington and one of the most conspicuous and heroic of the Spanish commanders in war against Napoleon, called the war of independence.

1852. BENJAMIN THOMPSON, a Massachusetts congressman, died at Charlestown, aged 75. He held many responsible offices, possessed great business talent, and his services were especially valuable at Washington on the committee of military affairs, during the Mexican war.

1854. George Leith Roussell, an eminent English physician and surgeon, died in London, of cholera, aged 57. He wrote upon typhus fever, cholera, and the effects of poisons.

SEPTEMBER 25.

275. The emperor Tacitus elected, after an interregnum of eight months. He ordered that ten copies of his kinsman's history should be placed in the libraries. *The* MS. was discovered in Westphalia.

1066. Battle of Stamford Bridge, between the English under Harold, and the Norwegians under Hafalgar and Tostig. The latter were defeated, and Hafalgar and Tostig slain. The Norwegian fleet also fell into the hands of the English. Judith, the wife of Tostig, afterwards married Guelph I, and became the lineal progenitor of the present royal family of England.

1154. King Stephen of England, died, and his adopted son Henry Fitzempress reigned in his stead.

1493. Columbus sailed from Cadiz with a fleet of seventeen ships, great and small, well furnished with all the necessaries for the voyage, and having on board 1,500 people, with horses, cattle, and implements to establish plantations.

1506. Philip I of Spain, died. He obtained the crown by marriage with Jane, the heiress of Ferdinand and Isabella, was a man of very moderate abilities, but regarded as the fairest man of his age.

1513. Nunez de Balboa, the Spaniard, discovered the sea, over Darien, and in his transport took corporal possession of the ocean in the name of his master.

1555. The famous *recess*, or peace of religion, established at Augsburg, the bond of union between the German states.

1586. The attainder of Gerald Fitzgerald, 16th earl of Desmond, and forfeiture of 574,628 acres. His head was fixed on London bridge.

1600. Anthony du Verdier died; historiographer of France, and author of a *Biography of French Authors*.

1602. Gaspard Peucer, an eminent German physician and mathematician, died. He was imprisoned ten years for his religious opinions, during which he committed his thoughts on the margins of old books, with an ink which he made of burnt crusts infused in wine.

1621. Mary Sidney, countess of Pembroke, an eminent poetess and patron of literature, died.

1626. Lancelot Andrews, bishop of Winchester, died; an eminent English prelate.

1638. De Vries sailed from Holland on his third expedition to America, with colonists, to settle Staten Island, which he had secured two years before.

1666. Schah Abas, king of Persia, died. He came to the throne at the age of 13; was valiant and enlightened, and promised by deeds of benevolence and liberality to rival the greatest heroes of antiquity, when he was cut off at the age of 37. He died of *lues Veneris*.

1689. Count Frontenac arrived at Canada to reassume the government of the province.

1732. Michael Ernest Ettmuller died; a German professor of anatomy at Leipsic, and author of several learned and curious treatises on medical subjects.

1758. Robert Clayton, a learned English prelate and antiquary, died.

1764. Robert Dodsley, an eminent English bookseller and author, died. He commenced life as a footman, but his natural abilities brought him into notice, and recommended him to assistance.

1765. Richard Pococke, bishop of Meath, died; a celebrated traveler, and author of the *Description of the East*, with observations on Palestine.

1777. John Henry Lambert, a German mathematician, died. He was the son of a poor tailor, but became one of the most learned men of his time by his own unaided exertions.

1777. The American colonel, Ethan Allen, captured near Montreal by the British. He had 15 men killed, and surrendered 38, of whom 7 were put to death.

1786. Edward Ives, a celebrated English traveler, died. The account which he published of his travels through Europe and Asia contains much information.

1791. William Bradford died; an eminent printer of Philadelphia, and an officer in the revolutionary war.

1792. James Cazotte, mayor of Pierry, in France, guillotined. He had previously been saved from the mob by the heroic conduct of his daughter, a girl of 17, who shared his misfortunes.

1804. Joseph Willard, president of Harvard college, died; whose attainments in Greek learning have been equaled by few in America.

1806. Bonaparte left Paris, to open the campaign against Prussia.

1806. Action between the British squadron, admiral Hood, and a French squadron. Several French frigates were captured; Hood lost his right arm.

1808. Richard Porson, an eminent English professor, died. He possessed great reputation as a Greek scholar and critic, and yet his learning scarcely produced him a living.

1814. The pope issued a bull prohibiting all secret societies, particularly those of freemasons.

1815. JOHN SINGLETON COPLEY, a distinguished American painter, died in London.

1815. First daily paper printed at Albany, N. Y.

1839. Treaty between France and Texas signed at Paris.

1840. Marshal MCDONALD, one of Bonaparte's distinguished generals, died at his chateau near Guise, in France. He was a kinsman of the celebrated Flora McDonald who was instrumental in aiding the escape of the pretender from the Isle of Skye.

1842. RICHARD COLLEY WELLESLY, marquis of Wellesly, and eldest son of the earl of Mornington, died, aged 82.

1854. WILLIAM HENRY PARTLETT, an English artist, died at sea, aged 44; author of *Views in Switzerland*, and other similar works of merit.

1855. JOHN GIFFORD, a British admiral, died at Southampton, aged 90. He had been in the service more than 75 years, was present at the relief of Gibraltar in 1781, and distinguished himself in many important engagements.

SEPTEMBER 26.

33. St. STEPHEN is said to have been stoned this day, Paul consenting.

329. Constantinople founded, about the same day that Solomon dedicated his temple at Jerusalem, 1005 B. C.

1087. WILLIAM II, surnamed Rufus, proclaimed and crowned king of England.

1415. Harfleur, a town in France, surrendered unconditionally to Henry V of England, after a siege of five weeks, and their defences had been demolished.

1417. FRANCIS ZABARELLA, an Italian cardinal, died; noted for his great learning and virtues.

1534. CLEMENT VII (*Julius de Medicis*), pope, died. It was in consequence of his refusing to ratify the acts of Henry VIII, and the issuing of a bull of excommunication against that monarch, that England was separated from the Roman church.

1635. ADRIAN METIUS died; a learned Dutch mathematician and author.

1722. WILLIAM MASSIEU died; a French writer, much admired, who after becoming blind met his death by a stroke of apoplexy.

1747. The leaden coffin of the noted Dr. Sacheverel, and Sally Salisbury, with 150 others, stolen from the church.

1766. The dividends on East India stock advanced in England from 6 to 10 per cent, in consequence of the success of lord Clive.

1776. Congress appointed Benj. Franklin, Silas Dean and Thomas Jefferson, commissioners to the court of France. They were the first persons appointed by the United States to act in the capacity of ministers plenipotentiary, but as the country had not yet been acknowledged by any power, they were designated by the humble title of commissioners.

1777. The British army under lord Howe entered Philadelphia. Washington's army lay at Skippack creek, 18 miles distant from the city.

1780. The advance of Cornwallis' army, consisting of Tarleton's legion, engaged the Americans at Charlotte court house, under Col. Davis.

1789. EDMUND RANDOLPH commissioned the first attorney-general of the United States.

1799. Zurich, in Switzerland taken by the French under Massena, and Lavater, while occupied in the streets assisting the distressed, received a shot in the side, of which he ultimately died. (Jan. 2.)

1811. A well 400 feet deep and 5 in diameter, exhibiting a fine specimen of ancient masonry, was discovered in the keep at Dover castle.

1812. GEORGE FREDERICK COOKE, an eminent English tragedian, died at New York, aged 57.

1812. The Russian army under Essen, entered Miltau, the French and Prussians under Macdonald, having previously evacuated it, leaving behind a vast quantity of provisions, and the whole mass of pelisses, which were the sum of the requisition upon Courland, and of vast importance to an army in so cold a region.

1813. Privateer schooner Saratoga, of New York, 10 guns and 116 men, captured by boarding, British packet ship Morgiana, 18 guns, 50 men, off Surinam.

1814. American privateer brig, Gen. Armstrong, attacked in Fayal roads, a neutral port, by the boats of three British ships. They were twice beaten off and several of the boats sunk. Capt. Reid was obliged to scuttle his vessel, and the British commander threatened to burn the town if she was not delivered up. American loss, 2 killed, 7 wounded; British loss, 120 killed, 130 wounded.

1815. Treaty of peace and alliance signed at Paris between the emperors of Austria, Russia and Prussia.

1822. JOHN OWEN, an eminent English divine, died. He was one of the originators of the British Foreign Bible Society, to whose establishment and extension he devoted his life with the greatest zeal.

1828. A monument erected at Charlestown, Mass., to the memory of John Harvard, founder of Harvard college, 190 years after his death. It is a monolith, 15 feet high and 4 feet square at the bottom; the expense of which was defrayed by a contribution of one dollar from each of the graduates of the college.

1828. John G. C. Brainard, an American poet of considerable note, died, aged 32.

1842. Richard Riker, for many years recorder of the city of New York, died, aged 69. He was a gentleman of the old school, and much respected.

1847. The valuable library of the royal society of Icelandic literature in Copenhagen was destroyed by fire. More than 2,000 unpublished MSS. were consumed.

1854. The French police organized at Paris on the plan of that of London; the number to be 2,900, to do duty day and night, under charge of two commissioners, at an annual cost of about $1,200,000.

1855. The corner stone of the Masonic hall laid in Philadelphia with ceremony, over 4,000 masons marching in procession.

SEPTEMBER 27.

489. Theodoric, the Ostrogoth, defeated Odoacer, king of Italy, near Verona, who fled to Ravenna.

642. Sigebert, king of the East-Angles, assassinated. He was a munificent prince, noted as the founder of churches, schools and monasteries; supposed to have been the founder of Cambridge university.

1087. William II, surnamed Rufus, crowned at Westminster. In his reign Malcolm of Scotland was slain at Alnwich by the earl of Northumberland, whose spear piercing Malcolm's eye, gave to Northumberland the surname of Percy (p' eye).

1106. Battle before the walls of Tinchebrai, between the two brothers, Henry of England and Robert of Normandy, in which the latter was defeated and imprisoned nearly thirty years.

1415. The reduction of Harfleur, in France, by Henry V, of England; he rifled the town of its affluent stores, and dismissed the inhabitants with five pennies.

1540. Pope Paul III confirmed the order of the Jesuits, and authorized its establishment.

1563. Nicholas Episcopius (or rather Bishop), a celebrated printer of Basil, died at London, where he had fled from France to avoid persecution.

1566. Mark Jerome Vida, a celebrated Latin poet, died, aged 96. Many tributes of praise have been paid to his genius and merits.

1615. Arabella Stuart died insane in the Tower of London.

1700. Innocent XII (*Anthony Pignatelli*), pope, died. He protested against the system adopted by his predecessors, of paying particular honors to the relations of the popes, and condemned Fenelon's *Maxims of the Saints*.

1715. Thomas Burnet, a learned and ingenious English writer, died; author of the *Sacred Theory of the Earth*, which was very popular.

1719. George Smalridge, bishop of Bristol, died; an elegant theological writer.

1729. Great fire in Constantinople, which consumed 12,000 houses. 7000 persons are said to have perished in the flames.

1730. Lawrence Eusden, an English divine and poet, died. He was preferred to the laureateship.

1731. A gang of felons, 130 in number, were taken from Newgate, and put aboard a ship to be transported to America, to colonize the country. In the next century they sent their felons to Botany Bay, and their paupers to America, several shiploads having been discharged on the coast, entirely destitute, directly from poorhouses.

1736. Rene Duguay Trouin died; a celebrated French admiral, who displayed the greatest skill, united with the most consummate wisdom.

1741. Dominic Perennin died at Pekin; a French Jesuit, who was sent on a mission to China, where he was well received by the emperor.

1743. The first act of governor Clinton was to dissolve the legislature, and issue writs the same day for convening another.

1749. John Sargent, a noted missionary among the Indians, died at Stockbridge.

1751. A mosaic pavement and other relics of Roman antiquity discovered at Avenches, in the canton of Bern.

1759. Isaac Maddox, bishop of Worcester, died. He rose to preferment from a very low station in life, and was conspicuous for the many benevolent institutions which he promoted.

1772. James Brindley died; an extraordinary mechanical genius, particularly successful in planning and executing projects of internal navigation, which were done without any drawing or model.

1775. Edward Lovibond died; an English poet of considerable talents.

1777. The American frigate Delaware, 32 guns, anchored within 500 yards of the unfinished British batteries at Philadelphia and seconded by another frigate and some smaller vessels commenced a heavy fire upon them. She grounded and struck her colors, and the other vessels were compelled to retire.

1782. HYDER ALLY defeated by the British under sir Eyre Coote.

1783. STEPHEN BEZOUT died; a French writer on mathematics, navigation and algebra.

1799. Rome, the eternal city, surrendered to the British.

1805. WILLIAM MOULTRIE, a distinguished officer of the revolution, died. He was a member of congress at the commencement of the war, and made a brave defence of Sullivan's island in 1776.

1810. Battle of Sierra Busaco, in Portugal; the French under Massena defeated with a loss of about 5000, by the British and Portuguese under Wellington, who lost 1000.

1811. Battle of Aldea de Ponte; the French under Marmont attacked the British general Cole; but were unsuccessful.

1811. BONAPARTE established a maritime conscription in the Hanseatic towns.

1812. Americans under colonel Newman defeated a party of Indians under king Paine, who was killed. A second attack was made by 200 Indians to recover his body, in which they succeeded, but with great loss.

1813. Americans under general Harrison landed in Canada, and in one hour took possession of Malden, evacuated by general Proctor after burning the fort and stores.

1832. Battle of Galeneta, in Mexico, between the partisans of general Montezuma, 5000 men, and those of Bustamente, 3500, in which the former were completely defeated.

1833. Deaths at Tampico, Mexico, by cholera and yellow fever, during the season to this date 2000, out of a population of 5200.

1833. RAMMOHUN ROY, a learned Bramin, died in England. He published works in Sanscrit, Arabic, Persian, Bengalee and English, and was acquainted with ten languages.

1835. GERVAISE DE LA RUE, a celebrated French antiquary, died at a very great age. He wrote various learned works relating to the poetry and literature of the middle ages.

1841. NICHOLAS BROWN, a wealthy and munificent merchant, died at Providence, aged 73. He graduated in 1786 at the college of Rhode Island, of which institution he afterwards became the benefactor, in consequence of which its name was changed in 1804 to Brown University.

1848. MICHAEL HOFFMAN, an American statesman, died at Brooklyn, N. Y., aged 60. He was a physician in Herkimer co., and was long a member of congress from that district. He held other offices, and was noted for stern integrity.

1848. Count LAMBERG, the imperial commissioner, appointed to take chief command in Hungary, was slain by the Hungarian population at Pesth, where he had recently arrived.

1849. Great fire at Owego, N. Y., which destroyed the place so completely that but three shops were left standing.

1849. The fortress of Comorn, in Hungary, one of the strongest in Europe, taken by the Austrains.

1854. The steamer Arctic, captain Luce, when about 50 miles distant from cape Race, came in collision with the French screw steamer Vesta, in a dense fog, by which her bows were stove in, and she filled and sunk in about five hours. The Arctic had 410 persons on board, including the crew, of which 22 passengers and 65 of the crew were saved, and 212 passengers and 110 of the crew were lost; of the 61 women and 19 children on board, not one was saved. The conduct of the crew is said to have been selfish, mutinous and dastardly.

1855. JOHN ADAMSON died at New-Castle-upon-Tyne, aged 68; an English author of a work upon the life and writings of Camoens, and devoted to literary and scientific pursuits, and to antiquarian research.

SEPTEMBER 28.

490 B. C. Battle of Marathon is said to have occurred at the full of the moon on this Julian day. (See Aug. 6.)

351. Battle of Murza, on the Drave, in which the emperor Constantius defeated Magnentius in a most desperate conflict.

855. LOTHAIRE I, emperor of Germany, died. He seized the person of his father, and confined him in a monastery, and waged a bloody war with his brother, during which 100,000 men fell in a single battle.

1014. Nearly the whole of Flanders was immersed by a storm.

1066. WILLIAM OF NORMANDY (*the Conqueror*) arrived at the coast of England, on his memorable invasion.

1197. HENRY VI, emperor of Germany, died. He had the meanness to detain Richard of England, who had been shipwrecked on the coast of Dalmatia. With the large sum of money obtained for the ransom of his illustrious captive he made war against Sicily, and plundered and desolated the country.

1396. Battle of Nicopolis; the Turks under Bajazet achieved a famous victory over the king of Hungary. The greater part of an army of 100,000 confederate Christians were slain, or driven into the Danube, and Sigismund, escaping by the river and the Black sea, returned after a long circuit to his exhausted kingdom. A *gout* preserved Europe.

1567. John Staininger died at Braunau, in Austria; he was remarkable for the length of his beard, which reached to the ground.

1582. George Buchanan, a learned Scottish historian, has his death placed on this day by several authorities. (See Feb. 28.)

1618. Joshua Sylvester, an English poet, died.

1667. James Golius, an eminent Dutch orientalist, died. He traveled into several countries, and published some learned works.

1670. The London royal exchange, having been rebuilt, was opened.

1687. The Venetians under Morosini bombarded Athens, when a bomb fired the powder magazine kept by the Turks in the Parthenon. This noble building, which had stood nearly 2000 years, and was then nearly perfect, was by this calamity reduced to a ruin, and with it perished the ever memorable remains of the genius of Phidias. In attempting to remove the chariot of victory, which stood on the west pediment of the Parthenon, it fell and was dashed to pieces. Though the ancient edifices of the Greeks' suffered much from the Turks, the siege of Morosini did infinitely more damage to the Parthenon than it had sustained during the 2000 years of its existence. A fine basso relievo, supposed to belong to the frieze of the building, has lately been discovered.

1708. The French defeated near Wynnendale, yet by means of 2000 horsemen each with a bag of powder behind him, contrived to throw supplies into Lisle.

1728. Henry Brown obtained a patent from the English government for an improvement in the manufacture of cannon.

1742. Hugh Boulter, primate of Ireland, died, leaving behind him an enviable reputation. During the great scarcity of 1741 in Ireland, 2500 persons were daily supported at his expense.

1742. John Baptist Massillon, a famous French ecclesiastic, died. His name has almost become proverbial as a powerful master of eloquence. (18th ?)

1763. John Byrom, an English poet, died. He was also famous as the inventor of a system of short hand writing.

1768. The commissioners of the customs having solicited the presence of a regular force in Boston, two British regiments, escorted by seven armed vessels, arrived from Halifax and took up quarters in the town.

1776. Cadwallader Colden, lieutenant-governor of New York under the British dynasty, died, aged 88. He was a Scottish physician; his publications were numerous in botany, medicine, history and philosophy.

1777. General Wayne, with a detachment of 1500 men, on the left wing of the British army, was surprised and defeated with a loss of about 300.

1778. A regiment of American cavalry stationed at Tappan on the Hudson river, was surprised while sleeping, by the British under general Gray, who rushed upon them with their bayonets, and giving them no quarter, 67 were killed, wounded and taken.

1779. The famed Houghton collection of pictures (lord Walpole's) was purchased by the empress of Russia, and shipped for Petersburg.

1780. Americans under general Marion attacked a party of tories at Black Mingo; several were killed and others taken.

1789. Thomas Day, an eminent English writer and eloquent speaker, killed by a fall from his horse.

1791. The French ships Recherche and L'Esperance under admiral D'Entrecasteaux and Hunon Kermadoc, sailed from Brest in search of La Perouse. The expedition was extremely unfortunate, both commanders dying on the voyage, and the ships and crews were seized by the Dutch governor at Java.

1795. The British under general Stuart took Jaffnapatam in the East Indies.

1803. Ralph Griffiths, an English writer, died; known in the republic of letters as the projector of the *Monthly Review*, begun 1749, and which became so popular as to procure him a comfortable independence, upon which he retired.

1839. William Dunlap, a portrait and historical painter, died at New York, aged 74. He also wrote several valuable historical works, besides biographies and dramas.

1842. Captain Enoch Preble, a skillful seaman and eminent philanthropist, died at Portland, Me.

1843. Shobal L. Vai Clevenger, an American sculptor of high reputation, died at sea, aged 31.

1848. Edward R. Tyler, editor of the *New Englander*, died in New Haven, Ct. aged 48. He was for many years engaged with ability and usefulness as a congregational minister at Middletown and at Colebrook.

1850. The North Star, which was sent out from England in 1849, arrived at Spithead on her return. She was imprisoned in the ice from Oct. 1, 1849 to Aug. 1, 1850.

1852. WILLIAM FINDEN, a celebrated English engraver, died at London of heart disease, aged 66.

1853. A deputation from the protestant alliance waited upon lord Clarendon to state the case of Miss Cunningham, arrested at Lucca for distributing an Italian version of the *Bible* and *Pilgrim's Progress*, and to urge the government to procure her immediate liberation.

1853. The ship Annie Jane, from Liverpool, was driven on the Barva island, one of the Hebrides, and of 450 passengers 348 were drowned.

1854. The United States sloop of war Albany, James T. Gerry, commander, sailed from Aspinwall and was never more heard of.

1854. GEORGE FIELD, an English philosopher, died, aged 77; well known for his success in the application of science to the arts.

SEPTEMBER 29.

1066. WILLIAM (*the Conqueror*) landed in England, at Pevensey, in Sussex, and made the conquest of the country, and revolutionized its institutions.

1399. RICHARD II resigned his right to the crown, publicly acknowledging his incapacity to reign.

1494. COLUMBUS met with his brother Bartholomew at the town of Isabella in the West Indies, after a separation of fourteen years, during which the latter had paid an unsuccessful visit to the court of England.

1513. Fall of Tournay, in Belgium, which closed the campaign of the English under Henry VIII.

1526. Rome taken by the partisans of cardinal Calonna, when the palace of the Vatican, the church of St. Peter, and the pope's ministers and servants were plundered.

1560. GUSTAVUS VASA, king of Sweden, died. He recovered the kingdom from the Danish yoke, and established the protestant religion in his country.

1564. The earl of LEICESTER was ennobled, on which occasion it is said coaches were first brought to London.

1604. The act of king JAMES against *witches* went into operation.

1622. CONRAD VORSTIUS died; a learned German protestant divine and polemical writer, who succeeded Arminius in the divinity chair at Leyden.

1720. The great *South sea bubble*, a scheme for paying off the national debt of England, burst and involved an incredible number of people in utter ruin. The capital of the company was about $168,-000,000.

1759. Volcano of Jorullo, in Mexico, by which a mountain was thrown up in a single night to the height of 1224 feet in the midst of a large plain. The volcano is surrounded by numerous conical hills, from which smoke is continually issuing.

1760. The astronomer MASKELYNE was sent by the English government to St. Helena, and Mr. MASON to Bencoolen, to observe the transit of Venus on the 6th June, 1761. Three astronomers were sent from France for a like purpose.

1764. Battle between the Irish White boys and English troops near Kilkenny. Several killed on both sides.

1772. JOHN BENJAMIN MICHAELIS, one of the minor German poets, died in his 25th year.

1778. American frigate Raleigh, after gallantly engaging two British men of war some time, ran on shore, and was captured.

1791. The national assembly of France dissolved itself.

1793. FRANCIS ROZIER, an eminent French agriculturist, killed by a bomb at Lyons, which fell on his bed, while he was asleep. He published a work on agriculture in 10 volumes quarto.

1793. The French convention decreed the incorporation with the French republic of all the Austrian possessions on the west side of the Rhine.

1809. CHARLES FRANCIS DUPUIS, a French philosopher, died; having filled several important professorships and civil offices. He published a work on the origin of all modes of religious worship, in 3 volumes quarto.

1813. The Americans under general HARRISON took possession of Sandwich and Detroit.

1825. DANIEL SHAYS, noted for the part he took in the celebrated rebellion of 1786, which bears his name, died at Sparta, aged 84. He had been an officer in the revolutionary army, and enjoyed a pension.

1827. Captains PARRY and FRANKLIN reached the admiralty, from the arctic and overland American expeditions. The latitude made by Parry was 82¾ degrees.

1833. FERDINAND VII, king of Spain, died, and was buried with great pomp in the Escurial. His reign was a period of disaster to Spain, during which she sank rapidly into insignificance as a European kingdom. He received a superior education, but was a superstitious and weak minded man, the victim or the tool of artful ministers or bigoted priests. His first wife, an accomplished woman, was poisoned in 1806, the second died 1808; the third 1829; the fourth by whom alone he had issue, outlived him. It was during his reign that the inquisition was re-established and six years afterwards permanently abolished. In his latter years he seemed to take little or no interest in public affairs, but continued to reign, nominally, goaded on one side by the liberals, and on the other by the absolutists, or apostolical party as they called themselves, who were for ruling by terror.

1840. JOHN MARSHALL, author of various works on manufactures, commerce and statistics, died at London, aged 58.

1843. RICHARD HARLAN, a noted writer on natural history, died of apoplexy at New Orleans. His parents were among the first quaker families that emigrated from England.

1848. GEORGE F. RUXTON, a British officer, died at St. Louis, Mo., aged 38 (Allen says 88). He wrote the series in *Blackwood's Magazine* on life in the far west, and also a book of adventures in Mexico and the Rocky mountains.

1854. Marshal DE SAINT ARNAUD, a commander of the French forces in the Crimea, died at Balaclava, aged 53. He served in Algeria, and conducted an expedition against the Kabyles; also executed the *coup d'état* for Louis Napoleon. He is represented as a man of deep religious impressions, was courted by the clergy, and had been much engaged in building chapels.

1855. The Russians, 35,000 strong, attacked Kars, gained possession of the redoubt four times, and were four times driven back, and at length retreated, leaving 4,000 dead in the trenches and around the city. Loss of the garrison about 800.

SEPTEMBER 30.

610 B. C. A total eclipse of the sun, foretold by the skill of Thales, which determined the battle between the Lydians and Medes.

480 B. C. The Carthagenians were overthrown at Gelo by Himera.

480 B. C. The great victory of Themistocles over the Persians at Salamis, is also placed upon this day by some authorities. (See Aug. 20.)

61 B. C. The great and unrivaled triumph of Pompey, which continued two days, for having concluded a war of 30 years, in which he had vanquished, slain and captured 2,183,000 men; sunk or taken 846 ships; reduced under the empire 1538 towers and fortresses, and subdued all the countries between the Mœotian lake and the Red sea. The golden vine of Aristobulus, king of the Jews, a little chapel of pearl consecrated to the Muses, surmounted by a sun-dial, and twenty kings and princes, with a string of barbaric gods, were among the trophies which preceded the car of the conqueror.

420. JEROME, one of the fathers of the Christian church, died. He was famous for his eloquence, his virtue and his extensive learning.

788. ABDURRAHMAN I, founder of the dynasty of Beni Umeggah in Spain, died, aged 62. On the defeat of his house in the east, he subdued Spain and founded a dynasty which continued 300 years.

1139. A revolt from king Stephen in favor of the empress Maud, daughter of Henry I, of England.

1283. DAVID, brother of Llewellyn of Wales, executed by Edward as a traitor. This opened the way for the title of prince of Wales to the princes of England.

1291. RODOLPH I, emperor of Germany, died. He added Austria, Styria and Carniola to his dominions by conquest.

1400. OWEN GLENDOWER erected his standard as prince of Wales.

1435. ISABELLA of Bavaria, queen of France, died. She was a licentious and intriguing woman, who preferred the interests of England to the prosperity of her own country.

1517. LUTHER maintained his ninety-five propositions at Wittemberg.

1572. Pope PIUS V died. He issued the famous bull, absolving the subjects of queen Elizabeth from their allegiance, but the lioness of England heeded not such bellowings.

1628. FULK GREVILLE, lord Brooke, assassinated; a literary character of considerable celebrity in the reigns of Elizabeth and James I.

1630. ISAAC JOHNSON, one of the principal founders of the city of Boston, died. He was the first magistrate who died in the colony, and was buried on his own lot. The first burying place in Boston was laid out around his grave. The spot is now built upon, being bounded by Tremont, Cornhill, Court and School streets.

1632. THOMAS ALLEN died; an Englishman, eminent for his knowledge of mathematics and philosophy.

1659. JUAN DE PALAFOX, an illustrious Spanish ecclesiastic, died. He was appointed bishop of Los Angelos in America, where he displayed an admirable character.

1662. A rencontre between the French and Spanish ambassadors, at which many were killed. The contest was precedency.

1682. Colonel THOMAS DONGAN preferred by the duke of York to the government of his province of New York in America.

1707. John Reinhold de Palkul, a Livonian gentleman, who resented the oppression his country suffered from the Swedes, was basely broken on the wheel, by order of Charles XII.

1719. Bernard Renau D'Elisagaray, a French mathematician, died. He obtained a pension for his improvements in the construction of ships.

1747. Thomas Hall died, aged 6 years; four feet six inches high, and weighing upwards of seven stone. He died as if of extreme old age.

1761. John Dollond died; an eminent English optician and inventor of the achromatic telescope.

1770. George Whitefield, one of the founders of the sect of the methodists, died at Newburyport, Mass., aged 55. He visited America seven times, and preached in all parts of the Atlantic states with great power and success.

1775. British ship Rose, captain Wallace, cannonaded Stonington. The town was considerably injured, 2 persons killed and a loaded schooner and two sloops carried off.

1779. Colonel John White, with 6 volunteers and his servant, captured a company of 141 British, posted on the Ogeeche river, and brought them safe to an American post 25 miles distant. He also took 5 vessels, one of 12 and another of 10 guns. The exploit was effected by kindling large fires round the post, and making such other parade as demonstrated a large encampment.

1781. Yorktown invested by the American and French armies under Washington and Rochambeau, assisted by the French fleet under count d'Estaing.

1789. Nova Castella and several villages in Italy destroyed by an earthquake.

1790. General Harmer with 320 regulars and 1133 militia, defeated the Indians at Miami village, in Ohio, but with the loss of 141 killed and 31 wounded. The loss of the Indians was estimated at about 100 killed and 300 wigwams burnt. They also destroyed 20,000 barrels of corn, and a great quantity of other provisions.

1793. A furious riot occurred at Bristol, England, on the erection of a new toll gate on the bridge. Several persons were killed and wounded by the military. But the tumults were allayed by the Bristoleans' agreeing to raise the money some other way than by toll.

1795. George Butt, an English prelate and poet, died.

1797. The state road having been completed, the first stage started from fort Schuyler (Utica) and arrived at Geneva in the afternoon of the third day, with four passengers.

1811. Thomas Percy, a learned English prelate, died. Besides his *Reliques of Ancient English Poetry*, a valuable work, he published translations from the Chinese, Icelandic and Hebrew languages.

1824. William Windham Sadler, an English æronaut, killed by a fall from his balloon. The accident occurred by the car being driven against the chimney in the descent. He was a skillful chemist and engineer, cut off at the early age of 28.

1826. Joseph Peter Picot Cloriviere, director of the monastery in Georgetown, D. C., died. He was a royalist of France, and the reputed inventor of the infernal machine for which he had to leave his country.

1826. A magazine of powder near Ostend, containing 1,300 barrels, or about 60 tons, exploded, damaging many houses by the concussion, and destroyed several lives.

1830. Independence of the South American republics acknowledged by France.

1849. Silas Jenison, for several years governor of Vermont, died at Shoreham, an esteemed and valuable citizen.

1849. Mrs. Maury died in Virginia; an artist, linguist and authoress, known in the United States by her *Statesmen of America*.

1849. Robert Goldsborough, for many years president of the medical and chirurgical society of Maryland, died at Centreville.

OCTOBER.

OCTOBER 1.

2016 B. C. The call of Abraham is placed by Eusebius upon this day, A. M. 1921. The Cæsarian era used by the Syrians, commenced from the same Julian day, first of their month Tisri, B. C. 48.

325. CONSTANTINE ordered that those criminals hitherto employed by a barbarious custom in the gladiator shows, should be sent to the mines.

829. MICHAEL II (*the Stammerer*), emperor of the East, died. He was of obscure origin, and dragged from prison to the throne on the death of Leo. He compelled the Christians to observe the sabbath and other holy days of the Jewish law.

1240. Dedication of the cathedral church of St. Paul's, at London.

1500. JOHN ALCOCK, a distinguished English prelate, died. His great learning recommended him to preferment, and he was appointed president of Wales and chancellor of England. He founded Jesus college.

1621. By an act of the British parliament, no tobacco was to be imported after this date but from Virginia and the Somer isles, and none to be planted in England. The merchant was to receive no more than eight, and the retailer ten shillings the pound, but they who sold by the pipe might make the most they could!

1664. Articles of capitulation were agreed to between the English under sir Robert Carr, and the Dutch and Swedes, on Delaware bay and river; which completed the subjection of New Netherland to the British crown.

1670. JAQUES DE PAULMIER, an eminent French physician, died. Besides some prose works he wrote poems in several European languages.

1684. Review of the marines at Putney heath, which were first established in England this year.

1684. PETER CORNEILLE, the great French poet, died. His dramas were eminently successful, and his poems are among the sublimest effusions of the French muse.

1728. Mr. PHILIPSE, speaker of the New York assembly, held a treaty with the Six Nations at Albany, and renewed the ancient covenant. He gave them great presents, and engaged them in the defence of Oswego.

1746. Battle of Roucoux, between the allies, who were defeated with the loss of 5,000 men and prince Tingray killed, and the French, whose loss was nearly equal.

1748. Action between the British fleet, admiral Knowles, 7 ships, and the Spanish fleet, under Spinola, 6 ships and a frigate. The latter were defeated with the loss of two ships.

1756. Battle of Lowositz, between the king of Prussia and the Austrians under Braun. Each army sustained a loss of about 2,500.

1761. Schweidnitz, a strong fortress in Silesia taken from the Prussians by a skillful coup-de-main of the Austrians under Laudohn. The governor and about 3,000 men were made prisoners.

1768. British troops landed at Boston from Halifax, and one regiment was quartered at Faneuil hall. (Sept. 30. ?)

1777. ALEXANDER SUMOROKOF, founder of the Russian theatre, died at Moscow. He wrote a number of plays and historical works.

1778. WILLIAM BUTLER made a successful expedition against the Indian towns, and returned to Schoharie on the 16th.

1795. ROBERT BAKEWELL, an eminent English agriculturist and cattle breeder, died. His improvements in the breeds of domestic animals were unprecedented; a single ram selling for nearly $4,000.

1796. JAMES FORDYCE died; a popular and eloquent Scottish preacher, who left behind him several excellent moral and religious works.

1799. JOHN WILLIAM BRUGUIERES, an eminent French botanist and mineralogist, died.

1800. Treaty of St. Ildefonso, by which Spain ceded Louisiana to France.

1802. Ratification of a treaty between Bonaparte and the bey of Tripoli, effected by Col. Sebastiana, who the same day concluded a treaty between the Swedes and the bey, by which the Swedes engaged to pay 150,000 piasters for the captives, and an annuity of 8,000 more.

1807. The first steam boat sailed from New York to Albany. It was 130 feet in length, called the Clermont, and made 5 miles an hour.

1831. BLACKHOOF, a chief of the Shawnee tribe of Indians, died at Wapaghkonnetto, aged 114. He was at the defeats of Braddock, St. Clair, Harmer and Crawford, and probably the last survivor of the former disaster.

1838. The law abolishing imprisonment for debt in England went into operation.

1841. The Chinese island of Chusan recaptured by the British forces under sir H. Gough, with the loss of only 2 killed and 24 wounded.

1842. The war in Affghanistan closed by the capture of Ghuznee and Cabul, and the withdrawal of the British troops.

1847. A telescopic comet was discovered by a lady of Nantucket, Mass., in the constellation Cepheus.

1847. A violent tornado unroofed the steam factory in Portsmouth, N. H.; weight not less than 70,000 pounds. It separated into 3 sections, one falling within 100 feet, another 200, the rafters coming down endways and sinking 4 feet in the earth; the largest section weighing 30,000 pounds, was carried 300 feet.

1848. JAMES BIDDLE, United States commodore, died at Philadelphia, aged 65.

1849. Hudson river rail road opened to Peekskill.

1850. Whitehall and Rutland rail road opened.

1853. The Turkish divan resolved on the most vigorous measures against Russia, and the sultan signed the declaration of war, and permitted the allied fleets to pass the Dardanelles.

1854. The shores around the harbor of Vera Cruz strewn with an immense number of dead fish, supposed to have been killed by the gas evolved in some submarine volcanic eruption.

1854. The steamer Yankee Blade from San Francisco to Panama, struck a reef of rocks, and was wrecked. Although there were 800 passengers on board, all but 15 were saved; $153,000 of specie was lost.

OCTOBER 2.

331 B. C. DARIUS, king of Persia defeated by Alexander at Arbela, losing 300,000 men. This defeat of Darius decided the fate of Persia.

322 B. C. ARISTOTELES, the celebrated Greek philosopher, died. It is said that he threw himself into the Euripus because he could not satisfactorily explain the cause of the tides. He was the first person on record who was possessed of a private library.

1346. The Scots under king DAVID took Liddel castle in Cumberland, after a siege of six days, beheaded the governor, plundered the abbey of Lanercrost, and then directed his march towards Durham.

1394. RICHARD II having made a truce with France, landed in Ireland with a large force; he succeeded in reducing the natives to obedience, who in the absence of the English barons and knights, had intercepted and refused the revenues. The country was divided, at that time, into different kingdoms.

1410. The heroic earl of WARWICK was *retained* under covenant by prince Henry, at a *wage* of 250 marks. Whenever he should be in the king's court, he was to have four esquires and six yeomen with him, and diet for them all; and the prince should have a third part of what he acquired in battle, and the third of the thirds of what should be taken by Richard the earl's men at arms.

1629. PETER BERULLE, a French bishop, distinguished for his learning and exemplary piety and virtues, died at the altar while performing mass.

1661. BARTEN HOLYDAY, an English divine, died; known as the author of several literary and theological works.

1693. CHARLES PATIN, a distinguished French physician, died at Padua. At the age of 14 he maintained a disputation for five hours in Greek and Latin, and took the degree of master of arts.

1710. The conquest of Port Royal, or Annapolis Royal completed by the British and colonial forces under colonel Nicholson.

1711. Memorable fire in Boston, which swept down Cornhill, and other streets, and was attended with loss of life and limb.

1724. FRANCIS TIMOLEON DE CHOISI, a French ecclesiastic, died. He was sent by the French government to convert the emperor of Siam, who had expressed a wish to embrace Christianity. He wrote several historical and other works.

1746. The French East India squadron destroyed at Madras by a hurricane.

1780. JOHN ANDRE, a British officer, hanged at Tappan, New York, as a spy, while Arnold made his escape to the British head quarters, where he received £10,000 and a commission in the army, as a reward for his treachery.

1780. A violent hurricane in the West Indies, which devastated the island of Jamaica. In one town of 200 inhabitants, not a vestige of man, beast or habitation was left. Twelve men of war were lost, and in most of them their entire crews perished.

1782. CHARLES LEE, a major-general in the revolutionary army, died. He was an officer in the British army at the age of 11, and distinguished himself in 1762 under Burgoyne in Portugal. He joined the American army at the outbreak of the war, but was suspended after the battle of Monmouth, for some improper conduct.

1786. AUGUSTUS KEPPEL, a distinguished British admiral, died. He accompanied Anson in his voyage round the world.

1801. AUGUSTUS FERDINAND VELTHEIM, an eminent German mineralogist, died; he published several valuable scientific works.

1803. SAMUEL ADAMS, governor of Massachusetts, died, aged 82; distinguished as a writer and a patriot, and for his influence in forwarding the American revolution; of stern integrity, dignified manners and great suavity of temper. He and John Hancock were proscribed when a pardon was offered to every one else.

1812. British cannonaded Ogdensburg.

1841. JAMES FRASER, the founder and publisher of *Fraser's Magazine*, died in London; when literature lost an earnest supporter, and literary men a generous patron.

1842. The United States sloop-of-war Concord was lost on the rocks in the Mozambique channel, and one or two of the crew perished.

1842. WILLIAM ELLERY CHANNING, an eminent unitarian preacher of Boston, died at Bennington, Vt. He was born 1780, and ordained 1803 at the Federal street church. He was honored throughout Christendom, for his learning and eloquence.

1846. BENJAMIN WATERHOUSE, an eminent American botanist, died, aged 92. He completed his studies in Europe, and graduated at Leyden; on his return home was elected to a professorship in Harvard university.

1848. HENRY BURBECK, an officer of the revolution, died at New London, aged 94. He retired from the public service in 1815, having spent 38 years in almost incessant activity.

OCTOBER 3.

382. The Goths submitted to the Roman empire under Theodosius.

1003. ABDULMALIK IBN SHOHEYD executed; a poet and historian of Cordova, who for his military services was made governor of Toledo. He wrote a history of the Spanish Arabs in 100 vols.; was put to death by order of Hisham II.

1187. Jerusalem acquired by the arms of Saladin the Turk.

1405. HENRY IV granted to sir John Stanley the isle of Man in the Irish sea.

1573. The Spaniards abandoned the famous siege of Leyden; during which Kanava obtained celebrity for her patriotism.

1594. Battle of Glenlivet, in which the forces of James V under the duke of Argyle were defeated by the Scotch.

1689. QUIRINUS KUHLMAN, a German fanatic, burnt at Moscow for some seditious prophecies.

1690. ROBERT BARCLAY, an eminent Scottish writer, of the society of quakers, died. His *Apology for the Quakers* is esteemed the standard of their doctrines, and has been published in many of the European languages.

1691. The English and Irish war ended by the fall of Limerick.

1733. CHARLES ST. YVES, a skillful French oculist, died; author of a valuable treatise on the diseases of the eye.

1751. JAMES LOGAN died; a learned quaker, who accompanied Penn to America in 1699, and assisted in the government of the colony. His library contained 3,000 volumes, and was the largest in the colony; he understood several ancient and modern languages, and his writings were republished in Europe.

1768. FERDINAND WARNER, an English divine, died; celebrated for his theological, biographical, historical and medical writings.

1793. The last two males natives of Pitcairn's island murdered by the three survivors of the British ship Bounty.

1794. The fortress of Juliers opened its gates to the victorious French, on the famous victory over the Austrians on the banks of the Roer, which delivered all the German provinces on the west side of the Rhine into the hands of the republicans.

1803. VICTOR ALFIERI, an eminent Italian dramatic poet, died. Within less than seven years he produced fourteen dramas, besides various other works in prose and verse, including a translation of Sallust. His posthumous works were published in 13 vols., two of which are occupied by his auto-biography.

1811. First newspaper issued at Buffalo, N. Y.

1813. Battle of Wartenburg, a small town on the left bank of the Elbe, between the Prussian army of 24,000 under Blucher, and the French under Bertrand, of 20,000. The former made a memorable march from Bautzen to the Elbe. The river was wide and rapid, and the pontoons were thrown over under the fire of the French, who were defeated with much loss.

1815. Juan Diez Porlier, a celebrated Spanish partisan general, hanged at Corunna. He distinguished himself at the battle of Trafalgar, and rendered the king important services in the war with the French.

1826. Levin Augustus Benningsen, a German military officer of great abilities, died. He entered the Russian service, and was in several important campaigns against the French.

1838. Blackhawk (*Muck-ker-ta-me-scheck-ker-kirk*), a celebrated Indian chief and warrior, died at his camp on the river Des Moines.

1843. Lewis F. Linn, senator of the United States from Missouri, died at St. Genevieve.

1848. The emperor of Austria dissolved the Hungarian diet, proclaimed martial law for that province, and appointed the Ban Jellachich to the supreme government.

1852. A severe gale swept over the Atlantic ocean and English channel, causing a great destruction of property and loss of life.

1853. James Talmadge died in New York, aged 75. He was lieutenant-governor of New York in 1824, and devoted the last twenty years of his life to the American institute as its president.

1855. Robert Adair, a British ambassador to various courts of Europe, died at London, aged 92.

OCTOBER 4.

633. Edwin (*the Great*), king of Britain, killed at Hatfield. He wielded the sovereignty 17 years, during which the *cumulus* of heathenism began to break up in large masses.

1226. Francis, of Assisi, died; founder of the order of Franciscans, or gray friars.

1253. Robert Grosseteste, an English prelate, died. He wrote several voluminous works, possessed great learning, and a clear and vigorous intellect.

1434. Cosmo de Medici reentered Florence from exile, and was received with the most extravagant demonstrations of public joy, and became, in fact, the prince of the state, accumulated enormous wealth, and lived in regal magnificence.

1489. John Wesselius, a Dutch ecclesiastic, died. His learning and abilities were so great, that the pope sent for him to Rome, and offered him what he should ask for. He merely requested a Greek and Hebrew Bible in the Vatican.

1535. Was published the first edition of the *Whole Bible* in the English language, being the translation of Miles Coverdale.

1590. James Cujacius, an eminent French lawyer, died. He rose from obscurity, and by his indefatigable industry, without the assistance of a master, perfected himself in Greek and Latin literature, and particularly in civil law. His works were published at Paris, in 10 vols. folio.

1595. John Maitland, lord Thirlstane, an eminent statesman under James VI of Scotland, died.

1609. Henry Hudson, having explored the river to where it divided itself into several branches, returned to its mouth on this day—put to sea with all sails set, to report the tidings of his valuable discovery.

1660. Francis Albano, an eminent Italian painter, died at Bologna, aged 82. He particularly excelled in expressing the delineations of female and infantine beauty; his pieces are dispersed in the cabinets of Europe, and highly esteemed.

1691. Louis Abelly died; a French ecclesiastic, who devoted himself principally to literature, and left numerous works behind him.

1692. Charles Fleetwood, lord deputy under Cromwell, died, aged 74. He married the widow of the gloomy Ireton; hesitating to declare at once for the king, he was allowed to end his days in obscurity.

1693. Battle near Marseilles, in France, between the French under Catinat, and the allies under Victor Amadeus and Eugene of Savoy. The allies were defeated, with the loss of all their artillery, and 8,000 men; the duke of Schomberg was mortally wounded.

1704. Alexander Selkirk, a Scottish mariner, put ashore on the desert island of Juan Fernandez, by orders of captain Pradling, with whom he had a quarrel. He was allowed a fowling piece and ammunition, and a very few necessaries. In this desolate situation he continued three years, subsisting on goats, fish and fruits.

1743. John Baptist du Halde, a learned French Jesuit, died. He is the author of a description of China and Tartary, a valuable work, compiled from the curious and interesting observations of the missionaries of his fraternity.

1744. Henry Carey, an English dramatic poet, and music composer, died by suicide. Besides his poems, he wrote *Chrononhotonthologos*, to ridicule the style of tragedy then in vogue, and produced the *Dragon of Wantley*, as a burlesque on Italian opera.

1777. Battle of Germantown, in which the Americans were defeated, with the loss of 200 killed, 600 wounded, and 400 taken. British loss, killed and wounded, 600. The disastrous termination of this affair, was owing to the darkness of the day, which embarrassed the operations of the Americans.

1780. The ships Resolution and Discovery, the circumnavigating ships which sailed under Cook and Clerke, returned, but without either of their original commanders. Both were dead.

1790. ANN LETTS died, at South river, N. J., aged 107.

1794. Battle of Maciejowice, in Poland; the forces under Kosciusko overthrown.

1795. The Parisians attacked the national convention, on account of the re-election of two-thirds of the members of that body. They were repulsed by the troops under Bonaparte, who now first signalized himself. About 8,000 of the citizens were killed.

1799. Brunnen, in Switzerland, taken from the French by the Russians under Suwarrow. This affair, however, terminated the progress of the invaders.

1806. SAMUEL HORSLEY, a learned English prelate, died. He engaged in a sectarian controversy with Priestley.

1812. Ogdensburgh attacked by the British, who were repulsed.

1812. American entrenched camp of Col. Newman attacked by the Indians, who were repulsed, with the loss of 30 warriors, among them three principal chiefs and their young king.

1813. American general HARRISON attacked by the Indians, at Chatham, whom he repulsed, and pursued four miles. He took on this occasion 2,000 stand of arms, a quantity of clothing, and several cannon; also three vessels laden with munitions.

1814. SAMUEL JACKSON PRATT, a once popular English novelist and miscellaneous writer, died.

1815. CHRISTOPHER PHILIP OBERKAMPF died; founder of the manufactory of printed linens at Jouy, and of the cotton manufacture of Essonne, in France. He commenced a small business under great disadvantages, and in a short time collected a population of 1500 in a spot which had been almost a desert. His manufactures became of so much importance to the country, that the king granted him letters of nobility, and a statue was decreed him by the council-general, a mark of generosity which he declined.

1821. JOHN RENNIE died; a celebrated Scottish civil engineer and mechanist. The canals, bridges, and other public works in England, attest his abilities.

1830. YORK, count von Wartenburg, a Prussian field-marshal, died. He was one of the most distinguished generals in the wars against Napoleon.

1830. The independence of Belgium declared by the central committee at Brussels: "The provinces of Belgium, violently separated from Holland, shall constitute an independent state."

1833. RICHARD HEBER died; an Englishman of talents and learning, distinguished for his zeal in collecting books, a business which he followed assiduously during the last thirty years of his life. He left immense collections of rare and valuable works in various languages, in various cities in Europe.

1835. Third centenary, or three hundredth year from the printing of the first English Bible, that of Coverdale, generally celebrated in the different churches and chapels in England. This Bible, as appears from the colophon, was finished on this day, 1535.

1835. TELESFORO DE TRUEBE Y COSIA, a Spanish dramatist, died at Paris, aged 30. He resided principally in England, where he produced several dramas and novels. He wrote dramas in English, Spanish, and French, which were successfully produced at the several national theatres.

1851. EMANUEL GODOY (*Prince of Peace*), minister of Charles VI and VII of Spain, died at Paris, in the 87th year of his age.

1853. The Great Republic, a mammoth clipper of 4000 tons, and the largest merchant vessel in the world, was launched at East Boston, Mass.

1854. The greater part of the town of Memel, a Prussian seaport, was destroyed by fire, including its churches, custom-house, bank, and court-houses; loss estimated at $5,000,000.

OCTOBER 5.

678. JUSTIN II, emperor of the east, died. He was a weak prince, but had a wife to govern him and the empire with ability.

610. PHOCAS, a Chalcedonian noble who seized on the empire of the east by the murder of the emperor Maurice and his children, beheaded by Heraclius, governor of Africa, who conspired against him.

1056. HENRY III, emperor of Germany, died. After making war against Poland, Hungary and Bohemia, he passed into Italy, expelled three popes, and was crowned by a fourth.

1540. ELIAS EOBANUS died; an elegant German scholar and good poet.

1555. EDWARD WATTON, an English physician, died. He took his decree at Padua and practiced with great success in London. He is said to have been the first who paid particular attention to natural history.

1571. CLAUDE D'ESPENCE, an eloquent French ecclesiastic, died.

1582. The Gregorian, or *new style*, commenced in Spain, Portugal and part of Italy, this day being accounted the 15th.

1675. Springfield, Mass., attacked by the Indians. The Springfield Indians had so resolutely resisted the persuasions of Philip to join his exterminating expeditions, that the inhabitants felt the greatest security. They were not aware of any defection, till news was received from Windsor that 300 of Philip's Indians were concealed in their fort. The timely arrival of forces from the neighboring towns alone saved the village from entire destruction.

1690. Sir WILLIAM PHIPPS arrived before Quebec with a British force. He summoned the place on the following day, but the French governor, count Frontenac, refused to surrender; the fleet being dispersed in a storm, the expedition failed in consequence.

1710. An expedition of British and provincials appeared before Port Royal, in Canada, with 5 frigates and a bomb ketch. The force being equal to its reduction, Subcrease, the French governor, only waited the compliment of a few shot and shells as a decent pretence for surrender, when the place fell into new hands, and was called Annapolis in honor of the queen.

1733. *Zenger's Weekly Journal* (2d paper at New York), was issued.

1740. JOHN PHILIP BARATIER, a German youth of most extraordinary genius, died at the age of 20. At the age of 4, besides his native language, he spoke French and Latin; at 6 Greek; at 8 Hebrew. He acquired also various branches of learning, and prepared a large work on Egyptian antiquities.

1759. Battle of St. Francis, an Indian village on the St. Lawrence, in lower Canada. Innumerable expeditions had been fitted out from this place to massacre and plunder the English settlements in New England, and the village was enriched by the scalps taken at those times. Major Rogers, an intrepid soldier, with 200 rangers, was despatched by general Amherst from Crown point to destroy the place. After a fatiguing march of twenty-one days he came upon the village when the savages were holding a dance, and made a grand assault at break of day, after their own manner. The Indians were taken so unexpectedly that little resistance could be made.

1763. AUGUSTUS III, king of Poland, died.

1768. Great hurricane at Havana, destroyed 96 public edifices, and 4,048 houses; 1,000 inhabitants perished almost instantaneously.

1789. The estates general of France met at Versailles. This was indisputably the first day of the revolution, although the object of the meeting was to prevent such a catastrophe.

1803. The Constitution and Nautilus anchored in the bay of Tangiers, within half a mile of the circular battery, and amused the emperor of Morocco with the sound of their guns. This procured the release of the American consul, who had been confined to his house, guarded by two sentinels; and also the discharge of the American brig Hannah, of Salem, which had been wrongfully seized at Mogadore.

1804. A British squadron under Com. Moore attacked and captured Spanish ships La Medee 42 guns, La Fama 36 guns, and La Clara 36 guns; a frigate of 36 guns, La Marcedes, blew up, on board of which were several families returning to Spain, 280 men, and $811,000. On board the captured ships were found, besides a very valuable cargo of merchandise, 2,538,885 dollars, 3,593 bars tin, and 774 pigs copper.

1805. CHARLES CORNWALLIS, governor-general of India, died. Although overthrown at Yorktown, his character for courage, prudence and sagacity was unaffected, and he was afterwards sent as civil and military governor to Ireland.

1813. Battle of the Thames; the combined British and Indian forces under Proctor and Tecumseh, defeated by the Americans under general Harrison. On this occasion the celebrated Tecumseh was slain, as was believed in a personal rencounter with colonel R. M. Johnson; the latter received five wounds in this battle. American loss 7 killed, 22 wounded.

1813. Action on lake Ontario between the American fleet under commodore Chauncey, and the British squadron; five schooners of the latter were captured, and one sloop burnt.

1821. CLAUDIUS JOHN RICH, a learned English orientalist, died at Shiraz, in Persia, a victim to his ardor in the pursuit of science. He wrote *Memoirs of Ancient Babylon*, whose ruins he explored with indefatigable industry. His manuscripts, coins and gems were purchased by government, and are deposited in the British Museum.

1825. BERNARD GERMAIN STEPHEN DE LACEPEDE, a French naturalist, died. He was unmolested during the reign of terror, and Bonaparte heaped honors upon him. He holds a high station among modern naturalists.

1835. HORTENSE EUGENIE, duchess of St. Leu and ex-queen of Holland, died. She was the daughter of Josephine by her first husband, and married Louis Bonaparte.

1839. Destructive fire in Philadelphia,

destroyed 52 buildings; said to have been the greatest fire ever known in Philadelphia.

1839. A fire at Aikin, S. C., destroyed 36 houses and stores, forming the whole business portion of the village.

1847. The first election of officers in Liberia, under the new constitution, took place. Gov. Roberts was chosen president of the republic.

1853. MAHLON DICKERSON, a New Jersey statesman, died, aged 83. He filled a great variety of public offices with distinguished ability.

1855. WILLIAM HENRY PERCY, a British rear admiral, died at London, aged 67.

1855. THOMAS LIVINGSTON MITCHELL, surveyor-general of New South Wales, died, aged 63. He surveyed the battle fields of the Peninsular war, in which he served, and was knighted in 1839 for his discoveries and surveys.

1855. Two asteroids, being the 36th and 37th, were discovered, one by Luther, at Bilk, the other by Goldsmith, in Prussia.

OCTOBER 6.

877. CHARLES II (*the Bald*), of France, poisoned. He succeeded to the French crown 840, and was elected emperor by the pope 875. The feudal government may be said to have begun under him.

1274. The English parliament restrained usury. The Jews in consequence were obliged to wear a badge.

1285. PHILIP III (*the Bold*), of France, died. He was proclaimed king while in Africa with his father on a crusade, where he defeated the Saracens, and concluded a truce with them for 10 years.

1470. HENRY VI, of England, released from the tower of London and again proclaimed king. He was imprisoned the second time in the following year and murdered.

1552. IVAN IV, czar of Russia, took the city of Kazan, and added that kingdom to his empire.

1713. *The Englishman* appeared, conducted by the same authors as *The Spectator*, but was more political in its character.

1748. The British under admiral Boscawen raised the siege of Pondicherry, in Hindostan, after a loss by battle and sickness of 1,065. Loss of the French garrison 200, and 50 sepoys.

1761. WILLIAM PITT, the British statesman, having resigned the ministry, a pension of £3,000 was settled upon him for three lives, and the title of baroness of Chatham conferred upon his wife.

1762. The British under admiral Cornish and general Draper, took Manilla, the capital of the Philippine islands, by storm. Several ships and a large quantity of military stores fell into their hands. The town was ransomed by four millions of dollars.

1767. FRANCIS WISE, an English divine and antiquary, died. His researches led to the publication of several learned works.

1777. The British under sir Henry Clinton, about 3,000 men, attacked and carried forts Clinton and Montgomery, defended by governor Clinton. The post having been designed principally to prevent the passing of ships, the works on the land side were incomplete and untenable, and were carried by the bayonet. Most of the garrison effected their escape, with the loss of 300; British lost about an equal number. Count Grabouski, a Polish nobleman in the American service, was killed.

1778. WILLIAM WORTHINGTON died; an English prelate and theological writer of merit.

1780. HENRY LAURENS, who had been taken on his passage from America to Holland, was committed to the tower of London for high treason. He was afterwards liberated.

1783. Treaty of peace between Great Britain and the United States proclaimed.

1789. LAFAYETTE preserved the royal family from the popular excitement. The king was then conducted to Paris, where he accepted the "declaration of the rights of man."

1794. British, general Graham, surrendered Guadaloupe by capitulation to the French.

1794. Fall of the *mountain party* in the French national convention.

1802. SIMON DE MAGISTRIS died at Rome; well known for his deep acquaintance with the Hebrew, Greek and Latin, and whose services to literature were liberally rewarded by the pope.

1813. Moravian town, on the river Thames, destroyed by the Americans under general Harrison, after which he marched to Detroit, where peace was negotiated with a number of vanquished tribes of Indians.

1821. ALEXANDER MURRAY, a distinguished naval officer, died. He fought in 13 battles in the army and navy during the war of the revolution. On the organization of the navy under the new government, he was one of the first officers recalled into service. To the highest firmness and resolution he united a remarkable mildness and serenity of temper.

1836. WILLIAM MARSDEN, a learned English orientalist, died. He published a dictionary and grammar of the Malayan language, and other works of acknowledged merit.

1839. Jesse Buel, an eminent agriculturist, died. He was several years member of the legislature and a candidate for governor of New York in 1836. He was also a practical printer, and had filled the office of printer to the state. He was a useful citizen, and highly esteemed in public and private life.

1841. A revolution in Mexico; Santa Anna entered the capital at the head of 10,000 men; displaced Bustamente, and established himself at the head of the government.

1843. James Leonard Cathcart died at Washington, aged 77. He entered the continental navy at an early age, was a midshipman during the revolution, and was captured by the Algerines and held eleven years in captivity. He turned his knowledge of that country to good account afterwards in the service of the government in quelling piracies, &c.

1848. Insurrection in Vienna; the emperor with his family left the city, escorted by a few troops.

1853. Simeon Greenleaf, a distinguished law teacher, died at Cambridge, Mass., aged 70. His law works attest his diligence and ability in his profession.

1857. Samuel Hueston, for many years publisher of the *Knickerbocker Magazine*, died in New York.

OCTOBER 7.

929. Charles III (*the Simple*), of France, died. His abilities were unequal to his station; he was defeated in battle by Hugh, and confined seven years in prison, in the castle of Peronne, where he died.

1492. The ship Nina, rigged with latteen sails and usually ahead of the others, supposing she had discovered land, hoisted her flag and fired a Lombardo. This was soon found to be an illusion; the insubordination broke forth among the crews, when Columbus, with the two Pinzons, commanders, was compelled to enter into an *agreement* with those murmurers, to return in case land was not discovered in three days.

1521. Date of king Henry VIII's diploma from the pope as Defender of the Faith, for his treatise *De Septem Sacramentis*.

1565. Thomas Chaloner, a noted English ambassador, died. He wrote a work on *The right ordering of the English Republic*, and has the honor of having discovered the first alum mines in England.

1571. Battle of Lepanto, a naval action between the Turks, and Venitians assisted by the Germans and Spaniards under Don John of Austria. The Turks were utterly defeated with the loss of 25,000 killed, 10,000 taken, and all their great commanders slain, and 200 galleys taken or destroyed. The Christians lost about 10,000 men. This was the greatest sea fight of modern times, and being the first signal victory achieved over the Turks, diffused the greatest joy over Christendom.

1577. George Gascoine, a celebrated English poet in the time of Elizabeth, died. He served with credit in the wars of the Low Countries; and wrote the first English comedy in prose.

1612. Giovanni Battista Guarini, a celebrated Italian poet, died. The *Pastor Fido* has immortalized his name.

1651. James Sirmond died; a French Jesuit and a voluminous theological writer.

1681. Nicholas Heinsius (*the Swan of Holland*), died. He was eminent as a statesman, poet and critic.

1708. Battle near Lesno, between 40,000 Russians under Peter the great, and 16,000 Swedes under Lewenhaupt, who was marching with men and supplies to relieve Charles XII. He was defeated after five engagements, which were fought in three days, and reached Charles with only 5,000 men. The Russians took 5,000 carriages, and much of the artillery and baggage.

1753. Sir Danvers Osborn arrived at New York from England, to supersede Clinton as governor of the province. (See Oct. 12.)

1759. Joseph Ames, a celebrated typographical historian, died. He was originally a ship chandler, who late in life took to the study of antiquities, and became secretary of the society of antiquaries.

1763. The king of France, viewing the extensive and valuable acquisitions in America secured by the treaty with Great Britain, granted letters patent under the great seal, to erect within the countries and islands ceded to him, four distinct and separate governments, namely, Quebec, East Florida, West Florida, and Granada.

1765. First congress of American colonies met at New York.

1777. Second battle of Stillwater, which was an attempt of the British to secure a retreat to the lakes. Darkness put an end to the action, after the Americans had gained decisive advantages. A great number of the enemy were killed; 200 taken, including several officers of distinction; 9 cannons and the encampment of a German brigade, with all their equipage. The loss of the Americans was inconsiderable. British general Frazer and lieutenant-colonel Breyman were killed.

1780. Battle of King's mountain, South Carolina, in which 300 British were killed and wounded, and 800 prisoners, and 1500 stand of excellent arms taken. Maj.

Ferguson, who commanded the British, was killed, gallantly defending his post.

1787. HENRY MELCHIOR MUEHLENBERG died; pastor of the first Lutheran church in Pennsylvania, and distinguished for his learning.

1788. JOHN BROWN, an English physician, died; known as the founder of the Brunonian system of medicine, which classes all diseases under two heads, those of deficient and those of redundant excitement.

1792. GEORGE MASON, a distinguished Virginia statesman, died at his domain of Gunston hall.

1794. ANTOINE JOSEPH GORSAS, a Girondist, guillotined at Paris. He was a school master, a man of letters, and the editor of a paper, through which he became one of the first instigators of the revolution, and actively promoted some of its important events.

1794. Bois-le-duc, one of the strongest bulwarks of the famous Dutch barrier along the left bank of the Meuse, surrendered to the French revolutionary army; by which several other fortresses were hemmed in and rendered useless.

1795. JOHN GEORGE ZIMMERMAN, a Swiss philosopher, died at Hanover, where he was first physician to his Brittanic majesty. His work on *Solitude* is a popular book in our own language.

1796. THOMAS REID, professor of moral philosophy at Glasgow, died, aged 89; highly distinguished as a mathematician and metaphysician.

1807. BONAPARTE called for a second conscription of 80,000 men for this year.

1810. Coimbra in Portugal, held by the French, was attacked by the British under colonel Trant and carried. Trant took 80 officers and 5,000 men prisoners, mostly sick and wounded.

1812. Battle of the Moskwa. The French army of 150,000 under Napoleon was opposed by a Russian army of about the same number, under Kutusoff. The attack began early in the morning and continued until late in the afternoon, when the Russian army retreated, no pursuit being made by the French; while the field of battle was strewed with 50,000 dead and dying. The Russians acknowledged a loss of 25,000, among whom was Bagration.

1840. WILLIAM I, king of the Netherlands, published a proclamation announcing his voluntary abdication of the throne in favor of his son William II. He is said to have retired with a private fortune of nearly forty-three millions of dollars, and abdicated in consequence of his determination to marry the countess d'Oultremont, a lady of the Roman catholic faith.

1841. FREDERICK JOHN, lord Monson, died, aged 32; a patron and amateur of art, a lover of literature and science, and a truly benevolent and public spirited man. A journal of his *Tour in Germany* was privately printed in 1839, and some beautiful views of the passes of the Tyrol were drawn on stone from his sketches.

1841. Revolutionary movement in Spain in favor of Christina and absolute government. By the prompt movement of the regent Espartero the insurrection was entirely quelled, and general Diego Leon was executed.

1849. EDGAR A. POE, favorably known as an American poet and magazine writer, died at Baltimore, aged 37.

1849. LOUIS BATTHYANYI, prime minister of Hungary, was shot at Pesth, at the sole urgency of general Haynau.

1850. Disunion meetings were held at Natchez and Yazoo city, at both of which the disorganizing resolutions were opposed and voted down.

1854. CALEB BUTLER died, aged 78; principally known by his history of the town of Groton, Mass.

OCTOBER 8.

66. CESTIUS, the Syrian prefect, in his fatal retreat, was defeated by the Jews at the pass of Bethhoran. Nero received this disastrous news at Achaia, and called in Vespasian.

451. Fourth œcumenical council assembled at Chalcedon, where the heretic Eutyches was finally condemned.

622. MAHOMET made his public entry into Medina. He was mounted on a she camel, and an umbrella shaded his reverend shoulders.

1200. JOHN, king of England, and his *new* queen, Isabella, were inaugurated. The devil was to be released at that year's close, said the *lipticians* on the canon.

1202. The Venetian crusade sailed, under Boniface, of Montferrat.

1635. JOHN WINTHROP, son of the governor of Massachusetts, arrived from England with a commission from the patentees as "governor of the river Connecticut, and places thereto adjoining," bringing men, ordnance, ammunition, and £2000 sterling for the erection of a fort.

1636. JOHN EVERARD, better known by his bibliographical name, Johannes Secundus, a Dutch *Latin* poet, died. His works have gone through many editions, and the *Kisses of Johannes Secundus* have been translated into various languages. He also distinguished himself by his skill in painting, sculpture, and engraving.

1684. GERAUD DE CORDEMOI died; a

French academician, and a great partisan of Descartes' systems.

1729. RICHARD BLACKMORE, an English physician, died. He was an indefatigable writer, and has left a great number of works, theological, poetical, and medical.

1744. JOHN BALCHEN, a celebrated English admiral, perished at sea, in the Victory man-of-war, 110 guns, and 1100 seamen, all of whom were lost.

1754. HENRY FIELDING, an eminent English novelist, died, aged 48.

1755. The remains of Braddock's army, in 33 transports, passed the city of New York on their way to winter quarters at Albany.

1767. BURCHARD CHRISTOPHER DE MUNICH died; a German who learned the art of war under Eugene and Marlborough, and distinguished himself in the service of Peter I of Russia.

1774. Congress resolved to support Massachusetts, if the acts of parliament were attempted to be carried into execution by force. The general court of Massachusetts met at Salem on the same day, although general Gage had ordered them not to assemble, resolved themselves into a provincial congress, and chose John Hancock president.

1785. L'EVESQUE DE BURIGNY, a French author, died, aged 94. He wrote a work on the authority of the pope, a learned history of pagan philosophy, and several other works, historical and biographical.

1785. *The Lounger* appeared at Edinburgh, conducted principally by Henry Mackenzie.

1791. A jury at Sudberry, England, not being able to agree, oppressed by hunger, broke open the doors and went home.

1792. PIETRO ANTONIO CREVENNA, an Italian bibliographer, died. He collected a choice library, which he sold by auction in 1790. The learned catalogues of his books, prepared by himself and others, have given to the works which belonged to him, great value, in the eyes of amateurs, and the catalogues themselves have bibliographical authority.

1793. JOHN HANCOCK, the master spirit of the American revolution, died. He was president of the congress which issued the declaration of independence, and his name stands out in bold relief on that document.

1793. Lyons, in France, surrendered to the republicans, and a most terrible massacre of the inhabitants ensued. The convention decreed that the walls should be razed, and Lyons called La ville affranchie.

1795. ANDREW KIPPIS, a very celebrated English biographer, died. His connection with the publication of the *Biographia Britannica*, will carry down his name with distinguished reputation to posterity.

1809. JAMES ELPHINSTONE, a Scottish grammarian, died. He undertook the reformation of English orthography by spelling words as they are pronounced.

1820. HENRY CHRISTOPHE, king of Hayti, shot. He was a slave, and served in the American war. His activity in the revolution of the slaves in the island of St. Domingo, led to his elevation.

1822. Eruption of mount Galongoon, in the island of Java. It commenced at 2 o'clock in the afternoon of a fine day, by a loud explosion, which was followed by a thick cloud, that wrapped the whole country in darkness, while immense columns of mud, boiling hot, and mixed with burning brimstone, were projected from the mountain like a water spout, with such prodigious violence, that large quantities fell at the distance of 40 miles. The destruction was at its height at 4 o'clock, and had ceased at 5, having in the short space of three hours, laid a fruitful and thickly peopled country under a crust of boiling mud, in some places to the depth of sixty feet. Five millions coffee trees were destroyed, 87 canals, numerous rice fields, 114 villages, and upwards of 4000 inhabitants. The scene presented a bluish, half-liquid waste, where bodies of men, women and children, partly boiled and partly burned, were strewed about in every variety of death. It was followed by a rain storm of four days' duration, which inundated the country, when another eruption took place, more violent than the first.

1822. The first boats passed from the west and the north, through the Erie and Champlain canals, into the tide waters of the Hudson at Albany, amidst the acclamations of thousands of spectators.

1831. Great earthquake in South America. The town of Arica was utterly ruined, and the shock was felt along the coast, including seven degrees of latitude, shaking to its centre the immense breadth of the main Cordillera. It was attended by a violent vertical movement of the earth, during about 70 seconds, which threw down or shattered the houses, and in some cases pieces were detached from the middle of walls, leaving the rest of the edifice uninjured.

1832. OTHO proclaimed and installed king of restored Greece, at the palace of Preysing, in Bavaria.

1837. CHARLES FOURIER, founder of the system of social and industrial reform which bears his name, died at Paris.

1841. JOHANN HEINRICH DANNECKER, the Nestor of German sculptors, died at Stuttgardt, aged 82.

1848. The populace of Vienna, which had

been in a state of insubordination two days, became calm, and the emperor was invited to return.

1851. The Hudson river rail road was opened throughout, from New York to Albany.

1853. Thomas Childs, one of the bravest and most distinguished officers in the United States army, died at Tampa bay.

1854. Gideon Tomlinson, a Connecticut statesman, died, aged 74.

1854. The steam boat E. K. Collins, from Saut St. Marie to Cleveland, took fire on the lake and was burned, by which 23 persons lost their lives.

1855. Samuel Dickinson Hubbard, sometime post master general of the United States, died at Middletown, Ct., aged 55.

1855. The grand jury in New York city returned indictments against several city officers, for corruption and malversation in office.

OCTOBER 9.

1047. Clement II, pope, died. He was a Saxon, elected the year previous, and distinguished for his zeal against Simony.

1192. King Richard of England embarked from Palestine in a single ship for Europe.

1253. Robert Greathead, bishop of Lincoln, and a learned and voluminous writer, died.

1326. Hugh Spencer, a favorite of Edward II, hanged at Bristol, which city he defended against the forces of queen Isabella.

1555. Justus Jonas died; a learned coadjutor of Luther and the other reformers, and author of a *Defence of the Marriage of the Priests*, and other works.

1563. Gabriel Fallopius, a celebrated Italian physician and anatomist, died at Padua. He possessed great powers of mind, which he cultivated by intense application.

1642. The first commencement was held at Harvard college, when nine candidates took the degree of A. B.

1646. The whole order of English bishops abolished by an ordinance of parliament.

1665. Gov. Stuyvesant submitted to the states general his report in relation to the surrender of New York to the English.

1682. Henry Blount died; an English traveler, who made the tour of Europe and part of Asia, and published an account of his travels on his return.

1688. Claude Perrault, a distinguished French physician and architect, died.

1690. John Maynard, an eminent English lawyer, died; celebrated for his eloquence, integrity and public spirit.

1705. John Christopher Wagenseil died; a learned German polemical writer, and professor of history and oriental languages at Altorf.

1707. A fleet of English merchantmen attacked off the Lizard point; the Devonshire man-of-war blown up.

1711. The British fleet returning from its unsuccessful expedition against Canada, arrived at Portsmouth, N. H., when in addition to their other misfortunes, the Edgar 70 gun ship blew up, having on board 400 men besides many persons who came to visit their friends.

1718. Richard Cumberland, a learned English divine and mathematician, died.

1733. Seven hundred British troops withdrawn from Gibraltar to defend the planters of Jamaica from their runaway slaves.

1745. Ath surrendered to the French after a severe and destructive bombardment. This gave France the command of Flanders.

1747. David Brinard, an eminent American missionary among the Indians, died at Northampton, a victim to his extreme mortification and inextinguishable zeal for the success of his mission. He rode about 4,000 miles in 1744, on pastoral duties.

1747. Jonas Surrington died near Bergen in Norway, aged 159, retaining the perfect use of his faculties to the last.

1759. The architect Smeaton finished the Eddystone light house; not an accident occurred to sadden the joy.

1760. Berlin in Prussia, taken and sacked by the Russians and Austrians.

1772. Christian Jacobson Drackenburg died at Aarhus, Denmark, aged 146; "a celebrated and well-known character."

1779. The people of Manchester rioted on account of Arkwright's machinery for spinning.

1779. The French and Americans, about 4,500 men under count d'Estaing and Gen. Lincoln, made an unsuccessful assault upon Savannah, and were compelled to retreat with considerable loss. The brave count Pulaski was mortally wounded in this affair. (Holmes says Oct. 11.)

1781. The French and Americans opened their batteries upon the British at Yorktown.

1791. Abraham J. Lansing, the original proprietor of Lansingburgh, N. Y., died, aged 72, at his seat in that town.

1803. Deluge in the island of Madeira; the city of Funchal, with all its inhabitants, was swept into the ocean, leaving the rocky basis of the island bare. But one human being escaped, which was an infant. The event is supposed to have been occasioned by a water spout, which had burst against the side of a mountain, and discharged itself down the declivities upon the city.

1805. Battle of Guntzburg; the Austrians under prince Ferdinand, defeated by the French under Bonaparte, with the loss of 2,000 prisoners, besides killed and wounded.

1806. Battle of Schleitz in Saxony; 10,000 Prussians defeated by Bernadotte; being the recommencement of hostilities between the French and Prussians.

1809. Great storm at Boston and vicinity, by which a vast number of vessels were lost.

1812. Lieut. ELLIOTT, of the United States navy, with 50 volunteers, attacked and carried two British vessels, the Caledonia and Detroit, on lake Erie. One of these was burnt, with a cargo valued at $200,000.

1813. British broke up their cantonments before fort George, and marched rapidly for Burlington bay.

1822. RICHARD EARLOM, an English engraver of great skill, died. His flower pieces are highly valued.

1826. CHARLES MILLS, an eminent English historian, died. His histories of the crusades, of chivalry and of Muhammedanism, are valuable acquisitions to literature.

1831. CAPO D'ISTRIAS, president of Greece, assassinated by one of his own countrymen.

1836. JAMES SAUMAREZ, an English admiral, died; distinguished in the naval history of his country, and eminent for his private virtues.

1842. JOSHUA STOW, sometime chief judge in Middlesex county court, Conn., died at Middletown.

1845. DAVID BAILLIE WARDEN died at Paris, aged 67. He was a native of Ireland, was sometime consul of the United States at Paris, where he collected a valuable library of American history, was a member of the French academy, and a man of letters and varied learning.

1847. Sweden abolished slavery in the island of St. Bartholomew and all her dependencies.

1849. TIMOTHY DWIGHT SPRAGUE, editor of the *American Literary Magazine*, died at Andover, Mass., aged 30.

1849. A riot in Philadelphia, between a set of whites called killers, and some negroes. It was continued the next day, until put down. Four houses were burned, 4 persons killed, and 11 wounded.

1854. WILLIAM DARBY, an eminent American geographer and statistician, died at Washington, aged 79.

1855. A treaty was ratified between Japan and Great Britain, by admiral sir James Stirling.

OCTOBER 10.

432 B. C. Battle of Potidæa, on its revolt from the Athenians, in which Socrates and Alcibiades were nobly distinguished for their prowess and friendship. In that year Anaxagoras, Phidias and Aspasia were prosecuted, the first for his impiety.

324. CONSTANTIUS, the second and favorite son of Constantine, was installed by his father *cæsar* of the Gallic provinces.

1571. "The field of Tulliangus was stricken" between Adam Gordon and Arthur Forbes, brother of lord Forbes, where the said Arthur was slain, with sundry others of his kin; on the other side John Gordon of Buckie, with divers hurt on both sides. A Scottish foray.

1582. The new style adopted in France, this day being made the 20th.

1615. Battle between Champlain and the Iroquois, in western New York.

1632. THOMAS ALLEN died; an Englishman illustrious for his knowledge of mathematics and philosophy. He published, among other works, the second and third books of Ptolemy on the judgment of the stars.

1706. PAUL PEZRON, a learned Frenchman, died. He occupied himself with the study of the Greek and Latin historians, and in tracing the origin of the language of the Goths, and made up a new system of chronology.

1710. DAVID GREGORY, an eminent Scottish mathematician, died. He displayed great powers in the elements of optics, and physical and geometrical astronomy, improving the discoveries of others by new and elegant demonstrations. He proposed to publish all the works of the ancient mathematicians, but did not live to finish the series.

1742. Sixty persons killed by the falling of the roof of the church in Fearn Russhire, in the time of worship.

1744. JOHN HENRY SCHULZE, a German physician, died; professor of medicine at Halle, and author of a history of medicine from the creation to the year of Rome 535.

1747. JOHN POTTER, primate of England, died. Besides theological and other works he wrote *Antiquities of Greece*, two vols., which have passed through several editions.

1747. British fleet of 14 ships, admiral Hawke, engaged the French fleet under M. de Letender, and captured 7 ships of the line, and a 50 gun ship.

1772. WILLIAM WILKIE died; a Scottish

divine and poet, and professor of philosophy at St. Andrews.

1774. Battle between the Americans, 1400 men, from Virginia, under colonel Lewis, and about 600 Ohio Indians. The Indians made the attack; 400 of the Virginians were killed and 100 wounded.

1775. British general GAGE sailed from Boston for Great Britain, and the command of the army devolved upon general Howe.

1775. LOUIS NICHOLAS VICTOR MUYS, minister of war and. marshal of France, died. He signalized himself at several important engagements, which led to his promotion.

1780. Hurricane in the West Indies, which continued about 48 hours. Several towns were leveled with the dust, and many thousand persons lost their lives. Several hundred vessels in the different ports were driven to sea or dashed to pieces.

1783. HENRY BROOKE, an eminent Irish writer, died. His tragedy of Gustavus Vasa, though forbidden the stage for its tone of freedom and liberty, met with a rapid sale.

1787. The Prussians under the duke of Brunswick took the city of Amsterdam by capitulation. It is said that before the surrender water sold for an English shilling a quart.

1792. Lord MULGRAVE died at Liege, aged 48. He was captain Phipps in the British service, and was celebrated for his voyage towards the North pole.

1794. Battle of Fersen, or Macekowice, between the Russians and the Poles under Kosciusko. The contest was bloody and fatal to the patriots. The victory was wavering, and the expected reinforcements not appearing, Kosciusko at the head of his principal officers, made a furious charge and plunged into the midst of the Russians. He had three horses killed under him, and finally fell covered with wounds, and was captured.

1797. CARTER BRAXTON died; a signer of the declaration of independence from Virginia.

1800. Explosion of an infernal machine intended to have destroyed Bonaparte, then first consul, as he proceeded to the opera. The coachman being intoxicated, drove faster than was his custom, and the engine exploded half a minute after the carriage had passed, killed 20 persons, and wounded 53, and shattered the windows on both sides of the street.

1806. JEREMIAH JAMES OBERLIN, an eminent archæologist of Strasburg, died. He was an accurate and industrious scholar, and besides various original works, published good editions of several of the Latin classics.

1806. Sanguinary battle at the bridge of Saalfeld in Saxony; the French under Suchet defeated the Prussians, and their general, prince Ferdinand Louis, was killed.

1812. Veraya, in Russia, garrisoned by the French, taken by the Russians under Dorochoff; 500 French were killed and 400 captured. The standard of Westphalia and 500 muskets were taken, and the place having been made a depot for provisions, great quantities fell into the hands of the Russians.

1824. FRANCIS BALTHAZAR SOLVYNS, a celebrated Dutch painter and engraver, died. He spent 15 years in Hindostan, studying the languages, manners and customs of the east, on which he published a work in folio.

1832. JAMES STEPHEN, an English statesman and philanthropist, died. He suggested and arranged the whole system of continental blockade, which for a long time occasioned great embarrassment to Bonaparte.

1834. THOMAS SAY, an eminent naturalist, died at New Harmony. He early abandoned his mercantile pursuits to devote himself to the study of nature. Perhaps no man has done more to make known the zoology of this country than he.

1836. MARTHA RANDOLPH, last surviving daughter of Thomas Jefferson, a lady of distinguished talents and virtues, died in Albemarle county, Va., aged 70.

1840. The Egyptian army under Ibrahim Pacha and Soliman Pacha defeated near Beyrout, in Syria, by the allied British and Turkish troops under Selim Pacha, com. Napier and colonel Hodges, with the loss of 7000 men.

1841. JOHN BAYLEY, a noted justice of the King's bench and baron of the exchequer, died in England, aged 78.

1841. CARL FREDERICH SCHINKEL, the most eminent architect in Prussia, died at Berlin, aged 61.

1849. A memorial for the annexation of Canada to the United States, received in five hours the signatures of 300 merchants, land owners, and professional men, at Montreal.

1849. The *initial point* of the boundary line between the United States and Mexico settled, and a monument with inscriptions erected in north latitude 32° 31′ 59″.58, and in longitude 119° 35′ 0″.15 west from Greenwich.

1854. GORDON DRUMMOND, a British officer who saw much service in the war with the United States in 1812, died in London, aged 82. He commanded the British troops at the battle of Niagara.

OCTOBER 11.

1347. Louis V, emperor of Germany, killed by a fall from his horse. This event prevented a new civil war, which threatened the happiness of Germany.

1441. The government of Venice prohibited the printing and vending of playing cards by foreigners in those dominions.

1492. Columbus discovered the Bahama islands, his first discovery of land.

1521. Leo X issued a decree, conferring upon Henry VIII of England the title of Defender of the Faith.

1531. Ulricus Zuinglius, an able and zealous Swiss reformer, killed in a skirmish with his popish opponents.

1611. John Cowell, an English lawyer and antiquary, died; author of some works on the law.

1612. The remains of Mary, queen of Scots, removed to a vault in Henry VIII's chapel, where a most magnificent monument was erected to her memory.

1614. Charter granted to "the United New Netherland company," giving it the exclusive right to visit and trade with the countries in America, lying between the 40th and 45th degrees of north latitude. This country was now for the first time called New Netherland.

1643. John du Verger de Haurane died; an eminent French ecclesiastic, who formed a new system of faith, which becoming popular, drew upon him the resentment of Richelieu.

1698. Treaty between England, France and Holland, for the partition of Spain.

1698. William Molyneux, an eminent Irish mathematician, died. He was ardently devoted to science, founded the philosophical society of Ireland, and invented a telescope dial.

1702. Battle of Vigo; the British admiral Rooke attacked the French fleet and Spanish batteries. The French destroyed 8 ships, and the British burnt 6 galleons richly laden with goods and plate, valued at 14,000,000 pieces of eight; they also razed the fortifications, and brought off 10 ships of war and 11 galleons, with 7,000,000 pieces of eight.

1705. William Amontons, an eminent French mechanic, died. He suggested some improvements in barometers and thermometers, and invented a method of communicating intelligence, which has since been adopted under the name of telegraph.

1709. Mons taken by the allies.

1727. Edward Colston, an English philanthropist, died. He acquired wealth by commerce with Spain, with which he endowed numerous charitable institutions.

1736. Great storm on the river Ganges; 300,000 lives are supposed to have been lost.

1750. John Baptist Joseph Languet died; the celebrated vicar of St. Sulpice at Paris, who refused all preferments, and devoted the revenues which he collected to the institution and support of judiciously planned charitable establishments.

1752. Thomas Stackhouse, a learned, pious but necessituous divine, died.

1776. The Americans under general Arnold attacked on lake Champlain by the British under captain Pringle. Arnold lost two gondolas taken and one blown up, and was forced to retreat, owing to the inferiority of his force.

1779. Several individuals who had voluntarily remained in King's bench prison, London, for the purpose of letting their rooms, were turned out.

1790. Henry Cullen, an eminent physician of Edinburgh, died.

1791. The bank of Providence, the first bank in Rhode Island, began to discount.

1797. Battle off Camperdown, between the British fleet, 17 vessels, admiral Duncan, and Dutch fleet, 23, admiral Winter. The Dutch were defeated with the loss of 9 ships.

1808. John Page, governor of Virginia, died; a patriot, statesman and philosopher.

1817. Andrew Pickens, a distinguished revolutionary officer, died, aged 78. He commenced his military career in the French war which terminated in 1763. He was one of those who indefatigably kept up the spirit of resistance in South Carolina, till the enemy was expelled.

1820. The printers of London went in grand procession to Brandenburgh house to present an address to queen Caroline. It was printed on white satin, and was a superior specimen of typographical skill.

1837. Samuel Wesley, a distinguished English musician, died. "His compositions are grand and masterly; his melodies sweet, varied and novel; his harmonies bold, imposing, unexpected and sublime; his resources boundless."

1841. William Liddiard, an admired and popular English writer in prose and verse, died at Clifton, aged 68.

1841. George Mairs, an eminent preacher of the Associate reformed presbyterian church, died at Argyle, N. Y., aged 81.

1846. Great hurricane in Havana, which began on the previous evening, wrecked or severely injured nearly 100 vessels, destroyed 1275 houses, and injured as many more.

1848. The Hungarian army advanced

to within six miles of Vienna; their videttes being visible from the city towers.

1855. The propeller Arctic and the barque Release, under command of Lieut. Hartstene, forming the arctic expedition in search of Dr. Kane and his companions, arrived in New York, bringing with them the objects of their search.

OCTOBER 12.

638. Honorius I, pope, died. He presided over the church with great zeal and wisdom.

1303. Boniface III (*Benedict Cajetan*), pope, died. His ambition and insolence were unbounded, and he hurled the thunders of the Vatican against the kings of France and Denmark; but the former despising his threats, had him seized.

1307. All the knights templars in France ordered to be arrested, and on the following day the grand master, the templars and all their possessions were seized.

1424. John de Troeznou Zisca, a famous Bohemian patriot, died. He was the formidable general of the Hussites, who undertook to avenge the death of their leader; he also defended his country against the emperor Sigismund, and performed prodigies of valor after he had lost both his eyes.

1428. The siege of Orleans commenced, memorable as one of the most extraordinary incidents in history.

1492. Columbus landed on the island of Guanahani, of which he had seen the first twinkling on the previous night; thus in the space of 36 days completing a voyage which he had been 20 years in projecting, which opened to Europeans a new world, which enlarged the empire of Spain, and stamped with immortality the name of Columbus.

1573. Great naval victory of the Dutch over the Spaniards.

1576. Maximilian II died. He was elected king of the Romans 1562, and afterwards succeeded his father as king of Hungary and Bohemia, and emperor of Germany.

1621. Peter Matthieu, a French historian, died. He was historiographer tot he king, and wrote the history of France, and of several of the French kings.

1646. Francis Bassompierre, marshal of France, died; a distinguished statesman, whom Richelieu confined 10 years in the Bastile, during which he wrote his own memoirs.

1649. The fall and massacre of Wexford under Oliver Cromwell.

1653. Humphrey Chetham, a great patron of learning and libraries, died, aged 73, at Mânchester, England, endowing the city with munificent bequests.

1711. King Charles III, of Spain, elected emperor of Germany at Frankfort, by the name of Charles IV.

1716. Ludolf Kuster, a learned German critic, died.

1753. Sir Danvers Osborne, who had arrived at New York on the 7th to succeed Clinton as governor of the province, was found in the morning suspended by the neck in the garden, and dead.

1764. Rene Michael Slodtz, an eminent French sculptor, died.

1793. St. Domingo ceded by its inhabitants to the British.

1798. British fleet, admiral Warren, intercepted the French fleet and captured several ships laden with troops and stores destined for Ireland. Theobald Wolfe Tone, the founder of the united Irishmen, was on board, and taken.

1822. The independence of Brazil, under don John, was proclaimed.

1834. Thos. S. Grimke, of South Carolina, died of an attack of cholera. He distinguished himself in a speech against the test oath of his native state.

1842. Bartlett Bennett, one of the early pioneers of Kentucky, and a baptist preacher, died at Cincinnati, aged 99.

1851. Lewis Warrington, an American commodore, died, aged 69. His services in the Tripoli war and the war of 1812 made his name familiar to the American people, as a brave, energetic and skillful captain.

1851. Samuel Beazley, a distinguished English architect died, aged 66. He was not only the designer of more theatres than any other modern architect, but also a dramatic compiler.

1855. General Walker took possession of Grenada, with a loss to the enemy of 15 killed and several wounded.

OCTOBER 13.

49. Tiberius Drusus Claudius, emperor of Rome, died of poison administered by his wife. He succeeded Caligula, and became contemptible for his vices and weakness.

409. Irruption of the Vandals into Spain, who, dividing her prolific territories, turned their swords into ploughshares.

643. Oswy, of Northumberland, and 10th king of Britain, ascended the throne. The great controversy for the celebration of Easter, was decided by him.

1164. The great council opened at Northampton, England, for the trial of Thomas Becket, by whose sentence he was placed at the king's mercy.

1269. The bones of Edward the Confessor enshrined in gold.

1417. GREGORY XII (*Angelo Corario*), pope, died, aged 92. He was elected during the schism of the west, while the opposite party supported Benedict XIII. They were both deposed, and another elected.

1503. THEODORE BEZA, a learned French protestant, died. He was professor of Greek at Lausanne, in Switzerland.

1515. Battle of Marignon, in Italy; the Swiss defeated by the French under Francis I.

1698. The French missionary GERBILLON, returned to Pekin from his eighth and last journey, from thence into Tartary, journals of all which are published in Du Halde's *History of China*.

1705. The parliament of Scotland convened for the last time.

1754. JACOB POWELL died at Stebbing, England. He weighed five hundred and sixty pounds. His body was five yards in circumference, and his limbs were in proportion. He had sixteen men to carry him to his grave.

1771. JOHN GILL, an eminent English Calvinistic divine, died. He was a learned orientalist and voluminous writer on theological subjects; his greatest work is a commentary on the Bible.

1777. Esopus, on the Hudson river, burnt by the British under general Vaughan; not a house escaped.

1782. Battle in Persia for the sovereignty, between Abdul Fatcan and Murat Kan, the lord regent. The latter and his three sons were slain, and Abdul caused himself to be proclaimed king.

1793. The allies under Wurmzer invested Landau, and carried the lines of Weissembourg; the French retreated with loss.

1797. BENJAMIN HAMMETT fined £1,000 sterling, for refusing the office of lord mayor of London.

1812. Battle of Queenston, in Canada; the Americans, under colonel Van Rensselaer, attacked and carried the heights and fort; but owing to the refusal of 1,200 militia to cross over to their support, and the arrival of British regulars and Indians from fort George, the Americans, to the number of 764, were obliged to surrender. General Brock was killed in this affair, and Van Rensselaer was wounded by four balls. American loss, 90 killed, 82 wounded.

1815. JOACHIM MURAT, king of Naples, shot. He was a soldier of fortune, who emerged from obscurity during the French revolution, became a distinguished general in the armies of France, married a sister of Napoleon, and was placed upon the throne of Naples.

1815. NAPOLEON BONAPARTE landed at St. Helena, a perpetual exile.

1822. ANTONIO CANOVA died; the most eminent sculptor of the age. His statues are in possession of the noble and the rich throughout Europe.

1828. VINCENT MONTI died; one of the most celebrated poets of modern Italy.

1836. JACOB SPENCER, a revolutionary pensioner, died at Washington, N. J., aged nearly 100. He had had seven wives, and left but one child living.

1845. DOUGLAS HOUGHTON, state geologist of Michigan, died, aged 36. He was prosecuting a combined geological and linear survey of the region near lake Superior, on a plan suggested by himself.

1845. W. K. ARMISTEAD, a general officer in the United States service, died at Upperville, Va., aged about 60. He had served long in the engineer department, and in 1840-41 had chief command in the campaign against the Florida Indians.

1846. Right honorable HENRY STEPHEN FOX, late her Britannic majesty's minister plenipotentiary to the United States, died at Washington, D. C. He was much respected as well for his prudence and urbane manners, as for his decision and diplomatic talent.

1847. A body of 200 German catholics met at the Tabernacle, in New York, and made a public and formal secession from the Romish church.

1853. TRISTRAM BURGESS, a Rhode Island statesman, died, aged 83. He stood in the front rank of the public men of his day.

1853. THOMAS KEMPER DAVIS died at Boston. He stood high in his profession as a lawyer, and having acquired a fortune, devoted himself to and became learned in English and classical literature.

1854. Howard college, at Marion, Ala., destroyed by fire.

OCTOBER 14.

1066. Battle of Hastings, and defeat of Harold by William of Normandy, which placed the latter upon the throne of England. The battle lasted from morning till sunset. William had three horses killed under him, and there fell about 15,000 Normans; but on the side of the vanquished, the loss was much greater, and included Harold and his two brothers, who were slain.

1066. The first earl created in England. Alfred in 920 used this word as king is now used.

1292. EDWARD I, of England, declared John Baliol king of Scotland.

1519. The Spaniards under Cortez entered without opposition the strong and populous city of Cholula, where a plot was laid for their destruction, but which resulted in a terrible massacre of the inhabitants.

1529. A placard appeared at Brussels, whereby all such as had any prohibited books in their custody, not brought forth to be burnt, should be put to death.

1537. JANE SEYMOUR, third queen of Henry VIII, died.

1644. Birthday of WILLIAM PENN, the first proprietor of Pennsylvania, son of admiral sir William Penn.

1645. Battle of Basing, in which Cromwell at the head of the parliamentary forces stormed and took, after an action of only three-quarters of an hour, the fortress of Basing house, which the royalists considered almost impregnable. There was immense booty taken with the place, of every kind. The plunder of treasure and furniture amounted to more than $1,000,000; in one room was found a bed which cost nearly $6,000. The mansion was set fire to and destroyed, with most of the valuable paintings, papers, &c., by the roundheads, who acted up to the scripture, "cursed is he that doeth the work of the Lord negligently."

1656. Act of the Massachusetts authorities, prohibiting the immigration of quakers, and subjecting such as should arrive to 20 lashes, and imprisonment at hard labor until transported, and if they returned to suffer death.

1660. PAUL SCARRON died; an eminent French comic writer and satirist.

1660. HUGH PETERS, chaplain to Oliver Cromwell, hanged at London. His death was the result of the most infamous trial on record. He was 7 years in New England as minister, first at Salem then in the Great church at Boston.

1734. Birthday of FRANCIS LIGHTFOOT LEE, a distinguished statesman and signer of the declaration of independence. The day of his death is not known.

1736. GEORGE CLARKE delivered his first speech to the assembly, as governor of the province of New York; and consented to introduce the practice which has ever since prevailed, of absenting himself from the council while they sit as a branch of the legislature.

1747. Six ships of war taken by admiral Hawke off the the isle of Aix.

1756. JOHN HENLEY, an eccentric English writer, died. He acquired the appellation of *orator Henley*, and entertained the public by theological orations on Sundays, and political and miscellaneous subjects on Wednesdays; also by a weekly paper called *The Hyp Doctor*.

1758. Battle of Hochkirchen; the Prussians under their king Frederick II, defeated by the Austrians under marshal Daun, with the loss of 7,000 men, all their tents, and baggage, &c. James Keith, a brave and experienced Scottish general, who had distinguished himself in the memorable wars of the king of Prussia, was killed, and general Geist mortally wounded.

1761. Volcanic phenomenon seen at Great Malvern in Worcestershire, Eng.

1781. Two British redoubts at Yorktown taken, and included in the second parallel, which greatly facilitated the subsequent operations of the besiegers.

1783. ANTONIO NUNES RIBEIRO SANCHEZ, an eminent Portuguese physician and writer, died.

1791. GREGORY ALEXANDER POTEMPKIN, a Russian statesman, died. He was descended from a Polish family, was the favorite of Catharine, and her minister of war.

1805. Battle of Ulm; the French under Bonaparte captured the bridge and the Austrian position of Elchingen.

1806. Battle of Jena, or Auerstadt, in Saxony, between the French under Bonaparte and the Prussians under king Frederick William. The Prussian line extended 18 miles, and numbered 150,000 strong; the total number of men engaged on both sides was over 250,000, and the number of cannon employed over 700. The Prussians were defeated with the loss of 20,000 killed and wounded, and 40,000 taken prisoners; together with 300 cannon, and immense magazines of stores. The French admitted a loss of only 1,200 killed and 3,000 wounded.

1813. BONAPARTE arrived at Leipsic, in Germany, having in the course of four days assembled there an army whose numbers are variously stated at from 150 to 400,000 men, with 600 cannon, and commanded by the ablest generals of the age.

1831. LOUIS PONS, an eminent Italian astronomer, died at Florence.

1836. JAMES WILD, an English geographer, died; distinguished for his numerous maps and charts.

1841. HEYER embarked at Boston for India, as the first missionary of the Lutheran church in the United States. He established a mission at Guntoor.

1842. Grand celebration in New York of the completion of the Croton water works; more than 15,000 persons joined in the procession.

1843. A check was put on the progress of Irish agitation by the arrest of Daniel O'Connell and his son on a charge of conspiracy and other misdemeanors.

1845. WILLIAM PRIDGEN died, in Bladen county, N. C., aged 123. He was a volunteer in the revolutionary army, although even then exempt from service by his age.

His grand children were aged people at the time of his death.

1850. The convention for amending the constitution of Virginia assembled at Richmond.

1854. Hugh A. Garland, an eminent lawyer of St. Louis, died; author of a life of John Randolph.

1854. Samuel Phillips died at Brighton, England, aged 39. He was some time the literary reviewer for *The Times* and author of *Readings on the Rail.*

OCTOBER 15.

55 b. c. Titus Lucretius Carus, one of the best of the Latin poets, died.

1564. Andreas Vesalius, a celebrated Dutch anatomist, died. He revived the study of anatomy in Europe, which had been neglected; and impeded by the prejudices of ignorance.

1608. Birthday of Evangeliste Torricelli, the Italian mathematician, and inventor of the barometer.

1634. About sixty men, women and children, with their horses, cattle and swine commenced a journey from the vicinity of Boston, through the wilderness to Connecticut river. After a tedious journey of fourteen days through swamps and over mountains and rivers, they arrived at the place of their destination, and commenced the settlements of Hartford, Windsor and Weathersfield.

1644. Gabriel du Pineau, an eminent French *avocat*, died; celebrated for his genius and eloquence; his counsel was often sought by the court, and he acquired the title of father of the people.

1651. John Owen, an eminent English divine, died. His works amount to 7 vols. folio, 20 quarto, and 30 octavo.

1651. King Charles II, who since his defeat at Worcester had wandered about from one royalist family to another, sleeping in their barns at night and concealing himself in the woods by day, escaped to France. A large oak on which he frequently stood in the woods near Whiteladies, obtained the name of the royal oak.

1671. John Amos Comenius, an eminent German protestant divine and grammarian, died.

1711. The Edgar, admiral Hovenburgh's ship, blown up with 400 seamen on board, the officers being on shore.

1728. Bernard de la Monnoye, an elegant French poet, died. He also wrote in Greek, Latin and Italian.

1743. John Ozell, an indefatigable English writer, died; he is immortalized by Pope in the *Dunciad.*

1760. Battle of Campen; the French defeated the prince of Brunswick, who had a horse killed under him, and lost 1,600 men, chiefly British troops.

1764. Gibbon says that on this day, as he sat musing among the ruins of the Roman capitol, while the barefooted friars were singing vespers in the temple of Jupiter, he first conceived the idea of writing the *Decline and Fall of the Roman Empire.*

1778. Pulaski's infantry surprised in the night by the British, and 50 killed, including baron de Bose. The timely arrival of Pulaski with the cavalry alone saved them from utter destruction.

1783. Pilatre de Rozier, the first aerial adventurer, made his first ascension from a garden in Paris. The balloon was of an oval shape.

1793. Battle of Tirlemont; the French defeated by the Austrians under Clairfait, with the loss of 2,000 killed, and 24 cannon, &c.

1793. Battle of Maubege; the French under Jourdan defeated the prince of Coburg, being his first defeat in a pitched battle, and compelled him to repass the Sambre.

1797. Celebration at Mantua of the birthday of the poet Virgil, when handsome dowries, raised by voluntary contributions among the "friends of learning and rural felicity," were distributed among fifty poor girls, who were the same day married to fifty industrious but poor young men.

1806. Paul Joseph Barthez, a learned French physician, died. He founded the celebrated medical school at Montpellier, and acquired so great reputation that he became a member of almost every learned society, and some of his works were translated into most of the European languages.

1808. James Anderson, an eminent Scottish writer, died. His first literary productions were on agriculture, which produced a greatly increased attention to the subject. His learning and research were conspicuous in the various subjects on which he wrote, and he was an original and accurate thinker.

1812. Action between United States frigate President, commodore Rodgers, and British packet Swallow; the latter was captured, with nearly $200,000 on board.

1814. Skirmish between detachments of the armies of the American generals Brown and Izard, each of whom had advanced to reconnoitre the British works. Four men were killed before the mistake was discovered.

1838. Letitia Elizabeth McLean (better known as *L. E. L.*), died at Cape-Coast castle, Africa, of which settlement her husband was governor. Her writings consist of poems and novels.

OCTOBER 16.

1529. The Turks under Solyman abandoned the famous siege of Vienna.

1555. Hugh Latimer and Nicholas Ridley, English bishops, burnt at Oxford.

1586. Philip Sidney, an English statesman, soldier and scholar, died of a wound received at the battle of Zutphen.

1660. Hugh Peters, a famous English prelate, executed for conspiring, with Cromwell, the king's death.

1678. Cæsar Egasse du Boulai died; register and historiographer of the university of Paris, of which he wrote a history in 6 vols. folio.

1679. Roger Boyle died; an eminent Irish general, statesman and writer.

1725. Ralph Thoresby died; an eminent English topographer and antiquary.

1725. First newspaper published in New York.

1726. The public granaries plundered by the turners of Cornwall for want of provisions.

1756. Battle of Pirna; the Saxons defeated by Frederick II, of Prussia, with the loss of 17,000 prisoners.

1760. Nicholas d'Assas, a French officer, killed at Klosterkamp. On going out to examine the posts, he was captured, and threatened with immediate death if he alarmed his regiment. Without a moment's hesitation he summoned all his strength, and exclaimed "Onward Auverne! here is the enemy!" The threat was immediately executed, but the patriot had gained his object; the attack was unsuccessful. A pension of 1,000 livres was decreed to his family forever.

1767. Burchard Christopher Munich, a German officer in the service of Russia, died. He was promoted by Peter I and Anne; banished by Elizabeth to Siberia, and recalled by Peter II, after an absence of 20 years, when he appeared at court in the same sheepskin dress which he had worn in his exile.

1774. Robert Ferguson, an excellent Scottish poet, died at the age of 24 in a lunatic asylum.

1778. Pondicherry, after a gallant resistance by the French, surrendered to the British.

1779. The fortress of St. Fernando de Omoa, in the bay of Honduras, taken by the British by assault. In the fort was found 250 quintals of quicksilver, and on board the vessels 3,000,000 piasters.

1780. The town of Royalton, Vt., was attacked by a party of 300 Indians of various tribes from Canada, and many of the houses burnt.

1781. A sortie consisting of 360 men under Col. Abercrombie, at Yorktown, forced two American batteries and spiked 11 cannon; but the guards from the trenches immediately repulsed them and restored the cannon. In the afternoon the Americans opened several batteries in their second parallel; and in the whole line of batteries nearly 100 pieces of heavy ordnance were now mounted. The works of the besieged were in no condition to sustain the fire which might be expected next day.

1783. The inhabitants of Canada were surprised by a very extraordinary phenomenon. About 2 o'clock P. M., an unusual darkness, equal it is said to the darkest night, took place. Its approach was instantaneous. This continued about 40 minutes, when there was a short interval of light, but soon was succeeded by darkness, horrible as before, though not of so long duration. The whole is said to have continued upwards of an hour, and to have extended, more or less, throughout the province.

1793. The French convention constituted death only *an eternal sleep!* It was afterwards restored, however, to its original condition!

1793. Marie Antoinette, queen of France, and sister of the emperor of Austria, guillotined. She was tried and condemned at 4 o'clock in the morning, dragged to the scaffold in an open tumbril, amid the scoffs and insults of the populace, and beheaded at the age of 38.

1793. John Hunter, a very eminent British surgeon and anatomical writer, died. From a humble assistant of his brother he became the first surgeon in the world, both in theory and practice.

1796. Victor Amadeus, king of Sardinia, died in his 71st year, and 23d of his reign.

1806. Erfurt, the capital of Upper Thuringia, surrendered to the French; 14,000 prisoners, 28 cannon, and immense magazines of stores were taken.

1813. Battle of Leipsic, between the French under Bonaparte, Ney, Murat, &c., and the allies under Blucher, Benningsen, Bernadotte, &c. It was a conflict between the best disciplined armies, commanded by the ablest generals in the world. Night alone put an end to the carnage, and the armies retired to rest on the ground which they occupied in the morning. The number of men engaged was 150,000 French and 230,000 allies.

1817. Thaddeus Kosciusko, the famous Polish general, died in Switzerland; one of the noblest characters of his age.

1836. Francis J. M. Reynouard, an eminent French philologist, died. He was one of the conductors of the *Journal des*

Savans, distinguished as a scholar, poet, historian, philologist and archæologist.

1837. MATTHIEU DUMAS, peer of France, a lieutenant-general in the French army, and an old companion in arms of Lafayette, died at Paris, aged 84.

1839. DEASE and SIMPSON accomplished an expedition which established the fact of a north-west passage, and gave to the world some new and interesting discoveries respecting the geography of the northern coast of America, and the arctic regions. The intervening space between the discoveries of Parry and Ross were traversed, and a curious point of science established; yet it can not be supposed that the passage can ever be of the smallest utility to navigation.

1842. BENJAMIN EATON, said to have been the last survivor of Washington's life guard, died at Cuddeback, Orange co., N. Y., aged 85. He joined in the pursuit at Lexington, and served till 1779, with an absence of only 20 days.

1848. The emperor of Austria issued a proclamation against Vienna, and appointed count Windischgratz to command his armies in Austria.

OCTOBER 17.

940. ATHELSTAN, king of England, died. He was bountiful, wise and affable; ascended the throne at the age of 30; became distinguished by the titles of *conqueror* and *faithful*, and left behind him a name of great renown, respected at home and abroad.

1346. Battle of Nevil's Cross; the Scots under king David Bruce signally defeated by the English under Philippa and lord Percy. Bruce was taken prisoner and 15,000 of his men slain.

1492. COLUMBUS named the more civilized island Fernandino, now Largo. The men wore cotton mantles, and the women a band of that manufacture round the waist.

1509. PHILIP DE COMINES, an excellent French historian, died, leaving behind him *Memoirs of his Own Times*.

1552. ANDREW OSIANDER died; a Bavarian, one of Luther's first disciples; a professor at Konigsburg, and a voluminous writer.

1616. JOHN PITS, an English biographer, died. He collected the lives of the kings, bishops, apostolical men and writers of England in four large volumes.

1662. The seaport Dunkirk, in France, sold to the English for five million livres. The annual charge of the place (£120,000) far exceeded its intrinsic importance.

1678. EDMUNDBURY GODFREY, before whom Oates gave evidence of the popish plot against the king of England, was found in a field with his sword through his body; verdict of the jury was, that he had been strangled.

1683. An assembly of the representatives of the freeholders of the province of New York, first met in assembly under governor Dongan.

1740. The Czarina ANNE, empress of Russia, died.

1748. Peace of Aix-la-Chapelle, between England, France and Spain. The British took, during the war, 1,249 Spanish and 2,185 French prizes; total 3,434. The Spaniards captured 1,360, and the French 1,878 British vessels; total 3,238.

1758. ROLAND MICHAEL BARRIA DE GALISSONIERE, a French admiral, died. After serving with distinction in the navy, he was made governor of Canada.

1758. JOHN WARD, an English dissenting minister, died; remembered for the assistance he rendered to many of the learned works of his day.

1775. Two men and eleven horses killed by the lightning which proceeded from a volcanic steam cloud of the Katlagia burning mountain, in the island of Iceland.

1777. BURGOYNE, after losing 3,461 men at Stillwater and other places, surrendered the remainder of his army (5,752), to the Americans under Gen. Gates, conditioned not to serve again in North America during the present contest. Thus was extinguished an army of 9,213 men, including volunteers. The army of Gates amounted to 10,557 effective men.

1781. Several new batteries were opened by the Americans in the second parallel, against Yorktown. In the judgment of Cornwallis and his engineers, the place was no longer tenable; and in a letter to Washington he requested a cessation of hostilities to prepare for a capitulation.

1781. EDWARD HAWKE, a brave and intrepid English admiral, died.

1793. Battle of Cholet, the Vendeans defeated by the French. The actions of *Hagenau* and *Brumpt* took place on the same day, in both of which the allies defeated the French.

1797. Treaty of Campio Formio between Bonaparte and the emperor of Austria.

1803. Agra in Hindostan taken by the British.

1805. Ulm surrendered by the Austrian general Mack to Bonaparte, and was delivered up on the 20th. The archduke with a corps of 17,000 Austrians effected his escape the night before by a masterly piece of generalship, leaving 40,000 behind who became prisoners to the French.

1806. Battle of Halle; prince Eugene of Wirtemburg defeated by the French under

Bernadotte; 34 cannon and 5,000 prisoners were taken.

1806. JACQUES DESSALINES, the black emperor of Hayti, assassinated.

1829. The Delaware and Chesapeake canal opened.

1834. Both houses of the British parliament destroyed by fire. They were not very remarkable for elegance or convenience; but with them was destroyed the celebrated tapestry that hung upon the walls of the house of lords, representing the defeat of the famous Spanish armada, a relic of great value in the eyes of the antiquary.

1837. JOHN HUMMEL, an eminent musical composer, founder of the modern school of pianoforte music, died at Weimar, in Germany.

1848. Vienna in a state of siege; the imperial troops drawn close around the city, and deputations passed from the diet at Vienna to the emperor at Olmutz. Kossuth withdrew the Hungarian army within their own frontier.

1853. A party of 45 men under colonel Walker, sailed from San Francisco for the purpose of establishing a republic in lower California.

1854. The allies opened their first fire from the fleet and batteries upon Sebastopol. The loss of the Russians was 500 killed; of the allies 90, and 300 wounded.

OCTOBER 18.

447 B. C. Battle of Coronea; the Bœotians gained a great and most important victory over the Athenians. Clinias, the father of Alcibiades, and Tolmides, fell.

33. AGRIPPINA, the virtuous wife of Germanicus Cæsar, died in exile of starvation. She was banished after the death of her husband.

1216. JOHN (*Lackland*), king of England, died, aged 47. No prince in English history has been transmitted to posterity in darker colors; ingratitude, cruelty, and perfidy, were habitual in his character.

1547. JAMES SADOLET, a polite and learned Italian writer and cardinal, died.

1564. Captain JOHN HAWKINS sailed from Plymouth, England, with four sail for the African coast; which was the first slave trade adventure, and the opening of that infernal commerce. The negroes were taken to Hispaniola, and sold to the Spaniards.

1605. JOHN RIOLAN died; a Paris physician and writer on anatomy and medicine.

1631. Corn made a legal tender in Massachusetts, unless money or beaver were expressly stipulated.

1633. A royal declaration ordered to be read in churches, reviving in England, wakes, lawful sports and recreations, after divine service on sabbaths.

1744. The duchess dowager of Marlborough died in her 85th year, leaving many legacies. She was the famous Sarah Jennings in queen Anne's days.

1757. RENE ANTHONY FERCHAULT DE REAUMUR, a French philosopher, died. He gave a new construction to the thermometer which bears his name, and wrote much on the various branches of natural philosophy.

1770. JOHN MANNERS died; an English nobleman, who distinguished himself at the head of the British forces in the German war, under Ferdinand of Brunswick.

1775. The Americans took Chamblee, in Canada, and for the first time captured the British colors; they also took 4 tons of powder.

1775. Falmouth, a town in the northeast part of Massachusetts, burnt. The inhabitants had obstructed some British movements, whereupon an armed vessel was sent to reduce the town to ashes. Of the dwelling houses, 139 were burnt, and 278 stores.

1783. FRANCIS XAVIER D'OLIVEYRA, a Portuguese statesman, died in England.

1783. The American army disbanded by proclamation.

1799. Treaty for the evacuation of Holland by the British and Russians.

1799. Three British frigates captured the Spanish galleon Santa Brigida, 36 guns and 320 men, with 1,500,000 Spanish dollars on board, and a cargo of merchandise, ivory, &c., of equal value.

1801. The Batavian republic again divided into the old provinces; the legislature was diminished to 35 deputies; the executive power extended to a council of twelve men.

1806. The French under Davoust took possession of Leipsic, in Saxony. They found there 15,000 quintals of flour, and British goods to an immense amount; sixty millions were offered as a ransom for the latter.

1809. Battle of Salamanca; the Spaniards defeated the French under Ney, and forced them to fall back with the loss of 1,500 men.

1811. The ladies of Cadiz formed a society to supply the wants of the Spanish soldiers.

1812. Action between the United States sloop of war Wasp, 18 guns, captain Jones, and British sloop of war Frolic, 22 guns; the latter captured in 45 minutes, with the loss of 30 killed, 50 wounded; Wasp had 5 killed, 5 wounded. Same day British ship Poictiers, 74 guns, came up with and captured both of them, the Wasp being too much damaged in her rigging to escape.

1812. Battle of Poltosk; the Russians under Witgenstein and Steingel attacked the French and Germans under St. Cyr, and compelled them to retire within their entrenchments.

1812. Battle of Garalavitz; the Russians under Benningsen defeated the French, 50,000, under Murat, killed 2,500, took 1,000 prisoners, 38 cannon, 40 ammunition wagons, and a large amount of spoil, besides the great standard of honor belonging to the regiment of cuirassiers.

1812. The French abandoned the city of Moscow; Napoleon, on learning the defeat of Murat, determined to march to his support with the whole French army.

1813. Second day's battle of Leipsic; the two great armies had paused one day to prepare for this grand contest. The forces of Napoleon were not less than 180,000; those of the allies had been swelled to near 300,000. The carnage was fearful, and the French were compelled to yield before an overwhelming superiority of numbers. The loss of Bonaparte on this day, including defections and prisoners, was not less than 80,000 men, 200 cannon, and an immense amount of baggage.

1813. Theodore Koerner, the German poet, was killed in the battle of Leipsic. He is particularly celebrated for the spirited poems which he composed in the campaign against Napoleon, in which he fell.

1814. Union of Norway and Sweden.

1815. Bonaparte, the exiled emperor of France, with his suit, landed at St. Helena.

1817. Stephen Henry Mehul, an eminent French musical composer, died.

1827. The last lottery authorized by the British government, drawn in London. In that lottery there were six prizes of $133,200 dollars each.

1833. Captain John Ross, who left England in 1829 in search of a north-west passage from the Atlantic to the Pacific ocean, returned on this day, after an absence of four years, and when all hopes of his return had been given up.

1840. The ceremony of the exhumation of the body of Napoleon Bonaparte was performed at St. Helena, with great parade, in order to be conveyed to Paris. The body, which had been embalmed by French physicians previous to interment, in 1821, was found in a state of complete preservation. (See Dec. 15.)

1841. A great flood of the Thames, caused by a succession of northerly gales; the water rose much higher than during the inundations of 1821 and 1828, and much property was destroyed.

1843. Ebenezer Elmer, an officer of the revolution, and the last survivor of the Jersey line, died at Bridgeton, aged 91.

1844. Destructive gale at Buffalo, carrying away part of the pier which protected the harbor, sinking vessels, and submerging a part of the city, by which more than fifty lives were lost.

1849. Leonidas Wetmore, an officer in the U. S. infantry, died on board a steam boat in the Mississippi. He was actively engaged in the Florida war, and participated in most of the hard fought battles of the Mexican campaign.

1850. Daniel Clark Sanders, formerly president of the university of Vermont, died, aged 82. He published a history of the Indians, and kept a meteorological register to the day of his death.

1852. Commodore McCauley, commander of the United States naval forces in the Pacific, by proclamation, withdrew his protection from American vessels proceeding to the Lobos islands for guano.

1854. Francis Burt, governor of the territory of Nebraska, died at Bellevue, aged 45. He was a native of South Carolina, and resigned the office of third auditor of the treasury at Washington for the governorship, which he held hardly two weeks after his arrival.

OCTOBER 19.

202 B. C. Battle of Zama, in which Hannibal was defeated by Scipio.

125 B. C. The era of Tyre began, with the month Hyperberetæus. The months are the same as those used in the Grecian era; the year similar to the Julian.

1453. The fall of Bordeaux, after a siege of seven weeks, when Guienne, an English province, was incorporated with the French monarchy.

1492. Columbus discovered the island of Isabella.

1608. Geoffrey Fenton, an eminent English writer, died. He served queen Elizabeth in Ireland, where he was promoted.

1619. James Arminius, founder of the Arminians, died. He was professor of divinity at Leyden; his writings are all on controversial and theological subjects.

1630. First general court of the Massachusetts colony held at Boston. Many of the first planters attended and were made free of the colony. The number of freemen this year was 110.

1640. Albertus Miræus, a learned German writer, died.

1645. Newcastle in England, a fortress of considerable strength, taken by the Scots under Leven. The place had been besieged ten weeks when the Scottish general directed a furious cannonade against the walls; at nightfall the besiegers advanced to the onset, and after two hours' hard fighting at the breaches, forced their entry.

1655. The kirk of Scotland refused to observe the *fast day* ordered by the protector, on the ground that the church should receive no directions from civil magistrates when to keep fasts.

1660. Colonels AXTEL and HACKER executed for the murder of Charles I of England. Axtel commanded the guard that attended the king to the scaffold.

1675. Attack on Hadley, Mass., by the Indians to the number of seven or eight hundred. Nearly all the towns on that river had been either totally destroyed or greatly injured during this season by the savages. They attacked this place in all quarters, but were so warmly received at all points, that after burning a few barns and outhouses, they hastened away as fast as they had come on. The town happened to be garrisoned, and the companies stationed at the neighboring towns hastened to their relief. This was the last attempt upon these settlements this season, the Indians retiring to their general rendezvous at Narragansett. Great numbers of them had been killed, and a greater number had perished by other means.

1682. THOMAS BROWN, an eminent English physician and writer, died.

1690. ISAAC BENSERADE, a French poet, died.

1745. JONATHAN SWIFT, the eccentric dean of St. Patrick's, died, aged 78, in a state of idiocy, leaving £10,000 to found a hospital for lunatics and idiots.

1749. WILLIAM GED, an ingenious Scottish artist, died; memorable for a new invention in the art of printing, called stereotyping.

1762. Dark day at Detroit; "one of the darkest days that ever was known."

1763. A patrol of horse commanded by sir John Fielding, established on the roads leading to London, to clear them of robbers and highwaymen.

1769. A terrible eruption of Vesuvius.

1780. Engagement at Palatine Bridge, N. Y.; colonel Brown killed.

1781. CORNWALLIS surrendered to the French and American army at Yorktown. Above 7000 prisoners, the military chest, a frigate, with a number of transports and the public stores, and 1500 seamen, fell into the hands of the captors. The allied army consisted of 7000 French, 5500 continental troops, and 3500 militia.

1789. FRANÇOIS, a baker in Paris, murdered in the street by a mob, because the return of the king had not lessened the price of bread. The great barbarity shown by the actors in this affair called down on them the severity of the national guards under Lafayette.

1794. Battle of Puffleck; the duke of York defeated by the French under Pichegru. The emigrant legion under Rohan were cut to pieces.

1806. HENRY KIRKE WHITE, an admired English poet, died, aged 21.

1807. WILLIAM GORDON died; an English author of a history of the American revolution, &c.

1810. The French burned all British merchandise in the country.

1812. Second battle of Poltosk; the French defeated and compelled to retreat with great loss.

1812. BONAPARTE, at the head of the French army, left Moscow. The palace of the Kremlin blown up.

1813. Last day's battle of Leipsic, in which above half a million of men and at least 2000 cannon were engaged in the work of death. The French emperor finding it in vain to stem the torrent of so vast a superiority of force as now bore down upon him, began a retreat, which was disastrous in the extreme. The only bridge by which the army could cross was blown up, leaving 25,000 men to surrender at discretion. On arriving at Erfurt, Bonaparte found his army reduced to 80,000; having lost by death and defection since the campaign opened, 200,000.

1814. Battle of Lyon's creek; the Americans, 900 men, under general Bissell, attacked by a select British corps of 1200 men, who were compelled to retreat.

1825. GIROLAMO LUCCHESINI, a Prussian minister of state and author, died. He combined the qualities of an experienced courtier with the practical knowledge of a statesman, was learned without pedantry, and possessed a great memory.

1826. FRANCIS JOSEPH TALMA, an eminent French tragedian and writer, died. He was a man of great natural talent, and esteemed by men of rank and talent; he was a great favorite with Napoleon.

1842. The town of Monterey in California was captured by the United States squadron under commodore Jones, under the belief that war existed. But it was soon restored to Mexico.

1845. HANNAH GOUGH died in New York, aged 110.

1847. A volcano burst forth with great violence on one of the high peaks of Lookout mountain, in the Alleghanian chain, in Georgia.

1847. The corner stone of a monument to the memory of general Washington laid in the city of New York.

1848. The Mormon temple at Nauvoo was fired by an incendiary, and totally destroyed.

1849. Frederick Strickland, a young Englishman, son of Thomas Strickland, bart., perished in the snow near the Notch house, in New Hampshire.

1852. A decree of the president issued for the convoking of the French senate for the purpose of deliberating on the restoration of the empire.

1853. Ichabod Bartlett, a New Hampshire statesman, died at Portsmouth, aged 67.

OCTOBER 20.

480 b. c. The battle of Salamis is, by respectable authority, placed upon this day. (See Sept. 30.)

1422. Charles VI of France, died. He succeeded to the kingdom at the age of 13, and during a reign of 42 years the kingdom, by foreign invasions and internal factions, was ruined, and passed into the hands of the English.

1524. Thomas Linacre, a learned English physician and divine, died. He was the best Greek and Latin scholar of his age, and founded the college of physicians.

1579. The Scottish parliament decreed that every householder, having lands or goods worth £500, should be obliged to have a Bible, which at this time was printed in folio, and a psalm book in his house, "for the better instruction of themselves and their families in the knowledge of God."

1687. The destruction of Lima in Peru by an earthquake.

1713. Archibald Pitcairne, an able Scottish physician, died. He disputed the right of Harvey to the discovery of the circulation of the blood, which he asserted was fully known to Hippocrates.

1714. Several people killed by the falling of scaffolds on which multitudes were standing to see the coronation of George I of England.

1719. Birthday of Godfrey Achenwall, a Prussian traveler, historian and political economist. He first gave a distinct character to the science of statistics, and gave it that name. He died 1772.

1728. A fire commenced in Copenhagen, the capital of Denmark, and lasted three days; most of the city was burnt down.

1740. Charles VI, emperor of Germany, died. He was the sixteenth and last prince of the ancient house of Austria, and was succeeded by his eldest daughter, Maria Theresa.

1741. The Prussians became masters of Silesia.

1786. A basket maker contrived by a singular scaffolding of twigs to bring down the weathercock from the old abby church of St. Albans, in England.

1796. The university of Oxford and the marquis of Buckingham each presented 2000 copies of the Bible for distribution among the French clergy.

1799. Rome capitulated to the English.

1807. The ports of Portugal shut against British shipping.

1807. Copenhagen evacuated by the British, who brought off the stores in the arsenal, amounting to 92 cargoes, and the ships of war.

1814. Philip Astley, founder of the royal amphitheatre, London, died, aged 72. He served seven years in Germany, in the English cavalry, and on his return began to exhibit equestrian performances. He erected several amphitheatres in England and Paris, wrote a treatise on horsemanship, and two works of a military character.

1815. Great hurricane at Jamaica, which continued 3 days and wrecked one hundred vessels.

1826. Boissy d'Anglas, died at his residence in France, whose name is so closely interwoven with the French revolution. He was a member of the council of 500, and subsequently the president of that body. His hostility to the Directory produced a sentence of deportation to Guiana, but he contrived to elude the exile.

1827. Battle of Navarino, in which the fleet of the pacha of Egypt was annihilated by the combined squadrons of Great Britain, Russia and France, under admiral Codrington.

1841. A fire broke out in the tower at London, and entirely consumed the building called the small armory; about 200,000 stand of arms, and a great number of trophies of various kinds were destroyed.

1853. Selim Pasha defeated a Russian corps of 15,000 men on the frontiers of Georgia. The Turks at this time had a fleet of 22 ships of the line and 9 war steamers, mounting 1116 guns, and the Egyptian contingent consisting of 10 ships of war and 2 steamers, mounting 614 guns.

OCTOBER 21.

1097. The siege of Antioch opened by the crusaders. (See June 3.) Baldwin founded the principality of Edessa in this year.

1217. The fortress of Alcazar-do-Sal taken from the Moors, after a hard fought battle, by the Portuguese under Alphonso II, assisted by William, earl of Holland, with a portion of the fleet and forces bound for the crusade.

1439. Ambrose of Portico, in Romania, died; distinguished by his fluency in the Greek tongue, at the councils of Basil, Ferrara, &c.

1441. Margery Jourdemain, the witch of Eye, condemned to be burnt for furnishing *love potions* to Eleanor Cobham, wife of that duke of Gloucester so eminent as a patron of science and letters.

1558. Julius Cæsar Scaliger died; an Italian physician, eminent as a Latin critic and poet.

1583. Laurent Joubert, a French physician and medical writer, died.

1593. Nymegen, a strong city of Holland, surrendered to Maurice of Nassau, who added a new fort to it.

1621. Anthony Montchrestien de Vateville, a French poet, torn to pieces and burnt by order of the authorities, for sedition and other crimes.

1662. Henry Lawes, an English musician, died. He was originally a choir boy of Salisbury church, first introduced the Italian style of music in England, and composed the notes for Milton's *Comus*.

1687. Edmund Waller, an eminent English poet and political writer, died.

1692. A commission was granted by William and Mary to Benjamin Fletcher, governor of New York, conferring on him the government of Pennsylvania, and depriving Penn of that office. He was however, restored again in two years after.

1716. James Gronovius died; a Dutch writer on the belles-lettres, and a man of learning.

1766. Cumana, the capital of New Andalusia in South America, entirely destroyed by an earthquake.

1771. Tobias Smollet, a Scottish physician, died; better known as a historian and novelist.

1771. William Clarke, an English divine and antiquary, died.

1774. The provincial congress of Massachusetts determined to raise and enlist men for the defence of the province for the first time, under the name of minute men.

1777. Samuel Foote died; a celebrated English dramatist and actor, called the English Aristophanes.

1783. Congress insulted at Philadelphia by a band of mutineers, whom the authorities were unable to quell, adjourned to Princeton; a circumstance which doubtless led to the agitation of the question of a permanent seat of government.

1794. Coblentz surrendered to the French revolutionists. The fortifications of this city, celebrated for having been the court of the emigrant princes, had been vastly augmented during the course of the war, but the Austrian commander evacuated it on the first appearance of the French.

1794. Anthony Petit, an eminent French physician, died. He was a copious and learned writer.

1800. Simeon Thayer, an officer of the revolution, died. He was in the army led by Arnold through the wilderness to Quebec, was wounded by a cannon ball at Monmouth, and was the brave volunteer defender of Mud fort on the Delaware.

1803. Frederick Cavendish, an English field marshal died.

1805. Battle of Trafalgar; the British fleet, 27 sail and 4 frigates, defeated, after an action of 4 hours, the combined French and Spanish fleets of 33 sail. Admiral Horatio Nelson was killed, and the French admiral Villeneuve was captured. British loss 423 killed, 1164 wounded. The French and Spanish fleet was completely overthrown; but 14 escaped from the battle, and nearly the whole of those were afterwards wrecked or captured.

1841. John Forsyth, an eminent American statesman, died. As a member of the Union convention of Georgia in 1832, he was principally instrumental in preventing that state from pledging itself to nullification. He was a man of talent and eloquence and long distinguished in public life by the many important offices which he held.

1849. Charles E. Horn, a well known musical composer of Boston, died.

1852. Saul Alley, long known as a leading merchant and capitalist of New York, died aged 74.

OCTOBER 22.

50 b. c. The civil wars of the Romans began in which Cesar and Pompey were arrayed against each other.

615. Columbanus, an Irish missionary and reformer of monastic life, died in Italy. In his character he was intrepid, violent and fearless.

741. Charles Martel, duke of Austrasia, died. He was the actual sovereign of France during 25 years, under the titles of mayor of the palace, and duke of the Franks. He repeatedly vanquished the Suevians, Frisons, Allemans and Saxons, and at the famous battle near Poictiers defeated the Saracens with such great slaughter, that it is said 375,000 of them were destroyed.

1322. Hugh, the illuminator, died at Cairo in Egypt, on his way from Dublin to the holy land.

1495. JOHN II (*the Great*) of Portugal, died. He carried war into Africa against the Moors, and extended the settlements of the Portuguese in Africa and India.

1658. Interment of Oliver Cromwell, with great pomp. "It was the joyfulest funeral I ever saw," says Evelyn; "for there were none that cried but dogs, which the soldiers hooted away with a barbarous noise, drinking and taking tobacco in the streets as they went."

1685. Edict of Nantes revoked by the imbecile Louis XIV, who imagined the protestants in his kingdom were nearly extirpated. The protestants were now deprived of their religious and civil rights, which they had enjoyed nearly a century. They were driven in great numbers into different countries of Europe by the persecutions which followed, where they established the silk and other manufactures, to the great prejudice of their own country.

1707. CLOUDESLEY SHOVEL, a celebrated English admiral, wrecked off the Scilly isles, as he was returning with his fleet from the coast of Spain; 900 seamen also perished with him.

1708. HERMAN WITSIUS died; a learned Dutch divine, and theological writer.

1710. Birthday of MARIE ANNE LE PAGE DU BOCCAGE, a French lady greatly celebrated for her writings.

1724. WILLIAM WOLLASTON died; a celebrated English divine, author of the *Religion of Nature.*

1726. The island of Jamaica visited by a fearful hurricane which destroyed much property on the plantations and a fleet of ships.

1746. The assembly of New York brought in a bill to raise £2,250 by lottery towards erecting a college.

1757. Alum first discovered in Ireland.

1764. Battle of Buxar, in Bengal; the British defeated Mir Cassim, who lost 4,000 killed, 133 cannon, and all his tents, &c., taken.

1775. PEYTON RANDOLPH, first president of the American congress, died. He was a native of Virginia, and one of the most distinguished lawyers and patriots of that state.

1777. Battle of Red Bank; the Hessians under count Donop in their attack upon the American fort, were defeated with the loss of about 500 killed. Donop was mortally wounded. Fort Mifflin was attacked at the same time by water, without success, and two British men-of-war were lost.

1784. Treaty at fort Stanwix (now Rome) between the Six Nations and the United States.

1788. GEORGE III, king of England, became insane.

1791. JOHN DAVID MICHAELIS, a German theological writer, died. His works are 49 in number.

1793. British took possession of Grand Ance and Nicola Mole, in St. Domingo.

1802. SAMUEL ARNOLD, an eminent English musical composer, died in London.

1812. VINZINGERODE, the Russian general, with his aid Narishkin, rode up to Warsaw with a white flag to offer terms, was made prisoner, and despatched towards Hesse; but was retaken by a party of Cossacks.

1812. The city of Moscow wholly evacuated by the French, after a possession of 1 month and 8 days. Russian troops entered it immediately afterwards, in time to preserve the Kremlin, which had been undermined to be blown up; and within a few hours, so completely had the Russian peasants baffled Napoleon, that the town swarmed with people and the markets were stocked with provision.

1818. JOACHIM HEINRICH CAMPE, a German theologian, died. His philosophical works, as well as those which he composed for the instruction of youth, display a noble and philanthropic spirit; some of them have been translated into most of the European languages.

1824. CHARLES VAN ESS, a German ecclesiastic, died. He wrote some historical works, and a translation of the New Testament was published under his name.

1840. HENRY RICHARD VASSALL, lord Holland, an English statesman, died. He was a man of literary accomplishments, and particularly distinguished for his knowledge of Spanish literature. He is characterized as a wit without a particle of ill-nature, and a man of learning without a taint of pedantry.

1841. ROBERT BISSETT SCOTT, an English writer on military jurisprudence and a military advocate, died at London, aged 67.

1846. BATIS STONE, another of those long lived patriots cf the revolution of the American colonies, died at Philadelphia, aged over 103 years. Though in nearly every battle he escaped unwounded.

1846. The steamship Great Britain ran aground on the coast of Ireland, and became too deeply imbedded to be lifted by subsequent tides. The passengers and most of the cargo saved.

1848. ALEXANDER G. MCNUTT, an eminent Mississippi lawyer, died, aged 47.

1850. The city council of Chicago passed resolutions nullifying the fugitive slave law, and releasing the police from the obedience of it. They subsequently reconsidered this action.

1855. WILLIAM MOLESWORTH, a Welsh baronet, died, aged 45. He began to make a figure before the public at a very early age, and distinguished himself in parliament and elsewhere.

OCTOBER 23.

439. Carthage, foremost in effeminacy, and second in importance among the western cities, was taken from the Romans and spoliated by Genseric, the Vandal, 585 years after the destruction of her republic by the younger Scipio.

472. FLAVIUS ANICIUS OLYBRIUS, emperor of the west, died, after a very brief reign.

524. ANICIUS MANLIUS TORQUATUS SEVERINUS BŒTHIUS, a celebrated Roman philosopher, executed. He fell under the displeasure of Theodoric.

1340. NICOLAS, of Lyra, a Norman Jew, died. He was converted to Christianity, taught divinity at Paris with great reputation, and wrote commentaries on the Bible and controversies with the Jews.

1389. The first charter to the town of Linlithgow, in Scotland, was given by Robert II. Here yet stands the old palace in which the unfortunate Mary, queen of Scotland, sometime resided.

1526. Date of the bishop of London's charge to his clergy, to destroy the English copy of the New Testament, as ruinous to the souls of their people.

1616. ACHILLE DE HARLEY, president of the parliament of Paris, died. He acquired great respect by the learning, firmness and dignity with which he sustained his office.

1641. Rebellion in Ireland; the catholics under Phelim O'Neil, rose against the protestants, and cruelly massacred men, women and children to the number of 40,000, and by some accounts more than 100,000.

1642. Battle of Edgehill, between the royalists, under Charles I and prince Rupert, and the parliament forces, under the earl of Essex. About 5,000 men fell on the occasion, among whom was general Bertie; the victory was undecided.

1667. The foundation stone of the first pillar in the Royal Exchange, London, laid by the king.

1679. The *Meal Tub* plot discovered in England.

1706. JOHN FOY VAILLANT, a celebrated French physician, medalist and traveler, died.

1707. The first parliament of Great Britain met after the union with Scotland.

1708. The town of Lisle surrendered, and the garrison retired into the castle, except the horse, which were allowed to march away. The allies acknowledged a loss of 12,000 men in taking the town only.

1713. ARCHIBALD PITCAIRNE, an eminent physician and scholar, died at Edinburgh.

1730. ANNE OLDFIELD, a very celebrated English actress, died; and after lying in state in Jerusalem chamber, was buried at Westminster with great pomp.

1764. JOHN LECLAIR, an eminent French music composer, assassinated at Paris.

1785. WILLIAM COCHRANE, a Scottish painter, died. His pieces acquired great celebrity.

1789. Two robbers seized by the citizens of Paris, and hung on the spot, under pretence that the authorities were too slow and dilatory.

1801. JOHN GOTTLIEB NAUMANN, an eminent German music composer, died. He was found in obscurity at the age of 13, and taken to Italy, where he commenced his career. His operas are very numerous.

1814. British ship Bulwark captured American privateer, Harlequin, 10 guns, 115 men.

1825. PLINY FISK, a zealous American missionary, died at Beyrout, in Syria. Although extremely indigent, he procured a regular education, subsisting two years upon bread and milk, and carrying his corn to mill upon his shoulders. Yet so great was his application, that he enabled himself to preach in Italian, French, modern Greek and Arabic.

1826. Date of JAMES SMITHSON'S will, which ultimately placed in the hands of the United States of America, a large sum for the diffusion of knowledge among men.

1841. GEORGE FREDERICK BELTZ, author of several works on antiquities and heraldry, died at Basle.

1844. The steam boat, Lucy Walker, stopping at New Albany, on her route from Louisville to New Orleans, exploded her three boilers at once, killing between 50 and 60 persons, and wounding others.

1848. General WINDISCHGRATZ, summoned the city of Vienna to surrender.

OCTOBER 24.

996. HUGH CAPET, king of France, died. He acquired the throne by his merits and courage, and became the head of the third race of the French monarchy.

1553. JOHN WAYLAND, queen Mary's "allowed printer," received his charter; yet Thomas Green, a journeyman of his, was imprisoned and whipped, for printing a book entitled *Antichrist*.

1601. TYCHO BRAHE, the Danish astronomer, died. He chose the study of astronomy when it was a science of small repute; and though he immortalized his name, yet it is to be regretted that he should have been led into so visionary a scheme as his *system* exhibits, from a mere spirit of opposition to Copernicus.

1612. Sir PECKSAEL BROCAS, for his adulteries, was compelled to stand at St. Paul's cross, in London, arrayed in a white sheet with a stick in his hand.

1644. The English parliament issued an ordinance, that no quarter should be given to any Irish papist, who should be found in hostility to the parliament.

1648. German thirty years' war concluded by the treaty of Westphalia. It commenced 1618, having grown out of the reformation. It spread from one end of Germany to the other, and left the country a scene of desolation and disorder, wasted by fire, sword and plague, which was followed by a great scarcity, owing to a deficiency of laborers. The art of war was the only one that had gained any thing, and that principally by the genius of Gustavus Adolphus, who made an era in military tactics, and was the first who had a train of artillery in his army.

1655. PETER GASSENDI, a celebrated French philosopher, died. He was at once a theologian, metaphysician, philosopher, astronomer, naturalist and mathematician; eminent in some, and above mediocrity in all those sciences.

1678. Desperate action between the English ship, Concord, captain Grantham, and the Algerine admiral ship, Rose, commanded by Canary, a Spanish renegado, who was beat off.

1682. WILLIAM PENN first arrived in America, and landed at New Castle, Delaware, with 100 passengers. Next day possession of the country was given him.

1819. Erie canal opened from Utica to Rome.

1812. Battle of Ouschatch; the Russians under Steingel and Sassanoff defeated the Bavarians, who lost 300 killed and 200 taken.

1821. A new organization of the Spanish church introduced, abolishing all the monasteries but ten or twelve, declaring all legacies and gifts to monasteries, churches and hospitals, unlawful, and curtailing the whole ecclesiastical establishment, so as to effect a saving of 44½ million dollars to the nation. The old order of things was restored to its former footing two years afterwards, on the restoration of the king to absolute power.

1821. ELIAS BOUDINOT, first president of the American Bible society, died. He was president of Congress in 1782, a man of great excellence of character, and left his large estate principally to charitable purposes.

1838. JOSEPH LANCASTER, promulgator of the Lancasterian system of mutual instruction, died in New York, aged 68.

1842. Great storm of wind and rain in the island of Madeira; 200 houses were swept away at Funchal, the capital.

1842. A destructive fire occurred at Canton, China, by which more than 1,400 houses were burnt.

1845. WILLIAM RUDE, of Cumberland, R. I., died, aged 98. He was at the battle of Bunker hill, and nearly every other during the revolutionary struggle, but escaped unhurt.

1845. England and France, having engaged by a public armed intervention to put a stop to the war between Buenos Ayres and Montevideo, declared a strict blockade of the port of Buenos Ayres.

1846. HENRY, an African, died in Woodford county, Ky., aged 112. At the age of 84 he married his fourth wife, and raised a family of 7 children.

1852. DANIEL WEBSTER, the greatest of American orators, died at Marshfield, aged 70. As a statesman, in the most complete meaning of the term, few Americans have ever equaled and none surpassed him.

1854. PIERRE SOULE, the United States minister to Spain, on landing at Calais from England, en route for Spain, was stopped by the French police, and returned to London.

1855. ROBERT H. MORRIS, a distinguished New York politician, died at Astoria, aged 51.

1855. JAMES OLIVER VAN DE VELDE, second bishop of Natchez, died, aged 63. He was a Belgian, who early united with the Jesuits, and was sent to America. He was sometime president of the catholic college at St. Louis, and afterwards bishop of Chicago. He was held in very high estimation by all denominations.

OCTOBER 25.

322 B. C. DEMOSTHENES, the Athenian orator, died at the isle of Calauria, as is supposed by poison, to save himself from falling into the hands of his enemies alive.

1154. STEPHEN, king of England, died. He usurped the throne, which belonged to Matilda, wife of Henry IV, of Germany, whose son Henry II, succeeded him.

1400. GEOFFREY CHAUCER, the father of English poetry, died.

1415. Battle of Agincourt, in France; the English army had been reduced by disease and sword from 30,000 to 15,000, when on ascending the heights of Blangi they saw the French army of 50,000 men drawn up to oppose their progress. There was no alternative but to give battle, which resulted in the defeat of the French, who lost 10,000 killed, and 14,000 taken prisoners; while the loss of the English was but 40 men.

1499. The bridge of Notre Dame, at Paris, fell.

1555. CHARLES V resigned the sovereignty of the Low Countries, in the presence of the states at Brussels, in favor of his bigoted son Philip.

1691. GEORGE LEGGE, an able English naval officer, died in the Tower, whither he had been sent on suspicion of favoring the revolution.

1692. PETER SCHUYLER was admitted by Gov. Fletcher to the council board, his peculiar qualifications being required by the administration.

1701. Philadelphia first chartered by William Penn; Edward Shippen was appointed mayor.

1714. SEBASTIAN LE CLERC died; a French engraver, who rose from obscurity to eminence.

1731. Several valuable manuscripts destroyed in the Cottonian library at Westminster, by a fire.

1735. CHARLES MORDAUNT, a renowned English naval officer, died. To bravery and heroism he added a penetrating genius and a mind highly polished.

1751. An extraordinary eruption of Mt. Vesuvius.

1757. AUGUSTINE CALMET, a learned French ecclesiastic, died. He was well acquainted with the oriental languages and published several learned works, which are still in use.

1760. GEORGE II, of England, died suddenly at Kensington from the extraordinary circumstance of a rupture of the right ventricle of the heart, in the 77th year of his age and the 34th of his reign.

1764. WILLIAM HOGARTH died; one of the most original of painters. He was originally destined for a copperplate engraver, to which art he served an apprenticeship.

1779. The British evacuated Newport, R. I.; to the honor of Gen. Pigot, no wanton injury was committed.

1780. JOHN HANCOCK chosen first governor of Massachusetts, under their new constitution.

1780. Gen. MARION attacked near the high hills of Santee, 200 British and tories, under Col. Tyne; killed or took nearly half of them, and most of their horses, &c.

1781. Americans under Col. Willett, of New York, defeated 600 British under major Ross.

1788. WILLIAM JULIUS MICKLE, an English poet, died. He commenced life as a brewer, but failing in business took up literature' in which he succeeded.

1793. Battle of Wazenau; the Austrians under Wurmzer defeated the French, who lost 3,000 men, all their baggage and 10 cannon.

1794. Venlo, an important fortress on the Meuse, surrendered to the French republicans; the commandant, Gen. Puffer, first requiring the French Gen. Lourent to assure him upon the honor of the French nation, that the garrison had no hopes left of being relieved by the allied powers.

1798. NELSON arrived at Malta with 14 ships of war and summoned Valetta to surrender, offering to transport the French home. The offer being refused the place was invested, and the siege left in charge of Capt. Ball, Nelson being forced to depart to refit his ships, which were damaged at the recent battle of Aboukir.

1806. HENRY KNOX died; major-general in the army of the United States during the war of the revolution, and secretary of war under Washington.

1806. The French under Davoust entered Berlin, the capital of Prussia, where they found 500 cannon, several hundred thousand pounds of powder and some thousands of muskets.

1806. Spandau, a fortress nine miles from Berlin, surrendered to the French under Victor; they found there oats and provisions for the French army for two months, and ammunition sufficient to double the stores of the artillery.

1806. A battalion of Saxons under baron Hund surrendered to the French at Little Somerda, in Thuringia.

1812. Action between American frigate United States, 54 guns, Com. Decatur, and British frigate Macedonian, 49 guns. The latter was captured after an action of an hour and a half, with the loss of 104 killed and wounded. American loss 12.

1813. Action between the United States frigate Congress, Capt. Smith, and British ship Rose, in which the latter was captured and destroyed.

1813. British and Indians repulsed in an attack upon the United States troops under Gen. Izard.

1826. First daily paper at Rochester, N. Y., issued.

1836. The Luxor obelisk erected in Paris in the Place of Louis XV, in the presence of the royal family and about 250,000 spectators.

1842. SAMPSON SALTER BLOWERS died at Halifax, aged 100. He was born in Boston, and studied law under Gov. Hutchinson; but adhering to the British party was proscribed. He was nearly 40 years a supreme court judge.

1844. The Providence theatre burnt, destroying the valuable scientific apparatus used by Dr. Lardner in his lectures.

1847. Tobasco was bombarded by a

portion of the Gulf squadron under Com. Perry, and all the vessels in the port were captured or destroyed. Com. Perry lost 1 killed, 3 wounded and 2 drowned.

1848. DIXON H. LEWIS, an important member of congress from Alabama during a quarter of a century, died at New York, aged 46.

1849. TOBIAS E. STANSBURY, a revolutionary officer, died near Baltimore, aged 93. A great portion of his long life was spent in the service of his country.

1849. BENJAMIN ABBOT, for half a century an eminent New England teacher, died at Exeter, N. H., aged 87. As principal of Phillips Exeter academy, he directed the studies of pupils who became eminent men in the land.

1852. The grand duke of Tuscany refused to give audience to an English protestant deputation in favor of Rosa and Francisco Madiai, under confinement for distributing Bibles.

1854. LEWIS EDWARD NOLAN, a distinguished British cavalry officer, was killed at Balaclava. He was well versed in all the languages of modern Europe, and a military writer.

1855. The Russians under Gen. Liprandi, 30,000 strong, attacked the allies at Balaclava, carried and maintained two Turkish redoubts, and captured several guns; but were repulsed by the English and French.

OCTOBER 26.

1656 A. M. NOAH entered the ark on the 10th day of 2d month, answering to this day of our month. The ark was 525 feet long, 87 broad, and 52 deep; requiring about 245,000 cubic feet of timber; its capacity two millions cubic feet of space; was commenced about 1556 and completed 1656, having been 100 years in building.

1331. ISMAEL ABULFEDA, prince of Hamath, in Syria, died. Before he began his reign he distinguished himself by his researches in geography, and published in Arabic an account of the regions beyond the Oxus.

1455. The charter of the beautiful town of Kirkcudbright in Scotland was given. This town was much frequented in time of persecution.

1522. Donna MARIA PACHECO, the widow of Padilla, retired into the citadel of Toledo, which she defended four months against the royalists.

1594. WILLIAM ALLEN, usually called the great English cardinal, died, and was buried at Rome.

1645. Bloody battle of Routon Heath, in which king Charles was defeated and many of his officers slain.

1701. Birth day of HELEN and JUDITH, the united twin sisters, at Tzoni, in Hungary. They possessed a musical genius, were exhibited in England in 1708, and died 1723.

1703. Great storm in England, by which large tracts of country were overflowed, trees torn up by the roots, immense numbers of cattle perished, and 8000 human lives were lost on the Thames, Severn and coast of Holland alone.

1723. GODFREY KNELLER, an eminent German painter, died in England, where he was greatly honored for his skill in portraits.

1724. HILKIAH BEDFORD, who was tried and fined for publishing a work entitled the hereditary right of the crown of England, died at London.

1727. LEWIS DE SACY died; an eloquent *avocat* of the parliament of Paris, and a learned member of the French academy.

1728. A dispatch was received in England that more than two thirds of the city of Copenhagen in Denmark was burned down. The fire commenced on the 20th and continued three days.

1751. PHILIP DODDRIDGE, an eminent English dissenting minister, died; author of the *Rise and Progress of Religion in the Soul*, a standard work.

1773. Conspiracy of Palermo.

1774. The first congress of North America, having finished their delibrations, adjourned.

1788. THOMAS REED died at Bordentown, N. J.; a captain in the navy of the revolution.

1794. SUWARROW, having defeated the Polish van guard, invested Praga, the suburb of Warsaw.

1795. The French national assembly dissolved itself, after three years' duration.

1796. MOREAU crossed the Rhine.

1798. A violent insurrection was raised against the French at Cairo in Egypt.

1800. Earthquake at Constantinople, destroyed the royal palace and many other buildings.

1803. EDMUND PENDLETON, a distinguished Virginia statesman, died. He was a member of the first congress.

1803. JOHN PENN, one of the signers of the declaration of American independence from Virginia, died.

1807. Treaty of Fontainbleau, between Bonaparte and Spain, for the conquest of Portugal.

1807. Russia declared war against Great Britain.

1811. Saguntum surrendered by the Spanish to the French under Suchet. Same day the Spaniards defeated the

French at Puycezda, and pursued them into the French territories, where they levied heavy contributions.

1816. Doctorow, the Russian general, died at Moscow.

1822. It was ordered in the Netherlands that the national language alone, the Dutch or Flemish, should be used in schools.

1825. Canal celebration at Albany.

1831. Cholera first appeared in England at Sunderland.

1836. George Coleman (*the Younger*) died in London, aged 74. He was the author of numerous comedies which were eminently successful, but failed to procure him a decent livelihood, so that many of the last years of his life were spent in great poverty.

1836. Charles Day, a wealthy blacking manufacturer, of the firm of Day & Martin, died in London. He had been totally blind for many years. He left an estate valued at about two millions of dollars, and directed about half a million to be devoted to establish a charity, to be called The Poor Blind Man's Friend.

1837. Harlem, N. Y., rail road completed.

1841. Thomas Cadwallader died at Philadelphia, aged 61. He was a lawyer by profession, and a brigadier general in the last war with Great Britain. He was distinguished for his military talents, and greatly respected for his private virtues and public usefulness.

1842. David Trimble, distinguished as a statesman and patriot, died at Trimble Furnace, Kentucky. Few had been more useful than he in developing the resources of that important state.

1843. Alden Bradford, a New England historian, died at Boston, aged 78. He was secretary of the commonwealth from 1812 to 1824.

1845. Disturbances and civil war in Hayti; the Dominicans surprised the Haytien garrison at Laxaron, the chief frontier town on the cape side of the island, and after killing 128 men, took the fort, which they soon after evacuated.

1850. John McDonough died at New Orleans, aged 72, who by untiring industry and the narrowest economy amassed immense wealth, which was principally divided between the cities of New Orleans and Baltimore.

1850. The northwest passage discovered by captain McClure, of the Investigator.

1851. Richard Cowling Taylor, an English naturalist and antiquary, died at Philadelphia, aged about 60.

1852. A violent storm at Athens; one of the columns of the temple of Jupiter Olympus overthrown.

OCTOBER 27.

42 b. c. Battle of Philippi, and death of Marcus Junius Brutus. This eventful day threw into the hands of two autocratical magistrates, of no tried reputation, and rivals by nature, the universal rule, with the liberties of their country. There were just twenty days between the deaths of Cassius, "the last of the Romans," and his friend Brutus, in the two great battles of Philippi.

251. Valerian elected in full senate to the restored Roman censorship, an office which had dropt with the life of Titus, from the modesty of his successors. The Roman virtue stood below correction.

1492. Columbus discovered Cuba, and made a landing on the following day.

1553. Michael Servetus, a learned and ingenious Spaniard, burnt at Geneva by the Calvinists, for the heresy of Arianism.

1617. Ralph Winwood died; an English statesman, and secretary of state under James I.

1644. Second battle of Newberry, in England; the royalists under Charles I defeated by the parliament army. Night favored the escape of the vanquished.

1650. The prince of Orange died of the small pox.

1675. Giles Personne Roberval, a French mathematician, died; author of a work on mechanics, &c.

1722. Third immigration of Palatines to the United States.

1775. The British under lord Dunmore, the royal governor of Virginia, cannonaded Hampton, but were repulsed.

1795. The French directory, which succeeded the national assembly, entered upon the duties of their appointment as the executive government.

1802. Henry Hunter, an eminent Scottish divine and author, died.

1805. Walter Blake Kirwan died; an Irish divine, eminent for his popularity as a preacher, which was so great that it was often necessary to keep off the crowds from the churches in which he preached by guards and palisades. He died exhausted by his labors.

1810. Bonaparte ordered all British goods found in France to be burned. Not the surest way to discourage manufactures.

1822. William Lowndes, a distinguished statesman of South Carolina, died. He was respected and beloved even by his political enemies, and stood in the first rank of American statesmen.

1830. Hard fighting at Antwerp, between the Dutch and Belgians; the former were driven into the citadel, where they commenced cannonading the town, and did great execution.

1840. JOHN THOMSON, a Scottish clergyman, died; distinguished as a landscape painter.

1844. WILLIAM CAMPBELL died at Cherry Valley, N. Y., aged 77. He was the only member of his family that escaped death or captivity at the massacre of Cherry Valley in 1778. He lived to fill many important stations with fidelity and ability.

1846. RANDOLPH RIDGELY, an officer in the Mexican war, was killed by a fall from his horse. He had greatly distinguished himself at the battles of Palo Alto and Resaca de la Palma.

1851. WILLIAM WYON, a celebrated British medalist and die sinker, died at Brighton, aged 57. He belonged to a family of German descent, who wrought the great seals of England, Scotland and Ireland.

1853. Captain J. W. GUNNISON, of the corps of topographical engineers, with seven other members of the party of exploration, while attempting to survey the lakes in Utah territory, were massacred by the Indians.

OCTOBER 28.

312. Battle of Saxa Rubra, and overthrow of the tyrant Maxentius, by Constantine. The whole race of Maxentius was extirpated, and the prætorian guards abolished at Rome.

900. ALFRED (*the Great*), king of England, died, aged 51, in the 28th year of his reign. To him is ascribed the mode of trial by jury.

1216. The crown and other regalia of England being lost, Henry III was crowned with a plain circle of gold on his temples.

1485. RODOLPHUS AGRICOLA, a Dutch author, died. He was one of the most learned men of his age.

1541. Great storm accompanied by an earthquake, at Algiers, which destroyed 86 Spanish ships and 15 galleys with their crews, belonging to a powerful fleet fitted out for the reduction of that place by the emperor Charles V. He was compelled to raise the siege and return to his own dominions.

1572. Earl Mar, regent of Scotland, died, and was succeeded by Morton.

1592. AUGIER GHISLEN BUSBEQUIUS, a celebrated Flemish ambassador, died. He was learned and venerated.

1597. ALDUS MANUTIUS, an eminent Venitian printer, died. He was the third of a line of illustrious printers, celebrated for the elegance and correctness of their editions, and in his youth bid fair to excel his predecessors. But he met with reverses, and was compelled to sell the excellent library collected by his ancestors, of 80,000 volumes, to maintain himself. He wrote several learned works.

1646. WILLIAM DOBSON, an English painter, died. He was drawn from obscurity by Vandyke, after which he rose to great celebrity; but becoming addicted to pleasure before he had acquired a fortune, he became involved, and died at the age of 36.

1652. WILLIAM MEAD, an English physician, died, aged 149.

1652. Action between the English fleet under Blake and Penn, and the Dutch fleet under De Witt and De Ruyter. Three ships of the latter were destroyed and one taken.

1670. JOHN HACKET, an English prelate, died; eminent for his learning and exemplary virtues.

1681. Algiers bombarded by the French fleet under admiral Duquesne and Bernard Renaud. It is said that bomb vessels were first used on this occasion, being the invention of Renaud, who had five of them built.

1685. MICHAEL LE TELLIER, a French statesman, died. He had sufficient influence with the king, Louis XIV, to procure the revocation to the edict of Nantes. He lived to triumph in the cruel measures which followed but a few days.

1687. JAMES ATKINS, a learned Scottish bishop, died, He wrote against the presbyterians, but his writings are now almost unknown.

1699. Pope INNOCENT XII died.

1701. WILLIAM PENN granted a charter of privileges to Pennsylvania and the counties, now state of Delaware, in which the liberty of conscience was fully recognized.

1703. JOHN WALLIS, an eminent English divine and mathematician, died. His works are numerous; and though his theological writings are respectable, yet it is from his mathematical labors that he derives a lasting celebrity.

1704. JOHN LOCKE, the illustrious English philosopher, died.

1708. GEORGE of Denmark, husband of Anne, queen of England, died; "an illustrious instance of conjugal affection among the great."

1710. EZEKIEL SPANHEIM died; an eminent Swiss writer on history and antiquities.

1740. ANNA IWANOWNA, empress of Russia, died.

1741. BALTHAZAR GIBERT, a French writer, died. He was 50 years professor of rhetoric at the college of Mazarin.

1746. Earthquake at Lima, by which that city and the port of Callao were destroyed. The sea first receded, then rushed upon the shore, carrying everything before it. Of 23 ships in the harbor 19 were sunk, and 4 carried a considerable way up the country, and Callao became a part of the ocean.

1748. Gov. CLINTON signed the bill reviving the act to raise £1,800 by lottery, to build a college.

1776. Battle of White Plains. The brunt of this battle was sustained by the troops under McDougal, 600 men, who nobly sustained their post, though deserted by 4 regiments of militia, who fled on the approach of the British light horse. Both armies laid on their arms awaiting another attack.

1788. First court held at Plattsburgh, Clinton county, N. Y.

1791. GEORGE LOUIS OEDER, an eminent German physician and botanist, died.

1792. JOHN SMEATON, an eminent English mechanic and engineer, died; celebrated as the builder of the Eddystone lighthouse.

1793. Hurricane on the island of Cuba; several vessels driven out to sea, and 520 houses in Havana totally destroyed.

1800. ARTEMAS WARD, the first major-general in the American revolutionary army, died. He graduated at Harvard, was subsequently a member of congress, and noted for incorruptible integrity.

1806. CHARLOTTE SMITH, an English poetess and novelist, died. She long enjoyed great popularity.

1806. Battle of Prentzlow, in Brandenburg; the Prussian army of 16,000 compelled to surrender to the French under Murat. This was the remnant of the king's guard which escaped from the battle of Jena, and included several princes.

1823. WASSIL WASSILIJEWITSCH CAPNIST, a Russian counselor of state, died. He is better known as a poet and dramatic writer, in which he is entitled to much praise.

1838. The Mormons, comprising about 700 men under arms, with their leaders, surrendered at Far-West, Missouri, to a body of 3,000 militia, under Gen. Atchinson. The whole number captured was 5,000, miserably destitute of the means of subsistence.

1844. The Royal Exchange at London opened in an imposing manner, the queen being present and presiding at the ceremony.

1848. HARRISON GRAY OTIS, a Massachusetts statesman, died, aged 83; having filled with distinguished success the principal political offices in the gift of the people of the state.

1848. WINDISCHGRATZ, besieging the city of Vienna, entered the suburbs and began an attack; a succession of conflicts ensued, which lasted several days before the city was completely mastered.

1849. DAVID B. DOUGLAS, an eminent civil and military engineer, died at Geneva, N. Y., aged 56. He distinguished himself in the war of 1812, before he was 21 years of age. He was a man of extensive and varied learning.

1851. A meeting of cotton planters was held at Macon, Georgia, to devise ways and means to prevent fluctuations in the price of cotton. Little harmony of views or concord of action was manifested.

1854. A fire at Cleveland, Ohio, consumed property to the amount of $2,000,000.

1854. The Turks in the principalities attacked the Russians, and after a contest of two hours compelled them to cross the Danube and destroy the bridges.

OCTOBER 29.

1038. ANGELOTH, archbishop of Canterbury, died. He is noted for having refused to crown Harold, although he had enjoyed the patronage of his father Canute.

1268. CONRADINO, emperor of Germany, beheaded at Naples, at the age of 16. In a hazardous attempt to recover a part of his possessions which had been wrested from him, he fell into the power of his enemy.

1618. WALTER RALEIGH, an illustrious English nobleman, beheaded at the age of 66. He is memorable as a "statesman, seaman, soldier, chemist and chronologist." He obtained the patent of Virginia in 1584.

1666. JAMES SHIRLEY, an English dramatic writer, died. His death was occasioned by the great fire of London; both himself and his wife died of fright, and were buried in one grave. He wrote 37 plays and a volume of poems.

1666. EDMUND CALAMY, an eminent English divine, died, it is said by reason of the great fire at London.

1691. MELCHIZEDEC THEVENOT died; librarian to the king of France, and a celebrated writer of travels.

1727. Earthquake in New England. No event of the kind had been witnessed by the English, of equal violence, since their settlement of the country, and consequently they were greatly alarmed. It was felt along the coast 700 miles, though of only 2 minutes' duration; and the island of Martinique was in danger of being entirely destroyed by an earthquake the same day, which was felt at intervals during eleven hours.

1745. Battle of Freybourg; the Prussians under prince Henry defeated the allies, who lost 8,000 men.

1757. Edward Vernon, a renowned English admiral, died.

1776. The British and Hessians repulsed in an attack on the Americans under Col. Glover, at White Plains.

1777. John Hancock resigned his office as president of Congress.

1777. The whole force of the Americans under Washington was 12,480 men, of whom 8,963 were regulars then called continentals.

1778. Americans under major Talbot captured the British schooner Pigott, and brought her into Stonington.

1783. John le Rond d'Alembert, a distinguished French philosopher, died.

1792. Three of the mutineers of the ship Bounty were executed at Portsmouth.

1793. The Austrians under Clairfait defeated the French in their intrenched camp before Mentz; the camp was carried, 106 cannon, 200 ammunition wagons, and 2,000 men were taken prisoners.

1795. The citizens of London obstructed the king on his way to the parliament house, clamoring for bread, peace, no Pitt. A bullet pierced the glass of the king's coach.

1804. George Morland died; an exquisite English painter, principally of rustic scenes.

1810. Battle of Aculco, Mexico; the Spanish patriots under the first Aldamo, defeated by the king's troops under Gen. Callejas, with the loss of 6,000.

1812. Mallet, with 12 of his confederates in a plot to subvert the Bonaparte dynasty, were tried and shot in the plains of Grenille.

1814. Holland, in consideration of its relinquishment of all its claims to the cape of Good Hope, and to the colonies of Demarara, Essequebo and Berbice, all the other colonies which she possessed previous to 1794, in Asia, Africa and America, were restored by Great Britain.

1814. Steam frigate Fulton launched at New York.

1814. The sloop of war Peacock, Capt. Warrington, returned from a cruise of 147 days, during which she had captured and destroyed 14 British vessels.

1824. Charles Pinckney, an American orator and statesman, died. He was a patriot of the revolution, and a member of the convention which framed the constitution.

1825. The first boat on the Erie canal, from Albany, reached Buffalo, on which occasion a celebration took place.

1828. Luke Hansard, a very eminent English printer, died; distinguished also for his piety.

1831. Riots at Bristol, England, during which the jails were broken open and burnt, the mansion house and custom house destroyed, the toll-gates pulled down, and many private houses plundered and set on fire, by which some hundreds of people were burnt to death.

1841. Thomas Philips, an eminent English vocalist, died by a rail road accident, aged 66.

1842. Allan Cunningham, an eminent Scottish poet, died in London, aged 56.

1850. The statue of John C. Calhoun, which had been lost by the wreck of a vessel, was recovered almost without injury.

1850. The Portuguese frigate Donna Maria II, of 32 guns, accidentally blown up in the harbor of Macao, and completely destroyed; of 244 men on board, 188 perished.

1852. The remains of Daniel Webster were buried at Marshfield, Mass., many thousands of citizens of Boston and adjoining towns being present.

1854. Josiah Butler, an eminent New Hampshire statesman and judge, died at Deerfield, aged 74.

1854. W. W. Farmer, lieutenant-governor of Louisiana, died at Baton Rouge, aged 45; for many years a prominent man in the state.

OCTOBER 30.

69. Cremona, in Italy, sacked and burned, 286 years after its foundation.

1270. The seventh and last crusade ended by the treaty of Barbary.

1270. Conflict on London bridge, between the retainers of the bishop of Winchester (bad Beaufort) and the duke of Gloucester.

1485. Coronation of Henry VII, two months after Bosworth field, when was instituted the *Yoemen of the Guard*, consisting of 50 archers. At that time there raged in London a malady called the sweating sickness, which terminated fatally in twenty-four hours.

1553. James Sturmius, a learned German ambassador, died. He contributed greatly to the reformation of Strasburg, where he erected a college, and assisted in the publication of a history of the reformation.

1574. Mary of Cleves, wife of Henry I, prince of Conde, died, aged 18, probably by poison. She was loved so ardently by the duke of Anjou, afterwards Henry III, that when he came to the throne he determined to annul her marriage; but her sudden death intervened.

1602. John James Boisard, a French antiquary, died. He pursued his favorite study in Italy and the isles of the Adriatic; but many of his materials were destroyed by the ravages of war.

1605. George Clifford, earl of Cumberland, died; a celebrated English navigator.

1632. Henry de Montmorency, admiral of France, beheaded for conspiracy. He distinguished himself by his valor, and was made admiral at the age of 18.

1655. John Seldon, the learned English antiquary, died.

1680. Antoinette de la Porte Bourignon, a celebrated French enthusiast, died, aged 64. She was so very deformed at her birth, that a consultation was had about stifling her as a monster. But she early developed great powers of mind, became a traveling preacher, wandered about incessantly, and was expelled from many countries. Her reveries fill 22 volumes.

1732 Shipped for transportation to Virginia, 68 men and 50 women, felon convicts.

1750. John Mottley died; an English dramatic writer and historian of Peter the Great of Russia.

1760. Great earthquake in Syria and Barbary; 6000 persons killed in Damascus.

1762. British king's ships Panther and Argo captured Spanish galleon Santissima Trinidad, from Manilla, valued at three millions of dollars.

1781. The Oneida Indians, part of Col. Willet's force, defeated the British, colonel John Butler; when that execrable savage, Butler, was killed.

1782. Anthony Terrasson, a distinguished French advocate, and professor of the royal college, died. He wrote a history of Roman jurisprudence, and other works.

1787. Ferdinand Galiani, a noble Italian writer, died. His genius and learning were employed on useful and practical subjects.

1793. Twenty-two deputies of the French national convention of the Girondists, convicted and sentenced to death. De Valaze, a lawyer, on hearing his sentence, with great sang froid, drew a poignard and stabbed himself to the heart.

1802. Charles Alexander de Calonne, a French statesman, died. He succeeded Necker as comptroller of the finances.

1804. Samuel Ayscough, assistant librarian in the British Museum, died. He is chiefly memorable for his patient industry in arranging the collections. He published a catalogue of the manuscripts, and a catalogue of the ancient charters in that institution; the latter amounting to 1,600.

1805. Anquetil du Perron, a learned Frenchman, died. His death is also placed, by different authorities, in November and January. (See Jan. 15, 1805.)

1808. John Whitaker died; an able English theologian, historian, critic, politician, and poet.

1810. Battle of Los Cruces, in Mexico, between the revolutionists under Hidalgo, and a corps of Spaniards, in which the latter were defeated. This was the first battle of the revolution.

1813. Sarah Rodgers, a celebrated painter, died at Philadelphia.

1822. The Caledonian canal, uniting the British sea with the Atlantic ocean, was opened. It is a great national work, but not much in requisition.

1822. Iturbide dissolved the Mexican congress in the same manner as Cromwell dissolved the long parliament, and the same day formed a new legislative assembly, composed of persons favorable to his plans. This step was fatal to his reign.

1825. Charles Robert Maturin, an Irish divine, dramatist, and poet, died. His genius was great, but not always under the control of a pure taste.

1840. Earthquake at Zante, which demolished 240 houses in the town, and injured nearly all the rest. The villages and country houses of the island were destroyed, or greatly injured.

OCTOBER 31.

1448. John Palæologus, emperor of Constantinople, died. He reigned 29 years, and resisted the invasion of the Turkish foe, who pressed upon his borders.

1517. Commencement of the reformation by Martin Luther, who on this day published his 95 theses against the papal indulgences, &c.

1579. John Stadius, a German historian and mathematician, died at Paris. He tarnished his scientific knowledge with astrological calculations.

1659. John Bradshaw died; celebrated as president of the tribunal which tried and condemned the king, Charles I. He was afterwards deprived of his office by Cromwell, to whose usurpations he was opposed; at the restoration his bones were dug up and hanged at Tyburn.

1665. An act called the "five mile act," passed by the English parliament, prohibiting nonconforming ministers from going within 5 miles of a town sending a member to parliament. This was to prevent them entering the pulpits of episcopalians vacated on account of the plague.

1678. From the evidence of Oates and others, the commons of England passed a resolution that there existed a hellish plot of the papists to assassinate king Charles.

1732. Victor Amadeus, king of Sardinia and duke of Savoy, died.

1735. General Oglethorpe re-embarked

for America, accompanied by John Wesley and other missionaries, with several families of settlers.

1751. JAMES LOGAN, governor of Pennsylvania after the death of the proprietor, died. He was a native of Ireland, distinguished for his talents and learning, and came to America with Penn.

1760. The foundation stone of Blackfriars bridge over the Thames was laid.

1765. WILLIAM AUGUSTUS, duke of Cumberland, died. He was the second son of George II of England, and commanded at many important battles in the German wars.

1782. LOUIS ELIZABETH DE LA VERGNE, a celebrated French general, died. He was the friend of learned men, and the author of numerous works.

1793. JEAN PIERRE BRISSOT DE WARVILLE, and 20 others, Girondists, condemned on the previous day, were guillotined at Paris. They were generally opposed to the death of the king and the violent and bloody measures pursued by Marat and Robespierre.

1803. The United States frigate Philadelphia, captain Bainbridge, grounded on a rock three and a half miles from Tripoli, and was taken after an action of 4 hours, having thrown over all her guns in the vain hope of getting off.

1806. Battle of Strelitz; the French general Savery with 600 horse took the place, and captured the hereditary prince of Mecklenbenburg-Strelitz.

1806. Battle of Anklan; the Bavarians defeated the Prussians under general Bila, and took him and 4,000 men prisoners.

1806. About this time a revolution took place at St. Domingo; the black king of Hayti, Dessalines, was killed, and succeeded by Christophe.

1812. The Cossacks under Platoff defeated the French rear guard near Kolotsk with terrible slaughter.

1812. The French defeated by Witgenstein at Tchasniki, with the loss of 900 killed and 800 taken.

1832. ANTONIO SCARPA, professor of anatomy at Pavia, died, aged 86. He stood, for nearly half a century, by the common consent of his countrymen, at the head of anatomy and surgery in Italy.

1838. NOAH WORCESTER, an eminent philanthropist and founder of the Massachusetts Peace society, died. He was an extraordinary man, and entirely self-taught. In 1815 he published *A Solemn View of the Custom of War*, which produced a strong impression, and has been circulated in different languages in Europe.

1842. SOLOMON HERSCHELL, chief rabbi of the German and Polish Jews in London, died, aged 82, and was buried with great solemnity. He was a majestic figure, with a look of one of the old fathers, and an object of considerable mark in the streets of London.

1847. A quarrel took place between the police in Rio de Janeiro and some sailors belonging to the United States vessels of war lying in the harbor. The sailors and an officer were imprisoned, which led to a serious difficulty between the two governments.

1848. STEPHEN WATTS KEARNEY, the conqueror of New Mexico, died at St. Louis, aged 54. He had been in the army since 1812, and his character and bearing as an officer were unsurpassed.

1849. The French cabinet, on being informed that they were wanting in dignity, resigned their commissions to their president.

1849. A remarkable meteoric stone fell at Charlotte, North Carolina.

1850. Queen ISABELLA opened the Cortez at Madrid in the new palace on the Plaza de Cervantes.

1855. RIVAS sworn into office as president of Nicaragua, Walker declining in his favor at Grenada.

NOVEMBER.

NOVEMBER 1.

51 B. C. CICERO sat down before Pindenissum, a city in Cilicia.

79. Pompeii and Herculaneum buried by an eruption of Vesuvius.

1290. The persons of all the English Jews, 16,511, were banished, and their estates and treasures confiscated to the crown.

1399. JOHN V (*the Conqueror*), duke of Brittany, died.

1483. HENRY STAFFORD, duke of Buckingham, beheaded. He was the vile instrument of the third Richard's usurpation, and was executed by that king's order, without any legal process.

1596. PETER PITHOU, a learned and eloquent French civilian, died. He visited England, and published some valuable works on law, history, and classical literature, and restored *Phædrus* and other ancient books which had long been lost.

1607. Sir JAMES MELVILLE died. He was a courtier, in the strictest sense of that word. To him the court was the world, and its rules of action his.

1653. The parliament of the English commonwealth chose a new council of state.

1678. WILLIAM CODDINGTON, governor of Rhode Island, died. He became dissatisfied with the ecclesiastical government in Massachusetts, and in 1638 associated himself with 170 others, who purchased Rhode Island of the natives. He was a man of learning, and contributed more than any other, perhaps, to the establishment of the colony of Rhode Island, and laying the foundation of civil and religious liberty in America.

1683. The counties of Albany, Dutchess, Kings, Orange, Queens, Suffold, Richmond, Ulster, and Westchester, N. Y., erected.

1700. CHARLES II, king of Spain, died. He was the last of the eldest branches of the Austrian princes who reigned in Spain.

1710. Lord HAVERSHAM, a noted British peer, died. He was a "constant" speaker in the house of lords.

1714. JOHN RADCLIFFE, an English physician of great eminence, died. The university of Oxford is indebted to him for the library and infirmary which bears his name, and for an annuity of £600 for two traveling fellowships.

1724. HUMPHREY PRIDEAUX died; an English divine, historian, and critic.

1730. LOUIS FERDINAND MARSIGLI, an Italian nobleman, died. He was famous in arms and in letters, and founded the academy of arts and sciences at Bologna, called the Institute.

1755. Earthquake at Lisbon, by which it is supposed about 50,000 persons perished. Every building worthy of notice was prostrated. Peerless pool was lifted from its bed; the Mios lake in Norway vibrated with the canals of Amsterdam; the fountains of Tangier were stopped, and artificial tides flowed every fifteen minutes at Gibraltar.

1765. Stamp act went into operation in America. The great dissatisfaction it created, was manifested by the tolling of bells, and other solemnities.

1769. LA SALLE arrived at the mouth of the Miami, having seventeen men in his company, the rest being dismissed, to return with furs to Niagara, when he embarked at the bay of Puans.

1770. ALEXANDER CRUDEN died; a Scottish writer, and corrector of the press, whose literary labors were notable. He was found dead on his knees, in the attitude of prayer.

1771. JOHN EYRE sentenced to be transported beyond seas, for stealing a few quires of paper. He was worth £30,000, yet committed and confessed the deed.

1775. PETER JOSEPH BERNARD died; a French writer of operas and other lighter pieces, which for their ease and elegance, procured for him the name of *le gentil Bernard*.

1783. CHARLES LINNÆUS (*the Younger*) died. He succeeded his father as professor of botany at Upsal.

1793. GEORGE GORDON died; an Englishman who led the opposition to the papists in 1780, which gave rise to the riots of that year. His life from that time was spent in legal censures and imprisonments, and he finally died in Newgate prison.

1794. Henry Hoogeveen died; an eminent Dutch philologist, of great learning and industry.

1794. Rhinefield, a fortress built on a rock on the left bank of the Rhine, abundantly provided and defended by 2000 men, surrendered at the first summons of the French.

1805. Captain Wright, of the British navy, died in the Temple at Paris. Bonaparte is accused of having suffered him to be put to the torture and strangled.

1806. French entered Kustrin, where they took 4000 Prussian prisoners, 90 cannon, and sufficient stores to supply the army two months.

1806. French under Mortier took Cassel and all Hesse.

1813. Four large British vessels, and a number of boats, attacked the advance guard of the United States army, under general Wilkinson, and were repulsed.

1815. John Coakley Lettsom, a distinguished London physician, died. He was long known by his public and private benevolence, his skill, and his numerous writings, moral and medical.

1818. The first steam boat on the lakes, called from an Indian chief, Walk-in-the-Water, left Buffalo on her first trip. The boat cost $70,000, including the sum paid Fulton and Livingston for patent.

1819. *The North Georgian Gazette and Winter Journal*, first published on board the Hecla discovery ship, in Winter harbor, off Melville island, in the Polar sea. The 21st number closed its polar existence, but it rose again in London.

1834. John Howard died in Fayette co., Ga., aged 103. He was in the revolutionary army, and received five wounds at the battle of Guilford. His sight continued good till his hundredth year, and he never used spectacles.

1835. Thomas Taylor died; an English author, long known by the appellation of *the Platonist*. His works comprise 23 vols. quarto, and 40 vols. octavo; the greatest of which are complete translations of Aristotle and Plato, illustrated copiously from the ancient commentators.

1835. William Motherwell, a Scottish poet of considerable reputation, died.

1842. Louis D. Jose, usually called *Portuguese Joe*, was burnt to death in the hotel at New Orleans in which he kept the bar. He was captain of the maintop on board the ship Saratoga, at the battle on lake Champlain, and nailed the colors to the mast after they had been shot away by the British.

1843. John Parish Robertson, a Scottish merchant in South America, died at Calais. He established an extensive business, and introduced many useful improvements, which the distracted partisans of that country could not appreciate; he was deprived of a large property which he had accumulated, and retired to England, where he produced two works on South America, of some merit.

1845. Samuel Harrison Smith, well known as the editor of the *Philadelphia New World*, and the first to establish the *National Intelligencer*, died at Washington.

1849. Jabez W. Huntington, of Connecticut, a distinguished senator of the United States, died at Norwich, Conn.

1849. Elizur Goodrich, professor of law in Yale college, and some time mayor of New Haven, died, aged 88. His removal from the office of collector of customs, at New Haven, immediately on the accession of Jefferson, gave occasion to the famous letter of that president, in which he avowed his principle of removal for political opinions.

1849. Jeffrey Chipman died at Kalamazoo, Mich., aged 60. He was a native of Rutland, Vt., and afterwards a magistrate at Canandaigua, N. Y., before whom William Morgan, the apostate free mason, was arraigned for larceny, and committed to Ontario jail, whence he was abducted. In all the subsequent trials, J. Chipman was the first witness called.

1852. Battle of Hermasillo; the French count Boulbon de Raousset, who led an enterprise upon Sonora, was defeated, and his expedition wholly overthrown.

1855. Accident on the Missouri and Pacific rail road; an excursion train going to celebrate the opening of the road, was precipitated through a bridge thirty feet into the river, by which the chief engineer of the road, Thomas S. O'Sullivan, and 24 others, were killed, and a great number injured, many of them prominent citizens of St. Louis.

NOVEMBER 2.

1656. a. m. The deluge began on the 17th day of the 2d month, answering to our November 2, on the supposition that the original civil year of the Hebrews began on the 16th of September, and contained 354 days.

285. b. c. Ptolemy Philadelphus, of Egypt, so memorable as a patron of learning, commenced his reign upon this Julian day; the year following that in which Pyrrhus was driven from Macedonia. It is the date of the *Septuagint*.

1502. Columbus entered the harbor which he named Porto Bello. The cazique was painted black, but all his subjects red. They all wore small golden ornaments in their nostrils; and the men a shell, and the women a fillet of cotton about their loins.

1552. Claude d'Annebaut, a French admiral, died; distinguished for his bravery and wisdom.

1600. Richard Hooker, an eminent English divine, died. His *Laws of Ecclesiastical Polity* in 8 books, procured him great fame and popularity.

1610. Richard Bancroft died; chaplain to queen Elizabeth, bishop of London, and archbishop of Canterbury.

1655. A committee appointed by the council of the lord protector of England to encourage trade and commerce.

1692. Alexander Menzikoff, a Russian prince, died in exile. He rose from the occupation of a pastry cook, and fell back to his orginal level in consequence of his pride and ostentation.

1716. Engelbert Kœmpfer, an eminent German botanist, died. Besides his works on botany, he wrote a *History of Japan*.

1726. Sophia Dorothea, queen of George I of England, died at the castle of Ahlen in Hanover, in which she had been immured since 1694 on a charge of an intrigue with count Koningsmarke; a charge which was never proved and generally disbelieved. She was often solicited to rejoin her husband. To the English who also made the proposal, she said, "If I am guilty I am not fit to be your queen; if I am innocent your king is not fit to be my husband."

1758. The Belliqueux, a French ship of war from Quebec, driven into Lundy road where she was taken possession of by the English; value estimated at £150,000.

1759. Charles Hanbury Williams, an English poet and ambassador, died.

1772. Town meeting in Boston, at which committees of correspondence were appointed by the "Sons of Liberty." Adams and Warren were among the originators of this plan, which was soon followed by the other states. These committees were undoubtedly the origin of the congress.

1783. Washington issued from head quarters, Rocky Hill, near Princeton, his farewell orders to the American armies.

1783. Charles Colle, a distinguished French comic writer, died.

1788. John Henderson, an English scholar, died. He displayed at a very early period of life, an uncommon thirst after knowledge, which he gratified with unremitted ardor. "The virtues of his heart were superior even to the astonishing powers of his understanding;" he died however, the victim of intemperance.

1794. François Joachim de Pierres Bernis, a French ecclesiastic, and courtier, died, aged 80. His talents and judgment were of a high order.

1812. Battle of Ghatz; the Cossacks under Platoff defeated a division of the French, and took 70 wagons, 20 cannons and some thousands of exhausted and helpless prisoners. Denizoff defeated another French division the same day, captured 40 loaded wagons and 1000 prisoners.

1818. Samuel Romilly, a learned English statesman, died by his own hand, in consequence of the death of his wife.

1825. The city of Albany celebrated the opening of the Erie canal with great ceremony.

1828. Thomas Pinckney, a general in the United States army, died. It was under his command that the Indian war in which general Jackson distinguished himself, was undertaken and brought to a successful issue.

1840. Anthony Carlisle, an eminent English surgeon, died. He was also a man of high literary and scientific attainments, and president of the royal college of surgeons.

1850. Samuel Young, a New York statesman, died at Ballston, aged 71. His official career was illustrated by the most remarkable integrity, by talents of the highest order, and by a character of the most marked individuality.

NOVEMBER 3.

361. Constantius, the last of the sons of Constantine the great, died, after a reign of 23 years, and was succeeded by Julian.

461. Leo I (*the Great*) pope, died. Rome was pillaged fourteen days by Genseric during his reign.

1327. James II (*the Just*), king of Arragon, died, aged 65; deservedly regretted for his moderation, courage, benevolence and magnanimity. He conquered Sicily, and waged a long war against the Moors and the people of Navarre. He had the good fortune to unite Valencia and Catalonia to his crown.

1369. That famous code of Godfrey, called the *Assize of Jerusalem*, restored by John d'Ibilen, count of Jaffa, was finished under the revision of sixteen native commissioners for the use of the Latin kingdom of Cyprus.

1493. Columbus, on his second voyage to the new world, descried land, which in honor of the day he called Dominica.

1580. Sir Francis Drake returned from his voyage round the world.

1603. Henry IV of France granted to Pierre du Gast, sieur de Monts, a patent of the American territory, from the 40th to the 46th degree of north latitude, with power to colonize and rule it, and to subdue and Christianize its native inhabitants; and the exclusive right to the commerce of peltry in Acadie and the gulf of St. Lawrence.

1611. Antonio Perez, a distinguished Spanish statesman and author, died at Paris, where he retired when disgraced at the court of Spain. He twice escaped the inquisition, and even eluded the emissaries sent to murder him, but although highly esteemed by the learned men of France and England, he died miserably poor.

1640. The long parliament of England began; Wm. Lenthal was chosen speaker.

1643. John Bainbridge died at Oxford; a physician and astronomer of high reputation.

1669. Charles Drelincourt, a French Calvinistic divine, died. His *Consolations against the Fear of Death* have passed through numerous editions, and been translated into several languages.

1680. The great comet of this year approached so near the earth as in many places to occasion no small alarm.

1710. Luke Rotgans, a Dutch poet, died. After being engaged two years in the wars of Holland he retired to his country seat to devote himself to poetry.

1739. Charles Jervas, an English painter, died. He is immortalized more by Pope's panegyric than by his own pictures.

1741. Behring wrecked on the island which bears his name.

1760. Battle of Torgau; the Austrians under Daun defeated by Frederick II of Prussia, with the loss of 20,000 men, 8,000 of whom were taken. Prussian loss 13,000.

1762. The remarkable peace between England and France was signed at Fontainebleau.

1771. First newspaper printed in Albany, N. Y.

1771. An attempt was made by count Pulaski and some other Polish nobleman to carry off Stanislaus Augustus, the king. They took him prisoner, but after wandering about all night, in the morning they found themselves near where they set out, and were obliged to liberate their captive.

1774. Gloucester Ridley, an eminent English divine, died. He commenced life as an actor..

1775. St. Johns surrendered to the Americans. General Carleton in attempting to cross the St. Lawrence with 800 men, was attacked by 300 Green Mountain boys under colonel Warren and compelled to retire; which induced the garrison to capitulate. They found 17 brass and 22 iron cannons, 2 howitzers, 7 mortars, 800 stand of arms, &c.

1775. Valentine Jaimerai Duval, an extraordinary French character, died. He at first gained his subsistence by watching poultry and sheep; but by perseverance and labor he obtained books and maps, became one of the most learned men of his time, and enjoyed the patronage of princes and the notice of the learned.

1787. Robert Lowth, an eminent English bishop, died; known by his translation of Isaiah, "the sublimest poetry in the world."

1793. Mary Olympe de Gouges, a French authoress, guillotined. Becoming disgusted with the brutalities of the revolutionists, she turned her pen against them, and fell a victim to their vengeance.

1797. William Enfield, an eminent English dissenting minister died; known by many ingenious and useful publications.

1812. Battle near Wiazma; the French under Ney, Davoust, and Beauharnois defeated by the Russians with the loss of 6,000 killed, and 3,500 taken prisoners, and 28 cannon. Of the wounded French, all who fell must have unquestionably perished, as in the night the Russian winter set in, with a degree of iron severity almost unknown to the oldest inhabitants; on the following morning all was buried under a deep, wide waste of snow.

1832. John Leslie died; an eminent Scottish chemist, mathematician, and natural philosopher, inventor of the differential thermometer, and author of various scientific works. He rose from humble life, and received the honor of knighthood for his acquirements.

1834. Dr. Horner, died at Zurich, Switzerland. He accompanied Krusenstern in his first Russian voyage round the world, and wrote the *Natural History of Russia.*

1839. Carter Berkley, an eminent Virginia physician, aged 72, died while feeling the pulse of a dying patient. He was a lineal descendant of sir William Berkley, and an excellent character.

1840. St. Jean d'Acre bombarded by the allied British and Turkish fleets. The firing commenced at half past 2 P. M., and ceased at 6. The magazine, containing 500 barrels of powder, was blown up, over which about 2,000 soldiers were stationed, who were nearly all buried in the ruins. The number of killed in the town is unknown; loss of the British and allies 18 killed and 42 wounded. The Egyptians evacuated the place on the following morning, and it was possessed by the conquerors, who found 121 mounted guns and 20 mortars on the walls, and 97 brass field pieces and 97 mortars in store, besides stores of all kinds and the military chest, valued altogether at about one million pounds.

NOVEMBER 4.

1493. COLUMBUS discovered the island of Guadaloupe, the largest of the Carib or Cannibal islands, called by the natives Carucueria. The drinking vessels of this fierce people were formed of human skulls. They here saw the pine apple.

1611. NICHOLAS LE FEVRE (or *Faber*), a learned and ingenious French writer, died. He was more ready to assist others than to appear as an author himself.

1613. EDWARD BREREWORD, a learned English antiquary, died.

1631. Lady MARY, eldest daughter of king Charles I, and subsequently the wife of William prince of Orange, born.

1673. The house of commons, in England, sent for to the house of lords, and prorogued, for addressing the king against a standing army.

1677. The marriage portion of the princess Mary was £40,000. She married the prince of Orange.

1680. JOSEPH GLANVIL, an eminent English divine, died; celebrated for his controversies.

1688. WILLIAM III entered Torbay with 50 sail of the line and 400 transports.

1694. The Hannibal, of London, arrived at Barbadoes with a cargo of negroes. Of 692 captives, 320 died on the passage; the rest, Philips, the master, says, "came out £19 per head, one with another." The official return of the population, four years afterwards was, 2,330 whites, 42,000 slaves.

1698. A colony from Scotland settled at New Edinburgh, on the coast of Darien.

1702. JOHN BENBOW, a brave English admiral, died in the West Indies, after an inglorious defeat, owing to the cowardice of his officers.

1702. EDWARD SHERBURNE, an English writer, died, aged 85. Besides his original works, he translated Seneca's tragedies and other Latin authors.

1713. FRANCIS PETIT DE LA CROIX, a French ambassador, died. He was an expert linguist in Turkish and Arabic, and rendered great services to literature by his dictionaries and other works on those languages.

1749. A ball of fire burst about 40 yards above the British ship Montague, admiral Chambers, knocking down five men, shattering the maintop mast, and otherwise injuring the ship. The ball was first visible about three miles from the ship, at midday, and rose before it burst.

1749. At Stoke, in Glocestershire, about 6 P. M., the inhabitants were surprised by a brilliant light surpassing that of the sun. It was seen but for a few minutes.

1764. CHARLES CHURCHILL, an eminent English poet, died. He was endowed with great natural abilities, and his poems, though they have lost something by time, are still preserved from oblivion.

1788. DEBORAH GODFREY died at Stepney, England, aged 80; celebrated as the mother of 34 children, all of whom lived to the age of maturity.

1791. The United States army, 1,400 men, under general St. Clair, defeated by the Indians, near the Miami villages. The Indians made the attack immediately after the soldiers had been dismissed, from the parade, and with so much intrepidity, that most of the officers were killed before they could form their men. The loss of the Americans was 894, being nearly two-thirds of the force. The Indians took 7 cannon, 200 oxen and a great number of horses. Their force was between three and four thousand, and their loss only 56. (Other and more reliable accounts say 1,500 Indians instead of 3,000.

1793. RICHARD TICKELL, an eminent English writer, was killed by a fall from a window of his apartments.

1794. Praga carried by storm by the Russians under Suwarrow; upon which Warsaw was compelled to surrender, and a massacre of the Poles followed, which issued in blotting out Poland from the nations of Europe.

1797. Earthquake at Quito; nearly 40,000 of the natives perished, either buried under the ruins of their own houses, swallowed up in the crevices of the earth, or drowned in the lakes which were suddenly formed.

1806. GEORGE MASON, an English writer, died. He made a valuable collection of English and foreign literature.

1825. The first boat down the Erie canal, arrived at New York.

1836. CHARLES X, ex-king of France, died at Goritz, in Illyria, an exile. He succeeded Louis XVIII, but lost the throne by his arbitrary measures.

1837. BARON ALBERT died at Paris, aged 70; a celebrated French physician, and author of numerous works in his profession.

1838. Martial law established at Montreal, in consequence of a rebellion against the government, which became general, throughout Canada and caused serious disturbances.

1839. Riot of 10,000 chartists from the mines and colleries, who attacked Newport, England, led on by John Frost, an ex-magistrate. About 20 of the rioters were killed, and Frost taken prisoner.

1845. ELEAZER BLACKMAN, the last survivor of the massacre at Wyoming, died at Hanover, Pa.

1848. The new constitution of France, adopted in the general assembly, by 739 to 30.

1853. LUCIEN B. WEBSTER, a United States officer, died at fort Brown, Texas. He served on the eastern frontier in the time of the Aroostook trouble, and also distinguished himself at Buena Vista.

1853. Battle of Oltenitza, between the Turks and Russians, in which the latter lost 1,200 killed and wounded.

NOVEMBER 5.

1500. COLUMBUS arrived at Cadiz in fetters; when the king and queen, ashamed of the orders they had given, commanded him to be released. Notwithstanding the apologies of his sovereigns, Columbus never forgot this ignominy. He preserved his fetters, hung them up in his apartment, and ordered them to be buried with him.

1548. There fell in Thuringia what is described as a ball of fire, which was attended with a great noise; and a reddish substance like coagulated blood was after wards found on the ground.

1605. Gunpowder plot discovered; a conspiracy for blowing up the English parliament, headed by Catesby. In the cellar was found 40 barrels of powder and Guy Fawkes.

1607. The famous grace *Non Nobis Domini*, composed by Bird, was first sung, on the second anniversary of the gunpowder plot.

1612. Prince HENRY died, aged 19. His funeral expenses were £16,016, yet his father, king James, would allow no mourning for him.

1630. JOHN KEPLER, a celebrated German astronomer, died. His genius and discoveries have been highly commended; but he maintained some very peculiar notions; among others, that the globe is a huge animal, which breathes out the winds through the holes in the mountains, as through its mouth and nostrils.

1635. THOMAS PARR, an English peasant, died at the age of 152. His habits were extremely temperate, and it is supposed that his death was hastened by a change of diet. JAMES BOWLES died in England in 1656, at the same age.

1678. JOHN BAPTIST NANI, a Venitian nobleman and ambassador, died. He wrote a history of Venice, and an account of his embassy to France.

1690. THOMAS BARTHOLINE died; an eminent professor of law and history at Copenhagen. His three brothers were professors in the same university, and his sister an excellent Danish poetess.

1702. The earl of Marlborough taken by a French party, but not being known, on producing a French pass, he was suffered to escape.

1714. BERNARDIN ROMAZZINI, an Italian physician, died at Padua, aged 81. Although blind he discharged the duties of professor of medicine with great applause in the university.

1732. JAMES OGLETHORPE, with several colonists, embarked for Georgia, in America.

1757. Battle of Rossbach, a village in Prussian Saxony; a decisive victory obtained by Frederick the great over the French and Austrians under Soubise.

1764. CHARLES CHURCHILL, the celebrated English poet, died at Boulogne.

1774. The militia of Virginia, assembled at fort Gower under lord Dunmore, the royal governor, declared their determination to support their countrymen, when called upon, and not the king, if he proceeded to execute the late obnoxious laws by force.

1780. VASILI EVDOKIMOVITCH ADADUROR, a Russian mathematician, died. He instructed Catharine II in the Russian language.

1782. The America, a 74 gun ship, built at Portsmouth, N. H., by order of congress, was launched. This was the first line of battle ship ever built in America.

1798. LEWIS GALVANI, an Italian philosopher, died at Bologna; celebrated as the discoverer of that kind of electricity called, after him, Galvanism. (See Feb. 5, 1799.)

1807. MARIA ANGELICA KAUFFMAN, an eminent French painter, and royal academician in London, died at Rome. She is styled by the Germans, "the painter of the soul;" and her mental acquirements and moral conduct were no less distinguished than her talents as an artist.

1816. GOUVERNEUR MORRIS, an American statesman and orator, died at his seat of Morrisiana, near New York.

1817. CHARLOTTE AUGUSTA, wife of prince Leopold of Coburg, and daughter of George IV of England and queen Caroline, died. The domestic life of the two former is held to be a *pattern*—not so the latter.

1831. PHILIP VAN COURTLAND, an officer of the revolutionary war, died at New York, aged 82.

1839. The British war ships Volage and Hyacinth proceeding to Chumpee in violation of the Chinese proclamation, were approached by 29 Chinese war junks, which they attacked. Six of the junks were sunk or blown up, and upwards of 500 men killed. The English suffered no injury. This was the beginning of the Chinese war.

1840. George R. T. Hewes, one of the persons who assisted in throwing the tea overboard in Boston harbor in the beginning of the revolution, died at German Flats, aged 106.

1854. George Cathcart, an eminent British general, killed at the battle of Inkerman, aged 60.

1854. Charles Kemble, an eminent English comedian, died at London, aged 74; the last surviving brother of this distinguished family.

1854. Battle of Inkerman, in which 50,000 Russians engaged 14,000 British and French. Russians lost about 9,000 besides prisoners; allies lost about 4,000.

1854. By the cholera which prevailed this season, the number of deaths up to this day were: in New York, 2,425; in Philadelphia, 575; in Boston, 255; in Pittsburg, 600.

1855. Battle at the river Ingour; Omar Pasha with 20,000 Turks defeated 10,000 Russians.

NOVEMBER 6.

606 b. c. The memory of the book of Jeremiah torn and burnt by king Jehoiakim, was observed as a fast, on the 6th of the Hebrew month *Caslew*.

63 b. c. Cataline assembled the conspirators on the evening of this day, to fire the capital and cut off the principal citizens and the senate.

644. Omar I, the second caliph after Mahomet, assassinated. His reign was signalized by many important events. The most extraordinary success attended the arms of the new religion; 36,000 towns and villages were conquered; the Alexandrian library and 4,000 Christian temples were destroyed; 400 mosques were built, and the ancient canal between the Nile and the Red sea was restored.

1406. Pope Innocent VII died.

1457. Gutenberg ceded to Faust all the moulds, types, presses and utensils of the office, as surety for the sums advanced by the latter to carry on the business of printing and experimenting. The partnership was dissolved, and Gutenberg, with the assistance of Conrad Humery, opened another office in the same city.

1460. John Fastolff, a brave English general, died, aged 80. Shakspeare has abused the character of this brave, generous and wealthy man, under the name of Falstaff. It is impossible for two characters to be more at variance than the real and fictitious Falstaff.

1620. Richard Carew, an English antiquary, died. His memory is extravagantly lauded, as another Livy, &c.

1622. King James issued "a proclamation, prohibiting interloping and disorderly trading to New England, in America." This remarkable edict was intended to protect the trade of the colony, but so far from proving beneficial to the company, really brought on its dissolution.

1632. Battle of Lutzen, and death of Gustavus Adolphus. The imperial troops, 40,000 men, under Wallenstein, were defeated by the Swedes, 27,000, under Gustavus. The famous general Papenheim was mortally wounded.

1644. Thomas Roe, an English statesman, died. During his residence at the court of Constantinople, he made a valuable collection of manuscripts, which were presented to the Bodleian library.

1656. John IV (*the Fortunate*), of Portugal, died. He undertook the emancipation of his country from the Spanish yoke, in which he was successful and was placed upon the throne.

1656. John Baptist Morin, a celebrated French physician, died. He acquired great reputation as an astrologer, and consulted the stars for Richelieu and Mazarin.

1714. Charles Davenant, an English writer, died. Besides his works on political economy, his tragedy was received with great applause.

1769. Claude Simeon Passemant died. He was brought up to a trade in Paris, which he quitted for higher pursuits. Among his ingenious labors, are mentioned an astronomical pendulum with a moving celestial sphere, a burning mirror, and some globes.

1790. James Bowdoin, governor of Massachusetts, died. He was constantly employed in the public service on the side of his country, and was honored at home and abroad for his literary acquirements.

1792. Battle of Gemappe, in which the French revolutionists under Dumourier, after a bloody action, gained a decisive victory over the Austrians; and a short time after every town in the Netherlands except Luxemburg was in the hands of the French.

1793. Louis Joseph Philip, duke of Orleans, guillotined at Paris. His character and morals were infamous. He gave his vote for the death of the king, an act which shocked even the most abandoned of his friends.

1806. Battle of Lubec; the French under Bernadotte and Soult carried the town by assault. Blucher retreated with the loss of 5,500 prisoners, 5,000 killed and wounded, and 300 wagons.

1813. The American army under general Wilkinson disembarked the whole of the troops and passed Prescott. A heavy cannonade was opened by the British on the flotilla of 300 boats, not one of which was touched, however.

1832. Grand festival in Sweden in honor of Gustavus Adolphus, it being the 200th anniversary of the battle of Lutzen.

1839. WILLIAM B. CONWAY, secretary of Iowa territory, died; well known as a poet, and a man of literary talent and taste.

1840. THOMAS PRINCE, a colored man, died in New York, aged 111. He is said to have been "as quick as a man in the prime of life;" he died suddenly, without sickness.

1842. WILLIAM HONE, the well known author of the *Every Day Book*, died at Tottenham, England. His political satires gave him some distinction.

1852. DANIEL DRAKE, an eminent physician, of Cincinnati, died, aged 67. He published a work on the *Diseases of the Valley of North America*, and earned the reputation of a man of high talent, unsparing labor and prodigal research.

1853. The first presbyterian Chinese church organized at San Francisco.

NOVEMBER 7.

63 B. C. CICERO, with the authority of a consul, summoned the senate to the temple of Jupiter, where it was assembled only in times of public alarm, and delivered his famous invective in the presence of Cataline.

3 B. C. CAIUS CILNIUS MAECENAS the friend and counselor of Augustus, died. To him Virgil dedicated his *Georgics*, and Horace his *Odes*.

1280. The statute in English law called *quo warranto*, passed.

1297. WALLACE granted a protection to the monks of Hexham, for their lives and possessions. "Abide with me, for there alone can you be secure; for my people are evil doers, and I can not punish them."

1492. A marvelous *thunder stone* fell about mid-day at Ensisheim, in Alsace, which weighed as is learnedly attested, 255 pounds.

1594. MARTIN FROBISHER, the English navigator, wounded at Croyson near Brest, of which he died.

1609. The Half Moon, under Henry Hudson, on her return from the discovery of New York and Albany, arrived at Dartmouth, in England, whence he forwarded tidings of his arrival and an account of his discoveries, to the directors of the East India company at Amsterdam.

1665. The first *Gazette* in England was published at Oxford, where the court had retired, during the great plague. It was removed to London in the February following, and took the title of *London Gazette*. (Quære.)

1696. Third frame of government of Pennsylvania passed by Gov. Matthews.

1704. ANDREW ACOLUTH (*Acoluthus*), a German linguist of extraordinary acquirements, died.

1724. JOHN KYRLE, the celebrated *Man of Ross*, died, aged 90. He is immortalized by Pope, and more by his own beneficent actions.

1724. The president and vice-president of Thorn, in Poland, sentenced to be beheaded for neglect of duty, it being alleged that they had suffered religionists to riot. The sentences against the protestants were so severe and harsh, that all the protestant powers of Europe interposed for a reversal, but without success.

1752. *The Adventurer*, by Dr. Hawkesworth, appeared.

1775. Lord DUNMORE declared Virginia to be in a state of rebellion; he proclaimed martial law, and invited the slaves to join him.

1783. The last person publicly burned by the Spanish inquisition. This was a woman, who perished at Seville. The victims of that diabolical institution were afterwards doomed to die in dungeons, where the shrieks of agonizing nature could only be heard by those whose interest it was to conceal them.

1794. Nymegen, which had been pronounced by British engineers strong enough to check the irruption of the *sans cullotes* into Holland, was evacuated by the British and Dutch, who succeeded in crossing the Waal.

1805. LEWIS and CLARK's party arrived at the mouth of the Columbia river, in sight of the ocean.

1806. The Prussian general BLUCHER, surrendered to the French, with 16,000 men and 80 cannon. This was the last body of the Prussians left after the battle of Jena, and closed all opposition to the views of Bonaparte in Prussia.

1811. Battle of Tippecanoe; the Indians under the Shawnee prophet, brother of Tecumseh, were defeated by the United States troops under Gen. Harrison. The Indians lost 300 killed; American loss, 188 killed and wounded.

1812. Battle of Dorogobouche; the Russians attacked the retreating French army, which, after a desperate and sanguinary contest, retreated to the river Dnieper. The field presented to the victors a continued line of dead and dying, the snow being absolutely blackened with the bodies of man and beast, destroyed by ball or sword, cold or famine.

1814. Pensacola, in Florida, taken by the Americans under Gen. Jackson, who kept possession of it until the Spaniards could obtain a sufficient force to maintain their neutrality from violation by the British.

1836. A great balloon journey from London to Weilburg, in Nassau, a distance of nearly 600 miles, which was traversed in 18 hours. It carried upwards of a ton ballast, besides a quantity of wine and other stores; its greatest elevation was 2 miles.

1837. The press of the *Alton Observer*, an anti-slavery newspaper, destroyed for the third time at Alton, Illinois, by the mob. The Rev. Elijah P. Lovejoy, the editor, was killed, and also one of the mob.

1838. Anne Grant, a Scottish authoress, died, aged 84. She was distinguished for her literary taste and conversational powers. The scene of her *American Lady*, is laid in the city of Albany.

1842. William McPheeters, a distinguished American divine, and for many years a successful teacher of youth, died at Raleigh, N. C.

1848. Agreeably to an act of the American congress, all the states voted for electors for president and vice-president.

1856. The first marriage of a Hindoo widow was celebrated at Calcutta, the parties being of high rank.

NOVEMBER 8.

532. Pope Boniface II died; his father was a Goth; he was elected to the pontifical office in 530.

1226. Louis VIII (*the Lion*), king of France, died. He was distinguished for his valor, and waged successful war against the English and other nations. He finally lost the greater part of his army by contagious disease, and perished by it himself.

1231. Abdu-l-lattif, an Arabian physician, historian and traveler, died, aged 69. He wrote upwards of 160 works, of which a history of Egypt is highly esteemed.

1308. John Duns (*Duns Scotus*), a celebrated theologian, died. He affected to maintain opinions contrary to those of Thomas Aquinas, which produced two parties in the schools, the Thomists and the Scotists.

1512. Amery d'Amboise, a French admiral, died; famous for the naval victory he obtained over the sultan of Egypt, two years before his death.

1517. Francis Ximenes, a Spanish ecclesiastic, died, aged 81. He was eminent as a statesman, warrior and patron of learning, and was at the head of the Spanish government many years. He was the publisher of the *Complutensian Polyglott*.

1519. The Spaniards under Cortez entered the city of Mexico.

1520. A general massacre of all the nobility of Sweden, except Gustavus Vasa, whose providential escape led to a revolution, and the separation of the union between Denmark, Sweden and Norway, and the deposition of Christian II, by whom the bloody deed was instigated.

1608. The Bodleian library at Oxford, England, first opened to the public.

1674. John Milton, an illustrious English poet, died. He also wrote many political and controversial tracts, and a *History of Britain*, which occupied him many years.

1690. Belgrade retaken by the Turks.

1777. British attacked Mud fort, now fort Mifflin. It was gallantly defended by a few militia under Col. Smith, who repulsed the enemy.

1781. Lewis Poulle, a French ecclesiastic, died; celebrated for his eloquence, and for his poetry.

1792. The French under Dampierre, took Ath, which contained several large magazines. They also took possession of Nieuwpoort, Ostend and Bruges on the same day. At the same time another army of the French took Tournay, and all Flanders submitted to them.

1793. Mary Jane Philipon Roland, an eminent French lady, guillotined. She was a woman of great information and superior talents. She published her travels in England and Switzerland, was the soul of the republican party, and secretly governed many of the public measures which were proposed in the convention before it fell into the foulest hands.

1799. Bonaparte affected a revolution in Paris, and the councils of Ancients, and Five Hundred, adjourned to St. Cloud.

1805. Battle of Marientzel; the French under Davoust defeated the allies, took 16 cannon and 3,000 prisoners.

1806. Magdeburg, in Lower Saxony, surrendered to the French under Ney. He took 20 generals, 16,000 men, 800 pieces of artillery, 1,000,000 pounds of powder, and a vast bridge equipage, and immense magazines of all kinds.

1808. A Mr. Dowler, of Towcetser, England, completed, on a wager, a pedestrian performance of 500 miles in 7 days.

1809. The French attacked, carried and plundered the town of Hostalrick, but were forced to retire by Gen. Quadrado, who retook the plunder.

1809. The functions of the British minister, Francis James Jackson, ceased by order of President Madison, and he was debarred all intercourse with the American government.

1813. Battle of Tallegada; the Indians defeated by Gen. Jackson.

1814. British ship Leander captured American privateer schooner Gen. Putnam, 8 guns and 57 men; her guns were thrown overboard during this and a former chase.

1828. THOMAS BEWICK, one of the most celebrated engravers on wood in England, died. Engraving the cuts for the celebrated Dr. Hutton's mensuration first introduced him to notice while yet an apprentice.

1837. EDWARD DORR GRIFFIN, an eminent American divine, died; 15 years president of Williams college.

1853. A new planet in the constellation Taurus was discovered by Mr. Hind, an English astronomer. It was the ninth planet discovered by Mr. Hind in the course of seven years, and raised the number of that extraordinary group of worlds between Mars and Jupiter to twenty-seven.

NOVEMBER 9.

2348 B. C. The great flood began, according to Polyhistor, from Berosus, upon the 15th, or the ides, of the Assyrian month Doesia, agreeing with this day. This event was prefigured to the patriarch in a vision, when the deity enjoined him to commit to writing a history of all things, which he was to bury in the city of the sun, at Sipara. The same uninspired authority informs us, that Noah was the tenth king of the Chaldea, and that he reigned 18 sari.

1606. JEROME MERCURIALIS died; an Italian physician of great abilities, and author of several works.

1616. ARGAL returned to Virginia from his expedition against the French settlements in Acadia. At St. Savior he broke in pieces the cross which the Jesuits had erected, and set up another inscribed with the name of the king of Great Britain; at St. Croix he destroyed all the remains of De Monts' settlement; at Port Royal the entire settlement was reduced to ashes in the short space of two hours.

1620. The *pilgrims*, after a boisterous passage, at break of day discovered the land of cape Cod. Finding that they had been carried north of their destination (see Sept. 6) they sailed southward; but falling among shoals, and the season being late, the captain gladly took advantage of their solicitude to put about, for he had been clandestinely promised a reward by the Dutch if he would not carry them to Hudson's river. Stearing northward again they were clear of the danger before night, and the next day, a storm coming on, they dropped anchor in cape Cod harbor.

1623. WILLIAM CAMDEN, an illustrious English historian, died. He is styled the Pausanias of England.

1641. FRANCIS DE ST. PREUIL, a distinguished French officer, and governor of Arras, beheaded at Amiens.

1677. GILBERT SHELDON, archbishop of Canterbury, died. It appeared, after his death, that he had bestowed, during 14 years, about $250,000 in private and public charities.

1704. Admiral LEAKE obliged the French and Spanish blockading squadron to retire from Gibraltar.

1732. ROBERT STEPHENS died; an eminent English antiquary and historiographer royal.

1775. ARNOLD, at the head of 1,000 men, arrived before Quebec. The unexpected appearance of an army, emerging out of the depths of an unexplored wilderness, threw the city into the greatest consternation; but want of boats to cross gave the citizens time to rally, and the critical moment was lost. The sufferings of this detachment were incredible. They ate their horses and dogs, and, after soaking their cartouch boxes, belts and leather breeches, absolutely ate them.

1794. The Jacobin society attacked by the Parisian mob, and several persons severely wounded by stones thrown into the windows of the hall of their sitting.

1794. MAASTRICHT, after a bombardment of some days, capitulated to the French; 8,000 men surrendered prisoners of war. The place was invested on the 10th Sept. by 50,000 republicans, and the first parallel was opened on the 23d October.

1799. The celebrated but bloodless revolution at Paris, of the 18th Brumaire, which, dissolving the directory, invested Bonaparte with the supreme authority. "You are the wisdom of the nation;" he addressed the council, "I come, surrounded by the generals of the republic, to promise you their support. Let us lose no time in looking for precedents. Nothing in history resembles the close of the 18th century—nothing in the 18th century resembles this movement. Your wisdom has devised the necessary measure; our arms shall put it in execution."

1802. THOMAS GIRTEN, an English artist, died. He introduced the practice of drawing upon cartridge paper, by which he avoided certain appearances incident to the drawings on white paper.

1803. BENJAMIN LEDYARD, an officer in the revolutionary war, died at Scipio, N Y. He was a meritorious soldier; at the time of his death held the office of clerk of Cayuga county.

1806. Eleazer Brooks, an officer of the revolution, died at Concord, Mass. He commanded a regiment at White Plains and Stillwater, and distinguished himself by his cool courage and determined bravery.

1806. Bonaparte livied a contribution on the Prussian dominion and its allies of 160,000,000.

1812. Bonaparte, on his retreat from Moscow, had his head quarters at Smolensk. When he left Moscow his army amounted to 100,000; it now scarcely numbered 60,000.

1813. British repulsed in an attack on Ogdensburgh.

1813. Commodore Chauncey's squadron, the whole carrying but 36 guns, again discovered the Royal George, 26 guns, and chased her under the batteries, which he engaged one hour and forty-five minutes. He had 1 killed and 3 wounded.

1839. Gilbert Y. Francis died at New Orleans, of yellow fever. His life was romantic and eventful. He was in early life attached to the navy; then to the stage; had traveled over the four quarters of the globe; was two years a prisoner in the great desert of Arabia; a slave to the bashaw of Tunis; lieutenant of a guerilla party in Spain; master of a Dutch luggar trading to the Malaccas; overseer of a sugar estate in Jamaica; a cutter of logwood in the forest of Campeachy; a prisoner among banditti in Mexico; a captive among the Camanches; ransomed by some Oregon fur traders; employed by the governor of the Russian settlements to command a brig in the wheat trade with Chili; married in Virginia; and was extensively engaged in the Texan operations when death arrested him.

1848. The king of Prussia prorogued the general assembly, at Berlin, naming Brandenburgh as the place of next meeting.

1848. Blum, a distinguished publisher at Leipsic, shot, at Vienna, as an insurrectionist and deputy for Frankfort.

1851. William Croswell, an episcopal clergyman of Boston, died, aged 47. He was a man of eminent ability, piety, modesty and worth, and his poetical productions are of a high order of merit.

1853. The ceremony of inaugurating the Washington aqueduct took place at the great falls of the Potomac, president Pierce turning the first turf.

1854. Elizabeth Hamilton, widow of Alexander Hamilton, died at Washington, aged 93. She was a daughter of general Philip Schuyler, of Albany; married lieutenant colonel Hamilton, then an aid of general Washington, in 1780, with whom she lived 24 years, and survived him nearly half a century.

1856. N. Cabet, founder of the Icarian community at Nauvoo, Illinois, died at St. Louis, aged about 69.

NOVEMBER 10.

1757 A. M. The waters of the deluge had subsided, and the earth became dry on the 27th of the 2d month, corresponding with this date (Nov. 10).

570. Birthday of Mahomet, as settled by the Benedictines: by other authority, April 21, 571.

1202. Siege of Jadera, now Zara, by the Venitian crusaders. It was a Roman city, colonized by Augustus.

1270. Edward I joined the African crusade before Tunis, a few weeks after the death of Louis, in his tent.

1444. Battle of Varna, between the Turks under Amurath, and the Christians under Ladislaus of Hungary, in which the latter were defeated, and Ladislaus and 10,000 slain.

1549. Paul III (*Alexander Farnese*), pope, died. It was with him that Henry VIII came to a rupture, which severed the church of England from that of Rome.

1558. Last auto-da-fé in the reign of queen Mary of England. It is supposed that in about three years 280 persons perished at the stake.

1567. Anne de Montmorency, marshal of France, killed at the battle of St. Denis, after performing prodigies of valor. He commanded at many memorable battles.

1624. Henry Wroitesley, earl of Southampton, one of the most steady patrons of men of learning, died at Bergen-op-Zoom, in Holland.

1683. John Collins, an eminent English mathematician, died; the intimate correspondent of the learned men of his times.

1715. Godfrey Olearius, a learned German divine and historian, died.

1721. John Mapletoft, an eminent English physician and divine, died, aged 91.

1722. The Royal Anne galley, cast away near Lizard point, and lord Bellhaven, governor of Barbadoes, with other passengers and ship's crew, perished. A boy and two sailors only saved.

1735. Thomas Dean, of Malden, a writer and printer, died in Kent, aged 102.

1750. Edward Bright, an English grocer, died, aged 29. His height was 5 feet 10 inches, his bulk round the body, 6 feet 11 inches, and his weight, 537 pounds.

1758. The oldest lion in the Tower of

London died. Said to be 68 years old. It had been presented to James II, by one of the Barbary states.

1769. Capt. Hollymore died, at Vauxhall, Eng. His mother had prepossessed him when a child, that he should die on the 10th of November, 1769, and in consequence of that prepossession, he made his will, and gave orders about his funeral; and though seemingly in perfect health when he went to bed, was found dead next morning, without the least sign of violence of any kind.

1781. Negapatam, in the East Indies, surrendered by the Dutch to the British, with 8000 prisoners.

1794. The French convention closed the hall of the Jacobins, and banished the society. They also banished the emigrants forever from France, and confiscated their estates.

1795. The schooner White Fish arrived at Philadelphia, from Presque isle, on lake Erie. The White Fish was 17½ feet keel, and 5 feet 7 inches beam, and performed her remarkable voyage in 7 weeks, passing the falls of Niagara 10 miles by land, and proceeding by lake Ontario, the Oswego river, lake Oneida, Wood creek, the Mohawk and Hudson rivers, to her place of destination—947 miles. The vessel was built and navigated by two young men, who made their unique voyage without chart or compass.

1797. Catharine II, of Russia, died. She seized her husband and probably had him murdered, by which she became sole mistress of the throne. She possessed many bad qualities, mixed with some good ones.

1797. Frederick William II, of Prussia, died.

1802. An island in latitude 5° 49′ N. longitude, 162° 23′ W. from London, discovered by captain Sowle, of the Palmyra, of Providence, R. I., which he called Palmyra island.

1808. Guy Carleton, a distinguished British officer in America, and governor of Canada, died. His great exertions saved Canada, when besieged by the Americans under Montgomery and Arnold.

1812. United States schooner Growler, lieutenant Mix, having under convoy a British prize schooner, by a masterly manoeuvre saved his prize and captured another British schooner, under convoy of two armed ships, on lake Ontario. The schooner had $12,000 on board, and the private property and baggage of general Brock.

1813. The British under lord Wellington attacked the French position at Anhoue, in Spain, and took 51 cannon and 1400 prisoners. British loss, 2484, exclusive of the loss of the Spanish; French loss, 3000.

1825. Com. McDonough, who commanded the fleet at Plattsburgh in 1814, died of consumption at Middletown, Conn.

1832. John Gaspard Spurzheim, the celebrated German phrenologist, died. He came to America in the same year of his death, after having traveled through several countries on the continent, for the purpose of propagating the science, and making investigations.

1834. Earl Spencer, an English statesman, died. He was much respected for his talents and virtues, and possessed the finest private library in Europe.

1835. Andrew Ljungstedt died; a Swedish author of great learning, who resided at Macao, in China, 40 years, and wrote a history of the Portuguese settlements in China.

1837. Albert Pawling died, aged 88; an officer in the revolutionary army, and engaged in several battles. He was the first sheriff of Rensselaer county, and first mayor of Troy.

1838. Santa Cruz, president of Bolivia, and protector of Peru, entered Lima at the head of a large army—Gomarra, with the Chilian army, having evacuated it.

1843. John Trumbell, a celebrated American painter, and aid to general Washington during the war of the revolution, died in New York, aged 87. He was buried in New Haven, where fifty-five of his paintings are preserved in the college. His *chef-d'œuvre* is the great painting of the signers of the declaration of independence.

1851. William G. Belknap, an officer of the United States army, died, aged 56. He distinguished himself at Buena Vista.

1852. The punishment of death re-established in Tuscany, for treason, crimes against religion, murder, and robbery with violence.

1852. A treaty was ratified between the courts of Vienna and Rome, stipulating that the latter should support in the territories of the pope, 12,000 infantry and 1400 cavalry, for whom $18,000 per month was to be paid by the papal government.

1852. Gideon Algernon Mantell, an eminent English geologist, died in London, aged 62.

1853. Thomas M. Nelson, an officer in the war of 1812, died at Columbus, Ga., aged 71.

1853. Maria, queen of Portugal, died in childbed. She was buried on the 19th with great solemnity, and demonstrations of public regret.

NOVEMBER 11.

397. St. Martin, the apostle of Gaul, died. He was a soldier, converted to Christianity, and made bishop of Tours. The festival of Martinmas was instituted in honor of him, in the year 560.

619. St. John (*the Almoner*) died. He was a native of Cyprus, raised to the see of Alexandria.

1100. Nuptials of Henry I of England (*Beauclerk*) and Maud, the fair daughter of Malcolm, king of Scots, and niece of Edgar Atheling, "of the right kingly kin of England."

1213. Date of the most ancient writ, summoning four discreet knights of the counties, to meet king John at Oxford, in 15 days from All Saints, *ad loquendum nobiscum de negotiis regni nostri.*

1400. Timour the Mogul sacked Aleppo, the capital of the Mamelukes. He thus addressed one of the cadhis: "I am not a man of blood; and God is my witness, that in all my wars, I have never been the aggressor, and that my enemies have always been the authors of their own calamities."

1462. Anne of Cyprus, died. She married Lewis, duke of Savoy, and showed herself able, active and discriminating at the head of public affairs.

1572. Tycho Brahe observed a new star in Cassiopeia, a phenomenon which had not been recorded since the age of Hipparchus. In splendor it was equal to Jupiter and Venus, and did not change its position in two years.

1620. The Plymouth pilgrims signed an instrument for their government, which was to go into force on their landing. It had the signatures of 41 of their number; and they with their families amounted to 101 persons. John Carver was chosen governor for one year. Thus did these intelligent colonists, says Holmes, find means to erect themselves into a republic, even though they had commenced their enterprise under the sanction of a royal charter; "a case that is rare in history, and can be effected only by that perseverance which the true spirit of liberty inspires."

1621. Robert Cushman arrived at Plymouth, in a ship from England, bringing 35 persons to remain in the colony, and a charter procured in London.

1623. Philip de Mornay, baron du Plesis Marly, died; an illustrious French protestant, a political and polemical writer, and privy counselor of the king.

1671. Thomas Fairfax, one of the principal generals in the civil wars of England, died.

1673. Battle of Choczin; the Turks defeated by John Sobieski, with the loss of 28,000.

1692. The negroes of the Barbadoes conspired against their masters for which many of them were executed.

1714. George I issued an order of council against the clergy meddling with state affairs in their sermons.

1750. Apostolo Zeno, a learned Venitian, died. He was a poet, and historian to Charles VI; his works are numerous and popular.

1778. A body of tories, Indians and British regulars, under the notorious John Butler, attacked fort Alden, at Cherry Valley. After an attack of 3 hours, they retreated, having killed 10 soldiers, and massacred 32 inhabitants, mostly women and children.

1793. John Sylvain Bailly, a famous French astronomer, died. He was induced to leave his studies for political distinction, and lost his life by manifesting some regard for justice.

1793. The amount of gold and silver collected in Paris from all parts of the republic, for the purpose of carrying on the measures of the government vigorously, was about two hundred millions of dollars.

1794. A treaty was concluded at Canandaigua between the United States by Timothy Pickering, and the Six Nations by 58 of their chiefs, among whom were Red Jacket and Cornplanter.

1794. Marquis Lafayette escaped from the prison at Olmutz.

1797. Joseph Toaldo, an Italian physician, died. He was professor of mathematics at Padua, and bestowed much attention on subjects of electricity, astronomy and meteorology.

1805. Battle of Diernsten; the French under Mortier defeated the Russians after a sanguinary battle.

1807. Three British orders in council restricting neutral trade with France and her allies. This was termed a paper blockade, was strongly resisted by America, and finally, with other aggressions, brought on a war in 1812.

1807. The decree of Napoleon restricting the trade of Holland went into operation, by which the commerce of that country, after a long declension, was totally ruined.

1813. Battle of Williamsburg, in Canada. The Americans under general Boyd, 1700, attacked the British, 2170. The victory was claimed by both parties, though it seems to have been with the British. American loss, killed 102, wounded 237; British loss, officially stated at 180—thought to exceed 500.

1817. Francisco Espoz y Mina, one of the most distinguished of the Spanish patriots, executed in Spain.

1835. Great tempest on lake Erie; a number of lives and vessels lost; the water rose higher than it was ever known before at Buffalo, and did great damage.

1837. Thomas Green Fessenden, an American poet and agricultural writer, died. He conducted the *New England Farmer* many years; was a man of extensive information and considerable literary acquirements.

1849. Henry Maynadier, a revolutionary officer and army surgeon, died at Annapolis, Maryland, aged 93.

1855. Thomas Wilde, baron Truro, died at London. As one of the best pleaders at the English bar, he was employed as one of the counsel for queen Caroline. He filled many offices of distinction and became lord chancellor in 1850.

1855. Jeddo, in the island of Japan destroyed by an earthquake.

NOVEMBER 12.

606. Boniface III, pope, died. He established the superiority of the popes over the patriarchs of Constantinople.

1035. Canute (*the Great*), king of Denmark, died. He took part of England from Edmund Ironsides, and afterwards seized the whole kingdom.

1041. The people rose on the tax collectors of Hardi Canute of England, and slew them.

1493. Columbus arrived at Navidad, on the north side of Hispaniola, where he had left a colony on his first voyage, and had the mortification to find that the people were all dead, and the fort destroyed.

1550. Paul Fagius (*Buchlin*), a learned protestant German minister, died in England. He undertook a new translation and illustration of the Old Testament under Cromwell, but died before he had made much progress.

1555. Stephen Gardiner, bishop of Winchester and chancellor of England, died. In his character as a minister, he had a large portion of haughtiness, boundless ambition and deep dissimulation; for he looked upon religion as an engine of state, and made use of it as such.

1562. Peter Martyr, a distinguished commentator on the Bible, died at Zurich.

1589. The first notice of the appointment of a licenser of stage plays, &c., in London.

1595. John Hawkins, an English admiral, died. He signalized himself in the reign of Elizabeth, by his encounters with the Spanish armada, and his expeditions to the West Indies.

1606. The expedition of the Plymouth company under Challons (See Aug. 12), on its passage from the West Indies towards the American coast, was captured by a Spanish fleet and carried into Spain, where the vessel was confiscated.

1684. Birthday of admiral Edward Vernon. The anniversary of his birthday was kept with great enthusiasm formerly, in England, especially about the year 1740.

1688. Andrew Anderson commenced an auction sale of books, the first of the kind in Scotland.

1722. Adrian Van der Werf, a Dutch portrait painter of great reputation, died. He was held in great esteem, received a pension and the honor of knighthood.

1746. Jacq. Alexander Cæsar Charles, in his lifetime so well known as a natural philosopher, was born at Baujency, in France. He was the first to make use of hydrogen gas instead of heated air in balloons.

1775. Montreal surrendered to the Americans; general Prescott, and several officers with 120 privates were intercepted. Eleven sail of vessels, with all their contents, fell into the hands of the provincials.

1775. British ships Tamarand and Cherokee attacked the United States schooner Defence, off South Carolina. This was the commencement of open hostilities in that state. The Defence sustained but little injury.

1780. Battle of Broad river; a band of American volunteers under Sumpter attacked by the British under major Wemys, who were defeated and Wemys taken.

1783. The crew of the British ship Antelope, wrecked on the Pelew island (see Aug. 10), sailed for China in a vessel which they had constructed, taking the king's son, Lee Boo.

1793. Bailly, late mayor of Paris, beheaded. He was a patriot and man of science. The first to take the famous oath never to separate till they had obtained a free constitution.

1799. Meteoric shower observed at Cumana, in South America; thousands of falling stars were seen to succeed each other during four hours.

1805. Robert Holmes, an English divine, died. He was distinguished as a poet and scholar, and for his devotion to Biblical criticism.

1812. The Russians under Orloff Denizoff attacked a strong body of French with a large convoy of provisions, cattle, horses, &c., on their way to Smolensk. He killed 1500 and took 1300 prisoners, 400 wagons of biscuit, brandy and wine, and 200 head of cattle and 1000 horses destined for the artillery. Few of those who escaped ever reached Smolensk, for the inclemency of the weather destroyed what the sword had spared. It was a dreadful blow to the French army, which was reduced to such extremities that the smallest assistance was invaluable.

1813. British frigate Lacedemonian captured Philadelphia sloop Betsey off Carrituck. The British took out the crew, leaving the captain and one man and a boy on board, in charge of a prize master and five men. In the night the two Americans rose upon the crew, recaptured the vessel, and brought her safe to Washington, N. C., with their six prisoners.

1820. William Hayley, an English poet and miscellaneous writer, died.

1824. County of Orleans, in western New York, erected.

1832. Barnaba Oriani, an Italian astronomer, died, aged 80. He was director of the observatory, and one of the most accomplished astronomers of the day.

1845. Maria Brooks, an American poetess, died, aged about 50. Her principal poem is *Zophies*, which is pronounced one of the most original, passionate and harmonious works of the imagination ever conceived. Southey pronounced her "the most impassioned and imaginative of poetesses."

1848. Revolutionary movements in Prussia. The burger guard at Berlin refused to comply with the king's proclamation to give up their arms.

1849. The American ship Caleb Grimshaw took fire at sea, and burnt four days, when 339 of her passengers were rescued; 60 who left the vessel on a raft, perished.

NOVEMBER 13.

36 B. C. Octavius Cæsar received the *oration* for his great naval victory over Sextus, the younger Pompey, in the Sicilian war.

1002. Massacre of the Danes, throughout England, by order of king Ethelred, one of those infamous shifts by which coward tyranny secures its sinister purposes. Neither age nor sex was spared, and among the victims was Gunilda, sister of Sweyn, king of Denmark. Her husband and children were butchered before her eyes. In the following year Sweyn invaded England and swept the country with fire and sword.

1004. Abbon de Fleury, a French ecclesiastic of note, who encouraged learning among the monastics, died of a wound he received in attempting to allay a brawl.

1499. Vincent Yanes Pinzon sailed from Palos, in Spain, for America, with four caravals, and was the first Spaniard who ventured to cross the equinoctial line. He explored a part of the coast of South America, and named the river which is still called Amazon—so named from the Spaniards observing that the women fought with the same bravery as the men in the common defence.

1503. Francisco Almeida, the first Portuguese viceroy of India, having surrendered his office to Albuquerque, sailed from Cochin for Portugal.

1539. The Bible, called *Matthew's Bible*, was permitted to be read in private houses, "of the royal liberality and goodness."

1549. Pope Paul III died, and was succeeded by cardinal de Monte, who took the name of Julius III.

1553. Arraignment of lady Jane Grey at Guildhall.

1558. Cardinal Pole, since the death of bishop Cranmer, bishop of Canterbury, died.

1620. The Plymouth colonists disembarked on cape Cod, and proceeded to make discovery of the country, and search for a convenient place of settlement. In the course of this search they found baskets of corn concealed under heaps of sand, a quantity of which they brought away in a great kettle found at the ruins of an Indian house. This gave them seed for a future harvest, and preserved the infant colony from starvation.

1624. Thomas Erpenius died at Leyden; a most learned Dutch writer, and incomparably skilled in the oriental tongues.

1646. A new volcano in the island of Palma, one of the Canaries, near Teneriffe.

1647. Battle of Knockinoss, in Ireland, during the rebellion, when the Irish army of 8,500 strong, under lord Taafe and sir Alexander MacDonnel, were routed by 5,200 under lord Inchiquin. The Irish left 4,000 in the field of battle. The British parliament voted lord Inchiquin £1,000 for his conduct on the occasion.

1650. Thomas May, an English dramatic poet and historian, died.

1654. William Habington, an English poet and historian, died.

1690. Lewis de Wolzogen died; a divine of Amsterdam, and a zealous partisan of the Socinians.

1712. John Ernest Grabe, a Prussian divine, died in England, where he published an edition of the *Septuagint*, and wrote some valuable works on divinity.

1712. Arthur Maynwaring, a learned Englishman, died. He was a member of parliament under queen Anne, and wrote in prose and verse.

1715. Battle of Dumblane between the

king's troops under the duke of Argyle, and those of the pretender under the earl of Mar, not decisive.

1715. Defeat of the pretender's forces at Preston, and many persons taken, among whom was their leader Mr. Foster.

1726. SOPHIA DOROTHY, only child of the duke of Zell, and wife of George I, of England, died. The malice of another subjected her to 32 years' captivity.

1770. GEORGE GRENVILLE, a celebrated English statesman, died. He was distinguished for his eloquence in the senate.

1771. Eruption of Solway Moss, in England. It is about seven miles in circumference, and composed of mud and putrid fibres of heath, diluted by internal springs. It burst its barrier in the night, and laid a large tract of country in ruin.

1781. JOHN MOODY hanged at Philadelphia as a spy. He intended to have seized the books and papers of congress.

1798. JEAN FRANCOIS CALLET, a French mathematician, died. It was to prevent the occurrence of errors in his tables that Didlot attempted the art of stereotyping.

1805. BONAPARTE entered Vienna; the commencement of a favorite plan of his to dictate peace to the conquered monarchs of Europe in their own capitals.

1810. JAMES ALLEN, the Northumbrian piper, died.

1812. BONAPARTE on his retreat from Moscow, quitted Smolensk for Krasnoy. His army was now reduced to 43,000.

1813. The junta, under the title of national assembly, declared the independence of Mexico.

1817. JOHN PHILPOT CURRAN, an eminent Irish barrister, died; celebrated for his eloquence and wit.

1832. A French army of 75,000 men entered Belgium and marched for Antwerp to assist in establishing the independence of the country.

1833. Remarkable meteoric phenomenon, which extended over a large portion of North America. The first appearance was that of fireworks of the most imposing grandeur, covering the entire vault of heaven with myriads of fire balls resembling sky rockets, and showers of fiery snow driven with inconceivable velocity to the north-west. Similar phenomena were witnessed in Arabia on this day the previous year. It was observed again on this day, 1837, at New York and New Haven.

1835. HENRY FREDERICK STORK died at St. Petersburg. He was an eminent writer as well on belles lettres as political economy.

1835. CHARLES AUGUSTUS BOTTIGER died; an eminent German scholar and archæologist, author of various learned works, and aulic counselor to the king of Saxony.

1836. CHARLES SIMEON, a most able and zealous English prelate, died at Cambridge. His works were published in 21 large octavo volumes. His funeral was attended with great solemnity by the whole town; the shops were closed and 1,300 persons joined the procession in the deepest mourning.

1839. The town of Kelat, in Beloochistan, taken by the British army. Mehrab Khan was killed, his principal sirdirs killed or taken, and hundreds of others captured.

1854. A great tempest raged over the Black sea, which continued several days; 18 British and 12 French ships were lost near Balaclava, together with 340 men and a large amount of property.

NOVEMBER 14.

332. B. C. Era of the accession of Alexander the great to the Persian rule.

565. JUSTINIAN I, emperor of Rome, died. He built St. Sophia's church at Constantinople, and reduced the Roman laws into a code, which was called the Digests or Pandects.

1318. The greatest earthquake ever known in England.

1524. FRANCISCO PIZARRO sailed from Panama for the conquest of Peru. Diego de Almagro, and Hernando de Luque a priest, associated with him under bonds and oaths for mutual protection. This expedition was a failure; they were repulsed and compelled to leave the country. More than six years afterwards the attempt was renewed with success.

1556. JOHN DE LA CASA, an Italian writer, died. Besides some beautiful Italian poems, he wrote the lives of cardinals Contarini and Bembo, and various other works.

1574. An aurora borealis appeared in England.

1672. FRANCIS DE LA BOE SYLVIUS, an eminent Dutch physician, died. He was professor of medicine at Leyden, where he ably demonstrated the truth of Harvey's discovery of the circulation of the blood.

1690. Capt. JAMES CAMPBELL, brother of the duke of Argyle, with the assistance of sir J. Johnstone, seized a rich heiress and married her, for which Johnstone was afterwards hung and Campbell divorced.

1716. GODFREY WILLAM LEIBNITZ, a German philosopher, died. He had in his life the singular felicity of being esteemed the greatest and most learned man in Europe.

1736. GEORGE SALE, a learned Englishman, died. He was well skilled in oriental literature, and contributed much to the completion of the *Universal History*, but his chief work is a translation of the *Koran.*

1770. Bruce discovered the sources of the mighty Nile.

1785. A chebeck with 19 men and 23 passengers, passing from Majorca to Ivica, was attacked by an Algerine pink, and boarded by about 100 men, in spite of the firing of two cannon and the musketry. A bloody engagement ensued, in which all the Moors but 6 or 7 were killed. These were assaulted by a volley of hail shot, which fired some powder casks, and blew up the vessel, destroying all on board but the captain and 3 passengers, who got to Ivica in a boat, badly wounded.

1800. Marquis de Bouille, a celebrated French general, died; during the American war he served with credit in the West Indies, but being opposed to the enormities of the French revolution he was compelled to seek an asylum in England.

1804. Jacob Bryant, an English philologist and antiquary, died. He was a learned and indefatigable writer, but fond of paradox.

1809. Bonaparte was congratulated on his return from Austria, by the public bodies of Paris, as "the greatest of heroes, who ever achieved victories but for the happiness of the world."

1809. Frederick Morton Eden, an English diplomatist and writer on political economy, died.

1812. Battle of Smolnya; the French under Victor and Oudinot defeated by the Russians under Wittgenstein, with the loss of 1,500 dead on the field, and 800 prisoners. Russian loss 1,000.

1825. Jean Paul Frederick Richter, a German writer of the first rank in belles lettres, died. He is known as Jean Paul among the Germans, and his numerous works are held in very high repute.

1827. Thomas Addis Emmett, an eminent Irish lawyer, died in New York, aged 63.

1828. Andre Joseph Abrial died; a French statesman under Napoleon and his successor.

1831. George William Frederick Hegel, the distinguished German philosopher, died by cholera at Berlin. His philosophy partakes of much of German mysticism.

1832. Charles Abbott, lord Tenterden, died, aged 70. He was the son of a London hairdresser, who by great application became one of the most learned jurists of England.

1832. Charles Carrol died, aged 96; the last of the signers of the declaration of independence. He studied the law in France and England, and returned to America at the age of 27, where he was soon known as an advocate for liberty, and as one of the best political writers in Maryland. He quitted public life in 1810.

1835. James Freeman, pastor of the Stone chapel society, in Boston, died. He was chosen pastor of the episcopal society that worshiped there in 1783. Having rejected the trinitarian doctrine, the greater part of his hearers responded to his sentiments and resolved to alter their liturgy and retain their minister. Thus did the first episcopal church in New England become the first unitarian church in the new world. He was a man of talent and learning, and one of the founders of the Massachusetts historical society.

1840. John A. G. Davis, professor of law in the university of Virginia, died of a pistol shot discharged by a disguised student. He was a man of extraordinary intellect, of untiring industry, of amiable and philanthropic character. He published a valuable treatise on criminal law.

1840. Zachariah Lewis, senior vice-president of the American Bible society, died at Brooklyn, N. Y. He was educated for the ministry, and was for 17 years editor of the *Commercial Advertiser* and *New York Spectator.*

1855. Tobias Watkins died at Washington, aged 75. He was a physician by education, had contributed largely to the public press, and figured as a politician.

NOVEMBER 15.

26. Agrippina, the mother of Nero, perished by order of her ungrateful son. She married the emperor Claudius, whom she poisoned to raise Nero to the throne.

1213. The first regular English parliament assembled by writ at Oxford.

1280. Albertus Magnus, a Swabian philosopher of extraordinary genius, died. His writings have been collected in 21 vols. folio.

1577. Francis Drake sailed from England with five ships and 164 men, professedly on a voyage to Egypt, but really with the intention of sailing into the Pacific, where no English flag had ever been.

1591. Barnabas Brissonius strangled at Paris. He was an eminent French lawyer, and ambassador to England.

1647. John Victor Rossi (*Janus Nicius Erythræus*) died; a Roman of noble birth, who devoted himself to literary pursuits.

1653. Aloysius Juglaris, an Italian Jesuit, died. He wrote 100 panegyrics on Jesus Christ, and 40 on Lewis XIII!

1680. The bill excluding James, duke of York, from the succession to his brother's throne, passed by the commons, was defeated in the house of lords, all the bishops voting against it.

1695. In the neighborhood of Limerick and Tipperary, Ireland, a shower of matter fell resembling butter or grease, and was gathered into pots by some of the inhabitants. When laid on the hand it melted, but placed by the fire it dried and became hard, emitting an offensive odor.

1712. A duel was fought in Hyde Park, London, when the duke of Hamilton and lord Mohun were both killed.

1745. The town of Carlisle surrendered to the troops of the pretender to the English throne.

1747. John Peter de Mendajors, a French historian, died. He wrote a history of Gaul.

1751. Henry Saint John, viscount Bolingbroke, a celebrated English politician and philosopher, died, aged 80. A panegyrist has observed that in his writings he united the wisdom of Socrates, the dignity and ease of Pliny, and the wit of Horace.

1761. John Sauve de la Noue, a French actor and dramatic writer, died. It was on his account that Voltaire wrote the *Princess of Navarre*, that he might act the chief character.

1763. The British parliament by a vote 273 to 111, resolved that the *North Briton*, a paper conducted by the noted Wilkes, was a scandalous and seditious libel, and ordered it to be burned by the common hangman. Great riot in consequence.

1777. Fort Mifflin evacuated by the Americans, after a most noble and gallant defence. The British fired 1,030 cannon shot at the fort during the day.

1787. Christopher Gluck, an eminent German musical composer, died. He introduced a new style of music into Paris.

1793. John Nicholas Houchard guillotined at Paris. He raised himself to the highest rank in the army, and displayed his abilities in several important victories.

1793. Jean Marie Baptiste Roland de la Platiere stabbed himself to the heart on receiving news that his wife had been guillotined. His knowledge of commerce and political economy led to his appointment of minister under Louis, and under the republic.

1793. Fort Lewis taken by the Austrians under Wurmzer, and 4,000 French and 112 cannons captured.

1794. John Witherspoon, a signer of the declaration, died. He was a Scotchman, who came over to take the presidency of Nassau Hall. His influence upon literature was greatly beneficial, and his talents as a preacher of the most popular kind.

1797. Joseph Milner, a learned Scottish divine and historian, died, aged 54.

1802. George Romney died; an eminent English painter.

1811. Frederick James Bast, an eminent German scholar, died. He took advantage of a diplomacy at Paris to make some valuable researches among the treasures of the Vatican which had recently been transported there.

1812. The Cossacks under Platoff fell in with 12 pieces of French cannon, and an immense train of carriages filled with plunder, abandoned by the French army. The horses lay dead in their harnesses, and mingled with them lay hundreds of human bodies, which had perished from the intense severity of the cold, from hunger and fatigue, in their retreat from Moscow.

1816. The bells of Notre Dame, Paris, were *formally baptized* under the names of the duke and Duchess of Angouleme.

1827. George Tomline, an eminent English bishop, died. His works display great erudition.

1828. Cayuga and Seneca canal completed.

1848. General Messenhausen, the commander of the national guard at Vienna, executed.

1849. The steam boat Louisiana exploded her boilers at New Orleans, when 60 persons were killed, and a great many wounded who afterwards died.

1852. The Lobos islands difficulty between the United States and Peru was settled, by the withdrawal of the American pretensions.

1852. John Hamilton Reynolds, an eminent English poet, contemporary with Byron, died in the Isle of Wight, aged 56.

NOVEMBER 16.

534. Justinian published his immortal *Code* of civil ordinances, amended in conformity with the Pandects which issued from the legal armory in the year preceding. It is called the second edition, although enriched with two hundred of his own laws, and fifty decisions of obscure points in jurisprudence.

1093. Margaret, of Scotland, died. She was the sister of Edgar Atheling, fled to Scotland on the invasion of William the Conqueror, and married Malcolm, king of the country. She was an amiable and benevolent princess.

1272. Henry III, eighth king of England, died. He succeeded John; was defeated in his wars abroad, and imprisoned by his barons at home.

1272. Edward I, of England, commenced his reign, and immediately expelled the Jews from the kingdom; their libraries were dispersed, their goods seized, and many of them barbarously murdered.

1326. EDWARD II, king of England, taken prisoner and delivered into the hands of his queen Isabella, by whom he was imprisoned and finally put to death.

1499. PERKIN WARBECK, an aspirant to the crown of England, executed at Tyburn. He gave himself out as the second son of Edward IV, who was supposed to have been murdered in the Tower by Richard III, and made a descent upon England, but was worsted and captured.

1538. Proclamation of HENRY VIII, following the formal trial and condemnation of the shrine and goods of Thomas Becket, declaring that he was no saint, but a rebel to his prince, and his bones were caused to be burnt by the hangman.

1603. PETER CHARRON, a learned French ecclesiastic, died. His *Book of Wisdom*, spread his fame through the country, and has been twice translated into English.

1613. TRAJAN BOCCALINI, an Italian wit, died at Venice; probably assassinated by the emissaries of the court of Spain. His works have been translated into several languages.

1644. HUGH MCMABONE executed at Tyburn for conspiring the Irish massacre.

1695. PETER NICOLE, an eminent French divine, died. He is the author of more than one hundred works.

1745. WILLIAM BROOME, a celebrated English poet, died.

1745. A party of French and Indians from Crown Point surprised the village of Saratoga, leaving the country uncovered to Schenectady and Albany.

1773. Destruction of the tea in Boston harbor. The duty imposed by the British parliament was 3 cents per pound; the quantity destroyed 342 chests.

1773. JOHN HAWKESWORTH, an English writer, died. He compiled a narrative of the discoveries in the South seas, and wrote the *Adventurer*.

1773. JOHN BRADLEY BLAKE, an English chemist, botanist and mathematician, died. He went to China, from whence he sent home all the valuable seeds and plants of the country, and began a collection of its ores and fossils, but his application destroyed his health.

1776. JAMES FERGUSON, the celebrated Scottish astronomer, died. He was an extraordinary instance among self taught men, having emerged from a shepherd's boy, to the highest rank in science.

1776. Fort Washington surrendered to the British under general Cornwallis. Col. Magaw, finding the fort too small to contain all the men, the ammunition nearly exhausted, and the force of the assailants too great to be resisted, surrendered the garrison, 2,800 men, prisoners of war. It is supposed that 1,200 of the British were killed or wounded.

1796. Battle of Arcola, which lasted two days, terminated in favor of the French. This determined the fate of Mantua.

1806. SCHAH ALLUM, the great mogul or emperor of Delhi, died, aged 82.

1811. Serious riots in Nottingham, Eng.; the journeymen weavers destroyed the articles ot machinery which diminished labor.

1812. The French under DAVOUST left Smolensk, having set fire to it in every quarter, and blown up the fortifications; and amidst this immense burning shower they issued forth like destroying angels, to join Bonaparte at Krasnoy.

1813. WILLIAM FRANKLIN died in England, aged 82. He was the son of Dr. Benjamin Franklin, and formerly British governor of New Jersey.

1838. Battle near Prescott, Canada, between 100 insurgents posted at a windmill, and 1,000 British troops. The former surrendered unconditionally. Their loss in 4 days was 102 killed, and 162 taken prisoners; the rest escaped into the woods.

1847. Poland blotted from among the nations of Europe, by Prussia, Austria and Russia.

1848. Great popular movements in Italy. Count Rossi, the prime minister, slain, as he entered the senate chamber at Rome. The pope's palace besieged.

1855. The powder in the French siege train, at Sebastopol, 100,000 pounds, exploded, killing and wounding a great number.

NOVEMBER 17.

375. VALENTINIAN I, emperor of Rome, died. He rose by his merit to the throne, and divided the empire with his brother Valens. He defeated the Germans, and restored tranquility to his African provinces. In giving audience to the ambassadors of the Quadi, whose country he had subdued, he ruptured a blood vessel in a fit of passion, which proved fatal.

537. BELISARIUS, who was then defending Rome against the Goths, exiled pope Sylverius for treachery.

1292. The government of Scotland was adjudged to John Baliol, by the forty peers assembled at the congress in Berwick castle.

1307. The Swiss patriots met at night in the field of Rutli, to concert measures for their independence.

1338. EDWARD III, of England, issued a writ, permitting the coinage of money by the abbots of Reading.

1372. JOHN DE MANDEVILLE, the English

warrior and traveler, died, aged 72. He received an education unusual for those times, and in 1327, went to Palestine, and joined the Turks. He afterwards served in India under the Sultan, and in Southern China, under the khan of Cathay. He resided three years at Pekin, and appears to have traveled over a large part of Asia. On his return to England, after an absence of about 33 years, he wrote a narrative of his travels.

1494. John Picus, earl of Mirandula, an Italian nobleman, and a prodigy of learning, died, aged 32. At the age of 23 he published 900 propositions in logic, mathematics, physics and divinity, drawn from classical, Jewish and Arabian authors, and challenged through Italy any philosopher or divine to enter the lists with him in disputation. He declared war against the astrologers, because they had foretold his death at the age of 32, which proved true.

1558. Mary, queen of England, died. She was the daughter of Henry VIII and Catharine of Arragon; was learned, but bigoted, jealous and resentful. Her memory is rendered detestable by the blood of the protestants whom she caused to be burnt.

1562. Anthony of Navarre (*Pantagruel*), a Spanish prince, died of a wound received in battle. He was weak and irresolute; his son was afterwards the celebrated Henry IV, of France.

1604 Trial of sir Walter Raleigh for treason.

1615. Thomas Chaloner, an English nobleman, tutor of the prince of Wales, died. He is celebrated for the discovery of the first alum mines known in England.

1640. Henry de Schomberg, a distinguished French officer, died. For his distinguished services he was promoted; and also figured as a minister to Germany and England, and as a historian.

1664. Nicholas Perret, a learned Frenchman, died; celebrated for his excellent translations of the Greek and Latin classics.

1664. A comet visible in New England, which appeared first in the east *bearded*, and disappeared in the west with a *tail*.

1665. John Earle, an English bishop, died; known by a work called the *Microcosmography, or a Piece of the World*, which has often been reprinted.

1679. In commemoration of queen Elizabeth's birth, the effigies of the pope, the devil, sir George Jeffries, Mr. L'Estrange, &c., were carried in procession, and burnt in Temple bar, by a *whig mob*, as it was then called.

1690. Fabian Phillips, a learned English antiquary, died.

1708. Jean Francois Foy Vaillant, a French antiquary and medalist, died. His father was the founder of the medalists in France, to whom Louis XIV was indebted for half his cabinet.

1747. Alain Rene Lesage, the French novelist and dramatic writer, died.

1747. Great tumults in Boston, on account of the British commodore, Knowles, having ordered several inhabitants of that city to be impressed there.

1768. Thos. Pelham Holles, duke of Newcastle, died in his 76th year. He played a bustling if not a brilliant part in the political movements of his day.

177– Bruce, the traveler, in passing the Taranta mountain, in Abyssinia, encountered an extraordinary phenomenon. The mountain tops were hid in the clouds, and loud thunder was heard. The river scarcely ran at the time of passing it, when suddenly a noise was heard in the mountain above, louder than the loudest thunder. His guides flew to the baggage, and removed it to the top of a green hill, which was no sooner done than the river was seen coming down in a stream about the height of a man, and the breadth of the whole bed it used to occupy. An antelope, surprised by the torrent, was driven to the station where they stood.

1775. Americans, under colonel Easton, took at the point of Sorel river, Canada, 11 British vessels with stores.

1782. Edward Drinker, a quaker of Philadelphia, died, aged 103. He had been the subject of seven crowned heads, and lived to see a village become a great city.

1793. Battle of Sarbruck; the Prussians defeated by the French under Pichegru.

1794. N. Dugomier, a French revolutionary general, killed at the battle of St. Sebastian, in which his army was victorious over the Spaniards. His name was inscribed in the Pantheon.

1794. James Bentham, an English prelate and historian, died. He also directed his attention to the introduction of turnpike roads, against the popular prejudice, and to the rendering of unfruitful into valuable fields by drainage.

1795. Alexander Abercromby died; a Scottish jurist, and a cooperator with Mackenzie in establishing the *Mirror* and *Lounger*, to which he contributed.

1800. Battle of Mincio, in Italy; the Austrians defeated by the French under general Brune, with the loss of 24 cannon, and 4,000 men.

1804. Launch of the Hibernia, at Plymouth, England, of 130 guns; length of keel 167 feet, tonnage 2499—the largest man-of-war that had ever been built in England.

1812. Battle of Koutovo, near Krasnoy,

in Russia; the Cossacks under Miloradovitch surrounded the French under Davoust, and defeated them with horrible slaughter. The French general, however, maintained his reputation for bravery, and cut his way through, with the loss of 4,000 killed, and 9 prisoners, and 70 cannon. The wretched beings who escaped the swords and bayonets of their conquerors sought shelter in the woods which skirt the Dnieper, and there, wounded, starving and naked, died in great numbers.

1812. British gun boats cannonaded Ogdensburgh.

1818. CHARLOTTE, queen of England, died, aged 75.

1823. THOMAS ERSKINE, an English nobleman, and one of the most celebrated of modern forensic orators, died.

1832. THOS. TAYLOR, styled the patriarch of the states-right party of South Carolina, died at Columbus.

1835. Remarkable aurora borealis; in extent and magnificence one of the grandest forms of this mysterious phenomenon. It attracted notice throughout the United States and Canada, and on the 18th was seen in Europe.

1854. DUDLEY COUTTS STUART died at Stockholm, Sweden, aged 51; well known in England and elsewhere, for his devotion to Poland and the Polish exiles.

NOVEMBER 18.

1247. ROBIN HOOD, the leader of a band of robbers who infested the recesses of Sherwood forest, England, died. The chief, with his formidable band, continued their plundering life with success, and with little opposition, from the year 1189 to 1247. It has been attempted to identify him with Robert, earl of Huntington, whom the malice of his enemies banished from the court of Richard I. The following epitaph is said to have been engraven upon his tombstone at Kirklees:

Hear undernead dis laitl stean
laiz robert earl of huntington
nae arcir ner as hie sae geud
an pipl kauld im Robin Heud
sick utlawz as he an is men
vil England nivir si agen
obit 24 kal. dekembris 1247.

1518. CORTEZ sailed from Cuba for the discovery and conquest of Mexico. His force consisted of 10 vessels, 10 pieces cannon, 18 horsemen, 600 infantry—13 only of whom were musqueteers, and the rest cross bowmen.

1558. REGINALD POLE, an English cardinal, died. He entered college at the age of 12, and took his first degree at the age of 15. Refusing to sanction the divorces of Henry VIII, he was obliged to reside in Italy for safety. On the accession of Mary, however, he was restored.

1559. CUTHBERT TONSTALL, a learned catholic bishop of London, died, aged 85.

1624. JACOB BOEHMEN died; a noted Teutonic philosopher and visionary.

1636. King CHARLES I restored to sir Hugh Middleton a portion of his private property, expended on bringing a supply of water into the city of London. Middleton survived this event but a short time.

1665. BLAISE FRANCIS DE PAGAN, a valiant French officer and eminent mathematician, died. He lost his eyesight in the service of his country, after which he devoted himself to study, and wrote several works on fortifications, astronomy, &c.

1682. JOHN FINCH (*Heneage?*), earl of Nottingham and lord high chancellor of England, died. He was distinguished for his wisdom and eloquence and styled the English Cicero.

1751. ABRAHAM VATER died; an eminent German physician and anatomist, famous for his anatomical preparations, which form a curious cabinet at Wirtemberg.

1755. A great earthquake, extending from New England to the West Indies, damaging the houses throughout the whole extent of the coast. In the harbor of St. Martin the sea withdrew leaving the vessels dry and the fish on the banks; when it came in the water overflowed the lowlands.

1776. Fort Lee, near Haversack, N. Y., evacuated by the Americans under general Greene. The British, 6000 men under Cornwallis, advancing to its reduction, it was found that the conflict would be too unequal to attempt its defence. The British took several hundred barrels of flour, most of the cannon, baggage, &c.—— Same day congress agreed upon a lottery to defray the expenses of the campaign, being the first lottery they sanctioned.

1777. Fort Mercer at Red Bank, on the Delaware, evacuated by the Americans on the approach of the British under Cornwallis.

1777. The British under governor Tryon burnt the houses at Philip's manor, N. Y., with circumstances of great barbarity; the women and children being turned out in a severe cold night, almost naked, and the men made prisoners and led with halters round their necks in triumph to the British camp.

1777. WILLIAM BOWYER, an eminent English printer, died. He was noted for the accuracy of his editions, and was a distinguished member of the antiquarian society, whose transactions he enriched with many valuable communications.

1784. M. LE ROY fixed a conductor on the Etoile galley, being the first conductor of lightning that had ever been placed on a French ship.

1785. Mrs. KELLY, the noted Irish fairy, died. She was only 34 inches long. Her child, which lived only two hours, was 22 inches.

1789. JOHN ELWES, the celebrated English miser, died, worth nearly five millions of dollars. This singular man, although he denied himself the necessaries of life, served twelve years in parliament, a most independent and incorruptible member. He would travel a whole day, eating only a hard boiled egg, and at night play for thousands in the most splendid apartments from whence he has been known to issue at four in the morning, and stand in a cold rain to dispute with a butcher for a shilling a head on his cattle.

1793. Battle of Bliescastle; the French general Pichegru stormed the Prussian camp.

1793. Battle of Dol; the French royalists defeated the conventional troops.

1803. Cape Francois surrendered to the blacks under Christophe.

1804. PHILIP SCHUYLER, a major general in the revolutionary army, died at Albany, aged 73. He was a member of the old congress, and of the federal congress.

1809. The French under Suchet attacked the Spaniards under Gen. Blake, posted on the heights of Beclhithe, and forced them to fall back.

1811. All differences between the United States and Great Britain on account of the attack made on the United States frigate Chesapeake amicably adjusted.

1813. Americans under general White, with a few Cherokee Indians, attacked Grayson's Farm, one of the Hillibee towns, of 20 houses, which they burnt, and killed 60 Creek warriors and captured about 256 more, without the loss of a man.

1824. Destructive hurricane on the coast of England. The river Neva overflowed its banks, and damaged the city of St. Petersburg.

1832. Violent eruption of mount Etna; the town of Bronte, containing 10,000 inhabitants, destroyed.

1848. The great dam at Hadley Falls, in Massachusetts, near Springfield, carried away by a flood.

1849. BENJAMIN SMITH, a very eminent and industrious American statesman, of Rhode Island, died at North Kingston.

1851. ERNEST AUGUSTUS, duke of Cumberland and king of Hanover, died, aged 81. He was the fifth son of George III, and distinguished himself as an officer on the continent during the last century.

1852. Duke of WELLINGTON'S funeral obsequies took place at London, with great pomp. The religious ceremonies were observed in St. Paul's cathedral, which was elaborately decorated for the purpose. The body was deposited in the crypt near that of Nelson.

1852. A convention was signed at London by England, France, Prussia, Bavaria and Greece, by which none but a prince of the Greek religion was thereafter to ascend the throne of Greece.

1854. GEORGE WILLIAM MAREBY, inventor of several kinds of apparatus for saving lives in shipwreck, died in England, aged 89.

NOVEMBER 19.

1231. ELIZABETH OF THURINGIA, a saint of the church, died. She was distinguished by the mild virtues of her sex, and when the country was oppressed with famine and pestilence, she caused hospitals to be erected, and fed and clothed a multitude of the poor, wandering about in a humble dress relieving the sorrows of the wretched. She was regarded as a saint during her life, and four years after her death was canonized. Her monument is one of the most splendid remains of Gothic architecture in Germany.

1530. The diet at Augsburg issued a severe decree against the protestants, which was sanctioned by the emperor Charles V.

1590. JEROME ZANCHIUS, a German protestant theologian, died. His commentaries on St. Paul's epistles were published after his death. He was a professor of theology at Heidelburg, and sustained the character of a learned, pious and benevolent man.

1628. JOHN FELTON, the assassin who killed the duke of Buckingham, favorite of Charles I of England, executed at Tyburn. The king proposed the rack previous to execution, that his accomplices might be discovered. But the judges unanimously declared that the English law did not allow of torture. This was the first adjudication on this subject.

1649. CASPAR SCIOPPIUS, a learned German, died, aged 73. He acquired the name of the grammatical cur, from his indiscreet attacks upon every person of eminence. His talents and acquirements were extraordinary, and his works more numerous than his years.

1665. NICHOLAS POUSSIN, an eminent French painter, died. He was long unable to maintain himself by his pencil, till his genius finally burst through the clouds of prejudice, and established his character as a great and sublime artist.

1672. John Wilkins, bishop of Chester, died; a most ingenious and learned English theologian, critic and mathematician.

1674. Samuel Danforth, the colleague of John Elliot, the Indian missionary, died at Roxbury, Mass. When he was contracted in marriage the celebrated John Cotton preached the sermon, customary in New England on such occasions, before the nuptial ceremony. He published several almanacs, and an astronomical account of the comet which appeared in 1764.

1677. Francis Junius, a German linguist, died in England. He was highly distinguished for his skill and researches in the Anglo Saxon and Gothic languages, which he pursued at Oxford, England.

1703. The Iron Mask (*Masque de Fer*), died at the Bastile in Paris, after an imprisonment of forty-two years. This mysterious personage is supposed to have been the twin brother of the king, and various authors have attempted to prove his identity with other characters of that day. It was at first believed that the mask which he was compelled to wear constantly on pain of instant death, was made of iron. But it was composed of black velvet, strengthened with whalebone, and fastened behind the head with a padlock. He was confined for imperious reasons of state, but was treated with the utmost deference and respect.

1731. William Edie, bellman of Canongate, in Edinburgh, died, aged 120. He had buried the inhabitants of Canongate thrice. He was 90 years a freeman, and married his second wife, a young woman, after he was 100 years old.

1741. Anthony Banier, a celebrated French mythologist, died. His *Mythology and Fables of the Antients* has been translated into English.

1744. A single battalion of Prussians under Wedel disputed the passage of the Elbe at Solnitz for five hours, against the whole Austrian army; and, under the fire of fifty cannons, thrice repulsed the Austrian grenadiers. Wedel lost two officers and 100 men killed, and acquired the title of Leonidas.

1761. Noel Anthony Pluche, a French writer on natural history, died. His *Spectacle de la Nature* is known to all the world.

1789. Junction of the Thames and Severn rivers by canal.; an important event in English inland commerce. This canal ascends the vale of Calford to the height of 343 feet by 40 locks; there entering a tunnel through the hill of Saperton, for the length of two miles and three furlongs, and descends to the Thames by 22 locks.

1790. James Hay Beattie died; a Scotchman of eminent talents, who was made assistant professor of moral philosophy and logic at Aberdeen at the age of 19.

1793. A number of persons met in Edinburgh and held a *convention* similar to that in France, but were arrested and sent to prison.

1794. The treaty signed at London between England and America, called Jay's treaty.

1801. Joseph de Beauchamp, a French theologian and astronomer, died. During a residence in the Levant, he made many astronomical observations, constructed a map of the Tigris and Euphrates, and surveyed the Black sea.

1806. Richard Weston died; an English thread hosier, who became eminent as a horticulturist, and published some useful tracts on that subject.

1806. Hameln, on the Weser, captured by the French, who took Von Schoeler and five other generals, 9,000 Prussians, some other troops, and great quantities of ammunition and stores.

1806. Mortier entered Hamburg and confiscated all British property found there.

1806. Nicholas Claude Ledoux, a fortunate though vain French architect, died.

1809. Battle of Ocana; the French under Soult defeated 50,000 Spaniards. Joseph Bonaparte commanded in person in this battle under Soult.

1812. Battle of Koutovo; the French under Ney attacked in the defiles near Krasnoy, on the very spot where Davoust had been defeated two days before. Although the French fought with the greatest courage and most desperate intrepidity, they were defeated with terrible slaughter, and the loss of all their cannon, baggage and colors. Scarcely had this second victory been obtained, when the last columns of the rear guard appeared in sight, and were compelled to surrender, 100 officers and 11,000 men.

1812. Americans under colonel Pike made an incursion into Canada, assaulted and carried a British post, burnt their blockhouse, and returned with only five wounded.

1813. American Com. Porter took possession of an island in the South sea, called by the natives Nooaheevah, which he called *Madison's island*, in honor of the president.

1816. Eclipse of the sun observed at Paris. It was total at Copenhagen.

1818. Abdullah ibn Saud, the last emir of the Wahhabis, was beheaded at Constantinople, which put an end to the temporal power of that sect.

1835. Charles Coote, an English author, died. He was for some years editor of the *Critical Review*, and wrote various historical and other works of merit.

1850. Richard M. Johnson, a Kentucky soldier and statesman, died at Frankfort, aged 70.

1853. Samuel H. Crafts died at Craftsbury, Vt., aged 84. On the organization of the town, which was settled by and named in honor of his father, in 1792, he was chosen town clerk, and held the office 37 years; and he filled every public office in the gift of Vermont during some part of his lifetime.

1855. Thomas Copeland, an eminent English surgeon and medical writer, died at Brighton, aged 74.

1855. Theodric Romeyn Beck, an eminent medical writer, died at Albany, N. Y., aged 64. He was one of the originators and most ardent supporters of the geological survey of the state; but is best known by his *Medical Jurisprudence*. He was a member of many scientific societies at home and abroad, and his whole life was one of uninterrupted and efficient labor.

NOVEMBER 20.

63. Shipwreck of St. Paul. It was a fortnight from the fast, and about the present day, that Paul, by the occular testimony of Luke, was cast upon the shores of Malta, where they wintered three months until the period of navigation in March. Josephus, the Jewish historian, was wrecked in the same sea, and in or very near the same year.

303. Diocletian and Maximian celebrated in a grand triumph their victories and those of the two Cæsars, their associates, in Persia and Britain, on the Rhine, the Danube and the Nile; the last spectacle of the kind that Rome ever beheld.

870. Edmund (*the Saint*), king of East Anglia, murdered by the Danes, who had him tied to a tree and shot to death with arrows. His kingdom comprised the present counties of Norfolk, Suffolk and part of Cambridgeshire.

1185. Abdurrahman, surnamed Abn Zeyd, died. He was a Moslem divine and poet, and left several valuable works.

1191. Baldwin, archbishop of Canterbury, died at Acre, in Palestine, whither he had followed the crusaders, whose cause he had exerted himself to promote.

1347. Stephen Colonna defeated and killed at Rome by the tribune Rienzi.

1411. Johannes Cantacuzenus, a Byzantine historian, died. His knowledge in literature and arms was so great that he became the favorite of the court and the people, and was finally persuaded to accept the throne, from which he retired again on the restoration of order.

1481. The *Last Siege and conquest of Jerusalem*, translated from the French "by me simple person, William Caxton," was printed at London in the Abby; one of the earliest specimens of English typography.

1497. The Portuguese admiral, Vasquez de Gama, doubled the cape of Good Hope, which, until then, had been considered the utmost boundary of navigation, and called the cape of Tempests.

1549. Kett, a tanner, rebelled against Edward, and was taken by Dudley, earl of Warwick, and hung in chains on the top of Norwich castle.

1571. The field of Craibstone stricken by John Master of Forbes, and Adam Gordon, brother to lord Huntley, where the said John lost the field, and was taken, and sundry of his friends slain, to the number on both sides of three score, or thereby, and good Duncan Forbes slain the same day.

1572. The first presbyterian meeting house in England erected at Wandsworth in Surrey.

1591. Christopher Hatton, chancellor of England under Elizabeth, died. He was a man of learning and great integrity, and though placed in so high a situation, had not been bred to the law. It was by his advice that the unfortunate Mary submitted to her fatal trial.

1660. The bishops of England again took their seats in the house of lords, verifying the adage of the king's grandfather, "no bishop no king."

1672. The island of Tobago taken from the Dutch by the English.

1683. A book entitled *Julian the Apostate*, burnt by the hangman, and its author, Samuel Johnson, a clergyman, fined 500 marks for an alleged libel on the duke of York.

1729. Nicholas Gervais, a French missionary, massacred in Guiana with all his attendants.

1737. Queen Caroline of England died, aged 55. Her favorite study was theology, and she has been accused of scepticism; at her death she refused the sacrament, but joined cordially in the Lord's prayer.

1759. Naval battle off Belleisle; the French fleet under M. de Conflans defeated by the British under admiral Hawke. The French lost several large ships, and abandoned the project of invading Great Britain.

1769. Charles Hugh le Fevre de St. Mark, a French miscellaneous writer, died at Paris.

1773. Charles Jennens died; an English gentleman of considerable fortune, who compiled the works of some of Handel's oratories, and began an edition of Shakspeare's works, which he did not live to complete.

1780. Battle of Blackstocks; the British under Tarleton attacked the American general Sumpter, but was repulsed with the loss of more than 30 killed or wounded. Sumpter and 4 others were wounded and 3 killed.

1789. Richard Burn, an English vicar, died; author of a work on ecclesiastical law, and on the office of justice of the peace, which have gone through several editions.

1789. North Carolina adopted the federal constitution, ayes 193, noes 75. This was the 12th pillar in the political edifice.

1789. A deputation was admitted to the French national assembly from the city of Issondein, with a patriotic offer of all the silver buckles of the inhabitants, to the value of 115 marks. Whereupon M. Dailly moved that all the members of the assembly should make a similar sacrifice, which was instantly agreed to.

1792. Battle of Cumptich, in which the French under Dumourier, after a long and bloody action, defeated the Austrians under the duke of Saxe Teschen, who exhibited great judgment and intrepidity in conducting his retreat.

1794. Figueras, an extensive and well provided fortress on the frontier of Spain, was taken by the French, when 9000 Spaniards were taken prisoners.

1798. Two French frigates attacked and captured U. S. schooner Retaliation.

1804. Archibald Maclain, an Irish protestant clergyman, died. He translated Mosheim's ecclesiastical history.

1804. The American expedition under Lewis and Clark went into winter quarters at fort Mandan, on the Missouri river, lat. 47° 21′ N.

1812. Bonaparte evacuated Orcha on his retreat from Moscow. He left there 23 cannon, some prisoners, and an immense number of sick and wounded, who fell into the hands of the Cossacks.

1813. John Baptist Bodoni, the celebrated printer of Parma, and probably the most distinguished in his profession during the last century, died.

1815. France ceded to the kingdom of the Netherlands whatever it still retained of the Austrian Netherlands, particularly a rich mineral district situated in the center of the Ardennes, and the fortresses of Marienburg and Philippeville.

1840. A series of extensive hurricanes and storms, which commenced on the 13th, and swept over England, Ireland and a part of France, ceased their fury. The destruction of lives and property, on land and at sea, was immense.

1843. Ferdinand Rudolph Hassler, aged 74, died at Philadelphia. He was director of the United States coast survey.

NOVEMBER 21.

53 b. c. Marcus Licinius Crassus, one of the triumvirs with Cæsar and Pompey, killed at Haran in Syria. He was surnamed *Dives*, the rich, on account of his vast fortune. He once gave an entertainment to the whole people, in which 10,000 tables were set, and besides distributed corn enough to last each family three months. He perished, with a great part of his army, in an expedition against the Parthians, undertaken from motives of avaricë and ambition.

533. The famous institutes, or system of elementary law, were completed by the delegates of Justinian. They were divided into four books, proceeding methodically, from 1, *persons* to 2, *things*; and from things to 3, *actions*, and 4, *private wrongs*, terminated, as in Blackstone, by the principles of *criminal* law.

1555. George Agricola died; a physician of Glaucen, in Misnia, known for his learning and works on minerals.

1579. Thomas Gresham, an eminent London merchant, died. His knowledge of commerce was considered complete, and he acquired a great fortune. He transacted the queen's commercial affairs, and his house was sometimes appointed for the reception of foreign princes. The first royal exchange was planned and executed by his munificence.

1616. Richard Field died; an English divine, eminent for his learning, benevolence and piety.

1638. A general assembly of the Scottish church met at Glasgow. It is said that not a few of the 260 commissioners of whom it was composed could neither read nor write.

1640. John, duke of Braganza, proclaimed king of Portugal. He recovered the independence of that kingdom, which had been annexed to Spain by Philip II in 1580.

1692. Thomas Shadwell died; an English dramatic writer, historiographer and poet laureate.

1695. Henry Purcell died; a very eminent English musician and composer.

1736. Battle of Porto Bello. A squadron was fitted out in England for the purpose of destroying the Spanish settlements in the West Indies, and placed under admiral Vernon. The attack was made on Porto Bello by the English, and after a furious engagement on both sides, the town surrendered.

1763. Public notice given in London that East and West Florida should be laid out into townships, and granted to those who would actually settle there.

1775. JOHN HILL, an English apothecary and writer, died. He published a system of botany, and was engaged in a great number of literary labors at the same time. He was also famous for several medicines which he prepared.

1777. Congress recalled Silas Deane from Paris, and appointed John Adams to succeed him.

1780. At the bank of England 471,000 three per cent stock was transferred to Mr. Van Otten on account of the landgrave of Hesse, so much being due on Hessian soldiers lost in the American war, at 30*l* per man. The number of men lost was 15,700.

1781. JEAN FREDERICK PHELLIPEAUX DE MAUREPAS died; a French statesman, eminent for his genius, activity and profound sagacity.

1782. JAMES DE VAUCANSON, a celebrated mechanician, died. He constructed with wonderful ingenuity various automata, and improved and simplified the machinery of silk mills, and advanced the interests of commerce and science by many other curious and useful inventions.

1783. The marquis D'ARLANDES and PILATRE ROSIER made an aerial voyage in a machine called a *Montgolfier*, in honor of the inventors, it being the first balloon raised by rarefied air.

1803. JOHN BUCKLER (*Schinderhannes*), the famous German robber, executed, with 19 of his band. He was the son of indigent parents, and entered into the service of an executioner. His first crime was a petty theft, which grew into the most extensive and expert robberies. He never committed murder, and expected pardon on that account, to the last moment.

1806. BONAPARTE'S famous Berlin decree, declaring the British ports in a state of blockade.

1807. ABRAHAM NEWLAND died at Highburg, in England; he was 60 years cashier of the bank of England.

1812. Battle of Borisoff; the French and Poles defeated by the Russians with great loss.

1812. Fort Niagara bombarded by the British from fort George and five other batteries. Above 2000 red hot shot and 180 shells were fired; which was returned with so much spirit, that the British had the worst of the battle. American loss 4 killed, 7 wounded.

1832. The emperor of Russia issued orders for the transportation of 5000 families of Polish gentlemen from the province of Podolia to the Steppes, on the line of the Caucasus. The university of Warsaw was abolished, except the faculties of divinity and medicine, and the library and collection of medals transported to St. Petersburg.

1832. Battle of Konich, between 75,000 Turks and 40,000 Egyptians, in which the former were defeated, and the grand vizier taken prisoner.

1832. Great riots at Lyons in France, which originated in a strike for higher wages by the operatives engaged in the silk manufacture, by which 30,000 persons were thrown out of employment, and the city was for some time at the mercy of the mob.

1835. JAMES HOGG (*the Ettrick Shepherd*), a Scottish poet, died. He was the son of a very poor shepherd, but his poems raised him to a high standing as a poet, and caused his society to be sought by the learned and the great.

1835. ALEXANDER CHEMIOTTE, one of the most learned orientalists of Europe, died. He wrote a history of all the Arabian emperors under the Abassides, and other works.

1848. LYNE STABLING died; one of the original proprietors of the soil on which the city of Columbus is located, and among its earliest inhabitants. He was one of the most wealthy men of the state, and was distinguished by private charities and public munificence.

1851. JAMES E. DE KAY, an eminent geologist, died at Oyster bay, aged 59. He was educated for a physician, but devoted himself from early years to natural history, and contributed the department of zoology to the publication of the New York survey.

1852. MARY BERRY, an English authoress, died aged 90; embalmed to posterity by the personal attentions and epistolary intercourse of Horace Walpole.

1856. SAMUEL SWARTWOUT died, aged 73. He was a noted politician, and during the presidency of Jackson was collector of the port of New York.

NOVEMBER 22.

1200. King JOHN, of England, held a famous parliament at Lincoln, where William, king of Scotland, did him homage in the sight of the people.

1419. BELTHAZAR COSA (John XXIII), pope, died. There was much opposition to his elevation, by rival claimants, and he was finally deposed and imprisoned three years. His liberty was purchased by acknowledging the election of Martin V.

1586. Sentence of death was announced to MARY queen of Scots, by lord Burkhurst, at Fotheringay.

1633. LEONARD CALVERT, brother of lord Baltimore, with 200 persons of good families, Roman catholics, embarked at Cowes, in the Isle of Wight, for America, to settle Maryland.

1652. The province of Maine was, by the request of its inhabitants, taken under the protection of Massachusetts; it was made a county, by the name of Yorkshire, and sent deputies to the general court at Boston.

1680. A brilliant comet appeared in England. First seen at Bristol.

1685. CLAUDE NICOLE, a French lawyer, died. He was a good linguist and poet, and translated several of the classics.

1714. SAMUEL REYHER died; professor of mathematics and jurisprudence at Kiel, and counselor of state to the duke of Saxe Gotha. His writings are theological.

1723. PHILIP, regent of France, duke of Orleans, &c., died at Versailles, aged 50.

1747. JOSEPH TRAPP, an able English divine, died; leaving behind him an excellent character as a critic, a scholar, a preacher and a man.

1771. Mr. STEPHEN was expelled from the Temple in London, by the benches, for writing a book on the impolicy of imprisonment for debt.

1774. ROBERT CLIVE, baron Plassy, a wealthy English nobleman, died by suicide; a striking instance of the insufficiency of wealth or external honors alone to produce happiness. While a colonel in the service of the East India company, he retook Calcutta from the nabob Surajah Dowlah, and defeated his immense army in the plains of Plassy, and thereby laid the foundation of the present extensive British empire in Hindostan. He was made governor of India, and died immensely rich.

1775. CHARLES HENRY DE FUSSE DE VOISENON, a French ecclesiastic, died. He abandoned his profession for the pleasures of the world and of authorship, and his works were collected in 5 vols.

1775. The Americans, about 1000 in number, took possession of Cobble or Miller's hill, near Boston, and erected entrenchments on it.

1784. PAUL FRISI, an Italian mathematician and philosopher, died at Milan. He was self-taught; and introduced into the Milanese the use of conductors to secure buildings from lightning, and contributed greatly to root out the superstitious notions of the people respecting sorcerers and magic. His works on hydraulics, astronomy, and many other sciences, are numerous and valuable.

1795. Battle of Loano, in Italy; the French under Scherer defeated the Austrians and obliged them to retreat with the loss of 8,000.

1798. THEOBALD WOLFE TONE, an Irishman having a commission in the French army, committed suicide in prison. He had been taken in arms against the British government, tried by a court martial, and sentenced to death.

1807. British Admiral SMITH declared Lisbon and the river Tagus in a state of blockade.

1812. Action between the United States brig Vixen, 14 guns, 120 men, Lieut. Reed, and British frigate Southampton, 32 guns, Capt. Yeo. The Vixen was captured, and Lieut. Reed died in the West Indies before he could be exchanged.

1814. LAVALETTE, the French general, sentenced to death for joining Bonaparte the preceding March.

1814. EDWARD RUSHTON, an independent politician, bookseller and elegant writer, died. He nearly lost his sight on the west coast of Africa.

1815. JAMES LACKINGTON, a celebrated London bookseller, but chiefly distinguished for his work on the evil consequences of girls being educated at boarding schools, died.

1821. ANSELM MARIE FUGGER, prince of Babenhausen, died. He was one of that great German family whose ancestor was a weaver, and which now consists of counts and princes, and whose property amounts to about 440 square miles, with 40,000 inhabitants.

1824. FRANCIS LEVAILLANT, the celebrated traveler, died at Paris, aged 70. He was born in the Dutch colony of Surinam. He early manifested a passion for the study of ornithology, and was encouraged by the patronage of Tenemink, of Amsterdam, to proceed to Africa in pursuit of that science. His long life was spent in research, and though he has added much to the stock of knowledge in that department, he was so unfortunate as to lose a great part of his valuable collections at sea.

1848. Great battle fought between the English and Seikhs near Ramuggur, in India, the British claiming the dearly bought victory.

1852. The shock of an earthquake was felt very severely at Exeter, N. H., and along the valley of the Merrimack, and in Salem and Newburyport, Mass., and in other places.

1852. The voting concluded throughout France and Algeria, upon the decree of the senate, relative to the reestablishment of the empire. The result was 7,824,189 votes in favor of the same, and 253,145 in the negative, and 63,326 void ballots.

NOVEMBER 23.

100. Clemens Romanus (*St. Clement*) died; a pupil of St. Paul and one of the fathers of the church. His epistle to the church of Corinth, though valuable for its antiquity, is excluded from the canon.

946. Edred. the successor of Edmund I of England, died of quinsy.

1585. Thomas Tallis died; "one of the greatest musicians that England ever bred."

1610. Bernard de Girard de Haillan, a French historian, died. His history reaches from Pharamond to the death of Charles VII, and he was the first who composed a body of French history in French.

1616. Richard Hakluyt died; famous in English history for his naval skill. He is author of a collection of voyages and discoveries in 3 vols. folio, and of several other useful works.

1665. Valentine Greatbreakes, an Irishman, appeared in England announcing his power to cure many diseases by stroking the patient. Flamstead, the astronomer, is said to have, when young, submitted to his art.

1679. William Wilde, an eminent English lawyer, died. He published *Yelverton's Reports*, was created baronet, and made a judge of the common pleas, and afterwards promoted to the king's bench.

1683. A partition line agreed upon by governor Dongan and governor Treat, between New York and Connecticut, beginning at the mouth of Byam brook, in the sound, thence running up the brook to the road across the same, thence in a northerly line into the country, keeping at a distance of 20 miles from Hudson's river. (See May 14, 1731.)

1709. William Bentinck, earl of Portland, favorite of William III, and an eminent statesman, died.

1758. Battle of Crefelt; the French under St. Germaine defeated by the allies under the duke of Brunswick, with the loss of 6,000, among whom was the count de Gisors. The allies lost 1,500.

1763. Anthony Francis d'Exiles, a French writer, died. He was educated among the Jesuits, but entered the army. He translated Richardson's novels into French.

1775. The British lieutenant-colonel John Connelly captured near Hagerstown by the Americans, on his way to Detroit with papers and despatches of great importance.

1794. Joachim Ibarra, an eminent Spanish printer, died. He raised the art of typography to an excellence before unequaled in Spain. As he never left his country, most of the improvements he introduced were of his own invention.

1794. Fort St. Fernando de Figueres capitulated to the French; 9,107 prisoners, 171 cannon, and great quantities of ammunition and stores were taken.

1795. Manheim surrendered to the imperialists under Wurmzer with more than 10,000 men.

1795. Battle of Geresio, in Italy; the Austrians defeated by the French under Angereau and Chastel.

1796. Battle of Castella Nuovo, in Italy; the Austrians defeated by the French under Massena, with the loss of 6,000. This closed the campaign, Bonaparte having defeated three armies and four generals.

1798. The king of Naples accompanied by the Austrian general Mack and 80,000 men, entered the Romish territories, but were soon compelled to retreat and act on the defensive.

1804. Stephen Borgia, an Italian cardinal eminent for his piety and learning, died at Lyons, while attending the pope on his journey to Paris.

1808. Battle of Tudela, in Spain; the French under Lannes, attacked and defeated the Spaniards under Castanos.

1812. American privateer Tom, of Baltimore, captured British packet Townsend. The British captain and 4 men were killed.

1812. The northern army under Gen. Dearborn went into winter quarters at Plattsburgh, Burlington and Greenbush.

1814. Elbridge Gerry, vice-president of the United States, died at Washington, aged 70. He was a signer of the declaration of independence, a member of the congress of 1776, and of the convention which formed the constitution. He transacted business as usual in the morning, was attacked about 10 o'clock, and died in 15 minutes.

1833. Jean Baptiste Jourdan, a celebrated French general of the revolution, died. In 1794 he conquered Belgium, and in 1796 subdued Franconia. "Jourdan," said Napoleon at St. Helena, "is a poor general, but he possessed the virtues rare among his competitors, of honor, integrity and humanity."

1849. The bones of Col. John Dixwell, the regicide, were removed from the grave of the centre churchyard, New Haven, where they were deposited in 1688, and reinterred with a view to the erection of a monument over them. The skeleton was in a good state of preservation.

1852. John Sergeant, an eminent Philadelphia lawyer, died, aged 73. For more than half a century he was known and honored for his ability and integrity.

NOVEMBER 24.

30. Eclipse of the sun in Palestine, accompanied by an earthquake, which overthrew several edifices at Niceas, in Bythinia. By the calculations of several eminent astronomers, it is demonstrated that this great eclipse, which is mentioned by Phlegon, and in the Grecian monuments, as having happened in the 202d Olympiad, took place on this day and year. Phlegon says, the day was changed into night at the 6th hour (noon), and the stars were seen. Between Cairo and Jerusalem it was wholly obscured for about two minutes, and by calculation, it is supposed, the middle of the eclipse happened at Jerusalem, an hour and fifteen minutes after noon.

62. Aulus Persius Flaccus, a Roman satirist, died, aged 28. He was a native of Etruria, studied at Rome, and imbibed the stoic philosophy of Cornutus, to whom he bequeathed his library and 25,000 crowns. His satires, animated and often beautiful, have been translated by several of the British poets.

1213. The possessions of the knights templars, in England appropriated by the crown, in obedience to a papal mandate, in trust for the knights hospitalers. That distinguished order was instituted in 1118, and consisted originally of nine poor knights, who for *Christ's love* protected the avenues of his shrine from infidels and robbers.

1230. Matthew de Montmorency, constable of France, died. He distinguished himself on many important occasions in the field, and proved himself equally capable as a statesman.

1516. James V 's charter of the town of Maybole, in Ayrshire, Scotland, bears this date. A room in the Red Lion inn in this town, is shown as having been that in which John Knox and the abbot Kennedy had the debate on the mass.

1567. The laird of Airth and the laird of Wemyss met upon the high street of Edinburgh, with their followers, when a furious encounter took place, "many being hurte on both sides by shote of pistoll." Three days afterwards a strict proclamation was issued, forbidding "the wearing of guns or pistolls, or aney sick like fyerwork ingyne, under ye paine of death, the king's guards and shouldours only excepted."

1572. John Knox, the celebrated Scottish reformer, died. He fiercely inveighed against the established religion, and succeeded in reforming the doctrines of the church in his country.

1638. Quinnipiack, now New Haven, purchased of Monauguin, sachem of the country, in consideration of protection from hostile Indians, and a payment of 12 coats of English cloth, 12 alchymy spoons, 12 hatches, 12 hoes, 2 dozen knives, 12 porringers, and 4 cases of French knives and scissors.

1675. Tea and coffee houses in London permitted by royal proclamation to be reopened, on condition that the keepers should prevent sedition, and the reading of libels in them.

1694. John Tillotson, archbishop of Canterbury, died, aged 65. He was a popular preacher, who exerted himself strenuously against popery, and was finally elevated to the highest dignity in the church.

1704. Landau surrendered to the imperialists after a loss of 4,000 men.

1728. Francis Masclef, a French ecclesiastic, died. A difference in theological opinions from his bishop led to his dismissal. From this time he devoted himself to study with so much application as to bring on a disease that hastened his death. His principal work was a Hebrew grammar, in which he discarded the vowel points, and embodied an elaborate argument against them.

1732. Ottomar Elliger, a distinguished Prussian painter, died by intemperance.

1751. George Graham, an ingenious watch maker, died. He was not only the most eminent of his profession, but the best mechanic of his time, and had a complete knowledge of practical astronomy.

1755. Lawrence Ricci, an illustrious Florentine, died. He embraced the order of the Jesuits, of which he was general at the time of its suppression; was imprisoned by the pope, and died in confinement.

1758. Pittsburgh evacuated by the French.

1759. Fort Du Quesne, now Pittsburgh, in Pennsylvania, taken by general Forbes.

1759. One of the most violent eruptions of mount Vesuvius ever known, which took place without any of the usual preceding symptoms.

1776. Theophilus Borden, an eminent French physician, died. He gained great reputation at Paris, where he published nine medical works.

1789. Assignats, the name given to paper money, first issued in France.

1790. Robert Henry, a Scottish clergyman, died; author of a history of Great Britain "on a new plan."

1814. Treaty of peace signed at Ghent, between the United States and Great Britain.

1819. Champlain canal declared to be navigable.

1828. Clarke Abel, a medical officer and naturalist, who accompanied the embassy of lord Amherst to China in 1816, died.

1835. William Duane died at Philadelphia; many years editor of the *Aurora*, one of the most able and distinguished papers which supported Mr. Jefferson and his measures.

1848. Pope PIUS IX, after a week's imprisonment in his palace, escaped in disguise to Mola di Geta.

1852. WALTER FORWARD, an eminent American statesman, died at Pittsburgh, aged 66. He was a native of Connecticut, but achieved his reputation at the west.

1854. The steamer Ocean, from Boston, for the Kennebec, came in collision in Boston harbor, with the Atlantic steamer Canada, took fire and was destroyed.

1855. LOUIS MATTHIEU, count Mole, formerly prime minister of Louis Philippe, died, aged 75. His abilities attracted the attention of Napoleon, and he filled various offices under the different rulers of France till his decease.

NOVEMBER 25.

165 B. C. Feast during eight days, commencing on the 25th of the Hebrew month Casleu, of the dedication of the temple, repaired and purified by the care of Judas Macabæus, being the anniversary of its profanation three years before by the order of Antiochus Epiphanes.

1185. LUCIUS III (*Humbaldo Allineigoli*), pope, died. He was twice compelled to fly from Rome to avoid the popular tumult. He established, with the countenance of the emperor Frederick, constitutions for the punishment of heretics, which may be considered as the origin of the inquisition.

1542. Battle of Solway Moss; the Scottish army under Sinclair defeated by an inferior force of English under Dacres and Musgrave.

1547. HENRY II, of France, caused the following to be proclaimed: "We forbid all booksellers, printers, &c., under pain of confiscation, to print any book relating to the holy scriptures."

1560. ANDREW DORIA, the famous Genoese admiral, died. He distinguished himself in the service of several Italian princes, and finally achieved the liberty of his own country, of which he refused to accept the sovereignty.

1624. RICHARD CRACKANTHORP, an eloquent English preacher, died. He was also an author of merit.

1626. EDWARD ALLEYN died; an actor of great reputation in the reigns of Elizabeth and James I, and founder of Dulwich college.

1651. HENRY IRETON, a republican general in the English civil war, died. He possessed great abilities and uncommon valor, and deserved the friendship of Cromwell, whose daughter he married. He died at the siege of Limerick, and was buried with great pomp in Westminster abbey; but at the restoration was dug up and exposed on Tyburn gibbet with Cromwell and Bradshaw.

1687. NICHOLAS STENO, an eminent Danish anatomist, died.

1694. ISMAEL BULLIALDUS, an astronomer of the isle of France, died.

1748. ISAAC WATTS, an English dissenting divine, died; author of several valuable works on subjects of divinity, and whose hymns and poetical version of the psalms are still in general use.

1758. Fort du Quesne taken by the British and provincial army, 8,000 men, under general Forbes; the French garrison, deserted by the Indians, being unequal to its maintenance. In compliment to the popular minister, William Pitt, it was named Pittsburgh, and has become an important place at the head of the Ohio.

1759. Battle of Chinchura, in the East Indies; the Dutch defeated by the British under colonel Forde.

1760. Tripoli nearly destroyed by an earthquake, shocks of which had continued nearly a month. Balbec was entirely ruined.

1766. ZACHARY GREY, an English scholar and divine, died. He was the author of thirty publications, the best known of which is an edition of *Hudibras*, with curious and interesting notes.

1770. PHILIP MORANT died; a learned and indefatigable English antiquary and biographer.

1774. HENRY BAKER, an ingenious English naturalist, died, aged 70.

1775. EUSEBIUS AMORT died; a distinguished Bavarian ecclesiastical and theological writer.

1780. NAPHTALI DAGGETT, fifth president of Yale college, died. He had previously been professor of divinity; was a good classical scholar and a learned divine.

1783. New York evacuated by the British. The Americans under general Knox took possession of it, and received general Washington and governor Clinton, who made a public entry into it.

1785. RICHARD GLOVER, an English poet, died. He was a merchant by profession, who made a proficiency in the belles lettres; and acquired an enviable reputation as a citizen.

1785. CHARLES DE MAUR, an eminent Spanish mathematician and engineer, died. He was employed in the army, and in the construction of canals and roads.

1789. A Jamaica paper of this date states, that 2,300 negroes had been imported into that island from Africa within the four weeks then preceding.

1792. Battle of Liege; the Austrians under Staray defeated by the French under Dumourier, and compelled to cross the river.

1795. STANISLAUS PONIATOWSKI, king of Poland, deposed by Catharine of Russia. He resigned his crown at Grodno, and was permitted to retire into Russia, where he died three years after.

1816. The new theatre, Philadelphia, illuminated with gas lights, under the direction of Dr. Kugler, being the first theatre on this continent thus illuminated.

1833. NICHOLAS ESTERHAZY died; prince of Este, field marshal and privy counselor of the emperor of Austria. He was at one time one of the richest subjects in Europe. The choice Tokay wine is made from his fruitful principality, upon whose estates were the largest flocks of sheep in Europe.

1835. ROBERT GOODACRE, a distinguished English lecturer on astronomy, died.

1837. St. Charles, in Canada, taken from the *patriots* by the British troops. The Canadian force consisted of between 3 and 4,000; their loss was 200 killed, 300 wounded and 30 taken prisoners.

1840. A negro woman, in Virginia, gave birth to a lusus naturæ, in the shape of a child with two heads, four arms and two chests; but from the umbilicus downwards, the formation was that of a single child; it did not survive. A living and perfect child was born at the same time.

1851. Battle at Cerralvo; between Carvajal, with 350 men, and Jarregui, the Mexican general, with 320 men and 2 pieces of artillery. Jarregui was driven with loss into a storehouse, which he held until aid arrived, and Carvajal's troops were dispersed.

1852. The canton of Ticino, in Switzerland, suppressed the order of Capuchin monks, and expelled all of that order under 65 years of age.

1853. J. W. GUNNISON, an eminent United States topographical engineer, was killed by a party of Utah Indians, while engaged in the survey of a route across to the Pacific.

1854. JOHN GIBSON LOCKHART, an eminent Scottish author, died at Abbottsford, aged 59. He succeeded Gifford as editor of the *Quarterly Review* in 1829, but is best known by his *Life of Walter Scott.*

1854. JOHN KITTO, author of many valuable works on Bibical literature, died at Stuttgart, aged 50.

1855. Admiral BRUAT, a noted French naval officer, died on board ship, aged 59. He had been governor of the French establishments in Oceanica, and was sent as commander of the French fleet in the Black sea.

1855. A revolution at Montevideo which lasted four days, in which 100 persons were killed, and many wounded.

1855. The town of Kars, after a siege of seven months, its garrison being reduced to extremities, surrendered to the Russians on honorable terms.

NOVEMBER 26.

380. GREGORY NAZIANZEN installed in the see of Constantinople, by the hand of Theodosius, upon the removal of Demophilus, and the fall of Arianism in the East soon followed.

1120. Prince WILLIAM, with Richard and Mary, children of Henry I, of England, with attendants and others, to the number of 180, wrecked in coming from Normandy, after which the king was never seen to laugh.

1504. ISABELLA, queen of Castile, died. Her reign was remarkable for the conquest of Grenada from the Moors and the discovery of America; but was disgraced by the introduction of the inquisition.

1678. STALEY, a catholic goldsmith, executed at Tyburn, London, for saying, as testified by a Scotchman, "Here's the hand that will kill the king."

1703. The great storm in England, the most violent on record. The Eddystone lighthouse was thrown down; 13 men-of-war and 1,500 seamen perished, with the admiral, Beaumont; bishop Kidder and a great number of persons were killed; and an immense number of animals, and a great amount of property destroyed.

1719. JOHN HUDSON died; an eminent English critic and keeper of the Bodleian library.

1763. ROBERT BOLTON, an English puritan, died; distinguished for his learning and eloquence, and the excellence of his writings.

1780. JEROME DAVID GAUBIUS died; a German professor of medicine, and lecturer on botany and chemistry.

1793. The French republican calendar was first used, but discontinued 31st Dec., 1805. The decade was seldom used in dates.

1799. JOSEPH BLACK, a celebrated Scottish chemist, died. He was professor of chemistry in the university of Edinburgh, and made important discoveries in that science.

1807. OLIVER ELLSWORTH, chief justice of the United States, died.

1812. Battle of Staroy-Borizoff, in Russia; a most sanguinary conflict, in which the French were defeated with great slaughter, after a conflict of four hours; 8,000 prisoners and a vast quantity of baggage were captured by the Russians; but the greatest trophy was two whole regiments of Saxon cavalry, fresh, and in excellent order.

1817. First newspaper in Wayne county issued.

1818. Field marshal COLLOREDO, Austrian minister of state, and director-general of artillery, died at Vienna, aged 84.

1826. JOHN NICHOLS, printer and editor of the *Gentleman's Magazine*, died at London.

1827. JOSE ALVAREZ, a famous Spanish sculptor, died at Madrid.

1829. BUSHROD WASHINGTON died; one of the judges of the supreme court of the United States.

1829. Great inundation of the Nile began, by which 30,000 persons perished.

1836. JOHN LOUDON MCADAM, died in Scotland, aged 80; the celebrated introducer of the system of road making which bears his name. He was 60 years of age when he commenced his public career as a reformer of roads; yet he became so great a benefactor that the British government made him a grant of nearly $50,000.

1842. ROBERT SMITH, a cabinet minister under presidents Jefferson and Madison, died at Baltimore, aged 85.

1851. PREISSNITZ, founder of the system of hydropathy, died at Graefenberg, in Bavaria, aged 52.

1851. Marshal SOULT, duke of Dalmatia, died in France, aged 82; terminating a long public career, both military and civil.

1852. An earthquake greatly damaged the city of St. Jago de Cuba.

1852. At Stafford house, in London, some English ladies, headed by the duchess of Sutherland, adopted an address to the women of America on the subject of negro slavery, which subsequently received 576,000 signatures.

NOVEMBER 27.

226 B. C. A solemn annual feast instituted at Rome, derived from the barbarians, when two Greeks and two Gauls, one of either sex, were inhumed alive, in the oxmarket. It was instituted upon the invasion of the Boian Gauls, in order to *fulfill* a sybilline prophecy, that those terrible nations should one day be masters of the capitol. At this period the city inrolled 770,000 infantry.

222 B. C. MARCELLUS carried off the *spoils* of Viridomarus, which is the last single handed triumph.

8 B. C. QUINTUS HORATIUS FLACCUS (*Horace*), an ancient lyric and satiric poet, died. He became the friend of Augustus, who offered him preferments, but he had the greatness of mind to refuse them all, and lived in retirement and study, free from the noise and hurry of ambition.

602. MAURITIUS TIBERIUS, emperor of Rome, died. He was a Cappadocian, distinguished himself at the head of the Roman armies, and was made emperor. But though valiant and successful, he was defeated by his own general Phocas, and put to death, together with his five sons.

1520. The Castilian insurgents under De Acuna, consisting of priests and men in holy orders, offered the royalists battle at Rio Seco; but the latter sued for terms, which not being accepted, the royalists struck a blow which turned the scale of fortune in their favor.

1520. FERNANDO MAGALHAENS entered the Pacific ocean, through the straits which bear his name. He navigated its waters three months and twenty days without finding an island; but during this course he enjoyed continuous fair weather, with such favorable winds, that he bestowed on the ocean the name of Pacific, which it still bears.

1627. The fall of a luminous stone or meteorolite, weighing 57 pounds, on Mt. Voisin, in Province, under a clear sky, observed by Gassendi.

1630. Great earthquake at Peru.

1666. Battle of Pentland hills, in which the persecuted covenanters were defeated by the king's troops.

1707. FITZ JOHN WINTHROP, governor of Connecticut, died. He was distinguished for his knowledge in philosophy and his skill in politics, and took a conspicuous part in the affairs of the colonies, both in peace and war.

1710. The British general Stanhope surprised at Briheuga, and compelled to surrender to the Spaniards with 2,000 men.

1714. Several persons tried for insulting the dissenters and breaking their windows at Bristol. This seemed to be an omen of the dawn of a more liberal day.

1754. ABRAHAM DEMOIVRE, a noted French mathematician, died. His abilities were so highly admired by the Royal society of London that they judged him a fit person to decide the famous contest between Newton and Leibnitz.

1778. General WASHINGTON broke up his camp and marched to Middlebrook, to go into winter quarters. The British expedition against Georgia, under colonel Campbell, 2,500 troops, sailed from Sandy Hook on the same day, escorted by a squadron under sir Hyde Parker.

1779. THOMAS, lord Lyttleton, a statesman of some merit, died in his 36th year. It is storied of him, that three days previous to his death a ghost admonished him that it would happen.

1781. Sortie from the garrison of Gibraltar, at 2 P. M., under Gen. Ross. They took and destroyed two mortar and three heavy cannon batteries, blew up several Spanish magazines, and returned before daylight with the loss of 4 killed, having destroyed property estimated at three millions.

1788. THOMAS HARMER died; an eminent English dissenting divine, and critical writer on Biblical literature.

1792. The national convention of France erected the duchy of Savoy into an 84th department of the French republic.

1807. The royal family of Portugal to avoid being made prisoners by Gen. Junot, who was approaching their capital, embarked at the mouth of the Tagus for Brazil.

1811. GASPAR MELCHIOR DE JOVELLANOS died; one of the most distinguished Spaniards of modern times, both as a statesman and a writer. The wretched state of the Spanish book trade does not allow a complete collection of his works to appear.

1812. Battle of Berezina; the Russian general Wittgenstein forced the French across the river, who were killed and drowned in great numbers in their flight. It is scarcely possible to calculate the loss of the French on this occasion. Cannon, bayonets, fire and water contributed to their destruction. A vast quantity of booty from Moscow fell into the hands of the Russians.

1812. British frigate Southampton, Capt. Yeo, and her prize the U. S. brig Vixen, totally lost on a reef of rocks 9 miles from the island of Conception. The officers and crews of both vessels were saved.

1812. A detachment of United States troops in ten boats made a successful attack upon the batteries opposite Black Rock, in Canada, spiked the cannon, and returned.

1814. Unsuccessful attack of the British on fort Kalunga, in the East Indies. British loss about 500.

1827. Eruption of the mud volcano of Jokmali, on the Caspian sea. The flames burst forth and blazed up to an extraordinary height for a period of three hours, so as to be seen at the distance of six German miles (31 Eng. ?), after which they scarcely rose three feet above the crater which discharged the mud.

1836. ANTOINE CHARLES HORACE VERNET died at Paris. He has produced some of the best paintings of the age. That of the battle of Fontenoy is much admired.

1838. The castle of San Juan de Ulloa. at Vera Cruz, Mexico, taken by a French naval force. The castle was reputed a very strong one, but was taken after a bombardment of 5 hours. The French lost 4 men killed; loss of the Mexicans upwards of 400.

1843. SUSAN JOHNSTON, widow of the late John Johnston, Esq., of Ireland, died at Sault St. Marie. She was daughter of Wabojeeg, chief of the Chippewa nation.

1850. HARDIN BIGELOW, mayor of Sacramento, died of cholera. He had distinguished himself by his vigor and bravery in quelling the squatter riots in Sacramento, and in enforcing the laws, by which he was wounded, and lost an arm.

1852. ADA AUGUSTA, countess of Lovelace, and daughter of Byron, died, aged 37. Her tastes turned to metaphysics and mathematics.

1855. ROBERT BUNYAN died at Lincoln, England, aged 80; the last male descendant in a direct line from the author of *Pilgrim's Progress*.

1856. H. TOLLENS, the great national poet of Holland, died at Ryswick, aged 77. His poetry, remarkable for its ardent patriotism, enjoyed extraordinary popularity among all classes of his countrymen.

NOVEMBER 28.

411. FLAVIUS JULIUS CONSTANTINE put to death by order of Constantius. He was a private Roman soldier, who invested himself with the imperial purple in Britain, and added Gaul and Spain to his dominions.

741. GREGORY III, pope, died. He was a charitable but magnificent pontiff, who added great splendor to the holy see.

1285. PETER III, king of Arragon, died. He is notorious for the massacre of the French in the island of Sicily, called the *Sicilian Vespers*, by which he became master of the kingdom.

1443. Revolt of Scanderbeg from the Turkish power, holding the standard of his native mountains.

1499. EDWARD PLANTAGENET, earl of Warwick, beheaded.

1523. Election of CLEMENT VII (*Julius de Medici*), to the disappointment and deep resentment of cardinal Wolsey; an event which had its weight in the establishment of the English reformation.

1631. EDMUND RICHER, an eminent French theological writer, died. He possessed great powers of mind, and a lively imagination; but his writings became obnoxious to the pope's legate, and drew on him persecution.

1655. Peace between England and France proclaimed.

1680. GIOVANNI LORENZO BERNINI died; an Italian famous for his skill in painting, sculpture, architecture and mechanics. He left a large fortune and was buried with great magnificence.

1708. ANTHONY VANDALE died; an eminent Dutch physician and critic.

1776. WASHINGTON retreated across the Passaic before Cornwallis. The diminution of the American army by the departure of those whose terms of service had expired, encouraged the British to pursue the remaining force with the prospect of annihilating it. The pursuit was urged with so much rapidity, that the rear of the army, pulling down bridges, was often within sight and shot of the van of the other, building them up.

1778. EDWARD ROWE MORES, an able English antiquary, died.

1782. Edict of the emperor JOSEPH II, absolving religious orders in the Low Countries from all foreign dependence whatever.

1785. WILLIAM WHIPPLE, one of the signers, died. He was a native of New Hampshire, and employed several years in commercial voyages. In 1775 he was a representative from Portsmouth, and in 1777 was placed at the head of a brigade raised to oppose Burgoyne, which he commanded at the battle of Saratoga.

1789. The iron, lead and woodwork of the Bastile were sold at Paris by auction.

1794. FREDERICK WILLIAM AUGUSTUS, baron Steuben, died at Steubenville, N. Y., aged 61. He came to America from France in 1777, and joined the revolutionary army. His sound judgment and experience, attained in the army of Frederick the Great, was of incalculable advantage to the Americans in establishing discipline and a uniform system of manoeuvres.

1799. KIEN LONG, emperor of China, died, aged 90. He received addresses from Voltaire and Peter Pindar.

1800. MATTHEW YOUNG, an Irish bishop and mathematician, died.

1801. DEODAT GUY SILVAIN TANCREDE DE DOLOMIEU, an eminent French geologist, died, of a disease taken during an imprisonment. He was indefatigable in the pursuit of his favorite science.

1806. The French under Murat entered Warsaw, the capital of ancient Poland, which had been overawed by the Russian soldiery, kept there for the purpose.

1812. LOGAN, the Mingo chief, died; so well known by his misfortunes.

1812. Battle of Tchatchovo; the Russians again defeated the French on the left bank of the Berezina. This was the last battle of consequence in Russia. Bonaparte fled the field, and was no more seen in any conflict during this campaign. His army was reduced to a wretched band of the shadows of men.

1818. ANN DAWSON died at Harrowgate, England, aged 161.

1825. MAXIMILIAN SEBASTIAN FOY, a distinguished French officer and orator, died. His funeral was attended by thousands of his countrymen, and a monument erected to his memory.

1828. MILLER RITCHIE, justly considered the father of fine English printing, died.

1840. London enveloped in dense fog, which arrested business in the city and on the river. Serious accidents and loss of life occurred. Such an event had not occurred before in 20 years; it was impossible to find the way along the streets without lighted flambeaux.

1849. THOMAS H. BLAKE, an early settler at Terre Haute, Ind., and a distinguished American statesman, died.

NOVEMBER 29.

92. AGRIPPA observed at Bethynia a conjunction of the moon with the Pleiades about 7 o'clock in the evening.

511. CLOVIS, the conqueror of Gaul and the real founder of the French monarchy, died. He fixed the royal residence at Lusatia, the modern Paris, which was originally situated on the isle of France, in the Seine.

1268. CLEMENT IV (*Guy de Foulques*), pope, died. He was a Frenchman, of great moderation, prudence and impartiality.

1290. ELEANOR, queen of England, died. She was a Castilian princess, characterized as pious, prudent and charitable, elegant in her person, and gentle in her manners.

1314. PHILIP IV (*the Fair*), of France, died. He engaged in a long and bloody war with England, Germany and Flanders, and in a single engagement with the latter 25,000 of his enemies were slain.

1330. RODGER MORTIMER, earl of March, hanged near London. He was engaged as a principal actor in a complicated scene of guilt with Isabella queen of Edward II.

1378. CHARLES IV, emperor of Germany, died. His reign is famous for the *golden bull*, enacted by the diet of Nuremberg. He founded the university of Prague, and deserves the respect of the learned for the patronage he extended to literature.

1526. JOHN DE MEDICIS died, aged 28; a warrior in the service of Francis I of France, and surnamed the invincible.

1530. THOMAS WOLSEY, an English cardinal, died in disgrace. From a butcher's boy he rose to be archbishop of York, and prime minister of England. He even aspired to the popedom. At the height of his fortune he had in his retinue 800 servants, among whom were ten lords, fifteen knights and forty esquires. His expenses exceeded the revenues of the crown. All this he owed to the capricious favor of the king, Henry VIII, who suddenly stripped him of all his possessions.

1599. CHRISTOPHER BARKER, printer to queen Elizabeth, died at Windsor. His books were specimens of good workmanship of that time.

1632. The king of Bohemia died; on whose youngest daughter, Sophia, by Elizabeth, sister of Charles I, and her issue, the crown of England was finally settled.

1643. WILLIAM CARTWRIGHT, an English dramatic poet, died.

1652. The Dutch fleet under Van Tromp defeated the English, and Van Tromp sailed through the channel with a broom at the mast head.

1661. BRIAN WALTON, an English bishop, died; editor of the Polyglot Bible, in 6 vols.

1662. Count D'ESTRADES took possession of Dunkirk, purchased by the French king of Charles II of England.

1682. Prince RUPERT, son of Frederick, king of Bohemia, died. He acquired military fame in the English civil war, but is better known for his discoveries in the arts and sciences. He invented what is called after him prince's metal, and discovered the art of engraving in mezzotint.

1694. MARCELLO MALPIGHI, an Italian physician, died. His discoveries in anatomy were curious and important. By his delicate dissections he found out the lobules of the liver, and the nature of the formation and mechanism of the kidneys, and of the veins and heart.

1695. ANTHONY WOOD, a famous English antiquary, died.

1710. Battle of Villa Visciosa; the left wing of the allies under Staremberg defeated by the French and Spaniards under the duke de Vendome; but the victors instead of following the blow began to plunder the baggage; Staremberg with his right wing fought their left with such valor and perseverance till night, that they retired in disorder with the loss of 6000 killed, leaving him master of the field and all their artillery.

1732. The city of Aveline and nearly all of the city of Oriano, inNaples, destroyed by an earthquake.

1759. WILLIAM DICKINS died at Kysoe, England. His life is remarkable for a single feat. While engaged in building the spire of a church, he fell from the height of 132 feet. In his descent he struck the battlements with such force as to fracture his leg and foot severely, and bring part of the stone work to the ground with him. He sustained so little injury in other respects, that he was soon enabled to reascend and finish his work. He lived 40 years afterwards.

1775. Captain MANLY, of Marblehead, in a privateer, took an ordnance brig from Woolwich containing a large brass mortar, several pieces of fine brass cannon, a large quantity of small arms and ammunition, with all kinds of tools, utensils and machines necessary for camps and artillery; and a few days after three ships from London, Glasgow and Liverpool, with various stores for the British army.

1780. MARIA THERESA, archduchess of Austria, queen of Hungary, and empress of Germany, died. She will ever rank high among illustrous women, and among those sovereigns who have been the benefactors of mankind.

1781. The British evacuated Dorchester on the approach of the Americans under general Greene; by which all the rice plantations between the Edisto and Ashley rivers were saved to the Americans.

1792. DAVID DALRYMPLE, lord Hailes, died. He was noted for his knowledge of law, and as an antiquarian, and was intimate with the most eminent men of the age.

1793. ANTHONY PETER JOSEPH MARIE DE BARNAVE, a French avocat, guillotined. He displayed great eloquence and strong powers of mind in the national assembly; but failing to keep pace with the terrorists, was imprisoned fifteen months, and finally brought to the block.

1793. M. F. DUPORT DU TERTRE guillotined at Paris; a modest and studious man, whose philosophical ideas led him to declare in favor of the revolution, in which he always displayed great moderation.

1793. The Austrians under Wurmzer defeated the French with great slaughter, and drove them beyond Strasburg. Loss of the French estimated at 15,000.

1793. Battle near Lautern; the duke of Brunswick defeated the French in two attacks, with great slaughter.

1794. CAESAR BONESANA BECCARIA, an Italian philosopher, died. He published a treatise on crimes and punishments, which became a popular work, and was translated into various languages.

1802. Ohio admitted into the Union.

1807. The royal family and court of Portugal emigrated to Brazil, on the invasion of the Portuguese kingdom by the French.

1812. British schooner Subtle, in chase of the American privateer Favorite, upset in a squall, and sunk before the Favorite could come to her assistance. All the crew perished.

1812. The American troops, 1400, embarked for the invasion of Canada under general Smyth.

1812. Battle of Autosse, between 950 Georgia militia and about 400 friendly Indians and a body of Creek Indians. The Creeks were defeated with the loss of 200 killed, among whom was the Autosse and Talisse kings.

1813. Giambattista Bodoni, a celebrated Italian printer, died. He was placed at the head of an establishment at Parma, in 1766, which he made the first of the kind in Europe, and gained the reputation of having surpassed all the splendid and beautiful productions of his predecessors in the art.

1814. The first newspaper printed by steam power. This was the *Times*, of London. The machine was the invention of a Saxon by the name of König, and printed at the rate of 1100 papers per hour.

1830. Revolt of Poland commenced at Warsaw, in consequence of the severe and insulting conduct of the grand duke Constantine. The insurrection extended quickly through the country, and into Lithuania and other parts of ancient Poland.

1842. Edmund Hawley died at Hawley, Mass., aged 96. He erected the first frame house in that town (then called No. 7), was a soldier of the revolution, and a justice of the peace for more than 50 years.

1847. The presbyterian mission station of Wallah Wallah valley, in Oregon, assaulted by Indians and several of the missionaries slain.

NOVEMBER 30.

406 b. c. Euripides, the Greek tragic poet, died at Barmiscus, in Macedonia. He wrote 92 tragedies which were greatly esteemed, but of which only 19 are extant.

69. Andrew, one of the apostles, suffered martyrdom at Patræ in Achaia, upon the cross. He is the patron saint of Scotland.

1016. Edmund II (*Ironside*), king of England, assassinated.

1093. Malcolm III, king of Scots, who was the son of the gracious Duncan immortalized by Shakspeare in Macbeth, was slain in his 70th year.

1292. John Baliol crowned king of Scotland at Scone, after swearing fealty to the king of England.

1603. William Gilbert, a learned English physician, died. He discovered some or the properties of the loadstone.

1654. John Selden died; an English antiquary, historian and law writer, of most extensive learning.

1672. The English East India company lost the island of St. Helena; the Dutch taking it.

1700. Battle of Narva; the Russians under Peter the great defeated by the Swedes under Charles XII. The forces of the two armies were unequal; that of the Russians differently stated from 80 to 100,000, while that of the Swedes varies from 8 to 20,000. Charles had a horse killed under him, and was struck in the neck by a ball.

1718. Charles XII, king of Sweden. killed by a musket shot while attacking one of the forts in Frederickshall, Norway.

1733. In consequence of a vast exportation of grain from England, freights nearly doubled and the price of wheat rose in some places to four shillings per bushel.

1750. The nunneries of Begging Friars suppressed in Ireland by the pope for vile and disorderly practices.

1750. Maurice of Saxe, marshal of France, died.

1751. Nicholas Boindin, a French dramatist, died. He left the pursuit of arms for that of literature, and became celebrated for his comedies.

1761. John Dollond died; an eminent English optician, and inventor of the achromatic telescope.

1781. Theodore Tronchin, an eminent physician of Genēva, died. He was the pupil of Boerhaave, and the author of several medical works.

1782. Preliminary articles of peace signed at Paris between England and America.

1793. Treaty between the United States and the Creek Indians.

1793. Jean Pierre Brissot guillotined; a very eminent Welch writer on philosophy, politics and legislation.

1793. William Lewis died in the act of drinking a cup of French ale, called a *tumbler maur*. He made it a rule to read a certain number of chapters in the Bible in the morning, and to drink eight gallons of ale in the evening. He weighed 40 stone, and his bulk was enormous. A machine in the form of a crane was constructed to hoist him on the carriage, and to let him into his grave. He had drank beer enough in his day to float a 74 gun ship.

1801. Joseph Francis Maurice de Lascy, a Russian officer in the service of Austria, died. He gradually rose to a high rank by his talents displayed at several important battles.

1803. French port of St. Domingo evacuated by capitulation; the French under Rochambeau went as prisoners of war on board the British squadron, and the black prince Dessalines took possession. Almost all the whites that remained were massacred.

1811. British ship Rover captured French corvette Le Compte Reginaud, 14 guns, with a valuable cargo of sugar, coffee and spices. She had before belonged to the British navy.

1812. Harriet Newell, an American missionary, died at the Isle of France. She was a woman of great excellence of character, who was the means of greatly exciting and extending the missionary spirit.

1813. The hereditary stadtholder of Holland arrived at the Hague from England to assume the sovereignty of the country.

1815. Fall of meteoric stones at the village of Chassigny, near Langres.

1828. John Bell, a distinguished citizen of New Hampshire, died. He was a leading member of the senate during the revolutionary war, and possessed great judgment, decision and integrity.

1830. The two Landers in descending the Niger, reached the sea, completing the discovery of that river; having ascertained that the Benin, the Nun and the New Calabar rivers, are all mouths of the great river Niger, with a direct communication with the Tschad lake.

1833. Gwyllym Lloyd Wardle, an English statesman, died at Florence. He obtained great notoriety for his successful motion in the British parliament in 1809 for inquiring into the conduct of the duke of York as commander-in-chief.

1833. William Macleod Bannatyne died, aged 90; a celebrated Scottish justice, one of the contributors to the *Mirror* and *Lounger*, and the last survivor of that phalanx of genius which shed a brilliant lustre on the periodical literature of Scotland near the close of the 18th century.

1838. Battle of Tampico; the Mexicans under general Piedra defeated by the federalists under general Urrea, with the loss of 500.

1848. Major John Roberts died. He served in the revolutionary war, and negotiated the exchange of prisoners obtained by the convention of Saratoga, 1777.

1850. Sereno Edwards Dwight, a noted New England preacher, died, aged 65. He published a life of Edwards, whose works he edited.

1853. Anson G. Phelps, a prominent, wealthy and benevolent merchant, died in New York, aged 74.

1853. Battle at Sinope; the Turkish squadron, consisting of 3 frigates, 2 steamers and some transports, was destroyed by the Russians; 5000 Turks were killed, and Osman Pasha was taken prisoner.

1856. Henderson Yoakem, the historian of Texas, died at Houston, aged 46. He possessed a high order of legal attainments.

DECEMBER.

DECEMBER 1.

627. Battle of Nineveh; the Romans under Heraclius defeated the Persians after a contest from daylight to the eleventh hour; 28 standards were wrenched from the hands of the conquered, and the cities and palaces of Assyria were opened for the first time to the Romans.

801. ALCUIN, preceptor of Charlemagne, presented his illustrious pupil with a magnificent folio Bible, bound in velvet, the leaves of vellum, and the writing in double columns, and containing 449 leaves. Prefixed is a richly ornamented frontispiece, in gold and colors. It is enriched with four large paintings exhibiting the state of the art at this early period; there are moreover thirty-four large initial letters, painted in gold and colors, and containing seals, historical allusions, and emblematical devices, besides some smaller painted capitals. (See April 27th, 1836.)

1135. HENRY I, king of England, died of a surfeit of lampreys. He is characterized as wise and valiant, and ranks among the most accomplished of the English kings.

1252. BLANCHE, (*of Castile*,) queen of France, died. She married Lewis VIII of France, after whose death she was regent of the kingdom during the minority of her son, and governed with spirit and ability.

1521. LEO X (*John de Medicis*), pope, died. He was the patron of learning and learned men; but is to be remembered as the cause of the reformation, in attempting to raise money by an unlimited sale of indulgencies.

1581. EDMUND CAMPRIAN executed. He was a learned English writer, who became a Roman catholic, and was hanged with three others for aiding the cause of the pope, and drawn and quartered.

1640. MICHAEL VASCONCELLOS, a Portuguese statesman devoted to the interests of Spain, was murdered during a political convulsion, and his body treated with ignominy.

1640. Portugal, of which Philip II of Spain had made himself master in 1580, became an independent kingdom by a revolution, which placed John, duke of Braganza, on the throne.

1666. JAMES WARE died, a celebrated antiquary and historian, of Ireland.

1722. ANNA LOUISA KARSCHIN, a German poetess, born. She was deprived of almost every literary advantage by the peculiar circumstances under which she was placed, until she attracted the attention of some influential persons, who published some of her poems. She acquired the title of the *German Sappho*, and died in October, 1791.

1723. SUSANNAH CENTLIVRE, author of several English dramas, died. She was born in Ireland, and becoming an orphan at an early age, set out for London on foot. Her adventures were romantic. Several of her dramas still keep possession of the stage.

1750. A wager was decided at Malden, England, that five men could be buttoned within the waistcoat of a person who had died a short time previous, without breaking a stitch or straining a button. Upon trial, the five persons were buttoned into the waistcoat, and two more with them. The person who wore it died at the age of twenty-nine, and weighed at the time of his death 646 pounds, and notwithstanding his corpulency, he was remarkably agile. There is a print representing the ludicrous appearance of the seven persons buttoned up in the vest.

1775. General MONTGOMERY, having sent several small detachments into the country to strengthen his interest with the Canadians, proceeded with the residue to Point aux Trembles, where he joined Arnold and marched directly upon Quebec.

1783. M. CHARLES, having made some improvements on balloons, ascended at Paris in one filled with inflammable air, the first which had been so filled. He ascended to the height of 9,000 feet. His predecessors had only reached a few hundred feet.

1787. The people at Worcester, England, rioted under the apprehension, that machines were to be introduced for spinning cotton.

1789. General WASHINGTON addressed a diplomatic letter from New York to his *great and magnanimous friend* Sidi Mohammed, emperor of Morocco, inclosing a copy of the new American constitution.

1793. The commune of Paris ordered all the churches to be closed. But the act exciting general abhorrence was soon repealed.

1795. Battle of Mainz; the Austrians under Clairfait attacked and carried the French entrenchments, took 106 cannon, 200 ammunition wagons and 2000 prisoners.

1795. Kreutznach carried by storm twice by the French under Pichegru, who was at length obliged to retire by the Austrians.

1795. At Lauterbach two whole battalions of French were cut to pieces by the Austrians.

1797. OLIVER WOLCOTT, governor of Connecticut, died, aged 71. He was one of the signers of the declaration of independence, for which he was a bold advocate, and was in the army of general Gates at the surrender of Burgoyne. He was remarkable for intrepidity, integrity, strong and bold conceptions, and great decision of character.

1803. THOMAS ASTLE, an eminent English antiquary, died.

1808. Battle of the Samo-Sierra, a narrow pass which the Spaniards had fortified with 12,000 men and 16 pieces of cannon, which completely swept the road leading to Madrid. The French began the attack at daybreak. Three battalions scattered themselves over the opposite sides of the defiles and a warm skirmishing fire commenced. At this moment Bonaparte came up. He rode into the mouth of the pass, surveyed the scene for a moment, and perceiving that his infantry were making no progress, at once conceived the daring idea of causing his Polish lancers to charge right up the causeway in face of the battery. The smoke of the skirmishers on the hill sides mingled with the thick fogs and vapors of the morning, and under this veil the brave Krazinski led his troopers fearlessly up the ascent. The Spanish infantry fired as they passed them, threw down their arms, abandoned their guns and fled.

1814. Action between American privateer schooner Kemp, of Baltimore, and 9 British merchantmen, several of which were captured.

1814. GILLIS MCKERHNIE died at Gourock, Scotland, aged 104, supposed to be the last of the warriors that fought with prince Charles in 1754.

1825. ALEXANDER PAULOWITZ, emperor of Russia, died at Taganrog. His efforts to improve his country and people were unceasing and most extensive. It was during his reign that Russia was invaded by the most formidable army ever assembled in Europe, but which in a few months returned in the most wretched defeat ever known.

1840. Battle of Kotriah, in Scinde, between 4,000 Beloochees, posted among the hills, and commanded by Nusser Khan, and 900 Sepoys with 2 field pieces, under lieutenant colonel Marshall. Of the former 500 were slain, and 6 chiefs and 132 followers captured.

1848. Hungary declared itself an independent republic.

1849. EBENEZER ELLIOTT, called the *corn law rhymer*, died in England.

1852. The French senate went in a body to St. Cloud to announce officially to Louis Napoleon the result of the election, and to hail him as emperor.

DECEMBER 2.

1469. PIETRO DE MEDICI, governor of Florence, died, aged 53. He was of weak constitution, but well meaning and prudent, and was assisted by his son Lorenzo in affairs of state. Under his reign an attempt was made to wrest the reins of government from the family.

1549. MARGARET DE VALOIS, a French princess, died; noted for her learning and the encouragement she gave to commerce, agriculture and the arts among her subjects.

1552. FRANCIS XAVIER died; a French missionary, denominated the apostle of the Indies. He was one of the most zealous disciples of Ignatius Loyola; performed his mission in Hindostan, the Moluccas, and Japan, and was on the point of landing in China, when he died.

1554. FERDINAND CORTES, the conqueror of Mexico, died, aged 63, leaving a character eminent for bravery and ability, but infamous for perfidy and cruelty.

1581. JOHN DEE, an English mathematician and sorcerer, died. He was a man of uncommon abilities, learning and application, but deluded himself with experiments in the occult sciences, which he continued till he reached the age of 80.

1594. GERARD MERCATOR, a Dutch mathematician, died. He was self-educated, but attained great eminence, and published numerous valuable maps and charts which he engraved and published himself, and which have been of great use to his successors.

1615. LEWIS DE BERTHON DE CRILLON, a French general and knight, died. He distinguished himself by his valor at the siege of Calais, at the age of 15, and during a long series of wars and perilous times displayed so much courage as to acquire the title of the brave Crillon.

1723. PHILIP, duke of Orleans, regent of France during the minority of Louis XV, died at Versailles in the 50th year of his age. He was a man of talent and political tact, but these qualities were much obscured by his love of pleasure.

1779. ALEXANDER ALBANI died; a Roman cardinal and a man of great merit.

1784. FRANCIS ARNAUD died; abbot of Grand Champs, in France, and distinguished by his literary labors.

1789. HERSCHELL announced the discovery of a 7th satellite to Saturn.

1791. HENRY FLOOD, the famed Irish orator and reformer, died. As a member of the house of commons his whole energies were devoted to the promotion of the political interests and internal resources of Ireland.

1792. Frankfort treacherously given up to the Austrians, when 1,300 Frenchmen were massacred by the Hessians, and several whose lives were spared had their hands cut off.

1792. The French under Dumourier took possession of Louvain.

1794. The United States concluded a treaty with the Oneida, Tuscarora and Stockbridge Indians, residing in the Oneida country. The former engaged to pay the Indians $5,000 for their losses in the late war; to build them a complete grist and saw mill, and hire faithful men to attend said mills for three years, and instruct some of their young men in those arts; to provide teams for carrying on the work of the mills, and to apply $1,000 to rebuild the church burnt in the war.

1796. The adventurous MUNGO PARK departed from Pisania, 200 miles from the Gambia's mouth, to explore the interior of Africa.

1804. NAPOLEON BONAPARTE inaugurated emperor of France at the cathedral of Notre-Dame, at Paris, and was enthroned with Josephine.

1805. JOSEPH BERNARD DE CHABERT, a French navigator, astronomer and geographer, died. He lost his eye sight by intense application, but his powerful memory enabled him to make many additions to the stores of scientific facts.

1805. Battle of Austerlitz; the French under Bonaparte defeated the Austro-Russian armies, under Alexander I and Francis I, who had united to check the ambition of Napoleon. The defeat was attended with the loss of 35,000 killed or drowned, 20,000 prisoners, and their whole pack of artillery.

1806. BONAPARTE decreed at Posen, a monument to the French soldiers who fell at the great battles of Ulm, Austerlitz and Jena.

1812. British again cannonaded Black Rock; the fire was returned with so much spirit that their batteries were entirely silenced.

1816. French general VANDAMME, resident at Ghent, arrested and sent to Brussels.

1816. Meeting of the citizens of London at Spafields; about 20,000 assembled to receive the report of Mr. Hunt, who had been appointed to present a petition to the prince regent, praying that two or three hundred thousand pounds should be appropriated out of the civil list fund for the relief of the poor. Only five thousand was granted, whereupon great disturbances took place.

1848. FERDINAND I, emperor of Austria, abdicated the throne, and Francis Joseph, his nephew was proclaimed emperor.

1849. ADELAIDE, the queen dowager of England, died.

1851. LOUIS NAPOLEON decreed in the name of the French people, that the national assembly and council of state were dissolved, that universal suffrage was reestablished, that the first military division was in a state of siege, and that the French people were convoked in the electoral colleges from December 14 to Dec. 21.

1852. LOUIS NAPOLEON publicly proclaimed emperor at the Hotel de Ville in Paris, under the name of Napoleon III. The emperor entered Paris from St. Cloud, and took up his residence in the Tuilleries. 80,000 troops were under arms, and the day was celebrated as a grand holiday in Paris, and in the evening there was a grand illumination.

1853. The steamer Winfield Scott, having on board 500 passengers and $1,100,000 in gold, was lost in a fog at night, about 500 miles from San Francisco; the passengers and treasure were saved.

DECEMBER 3.

69 B. C. The senate published a general thanksgiving in the name of Cicero for preserving the city from the Catalinian conspiracy. It was the first that had ever been decreed to any man in the gown; all other thanksgivings having been appointed for some particular *service* only.

1553. PEDRO DE VALDIVIA, having conquered the greater portion of Chili, and founded the city of Conception, was attacked by the Araucanians, defeated and made prisoner.

1557. The bond or covenant signed at Edinburgh, by the duke of Argyle and others, renouncing the *congregation of Sa-*

tan, with all the superstitions, abominations and idolatry thereof.

1586. In Verde, in Hanover, there fell large quantities of matter, partly red, partly blackened, accompanied by lightning and thunder, a fiery meteor, which burst with a loud noise. This matter burnt the boards on which it fell.

1610. The new bell of the cathedral church of Lincoln, called *Great Tom*, placed in the steeple of St. Mary. It is the largest bell in England, being seven feet in diameter at the mouth.

1632. De Vries, on his second voyage, arrived at the Delaware river. He found that the little colony, left here two years before (see Dec. 12), had been destroyed by the Indians, and the ground strewed with the skulls and bones of his murdered countrymen.

1647. Buonaventura Cavalieri, an Italian astronomer, died. He was the pupil of Galileo, and enjoyed a remarkable reputation in his day, but has descended to posterity solely through his method of *indivisibles*, one of the predecessors of the doctrine of fluxions.

1658. John Micrelius, professor of divinity at Stettin, died; a distinguished theological disputant.

1688. The abdication or flight of James II, and revolution in England.

1699. Captain Dampier arrived at the island of Papua or New Guinea, in Australasia, and named its eastern extremity New Britain.

1705. Pedro, king of Portugal, died in the 58th year of his age. Juan IV succeeded.

1758. Daring attempt to assassinate Joseph, king of Portugal. It was for this offence that the Jesuits were expelled the kingdom and their property confiscated—a judgment perhaps unequal to the crime.

1775. The continental flag was displayed for the first time, on board the flag ship of Esek Hopkins, who was commander-in-chief of the first American fleet.

1787. Delaware adopted the federal constitution, being the first state to do so. (7th?)

1798. Coni, the strongest fortification in Italy, was taken by the Austrians.

1800. Battle of Hohenlinden; the Austrians under the archduke John, defeated by the French under Moreau in a severe snow storm, with great slaughter, and night alone saved them from complete destruction. The Austrians lost nearly the whole of their baggage, a great number of cannon and ammunition wagons, 3 generals, and from 10 to 15,000 prisoners.

1809. Intelligence was received at London, that the Ionian isles, the principal of which are Zante, Ithaca and Cerigo, had submitted to the British. They form an independent state under the British government, and contain about 200,000 persons, who carry on a considerable commerce.

1810. The French, under general Decaen, surrendered the isle of Man to the British general, Abercrombie, with 209 pieces of ordnance.

1812. The 29th bulletin of the retreating French army was dated at Molodechno, describing their severe privations.

1814. The mayor of Lyons, in France, published an order forbidding all artists to engrave or paint the likeness of Napoleon Bonaparte.

1815. John Carroll, first catholic bishop in the United States, died, aged 80. He was born in the state of Maryland, and educated in France, where he became a Jesuit. On his return to America he rose from a parish priest to the dignity of archbishop.

1818. Illinois admitted into the union.

1821. Royal dance of torches, at Berlin, on the occasion of the marriage of the prince royal with the princess of Bavaria.

1823. John Baptist Belzoni, one of the most eminent travelers in Egypt, died. He was an Italian, who came to England, where he obtained a subsistence by exhibiting feats of strength and activity at the amphitheatre. He was afterwards engaged in exploring and bringing to light the antiquities of Egypt.

1826. John Flaxman, the celebrated English sculptor, died. His death is differently placed on the 7th and 9th.

1834. Simeon De Witt died, aged 79; surveyor-general of the state of New York. He had filled this office from the time of its establishment to that of his death, 50 years, with the highest satisfaction and ability, and was distinguished for his attainments in astronomy, engineering and physical science.

1838. John Bleecker Van Schaick, a poet of some merit, died at Albany, aged 35.

1839. Frederick VI, king of Denmark, died. He was a benefactor to his country, which is indebted to him for the liberty of the press, emancipation from the last remains of feudal authority, abolition of the slave trade, in which Denmark set the example to the rest of Europe, reforms of the laws, the establishment of schools for general education, the introduction of popular representation, and system, order and economy in the financial affairs of the kingdom.

1839. Pope Gregory XVI issued a bull for abolishing the slave trade; "urgently invoking all Christians of whatever condition, that none henceforth dare subject to slavery, unjustly persecute or despoil of their goods, Indians, negroes, or other classes of men, or be accessories to others in so doing; and on no account henceforth to exercise that inhuman traffic, by which negroes are reduced to slavery, as if they were not men but automata, or chattels," &c.

1849. WILLIAM L. HUNTER, a Rhode Island diplomat, died, aged 75. He studied medicine in London under his kinsman, John Hunter, but subsequently adopted the law. He was chargé at Brazil more than ten years.

1851. All attempts to oppose the assumption of power by Louis Napoleon were unsuccessful; the few barricades that were erected were soon torn or battered down.

1854. The people of Mexico completed three days' balloting, and decided with great unanimity that the republic should continue to be governed by Santa Anna.

DECEMBER 4.

1137. LOTHAIRE II, emperor of Germany, died. He was king of Saxony when he was made king of Germany, and finally invested with the title of emperor.

1139. ROGER, prior of Hexham, died; author of a history of the campaign of the Scottish army under king David.

1214. WILLIAM (*the Lion*), of Scotland, died. He confederated with Henry of England against his father, and his inconsiderate valor at the siege of Alnwick, as well as many other rash acts, brought misfortunes on himself and disgrace upon his people.

1334. JOHN XXII (*James d'Eusse*), pope, died. He rose under the patronage of Charles II, of Naples. He attempted the suppression of the Cordeliers; was an active pontiff, and respected for his frugality, prudence and sanctity.

1402. CHARLES VI granted letters patent to the priests to enact mysteries, or as they came to be called moralities, such as the conception of the Savior, &c.

1642. JOHN ARMAND DU PLESSIS DE RICHELIEU, a celebrated French cardinal and statesman, died. He was a man of great capacity and boundless ambition, whose ministery forms an era in the French government, and prepared the way for the power and grandeur of the reign of Lewis XIV.

1649. WILLIAM DRUMMOND, a Scottish poet and historian, died. He preceded Waller in polishing English versification.

1654. The expedition under Venables and Penn, sailed for America.

1664. The English, under the duke of York, destroyed 130 of the Bordeaux fleet.

1672. The king of England shut up the exchequer, and suspended payment.

1679. THOMAS HOBBES, a celebrated English writer, died. He published his religious, political and moral principles in a complete system, which he called the *Leviathan*. It is said that few writings have had a more pernicious influence in spreading irreligion and infidelity than his, and yet that none of them were directly leveled against revealed religion.

1679. JOHN BIRKENHEAD died; professor of moral philosophy at Oxford, a zealous royalist, and a popular courtier.

1680. THOMAS BARTHOLINE, a learned Danish physician, died. He lost his library by fire, but that his pursuits might not be interrupted he was made librarian to the university. His works are chiefly medical.

1717. Mr. SHIPPEN, a member of the British parliament, from *Salt Ash*, sent to the tower for saying, "The king's speech was fitted rather for the meridian of Germany than England." The king had little acquaintance with the English language.

1732. JOHN GAY, a celebrated English poet, died; whose fables will ever be admired. His play of the *Beggar's Opera* was received with greater favor than had ever been known on any former occasion.

1746. Genoa surrendered to the Austrians, and was subjected to the most cruel contributions.

1777. Sir WILLIAM HOWE marched the British army from Philadelphia, to Whitemarsh, for the purpose of attacking Washington, but marched back again without making the attack.

1783. WASHINGTON took leave of the officers of the American army in New York.

1789. The city and suburbs of London, overspread with a dense fog, so that the stages traveling between the city and the surrounding villages, were at five in the afternoon, obliged to be preceded by men with lanterns, a thing unprecedented in the memory of any one living.

1792. WILLIAM FORDYCE, an eminent Scottish physician and philanthropist, died in London where he enjoyed an extraordinary reputation.

1798. Minister PITT's bill, establishing the ten per cent income tax, was introduced into the British parliament.

1808. CHARLES LOUIS FERNOW died; a distinguished German writer on the fine arts. His father was a common laborer, and his early years were those of a talented youth struggling with poverty and other difficulties. After finishing an apprenticeship as an apothecary, he maintained himself by portrait painting and teaching drawing; and finally devoted his attention to the history of the fine arts and Italian literature. His productions are valuable.

1808. Madrid, being invested by Bonaparte, surrendered. The Spaniards were disarmed, and the town filled with the French army. The pavement had been taken up; the streets barricadoed; the houses on the outskirts loopholed; but in a few days tranquility seemed completely re-established; the French soldiery observed excellent discipline; the shops were re-opened, and the theatres frequented as usual. Such is in most cases the enthusiasm of a great city.

1808. The inquisition abolished by Bonaparte this day.

1815. Christian Godfrey Gruner, a celebrated German physician, died. He was one of the most prolific writers on medical science; having written 50 large works, and as many essays.

1819. Alabama admitted into the union.

1823. Susan Huntington died at Boston; an intelligent American authoress, whose *Life of Wisner* has passed through several additions in Europe and America.

1826. Abraham Robertson, an eminent English astronomer, died.

1829. Abolition of the rite of suttee, or immolation of Hindoo widows on the funeral pile of their husbands; the British government interposed to prevent its continuance.

1829. Commencement of a revolution in Mexico; Bustamente, the vice-president, issued a proclamation against the government of Guerero, demanding the resignation of his extraordinary powers.

1830. William B. Giles, died at his seat in Amelia county, Virginia. He was chiefly instrumental in getting up the celebrated resolutions of Virginia, 1798-99, and the no less celebrated Virginia report.

1831. General Torrijos, with 54 of his partisans, taken and executed, at Malaga, in Spain.

1836. Richard Westall, an eminent English artist, died. He was the author of a great number of works and designs, and well known for his numerous beautiful illustrations of elegant literature.

1839. Samuel Butler, an English pre late, died. He was the author of various publications, and collected a library valued at £30,000.

1840. John Robinson, an English prelate, died, aged 66. He compiled a theological dictionary, and a work on the antiquities of Greece, ancient and modern history, and some others.

1845. Elisha Blackman, the last survivor of the Wyoming massacre, died at his residence, in Hanover, Wyoming valley, aged 89, and was buried with military honors.

1851. George Crabbe, an eminent English author, died near London, aged 73.

1852. An earthquake at Acapulco did great damage to the city, though without destroying any lives. Shocks were continued for a considerable time.

1853. Kalafat attacked by the Russians, who were repulsed with great slaughter.

DECEMBER 5.

1056. Macbeth, usurper of the Scottish throne, slain by Macduff, after a reign of 17 years.

1492. Columbus discovered the island of Hispaniola, called by the natives *Hayti*, or high country, from its mountains; *Quesqueya*, or the whole, from its dimensions; and *Bohio*, or house, from its very superior civilization.

1518. John James Trivulci, marshal of France, died. He was banished from Milan, his native country, and entered into the service of Charles VIII, under whom he distinguished himself repeatedly in battle.

1537. An order for the expulsion of all the gypsies from England.

1560. Francis II, of France, died, aged 17, after a reign of 17 months. He had lately married Mary, queen of Scots.

1639. Henry Wotton, an English statesman and poet, died, leaving many writings.

1712. Anne Mary de Tremouille Ursins died at Rome, aged 80. She was a woman of great powers of mind, who as maid of honor to the queen of Spain, possessed so much influence over the court as to give her the direction of the affairs of the nation.

1734. Peter Tillemans died; a distinguished landscape painter of Antwerp, who settled in England and enjoyed there the patronage of the great.

1754. Battle of Leuthen, or Lissa; the Austrians and Saxons under count Daun defeated by the Prussians under Frederick II, with the loss of 6,000 killed, 21,000 taken prisoners, 134 cannon, and 4,000 baggage and ammunition wagons.

1775. The Americans under Gen. Montgomery and Arnold appeared before Quebec.

1784. Phillis Peters, known to the literary world by her miscellaneous writings, died at Boston. She was an African who acquired the English language, and made some progress in Latin.

1784. A violent storm off the coast of England, which destroyed a vast amount of shipping. A British fleet of 150 sail went out of Yarmouth road that morning, and was totally dispersed, all the sails torn in shreds, and a great many of the ships foundered, their crews in some instances being lost entirely.

1788. Admiral Greig, a Scottish naval commander in the service of Russia, was buried at Revel with great honors.

1792. Johann Wolfgang Theophilus Mozart, a celebrated German musician, died. His works will ever rank with those of the greatest masters.

1793. Armand Guy Simon de Kersaint, a French count, and naval officer of high merit, beheaded at Paris.

1793. John Paul Rabaut de St. Etienne, a French protestant minister, guillotined for his bold and eloquent defence of the king.

1793. Battle of Martigne; the French under Danican defeated by the Vendeans.

1795. John Bewick died; an English engraver on wood, of great excellence; who with his brother carried the art to a state of perfection before unknown.

1806. The French under Murat crossed the Vistula and occupied Praga.

1808. William Hawes, an English physician and philanthropist, died. He was the founder of the Royal humane society, for the recovery of persons apparently dead by drowning, strangulation or suffocation; an institution which has renewed the lives of thousands that would otherwise have perished.

1813. Charles John Maria Denina, an Italian historian, died at Paris; the author of many excellent works.

1815. A foot-ball match at Carterhaugh, Ettrick forest, between the Ettrick men and the men of Yarrow. One party was backed by the earl of Home, the other by sir Walter Scott, sheriff of the forest, who wrote two songs for the occasion.

1819. Frederick Leopold Stolberg, a German writer, died. His works consist of travels, history, poems, dramas and translations.

1835. Thomas Pringle, the first editor of *Blackwood's Magazine*, and for many years secretary to the London anti-slavery society, died at London.

1837. James Marshman, an eminent and learned baptist missionary, died at Serampore, aged 70. He was the son of a poor English weaver, who having received his education, went to India in 1799. He published a Chinese grammar, and a translation of the entire scriptures.

1838. The French evacuated the city of Vera Cruz. In an engagement between the French and the Mexicans, Santa Anna, who commanded the Mexicans, was wounded so as to oblige an amputation of his leg.

1851. Kossuth, the Hungarian general, arrived at Staten island, and the next day, as the guest of the city of New York, reviewed the troops, which formed a military and civic procession in his honor.

1853. The steamer Humboldt, of the New York and Havre line, run upon a rock in attempting to enter the harbor at Halifax, and was lost.

DECEMBER 6.

342. St. Nicholas, an eminent Grecian bishop, and the patron of children, died. At the council of Nice he was said to be like a sun among so many stars.

884. Carloman, king of France, died.

1139. Alphonso I, king of Portugal, died; celebrated for the defeat of five Moorish kings at the battle of Ourique.

1216. Hertford, in England, taken by the French under Louis the dauphin.

1352. Clement VI (*Peter Roger*), pope, died. He was a doctor of the Paris university, and is represented by Petrarch as a worthy, generous and learned prelate; but is differently represented by others.

1527. Pope Clement VII escaped in disguise from prison, although, by a treaty with the emperor Charles V, he would have been liberated the following day.

1540. Diet of Worms; conference between the popish and protestant divines; Melanchton and Eckius maintained the principal part of the dispute.

1540. Thomas Davidson, licensed by the "rycht excellent prince James V, king of Scots, to print the new actis and constitutionis of parliament."

1541. Emperor Charles V, obliged by a storm to relinquish his attempt on Algiers and return to Europe.

1557. John Macchabaeus (*or Macalpine*) died. He was a Scotchman, who resided sometime at Wirtemberg, with Luther and Melanchton. He was afterwards invited to Copenhagen, where he assisted in translating the Danish Bible.

1648. Colonel Pride prevented about 200 members of parliament from entering the house. This is usually called *Pride's purge*.

1670. Henry Jenkins, an Englishman, died at the remarkable age of 169. He retained his faculties to the last, and was once examined in court on a circumstance that happened 140 years before. As he was born before parochial registers were kept, no parish would support him, and he was obliged to beg for a subsistence.

1672. Jasper Mayne died; an English divine, poet and dramatic writer.

1675. John Lightfoot died; an eminent English divine, distinguished as an able scholar and an eloquent orator.

1688. Flight of Mary d'Este, queen of

James II, of England, with her child, afterwards the *pretender*.

1711. JANE SCHRIMSHAW died in Rosemary hospital, near London tower, aged 127.

1718. NICHOLAS ROWE died; an eminent English poet and dramatic writer.

1726. FLORENCE CARTON D'ANCOURT, an eminent French actor and dramatic writer, died. He was the author of 32 plays.

1734. ABIGAIL MASHAM, the favorite of queen Anne, died; noted in the history of the time for her political intrigues.

1776. The capture of Rhode Island by the British under Gen. Clinton and sir Peter Parker. "It is called the *Eden of America*," says an English work, "and celebrated (very naturally) for the beauty of its women."

1787. LA PEROUSE reached the Navigator's islands, in Polynesia.

1790. Kentucky was erected into an independent state.

1798. Turin and Piedmont relinquished to the French by the king of Sardinia.

1806. Thorn, in Prussia, taken by the French under marshal Ney, after a slight resistance.

1812. Boston privateer brig Montgomery, of 18 guns, captured British ship Surinam, 20 guns.

1815. A magazine at Dantzic containing 6,000 pounds of powder, with filled bombs and shells, blew up, destroying 700 houses and killing upwards of 600 persons.

1834. EDWARD IRVING, a celebrated and eccentric Scottish preacher, died. He was minister of the Caledonian church in London, and, by the force and eloquence of his discourses, attracted large congregations; the greatest orators and statesmen, the wealthy and fashionable hurried to hear him. But he became finally subject to the wildest vagaries, in respect to the *unknown tongues*, and was ejected from his place.

1835. NATHAN SMITH, an eminent lawyer of Connecticut, died at Washington. He was several years United States attorney for Connecticut, and senator in congress, and was respected for his integrity and ability.

1843. JOHN M. TAYLOR, commissary-general of the American army under Gen. Montgomery at Quebec, 1775, died at Philadelphia, aged 92.

1844. NATHAN ROGERS, an artist of merit and reputation, died, aged 57. He was a member of the national academy of design, and lent his aid to institutions of morals and charity.

1848. The king of Prussia dissolved his assembly and promulgated a new constitution.

1852. HORATIO GREENOUGH, an eminent American sculptor, died at Somerville, Mass., aged 47. He spent most of his life in Italy in the pursuit of his art, where he produced his colossal statue of Washington, and other works which stamp his fame.

1855. ANSELM ROTHSCHILD died at Frankfort, Germany; the founder of the great financial house of the Rothschilds.

DECEMBER 7.

424 B. C. The accession of Darius II (*Nothus*). This is also the date of the battles of Delium and Amphipolis, where Xenophon and Thucydides were present, and of the occupation of Cytheria by the Athenians.

43 B. C. MARCUS TULLIUS CICERO, the celebrated Roman orator, statesman and philosopher, assassinated at his villa, by Popilius, at the instigation of Antony.

983. Otho II (*the Bloody*), emperor of Germany, poisoned.

1154. Landing of Henry II in England from France.

1229. The *boy bishop* said vespers before Edward I at Heton near New Castle upon Tyne. On Childermas the scholars of St. Paul's and other schools were enjoined to hear the "Chylde Bishop's sermon."

1542. MARY STUART, sole daughter and heir to king James V, born.

1626. JOHN DAVIES, an eminent English lawyer and poet, died. His works on legal subjects are numerous and valuable.

1641. RALPH BROWNRIG, bishop of Exeter, died. He had the hardihood boldly to advise Cromwell to restore Charles II to his throne.

1657. CROMWELL sent an agent to the duke of Savoy to negotiate respecting his protestant subjects.

1666. Ten of the Scottish covenanters executed at Edinburgh.

1672. RICHARD BELLINGHAM, governor of Massachusetts, died. He had exercised the offices of governor or deputy for 23 years.

1683. ALGERNON SIDNEY, an English patriot and political writer, beheaded at the age of 66.

1721. BERNARD ALBINUS, a celebrated German physician, died. He was professor at Frankfort and Leyden.

1741. Revolution in Russia.

1776. British under Cornwallis marched to Princeton.

1787. The deputies of the Delaware state convention signed the constitution of the United States, which they had agreed by vote to adopt the day previous. She was the first state that ratified the instrument.

1796. WASHINGTON met both houses of congress for the last time as president of the United States.

1799. Battle of Sediman, in Egypt; the French under Dessaix defeated 3,000 Mamelukes and 10,000 Arabs under Murad Bey.

1805. Action off cape St. Mary between the British ship Polyphemus, 64 guns, and Spanish ships Santa Gertruyda, with twelve hundred thousand dollars on board, and El Felix, valued at nearly one million, both of which were captured.

1812. BONAPARTE in disguise with Caulincourt arrived at Wilna in a sledge.

1815. MICHAEL NEY, a French marshal, shot. His career under Bonaparte was distinguished during ten years, by great military skill and daring bravery. On the second restoration of the Bourbons he was condemned to death.

1822. JOHN AIKIN, an English surgeon, died; better known as a writer of great erudition. He edited the first twenty volumes of the *Monthly Magazine*, the *Athenæum*, various editions of the poets, and was one of the writers of the *General Biographical Dictionary* in 10 vols. quarto.

1832. VICTOR JACQUEMONT, a distinguished French naturalist, died at Bombay, aged 32.

1835. The rail road from Nuremberg to Furth, the first rail road in Germany, opened, and the journey made in 15 minutes. The monumental stone has the inscription: "Germany's first iron rail road, with steam power, 1835."

1842. THOMAS HAMILTON, the author of *Cyril Thornton*, a contributor to *Blackwood's Magazine*, &c., died at Pisa, in Italy.

1853. A statue inaugurated to marshal Ney at Paris, on the place where he was shot on this day of the month, in 1815.

DECEMBER 8.

1275. Meeting of *Stationarii*, or booksellers, at London. For a quarter of a century previous to this time, booksellers not unfrequently kept school in their porches. The portal at the north end of the cathedral in Rouen is still called *Le Portail des Libraires*, the porch of the booksellers.

1315. Battle of Morgarten, or Ægeri, in Switzerland; the Austrian army of 20,000 under the archduke Leopold, defeated by 1,600 mountaineers in the pass between the mountain and the lake.

1437. SIGISMUND, emperor of Germany, died. He volunteered his assistance to tranquilize the church, and proposed the famous council, which consisted of 14,000 ecclesiastics and 16,000 noblemen. His perfidy in allowing Huss and Jerome of Prague to be burnt, after giving them a passport of safety, armed against him the bravest of his subjects, and led to a civil discord and bloodshed of sixteen years' duration.

1493. Isabella, the first European town in America, founded by Columbus. All his men, provisions and utensils, were landed on a plain near a rock, on the island of Navidad, in the West Indies, and a fort erected. The town was named in honor of the Spanish queen, to whom the great navigator was much indebted.

1612. Great earthquake at Munster.

1643. JOHN PYM died; a celebrated English republican, distinguished for his virulence against Charles I.

1660. First time of the appearance of a female on the public stage; the character was Desdemona.

1661. An order of both houses of parliament was passed for hanging the carcasses of Oliver Cromwell, John Bradshaw, Henry Ireton and Thomas Pride upon the gallows at Tyburn, and then burying them under the gallows.

1677. NICHOLAS PAVILLON, an eminent French ecclesiastic, made bishop of Alet by Richelieu, and afterwards deposed, died in exile.

1691. RICHARD BAXTER, a celebrated English nonconformist divine, died. He wrote a vast number of books; his practical works were collected in 4 vols. folio.

1695. BARTHOLOMEW D'HERBELOT, a French orientalist, died. He wrote a *Universal Dictionary*, "containing whatever relates to the knowledge of the eastern world."

1709. THOMAS CORNEILLE, a French dramatist, died. He wrote 42 dramatic pieces, which were received with greater applause than those of his brother Peter, but have been lost and forgotten.

1741. VITUS BEHRING, a Danish navigator, died. He was a commodore in the Russian service, and was employed in exploring some of the northern coasts of America, where he died, after having made some important discoveries, among which was the strait that bears his name.

1745. JOHN ROQUE, a French traveler, died at Paris. He published an account of his travels in Arabia Felix, Palestine and Syria.

1746. CHARLES RATCLIFFE, earl of Derwentwater, executed at Towerhill, London. He had resided 30 years in France.

1751. LOUISA, youngest daughter of George II, queen of Denmark, died.

1775. A number of American whaleboats under captain Manly captured three British ships with various stores intended for the army.

1776. WASHINGTON retreated across the Delaware. The British, on the same day, blocked up commodore Hopkins' squadron and a number of privateers at Providence.

1792. HENRY LAURENS, a patriot of South Carolina, died. He was distinguished for talent and activity, and succeeded Hancock as president of congress. He was captured by the British on a mission to Holland, and confined a long time in the tower of London. At his death he left a property of about $250,000 to his son, on condition that he should burn his body on the third day after his death.

1803. HIPPOLYTUS THEODOROVITCH BOGDANOVITCH, a Russian poet, died. His poem of *Dushenka* procured him the favor of the queen and the whole nation. It is founded on the mythological story of Psyche, but so unlike any thing that had preceded it in that language that he immediately became the favorite of all classes.

1806. ANDREW DALSELL, professor of Greek at Edinburgh, died; an amiable and a learned man.

1821. EBENEZER COBB died at Kingston, Mass., aged 107. He was the cotemporary for ten years of Peregrine White, the first born child of English parents in America. His mode of living was extremely simple, having tasted tea but twice in his life. He shrewdly remarked, a short time before his death, that it was very unusual for persons of his age to die.

1847. The United States brig-of-war Somers thrown on her beam ends by a squall near Vera Cruz, and 2 officers with 39 out of 76 of her crew drowned. The French and Spanish men-of-war lying at Sacrificios rendered much assistance and received the thanks of congress.

1848. The first deposit of California gold made in the United States mint by David Carter.

1851. Battle of Longomilla, between the government troops of Chili under general Bulnes, late president, and the rebels under general Cruz, who was defeated and his troops dispersed.

1854. The immaculate conception of the Virgin Mary proclaimed by the pope, in St. Peter's church, Rome, as a dogma of the catholic faith.

DECEMBER 9.

493 B. C. MENENIUS AGRIPPA met the plebeian seceders, encamped on the Mons Sacer, near Rome, and delivered to them there the memorable apologue of the belly and the members.

1150. A great frost in England mentioned by Matthew Paris, began on this day and continued about two months and ten days, so that "both foot and horse crossed the Thames." In that year all the prelates in council were shut up by king Stephen for refusing to crown his son; more remarkable for the appearance of Gratian's twenty-four years' labor, the *Decretals*.

1165. MALCOLM IV, king of Scots, died of a lingering disease, at Jedburgh, after a short reign. His subjects were rebellious, but by his vigor he overcame them all.

1565. PIUS IV (*John Angelo de Medicis*) died. He was not of the Florence family, but brother of the famous marquis de Marignan, and distinguished as an ambassador. He evinced his zeal for the church by his enemity against the Turks and heretics.

1641. ANTHONY VANDYCK, the celebrated Dutch painter, died. He was a pupil of Rubens, and excelled his master in delicacy of coloring. His pictures preserve in high perfection the dress and costume of the times.

1669. CLEMENT IX (*Julius Rospigliosi*) died of grief, at the loss of Candia, which was taken by the Turks. His reign was disturbed by the schisms of the Jansenists.

1674. EDWARD HYDE, lord of Clarendon, died at Rouen, in France, in exile. His name is immortalized by the *History of the Rebellion*, a splendid monument of his genius and impartiality, which he finished in exile.

1680. Comet seen at Albany.

1683. JOHN OLDHAM, an eminent English poet, died of small pox. His genius lay chiefly in satire.

1694. PAUL SIGNERI died at Rome; a theological writer, and a popular preacher and active missionary of the Jesuits.

1702. HAAGEN SWENSDEN executed for stealing and marrying Mrs. Pleasant Rawlins, an heiress.

1708. JOHN HIGGINSON died; the first minister of Salem, Mass.

1788. JONATHAN SHIPLEY, bishop of St. Asaph, died. He was a distinguished prelate and eminent among his episcopal brethren for his firm and determinate opposition to the American war.

1798. JOHN REINHOLD FORSTER, an eminent English writer on natural history and philosophy, died at Halle, in Germany. He accompanied Cook in his second voyage round the world.

1804. The British under admiral POPHAM attacked fort Rouge at the entrance of Calais harbor with explosion vessels.

1808. The Chinese interdicted the English from trading until their soldiery were drawn from Macao.

1808. The British rejected the French and Russian proposals for peace.

1811. Americans under general Harrison left the battle ground at Tippecanoe, on their return to the United States.

1813. Battle on the Nieve, near Bayonne; the British under general Hope attacked the French under Soult, without obtaining any decisive advantage.

1814. Joseph Bramah, a very ingenious English engineer and mechanist, died.

1815. The exiled emperor Napoleon, took possession of the villa of Longwood. This year, at its dawn, found him sovereign of the little island of Elba; ere the vernal equinox he was again emperor of France; before the summer solstice he was finally defeated at Waterloo; the year closed over him a solitary exile.

1816. The bank of England commenced paying specie on one and two pound notes dated prior to 1812.

1824. Battle of Ayacucho, in Peru, between the royalists under La Serna, 9,310, and the patriots, 5,780, under Sucre, which terminated in the total defeat of the former, who lost 1800 killed, and their general taken prisoner. Loss of the patriots, 370 killed. This victory accomplished the delivery of Peru from the Spaniards.

1824. Jose La Serna, viceroy of Peru, wounded and taken prisoner at the battle of Ayacucho, which put an end to his authority in that state. He commenced his career in the artillery, and served at Saragossa under the celebrated Palafox. His skill in the art of war did not avail him against the determined bravery of the revolutionists.

1831. Disturbances in Ireland; the soldiers fired upon a mob of 2000 Irish; whereupon the mob rushed upon the soldiery and killed 19 out of 34.

1831. Ibrahim Pasha completely defeated before St. Jean d'Acre.

1833. John Jebb, bishop of Limerick, died. He was an accomplished author, a learned theologian, and an amiable man. His publications, though not numerous, were of high merit.

1835. President's message reached Boston in 26 hours and 50 minutes from Washington. It was formerly announced as an instance of extraordinary speed that the message reached Boston in 64 hours. In 1841 the message reached New York in 8 hours 53 minutes, and probably was in Boston within another 8 hours. Dr. Franklin once expressed an opinion that the time would come when the mail might be conveyed from Philadelphia to Boston in a fortnight, and *perhaps* in a week. The regular time is now 24 hours.

1842. Samuel Woodworth, well known as an American poet, died in New York. He was the author of the popular song, the *Old Oaken Bucket*.

1850. Bem, the Hungarian general, died at Aleppo.

1853. The men and women of Harbor creek, near Erie, Pa., turned out in large numbers, tore up the rail road track, burnt the ties and bridges over the culvert, and plowed down the track to its former level.

1854. The king of the Sandwich islands to prevent the overthrow of his government by lawless violence, accepted the aid of the naval forces of the United States, Great Britain and France.

1856. Father Matthew, called the apostle of temperance, died at Cork, Ireland, aged 66. He devoted himself in early life to the regeneration of his countrymen among the poorer classes who had fallen under the tyranny of strong drink.

DECEMBER 10.

590 b. c. The tenth day of the month Thanet was observed as a fast in memory of the investment of Jerusalem by Nebuchadnezzar. Zechariah promised the extinction of this day of grief, in joy and feasting, upon the restoration of the house of Judah, b. c. 518.

493 b. c. The immortal day when *tribunes* for the Roman people were first chosen; the anniversary also of their authority afterwards.

270 b. c. Epicurus, the Athenian philosopher, died on the 10th day of Gamelion, having three days before observed his 71st anniversary. He taught a rational philosophy and with his disciples lived conformably to the rules of wisdom and frugality, although his name is unjustly associated with folly and feasting. His academy was the best regulated society that had ever been seen.

536. Rome opened her gates to Belisarius; the garrison departed without molestation along the Flaminian way, and the city, after sixty years of servitude, was delivered from the yoke of the barbarians. Leutherius, the Gothic chief, was sent to bear the keys of the city to his imperial master.

1282. Llewellyn ap Grufydd, a Welsh prince, killed. He heroically resisted the invasion of Edward I of England; but fell, and the liberty of his country perished with him after an independence of 800 years.

1506. Bologna captured by pope Julius I, who entered in triumph.

1508. The league of Cambray formed against the Venitian power. The pope, the emperor of Germany, and the kings of France and Spain, were the parties to it.

1520. Luther destroyed the papal bull against himself, with the works of the anti reformers, in a public fire behind the walls of Wittemberg.

1548. Battle of Pinckney field, near

Musselburgh, in which 13,000 of the Scots were slain.

1577. On Sanctobertis eve a great number of persons paraded the streets of Perth in disguise. One clad in the devil's coat; the horse of another walked in men's shoes.

1586. ELIZABETH signed the warrant for the execution of Mary.

1626. EDMUND GUNTER, an English mathematician and astronomer, died. He distinguished himself by many important improvements in mathematical instruments for the use of navigation, &c.

1672. A monthly post established from New York to Boston.

1674. JOHN VAUGHAN, an eminent English law reporter, died; "more admired for his talents than loved for his courteous manners."

1681. The British factor, captain DREW, arrived at Chester, on the river Delaware, from England, with settlers for Pennsylvania; they remained there all winter, the river having frozen over that night. She was one of the three ships that left England with the first settlers. One of them, the Amity, arrived before her; the third was blown off the coast to the West Indies, and did not arrive until the next spring.

1688. JAMES IV deserted the English throne, embarked for France, and ordered his army to be disbanded.

1697. The peace of Ryswick, which had been signed in September, proclaimed in Boston, and the colonies had repose from war. Some of the Indians continued their hostilities, but finding themselves unsupported by the French, they took measures for peace.

1697. The population of New France, exclusive of Acadie, was 8,515, and could arm about 1,000 men.

1747. DUNCAN FORBES, an eminent Scottish lawyer, died. He wrote chiefly on theological subjects.

1757. Breslau retaken from the Austrians by Frederick II of Prussia. The Austrians lost 13 generals and 18,000 men prisoners.

1768. The royal academy of London instituted.

1792. JOHN JOSEPH SUE died; professor of anatomy at Paris, and a writer on anatomy and surgery.

1801. JONATHAN BATTISHILL, an eminent English musical composer, died. "To a profound knowledge he added great taste and a fine imagination."

1804. New York historical society instituted.

1807. Kingdom of Etruria dissolved and annexed to France.

1808. JAMES SULLIVAN, governor of Massachusetts, died. He rose to great usefulness unaided by opulence or family connexions.

1809. Gerona in Spain surrendered to the French after a siege of six months.

1813. French under SOULT endeavored to force the British under Wellington to repass the Nieve but were repulsed.

1813. The United States troops under general McClure burnt Newark adjoining fort George, destroyed that fort, removed the public stores, and retired to the south side of the Niagara river.

1817. Mississippi admitted into the confederacy.

1833. The house of assembly in Jamaica passed a bill for the abolition of slavery.

1834. ALEXANDER CHALMERS died; one of the most eminent biographers that Great Britain has produced. He commenced a laborious literary life in London and no man, it is said, ever edited so many books for the booksellers. He published a *General Biographical Dictionary* in 32 volumes.

1835. The fortress of San Antonio surrendered by the Mexicans to the Texans under colonel Milan; the captors found 1900 rounds of powder and ball, 24 pieces of cannon, and a large amount of military stores, &c.

1836. A decree of the queen of Portugal published, abolishing the slave trade in the Portuguese dominions.

1842. PLEASANT HENDERSON, a soldier of the revolution from North Carolina, died in Tennessee. He was a companion of Daniel Boone in many of his wanderings and was for more than thirty years a clerk of the North Carolina house of commons.

1842. ROWLAND HILL, viscount Hill, the well known coadjutor of the duke of Wellington in the peninsula campaigns, died in his 70th year, near Shrewsbury, England.

1845. JESSE D. ELLIOT, an American commodore, died at Philadelphia, aged 62. He contributed much to Perry's success on lake Erie.

1846. JAMES GRIERSON died at Masharene, New Brunswick, aged 105. He was one of the loyalists that left the United States during the revolution.

1848. LOUIS NAPOLEON elected president of the French; 5,534,520 voting for him.

1852. WILLIAM EMPSON, professor of law in the East India college at Hoxley, England, died, aged 62. He was editor of the *Edinburgh Review*.

1855. The emperor FAUSTIN I left Port-au-Prince with 30,000 men to subjugate the Dominican republic; his forces were completely routed and dispersed.

DECEMBER 11.

361. Julian, the new emperor, made his triumphial entry into the eastern capital, having traversed with victory the whole continent of Europe, from the Atlantic.

1282. Michael VIII (*Palæologus*), emperor of Rome, died. He was regent of the eastern empire, and took advantage of his situation to assume the supreme power. He retook Constantinople, which had been 58 years under the power of the French, and labored to reconcile the eastern and western churches.

1595. Philippe de Croi, duke of Aarschot, died; a Flemish nobleman and general, who, in an attempt to free his country of Spanish dictation, was unsuccessful, and exiled.

1620. The Plymouth adventurers, having sounded the harbor, and found it fit for shipping, went ashore and explored the adjacent land, where they saw cornfields and brooks; and judging the situation to be convenient for a settlement, they returned with the welcome intelligence to the ship.

1652. Dionysius Petavius died; a French Jesuit of great erudition, and an author.

1657. Writs issued by Cromwell to sixty individuals, to meet at Westminister, and compose a house of lords.

1697. Joachim Kuhnius, a learned Pomeranian, died. He was principal of the college of Octigen, and acquired great celebrity by his publications.

1699. The king of Sweden defeated the Muscovites at Narva.

1704. Roger L'Estrange, an English gentleman and scholar, died. He was unsuccessful in his enterprises in favor of Charles I; but on the restoration he returned to England, and printed the first regular English newspaper, 1663, under the title of the *Public Intelligencer*. He was the author of some political tracts, and translations from different languages.

1714. George I, and his cabinet, issued an order forbidding the clergy to meddle in their sermons with the affairs of state.

1718. Charles XII, of Sweden, killed; supposed to have been struck by a cannon ball in the trenches, at Frederickshall; a fortress which he was then besieging near the bay of Denmark.

1747. Edmund Curl died; one of the characters mentioned in Pope's *Dunciad*. His character for morality was not without blemish, and he was highly injurious to the literary world, in his profession of book maker and seller, by his piracies and forgeries. He lost his ears in the pillory, by sentence of the law, for issuing obscene publications.

1753. The dey of Algiers assassinated by a soldier, as he was distributing pay to about 300 in the court yard of his palace. The assassin seated himself in the chair of state, and was taking measures to secure his power, when he was shot with a carbine.

1756. Theodore Newhoff, king of Corsica, died in England, where he had been long confined in prison for debt.

1758. The old castle of the Douglasses, so famed in Scottish history, was accidentally burned to the ground.

1794. Assault on the works of Nijmegen, a strong city of Holland; general Bushe, of the allies, was killed by an 8lb. cannon ball.

1794. Battle of Roussilon; the Spaniards and Portuguese defeated the French, killed 800, took 600 prisoners, and 50 cannon.

1806. Saxony erected into a kingdom, under Frederick Augustus, by the treaty of Posen, between Bonaparte and the elector.

1807. The Dutch fleet burnt at Greisse, in Java, by the British squadron, under sir Edward Pellew.

1812. Wilna entered by the Russians, where they found vast magazines, 30 cannon, upwards of 5,000 in the hospitals, including some distinguished officers, and took about 10,000 prisoners.

1813. The French, under Soult, again repulsed in an attempt to force the British under lord Wellington to repass the Nieve.

1816. Indiana admitted as a new state into the Union of the United States.

1828. Beranger was sentenced by the French court of correctional police, to pay 10,000 francs ($1,800) fine, and to undergo nine months' imprisonment, for having attacked the dignity of the church, and of the king, in his poems.

DECEMBER 12.

1656 a. m. The rain of the deluge having ceased to fall, having continned 40 days, from the 17th of the 2d month, answering to our 2d Nov., q. v.

404 b. c. Darius II (*Nothus*), king of Persia, died, after a reign of nineteen years, and was succeeded by Artaxerxes Mnemon, his son. Cyrus, the younder, another of his sons, carried on several successful wars during the reign of Darius.

1271. Richard, king of the Romans, died, at Berkhamstead, England.

1600. John Craig, a Scottish ecclesiastic, died. He was at first a Dominican, and by his talents recommended himself to cardinal Pole. But, becoming a heretic, narrowly escaped been burnt. He afterwards became the coadjutor of Knox, the great reformer.

1611. THOMAS SUTTON, a rich English bachelor, died. He was the founder of the Charter house.

1630. DAVID PIETERSZEN DE VRIES, who had associated himself with Samuel Godyn, Kilian Van Rensselaer, Samuel Bloemart, and Jan de Laet, sailed from Texel for the South (Delaware) river, intending to plant a colony there. Godyn being informed that whales were plenty in those regions, and fish oil being 60 guilders the hogshead, the vessel was laden with utensils for fishing, and planters and cattle the the colony.

1653. OLIVER CROMWELL declared lord protector of England for life, and the same day dissolved the convention called Barebones's parliament, by the corporal of the guard and a file of soldiers.

1671. VOPISCUS FORTUNATUS POLEMPIUS, a Dutch physician and professor at Louvain, died, leaving several valuable works.

1676. WILLIAM MORICE, a learned Englishman, died; secretary of state under Charles II.

1680. The extraordinary comet of this year observed throughout Britain.

1685. JOHN PELL died; an English divine, and very eminent mathematician.

1688. JAMES II, of England, made his escape from London.

1731. JOHN HORSLEY died; author of a very learned and excellent work entitled *Britannia Romana*; being an ample account of the vestiges of the Romans in Britain.

1733. The bills of mortality in London this year, showed the death of 14,372 males, and 14,861 females.

1753. An act passed the provincial assembly, of New York, that mortgages should be subjected to public registry for the prevention of frauds. But this act, though a useful one, did not reach all the mischiefs intended to be prevented.

1757. COLLEY CIBBER, poet laureate to George II, died. He was also a very noted comedian. He wrote a curious apology for his life.

1764. JOHN OTHO TABOR died at Frankfort. He was a native of Lusatia, became counselor to the landgrave of Hesse Darmstadt, and wrote several works on law.

1776. The neighborhood of Philadelphia having became the seat of war, congress adjourned to Baltimore.

1777. ALBERT HALLER, an eminent Swiss physician, died. He was a voluminous writer, and one of the most acute, various and original men that have appeared since Boerhaave.

1781. Action between the British fleet, 12 sail, under Kempenfelt, and a French convoy, protected by 19 heavy ships of the line, and 2 armed *en flute*. Of the merchantmen, 20 were captured, having on board 1,100 troops, and about 600 seamen, besides valuable cargoes of military stores, cannon, &c.

1782. Action between British ship Mediator, and American ship Alexander, 24 guns, captain Gregory, and French ship Menagerie, 212 men, laden with powder, naval stores, &c. The two latter were captured without any loss on the part of the British.

1783. JOHN SCOTT died; an English quaker poet, called the poet of Arnwell.

1787. Pennsylvania (the second state), ratified the constitution of the United States, without amendments.

1789. RICHARD ALTON, an Austrian general, died. He commanded in the Low countries, in 1787, and though a strict disciplinarian and a man of bravery, betrayed so much weakness during the insurrection in Brabant, that he was sent for to answer charges, and died on the journey.

1793. Battle of Mans; the royalists of La Vendee defeated with great slaughter by the French under Marceau.

1804. JOHN BOYDELL died; a most distinguished encourager of the arts of painting and engraving, in England.

1809. Action at night between British sloop Trincomale, and French privateer Iphigene. The sloop was blown up and all on board but two perished; the privateer had her side stove in and her masts forced out by the shock, and lost 115 men.

1822. Napoli di Romania, the ancient Nauplia, surrendered to the Greeks, after a long and tedious blockade, during which the Turkish garrison was reduced to feed on the corpses of their companions. The crescent had been flying on the fortress uninterruptedly since 1714, at which time it was treacherously given up to the Coumourgi, and made the seat of the Turkish government for the Morea.

1830. BENJAMIN CONSTANT, a distinguished French author, and one of the greatest orators of his day, was honored with a magnificent funeral.

1834. The Carlists, of Spain, under Gen. Eraso, defeated at Soraida, by the troops of the queen, under general Mina.

1834. The government of Greece transferred from Napoli to Athens.

1836. JOHN DAVIDSON, an English traveler, murdered by the El Hareb tribe of Africans, on his way to Tombuctoo. He commenced traveling in 1826, and had visited North and South America, India, Egypt, as far as the second cataract, Syria, Palestine, Turkey, Greece, Italy, France and Germany, and had proceeded to within 25 days' journey of the city of Tombuctoo. He was conversant with the different languages of the east, and possessed extraordinary enterprise and great accomplishments as a traveler.

1838. Charles Philip Wrede, a Bavarian field-marshal, died. He distinguished himself under Bonaparte, in the war against Austria, and was severely wounded at the battle of Wagram. In the celebrated Russian campaign he commanded, with great credit, the Bavarian contingent army.

1840. J. D. E. Esquirol, who so successfully introduced a new mode of treating the insane, died.

1842. Elkanah Watson, a great friend of and writer on internal improvements, died at port Kent, Essex county, N. Y., aged 86.

1847. James Kent, so long distinguished as an American jurist and philanthropist, died at New York, aged 84.

1849. Isambard Brunel, the celebrated engineer of the Thames tunnel, died at London.

1856. Herman E. Ludewig, a Saxon scholar, died in Brooklyn, N. Y., aged 47. He is known by his *Literature of American Local History*.

DECEMBER 13.

405. b. c. Battle of Ægospotami. This celebrated Spartan victory of Lysander over a vast Athenian fleet, happily closed the 27 years' war in the Peloponesus. Conon fled to Cyprus, and the admiral took possession of Athens in the following spring.

126. b. c. A league of friendship referred to the Roman senate assembled in the temple of Concord, on behalf of the Jews, who had sent three ambassadors with a shield of gold as a mark of confederacy.

1250. Frederick II, emperor of Germany, died. He was successful in his wars against the Saracens, but was forced to return to wage war with the pope, whom he also conquered. He was deposed, however, in 1245 by Innocent IV.

1254. Innocent IV (*Sinibaldi de Fiesque*) died. He was early engaged in a quarrel with Frederick of Germany, whom he excommunicated and deposed. He was the first who invested the cardinals with a red hat as a mark of dignity.

1502. A water spout at Porto Bello greatly alarmed the Spaniards. Ferdinand Columbus says "if they had not dissolved it by saying the gospel of St. John, it had certainly sunk whatsoever it fell upon."

1521. Emanuel (*the Great*), king of Portugal, died. He distinguished himself by the liberal manner in which he patronized commercial enterprises, by which the cape of Good Hope was rounded, and Brazil visited.

1542. James V, of Scotland, died. He assumed the government at the age of 17, and was admired for his virtues.

1542. An act passed permitting those deemed the better sort to read the Bible in England.

1545. The great council of Trent opened.

1565. Conrad Gesner, a Swiss botanist, died. It has been said that botany owes to him its very existence as a science.

1577. Drake sailed from Plymouth, England, in the Golden Hind, on his voyage round the world, which he was the second navigator that accomplished.

1621. Robert Cushman having visited the colony of Plymouth with supplies, took in a cargo of beaver skins and clapboards, the first export from New England, which was valued at £500. The vessel was captured and carried into France.

1642. New Zealand discovered by Tasman.

1648. In order to enforce an ordinance of Cromwell, Capt. Bethan was appointed provost marshal, "with power to seize upon all ballad singers, and to suppress stage plays."

1702. The motto *semper eadem* first attached to the arms of England.

1721. Several alterations made in the form of the affirmation of the English quakers. About 20 years previous to this their affirmation was accepted instead of their oath.

1729. Anthony Collins died; an English polemical writer, whose numerous works were warmly attacked by the orthodox writers of the day.

1737. John Strype died, aged 94; an English divine, industrious as a historian and biographer.

1738. Philip Frowde died; a writer of English and Latin poetry, and of tragedy.

1754. Mahomet V, emperor of Turkey, died. He was more eminent for his pacific disposition than for his military exploits.

1759. At Leipsic the cold was so intense that ten sentinels were frozen to death.

1769. Christian Furchtegott Gellert, a German comic poet, died.

1775. Congress first determined to build a navy, to consist of 5 frigates of 32 guns, 5 of 28 guns, and 3 of 24 guns.

1776. American Gen. Lee surprised and made prisoner by a British patrole in New Jersey.

1783. Peter Wargentin died; a learned Swede, who published tables for computing the eclipses of Jupiter's satellites.

1784. Samuel Johnson, the English lexicographer, died; a writer of great eminence and celebrity.

1788. Charles III, king of Spain, died. His policy was censured for endangering the Spanish empire in America by supporting the independence of the British colonies.

1788. DAVID MACBRIDE, an Irish physician of great celebrity, died. His *Theory and Practice of Medicine* was formerly in great request.

1797. LEWIS LE GENDRE, a prominent actor in the French revolution, died. He proposed in the Jacobin club that the body of the king should be cut into 84 pieces, and one sent to each of the departments.

1803. FRANCIS LEWIS, one of the signers, died, aged 90. He was a merchant of New York, had visited Russia, and was employed in the importation of military stores, and other secret services.

1809. Desperate action between British frigate Junon, 40 guns, Capt. Shortland, and three French frigates of 88 guns in all. The Junon was captured, after losing 90 men killed and wounded; among the latter was the captain, who received several shots before surrendering. His vessel was so much shattered that the French burnt her the next day.

1811. A dog which had been accidentally shut into a house in Albany, on the 1st day of November, was taken out alive on this day, after a fast of 42 days, and recovered.

1813. Battle near Bayonne, between the French under Soult, and the allies under Wellington, in which the former were defeated and driven into the city with the loss of 6,500 men. British loss about half the number.

1814. CHARLES JOSEPH, prince De Ligne, an Austrian field marshal, died. He was born at Bruxelles, 1735, and devoted his early years to science and learning. His writings were numerous, of which 30 vols. have been published.

1850. The steam boat Anglo Norman, while on a pleasure trip for the day, at New Orleans, exploded both boilers, and nearly a hundred persons were either killed or wounded.

1854. A Russian decree ordered an additional levy of ten men in every thousand, in the eastern half of the Russian empire, Jews not excepted.

DECEMBER 14.

402. ANASTASIUS I, pope, died. He reconciled the eastern and western churches, and was much respected for his sanctity and virtue.

628. Pilgrimage of the emperor HERACLIUS at Jerusalem.

1417. JOHN OLDCASTLE, "the good lord Cobham," the first author and an early martyr of the reformation, hung alive in chains and burnt to death.

1622. VALENTINE SMALCIUS, a celebrated Socinian writer, died at Cracow.

1624. CHARLES HOWARD, an intrepid English admiral, died. He commanded the English fleet at the defeat of the Spanish armada.

1681. FRANCIS VAVASSEUR, a French Jesuit, died; distinguished as a teacher of rhetoric and belles lettres at Paris, and as a lecturer on the scriptures.

1704. JOSEPH DUCHE DE VANCY died; a French poet, author of several scripture tragedies.

1710. HENRY ALDRICH died; an eminent English scholar, divine, architect and musician.

1713. THOMAS RYMER, a famous English antiquary, died.

1715. THOMAS TENISON, archbishop of Canterbury, died; a celebrated polemical writer against popery.

1716. WILLIAM TRUMBULL died; an English statesman, ambassador to France and afterwards secretary of state.

1735. THOMAS TANNER, a learned English antiquary, died, leaving behind him a valuable work, upon which he had been employed 40 years.

1759. Prof. BRAUN ascertained the congelation of quicksilver.

1769. SAMUEL KNEELAND, an eminent Boston printer, died. He published the first edition of the Bible in America, which was in 4to, with a London imprint, to evade the patent which was held by English and Scottish publishers, *cum privilegio.*

1774. The citizens of New Hampshire attacked and carried the king's castle, and removed the powder.

1775. Gen. HOWE ordered the old North Meeting and 100 other wooden houses, to be taken down in Boston and used for fire wood.

1775. British lord DUNMORE defeated by the Americans at Norfolk, Va.

1776. British overran New Jersey.

1780. IGNATIUS SANCHO, an African author, died at London, aged 51. He was born on board of a slave ship. His *Letters* possess great originality. (15 ?)

1781. Gen. GREENE informed the board of war that he had been unable to advance on the British for ten days for want of ammunition; that he had not paper with which to make returns, no camp kettles, &c.; that he lay within a few miles of the enemy and had not six rounds per man; that he had been seven months in the field without taking off his clothes one night.

1782. British under Gen. LESLIE evacuated Charleston, S. C., and embarked under cover of the king's ship Caroline. The

Americans under Gen. Wayne took immediate possession of it.

1785. John Baptist Cypriani, a famous Italian painter, died. He settled in England, but his numerous pieces were spread over Europe by the graver of Bartolozzi.

1789. Caleb Elliott died of starvation. He was a visionary enthusiast who imagined that he was called upon to fast 40 days, and actually lived 16 days without food of any kind, having refused all sorts of sustenance.

1792. Arthur Lee, an American statesman, died. He was an ardent friend of the rights of the colonies, which he rendered essential services as agent at London, and afterwards as minister with Franklin in France. He is represented as a man of uniform patriotism, sound understanding, great probity, plain manners and strong passions.

1796. Anthony Wayne, commander-in-chief of the United States troops, died at Presque isle, aged 51. He distinguished himself in the wars of the revolution by his bravery and untiring patriotism.

1797. Great earthquake at Cumana; more than four-fifths of the city was entirely destroyed, and a number of persons perished.

1799. George Washington, the American hero and statesman, the man on whom, in times of danger, every eye was turned and all hopes were placed, expired without a struggle, at Mount Vernon, in the 68th year of his age.

1803. The British under Maj. Gen. Wellesley, since lord Wellington, carried by storm the almost impregnable fortress of Gawilghar, in the East Indies.

1807. An extraordinary large and brilliant meteor was seen in Connecticut, exploding at three different times, each explosion accompanied with a fall of meteoric stones, one of which was probably 200 pounds weight.

1814. British flotilla of 45 boats with 1,200 men and 43 cannon captured several American gun boats on lake Borgne near New Orleans, manned by 23 guns and 182 men, after an action of about three hours.

1815. The prince regent of Portugal at Rio de Janeiro, proclaimed the Brazils to be a separate kingdom.

1816. Charles Stanhope, an English statesman, died. He is better known by his numerous mechanical inventions, and as a man of science.

1818. Edward Law, lord Ellenborough, an eminent English lawyer, died.

1826. Conrad Malte-Brun, a Danish poet, political and philosophical writer, and geographer, died at Paris. He was forced to leave his own country for the tendency of his writings to liberty.

1829. Commencement of a civil war in Chili, by an action between the armies of Luctra and Pietro, in which the latter were defeated.

1843. Charles Goldsborough, author of the naval history of the United States, died at Washington, D. C., where he was engaged in the navy department.

1849. Edward Doubleday, a distinguished British naturalist, died at London, aged 39. He visited the United States in 1835, and returned with a large and rare collection of specimens in most of the branches of natural history, which he distributed to several of the public institutions of England.

1851. Joel R. Poinsett, an American statesman, died, aged 72. He was a native of South Carolina, was secretary of war under Mr. Van Buren, and opposed to the revolutionary schemes of some of the politicians of his native state.

1852. Madame d'Arusmont, better known as *Fanny Wright*, died at Cincinnati, aged 57. She was born at Dundee, Scotland, and came to America with considerable property, where she gained great notoriety by her lectures and writings.

1855. Joel Abbott, commanding the United States squadron in the East Indies, died at Hong Kong, China; a brave and energetic officer, who discharged his duties with signal ability and discretion.

DECEMBER 15.

337 b. c. Timoleon, an illustrious Corinthian, died at Syracuse. He went to the assistance of the Syracusans against the tyrant Dionysius, and became there a most benevolent and popular character.

215. b. c. Hieronymus, tyrant of Syracuse, slain. From his fall is dated the three years' siege of Marcellus, and the death of Archimedes at the end of it.

168. b. c. Antiochus Epiphanes set up his *abomination*, the statue of Jupiter, in the sacred temple, it being the anniversary of his own birthday.

533. Tribonian began the *Digests* or *Pandects*, that astonishing labor, which condensed within fifty books a body of three million sentences from dead civilians, and which he finished by the aid of seventeen associates in exactly three years.

882. John VIII, pope, died. He held a council at Troyes, but was called back to Italy by the invasion of the Saracens, who were so successful that they obliged him to pay an annual tribute. Three hundred of his letters are preserved.

1347. Abdication and exile of Rienzi the Roman tribune.

1582. The Gregorian style adopted at Paris, omitting ten days.

1683. Izaak Walton, an English writer, died, aged 90. He acquired a fortune and occupied his time in writing and angling; his little treatise called the *Complete Angler* is unique.

1692. George Adam Struvius died; professor of jurisprudence at Jena, and counselor of the king of Saxony.

1715. George Hicks died, an English divine, antiquary, critic and polemical writer of great learning and abilities.

1725. John Johnson, an English nonjuror divine, died. Although promoted to various dignities in the church, he entertained a contempt for its articles and liturgy.

1745. Battle of Kesseldorf; the Prussians under the prince of Anhalt, defeated the Austrians and Saxons, who lost 3,000 killed and 6,500 prisoners.

1751. Henry St. John, viscount Bolingbroke, for many years busily engaged in the politics, literature and philosophy of his times, died of cancer in the face, aged 73.

1764. Robert Lloyd, an English poet and miscellaneous writer, died in the Fleet prison.

1771. Benjamin Stillingfleet, a distinguished poet and naturalist, died.

1778. French admiral count d'Estaing, arrived from America at St. Lucia and attacked unsuccessfully the British fleet and batteries in the bay of Grand Cul de Sac, in which he sustained great loss.

1782. William Francis Berthier, a French Jesuit, died; known as the conductor for many years of the *Journal dé Travaux*, royal librarian and preceptor of Lewis XVI.

1782. American ship Commerce, 16 guns, Capt. Truxton, engaged a British brig of 18 guns and a schooner of 14 guns; he was obliged to make off on the appearance of two other British vessels. He saved his convoy, and they all arrived at St. Thomas in safety, a few hours after the action.

1794. Carrier, Pinard and Grand Maison guillotined at Paris. The former was noted for his refined cruelty to the numerous victims which power placed in his hands. On the fall of the mountain party he was consigned to punishment, which he well merited.

1810. Sarah Trimmer, an English authoress, died. She is well known by her various works designed for the use of children.

1814. Meeting of the Hartford convention, which consisted of 26 members from the new England states, to consult upon the exigencies of the times, and the defenceless condition of the coast.

1831. Hannah Adams, an American authoress, died. She was a native of Massachusetts, a woman of great excellence and purity of character, and a writer of very fair reputation. Her monument is to be seen in the Mount Auburn cemetery, near Boston.

1834. Andrew Frank, a colored man, died at Johnston, R. I., aged 104.

1836. The United States post office, the patent office and the Washington city post office, together with the contents of the two latter, destroyed by fire. In the patent office were 7,000 models of patents, out of 10,000 which had been granted by congress; 163 large folio volumes of records; 26 port folios containing 9,000 drawings, many of them beautifully executed and valuable.

1837. John Cox died, aged 85. He was a captain in the naval service of Virginia in the early part of the revolutionary war, and was one of the most efficient and distinguished patriots during the contest.

1837. Philip Sing Physic, a Philadelphia physician and surgeon of great eminence, died, aged 70. He was long a celebrated professor of anatomy and surgery in the university of Pennsylvania.

1840. The remains of Bonaparte were removed from Cherbourg, where they were disembarked, to the Church of the invalides at Paris. The procession was splendid beyond all precedent, the number assembled being computed at 500,000. The king and royal family were present at the ceremony, and 60,000 national guards were in attendance.

1842. John R. Watrous, an eminent physician and revolutionary surgeon, died at Colchester, Conn., aged 91.

1842. Benjamin Parkhurst died at Royalton, Vt., aged 97. He was the first settler of that town, living in it over 78 years, and of a family famed for longevity. His parents died at the age of 97. His grandfather reached 100, and his grandmother 104 years.

1848. The postal convention between Great Britain and the United States signed at London by lord Palmerston and Mr. Bancroft.

1854. Kamehameha III, king of the Sandwich islands, died, aged 41, and was succeeded by prince Alexander Liholiho, aged 20, under the title of Kamehameha IV.

DECEMBER 16.

714. Pepin (*the Fat*), mayor of Paris, died; a man of wisdom and vigor.

1215. A special excommunication of the English barons fulminated at Rome, and towered London laid under an interdict.

1515. Alfonzo Albuquerque died, Portuguese viceroy of India, surnamed *the Great* and *the Portuguese Mars*.

1653. William Gouge died; a minister of the famous assembly of divines, and appointed one of the annotators of the Bible.

1653. Oliver Cromwell appointed lord protector of England.

1656. Edmund Wingate died; an English writer on arithmetic and mathematics.

1657. Joshua Reynolds, commander of the English forces in Mardyke, was cast away with the whole ship's company, on Goodwin's sands.

1684. The statue of Charles II in the Royal Exchange at London, was erected by the Hamburg company.

1687. William Petty, an eminent English physician, died; chiefly celebrated for his knowledge in mathematics and mechanics, and for his writings on political arithmetic.

1703. Julius Mascaron, a most eminent preacher, died. His eloquence was astonishing, and it is related that his preaching had such an effect upon the Huguenots, that of 30,000 Calvinists which he found on coming to the see of Agen, 28,000 forsook their church.

1710. Gerona, the key of Catalonia in Spain, surrendered to the French.

1723. John Trenchard died; an eminent English patriot and political writer.

1745. Peter Francis Guyot des Fontaines died; a French critic, historical writer and translator.

1767. James Grainger, a Scottish physician and poet, died in the West Indies.

1770. Roger Long, an eminent English astronomer, died.

1773. Destruction of 340 chests of tea in Boston harbor by a party of citizens disguised as Indians. There was but one survivor of that event, in 1840.

1782. The British burnt fort Arbuthnot and a new fort on Sullivan's island.

1783. William James died; an English baronet, who rose from the humble occupation of a plowboy to the chief command of the East India company's marine forces.

1788. Oczakow taken from the Turks by storm by the Russians under prince Potemkin, who had about 1,000 killed in the assault.

1798. Thomas Pennant died; an Englishman of eminent knowledge in natural history and antiquities, and the author of a number of valuable books.

1800. Convention of the northern powers of Europe for an armed neutrality, signed at St. Petersburg between Russia and Sweden.

1809. The most ceremonious and extraordinary divorce in the world took place between Bonaparte and Josephine.

1809. Anthony Francis Fourcroy died; a very eminent French writer on chemistry, and a member of the Institute.

1811. An earthquake was experienced in the southern states and in Ohio and Pennsylvania. Charleston, Savannah, Pittsburgh and Circleville especially suffered from it.

1825. James Watt, the original publisher of the *Montrose, Arbroath and Brechin Review*, fell over board in Yarmouth Roads and was drowned.

1832. Robert C. Sands, an American author and editor, died. He was a man of genius, a scholar, and an elegant writer.

1835. The coldest day on record, from sunrise to sunset. The thermometer ranged from 12° to 16° below zero all day, in the vicinity of Boston. The winter was remarkable for the lowness of its mean temperature, the number of extremely cold days, and the great quantity and long duration of snow.

1835. Great fire in New York, the most destructive that ever took place in this country, by which the entire seat of the greatest commercial transactions of the city, was destroyed. The number of buildings destroyed was 529, including the Merchant's Exchange, valued at $150,000, and the Garden street church $50,000. The total loss was estimated at $17,000,000.

1848. A little after midnight the Park theatre at New York was burned to the ground.

1852. Samuel Lee, canon of Bristol, and the profoundest orientalist of the age, died, aged 69. He rose from the sphere of a carpenter's apprentice.

DECEMBER 17.

546. The Goths under Totilla captured and plundered Rome.

1413. William Gascoigne, a noted English judge, died. His opinions, arguments and decisions occur in the old law reports.

1468. The first book printed in England bears this date at Oxford, and contains 41 quarto leaves.

1500. Columbus was introduced at the court of Ferdinand and Isabella at Grenada.

1538. Luther notes in his *Table Talk*, that he invited the singers and musicians to supper. "I always loved music; who so has skill in this art, the same is of good kind, and fitted for all things,"—a divine saying.

1593. Henry May, an English mariner, returning from the East Indies, was wrecked on the islands of Bermudas, and was the first Englishman, who set foot on those islands. The carpenter's tools having been saved, they built a cedar bark of about 18 tons, payed the seams with lime and turtle's fat, procured some rigging from the ship, and put in thirteen live turtles for provisions, when, having remained there nearly five months, they sailed for Newfoundland.

1615. JACOB LE MAIRE, in his voyage to the straits, reports that he found this day at Port Desire, a skeleton of nearly 11 feet in length, entombed.

1657. JAMES NAYLOR, a quaker, accused of blasphemy, convicted and ordered to be whipped and pilloried and his tongue bored through with a red hot iron.

1719. Aurora borealis first noticed in this country, and filled the people with alarm and consternation. It was of course viewed as a sign of the last judgment.

1724. THOMAS GUY, founder of a hospital which bears his name, died in London, aged 81. He acquired great wealth as a bookseller, and left more than a million of dollars to one hospital, besides aiding others, and leaving nearly $400,000 to be divided among such as could prove themselves in any way related to him.

1731. ROBERT BOLTON died; an English puritan, distinguished for his learning and eloquence, and whose high reputation is sustained by his numerous writings.

1742. FRANCIS JOSEPH DE BEAUPOIL DE SAINT-AULAIRE, an ingenious French poet, died, aged 100. He wrote much in the manner of Anacreon, and it is remarkable, that his best pieces are those of his old age, when he had reached his 90th year.

1778. The theatre at Saragossa, in Spain, was burned, occasioning the death of 400 persons.

1788. The thermometer at Leipsic fell 27 degrees below zero.

1807. Milan decree issued by Bonaparte, denationalizing all such vessels as should submit to the British order in council.

1808. CHARLES JENKINSON, earl of Liverpool, died. He was a statesman of profound ability, but extremely unpopular, who rose from obscurity to wealth and rank.

1812. Mississinewa, an Indian town inhabited by Delawares and Miamis, attacked by 600 Americans under colonel Campbell. The town was burnt, with several others in the vicinity.

1812. British attacked Darby, Vt., and burnt the barracks and store houses, and carried off considerable quantities of stores.

1830. SIMON BOLIVAR, a distinguished South American general, died. He headed the revolution of the provinces against the mother country, and having achieved their independence was elected president of Colombia.

1832. Prof. ZAHN discovered a city buried under the lava, between Vesuvius and Pompeii.

1832. ROBERT C. SANDS, the assistant editor of the *New York Commercial Advertiser*, died by apoplexy while in the act of composing.

1843. JACOB MANN, supposed to be the oldest newspaper editor of the state of New Jersey, died in Morristown; having published the *Genius of Liberty* in 1798.

1852. WILLIAM JACOB, an English agricultural writer, died at London, aged 89.

1853. RALPH WARDLAW, an eminent minister of the congregational dissenters, died at Glasgow, aged 73.

DECEMBER 18.

69. VITELLUS abdicated the Roman empire, which "he had received against his will." The next day he desired to restore the dagger of his authority.

1551. GEORGE MARTINUSIUS (*Visinovitsch*), governor of Transylvania, assassinated by order of Ferdinand, king of the Romans and of Hungary. He was a native of Croatia, who rose from the humble occupation of a lighter of stoves.

1555. JOHN PHILPOT, archdeacon of Winchester, an English reformer, convicted of heresy and burnt at Smithfield.

1621. The famous resolution of the commons of England against the usurped royal prerogative was adopted. King James did indeed tear it from the records with his own hand, but it had its effect.

1665. BENEDICT VARCHI died; professor of morality at Padua, and distinguished for the purity and elegance of his language and writings.

1674. GABRIEL COSSART died. He assisted Labbe in his grand collection of councils, which occupied 28 vols. folio.

1678. ROBERT NANTEUIL, a celebrated French engraver and designer, died.

1682. HENEAGE FINCH, lord high chancellor of England, died. He was distinguished for his wisdom and eloquence.

1686. EDWARD BENDLOWES, an English poet, died in great want, the result of imprudence.

1692. VITUS LUDOVICUS DE SECHENDORF, a learned German, died; author of several works, among which is the best account of Luther.

1708. JOHN LOVELACE arrived at New York from England, as governor of the province.

1714. CÆSAR D'ESTREES, a French cardinal, died; an able negotiator and a benevolent man.

1733. JOHN POTENGER died; an English poet and miscellaneous writer.

1733. EMNAUEL MATTI died; a Spanish poet of eminence, and member of the Arcadia at Rome.

1737. The cliff at Scarborough sunk.

1741. Remarkable meteor seen at noon near Canterbury, Eng., accompanied by an inverted rainbow and three mock suns next morning.

1745. The Prussians under Frederick II entered Dresden. They captured the younger sons of the king of Poland, and took 415 officers and 1500 men prisoners.

1760. CHARLES HAYES, an ingenious English mathematical writer, died.

1771. PHILIP MILLA, an eminent Scottish botanist, died. He had charge of the apothecary company's physic garden at Chelsea, where he was visited by Linnæus.

1775. Battle of Great Bridge, near Norfolk, Va.

1776. The constitution of the state of North Carolina was adopted.

1778. The French under count d'Estaing made another attack upon the British batteries at Grand Cul de Sac, St. Lucia, and after being three times repulsed, were compelled to retire with the loss of 400 killed and 1100 wounded. British general Meadows was wounded.

1780. Society of antiquaries first instituted in Edinburgh, Scotland.

1785. The sloop Experiment, captain Dean, of Albany, sailed from New York for China. She returned in 1787, with a valuable cargo, and was the second vessel that sailed from America to China.

1787. The convention of New Jersey unanimously assented to and ratified the new federal constitution, without amendments.

1787. SOAME JENYNS, an English theological writer, died, aged 83. His writings are distinguished by purity of language, elegance of diction and critical knowledge.

1793. Toulon, which had revolted from the convention, after sustaining a murderous siege, was attacked by the revolutionists with a tremendous charge upon the fortifications. The English redoubt, defended by three thousand men and 20 pieces of cannon and several mortars, was carried in the space of an hour; and the town after being bombarded ten hours incessantly, was evacuated by the allies. Great efforts were made to carry away as many of the inhabitants as possible, but several thousand were left to the fury of their countrymen, who showed no mercy.

1796. The contemplated invasion of England, or rather Ireland, by an army of 25,000 under general Hoche, failed by a dispersion of the transport ships.

1799. Burial of WASHINGTON.

1799. JEAN ETIENNE MONTUCLA, an eminent French mathematician, died. His problems of the trisection of the angle, and the duplication of the cube, are curious and interesting.

1803. JOHN GODFREY HERDER, a German theological writer, died. Some of his writings have been translated.

1807. Counter declaration by the king of England against the emperor of Russia, and an order in council issued for granting letters of marque and reprisal against Russia.

1809. ALEXANDER ADAM, an eminent Scottish teacher, died. His *Roman Antiquities* is still in extensive use.

1810. LUCIEN BONAPARTE with his family and a suite of thirty-five persons, arrived at Plymouth, England, and voluntarily placed themselves under the protection of the British government.

1812. BONAPARTE arrived at Paris from his disastrous campaign in Russia.

1820. GUISEPPE BONZANIGA, royal sculptor of Turin, died. By a persevering application of 40 years he raised the art of carving in wood and ivory to a high degree of perfection, and founded an establishment from which numerous works of art have been produced that are much sought for in all Italy, and valued by connoisseurs.

1828. Lord LIVERPOOL, the English premier, was killed at the opening of the rail road at Liverpool.

1832. PHILIP FRENEAU, a poet of the American revolution, died in New Jersey, aged 80. His poems were collected in two volumes and have gone through several editions.

1832. Treaty of navigation and commerce concluded at St. Petersburg, between the United States and Russia.

1843. SMITH THOMPSON, one of the justices of the supreme court of the United States, died at Poughkeepsie, aged 76.

1845. SAMUEL MCCLURE died in Illinois. Having fought in the revolutionary wars, he at their close in removing his family to Kentucky was attacked by Indians, his wife taken prisoner, and his children slain. He escaped himself and returning severely punished the Indians and rescued his wife.

1847. TIMOTHY PITKIN, a celebrated historical writer and statesman, died at his residence, New Haven, Conn.

1855. SAMUEL ROGERS, the distinguished English poet, died, aged 92.

DECEMBER 19.

69. The Roman capitol burnt by Vitellius.

1567. The Burghley papers state from the diocesan's certificate, that there were then in London and its immediate vicinity, 3,838 Dutchmen, 720 Frenchmen, 137 Italians, 10 Venitians, 56 Spaniards, 25 Portuguese, 2 Grecians, 2 Blackmores, 1 Dane, and but 58 Scots.

1675. Attack on Narragansett, by the united forces of the New England colonies. The English having gained an entrance, and withstood the first fire of the Indians, poured in amain, and made such havoc with their enemies that they soon had possession of every part of the fort. The wigwams to the number of five or six hundred were fired. The loss of the Indians on this occasion was by their own account 1000 fighting men; the loss of old men, women and children could not be estimated, as they mostly perished in the flames. The loss of the English was 80 killed. The blow was irreparable to the Indians, who were deprived of their homes and provisions.

1728. White Kennet, an English prelate, died. He was an eloquent and popular preacher, and made a valuable collection of manuscripts.

1745. The avails of three nights' acting the *Beggar's Opera*, amounting to £600, given to encourage king George's army against France and the rebels.

1753. Styan Thirlby, an ingenious and learned English critic, died. He edited the works of Justin Martyr.

1777. Washington moved his troops from the Swedes ford to Valley Forge 16 miles from Philadelphia, where he hutted them. They were in great want of shoes and stockings. At one time his army was without bread four days; on the fifth day two regiments refused to perform duty, but finally returned to order on the prudent conduct and persuasion of Washington.

1793. The princess royal of France, the only remaining member of the family of the unhappy Louis XVI, was exchanged for the marquis Lafayette.

1793. The French troops entered Toulon, when such of the inhabitants as had favored the allies either put an end to their own existence or perished by the guillotine or musket.

1799. Charles Joseph Panckoucke, an eminent Parisian printer, died. He acquired great celebrity as an author and a man of letters, as well as by the excellence of his printing.

1806. Elizabeth Carter, a contributor to the *Rambler*, and a good Latin and Greek scholar, died at London.

1807. Frederick Melchoir, baron de Grimm, died. He is indebted for his fame to a correspondence with the duke of Saxe Gotha, from Paris, which was published in 16 vols.

1813. David Hartley, an English philanthropist, died. He is distinguished also as a politician and a projector. In parliament he steadily opposed the war with the colonies, and was one of the commissioners appointed to treat with Dr. Franklin at Paris.

1813. Fort Niagara captured by the British, who took the Americans by surprise. In the fort were 250 men and 25 cannon.

1813. Lewistown and Tuscarora village, near fort Schlosser, were burnt by the Indians.

1815. Benjamin Smith Barton, an eminent physician of Philadelphia, died. He held the professorships of natural history and botany, afterwards of materia medica, and succeeded Dr. Rush in theory and practice of medicine.

1831. The national assembly of Greece met at Argos, but in consequence of sedition was soon obliged to remove to Napoli.

1840. Felix Grundy, long a distinguished senator of the United States from Tennessee, died. He was a zealous supporter of the measures of general Jackson's administration.

1842. John Uncas, the last male descendant of the Mohegan chief of that name, died, aged 89, and was buried in the royal burying ground of the Mohegans in Connecticut.

1845. Charles Bowen, with his wife and oldest child, drowned by the sinking of the steamer Bellozane in the Mississippi. He was for many years publisher of the North American Review, the American Almanac, Token, &c., in Boston.

1851. J. M. William Turner, an unrivaled English landscape painter, died at Chelsea, aged 76. He was a man of miserly habits and great eccentricities.

1852. Sacramento in California inundated; the city submerged by the breaking through of a levee.

DECEMBER 20.

69. Aulus Vitellius, emperor of Rome, assassinated. After sharing in the debaucheries of Tiberius, and administering to the vices of Caligula, Claudius and Nero, he was proclaimed by his troops in Germany, in opposition to Otho. Though defeated in three battles, he triumphed in the fourth. He disgraced his reign by every species of licentiousness.

107. Ignatius, bishop of Antioch, torn in pieces by lions at Rome, by order of the emperor Trajan. His epistles are very interesting remains of ecclesiastical antiquity.

860. Ethelbald, who married his

mother-in-law, died, after having to the priests atoned for his offence by building and endowing many abbeys and monasteries.

912. ALPHONSO III (*the Great*), king of Asturias, in Spain, died. He wrote a chronicle of the Spanish monarchs, and a short time before his death obtained a memorable victory over the Moors.

1192. RICHARD of England seized in his disguise at Vienna.

1492. COLUMBUS cast anchor in the bay of St. Thomas; the anniversary also of the interment of his venerable bones more than three centuries after (1795) at Cuba.

1494. MATTEO MARIE BOJARDO, an Italian lyric poet, died.

1560. JOHN DRYANDER, a Hessian medical and mathematical writer, died. His discoveries in astronomy and his invention of mathematical instruments are important.

1560. First general assembly of the Scottish church was opened.

1603. MAHOMET III, sultan of Turkey, died of the plague. He began his reign by ordering 19 of his brothers to be strangled, and 10 of his father's wives to be drowned. He invaded Hungary with an army of 200,000 men, but after some successes his progress was checked, and he sued in vain for peace.

1686. Sir EDMUND ANDROS arrived in Boston with a commission from king James as governor of New England. He was received with satisfaction only as he was less dreaded than Kirk.

1697. THOMAS FIRMIN, an eminent English philanthropist, died. He devoted his time and money to charitable objects, and his benefactions were unequaled at the time when he lived.

1698. BARTHOLOMEW DU QUENTAL died; a Portuguese catholic priest, distinguished for his piety and learning.

1735. The Gentleman's Magazine announced the arrival of a dwarf in England from France, who at the age of 46, measured 21 inches in height.

1735. Part of the island of Portland sank into the sea.

1765. The dauphin of France died in his 36th year. He was a prince of benevolent character and exemplary piety, but little known in public life.

1766. Prayers were publicly read in all the popish chapels in Ireland for George III and family, being the first time prayers were made by Romanists for the protestant succession since 1688.

1770. JOHN SENAC died; physician to the king of France, counselor of state, and superintendent of the mineral waters of the kingdom. He wrote several works on anatomy and medicine.

1782. The United States frigate Charleston, 40 guns, captured by the British ships Quebec and Diomede, 76 guns, after a chase of 18 hours.

1790. The fortress of Ismael taken by storm by the Russians under Suwarrow; of 12,000 Turks all were put to the sword but 400.

1791. Bank of the United States commenced discounting in Philadelphia; $300,000 were discounted. Branches were established in New York, Boston, Baltimore and Charleston, which commenced business in January, 1792.

1793. JOHN STRANGEWAYS HUTTON died at Philadelphia, aged 110. He was born on Long Island in 1682.

1793. The first ambassador from the Porte arrived in London.

1795. The remains of Columbus removed to Cuba. In the presence of the dignitaries and military of San Domingo, assembled at the Metropolitan cathedral, a small vault was opened above the chancel, wherein were found the fragments of a lead coffin, a number of bones, and a quantity of mould, evidently the remains of a human body. These were carefully collected and put into a case of gilded lead secured by a lock, and enclosed in a coffin covered with black velvet, and ornamented with lace and fringe of gold. (See Jan. 15, 1849.)

1795. French under JOURDAN made an attack on Kayserslautern, but were repulsed with a loss of 2000 men.

1803. SAMUEL HOPKINS, an eminent New England minister, died. He published a work to show that it was the interest of all the American states to emancipate their slaves.

1804. RICHARD HUMPTON, adjutant general of the state of Pennsylvania, died. He was a native of England, who early entered the military service, and distinguished himself as a gallant soldier during the war of the revolution.

1809. JOSEPH JOHNSON, the fortunate publisher of Cowper's poems, died.

1815. CAMBACERES arrested and sent to prison at Paris.

1849. WILLIAM MILLER, the founder of the sect of Millerites, died at Hampton, Washington co., N. Y., aged 68. He was a native of Pittsfield, Mass., and during the last war with England served as a captain of volunteers on the northern frontier. He began to speak in public assemblies upon the subject of the Millenium in 1833, and in the ten years which preceded the time which he had set for the consummation of all prophecy he labored assiduously in the middle and northern states, averaging, it is said, nearly one sermon a day for more than half that period. He was uneducated, and not largely read in even the common English commentaries; his views were absurd and supported but feebly; yet he succeeded in building up a sect of some 30 or 40,000 disciples, which disappeared rapidly after the close of the "day of probation" in 1843, after which time Mr. Miller himself did not often advocate or defend his views in public.

1852. By a decree of the governor-general of British India, the province of Pegu was annexed to the British dominions.

1855. Thomas Cubitt, an eminent English builder, principally on works of great magnitude for the government, died, aged 68.

DECEMBER 21.

73. Festival of St. Thomas, the Christian apostle, whose counsels penetrated into India. He was killed by the Bramins, and buried at Meliapour, about ten miles from Madras.

1375. Giovanni Boccaccio, an eminent Italian writer, died; whose *Decameron* has been translated into all the European languages, although great pains were taken to suppress it.

1641. Maximilian de Bethune, duke de Sully, died; celebrated as the prime minister of Henry IV, and the most able and incorruptible statesman that France ever had. After the murder of the king he went into retirement, where he wrote his *Memoirs*, a minute history of his own times.

1667. Milton's widow disposed of her entire interest in the *Paradise Lost* for eight pounds; so that the sublimest poetical building in the world produced for its architect and his family, the sum of eighty dollars; ten pounds having been paid to the author in his life time!

1667. Sentence was executed upon many of those Scottish covenanters who had rebelled, it is supposed under persecution.

1670. The maiming of sir John Coventry for reflecting on the moral character of Charles II, which caused the Coventry act.

1705. Catharine, of Portugal, died; queen of Charles II, of England, by whom she was treated unkindly.

1706. Tumultuous meetings in Edinburgh, occured on account of signing the articles of union with England.

1719. First No. of the *Boston Gazette* issued by William Brooker.

1741. Bernard de Montfaucon, a very learned French Benedictine, died; famous for his knowledge of ecclesiastic and pagan antiquities.

1774. Thomas Broughton, a learned English divine, died; author of the *Bibliotheca Historica Sacra*, and one of the original writers for the *Biographia Britannica*.

1775. An act of parliament confiscating all American vessels found floating on the water, and for *impressing* the crews of American vessels into the British navy, without distinction of persons.

1777. There were at this time 300 American officers and 900 privates confined as prisoners of war in New York by the British. They were mostly confined in sugar houses and the most loathsome jails. In Philadelphia there were 500 privates and 50 officers. They were generally stripped of what clothing they had when taken, and were sometimes confined several days with scarcely any food in order to induce them to enlist to save their lives. Frequent instances occurred of persons thus perishing from hunger.

1780. James Harris died; an English gentleman of uncommon abilities and learning, whose writings have been greatly admired.

1782. Francis Philip de Reyrac, a French ecclesiastic, died; a learned and amiable character.

1791. Arnauld de Barquin, a French miscellaneous writer died; whose works are known in our language. His *Children's Friend* was honored with the prize of the French academy, as the most useful book issued in 1784.

1807. The Danish islands of St. Thomas and St. Johns, in the West Indies, surrendered to the British.

1811. Peter Parker, the British admiral, died, aged 89.

1815. William Vincent, a learned English divine, died. As an author he is principally known by his commentary on Arrian's voyages of Nearchus.

1815. Lavalette, one of Bonaparte's ministers, escaped from prison in the disguise of his wife's dress, she having been permitted to visit him.

1831. Trial of the French ministers for high treason. The excitement was so great that a strong guard was required to save them from the popular violence. Above 70,000 men were under arms at one time. Their sentence was imprisonment for life, with the additional penalty of civil death on Polignac.

1832. William Bray, an eminent English antiquary, died, aged 97.

1833. John P. Hungerford died; an officer in the revolutionary war, and afterwards a member of congress from Virginia.

1835. John Sinclair, an eminent British statesman, died, aged 82. He was also a very voluminous author, and was distinguished for his patriotism and philanthropy. During a public life of upwards of fifty years, there is scarcely any topic in the whole range of political, statistical or medical science, to which he did not turn his inquiring mind.

1840. FRANK HALL STANDISH, an English author, died at Cadiz, aged 42. He wrote biography, travels, sketches and poems.

1845. The battle of Punjaub, between the English forces and the Sikh army, was fought, which issued in the defeat of the Sikhs, and the annexation of a large portion of their territory to that of the English.

1848. The Asiatic cholera broke out with great violence among the United States troops at port Lavaca, Texas.

DECEMBER 22.

640. Alexandria taken from the Greeks, by the Saracens, under Amri, after a siege of 14 months. "I have taken," he addressed the caliph Omar, "the great city of the west. It is impossible for me to enumerate the variety of its riches and beauty; and I shall content myself with observing that it contains 4,000 palaces, 4,000 baths, 400 theatres, or places of amusement, 12,000 shops for the sale of vegetable food, and 40,000 tributary Jews." It is well known that the second Alexandrian library, established by Cleopatra, was then destroyed, to feed the baths. The collection consisted of 300,000 volumes, and those 200,000 rolls, brought by Mark Antony from Pergamus, with the accumulation of seven centuries.

937. A severe frost which lasted 120 days, began in England.

1332. Found in the library of St. Mary, at Florence, the whole of the New Testament in silk; at the end of it is this inscription in Greek: "By the hand of the sinner, and most unworthy, Mark, in the year of the world 7840."

1483. WILLIAM D'ESTOUTEVILLE, a Norman cardinal, died; who reformed the university of Paris.

1530. The famous protestant league of defence, against a decree of the imperial diet, was concluded this day.

1558. The great seal of England delivered to sir Nicholas Bacon, with the style of *lord keeper*, then first adopted.

1585. VIRGINIA ACCORAMBONI, celebrated for her beauty and poetical talents, was assassinated at Padua.

1592. ALEXANDER FARNESE, duke of Parma, and governor of the Low Countries, died of a wound given by Henry IV, of France, at the siege of Rouen.

1620. Landing of the first settlers at Plymouth. The total number of them was 101; of which 50 died during the winter.

1662. GEORGE PHILLIPS, with three others, styled fanatics, executed for conspiring the death of Charles II.

1681. RICHARD ALLEIN died; a puritan of great learning, whose writings are mostly on theology.

1694. FRANCIS NICHOLSON made governor of Maryland.

1699. The protestants of Germany here introduced the Gregorian or *new style* of supputation, by the omission of ten days, concluding this year.

1715. The Pretender (*Chevalier de St. George*), son of James II of Scotland, the deposed king of England, arrived at Peterhead, and was proclaimed king of England.

1719. ANDREW BRADFORD issued the first number of the *American Weekly Mercury*, the first paper printed in Pennsylvania, and the second in the United States.

1722. PIERRE VARIGNON, a distinguished French architect and mathematician, died. He was professor of mathematics, and an able writer on that science.

1723. JAMES BASNAGE, a French protestant minister, died. He was a man of talent and erudition. His works are numerous and valuable, particularly his *History of the Jews*, 15 vols.

1729. MICHAEL BARON, the Roscius of the French theatre, died.

1753. A MR. BRAITHWAITE died at Carlisle, England, at the age of 110. In 1652 he commenced singing in the cathedral, and at the time of his death had continued singing one hundred years.

1768. CHARLES LITTLETON, bishop of Carlisle, died; an eminent English antiquary.

1788. PERCIVAL POTT, a very eminent English surgeon, died.

1789. A number of ice islands, of great magnitude, discovered, which had been wafted from the southern polar regions. The ship Guardian struck them near the cape of Good Hope, on her passage to Botany bay. These islands were wrapt in darkness; they were 150 fathoms long, and more than 50 fathoms above the surface of the waves. A fragment from the summit of one of them broke off, and plunging into the sea, caused a tremendous commotion in the water, and dense smoke all around it.

1796. Kehl, a fortress on the Rhine, surrendered by the French, under Dessaix, to the Austrians, under the archduke Charles, after a siege of 51 days, and a blockade of 115. The garrison were permitted to withdraw, with their artillery and baggage, with drums beating and colors flying.

1798. BONAPARTE arrived at Suez, with several officers and men of science, and, having forded the Red sea, visited the fountains of Moses. Whilst here he received a deputation from the monks of mount Sinai, and countersigned the charter they had received from Mahomet.

1803. Louisiana taken possession of by the Americans.

1807. Embargo; the ports of the United States closed against British commerce.

1812. JAMES CLINTON, an American general, died. He was a firm and undeviating patriot of the revolution.

1812. PETER HENRY LARCHER, a French writer, died. He translated some of the principal Greek classics.

1813. The Indians attacked and defeated at Ecchanachaca, by the Americans under general Claiburn, who destroyed the town, 200 houses, with a large quantity of provisions.

1818. PHILIP FRANCIS, an English statesman, died. He was an active promoter of the impeachment of the famous Warren Hastings, and was considered by some as the author of *Junius's Letters.*

1822. WILLIAM LOWNDES, a distinguished orator and patriot, of South Carolina, died at sea.

1828. WILLIAM HYDE WOLLASTON died, aged 62; one of the ablest and most renowned of English chemists and natural philosophers. Very little of his personal history is known, his biography not having been written (1846).

1832. FRANCIS HUBER, a Swiss naturalist, died, aged 82. He lost his sight at the age of 17. Notwithstanding this difficulty in the way of scientific pursuits, with the assistance of his wife, he wrote and published a very accurate work on the habits of bees, and some other works.

1835. EDMUND FRY died in London, at a very advanced age. He was a member of the society of Friends, originally bred to the medical profession, but was more generally known as an eminent and learned type founder.

1835. DAVID HOSACK, an eminent physician, died at New York, where he was professor of the theory and practice of physic, and was held in high estimation as a man of talent, learning and worth.

1838. HUGH JAMES ROSE, a talented and eloquent English divine, died. Besides numerous works of which he was the author, he projected the *British Magazine*, and edited the *Theological Library*.

1842. 250 troops from Texas invading Mexico, were defeated and taken prisoners.

1854. MARTIN JOSEPH ROUTH, president of Magdalen college, died at Oxford, England, aged 99; a man of great learning, talent and virtues.

1854. The British parliament passed a law permitting the enlistment of foreigners, as officers and soldiers, in her majesty's service.

1855. VALERIAN KRASINSKI, one of the most distinguished members of the Polish emigration, and an eminent author, died at Edinburgh, Scotland.

DECEMBER 23.

486 B. C. The accession of Xerxes the magnificent to the Persian throne, *Nar. Era*, 263. When Darius Hystaspes, his father, was cut off, he had reigned 36 years, from the *thoth* of N. E. 227, corresponding with the first day of January B. C. 521. The year 485, in which he died, is remarkable for two facts, the conquest of Syracuse under Gelon, and a comic work by Epicharmus, who added the Greek letters *chi* and *theta* to his native alphabet.

176. MARCUS ANTONINUS entered Rome in triumph, after his German victories on the Danube, accompanied by his monstrous son Commodus.

400. Naval battle of the Hellespont, and defeat of Gainas the barbarian; who was despatched in Thrace.

558. CHILDEBERT I, king of France, died. His great military exploit was the defeat of the king of Burgundy.

679. DAGOBERT II, king of Austrasia, assassinated.

1588. HENRY DE LORRAINE, duke of Guise, assassinated by order of the king. He was a turbulent and seditious subject of Henry III, of France.

1620. The Plymouth settlers having fixed upon a place for a town, on a high ground facing the bay, where the land was cleared and the water excellent, as many as could conveniently went on shore, and felled and carried timber to the spot designated for the erection of a building for common use.

1622. REDEMPTUS BARENZANO, a Piedmontese monk, died. He was professor of philosophy at Anneci, and a correspondent of the great Bacon.

1631. MICHAEL DRAYTON, an English poet, died. His works which were numerous, and of great merit, were collected in 1748 in one volume folio.

1632. JOHN COTTON, the first minister of Boston, died. He was a good scholar and a pious, able and benevolent man.

1688. JAMES II, king of England, escaped from England to Calais, in France, and was declared to have abdicated his throne.

1715. The *Freeholder*, first No., appeared, in a great degree political. In this work the labors of Addison as an essayist were brought to a close.

1721. WILLIAM MUSGRAVE died; an eminent English physician and antiquary, and secretary of the Royal society.

1747. The colonial house and records at Boston destroyed by fire.

1757. British privateer *Terrible*, captain William *Death*, of 26 guns and 200 men, captured a large French ship, after an obstinate battle, in which he lost his brother and 16 men killed. A few days after he fell in with the privateer *Vengeance*, 36 guns and 360 men, who recaptured the prize, and having manned her, both ships bore down on the Terrible, whose main was shot away by the first broadside. After a desperate engagement, in which the French captain and his second were killed, with two-thirds of his company, the Terrible was boarded, when no more than 26 persons were found alive, 16 of whom had lost a leg or an arm, and the other 10 were badly wounded. The ship itself was so shattered that it could scarcely be kept above water. There was a strange combination of names in this affair; the *Terrible* was equipped at *Execution* dock; was commanded by *Death*, who had *Devil* for his lieutenant and *Ghost* for surgeon.

1777. WASHINGTON had 2,898 men unfit for duty, "owing to their being barefooted and otherwise naked." His whole force fit for duty amounted to 8,200.

1783. SAMUEL COOPER, one of the most celebrated divines and politicians of New England, died.

1783. General WASHINGTON delivered up his commission to congress at Annapolis.

1789. CHARLES MICHAEL DE L'EPEE, a celebrated French teacher of the deaf and dumb, died. He devoted his time and money to the education of indigent mutes. Sacrificing his own comfort to promote theirs. Some of his pupils obtained academical prizes by poetical and literary works.

1804. Battle of Biezun; the French under Grouchy defeated 8,000 Prussians, and took 500 prisoners and 5 cannon.

1814. Battle at Villaret's plantation, near New Orleans, between 2000 Americans under general Jackson and about 4000 British under general Keene. American loss 213; British loss 305.

1816. Bible societies prohibited in Hungary.

1825. SAMUEL PARKES, an English chemist, died. He was no less distinguished for his benevolence than for his ardor, diligence and perseverance in the pursuit of science.

1832. Civil war in Mexico terminated by a convention at Zalaveta, of delegates from the armies of Bustamente and Santa Anna.

1846. JAMES STEVENSON, one of the oldest of the Seneca chiefs, and a friend of Red Jacket, died on the Cattaraugus reservation, aged 81. He was the son of an English officer, who vainly tried to persuade his beautiful Indian wife to accompany him to England.

1854. Simoda, Japan, destroyed by an earthquake. A wave from the bay overflowed the town, and on its return left but 16 buildings out of a thousand standing.

DECEMBER 24.

361. GEORGE of Capadocia, Arian bishop of Alexandria, was assassinated in consequence of his oppression.

705. ÆLFRID, king of Northumberland, died.

1156. PETER (*the Venerable*), a French ecclesiastic, died. He was sprung of a noble family, and became general of the order of Cluni. He was a man of great learning and exemplary piety.

1247. ROBIN HOOD, the English outlaw, has his death placed on this day (See Nov. 18).

1460. Battle of Wakefield Green; the Lancasterians under Margaret queen of Henry IV, defeated Richard duke of York, who was slain.

1525. VASQUEZ DE GAMA, the Portuguese navigator, died at Cochin in Malabar. He discovered the course to the East Indies, by the cape of Good Hope.

1535. EURICIUS CORDUS died; a German physician and poet, the friend of Erasmus.

1560. At Lillebone, Lower Seine, France, a fiery meteor fell, attended with red rain.

1565. A Dutch church was opened at Norwich by order of queen Elizabeth.

1650. Edinburgh castle taken by Cromwell, said to be the first time ever reduced.

1664. A comet styled a blazing star appeared in England.

1704. First eruption on record of the peak of Teneriffe.

1728. Second newspaper established in Philadelphia, called the *Universal Instructor in all Arts and Sciences and Pennsylvania Gazette*, by Samuel Keimer. The first press had been established by Bradford about six weeks after the city was founded.

1736. Plot discovered to destroy the whole family of Brunswick Wolfenbuttel.

1740. DANIEL WATERLAND, an eminent English divine and polemical writer, died.

1771. CHARLES JOHN FRANCIS HENAULT, an eminent French chronologist, died. His great work, the result of forty years' study, has gone through many editions and been translated into the Chinese and several European languages.

1775. JOHN CAMPBELL, king's agent for the province of Georgia, died. He was an eminent writer on biography, history and politics.

1793. The French convention decreed

that the houses in Toulon should be leveled with the ground.

1794. South Hadley canal, or Connecticut river, opened. It was constructed to overcome a fall of 53 feet in the river; is upwards of 2 miles in length, including a cut of 300 feet in length through solid rock, 40 feet deep and 18 wide. The descent into the river was made by an inclined plane 230 feet in length, traversed by a carriage with six wheels, which was regulated by a water wheel. It was altogether quite an original affair.

1798. ROBERT MERRY, author of the *Pains of Memory*, died at Baltimore.

1800. An attempt to assassinate Bonaparte at Paris by an infernal machine.

1804. MARTIN VAHL, a Norwegian naturalist, died. He extended his researches over various parts of Europe and the African coast.

1805. American exploring party under Capts. Lewis and Clark, went into winter quarters in huts on the shore of the Pacific, near the mouth of Columbia river.

1806. Battle of Nasielsk; the Russians under Kaminski defeated by the French under Davoust.

1806. Battle of Kursonet, on the Wrka; 15,000 Cossacks defeated by the French under Nansouty.

1808. THOMAS BEDDOES, an eminent English physician, died. He is known by his perseverance in making experiments to cure consumption by the application of pneumatics.

1814. Preliminaries of the treaty of peace between England and the United States signed at Ghent.

1824. CHRISTOPHER ARETIN, a learned German writer, died. On the abolition of the monastries in 1803 he was appointed to examine their libraries.

1830. STEPHANIA FELICITE DE GENLIS, a celebrated French authoress, died, aged 84. For the last thirty years of her life, her inexhaustible pen continued to pour forth a variety of works of which space is here wanted to enumerate even their names. The whole of her literary progeny falls little short of an hundred volumes, and are characterized by fertility of imagination and purity of style.

1831. A volcanic island, recently formed near Sicily, disappeared.

1832. The citadel of Antwerp, with 3,500 troops, surrendered to the French, after a brave resistance of 26 days. The French had thrown up 14,000 metres of trenches, and fired 63,000 rounds, by which 695 were wounded and 108 killed.

1836. FRANCISCO ESPOZ Y MINA, a distinguished Spanish constitutional general, died.

1836. Great snow storm in England, which blocked up the roads so as to prevent all traveling, and many lives were lost. In some places the snow drifted to the depth of forty feet, and in others avalanches buried houses and their inhabitants.

1846. ERASTUS ROOT, a distinguished statesman in the state of New York, died while on a visit to New York city, aged 74.

1849. PATRICK FRAZER TYTLER, the Scottish historian, died.

1849. Great fire at San Francisco; property destroyed valued at a million and a half of dollars.

1851. The principal room of the library of Congress was destroyed by fire.

DECEMBER 25.

The commencement of what is usually called the vulgar era, was four years prior to the date now used as the beginning of the Christian era.

98. Christ mass was first used as a festival.

283. MARCUS AURELIUS CARUS, the Roman emperor, killed by lightning, beyond the Tigris.

400. GAINAS, a Goth of great valor, killed. He became a general under Arcadius, and desolated Thrace, because refused a church for the Arians.

496. CLOVIS, the first Christian king of France, crowned at Rheims; a glorious day among the Franks.

800. CHARLES, king of France, crowned at Rome emperor of the West. It was the commencement of a new Roman era, and he took the name of *Charlemagne*.

820. LEO V, emperor of Constantinople, assassinated. He was an Armenian, who became a general by his valor in the Roman armies, and prevailed on his troops to proclaim him emperor.

1066. WILLIAM, the conqueror, was crowned at London, amid a tumult, and the better to secure the obedience of the citizens, granted them a charter.

1440. GILLES DE RETZ, the famous *Bluebeard*, executed at Nantes for his horrible crimes. The ruins of his castle, La Verriere, are seen on the banks of the Erde, in the Lower Loire.

1476. GELEAS MARIE SFORZA, duke of Milan, assassinated. He rendered himself unpopular by his ferocity and debauchery.

1618. The first house erected at Plymouth, Mass., by the puritan settlers, after having spent more than a month in selecting a place for settlement. The company was divided into 19 families, and to each person was assigned a lot, half a rod in width, and three rods in length, for houses and gardens.

1658. CROMWELL dispersed several congregations, met to celebrate the birth of the Savior.

1676. MATTHEW HALE, a learned English judge, died. He was conversant with almost every branch of scie ce, and has left valuable works in law, philosophy and religion.

1678. JOHN NEWTON died; an English mathematician and chaplain to Charles II.

1698. JAMES HOUBRACKEN, the celebrated Dutch engraver, was born at Dordrecht.

1712. WILLIAM KING, an English poetical and political writer, died. His most useful work is an account of the heathen gods and heroes, necessary for the understanding of the ancient poets.

1715. JAMES, the pretender to the English throne, landed at Peterhead, and formed his court.

1740. JOHN SOANEN, an eminent French ecclesiastic, having been deposed from his bishopric, died in exile.

1741. ROBERT SANDERSON died; an English writer, distinguished as the continuator of *Rymer's Fœdera*, from the 16th to the 20th volume.

1758. JAMES HERVEY, an English divine of exemplary virtue and piety, died. His *Meditations* and *Letters* are well known.

1762. Great riot at Drury lane theatre, because the managers would not admit at half price after the 3d October.

1770. HENRY MILL, an ingenious English mechanic, died. He is said to have been unrivaled in the science of hydraulics.

1777. Vermont became an independent state. It was first settled in 1725, and claimed as part of New Hampshire.

1796. KOSCIUSKO, with other Polish prisoners, liberated by the emperor Paul, when he came to America.

1801. HESTER CHAPONE, an elegant English poetess and moral writer, died. Her works will long be popular.

1813. Violent eruption of mount Etna.

1816. Treaty between the United States and the dey of Algiers.

1822. A hurricane in Iceland, which overthrew the churches. The new volcano of Oefields Jokkelen, spouted burning stones and ashes.

1827. ENRICO ACERBI, an Italian surgeon and medical writer, died.

1837. JOHN AUSTIN died at Philadelphia, aged 67; a native of Barbadoes, formerly a surgeon in the British army, and a practitioner at Barbadoes and Demarara, where he was greatly esteemed.

1853. JOHN MACRAE WASHINGTON, a brave American military officer, was swept from the wreck of the San Francisco, aged 60. After the close of the Mexican war he commanded an expedition across the plains of Mexico to the Pacific, and acted as military governor one year.

DECEMBER 26.

795. ADRIAN I, pope, died. He was a Roman patrician, who on his elevation to tthe pontificate highly embellished St. Peter's church, and displayed his benevolence and humanity during a famine occasioned by the inundation of the Tiber.

1135. STEPHEN crowned king of England on St. Stephen's day.

1292. JOHN BALIOL performed homage to Edward of England at New Castle.

1300. EDWARD I of England forbade the circulation of crockards, pollards, rosaries, and other foreign coins, as sterlings. They were all called in and a new *sterling* money coined, so called from the Easterlings, who were the first coiners of silver of that fineness in England.

1530. ZAHIR-EDDIN MOHAMMED BABER, founder of the Tartar empire in Hindostan, died, aged 47. He made the first irruption into Hindostan in 1505, which was unsuccessful; but in 1524 he again undertook the invasion, defeated and killed the sultan in battle, and extended his conquests far and wide with astonishing rapidity. He was one of the most distinguished sovereigns that ever sat upon an Asiatic throne.

1552. CHARLES V raised the siege of Metz, with the loss of 30,000 men.

1679. THOMAS BLOUNT, an English barrister at law, died; distinguished for his talents and learning, and as a respectable writer.

1729. HONORE TOURNELY, a distinguished French ecclesiastic, died. He was professor of philosophy at Douay, and a popular preacher.

1731. ANTHONY HOUDART DE LA MOTTE, an ingenious French critic and miscellaneous author, died. His works consist of epic poetry, tragedy, comedy, lyric, pastoral, and fable; besides a vast variety of discourses, critical and academical.

1732. WILLIAM LELAND, of Lisnaken, in Ireland, died, aged 139. He was alike remarkable for his stature and longevity.

1762. EVERARD TITON DU TILLET, a French Jesuit, died; distinguished for his learning, and for a brazen Parnassus which he planned and erected in honor of Louis XIV.

1771. CLAUDE ADRIAN HELVETIUS, a French writer, died. He was a wealthy and benevolent man, but his works were irreligious.

1776. Battle of Trenton, New Jersey. The Americans under Washington crossed the Delaware on a cold and stormy night, and surprised the Hessians at sunrise. Col. Rhalle and 20 men were killed and the remainder surrendered, to the number of 1,000. Of the Americans 2 were killed and 2 frozen to death. This well judged and successful enterprise revived the depressed spirits of the colonists and produced an immediate and happy effect in recruiting the American army.

1780. JOHN FOTHERGILL, an eminent London physician, died. He was of the sect of quakers, and distinguished himself by his public and private benefactions, his encouragement of science, and attention to the health, the police and the conveniences of the city, as well as his great medical skill.

1782. HENRY HOME, lord Kaimes, died. He was one of the senators of the college of justice in Scotland, and eminent as a critical and philosophical writer.

1784. OTHO FREDERIC MULLER, a Danish naturalist, died. His works show much method and great accuracy.

1797. JOHN WILKES, a famous English politician and an elegant scholar, died. He was a member of parliament, lord mayor of London, and afterwards chamberlain.

1800. MARY ROBINSON died; an elegant English poetess, novelist and dramatic writer.

1806. Battle of Pultusk in Poland, between the Russians under Beningsen and the French under Lannes. The latter were defeated with the loss of 8,000; Russian loss 5,000. The French drew back with such haste that the advancing Cossacks were unable to overtake their rear guard next day. Lannes was glanced by a ball, and had two aids killed.

1806. Battle of Soldau; French under Ney defeated the Prussians under Lestocq.

1806. Battle of Alawa, in Prussian Poland; French under Marchand gained a brilliant victory.

1806. Battle of Golymin; Russians defeated by the French under Murat and Davoust. The Russians on this eventful day lost 80 cannon, 12,000 men, and a great amount of baggage, &c.

1811. Destruction of Richmond theatre, in consequence of the scenery taking fire, when 123 persons perished, among whom was the governor of the state, and a great number of females.

1812. JOEL BARLOW, an American poet and statesman, died at Garnowitch, in Poland, while on an embassy from the United States to Bonaparte. His principal work is the *Columbiad*, a poem.

1820. JOSEPH FOUCHE, duke of Otranto, died. He was one of the most flagrant of the French revolutionists; but had the adroitness to escape punishment by shifting his opinions with every variation of the public sentiment and policy.

1831. STEPHEN GIRARD, a wealthy Philadelphia banker, died. He was a native of France; was first a cabin boy, then mate of a ship, then keeper of a toy shop, afterwards a merchant, and finally a banker. He left an estate of ten or fifteen millions, which was bequeathed to charitable and public purposes.

1843. Rev. JAMES HARVEY LINSLEY, a writer in the *American Journal of Science*, died at Stratford.

1851. The town of Lagos, on the coast of Africa, destroyed by an English force, with a loss of 30 killed and 60 wounded, because the native chief refused to sign a treaty for the effectual suppression of the slave trade. The chief was deposed, and another substituted in his place.

1851. A large portion of the Chinese part of Hong-Kong destroyed by fire, including all the printing offices, the finest edifices and public buildings; involving the loss of nearly 500 houses and many human lives.

DECEMBER 27.

100. JOHN (*the Evangelist*) died at Ephesus, aged 94.

1552. CATHARINE VON BORA, wife of Martin Luther, died. She was rescued from a nunnery with eight others by the assistance of the great reformer. She survived him several years.

1585. PETER DE RONSARD died; a French elegiac and epigrammatic poet of a noble family.

1603. THOMAS CARTWRIGHT, an English puritan of great eminence and learning, died. He was a sharp and powerful controversialist, author of a practical commentary on the gospels and proverbs. He was obliged to quit the kingdom to avoid persecution, and died in great poverty.

1605. JOHN DAVIS, a famous English navigator, killed in a desperate fight with some Japanese near the coast of Malacca.

1669. SAMUEL CLARKE died; a celebrated English oriental scholar.

1689. PETER HALLE, an eminent French civilian and poet, died. He was offered the headship of five colleges, and accepted the professorship of canon law in the university of Paris, where he raised the character of that much neglected science.

1763. LAWRENCE NATTIER died; a Swabian, who published a work on antient gems.

1763. The Paxton boys broke into Lancaster jail and massacred fourteen friendly Indians.

1771. HENRY PITOT died: a celebrated French mathematician, and friend of the great Reaumur.

1779. The Spanish armament opened their batteries upon Gibraltar. It is supposed the general had no orders to fire until this time, but to remain on the defensive.

1784. Lee Boo, a prince of the Pelew islands, died in England, whither he had been sent to acquire an education.

1791. John Monro died; an English physician, celebrated for his skill in cases of insanity.

1800. Hugh Blair, a celebrated Scottish divine, died. His *Lectures on Rhetoric* delivered as professor at the Edinburgh university, are eminently distinguished by laborious investigation, sound sense and refined taste; and his printed sermons have had a success almost unparalleled in the annals of pulpit eloquence.

1808. The French under Lannes assaulted Saragossa, in Spain, and the convent of St. Eugratia carried. This was the second siege.

1814. Joanna Southcott, a noted English fanatic and imposter, died. At the age of 42 she claimed the character of a prophet, and for more than twenty years continued her rhapsodies, and drew after her several thousand adherents, who are not yet extinct.

1814. United States schooner Carolina, blown up on the Mississippi river by a red hot ball from the British batteries.

1820. John Keats, an English poet, died in Italy. He was originally a stable boy, subsequently apprenticed to a surgeon, but gave way to the ambition of becoming a poet. His poems though written at a very early age, possess merit.

1834. Charles Lamb, the poet Coleridge's friend, died. In some of his most popular works he was assisted by his sister Mary Lamb.

1835. Ephraim Williams, an eminent lawyer, died at Deerfield, Mass. He prepared the first volume of the Massachusetts reports.

1840. Jenny Kennison died at Brookfield, N. H., aged 110.

1842. Alexander Croke, quite a voluminous writer on law, politics, &c., died at Studley priory, England, aged 85.

1842. Francis Wrangham, distinguished as a poet and antiquary, died at Chester, England.

1851. Basil Montagu, an English author, died, aged 81. He edited the last and best edition of *Bacon's Works*, and was one of the earliest, most prominent and most zealous advocates of a mitigated penal code in England.

1853. The mammoth clipper Great Republic was burnt at her wharf in New York, together with several other vessels and five large flour warehouses.

1854. Thomas Wilson Dorr, the cause of what was called the Dorr war in Rhode Island, died at Providence, aged 49.

DECEMBER 28.

1065. St. Peter's church at Westminster dedicated by Edward the confessor.

1278. Injunction of the primate of England to the nunnery at Godstow, that public prayers on this day, Childermas, should not any more be said by little girls.

1377. Wickliff divulged his opinion upon the pope's mandate.

1499. Earl of Warwick, the last of the male line of the Plantagenets, beheaded on Tower hill.

1601. The town of Kinsale, head of the sea, in Ireland, garrisoned by Spaniards and Irish catholics, surrendered to the English armies.

1638. A Spanish ordinance establishing stamped paper in America.

1694. Mary II, queen of England, died of small pox, aged 33. She had reigned six years in conjunction with William III, and was greatly extolled for her virtues.

1697. Mary Beale, an English portrait painter, died. She is styled by Oldys "that masculine poet as well as painter, the incomparable Mrs. Beale."

1706. Peter Bayle, a most laborious and indefatigable French writer, died. He was an author of great ability, principally known by his *Critical Dictionary*.

1708. Joseph Pitton de Tournefort, a famous French botanist and natural historian, died.

1733. Kouli Khan defeated the Turks before Babylon, killing 20,000, with the loss of 10,000.

1737. Victor Marie d'Estrees, a French admiral, died. He was also a man of literature, and member of several learned bodies.

1737. Singular sinking and rising of land at Scarborough, in Yorkshire, England.

1757. Caroline Elizabeth, 3d daughter of Geo. II, of England, died.

1757. Leignitz taken by the Prussians under Frederick II, by which the Austrians and French were compelled to abandon Silesia, with the loss of 4,000 men.

1758. The French settlement of Goree taken by the British admiral Keppel.

1775. John Campbell, an eminent Scottish historical, biographical and political writer died.

1778. The French under count d'Estaing re-embarked their troops at St. Lucia, and sailed on the following day.

1788. John Logan, a Scottish divine and poet, died. He obtained much distinction as an eloquent preacher.

1797. War with the pope renewed by the French, occasioned by the assassination of Duplot, a French general, who was sent to Rome as an ambassador.

1811. Funeral at Richmond, Va., of those who perished at the burning of the theatre.

1814. United States privateer Prince of Neufchatel, 18 guns and 130 men, captured by British ship Leander, two frigates in company.

1814. British cannonaded unsuccessfully the Americans under Gen. Jackson. The cannonade continued 7 hours; the British loss estimated at 120 killed; American loss 9 killed, 8 wounded.

1817. Charles Barney, an eminent English scholar, died. He greatly distinguished himself by the depth of his literary researches, and by his extraordinary skill in the Greek language.

1817. American colonization society formed at Washington, having for its object the returning of free people of color to Africa.

1818. Alexander, emperor of Russia, gave to his peasant subjects the same right with his nobles to establish manufactures.

1825. J. D. Barbie-du-Bocage, a French geographer, died. He furnished plans and maps for the most celebrated works of the day, and published an atlas of 54 sheets to illustrate ancient history.

1825. John Thomas Serres, a French artist, died. His sea pieces possess much merit, and he is besides the author of the *Little Sea Torch*, a guide for coasting pilots.

1831. Insurrection of the slaves in Jamaica, in the course of which about 30,000 blacks were under arms, 4,000 of whom were killed. The amount of property destroyed was estimated at $15,000,000.

1835. Battle of Tampa bay; a company of 110 United States troops under major Dade, attacked by a large party of Seminole Indians, and all but three slain.

1853. A great snow storm commenced, which continued 36 hours, extending over the new England states, and causing great interruption to business and travel.

DECEMBER 29.

1170. Thomas Becket, archbishop of Canterbury, assassinated in his cathedral, aged 53.

1563. Sebastian Castalio, a French writer, died. His writings are very considerable, both for their number and quality, discover great knowledge of the languages, and are chiefly on scripture subjects.

1594. John Chastel, the son of a woolen draper at Paris, executed for an attempt to assassinate the king, Henry IV.

1674. Battle of Mulhausen; the French under Turenne, gained a victory over the Germans.

1680. William Stafford, an English nobleman, beheaded. He was convicted of high treason as a conspirator in the popish plot, said to have been contrived by the catholics for the assassination of Charles II.

1689. Thomas Sydenham died; an excellent English physician and medical writer.

1699. George Matthias Kœnig, a learned German writer, died; distinguished for his knowledge of belles lettres, divinity and oriental languages; principally known by a biographical dictionary which has been of great service to subsequent compilers.

1713. John Chardin, a famous French *voyageur*, died. He was driven to England on the revocation of the edict of Nantes, where he was knighted by Charles II. His *Voyages* have always been much esteemed as very curious and accurate.

1731. Brook Taylor, an English mathematician and philosopher, died. His works were valuable and often republished.

1737. Joseph Saurin, a French mathematician, died. He devoted his life to geometrical pursuits, and is conspicuous for a controversy with Rousseau who wised to palm upon him some of his own libelous verses against persons of distinction.

1755. Gabrielle Susanne Barbot de Villeneuve, a celebrated French novel writer, died.

1761. Elizabeth, queen of Russia, died. She was the daughter of Peter the Great, and ascended the throne, 1741.

1774. Toussaint Gaspard Taconnet died; a French actor and dramatic writer, noted for his eccentricity.

1778. Savannah taken by the British. A negro conducted the British by a private path to the rear of the Americans, who being attacked in front and flank, made a fatal retreat. Upwards of 100 Americans were killed, 453 taken; the town and fort, 48 cannon, 23 mortars, with ammunition and stores, the shipping in the river, and large quantities of provisions fell into the hands of the enemy.

1783. Samuel Cooper, a Boston clergyman, died. His sermons were evangelical and perspicuous, and unequaled in America at that time for taste and elegance.

1783. Daniel Wray, a learned English antiquary, died, aged 82.

1790. John George la Franc de Pompignan, a learned French prelate, died. He was author of sixteen works on different subjects.

1794. The town of Grave, considered a masterpiece of fortification, surrendered to the French under Pichegru, after a blockade of two months.

1797. General DUPHOT, assassinated by the populace at Rome, which was made a pretext of the French directory for dethroning the pope, Pius VI. Duphot had distinguished himself on several memorable occasions, and had repaired to Rome for the purpose of espousing the sister of Bonaparte, afterwards married to Murat.

1798. American government issued orders to the commanders of their armed vessels to repel by force the mustering and searching their vessels, and detaining them; but when overpowered by a superior force, to strike their colors and surrender ship and men.

1812. Action between United States frigate Constitution, 54 guns, 480 men, Capt. Bainbridge, and British frigate Java, 49 guns and 500 men including supernumerary officers, which resulted in the capture of the latter in 55 minutes. Loss of the Java 60 killed and 101 wounded including the captain, Lambert, mortally. Constitution lost 34 killed and wounded.

1825. JAMES LOUIS DAVID, a celebrated French painter, died. He was one of the wildest idolators of Robespierre and Marat, but finally lost his repugnance to monarchy under Bonaparte. He was banished on the restoration of the Bourbons, and died at Brussels. His works are numerous, and attest a splendid genius.

1832. Baron COTTA died. He was the originator of the daily political paper, the *Algemeine Zeitung*, so extensively circulated in Europe.

1832. JAMES HILLHOUSE, an American statesman, died at New Haven, Ct., aged 79. He took an active part in the revolution, and was eighteen years a member of congress. He was entrusted with the construction of the Farmington canal.

1834. T. R. MALTHUS, an English writer on political economy, died, His most celebrated work is an *Essay on Population*, which has passed through many editions, and been translated into various languages.

1836. DEBORAH TRIPP died at Poughkeepsie, aged 10 years and six months, and weighing 360 pounds. A few years before, herself and a younger sister were exhibited about the country for their extraordinary fatness. The younger sister died two or three years previous.

1837. WILLIAM MAVOR, a popular English author and compiler, died, aged 80. His *Voyages* and *Universal History*, in 25 vols. each, are well known, and his *English Spelling Book* passed through between four and five hundred editions.

1837. Tho imperial palace at St. Petersburg burnt, the weather at the time being 22° below zero. The palace was built in the reign of Elizabeth, at a cost of upwards of $5,000,000, and was the largest in Europe, sufficient to lodge 12,000 persons. The loss of treasures, pictures, statues, ornaments and furniture was immense.

1837. Steamer Caroline, a vessel in the service of the Navy island patriots, destroyed.

1839. Battle of Cagancha between the forces of Uruguay, under Rivera, and those of Buenos-Ayres under Echague. The latter had an army of 5,000 men, and was defeated with the loss of 800 killed, and prisoners, baggage, &c., taken. Rivera's loss about 200.

1845. Texas admitted into the union.

1848. Wisconsin admitted into the union.

1848. The Roman chambers were dissolved and a constituent assembly convened.

1849. Great crevasse in the Mississippi banks at Bonnet Carré, about forty miles above New Orleans.

1850. The British forces had an engagement with the Caffres, in South Africa, were defeated with considerable loss, and obliged to retreat to their fort.

1852. ROBERT FORREST, an eminent Scottish sculptor, died, aged 63. He was originally a stone mason, in the quarries of Clydesdale; but the products of his chisel are seen in the most conspicuous points of Glasgow and Edinburgh.

1855. The French imperial guard made a triumphal entry into Paris on its return from the Crimea.

DECEMBER 30.

944 B. C. The winter solstice fell upon this day, according to the marble, by the table of Petavius; which places the period of Homer thirty-seven years later.

1535. The society of the Jesuits founded by Ignatius Loyola, a Spanish monk, who entered into an agreement with five of his fellow students to undertake the conversion of unbelievers and a pilgrimage to Jerusalem. From this small beginning it became a powerful society under the energy and shrewd policy of its leaders, and was raised to a degree of historical importance unparalleled in its kind.

1567. Bonhill field, the ancient burial place of the dissenters, surveyed, "containing 23 acres, 1 rod and 6 poles; butting upon Chiswell street on the south, and on the north upon the highway that leadeth from Wenlock's barn to the well called St. Agnes the Cleere." It was also the common place of interment for the victims of the great plague in 1665. Bunyan, Watts, Owen, De Foe, George Fox, are among the distinguished men who rest there.

1568. The learned ROGER ASCHAM, died; sometime tutor to queen Elizabeth, and afterwards her Latin secretary.

1582. EMANUEL ALVAREZ died; a Portuguese Jesuit, distinguished as a grammarian.

1596. EMANUEL DE SAA, a Portuguese Jesuit, died: professor of theology at Coimbra and at Rome, and author of several valuable works.

1644. JOHN BAPTIST VAN HELMONT, a physician of Brussels, died. He was a man of great learning in physic and natural philosophy. His cures were so extraordinary that he was brought before the inquision as a man that did things beyond the reach of nature. He cleared himself of the inquisition, but to be more at liberty retired into Holland.

1655. Several persons wounded at the door of the parliament house, England, by a quaker, who pretended that he was inspired to slay all in the house.

1661. The earl of Argyle committed to Edinburgh castle for high treason.

1688. The prince of Orange received the sacrament to allay suspicions of his wishing to change the liturgy of the English church.

1691. ROBERT BOYLE, the distinguished philosopher and chemist, died. He was the seventh son and fourteenth child of Richard, earl of Cork, and secured immortal fame by his writings and discoveries in experimental philosophy.

1695. SAMUEL MORLAND, though a great favorite with king Charles, died in poverty. He constructed an arithmetical machine.

1721. PETER DE VALLEMONT, a French ecclesiastic, died; known by his *Elements of History*, and other works.

1730. JAMES SAURIN, an eminent French divine and theological and controversial writer, died in Holland, where he took shelter from persecution.

1747. EDWARD HOLDSWORTH, an English poet, died.

1765. SAMUEL MADDEN, an Irish divine and dramatic poet, died. He instituted the Dublin society, and set apart an annuity of £100 to be distributed as premiums for improvements in the useful arts.

1765. JAMES FRANCIS EDWARD (*the Pretender*), died at Rome. He was the son of James II of England, who was compelled to abdicate by his want of discretion in the government.

1774. PAUL WHITEHEAD died; an English poet of considerable eminence.

1777. LEOPOLD MAXIMILIAN, elector of Bavaria, died. The succession to his dominions occasioned a war between Germany and Prussia.

1781. JOHN TUBERVILLE NEEDHAM, professor of philosophy in the English college at Lisbon, died. He wrote various philosophical and critical works: though a learned man he was a very superstitious character.

1800. THOMAS DIMSDALE, an eminent English physician, died. His celebrity was such that he was invited to the court of Russia, where he inoculated the empress Catharine and her son with small pox.

1809. AUGUSTUS FRANCIS JULIAN HERBIN died; a native of France, distinguished as an oriental scholar.

1813. Buffalo burnt. Fort George, or Newark, in Upper Canada, having been wantonly burnt down by the American troops, a part of the British army crossed over from fort Erie, and utterly destroyed the village of Buffalo, in retaliation. It contained 100 houses.

1833. WILLIAM SOTHEBY, an English poet and translator, died. His translations from Virgil and Homer rank in the first class of that difficult and rarely successful branch of literature.

1834. The first reformed British parliament dissolved by royal proclamation.

1836. The plague continued to rage at Constantinople; having carried off during the summer and autumn no less than 100,000 citizens.

1837. An attack made by upwards of 100 Canadian loyalists upon the American steamboat Caroline, lying in the Niagara, at Schlosser, and of 34 Americans on board 22 lost their lives. The boat was towed into the current, with part of the men on board, and precipitated down the falls.

1853. JOHN AVERY PARKER, a distinguished merchant and a millionaire, died in New Bedford, Mass.

1853. The ship Staffordshire, captain Richardson, from Liverpool to Boston, struck on a rock south of Seal island, and sunk, carrying down 177 of the passengers and crew.

DECEMBER 31.

71 B. C. POMPEY and CRASSUS triumph at Rome. The former had closed the ten years' war in Lusitania, and Crassus the revolt of Spartacus at home. Marcus Lucullus triumphed the same year, bringing with him the Thracian colossus of Apollo.

192. LUCIUS AURELIUS COMMODUS, a dissipated emperor of Rome, strangled, and Pertinax elected. It was in the reign of this emperor, A. D. 190, that the Capitoline library at Rome was destroyed.

406. The Huns, 100,000 strong, entered Gaul, and laid desolate her seventeen luxurious provinces with havoc and flame,

from the banks of the Rhine to the Pyrenæan mountains.

535. The acquisition of Sicily from the Goths. Belisarius entered Syracuse in triumph, a city which once embraced 22 miles.

1384. JOHN WICKLIFFE died; professor of divinity in the university of Oxford, and father of the reformation of the English church from popery.

1460. Battle of Wakefield, in England; the duke of York and 3000 of his followers slain.

1563. CHARLES DE COSSE died; a French general of great military talents, and employed also as a diplomatist.

1583. THOMAS ERASTUS, a celebrated German physician and divine, died. He wrote several works on philosophy, physic and divinity; but is chiefly memorable for his work on excommunication, in which he denies the power of the church, and affirms its censures to be incapable of extending beyond the present life.

1600. The East India company established by a charter from Elizabeth, granted to the earl of Cumberland and 215 knights, aldermen and merchants. The original capital was £22,000, divided into shares of £50.

1616. JAMES LE MAIRE died at sea in returning with the Dutch navigator, Schouten. In this voyage, the straits that bear his name were discovered, between Staaten Land and Terra del Fuego.

1620. Era of the first settlement of New England. It being sabbath, they kept the day for the first time in their new house, and in grateful remembrance of the friends they found in the last town they left in their native country, they called it Plymouth.

1674. Battle of Mulhausen, in Alsace, in which the French marshal Turenne defeated the Austrians.

1679. JOHN ADOLPHUS BORELLI, a distinguished philosopher and mathematician, of Naples, died; author of thirteen treatises in Italian and Latin.

1704. The peak of Teneriffe formed a lateral eruption in the plain de los Infantes, preceded by tremendous earthquakes.

1718. JOHN FLAMSTEAD, an eminent English astronomer, died. He formed a new catalogue of the fixed stars, containing about three thousand.

1762. MARY COLLYER died; the translator of Gessner's poem of the *Death of Abel.*

1771. CHRISTIAN ADOLPHUS KLOTZ, professor of philosophy at Göttingen, died. He distinguished himself by his Latin poems, his numismatic treatises, his works on the study of antiquity, and on the value and mode of using ancient gems.

1775. Assault of the American forces under Montgomery and Arnold on Quebec. Montgomery was killed in advancing upon the barrier, at the head of the New York troops, and Arnold's division, after a desperate engagement, in which the Americans sustained the whole force of the garrison three hours were compelled to surrender themselves prisoners of war. They lost 100 killed, 300 taken.

1781. HENRY LAURENS, ambassador from the United States to France, liberated from the tower of London in exchange for general Burgoyne.

1791. JOHN ELLIS, a London scrivner, died; the last of that ancient profession. He was an alderman of London nearly half a century, and was besides a man of literature, whose conversation was highly extolled by Dr. Johnson.

1792. The quantity of gold coined at the royal mint of Mexico this year was $969,430; of silver, $23,225,611; total, $24,195,041; the largest sum which had been coined there since the conquest of the country.

1793. THOMAS JEFFERSON resigned the office of secretary of state to the United States.

1796. The thermometer 4° below zero in London. Several persons were frozen to death.

1799. JOHN FRANCIS MARMONTEL, a French novelist, died. He was admired for the vigor and delicacy of his writings, but was allowed to pass his last days in a state of retirement bordering on want.

1811. Tariffa, near Gibraltar, attacked by the French, who were repulsed with great loss by the British under colonel Skerritt.

1812. United States frigates President and Congress returned to Boston after an active cruise of three months, during which they passed over a space of about 8000 miles without meeting an adventure to test the courage and discipline of their crews. They, however, captured two British vessels, one laden with $300,000 specie and gold dust, the other with oil.

1816. Deaths in Boston this year, 904; in Paris, 19,992.

1820. JOSEPH LATHROP, an American clergyman, died. His publications were more numerous and highly esteemed than those of any contemporary theologian in American.

1826. WILLIAM GIFFORD, an English poet and reviewer, died. He rose from a shoemaker's bench to an editor's stool where he acquired fame and fortune. He was a very good poet and critic, but a poor shoemaker.

1832. Insurrection of the slaves in Jamaica. More than 150 plantations were destroyed, and the loss of property was estimated at more than four millions of dollars. About 2000 negroes are supposed to have been killed.

1835. Battle of Withlacoochie; about 250 United States troops and milit a engaged 300 Seminole Indians. Of the latter 40 were killed; of the former, 4 killed, 59 wounded.

1839. HYACINTHE LOUIS DE QUELEN, archbishop of Paris, died. At the revolution of 1830 his adherence to the Bourbons incensed the mob to level the archiepiscopal palace to the ground, by which he was reduced to poverty. He was a man of distinguished talents and learning.

1840. PRENTISS MELLEN, chief justice of Maine, died at Portland, aged 77. The first eleven volumes of the *Maine Reports* are a monument of his legal discrimination, great familiarity with practice, and high sense of justice.

1846. JAMES COCHRAN died at Batavia, Genesee co., N. Y., aged 83. To him the world owes the invaluable invention of making cut nails, yet he died poor.

1849. Hudson river rail road opened to Poughkeepsie.

1852. AMOS LAWRENCE, a wealthy and leading Boston merchant, died, aged 77. His charities amounted to several hundred thousands of dollars.

INDEX.

ALPHABETICAL INDEX TO NAMES OF PERSONS.

64

INDEX.

BATTLES, SIEGES AND OTHER MILITARY OPERATIONS.

GENERAL INDEX.

68

www.ingramcontent.com/pod-product-compliance
Lightning Source LLC
LaVergne TN
LVHW021305110826
845150LV00003B/485

* 9 7 8 1 4 2 5 5 5 9 9 8 4 *